THIRD EDITION

The Making of the West

PEOPLES AND CULTURES

THIRD EDITION

The Making of the West

of the West

PEOPLES AND CULTURES

**Volume II:
Since 1500**

Lynn Hunt
University of California, Los Angeles

Thomas R. Martin
College of the Holy Cross

Barbara H. Rosenwein
Loyola University Chicago

R. Po-chia Hsia
Pennsylvania State University

Bonnie G. Smith
Rutgers University

BEDFORD / ST. MARTIN'S
Boston ■ New York

For Bedford/St. Martin's

Executive Editor for History: Mary Dougherty
Director of Development for History: Jane Knetzger
Senior Developmental Editor: Heidi L. Hood
Senior Production Editor: Karen S. Baart
Senior Production Supervisor: Dennis Conroy
Executive Marketing Manager: Jenna Bookin Barry
Editorial Assistants: Lindsay DiGianvittorio and Katherine Flynn
Production Associate: Lindsay DiGianvittorio
Production Assistant: David Ayers
Copyeditor: Janet Renard
Text Design: Janis Owens
Page Layout: Boynton Hue Studio
Photo Research: Gillian Speeth
Indexer: Leoni Z. McVey & Associates, Inc.
Cover Design: Donna Lee Dennison
Cover Art: Jacques Émile Blanche (1861–1942) © Copyright ARS, NY. *André Gide and His Friends at the Moorish Coffeehouse of the Universal Exhibition of 1900.* Canvas, 1900. Photo Credit: Erich Lessing/Art Resource, NY. Musée des Beaux-Arts, Rouen, France.
Cartography: Mapping Specialists Limited
Composition: Aptara
Printing and Binding: R.R. Donnelley & Sons Company

President: Joan E. Feinberg
Editorial Director: Denise B. Wydra
Director of Marketing: Karen Melton Soeltz
Director of Editing, Design, and Production: Marcia Cohen
Managing Editor: Elizabeth M. Schaaf

Library of Congress Control Number: 2007927405

Manufactured in the United States of America.

5   6   12   11   10   09

For information, write: Bedford/St. Martin's, 75 Arlington Street, Boston, MA 02116 (617-399-4000)

ISBN-10: 0–312–45294–2   ISBN-13: 978–0–312–45294–0   (combined edition)
ISBN-10: 0–312–45295–0   ISBN-13: 978–0–312–45295–7   (Vol. I)
ISBN-10: 0–312–45296–9   ISBN-13: 978–0–312–45296–4   (Vol. II)
ISBN-10: 0–312–46508–4   ISBN-13: 978–0–312–46508–7   (Vol. A)
ISBN-10: 0–312–46509–2   ISBN-13: 978–0–312–46509–4   (Vol. B)
ISBN-10: 0–312–46510–6   ISBN-13: 978–0–312–46510–0   (Vol. C)
ISBN-10: 0–312–46663–3   ISBN-13: 978–0–312–46663–3   (high school edition)

Preface

WHEN A BOOK GOES INTO its third edition, authors feel affirmed but also encouraged to do even better. Instructors who have read and used our book confirmed that the new synthesis we offered in the first and second editions enabled them to bring the most current conceptualizations of the West into their classroom. From the start, our goal has been to create a text that demonstrates that the history of the West is the story of an ongoing process, not a finished result with only one fixed meaning. We wanted also to make clear that there is no one Western people or culture that has existed from the beginning until now. Instead, the history of the West includes many different peoples and cultures. To convey these ideas, we have written a sustained story of the West's development in a broad, global context that reveals the cross-cultural interactions fundamental to the shaping of Western politics, societies, cultures, and economies. Indeed, the first chapter opens with a section on the origins and contested meaning of *Western civilization*. In this conversation, we emphasize our theme of cultural borrowing between the peoples of Europe and their neighbors that has characterized Western civilization from the beginning. Continuing this approach in subsequent chapters, we have insisted on an expanded vision of the West that includes the United States and fully incorporates eastern Europe and Scandinavia. Through the depth and breadth embraced in our narrative, we have been able to offer sustained treatment of crucial topics such as Islam and provide a more thorough treatment of globalization than any competing text. Our aim has been to convey the relevance of Western history throughout the book as essential background to today's events, from debate over European Union membership to conflict in the Middle East. Instructors have found this synthesis essential for helping students understand the West in today's ever-globalizing world.

Equally valuable to instructors has been the way our book is organized with a chronological framework to help students understand how political, social, cultural, and economic histories have influenced each other over time. We know from our own teaching that introductory students need a solid chronological framework, one with enough familiar benchmarks to make the material easy to grasp. Each chapter treats all the main events, people, and themes of a period in which the West significantly changed; thus, students learn about political events and social and cultural developments as they unfolded. This chronological integration also accords with our belief that it is important, above all else, for students to see the interconnections among varieties of historical experience—between politics and cultures, between public events and private experiences, between wars and diplomacy and everyday life. Our chronological synthesis provides a unique benefit to students: it makes these relationships clear while highlighting the major changes of each age. For teachers, our chronological approach ensures a balanced account and provides the opportunity to present themes within their greater context. But perhaps best of all, this approach provides a text that reveals history as a process that is constantly alive, subject to pressures, and able to surprise us.

Despite gratifying praise from the many reviewers who helped shape this edition, we felt we could do even more to help students and instructors. First, we have further highlighted thematic coverage to help students discern major developments. The most extensive changes we made to this end appear in the Renaissance and Reformation chapters; we rewrote and reorganized the three chapters of the second edition to create a more meaningful two. Chapter 13 includes new coverage of Renaissance art and architecture and the Ottomans' influence on the West, while Chapter 14 offers new consideration of the European Reformation in the context of global exploration and the spread of print culture. We have worked to make key developments clearer in other chapters as well. We united and expanded the discussion of early Canaanites and Hebrews in Chapter 2, added extended coverage of the first and second crusades in Chapter 10, refocused a section on religious fervor and later crusades in Chapter 11, consolidated coverage of the scientific revolution in Chapter 15, and combined and strengthened a section on industrialization in Chapter 21.

A second way we have chosen to help students identify and absorb major developments is by adding and refining signposts to guide student reading. Most notably, we have added new chapter-opening focus questions. Posed at the end of the opening vignettes, these single questions encapsulate the essence of the era covered in the chapter and guide students toward the core message of the chapter. To further help students as they read, we have worked hard to ensure that chapter and section overviews outline the central points of each section in the clearest manner possible. In addition, we have condensed some material to better illuminate key ideas.

A third way we have made this book more useful is by adding a special feature called Seeing History. We know that today's students are attuned to visual sources of information, yet they do not always receive systematic instruction in how to "read" or think critically about such sources. Similarly, we know instructors often wish to use visual evidence as the basis of class discussion but do not have materials appropriate for introductory students readily at hand. We have crafted our Seeing History features to address these needs. Each single-page Seeing History feature contains a pair of images — such as paintings, sculpture, photographs, and artifacts — accompanied by background information and probing questions designed to guide students through the process of reading images as historical evidence and to help them explore different perspectives and significant historical developments.

Finally, as always, we have incorporated the latest scholarly findings throughout the book so that students and instructors alike have a text that they can confidently rely on. In the third edition, we have included new and updated discussions of topics such as the demography of the later Roman republic and its effect on social change, the social and political causes of the Great Famine of the early fourteenth century, the emergence of the plague in Europe, the development of new slave-trading routes in the seventeenth and eighteenth centuries, the refugee crisis following World War II, and the enlargement of the European Union, among others.

Aided by a fresh and welcoming design, new pedagogical aids, and new multimedia offerings that give students and instructors interactive tools for study and teaching, we believe we have created a new edition even more suited to today's Western civilization courses. In writing *The Making of the West: Peoples and Cultures*, we have aimed to communicate the vitality and excitement as well as the fundamental importance of history. Students should be enthused about history; we hope we have conveyed some of our own enthusiasm and love for the study of history in these pages.

Pedagogy and Features

We know from our own teaching that students need all the help they can get in absorbing and making sense of information, thinking analytically, and understanding that history itself is debated and constantly revised. With these goals in mind, we retained the class-tested learning and teaching aids that worked well in the first and second editions, but we have also done more to help students distill the central story of each age and give them more opportunities to develop their own historical skills.

The third edition incorporates more aids to help students sort out what is most important to learn while they read. *New chapter focus questions* guide them toward the central themes of the era and the most significant information they should take away from their reading. Boldface *key terms* have been updated to concentrate on likely test items and have been expanded to include people. To help students read and study, the key terms and people are defined in a *new running glossary* at the bottom of pages and collected in a comprehensive *glossary* at the end of the book.

The study tools introduced in the previous edition continue to help students check their understanding of the chapters and the periods they cover. *Review questions*, strategically placed at the end of each major section, help students recall and assimilate core points in digestible increments. The *Chapter Review section* provides a clear study plan with a table of important events, a list of key terms and people, section review questions repeated from within the chapter, and "Making Connections" questions that encourage students to analyze chapter material or make comparisons within or beyond the chapter. *Vivid chapter-opening anecdotes* with overviews and *chapter outlines*, *timelines*, and *conclusions* further reinforce the central developments covered in the reading.

But like a clear narrative synthesis, strong pedagogical support is not enough on its own to encourage active learning. To reflect the richness of the themes in the text and offer further opportunities for historical investigation, we include a rich assortment of *single-source documents* (two per chapter). Nothing can give students a more direct experience of the past than original voices, and we have endeavored to let those voices speak, whether it is Frederick Barbarossa replying to the Romans when they offer him the emperor's crown, Marie de Sévigné's description of the French court, or an ordinary person's account of the outbreak of the Russian Revolution.

Accompanying these primary-source features are our unique features that extend the narrative by revealing the process of interpretation, providing a solid introduction to historical argument and critical thinking, and capturing the excitement of historical investigation:

- **NEW** *Seeing History* features guide students through the process of reading images as historical evidence. Each of the ten features provides a pair of images with background information and questions that encourage visual analysis. Examples include comparisons of pagan and Christian sarcophagi, Persian and Arabic coins, Romanesque and Gothic naves, pre- and post–French Revolution attire, and Italian propaganda posters from World War I.

- *Contrasting Views* features provide three or four often conflicting primary-source accounts of a central event, person, or development, such as Julius Caesar, the First Crusade, Joan of Arc, Martin Luther, the English Civil War, and late-nineteenth-century migration.

- *New Sources, New Perspectives* features show students how historians continue to develop fresh insights using new kinds of evidence about the past, from tree rings to Holocaust museums.

- *Terms of History* features explain the meanings of some of the most important and contested terms in the history of the West and show how those meanings have developed — and changed — over time. For example, the discussion of *progress* shows how the term took root in the eighteenth century and has been contested in the twentieth.

- *Taking Measure* features introduce students to the intriguing stories revealed by quantitative analysis. Each feature highlights a chart, table, graph, or map of historical statistics that illuminates an important political, social, or cultural development.

The book's map program has been widely praised as the most comprehensive and inviting of any competing survey text. In each chapter, we offer three types of maps, each with a distinct role in conveying information to students. Four to five *full-size maps* show major developments, two to four *"spot" maps* — small maps positioned within the discussion right where students need them — aid students' understanding of crucial issues, and *"Mapping the West"* summary maps at the end of each chapter provide a snapshot of the West at the close of a transformative period and help students visualize the West's changing contours over time. For this edition, we have carefully considered each map, simplified where possible to better highlight essential information, and clarified and updated borders and labels where needed.

We have striven to integrate art as fully as possible into the narrative and to show its value for teaching and learning. ***Over 425 illustrations***, carefully chosen to reflect this edition's broad topical coverage and geographic inclusion, reinforce the text and show the varieties of visual sources from which historians build their narratives and interpretations. All artifacts, illustrations, paintings, and photographs are contemporaneous with the chapter; there are no anachronistic illustrations. Furthermore, along with the new Seeing History features, our substantive captions for the maps and art help students learn how to read visuals, and we have frequently included specific questions or suggestions for comparisons that might be developed. Specially designed visual exercises in the Online Study Guide supplement this approach. A new page design for the third edition supports our goal of intertwining the art and the narrative, and makes the new study tools readily accessible.

Supplements

As with previous editions, a well-integrated ancillary program supports *The Making of the West: Peoples and Cultures*. Each print and new media resource has been carefully revised to provide a host of practical teaching and learning aids. (Visit the online catalog at **bedfordstmartins.com/hunt/catalog** for ordering information and special packaging options.)

For Students

PRINT RESOURCES

Sources of THE MAKING OF THE WEST, **Third Edition** — Volumes I (to 1740) and II (since 1500) — by Katharine J. Lualdi, University of Southern Maine. This companion sourcebook provides written and visual sources to accompany each chapter of *The Making of the West*. Political, social, and cultural documents offer a variety of perspectives that complement the textbook and encourage students to make connections between narrative history and primary sources. Short chapter summaries and document headnotes contextualize the wide array of sources and perspectives represented, while discussion questions guide students' reading and promote historical thinking skills. The third edition features five or more written documents per chapter and one-third more visual sources. Available free when packaged with the text and now available in the e-book (see below).

NEW Trade Books. Titles published by sister companies Farrar, Straus and Giroux; Henry Holt and Company; Hill and Wang; Picador; and St. Martin's Press are available at a 50 percent discount when packaged with Bedford / St. Martin's textbooks. For more information, visit **bedfordstmartins.com/tradeup**.

NEW *The Bedford Glossary for European History.* This handy supplement for the survey course gives students historically contextualized definitions for hundreds of terms—from Abbasids to Zionism—that students will encounter in lectures, reading, and exams. Available free when packaged with the text.

Bedford Series in History and Culture. Over 100 titles in this highly praised series combine first-rate scholarship, historical narrative, and important primary documents for undergraduate courses. Each book is brief, inexpensive, and focused on a specific topic or period. Package discounts are available.

NEW MEDIA RESOURCES

NEW *The Making of the West e-Book with e-Sources.* This one-of-a-kind online resource integrates the text of *The Making of the West* with the written and visual sources of the companion sourcebook *Sources of THE MAKING OF THE WEST* and the self-testing and activities of the Online Study Guide into one easy-to-use e-book. With search functions stronger than in any competing text, this e-book is an ideal study and reference tool for students. Instructors can easily add their own documents, images, and other class material to customize the text.

Online Study Guide at bedfordstmartins.com/ hunt. The popular Online Study Guide for *The Making of the West* is a free and uniquely personalized learning tool to help students master themes and information presented in the textbook and improve their historical skills. Assessment quizzes let students evaluate their comprehension and provide them with customized plans for further study through a variety of activities. Instructors can monitor students' progress through the online Quiz Gradebook or receive e-mail updates.

A Student's Online Guide to History Reference Sources at bedfordstmartins.com/hunt. This Web site provides links to history-related databases, indexes, and journals, plus contact information for state, provincial, local, and professional history organizations.

The Bedford Research Room at bedfordstmartins .com/hunt. The Research Room, drawn from Mike Palmquist's *The Bedford Researcher*, offers a wealth of resources—including interactive tutorials, research activities, student writing samples, and links to hundreds of other places online—to support students in courses across the disciplines. The site also offers instructors a library of helpful instructional tools.

The Bedford Bibliographer at bedfordstmartins .com/hunt. *The Bedford Bibliographer*, a simple but powerful Web-based tool, assists students with the process of collecting sources and generates bibliographies in four commonly used documentation styles.

Research and Documentation Online at bedfordstmartins.com/hunt. This Web site provides clear advice on how to integrate primary and secondary sources into research papers, how to cite sources correctly, and how to format in MLA, APA, Chicago, or CBE style.

The St. Martin's Tutorial on Avoiding Plagiarism at bedfordstmartins.com/hunt. This online tutorial reviews the consequences of plagiarism and explains what sources to acknowledge, how to keep good notes, how to organize research, and how to integrate sources appropriately. The tutorial includes exercises to help students practice integrating sources and recognize acceptable summaries.

For Instructors

PRINT RESOURCES

Instructor's Resource Manual. This helpful manual by Malia Formes (Western Kentucky University), Dakota Hamilton (Humboldt State University), and Paul A. Townend (University of North Carolina Wilmington) offers both first-time and experienced teachers a wealth of tools for structuring and customizing Western civilization history courses of different sizes. For each chapter in the textbook, the *Instructor's Resource Manual* includes an outline of chapter themes; a chapter summary; lecture and discussion topics; film and literature suggestions; writing and class-presentation assignments; research topic suggestions; and in-class exercises for working with maps, illustrations, and sources. The new edition includes model answers for the review questions in the book as well as a chapter-by-chapter guide to all the supplements available with *The Making of the West*.

Transparencies. A set of over 200 full-color acetate transparencies for *The Making of the West* includes all full-sized maps and many images from the text.

NEW MEDIA RESOURCES

NEW HistoryClass. Bedford / St. Martin's online learning space for history gives you the right tools and the rich content to create your course, your way. An interactive e-book and e-reader enable you to easily assign relevant textbook sections and primary documents. Access to the acclaimed content library, Make History, provides unlimited access to thousands of maps, images, documents, and Web links. The tried-and-true content of the Online Study Guide offers a range of activities to help students access their progress, study more effectively, and improve their critical thinking skills. Customize provided content and mix in your own with ease — everything in HistoryClass is integrated to work together in the same space.

Instructor's Resource CD-ROM. This disc provides PowerPoint presentations built around chapter outlines, maps, figures; selected images from the textbook, plus jpeg versions of all maps, figures, and selected images; and questions for instructor use with i>clicker, a personal response system.

Computerized Test Bank — by Malia Formes, Western Kentucky University; available on CD-ROM. This fully updated test bank offers over 80 exercises per chapter, including multiple-choice, identification, timelines, map labeling and analysis, source analysis, and full-length essay questions. Instructors can customize quizzes, edit both questions and answers, as well as export them to a variety of formats, including WebCT and Blackboard. The disc includes answer keys and essay outlines.

Book Companion Site at bedfordstmartins.com/ hunt. The companion Web site gathers all the electronic resources for *The Making of the West*, including the Online Study Guide and related Quiz Gradebook, at a single Web address, providing convenient links to lecture, assignment, and research materials such as PowerPoint chapter outlines and the digital libraries at Make History.

NEW Make History at bedfordstmartins.com/ hunt. Comprising the content of Bedford / St. Martin's five acclaimed online libraries — Map Central, the Bedford History Image Library, DocLinks, HistoryLinks, and PlaceLinks, Make History provides one-stop access to relevant digital content including maps, images, documents, and Web links. Students and instructors alike can search this free, easy-to-use database by keyword, topic, date, or specific chapter of *The Making of the West* and download the content they find. Instructors can also create entire collections of content and store them online for later use or post their collections to the Web to share with students.

Content for Course Management Systems. A variety of student and instructor resources developed for this textbook is ready for use in course management systems such as Blackboard, WebCT, and other platforms. This e-content includes nearly all of the offerings from the book's Online Study Guide as well as the book's test bank.

Videos and Multimedia. A wide assortment of videos and multimedia CD-ROMs on various topics in European history is available to qualified adopters.

Acknowledgments

In the vital process of revision, the authors have benefited from repeated critical readings by many talented scholars and teachers. Our sincere thanks go to the following instructors, whose comments often challenged us to rethink or justify our interpretations and who always provided a check on accuracy down to the smallest detail.

Abel Alves, *Ball State University*
Gene Barnett, *Calhoun Community College*
Giovanna Benadusi, *University of South Florida*

Marjorie K. Berman, *Red Rocks Community College*

Gregory Bruess, *University of Northern Iowa*

James M. Burns, *Clemson University*

Kevin W. Caldwell, *Blue Ridge Community College*

William R. Caraher, *University of North Dakota*

Joseph J. Casino, *Villanova University, St. Joseph's University*

Sara Chapman, *Oakland University*

Michael S. Cole, *Florida Gulf Coast University*

Robert Cole, *Utah State University*

Theodore F. Cook, *William Patterson University*

Jo Ann Hoeppner Moran Cruz, *Georgetown University*

Luanne Dagley, *Pellissippi State Technical Community College*

Frederick H. Dotolo III, *St. John Fisher College*

Mari Firkatian, *University of Hartford*

David D. Flaten, *Tompkins Cortland Community College*

Ellen Pratt Fout, *The Ohio State University*

Rebecca Friedman, *Florida International University*

Helen Grady, *Springside School, Philadelphia, Pennsylvania*

Padhraig S. Higgins, *Pennsylvania State University*

Ronald K. Huch, *Eastern Kentucky University*

Michael Innis-Jiménez, *William Paterson University*

Jason M. Kelly, *Indiana University–Purdue University Indianapolis*

Nathaniel Knight, *Seton Hall University*

Elizabeth A. Lehfeldt, *Cleveland State University*

Charles Levine, *Mesa Community College*

Keith P. Luria, *North Carolina State University*

Kathryn Lynass, *Arizona State University*

Michael Mackey, *Community College of Denver*

John McManamon, *Loyola University*

Anthony Makowski, *Delaware County Community College*

John W. Mauer, *Tri-County Technical College*

Lynn Wood Mollenauer, *University of North Carolina–Wilmington*

Michelle Anne Novak, *Houston Community College*

Jason M. Osborne, *Northern Kentucky University*

James A. Ross-Nazzal, *Houston Community College–Southeast College*

Daniel Sarefield, *The Ohio State University*

Nancy E. Shockley, *New Mexico State University*

Dionysios Skentzis, *College of DuPage*

Daniel Stephen, *University of Colorado at Boulder*

Charles R. Sullivan, *University of Dallas*

Emily Sohmer Tai, *Queensborough Community College of the City University of New York*

David Tengwall, *Anne Arundel Community College*

Andrew Thomas, *Purdue University*

Paul A. Townend, *University of North Carolina–Wilmington*

David Ulbrich, *Ball State University*

Karen T. Wagner, *Pikes Peak Community College*

William Welch Jr., *Troy University*

David K. White, *McHenry County College*

James Theron Wilson, *Ball State University*

Many colleagues, friends, and family members have made contributions to this work. They know how grateful we are. We also wish to acknowledge and thank the publishing team at Bedford/St. Martin's who did so much to bring this revised edition to completion: president Joan Feinberg, editorial director Denise Wydra, publisher for history Mary Dougherty, director of development for history Jane Knetzger, senior editor Heidi Hood, senior editor Louise Townsend, senior editor Sara Wise, freelance editors Betty Slack and Dale Anderson, editorial assistant and production associate Lindsay DiGianvittorio, executive marketing manager Jenna Bookin Barry, senior production editor Karen Baart, managing editor Elizabeth Schaaf, art researcher Gillian Speeth, text designer Janis Owens, page makeup artist Cia Boynton, cover designer Donna Dennison, and copyeditor Janet Renard.

Our students' questions and concerns have shaped much of this work, and we welcome all our readers' suggestions, queries, and criticisms. Please contact us at our respective institutions or via **history@bedfordstmartins.com**.

Contents

CHAPTER 29
A New Globalism,
1989 to the Present   *951*

Maps and Figures

Maps

Figures

Special Features

Documents

Contrasting Views

New Sources, New Perspectives

Terms of History

Seeing History

Taking Measure

To the Student

This guide to your textbook introduces the unique features that will help you understand the fascinating story of Western Civilization.

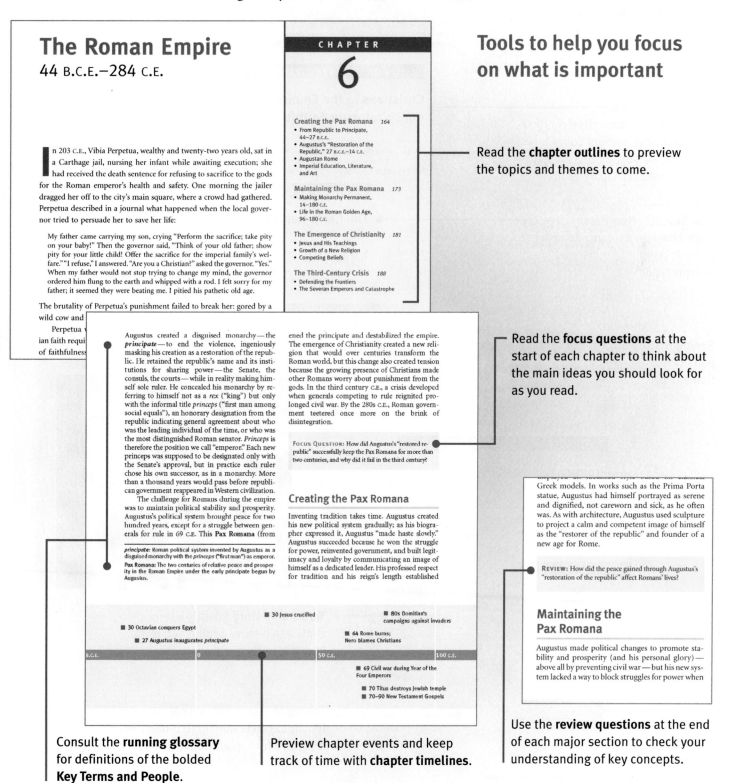

The Roman Empire
44 B.C.E.–284 C.E.

Tools to help you focus on what is important

CHAPTER

6

Creating the Pax Romana 164
• From Republic to Principate, 44–27 B.C.E.
• Augustus's "Restoration of the Republic," 27 B.C.E.–14 C.E.
• Augustan Rome
• Imperial Education, Literature, and Art

Maintaining the Pax Romana 173
• Making Monarchy Permanent, 14–180 C.E.
• Life in the Roman Golden Age, 96–180 C.E.

The Emergence of Christianity 181
• Jesus and His Teachings
• Growth of a New Religion
• Competing Beliefs

The Third-Century Crisis 188
• Defending the Frontiers
• The Severan Emperors and Catastrophe

Read the **chapter outlines** to preview the topics and themes to come.

I n 203 C.E., Vibia Perpetua, wealthy and twenty-two years old, sat in a Carthage jail, nursing her infant while awaiting execution; she had received the death sentence for refusing to sacrifice to the gods for the Roman emperor's health and safety. One morning the jailer dragged her off to the city's main square, where a crowd had gathered. Perpetua described in a journal what happened when the local governor tried to persuade her to save her life:

> My father came carrying my son, crying "Perform the sacrifice; take pity on your baby!" Then the governor said, "Think of your old father; show pity for your little child! Offer the sacrifice for the imperial family's welfare." "I refuse," I answered. "Are you a Christian?" asked the governor. "Yes." When my father would not stop trying to change my mind, the governor ordered him flung to the earth and whipped with a rod. I felt sorry for my father; it seemed they were beating me. I pitied his pathetic old age.

The brutality of Perpetua's punishment failed to break her: gored by a wild cow and

Perpetua
ian faith requi
of faithfulness

Augustus created a disguised monarchy—the *principate*—to end the violence, ingeniously masking his creation as a restoration of the republic. He retained the republic's name and its institutions for sharing power—the Senate, the consuls, the courts—while in reality making himself sole ruler. He concealed his monarchy by referring to himself not as a *rex* ("king") but only with the informal title *princeps* ("first man among social equals"), an honorary designation from the republic indicating general agreement about who was the leading individual of the time, or who was the most distinguished Roman senator. *Princeps* is therefore the position we call "emperor." Each new princeps was supposed to be designated only with the Senate's approval, but in practice each ruler chose his own successor, as in a monarchy. More than a thousand years would pass before republican government reappeared in Western civilization.

The challenge for Romans during the empire was to maintain political stability and prosperity. Augustus's political system brought peace for two hundred years, except for a struggle between generals for rule in 69 C.E. This **Pax Romana** (from

principate: Roman political system invented by Augustus as a disguised monarchy with the *princeps* ("first man") as emperor.
Pax Romana: The two centuries of relative peace and prosperity in the Roman Empire under the early principate begun by Augustus.

ened the principate and destabilized the empire. The emergence of Christianity created a new religion that would over centuries transform the Roman world, but this change also created tension because the growing presence of Christians made other Romans worry about punishment from the gods. In the third century C.E., a crisis developed when generals competing to rule reignited prolonged civil war. By the 280s C.E., Roman government teetered once more on the brink of disintegration.

> **FOCUS QUESTION:** How did Augustus's "restored republic" successfully keep the Pax Romana for more than two centuries, and why did it fail in the third century?

Creating the Pax Romana

Inventing tradition takes time. Augustus created his new political system gradually; as his biographer expressed it, Augustus "made haste slowly." Augustus succeeded because he won the struggle for power, reinvented government, and built legitimacy and loyalty by communicating an image of himself as a dedicated leader. His professed respect for tradition and his reign's length established

Read the **focus questions** at the start of each chapter to think about the main ideas you should look for as you read.

Greek models. In works such as the Prima Porta statue, Augustus had himself portrayed as serene and dignified, not careworn and sick, as he often was. As with architecture, Augustus used sculpture to project a calm and competent image of himself as the "restorer of the republic" and founder of a new age for Rome.

> **REVIEW:** How did the peace gained through Augustus's "restoration of the republic" affect Romans' lives?

Maintaining the Pax Romana

Augustus made political changes to promote stability and prosperity (and his personal glory)—above all by preventing civil war—but his new system lacked a way to block struggles for power when

30 Octavian conquers Egypt
27 Augustus inaugurates *principate*
30 Jesus crucified
64 Rome burns; Nero blames Christians
80s Domitian's campaigns against invaders

B.C.E.   0   50 C.E.   100 C.E.

69 Civil war during Year of the Four Emperors
70 Titus destroys Jewish temple
70–90 New Testament Gospels

Use the **review questions** at the end of each major section to check your understanding of key concepts.

Consult the **running glossary** for definitions of the bolded **Key Terms and People**.

Preview chapter events and keep track of time with **chapter timelines**.

Special features introduce the way historians work and help you learn to think critically about the past.

Numerous **individual primary-source documents** offer direct experiences of the past and the opportunity to consider sources historians use.

Contrasting Views provide three or four often conflicting eyewitness accounts of a central event, person, or development to foster critical thinking skills.

New Sources, New Perspectives show how new evidence leads historians to fresh insights—and sometimes new interpretations.

Seeing History pairs two visuals with background information and probing questions to encourage analysis of images as historical evidence.

DOCUMENT

Augustus, *Res Gestae* (My Accomplishments)

Augustus, the first Roman emperor, had an autobiographical report of his accomplishments displayed around the empire. These excerpt

5. I refused to accept the dictatorship offered to me [in 22 B.C.E.] by the people and by the senate, both in my

end to the civil wars, having gained possession of everything through the consent of everyone, I returned

CONTRASTING VIEWS

Christians in the Empire: Conspirators or Faithful Subjects?

Romans worried that new religions would disrupt the "peace with the gods" that guaranteed their national safety and prosperity. Groups whose religious beliefs seemed likely to offend the traditional deities

Christians—with hands outspread, because innocent, with head bare because we do not blush, yes! and without a prompter because we pray from the heart—are ever praying for all the em-

NEW SOURCES, NEW PERSPECTIVES

The Cairo Geniza

What do historians know about the daily life of ordinary people in the Middle Ages? Generally speaking, very little. We have writings from the intellectual elite and administrative

they wanted to study the evolution of their handwriting (a discipline called paleography). They also needed to organize the material. Dispersed among various libraries, the documents were a hodgepodge

a small group: "I have been earning hood, just managing to get by," man named Yahya sometime arou to a hoped-for benefactor. He co

SEEING HISTORY

Shifting Sculptural Expression: From Egypt to Greece

As Greek civilization revived during the Archaic Age (750–500 B.C.E.), artists drew inspiration from the older civilizations of Egypt and the Near East, with sculpture in particular emerging

TERMS OF HISTORY

Progress

Believing as they did in the possibilities of improvement, many Enlightenment writers preached a new doctrine about the meaning of human history. They challenged the traditional Christian belief that the original sin of Adam and Eve condemned hu-

TAKING MEASURE

Terms of History identify a term central to history writing and reveal how it is hotly debated.

Taking Measure data reveal how individual facts add up to broad trends and introduce quantitative analysis skills.

Art and maps extend the chapter, and help you analyze images and put events in geographical context.

MAP 12.1 Europe in the Time of Frederick II, r. 1212–1250
King of Sicily and Germany and emperor as well, Frederick ruled over territory that encircled—and threatened—the papacy. Excommunicated several times, Frederick spent much of his career fighting the pope's forces. In the process he made so many concessions to the German princes that the emperor thenceforth had little power in Germany. Meanwhile, rulers of smaller states, such as England, France, and Castile-León, were increasing their power and authority.

Full-size maps show major historical developments and carry informative captions.

to kill the king, defeat his army, to take the kingdom.

Italy the Lombard king con-ile papacy in the center of the ally independent dukes in the y royal officers, the dukes of leto in fact ruled on their own many Lom-ics, others, t kings and The "offi-ombards in he ruler in n signal a major political event, the conversion of the Lombards to Catholic Christianity occurred nly around tury. Partly w develop-l kings, un-Franks, or ons, never enlisted the full support lar group of churchmen. ng united religious support, wer still had strengths. Chief he traditions of leadership as-al dynasty, the kings' military

Lombard Italy, Early Eighth Century

"Spot" maps offer geographical details right where you need them.

MAPPING THE WEST

Major Religions in the West, c. 1150
The broad washes of color on this map tell a striking story: by 1150, there were three major religions, each corresponding to a broad region. To the west, north of the Mediterranean Sea, Catholic Christianity held sway; to the east, the Greek Orthodox Church was ascendant; all along the southern Mediterranean, Islam triumphed. Only a few places defied this logic: one was a tiny outpost of Catholic crusaders who ruled over a largely Muslim population. What this map does not show, however, are the details: Jewish communities in many cities, lively varieties of Islamic beliefs within the Muslim world, communities of Coptic Christians in Egypt, and scattered groups of heretics in Catholic lands.

Mapping the West summary maps provide a snapshot of the West at the close of each chapter.

ere generally quite status, churchmen diction of Henry's ensuing contest be-op, Thomas Becket test battle between he twelfth century. years, with Becket erics"—clergy sus-—to come before nchmen murdered edral. The desecra-cket into a martyr. murder remained e general outcry to d. In the end, both ded to address the igious society. (See , this page.) ting with an impe-host half of France, was in the hands of t theoretically, vas-11.1.) In England, e felt everywhere rts that traveled the ntry. On the conti-ion, but rebellions

The Murder of Thomas Becket
Almost immediately after King Henry II's knights murdered Archbishop Thomas Becket in his church at Canterbury, Becket was viewed as a martyr. In this early depiction of the event, one of the murderers knocks off Becket's cap, while another hits the arm of Becket's supporter, who holds the bishop's cross-staff. (British Library, London, UK/The Bridgeman Art Library.)

■ For more help analyzing this image, see the visual activity for this chapter in the Online Study Guide at bedfordstmartins.com/hunt.

Web references direct you to visual activities designed to help you analyze images.

Tools to help you remember the chapter's main points and do further research

Conclusion ●

Augustus created the principate and the Pax Romana by installing a disguised monarchy while insisting that he was restoring the republic. He succeeded because he ensured the army's loyalty and exploited the traditional patron-client system. The principate made the emperor the army's and the people's patron. Provincials fo[und] arrangement acceptable because it repl[aced] kind of top-down government that [they had] grown used to before Roman conquest. [The impe]rial cult provided a focus for building an[d maintain]ing loyalty to the emperor.

So long as the emperors had enoug[h revenue] to keep their millions of clients satisfie[d, peace] prevailed. They provided food to the p[oor and] baths and arenas for public entertainm[ent, and] paid their troops well. The emperors o[f the first] and second centuries expanded the m[ilitary to] protect their distant territories stretch[ing from] Britain to North Africa to Syria. By the se[cond cen]tury, peace and prosperity had created a[n age some call a] Golden Age. Long-term financial difficul[ties loomed,] however, because the army, now concentrating on defense, no longer brought money in through frequent conquests. Severe inflation made the situation desperate. Since the elites could no longer meet the demand for increased taxes without draining their fortunes, they lost their public-spiritedness and avoided their communal responsibilities. Loyalty to the state became too expensive.

The emergence of Christianity added to the instability because Roman officials doubted Chris-

Read the **chapter conclusions** to review how the chapters' most important themes and topics fit together and learn how they connect to the next chapter.

FOR FURTHER EXPLORATION ●

■ **For suggested references, including Web sites, for topics in this chapter**, see page SR-1 at the end of the book.

■ **For additional primary-source material from this period**, see Chapter 6 in *Sources of THE MAKING OF THE WEST*, Third Edition.

■ **For Web sites and documents related to topics in this chapter,** see *Make History* at bedfordstmartins.com/hunt.

For **print and Web resources for papers or further study**, consult the **For Further Exploration** boxes at the end of each chapter, which guide you to annotated lists of suggested references, additional primary-source materials, and related Web resources.

Answer the analytical **Making Connections** questions, which will help you link ideas within or across chapters.

Test your knowledge of the important concepts and historical figures in the **Key Terms and People** lists, which include page references to the text discussion and **running glossary** definition. These definitions are also in the **glossary** at the end of the book.

Answer the **Review Questions**, which repeat the chapter's end-of-section comprehension prompts.

Visit the **free online study guide**, which provides quizzes and activities to help you master the chapter material.

Review the **Important Events** chronologies to make sure you understand the relationships between major events in the chapter and their sequence.

CHAPTER REVIEW

KEY TERMS AND PEOPLE

principate (164)	Christ (181)
Pax Romana (164)	martyr (183)
Augustus (165)	apostolic succession (184)
praetorian guard (166)	orthodoxy (184)
Julio-Claudians (173)	heresy (184)
Colosseum (175)	Neoplatonism (188)
decurions (177)	debasement of coinage
Romanization (177)	(189)

REVIEW QUESTIONS

1. How did the peace gained through Augustus's "restoration of the republic" affect Romans' lives?

2. In the early Roman Empire, what was life like in the cities and in the country for the elite and for ordinary people?

3. Which factors supported the growth of Christianity, and which opposed it?

4. What were the causes and the effects of the Roman crisis in the third century C.E.?

MAKING CONNECTIONS

1. What were the similarities and differences between the crisis in the first century B.C.E. that undermined the republic and the crisis in the third century C.E. that undermined the principate?

2. If you had been a first-century Roman emperor under the principate, what would you have done about the Christians and why? What if you had been a third-century emperor?

For practice quizzes, a customized study plan, and other study tools, see the Online Study Guide at bedfordstmartins.com/hunt.

IMPORTANT EVENTS

30 B.C.E.	Octavian (the future Augustus) conquers Ptolemaic Egypt	70–90 C.E.	New Testament Gospels are written
27 B.C.E.	Augustus inaugurates the *principate*	80s C.E.	Domitian leads campaigns against multiethnic invaders on northern frontiers
30 C.E.	Jesus crucified in Jerusalem	161–180 C.E.	Multiethnic bands attack the northern frontiers
64 C.E.	Much of Rome burns in mammoth fire; Nero blames Christians	212 C.E.	Caracalla extends Roman citizenship to almost all free inhabitants of the provinces
69 C.E.	Civil war during the Year of the Four Emperors	249–251 C.E.	Decius persecutes Christians
70 C.E.	Titus captures Jerusalem and destroys the Jewish temple	230s–280s C.E.	Third-century crisis

How to Read Primary Sources

In each chapter of this textbook you will find many primary sources to broaden your understanding of the development of the West. Primary sources refer to firsthand, contemporary accounts or direct evidence about a particular topic. For example, speeches, letters, diaries, song lyrics, and newspaper articles are all primary sources that historians use to construct accounts of the past. Nonwritten materials such as maps, paintings, artifacts, and even architecture and music can also be primary sources. Both types of historical documents in this textbook — written and visual — provide a glimpse into the lives of the men and women who influenced or were influenced by the course of Western history.

To guide your interpretation of any source, you should begin by asking several basic questions, listed below, as starting points for observing, analyzing, and interpreting the past. Your answers should prompt further questions of your own.

1. **Who is the author?** Who wrote or created the material? What was his or her authority? (Personal? institutional?) Did the author have specialized knowledge or experience? If you are reading a written document, how would you describe the author's tone of voice? (Formal, personal, angry?)

2. **Who is the audience?** Who were the intended readers, listeners, or viewers? How does the intended audience affect the ways that the author presents ideas?

3. **What are the main ideas?** What are the main points that the author is trying to convey? Can you detect any underlying assumptions of values or attitudes? How does the form or medium affect the meaning of this document?

4. **In what context was the document created?** From when and where does the document originate? What was the interval between the initial problem or event and this document, which responded to it? Through what form or medium was the document communicated? (For example, a newspaper, a government record, an illustration.) What contemporary events or conditions might have affected the creation of the document?

5. **What's missing?** What's missing or cannot be learned from this source, and what might this omission reveal? Are there other sources that might fill in the gaps?

Now consider these questions as you read "Columbus Describes His First Voyage (1493)," the document on the next page. Compare your answers to the sample observations provided.

DOCUMENT

Columbus Describes His First Voyage (1493)

In this famous letter to Raphael Sanchez, treasurer to his patrons, Ferdinand and Isabella, Columbus recounts his initial journey to the Bahamas, Cuba, and Hispaniola (today Haiti and the Dominican Republic), and tells of his achievements. This passage reflects the first contact between native Americans and Europeans; already the themes of trade, subjugation, gold, and conversion emerge in Columbus's own words.

Indians would give whatever the seller required; . . . Thus they bartered, like idiots, cotton and gold for fragments of bows, glasses, bottles, and jars; which I forbad as being unjust, and myself gave them many beautiful and acceptable articles which I had brought with me, taking nothing from them in return; I did this in order that I might the more easily conciliate them, that they might be led to become Christians, and be inclined to entertain a regard for the King and Queen, our Princes and all Spaniards, and that I might induce them to take an interest in seeking out, and collecting, and delivering to us such things as they possessed in abundance, but which we greatly needed. They practise no kind of idolatry, but have a firm belief that all strength and power, and indeed all good things, are in heaven, and that I had descended from thence with these ships and sailors, and under this impression was I received after they had thrown aside their fears. Nor are they slow or stupid, but of very clear understanding; and those men who have crossed to the neighbouring islands give an admirable description of everything they observed; but they never saw any people clothed, nor any ships like ours. On my arrival at that sea, I had taken some Indians by force from the first island that I came to, in order that they might learn our language, and communicate to us what they know respecting the country; which plan succeeded excellently, and was a great advantage to us, for in a short time, either by gestures and signs, or by words, we were enabled to understand each other. These men are still travelling with me, and although they have been with us now a long time, they continue to entertain the idea that I have descended from heaven.

Source: Christopher Columbus, *Four Voyages to the New World.* Translated by R. H. Major (New York: Corinth Books, 1961), 8–9.

1. **Who is the author?** The title and headnote that precede each document contain information about the authorship and date of its creation. In this case, the Italian explorer Christopher Columbus is the author. His letter describes events in which he was both an eyewitness and a participant.

2. **Who is the audience?** Columbus sent the letter to Raphael Sanchez, treasurer to Ferdinand and Isabella — someone who Columbus knew would be keenly interested in the fate of his patrons' investment. Because the letter was also a public document written to a crown official, Columbus would have expected a wider audience beyond Sanchez. How might his letter have differed had it been written to a friend?

3. **What are the main ideas?** In this segment, Columbus describes his encounter with the native people. He speaks of his desire to establish good relations by treating them fairly, and he offers his impressions of their intelligence and naiveté — characteristics he implies will prove useful to Europeans. He also expresses an interest in converting them to Christianity and making them loyal subjects of the crown.

4. **In what context was the document created?** Columbus wrote the letter in 1493, within six months of his first voyage. He would have been eager to announce the success of his endeavor.

5. **What's missing?** Columbus's letter provides just one view of the encounter. We do not have a corresponding account from the native Americans' perspective nor from anyone else travelling with Columbus. With no corroboration evidence, how reliable is this description?

Note: You can use these same questions to analyze visual images. Start by determining who created the image — whether it's a painting, photograph, sculpture, map, or artifact — and when it was made. Then consider the audience for whom the artist might have intended the work and how viewers might have reacted. Consult the text for information about the time period, and look for visual cues such as color, artistic style, and use of space to determine the central idea of the work. As you read, consult the captions in this book to help you evaluate the images and to ask more questions of your own.

About the Authors

LYNN HUNT, Eugen Weber Professor of Modern European History at the University of California, Los Angeles, received her B.A. from Carleton College and her M.A. and Ph.D. from Stanford University. She is the author of *Revolution and Urban Politics in Provincial France* (1978); *Politics, Culture, and Class in the French Revolution* (1984); *The Family Romance of the French Revolution* (1992); and *Inventing Human Rights* (2007). She is also the coauthor of *Telling the Truth about History* (1994); coauthor of *Liberty, Equality, Fraternity: Exploring the French Revolution* (2001, with CD-ROM); editor of *The New Cultural History* (1989); editor and translator of *The French Revolution and Human Rights* (1996); and coeditor of *Histories: French Constructions of the Past* (1995), *Beyond the Cultural Turn* (1999), and *Human Rights and Revolutions* (2000). She has been awarded fellowships by the Guggenheim Foundation and the National Endowment for the Humanities and is a fellow of the American Academy of Arts and Sciences. She served as president of the American Historical Association in 2002.

THOMAS R. MARTIN, Jeremiah O'Connor Professor in Classics at the College of the Holy Cross, earned his B.A. at Princeton University and his M.A. and Ph.D. at Harvard University. He is the author of *Sovereignty and Coinage in Classical Greece* (1985) and *Ancient Greece* (1996, 2000) and is one of the originators of *Perseus: Interactive Sources and Studies on Ancient Greece* (1992, 1996, and www.perseus.tufts.edu), which, among other awards, was named the EDUCOM Best Software in Social Sciences (History) in 1992. He serves on the editorial board of STOA (www.stoa.org) and as codirector of its DEMOS project (online resources on ancient Athenian democracy). A recipient of fellowships from the National Endowment for the Humanities and the American Council of Learned Societies, he is currently conducting research on the comparative historiography of ancient Greece and ancient China.

BARBARA H. ROSENWEIN, professor of history at Loyola University Chicago, earned her B.A., M.A., and Ph.D. at the University of Chicago. She is the author of *Rhinoceros Bound: Cluny in the Tenth Century* (1982); *To Be the Neighbor of Saint Peter: The Social Meaning of Cluny's Property, 909–1049* (1989); *Negotiating Space: Power, Restraint, and Privileges of Immunity in Early Medieval Europe* (1999); *A Short History of the Middle Ages* (2001); *Emotional Communities in the Early Middle Ages* (2006); and *Reading the Middle Ages: Sources from Europe, Byzantium, and the Islamic World* (2006). She is the editor of *Anger's Past: The Social Uses of an Emotion in the Middle Ages* (1998) and coeditor of *Debating the Middle Ages: Issues and Readings* (1998) and *Monks and Nuns, Saints and Outcasts: Religion in Medieval Society* (2000). A recipient of Guggenheim and National Endowment for the Humanities fellowships, she is currently working on a general history of emotions in the West.

R. PO-CHIA HSIA, Edwin Erle Sparks Professor of History at Pennsylvania State University, received his B.A. from Swarthmore College and his M.A. and Ph.D. from Yale University. He is the author of *Society and Religion in Münster, 1535–1618* (1984); *The Myth of Ritual Murder: Jews and Magic in Reformation Germany* (1988); *Social Discipline in the Reformation: Central Europe 1550–1750* (1989); *Trent 1475: Stories of a Ritual Murder Trial* (1992); *The World of the Catholic Renewal* (1997); and *Noble Patronage and Jesuit Missions: Maria Theresa von Fugger-Wellenburg (1690–1762) and Jesuit Missionaries to China and Vietnam* (2006). He has edited or coedited *In and Out of the Ghetto: Jewish-Gentile Relations in Late Medieval and Early Modern Germany* (1995); *The German People and the Reformation* (1998); *Calvinism and Religious Toleration in the Dutch Golden Age* (2002); *A Companion to the Reformation World* (Blackwell Companion Series, 2004); *Cultural Translation in Early Modern Europe* (2007); and *Cambridge History of*

XXXII ABOUT THE AUTHORS

Christianity, Volume 6, *Reform and Expansion, 1500–1660* (2007). An academician at the Academia Sinica, Taiwan, he has also been awarded fellowships by the Woodrow Wilson International Society of Scholars, the National Endowment for the Humanities, the Guggenheim Foundation, the Davis Center of Princeton University, the Mellon Foundation, the American Council of Learned Societies, and the American Academy in Berlin. Currently he is working on the cultural contacts between Europe and Asia between the sixteenth and eighteenth centuries.

BONNIE G. SMITH, Board of Governors Professor of History at Rutgers University, earned her B.A. at Smith College and her Ph.D. at the University of Rochester. She is the author of *Ladies of the Leisure Class* (1981); *Confessions of a Concierge: Madame Lucie's History of Twentieth-Century France* (1985); *Changing Lives:* *Women in European History Since 1700* (1989); *The Gender of History: Men, Women, and Historical Practice* (1998); *Imperialism* (2000); and *Europe in the Contemporary World: 1900 to the Present* (2007). She is also the coauthor and translator of *What Is Property?* (1994); editor of *Global Feminisms since 1945* (2000) and *Women's History in Global Perspective* (3 vols. 2004–2005); coeditor of *History and the Texture of Modern Life: Selected Writings of Lucy Maynard Salmon, Gendering Disability* (2004); and general editor of *Oxford Encyclopedia of Women in World History* (4 vols. 2007). She has received fellowships from the Guggenheim Foundation, the National Endowment for the Humanities, the National Humanities Center, the Davis Center of Princeton University, and the American Council of Learned Societies. Currently she is studying the globalization of European culture since the seventeenth century.

Global Encounters and Religious Reforms
1492–1560

In Tlaxcala, New Spain (present-day Mexico), Indians newly converted to Christianity performed a pageant organized in 1539 by Catholic missionaries. The festivities celebrated a truce recently concluded between the Habsburg emperor Charles V and the French king Francis I. *The Conquest of Jerusalem*, as the drama was called, featured a combined army from Spain and New Spain fighting to protect the pope, defeat the Muslims, and win control of the holy city of Jerusalem. In the play, a miracle saves the Christian soldiers, and the Muslims give up and convert to Christianity. Although it is hard to imagine what the Indians made of this celebration of places and people far away, the event reveals a great deal about the Europeans: still preoccupied with battling the Muslims and still fighting among themselves, Europeans now pursued their interests worldwide. Yet even as their explorations and conquests transformed the New World, disputes over the "true" religion divided Europeans into hostile camps. Catholic missionaries saw their success in converting Indians as a sign of God's favor in the struggle against the Protestant reformers, who had begun to spread their message in Europe not long before the pageant in Tlaxcala took place.

Led first by the Portuguese and then Spanish explorers, Europeans sailed into contact with peoples and cultures hitherto unknown to Latin Christendom. Motivated by the desire to find gold, win personal glory, extend the reach of Christianity, and chart the unknown, European

Cortés

In this Spanish depiction of the landing of Hernán Cortés in Mexico in 1519, the ships and arms of the Spanish are a commanding presence, especially in comparison to the nakedness and lack of firearms among the Indians and the kneeling stance of their leader. A Spanish artist painted this miniature, which measures only 6⅛ inches by 4¼ inches. It probably accompanied an account of the Spanish conquest of Mexico. On the back of the picture is a small map of the west coast of Europe and Africa and the east coast of Central America. Europeans relied on such images, and especially on maps, to help them make sense of all the new information flooding into Europe from faraway places. Many Spaniards viewed Cortés's conquests as a sign of divine favor in a time of religious division. Some even believed that Cortés was born the same day, or at least the same year, as Martin Luther, the German monk who had initiated the Protestant Reformation just two years before Cortés's landing (in fact, Luther was born two years before Cortés). *(Erich Lessing/Art Resource, NY.)*

voyagers subjugated native peoples, declared their control over vast new lands, and established a new system of slavery linking Africa and the New World. Millions of Indians died of diseases unknowingly imported by the Europeans. The discovery of new crops—corn, potatoes, tobacco, coffee, and cocoa—and of gold and silver mines brought new patterns of consumption, and new objects of conflict, to Europe. This spiral of changes in ecology, agriculture, and social patterns is so momentous that historians now call it the Columbian exchange after Christopher Columbus, who started the process.

The invention of the printing press in the 1440s helped spread news of the European explorations, but it had an even more significant impact when it hastened the breakup of Christian unity under the impact of the Protestant Reformation. After the German Catholic monk Martin Luther criticized corrupt church practices in 1517, printed broadsheets, pamphlets, and books quickly spread his message and helped make the Protestant break with Roman Catholicism permanent. Religious division soon engulfed the German states and reached into Switzerland, France, and England. Responding to the desire for reform that fed the Protestant movement, Catholics undertook their own renewal. When radical Protestants threatened to overthrow the social and political order, more mainstream Protestants, like Catholics, insisted that the state oversee religious, moral, and social matters.

Confrontations between Protestants and Catholics complicated the long-standing rivalries between princes. Traditional sources of enmity between the Christian powers did not disappear, and the Ottomans continued their thrust into Hungary. Now, however, the Catholic Habsburg emperor had to wage war against Protestant German princes and religious divisions threatened the stability of the monarchy in England and Scotland. Divisions between Catholics and Protestants

would shape the course of European history for several generations.

> **FOCUS QUESTION:** Why did Christian unity break up in Europe just when Europeans began to expand their influence overseas in dramatic fashion?

Widening Horizons

The maritime explorations of Portugal and Spain brought Europe to the attention of the rest of the world. Fourteenth-century Mongols had been more interested in conquering China and Persia—lands with sophisticated cultures—than in invading Europe; Persian historians of the early fifteenth century dismissed Europeans as "barbaric Franks"; and China's Ming dynasty rulers, who sent maritime expeditions to Southeast Asia and East Africa around 1400, seemed unaware of the Europeans, even though Marco Polo and other Italian merchants had appeared at the court of the preceding Mongol Yuan dynasty. By the end of the fifteenth century, in contrast, Europeans could no longer be ignored. The Portuguese and Spanish, inspired by a crusading spirit against Islam and by riches to be won through trade in spices and gold, sailed across the Atlantic, Indian, and Pacific oceans. The English, French, and Dutch followed a century later, creating a new global exchange of people, crops, and diseases that would shape the modern world. As a result of these European expeditions, the people of the Americas for the first time confronted forces that threatened to destroy not only their culture but even their existence.

Portuguese Explorations

The first phase of European overseas expansion began in 1433 with Portuguese exploration of the West African coast and culminated in 1519–1522

■ 1492 Columbus reaches the Americas

■ 1516 Erasmus publishes Greek
New Testament; More, *Utopia*

1490	1500	1510	1520

■ 1494 Italian Wars begin;
Treaty of Tordesillas

■ 1517 Luther composes ninety-five theses

■ 1520 Luther publishes
three treatises; Zwingli
breaks from Rome

with Spanish circumnavigation of the globe. Looking back, the sixteenth-century Spanish historian Francisco López de Gómora described the Iberian maritime voyages to the East and West Indies as "the greatest event since the creation of the world, apart from the incarnation and death of him who created it."

The Portuguese hoped to find a sea route to the spice-producing lands of South and Southeast Asia in order to bypass the Ottoman Turks, who controlled the traditional land routes between Europe and Asia. Rumors of vast gold mines in West Africa and the legend of a mysterious Christian kingdom established by Prester John and surrounded by Muslims drew sailors to voyages despite the possibilities of shipwreck and death. Success in the voyages of exploration depended on several technological breakthroughs, including the caravel, a small, easily maneuvered three-masted ship that used triangular lateen sails adapted from the Arabs. (The sails permitted a ship to tack against headwinds.) Prince Henry the Navigator of Portugal (1394–1460) personally financed many voyages with revenues from a noble crusading order. The first triumphs of the Portuguese attracted a host of Christian, Jewish, and even Arab sailors, astronomers, and cartographers to the service of Prince Henry and King John II (r. 1481–1495). They compiled better tide calendars and books of sailing directions for pilots that enabled sailors to venture farther into the oceans and reduced — though did not eliminate — the dangers of sea travel.

Searching for gold and then slaves, the Portuguese gradually established forts down the West African coast. In 1487–1488, they reached the Cape of Good Hope at the tip of Africa; ten years later, Vasco da Gama led a Portuguese fleet around the cape and reached as far as Calicut, India, the center of the spice trade. His return to Lisbon with twelve pieces of Chinese porcelain for the Portuguese king set off two centuries of porcelain mania. Until the early eighteenth century, only the Chinese knew how to produce porcelain (in vases or dinnerware), so over the next two hundred years Western merchants would import no fewer than seventy million pieces of porcelain, still known today as "china." In 1512, Ferdinand Magellan, a Portuguese sailor in Spanish service, led the first expedition to circumnavigate the globe. By 1517, a chain of Portuguese forts dotted the Indian Ocean — at Mozambique, Hormuz (at the mouth of the Persian Gulf), Goa (in India), Colombo (in modern Sri Lanka), and Malacca (modern Malaysia) (Map 14.1).

The Voyages of Columbus

One of many sailors inspired by the Portuguese explorations, **Christopher Columbus** (1451–1506) opened an entirely new direction for discovery. Most likely born in Genoa of Italian parents, Columbus sailed the West African coast in Portuguese service between 1476 and 1485. Fifteenth-century Europeans already knew that the world was round (see "Seeing History," page 424). Columbus had studied *The Travels of Marco Polo*, written more than a century earlier, and wanted to sail west to reach "the lands of the Great Khan," unaware that the Mongol Empire had already collapsed in eastern Asia. Hugely underestimating the distance of such a voyage, Columbus dreamed of finding a new route to the East's gold and spices. After the Portuguese refused to fund his plan, Columbus turned to the Spanish monarchs Isabella of Castile and Ferdinand of Aragon, who agreed to finance his venture.

On August 3, 1492, with ninety men on board two caravels and one larger merchant ship for carrying supplies, Columbus set sail westward. His

---

Christopher Columbus: An Italian sailor (1451–1506) who opened up the New World by sailing west across the Atlantic in search of a route to Asia.

■ 1525 German Peasants' War

    ■ 1527 Charles V's imperial troops sack Rome   ■ 1540 Jesuits (Society of Jesus) established

            ■ 1529 Colloquy of Marburg   ■ 1545–1563 Catholic Council of Trent

■ 1555 Peace of Augsburg

    ■ 1559 Treaty of Cateau-Cambrésis

1530	**1540**	**1550**	**1560**

    ■ 1534 Henry VIII breaks with Rome;   ■ 1547 Charles V defeats Protestants at Mühlberg
Affair of the Placards in France

        ■ 1536 Calvin, *Institutes of the Christian Religion*

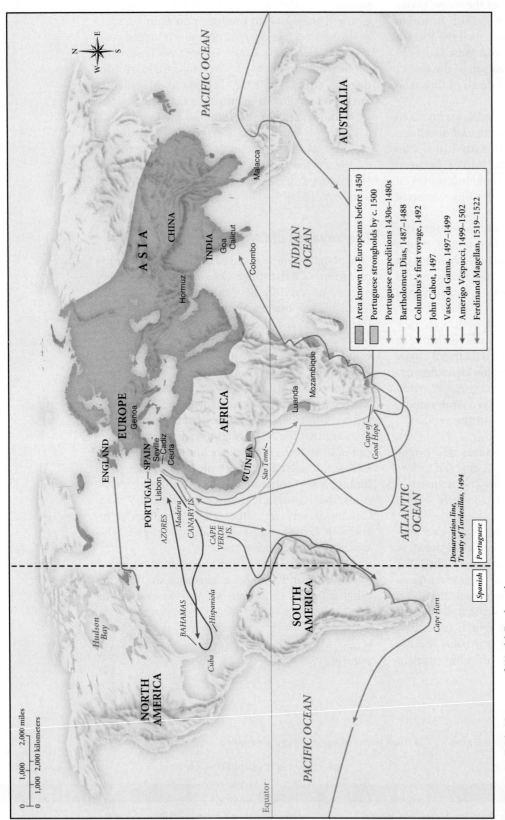

MAP 14.1 Early Voyages of World Exploration

Over the course of the fifteenth and early sixteenth centuries, European shipping dominated the Atlantic Ocean after the pioneering voyages of the Portuguese, who also first sailed around the Cape of Good Hope to the Indian Ocean and the Cape Horn to the Pacific. The search for spices and the need to circumnavigate the Ottoman Empire inspired these voyages.

Columbus Describes His First Voyage (1493)

In this famous letter to Raphael Sanchez, treasurer to his patrons, Ferdinand and Isabella, Columbus recounts his initial journey to the Bahamas, Cuba, and Hispaniola (today Haiti and the Dominican Republic), and tells of his achievements. This passage reflects the first contact between native Americans and Europeans; already the themes of trade, subjugation, gold, and conversion emerge in Columbus's own words.

Indians would give whatever the seller required; . . . Thus they bartered, like idiots, cotton and gold for fragments of bows, glasses, bottles, and jars; which I forbad as being unjust, and myself gave them many beautiful and acceptable articles which I had brought with me, taking nothing from them in return; I did this in order that I might the more easily conciliate them, that they might be led to become Christians, and be inclined to entertain a regard for the King and Queen, our Princes and all Spaniards, and that I might induce them to take an interest in seeking out, and collecting, and delivering to us such things as they possessed in abundance, but which we greatly needed. They practise no kind of idolatry, but have a firm belief that all strength and power, and indeed all good things, are in heaven, and that I had descended from thence with these ships and sailors, and under this impression was I received after they had thrown aside their fears. Nor are they slow or stupid, but of very clear understanding; and those men who have crossed to the neighbouring islands give an admirable description of everything they observed; but they never saw any people clothed, nor any ships like ours. On my arrival at that sea, I had taken some Indians by force from the first island that I came to, in order that they might learn our language, and communicate to us what they know respecting the country; which plan succeeded excellently, and was a great advantage to us, for in a short time, either by gestures and signs, or by words, we were enabled to understand each other. These men are still travelling with me, and although they have been with us now a long time, they continue to entertain the idea that I have descended from heaven.

Source: Christopher Columbus, *Four Voyages to the New World.* Translated by R. H. Major (New York: Corinth Books, 1961), 8–9.

contract stipulated that he would claim Castilian sovereignty over any new land and inhabitants and share any profits with the crown. Reaching what is today the Bahamas on October 12, Columbus mistook the islands to be part of the East Indies, not far from Japan. As the Spaniards explored the Caribbean islands, they encountered communities of peaceful Indians, the Arawaks, who were awed by the Europeans' military technology, not to mention their appearance. Although many positive entries in the ship's log testified to Columbus's personal goodwill toward the Indians, the Europeans' objectives were clear: find gold, subjugate the Indians, and propagate Christianity. (See Document, "Columbus Describes His First Voyage," above.)

Excited by the prospect of easy riches, many flocked to join Columbus's second voyage. When Columbus departed Cádiz in September 1493, he commanded a fleet of seventeen ships carrying some fifteen hundred men, many of whom believed that all they had to do was "to load the gold into the ships." Failing to find the imagined gold mines and spices, Columbus and his crew began capturing Caribs, enemies of the Arawaks, with the intention of bringing them back as slaves. In 1494, Columbus proposed setting up a regular slave trade based in Hispaniola. The Spaniards exported enslaved Indians to Spain, and slave traders sold them in Seville. When the Spanish monarchs realized the vast potential for material gain of their new dominions, they asserted direct royal authority by sending officials and priests to the Americas, which were named after the Italian Amerigo Vespucci, who led a voyage across the Atlantic in 1499–1502.

To head off looming conflicts between the Spanish and the Portuguese, Pope Alexander VI helped negotiate the Treaty of Tordesillas of 1494. It divided the Atlantic world between the two maritime powers, reserving for Portugal the West African coast and the route to India and giving Spain the oceans and lands to the west (see Map 14.1). The agreement allowed Portugal to claim Brazil in 1500, when it was accidentally "discovered" by Pedro Alvares Cabral (1467–1520) on a voyage to India.

A New Era in Slavery

The European voyages of discovery initiated a new era in slavery, both by expanding the economic scale of slave labor and by attaching race and color to servitude. Slavery had existed since antiquity and flourished in many parts of the world. Some slaves were captured in war or by piracy; others—

Expanding Geographic Knowledge: World Maps in an Age of Exploration

On the eve of Christopher Columbus's voyages, most Europeans knew that the world was round and many shared Columbus's view that new routes to Asia and its riches could be found by sailing west. Beyond that, however, geographic knowledge of what precisely lay on the other side of the Atlantic was sketchy at best. Even those regions familiar to Europe through trade and exploration—Africa and parts of Asia—were often shown inaccurately on maps of the day.

The hand-colored map at the top produced by a German geographer, Henricus Martellus, depicts the world as Europeans knew it just before Columbus's first voyage. How accurate is its rendition of Europe, the Mediterranean, and Africa? Note that the Americas are not shown as a separate continent, but rather are joined to the Asian landmass on the far right. (Scholars have identified several major Latin American rivers, including the Orinooko and the Amazon in part of lower right-hand quadrant of the map.) How does this map help explain Columbus's mistake about where he had landed in 1492? What else does it tell you about Europeans' perceptions of the world in this period?

By 1570, when Abraham Ortelius's map was printed, European knowledge of world geography had grown by leaps and bounds thanks to the voyages of exploration. Ortelius, a well-traveled and prominent geographer and cartographer, included this map in his Theatrum Orbis Terrarum (Theater of the World), considered to be the first modern atlas. Judging from this map, what areas of the world have come into greater focus? What areas are still inaccurately portrayed and rudimentary in some respects? How might you account for that? What advantages do accurate maps offer you, beyond knowing where you are headed? What else does the later map reveal about Europeans' knowledge of the world after less than a century of exploration?

World Map by Henricus Martellus, 1489. *(The Art Archive/British Library.)*

World Map by Abraham Ortelius, 1570. *(By permission of the British Library © British Library Board. All Rights Reserved. MAPS C2.c.3.)*

Africans — were sold by other Africans and Bedouin traders to Christian buyers; in western Asia, parents sold their children out of poverty into servitude; and many in the Balkans became slaves when their land was devastated by Ottoman invasions. Slaves could be Greek, Slav, European, African, or Turkish. Many served as domestics in European cities of the Mediterranean such as Barcelona or Venice. Others sweated as galley slaves in Ottoman and Christian fleets. Still others worked as agricultural laborers on Mediterranean islands. In the Ottoman army, slaves even formed an important elite contingent.

From the fifteenth century onward, Africans increasingly filled the ranks of slaves. Exploiting warfare between groups within West Africa, the Portuguese traded in gold and "pieces," as African slaves were called, a practice condemned at home by some conscientious clergy. Manoel Severim de Faria, for example, observed that "one cannot yet see any good effect resulting from so much butchery; for this is not the way in which commerce can flourish and the preaching of the gospel progress." Critical voices, however, could not deny the potential for profits that the slave trade brought to Portugal. Most slaves toiled in the sugar plantations of the Portuguese Atlantic islands and in Brazil. A fortunate few had somewhat easier lives as domestic servants in Portugal, where African freedmen and slaves, some thirty-five thousand in the early sixteenth century, constituted almost 3 percent of the population, a percentage that was much higher than in other European countries.

In the Americas, slavery would expand enormously in the following centuries. Even outspoken critics of colonial brutality toward indigenous peoples defended the development of African slavery. The Spanish Dominican Bartolomé de Las Casas (1474–1566), for example, argued that Africans were constitutionally more suitable for labor than native Americans and should therefore be imported to the plantations in the Americas to relieve the indigenous peoples, who were being worked to death.

Conquering the New World

In 1500, on the eve of European invasion, the native peoples of the Americas lived in a great diver-

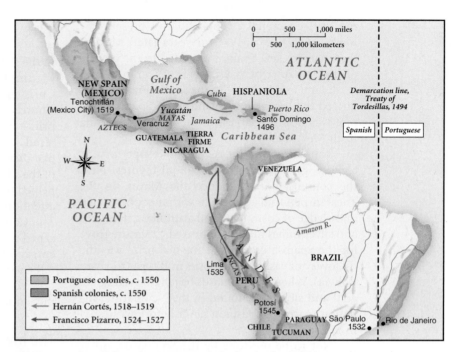

MAP 14.2 Spanish and Portuguese Colonies in the Americas, 1492–1560
The discovery of precious metals fueled the Spanish and Portuguese explorations and settlements of Central and South America, establishing the foundations of European colonial empires in the New World.

sity of social and political arrangements. Some were nomads roaming large, sparsely inhabited territories; others practiced agriculture in complexly organized states. Among the settled peoples, the largest groupings could be found in the Mexican and Peruvian highlands. Combining an elaborate religious culture with a rigid social and political hierarchy, the Aztecs in Mexico and the Incas in Peru ruled over subjugated Indian populations in their respective empires. From their large urban capitals, the Aztecs and Incas controlled large swaths of land and could be ruthless as conquerors.

The Spanish explorers organized their expeditions to the mainland of the Americas from a base in the Caribbean (Map 14.2). Two prominent commanders, **Hernán Cortés** (1485–1547) and Francisco Pizarro (c. 1475–1541), gathered men and arms and set off in search of gold. With them came Catholic priests intending to bring Christianity to supposedly uncivilized peoples. Some natives who resented their subjugation by the Aztecs joined Cortés and his soldiers. With a band of fewer than two hundred men, Cortés captured

---

Hernán Cortés: A Spanish explorer (1485–1547) who captured the Aztec capital, Tenochtitlán (present-day Mexico City), in 1519.

the Aztec capital, Tenochtitlán (present-day Mexico City), in 1519. Two years later, Mexico, then named New Spain, was added to the empire of the new ruler of Spain, Charles V, grandson of Ferdinand and Isabella. To the south, Pizarro conquered the Peruvian highlands. The Spanish Empire was now the largest in the world, stretching from Mexico to Chile.

The Aztecs and Incas fell to the superior war technology of the Spanish conquistadores. Next the conquistadores subdued the Mayas on the Yucatán peninsula, a people with a sophisticated knowledge of cosmology and arithmetic. The gold and silver mines in Mexico proved a treasure trove for the Spanish crown, but the real prize was the discovery of vast silver deposits in Potosí (today in Bolivia). When the Spaniards began importing the gold and silver they found in the New World, inflation soared in a fashion never before witnessed in Europe.

Not to be outdone by the Spaniards, other European powers joined the scramble for gold in the New World. In North America, the French went in search of a "northwest passage" to China. The French wanted to establish settlements in what became Canada, but the climate and the hostility of the indigenous peoples defeated them. Permanent European settlements in Canada and the present-day United States would succeed only in the seventeenth century, and by then the English had entered the contest for world mastery. Even before the French and the English, the Dutch entered the colonial competition. After they broke away from Spain late in the sixteenth century, the Dutch set about systematically and aggressively taking over Spanish and Portuguese trade routes. By the mid-seventeenth century, they had become the wealthiest people (per capita) in the world.

The discovery of the Americas resulted in a significant global movement of peoples, animals, plants, manufactured goods, and precious metals. Tobacco and cocoa were among the exotic items brought from the Americas to Europe. Voyages to the New World also brought diseases from Europe to the unsuspecting peoples of America. Without natural immunity, the Amerindians died in catastrophic numbers. Within fifty years of Columbus's first voyage, the indigenous populations of the Caribbean Islands had been wiped out.

REVIEW: Which European countries led the way in maritime exploration, and what were their motives?

The Protestant Reformation

In the sixteenth century, religious reformers led by Martin Luther shattered the unity of Western Christendom, supplied by the Roman Catholic Church since the fourth century. The invention of printing with movable type proved crucial to the rapid spread of the Protestant message. The popular piety that swept Europe in the closing decades of the 1400s, along with Christian humanism, also helped pave the way for the reformers by focusing attention on corrupt practices and clerical abuses. The Catholic church might nonetheless have escaped a schism had it not been for the drive, talent, and theological brilliance of Luther and other reformers such as Huldrych Zwingli and John Calvin. They turned reform into protest—hence the name of their movement, Protestantism.

The Invention of Printing

Printing with movable type, developed in the 1440s by Johannes Gutenberg, a German goldsmith, marked a revolutionary departure from the old practice of copying works by hand or stamping pages with individually carved wood blocks. Printing itself predated movable type: the Chinese had been printing by woodblock since the tenth century, and woodcut pictures made their appearance in Europe in the early fifteenth century. Movable type, however, allowed entire manuscripts to be printed more quickly. Single letters, made in metal molds, could be emptied out of a frame and new ones inserted to print each new page. Also, the large-scale production of paper had paved the way for the invention of printing. Papermaking came to Europe from China via Arab intermediaries. By the fourteenth century, paper mills in Italy were producing paper that was more fragile but also much cheaper than parchment or vellum, the animal skins that Europeans had previously used for writing.

The invention of movable type in the West no doubt owed something to the twenty-six-character alphabets found in most European languages; setting twenty-six characters in metal type was much easier than trying to set the hundreds or even thousands of different picture-like characters that made up written Chinese. (See Printing Press, page 427.) In 1467, two German printers established the first press in Rome; within five years, they had produced twelve thousand volumes, a feat that in the past would have required a thousand scribes working full-time.

In the 1490s, the German city of Frankfurt became an international meeting place for printers and booksellers, establishing a book fair that remains an unbroken tradition to this day. Early printed books attracted an elite audience; their expense made them inaccessible to most literate people, who comprised a minority of the population in any case. Gutenberg's famous two-volume Latin Bible was a luxury item, and only 185 copies were printed. Gutenberg Bibles remain today a treasure that only the greatest libraries possess.

The invention of mechanical printing dramatically increased the speed at which knowledge could be transmitted and freed individuals from having to memorize everything that they learned. Printed books and pamphlets, even one-page flyers, might create a wider community of scholars no longer dependent on personal patronage or church sponsorship for texts. Printing thus encouraged the free expression and exchange of ideas, and its disruptive potential did not go unnoticed by political and religious authorities. Rulers and bishops in the German states, the birthplace of the printing industry, moved quickly to issue censorship regulations, but their efforts could not prevent the outbreak of the Protestant Reformation.

Popular Piety and Christian Humanism

The Christianizing of Europe had taken many centuries to complete, and by 1500 most people in Europe believed devoutly. However, the vast majority of them had little knowledge of Catholic doctrine. More popular forms of piety such as processions, festivals, and marvelous tales of saints' miracles captivated ordinary believers.

Urban merchants and artisans, more likely than the general population to be literate and critical of their local priests, yearned for a faith more meaningful to their daily lives and for a clergy more responsive to their needs. They wanted priests to preach edifying sermons, to administer the sacraments conscientiously, and to lead moral lives, so they generously donated money to establish new preaching positions for university-trained clerics. The merchants resented the funneling of the Catholic church's rich endowments to the younger children of the nobility who took up religious callings to protect the wealth of their families. The young, educated clerics funded by the merchants often came from cities themselves. They formed the backbone of **Christian humanism** and sometimes became reformers, too.

Christian humanism: A general intellectual trend in the sixteenth century that coupled love of classical learning, as in Renaissance humanism, with an emphasis on Christian piety.

Printing Press
This illustration from a French manuscript of 1537 depicts typical printing equipment of the sixteenth century. An artisan is using the screw press to apply the inked type to the paper. Also shown are the composed type secured in a chase, the printed sheet (four pages of text printed on one sheet) held by the seated proofreader, and the bound volume. When two pages of text were printed on one standard-sized sheet, the bound book was called a folio. A bound book with four pages of text on one sheet was called a quarto ("in four"), and a book with eight pages of text on one sheet was called an octavo ("in eight"). The last is a pocket-size book, smaller than today's paperback. *(The Granger Collection, New York.)*

Humanism originated during the Renaissance in Italy among highly educated individuals attached to the personal households of prominent rulers. North of the Alps, however, humanists focused more on religious revival and the inculcation of Christian piety, through such means as the model school of the Brethren of the Common Life. The Brethren preached self-discipline and often criticized the local clergy for their inadequate training and lax morals. Two men, the Dutch scholar Desiderius Erasmus (c. 1466–1536) and the English lawyer Thomas More (1478–1535), stood out as representatives of these Christian humanists, who coupled their love of classical learning with the emphasis on Christian piety. They both longed for ideal societies based on peace and morality but faced a world that seemed bent on violent division instead.

Erasmus. Just as Cicero had dominated ancient Roman letters, Erasmus towered over the humanist world of early-sixteenth-century Europe. An intimate friend of kings and popes, he became known across Europe. Disseminated by the printing press, Erasmus's books made him famous. He devoted years to preparing a critical edition of the New Testament in Greek with a translation into Latin, which was finally published in 1516.

Only through education, Erasmus believed, could individuals reform themselves and society. He strove for a unified, peaceful Christendom in which charity and good works, not empty ceremonies, would mark true religion and in which learning and piety would dispel the darkness of ignorance. He elaborated many of these ideas in his *Handbook of the Militant Christian* (1503), an eloquent plea for a simple religion devoid of greed and the lust for power. In *The Praise of Folly* (1509), he satirized values held dear by his contemporaries. Modesty, humility, and poverty represented the true Christian virtues in a world that worshipped pomposity, power, and wealth. The wise

appeared foolish, he concluded, for their wisdom and values were not of this world.

He instructed the young future emperor Charles V to rule as a just Christian prince and expressed deep sorrow about the brutal fighting that had ravaged Europe for decades. A man of peace and moderation, Erasmus soon found himself challenged by angry younger men and radical ideas once the Reformation took hold; he eventually chose Christian unity over reform and schism. His dream of Christian pacifism crushed, he lived to see dissenters executed — by Catholics and Protestants alike — for speaking their conscience. Erasmus spent his last years in Freiburg and Basel, isolated from the Protestant community, his writings condemned by many in the Catholic church. After the Protestant Reformation had been secured, the saying arose that "Erasmus laid the egg that Luther hatched." Some blamed the humanists for the emergence of Luther and Protestantism, despite the humanists' decision to remain in the Catholic church.

Thomas More. If Erasmus found himself abandoned by his times, his good friend across the English Channel, Thomas More, to whom *The Praise of Folly* was dedicated, met with even greater suffering. Like the humanists of Italy, More chose to

Albrecht Dürer, *The Knight, Death, and the Devil*
Dürer's 1513 engraving of the knight depicts a grim and determined warrior advancing in the face of devils, one of whom holds out an hourglass with a grimace while another wields a menacing pike. An illustration for Erasmus's *The Handbook of the Militant Christian*, this scene is often interpreted as portraying a Christian clad in the armor of righteousness on a path through life beset by death and demonic temptations. Yet the knight in early-sixteenth-century Germany had become a mercenary, selling his martial skills to princes. Some waylaid merchants, robbed rich clerics, and held citizens for ransom. The most notorious of these robber-knights, Franz von Sickingen, was declared an outlaw by the emperor and murdered in 1522. *(Bridgeman-Giraudon/Art Resource, NY.)*

■ **For more help analyzing this image,** see the visual activity for this chapter in the Online Study Guide at **bedfordstmartins.com/hunt**.

serve his prince. In 1529, he became lord chancellor, the chief officer of the English government. King Henry VIII had his own issues with the papacy and, in 1532, broke with the Roman Catholic church. He pulled England out from under papal control and began appointing his own bishops. In protest against Henry's newly asserted control of the clergy, More resigned his position and was executed in 1535 for refusing to subscribe to Henry VIII's version of the Protestant Reformation. By executing More, Henry created a martyr revered for centuries by Catholics and by those who believed in liberty of conscience.

From any perspective, More was an audacious, even eccentric thinker. In his best-known work, *Utopia* (1516), he describes an ideal imaginary land that stands in stark contrast to his own society. A just, equitable, and hardworking community, Utopia (meaning both "no place" and "best place" in Greek) was the opposite of England. In Utopia, everyone worked the land for two years; and since Utopians enjoyed public schools, communal kitchens, hospitals, and nurseries, they had no need for money or private property. Dedicated to the pursuit of knowledge and natural religion, with equal distribution of goods and few laws, Utopians knew neither crime nor internal discord.

Yet even in More's Utopia some oddities existed—voluntary slavery, for example, and strictly controlled travel. Although premarital sex brought severe punishment, prospective marriage partners could examine each other naked before making their final decisions. Men headed Utopia's households and exercised authority over women and children. And Utopians did not shy away from declaring war on their neighbors to protect their way of life. More nonetheless created an imaginary society that was paradise when compared with a Christian Europe battered by division and violence. The Christian humanists offered stirring visions of a better future, but peace, moderation, unity, and any idea of Utopia would all be submerged in the coming flood of radical religious change.

Martin Luther and the Holy Roman Empire

The Protestant Reformation began when the crisis of faith of one man, **Martin Luther** (1483–1546), started an international movement. Luther was an improbable spiritual revolutionary. Son of a miner

---

Martin Luther: A German monk (1483–1546) who started the Protestant Reformation in 1517 by challenging the practices and doctrines of the Catholic church and advocating salvation through faith alone.

and a deeply pious mother, he began his studies in the law. Caught in a storm on a lonely road one midsummer's night, the young student grew terrified by the thunder and lightning. He implored the help of St. Anne, the mother of the Virgin Mary, and promised to enter a monastery if she protected him. Luther abandoned his law studies and entered the Augustinian order. There he experienced his religious crisis and its resolution: the doctrine of faith alone as the means to salvation.

Even though as a monk Luther took up all the practices offered by the church to achieve personal salvation, he did not feel saved. He prayed, he took the sacraments, and as a priest he even said Mass. He did all the good works that the church prescribed yet still felt bereft of God's love. He came to believe that the church gave external behavior more weight than spiritual intentions. The sacrament of penance was a case in point. Instead of emphasizing the remorse that led the sinner to confess his sins to a priest and then receive forgiveness from the priest in God's name, the church emphasized the penance imposed by the priest. Some priests abused their authority by demanding sexual or monetary favors before granting forgiveness. Luther found peace inside himself when he became convinced that sinners were saved only through faith and that faith was a gift freely given by God. No amount of good works, he believed, could produce the faith on which salvation depended. Shortly before his death, Luther recalled his crisis:

> Though I lived as a monk without reproach, I felt that I was a sinner before God with an extremely disturbed conscience. I could not believe that he was placated by my satisfaction [in penance]. I did not love, yes, I hated the righteous God who punishes sinners, and secretly . . . I was angry with God. . . . At last, by the mercy of God, meditating day and night, I gave heed to the context of the words, namely, "In [the gospel] the righteousness of God is revealed, as it is written, 'He who through faith is righteous shall live.'" There I began to understand that the righteousness of God is that by which the righteous live by a gift of God, namely by faith.

Just as Luther was working out his own personal search for salvation, a priest named Johann Tetzel arrived in Wittenberg, where Luther was a university professor, to sell indulgences. Penance normally consisted of spiritual duties (prayers, pilgrimages), but the church also asked for monetary substitutions, called indulgences. Indulgences could even be bought for a deceased relative, which would forgive that person's time in purgatory and release the soul for heaven. Luther denounced what he, like so many of the Church's other critics, saw as a corrupt practice, allowing sinners to buy rather than to earn forgiveness of their sins. But Luther's objections went far deeper. He believed that indulgences, like the sacrament of penance, were ultimately useless unless one had faith. No one, he felt, could be allowed to think that such a purchase had anything to do with salvation.

Armed with his sense of God's justice and grace, Luther composed ninety-five theses for academic debate in 1517. Among them were attacks on the sale of indulgences and the purchase of church offices. Printed, the theses became public and unleashed a torrent of pent-up resentment and frustration among the laypeople. What began as a theological debate in a provincial university soon engulfed the Holy Roman Empire. (See "Contrasting Views," page 431.) Luther's earliest supporters included younger Christian humanists and clerics who shared his critical attitude toward the church establishment. None of these Evangelicals, as they called themselves, came from the upper echelons of the church; many were from urban middle-class backgrounds, and most were university trained. The Evangelicals represented social groups most ready to challenge clerical authority—merchants, artisans, and literate urban laypeople. But illiterate artisans and peasants also rallied to Luther, sometimes with an almost fanatical zeal. They and he believed they were living in the last days of the world. Luther and his cause might be a sign of the approaching Last Judgment.

Initially, Luther presented himself as the pope's "loyal opposition," but in 1520, he burned his bridges with the publication of three fiery treatises. In *Freedom of a Christian*, written in Latin for the learned and addressed to Pope Leo X, Luther argued that faith, not good works, saved sinners from damnation, and he sharply distinguished between true Gospel teachings and invented church doctrines. Luther advocated "the priesthood of all believers," insisting that the Bible provided all the teachings necessary for Christian living and that a professional caste of clerics should not hold sway over laypeople. *Freedom of a Christian* circulated widely in an immediate German translation. Its principles "by faith alone," "by Scripture alone," and "the priesthood of all believers" became central features of the reform movement.

In his second treatise, *To the Nobility of the German Nation*, written in German, Luther ap-

Luther's World in the Early Sixteenth Century

pealed to German identity and to the nobles as the natural leaders of any reform movement. He denounced the corrupt Italians in Rome who were cheating and exploiting his compatriots and called on the German princes to defend their nation and reform the church. Luther's third treatise, *On the Babylonian Captivity of the Church*, condemned the papacy as the embodiment of the Antichrist.

From Rome's perspective, the "Luther Affair," as church officials called it, concerned only one unruly monk. When the pope ordered him to obey his superiors and keep quiet, Luther tore up the decree. Spread by the printing press, Luther's ideas circulated throughout the Holy Roman Empire, letting loose forces that neither the church nor Luther could control. Social, nationalist, and religious protests fused with lower-class resentments, much as in the Czech movement that Jan Hus had inspired a century earlier. Like Hus, Luther appeared before an emperor: in 1521, he defended his faith at the Imperial Diet of Worms before **Charles V** (r. 1519–1556), the newly elected Holy Roman Emperor who, at the age of nineteen, ruled over the Low Countries, Spain, Spain's Italian and New World dominions, and the Austrian Habsburg lands. Luther shocked Germans by declaring his admiration for the Czech heretic. But unlike Hus, Luther did not suffer martyrdom because he enjoyed the protection of Frederick the Wise, the elector of Saxony and Luther's lord. Frederick was one of the seven electors whom Charles V had bribed to become Holy Roman Emperor, and Charles had to treat him with respect. The emperor soon had cause to regret his reluctance to punish Luther.

Lutheran propaganda flooded German towns and villages. Hundreds of pamphlets lambasted the papacy and the Catholic clergy; others simplified the message of Luther for the common folk. Sometimes only a few pages in length, these broadsheets were often illustrated with crude satirical cartoons. City dwellers proved particularly receptive to Luther's teachings; they were literate and were eager to read the Bible for themselves. Magistrates began to curtail clerical privileges and

---

Charles V: Holy Roman Emperor (r. 1519–1556) and the most powerful ruler in sixteenth-century Europe; he reigned over the Low Countries, Spain, Spain's Italian and New World dominions, and the Austrian Habsburg lands.

CONTRASTING VIEWS

Martin Luther: Holy Man or Heretic?

When Martin Luther criticized the papacy and the Catholic church, he was hailed as a godly prophet by some and condemned as a heretic by others. Both Protestants and Catholics used popular propaganda to argue their cause. They spread their message to a largely illiterate or semiliterate society through pamphlets, woodcuts, and broadsheets in which visual images took on increasing importance, to appeal to a wide public. These polemical works were distributed in the thousands to cities and market towns throughout the Holy Roman Empire. A few were even translated into Latin to reach an audience outside of Germany.

The 1521 woodcut by Matthias Gnidias represents Luther standing above his Catholic opponent, the Franciscan friar Thomas Murner, who is depicted here as a crawling dragon, Leviathan, the biblical monster (Document 1). Another positive image of Luther, also published in 1521, depicts him as inspired by the Holy Spirit (Document 2). An anti-Luther image from a few years later represents him as a seven-headed monster (Document 3), signifying that the reformer is the source of discord within Christianity. This image appeared in a book published in 1529 by the Dominican friar Johannes Cochlaeus, one of Luther's vociferous opponents.

Visual examples of religious propaganda worked effectively to demonize enemies and to contrast sharply good and evil. The 1520s saw the most intense production of these cheap polemical visual prints, but the use of visual propaganda would continue for more than a century in the religious conflict.

Luther as Monk. *(The Granger Collection, New York.)*

1. Matthias Gnidias's Representation of Luther and Leviathan (1521)

LVTHERVS.

Luther and Leviathan

Dressed in a friar's robes, the Murner-Leviathan monster breathes "ignis, sumus, & sulphur"—fire, smoke, and sulphur. The good friar, Luther, holds the Bible in his hands, and is represented here as a prophet (foretelling the end of the world). The vertical Latin caption declares that the Lord will visit the earth with his sword and kill the Leviathan monster; he will trample underfoot lions and dragons; and the dragon, with a halter around its nostrils, will be dragged away on a hook.

2. Luther as Monk, Doctor, Man of the Bible, and Saint (1521)

This woodcut by an anonymous artist appeared in a volume that the Strasbourg printer Johann Schott published in 1521. In addition to being one of the major centers of printing, Strasbourg was also a stronghold of the reform movement. Note the use of traditional symbols to signify Luther's holiness: the Bible in his hands, the halo, the Holy Spirit in the form of a dove, and his friar's robes. Although the cult of saints and monasticism came under severe criticism during the Reformation, the representation of Luther in traditional symbols of sanctity stressed his conservative values instead of his radical challenge to church authorities.

3. The Seven-Headed Martin Luther by Johannes Cochlaeus (1529)

The seven heads are labeled (from left to right) doctor, Martin, Luther, ecclesiast, enthusiast, visitirer, and Barrabas. The term enthusiast represented a name of abuse, applied usually by the Catholic church to Anabaptists and religious radicals of all sorts. Visitirer is a pun in German on the word Tier, meaning "animal." Cochlaeus also mocks the new practice of Protestant clergy visiting parishes to check up on pastors' and parishioners' adherence to reformed doctrines and rituals in order to enforce Christian discipline. From left to right, Luther's many heads gradually reveal him to be a rebel, as Barrabas was condemned to die as a rabble-rouser by the Romans but instead was freed and his place taken by Jesus at the crucifixion. The number seven also alludes to the seven deadly sins.

Seven-Headed Luther. *(The Granger Collection, New York.)*

QUESTIONS TO CONSIDER

1. Why did Johannes Cochlaeus condemn Martin Luther? How did he construct a negative image of Luther?
2. Evaluate the visual representations of Luther as a godly man. Which one is more effective?

subordinate the clergy to municipal authority. Luther's message—that each Christian could appeal directly to God for salvation—spoke to townspeople's spiritual needs and social vision. From Wittenberg, the many streams of the reform movement quickly merged and threatened to swamp all before it.

Huldrych Zwingli and John Calvin

Separate reform movements sprang up in Swiss cities. In 1520, just three years after Luther's initial break with Rome, the chief preacher of Zurich, Huldrych Zwingli (1484–1531), openly declared himself a reformer. Like Luther, Zwingli attacked corruption in the Catholic church hierarchy, and he also questioned fasting and clerical celibacy. Under Zwingli's leadership, Zurich served as the center for the Swiss and southern German reform movement. Luther and Zwingli did not agree on all points of doctrine. Luther insisted that Christ was both truly and symbolically present in the Eucharist, the central Christian sacrament that Christians partook of in communion; Zwingli, however, viewed the Eucharistic bread and wine as symbols of Christ's union with believers.

Calvin's World in the Mid-Sixteenth Century

In 1529, troubled by these differences and other disagreements, Evangelical princes and magistrates assembled the major reformers in the Colloquy of Marburg, in central Germany. After several days of intense discussions, the reformers managed to resolve some differences over doctrine, but Luther and Zwingli failed to agree on the meaning of the Eucharist. The issue of the Eucharist would soon divide Lutherans and Calvinists as well.

Under the leadership of **John Calvin** (1509–1564), another wave of reform pounded at the gates of Rome. Born in Picardy, in northern France, Calvin studied in Paris and Orléans, where he took a law degree. A gifted intellectual attracted to humanism, Calvin could have enjoyed a brilliant career in government or the church. Instead, experiencing a crisis of faith, like Luther, he sought salvation through intense theological study. Calvin

read the works of the leading French humanists who sought to reform the church from within, and he also examined Luther's writings. Gradually, he came to question fundamental Catholic teachings.

On Sunday, October 18, 1534, Parisians found church doors posted with ribald broadsheets denouncing the Catholic Mass. Smuggled into France from the Protestant and French-speaking parts of Switzerland, the broadsheets provoked a wave of royal repression in the capital. In response to this so-called Affair of the Placards, the government arrested hundreds of French Protestants, executed some of them, and forced many more, including Calvin, to flee abroad.

On his way to Strasbourg, a haven for religious dissidents, Calvin detoured to Geneva—the French-speaking Swiss city-state where he would find his life's work. Genevans had renounced their allegiance to the Catholic bishop, and local supporters of reform begged Calvin to stay and labor there. Although it took some time for Calvin to solidify his position in the city, his supporters eventually triumphed and he remained in Geneva until his death in 1564.

Under Calvin's leadership, Geneva became a Christian republic on the model set out in his *Institutes of the Christian Religion*, first published in 1536. No reformer prior to Calvin had expounded on the doctrines, organization, history, and practices of Christianity in such a systematic, logical, and coherent manner. Calvin followed Luther's doctrine of salvation to its ultimate logical conclusion: if God is almighty and humans cannot earn their salvation by good works, then no Christian can be certain of salvation. Developing the doctrine of **predestination**, Calvin argued that God had ordained every man, woman, and child to salvation or damnation—even before the creation of the world. Thus, in Calvin's theology, God saved only the "elect"; he knew their identity eternally.

Predestination could terrify, but it could also embolden. A righteous life might be a sign of a person's having been chosen for salvation. Thus, Calvinist doctrine demanded rigorous discipline. The knowledge that only the elect, a small group,

---

John Calvin: French-born Christian humanist (1509–1564) and founder of Calvinism, one of the major branches of the Protestant Reformation; he led the reform movement in Geneva, Switzerland, from 1541 to 1564.

predestination: John Calvin's doctrine that God preordained salvation or damnation for each person before creation; those chosen for salvation were considered the "elect."

DOCUMENT

Ordinances for Calvinist Churches (1547)

The Calvinist churches, like others during the Protestant Reformation, emphasized the need for stricter moral regulation of individual behavior. These ordinances placed on churches in Geneva and surrounding areas show how all aspects of behavior, including popular entertainments, were subject to scrutiny.

Concerning the Times of Assembling at Church

That the temples be closed for the rest of the time [outside the time of services], in order that no one shall enter therein out of hours, impelled thereto by superstition; and if anyone be found engaged in any special act of devotion therein or nearby he shall be admonished for it: if it be found to be of a superstitious nature for which simple correction is inadequate then he shall be chastised.

Blasphemy.

Whoever shall have blasphemed, swearing by the body or by the blood of our Lord, or in similar manner, he shall be made to kiss the earth for the first offence; for the second to pay 5 sous, and for the third 6 sous, and for the last offence be put in the pillory for one hour.

Drunkenness.

1. That no one shall invite another to drink under penalty of 3 sous.
2. That taverns shall be closed during the sermon, under penalty that the tavern-keeper shall pay 3 sous, and whoever may be found therein shall pay the same amount.
3. If anyone be found intoxicated he shall pay for the first offence 3 sous and shall be remanded to the consistory [church council or governing body]; for the second offence he shall be held to pay the sum of 6 sous, and for the third 10 sous and be put in prison.
4. That no one shall make roiaumes [popular festivals] under penalty of 10 sous.

Songs and Dances.

If anyone sings immoral, dissolute or outrageous songs, or dance the virollet or other dance, he shall be put in prison for three days and then sent to the consistory.

Usury.

That no one shall take upon interest or profit more than five per cent., upon penalty of confiscation of the principal and of being condemned to make restitution as the case may demand.

Games.

That no one shall play at any dissolute game or at any game whatsoever it may be, neither for gold nor silver nor for any excessive stake [i.e., gambling], upon penalty of 5 sous and forfeiture of stake played for.

Source: George L. Burns, ed., in *Translations and Reprints from the Original Sources of European History*, 6 vols. (Philadelphia: University of Pennsylvania History Department, 1898–1912), vol. 1, 2–5.

---

would be saved should guide the actions of the godly in an uncertain world. Fusing church and society into what followers named the Reformed church, Geneva became a theocratic city-state dominated by Calvin and the elders of the Reformed church. Its people were rigorously monitored; detractors said that they were bullied. (See Document, "Ordinances for Calvinist Churches," above.)

Calvin tolerated no dissent. While passing through Geneva in 1553, the Spanish physician Michael Servetus was arrested because he had published books attacking Calvin and questioning the doctrine of the Trinity, the belief that there are three persons in one God—the Father, the Son (Christ), and the Holy Spirit. Upon Calvin's advice, the authorities executed Servetus. Despite the outcry over this action, Geneva became the new center of the Reformation, the place where pastors trained for missionary work and where books about Calvinist doctrines were produced and exported all over Europe. The Calvinist movement spread to France, the Low Countries, England, Scotland, the German states, Poland, Hungary, and eventually New England, becoming the established form of the Reformation in many of these countries.

The Anglican Church in England

England followed its own path, with reform led by the king rather than by men trained as Catholic clergy. Despite a tradition of religious dissent that went back to John Wycliffe, Protestantism gained few English adherents in the 1520s. King **Henry VIII** (r. 1509–1547) changed that when he broke

---

Henry VIII: The English king (r. 1509–1547) who first opposed the Protestant Reformation and then broke with the Catholic church, naming himself head of the Anglican church in the Act of Supremacy of 1534.

THE PROGRESS OF THE REFORMATION

1517	Martin Luther disseminates ninety-five theses attacking the sale of indulgences and other church practices
1520	Reformer Huldrych Zwingli breaks with Rome
1525	Peasants' War in German states divides reform movement
1529	Lutheran German princes protest the condemnation of religious reform by Charles V
1534	The Act of Supremacy establishes King Henry VIII as head of the Anglican church, severing ties to Rome
1534–1535	Anabaptists take over the German city of Münster in a failed experiment to create a holy community
1541	John Calvin establishes himself permanently in Geneva, making that city a model of Christian reform and discipline

with the Roman Catholic church for reasons that were both personal and political. The resulting Anglican church retained many aspects of Catholic worship but nonetheless aligned itself in the Protestant camp.

At first, Henry opposed the Reformation, even receiving the title Defender of the Faith from Pope Leo X for a treatise Henry wrote against Luther. A robust, ambitious, and well-educated man, Henry wanted to make his mark on history and, with the aid of his chancellors Cardinal Thomas Wolsey and Thomas More, he vigorously suppressed Protestantism and executed its leaders. But by 1527, the king wanted to divorce his wife, Catherine of Aragon (d. 1536), the daughter of Ferdinand and Isabella of Spain and the aunt of Charles V. The eighteen-year marriage had produced a daughter, Mary (known as Mary Tudor), but Henry desperately needed a male heir to consolidate the rule of the still-new Tudor dynasty. Moreover, he had fallen in love with Anne Boleyn, a lady at court and a strong supporter of the Reformation. Henry claimed that his marriage to Catherine had never been valid because she was the widow of his older brother, Arthur. Arthur and Catherine's marriage, which apparently was never consummated, had been annulled by Pope Julius II to allow the marriage between Henry and Catherine to take place. Now Henry asked the reigning pope, Clement VII, to declare his marriage to Catherine invalid.

Around "the king's great matter" unfolded a struggle for political and religious control. When Henry failed to secure papal approval of his divorce, he chose two Protestants as his new loyal servants: Thomas Cromwell (1485–1540) as chan-

cellor and Thomas Cranmer (1489–1556) as archbishop of Canterbury. Under their leadership, the English Parliament passed a number of acts that severed ties between the English church and Rome. The most important of these, the Act of Supremacy of 1534, made Henry the head of the Anglican church (the Church of England). Other legislation invalidated the claims of Mary, his daughter with Catherine, to the throne, recognized his marriage to Anne Boleyn, and allowed the English crown to embark on the dissolution of the monasteries. In an effort to consolidate support behind his version of the Reformation, Henry sold off monastic lands to the local gentry and aristocracy. Henry thus missed a golden opportunity to make the English crown as rich as its French counterpart by adding those lands to its own holdings.

By 1536, Henry had grown tired of Anne Boleyn, who had given birth to a daughter, the future Queen Elizabeth I, but had produced no sons. He ordered Anne beheaded on the charge of adultery, an act that he defined as treason. The king would go on to marry four other wives but father only one son, Edward. Thomas More had also been executed for treason, in 1535, and Cromwell suffered the same fate in 1540 after he lost the king's favor. When Henry died in 1547, the principle of royal supremacy in religious matters was firmly established, but much would now depend on who held the crown.

> **REVIEW:** How did Luther, Zwingli, Calvin, and Henry VIII challenge the Roman Catholic church?

Reshaping Society through Religion

The religious upheavals of the sixteenth century affected European society in two contradictory ways: first, the reformers and their followers challenged political authority and the social order, and second, in reaction to the more extreme manifestations of the first, they underlined the need for discipline in worship and social behavior. Peasant rebels and radical Protestants known as Anabaptists wanted to push the Reformation in a more populist direction. They took the phrase "priesthood of all believers" quite literally and sided with the poor and the downtrodden. Like Catholics, Protestant authorities then became alarmed by the subversive potential of religious reforms. They viewed the Reformation not as a political and social movement, but as a way of instilling greater discipline in individual worship and church organization. Bible reading became a potent tool in the creation of this new, internally motivated person. At the same time, the Roman Catholic church undertook reforms of its own and launched an offensive against the Protestant Reformation, sometimes called the Counter-Reformation.

Protestant Challenges to the Social Order

When Luther described the freedom of the Christian, he meant an entirely spiritual freedom. But others interpreted his call for freedom in social and political terms. During the 1520s and 1530s, two movements emerged in the Holy Roman Empire to demand more far-reaching changes. In 1525, peasants and urban artisans rose up against the Catholic church and landed nobility and armed themselves to pursue their goals. Anabaptists experimented with new social and political doctrines. Some rejected violence, but one Anabaptist group tried to create a perfect Christian community in the German town of Münster. The results were disastrous.

The Peasants' War of 1525.   The Catholic church was the largest landowner in the Holy Roman Empire: about one-seventh of the empire's territory consisted of ecclesiastical principalities in which bishops and abbots exercised both secular and churchly power. Luther's anticlerical message struck home with peasants who paid taxes to both their lord and the Catholic church. In the spring of 1525, many peasants in southern and central Germany, joined by urban workers, rose in rebellion (Map 14.3). In Thuringia (central/eastern Germany), the rebels followed an ex-priest, Thomas Müntzer (1468?–1525), who promised to chastise the wicked and thus clear the way for the Last Judgment.

The Peasants' War split the reform movement. Princes and city officials, ultimately supported by Luther, turned against the rebels. Catholic and Protestant princes joined hands to crush Müntzer and his supporters. All over the empire, princes

MAP 14.3 The Peasants' War of 1525
The centers of uprisings clustered in southern and central Germany, where the density of cities encouraged the spread of discontent and allowed for alliances between urban masses and rural rebels. The proximity to the Swiss Confederation, a stronghold of the Reformation movement, also inspired antiestablishment uprisings.

German Peasants' War of 1525
This colored woodcut depicts peasants attacking the pope, a monk, and a nobleman during the massive rural uprisings against the church that took place in southern and central Germany in 1525. Even the heavens show signs of trouble: a comet and clouds in the shape of a goat signify bloodshed and sin.
(The Granger Collection, New York.)

trounced peasant armies, hunted down their leaders, and uprooted all opposition. By the end of the year, more than 100,000 rebels had been killed and many others maimed, imprisoned, or exiled. Initially, Luther had tried to mediate the conflict, criticizing the princes for their brutality toward the peasants but also warning the rebels against mixing religion and social protest. Luther believed that God ordained rulers, who must therefore be obeyed even if they were tyrants. The kingdom of God belonged not to this world but to the next, he insisted. Luther considered Müntzer's mixing of religion and politics the greatest danger to the Reformation, nothing less than "the devil's work." When the rebels ignored Luther's appeal and continued to follow more radical preachers, Luther called on the princes to slaughter the rebels and restore the divinely ordained social order.

Fundamentally conservative in its political philosophy, the Lutheran church henceforth depended on established political authority for its protection. It lost supporters in rural areas and became an increasingly urban phenomenon. The ultimate victors were the German princes. They

defeated the peasants, sided with Luther, and confronted the Holy Roman Emperor, Charles V, who declared Roman Catholicism the empire's only legitimate religion. The fragmentation of the Holy Roman Empire only increased as people came to support their Protestant princes against Charles's Catholic orthodoxy.

Anabaptists. While Zwingli challenged the Roman Catholic church in public, some laypeople in Zurich secretly pursued their own path to reform. Taking their cue from the New Testament's descriptions of the first Christian community, these men and women believed that true faith came only to those with reason and free will. How could a baby knowingly choose Christ? Only adults could believe and accept baptism; hence, the **Anabaptists** (literally, "rebaptizers") rejected the validity of infant baptism and called for adult rebaptism. Many were pacifists who also refused to acknowledge the authority of law courts and considered themselves a community of true Christians unblemished by sin. The Anabaptist movement drew its leadership primarily from the artisan class and its members from the middle and lower classes — men and women attracted by a simple but radical message of peace and salvation.

Zwingli immediately attacked the Anabaptists for their refusal to bear arms and swear oaths of allegiance, sensing accurately that they were repudiating his theocratic (church-directed) order. When persuasion failed to convince the Anabaptists, Zwingli urged Zurich magistrates to impose the death sentence. Thus, the evangelical reformers themselves created the Reformation's first martyrs of conscience.

Despite condemnation in 1529 of the movement by the Holy Roman Emperor, Anabaptism spread rapidly from Zurich to many cities in southern Germany. In 1534, one Anabaptist group, believing the end of the world was imminent, seized control of the city of Münster. Proclaiming themselves a community of saints, the Münster Anabaptists abolished private property in imitation of the early Christians and dissolved traditional marriages, allowing men, like Old Testament patriarchs, to have multiple wives, to the consternation of many women. Besieged by a combined Protestant and Catholic army, the city fell in June 1535. The Anabaptist leaders died in battle or were executed, their bodies hung in cages affixed to the church tower. Their punishment was intended as a

Anabaptists: Sixteenth-century Protestants who believed that only adults could truly have faith and accept baptism.

warning to all who might want to take the Reformation away from the Protestant authorities and hand it to the people. The Anabaptist movement in northwestern Europe nonetheless survived under the determined pacifist leadership of the Dutch reformer Menno Simons (1469–1561), whose followers were eventually named Mennonites.

New Forms of Discipline

Faced with the social firestorms ignited by religious reform, the middle-class urbanites who supported the Protestant Reformation urged greater religious conformity and stricter moral behavior. To gain more control over religious ferment, Protestant rulers and clergy encouraged Bible reading and a new work ethic. Ordinary men and women who learned how to behave as virtuous Christians at home and in Sunday worship applied what they learned in their households and their businesses. Protestants did not have monasteries or convents or saints' lives to set examples; they sought moral examples in their own homes, in the sermons of their preachers, and in their own reading of the Bible. The new emphasis on self-discipline led to growing impatience with the poor, now viewed as lacking personal virtue, and greater emphasis on regulation of marriage, now seen as critical to social discipline in general. Although some of these attitudes had medieval roots, the Protestant Reformation fostered their spread and Catholics soon began to embrace them.

Reading the Bible. The only Bible authorized by the Catholic church was the Latin Bible, or Vulgate, even though it contained errors of translation from the Greek and Hebrew. In 1522, Martin Luther translated Erasmus's Greek New Testament into German, the first full vernacular translation in that language. A new Bible-centered culture began to take root, as more than 200,000 copies of Luther's New Testament were printed over twelve years, an immense number for the time. In 1534, Luther completed a translation of the Old Testament. Peppered with witty phrases and colloquial expressions, Luther's Bible was a treasure chest of the German language.

Found for the most part in urban and literate households, the German Bible occupied a central place in a family's history. Generations handed down valuable editions, and pious citizens often bound Bibles with family papers or other reading material. Bible reading became a common pastime undertaken in solitude or in family and church gatherings. To counter Protestant success, Catholic German Bibles soon appeared, thus sanctioning Bible reading by the Catholic laity, a sharp departure from medieval church practice. In the same year that Luther's German New Testament appeared in print, the French humanist Jacques Lefèvre d'Étaples (c. 1455–1536) translated the Vulgate (Latin) New Testament into French.

Catholic authorities did not always welcome translations, however. Sensing a potentially dangerous association between the vernacular Bible and heresy, England's Catholic church hierarchy had reacted swiftly against English-language Bibles. When William Tyndale (1495–1536) translated the Bible into English, he was burned at the stake as a heretic. After Henry VIII's break with Rome and adoption of the Reformation, in contrast, his government promoted an English Bible based on Tyndale's translation.

Public Relief for the Poor. In the early sixteenth century, secular governments began to take over institutions of public charity from the church. This development, which took place in both Catholic and Protestant Europe, grew out of two trends: a new upsurge in poverty brought about by population growth and spiraling inflation, and the rise of a work ethic that included growing hostility toward the poor.

By 1500, the cycle of demographic collapse and economic depression triggered by the Black Death of 1346–1353 had passed. Between 1500 and 1560, rapid economic and population growth created prosperity for some and stress — caused or heightened by increased inflation — for many. Wanderers and urban beggars were by no means novel, but the reaction to poverty was. Sixteenth-century moralists decried the crime and sloth of vagabonds. Rejecting the notion that the poor played a central role in the Christian idea of salvation and that charity and prayers united rich and poor, these moralists distinguished between the genuine poor, or "God's poor," and vagabonds; they insisted that the latter, who were able-bodied, should be forced to work.

The Reformation provided an opportunity to restructure relief for the poor. Instead of decentralized, private initiatives often overseen by religious orders, Protestant magistrates appointed officials to head urban agencies that would certify the genuine poor and distribute welfare funds to them. This development progressed rapidly in urban areas, where poverty was most visible, and transcended religious divisions. During the 1520s, cities in the Low Countries, Italy, and Spain passed ordinances that prohibited begging and instituted public charity. In 1526, the Spanish humanist Juan Luis Vives, a Catholic, wrote *On the Support of the Poor*, a Latin treatise urging authorities to establish public poor relief; the work was soon translated into French, Italian, German, and English. National laws followed. In 1531, Henry VIII asked justices of the peace (unpaid local magistrates) to license the poor in England and to differentiate between those who could work and those who could not. In 1540, Charles V imposed a welfare tax in Spain to augment that country's inadequate system of private charity. In Spain, however, the religious orders continued to dominate the system of almsgiving.

Reforming Marriage.   In their effort to establish order and discipline, Protestant reformers denounced sexual immorality and glorified the family. The early Protestant reformers like Luther championed the end of clerical celibacy and embraced marriage. Luther, once a celibate priest himself, married a former nun. The idealized patriarchal family provided protection against the forces of disorder and a place where reform values could be inculcated. Protestant magistrates established marital courts, passed new marriage laws, closed brothels, and inflicted harsher punishments for sexual deviance.

Prior to the Reformation, despite the legislation of church councils, marriages had largely been private affairs between families; some couples never even registered with the church. The Catholic church recognized any promise made between two consenting adults (with the legal age of twelve for females, fourteen for males) in the presence of two witnesses as a valid marriage. Many couples simply lived together as common-law husband and wife. Young men sometimes promised marriage in a passionate moment, only to renege later. The overwhelming number of cases in Catholic church courts involved young women seeking to enforce promises after they had exchanged their personal honor—that is, their virginity—for the greater honor of marriage.

The Reformation proved more effective than the late medieval church in suppressing common-law marriages. Protestant governments asserted greater official control over marriage, and Catholic governments followed suit. A marriage was legitimate only if registered by both a government official and a member of the clergy. In many Protestant countries, the new marriage ordinances also required parental consent, thus giving householders immense power in regulating not only marriage but also the transmission of family property.

In the fervor of the early Reformation years, the first generation of Protestant women attained greater marital equality than those of subsequent generations. Katharina Zell, wife of the reformer Matthew Zell, defended her equality by citing a Bible verse when a critic used St. Paul to support his argument that women should remain silent in church. Katharina retorted, "I would remind you of the word of this same apostle that in Christ there is no male nor female." Katharina helped feed and clothe the thousands of refugees who flooded Strasbourg after their defeat in the Peasants' War. In 1534, she published a collection of hymns. Outraged by the intolerance of a new breed of Protestant clergy, she reprimanded a prominent Lutheran pastor for his persecution of dissenters: "You young fellows tread on the graves of the first fathers of this church in Strasbourg and punish all who disagree with you, but faith cannot be forced."

The Disciplined Home
Proper table manners reflected discipline and morality in the godly household, an ideal of the religious reformers of the sixteenth century. The householder, the father patriarch, leads his wife and children in prayer before a meal. The orderly behavior parallels the comfort (oven, smoked glass windows, chandeliers, timber ceiling, and cabinets) of a well-off patrician family. *(Staatsbibliothek Bamberg, Germany.)*

Catholic Renewal

Like a slumbering giant finally awakened, the Catholic church decided in the 1540s to undertake drastic action to fend off the Protestant threat. Pope Paul III convened a general council of the

church in 1545 at Trent, a town on the border between the Holy Roman Empire and Italy. Meeting
sporadically over nearly twenty years (1545–1563),
the **Council of Trent** effectively set the course
of Catholicism until the 1960s. Catholic leaders
sought a renewal of religious devotion and spirituality as well as a clarification of church doctrine.
New religious orders set out to win converts overseas or to reconvert Catholics who had turned to
Protestantism. Catholic clergy emphasized the
pageantry of ritual and the decoration of churches
in order to counter the austerity of Protestant worship. At the same time, the church did not hesitate
to root out dissent by giving greater powers to the
Inquisition, including the power to censor books.
The papal Index, or list of prohibited books, was
established in 1557 and not abolished until 1966.

The Council of Trent. Italian and Spanish clergy
predominated among the 255 bishops, archbish-
ops, and cardinals attending the Council of Trent.
Though its deliberations were interrupted first by
an outbreak of the plague and then by warfare, the
council came up with a remarkably wide-ranging
series of decisions. It condemned the central doctrines of Protestantism. Salvation depended on
faith and good works, not faith alone. On the
sacrament of the Eucharist, the council reaffirmed
that the bread of communion "really, truly" becomes Christ's body—a rejection of all Protestant
positions on this issue so emphatic as to preclude
compromise. It reasserted the supremacy of clerical authority over the laity; the church's interpretation of the Bible could not be challenged, and
the Vulgate was the only authoritative version. The
council rejected divorce, permitted by Protestants,
and reaffirmed the legitimacy of indulgences. It
also called for reform from within, however, insisting that bishops henceforth reside in their dio-
ceses and decreeing that seminaries for the training
of priests be established in every diocese.

The Council of Trent marked a watershed;
henceforth, the schism between Protestant and
Catholic remained permanent, and all hopes of reconciliation faded. The focus of the Catholic church
turned now to rolling back the tide of dissent.

New Religious Orders. The energy of the
Catholic renewal expressed itself most vigorously
in the founding of new religious orders. Several
were founded in early-sixteenth-century Italy and

reflected an intense religious revival in the Italian
cities from the 1490s to the 1520s. The most important of these, the Society of Jesus, or **Jesuits**,
was established by a Spanish nobleman, Ignatius
of Loyola (1491–1556). Inspired by tales of chivalric romances and the national glory of the *recon-
quista*, Ignatius eagerly sought to prove himself as
a soldier. In 1521, while defending a Spanish border fortress against French attack, he sustained a
severe injury. During his convalescence, Ignatius
read lives of the saints; once he recovered, he abandoned his quest for military glory in favor of serving the church.

Attracted by his activist piety, young men
gravitated to this charismatic figure. Thanks to a
cardinal's intercession, Ignatius gained a hearing
before the pope, and in 1540 the church recognized
his small band. With Ignatius as its first general,
the Jesuits became the most vigorous defenders of
papal authority. The society quickly expanded; by
the time of Ignatius's death in 1556, Europe had
one thousand Jesuits. They established hundreds
of colleges throughout the Catholic world, educating future generations of Catholic leaders. Jesuit
missionaries played a key role in the global Portuguese maritime empire and brought Roman
Catholicism to Africans, Asians, and native Americans. Together with other new religious orders, the
Jesuits restored the confidence of the faithful in the
dedication and power of the Catholic church. They
also acquired a reputation for bringing controversy
in their wake and for being drawn to power as
counselors to powerful nobles and kings.

Missionary Zeal. To win new souls, Catholic
missionaries set sail throughout the globe. They
saw their effort as proof of the truth of Roman
Catholicism and the success of their missions as a
sign of divine favor, both particularly important
in the face of Protestant challenge. But the missionary zeal of Catholics brought conflicting messages to indigenous peoples: for some, the message
of a repressive and coercive alien religion; for others, a sweet sign of reason and faith. Frustrated in
his efforts to convert Brazilian Indians, a Jesuit
missionary wrote to his superior in Rome in 1563
that "for this kind of people it is better to be
preaching with the sword and rod of iron."

To ensure rapid Christianization, European
missionaries focused initially on winning over local elites. The recommendation of a Spanish royal

Council of Trent: A general council of the Catholic church that
met at Trent between 1545 and 1563 to set Catholic doctrine,
reform church practices, and defend the church against the
Protestant challenge.

Jesuits: Members of the Society of Jesus, a Catholic religious
order founded by Ignatius of Loyola (1491–1556) and approved
by the pope in 1540. Jesuits served as missionaries and educators all over the world.

official in Mexico City was typical. He wrote to the crown in 1525:

> In order that the sons of caciques [chiefs] and native lords may be instructed in the faith, Your Majesty must command that a college be founded wherein they may be taught . . . to the end that they may be ordained priests. For he who shall become such among them, will be of greater profit in attracting others to the faith than will fifty [European] Christians.

Nevertheless, this recommendation was not adopted and the Catholic clergy in Spanish America remained overwhelmingly European.

After an initial period of relatively little racial discrimination, the Catholic church in the Americas and Africa adopted strict rules based on color. For example, the first Mexican Ecclesiastical Provincial Council in 1555 declared that holy orders were not to be conferred on Indians, mestizos (people of mixed European-Indian parentage), or mulattoes (people of mixed European-African heritage); along with descendants of Muslims, Jews, and persons who had been sentenced by the Spanish Inquisition, these groups were deemed "inherently unworthy of the sacerdotal [priestly] office." Europeans' sense of racial superiority led them to perceive native Americans' and Africans' resistance to domination as "treachery."

In East Asia, as in the Americas, Christian missionaries under Portuguese protection concentrated their efforts on the elites, preaching the Gospel to Confucian scholar-officials in China and to the samurai (the warrior aristocracy) in Japan. However, European missionaries in Asia greatly admired Chinese and Japanese civilization and thus used the sermon rather than the sword to win converts (see the illustration on this page). The Jesuit Francis Xavier preached in India and Japan, his work greatly assisted by a network of Portuguese trading stations. He died in 1552, awaiting permission to travel to China. A pioneer missionary in Asia, Xavier had prepared the ground for future missionary successes in Japan and China. The efforts of the Catholic missionaries seemed highly successful: vast multitudes of native Americans had become nominal Christians by the second half of the sixteenth century, and thirty years after Francis Xavier's 1549 landing in Japan, the Jesuits could claim more than 100,000 Japanese converts.

REVIEW: How did the forces for radical change unleashed by the Protestant Reformation interact with the urge for social order and stability?

The Portuguese in Japan
In this sixteenth-century Japanese black-lacquer screen painting of Portuguese missionaries, the Jesuits are dressed in black and the Franciscans in brown. At the lower right corner is a Portuguese nobleman depicted with exaggerated "Western" features. The Japanese considered themselves lighter in skin color than the Portuguese, whom they classified as "barbarians." In turn, the Portuguese classified Japanese (and Chinese) as "whites." The perception of ethnic differences in the sixteenth century, however, depended less on skin color than on clothing, eating habits, and other cultural signals. Color classifications were unstable and changed over time: by the late seventeenth century, Europeans no longer regarded Asians as "whites."
(Laurie Platt Winfrey, Inc.)

A Struggle for Mastery

In the sixteenth century, conflicts generated by the Reformation posed new challenges to the ambitions of rulers. Even as courts continued to sponsor the arts and literature of the Renaissance, princes and kings seized opportunities to build stronger states by fighting wars. Wars justified increased taxes, and growing revenues fostered the creation of a central bureaucracy housed at court. Victory on the battlefield translated into territory and just as important into reputation and awe. But victory required skills in making war; monarchs eagerly sought new military technology and battlefield ploys. One major obstacle complicated these efforts at state building: religious division. Could states maintain their authority if individuals were allowed to choose their religion? Almost everywhere, violence failed to settle religious differences. By 1560, an exhausted Europe had achieved a provisional peace, but one fraught with the seeds of future conflict.

The High Renaissance Court

At the center of art patronage, dynastic competition, and religious division lay the court, the focus of princely power and intrigue and the agent of state building. Kings, princes, and popes alike used their courts to keep an eye on their leading courtiers (cardinals in the case of popes) and impress their other subjects. Briefly defined, the court was the ruler's household. Around the prince gathered a community of household servants, noble attendants, councilors, officials, artists, and soldiers. Renaissance culture had been promoted by this political elite, and that culture now entered its "high" or most sophisticated phase. Its acclaimed representative was Michelangelo Buonarroti (1475–1564), an immensely talented Italian artist who sculpted a gigantic nude statue (see right) for officials in Florence and then painted the ceiling of the Sistine Chapel for the recently elected Pope Julius II.

Italian artists also flocked to the French court of Francis I (r. 1515–1547), which swelled to the largest in Europe. In addition to the king's own household, the queen and the queen mother each had her own staff of maids and chefs, as did each of the royal chil-

dren. The royal household employed officials to handle finances and provide guard duty, clothing, and food; in addition, physicians, librarians, musicians, dwarfs, animal trainers, and a multitude of hangers-on bloated its size. By 1535, the French court numbered 1,622 members. Although Francis built a magnificent Renaissance palace at Fontainebleau, where he hired Italian artists to produce paintings and sculpture, the French court often moved from palace to palace. It took no fewer than eighteen thousand horses to transport the people, furniture, and documents—not to mention the dogs and falcons for the royal hunt. Hunting was no mere diversion; it represented a form of mock combat, essential in the training of a military elite. Francis himself loved war games and almost lost his own life when, storming a house during one mock battle, he was hit on the head by a burning log.

Two Italian writers helped define the new culture of courtesy, or proper court behavior, that developed in such a setting: Ludovico Ariosto (1474–1533), in service at the Este court in Ferrara, and Baldassare Castiglione (1478–1529), a servant of the duke of Urbino and the pope. Considered one of the greatest Renaissance poets,

Michelangelo's *David*
Michelangelo combined the classical nude statue with the biblical figure of David in this larger-than-life sculpture showing the young man preparing for action against the giant Goliath. Originally commissioned by church officials in Florence, the statue ended up standing in front of city hall as a commemoration of the recapture of the city-state's freedom. Michelangelo's intentions are not easy to decipher. David's slingshot is barely visible on his left shoulder, and his easy slouch seems incongruous for a coming battle. An earlier drawing by Michelangelo showed David standing on the head of the defeated Goliath, a much more common depiction. What do you deduce from this portrayal?
(Nimatallah/Art Resource, NY.)

Ariosto composed a long epic poem, *Orlando Furioso*, which represented court culture as the highest synthesis of Christian and classical values. The poem's tales of combat, valor, love, and magic captivated the court's noble readers. In *The Courtier*, Castiglione represented court culture as a synthesis of military virtues and literary and artistic cultivation. His characters debate the qualities of an ideal courtier in a series of eloquent dialogues. The true courtier, Castiglione asserts, is a gentleman who speaks in a refined language and carries himself with nobility and dignity in the service of his prince and his lady.

Princes faced greater challenges than did their courtiers, and courtesy was not always their most cherished virtue. The greatest writer on politics of the age, Niccolò Machiavelli (1469–1527), underlined the need for pragmatic, even cold calculation in his controversial essay *The Prince*. Was it better, he asked, for a prince to be feared by his people or loved?

> It may be answered that one should wish to be both, but, because it is difficult to unite them in one person, is much safer to be feared than loved. . . . Because this is to be asserted in general of men, that they are ungrateful, fickle, false, cowardly, covetous, and as long as you succeed they are yours entirely; they will offer you their blood, property, life and children . . . when the need is far distant; but when it approaches they turn against you.

Machiavelli insisted that princes could benefit their subjects only by maintaining a firm grip on power, if necessary through deceit and manipulation. *Machiavellian* has remained ever since a term for using cunning and duplicity to achieve one's ends.

Dynastic Wars

Even as the Renaissance developed in the princely courts and the Reformation took hold in the German states, the Habsburgs (the ruling family in Spain and then the Holy Roman Empire) and the Valois (the ruling family in France) fought each other for domination of Europe (Map 14.4). French claims provoked the Italian Wars in 1494, which soon escalated into a general conflict that involved most Christian monarchs and the Muslim Ottoman sultan as well. From 1494 to 1559, the Valois and Habsburg dynasties, both Catholic, remained implacable enemies. The fighting raged in Italy and the Low Countries. During the 1520s,

MAP 14.4 Habsburg-Valois-Ottoman Wars, 1494–1559
As the dominant European power, the Habsburg dynasty fought on two fronts: a religious war against the Islamic Ottoman Empire and a political war against the French Valois, who challenged Habsburg hegemony. The Mediterranean, the Balkans, and the Low Countries all became theaters of war.

Charles V and Francis I Make Peace
This fresco from the Palazzo Farnese in the town of Caprarola north of Rome shows French king Francis I and Holy Roman Emperor Charles V agreeing to the Truce of Nice in 1538, one of many peace agreements made and then broken during the wars between the Habsburgs and the Valois. Pope Paul III, who negotiated the truce, stands behind and between them. Charles is on the right pointing to Francis. The truce is the one celebrated in the Tlaxcala pageant described at the start of this chapter. *(The Art Archive/Palazzo Farnese Caprarola/Dagli Orti.)*

the Habsburgs enjoyed the upper hand. In 1525, the troops of Charles V crushed the French army at Pavia, Italy, counting among their captives the French king himself, Francis I. Forced to renounce all claims to Italian territory to gain his freedom, Francis furiously repudiated the treaty the moment he reached France, reigniting the conflict.

In 1527, Charles's troops captured and sacked Rome because the pope had allied with the French. Many of the imperial troops were German Protestant mercenaries, who pillaged Catholic churches and brutalized the Catholic clergy. Protestants and Catholics alike interpreted the sack of Rome by imperial forces as a punishment of God; even the Catholic church read it as a sign that reform was necessary. Finally, in 1559, the French gave up their claims in Italy and signed the Treaty of Cateau-Cambrésis, ending the conflict. As was common in such situations, marriage sealed the peace between rival dynasties; the French king Henry II married his sister to the duke of Savoy, an ally of the Habsburgs, and his daughter to the Habsburg king of Spain, Philip II.

The dynastic struggle (Valois versus Habsburg ruling family) had drawn in many other belligerents, who fought on one side or the other for their own benefit. Some acted purely out of power considerations, such as England, first siding with the Valois and then with the Habsburgs. Others fought for their independence, such as the papacy and the

Italian states, which did not want any one power to dominate Italy. Still others chose sides for religious reasons, such as the Protestant princes in Germany, who exploited the Valois-Habsburg conflict to extract religious concessions from the emperor in 1555. The Ottoman Turks saw in this fight an opportunity to expand their territory.

The Ottoman Empire reached its height of power under Sultan Suleiman I, known as **Suleiman the Magnificent** (r. 1520–1566). In 1526, a Turkish expedition destroyed the Hungarian army at Mohács (see the illustration on page 443). Three years later, the Ottomans laid siege to Vienna; though unsuccessful, the attack sent shock waves throughout Christian Europe. In 1535, Charles V led a campaign to capture Tunis, the lair of North African pirates loyal to the Ottomans. Desperate to overcome Charles's superior Habsburg forces, the French king Francis I forged an alliance with the Turkish sultan. Coming to the aid of the French, the Turkish fleet besieged the Habsburg troops holding Nice, on the southern coast of France. Francis even ordered all inhabitants of nearby Toulon to vacate the town so that he could turn it into a Muslim colony for eight months, complete with a mosque and slave market. The French alliance with the Turks scandalized many Christians, but it reflected the spirit of the times:

Suleiman the Magnificent: Sultan of the Ottoman Empire (r. 1520–1566) at the time of its greatest power.

The Siege of Vienna, 1529
This illustration from an Ottoman manuscript of 1588 depicts the Turkish siege of Vienna (the siege guns can be seen in the center of the picture). Sultan Suleiman I (Suleiman the Magnificent) led an army of more than 100,000 men against Vienna, capital of the Austrian Habsburg lands. Several attacks on the city failed, and the Ottomans withdrew in October 1529. They maintained control over Hungary, but the logistics of moving so many men and horses kept them from advancing any farther westward into Europe. *(The Art Archive/Topkapi Museum Istanbul/Dagli Orti.)*

the age-old idea of the Christian crusade against Islam now had to compete with a new political strategy that considered religion only one factor among many in power politics. Religion could be sacrificed, if need be, on the altar of state building.

Constantly distracted by the challenges of the Ottomans to the east and the German Protestants at home, Charles V could not crush the French with one swift blow. Years of conflict drained the treasuries of all rulers, because warfare was becoming more expensive. The formula that war raises revenues that in turn build governments could devolve into an absurdity if wars could not be won. The race for battlefield superiority was on.

Financing War

The sixteenth century marked the beginning of superior Western military technology. All armies grew in size and their firepower became ever more deadly, increasing the cost of war. Heavier artillery

pieces meant that the rectangular walls of medieval cities had to be transformed into fortresses with jutting ramparts and gun emplacements. Royal revenues could not keep up with war expenditures. To pay their bills, governments routinely devalued their coinage (the sixteenth-century equivalent of printing more paper money), causing prices to rise rapidly.

Charles V boasted the largest army in Europe, but like everyone else he sank into debt. Between 1520 and 1532, Charles borrowed 5.4 million ducats, primarily to pay his troops; from 1552 to 1556, his war loans soared to 9.6 million ducats. On his death in 1547, Francis I owed the bankers of Lyon almost 7 million French pounds — approximately the entire royal income for that year. The European powers literally fought themselves into bankruptcy. Taxation, the sale of offices, and outright confiscation failed to bring in enough money to satisfy the war machine. Both the Habsburg and the Valois kings

A STRUGGLE FOR MASTERY **445**

looked to the leading bankers to finance their costly wars.

Foremost among these financiers was the Fugger bank, the largest such enterprise in sixteenth-century Europe. Based in the southern German imperial city of Augsburg, the Fugger family and their associates built an international financial empire that helped to make kings. The enterprise began with Jakob Fugger (1459–1525), who became personal banker to Charles V's grandfather Maximilian I. Constantly short of cash, Maximilian granted the Fugger family numerous mining and minting concessions. To pay for the service of providing and accepting bills of exchange, the Fuggers charged substantial fees and made handsome profits. By the end of his life, Maximilian was so deeply in debt to Jakob Fugger that he had to pawn the royal jewels.

In 1519, Fugger assembled a consortium of German and Italian bankers to secure the election of Charles V as Holy Roman Emperor. For the next three decades, the alliance between Europe's biggest international bank and its largest empire remained very close. Between 1527 and 1547, the Fugger bank's assets more than doubled; more than half came from loans to the Habsburgs. Charles stayed barely one step ahead of his creditors, and his successor in Spain gradually lost control of the Spanish state finances. Debt forced the Valois and the Habsburgs to sign the Treaty of Cateau-Cambrésis in 1559, ending more than sixty years of warfare, but the cycle of financial crises and warfare continued until the late eighteenth century.

Divided Realms

All European rulers viewed religious division as a dangerous challenge to the unity and stability of their rule. Subjects who considered their rulers heretics or blasphemers could only cause trouble, as the Peasants' War of 1525 had amply demonstrated. Moreover, religious differences encouraged the formation of competing noble factions, which easily led to violence when weak monarchs or children ruled.

France.   King Francis I tolerated Protestants until the Affair of the Placards in 1534. Even then, the government did not try to root out Protestantism, and the Reformed (Calvinist) church grew steadily. During the 1540s and 1550s, many French noble families — including some of the most powerful — converted to Calvinism and afforded the Protestants a measure of protection, es-

pecially in southern and western France. Francis and his successor, Henry II (r. 1547–1559), succeeded in maintaining a balance of power between Catholics and Calvinists, but after Henry's death the weakened monarchy could no longer hold together the fragile realm. The real drama of the Reformation in France took place after 1560, when the country plunged into four decades of religious wars, whose savagery was unparalleled elsewhere in Europe.

England and Scotland.   Religious divisions at the very top threatened the control of the English and Scottish rulers. Before his death in 1547, Henry VIII had succeeded in making England officially Protestant, but would they remain Protestants and if so, what kind of Protestants would his subjects become? Each of his children offered answers to that question, and the answers could not have been more contradictory. The advisers of the boy king Edward VI (r. 1547–1553) furthered the Reformation by welcoming prominent religious refugees from the continent. The refugees had been deeply influenced by Calvinism and wanted to see England move in that austere direction. But Edward died at age fifteen, opening the way to his Catholic half-sister, Mary Tudor, who had been restored to the line of succession by an act of Parliament under Henry VIII in 1544.

When Mary (r. 1553–1558) came to the throne, she restored Catholicism and persecuted Protestants. Nearly three hundred Protestants perished at the stake, and more than eight hundred fled to the Protestant German states and Switzerland. Finally, when Anne Boleyn's daughter, Elizabeth, succeeded her half-sister Mary, becoming Queen Elizabeth I (r. 1558–1603), the English Protestant cause again gained momentum. Under Elizabeth's leadership, Anglicanism eventually defined the character of the English nation. Catholics were tolerated only if they kept their opinions on religion and politics to themselves. A tentative but nonetheless real peace returned to England.

Still another pattern of religious politics unfolded in Scotland, where powerful noble clans directly challenged royal power. Protestants formed a small minority in Scotland until the 1550s. The most prominent Scottish reformer, John Knox (1514–1572), spent many of his early years in exile in England and on the continent because of his devout Calvinism. At the center of Scotland's conflict over religion stood Mary of Guise, a native French woman and Catholic married to the king of Scotland, James V. After he died in 1542, she surrounded herself and her daughter Mary Stuart, also a Catholic and heir to the throne, with French advisers. When Mary Stuart married Francis, the son of Henry II and the heir to the French throne, in 1558 many Scottish noblemen, alienated by this pro-French atmosphere, joined the pro-English, anti-French Protestant cause.

John Knox helped bring matters to a head when he published in 1558 a diatribe against both Mary Tudor of England and Mary of Guise. The era's suspicion of female rulers and regents also played a part in the work, *The First Blast of the Trumpet against the Monstrous Regiment [Rule] of Women.* In 1560, Protestant nobles gained control of the Scottish Parliament and dethroned the regent Mary of Guise. Eventually they forced her daughter, Mary, by then known as queen of Scots, to flee to England, and installed Mary's infant son James as king. Scotland would turn toward the Calvinist version of the Reformation and thus establish the potential for conflict with England and its Anglican church.

The German States. In the German states, the Protestant princes and cities formed the Schmalkaldic League in 1531. Headed by the elector of Saxony and Philip of Hesse (the two leading Protestant princes), the league included most of the imperial cities, the chief source of the empire's wealth. Opposing the league were Emperor Charles V, the bishops, and the few remaining Catholic princes. Although Charles had to concentrate on fighting the French and the Turks during the 1530s, he eventually secured the western Mediterranean and then turned his attention back home to central Europe to try to resolve the growing religious differences in his lands.

In 1541, Charles convened an Imperial Diet at Regensburg in an effort to mediate between Protestants and Catholics, only to see negotiations between the two sides rapidly break down. Rather than accept a permanent religious schism, Charles prepared to fight the Protestant Schmalkaldic League. To this end, he secured French neutrality in 1544 and papal support in 1545. War broke out in 1547, the year after Martin Luther's death. Using seasoned Spanish veterans and German allies, Charles occupied the German imperial cities in the south, restoring Catholic elites and suppressing the Reformation. In 1547, he defeated the Schmalkaldic League's armies at Mühlberg and captured the leading Lutheran princes. Jubilant, Charles restored Catholics' right to worship in Protestant lands while permitting Lutherans to keep their own rites. Protestant resistance to the declaration was deep and widespread: many pastors went into exile, and riots broke out in many cities.

For Charles V, the reaction of his former allies proved far more alarming than Protestant resistance. His success frightened some Catholic powers. With Spanish troops controlling Milan and Naples, Pope Julius III (r. 1550–1555) feared that papal authority would be subjugated by imperial might. In the Holy Roman Empire, Protestant princes spoke out against "imperial tyranny." Jealously defending their traditional liberties against an overmighty emperor, the Protestant princes, led by Duke Maurice of Saxony, a former ally, raised another army to fight Charles. The princes declared war in 1552 and chased a surprised, unprepared, and practically bankrupt emperor back to Italy.

Forced to compromise, Charles V agreed to the **Peace of Augsburg** in 1555. The settlement recognized the Lutheran church in the empire; accepted the secularization of church lands but "reserved" the remaining ecclesiastical territories (mainly the bishoprics) for Catholics; and, most important, established the principle that all princes, whether Catholic or Lutheran, enjoyed the sole right to determine the religion of their lands and subjects. Significantly, Calvinist, Anabaptist, and other dissenting groups were excluded from the settlement. Ironically, the religious revolt of the common people had culminated in a princes' reformation. As the constitutional framework for the Holy Roman Empire, the Augsburg settlement preserved a fragile peace in central Europe until 1618, but the exclusion of Calvinists would prompt future conflict.

Exhausted by decades of war and disappointed by the disunity in Christian Europe, Emperor Charles V resigned his many thrones in 1555 and 1556, leaving his Netherlandish-Burgundian and Spanish dominions to his son, Philip II, and his Austrian lands to his brother, Ferdinand (who was also elected Holy Roman Emperor to succeed Charles). Retiring to a monastery in southern Spain, the most powerful of the Christian monarchs spent his last years quietly seeking salvation.

REVIEW: How did religious divisions complicate the efforts of rulers to maintain political stability and build stronger states?

Peace of Augsburg: The treaty of 1555 that settled disputes between Holy Roman Emperor Charles V and his Protestant princes. It recognized the Lutheran church and established the principle that all Catholic or Lutheran princes enjoyed the sole right to determine the religion of their lands and subjects.

Conclusion

Europe became a global power while at the same time undergoing a searing internal religious upheaval that permanently divided Christians. Even as Portuguese and Spanish explorers claimed new lands and Catholic missionaries gathered new souls for the church from Mexico to Japan, Luther, Calvin, and a host of others formed competing branches of Protestants in Europe. Lutherans, Calvinists, and Anglicans disagreed on many points of doctrine and church organization, but they all broke definitively from the Roman Catholic church. Protestant laypeople and priests established new Christian communities with new forms of ritual, new doctrines, new social prac-

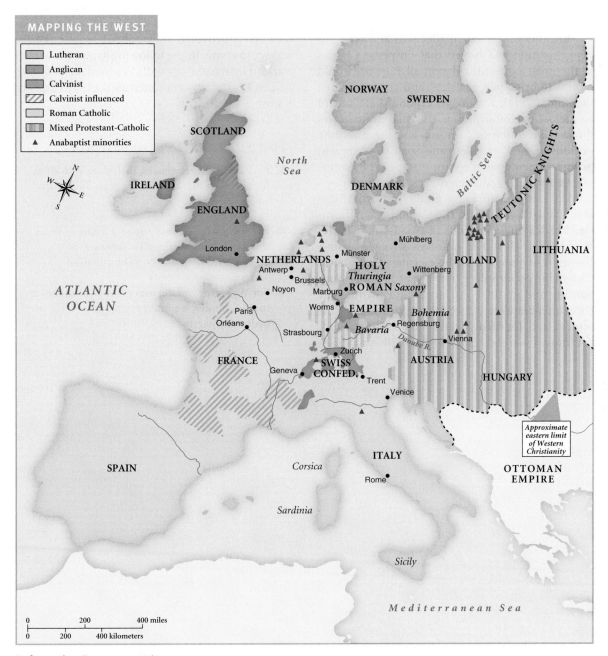

MAPPING THE WEST

Reformation Europe, c. 1560
The fortunes of Roman Catholicism were at their lowest point around 1560. Northern Germany and Scandinavia owed allegiance to the Lutheran church; England broke away under a national church headed by its monarchs; and the Calvinist Reformation would extend across large areas of western, central, and eastern Europe. Southern Europe remained solidly Catholic.

tices, and clergy with vastly different powers and personal lives from those of the Roman Catholic clergy. Catholic priests could not marry; Protestant clergymen could. Catholic clergymen said Mass and heard confessions; Protestant clergy preached the word of God and left confession and penance to the individual sinner, a matter between God and the human heart. Central to the Protestant cause was the belief that people are saved by faith alone; no amount of good works will bring salvation.

Erasmus and many intellectuals and artists of his generation had hoped that Emperor Charles V, the most powerful ruler in all Europe, would be able to bring peace, justice, and victory against the infidel Turks. For the generation that came of age before the Reformation, Christian humanism, the new invention of printing, and the maritime exploits of the Portuguese and Spanish seemed to promise a new golden age for Europe. The Protestant Reformation shattered their dream of powerful princes encouraging gradual improvement and change from within the Catholic church. Instead of leading a crusade against Islam, Charles V wore himself out in ceaseless struggle against Francis I of France and the German Protestants. Christianity split into a number of hostile camps battling one another with words and swords. The consequences were censorship, repression of dissenters, and, for many, death. After the brutal suppression of popular revolts in the 1520s and 1530s,

religious persecution became a Christian institution: Luther called on the princes to kill rebellious peasants in 1525, Zwingli advocated the drowning of Anabaptists, and Calvin supported the death sentence for Michael Servetus. Executions in Catholic lands provided Protestants with a steady stream of martyrs. The two peace settlements in the 1550s failed to provide long-term solutions: the Peace of Augsburg gradually disintegrated as the religious struggles in the empire intensified, and the Treaty of Cateau-Cambrésis provided only a brief respite. Worse was yet to come. In the following generations, civil war and international conflicts would set Catholics against Protestants in numerous futile attempts to restore a single faith.

FOR FURTHER EXPLORATION

- For suggested references, including Web sites, for topics in this chapter, see page SR-1 at the end of the book.

- For additional primary-source material from this period, see Chapter 14 in *Sources of THE MAKING OF THE WEST*, Third Edition.

- For Web sites and documents related to topics in this chapter, see *Make History* at bedfordstmartins.com/hunt.

CHAPTER REVIEW

KEY TERMS AND PEOPLE

Christopher Columbus
(421)

Hernán Cortés (425)

Christian humanism
(427)

Martin Luther (429)

Charles V (430)

John Calvin (432)

predestination (432)

Henry VIII (433)

Anabaptists (436)

Council of Trent (439)

Jesuits (439)

Suleiman
the Magnificent (443)

Peace of Augsburg (446)

MAKING CONNECTIONS

1. Why was Charles V ultimately unable to prevent religious division in his lands?

2. How did the different religious groups respond to the opportunity presented by the printing press?

> **For practice quizzes, a customized study plan, and other study tools,** see the Online Study Guide at bedfordstmartins.com/hunt.

REVIEW QUESTIONS

1. Which European countries led the way in maritime exploration and what were their motives?

2. How did Luther, Zwingli, Calvin, and Henry VIII challenge the Roman Catholic church?

3. How did the forces for radical change unleashed by the Protestant Reformation interact with the urge for social order and stability?

4. How did religious divisions complicate the efforts of rulers to maintain political stability and build stronger states?

IMPORTANT EVENTS

1492	Columbus reaches the Americas
1494	Italian Wars begin; Treaty of Tordesillas divides Atlantic world between Portugal and Spain
1516	Erasmus publishes Greek edition of the New Testament; More writes *Utopia*
1517	Luther composes ninety-five theses to challenge Catholic church
1520	Luther publishes three treatises; Zwingli breaks from Rome
1525	German Peasants' War
1527	Charles V's imperial troops sack Rome
1529	Colloquy of Marburg assembles to address disagreements between German and Swiss church reformers
1534	Henry VIII breaks with Rome; Affair of the Placards in France
1536	Calvin publishes *Institutes of the Christian Religion*
1540	Jesuits (Society of Jesus) established as new Catholic order
1545–1563	Catholic Council of Trent condemns Protestant beliefs and confirms church doctrine and sacraments
1547	Charles V defeats Protestants at Mühlberg
1555	Peace of Augsburg ends religious wars and recognizes Lutheran church in German states
1559	Treaty of Cateau-Cambrésis ends wars between Habsburg and Valois rulers

Wars of Religion and the Clash of Worldviews

1560–1648

I n May 1618, Protestants in the kingdom of Bohemia furiously protested the Holy Roman Emperor's attempts to curtail their hard-won religious freedoms. Protestants wanted to build new churches; the Catholic emperor wanted to stop them. Tensions boiled over when two Catholic officials tried to dissolve the meetings of Protestants. On May 23, a crowd of angry Protestants surged up the stairs of the royal castle in Prague, trapped the two Catholic deputies, dragged them screaming for mercy to the windows, and hurled them to the pavement below. One of the rebels jeered: "We will see if your [Virgin] Mary can help you!" But because they landed in a dung heap, the Catholic deputies survived. One of the two limped off on his own; the other was carried by his servants to safety. Although no one died, the defenestration (from the French for "window," *la fenêtre*) of Prague touched off the Thirty Years' War (1618–1648), which eventually involved almost every major power in Europe. Before it ended, the fighting had devastated the lands of central Europe and produced permanent changes in European politics and culture.

The Thirty Years' War grew out of the religious conflicts initiated by the Reformation. When Martin Luther began the Protestant Reformation in 1517, few could have predicted that he would be unleashing such dangerous forces, but religious turmoil and warfare followed almost immediately upon Luther's break with the Catholic church. From its establishment in 1555 until the early 1600s, the Peace of Augsburg maintained relative calm in the lands of the Holy Roman Empire by granting each ruler the right to determine the religion of his territory. But in western Europe, religious strife increased dramatically after 1560 as Protestants made inroads in France, the Spanish-ruled Netherlands, and England. All in all, nearly constant warfare marked the century

The Defenestration of Prague, 1618
In this copper-plate engraving by Swiss artist Matthäus Merian (1593–1650), Czech Protestants attack the Catholic deputies sent to disband their meeting. The attackers are about to throw the two Catholics out of the windows of the royal castle (that is, the Catholics are about to suffer "defenestration"). The defenestration touched off the Thirty Years' War. *(Bildarchiv Preussischer Kulturbesitz/Art Resource, NY.)*

between 1560 and 1648. These struggles often began as religious conflicts, but religion was rarely the sole motive; political ambitions, commercial competition, and long-standing rivalries between the leading powers inevitably raised the stakes of conflict.

Although particularly dramatic and deadly, the church-state crisis was only one of a series of upheavals that shaped this era. In the early seventeenth century, a major economic downturn led to food shortages, famine, and disease in much of Europe. These catastrophes hit especially hard in the central European lands devastated by the fighting of the Thirty Years' War and helped shift the balance of economic power to northwestern Europe, away from the Mediterranean and central Europe. The deepening sense of crisis prompted some to seek new, nonreligious grounds for all forms of authority, whether artistic, political, or philosophical. The emergence of a secular worldview that relied on new scientific methods of research would ultimately reshape Western attitudes over the long term.

> **FOCUS QUESTION:** What were the long-term political, economic, and intellectual consequences of the conflicts over religious belief?

Religious Conflicts Threaten State Power, 1560–1618

The Peace of Augsburg made Lutheranism a legal religion in the predominantly Catholic Holy Roman Empire, but it did not extend recognition to Calvinists. Although the followers of Martin Luther (Lutherans) and those of John Calvin (Calvinists) similarly refused the authority of the Catholic church, they disagreed with each other about religious doctrine and church organization. The rapid expansion of Calvinism after 1560 threatened to alter the religious balance of power in much of Europe. Calvinists challenged Catholic dominance in France, the Spanish-ruled Netherlands, Scotland, and Poland-Lithuania. In England, they sought to influence the new Protestant monarch, Elizabeth I. Calvinists were not the only source of religious contention, however. Philip II of Spain fought the Muslim Ottoman Turks in the Mediterranean and expelled the remnants of the Muslim population in Spain. To the east, the Russian tsar Ivan IV fought to make Muscovy the center of an empire based on Russian Orthodox Christianity.

French Wars of Religion, 1562–1598

Calvinism spread in France after 1555, when the Genevan Company of Pastors sent missionaries supplied with false passports and often disguised as merchants. The Calvinist pastors moved rapidly among their growing flock, which gathered in secret in towns near Paris or in the south. Calvinist nobles provided military protection to local congregations and helped set up a national organization for the French Calvinist — or Huguenot — church. In 1562, rival Huguenot and Catholic armies began fighting a series of wars that threatened to tear the French nation into shreds (Map 15.1).

Religious Division in the Nobility.   Armed struggle erupted because the French kings could not keep a lid on religious conflict. By the end of the 1560s, nearly one-third of the nobles had joined the Huguenots, and they could raise their own armies. Conversion to Calvinism in French noble families often began with the noblewomen, some of whom sought intellectual independence as well as spiritual renewal in the new faith. Charlotte de

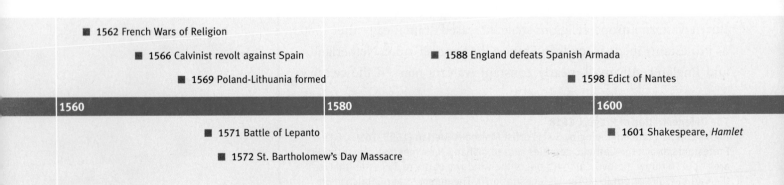

■ 1562 French Wars of Religion

■ 1566 Calvinist revolt against Spain

■ 1569 Poland-Lithuania formed

■ 1588 England defeats Spanish Armada

■ 1598 Edict of Nantes

1560	1580	1600

■ 1571 Battle of Lepanto

■ 1572 St. Bartholomew's Day Massacre

■ 1601 Shakespeare, *Hamlet*

Bourbon, for example, fled from a Catholic convent and eventually married William of Orange, the leader of the anti-Spanish resistance in the Netherlands. Calvinist noblewomen protected pastors, provided money and advice, and helped found schools and establish relief for the poor.

A series of family tragedies prevented the French kings from acting decisively to prevent the spread of Calvinism. King Henry II was accidentally killed during a jousting tournament in 1559 and his fifteen-year-old son, Francis, died soon after. Ten-year-old Charles IX (r. 1560–1574) became king, with his mother, **Catherine de Médicis**, as regent, or acting ruler. An ambassador commented on the weakness of Catherine's hold: "It is sufficient to say that she is a woman, a foreigner, and a Florentine to boot, born of a simple house, altogether beneath the dignity of the Kingdom of France." The Huguenots followed the lead of the Bourbon family, who were close relatives of the French king and stood first in line to inherit the throne if the Valois kings failed to produce a male heir. The most militantly Catholic nobles took their cues from the Guise family, who aimed to block Bourbon ambitions. Catherine tried to play the Bourbon and Guise factions against each other, but civil war erupted in 1562. Both sides committed terrible atrocities. Priests and pastors were murdered, and massacres of whole congregations became frighteningly commonplace.

Catherine de Médicis: Italian-born mother of French king Charles X; she served as regent and tried but failed to prevent religious warfare between Calvinists and Catholics.

MAP 15.1 Protestant Churches in France, 1562
Calvinist missionaries took their message from their headquarters in Geneva across the border into France. The strongest concentration of Protestants was in southern France. The Bourbons, leaders of the Protestants in France, had their family lands in Navarre, a region in southwestern France that had been divided between France and Spain.

■ 1618 Thirty Years' War   ■ 1635 French declare war on Spain

■ 1648 Peace of Westphalia

| 1620 | 1640 | 1660 |

■ 1625 Grotius, *The Laws of War and Peace*

■ 1633 Galileo forced to recant

Massacre Motivated by Religion
The Italian artist Giorgio Vasari painted *St. Bartholomew's Night: The Massacre of the Huguenots* for a public room in Pope Gregory XIII's residence. How did the artist celebrate what he saw as a Catholic victory over Protestant heresy? *(Scala/Art Resource, NY.)*

St. Bartholomew's Day Massacre, 1572. Although a Catholic herself, Catherine feared the rise of Guise influence, so she arranged the marriage of the king's Catholic sister, Marguerite de Valois, to Henry of Navarre, a Huguenot and Bourbon. Just four days after the wedding in August 1572, assassins tried but failed to kill one of the Huguenot nobles allied with the Bourbons. Perhaps herself implicated in the botched plot and panicked at the thought of Huguenot revenge, Catherine convinced her son to go on the offensive by ordering the death of Huguenot leaders who had come to Paris for the wedding. Violence almost immediately spiraled out of control. On St. Bartholomew's Day, August 24, a bloodbath began, fueled by years of growing animosity between Catholics and Protestants. (See Massacre Motivated by Religion, at left.) In three days, Catholic mobs murdered three thousand Huguenots in Paris. Wherever Calvinists lacked military protection, they were at risk. Ten thousand Huguenots died in the provinces over the next six weeks. The pope joyfully ordered the church bells rung throughout Catholic Europe; Spain's Philip II wrote Catherine that it was "the best and most cheerful news which at present could come to me."

The massacre settled nothing. Huguenot pamphleteers now proclaimed their right to resist a tyrant who worshipped idols (a practice that Calvinists equated with Catholicism). This right of resistance was linked to a political notion of contract; upholding the true religion was part of the contract imagined as binding the ruler to his subjects. Both the right of resistance and the idea of a contract fed into the larger doctrine of constitutionalism — that a government's legitimacy rested on its upholding a constitution or contract between ruler and ruled. Constitutionalism was used to justify resistance movements from the sixteenth century onward. Protestants and Catholics alike now saw the religious conflict as an international struggle for survival that required aid to their fellow Catholics or Protestants in other countries. In this way, the French Wars of Religion paved the way for wider international conflicts over religion in the decades to come.

Henry IV and the Edict of Nantes. The religious division in France grew even more dangerous when Charles IX died and his brother Henry III (r. 1574–1589) became king. Like his brothers before him, Henry III failed to produce an heir. Next in line to the throne was none other than the Protestant Bourbon leader Henry of Navarre, a distant cousin of the Valois ruling family and brother-in-law of Charles and Henry. Convinced that Henry III lacked the will to root out Protestantism, the Guises formed the Catholic League, which requested help from Spanish king Philip II. Henry III responded with a fatal trick: in 1588, he summoned the two Guise leaders to a meeting and had his men kill them. A few months later, a fanatical monk stabbed Henry III to death, and Henry of Navarre became Henry IV (r. 1589–1610), despite Philip II's attempt to block his ascension with military intervention.

Henry IV soon concluded that to establish control over war-weary France he had to place the interests of the French state ahead of his Protestant faith. In 1593, he publicly embraced Catholicism, reputedly explaining his conversion with the statement "Paris is worth a Mass." Within a few years he defeated the ultra-Catholic opposition and drove out the Spanish. In 1598, he made peace with Spain and issued the **Edict of Nantes**, in which he granted the Huguenots a large measure of religious toleration. The approximately 1.25 million Huguenots became a legally protected minority within an officially Catholic kingdom of some 20 million people. Protestants were free to worship in specified towns and were allowed their own troops, fortresses, and even courts. Few believed in religious toleration, but Henry IV followed the advice of those moderate Catholics and Calvinists called *politiques* who urged him to give priority to the development of a durable state. Although their opponents hated them for their compromising spirit, the politiques believed that religious disputes could be resolved only in the peace provided by strong government.

The Edict of Nantes ended the French Wars of Religion, but Henry still needed to reestablish monarchical authority and hold the fractious nobles in check. He used court festivities and royal processions to rally subjects around him, and he allowed rich merchants and lawyers to buy offices and, in exchange for an annual payment, pass their positions on to their heirs to sell them to someone else. This new social elite was known as the "nobility of the robe" (named after the robes that magistrates wore, much like those judges wear today). Income raised by the increased sale of offices reduced the state debt and also helped Henry strengthen the monarchy. His efforts did not, however, prevent his enemies from assassinating him in 1610 after nineteen unsuccessful attempts.

Challenges to Spain's Authority

Although he failed to prevent Henry IV from taking the French throne in 1589, Philip II of Spain (r. 1556–1598) was the most powerful ruler in Europe (Map 15.2). In addition to the western Habsburg lands in Spain and the Netherlands, Philip had inherited from his father, Charles V, all the Spanish colonies recently settled in the New World of the Americas. Gold and silver funneled from the colonies supported his campaigns against the Ottoman Turks and the French and the English Protestants. But all of the money of the New World could not prevent Philip's eventual defeat in the Netherlands, where Calvinist rebels established an independent Dutch Republic that soon vied with Spain, France, and England for commercial supremacy.

Philip II, the Catholic King. A deeply devout Catholic, **Philip II** came to the Spanish throne at age twenty-eight determined to restore Catholic unity in Europe and lead the Christian defense against the Muslims. In his quest, Philip benefited from a series of misfortunes. His four wives all died, but through them he became part of four royal families: Portuguese, English, French, and Austrian. His brief marriage to Mary Tudor (Mary I of England) did not produce an heir, but it and his subsequent marriage to Elisabeth de Valois, the sister of Charles IX and Henry III of France, gave him reason enough for involvement in English and French affairs. In 1580, when the king of Portugal died without a direct heir, Philip took over this neighboring realm with its rich empire in Africa, India, and the Americas.

Philip insisted on Catholic unity in his own possessions and worked to forge an international Catholic alliance against the Ottoman Turks. In 1571, he achieved the single greatest military victory of his reign when he joined with Venice and the papacy to defeat the Turks in a great sea battle off the Greek coast at **Lepanto**. Fifty thousand sailors and soldiers fought on the allied side, and eight thousand died. Spain now controlled the western Mediterranean. But Philip could not rest on his laurels. Between 1568 and 1570, the Moriscos — Muslim converts to Christianity who

---

Edict of Nantes: The decree issued by French king Henry IV in 1598 that granted the Huguenots a large measure of religious toleration.

politiques (poh lih TEEK): Political advisers during the sixteenth-century French Wars of Religion who argued that compromise in matters of religion would strengthen the monarchy.

Philip II: King of Spain (r. 1556–1598) and the most powerful ruler in Europe; he reigned over the western Habsburg lands and all the Spanish colonies recently settled in the New World.

Lepanto: A site off the Greek coast where, in 1571, the allied Catholic forces of Spain's king Philip II, Venice, and the papacy defeated the Ottoman Turks in a great sea battle; the victory gave the Christian powers control of the Mediterranean.

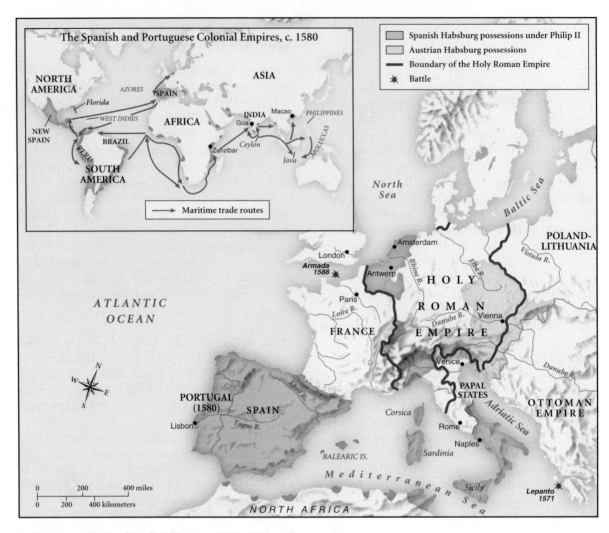

MAP 15.2 The Empire of Philip II, r. 1556–1598
Spanish king Philip II drew revenues from a truly worldwide empire. In 1580, he was
the richest European ruler, but the demands of governing and defending his control of
such far-flung territories eventually drained many of his resources.

remained secretly faithful to Islam — had revolted in the south of Spain, killing ninety priests and fifteen hundred Christians. Philip retaliated by forcing fifty thousand to leave their villages and resettle in other regions. In 1609, his successor, Philip III, ordered their expulsion from Spanish territory, and by 1614 some 300,000 Moriscos had been forced to relocate to North Africa.

The Revolt of the Netherlands.

The Calvinists of the Netherlands were less easily intimidated than the Moriscos: they were far from Spain and accustomed to being left alone. When Calvinists in the Netherlands attacked Catholic

The Netherlands during the Revolt, c. 1580

churches in 1566, smashing stained-glass windows and statues of the Virgin Mary, Philip sent an army to punish the rebels. Calvinist resistance continued despite this occupation, and in November 1576 Philip's long-unpaid armies sacked Antwerp, then Europe's wealthiest commercial city. In eleven days of horror known as the Spanish Fury, the Spanish soldiers slaughtered seven thousand people. Led by Prince William of Orange (whose name came from the lands he owned in southern France), the Netherlands' seven Protestant northern provinces formally allied with the ten Catholic southern provinces and drove out the Spaniards. The

Philip II of Spain
The king of Spain is shown here (kneeling in black) with his allies at the battle of Lepanto, the doge of Venice on his left and Pope Pius V on his right. El Greco painted this canvas, sometimes called *The Dream of Philip II*, in 1578 or 1579. The painting is typically mannerist in the way it crowds figures into every available space, uses larger-than-life or elongated bodies, and creates new and often bizarre visual effects. What can we conclude about Philip II's character from the way he is depicted here? *(© The National Gallery, London.)*

southern provinces nonetheless remained Catholic, French-speaking in parts, and suspicious of the increasingly strict Calvinism in the north. In 1579, they returned to the Spanish fold. Despite the assassination in 1584 of William of Orange, Spanish troops never regained control in the north. Spain would not formally recognize Dutch independence until 1648, but by the end of the sixteenth century the Dutch Republic (sometimes called Holland after the most populous of its seven provinces) was a self-governing state sheltering a variety of religious groups.

Religious toleration thrived because the central government did not have the power to enforce religious orthodoxy. Urban merchant and professional families known as regents controlled the towns and provinces. In the absence of a national bureaucracy, a single legal system, or a central court, each province governed itself and sent delegates to the one common institution, the States General, which carried out the wishes of the strongest individual provinces and their ruling families. Although the princes of Orange resembled a ruling family, their powers paled next to those of local elites. One-third of the Dutch population remained Catholic, and local authorities allowed them to worship as they chose in private. The Dutch Republic also had a relatively large Jewish population because many Jews had settled there after being driven out of Spain and Portugal. From 1597, Jews could worship openly in their synagogues. This openness to various religions would help to make the Dutch Republic one of Europe's chief intellectual and scientific centers in the seventeenth and eighteenth centuries.

Well situated for maritime commerce, the Dutch Republic developed a thriving economy based on shipping and shipbuilding. Dutch merchants favored free trade in Europe because they could compete at an advantage. Whereas elites in other countries focused on their landholdings, the Dutch looked for investments in trade. After the Dutch gained independence, Amsterdam became the main European money market for two centuries. The city was also a primary commodities market and a chief supplier of arms—to allies, neutrals, and even enemies. Dutch entrepreneurs

Queen Elizabeth I of England
The Anglican (Church of England) Prayerbook of 1569 included a hand-colored print of Queen Elizabeth saying her prayers. As queen, Elizabeth was also official head of the Church of England—the scepter or sword at her feet symbolizes her power. She named bishops and made final decisions about every aspect of church governance. *(HIP/Art Resource, NY.)*

■ **For more help analyzing this image,** see the visual activity for this chapter in the Online Study Guide at **bedfordstmartins.com/hunt**.

produced goods at lower prices than competitors and marketed them more efficiently. The Dutch controlled many overseas markets thanks to their preeminence in seaborne commerce: by 1670, the Dutch commercial fleet was larger than the English, French, Spanish, Portuguese, and Austrian fleets combined.

Elizabeth I's Defense of English Protestantism

As the Dutch revolt unfolded, Philip II became increasingly infuriated with **Elizabeth I** (r. 1558–1603), who had succeeded her half-sister Mary Tudor as queen of England. Philip had been married to Mary and had enthusiastically seconded Mary's efforts to return England to Catholicism. When Mary died in 1558, Elizabeth rejected Philip's proposal of marriage and promptly brought Protestantism back to England. Eventually, she provided funds and troops to the Dutch Protestant cause. As Elizabeth moved to solidify her personal power and the authority of the Anglican church (Church of England), she had to squash uprisings by Catholics in the north and at least two serious plots against her life. In the long run, however, her greater challenges came from the Calvinist Puritans and Philip II.

Puritanism and the Church of England. The **Puritans** were strict Calvinists who opposed all vestiges of Catholic ritual in the Church of England. After Elizabeth became queen, many Puritans returned from exile abroad, but Elizabeth resisted their demands for drastic changes in church ritual and governance. The Church of England's Thirty-Nine Articles of Religion, issued under her authority in 1563, incorporated elements of Catholic ritual along with Calvinist doctrines. Puritan ministers angrily denounced the Church of England's "popish attire and foolish disguising, . . . tithings, holy days, and a thousand more abominations." To accomplish their reforms, Puritans tried to undercut the crown-appointed bishops' authority by placing control of church administration in the hands of a local presbytery, that is, a group made up of the minister and the elders of the congregation. Elizabeth rejected this Calvinist presbyterianism.

Elizabeth I: English queen (r. 1558–1603) who oversaw the return of the Protestant Anglican church and, in 1588, the successful defense of the realm against the Spanish Armada.

Puritans: Strict Calvinists who opposed all vestiges of Catholic ritual in the Church of England.

The Puritans nonetheless steadily gained influence. Known for their emphasis on strict moral lives, the Puritans tried to close England's theaters and Sunday fairs. Every Puritan father—with the help of his wife—was to "make his house a little church" by teaching the children to read the Bible. At Puritan urging, a new translation of the Bible, known as the King James Bible after Elizabeth's successor, James I, was authorized in 1604. Believing themselves God's elect—those whom God has chosen for mercy and salvation—and England an "elect nation," the Puritans also pushed Elizabeth to help Protestants on the continent. Elizabeth initially resisted, but after Philip II annexed Portugal and began to interfere in French affairs, she sent funds to the Dutch rebels and in 1585 dispatched seven thousand soldiers to help them.

Triumph over Spain.   Although enraged by Elizabeth's aid to the Dutch rebels against his rule, Philip II bided his time as long as Elizabeth remained unmarried and her Catholic cousin Mary Stuart, better known as Mary, Queen of Scots, stood next in line to inherit the English throne. In 1568, Scottish Calvinists forced Mary to abdicate the throne of Scotland in favor of her one-year-old son James (eventually James I of England), who was then raised as a Protestant. After her abdication, Mary spent nearly twenty years under house arrest in England, fomenting plots against Elizabeth. In 1587, when a letter from Mary offering her succession rights to Philip was discovered, Elizabeth overcame her reluctance to execute a fellow monarch and ordered Mary's beheading.

Now determined to act, Philip II sent his armada (Spanish for "fleet") of 130 ships from Lisbon toward the English Channel in May 1588. The English scattered the Spanish Armada by sending blazing fire ships into its midst. A great gale then forced the Spanish to flee around Scotland. When the armada limped home in September, half the ships had been lost and thousands of sailors were dead or starving. Protestants throughout Europe rejoiced. Philip and Catholic Spain suffered a crushing psychological blow. A Spanish monk lamented, "Almost the whole of Spain went into mourning."

Retreat of the Spanish Armada, 1588

By the time Philip II died in 1598, his great empire had begun to lose its luster. The costs of fighting the Dutch, the English, and the French had mounted, and an overburdened peasantry could no longer pay the taxes required to meet rising expenses. In his novel *Don Quixote* (1605), the Spanish writer Miguel de Cervantes captured the disappointment of thwarted imperial ambition. Cervantes himself had been wounded at Lepanto. His novel's hero, a minor nobleman, wants to understand "this thing they call reason of state," but he reads so many romances and books of chivalry that he loses his wits and wanders the countryside hoping to re-create the heroic deeds of times past.

England could never have defeated Spain in a head-to-head battle on land, but Elizabeth made the most of her limited means and consolidated the country's position as a Protestant power. In her early years, she held out the prospect of marriage to many political suitors; but in order to maintain her—and England's—independence, she never married. Her chosen successor, James I (r. 1603–1625), came to the throne as king of both Scotland and England. Shakespeare's tragedies *Hamlet* (1601), *King Lear* (1605), and *Macbeth* (1606), written around the time of James's succession, might all be read as commentaries on the uncertainties faced by Elizabeth and James. But Elizabeth's story, unlike Shakespeare's tragedies, had a happy ending; she left James secure in a kingdom of growing weight in world politics.

The Clash of Faiths and Empires in Eastern Europe

In the east, the most contentious border divided Christian Europe from the Islamic realm of the Ottoman Turks. Even after their defeat at Lepanto in 1571, the Ottomans continued their attacks, seizing Venetian-held Cyprus in 1573. In the Balkans, the Turks allowed their Christian subjects to cling to the Orthodox faith rather than forcibly converting them to Islam. They also tolerated many prosperous Jewish communities, which grew with the influx of Jews expelled from Spain.

The Muscovite tsars officially protected the Russian Orthodox church, which faced no competition within Russian lands. Building on the base laid by his grandfather Ivan III, Tsar Ivan IV (r. 1533–1584) stopped at nothing in his endeavor to make Muscovy the center of a mighty Russian empire. Given to unpredictable fits of rage, Ivan tortured priests, killed numerous *boyars* (nobles), and murdered his own son with an iron rod during a quarrel. His epithet "the Terrible" reflects not only the terror he unleashed but also the awesome impression he evoked. Cunning and cruel, Ivan came to embody barbarism in the eyes of Westerners. One English visitor commented disapprovingly that the Russian government "is very similar to the Turkish, which they apparently try to imitate."

Ivan initiated Russian expansion eastward into Siberia and also tried to gain new territory to the west, when he tried, unsuccessfully, to seize parts of present-day Estonia and Latvia to provide Russia direct access to the Baltic Sea. Two formidable foes blocked Ivan's plans for expansion: Sweden (which then included much of present-day Finland) and Poland-Lithuania. Their rulers hoped to annex the eastern Baltic provinces themselves. Poland and the grand duchy of Lithuania united into a single commonwealth in 1569 and controlled an extensive territory stretching from the Baltic Sea to deep within present-day Ukraine and Belarus. Poland-Lithuania, like the Dutch Republic, was one of the great exceptions to the general trend toward greater monarchical authority; the country's nobles elected their king and placed severe limits on his authority. Noble converts to Lutheranism or Calvinism feared religious persecution by the Catholic majority, so the Polish-Lithuanian nobles insisted that their kings accept the principle of religious toleration as a prerequisite for election.

Poland-Lithuania threatened the rule of Ivan's successors in Russia. After Ivan IV died in 1584, a terrible period of chaos known as the Time of Troubles ensued, during which the king of Poland-Lithuania tried to put his son on the Russian throne. In 1613, an army of nobles, townspeople, and peasants finally expelled the intruders and put on the throne a nobleman, Michael Romanov (r. 1613–1645), who established an enduring new dynasty. With the return of peace, Muscovite Russia resumed the process of state building.

Russia, Poland-Lithuania, and Sweden in the Late 1500s

> **REVIEW:** How did state power depend on religious unity at the end of the sixteenth century and start of the seventeenth?

The Thirty Years' War, 1618–1648

Although the eastern states managed to avoid civil wars over religion in the early seventeenth century, the rest of Europe was drawn into the final and most deadly of the wars of religion, the Thirty Years' War. It began in 1618 with conflicts between Catholics and Protestants within the Holy Roman Empire and eventually involved most European states. By its end in 1648, many central European lands lay in ruins and the balance of power had shifted away from the Habsburg powers — Spain and Austria — toward France, England, and the Dutch Republic. Prolonged warfare created turmoil and suffering, but it also fostered the growth of armies and bureaucracies; out of the carnage would emerge centralized and powerful states that made increasing demands on ordinary people.

Origins and Course of the War

The fighting that devastated central Europe had its origins in a combination of religious dispute, ethnic competition, and political weakness. The Austrian Habsburgs officially ruled over the huge Holy Roman Empire, which comprised eight major ethnic groups. The emperor and four of the seven electors who chose him were Catholic; the other three electors were Protestants. The Peace of Augsburg of 1555 (see Chapter 14) was supposed to maintain the balance between Catholics and Lutherans, but it had no mechanism for resolving conflicts; tensions rose as the new Catholic religious order, the Jesuits, won many Lutheran cities back to Catholicism and as Calvinism, unrecognized under the peace, made inroads into Lutheran areas. By 1613, two of the three Protestant electors had become Calvinists.

These conflicts came to a head when the Catholic Habsburg heir Archduke Ferdinand was crowned king of Bohemia in 1617. The Austrian Habsburgs held not only the imperial crown of the Holy Roman Empire but also a collection of separately administered royal crowns, of which Bohemia was one. Once crowned, Ferdinand began to curtail the religious freedom previously granted to Protestants. The Czechs, the largest ethnic group in Bohemia, responded with the so-called defenestration of Prague and promptly established a Protestant assembly to spearhead resistance. A year later, when Ferdinand was elected emperor (as Ferdinand II, r. 1619–1637), the rebellious Bohemians deposed him and chose in his place the young Calvinist Frederick V of the Palatinate

(r. 1616–1623). A quick series of clashes ended in 1620 when the imperial armies defeated the out-manned Czechs at the battle of White Mountain, near Prague. Like the martyrdom of the religious reformer Jan Hus in 1415, White Mountain became an enduring symbol of the Czechs' desire for self-determination. They would not gain their independence until 1918.

White Mountain did not end the war, which soon spread to the German lands of the empire. Private mercenary armies (armies for hire) began to form during the fighting, and the emperor had little control over them. The meteoric rise of one commander, Albrecht von Wallenstein (1583–1634), showed how political ambition could trump religious conviction. A Czech Protestant by birth, Wallenstein offered in 1625 to raise an army for Ferdinand II and soon had in his employ 125,000 soldiers, who occupied and plundered much of Protestant Germany with the emperor's approval.

The Lutheran king of Denmark, Christian IV (r. 1596–1648), responded by invading northern Germany to protect the Protestants and to extend his own influence. Despite Dutch and English encouragement, Christian lacked adequate military support, and Wallenstein's forces defeated him. Emboldened by his general's victories, Ferdinand issued the Edict of Restitution in 1629, which outlawed Calvinism in the empire and reclaimed Catholic church properties confiscated by the Lutherans.

With Protestant interests in serious jeopardy, Gustavus Adolphus (r. 1611–1632) of Sweden marched into Germany in 1630. Declaring his support for the Protestant cause, he also intended to gain control over trade in northern Europe. His highly trained army of some 100,000 soldiers made Sweden, with a population of only one million, the supreme power of northern Europe. Hoping to block Spanish intervention in the war and win influence and perhaps territory in the Holy Roman Empire, the French monarchy's chief minister, Cardinal Richelieu (1585–1642), offered to subsidize the Lutheran Gustavus. This agreement between the Swedish Lutheran and French Catholic powers to fight the Catholic Habsburgs showed that state interests could outweigh all other considerations.

Gustavus defeated the imperial army and occupied the Catholic parts of southern Germany before he was killed at the battle of Lützen in 1632. Once again the tide turned, but this time it swept Wallenstein with it. Because Wallenstein was rumored to be negotiating with Protestant powers, Ferdinand dismissed his general and had him assassinated.

France openly joined the fray in 1635 by declaring war on Spain and soon after forged an alliance with the Calvinist Dutch to aid them in their ongoing struggle for official independence from Spain. Religion took a backseat to dynastic rivalry as the two Catholic powers France and Spain

---

The Violence of the Thirty Years' War
The French artist Jacques Callot produced this engraving of the Thirty Years' War as part of a series called *The Miseries and Misfortunes of War* (1633). It shows the rape, torture, and pillaging inflicted by soldiers on noncombatants they found in their path. *(The Granger Collection, New York.)*

DOCUMENT

The Horrors of the Thirty Years' War

Hans Grimmelshausen experienced the Thirty Years' War firsthand and then wrote about it in his novel The Adventures of a Simpleton *(published in 1669). He had been a Lutheran schoolboy when soldiers from an unidentified army looted his town. Later he served as a musketeer in the Catholic imperial armies and converted to Catholicism. In the novel, he writes from the point of view of a "simpleton," a naive peasant who does not understand what is happening around him as a group of cavalrymen ransack the village.*

What they did not intend to take along they broke and spoiled. Some ran their swords into the hay and straw, as if there hadn't been hogs enough to stick. Some shook the feathers out of beds and put bacon slabs, hams, and other stuff in the ticking, as if they might sleep better on these. Others knocked down the hearth and broke the windows, as if announcing an everlasting summer. They flattened out copper and pewter dishes and baled the ruined goods. They burned up bedsteads, tables, chairs, and benches, though there were yards of dry firewood outside the kitchen. Jars and crocks, pots and casseroles all were broken, either because they preferred their meat broiled or because they thought they'd eat only one meal with us. In the barn, the hired girl was handled so roughly that she was unable to walk away, I am ashamed to report. They stretched the hired man out flat on the ground, stuck a wooden wedge in his mouth to keep it open, and emptied a milk bucket full of stinking manure drippings down his throat; they called it a Swedish cocktail. He didn't relish it and made a very wry face. . . . Then they used thumbscrews, which they cleverly made out of their pistols, to torture the peasants, as if they wanted to burn witches. Though he had confessed to nothing as yet, they put one of the captured hayseeds in the bakeoven and lighted a fire in it. They put a rope around someone else's head and tightened it like a tourniquet until blood came out of his mouth, nose, and ears. In short, every soldier had his favorite method of making life miserable for peasants, and every peasant had his own misery.

Source: *The Adventures of Simplicius Simpliccissimus*, 2nd ed. Trans. George Schulz-Behrend (Columbia, S.C.: Camden House, 1993), 6–7.

pummeled each other. Advised by his minister Richelieu, who held the high rank of cardinal in the Catholic church, the French king Louis XIII (r. 1610–1643) hoped to profit from the troubles of Spain in the Netherlands and from the conflicts between the Austrian emperor and his Protestant subjects. The Swedes kept up their pressure in Germany, the Dutch attacked the Spanish fleet, and a series of internal revolts shook the cash-strapped Spanish crown. In 1640, peasants in the rich northeastern province of Catalonia rebelled, overrunning Barcelona and killing the viceroy; the Catalans resented government confiscation of their crops and demands that they house and feed soldiers on their way to the French frontier. The Portuguese revolted in 1640 and proclaimed independence like the Dutch. In 1643, the Spanish suffered their first major defeat at French hands. Although the Spanish were forced to concede independence to Portugal (part of Spain only since 1580), they eventually suppressed the Catalan revolt.

France, too, finally faced exhaustion after years of rising taxes and recurrent revolts. Richelieu died in 1642. Louis XIII followed him a few months later and was succeeded by his five-year-old son, Louis XIV. With yet another foreign queen mother—she was the daughter of the Spanish king—serving as regent and an Italian cardinal, Mazarin, providing advice, French politics once again moved into a period of instability, rumor, and crisis. All sides were ready for peace.

The Effects of Constant Fighting

When peace negotiations began in the 1640s, they did not come a moment too soon for the ordinary people of Europe. Some towns had faced up to ten or eleven prolonged sieges during the decades of fighting. Even worse suffering took place in the countryside. Peasants fled their villages, which were often burned down (see Document, "The Horrors of the Thirty Years' War," above). At times, desperate peasants revolted and attacked nearby castles and monasteries. War and intermittent outbreaks of plague cost some German towns one-third or more of their population. One-third of the inhabitants of Bohemia also perished.

Soldiers did not fare all that much better. An Englishman who fought for the Dutch army in 1633 described how he slept on the wet ground, got his boots full of water, and "at peep of day looked like a drowned ratt." Governments increasingly short of funds often failed to pay the troops, and frequent mutinies, looting, and pillaging resulted. Armies attracted all sorts of displaced people

MAP 15.3 The Thirty Years' War and the Peace of Westphalia, 1648
The Thirty Years' War involved many of the major continental European powers. The arrows marking invasion routes show that most of the fighting took place in central Europe in the lands of the Holy Roman Empire. The German states and Bohemia sustained the greatest damage during the fighting. None of the combatants emerged unscathed because even ultimate winners such as Sweden and France depleted their resources of men and money.

desperately in need of provisions. In the last year of the Thirty Years' War, the Imperial-Bavarian Army had 40,000 men entitled to draw rations—and more than 100,000 wives, prostitutes, servants, children, and other camp followers forced to scrounge for their own food.

The Peace of Westphalia, 1648

The comprehensive settlement provided by the **Peace of Westphalia**—named after the German province where negotiations took place—would serve as a model for resolving future conflicts among warring European states. For the first

time, a diplomatic congress convened to address international disputes, and those signing the treaties guaranteed the resulting settlement. A method still in use, the congress was the first to bring *all* parties together, rather than two or three at a time.

The Winners and Losers. France and Sweden gained most from the Peace of Westphalia. Although France and Spain continued fighting until 1659, France acquired parts of Alsace and replaced Spain as the prevailing power on the continent. Baltic conflicts would not be resolved until 1661, but Sweden took several northern territories from the Holy Roman Empire (Map 15.3).

The Habsburgs lost the most. The Spanish Habsburgs recognized Dutch independence after eighty years of war. The Swiss Confederation and the German princes demanded autonomy from the Austrian Habsburg rulers of the Holy Roman

---

Peace of Westphalia: The settlement (1648) of the Thirty Years' War; it established enduring religious divisions in the Holy Roman Empire by which Lutheranism would dominate in the north, Calvinism in the area of the Rhine River, and Catholicism in the south.

Empire. Each German prince gained the right to establish Lutheranism, Catholicism, or Calvinism in his state, a right denied to Calvinist rulers by the Peace of Augsburg in 1555. The independence ceded to German princes sustained political divisions that would remain until the nineteenth century and prepared the way for the emergence of a new power, the Hohenzollern Elector of Brandenburg, who increased his territories and developed a small but effective standing army. After losing considerable territory in the west, the Austrian Habsburgs turned eastward to concentrate on restoring Catholicism to Bohemia and wresting Hungary from the Turks.

The Peace of Westphalia permanently settled the distributions of the main religions in the Holy Roman Empire: Lutheranism would dominate in the north, Calvinism in the area of the Rhine River, and Catholicism in the south. Most of the territorial changes in Europe remained intact until the nineteenth century. In the future, international warfare would be undertaken for reasons of national security, commercial ambition, or dynastic pride rather than to enforce religious uniformity. As the politiques of the late sixteenth century had hoped, state interests now outweighed motivations of faith in political affairs.

Growth of State Authority.   Warfare increased the reach of states: as armies grew to bolster the war effort, governments needed more money and more supervisory officials. The rate of land tax paid by French peasants doubled in the eight years after France joined the war. In addition to raising taxes, governments deliberately depreciated the value of the currency, which often resulted in inflation and soaring prices. Rulers also sold new offices and manipulated the embryonic stock and bond markets. When all else failed, they declared bankruptcy. The Spanish government, for example, did so three times in the first half of the seventeenth century. From Portugal to Muscovy, ordinary people resisted new taxes by forming makeshift armies and battling royal forces. With their colorful banners, unlikely leaders, strange names (the Nu-Pieds, or "Barefooted," in France, for instance), and crude weapons, the rebels usually proved no match for state armies, but they did keep officials worried and troops occupied.

To meet these new demands, monarchs relied on advisers who took on the role of modern prime ministers. Continuity in Swedish affairs, especially after the death of Gustavus Adolphus, largely depended on Axel Oxenstierna, who held office for more than forty years. Louis XIII's chief minister, Cardinal Richelieu, proclaimed the priority of *raison d'état* (reason of state), that is, the state's interest above all else. He silenced Protestants within France because they had become too independent, and he crushed noble and popular resistance to Louis's policies. He set up intendants — delegates from the king's council dispatched to the provinces — to oversee police, army, and financial affairs.

To justify the growth of state authority and the expansion of government bureaucracies, rulers carefully cultivated their royal images. (See The Arts and State Power, at left.) James I of England

The Arts and State Power

King Philip IV of Spain commissioned Diego Velázquez to paint this portrait in 1634–1635. He hung the painting in the new palace, called Buen Retiro, that he built near Madrid in the 1630s. Philip's court at Buen Retiro included formal gardens, artificial ponds, a huge iron bird cage (which led some critics to call the whole thing a chicken coop), a zoo, and a courtyard for bullfights as well as rooms filled with sculptures and paintings. Note that Philip looks completely in control, almost impassive, even though the horse is rearing. In this way the artist emphasizes the king's mastery.

raison d'état (ray ZOHN day TAH): French for "reason of state," the political doctrine, first proposed by Cardinal Richelieu of France, which held that the state's interests should prevail over those of religion.

argued that he ruled by divine right and was accountable only to God: "The state of monarchy is the supremest thing on earth; for kings are not only God's lieutenant on earth, but even by God himself they are called gods." He advised his son to maintain a manly appearance (his own well-known homosexual liaisons did not make him seem less manly to his subjects): "Eschew to be effeminate in your clothes, in perfuming, preening, or such like." Appearance counted for so much that most rulers regulated who could wear which kinds of cloth and decoration, reserving the richest and rarest, such as ermine and gold, for themselves.

REVIEW: Why did a war fought over religious differences result in stronger states?

Economic Crisis and Realignment

The devastation caused by the Thirty Years' War deepened an economic crisis that was already under way. After a century of rising prices, caused partly by massive transfers of gold and silver from the New World and partly by population growth, in the early 1600s prices began to level off and even to drop, and in most places population growth slowed. With fewer goods being produced, international trade fell into recession. Agricultural yields also declined, and peasants and townspeople alike were less able to pay the escalating taxes needed to finance the wars. Famine and disease trailed grimly behind economic crisis and war, in some areas causing large-scale uprisings and revolts. Behind the scenes, the economic balance of power gradually shifted as northwestern Europe began to dominate international trade and broke the stranglehold of Spain and Portugal in the New World.

From Growth to Recession

Population grew and prices rose in the second half of the sixteenth century. Even though religious and political turbulence led to population decline in some cities, such as war-torn Antwerp, overall rates of growth remained impressive: in the sixteenth century, parts of Spain doubled in population and England's population grew by 70 percent. The supply of precious metals swelled, too. In the 1540s, new silver mines were discovered in Mexico and Peru. Spanish gold imports peaked in the 1550s,

silver in the 1590s. (See "Taking Measure," below.) This flood of precious metals combined with population growth to fuel an astounding inflation in food prices in western Europe—400 percent in the sixteenth century—and a more moderate rise in the cost of manufactured goods. Wages rose much more slowly, at about half the rate of the increase in food prices. Governments always overspent revenues, and by 1600 most of Europe's rulers faced deep deficits.

Recession did not strike everywhere at the same time, but the warning signs were unmistakable. Foreign trade slumped as war and an uncertain money supply made business riskier. After 1625, silver imports to Spain declined, in part because so many of the native Americans who worked in Spanish colonial mines died from disease and in part because the mines themselves were progressively depleted. Textile production fell in many countries and in some places nearly

TAKING MEASURE

The Rise and Fall of Silver Imports to Spain, 1550–1660
Gold and silver from the New World enabled the king of Spain to pursue aggressive policies in Europe and around the world. At what point did silver imports reach their highest level? Was the fall in silver imports precipitous or gradual? What can we conclude about the resources available to the Spanish king? *(From Earl J. Hamilton, American Revolution and the Price Revolution in Spain, 1501–1650 [Cambridge, MA: Harvard University Press, 1934].)*

Tree Rings and the Little Ice Age

Global cooling helped bring about the economic crisis of the seventeenth century. Glaciers advanced, average temperatures fell, and winters were often exceptionally severe. Canals and rivers essential to markets froze over. Great storms disrupted ocean traffic — in fact, one storm changed the escape route of the Spanish Armada. Even in the valleys far from the mountain glaciers, cooler weather meant lower crop yields, which quickly translated into hunger and greater susceptibility to disease, leading in turn to population decline. Some historians of climate refer to the entire period 1600–1850 as the little ice age because glaciers advanced during this time and retreated only after 1850; others argue that the period 1550–1700 was the coldest, but either time frame includes the seventeenth century. Given the current debates about global warming, how can we sift through the evidence to come up with a reliable interpretation? Since systematic records of European temperatures were kept only from the 1700s onward, how do historians know that the weather was cooler?

Information about climate comes from various sources. The advance of glaciers can be seen in letters complaining to the authorities. In 1601, for example, panic-stricken villagers in Savoy (in the French Alps) wrote, "We are terrified of the glaciers . . . which are moving forward all the time and have just buried two of our villages." Yearly temperature fluctuations can be determined from the dates of wine harvests; growers harvested their grapes earliest when the weather was warmest and latest when it was coolest. Scientists study ice cores taken from Greenland to determine temperature variations; such studies seem to indicate that the coolest times were the periods 1160–1300; the 1600s; and 1820–1850. The period 1730–1800 appears to have been warmer. Recently, scientists have developed techniques for sampling corals in the tropics and sediments on oceanic shelves to provide evidence of climate change.

But the most striking are data gathered from tree rings (the science is called dendrochronology or dendroclimatology). Timber samples have been taken from very old oak trees and also from ancient beams in buildings and archaeological digs and from logs left long undisturbed in northern bogs and riverbeds. In cold summers, trees lay down thinner growth rings; in warm ones, thicker rings. Information about tree rings confirms the conclusions drawn from wine harvest and ice core samples: the seventeenth century was relatively cold. Recent tree ring studies have shown that some of the coldest summers were caused by volcanic eruptions; according to a study of more than one hundred sites in North America and Europe, the five coldest summers in the past four

collapsed, largely because of decreased demand and a shrinking labor force. Even the relatively limited trade in African slaves stagnated, though its growth would resume after 1650 and skyrocket after 1700. African slaves were first transported to the new colony of Virginia in 1619, foreshadowing a major transformation of economic life in the New World colonies.

Demographic slowdown also signaled economic trouble. Despite population growth in some areas, Europe's total population may actually have declined, from 85 million in 1550 to 80 million in 1650. In the Mediterranean, growth had already stopped in the 1570s. The most sudden reversal occurred in central Europe as a result of the Thirty Years' War: one-fourth of the inhabitants of the Holy Roman Empire perished in the 1630s and 1640s. Population growth continued only in England, the Dutch Republic and the Spanish Netherlands, and Scandinavia.

Where the population stagnated or declined, agricultural prices dropped because of less demand, and farmers who produced for the market suffered. The price of grain fell most precipitously, causing many farmers to convert grain-growing land to pasture or vineyards. In some places, peasants abandoned their villages and left land to waste, as had happened during the plague epidemic of the late fourteenth century. The only country that emerged unscathed from this downturn was the Dutch Republic, thanks to a growing population and tradition of agricultural innovation. Inhabiting Europe's most densely populated area, the Dutch developed systems of field drainage, crop rotation, and animal husbandry that provided high yields of grain for both people and animals. Their foreign trade, textile industry, crop production, and population all grew. After the Dutch, the English fared best; unlike the Spanish, the English never depended on infusions of New World gold and silver to shore up their economy, and unlike most continental European countries, England escaped the direct impact of the Thirty Years' War.

The Frozen Thames
This painting by Abraham Hondius of the frozen Thames River in London dates to 1677. In the 1670s and 1680s the Thames froze several times. Diarists recorded that shopkeepers even set up their stalls on the ice. The expected routines of daily life changed during the cooling down of the seventeenth century, and contemporaries were shocked enough by the changes to record them for posterity. *(© Museum of London.)*

hundred years were in 1601, 1641, 1669, 1699, and 1912 (four out of five in the seventeenth century), and all but the summer of 1699 came in years following recorded eruptions.

QUESTIONS TO CONSIDER
1. What were the historical consequences of global cooling in the seventeenth century?
2. Why would trees be especially valuable sources of information about climate?

FURTHER READING
Climate of the Past: **http://www.clim-past .net/recentpapers.html**
Jones, P. D., ed. *History and Climate: Memories of the Future?* 2001.

Historians have long disagreed about the causes of the early-seventeenth-century recession. Some cite the inability of agriculture to support a growing population by the end of the sixteenth century; others blame the Thirty Years' War, the states' demands for more taxes, the irregularities in money supply resulting from rudimentary banking practices, or the waste caused by middle-class expenditures in the desire to emulate the nobility. To this list of causes, recent researchers have added climatic changes. (See "New Sources, New Perspectives," page 466.) Cold winters and wet summers meant bad harvests, and these natural disasters ushered in a host of social catastrophes. When the harvest was bad, prices shot back up and many could not afford to feed themselves.

Consequences for Daily Life

The recession of the early 1600s had both short-term and long-term effects. In the short term, it aggravated the threat of food shortages, increased the outbreaks of famine and disease, and caused people to leave their families and homes. In the long term, it deepened the division between prosperous and poor peasants and fostered the development of a new pattern of late marriages and smaller families.

Famine and Disease. When grain harvests fell short, peasants immediately suffered because, outside of England and the Dutch Republic, grain had replaced more expensive meat as the essential staple of most Europeans' diets. By the end of the sixteenth century, the average adult European ate more than four hundred pounds of grain per year. Peasants lived on bread, soup with a little fat or oil, peas or lentils, garden vegetables in season, and only occasionally a piece of meat or fish. Usually the adverse years differed from place to place, but from 1594 to 1597 most of Europe suffered from shortages; the resulting famine triggered revolts from Ireland to Muscovy.

The Life of the Poor

This mid-seventeenth-century painting by the Dutch artist Adriaen Pietersz van de Venne depicts the poor peasant weighed down by his wife and child. An empty food bowl signifies their hunger. In retrospect, this painting seems unfair to the wife of the family; she is shown in clothes that are not nearly as tattered as her husband's and is portrayed entirely as a burden, rather than as a help in getting by in hard times. In reality, many poor men abandoned their homes in search of work, leaving their wives behind to cope with hungry children and what remained of the family farm. *(Allen Memorial Art Museum, Oberlin College, Mrs. F. F. Prentiss Fund, 1960. Inv # 1960.94.)*

Most people, however, did not respond to their dismal circumstances by rebelling. They simply left their huts and hovels and took to the road in search of food and charity. Men left their families to search for better conditions in other parishes or even other countries. Those left behind might be reduced to eating chestnuts, roots, bark, and grass. Overwhelmed officials recorded pitiful tales of suffering. Women and children died while waiting in line for food at convents or churches. In eastern France in 1637, a witness reported, "The roads were paved with people. . . . Finally it came to cannibalism." Compassion sometimes gave way

to fear when hungry vagabonds, who sometimes banded together to beg for bread, became more aggressive, occasionally threatening to burn a barn if they were not given food.

Successive bad harvests led to malnutrition, which weakened people and made them more susceptible to such epidemic diseases as the plague, typhoid fever, typhus, dysentery, smallpox, and influenza. Disease did not spare the rich, although many epidemics hit the poor hardest. The plague was feared most: in one year it could cause the death of up to half of a town's or village's population, and it struck with no discernible pattern. Nearly 5 percent of France's entire population died just in the plague of 1628–1632.

The Changing Status of the Peasantry. Economic crisis widened the gap between rich and poor. Peasants shouldered many burdens, including rent and various fees for inheriting or selling land and tolls for using mills, wine presses, or ovens. States collected direct taxes on land and sales taxes on such consumer goods as salt, an essential preservative. Protestant and Catholic churches alike exacted a tithe (a tax equivalent to one-tenth of the parishioner's annual income); often the clergy took their tithe in the form of crops and collected it directly during the harvest. Any reversal of fortune could force peasants into the homeless world of vagrants and beggars, who numbered as much as 2 percent of the total population.

In England, the Dutch Republic, northern France, and northwestern Germany, the peasantry was disappearing. Improvements gave some peasants the means to become farmers who rented substantial holdings, produced for the market, and in good times enjoyed relative comfort and higher status. Those who could not afford to plant new crops such as maize (American corn) or to use techniques that ensured higher yields became simple laborers with little or no land of their own. One-half to four-fifths of the peasants did not have enough land to support a family. They descended deeper into debt during difficult times and often lost their land to wealthier farmers or to city officials intent on developing rural estates.

As the recession deepened, women lost some of their economic opportunities. Widows who had been able to take over their late husbands' trade now found themselves excluded by the urban guilds or limited to short tenures. Many women went into domestic service until they married, some for their entire lives. When town governments began to fear the effects of increased mobility from country to town and town to town, they carefully regulated the work of female servants, requiring women to stay in their positions unless they could prove mistreatment by a master.

Effects on Marriage and Childbearing. European families reacted to economic downturn by postponing marriage and having fewer children. When hard times passed, more people married and had more children. But even in the best of times, one-fifth to one-quarter of all children died in their first year, and half died before age twenty. Childbirth still carried great risks for women, about 10 percent of whom died in the process. Even in the richest and most enlightened homes, childbirth often occasioned an atmosphere of panic. To allay their fears, women sometimes depended on magic stones, special pilgrimages, or prayers. Midwives delivered most babies; physicians were scarce, and even those who did attend births were generally less helpful than midwives. The Englishwoman Alice Thornton described in her diary how a doctor bled her to prevent a miscarriage after a fall (bloodletting, often by the application of leeches, was a common medical treatment); her son died anyway in a breech birth that almost killed her, too.

It might be assumed that families would have more children to compensate for high death rates, but beginning in the early seventeenth century and continuing until the end of the eighteenth, families in all ranks of society started to limit the number of children. Because methods of contraception were not widely known, they did this for the most part by marrying later; the average age at marriage during the seventeenth century rose from the early twenties to the late twenties. The average family had about four children. Poorer families seem to have had fewer children, wealthier ones more. Peasant couples, especially in eastern and southeastern Europe, had more children than urban couples because cultivation still required intensive manual labor—and having children was the most economical means of securing enough laborers.

The consequences of late marriage were profound. Young men and women were expected to put off marriage (and sexual intercourse) until their mid to late twenties—if they were among the lucky 50 percent who lived that long and not among the 10 percent who never married. Because both Protestant and Catholic clergy alike stressed sexual fidelity and abstinence before marriage, the number of births out of wedlock was relatively small (2–5 percent of births); premarital intercourse was generally tolerated only after a couple had announced their engagement.

The Economic Balance of Power

Just as the recession produced winners and losers among ordinary people, so too it created winners and losers among the competing states of Europe. The economies of southern Europe declined during this period, whereas those of the northwest emerged stronger. Competition in the New World reflected and reinforced this shift as the English, Dutch, and French rushed to establish trading outposts and permanent settlements to compete with the Spanish and Portuguese.

Regional Differences. The new powers of northwestern Europe with their growing Atlantic trade gradually displaced the Mediterranean economies, which had dominated European commerce since the time of the Greeks and Romans. With expanding populations and geographical positions that promoted Atlantic trade, England and the Dutch Republic vied with France to become the leading mercantile powers. Northern Italian industries were eclipsed; Spanish commerce with the New World dropped. Amsterdam replaced Seville, Venice, Genoa, and Antwerp as the center of European trade and commerce. Even the plague contributed to this difference. Whereas central Europe and the Mediterranean countries took generations to recover from its ravages, northwestern Europe quickly replaced its lost population, no doubt because this area's people had suffered less from the effects of the Thirty Years' War and from the malnutrition related to the economic crisis.

All but the remnants of serfdom had disappeared in western Europe, yet in eastern Europe nobles reinforced their dominance over peasants, and the burden of serfdom increased. The price rise of the sixteenth century prompted Polish and eastern German nobles to increase their holdings and step up their production of grain for western markets. They demanded more rent and dues from their peasants, whom the government decreed must stay in their villages. In the economic downturn of the first half of the seventeenth century, peasants who were already dependent became serfs—completely tied to the land. A local official might complain of "this barbaric and as it were Egyptian servitude," but he had no power to fight the nobles. In Muscovy, the complete enserfment of the peasantry would eventually be recognized in the Code of Laws in 1649. Although enserfment produced short-term profits for landlords, in the long run it retarded economic development in eastern Europe and kept most of the population in a stranglehold of illiteracy and hardship.

Competition in the New World. Economic realignment also took place across the Atlantic ocean. Because Spain and Portugal had divided between themselves the rich spoils of South America, other prospective colonizers had to carve niches in seemingly less hospitable places, especially North America and the Caribbean (Map 15.4). Eventually, the English, French, and Dutch would dominate commerce with these colonies. Many European states, including Sweden and Denmark, rushed to join the colonial competition as a way of increasing national wealth. To this end, they chartered private joint-stock companies to enrich investors by importing fish, furs, tobacco, and precious metals, if they could be found, and to develop new markets for European products.

In establishing permanent colonies, the Europeans created whole new communities across the Atlantic. Careful plans could not always surmount the hazards of transatlantic shipping, however. Originally, the warm climate of Virginia made it an attractive destination for the Pilgrims, a small English sect that attempted to separate from the Church of England. But the *Mayflower*, which had sailed for Virginia with Pilgrim emigrants, landed far to the north in Massachusetts, where in 1620 the settlers founded New Plymouth Colony. By the 1640s, the British North American colonies had more than fifty thousand people — not including the Indians, whose numbers had been decimated in epidemics and wars — and the foundations of representative government in locally chosen colonial assemblies.

In contrast, French Canada had only about three thousand European inhabitants by 1640. Though thin in numbers, the French rapidly moved into the Great Lakes region. Fur traders sought beaver pelts to make the hats that had taken Paris fashion by storm. Jesuit missionaries lived with native American groups, learning their languages and describing their ways of life. Both England and France turned their attention to the Caribbean in the 1620s and 1630s when they occupied the islands of the West Indies after driving off the native Caribs. These islands would prove ideal for a plantation economy of tobacco and sugarcane.

Even as the British and French moved into North America and the Caribbean, Spanish explorers traveled the Pacific coast up to what is now northern California and pushed into New Mexico. On the other side of the world, in the Philippines, the Spanish competed with local Muslim rulers and indigenous tribal leaders to extend their control. Catholic missionaries printed tracts in Spanish and the islands' native Tagalog and established a university in 1611. Spanish officials

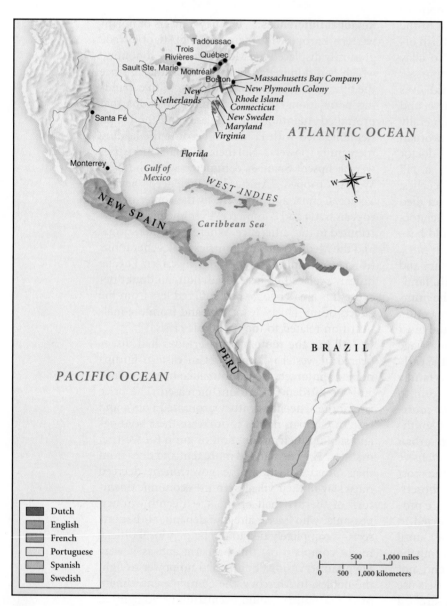

MAP 15.4 European Colonization of the Americas, c. 1640
Europeans coming to the Americas established themselves first in coastal areas. The English, French, and Dutch set up most of their colonies in the Caribbean and North America because the Spanish and Portuguese had already colonized the easily accessible regions in South America. Vast inland areas still remained unexplored and uncolonized in 1640.

"Savages" of the New World
The half-dressed savage appears much like a noble Italian in Paolo Farinati's 1595 painting *America*; he holds a crucifix in his right hand, signifying his conversion to Christianity. But to his left, a figure is roasting human flesh. Europeans were convinced that many native peoples were cannibals. What can we conclude from this painting about European attitudes toward peoples of the New World? *(Villa della Torre, Mezzane de Sotto, Verona.)*

worked closely with the missionaries to rule over a colony composed of indigenous peoples, Spaniards, and some Chinese merchants.

> **REVIEW:** What were the consequences of economic recession in the early 1600s?

The Rise of Secular and Scientific Worldviews

The countries that moved ahead economically in the first half of the seventeenth century—England, the Dutch Republic, and to some extent France—turned out to be the most receptive to new secular worldviews. In the long-term process known as **secularization**, religion became a matter of private conscience rather than public policy. Secularization did not entail a loss of religious faith, but it did prompt a search for nonreligious explanations for political authority and natural phenomena. During the late sixteenth and early seventeenth centuries, art, political theory, and science all began to break their bonds with religion. The visual arts, for example, more frequently depicted secular subjects. Scientists and scholars sought laws in nature to explain politics as well as

movements in the heavens and on earth. A scientific revolution was in the making. Yet traditional attitudes did not disappear. Belief in magic and witchcraft pervaded every level of society. People of all classes believed that the laws of nature reflected a divine plan for the universe. They accepted supernatural explanations for natural phenomena, a view only gradually and partially undermined by new ideas.

The Arts in an Age of Crisis

Two new forms of artistic expression—professional theater and opera—provided an outlet for secular values in an age of conflict over religious beliefs. The greatest playwright of the English language, William Shakespeare, never referred to religious disputes in his plays, and he always set his most personal reflections on political turmoil and uncertainty in faraway times or places. Religion played an important role in the new mannerist and baroque styles of painting, however, even though many rulers commissioned paintings on secular subjects for their own uses.

Theater in the Age of Shakespeare.   The first professional acting companies performed before paying audiences in London, Seville, and Madrid in the 1570s. In previous centuries, traveling companies made their living by playing at major religious festivals and by repeating their performances in small towns and villages along the way. A huge outpouring of playwriting followed upon the formation of permanent professional theater

---

secularization: The trend toward making religious faith a private domain rather than one directly connected to state power and science; it prompted a search for nonreligious explanations for political authority and natural phenomena.

companies. The Spanish playwright Lope de Vega (1562–1635) alone wrote more than fifteen hundred plays. Theaters were extremely popular despite Puritan opposition in England and Catholic objections in Spain. Shopkeepers, apprentices, lawyers, and court nobles crowded into open-air theaters to see everything from bawdy farces to profound tragedies.

The most enduring and influential playwright of the time was the Englishman William Shakespeare (1564–1616), who wrote three dozen plays, comedies as well as tragedies, and acted in one of the chief troupes. Although Shakespeare's plays were not set in contemporary England, they reflected the concerns of his age: the nature of power and the crisis of authority. His tragedies in particular show the uncertainty and even chaos that result when power is misappropriated or misused. In *Hamlet* (1601), for example, Hamlet's mother marries the man who murdered his royal father and usurped the crown. In the end, Hamlet, his mother, and the usurper all die. One character in the final act describes the tragic story of Prince Hamlet as one "Of carnal, bloody, and unnatural acts;/Of accidental judgments, casual slaughters;/Of deaths put on by cunning and forced cause." Like many real-life people, Shakespeare's tragic characters found little peace in the turmoil of their times.

Mannerism and the Baroque in Art. Although painting did not always touch broad popular audiences in the ways that theater could, new styles in art and especially church architecture helped shape ordinary people's experience of religion. In the late sixteenth century, the artistic style known as mannerism emerged in the Italian states and soon spread across Europe. Mannerism was an almost theatrical style that allowed painters to distort perspective to convey a message or emphasize a theme. The most famous mannerist painter, called El Greco because he was of Greek origin, trained in Venice and Rome before he moved to Spain in the 1570s. The religious intensity of El Greco's pictures found a ready audience in Catholic Spain, which had proved immune to the Protestant suspicion of ritual and religious imagery (see Philip II of Spain, page 457).

The most important new style was the **baroque**, which, like mannerism, originated in the Italian states. In place of the Renaissance emphasis on harmonious design, unity, and clarity, the

---

baroque (buh ROHK): An artistic style of the seventeenth century that featured curves, exaggerated lighting, intense emotions, release from restraint, and even a kind of artistic sensationalism.

baroque featured curves, exaggerated lighting, intense emotions, release from restraint, and even a kind of artistic sensationalism. Like many other historical designations, the word *baroque* was not used as a label by people living at the time; in the eighteenth century, art critics coined the word to mean shockingly bizarre, confused, and extravagant, and until the late nineteenth century, art historians and collectors largely disdained the baroque.

Closely tied to Catholic resurgence after the Reformation, the baroque melodramatically reaffirmed the emotional depths of the Catholic faith and glorified both church and monarchy (see "Seeing History," page 473). The style spread from Rome to other Italian states and then into central Europe. The Catholic Habsburg territories, including Spain and the Spanish Netherlands, embraced the style. The Spanish built baroque churches in their American colonies as part of their massive conversion campaign.

Opera. A new secular musical form, the opera, grew up parallel to the baroque style in the visual arts. First influential in the Italian states, opera combined music, drama, dance, and scenery in a grand sensual display, often with themes chosen to please the ruler and the aristocracy. Operas could be based on typically baroque sacred subjects or on traditional stories. Like many playwrights, including Shakespeare, opera composers often turned to familiar stories their audiences would recognize and readily follow. One of the most innovative composers of opera was Claudio Monteverdi (1567–1643), whose work contributed to the development of both opera and the orchestra. His earliest operatic production, *Orfeo* (1607), was based on Greek mythology. It required an orchestra of about forty instruments, and unlike previous composers, Monteverdi wrote parts for specific instruments as well as voices.

The Natural Laws of Politics

In reaction to the religious wars, writers not only began to defend the primacy of state interests over those of religious conformity but also insisted on secular explanations for politics. Machiavelli had pointed in this direction with his advice to Renaissance princes in the early sixteenth century, but this secular intellectual movement gathered steam in the aftermath of the religious violence unleashed by the Reformation. Adherents believed that religious toleration could not take hold until government could be organized on some principle other than one king, one faith. The French

Religious Differences in Painting of the Baroque Period: Rubens and Rembrandt

Although the arts rarely reflect rigid religious or political divisions, artists do respond to the times in which they live. Protestant artists could not ignore the growing influence of the baroque style, but they also sought to distinguish themselves from it because of its association with the Catholic Counter-Reformation. The baroque style emphasized intense emotions, monumental decors, and even a kind of artistic sensationalism. Protestant artists, like Protestant preachers, wanted to produce strong reactions, too, but they placed more emphasis on the inner experience than on public display.

Here you see two paintings on the same biblical theme, one by Peter Paul Rubens (1577–1640), the great Catholic pioneer of the baroque style, and one by Rembrandt van Rijn (1606–1669), a Dutch Protestant. The subject of the paintings, taken from the Old Testament, is a scandalous one: when King David saw Bathsheba bathing, he fell in love with her, seduced her, and arranged for her husband to be killed in battle so that he might marry her.

Even though the central figure is the same in each painting, the artists' treatments are not. Look at the differences in settings, the number of people in the pictures, the colors, the lighting, and especially the facial expressions. In the Rubens, Bathsheba is about to receive a letter of summons from King David (shown on the balcony above), whereas in the Rembrandt she has just read the letter. What are the differences in feeling conveyed in the two depictions of Bathsheba? Why would Rembrandt draw attention to the sadness felt by Bathsheba, and how might this relate to the Protestant emphasis on each person's individual relationship to God? How do the setting and the lighting reinforce this emphasis on inwardness in the Rembrandt painting? Do not assume, however, that every difference in approach can be attributed to religious differences. Rembrandt created his own sensation by depicting Bathsheba almost entirely nude (and using his own mistress as the model).

Peter Paul Rubens, *Bathsheba at the Fountain*, c. 1635.
(© Gemaeldegalerie Alte Meister, Dresden, Germany/The Bridgeman Art Library.)

Rembrandt van Rijn, *Bathsheba at Her Bath*, 1654.
(© Louvre, Paris, France/Giraudon/The Bridgeman Art Library.)

politiques Michel de Montaigne and Jean Bodin started the search for those principles, and the Dutch legal scholar Hugo Grotius developed ideas on government that would influence John Locke and the American revolutionaries of the eighteenth century.

Montaigne and Bodin. Michel de Montaigne (1533–1592) was a French magistrate who resigned his office in the midst of the wars of religion to write about the need for tolerance and open-mindedness. Although himself a Catholic, Montaigne painted on the beams of his study the statement "All that is certain is that nothing is certain." To capture this need for personal reflection in a tumultuous age of religious discord, he invented the essay as a short and pithy form of expression. He revived the ancient doctrine of skepticism, which held that total certainty is never attainable — a doctrine, like toleration of religious differences, that was repugnant to Protestants and Catholics alike, both of whom were certain that their religion was the right one. He also questioned the common European habit of calling the native peoples of the New World barbarous and savage: "Everyone gives the title of barbarism to everything that is not in use in his own country."

The French Catholic lawyer Jean Bodin (1530–1596) sought systematic secular answers to the problem of disorder in *The Six Books of the Republic* (1576). Comparing the different forms of government throughout history, he concluded that there were three basic types of sovereignty: monarchy, aristocracy, and democracy. Only strong monarchical power offered hope for maintaining order, he insisted. Bodin rejected any doctrine of the right to resist tyrannical authority: "I denied that it was the function of a good man or of a good citizen to offer violence to his prince for any reason, however great a tyrant he might be" (and, it might be added, whatever his ideas on religion). While Bodin's ideas helped lay the foundation for absolutism, the idea that the monarch should be the sole and uncontested source of power, his systematic discussion of types of governments implied that they might be subject to choice and undercut the notion that monarchies were ordained by God, as most rulers maintained.

Grotius and Natural Law. During the Dutch revolt against Spain, Hugo Grotius (1583–1645) furthered secular thinking by attempting to systematize the notion of "natural law" — laws of nature that give legitimacy to government and stand above the actions of any particular ruler or religious group. Grotius argued that natural law stood beyond the reach of either secular or divine authority; it would be valid even if God did not exist (though Grotius himself believed in God). By this account, natural law — not scripture, religious authority, or tradition — should govern politics. Such ideas got Grotius into trouble with both Catholics and Protestants. His work *The Laws of War and Peace* (1625) was condemned by the Catholic church, while the Dutch Protestant government arrested him for taking part in religious controversies. Grotius's wife helped him escape prison by hiding him in a chest of books. He fled to Paris, where he got a small pension from Louis XIII and served as his ambassador to Sweden. The Swedish king Gustavus Adolphus claimed that he kept Grotius's book under his pillow even while at battle. Grotius was one of the first to argue that international conventions should govern the treatment of prisoners of war and the making of peace treaties.

Grotius's conception of natural law also challenged the widespread use of torture. Most states and the courts of the Catholic church used torture when a serious crime had been committed and the evidence seemed to point to a particular defendant but no definitive proof had been established. The judges ordered torture — hanging the accused by the hands with a rope thrown over a beam, pressing the legs in a leg screw, or just tying the hands very tightly — to extract a confession, which had to be given with a medical expert and notary present and had to be repeated without torture. Children, pregnant women, the elderly, aristocrats, kings, and even professors were exempt.

To be in accord with natural law, Grotius argued, governments had to defend natural rights, which he defined as life, body, freedom, and honor. Grotius did not encourage rebellion in the name of natural law or rights, but he did hope that someday all governments would adhere to these principles and stop killing their own and one another's subjects in the name of religion. Natural law and natural rights would play an important role in the founding of constitutional governments from the 1640s forward and in the establishment of various charters of human rights in our own time.

The Scientific Revolution

Although the Catholic and Protestant churches encouraged the study of science and many prominent scientists were themselves clerics, the search for a secular, scientific method of determining the laws of nature undermined traditional accounts of natural phenomena. Christian doctrine had incorporated the scientific teachings of ancient philosophers, especially Ptolemy and Aristotle; now these came into question. A revolution in astronomy contested the Ptolemaic view, endorsed by the Catholic church, which held that the sun revolved around the earth. Startling breakthroughs took place in medicine, too, which laid the foundations for modern anatomy and pharmacology. Supporters of these new developments argued for a **scientific method** that would combine experimental observation and mathematical deduction. The use of scientific method culminated in the astounding breakthroughs of Isaac Newton at the end of the seventeenth century. Newton's ability to explain the motion of the planets, as well as everyday objects on earth, gave science enormous new prestige.

The Revolution in Astronomy. The traditional account of the movement of the heavens derived from the second-century Greek astronomer Ptolemy, who put the earth at the center of the cosmos. Above the earth were fixed the moon, the stars, and the planets in concentric crystalline spheres; beyond these fixed spheres dwelt God and the angels. The planets revolved around the earth at the command of God. In this view, the sun revolved around the earth; the heavens were perfect and unchanging, and the earth was "corrupted." Ptolemy insisted that the planets revolved in perfectly circular orbits (because circles were more "perfect" than other figures). To account for the actual elliptical paths that could be observed and calculated, he posited orbits within orbits, or epicycles.

In 1543, the Polish clergyman Nicolaus Copernicus (1473–1543) began the revolution in astronomy by publishing his treatise *On the Revolution of the Celestial Spheres.* Copernicus attacked the Ptolemaic account, arguing that the earth and planets revolved around the sun, a view known as **heliocentrism** (a sun-centered universe). He discovered that by placing the sun instead of the earth at the center of the system of spheres, he could eliminate many epicycles from the calculations. In other words, he claimed that the heliocentric view simplified the mathematics. Copernicus died soon after publishing his theories, but when the Italian monk Giordano Bruno (1548–1600) taught helio-

centrism, the Catholic Inquisition (set up to seek out heretics) arrested him and burned him at the stake.

Copernicus's views began to attract widespread attention in the early 1600s, when astronomers systematically collected evidence that undermined the Ptolemaic view. A leader among them was the Danish astronomer Tycho Brahe (1546–1601), who designed his own instruments and observed a new star in 1572 and a comet in 1577. These discoveries called into question the traditional view that the universe was unchanging. Brahe still rejected heliocentrism, but the assistant he employed when he moved to Prague in 1599, Johannes Kepler (1571–1630), was converted to the Copernican view. Kepler continued Brahe's collection of planetary observations and used the evidence to develop his three laws of planetary motion, published between 1609 and 1619. Kepler's laws provided mathematical backing for heliocentrism and directly challenged the claim long held, even by Copernicus, that planetary motion was circular. Kepler's first law stated that the orbits of the planets are ellipses, with the sun always at one focus of the ellipse.

The Italian Galileo Galilei (1564–1642) provided more evidence to support the heliocentric view and also challenged the doctrine that the heavens were perfect and unchanging. After learning in 1609 that two Dutch astronomers had built a telescope, he built a better one and observed the earth's moon, four satellites of Jupiter, the phases of Venus (a cycle of changing physical appearances), and sunspots. The moon, the planets, and the sun were no more perfect than the earth, he insisted, and the shadows he could see on the moon could only be the product of hills and valleys like those on earth. Galileo portrayed the earth as a moving part of a larger system, only one of many planets revolving around the sun, not as the fixed center of a single, closed universe.

Because he recognized the utility of the new science for everyday projects, Galileo published his work in Italian, rather than Latin. But he meant only to instruct an educated elite of merchants and aristocrats. The new science, he claimed, suited "the minds of the wise," not "the shallow minds of the common people." After all, his discoveries challenged the commonsensical view that it is the sun that rises and sets while the earth stands still. If the Bible was wrong about motion in the universe, as Galileo's position implied, the error came from the Bible's use of common language to appeal to the lower orders. The Catholic church was not mollified by this explanation. In 1616, the church for-

---

scientific method: The combination of experimental observation and mathematical deduction that was used to determine the laws of nature and became the secular standard of truth.

heliocentrism: The view articulated by Polish clergyman Nicolaus Copernicus that the earth and planets revolve around the sun.

The Trial of Galileo
In this anonymous painting of the trial held in 1633, Galileo appears seated on a chair in the center facing the church officials who accused him of heresy for insisting that the sun, not the earth, was the center of the universe (heliocentrism). Catholic officials forced him to recant or suffer the death penalty. *(Erich Lessing/Art Resource, NY.)*

bade Galileo to teach that the earth moves; then, in 1633, it accused him of not obeying the earlier order. Forced to appear before the Inquisition, he agreed to publicly recant his assertion about the movement of the earth to save himself from torture and death. (See Document, "Sentence Pronounced against Galileo," page 477, and painting, The Trial of Galileo, above.) Afterward, he lived under house arrest and could publish his work only in the Dutch Republic, which had become a haven for iconoclastic scientists and thinkers.

Breakthroughs in Medicine. Just as astronomical knowledge was based on Ptolemy's work, medical knowledge in Europe was, until the mid-sixteenth century, based on the writings of the second-century Greek physician Galen, Ptolemy's contemporary. Galen derived his knowledge of the anatomy of the human body from partial dissections. In the same year that Copernicus challenged the traditional account in astronomy (1543), the Flemish scientist Andreas Vesalius (1514–1564) did the same for anatomy. Drawing on public dissections (which had been condemned by the Catholic church since 1300) he performed himself, Vesalius refuted Galen's work in his illustrated anatomical text, *On the Construction of the Human Body*. The German physician Paracelsus (1493–1541) went even further than Vesalius. In 1527, he burned Galen's text at the University of Basel, where he was a professor of medicine. Paracelsus performed operations (at the time, most academic physicians

taught medical theory, not practice) and pursued his interests in magic, alchemy, and astrology. He also experimented with new drugs and thus helped establish the modern science of pharmacology.

Like Vesalius, the Englishman William Harvey (1578–1657) used dissection to examine the circulation of blood within the body, demonstrating how the heart worked as a pump. The heart and its valves were "a piece of machinery," Harvey insisted. They obeyed mechanical laws just as the planets and earth revolved around the sun in a mechanical universe. Nature could be understood by experiment and rational deduction, not by following traditional authorities.

Scientific Method: Bacon and Descartes. In the 1630s, the European intellectual elite began to accept the new scientific views. Ancient learning, the churches and their theologians, and long-standing popular beliefs all seemed to be undercut by the scientific method. Two men were chiefly responsible for spreading the reputation of the scientific method in the first half of the seventeenth century: the English Protestant politician Sir Francis Bacon (1561–1626) and the French Catholic mathematician and philosopher René Descartes (1596–1650). They represented the two essential halves of the scientific method: inductive reasoning through observation and experimental research, and deductive reasoning from self-evident principles.

In *The Advancement of Learning* (1605), Bacon attacked reliance on ancient writers and optimisti-

DOCUMENT

Sentence Pronounced against Galileo (1633)

In 1633, the Roman Inquisition, a committee of cardinals of the Catholic church, considered the case against Galileo and pronounced its final judgment. It found Galileo guilty of heresy against Catholic doctrine for defending heliocentrism but allowed him to recant and thus avoid the death penalty usual in cases of heresy. In 1980, Pope John Paul II appointed a commission to review the evidence and verdict. Four years later, the commission published its findings and concluded that the judges who condemned Galileo were wrong.

We say, pronounce, sentence, and declare that you, the above-mentioned Galileo, because of the things deduced in the trial and confessed by you as above, have rendered yourself according to this Holy Office [Inquisition] vehemently suspected of heresy, namely of having held and believed a doctrine which is false and contrary to the divine and Holy Scripture: that the sun is the center of the world and does not move from east to west, and the earth moves and is not the center of the world, and that one may hold and defend as probable an opinion after it has been declared and defined contrary to Holy Scripture. Consequently you have incurred all the censures and penalties imposed and promulgated by the sacred canons and all particular and general laws against such delinquents. We are willing to absolve you from them provided that first, with a sincere heart and unfeigned faith, in front of us you abjure, curse, and detest the above-mentioned errors and heresies, and every other error and heresy contrary to the Catholic and Apostolic Church, in the manner and form we will prescribe to you.

Furthermore, so that this serious and pernicious error and transgression of yours does not remain completely unpunished, and so that you will be more cautious in the future and an example for others to abstain from similar crimes, we order that the book *Dialogue* [*Dialogue Concerning the Two Chief World Systems*, published in 1632] by Galileo Galilei be prohibited by public edict.

Source: Maurice A. Finocchiaro, ed., *The Galileo Affairs: A Documentary History* (Berkeley: University of California Press, 1989), 291.

---

cally predicted that the scientific method would lead to social progress. The minds of the medieval scholars, he said, had been "shut up in the cells of a few authors (chiefly Aristotle, their dictator) as their persons were shut up in the cells of monasteries and colleges," and they could therefore produce only "cobwebs of learning" that were "of no substance or profit." Advancement would take place only through the collection, comparison, and analysis of information. Knowledge, in Bacon's view, must be empirically based (that is, gained by observation and experiment). Claiming that God had called the Catholic church "to account for their degenerate manners and ceremonies," Bacon looked to the Protestant English state, which he served as lord chancellor, for leadership on the road to scientific advancement.

Although Descartes agreed with Bacon's denunciation of traditional learning, he saw that the attack on tradition might only replace the dogmatism of the churches with the skepticism of Montaigne—that nothing at all was certain. Descartes aimed to establish the new science on more secure philosophical foundations, those of mathematics and logic. In his *Discourse on Method* (1637), he argued that mathematical and mechanical principles provided the key to understanding all of nature, including the actions of people and states. All prior assumptions must be repudiated in favor of one elementary principle: "I think, therefore I am." Everything else could—and should—be doubted, but even doubt showed the certain existence of someone thinking. Begin with the simple and go on to the complex, Descartes asserted, and believe only those ideas that present themselves "clearly and distinctly." He insisted that human reason could not only unravel the secrets of nature but also prove the existence of God. Although he hoped to secure the authority of both church and state, his reliance on human reason rather than faith irritated authorities, and his books were banned in many places. He moved to the Dutch Republic to work in peace. Scientific research, like economic growth, became centered in the northern, Protestant countries, where it was less constrained by church control than in the Catholic south.

Newton and the Consolidation of the Scientific Revolution. The power of the new scientific method was dramatically confirmed in the grand synthesis of the laws of movement developed by the English natural philosopher Isaac Newton (1642–1727). Born five years after the publication of Descartes's *Discourse on Method* and educated at Cambridge University, where he later became a professor, Newton attacked an astounding variety of problems in mathematics, mechanics, and optics. For example, he established the basis for the new mathematics of moving bodies, the infinitesimal calculus. After years of labor, he finally brought his most significant mathematical and mechanical discoveries together in his masterwork, *Principia Mathematica* (1687). In it, he developed his law of universal gravitation, which explained both movement on earth and the motion of the planets. His law held that every body in the universe exerts over every other body an attractive force directly proportional to the product of their masses and inversely proportional to the square of the distance between them. This law of universal gravitation explained Kepler's elliptical planetary orbits just as it accounted for the way an apple fell to the ground.

To establish his law of universal gravitation, Newton first applied mathematical principles to formulate three fundamental physical laws: (1) in the absence of force, motion continues in a straight line; (2) the rate of change in the motion of an object is a result of the forces acting on it; and (3) the action of one object on another has an equal and opposite reaction. Newtonian physics thus combined mass, inertia, force, velocity, and acceleration—all key concepts in modern science—and made them quantifiable. Newton knew that the stakes were high: "From the same principles [of motion] I now demonstrate the frame of the System of the World."

Once set in motion, in Newton's view, the universe operated like a masterpiece made possible by the ingenuity of God. Newton saw no conflict between faith and science. He believed that by demonstrating that the physical universe followed rational principles, natural philosophers could prove the existence of God and so liberate humans from doubt and the fear of chaos. Even while laying the foundation for modern physics, optics, and mechanics, Newton spent long hours trying to calculate the date of the beginning of the world and its end with the second coming of Jesus. Others, less devout than Newton, envisioned a clockwork universe that had no need for God's continuing intervention.

Some scientists, especially those on the continent, were reluctant to accept Newton's planetary theories. The Dutch scientist Christian Huygens, for example, declared the concept of attraction (action at a distance) "absurd." But within a couple of generations, Newton's work had gained widespread assent, partly because of experimental verification.

Magic and Witchcraft

Despite the new emphasis on clear reasoning, observation, and independence from past authorities, magic and science were still closely linked even in the greatest minds. Many scholars, like Paracelsus and Newton, studied alchemy alongside other scientific pursuits. Elizabeth I maintained a court astrologer who was also a serious mathematician, and many writers distinguished between "natural magic," which was close to experimental science, and demonic "black magic." The astronomer Tycho Brahe defended his studies of alchemy and astrology as part of natural magic.

In a world in which most people believed in astrology, magical healing, prophecy, and ghosts, it is hardly surprising that many of Europe's learned people also firmly believed in witchcraft, that is, the exercise of magical powers gained by a pact with the devil. The same Jean Bodin who argued against religious fanaticism insisted on death for witches—and for those magistrates who would not prosecute them. In France alone, 345 books and pamphlets on witchcraft appeared between 1550 and 1650. Trials of witches peaked in Europe between 1560 and 1640, the very time of the celebrated breakthroughs of the new science. Montaigne was one of the few to speak out against executing accused witches: "It is taking one's conjectures rather seriously to roast someone alive for them," he wrote in 1580.

Belief in witches was not new in the sixteenth century. Witches had long been blamed for de-

Giving a Child to Satan
This woodcut from Francesco Maria Guazzo's *Compendium Maleficarum* of 1608 shows witches giving a child to the devil. Many believed that witches made a pact with the devil to carry out his evil deeds. *(The Art Archive/Dagli Orti [A].)*

stroying crops and causing personal catastrophes ranging from miscarriage to madness. What was new was official persecution by state and religious authorities. In a time of economic crisis, plague, warfare, and the clash of religious differences, witchcraft trials provided an outlet for social stress and anxiety, legitimated by state power. Denunciation and persecution of witches coincided with the spread of reform, both Protestant and Catholic. Witch trials concentrated especially in the German lands of the Holy Roman Empire, the boiling cauldron of the Thirty Years' War.

The victims of the persecution were overwhelmingly female: women accounted for 80 percent of the accused witches in about 100,000 trials in Europe and North America during the sixteenth and seventeenth centuries. About one-third were sentenced to death. Before 1400, when witchcraft trials were rare, nearly half of those accused had been men. Why did attention now shift to women? Official descriptions of witchcraft oozed lurid details of sexual orgies, incest, homosexuality, and cannibalism, in which women acted as the devil's sexual slaves. Social factors help explain the prominence of women among the accused. Accusers were almost always better off than those they accused. The poorest and most socially marginal people in most communities were elderly spinsters and widows. Because they were thought likely to hanker after revenge on those more fortunate, they were singled out as witches.

Witchcraft trials declined when scientific thinking about causes and effects raised questions about the evidence used in court: how could judges or jurors be certain that someone was a witch? The tide turned everywhere at about the same time, as physicians, lawyers, judges, and even clergy came to suspect that accusations were based on popular superstition and peasant untrustworthiness. As early as the 1640s, French courts ordered the arrest of witch-hunters and released suspected witches. In 1682, a French royal decree treated witchcraft as fraud and imposture, meaning that the law did not recognize anyone as a witch. In 1693, the jurors who had convicted twenty witches in Salem, Massachusetts, recanted, claiming: "We confess that we ourselves were not capable to understand. . . . We justly fear that we were sadly deluded and mistaken." The Salem jurors had not stopped believing in witches; they had simply lost confidence in their ability to identify them. This was a general pattern. Popular attitudes had not changed; what had changed was the attitudes of the elites. When physicians and judges had believed in witches and carried out official persecutions, with torture, those accused of witchcraft had gone to their deaths in record numbers. But when the same groups distanced themselves from popular beliefs, the trials and the executions stopped.

> **REVIEW:** How could belief in witchcraft and the rising prestige of scientific method coexist?

Conclusion

The witchcraft persecutions reflected the traumas of these times of religious war, economic decline, and crises of political and intellectual authority. Faced with new threats, some people blamed poor widows or struggling neighbors for their problems; others joined desperate revolts, and still others emigrated to the New World to seek a better life. Even rulers confronted frightening choices: forced abdication, death in battle, or assassination often accompanied their religious decisions, and economic shocks could threaten the stability of their governments.

Deep differences over religion shaped the destinies of every European power in this period. These quarrels came to a head in the Thirty Years' War (1618–1648), which cut a path of destruction through central Europe and involved most of the European powers. Repulsed by the effects of religious violence on international relations, European rulers agreed to a peace that effectively removed disputes between Catholics and Protestants from the international arena. The growing separation of political motives from religious ones did not mean that violence or conflict had ended, however. Struggles for religious uniformity within states would continue, though on a smaller scale. Larger armies required more state involvement, and almost everywhere rulers emerged from these decades of war with expanded powers that they would seek to extend further in the second half of the seventeenth century. The growth of state power directly changed the lives of ordinary people: more men went into the armies, and most families paid higher taxes. The constant extension of state power is one of the defining themes of modern history; religious warfare gave it a jump-start.

For all their power and despite repeated efforts, rulers could not control economic, social, or intellectual trends. The economic downturn of the seventeenth century produced unexpected consequences for European states even while it made life miserable for many ordinary people; economic power and vibrancy shifted from the Mediterranean world to northwestern Europe because England, France, and the Dutch Republic,

MAPPING THE WEST

Legend:
- Catholic
- Orthodox
- Lutheran
- Calvinist
- Anglican
- Islamic
- ▬▬ Boundary of the Holy Roman Empire
- Stripes = mixed religions

The Religious Divisions of Europe, c. 1648

The Peace of Westphalia recognized major religious divisions within Europe that have endured for the most part to the present day. Catholicism dominated in southern Europe, Lutheranism had its stronghold in northern Europe, and Calvinism flourished along the Rhine River. In southeastern Europe, the Islamic Ottoman Turks accommodated the Greek Orthodox Christians under their rule but bitterly fought the Catholic Austrian Habsburgs for control of Hungary.

especially, suffered less from the fighting of the Thirty Years' War and recovered more quickly from the loss of population and production during bad times.

In the face of violence and uncertainty, some began to look for secular alternatives in art, politics, and science. Although it would be foolish to claim that everyone's mental universe changed because of the clash between religious and secular worldviews, a truly monumental shift in attitudes had begun. Secularization encompassed the growing popularity of nonreligious forms of art, such as theater and opera; the search for nonreligious foundations of political authority; and the establishment of scientific method as the standard of truth. Proponents of these changes did not renounce their religious beliefs or even hold them less

fervently, but they did insist that attention to state interests and scientific knowledge could diminish religious violence and popular superstitions.

FOR FURTHER EXPLORATION

- **For suggested references, including Web sites, for topics in this chapter,** see page SR-1 at the end of the book.

- **For additional primary-source material from this period,** see Chapter 15 in *Sources of THE MAKING OF THE WEST*, Third Edition.

- **For Web sites and documents related to topics in this chapter,** see *Make History* at **bedfordstmartins.com/hunt**.

CHAPTER REVIEW

KEY TERMS AND PEOPLE

Catherine de Médicis
  (453)

Edict of Nantes (455)

politiques (455)

Philip II (455)

Lepanto (455)

Elizabeth I (458)

Puritans (458)

Peace of Westphalia
  (463)

raison d'état (464)

secularization (471)

baroque (472)

scientific method (475)

heliocentrism (475)

REVIEW QUESTIONS

1. How did state power depend on religious unity at the end of the sixteenth century and start of the seventeenth?

2. Why did a war fought over religious differences result in stronger states?

3. What were the consequences of economic recession in the early 1600s?

4. How could belief in witchcraft and the rising prestige of scientific method coexist?

MAKING CONNECTIONS

1. How did the balance of power shift in Europe between 1560 and 1648? What were the main reasons for the shift?

2. Relate the new developments in the arts and sciences to the political and economic changes of this period of crisis.

> **For practice quizzes, a customized study plan, and other study tools,** see the Online Study Guide at bedfordstmartins.com/hunt.

IMPORTANT EVENTS

1562	French Wars of Religion begin	1598	French Wars of Religion end with Edict of Nantes
1566	Revolt of Calvinists in the Netherlands against Spain begins	1601	William Shakespeare, *Hamlet*
1569	Formation of commonwealth of Poland-Lithuania	1618	Thirty Years' War begins
1571	Battle of Lepanto marks victory of West over Ottomans at sea	1625	Hugo Grotius publishes *The Laws of War and Peace*
1572	St. Bartholomew's Day Massacre of French Protestants	1633	Galileo Galilei is forced to recant his support of heliocentrism
1588	English defeat of the Spanish Armada	1635	French join the Thirty Years' War by declaring war on Spain
		1648	Peace of Westphalia ends the Thirty Years' War

State Building and the Search for Order
1648–1690

In May 1664, King Louis XIV of France organized a weeklong series of entertainments for his court at Versailles, where he had recently begun construction of a magnificent new palace. More than six hundred members of his court attended the series of spectacles called "The Delights of the Enchanted Island." The carefully orchestrated activities opened with an elaborate parade of the king and his courtiers, accompanied by an eighteen-foot-high float in the form of a chariot dedicated to Apollo, Greek god of the sun and Louis's personally chosen emblem. The king's favorite artists presented works specially prepared for the occasion, including ballets, plays, and musical concerts. Equestrian tournaments, visits to the king's personal collection of wild animals and birds, and a huge fireworks display captivated the audience. Every detail of the festivities appeared in an official program published the same year.

Louis XIV spared no expense in promoting his image, especially to those most dangerous to him, the leading nobles of his kingdom. Other mid-seventeenth-century rulers followed his example or explicitly rejected it, but they could not afford to ignore it. All governments faced the daunting task of rebuilding authority after the wars over religion and the economic recession of the early seventeenth century. As part of his campaign to underline his majesty, Louis encouraged leading nobles to dispense huge sums to entertain him and his court. He always spent even more in order to show that he was richer and more powerful than any noble or than any other monarch.

Louis XIV's model of state building was known as absolutism, a system of government in which the ruler claims sole and uncontestable power. Although absolutism exerted great influence beginning in the mid-1600s, especially in central and eastern Europe, it faced competition

Louis XIV and His Bodyguards
One of Louis XIV's court painters, the Flemish artist Adam Frans van der Meulen, depicted the king arriving at the palace of Versailles, still under construction (the painting dates from 1669). None of the gardens, pools, or statues had been installed. Louis is the only figure facing the viewer, and his dress is much more colorful than that of anyone else in the painting. *(Réunion des Musées Nationaux/Art Resource, NY.)*

483

from **constitutionalism**, a system in which the ruler shares power with an assembly of elected representatives. Constitutionalism led to weakness in Poland-Lithuania, but it provided a strong foundation for state power in England, the Dutch Republic, and the British North American colonies. Constitutionalism triumphed in England, however, only after one king had been executed as a traitor and another had been deposed. The English conflicts over the nature of authority found their most enduring expression in the writings of Thomas Hobbes and John Locke, which laid the foundations of modern political science.

Whether absolutist or constitutionalist, nations faced similar challenges in the mid-seventeenth century. Competition in the international arena required resources, and all states raised taxes in this period, provoking popular protests and rebellions. Monarchs still relied on religion to justify their divine right to rule, but they increasingly sought secular defenses of their powers, too. **Absolutism** and constitutionalism were the two main responses to the threat of disorder and breakdown left as a legacy of the wars over religion.

The search for order took place not only in government and politics but also in intellectual, cultural, and social life. Artists sought means of glorifying power and expressing order and symmetry in new fashion. As states consolidated their power, elites endeavored to distinguish themselves more clearly from the lower orders. The upper classes emulated the manners developed at court and tried in every way to distance themselves from anything viewed as vulgar or lower class. Officials, clergy, and laypeople all worked to reform the poor, now seen as a major source of disorder. Whether absolutist or constitutionalist, seventeenth-century states all aimed to extend control over their subjects' lives.

> **FOCUS QUESTION:** What were the most important differences between absolutism and constitutionalism, and how did they establish order?

Louis XIV: Absolutism and Its Limits

French king **Louis XIV** (r. 1643–1715) personified the absolutist ruler, who in theory shared his power with no one. Louis personally made all important state decisions and left no room for dissent. In 1655, he reputedly told the Paris high court of justice, *"L'état, c'est moi"* ("I am the state"), emphasizing that state authority rested in him personally. Louis cleverly manipulated the affections and ambitions of his courtiers, chose as his ministers middle-class men who owed everything to him, built up Europe's largest army, and snuffed out every hint of religious or political opposition. Yet the absoluteness of his power should not be exaggerated. Like all other rulers of his time, Louis depended on the cooperation of many people: local officials who enforced his decrees, peasants and artisans who joined his armies and paid his taxes, creditors who loaned crucial funds, clergy who preached his notion of Catholicism, and nobles who joined court festivities rather than staying home and causing trouble.

---

constitutionalism: A system of government in which rulers share power with parliaments made up of elected representatives.

absolutism: A system of government in which the ruler claims sole and uncontestable power.

Louis XIV: French king (r. 1643–1715) who personified the absolutist ruler; in theory he shared his power with no one, but in practice he had to gain the cooperation of nobles, local officials, and even the ordinary subjects who manned his armies and paid his taxes.

■ **1642–1646** English civil war

■ **1649** Charles I beheaded; new Russian legal code

■ **1651** Hobbes, *Leviathan*

■ **1660** Monarchy restored in England

1640 · · · **1650** · · · **1660**

■ **1648** Peace of Westphalia; Fronde revolt in France; Ukrainan Cossacks rebel; Dutch Republic recognized as independent

■ **1661** Barbados institutes slave code

The Fronde, 1648–1653

Louis XIV's absolutism built on a long French tradition of increasing centralization of state authority, but before he could establish his preeminence he had to weather a series of revolts known as the Fronde. Derived from the French word for a child's slingshot, the term was used by critics to signify that the revolts were mere child's play. In fact, however, they posed an unprecedented threat to the French crown. Louis was only five when he came to the throne in 1643 upon the death of his father, Louis XIII, who with his chief minister, Cardinal Richelieu, had steered France through increasing involvement in the Thirty Years' War, rapidly climbing taxes, and innumerable tax revolts. Louis XIV's mother, Anne of Austria, and her Italian-born adviser and rumored lover, Cardinal Mazarin (1602–1661), ruled in the young monarch's name.

To meet the financial pressure of fighting the Thirty Years' War, Mazarin sold new offices, raised taxes, and forced creditors to extend loans to the government. In 1648, a coalition of his opponents presented him with a charter of demands that, if granted, would have given the parlements (high courts) a form of constitutional power with the right to approve new taxes. Mazarin responded by arresting the leaders of the parlements. He soon faced the series of revolts that at one time or another involved nearly every social group in France.

The Fronde posed an immediate menace to the young king. Fearing for his safety, his mother and members of his court took Louis and fled Paris. With civil war threatening, Mazarin and Anne agreed to compromise with the parlements. The nobles saw an opportunity to reassert their claims to power against the weakened monarchy and renewed their demands for greater local control, which they had lost when the French Wars of Religion ended in 1598. Leading noblewomen often played key roles in the opposition to

Louis XIV, Conqueror of the Fronde
In this painting of 1654, Louis XIV is depicted as the Roman god Jupiter, who crushes the discord of the Fronde (represented on the shield by the Medusa's head made up of snakes). When the Fronde began, Louis was only ten years old; at the time of this painting, he was sixteen. The propaganda about his divine qualities had already begun. *(Réunion des Musées Nationaux/Art Resource, NY.)*

Mazarin, carrying messages and forging alliances, especially when male family members were in prison. While the nobles sought to regain power and local influence, the middle and lower classes chafed at the repeated tax increases. Conflicts erupted throughout the kingdom as nobles, parlements, and city councils all raised their own

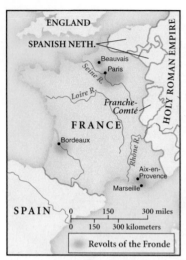

The Fronde, 1648–1653

armies to fight either the crown or each other, and rampaging soldiers devastated rural areas and disrupted commerce. The urban poor, such as those in the southwestern city of Bordeaux, sometimes revolted as well.

Neither the nobles nor the judges of the parlements really wanted to overthrow the king; they simply wanted a greater share in power. Mazarin and Anne eventually got the upper hand because their opponents failed to maintain unity in fighting the king's forces. But Louis XIV never forgot the humiliation and uncertainty that marred his childhood. His own policies as ruler would be designed to prevent the recurrence of any such revolts. Yet, for all his success, peasants would revolt against the introduction of new taxes on at least five more occasions in the 1660s and 1670s, requiring tens of thousands of soldiers to reestablish order. Absolutism was in part a fervent hope and not always a reality.

Court Culture as an Element of Absolutism

When Cardinal Mazarin died in 1661, Louis XIV, then twenty-two years old, decided to rule without a first minister. He described the dangers of his situation in memoirs he wrote later for his son's instruction: "Everywhere was disorder. My Court as a whole was still very far removed from the sentiments in which I trust you will find it." Louis listed many other problems in the kingdom, but none occupied him more than his attempts to control France's leading nobles, some of whom came from families that had opposed him militarily during the Fronde.

Typically quarrelsome, the French nobles had long exercised local authority by maintaining their own fighting forces, meting out justice on their estates, arranging jobs for underlings, and resolving their own conflicts through dueling. Louis set out to domesticate the warrior nobles by replacing violence with court ritual, such as the festivities at Versailles described at the beginning of this chapter. Using a systematic policy of bestowing pensions, offices, honors, gifts, and the threat of disfavor or punishment, Louis induced the nobles to cooperate with him and made himself the center of French power and culture. The aristocracy increasingly vied for his favor, attended the ballets and theatricals he put on, and learned the rules of etiquette he supervised—in short, became his clients, dependent on him for advancement. Great nobles competed for the honor of holding his shirt when he dressed, foreign ambassadors squabbled for places near him, and royal mistresses basked in the glow of his personal favor. Far from the court, however, nobles could still make considerable trouble for the king, and royal officials learned to compromise with them.

Those who did come to the king's court were kept on their toes. The preferred styles changed without notice, and the tiniest lapse in attention to etiquette could lead to ruin. Madame de

Louis XIV Visits the Royal Tapestry Workshop

This tapestry was woven at the Gobelins tapestry workshop between 1673 and 1680. It shows Louis XIV (wearing a red hat) and his minister Colbert (dressed in black, holding his hat) visiting the workshop on the outskirts of Paris. The workshop artisans scurry to show Louis all the luxury objects they manufacture. Louis bought the workshop in 1662 and made it a national enterprise for making tapestries and furniture. (Bridgeman-Giraudon/Art Resource, NY.)

DOCUMENT

Marie de Sévigné, Letter Describing the French Court (1675)

Marie de Rabutin-Chantal, marquise de Sévigné (1626–1696), was the most famous letter writer of her time. A noblewoman born in Paris, she frequented court circles and wrote about her experiences to her friends and relatives, especially her daughter. Although not published in her lifetime, her letters soon gained fame and were copied and read by those in her circle. She wrote her later letters with this audience in mind and so downplayed her own personal feelings, except those of missing her daughter to whom she was deeply attached. This letter from 1675 to her daughter recounts court intrigue surrounding Louis XIV's mistress and the shock when one of France's leading generals was killed in battle. Though Sévigné enjoyed spending time at Louis XIV's court, she could also write about it with biting wit.

They [the king and his court] were to set off today for Fontainebleau [one of the king's castles near Paris], where the entertainments were to become boring by their very multiplicity. Everything was ready when a bolt fell from the blue that shattered the joy. The populace says it is on account of *Quantova* [Sévigné's nickname for the king's mistress, Madame de Montespan, who gave birth to seven children fathered by Louis XIV], the attachment is still intense. Enough fuss is being made to upset the curé [priest] and everybody else, but perhaps not enough for her, for in her visible triumph there is an underlying sadness. You talk of the pleasures of Versailles, and at the time when they were off to Fontainebleau to plunge into joys, lo and behold M. De Turenne [commander of the French armies during the Dutch War] killed, general consternation, Monsieur le Prince [de Condé, another leading general], rushing off to Germany, France in desolation. Instead of seeing the end of the campaigns and having your brother back [Sévigné's son served in the army], we don't know where we are. There you have the world in its triumph and, since you like them, surprising events.

Source: *Madame de Sévigné: Selected Letters,* translated Leonard Tancock (New York: Penguin Books, 1982), 165.

Lafayette described the court in her novel *The Princess of Clèves* (1678): "The Court gravitated around ambition. Nobody was tranquil or indifferent—everybody was busily trying to better his or her position by pleasing, by helping, or by hindering somebody else." Elisabeth Charlotte, duchess of Orléans, the German-born sister-in-law of Louis, complained that "everything here is pure self-interest and deviousness." (See Document, "Marie de Sévigné, Letter Describing the French Court," above.)

Politics and the Arts.   Louis XIV appreciated the political uses of every form of art. Mock battles, extravaganzas, theatrical performances, even the king's dinner—Louis's daily life was a public performance designed to enhance his prestige. Calling himself the Sun King, after Apollo, Greek god of the sun, Louis stopped at nothing to burnish this radiant image. He played Apollo in ballets performed at court; posed for portraits with the emblems of Apollo (laurel, lyre, and tripod); and adorned his palaces with statues of the god. He also emulated the style and methods of ancient Roman emperors. At a celebration for the birth of his first son in 1662, Louis dressed in Roman attire, and many engravings and paintings showed him as a Roman emperor. Commissioned histories vaunted his achievements, and coins and medals spread his likeness throughout the realm.

The king's officials treated the arts as a branch of government. The king gave pensions to artists who worked for him and sometimes protected writers from clerical critics. The most famous of these was the playwright Molière, whose comedy *Tartuffe* (1664) made fun of religious hypocrites and was loudly condemned by church leaders. Louis forced Molière to delay public performances of the play after its premiere at the festivities of May 1664 but resisted calls for his dismissal. Louis's ministers set up royal academies of dance, painting, architecture, music, and science and took control of the Académie française (French Academy), which to this day decides on correct usage of the French language. Louis's government also regulated the number and locations of theaters and closely censored all forms of publication.

Music and theater enjoyed special prominence. Louis commissioned operas to celebrate royal marriages, baptisms, and military victories. His favorite composer, Jean-Baptiste Lully, wrote sixteen operas for court performances as well as many ballets. Louis himself danced in the ballets if a role seemed especially important. Playwrights often presented their new plays first to the court. Pierre Corneille and Jean-Baptiste Racine wrote tragedies set in Greece or Rome that celebrated the new aristocratic virtues that Louis aimed to inculcate: a reverence for order and self-control. All the characters were regal or noble, all the language lofty, all the behavior aristocratic.

The Palace of Versailles.   Louis glorified his image as well through massive public works projects. Veterans' hospitals and new fortified towns on the frontiers represented his military might. Urban improvements, such as the reconstruction of the Louvre palace in Paris, proved his wealth. But his most ambitious project was the construction of a new palace at Versailles, twelve miles from the turbulent capital (see illustration below).

Building began in the 1660s. By 1685, the frenzied effort engaged thirty-six thousand workers, not including the thousands of troops who diverted a local river to supply water for pools and fountains. The gardens designed by landscape architect André Le Nôtre reflected the spirit of Louis XIV's rule: their geometrical arrangements and clear lines showed that art and design could tame nature and that order and control defined the exercise of power. Le Nôtre's geometrical landscapes were later imitated in places as far away as St. Petersburg in Russia and Washington, D.C. Versailles symbolized Louis's success in reining in the nobility and dominating Europe, and other monarchs eagerly mimicked French fashion and often conducted their business in French.

Yet for all its apparent luxury and frivolity, life at Versailles was often cramped and cold. Fifteen thousand people crowded into the palace's apartments, including all the highest military officers, the ministers of state, and the separate households of each member of the royal family. Refuse collected in the corridors during the incessant building, and thieves and prostitutes overran the grounds. By the time Louis actually moved from the Louvre to Versailles in 1682, he had reigned as monarch for thirty-nine years. After his wife's death in 1683, he secretly married his mistress, Françoise d'Aubigné, marquise de Maintenon, and

The Palace of Versailles
This painting by Jean-Baptiste Martin from the late seventeenth century gives a good view of one section of the palace and especially the geometrically arranged gardens. What would observers conclude about Louis XIV when they viewed this scene?
(Réunion des Musées Nationaux/Art Resource, NY.)

conducted most state affairs from her apartments at the palace. Her opponents at court complained that she controlled all the appointments, but her efforts focused on her own projects, including her favorite: the founding in 1686 of a royal school for girls from impoverished noble families. She also inspired Louis XIV to increase his devotion to Catholicism.

Enforcing Religious Orthodoxy

Louis believed that he reigned by divine right. He served as God's lieutenant on earth and even claimed certain godlike qualities. As Bishop Jacques-Benigne Bossuet (1627–1704) explained, "We have seen that kings take the place of God, who is the true father of the human species. We have also seen that the first idea of power which exists among men is that of the paternal power; and that kings are modeled on fathers." The king, like a father, should instruct his subjects in the true religion, or at least make sure that others did so. In religious questions, too, the king's endeavors to gain more complete control showed both his wide-ranging ambition and the nature of the obstacles he faced.

Louis's campaign for religious conformity first focused on the Jansenists, Catholics whose doctrines and practices resembled some aspects of Protestantism. Following the posthumous publication of the book *Augustinus* (1640) by the Flemish theologian Cornelius Jansen (1585–1638), the Jansenists stressed the need for God's grace in achieving salvation. They emphasized the importance of original sin and resembled the English Puritans in their austere religious practice. Prominent among the Jansenists was Blaise Pascal (1623–1662), a mathematician of genius, who wrote his *Provincial Letters* (1656–1657) to defend Jansenism against charges of heresy. Many judges in the parlements likewise endorsed Jansenist doctrine.

Some questioned Louis's understanding of the finer points of doctrine: according to his sister-in-law, Louis himself "has never read anything about religion, nor the Bible either, and just goes along believing whatever he is told." But Louis rejected any doctrine that gave priority to considerations of individual conscience over the demands of the official church hierarchy, especially when that doctrine had been embraced by some noble supporters of the Fronde. Louis preferred teachings that stressed obedience to authority. Therefore, in 1660 he began enforcing various papal bulls (decrees) against Jansenism and closed down Jansenist theological centers. Jansenists were forced underground for the rest of his reign.

After many years of escalating pressure on the Calvinist Huguenots, Louis decided in 1685 to eliminate all of the Calvinists' rights. Louis considered the Edict of Nantes (1598), by which his grandfather Henry IV granted the Protestants religious freedom and a degree of political independence, a temporary measure, and he fervently hoped to reconvert the Huguenots to Catholicism. His **revocation of the Edict of Nantes** closed their churches and schools, banned all their public activities, and exiled those who refused to embrace the state religion. Tens of thousands of Huguenots responded by emigrating to England, Brandenburg-Prussia, the Dutch Republic, or North America. Many now wrote for publications attacking Louis XIV's absolutism. Protestant European countries were shocked by this crackdown on religious dissent and would cite it in justification of their wars against Louis.

Extending State Authority at Home and Abroad

Louis XIV could not have enforced his religious policies without the services of a nationwide bureaucracy. **Bureaucracy** — a network of state officials carrying out orders according to a regular and routine line of authority — comes from the French word *bureau*, for "desk," which came to mean "office," both in the sense of a physical space and a position of authority. Louis personally supervised the activities of his bureaucrats and worked to ensure his supremacy in all matters. But he always had to negotiate with nobles and local officials who sometimes thwarted his will.

Bureaucracy and Mercantilism.　Louis extended the bureaucratic forms his predecessors had developed, especially the use of intendants, officials who held their positions directly from the king rather than owning their offices, as crown officials had traditionally done. Louis handpicked an intendant for each region to represent his rule against entrenched local interests such as the parlements, provincial estates, and noble governors; they supervised the collection of taxes, the financing of public works, and the provisioning of the army. In 1673, Louis decreed that the parlements could no longer vote against his proposed laws or even speak against them. His

---

revocation of the Edict of Nantes: French king Louis XIV's decision to eliminate the rights of Calvinists granted in the edict of 1598; Louis banned all Calvinist public activities and forced those who refused to embrace the state religion to flee.

bureaucracy: A network of state officials carrying out orders according to a regular and routine line of authority.

intendants reduced local powers over finances and insisted on more efficient tax collection.

Louis's success in consolidating his authority depended on hard work, an eye for detail, and an ear to the ground. In his memoirs he described the tasks he set for himself:

> to learn each hour the news concerning every province and every nation, the secrets of every court, the mood and weaknesses of each Prince and of every foreign minister; to be well-informed on an infinite number of matters about which we are supposed to know nothing; to elicit from our subjects what they hide from us with the greatest care; to discover the most remote opinions of our courtiers and the most hidden interests of those who come to us with quite contrary professions [claims].

To gather all this information, Louis relied on a series of talented ministers, usually of modest origins, who gained fame, fortune, and even noble status from serving the king. Most important among them was Jean-Baptiste Colbert (1619–1683), the son of a wool merchant turned royal official. Colbert had managed Mazarin's personal finances and worked his way up under Louis XIV to become head of royal finances, public works, and the navy. He founded a family dynasty that eventually produced five ministers of state, an archbishop, two bishops, and three generals.

Colbert used the bureaucracy to establish a new economic doctrine, **mercantilism**. According to mercantilist policy, governments must intervene to increase national wealth by whatever means possible. Such government intervention inevitably increased the role and eventually the number of bureaucrats needed. Under Colbert, the French government established overseas trading companies, granted manufacturing monopolies, and standardized production methods for textiles, paper, and soap. A government inspection system regulated the quality of finished goods and compelled all craftsmen to organize into guilds, in which masters could supervise the work of the journeymen and apprentices. To protect French production, Colbert rescinded many internal customs fees but enacted high foreign tariffs, which cut imports of competing goods. To compete more effectively with England and the Dutch Republic, Colbert also subsidized shipbuilding, a policy that dramatically expanded the number of seaworthy vessels. Such mercantilist measures aimed to ensure France's prominence in world markets and to provide the resources needed to fight wars against the increasingly long list of en-

emies. Although later economists questioned the value of this state intervention in the economy, virtually every government in Europe embraced mercantilism.

Colbert's mercantilist projects extended to Canada, where in 1663 he took control of the trading company that had founded New France. He aimed to regulate all economic activity in the colonies. For example, he forbade colonial businesses from manufacturing anything already produced in mainland France. With the goal of establishing permanent settlements like those in the British North American colonies, he transplanted several thousand peasants from western France to the present-day province of Quebec, which France had claimed since 1608. He also tried to limit expansion westward, without success. Despite initial interruption of French fur-trading convoys by the Iroquois, in 1672 fur trader Louis Jolliet and Jesuit missionary Jacques Marquette reached the upper Mississippi River and traveled downstream as far as Arkansas. In 1684, French explorer Sieur de La Salle went all the way down to the Gulf of Mexico, claiming a vast territory for Louis XIV and calling it Louisiana after him. Colbert's successors embraced the expansion he had resisted, thinking it crucial to competing successfully with the English and the Dutch in the New World.

The Army and War.   Colonial settlement occupied only a small portion of Louis XIV's attention, however, for his main foreign policy goal was to extend French power in Europe. In pursuing this purpose, he inevitably came up against the Spanish and Austrian Habsburgs, whose lands encircled his. To expand French power, Louis needed the biggest possible army. His powerful ministry of war centralized the organization of French troops. Barracks built in major towns received supplies from a central distribution system. The state began to provide uniforms for the soldiers and to offer veterans some hospital care. A militia draft instituted in 1688 supplemented the army in times of war and enrolled a hundred thousand men. Louis's wartime army could field a force as large as that of all his enemies combined.

Absolutist governments always tried to increase their territorial holdings, and as Louis extended his reach, he gained new enemies. In 1667–1668, in the War of Devolution (so called because Louis claimed that lands in the Spanish Netherlands should devolve to him since the Spanish king had failed to pay the dowry of Louis's Spanish bride), Louis defeated the Spanish armies

---

mercantilism: The doctrine that governments must intervene to increase national wealth by whatever means possible.

but had to make peace when England, Sweden, and the Dutch Republic joined the war. In the Treaty of Aix-la-Chapelle in 1668, he gained control of a few towns on the border of the Spanish Netherlands. Pamphlets sponsored by the Habsburgs accused Louis of aiming for "universal monarchy," or domination of Europe.

In 1672, Louis XIV opened hostilities against the Dutch because they stood in the way of his acquisition of more territory in the Spanish Netherlands. He declared war again on Spain in 1673. By now the Dutch had allied themselves with their former Spanish masters to hold off the French. Louis also marched his troops into territories of the Holy Roman Empire, provoking many of the German princes to join with the emperor, the Spanish, and the Dutch in an alliance against Louis, now denounced as a "Christian Turk" for his imperialist ambitions. But the French armies more than held their own. Faced with bloody but inconclusive results on the battlefield, the parties agreed to the Treaty of Nijmegen of 1678–1679, which ceded several Flemish towns and the Franche-Comté region to Louis, linking Alsace to the rest of France. French government deficits soared, and in 1675 increases in taxes touched off the most serious antitax revolt of Louis's reign.

Louis had no intention of standing still. Heartened by the Habsburgs' seeming weakness, he pushed eastward, seizing the city of Strasbourg in 1681 and invading the province of Lorraine in 1684. In 1688, he attacked some of the small German cities of the Holy Roman Empire. As Louis's own mental powers diminished with age, he apparently lost all sense of measure. His armies laid waste to German cities such as Mannheim; his government ordered the local military commander to "kill all those who would still wish to build houses there." Between 1689 and 1697, a coalition known as the League of Augsburg—made up of England, Spain, Sweden, the Dutch Republic, the Austrian emperor, and various German princes—fought Louis XIV to a stalemate. When hostilities ended in the Peace of Rijswijk in 1697, Louis returned many of his conquests made since 1678 with the exception of Strasbourg (Map 16.1). Louis never lost his taste for war, but his allies learned how to set limits on his ambitions. (See Chapter 17 for the end of Louis's reign.)

Louis was the last French ruler before Napoleon to accompany his troops to the battlefield. In later generations, as the military became more professional, French rulers left the fighting to their generals. Although Louis had eliminated

WARS OF LOUIS XIV

1667–1668	**WAR OF DEVOLUTION**
	Enemies: Spain, Dutch Republic, England, Sweden
	Ended by Treaty of Aix-la-Chapelle in 1668, with France gaining towns in Spanish Netherlands (Flanders)
1672–1678	**DUTCH WAR**
	Enemies: Dutch Republic, Spain, Holy Roman Empire
	Ended by Treaty of Nijmegen, 1678–1679, which gave several towns in Spanish Netherlands and Franche-Comté to France
1688–1697	**WAR OF THE LEAGUE OF AUGSBURG**
	Enemies: Holy Roman Empire, Sweden, Spain, England
	Ended by Peace of Rijswijk, 1697, with Louis returning all his conquests made since 1678 except Strasbourg

the private armies of his noble courtiers, he constantly promoted his own military prowess in order to keep his noble officers under his sway. He had miniature battle scenes painted on his high heels and commissioned tapestries showing his military processions into cities, even those he did not take by force. He seized every occasion to assert his supremacy, insisting that other fleets salute his ships first.

War required money and men, which Louis obtained by expanding state control over finances, conscription, and military supply. Thus, absolutism and warfare fed each other as the bureaucracy created new ways to raise and maintain an army and the army's success in war justified further expansion of state power. But constant warfare also eroded the state's resources. Further administrative and legal reform, the elimination of the buying and selling of offices, and the lowering of taxes—all were made impossible by the need for more money.

Ordinary people suffered the most for Louis's ambitions. By the end of the Sun King's reign, one in six Frenchmen had served in the military. Louis XIV's armies swelled to twice the size of the armies France fielded during the Thirty Years' War. In addition to the higher taxes paid by everyone, those who lived on the routes leading to the battlefields had to house and feed soldiers; only nobles were exempt from this requirement. Fulfilling these

MAP 16.1 Louis XIV's Acquisitions, 1668–1697
Every ruler in Europe hoped to extend his or her territorial control, and war was often the result. Louis XIV steadily encroached on the Spanish Netherlands to the north and the lands of the Holy Roman Empire to the east. Although coalitions of European powers reined in Louis's grander ambitions, he nonetheless incorporated many neighboring territories into the French crown.

demands could be difficult, if not impossible, especially during the months from November to March when weather made military campaigns difficult. Soldiers had to be fed, even when locals found themselves living off the food stored from the previous fall harvest. When food fell short, soldiers sometimes gave in to the temptation to pillage, extort, or steal from local residents.

REVIEW: How "absolute" was the power of Louis XIV?

Absolutism in Central and Eastern Europe

Central and eastern European rulers saw in Louis XIV a powerful model of absolutist state building, yet they did not blindly emulate the Sun King, in part because they confronted conditions peculiar to their regions. The ruler of Brandenburg-Prussia had to rebuild lands ravaged by the Thirty Years' War and unite far-flung territories. The Austrian Habsburgs needed to govern a mosaic of ethnic

TAKING MEASURE

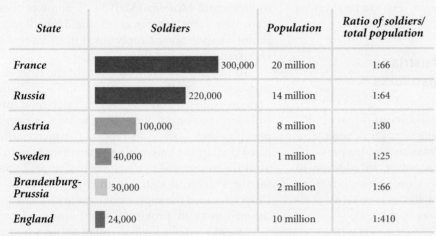

State	Soldiers	Population	Ratio of soldiers/ total population
France	300,000	20 million	1:66
Russia	220,000	14 million	1:64
Austria	100,000	8 million	1:80
Sweden	40,000	1 million	1:25
Brandenburg-Prussia	30,000	2 million	1:66
England	24,000	10 million	1:410

*Figures for the end of the seventeenth century, ranging from 1688 for Prussia to 1710 for France

The Seventeenth-Century Army
The figures in this chart are only approximate, but they tell an important story. What conclusions can you draw about the relative weight of the military in the different European states? Why would England have such a smaller army than the others? Is the absolute or the relative size of the military the most important indicator? *(From André Corvisier,* Armées et sociétés en Europe de 1494 à 1789 *(Paris: Presses Universitaires de France, 1976), 126.)*

and religious groups while fighting off the Ottoman Turks. The Russian tsars wanted to extend their power over an extensive but relatively impoverished empire. The great exception to absolutism in eastern Europe was Poland-Lithuania, where a long crisis virtually destroyed central authority and pulled much of eastern Europe into its turbulent wake.

Brandenburg-Prussia: Militaristic Absolutism

Brandenburg-Prussia began as a puny state on the Elbe River, but it had a remarkable future. In the nineteenth century, it would unify the disparate German states into modern-day Germany. The ruler of Brandenburg was an elector, one of the seven German princes entitled to select the Holy Roman Emperor. Since the sixteenth century the ruler of Brandenburg had also controlled the duchy of East Prussia; after 1618, the state was called Brandenburg-Prussia. Despite meager resources, **Frederick William of Hohenzollern**, who was the Great Elector of Brandenburg-Prussia (r. 1640–1688), succeeded in welding his scattered lands into an absolutist state.

Pressured first by the necessities of fighting the Thirty Years' War and then by the demands of re-

construction, Frederick William was determined to force his territories' estates (representative assemblies) to grant him a dependable income. The Great Elector struck a deal with the Junkers (nobles) of each province: in exchange for allowing him to collect taxes, he gave them complete control over their enserfed peasants and exempted them from taxation. The tactic worked. By the end of his reign, the estates met only on ceremonial occasions.

Supplied with a steady income, Frederick William could devote his attention to military and bureaucratic consolidation. Over forty years he expanded his army from eight thousand to thirty thousand men. (See "Taking Measure," above.) The army mirrored the rigid domination of nobles over peasants that characterized Brandenburg-Prussian society: peasants filled the ranks, and Junkers became officers. Nobles also took positions as bureaucratic officials, but military needs always had priority. The elector named special war commissars to take charge not only of military affairs but also of tax collection. To hasten military dispatches, he also established one of Europe's first state postal systems.

As a Calvinist ruler, Frederick William avoided the ostentation of the French court, even while following the absolutist model of centralizing state power. He boldly rebuffed Louis XIV by welcoming twenty thousand French Huguenot refugees after Louis's revocation of the Edict of Nantes. In pursuing foreign and domestic policies that promoted state power and prestige, Frederick William adroitly switched sides in Louis's wars and would

---

Frederick William of Hohenzollern: The Great Elector of Brandenburg-Prussia (r. 1640–1688) who brought his nation through the end of the Thirty Years' War and then succeeded in welding his scattered lands into an absolutist state.

stop at almost nothing to crush resistance at home. In 1701, his son Frederick I (r. 1688–1713) persuaded Holy Roman Emperor Leopold I to grant him the title "king in Prussia." Prussia had arrived as an important power.

An Uneasy Balance: Austrian Habsburgs and Ottoman Turks

Holy Roman Emperor Leopold I (r. 1658–1705) ruled over a variety of territories of different ethnicities, languages, and religions, yet in ways similar to his French and Prussian counterparts, he gradually consolidated his power. In addition to holding Louis XIV in check on his western frontiers, Leopold confronted the ever-present challenge of the Ottoman Turks to the east.

The Austrian Version of Absolutism.

Like all the Holy Roman Emperors since 1438, Leopold was an Austrian Habsburg. He was simultaneously duke

of Upper and Lower Silesia, count of Tyrol, archduke of Upper and Lower Austria, king of Bohemia, king of Hungary and Croatia, and ruler of Styria and Moravia (Map 16.2). Some of these territories were provinces in the Holy Roman Empire; others were simply ruled from Vienna as Habsburg family holdings.

In response to the weakening of the Holy Roman Empire by the ravages of the Thirty Years' War, the emperor and his closest officials took control over recruiting, provisioning, and strategic planning and worked to replace the mercenaries hired during the war with a permanent standing army that promoted professional discipline. To pay for the army and staff his growing bureaucracy, Leopold gained the support of local aristocrats and chipped away at provincial institutions' powers.

Intent on replacing Bohemian nobles who had supported the 1618 revolt against Austrian authority, the Habsburgs promoted a new nobility made up of Czechs, Germans, Italians, Spaniards, and

MAP 16.2 State Building in Central and Eastern Europe, 1648–1699
The Austrian Habsburgs had long contested the Ottoman Turks for dominance of eastern Europe, and by 1699 they had pushed the Turks out of Hungary. In central Europe, the Austrian Habsburgs confronted the growing power of Brandenburg-Prussia, which had emerged from relative obscurity after the Thirty Years' War to begin an aggressive program of expanding its military and its territorial base. As emperor of the Holy Roman Empire, the Austrian Habsburg ruler governed a huge expanse of territory, but the emperor's control was in fact only partial because of guarantees of local autonomy.

even Irish who used German as their common tongue, professed Catholicism, and loyally served the Austrian dynasty. Bohemia became a virtual Austrian colony. "Woe to you," lamented a Czech Jesuit in 1670, addressing Leopold, "the nobles you have oppressed, great cities made small. Of smiling towns you have made straggling villages." Austrian censors prohibited publication of this protest for over a century.

Battle for Hungary. Austria had fought the Turks for control of Hungary for more than 150 years. In 1682, when war broke out again, Leopold I's Austria controlled the northwest section of Hungary; the Turks occupied the center; and in the east, the Turks demanded tribute from the Hungarian princes who ruled Transylvania. In 1683, the Turks pushed all the way to the gates of Vienna and laid siege to the Austrian capital. With the help of Polish cavalry, the Austrians finally broke the siege and turned the tide in a major counteroffensive (see illustration at right). By the Treaty of Karlowitz of 1699, the Ottoman Turks surrendered almost all of Hungary to the Austrians, marking the beginning of the decline of Ottoman power.

Hungary's "liberation" from the Turks came at a high price. The fighting laid waste vast stretches of Hungary's central plain, and the population may have declined by as much as 65 percent in the seventeenth century. Once the Turks had been beaten back, Austrian rule over Hungary tightened. In 1687, the Habsburg dynasty's hereditary right to the Hungarian crown was acknowledged by the Hungarian diet, a parliament revived by Leopold in 1681 to gain the cooperation of Hungarian nobles. The diet was dominated by a core of pro-Habsburg Hungarian aristocrats who would support the dynasty until it fell in 1918; Austrians and Hungarians looked down on the other ethnic groups, such as Croats and Romanians, who had enjoyed considerable autonomy under the Ottoman Turks. To root out remaining Turkish influence and assert Austrian superiority, Leopold systematically destroyed Turkish buildings and rebuilt Catholic churches, monasteries, roadside shrines, and monuments in the flamboyant Austrian baroque style.

Ottoman State Authority. The Ottoman Turks also pursued state consolidation, but in a very different fashion from Leopold I and other European rulers. The Ottoman state extended its authority through a combination of settlement and military control. Hundreds of thousands of Turkish families moved with Turkish soldiers into the Balkan peninsula in the 1400s and 1500s. As locals con-

The Siege of Vienna, 1683
This detail from a painting by Franz Geffels shows the camp of the Ottoman Turks. The Turkish armies had surrounded Vienna since July 14, 1683. Jan Sobieski led an army of Poles who joined with Austrians and Germans to beat back the Turks on September 12, 1683.
(© The Art Archive/Corbis.)

verted to Islam, administration passed gradually into their hands. The Ottoman state would last longer than the French absolutist monarchy. Nevertheless, the seventeenth century marked a period of cultural decline in the eyes of the Turks themselves.

The Ottoman rulers, the sultans, were often challenged by mutinous army officers, but they rarely faced peasant revolts. Rather than resisting state authorities, Ottoman peasants periodically worked for the state as mercenaries. The sultans played elites off each other, absorbing some into the state bureaucracy and pitting one level of authority against another. Despite frequent palace coups and assassinations of sultans, the Ottoman state survived. This constantly shifting social and political system explains how the Ottoman state could appear weak in Western eyes and still pose a massive military threat on Europe's southeastern borders.

Russia: Setting the Foundations of Bureaucratic Absolutism

Seventeenth-century Russia seemed a world apart from the Europe of Leopold I and Louis XIV. Straddling Europe and Asia, the Russian lands stretched across Siberia to the Pacific Ocean. Western visitors either sneered or shuddered at the "barbarism" of Russian life, and Russians reciprocated by nursing deep suspicions of everything foreign. But under the surface, Russia was evolving as an absolutist state; the tsars wanted to claim unlimited autocratic power, but like their European counterparts they had to surmount internal disorder and come to an accommodation with noble landlords.

Serfdom and the Code of 1649. When Tsar Alexei (r. 1645–1676) tried to extend state authority by imposing new administrative structures and taxes in 1648, Moscow and other cities erupted in bloody rioting. The government immediately doused the fire. In 1649, Alexei convened the Assembly of the Land (consisting of noble delegates from the provinces) to consult on a sweeping law code to organize Russian society in a strict social hierarchy that would last for nearly two centuries. The code of 1649 assigned all subjects to a hereditary class according to their current occupation or state needs. Slaves and free peasants were merged into a serf class. As serfs, they could not change occupations or move; they were tightly tied to the

soil and to their noble masters. To prevent tax evasion, the code also forbade townspeople to move from the community where they resided. Nobles owed absolute obedience to the tsar and were required to serve in the army, but in return no other group could own estates worked by serfs. Serfs became the chattel of their lord, who could sell them like horses or land. Their lives differed little from those of the slaves on the plantations in the Americas.

Some peasants resisted enserfment. In 1667, **Stenka Razin**, the head of a powerful band of pirates and outlaws in southern Russia, led a rebellion that promised liberation from "the traitors and bloodsuckers of the peasant communes"—the great noble landowners, local governors, and Moscow courtiers. Captured four years later by the tsar's army, Razin was taken to Moscow, where he was dismembered in front of the public and his body thrown to the dogs (see illustration at left). Thousands of his followers also suffered grisly deaths, but his memory lived on in folk songs and legends. Landlords successfully petitioned for the abolition of the statute of limitations on runaway serfs, the use of state agents in searching for runaways, and harsh penalties against those who harbored runaways. The increase in Russian state authority went hand in hand with the enforcement of serfdom.

The Tsar's Absolute Powers. To extend his power and emulate his western rivals, Tsar Alexei wanted a bigger army, exclusive control over state policy, and a greater say in religious matters. The size of the army increased dramatically from 35,000 in the 1630s to 220,000 by the end of the century. The Assembly of the Land, once an important source of noble consultation, never met again after 1653. Alexei also imposed firm control over the Russian Orthodox church. In 1666, a church council reaffirmed the tsar's role as God's direct representative on earth. The state-dominated church took action against a religious group called the Old Believers, who rejected church efforts to bring Russian worship in line with Byzantine tradition. Whole communities of Old Believers starved or burned themselves to death rather than submit. Religious schism opened a gulf between the Russian people and the crown.

Stenka Razin in Captivity

After leading a revolt of thousands of serfs, peasants, and members of non-Russian tribes of the middle and lower Volga region, Stenka Razin was captured by Russian forces and led off to Moscow, as shown here, where he was executed in 1671. He has been the subject of songs, legends, and poems ever since. *(RIA Novosti.)*

Stenka Razin: The head of a powerful band of pirates and outlaws in southern Russia, who in 1667 led a rebellion that promised peasants liberation from noble landowners and officials; Razin was captured by the tsar's army in 1671 and publicly executed in Moscow.

Nevertheless, modernizing trends prevailed. As the state bureaucracy expanded, adding more officials and establishing regulations and routines, the government intervened more and more in daily life. Decrees regulated tobacco smoking, card playing, and alcohol consumption and even dictated how people should leash and fence their pet dogs. Tsar Alexei set up the first Western-style theater in the Kremlin, and his daughter Sophia translated French plays. The most adventurous nobles began to wear German-style clothing. Some even argued that service and not just birth should determine rank. Russia's long struggle over Western influences had begun.

Poland-Lithuania Overwhelmed

Unlike Russia and the other eastern European powers, Poland-Lithuania did not follow the absolutist model. Decades of war weakened the monarchy and made the great nobles into virtually autonomous warlords. The great nobles dominated the Sejm (parliament), and to maintain an equilibrium among themselves, they each wielded an absolute veto power. This "free veto" constitutional system deadlocked parliamentary government. The monarchy lost its room to maneuver, and with it much of its remaining power.

In 1648, Ukrainian Cossack warriors revolted against the king of Poland-Lithuania, inaugurating two decades of tumult known as the Deluge. *Cossack* was the name given to runaway serfs and poor nobles who formed outlaw bands in the no-man's-land of southern Russia and Ukraine (Stenka Razin was a Cossack). The Polish nobles who claimed this potentially rich land scorned the Cossacks as troublemakers, but to the Ukrainian peasant population they were liberators. In 1654, the Cossacks offered Ukraine to Russian rule, provoking a Russo-Polish war that ended in 1667 when the tsar annexed eastern Ukraine and Kiev. Neighboring powers tried to profit from the chaos in Poland-Lithuania; Sweden, Brandenburg-Prussia, and Transylvania sent armies to seize territory.

Many towns were destroyed in the fighting, and as much as a third of the Polish population perished. The once prosperous Jewish and Protestant minorities suffered greatly: some fifty-six thousand Jews were killed by either the Cossacks, the Polish peasants, or the Russian troops, and thousands more had to flee or convert to Christianity. One rabbi wrote, "We were slaughtered each day, in a more agonizing way than cattle: they are butchered quickly, while we were being executed slowly." Surviving Jews moved from towns to shtetls (Jewish villages), where they took up petty trading, moneylending, tax gathering, and tavern leasing—activities that fanned peasant anti-Semitism. Desperate for protection amid the war, most Polish Protestants backed the violently anti-Catholic Swedes, and the victorious Catholic majority branded them as traitors. Some Protestant refugees fled to the Dutch Republic and England. In Poland-Lithuania it came to be assumed that a good Pole was a Catholic. The commonwealth had ceased to be an outpost of toleration.

Poland-Lithuania in the Seventeenth Century

The commonwealth revived briefly when a man of ability and ambition, Jan Sobieski (r. 1674–1696), was elected king. He gained a reputation throughout Europe when he led twenty-five thousand Polish cavalrymen into battle in the siege of Vienna in 1683. His cavalry helped rout the Turks and turned the tide against the Ottomans. Married to a politically shrewd French princess, Sobieski openly admired Louis XIV's France. Despite his efforts to rebuild the monarchy, he could not halt Poland-Lithuania's decline into powerlessness. The Polish version of constitutionalism fatally weakened the state and made it prey to neighboring powers.

> **REVIEW:** Why did absolutism flourish everywhere in eastern Europe except Poland-Lithuania?

Constitutionalism in England

In the second half of the seventeenth century, western and eastern European states began to move in different directions. In eastern Europe, nobles lorded over their serfs but owed almost slavish obedience in turn to their rulers. In western Europe, even in absolutist France, serfdom had almost entirely disappeared and nobles and rulers alike faced greater challenges to their control. The greatest challenges of all would come in England.

This outcome might seem surprising, for the English monarchs enjoyed many advantages compared with their continental rivals: they needed less money for their armies because they had stayed out of the Thirty Years' War, and their island kingdom's population was only one-fourth the size of France's and of relatively homogeneous ethnicity, making it, in theory at least, easier to rule. Yet the English rulers failed in their efforts to install absolutist policies. The English revolutions of 1642–1660 and 1688–1689 overturned two kings, confirmed the constitutional powers of an elected parliament, and laid the foundation for the idea that government must guarantee certain rights to the people under the law.

England Turned Upside Down, 1642–1660

Disputes about the right to levy taxes and the nature of authority in the Church of England had long troubled the relationship between the English crown and Parliament. For more than a hundred years, wealthy English landowners had been accustomed to participating in government through Parliament and expected to be consulted on royal policy. Although England had no single constitutional document, a variety of laws, judicial decisions, charters and petitions granted by the king, and customary procedures all regulated relations between king and Parliament. When Charles I tried to assert his authority over Parliament, a civil war broke out. It set in motion an unpredictable chain of events, which included an extraordinary ferment of religious and political ideas. Some historians view the English civil war of 1642–1646 as the last great war of religion because it pitted Puritans against those trying to push the Anglican church toward Catholicism; others see in it the first modern revolution because it gave birth to democratic political and religious movements.

Charles I versus Parliament. When Charles I (r. 1625–1649) succeeded his father, James I, he faced an increasingly aggressive Parliament that resisted new taxes and resented the king's efforts to extend his personal control. In 1628, Parliament forced Charles to agree to the Petition of Right, by which he promised not to levy taxes without its consent. Charles hoped to avoid further interference with his plans by simply refusing to call Parliament into session between 1629 and 1640. Without it, the king's ministers had to find every loophole possible to raise revenues. They tried to turn "ship money," a levy on seaports in times of emergency, into an annual tax collected everywhere in the country. The crown won the ensuing court case, but many subjects still refused to pay what they considered to be an illegal tax.

Religious tensions brought conflicts over the king's authority to a head. The Puritans had long agitated for the removal of any vestiges of Catholicism, but Charles, married to a French Catholic, moved Anglicanism in the opposite direction in the 1630s. With Charles's encouragement, the archbishop of Canterbury, William Laud (1573–1645), imposed increasingly elaborate ceremonies on the Anglican church. Angered by these moves toward "popery," the Puritans poured forth reproving pamphlets and sermons. In response, Laud hauled them before the feared Court of Star Chamber, which the king personally controlled. The court ordered harsh sentences for Laud's Puritan critics; they were whipped, pilloried, branded, and even had their ears cut off and their noses split. When Laud tried to apply his policies to Scotland, however, they backfired completely: the stubborn Presbyterian Scots rioted against the imposition of the Anglican prayer book—the Book of Common Prayer—and in 1640 they invaded the north of England. To raise money to fight the war, Charles called Parliament into session and unwittingly opened the door to a constitutional and religious crisis.

The Parliament of 1640 did not intend revolution, but reformers in the House of Commons (the lower house of Parliament) wanted to undo what they saw as the royal tyranny of the 1630s. Parliament removed Laud from office, ordered the execution of an unpopular royal commander, abolished the Court of Star Chamber, repealed recently levied taxes, and provided for a parliamentary assembly at least once every three years, thus establishing a constitutional check on royal authority. Moderate reformers expected to stop there and resisted Puritan pressure to abolish bishops and eliminate the Anglican prayer book. But their hand was forced in January 1642, when Charles and his soldiers invaded Parliament and tried unsuccessfully to arrest those leaders who had moved to curb his power. Faced with mounting opposition within London, Charles quickly withdrew from the city and organized an army.

Civil War and the Challenge to All Authorities. The ensuing civil war between king and Parliament lasted four years (1642–1646) and divided the country. The king's army of royalists, known as Cavaliers, enjoyed the most support in northern and western England. The parliamentary forces, called Roundheads because they cut their hair short, had their stronghold in the southeast, including London. Although Puritans dominated on the parliamentary side, they were divided among themselves about the proper form of church government: the Presbyterians wanted a Calvinist church with some central authority, whereas the

Independents favored entirely autonomous congregations free from other church government (hence the term *congregationalism*, often associated with the Independents). The Puritans put aside their differences for the sake of military unity and united under an obscure member of the House of Commons, the country gentleman Oliver Cromwell (1599–1658), who sympathized with the Independents. After Cromwell skillfully reorganized the parliamentary troops, his New Model Army defeated the Cavaliers at the battle of Naseby in 1645. Charles surrendered in 1646.

England during the Civil War

Area supporting Parliament in 1643

Area supporting Royalists in December 1643

✴ Battle

Although the civil war between king and Parliament had ended in victory for Parliament, divisions within the Puritan ranks now came to the fore: the Presbyterians dominated Parliament, but the Independents controlled the army. The disputes between the leaders drew lower-class groups into the debate. (See "Contrasting Views," page 500.) When Parliament tried to disband the New Model Army in 1647, disgruntled soldiers protested. Called **Levellers** because of their insistence on leveling social differences, the soldiers took on their officers in a series of debates about the nature of political authority. The Levellers demanded that Parliament meet annually, that members be paid so as to allow common people to participate, and that all male heads of households be allowed to vote. Their ideal of political participation excluded servants, the propertyless, and women but offered access to artisans, shopkeepers, and modest farmers. Cromwell and other army leaders rejected the Levellers' demands as threatening to property owners. Cromwell insisted, "You have no other way to deal with these men but to break them in pieces. . . . If you do not break them they will break you."

Just as political differences between Presbyterians and Independents helped spark new political movements, so too their conflicts over church organization fostered the emergence of new religious doctrines. The new sects had in common only their emphasis on the "inner light" of individual religious inspiration and a disdain for hierarchical authority. Their emphasis on equality

before God and greater participation in church governance appealed to the middle and lower classes. The Baptists, for example, insisted on adult baptism because they believed that Christians should choose their own church and that every child should not automatically become a member of the Church of England. The Quakers demonstrated their beliefs in equality and the inner light by refusing to doff their hats to men in authority. Manifesting their religious experience by trembling, or "quaking," the Quakers believed that anyone — man or woman — inspired by a direct experience of God could preach.

Parliamentary leaders feared that the new sects would overturn the whole social hierarchy. Rumors abounded, for example, of naked Quakers

---

The World Turned Upside Down

The print from 1647 conveys the anxieties many people felt in the midst of religious and political upheaval. Nothing is as it should be: the feet are where the hands should be, the cart comes before the horse, a fish flies, and the wheelbarrow pushes the person. *(By permission of the British Library.)*

Levellers: Disgruntled soldiers in Cromwell's New Model Army who wanted to "level" social differences and extend political participation to all male property owners.

The English Civil War

The civil war between Charles I and Parliament (1642–1646) excited furious debates about the proper forms of political authority, debates that influenced political thought for two centuries or more. The Levellers, who served in the parliamentary army, wanted Parliament to be more accountable to ordinary men like themselves (Document 1). After the restoration of the monarchy in 1660, Lucy Hutchinson wrote a memoir in which she complained that Puritan *had become a term of political slander. Her memoir shows how religious terms had been politicized by the upheaval (Document 2). Thomas Hobbes, in his famous political treatise* Leviathan *(1651), develops the consequences of the civil war for political theory (Document 3).*

1. The Levellers, "The Agreement of the People, as Presented to the Council of the Army" (October 28, 1647)

Note especially two things about this document: (1) it focuses on Parliament as the chief instrument of reform, and (2) it claims that government depends on the consent of the people.

Since, therefore, our former oppressions and scarce-yet-ended troubles have been occasioned, either by want of frequent national meetings in Council [Parliament], or by rendering those meetings ineffectual, we are fully agreed and resolved to provide that hereafter our representatives be neither left to an uncertainty for the time nor made useless to the ends for which they are intended. In order whereunto we declare: — That the people of

England, being at this day very unequally distributed by Counties, Cities, and Borough for the election of their deputies in Parliament, ought to be more indifferently [equally] proportioned according to the number of the inhabitants. . . . That the power of this, and all future Representatives of this Nation, is inferior only to theirs who choose them, and doth extend, without the consent or concurrence of any other person or persons [the king], to the enacting, altering, and repealing of laws, to the erecting and abolishing of offices and courts, to the appointing, removing, and calling to account magistrates and officers of all degrees, to the making of war and peace, to the treating with foreign States [in other words, Parliament is the supreme power, not the king]. . . . These things we declare to be our native rights, and therefore are agreed and resolved to maintain them with our utmost possibilities against all opposition whatsoever.

Source: Samuel Rawson Gardiner, ed., *The Constitutional Documents of the Puritan Revolution, 1625–1660* (Oxford: Clarendon Press, 1906), 333–35.

2. Lucy Hutchinson, Memoirs of the Life of Colonel Hutchinson (1664–1671)

Lucy Hutchinson wrote her memoir to defend her Puritan husband, who had been imprisoned upon the restoration of the monarchy.

If any were grieved at the dishonour of the kingdom, or the griping of the poor, or the unjust oppressions of the subject by a

running through the streets waiting for "a sign." Some sects did advocate sweeping change. The Diggers promoted rural communism — collective ownership of all property. Seekers and Ranters questioned just about everything. One notorious Ranter, John Robins, even claimed to be God. A few men advocated free love. These developments convinced the political elite that tolerating the new sects would lead to skepticism, anarchism, and debauchery.

In keeping with their notions of equality and individual inspiration, many of the new sects provided opportunities for women to become preachers and prophets. The Quakers thought women especially capable of prophecy. One such prophet, Anna Trapnel, explained her vocation: "For in all that was said by me, I was nothing, the Lord put all in my mouth, and told me what I should say." Women presented petitions, participated promi-

nently in street demonstrations, distributed tracts, and occasionally even dressed as men, wearing swords and joining armies. The duchess of Newcastle complained in 1650 that women were "affecting a Masculinacy . . . practicing the behaviour . . . of men." The outspoken women in new sects like the Quakers underscored the threat of a social order turning upside down.

Oliver Cromwell. At the heart of the continuing political struggle was the question of what to do with the king, who tried to negotiate with the Presbyterians in Parliament. In late 1648, Independents in the army purged the Presbyterians from Parliament, leaving a "rump" of about seventy members. This Rump Parliament then created a high court to try Charles I. The court found him guilty of attempting to establish "an unlimited and tyrannical power" and pronounced a death sentence. On thousand ways invented to maintain the riots of the courtiers and the swarms of needy Scots the king had brought in to devour like locusts the plenty of this land, he was a puritan; if any showed favour to any godly, honest person, kept them company, relieved them in want, or protected them against violent and unjust oppression, he was a puritan. . . . In short, all that crossed the views of the needy courtiers, the proud encroaching priests, the thievish projectors [speculators], the lewd nobility and gentry . . . all these were puritans; and if puritans, then enemies to the king and his government, seditious, factious hypocrites, ambitious disturbers of the public peace, and finally the pest of the kingdom.

Source: Christopher Hill and Edmund Dell, eds., *The Good Old Cause: The English Revolution of 1640–1660, Its Causes, Course and Consequences* (London: Lawrence and Wishart, 1949), 179–80.

3. Thomas Hobbes, *Leviathan* (1651)

In this excerpt, Hobbes depicts the anarchy of a society without a strong central authority, but he leaves open the question of whether that authority should be vested in "one Man" or "one Assembly of men," that is, a king or a parliament.

During the time men live without a common Power to keep them all in awe, they are in that condition which is called Warre; and such a warre, as is of every man, against every man. . . . In such condition, there is no place for Industry; because the fruit thereof is uncertain: and consequently no Culture of the Earth; no Navigation, nor use of the commodities that may be imported by Sea; no commodious Building; no Instrument of moving, and

removing such things as require much force; no Knowledge of the face of the Earth; no account of Time; no Arts; no Letters; no Society; and which is worst of all, continuall feare, and danger of violent death; and the life of man, solitary, poore, nasty, brutish, and short. The only way to erect such a Common Power, as may be able to defend them from the invasion of Forraigners, and the injuries of one another, and thereby to secure them in such sort, as that by their owne industrie, and by the Fruites of the Earth, they may nourish themselves and live contentedly; is, to conferre all their power and strength upon one Man, or upon one Assembly of men, that may reduce all their wills, by plurality of voices, unto one Will. . . . This is more than Consent, or Concord; it is a reall Unitie of them all, in one and the same Person, made by Covenant of every man with every man. . . . This done, the Multitude so united in one Person, is called a COMMON-WEALTH, in latine CIVITAS. This is the Generation of that great LEVIATHAN, or rather (to speake more reverently) of that *Mortall God*, to which wee owe under the *Immortall God*, our peace and defence.

Source: Thomas Hobbes, *Leviathan*, ed. Richard E. Flathman and David Johnston (New York: Norton, 1997), 70, 95.

QUESTIONS TO CONSIDER
1. Why would both the king and the parliamentary leaders find the Levellers' views disturbing?
2. Why did Hobbes's arguments about political authority upset supporters of both monarchy and Parliament?

January 30, 1649, Charles was beheaded before an enormous crowd, which reportedly groaned as one when the axe fell. Although many had objected to Charles's autocratic rule, few had wanted him killed. For royalists, Charles immediately became a martyr, and reports of miracles, such as the curing of blindness by the touch of a handkerchief soaked in his blood, soon circulated.

The Rump Parliament abolished the monarchy and the House of Lords (the upper house of

Execution of Charles I
This print of the execution of English king Charles I appeared on the first page of the fictitious confessions of his executioner, Richard Brandon, who supposedly claimed to feel pains in his own neck from the moment he cut off Charles's head. (© *British Library, London, UK/The Bridgeman Art Library.*)

Printed in the year Year, of the Hang-mans down-fall, 1649.

Oliver Cromwell

In this painting of 1649, Robert Walker deliberately evokes previous portraits of English kings. Cromwell is shown preparing for battle in Ireland (note the shore and sea on Cromwell's right); he holds the baton of military command, and a young page is tying on a sash, symbol of his rank. Cromwell lived an austere life; he is depicted here without any sign of luxury. When he died, he was buried in Westminster Abbey, but in 1661 his body was exhumed and hanged in its shroud. His head was cut off and displayed outside Westminster Hall for nearly twenty years. *(National Portrait Gallery, London.)*

Parliament) and set up a Puritan republic with Oliver Cromwell (see illustration above) as chairman of the Council of State. Cromwell did not tolerate dissent from his policies. He saw the hand of God in events and himself as God's agent. Pamphleteers and songwriters ridiculed his red nose and accused him of wanting to be king, but few challenged his leadership. When his agents discovered plans for mutiny within the army, they executed the perpetrators; new decrees silenced the Levellers. Although Cromwell allowed the various Puritan sects to worship rather freely and permitted Jews with needed skills to return to England for the first time since the thirteenth century, Catholics could not worship publicly, nor could Anglicans use the Book of Common Prayer. The elites—many of them were still Anglican—were troubled by Cromwell's religious policies but pleased to see some social order reestablished.

The new regime aimed to extend state power just as Charles I had before. Cromwell laid the foundation for a Great Britain made up of England, Ireland, and Scotland by reconquering Scotland and subduing Ireland. Anti-English rebels in Ireland had seized the occasion of troubles between king and Parliament to revolt in 1641. When his position was secured in 1649, Cromwell went to Ireland with a large force and easily defeated the rebels, massacring whole garrisons and their priests. He encouraged expropriating the lands of the Irish "barbarous wretches," and Scottish immigrants resettled the northern county of Ulster. This seventeenth-century English conquest left a legacy of bitterness that the Irish even today call "the curse of Cromwell." In 1651, Parliament turned its attention overseas, putting mercantilist ideas into practice in the first Navigation Act, which allowed imports only if they were carried on English ships or came directly from the producers of goods. The Navigation Act was aimed at the Dutch, who dominated world trade; Cromwell tried to carry the policy further by waging naval war on the Dutch from 1652 to 1654.

At home, however, Cromwell faced growing resistance. His wars required a budget twice the size of Charles I's, and his increases in property taxes and customs duties alienated landowners and merchants. The conflict reached a crisis in 1653: Parliament considered disbanding the army, whereupon Cromwell abolished the Rump Parliament in a military coup and made himself Lord Protector. He now silenced his critics by banning newspapers and using networks of spies to read mail and keep tabs on his enemies. When Cromwell died in 1658, the diarist John Evelyn claimed, "There were none that cried but dogs." Cromwell intended that his son should succeed him, but his death only revived the prospect of civil war and political chaos. In 1660, a newly elected, staunchly Anglican Parliament invited Charles II, the son of the executed king, to return from exile.

The Glorious Revolution of 1688

The traditional monarchical form of government was reinstated in 1660, restoring Charles II (r. 1660–1685) to full partnership with Parliament. He promised "a liberty to tender consciences" in an attempt to extend religious toleration, especially to Catholics, with whom he sympathized. His successor James II (r. 1685–1688) pursued even more aggressive pro-Catholic policies, bringing dissent once more to a boil. In response, Parliament deposed James and installed his Protestant daughter, Mary, and her Dutch husband, William, as joint monarchs. This Glorious Revolution marked the final triumph of constitutionalism over absolutism in England.

The Restored Monarchy. Charles II moved quickly to reestablish royal authority. More than a thousand Puritan ministers lost their positions, and attending a service other than one conforming with the Anglican prayer book was illegal after 1664. Natural disasters also marred the early years of his reign. The plague stalked London's rat-infested streets in May 1665 and claimed more than thirty thousand victims by September. Then in 1666, the Great Fire (see illustration on this page) swept the city. Some in Parliament feared, not without cause, that the English government would come to resemble French absolutism. In 1670, Charles II made a secret agreement, soon leaked, with Louis XIV in which he promised to announce his conversion to Catholicism in exchange for money for a war against the Dutch. Charles never proclaimed himself a Catholic, but in his Declaration of Indulgence (1673) he did suspend all laws against Catholics and Protestant dissenters. Parliament refused to continue funding the Dutch war unless Charles rescinded his Declaration of Indulgence. Asserting its authority further, Parliament passed the Test Act in 1673, requiring all government officials to profess allegiance to the Church of England and in effect disavow Catholic doctrine. Then in 1678, Parliament precipitated the so-called Exclusion Crisis by explicitly denying the throne to a Roman Catholic. This action was aimed at the king's brother and heir, James, an open convert to Catholicism. Charles refused to allow it to become law.

The dynastic crisis over the succession of a Catholic gave rise to two distinct factions in Parliament: the Tories, who supported a strong, hereditary monarchy and the restored ceremony of the Anglican church, and the Whigs, who advocated parliamentary supremacy and toleration of Protestant dissenters such as Presbyterians. Both labels were originally derogatory: *Tory* meant an Irish Catholic bandit; *Whig* was the Irish Catholic

Great Fire of London, 1666
This view of London shows the three-day fire at its height. The writer John Evelyn described the scene in his diary: "All the sky was of a fiery aspect, like the top of a burning oven, and the light seen above 40 miles round about for many nights. God grant mine eyes may never behold the like, who now saw above 10,000 houses all in one flame; the noise and cracking and thunder of people, the fall of towers, houses, and churches, was like an hideous storm." Everyone in London at the time felt overwhelmed by the catastrophe, and many attributed it to God's punishment for the upheavals of the 1640s and 1650s. (©Museum of London.)

designation for a Presbyterian Scot. The Tories favored James's succession despite his Catholicism, whereas the Whigs opposed a Catholic monarch. The loose moral atmosphere of Charles's court also offended some Whigs, who complained tongue in cheek that Charles was father of his country in much too literal a fashion (he had fathered more than one child by his mistresses but produced no legitimate heir).

Parliament's Revolt against James II. When he succeeded his brother, James seemed determined to force Catholicism on his subjects. Tories and Whigs joined together when a male heir—who would take precedence over James's two adult Protestant daughters—was born to James's second wife, an Italian Catholic, in 1688. They invited the Dutch ruler **William, prince of Orange**, and his wife, James's older daughter, Mary, to invade England. Mary was brought up as a Protestant and was willing to act with her husband against her father's pro-Catholic policies. James fled to France, and hardly any blood was shed. Parliament offered the throne jointly to William (r. 1689–1702) and Mary (r. 1689–1694) on the condition that they accept a bill of rights guaranteeing Parliament's full partnership in a constitutional government.

In the Bill of Rights (1689), William and Mary agreed not to raise a standing army or to levy taxes without Parliament's consent. They also agreed to call meetings of Parliament at least every three years, to guarantee free elections to parliamentary seats, and to abide by Parliament's decisions and not suspend duly passed laws. The agreement gave England's constitutional government a written, legal basis by formally recognizing Parliament as a self-contained, independent body that shared power with the rulers. Victorious supporters of the coup declared it the **Glorious Revolution** because it was achieved with so little bloodshed (at least in England).

The propertied classes who controlled Parliament prevented any resurgence of the popular turmoil of the 1640s. The Toleration Act of 1689 granted all Protestants freedom of worship, though non-Anglicans were still excluded from the universities; Catholics got no rights but were more often left alone to worship privately. When the Catholics in Ireland rose to defend James II, William and Mary's troops brutally suppressed them. With the Whigs in power and the Tories in opposition, wealthy landowners now controlled political life throughout the realm. The factions' differences, however, were minor; essentially, the Tories had less access to the king's patronage. A contemporary reported that King William had said "that if he had good places [honors and land] enough to bestow, he should soon unite the two parties."

Social Contract Theory: Hobbes and Locke

Out of the turmoil of the English revolutions came a major rethinking of the foundations of all political authority. Although Thomas Hobbes and John Locke wrote in response to the upheavals of their times, they offered opposing arguments that were applicable to any place and any time, not just England of the seventeenth century. Hobbes justified absolute authority; Locke provided the rationale for constitutionalism. Yet both argued that all authority came not from divine right but from a **social contract** among citizens.

Hobbes. Thomas Hobbes (1588–1679) was a royalist who sat out the English civil war of the 1640s in France, where he tutored the future king Charles II. Returning to England in 1651, he published his masterpiece, *Leviathan* (1651), in which he argued for unlimited authority in a ruler. Absolute authority could be vested in either a king or a parliament; it had to be absolute, Hobbes insisted, in order to overcome the defects of human nature. Believing that people are essentially self-centered and driven by the "right to self-preservation," Hobbes made his case by referring to science, not religion. To Hobbes, human life in a state of nature—that is, any situation without firm authority—was "solitary, poor, nasty, brutish, and short." He believed that the desire for power and natural greed would inevitably lead to unfettered competition. Only the assurance of social order could make people secure enough to act according to law; consequently, giving up personal liberty, he maintained, was the price of collective security. Rulers derived their power, he concluded, from a contract in which absolute authority protects people's rights.

William, prince of Orange: Dutch ruler who, with his Protestant wife, Mary (daughter of James II), ruled England after the Glorious Revolution of 1688.

Glorious Revolution: The events of 1688 when Tories and Whigs replaced England's monarch James II with his Protestant daughter, Mary, and her husband, Dutch ruler William of Orange; William and Mary agreed to a Bill of Rights that guaranteed rights to Parliament.

social contract: The doctrine that all political authority derives not from divine right but from an implicit contract between citizens and their rulers.

Hobbes's notion of rule by an absolute authority left no room for political dissent or nonconformity, and it infuriated both royalists and supporters of Parliament. He enraged royalists by arguing that authority came not from divine right but from the social contract. Parliamentary supporters resisted Hobbes's claim that rulers must possess absolute authority to prevent the greater evil of anarchy; they believed that a constitution should guarantee shared power between king and Parliament, and protect individual rights under the law. Like Machiavelli before him, Hobbes became associated with a cynical, pessimistic view of human nature, and future political theorists often began their arguments by refuting Hobbes.

Locke. Rejecting both Hobbes and the more traditional royalist defenses of absolute authority, John Locke (1632–1704) used the notion of a social contract to provide a foundation for constitutionalism. Locke experienced political life firsthand as physician, secretary, and intellectual companion to the earl of Shaftesbury, a leading English Whig. In 1683, during the Exclusion Crisis, Locke fled with Shaftesbury to the Dutch Republic. There he continued work on his *Two Treatises of Government*, which, when published in 1690, served to justify the Glorious Revolution of 1688. Locke's position was thoroughly anti-absolutist. He denied the divine right of kings and ridiculed the common royalist idea that political power in the state mirrored the father's authority in the family. Like Hobbes, he posited a state of nature that applied to all people. Unlike Hobbes, however, he thought people were reasonable and the state of nature peaceful.

Locke insisted that government's only purpose was to protect life, liberty, and property, a notion that linked economic and political freedom. Ultimate authority rested in the will of a majority of men who owned property, and government should be limited to its basic purpose of protection. A ruler who failed to uphold his part of the social contract between the ruler and the populace could be justifiably resisted, an idea that would become crucial for the leaders of the American Revolution a century later. For England's seventeenth-century landowners, however, Locke helped validate a revolution that consolidated their interests and ensured their privileges in the social hierarchy.

Locke defended his optimistic view of human nature in the immensely influential *Essay Concerning Human Understanding* (1690). He denied the existence of any innate ideas and asserted instead that each human is born with a mind that is a tabula rasa (blank slate). Not surprisingly, Locke devoted considerable energy to rethinking educational practices; he believed that education crucially shaped the human personality by channeling all sensory experience. Everything humans know, he claimed, comes from sensory experience, not from anything inherent in human nature. Locke's views promoted the belief that "all men are created equal," a belief that challenged absolutist forms of rule and ultimately raised questions about women's roles as well. Although Locke himself owned shares in the Royal African Company and justified slavery, his writings were later used by abolitionists in their campaign against slavery.

> **REVIEW:** What differences over religion and politics caused the conflict between king and Parliament in England?

Outposts of Constitutionalism

When William and Mary came to the throne in England in 1689, the Dutch and the English put aside the rivalries that had brought them to war against each other in 1652–1654, 1665–1667, and 1672–1674. Under William, the Dutch and the English together led the coalition that blocked Louis XIV's efforts to dominate continental Europe. The English and Dutch had much in common: oriented toward commerce, especially overseas, they were the successful exceptions to absolutism in Europe. Also among the few outposts of constitutionalism in the seventeenth century were the British North American colonies, which developed representative government while the English were preoccupied with their revolutions at home. Constitutionalism was not the only factor shaping this Atlantic world; as constitutionalism developed in the colonies, so too did the enslavement of black Africans as a new labor force.

The Dutch Republic

When the Dutch Republic gained formal independence from Spain in 1648, it had already established a decentralized, constitutional state. Rich merchants called regents effectively controlled the internal affairs of each province and through the Estates General named the *stadholder*, the executive officer responsible for defense and for representing the state at all ceremonial occasions. They

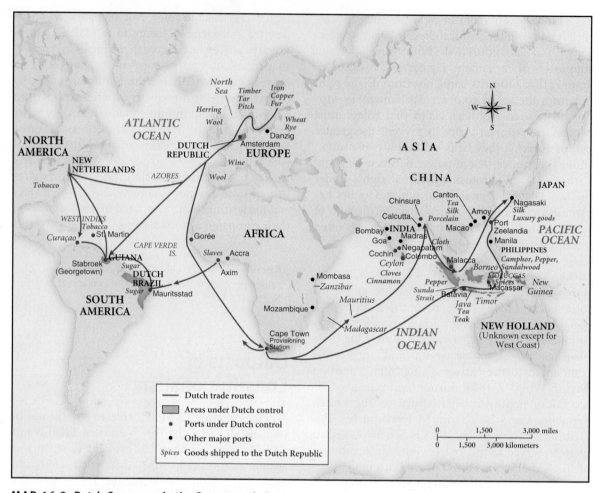

MAP 16.3 Dutch Commerce in the Seventeenth Century
Even before gaining formal independence from the Spanish in 1648, the Dutch had begun to compete with the Spanish and Portuguese all over the world. In 1602, a group of merchants established the Dutch East India Company, which soon offered investors an annual rate of return of 35 percent on the trade in spices with countries located on the Indian Ocean. Global commerce gave the Dutch the highest standard of living in Europe and soon attracted the envy of the French and the English.

almost always chose one of the princes of the house of Orange, but the stadholder resembled a president more than a king.

The decentralized state encouraged and protected trade, and the Dutch Republic soon became Europe's financial capital. The Bank of Amsterdam offered borrowers lower interest rates than those available in England and France. Praised for their industriousness, thrift, and cleanliness — and maligned as greedy, dull "butter-boxes" — the Dutch dominated overseas commerce with their shipping (Map 16.3). They imported products from all over the world: spices, tea, and silk from Asia; sugar and tobacco from the Americas; wool from England and Spain; timber and furs from Scandinavia;

grain from eastern Europe. A widely reprinted history of Amsterdam that appeared in 1662 described the city as "risen through the hand of God to the peak of prosperity and greatness. . . . The whole world stands amazed at its riches and from east and west, north and south they come to behold it."

The Dutch rapidly became the most prosperous and best-educated people in Europe. Middle-class people supported the visual arts, especially painting, to an unprecedented degree. Artists and engravers produced thousands of works, and Dutch artists were among the first to sell to a mass market. Whereas in other countries kings, nobles, and churches bought art, Dutch buyers were mer-

A Typical Dutch Scene from Daily Life
Jan Steen painted *The Baker Arent Oostward and His Wife* in 1658. Steen ran a brewery and tavern in addition to painting, and he was known for his interest in the details of daily life. Dutch artists popularized this kind of "genre" painting, which showed ordinary people at work and play.
(Rijksmuseum, Amsterdam.)

■ **For more help analyzing this image,** see the visual activity for this chapter in the Online Study Guide at **bedfordstmartins.com/hunt**.

chants, artisans, and shopkeepers. Engravings, illustrated histories, and oil paintings were all relatively inexpensive. One foreigner commented that "pictures are very common here, there being scarce an ordinary tradesman whose house is not decorated with them." Dutch artists focused on familiar daily details because for them ordinary people had religious as well as political significance; even children at play could be infused with radiant beauty. The family household, not the royal court, determined the moral character of this intensely commercial society. Relative prosperity decreased the need for married women to work, so Dutch society developed the clear contrast between middle-class male and female roles that would become prevalent elsewhere in Europe and in America more than a century later. As one contemporary Dutch writer explained, "The husband must be on the street to practice his trade; the wife must stay at home to be in the kitchen."

Extraordinarily high levels of urbanization and literacy created a large reading public. Dutch presses printed books censored elsewhere (printers or authors censored in one province simply shifted operations to another), and the University of Leiden attracted students and professors from all over Europe. Dutch tolerance extended to the works of Benedict Spinoza (1633–1677), a Jewish

philosopher and biblical scholar who was expelled by his synagogue for alleged atheism but left alone by the Dutch authorities. Spinoza strove to reconcile religion with science and mathematics, but his work scandalized many Christians and Jews because he seemed to equate God and nature. Like nature, Spinoza's God followed unchangeable laws and could not be influenced by human actions, prayers, or faith.

Dutch learning, painting, and commerce all enjoyed wide renown in the seventeenth century, but this luster proved hard to maintain. The Dutch lived in a world of international rivalries in which strong central authority gave their enemies an advantage. Though inconclusive, the naval wars with England between 1652 and 1674 drained the state's revenues. Even more dangerous were the land wars with France, which continued into the eighteenth century. The Dutch survived these challenges but increasingly depended on alliances with other powers, especially England after the Glorious Revolution. At the end of the seventeenth century, the Dutch elites became more exclusive, more preoccupied with ostentation, and less tolerant of deviations from strict Calvinism. Rather than encouraging native Dutch styles, they became more concerned with imitating French ones. The Dutch "golden age" was over.

Freedom and Slavery in the New World

The Dutch also lost ground to the French and English in the New World colonies. While the Dutch concentrated on shipping, including the slave trade, the seventeenth-century French and English established settler colonies that would eventually provide fabulous revenues to the home countries. Many European governments encouraged private companies to vie for their share of the slave trade, and slavery began to take clear institutional form in the New World in this period. While whites found in the colonies greater political and religious freedom than in Europe, they subjected black Africans to the most degrading forms of bondage.

The Rise of the Slave Trade.

After the Spanish and Portuguese had shown that African slaves could be transported and forced to labor in South and Central America, the English and French endeavored to set up similar labor systems in their new Caribbean island colonies. White planters with large tracts of land bought African slaves to work fields of sugarcane; and as they gradually built up their holdings, the planters displaced most of the original white settlers, who moved to mainland North American colonies. After 1661, when Barbados instituted a slave code that stripped all Africans of rights under English law, slavery became codified as an inherited status that applied only to blacks. The result was a society of extremes: the very wealthy whites (about 7 percent of the population in Barbados) and the enslaved, powerless black majority. The English brought few of their religious or constitutional practices to the Caribbean.

Other Caribbean colonies followed a similar pattern of development. Louis XIV promulgated a "black code" in 1685 to regulate the legal status of slaves in the French colonies and to prevent non-Catholics from owning slaves. The code supposedly set limits on the violence planters could exercise and required them to house, feed, and clothe their slaves. But white planters simply ignored provisions of the code that did not suit them, and in any case, because the code defined slaves as property, slaves could not themselves bring suit in court to demand better treatment.

The governments of England, France, Spain, Portugal, the Dutch Republic, and Denmark all encouraged private companies to traffic in black Africans, while the highest church and government authorities in Catholic and Protestant countries alike condoned the gradually expanding slave trade. In 1600, about 9,500 Africans were exported from Africa to the New World every year; by 1700, this number had increased nearly fourfold to 36,000 annually. Historians advance several different ideas about which factors increased the slave trade: some claim that improvements in muskets made European slavers more effective; others cite the rising price for slaves, which made their sale more attractive for Africans; still others focus on factors internal to Africa such as the increasing size of African armies and their use of muskets in fighting and capturing other Africans for sale as slaves. The way had been prepared for the development of an Atlantic economy based on slavery.

Constitutional Freedoms in the English Colonies.

Virtually left to themselves during the upheavals in England, the fledgling English colonies in North America developed representative government on their own. Almost every colony had a governor and a two-house legislature. The colonial legislatures constantly sought to increase their power and resisted the efforts of Charles II and James II to reaffirm royal control. William and Mary reluctantly allowed emerging colonial elites more control over local affairs. The social and political elite among the settlers hoped to impose an English social hierarchy dominated by rich landowners. Ordinary immigrants to the colonies, however, took advantage of plentiful land to carve out their own farms using white servants and, later, in some colonies, African slaves.

For native Americans, the expanding European presence meant something else altogether. They faced death through disease and warfare and the accelerating loss of their homelands. Unlike white settlers, many native Americans believed that land was a divine gift provided for their collective use and not subject to individual ownership. Europeans' claims that they owned exclusive land rights consequently resulted in frequent skirmishes. In 1675–1676, for instance, three tribes allied under Metacomet (called King Philip by the English) threatened the survival of New England settlers, who savagely repulsed the attacks and sold their captives as slaves. Whites could portray native Americans as "noble savages," but when threatened they often depicted them as conspiring villains and sneaky heathens who were akin to Africans in their savagery. The benefits of constitutionalism were reserved for Europeans.

REVIEW: Why did constitutionalism thrive in the Dutch Republic and the British North American colonies, even as their participation in the slave trade grew?

The Search for Order in Elite and Popular Culture

Constitutionalism's emphasis on a social contract fostered the guarantee of individual freedoms, yet the constitutional governments pursued profits in the burgeoning slave trade just as avidly as the absolutist ones. Freedom did not mean liberty for everyone. One of the great debates of the time—and thereafter—concerned the meaning of freedom: for whom, under what conditions, with what justifiable limitations could freedom be claimed? Freedom of the press found its first champion in the English poet John Milton, and freedom to choose one's own religion began to attract adherents too. These freedoms posed their own dilemmas: should publishers be allowed to print anything they wished and would religious toleration undermine the state's authority or even promote skepticism about religion in general?

Poetry, painting, architecture, and even science at this time all reflected in some measure the attempts to ground authority—to define the relation between freedom and order—in new ways. Authority concerned not just rulers and subjects but also the hierarchy of groups in society. As European states consolidated their powers, elites worked to distinguish themselves from the lower classes. They developed new codes of correct behavior for themselves and tried to teach order and discipline to their social inferiors. Their repeated efforts show, however, that popular culture had its own dynamics which resisted control from above.

Freedom and Constraint in the Arts and Sciences

Most Europeans feared disorder above all else. The French mathematician Blaise Pascal vividly captured their worries in his *Pensées* (Thoughts) of 1660: "I look on all sides, and I see only darkness everywhere." Though Pascal made important contributions to the mathematical theory of probabilities, he was skeptical about the human ability to forge order out of chaos: "Nature presents to me nothing which is not a matter of doubt and concern. . . . It is incomprehensible that God should exist, and incomprehensible that He should not exist." Pascal urged his readers to accept the wager that God existed. Reason could not determine whether God existed or not, Pascal concluded. Poets, painters, and architects all grappled with similar issues of faith, reason,

and authority, but most of them came to more positive conclusions than Pascal about human capacities.

Milton. The English Puritan poet John Milton (1608–1674) wrestled with the inevitable limitations on individual liberty. In 1643, in the midst of the civil war between king and Parliament, he published writings in favor of divorce. When Parliament enacted a censorship law aimed at such literature, Milton responded in 1644 with one of the first defenses of freedom of the press, *Areopagitica*. (See Document, "John Milton, Defense of Freedom of the Press," page 511.) In it, he argued that even controversial books about religion should be allowed because the state could not command religious belief. Milton favored limited

Gian Lorenzo Bernini, *Ecstasy of St. Teresa of Ávila* (c. 1650)
This ultimate statement of baroque sculpture captures all the drama and even sensationalism of a mystical religious faith. Bernini based his figures on a vision reported by St. Teresa in which she saw an angel: "In his hands I saw a great golden spear, and at the iron tip there appeared to be a point of fire. This he plunged into my heart several times so that it penetrated my entrails. When he pulled it out I felt that he took them with it, and left me utterly consumed by the great love of God." *(Scala/Art Resource, NY.)*

French Classicism
This painting by Nicolas Poussin, *Discovery of Achilles on Skyros* (1649–1650), shows the French interest in classical themes and ideals. In the Greek story, Thetis dresses her son Achilles as a young woman and hides him on the island of Skyros so he would not have to fight in the Trojan War. When a chest of treasures is offered to the women, Achilles reveals himself (he is the figure on the far right) because he cannot resist the sword. In telling the story, Poussin emphasizes harmony and almost a sedateness of composition, avoiding the exuberance and emotionalism of the baroque style. *(Photograph © 2007 Museum of Fine Arts, Boston.)*

religious toleration; that is, he wanted religious freedom for the many varieties of Protestants, but not for Catholics or non-Christians. Milton served as secretary to the Council of State during Cromwell's rule and earned the enmity of Charles II by writing a justification for the execution of his father, Charles I.

Forced into retirement after the restoration of the monarchy, Milton published his epic poem *Paradise Lost* in 1667. He used the biblical Adam and Eve's fall from grace to meditate on human freedom and the tragedies of rebellion. Although Milton wanted to "justify the ways of God to man," his Satan, the proud angel who challenges God and is cast out of heaven, is so compelling as to be heroic. In the end, Adam and Eve embrace moral responsibility for their actions. Individuals learn the limits to their freedom, yet personal liberty remains essential to their humanity.

The Varieties of Artistic Style. The dominant artistic styles of the time—the baroque and the classical—both submerged the ordinary individual in a grander design. The baroque style proved to be especially suitable for public displays of faith and power that overawed individual beholders. The combination of religious and political purposes in baroque art is best exemplified in the architecture and sculpture of Gian Lorenzo Bernini (1598–1680), the papacy's official artist. His architectural masterpiece was the gigantic square facing St. Peter's Basilica in Rome. Bernini's use of freestanding colonnades and a huge open space was meant to impress the individual observer with

the power of the popes and the Catholic religion. He also sculpted tombs for the popes and a large statue of Constantine, the first Christian emperor of Rome—perfect examples of the marriage of power and religion.

Although France was a Catholic country, French painters, sculptors, and architects, like their patron Louis XIV, preferred the standards of **classicism** to those of the baroque. French artists developed classicism to be a French national style, distinct from the baroque style that was closely associated with France's enemies, the Austrian and Spanish Habsburgs. As its name suggests, classicism reflected the ideals of the art of antiquity: geometric shapes, order, and harmony of lines took precedence over the sensuous, exuberant, and emotional forms of the baroque. Rather than being overshadowed by the sheer power of emotional display, in classicism the individual could be found at the intersection of converging, symmetrical, straight lines (see illustration above). These influences were apparent in the work of the leading French painters of the period, Nicolas Poussin (1594–1665) and Claude Lorrain (1600–1682), both of whom worked in Rome and tried to recreate classical Roman values in their mythological scenes and Roman landscapes.

Art could also serve the interests of science. One of the most skilled illustrators of insects and

---

classicism: A style of painting and architecture that reflected the ideals of the art of antiquity; in classicism, geometric shapes, order, and harmony of lines take precedence over the sensuous, exuberant, and emotional forms of the baroque.

DOCUMENT

John Milton, Defense of Freedom of the Press (1644)

In Areopagitica (1644), the English poet John Milton rebuked Parliament for passing a bill to restrict freedom of the press by requiring licensing of every publication. The title came from Areopagus, the name of a court in ancient Athens. Milton argued that freedom of thought was essential to human dignity.

I deny not but that it is of greatest concernment in the church and commonwealth to have a vigilant eye how books demean themselves as well as men; and thereafter to confine, imprison, and do sharpest justice on them as malefactors. For books are not absolutely dead things, but do contain a potency of life in them to be as active as that soul was whose progeny they are; nay, they do preserve as in a vial the purest efficacy and extraction of that living intellect that bred them. I know they are as lively and as vigorously productive as those fabulous dragon's teeth; and being sown up and down, may chance to spring up armed men. And yet, on the other hand, unless wariness be used, as good almost kill a man as kill a good book:

who kills a man kills a reasonable creature, God's image; but he who destroys a good book, kills reason itself, kills the image of God, as it were, in the eye. Many a man lives a burden to the earth; but a good book is the precious lifeblood of a master spirit, embalmed and treasured up on purpose to a life beyond life. 'Tis true, no age can restore a life, whereof perhaps there is no great loss; and revolutions of ages do not oft recover the loss of a rejected truth, for the want of which whole nations fare the worse. We should be wary, therefore, what persecution we raise against the living labors of public men, how we spill that seasoned life of man preserved and stored up in books; since we see a kind of homicide may be thus committed, sometimes a martyrdom; and if it extend to the whole impression, a kind of massacre, whereof the execution ends not in the slaying of an elemental life, but strikes at that ethereal and fifth essence, the breath of reason itself, slays an immortality rather than a life. But lest I should be condemned of introducing license, while I oppose licensing, I refuse not the pains to be so much histor-

ical as will serve to show what hath been done by ancient and famous commonwealths against this disorder, till the very time that this project of licensing crept out of the Inquisition, was caught up by our prelates, and hath caught some of our presbyters. [. . .] As therefore the state of man now is, what wisdom can there be to choose, what continence to forbear without the knowledge of evil? He that can apprehend and consider vice with all her baits and seeming pleasures, and yet abstain, and yet distinguish, and yet prefer that which is truly better, he is the true warfaring Christian. I cannot praise a fugitive and cloistered virtue, unexercised and unbreathed, that never sallies out and sees her adversary, but slinks out of the race where that immortal garland is to be run for, not without dust and heat. Assuredly we bring not innocence into the world, we bring impurity much rather: that which purifies us is trial, and trial is by what is contrary.

Source: John Milton, *Milton's Prose Writing* (London: J. M. Dant, 1961), 149–50, 158.

---

flowers was Maria Sibylla Merian (1646–1717), a German-born painter-scholar whose engravings were widely celebrated for their brilliant realism and microscopic clarity. Merian eventually separated from her husband and joined a sect called the Labadists (after its French founder, Jean de Labadie), whose members did not believe in formal marriage ties. After moving with her daughters to the Labadists' community in the northern Dutch province of Friesland, Merian went with missionaries from the sect to the Dutch colony of Surinam, in South America, and painted watercolors (see illustration, page 512) of the exotic flowers, birds, and insects she found in the jungle around the cocoa and sugarcane plantations. Many women became known for their still lifes, and especially their paintings of flowers, during this time.

Public Interest in Science. Despite the initial religious controversies associated with the scientific

revolution, absolutist rulers quickly saw the potential of the new science for enhancing their prestige and glory. Frederick William, the Great Elector of Brandenburg-Prussia, for example, set up agricultural experiments in front of his Berlin palace, and various German princes supported the work of Gottfried Wilhelm Leibniz (1646–1716), who claimed that he, and not Isaac Newton, had invented the calculus. A lawyer, diplomat, mathematician, and scholar who wrote about metaphysics, cosmology, and history, Leibniz also helped establish scientific societies in the German states.

Government involvement in science was greatest in France, where science became an arm of mercantilist policy; in 1666, Colbert founded the Royal Academy of Sciences, which supplied fifteen scientists with government stipends. It met in the King's Library in Paris, where for the first years the members devoted themselves to alchemical experiments and the study of mechanical devices.

European Fascination with Products of the New World
In this painting of a banana plant, Maria Sibylla Merian offers a scientific study of one of the many exotic plants and animals found by Europeans who traveled to the colonies overseas. Merian was fifty-one when she traveled to the Dutch South American colony of Surinam with her daughter. *(Courtesy of Hunt Institute for Botanical Documentation, Carnegie Mellon University, Pittsburgh, PA.)*

Constitutional states supported science informally but provided an environment that encouraged its spread. The Royal Society of London, the counterpart to the one in Paris, grew out of informal meetings of scientists at London and Oxford rather than direct government involvement. It received a royal charter in 1662 but maintained complete independence. The society's secretary described its business to be "in the first place, to scrutinize the whole of Nature and to investigate its activity and powers by means of observations and experiments; and then in course of time to hammer out a more solid philosophy and more ample amenities of civilization." Whether the state paid for the work or not, thinkers of the day now tied science explicitly to social progress.

Because of their exclusion from most universities, women only rarely participated in the new scientific discoveries. In 1667, nonetheless, the Royal Society of London invited Margaret Cavendish, a writer of poems, essays, letters, and philosophical treatises, to attend a meeting to watch the exhibition of experiments. Labeled "mad" by her critics, she attacked the use of telescopes and microscopes because she detected in the new experimentalism a mechanistic view of the world that exalted masculine prowess and challenged the Christian belief in freedom of the will. Yet she urged the formal education of women, complaining that "we are kept like birds in cages to hop up and down in our houses." "Many of our Sex may have as much wit, and be capable of Learning as well as men," she insisted, "but since they want Instructions [lack education], it is not possible they should attain to it."

Women and Manners

Although excluded from the universities and the professions, women played important roles not only in the home but also in more formal spheres of social interaction, such as the courts of rulers. Women often took the lead in teaching manners or social etiquette. Poetry and painting might imaginatively explore the place of the individual within a larger whole, but real-life individuals had to learn to navigate their own social worlds. Women's importance in refining social relationships quickly became a subject of controversy.

The Cultivation of Manners. The court had long been a central arena for the development of manners. Under the tutelage of their mothers and wives, nobles learned to hide all that was crass and to maintain a fine sense of social distinction. In some ways, aristocratic men were expected to act more like women; just as women had long been expected to please men, now aristocratic men had to please their monarch or patron by displaying proper manners and conversing with elegance and wit. The art of pleasing included foreign languages (especially French), dance, a taste for fine music, and attention to dress.

As part of the evolution of new aristocratic ideals, nobles learned to disdain all that was lowly. The upper classes began to reject popular festivals and fairs in favor of private theaters, where seats were relatively expensive and behavior was formal. Clowns and buffoons now seemed vulgar; the last king of England to keep a court fool was Charles I. Chivalric romances that had entranced the nobility since the time of Cervantes's *Don Quixote* (1605) now passed into popular literature.

The greatest French playwright of the seventeenth century, Molière (the pen name of Jean-Baptiste Poquelin, 1622–1673), wrote sparkling comedies of manners that revealed much about the new aristocratic behavior. His play *The Middle-Class Gentleman*, first performed for Louis XIV in 1670, revolves around the yearning of a rich, middle-class Frenchman, Monsieur Jourdain, to learn to act like a *gentilhomme* (meaning both "gentleman" and "nobleman"). Monsieur Jourdain buys fancy clothes; hires private instructors in dancing, music, fencing, and philosophy; and lends money to a debt-ridden noble in hopes that the noble will marry his daughter. Only his sensible wife and his daughter's love for a worthier commoner stand in his way. The message for the king's courtiers seemed to be a reassuring one: only true nobles by blood can hope to act like nobles. But the play also showed how the middle classes were learning to emulate the nobility; if one could learn to act nobly through self-discipline, could not anyone with some education and money pass himself off as noble?

As Molière's play demonstrated, new attention to manners trickled down from the court to the middle class. A French treatise on manners written in 1672 explained proper behavior:

> If everyone is eating from the same dish, you should take care not to put your hand into it before those of higher rank have done so. . . . Formerly one was permitted . . . to dip one's bread into the sauce, provided only that one had not already bitten it. Nowadays that would be a kind of rusticity. Formerly one was allowed to take from one's mouth what one could not eat and drop it on the floor, provided it was done skillfully. Now that would be very disgusting.

The key words *rusticity* and *disgusting* reveal the association of unacceptable social behavior with the peasantry, dirt, and repulsion. Similar rules governed spitting and blowing one's nose in public. Once the elite had successfully distinguished itself from the lower classes through manners, scholars became more interested in studying popular expressions. They avidly collected proverbs, folktales, and songs — all of these now curiosities.

Debates about Women's Roles.   Courtly manners often permeated the upper reaches of society by means of the **salon**, an informal gathering held regularly in private homes and presided over by a socially eminent woman. In 1661, one French author claimed to have identified 251 Parisian women as hostesses of salons. The French government occasionally worried that these gatherings might challenge its authority, but the three main topics of conversation were love, literature, and philosophy. Hostesses often worked hard to encourage the careers of budding authors. Before publishing a manuscript, many authors, including court favorites like Corneille and Racine, would read their compositions to a salon gathering.

Some women went beyond encouraging male authors and began to write on their own, but they faced many obstacles. Marie-Madeleine Pioche de La Vergne, known as Madame de Lafayette, wrote several short novels that were published anonymously because it was considered inappropriate for aristocratic women to appear in print. Following the publication of *The Princess of Clèves* in 1678, she denied having written it. Hannah Woolley, the English author of many books on domestic conduct, published under the name of her first husband. Women were known for writing wonderful letters, but the correspondence circulated only in handwritten form. In the 1650s, despite these limitations, French women began to turn out best sellers of a new type of literary form, the novel. Their success prompted the philosopher Pierre Bayle to remark in 1697 that "our best French novels for a long time have been written by women."

The new importance of women in the world of manners and letters did not sit well with everyone. Although the French writer François Poulain de la Barre, in a series of works published in the 1670s, used the new science to assert the equality of women's minds, most men resisted the idea. Clergy, lawyers, scholars, and playwrights attacked women's growing public influence. Women, they complained, were corrupting forces and needed restraint. Only marriage, "this salutary yoke," could control their passions and weaknesses. Women were accused of raising "the banner of prostitution in the salons, in the promenades, and in the streets." Molière wrote plays denouncing women's pretension to judge literary merit. English playwrights derided learned women by creating characters with names such as Lady Knowall, Lady Meanwell, and Mrs. Lovewit.

A real-life target of the English playwrights was Aphra Behn (1640–1689), one of the first professional woman authors, who supported herself by journalism, wrote plays and poetry, and translated scientific works. Her short novel *Oroonoko* (1688) told the story of an African prince mistakenly sold into slavery. The story was so successful that it was adapted by playwrights and performed repeatedly in England and France for the next hundred years.

Women also played important roles in the new colonies. In order to establish more permanent

---

salon: An informal gathering held regularly in private homes and presided over by a socially eminent woman; salons spread from France in the seventeenth century to other countries in the eighteenth century.

and settled colonies, governments promoted the emigration of women so that male colonists would set up orderly Christian white households rather than pursuing sexual relations with native or slave women.

Reforming Popular Culture

Controversies over female influence had little effect on the unschooled peasants who made up most of Europe's population. Their culture had three main elements: their religion, which shaped every aspect of life and death; the knowledge needed to work at farming or in a trade; and popular forms of entertainment such as village fairs and dances. What changed most noticeably in the seventeenth century was the social elites' attitude toward lower-class culture. The division between elite and popular culture widened as elites insisted on their difference from the lower orders and tried to instill new forms of discipline in their social inferiors. These efforts did not always succeed, however, as villagers tenaciously clung to their own traditions.

Popular Religion.   In the seventeenth century, Protestant and Catholic churches alike pushed hard to change popular religious practices. Their campaigns against popular "paganism" began during the sixteenth-century Protestant Reformation and Catholic Counter-Reformation but reached much of rural Europe only in the seventeenth century. Puritans in England tried to root out maypole dances, Sunday village fairs, gambling, taverns, and bawdy ballads because they interfered with sober observance of the Sabbath. In Lutheran Norway, pastors denounced a widespread belief in the miracle-working powers of St. Olaf. The word *superstition* previously meant "false religion" (Protestantism was a superstition for Catholics, Catholicism for Protestants); in the seventeenth century, it took on its modern meaning of irrational fears, beliefs, and practices, which anyone educated or refined would avoid.

The Catholic campaign against superstitious practices found a ready ally in Louis XIV. While the Sun King reformed the nobles at court through etiquette and manners, Catholic bishops in the French provinces trained parish priests to reform their flocks by using catechisms in local dialects and insisting that parishioners attend Mass. The church faced a formidable challenge. One bishop in France complained in 1671, "Can you believe that there are in this diocese entire villages where no one has even heard of Jesus Christ?" In some places, believers sacrificed animals to the Virgin, prayed to

the new moon, and worshiped at the sources of streams as in pre-Christian times.

Like its Protestant counterpart, the Catholic campaign against ignorance and superstition helped extend state power. Clergy, officials, and local police worked together to limit carnival celebrations, to regulate pilgrimages to shrines, and to replace "indecent" images of saints with more restrained and decorous ones. In Catholicism, the cult of the Virgin Mary and devotions closely connected with Jesus, such as the Holy Sacrament and the Sacred Heart, took precedence over the celebration of popular saints who seemed to have pagan origins or were credited with unverified miracles. Reformers everywhere tried to limit the number of feast days on the grounds that they encouraged lewd behavior.

New Attitudes toward Poverty.   The campaign for more disciplined religious practices helped generate a new attitude toward the poor. Poverty previously had been closely linked with charity and virtue in Christianity; it was a Christian duty to give alms to the poor, and Jesus and many of the saints had purposely chosen lives of poverty. In the sixteenth and seventeenth centuries, the upper classes, the church, and the state increasingly regarded the poor as dangerous, deceitful, and lacking in character. "Criminal laziness is the source of all their vices," wrote a Jesuit expert on the poor. The courts had previously expelled beggars from cities; now local leaders, both Catholic and Protestant, tried to reform their character. Municipal magistrates collected taxes for poor relief, and local notables organized charities; together they transformed hospitals into houses of confinement for beggars. In Catholic France, upper-class women's religious associations, known as confraternities, set up asylums that confined prostitutes (by arrest if necessary) and rehabilitated them. Confraternities also founded hospices where orphans learned proper behavior and respect for their betters. Such groups advocated harsh discipline as the cure for poverty.

As hard times increased the numbers of the poor and the rates of violent crime as well, attitudes toward the poor hardened. The elites tried to separate the very poor from society either to change them or to keep them from contaminating others. Hospitals became holding pens for society's unwanted members; in them, the poor joined the disabled, the incurably diseased, and the insane. The founding of hospitals demonstrates the connection between elites' attitudes and state building. In 1676, Louis XIV ordered every French city to establish a hospital, and his government took charge of the finances. Other rulers soon followed the same path.

Popular Resistance to Reform.   Even as elites set themselves apart and reformers from church and state tried to regulate popular activities, villagers and townspeople pushed back with reassertions of their own values. For hundreds of years, peasants had maintained their own forms of village justice — called variously "rough music," "ride on a donkey," "skimmington," "charivari," or in North America, "shivaree." If a young man married a much older woman for her money, for example, villagers would serenade the couple by ringing bells, playing crude flutes, banging pots and pans, and shooting muskets. If a man was rumored to have been physically assaulted by his wife, a reversal of the usual sex roles, he (or effigies of him and his wife) might be ridden on a donkey facing backward (to signify the role reversal) and pelted with dung before being ducked in a nearby pond or river. Anyone who transgressed the local customs governing family life — adulterers, for example — might suffer a similar fate. Processions sometimes included the display of horned animal heads (a symbol of adultery) or obscene drawings, and people made up mocking ryhmes and songs for various occasions. Some villagers singled out rebellious women, wife beaters, and fathers deemed excessively cruel to their children. Others directed their mockery at tax officials, gamekeepers on big estates who tried to keep villagers from hunting, or unpopular preachers.

No matter how much care went into controlling religious festivals, such events almost invariably opened the door to popular reinterpretation and sometimes drunken celebration. When the Spanish introduced Corpus Christi processions to their colony in Peru in the seventeenth century, elite Incas dressed in royal costumes to carry the banners of their parishes. Their clothing and ornaments combined Christian symbols with their own indigenous ones. They thus signaled their conversion to Catholicism but also reasserted their own prior identities. The Corpus Christi festival, held in late May or early June, conveniently took place about the same time as Inca festivals from the pre-Spanish era. Carnival, the days preceding Lent on the Christian calendar (Mardi Gras, or Fat Tuesday, is the last of them), offered the occasion for public revelry of all sorts. Although Catholic clergy worked hard to clamp down on the more riotous aspects of Carnival, many towns and villages still held parades, like those of modern New

Corpus Christi Procession in Peru
This painting shows a Catholic procession by Incas that took place in the late 1670s in Cuzco, Peru. The Inca in front is wearing his native dress and he is followed by a float and religious figures carrying traditional Catholic imagery. *(Museo del Arzobispo, Cuzco, Peru.)*

Orleans or Rio de Janeiro, that included companies of local men dressed in special costumes and gigantic stuffed figures, sometimes with animal skins or heads, or elaborate masks.

> **REVIEW:** How did elite and popular culture become more separate in the seventeenth century?

Conclusion

The search for order took place on various levels, from the reform of the disorderly poor to the establishment of bureaucratic routines in government. The absolutist government of Louis XIV served as a model for all those who aimed to increase the power of the central state. Even Louis's rivals — such as the Holy Roman Emperor Leopold I and Frederick William, the Great Elector of Brandenburg-Prussia — followed his lead in centralizing authority and building up their armies. Whether absolutist or constitutionalist in form, seventeenth-century states aimed to penetrate more deeply into the lives of their subjects. They wanted more men for their armed forces; higher taxes to support their projects; and more control over foreign trade, religious dissent, and society's unwanted.

Some tears had begun to appear, however, in the seamless fabric of state power. The civil war

MAPPING THE WEST

- Austrian territory by 1699
- Brandenburg-Prussian territory by 1688
- Spanish Habsburg lands
- Venetian possessions
- Ottoman Empire
- Boundary of the Holy Roman Empire

Europe at the End of the Seventeenth Century

Size was not necessarily an advantage in the late 1600s. Poland-Lithuania, a large country on the map, had been fatally weakened by internal conflicts. In the next century it would disappear entirely. While the Ottoman Empire still controlled an extensive territory, outside of Anatolia its rule depended on intermediaries. The Austrian Habsburgs had pushed the Turks out of Hungary and back into the Balkans. The tiny Dutch Republic, meanwhile, had become very rich through international commerce and was the envy of far larger nations.

between Charles I and Parliament in England in the 1640s opened the way to new demands for political participation. When Parliament overthrew James II in 1688, it also insisted that the new king and queen, William and Mary, agree to a Bill of Rights. Left on their own during the turmoil in England, the English North American colonies developed distinctive forms of representative government. In the eighteenth century, new levels of economic growth and the appearance of new social groups would exert pressures on the European state system. The success of seventeenth-century rulers created the political and economic conditions in which their critics would flourish.

FOR FURTHER EXPLORATION

- **For suggested references, including Web sites, for topics in this chapter,** see page SR-1 at the end of the book.

- **For additional primary-source material from this period,** see Chapter 16 in *Sources of* THE MAKING OF THE WEST, Third Edition.

- **For Web sites and documents related to topics in this chapter,** see *Make History* at bedfordstmartins.com/hunt.

CHAPTER REVIEW

KEY TERMS AND PEOPLE

constitutionalism (484)
absolutism (484)
Louis XIV (484)
revocation of the Edict
 of Nantes (489)
bureaucracy (489)
mercantilism (490)
Frederick William
 of Hohenzollern (493)

Stenka Razin (496)
Levellers (499)
William, prince
 of Orange (504)
Glorious Revolution
 (504)
social contract (504)
classicism (510)
salon (513)

REVIEW QUESTIONS

1. How "absolute" was the power of Louis XIV?

2. Why did absolutism flourish everywhere in eastern Europe except Poland-Lithuania?

3. What differences over religion and politics caused the conflict between king and Parliament in England?

4. Why did constitutionalism thrive in the Dutch Republic and the British North American colonies, even as their participation in the slave trade grew?

5. How did elite and popular culture become more separate in the seventeenth century?

MAKING CONNECTIONS

1. What accounts for the success of absolutism in some parts of Europe and its failure in others?

2. How did religious differences in the late seventeenth century still cause political conflict?

3. Why was the search for order a major theme in science, politics, and the arts during this period?

For practice quizzes, a customized study plan, and other study tools, see the Online Study Guide at bedfordstmartins.com/hunt.

IMPORTANT EVENTS

1642–1646	Civil war between King Charles I and Parliament in England
1648	Peace of Westphalia ends Thirty Years' War; the Fronde revolt challenges royal authority in France; Ukrainian Cossack warriors rebel against the king of Poland-Lithuania; Spain formally recognizes independence of the Dutch Republic
1649	Execution of Charles I of England; new Russian legal code assigns all to hereditary class
1651	Thomas Hobbes publishes *Leviathan*
1660	Monarchy restored in England
1661	Slave code set up in Barbados
1667	Louis XIV begins first of many wars that continue throughout his reign
1678	Madame de Lafayette anonymously publishes her novel *The Princess of Clèves*
1683	Austrian Habsburgs break the Turkish siege of Vienna
1685	Louis XIV revokes toleration for French Protestants granted by the Edict of Nantes
1688	Parliament deposes James II and invites his daughter, Mary, and her husband, William of Orange, to take the throne
1690	John Locke publishes *Two Treatises of Government* and *Essay Concerning Human Understanding*

The Atlantic System and Its Consequences
1690–1740

Johann Sebastian Bach (1685–1750), composer of mighty organ fugues and church cantatas, was not above amusing his Leipzig audiences, many of them university students. In 1732, he produced a cantata about a young woman in love — with coffee. Her old-fashioned father rages that he won't find her a husband unless she gives up the fad. She agrees, secretly vowing to admit no suitor who will not promise in the marriage contract to let her brew coffee whenever she wants. Bach offers this conclusion:

> The cat won't give up its mouse,
> Girls stay faithful coffee-sisters
> Mother loves her coffee habit,
> Grandma sips it gladly too —
> Why then shout at the daughters?

Bach's era might well be called the age of coffee. European travelers at the end of the sixteenth century had noticed Middle Eastern people drinking a "black drink," *kavah*, and the Turks took coffee beans with them on their military campaigns in eastern Europe. Few Europeans sampled the drink at first, and the Arab monopoly on its production kept prices high. This changed around 1700 when the Dutch East India Company introduced coffee plants to Java and other Indonesian islands. Coffee production then spread to the French Caribbean, where African slaves provided the plantation labor. In Europe, imported coffee spurred the development of a new kind of meeting place: the first coffeehouse opened in London in 1652, and the idea spread quickly to other European cities. Men gathered in coffeehouses to drink, read newspapers, and talk politics. As a London newspaper commented in 1737, "There's scarce an Alley in City and Suburbs but has a Coffeehouse in it, which may be called the School of Public Spirit, where every Man over Daily and Weekly Journals, a Mug, or a Dram . . . devotes himself to that glorious one, his Country."

London Coffeehouse
This gouache (a variant on watercolor painting) from about 1725 depicts a scene from a London coffeehouse located in the courtyard of the Royal Exchange (merchants' bank). Middle-class men (wearing wigs) read newspapers, drink coffee, smoke pipes, and discuss the news of the day. The coffeehouse draws them out of their homes into a new public space. (© *British Museum, London/The Bridgeman Art Library.*)

European consumption of coffee, tea, chocolate, and other novelties increased dramatically as European nations forged worldwide economic links. At the center of this new global economy was the **Atlantic system**, the web of trade routes that bound together western Europe, Africa, and the Americas. Europeans bought slaves in western Africa, transported them to be sold in the colonies in North and South America and the Caribbean, bought raw commodities such as coffee and sugar that were produced by the new colonial plantations, and then sold those commodities in European ports for refining and reshipment. This Atlantic system, which first took clear shape in the early eighteenth century, became the hub of European expansion throughout the world.

Coffee drinking is just one example of the many new social and cultural patterns that took root between 1690 and 1740. Improvements in agricultural production at home reinforced the effects of trade overseas; Europeans now had more disposable income for extras, and they spent their money not only in the new coffeehouses and cafés that sprang up all over Europe but also on newspapers, musical concerts, paintings, and novels. A new middle-class public began to make its presence felt in every domain of culture and social life.

Although the rise of the Atlantic system gave Europe new prominence in the global context, European rulers still focused most of their political, diplomatic, and military energies on their rivalries within Europe. A coalition of countries succeeded in containing French aggression, and a more balanced diplomatic system emerged. In eastern Europe, Prussia and Austria had to contend with the rising power of Russia under Peter the Great. In western Europe, both Spain and the Dutch Republic declined in influence but continued to vie with Britain and France for colonial spoils in the Atlantic. The more evenly matched competition among the great powers encouraged the development of diplomatic skills and drew attention to public health as a way of encouraging population growth.

In the aftermath of Louis XIV's revocation of the Edict of Nantes in 1685, a new intellectual movement known as the Enlightenment began to germinate. An initial impetus came from French Protestant refugees who published works critical of absolutism in politics and religion. Increased prosperity, the growth of a middle-class public, and the decline in warfare after Louis XIV's death in 1715 helped fuel this new critical spirit. Fed by the popularization of science and the growing interest in travel literature, the Enlightenment encouraged greater skepticism about religious and state authority. Eventually, the movement would question almost every aspect of social and political life in Europe. The Enlightenment began in western Europe in those countries—Britain, France, and the Dutch Republic—most affected by the new Atlantic system. It too was a product of the age of coffee.

FOCUS QUESTION: What were the most important consequences of the growth of the Atlantic system?

Atlantic system: The network of trade established in the 1700s that bound together western Europe, Africa, and the Americas. Europeans sold slaves from western Africa and bought commodities that were produced by the new colonial plantations in North and South America and the Caribbean.

The Atlantic System and the World Economy

Although their ships had been circling the globe since the early 1500s, Europeans did not draw most of the world into their economic orbit until the 1700s. Western European trading nations sent

---

■ **1690s** Development of Caribbean plantations

■ **1694** Bank of England established; Astell, *A Serious Proposal to the Ladies*

■ **1697** Bayle, *Historical and Critical Dictionary*

■ **1699** Turks forced to recognize Austrian rule over Hungary, Transylvania

■ **1703** Building of St. Petersburg begins; first Russian newspaper

■ **1713–1714** Peace of Utrecht

■ **1714–1727** King George I of England

■ **1715** Death of Louis XIV

1690   **1700**   **1710**

ships loaded with goods to buy slaves from local rulers on the western coast of Africa; the slaves were then transported to the colonies in North and South America and the Caribbean and sold to the owners of plantations producing coffee, sugar, cotton, and tobacco. Money from the slave trade was used to buy the raw commodities produced in the colonies and ship them back to Europe, where they were refined or processed and then sold within Europe and around the world. The Atlantic system and the growth of international trade thus helped create a new consumer society.

Slavery and the Atlantic System

Spain and Portugal dominated Atlantic trade in the sixteenth and seventeenth centuries, but in the eighteenth century European trade in the Atlantic rapidly expanded and became more systematically interconnected (Map 17.1). By 1630, Portugal had already sent sixty thousand African slaves to Brazil to work on the new **plantations** (large tracts of lands that produced staple crops, were farmed by slave labor, and were owned by colonial settlers from western Europe), which were producing some fifteen thousand tons of sugar a year. Realizing that plantations producing staples for Europeans could bring fabulous wealth, the European powers grew less interested in the dwindling trade in precious metals and more eager to colonize. In the 1690s, large-scale planters of sugar, tobacco, and coffee began displacing small farmers who relied on one or two servants. Planters and their plantations won out because cheap slave labor allowed them to produce mass quantities of commodities at low prices.

---

plantation: A large tract of land that produced staple crops such as sugar, coffee, and tobacco; was farmed by slave labor; and was owned by a colonial settler.

State-chartered private companies from Portugal, France, Britain, the Dutch Republic, Prussia, and even Denmark exploited the 3,500-mile coastline of West Africa for slaves. Before 1675, most blacks taken from Africa had been sent to Brazil, but by 1700 half of the African slaves were landing in the Caribbean (Figure 17.1). Thereafter, the plantation economy began to expand on the North American mainland. The numbers stagger the imagination. Before 1650, slave traders transported about seven thousand Africans each year

---

FIGURE 17.1 African Slaves Imported into American Territories, 1701–1810

During the eighteenth century, planters in the newly established Caribbean colonies imported millions of African slaves to work the new plantations that produced sugar, coffee, indigo, and cotton for the European market. The vast majority of African slaves transported to the Americas ended up in either the Caribbean or Brazil. Why were so many slaves transported to the Caribbean islands, which are relatively small compared to Spanish or British North America? *(Adapted from Philip D. Curtin, The Atlantic Slave Trade: A Census [Madison: University of Wisconsin Press, 1969].)*

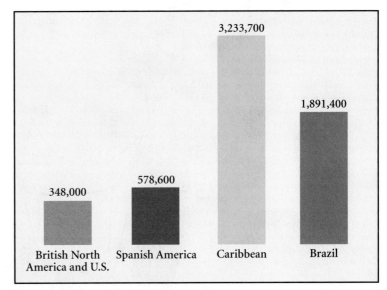

- 1720 Last plague outbreak in western Europe

- 1721 Treaty of Nystad; Montesquieu, *Persian Letters*

- 1733 War of the Polish Succession; Voltaire, *Letters Concerning the English Nation*

1720   **1730**   **1740**

- 1719 Defoe, *Robinson Crusoe*

- 1741 Handel, *Messiah*

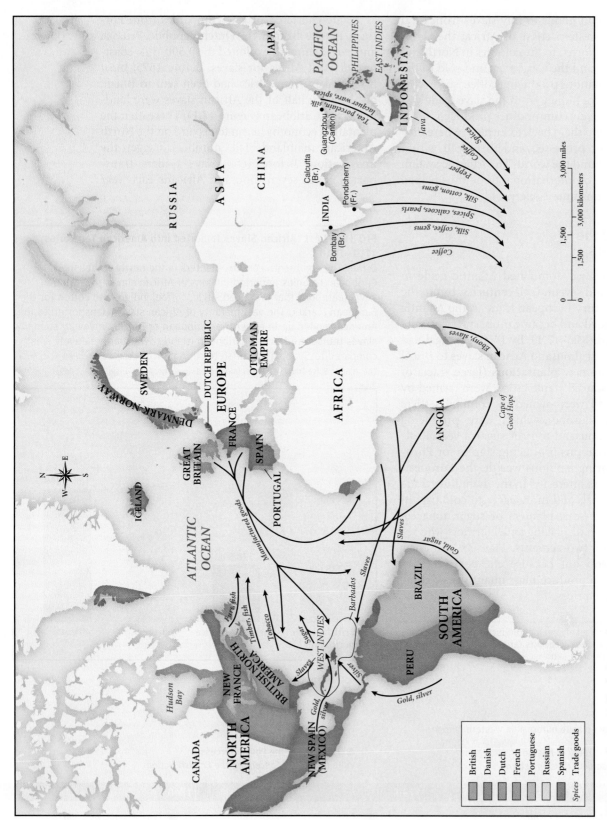

MAP 17.1 European Trade Patterns, c. 1740

By 1740, the European powers had colonized much of North and South America and incorporated their colonies there into a worldwide system of commerce centered on the slave trade and plantation production of staple crops. Europeans still sought spices and luxury goods in China and the East Indies, but outside of Java, few Europeans had settled permanently in these areas.

■ How did control over colonies determine dominance in international trade in this period?

across the Atlantic; this rate doubled between 1650 and 1675, nearly doubled again in the next twenty-five years, and kept increasing until the 1780s (Figure 17.2, below). In all, more than eleven million Africans, not counting those who were captured but died before or during the sea voyage, were transported to the Americas before the slave trade began to wind down after 1850. Many individual traders gained spectacular wealth, but companies did not always make profits. The English Royal African Company, for example, delivered 100,000 slaves to the Caribbean and imported thirty thousand tons of sugar to Britain yet lost money after the few profitable years following its founding in 1672.

The Life of the Slaves. The balance of white and black populations in the New World colonies was determined by the staples produced. Because they did not own plantations, New England merchants and farmers bought few slaves. Blacks — both slave and free — made up only 3 percent of the population in eighteenth-century New England, compared with 60 percent in South Carolina. On the whole, the British North American colonies contained a higher proportion of African Americans

from 1730 to 1765 than at any other time in American history. The imbalance of whites and blacks was even more extreme in the Caribbean, where most indigenous people had already died fighting Europeans or the diseases brought by them. By 1713, the French Caribbean colony of St. Domingue (on the western part of Hispaniola, present-day Haiti) had four times as many black slaves as whites; by 1754, slaves there outnumbered whites more than ten to one.

Enslaved women and men suffered terribly. Most had been sold to European traders by Africans from the west coast who acquired them through warfare or kidnapping. The vast majority were between fourteen and thirty-five years old. Before they were crammed onto the ships for the three-month trip, their heads were shaved, they were stripped naked, and some were branded with red-hot irons. Men and women were separated. Men were shackled with leg irons. Sailors and officers raped the women whenever they wished and beat those who refused their advances. In the cramped and appalling conditions of the voyage, as many as one-fourth of the slaves died.

Those who survived the transit were forced into degrading and oppressive conditions. Upon

---

FIGURE 17.2 Annual Imports in the Atlantic Slave Trade, 1450–1870
The importation of slaves to the American territories reached its height in the second half of the eighteenth century and began to decline around 1800. Yet despite the abolition of the slave trade by the British in 1807, commerce in slaves did not seriously diminish until after the revolutions of 1848.
(Adapted from Philip D. Curtin, The Atlantic Slave Trade: A Census *(Madison: University of Wisconsin Press, 1969). Reprinted by permission of the University of Wisconsin Press.)*

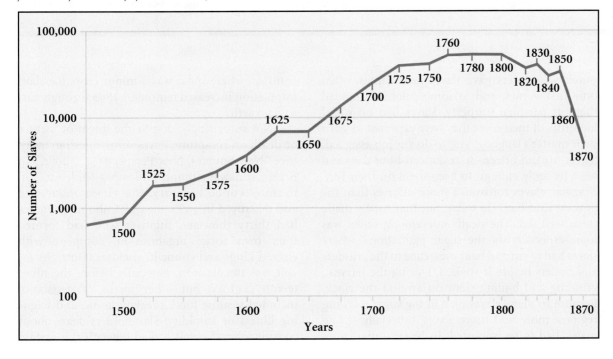

Oral History and the Life of Slaves

Historians have found it difficult to reconstruct slave life from the point of view of the slaves themselves, in part because slaves newly imported from Africa to the New World did not speak the language of their captors. Scholars have attempted to fill in this blank by using a variety of overlapping sources. The most interesting and controversial of these sources are oral histories taken from descendants of slaves. In some former slave societies, these descendants still tell stories about their ancestors' first days under slavery. The controversy comes from using present-day memories to shed light on eighteenth-century lives.

One of the regions most intensively studied in this fashion is Suriname (formerly Dutch Guiana), on the northeast coast of South America between present-day Guyana and French Guiana. This region is a good source of oral histories because 10 percent of the African slaves transported there between the 1680s and the 1750s escaped from the plantations and fled into the nearby rain forests. There they set up their own societies and developed their own language, in which they carried on the oral traditions of the first runaway slaves. The descendants of the runaway slaves recounted the following details:

> In slavery, there was hardly anything to eat. It was at the place called Providence Plantation. They whipped you there till your ass was burning. Then they would give you a bit of plain rice in a calabash [a bowl made from a hard-shelled tropical American fruit]. . . . And the gods told them that this is no way for human beings to live. They would help them. Let each person go where he could. So they ran.

From other sources, historians have learned that there was a major slave rebellion at Providence Plantation in Suriname in 1693.

By comparing such oral histories to written accounts of plantation owners, missionaries, and Dutch colonial officials, historians have been able to paint a richly detailed picture not only of slavery but also of runaway slave societies, which were especially numerous in South America. At the end of the eighteenth century, a Portuguese-speaking Jew named David de Ishak Cohen Nassy wrote his own history of plantation life based on records from the local Jewish community that are now lost. Because the Dutch, unlike most other Europeans, allowed Jews to own slaves, Portuguese-speaking Jews from Brazil owned about one-third of the plantations and slaves in Suriname. Nassy gave the following account of Suriname's first slave revolt:

> There was in the year 1690 a revolt on a plantation situated on the Cassewinica Creek, behind Jews Savannah, belonging to a Jew named Imanuël Machado, where, having killed their master, [the slaves] fled, carrying away with them everything that was there. . . . The Jews . . . in an expedition which they undertook against the rebels, killed many of them and brought back several who were punished by death on the very spot.

The oral histories told about the revolt from the runaway slaves' perspective:

> There had been a great council meeting [of runaway slaves] in the forest. . . . They decided to burn a different one of [Machado's] plantations from the place where he had whipped Lanu [one of the runaway slaves] because they would find more tools there. This was the Cassewinica Plantation, which had many slaves. They knew all about this plantation from slavery times. So, they at-

purchase, masters gave slaves new names, often only first names, and in some colonies branded them as personal property. Slaves had no social identities of their own; they were expected to learn their master's language and to do any job assigned. Slaves worked fifteen- to seventeen-hour days and were fed only enough to keep them on their feet. Brazilian slaves consumed more calories than the poorest Brazilians do today, but that hardly made them well fed. The death rate among slaves was high, especially on the sugar plantations, where slaves had to cut and haul sugarcane to the grinders and boilers before it spoiled. During the harvest, grinding and boiling went on around the clock. Because so many slaves died in the sugar-growing regions, more and more slaves, especially strong males, had to be imported. In North America, in contrast, where sugar was a minor crop, the slave population increased tenfold by 1863 through natural growth.

Not surprisingly, despite the threat of torture or death on recapture, slaves sometimes ran away. (See "New Sources, New Perspectives," above.) In Brazil, runaways found *quilombos* (hideouts) in the forests or backcountry. When it was discovered and destroyed in 1695, the quilombo of Palmares had thirty thousand fugitives who had formed their own social organization, complete with elected kings and councils of elders. Outright revolt was uncommon, especially before the nineteenth century, but other forms of resistance included stealing food, breaking tools, and feigning illness or stupidity. Slaveholders' fears about conspiracy and revolt lurked beneath the surface

Slaves of Suriname in the 1770s

John Gabriel Stedman published an account of his participation in a five-year expedition against the runaway slaves of Suriname that took place in the 1770s. He provided drawings such as the one reproduced here, which shows Africans who have just come off a slave ship. *(The New York Public Library/Art Resource, NY.)*

the main town of the colony in exchange for agreeing to return all future runaways. The runaways had not destroyed the slave system, but they had gained their own independence alongside it. From their oral histories it is possible to retrace their efforts to build new lives in a strange place, in which they combined African practices with New World experiences.

Source: Richard Price, *Alabi's World* (Baltimore: Johns Hopkins University Press, 1990), 17, 9.

QUESTIONS TO CONSIDER

1. What did the runaway slaves mentioned in these accounts aim to accomplish when they attacked plantations?
2. Why would runaway slaves make an agreement with the Dutch colonial officials to return future runaways?
3. Can oral histories recorded in the twentieth century be considered accurate versions of events that took place in the eighteenth century? How can they be tested?

FURTHER READING

Price, Richard. *Alabi's World.* 1990.
Stedman, John Gabriel. *Narrative of a Five Years' Expedition Against the Revolted Negroes of Surinam.* Edited, and with an introduction and notes, by Richard Price and Sally Price. 1988.

tacked. It was at night. They killed the head of the plantation, a white man. They took all the things, everything they needed.

The runaway slaves saw the attack as part of their ongoing effort to build a life in the rain forest, away from the whites.

Over the next decades, the runaway slaves fought a constant series of battles with plantation owners and Dutch officials. Finally, in 1762, the Dutch granted the runaway slaves their freedom in a peace agreement and allowed them to trade in

---

of every slave-based society. In 1710, the royal governor of Virginia reminded the colonial legislature of the need for unceasing vigilance: "We are not to Depend on Either Their Stupidity, or that Babel of Languages among 'em; freedom Wears a Cap which Can Without a Tongue, Call Togather all Those who Long to Shake off the fetters of Slavery." Masters defended whipping and other forms of physical punishment as essential to maintaining discipline. Laws called for the castration of a slave who struck a white person.

Effects of the Slave Trade on Europe. Plantation owners often left their colonial possessions in the care of agents and merely collected the revenue so that they could live as wealthy landowners back home, where they built opulent mansions and

gained influence in local and national politics. William Beckford, for example, had been sent from Jamaica to school in England as a young boy. When he inherited sugar plantations and shipping companies from his father and older brother, he moved the headquarters of the family business to London in the 1730s to be close to the government and financial markets. His holdings formed the single most powerful economic interest in Jamaica, but he preferred to live in England, where he could buy works of art for his many luxurious homes, hold political office (he was lord mayor of London and a member of Parliament), and even lend money to the government.

The slave trade permanently altered consumption patterns for ordinary people. Sugar had been prescribed as a medicine before the end of the

Caribbean Sugar Mill

This seventeenth-century engraving of a sugar mill or grinder makes the work seem much less difficult than it was in practice. Slaves cut the sugarcane and then hauled it from the fields to the mill, where it was crushed. Many slaves lost fingers or hands in the process. The slaves then collected the juice (bottom center) and carried it to the boilers, shown at the bottom left and right. The sap was poured into molds and dried. Then the bricks of raw sugar were exported to Europe for refining.

(The Granger Collection, New York.)

sixteenth century, but the development of plantations in Brazil and the Caribbean made it a standard food item. By 1700, the British were sending home fifty million pounds of sugar a year, a figure that doubled by 1730. During the French Revolution of the 1790s, sugar shortages would become a cause for rioting in Paris. Equally pervasive was the spread of tobacco; by the 1720s, Britain was importing two hundred shiploads of tobacco from Virginia and Maryland annually, and men of every country and class smoked pipes or took snuff.

The Origins of Modern Racism. The traffic in slaves disturbed many Europeans. As a government memorandum to the Spanish king explained in 1610: "Modern theologians in published books commonly report on, and condemn as unjust, the acts of enslavement which take place in provinces of this Royal Empire." Between 1667 and 1671, the French Dominican monk Father Du Tertre published three volumes in which he denounced the mistreatment of slaves in the French colonies.

In the 1700s, however, slaveholders began to justify their actions by demeaning the mental and spiritual qualities of the enslaved Africans. White Europeans and colonists sometimes described black slaves as animal-like, akin to apes. A leading New England Puritan asserted about the slaves: "Indeed their *Stupidity* is a *Discouragement*. It may seem, unto as little purpose, to *Teach*, as to *wash an Aethiopian* [Ethiopian]." One of the great para-

doxes of this time was that talk of liberty and self-evident rights, especially prevalent in Britain and its North American colonies, coexisted with the belief that some people were meant to be slaves. Although Christians believed in principle in a kind of spiritual equality between blacks and whites, the churches often defended or at least did not oppose the inequities of slavery.

World Trade and Settlement

The Atlantic system helped extend European trade relations across the globe. The textiles that Atlantic shippers exchanged for slaves on the west coast of Africa, for example, were manufactured in India and exported by the British and French East India Companies. As much as one-quarter of the British exports to Africa in the eighteenth century were actually re-exports from India. To expand its trade in the rest of the world, Europeans seized territories and tried to establish permanent settlements. The eighteenth-century extension of European power prepared the way for western global domination in the nineteenth and twentieth centuries.

The Americas. In contrast to the sparsely inhabited trading outposts in Asia and Africa, the colonies in the Americas bulged with settlers. The British North American colonies, for example, contained about 1.5 million nonnative (that is, white settler and black slave) residents by 1750.

While the Spanish competed with the Portuguese for control of South America, the French competed with the British for control of North America. Spanish and British settlers came to blows over the boundary between the British colonies and Florida, which was held by Spain.

Local economies shaped colonial social relations; men in French trapper communities in Canada, for example, had little in common with the men and women of the plantation societies in Barbados or Brazil. Racial attitudes also differed from place to place. The Spanish and Portuguese tolerated intermarriage with the native populations in both America and Asia. Sexual contact, both inside and outside marriage, fostered greater racial variety in the Spanish and Portuguese colonies than in the French or the English territories (though mixed-race people could be found everywhere). By 1800, **mestizos**, children of Spanish men and Indian women, accounted for more than a quarter of the population in the Spanish colonies, and many of them aspired to join the local elite. However, greater racial diversity seems not to have improved the treatment of slaves.

Where intermarriage between colonizers and natives was common, conversion to Christianity proved most successful. Even while maintaining their native religious beliefs, many Indians in the Spanish colonies had come to consider themselves devout Catholics by 1700. Indian carpenters and artisans in the villages produced innumerable altars, retables (painted panels), and sculpted images to adorn their local churches, and individual families put up domestic shrines. Yet the clergy remained overwhelmingly Spanish: the church hierarchy concluded that the Indians' humility and innocence made them unsuitable for the priesthood.

In the early years of American colonization, many more men than women emigrated from Europe. Although the sex imbalance began to decline at the end of the seventeenth century, it remained substantial; two and a half times more men than women were among the immigrants leaving Liverpool, England, between 1697 and 1707, for example. Women who emigrated as indentured servants ran great risks: if they did not die of disease during the voyage, they were likely to give birth to illegitimate children (the fate of at least one in five servant women) or be virtually sold into marriage. Upper-class women were often kept in seclusion, especially in the Spanish and Portuguese colonies.

The uncertainties of life in the American colonies provided new opportunities for European women and men willing to live outside the law, however. In the 1500s and 1600s, the English and Dutch governments had routinely authorized pirates to prey on the ships of their rivals, the Spanish and Portuguese. Then, in the late 1600s, English, French, and Dutch bands made up of deserters and crews from wrecked vessels began to form their own associations of pirates, especially in the Caribbean. Called **buccaneers** from their custom of curing strips of beef, called *boucan* by the native Caribs of the islands, the pirates governed themselves and preyed on everyone's shipping without regard to national origin. After 1700, the colonial governments tried to stamp out piracy. As one British judge argued in 1705, "A pirate is in perpetual war with every individual and every state. . . . They are worse than ravenous beasts."

Africa and Asia.   White settlements in Africa and Asia remained small and almost insignificant, except for their long-term potential. Europeans had little contact with East Africa and almost none with Africa's vast interior. A handful of Portuguese trading posts in Angola and a few Dutch farms on the Cape of Good Hope provided the only toeholds for future expansion. In China, the emperors had welcomed Catholic missionaries at court in the seventeenth century, but the priests' credibility diminished as they squabbled among themselves and associated with European merchants, whom the Chinese considered pirates. "The barbarians [Europeans] are like wild beasts," one Chinese official concluded. In 1720, only one thousand Europeans resided in Guangzhou (Canton), the sole place where foreigners could legally trade for spices, tea, and silk (see Map 17.1, page 522).

Europeans exercised more influence in Java (in what was then called the East Indies) and in India. Dutch coffee production in Java and nearby islands increased phenomenally in the early 1700s, and many Dutch settled there to oversee production and trade. Dutch, English, French, Portuguese, and Danish companies competed in India for spices, cotton, and silk; by the 1740s, the English and French had become the leading rivals in India, just as they were in North America. Both countries extended their power as India's Muslim rulers lost control to local Hindu princes, rebellious Sikhs, invading Persians, and their own

---

mestizo: A person born to a Spanish father and a native American mother.

buccaneers: Pirates of the Caribbean who governed themselves and preyed on international shipping.

India Cottons and Trade with the East
This colored cotton cloth (now faded with age) was painted and embroidered in Madras in southern India sometime in the late 1600s. The male figure with a mustache may be a European, but the female figures are clearly Asian. Europeans—especially the British—discovered that they could make big profits on the export of Indian cotton cloth to Europe. They also traded Indian cottons in Africa for slaves and sold large quantities in the colonies.
(V & A Images/Victoria and Albert Museum, London.)

provincial governors. A few thousand Europeans lived in India, though many thousand more soldiers were stationed there to protect them. The staple of trade with India in the early 1700s was calico — lightweight, brightly colored cotton cloth that caught on as a fashion in Europe (see the image above).

Europeans who visited India were especially struck by what they viewed as exotic religious practices. In a book published in 1696 of his travels to western India, an Anglican minister described the fakirs (religious mendicants, or beggars of alms), "some of whom show their devotion by a shameless appearance, walking naked, without the least rag of clothes to cover them." Such writings increased European interest in the outside world but also fed a European sense of superiority that helped excuse the more violent forms of colonial domination (see The Exotic as Consumer Item, page 529).

The Birth of Consumer Society

As worldwide colonization produced new supplies of goods, from coffee to calico, population growth in Europe fueled demand for them. Beginning first in Britain, then in France and the Italian states, and finally in eastern Europe, population surged, growing by about 20 percent between 1700 and 1750. The gap between a fast-growing northwest and a more stagnant south and central Europe now diminished as regions that had lost population during the seventeenth-century downturn recovered. Cities, in particular, grew. Between 1600 and 1750,

London's population more than tripled and Paris's more than doubled.

Although contemporaries could not have realized it then, this was the start of the modern population explosion. It appears that a decline in the death rate, rather than a rise in the birthrate, explains the turnaround. Three main factors contributed to increased longevity: better weather and hence more bountiful harvests, improved agricultural techniques, and the plague's disappearance after 1720.

By the early eighteenth century, the effects of economic expansion and population growth brought about a **consumer revolution**. For example, the British East India Company began to import into Britain huge quantities of calico; British imports of tobacco doubled between 1672 and 1700; and at Nantes, the center of the French sugar trade, imports quadrupled between 1698 and 1733. Tea, chocolate, and coffee became virtual necessities. In the 1670s, only a trickle of tea reached London, but by 1720 the East India Company had sent nine million pounds to England—a figure that rose to thirty-seven million pounds by 1750. In 1700, England had two thousand coffeehouses; by 1740, every English country town had at least two. Paris got its first cafés at the end of the seventeenth century; Berlin opened its first coffeehouse in 1714; and Bach's Leipzig boasted eight by 1725.

---

consumer revolution: The rapid increase in consumption of new staples produced in the Atlantic system as well as of other items of daily life that were previously unavailable or beyond the reach of ordinary people.

The Exotic as Consumer Item
This painting by the Venetian artist Rosalba Carriera (1675–1757) is titled *Africa*. The young black girl wearing a turban represents the African continent. Carriera was known for her use of pastels. In 1720, she journeyed to Paris, where she became an associate of Antoine Watteau and helped inaugurate the rococo style in painting. Why might the artist have chosen to paint an African girl? *(Staatliche Kunstsammlungen Dresden, Gemaldegalerie Alte Meister.)*

■ **For more help analyzing this image,** see the visual activity for this chapter in the Online Study Guide at **bedfordstmartins.com/hunt**.

A new economic dynamic steadily took shape that would influence all of subsequent history. More and more people escaped the confines of a subsistence economy, in which peasants produced barely enough to support themselves from year to year. As ordinary people gained more disposable income, demand for nonessential consumer goods rose (see Document, "The Social Effects of Growing Consumption," page 530). These included not only the new colonial products such as coffee and tea but also tables, chairs, sheets, chamber pots, lamps, mirrors, and for the better off still, coffee- and teapots, china, cutlery, chests of drawers, desks, clocks, and pictures for the walls. Rising demand created more jobs and more income and yet more purchasing power in a mutually reinforcing cycle. In the English economic literature of the 1690s, writers reacted to these developments by expressing a new view of humans as consuming animals with boundless appetites. Many authors attacked the new doctrine of consumerism, but they could not hold back the fast-growing market for consumption. Change did not occur all at once, however. The consumer revolution spread from the cities to the countryside, from England to the continent, and from western Europe to eastern Europe only over the long run.

> **REVIEW:** How was consumerism related to slavery in the early eighteenth century?

New Social and Cultural Patterns

The rise of consumption was fueled in part by a revolution in agricultural techniques that made it possible to produce larger quantities of food with a smaller agricultural workforce. As population increased, more people moved to the cities, where they found themselves caught up in innovative urban customs such as attending musical concerts and reading novels. Along with a general increase in literacy, these activities helped create a public that responded to new writers and artists. As always, people's experiences varied depending on whether they lived in wealth or poverty, in urban or rural areas, or in eastern or western Europe.

Agricultural Revolution

Although Britain, France, and the Dutch Republic shared the enthusiasm for consumer goods, Britain's domestic market grew most quickly. In Britain, as agricultural output increased 43 percent over the course of the 1700s, the population increased by 70 percent. The British imported grain to feed the growing population, but they also benefited from the development of techniques that together constituted an **agricultural revolution**. No new machinery propelled this revolution—just increasingly aggressive attitudes toward investment and management. The Dutch and the Flemish had pioneered many of these techniques in the 1600s, but the British took them further.

Four major changes occurred in British agriculture that eventually spread to other countries. First, farmers increased the amount of land under cultivation by draining wetlands and by growing crops on previously uncultivated common lands

---

agricultural revolution: Increasingly aggressive attitudes toward investment in and management of land that increased production of food in the 1700s.

DOCUMENT

The Social Effects of Growing Consumption

Daniel Defoe's adventures in real life are matched only by those of his famous fictional characters Robinson Crusoe and Moll Flanders. Though never shipwrecked like Crusoe, Defoe spent time in bankruptcy, in exile, and in prison (for writing a pamphlet satirizing Anglican treatment of dissenters). He turned his hand to various forms of commerce, in hosiery, woolens, wine, and political secrets, but most of all to mad scribbling on almost any topic imaginable. He published hundreds of books and pamphlets. In the 395-page book from which this excerpt is taken, he describes the recent fabulous growth in the import and export trade of Great Britain and contrasts the wealth gained by the "industrious" classes to the contempt shown them by the aristocracy [Gentry or Gentlemen].

Our People in general being in good Circumstances, I mean the middling, trading, and industrious People, living tolerably well, their well-faring gives Occasion to the vast Consumption of the foreign, as well as home Produce, the like of which is not to be equalled by any Nation in the World; the Particulars we shall enquire into in their Order.

How far the Multitudes of our People are encreased by these very Articles, and that to such a Degree as is scarce conceivable, is worth our Enquiry, were it not too tedious for this Place. What populous Towns are rais'd by our Manufactures, from with few Years! How are our Towns built into Cities, and small Villages (hardly known in ancient Times) grown up into populous Towns! . . .

Well might I say, as in the foregoing Chapter, That it is a Scandal upon the Understanding of the Gentry, to think contemptibly of the trading part of the Nation; seeing however the Gentlemen may value themselves upon their Birth and Blood, the Case begins to turn against them so evidently, as to Fortune and Estate, that tho' they say, the Tradesmen cannot be made Gentlemen; yet the Tradesmen are, at this Time, able to buy the Gentlemen almost in every part of the Kingdom. . . .

The ancient Families, who having wasted and exhausted their Estates, and being declin'd and decay'd in Fortune by Luxury and high Living, have restor'd and rais'd themselves again, by mixing Blood with the despis'd Tradesmen, marrying the Daughters of such Tradesmen. . . .

I might add here, that it would be worth the while for those Gentlemen, who talk so much of their antient Family Merit, and look so little at preserving the Stock, by encreasing their own: I say, it would be worth their while to look into the Roll of our Gentry, and enquire what is become of the Estates and those prodigious Numbers of lost and extinct Families, which now even the Heralds themselves can hardly find; let them tell us if those Estates are not now purchased by Tradesmen and Citizens, or the Posterity of such; and whether those Tradesmens Posterity do not now fill up the Vacancies, the Gaps, and Chasms in the great Roll or Lift of Families, as well of the Gentry, as of the Nobility themselves; and whether there are many Families left, who have not been either restored *as in our first Head*, or supply'd, *as in the second*, by the Succession of Wealth, and new Branches from the growing Greatness of Trade.

Trade, in a word, raises antient Families when sunk and decay'd: And plants new Families, where the old ones are lost and extinct.

Source: Daniel Defoe, *A Plan of the English Commerce. Being a complete prospect of the trade of this nation, as well home as foreign. In three parts,* 2nd ed. (London, 1737), 79–83.

(acreage maintained by the community for grazing). Second, those farmers who could afford it consolidated small, scattered plots into larger, more efficient units. Third, livestock raising became more closely linked to crop growing, and the yields of each increased. (See "Taking Measure," page 531.) For centuries, most farmers had rotated their fields in and out of production to replenish the soil. Now farmers planted carefully chosen fodder crops such as clover and turnips that added nutrients to the soil, thereby eliminating the need to leave a field fallow (unplanted) every two or three years. With more fodder available, farmers could raise more livestock, which in turn produced more manure to fertilize grain fields. Fourth, selective breeding of animals combined with the increase in fodder to improve the quality and size of herds. New crops had only a slight impact; potatoes, for example, were introduced to Europe from South America in the 1500s, but because people feared they might cause leprosy, tuberculosis, or fevers, they were not grown in quantity until the late 1700s. By the 1730s and 1740s, agricultural output had increased dramatically, and prices for food had fallen because of these interconnected innovations.

Changes in agricultural practices did not benefit all landowners equally. The biggest British landowners consolidated their holdings in the "enclosure movement." They put pressure on small farmers and villagers to sell their land or give up their common lands. The big landlords then fenced off (enclosed) their property. Because enclosure eliminated community grazing rights, it frequently sparked a struggle between the big landlords and villagers, and in Britain it normally required an act of Parliament. Such acts became increasingly common in the second half of the eighteenth century, and by the century's end six million acres of common lands had been enclosed and developed. "Improvers" produced more food more efficiently than small farmers could and thus supported a growing population.

Contrary to the fears of contemporaries, small farmers and cottagers (those with little or no property) were not forced off the land all at once. But most villagers could not afford the litigation involved in resisting enclosure, and small landholders consequently had to sell out to landlords or farmers with larger plots. Landlords with large holdings leased their estates to tenant farmers at constantly increasing rents, and the tenant farmers in turn employed the cottagers as salaried agricultural workers. In this way the English peasantry largely disappeared, replaced by a more hierarchical society of big landlords, enterprising tenant farmers, and poor agricultural laborers.

The new agricultural techniques spread slowly from Britain and the Low Countries (the Dutch Republic and the Austrian Netherlands) to the rest of western Europe. Outside a few pockets in northern France and the western German states, however, subsistence agriculture (producing just enough to get by rather than surpluses for the market) continued to dominate farming in western Europe and Scandinavia. In southwestern Germany, for example, 80 percent of the peasants produced no surplus because their plots were too small. Unlike the populations of the highly urbanized Low Countries (where half the people lived in towns and cities), most Europeans, western and eastern, eked out their existence in the countryside and could barely participate in the new markets for consumer goods.

In eastern Europe, the condition of peasants worsened in the areas where landlords tried hardest to improve crop yields. To produce more for the Baltic grain market, aristocratic landholders in Prussia, Poland, and parts of Russia drained wetlands, cultivated moors, and built dikes. They also forced peasants off lands that the peasants had worked for themselves, increased compulsory labor services (the critical element in serfdom), and began to manage their estates directly. Some eastern landowners grew fabulously wealthy. The Potocki family in the Polish Ukraine, for example, owned three million acres of land and had 130,000

Relationship of Crop Harvested to Seed Used, 1400–1800
The impact and even the timing of the agricultural revolution can be determined by this figure, based on yield ratios (the number of grains produced for each seed planted). Britain, the Dutch Republic, and the Austrian Netherlands all experienced huge increases in crop yields after 1700. Other European regions lagged behind right into the 1800s. Why is crop yield such an important measure? *(From Peter J. Hugill, World Trade since 1431: Geography, Technology, and Capitalism (Johns Hopkins University Press, 1995), 56.)*

serfs. In parts of Poland and Russia, the serfs hardly differed from slaves in status, and their "masters" ran their huge estates much like American plantations (see the image on page 532).

Social Life in the Cities

Because of emigration from the countryside, cities grew in population and consequently exercised more influence on culture and social life. Between

Treatment of Serfs in Russia
Visitors from western Europe often remarked on the cruel treatment of serfs in Russia. This drawing by one such visitor shows the punishment that could be inflicted by landowners. Serfs could be whipped for almost any reason, even for making a soup too salty or neglecting to bow when the lord's family passed by. Their condition worsened in the 1700s, as landowners began to sell serfs much like slaves. Although life for Russian serfs was more brutal than for peasants elsewhere, upper classes in every country regarded the serfs as dirty, deceitful, and brutish. *(New York Public Library/Art Resource, NY.)*

1650 and 1750, cities with at least ten thousand inhabitants increased in population by 44 percent. From the eighteenth century onward, urban growth would be continuous. Along with the general growth of cities, an important south-to-north shift occurred in the pattern of urbanization. Around 1500, half of the people in cities of at least ten thousand residents could be found in the Italian states, Spain, or Portugal; by 1700, the urbanization of northwestern and southern Europe was roughly equal. Eastern Europe, despite the huge cities of Istanbul and Moscow, was still less urban than western Europe. London was by far the most populous European city, with 675,000 inhabitants in 1750; Berlin had 90,000 people, Warsaw only 23,000.

Urban Social Classes. Many landowners kept a residence in town, so the separation between rural and city life was not as extreme as might be imagined, at least not for the very rich. At the top

of the ladder in the big cities were the landed nobles. Some of them filled their lives only with conspicuous consumption of fine food, extravagant clothing, coaches, books, and opera; others held key political, administrative, or judicial offices. However they spent their time, these rich families employed thousands of artisans, shopkeepers, and domestic servants. Many English peers (highest-ranking nobles) had thirty or forty servants at each of their homes.

The middle classes of officials, merchants, professionals, and landowners occupied the next rung down on the social ladder. London's population, for example, included about twenty thousand middle-class families (constituting, at most, one-sixth of the city's population). In this period the middle classes began to develop distinctive ways of life that set them apart from both the rich noble landowners and the lower classes. Unlike the rich nobles, the middle classes lived primarily in the cities and towns, even if they owned small country estates. They ate more moderately than nobles but much better than peasants or laborers. For breakfast the British middle classes ate toast and rolls and, after 1700, drank tea. Dinner, served midday, consisted of roasted or boiled beef or mutton, poultry or pork, and vegetables. Supper was a light meal of bread and cheese with cake or pie. Beer was the main drink in London, and many families brewed their own. Even children drank beer because of the lack of fresh water.

Below the middle classes came the artisans and shopkeepers (most of whom were organized in professional guilds), then the journeymen, apprentices, servants, and laborers. At the bottom of the social scale were the unemployed poor, who survived by intermittent work and charity. Women married to artisans and shopkeepers often kept the accounts, supervised employees, and ran the household as well. Every middle-class and upper-class family employed servants; artisans and shopkeepers frequently hired them too. Women from poorer families usually worked as domestic servants until they married. Four out of five domestic servants in the city were female. In large cities such as London, the servant population grew faster than the population of the city as a whole.

Signs of Social Distinction. Social status in the cities was readily visible. Wide, spacious streets graced rich districts; the houses had gardens, and the air was relatively fresh. In poor districts, the streets were narrow, dirty, dark, humid, and smelly, and the houses were damp and crowded. The poorest people were homeless, sleeping under

Vauxhall Gardens, London
This hand-colored print from the mid-eighteenth century shows the newly refurbished gardens near the
Thames River. Prosperous families show off their brightly-colored clothes and listen to a public concert
by the orchestra seated just above them. These activities helped form a more self-conscious public.
(© Bibliothèque des Arts Décoratifs, Paris, France/The Bridgeman Art Library.)

bridges or in abandoned buildings. A Neapolitan prince described his homeless neighbors as "lying like filthy animals, with no distinction of age or sex." In some districts, rich and poor lived in the same buildings; the poor clambered up to shabby, cramped apartments on the top floors.

Like shelter, clothing was a reliable social indicator. The poorest workingwomen in Paris wore woolen skirts and blouses of dark colors over petticoats, a bodice, and a corset. They also donned caps of various sorts, cotton stockings, and shoes (probably their only pair). Workingmen dressed even more drably. Many occupations could be recognized by their dress: no one could confuse lawyers in their dark robes with masons or butchers in their special aprons, for example. People higher on the social ladder were more likely to sport a variety of fabrics, colors, and unusual designs in their clothing and to own many different outfits. Social status was not an abstract idea; it permeated every detail of daily life.

The Growth of a Literate Public. The ability to read and write also reflected social differences. People in the upper classes were more literate than those in the lower classes; city people were more literate than peasants. Protestant countries appear to have been more successful at promoting education and literacy than Catholic countries, perhaps because of the Protestant emphasis on Bible reading. Widespread literacy among the lower classes was first achieved in the Protestant areas of Switzerland and in Presbyterian Scotland, and rates were also very high in the New England colonies and the Scandinavian countries. In France, literacy doubled in the eighteenth century thanks to the spread of parish schools, but still only one in two men and one in four women could read and write. Most peasants remained illiterate. Although some Protestant German states encouraged primary education, schooling remained woefully inadequate almost everywhere in Europe: few schools existed, teachers received low wages, and no country had yet established a national system of control or supervision.

Despite the deficiencies of primary education, a new literate public arose especially among the middle classes of the cities. More books and periodicals were published than ever before, another aspect of the consumer revolution. The trend began in the 1690s in Britain and the Dutch Republic and gradually accelerated. In 1695, the British government allowed the licensing system, through which it controlled publications, to lapse, and new newspapers and magazines appeared almost immediately. The first London daily newspaper came out in 1702, and in 1709 Joseph Addison and Richard Steele published the first literary magazine, *The Spectator*. They devoted their magazine to the cultural improvement of the increasingly influential middle class. By the 1720s, twenty-four

provincial newspapers were published in England. In the London coffeehouses, an edition of a single newspaper might reach ten thousand male readers. Women did their reading at home. Except in the Dutch Republic, newspapers on the continent lagged behind and often consisted mainly of advertising with little critical commentary. France, for example, had no daily paper until 1777.

New Tastes in the Arts

The new literate public did not just read newspapers; its members now pursued an interest in painting, attended concerts, and besieged booksellers in search of popular novels. Because increased trade and prosperity put money into the hands of the growing middle classes, a new urban audience began to compete with the churches, rulers, and courtiers as chief patrons for new work. As the public for the arts expanded, printed commentary on them emerged, setting the stage for the appearance of political and social criticism. New artistic tastes thus had effects far beyond the realm of the arts.

Rococo Painting. Developments in painting reflected the tastes of the new public, as the **rococo** style challenged the hold of the baroque and classical schools, especially in France. Like the baroque, the rococo emphasized irregularity and asymmetry, movement and curvature, but it did so on a much smaller, subtler scale. Many rococo paintings depicted scenes of intimate sensuality rather than the monumental, emotional grandeur favored by classical and baroque painters. Personal portraits and pastoral paintings took the place of heroic landscapes and grand, ceremonial canvases. Rococo paintings adorned homes as well as palaces and served as a form of interior decoration rather than as a statement of piety. Its decorative quality made rococo art an ideal complement to newly discovered materials such as stucco and porcelain, especially the porcelain vases now imported from China.

Rococo, like *baroque*, was an invented word (from the French word *rocaille*, meaning "shellwork") and originally a derogatory label, meaning "frivolous decoration." But the great French rococo painters, such as Antoine Watteau (1684–1721) and François Boucher (1703–1770), were much more than mere decorators. Although both em-

Rococo Painting

The rococo emphasis on interiors, on decoration, and on intimacy rather than monumental grandeur are evident in François Boucher's painting *The Luncheon* (1739). The painting also draws attention to new consumer items, from the mirror and the clock to chocolate, children's toys, a small Buddha statue, and the intricately designed furniture. *(The Art Archive/Galleria Degli Uffizi/Dagli Orti (A).)*

---

rococo: A style of painting that emphasized irregularity and asymmetry, movement and curvature, but on a smaller, more intimate scale than the baroque.

phasized the erotic in their depictions, Watteau captured the melancholy side of a passing aristocratic style of life, and Boucher painted middle-class people at home during their daily activities. Both painters thereby contributed to the emergence of new sensibilities in art that increasingly attracted a middle-class public.

Music for the Public. The first public music concerts were performed in England in the 1670s, becoming much more regular and frequent in the 1690s. City concert halls typically seated about two hundred, but the relatively high price of tickets limited attendance to the better-off. Music clubs provided entertainment in smaller towns and villages. On the continent, Frankfurt organized the first regular public concerts in 1712; Hamburg and Paris began holding them within a few years. Opera continued to spread in the eighteenth century; Venice had sixteen public opera houses by 1700, and the Covent Garden opera house opened in London in 1732.

The growth of a public that appreciated and supported music had much the same effect as the extension of the reading public: like authors, composers could now begin to liberate themselves from court patronage and work for a paying audience. This development took time to solidify, however, and court or church patrons still commissioned much eighteenth-century music. Bach, a German Lutheran, wrote his *St. Matthew Passion* for Good Friday services in 1729 while he was organist and choirmaster for the leading church in Leipzig. He composed secular works (like the "Coffee Cantata") for the public and a variety of private patrons.

The composer George Frideric Handel (1685–1759) was among the first to grasp the new directions in music. A German by birth, he wrote operas in Italy and then moved in 1710 to Britain, where he wrote music for the court and began composing oratorios. The oratorio, a form Handel introduced in Britain, combined the drama of opera with the majesty of religious and ceremonial music and featured the chorus over the soloists. The "Hallelujah Chorus" from Handel's oratorio *Messiah* (1741) is perhaps the single best-known piece of Western classical music. It reflected the composer's personal, deeply felt piety but also his willingness to combine musical materials into a dramatic form that captured the enthusiasm of the new public. In 1740, a poem about Handel published in the *Gentleman's Magazine* exulted: "His art so modulates the sounds in all, / Our passions, as he pleases, rise and fall." Music had be-

come an integral part of the new middle-class public's culture.

Novels. Nothing captured the imagination of the new public more than the novel, the literary genre whose very name underscored the eighteenth-century taste for novelty. More than three hundred French novels appeared between 1700 and 1730. During this unprecedented explosion, the novel took on its modern form and became more concerned with individual psychology and social description than with the adventure tales popular earlier (such as Miguel de Cervantes's *Don Quixote*). The novel's popularity was closely tied to the expansion of the reading public, and novels were available in serial form in periodicals or from the many booksellers who served the new market.

Women figured prominently in novels as characters, and women writers abounded. The English novel *Love in Excess* (1719) quickly reached a sixth printing, and its author, Eliza Haywood (1693?–1756), earned her living turning out a stream of novels with titles such as *Persecuted Virtue, Constancy Rewarded*, and *The History of Betsy Thoughtless* — all showing a concern for the proper place of women as models of virtue in a changing world. When her husband deserted her and her two children, Haywood first worked as an actress but soon turned to writing plays and novels. In the 1740s, she began publishing a magazine, *The Female Spectator*, which argued in favor of higher education for women.

Haywood's male counterpart was Daniel Defoe (1660–1731), a merchant's son who had a diverse and colorful career as a manufacturer, political spy, novelist, and social commentator (see Document, "The Social Effects of Growing Consumption," page 530). Defoe wrote about schemes for national improvement, the state of English trade, the economic condition of the countryside, the effects of the plague, and the history of pirates; he is most well known, however, for his novels *Robinson Crusoe* (1719) and *Moll Flanders* (1722). The story of the adventures of a shipwrecked sailor, *Robinson Crusoe* portrayed the new values of the time: to survive, Crusoe had to employ fearless entrepreneurial ingenuity. He had to be ready for the unexpected and be able to improvise in every situation. He was, in short, the model for the new man in an expanding economy. Crusoe's patronizing attitude toward the black man Friday now draws much critical attention, but his discovery of Friday shows how the fate of blacks and whites had become intertwined in the new colonial environment.

Religious Revivals

Despite the novel's growing popularity, religious books and pamphlets still sold in huge numbers, and most Europeans remained devout, even as their religions were changing. In this period, a Protestant revivalist movement known as **Pietism** rocked the complacency of the established churches in the German Lutheran states, the Dutch Republic, and Scandinavia. Pietists believed in a mystical religion of the heart; they wanted a deeply emotional, even ecstatic religion. They urged intense Bible study, which in turn promoted popular education and contributed to the increase in literacy. Many Pietists attended catechism instruction every day and also went to morning and evening prayer meetings in addition to regular Sunday services. Although Pietism appealed to both Lutherans and Calvinists, it had the greatest impact in Lutheran Prussia, where it taught the virtues of hard work, obedience, and devotion to duty.

Catholicism also had its versions of religious revival, especially in France. A Frenchwoman, Jeanne Marie Guyon (1648–1717), attracted many noblewomen and a few leading clergymen to her own Catholic brand of Pietism, known as Quietism. Claiming miraculous visions and astounding prophecies, she urged a mystical union with God through prayer and simple devotion. Despite papal condemnation and intense controversy within Catholic circles in France, Guyon had followers all over Europe.

Even more influential were the Jansenists, who gained many new adherents to their austere form of Catholicism despite Louis XIV's harassment and repeated condemnation by the papacy. Under the pressure of religious and political persecution, Jansenism took a revivalist turn in the 1720s. At the funeral of a Jansenist priest in Paris in 1727, the crowd who flocked to the grave claimed to witness a series of miraculous healings. Within a few years, a cult formed around the priest's tomb and clandestine Jansenist presses were reporting new miracles to the reading public. When the French government tried to suppress the cult, one enraged wit placed a sign at the tomb that read, "By order of the king, God is forbidden to work miracles here." Some believers fell into frenzied convulsions, claiming to be inspired by the Holy Spirit through the intercession of the dead priest. After

midcentury, Jansenism became even more politically active as its adherents joined in opposition to the crown's policies on religion.

> **REVIEW:** How were new social trends reflected in cultural life in the late 1600s and early 1700s?

Consolidation of the European State System

The spread of Pietism and Jansenism reflected the emergence of a middle-class public that now participated in every new development, including religion. The middle classes could pursue these interests because the European state system gradually stabilized despite the increasing competition for wealth in the Atlantic system. Warfare settled three main issues between 1690 and 1740: a coalition of powers held Louis XIV's France in check on the continent, Great Britain emerged from the wars against Louis as the preeminent maritime power, and Russia defeated Sweden in the contest for supremacy in the Baltic. After Louis XIV's death in 1715, Europe enjoyed the fruits of a more balanced diplomatic system, in which warfare became less frequent and less widespread. States could then spend their resources establishing and expanding control over their own populations, both at home and in their colonies.

French Ambitions Thwarted

Lying on his deathbed in 1715, the seventy-six-year-old Louis XIV watched helplessly as his accomplishments began to unravel. Not only had his plans for territorial expansion been frustrated, but his incessant wars had exhausted the treasury, despite new taxes. In 1689, Louis's rival, William III, prince of Orange and king of England and Scotland (r. 1689–1702), had set out to forge a European alliance that eventually included Britain, the Dutch Republic, Sweden, Austria, and Spain. The allies fought Louis to a stalemate in the War of the League of Augsburg, sometimes called the Nine Years' War (1689–1697), and when hostilities resumed four years later, they finally put an end to Louis's expansionist ambitions.

The War of the Spanish Succession, 1701–1713.
When the mentally and physically feeble Charles II (r. 1665–1700) of Spain died without a direct heir, all of Europe poised for a fight over the spoils.

Pietism: A Protestant revivalist movement of the early eighteenth century that emphasized deeply emotional individual religious experience.

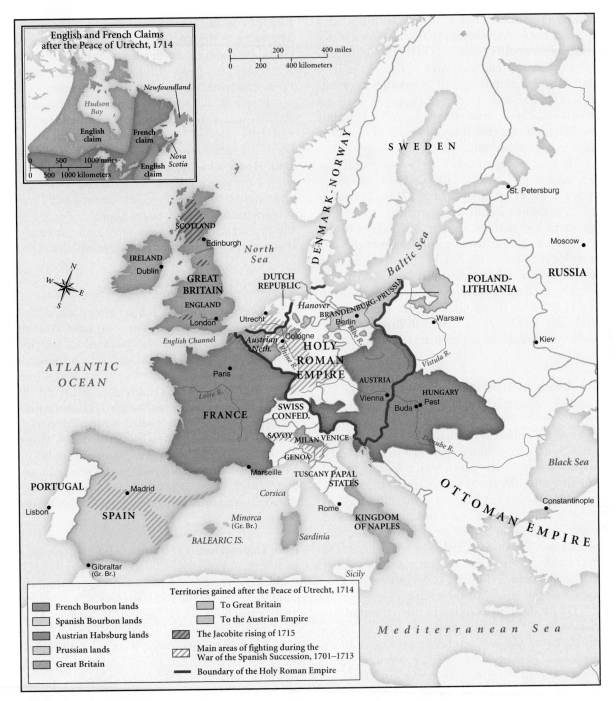

MAP 17.2 Europe, c. 1715

Although Louis XIV succeeded in putting his grandson Philip on the Spanish throne, France emerged considerably weakened from the War of Spanish Succession. France ceded large territories in Canada to Britain, which also gained key Mediterranean outposts from Spain as well as a monopoly on providing slaves to the Spanish colonies. Spanish losses were catastrophic. Philip had to renounce any future claim to the French crown and give up considerable territories in the Netherlands and Italy to the Austrians.

■ How did the competing English and French claims in North America around 1715 create potential conflicts for the future?

The Spanish succession could not help but be a burning issue. Even though Spanish power had declined since Spain's golden age in the sixteenth century, Spain still had extensive territories in Italy and the Netherlands as well as colonies overseas. Before Charles died, he named Louis XIV's second grandson, Philip, duke of Anjou, as his heir, but the Austrian emperor Leopold I refused to accept Charles's deathbed will.

In the ensuing war, the French lost several major battles and had to accept disadvantageous terms in the **Peace of Utrecht** of 1713–1714 (Map 17.2). Although Philip was recognized as king of Spain, he had to renounce any future claim to the French crown, thus barring unification of the two kingdoms. Spain surrendered its territories in Italy and the Netherlands to the Austrians and Gibraltar to the British; France ceded possessions in North America (Newfoundland, the Hudson Bay area, and most of Nova Scotia) to Britain. France no longer threatened to dominate European power politics.

The Death of Louis XIV and the Regency. At home, Louis's policy of absolutism had fomented bitter hostility. Nobles fiercely resented his promotions of commoners to high office. The duke of Saint-Simon complained that "falseness, servility, admiring glances, combined with a dependent and cringing attitude, above all, an appearance of being nothing without him, were the only ways of pleasing him." Archbishop Fénelon, who tutored the king's grandson, called for reform. An admirer of Guyon's Quietism, Fénelon severely criticized the "steady stream of extravagant adulation, which reaches the point of idolatry"; the constant, bloody wars; and the misery of the people.

On his deathbed, Louis XIV offered sound advice to his five-year-old great-grandson and successor, Louis XV (r. 1715–1774): "Do not imitate my love of building nor my liking for war." After being named regent, the duke of Orléans (1674–1723), nephew of the dead king, revived some of the parlements' powers and tried to give leading nobles a greater say in political affairs. To raise much-needed funds, in 1719 the regent encouraged the Scottish financier John Law to set up an official trading company for North America and a state bank that issued paper money and stock (without them, trade depended on the available supply of gold and silver). The bank was supposed to offer lower interest rates to the state, thus cut-

ting the cost of financing the government's debts. The value of the stock rose rapidly in a frenzy of speculation, only to crash a few months later. With it vanished any hope of establishing a state bank or issuing paper money for nearly a century.

France finally achieved a measure of financial stability under the leadership of Cardinal Hercule de Fleury (1653–1743), the most powerful member of the government after the death of the regent. Fleury aimed to avoid adventure abroad and keep social peace at home; he balanced the budget and carried out a large project for road and canal construction. Colonial trade boomed. Peace and the acceptance of limits on territorial expansion inaugurated a century of French prosperity.

British Rise and Dutch Decline

The British and the Dutch had formed a coalition against Louis XIV under their joint ruler William III, who was simultaneously stadholder (elected head) of the Dutch Republic and, with his English wife, Mary (d. 1694), ruler of England, Wales, and Scotland. After William's death in 1702, the British and Dutch went their separate ways. Over the next decades, England incorporated Scotland and subjugated Ireland, becoming "Great Britain." At the same time, Dutch imperial power declined; by 1700, Great Britain dominated the seas and the Dutch, with their small population of less than two million, came to depend on alliances with bigger powers.

From England to Great Britain. English relations with Scotland and Ireland were complicated by the problem of succession: William and Mary had no children. To ensure a Protestant succession, Parliament ruled that Mary's sister, Anne, would succeed William and Mary and that the Protestant House of Hanover in Germany would succeed Anne if she had no surviving heirs. Catholics were excluded. When Queen Anne (r. 1702–1714) died leaving no children, the elector of Hanover, a Protestant great-grandson of James I, consequently became King George I (r. 1714–1727). The House of Hanover — renamed the House of Windsor during World War I — still occupies the British throne.

Support from the Scots and Irish for this solution did not come easily, because many in Scotland and Ireland supported the claims to the throne of the deposed Catholic king, James II, and, after his death in 1701, his son James Edward. Out of fear of this Jacobitism (from the Latin *Jacobus* for "James"), Scottish Protestant leaders agreed to the Act of Union of 1707, which abolished the

---

Peace of Utrecht: Treaties drawn up in 1713–1714 that ended the War of the Spanish Succession.

Scottish Parliament and affirmed the Scots' recognition of the Protestant Hanoverian succession. The Scots agreed to obey the Parliament of Great Britain, which would include Scottish members in the House of Commons and the House of Lords. A Jacobite rebellion in Scotland in 1715, aiming to restore the Stuart line, was suppressed. The threat of Jacobitism nonetheless continued into the 1740s (see Map 17.2, page 537).

The Irish — 90 percent of whom were Catholic — proved even more difficult to subdue. When James II had gone to Ireland in 1689 to raise a Catholic rebellion against the new monarchs of England, William III responded by taking command of the joint English and Dutch forces and defeating James's Irish supporters. James fled to France, and the Catholics in Ireland faced yet more confiscation and legal restrictions. By 1700, Irish Catholics, who in 1640 had owned 60 percent of the land in Ireland, owned just 14 percent. The Protestant-controlled Irish Parliament passed a series of laws limiting the rights of the Catholic majority: Catholics could not bear arms, send their children abroad for education, establish Catholic schools at home, or marry Protestants. Catholics could not sit in Parliament, nor could they vote for its members unless they took an oath renouncing

Catholic doctrine. These and a host of other laws reduced Catholic Ireland to the status of a colony; one English official commented in 1745, "The poor people of Ireland are used worse than negroes." Most of the Irish were peasants who lived in primitive housing and subsisted on a meager diet that included no meat.

The Parliament of Great Britain was soon dominated by the Whigs. In Britain's constitutional system, the monarch ruled with Parliament. The crown chose the ministers, directed policy, and supervised administration, while Parliament raised revenue, passed laws, and represented the interests of the people to the crown. The powers of Parliament were reaffirmed by the Triennial Act in 1694, which provided that Parliaments meet at least once every three years (this was extended to seven years in 1716, after the Whigs had established their ascendancy). Only 200,000 propertied men could vote, out of a population of more than five million, and, not surprisingly, most members of Parliament came from the landed gentry. In fact, a few hundred families controlled all the important political offices.

George I and George II (r. 1727–1760) relied on one man, Sir **Robert Walpole** (1676–1745), to help them manage their relations with Parliament.

Sir Robert Walpole at a Cabinet Meeting
Sir Robert Walpole and George II developed the institution of a cabinet, which brought together the important heads of departments. Their cabinet was the ancestor of modern cabinets in both Great Britain and the United States. Because of its modest size, its similarities to modern forms should not be overstated, however. How would discussions in the new coffeehouses (shown in the opening illustration to this chapter) influence the kinds of decisions made by Walpole and his cabinet? (© *The Fotomas Index, U.K./The Bridgeman Art Library.*)

Robert Walpole: The first, or "prime," minister of the House of Commons of Great Britain's Parliament. Although appointed initially by the king, through his long period of leadership (1721–1742) he effectively established the modern pattern of parliamentary government.

From his position as First Lord of the Treasury, Walpole made himself into the first, or "prime," minister, leading the House of Commons from 1721 to 1742 (see illustration, page 539). Although appointed initially by the king, Walpole established an enduring pattern of parliamentary government in which a prime minister from the leading party guided legislation through the House of Commons. Walpole also built a vast patronage machine that dispensed government jobs to win support for the crown's policies. Walpole's successors relied more and more on the patronage system and eventually alienated not only the Tories but also the middle classes in London and even the North American colonies.

The partisan division between the Whigs, who supported the Hanoverian succession and the rights of dissenting Protestants, and the Tories, who had backed the Stuart line and the Anglican church, did not hamper Great Britain's pursuit of economic, military, and colonial power. In this period, Great Britain became a great power on the world stage by virtue of its navy and its ability to finance major military involvement in the wars against Louis XIV. The founding in 1694 of the Bank of England—which, unlike the French bank, endured—enabled the government to raise money at low interest for foreign wars. By the 1740s, the government could borrow more than four times what it could in the 1690s.

The Dutch Eclipse. When William of Orange (William III of England) died in 1702, he left no heirs, and for forty-five years the Dutch lived without a stadholder. The merchant ruling class of some two thousand families dominated the Dutch Republic more than ever, but they presided over a country that counted for less in international power politics. In some areas, Dutch decline was only relative: the Dutch population was not growing as fast as others, for example, and the Dutch share of the Baltic trade decreased from 50 percent in 1720 to less than 30 percent by the 1770s. After 1720, the Baltic countries—Prussia, Russia, Denmark, and Sweden—began to ban imports of manufactured goods to protect their own industries, and Dutch trade in particular suffered. The output of Leiden textiles dropped to one-third of its 1700 level by 1740. Shipbuilding, paper manufacturing, tobacco processing, salt refining, and pottery production all dwindled as well. The Dutch East India Company saw its political and military grip loosened in India, Ceylon, and Java.

The biggest exception to the downward trend was trade with the New World, which increased with escalating demands for sugar and tobacco. The Dutch shifted their interest away from great power rivalries toward those areas of international trade and finance where they could establish an enduring presence.

Russia's Emergence as a European Power

The commerce and shipbuilding of the Dutch and British so impressed Russian tsar Peter I (r. 1689–1725) that he traveled incognito to their shipyards in 1697 to learn their methods firsthand. Known to history as **Peter the Great**, he dragged Russia kicking and screaming all the way to great-power status. Although he came to the throne while still a minor (on the eve of his tenth birthday), grew up under the threat of a palace coup, and enjoyed little formal education, his accomplishments soon matched his seven-foot-tall stature. Peter transformed public life in Russia and established an absolutist state on the Western model. His attempts to create a society patterned after western Europe, known as **Westernization**, ignited an enduring controversy: Did Peter set Russia on a course of inevitable Westernization required to compete with the West? Or did he forever and fatally disrupt Russia's natural evolution into a distinctive Slavic society?

Westernization. To pursue his goal of Westernizing Russian culture, Peter set up the first greenhouses, laboratories, and technical schools and founded the Russian Academy of Sciences. He ordered translations of Western classics and hired a German theater company to perform the French plays of Molière. He replaced the traditional Russian calendar with the Western one,[1] introduced Arabic numerals, and brought out the first public newspaper. He ordered his officials and the nobles to shave their beards (see the illustration on page 541) and dress in Western fashion, and he even

---

[1] Peter introduced the Julian calendar, then still used in Protestant but not Catholic countries. Later in the eighteenth century, Protestant Europe abandoned the Julian for the Gregorian calendar. Not until 1918 was the Gregorian calendar adopted in Russia, at which point Russia's calendar had fallen thirteen days behind Europe's.

Peter the Great: Russian tsar Peter I (r. 1689–1725), who undertook the Westernization of Russia and built a new capital city named after himself, St. Petersburg.

Westernization: The effort, especially in Peter the Great's Russia, to make society and social customs resemble counterparts in western Europe, especially France, Britain, and the Dutch Republic.

Peter the Great Modernizes Russia

In this popular print, a barber forces a protesting noble to conform to western fashions. Peter the Great ordered all nobles, merchants, and middle-class professionals to cut off their beards or pay a huge tax to keep them. An early biographer of Peter claimed that those who lost their beards saved them to put in their coffins, in fear that they would not enter heaven without them. Most western Europeans applauded these attempts to modernize Russia, but many Russians deeply resented the attack on traditional ways. Why was everyday appearance such a contested issue in Russia? *(The Visual Connection.)*

issued precise regulations about the suitable style of jacket, boots, and cap (generally French or German).

Peter encouraged foreigners to move to Russia to offer their advice and skills, especially for building the capital city. Named St. Petersburg after the tsar, the new capital symbolized Russia's opening to the West. Construction began in 1703 in a Baltic province that had been recently conquered from Sweden. By the end of 1709, forty thousand recruits a year found themselves assigned to the work. Peter ordered skilled workers to move to the new city and commanded all landowners possessing more than forty serf households to build houses there. In the 1720s, a German minister described St. Petersburg "as a wonder of the world, considering its magnificent palaces, . . . and the short time that was employed in the building of it." By 1710, the permanent population of the capital reached eight thousand. At Peter's death in 1725, it had forty thousand residents.

As a new city far from the Russian heartland around Moscow, St. Petersburg represented a decisive break with Russia's past. Peter widened that gap by every means possible. At his new capital he tried to improve the traditionally denigrated, secluded status of women by ordering them to dress in European styles and appear publicly at his dinners for diplomatic representatives. Imitating French manners, he decreed that women attend his new social salons of officials, officers, and merchants for conversation and dancing. A foreigner headed every one of Peter's new technical and vocational schools, and for its first eight years the new Academy of Sciences included no Russians. Every ministry was assigned a foreign adviser. Upper-class Russians learned French or German, which they spoke even at home. Such changes affected only the very top of Russian society, however; the mass of the population had no contact with the new ideas and ended up paying for the innovations either in ruinous new taxation or by building St. Petersburg, a project that cost the lives of thousands of workers. Serfs remained tied to the land, completely dominated by their noble lords.

Peter the Great's Brand of Absolutism.

Peter also reorganized government and finance on Western models and, like other absolute rulers, strengthened his army. With ruthless recruiting methods, which included branding a cross on every recruit's left hand to prevent desertion, he forged an army of 200,000 men and equipped it with modern weapons. He created schools for artillery, engineering, and military medicine and built the first navy in Russian history. Not surprisingly, taxes tripled.

The tsar allowed nothing to stand in his way. He did not hesitate to use torture, and he executed thousands. He allowed a special guard regiment

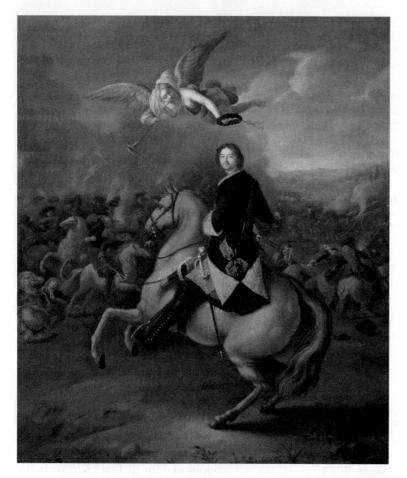

Peter the Great
In this painting by Gottfried Danhauer (1680–1733/7), the Russian tsar appears against the background of his most famous battle, Poltava. The angel holds a laurel wreath, symbol of victory, over his head. *(© Tretyakov Gallery, Moscow, Russia/The Bridgeman Art Library.)*

unprecedented power to expedite cases against those suspected of rebellion, espionage, pretensions to the throne, or just "unseemly utterances" against him. Opposition to his policies reached into his own family: because his only son, Alexei, had allied himself with Peter's critics, the tsar threw him into prison, where the young man mysteriously died.

To control the often restive nobility, Peter insisted that all noblemen engage in state service. A Table of Ranks (1722) classified them into military, administrative, and court categories, a codification of social and legal relationships in Russia that would last for nearly two centuries. All social and material advantages now depended on serving the crown. Because the nobles lacked a secure independent status, Peter could command them to a degree that was unimaginable in western Europe. State service was not only compulsory but also permanent. Moreover, the male children of those in service had to be registered by the age of ten and begin serving at fifteen. To increase his authority over the Russian Orthodox church, Peter allowed the office of patriarch (supreme head) to remain vacant, and in 1721 he replaced it with the

Holy Synod, a bureaucracy of laymen under his supervision. To many Russians, Peter was the devil incarnate.

Changes in the Balance of Power in the East.
Peter the Great's success in building up state power changed the balance of power in eastern Europe. Overcoming initial military setbacks, Russia eventually defeated Sweden and took its place as the leading power in the Baltic region. Russia could then compete with Prussia, Austria, and France in the rivalries between great powers.

Sweden had dominated the Baltic region since the Thirty Years' War (1618–1648), and though the monarchy lost some of its power under Queen Christina (r. 1632–1654), the daughter of Gustavus Adolphus, the Swedish kings quickly recovered their position. When Peter the Great joined an anti-Swedish coalition in 1700 with Denmark, Saxony, and Poland, Sweden's Charles XII (r. 1697–1718) stood up to the test. Still in his teens at the beginning of the Great Northern War, Charles first defeated Denmark, then destroyed the new Russian army, and quickly marched into Poland and Saxony. After defeating the Poles and occupying Saxony, Charles invaded Russia. Here Peter's rebuilt army finally defeated the Swedish king at the battle of Poltava (1709).

The Russian victory resounded everywhere. The Russian ambassador to Vienna reported, "It is commonly said that the tsar will be formidable to all Europe, that he will be a kind of northern Turk." Prussia and other German states joined the anti-Swedish alliance, and when Charles XII died in battle in 1718, negotiations finally ended the Great Northern War. By the terms of the Treaty of Nystad (1721), Sweden ceded its eastern Baltic provinces — Livonia, Estonia, Ingria, and southern Karelia — to Russia. Sweden also lost territories on the north German coast to Prussia and the other allied German states (Map 17.3). An aristocratic reaction against Charles XII's incessant demands for war supplies swept away Sweden's absolutist regime, essentially removing Sweden from great power competition.

Prussia had to make the most of every military opportunity, as it did in the Great Northern War, because it was much smaller in size and population than Russia, Austria, or France. King Frederick William I (r. 1713–1740) doubled the size of the Prussian army; though still smaller than those of his rivals, it was the best-trained and most up-to-date force in Europe. By 1740, Prussia had Europe's highest proportion of men at arms (1 of every 28 people, versus 1 in 157 in France and 1 in 64 in Russia) and the highest proportion of nobles in the military (1 in 7 noblemen, as compared with 1 in 33 in France and 1 in 50 in Russia).

The army so dominated life in Prussia that the country earned the label "a large army with a small state attached." Frederick William, known as the "Sergeant King," was one of the first rulers to wear a military uniform as his everyday dress. He subordinated the entire domestic administration to the army's needs. He also installed a system for recruiting soldiers by local district quotas. He financed the army's growth by subjecting all the provinces to an excise tax on food, drink, and manufactured goods and by increasing rents on crown lands. Prussia was now poised to become one of the major players on the continent, but it could not enter into military engagements foolishly given the size of its forces and chose to sit on the sidelines during the next conflict.

War broke out in 1733 when the king of Poland-Lithuania died. France, Spain, and Sardinia joined in the War of Polish Succession (1733–1735) against Austria and Russia, each side supporting rival claimants to the Polish throne. Although Peter the Great had been followed by a series of weak rulers, Russian forces were still strong enough to drive the French candidate out of Poland-Lithuania, prompting France to accept the Austrian candidate. In exchange, Austria gave the province of Lorraine to the French candidate, the father-in-law of Louis XV, with the promise that the province would pass to France on his death.

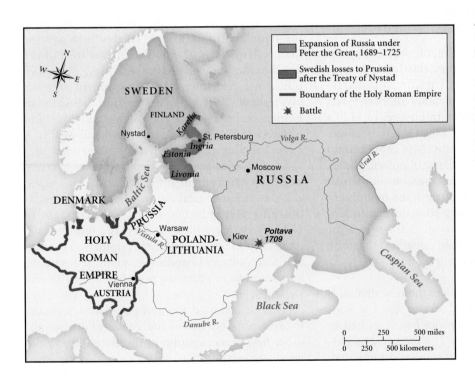

MAP 17.3 Russia and Sweden after the Great Northern War, 1721
After the Great Northern War, Russia supplanted Sweden as the major power in the north. Although Russia had a much larger population from which to draw its armies, Sweden made the most of its advantages and gave way only after a great military struggle.

France and Britain went back to pursuing their colonial rivalries. Prussia and Russia concentrated on shoring up their influence within Poland-Lithuania.

Austria did not want to become mired in a long struggle in Poland-Lithuania because its armies still faced the Turks on its southeastern border. Even though the Austrians had forced the Turks to recognize their rule over all of Hungary and Transylvania in 1699 and occupied Belgrade in 1717, the Turks did not stop fighting. In the 1730s, the Turks retook Belgrade, and Russia now claimed a role in the struggle against the Turks. Moreover, Hungary, though "liberated" from Turkish rule, proved less than enthusiastic about submitting to Austria. In 1703, the wealthiest Hungarian noble landlord, Ferenc Rákóczi (1676–1735), raised an army of seventy thousand men who fought for "God, Fatherland, and Liberty" until 1711. They forced the Austrians to recognize local Hungarian institutions, grant amnesty, and restore confiscated estates in exchange for confirming hereditary Austrian rule.

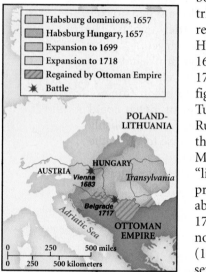

Legend:
- Habsburg dominions, 1657
- Habsburg Hungary, 1657
- Expansion to 1699
- Expansion to 1718
- Regained by Ottoman Empire
- ✹ Battle

Austrian Conquest of Hungary, 1657–1730

The Power of Diplomacy and the Importance of Population

No single power emerged from the wars of the first half of the eighteenth century clearly superior to the others, and the Peace of Utrecht explicitly declared that maintaining a balance of power was crucial to maintaining peace in Europe. In 1720 a British pamphleteer wrote, "There is not, I believe, any doctrine in the law of nations, of more certain truth . . . than this of the balance of power." Diplomacy helped maintain the balance, but in the end this system of equilibrium often rested on military force, such as the leagues formed against Louis XIV or the coalition against Sweden. In the search for ever larger armies, states could not afford to ignore the general health of their populations.

Diplomatic Services. To meet the new demands placed on it, the diplomatic service, like the military and financial bureaucracies before it, had to develop regular procedures. The French set a pattern that the other European states soon imitated.

By 1685, France had embassies in all the important capitals. Nobles of ancient families served as ambassadors to Rome, Madrid, Vienna, and London, whereas royal officials were chosen for Switzerland, the Dutch Republic, and Venice. The ambassador selected and paid for his own staff. This practice could make the journey to a new post cumbersome, because the staff might be as large as eighty people, and they brought along all their own furniture, pictures, silverware, and tapestries. It took one French ambassador ten weeks to get from Paris to Stockholm.

Despite a new emphasis on honest and informed negotiation, rulers still employed secret agents and often sent covert instructions that negated the official ones sent by their own foreign offices. This behind-the-scenes diplomacy had some advantages because it allowed rulers to break with past alliances, but it also led to confusion and sometimes scandal, for the rulers often engaged unreliable adventurers as their confidential agents. Still, the diplomatic system in the early eighteenth century proved successful enough to ensure a continuation of the principles of the Peace of Westphalia (1648); in the midst of every crisis and war, the great powers would convene and hammer out a written agreement detailing the requirements for peace.

Public Health. Adroit diplomacy could smooth the road toward peace, but success in war still depended on sheer numbers—of men and of muskets. Because each state's strength depended largely on the size of its army, the growth and health of the population increasingly entered into government calculations. The publication in 1690 of the Englishman William Petty's *Political Arithmetick* quickened the interest of government officials everywhere. Petty offered statistical estimates of human capital—that is, of population and wages—to determine Britain's national wealth. A large, growing population could be as vital to a state's future as access to silver mines or overseas trade, so government officials devoted increased effort to the statistical estimation of total population and rates of births, deaths, and marriages. In 1727, Frederick William I of Prussia founded two university chairs to encourage population studies, and textbooks and handbooks advocated state intervention to improve the population's health and welfare.

Physicians used the new population statistics to explain the environmental causes of disease, another new preoccupation in this period. Petty devised a quantitative scale that distinguished healthy from unhealthy places largely on the basis of air quality, an early precursor of modern environmental studies. Cities were the unhealthiest places because excrement (animal and human) and garbage accumulated where people lived densely packed together. Medical geographers gathered and analyzed data on climate, disease, and population, searching for correlations to help direct policy. As a result of these efforts, local governments undertook such measures as draining low-lying areas, burying refuse, and cleaning wells, all of which eventually helped lower the death rates from epidemic diseases.

Not all changes came from direct government intervention. Hospitals, founded originally as charities concerned foremost with the moral worthiness of the poor, gradually evolved into medical institutions that defined patients by their diseases. The process of diagnosis changed as physicians began to use specialized Latin terms for illnesses. The gap between medical experts and their patients increased, as physicians now also relied on postmortem dissections in the hospital to gain better knowledge, a practice most patients' families resented. Press reports of body snatching and grave robbing by surgeons and their apprentices outraged the public well into the 1800s.

Despite the change in hospitals, individual health care remained something of a free-for-all in which physicians competed with bloodletters, itinerant venereal-disease doctors, bonesetters, druggists, midwives, and "cunning women," who specialized in home remedies. The medical profession, with nationwide organizations and licensing, had not yet emerged, and no clear line separated trained physicians from quacks. In any case, trained physicians were few in number and almost nonexistent outside cities. Patients were as likely to catch a deadly disease in the hospital as to be cured there. Antiseptics were virtually unknown. Because doctors believed most insanity was caused by disorders in the system of bodily "humors," their prescribed treatments included blood transfusions; ingestion of bitter substances such as coffee, quinine, and even soap; immersion in water; various forms of exercise; and burning or cauterizing the body to allow black vapors to escape.

Hardly any infectious diseases could be cured, though inoculation against smallpox spread from the Middle East to Europe in the early eighteenth century, thanks largely to the efforts of Lady Mary Wortley Montagu (1689–1762). In 1716, Montagu accompanied her husband to Constantinople, where he took up a post as British ambassador to the Ottoman Empire. She returned in 1718, after witnessing firsthand the Turkish use of inoculation. When a new smallpox epidemic threatened England in 1721, she called on her physician to inoculate her daughter. Two patients died after inoculation in the following months, prompting clergymen and physicians to attack the practice, which remained in dispute for decades. Inoculation against smallpox began to spread more widely after 1796, when the English physician Edward Jenner developed a serum based on cowpox, a milder disease. Many other diseases spread quickly in the unsanitary conditions of urban life. Ordinary people washed or changed clothes rarely, lived in overcrowded housing with poor ventilation, and got their water from contaminated sources such as refuse-filled rivers.

Public bathhouses had disappeared from cities in the sixteenth and seventeenth centuries because they seemed a source of disorderly behavior and epidemic illness. In the eighteenth century, even private bathing came into disfavor because people feared the effects of contact with water. Fewer than one in ten newly built private mansions in Paris had baths. Bathing was hazardous, physicians insisted, because it opened the body to disease. One manners manual of 1736 admonished, "It is correct to clean the face every morning by using a white cloth to cleanse it. It is less good to wash with water, because it renders the face susceptible to cold in winter and sun in summer." The upper classes associated cleanliness not with baths but with frequently changed linens, powdered hair, and perfume, which was thought to strengthen the body and refresh the brain by counteracting corrupt and foul air.

REVIEW: What events and developments led to greater stability and less warfare in the European state system?

The Birth of the Enlightenment

Economic expansion, the emergence of a new consumer society, and the stabilization of the European state system all generated optimism about the future. The intellectual corollary was the **Enlightenment**, a term used later in the eighteenth century to describe the loosely knit group of writers

Enlightenment: The eighteenth-century intellectual movement whose proponents believed that human beings could apply a critical, reasoning spirit to every problem.

and scholars who believed that human beings could apply a critical, reasoning spirit to every problem they encountered in this world. The new secular, scientific, and critical attitude first emerged in the 1690s, scrutinizing everything from the absolutism of Louis XIV to the traditional role of women in society. After 1740, criticism took a more systematic turn as writers provided new theories for the organization of society and politics; but as early as the 1720s, established authorities realized they faced a new set of challenges. Even while slavery expanded in the Atlantic system, Enlightenment writers began to insist on the need for new freedoms in Europe.

Popularization of Science and Challenges to Religion

The writers of the Enlightenment glorified the geniuses of the new science and championed the scientific method as the solution for all social problems. (See "Terms of History," page 547.) One of the most influential popularizations was the French writer Bernard de Fontenelle's *Conversations on the Plurality of Worlds* (1686). Presented as a dialogue between an aristocratic woman and a man of the world, the book made the Coperni-

can, heliocentric view of the universe available to the literate public. By 1700, mathematics and science had become fashionable pastimes in high society, and the public flocked to lectures explaining scientific discoveries. Journals complained that scientific learning had become the passport to female affection: "There were two young ladies in Paris whose heads had been so turned by this branch of learning that one of them declined to listen to a proposal of marriage unless the candidate for her hand undertook to learn how to make telescopes." Such writings poked fun at women with intellectual interests, but they also demonstrated that women now participated in discussions of science.

The New Skepticism.   Interest in science spread in literate circles because it offered a model for all forms of knowledge. As the prestige of science increased, some developed a skeptical attitude toward attempts to enforce religious conformity. A French Huguenot refugee from Louis XIV's persecutions, Pierre Bayle (1647–1706), launched an internationally influential campaign against religious intolerance from his safe haven in the Dutch Republic. His *News from the Republic of Letters* (first published in 1684) bitterly criticized the poli-

A Budding Scientist
In this engraving, *Astrologia*, by the Dutch artist Jacob Gole (c. 1660–1723), an upper-class woman looks through a telescope to do her own astronomical investigations. Women with intellectual interests were often disparaged by men, and women were not allowed to attend university classes in any European country. Yet because many astronomical observatories were set up in private homes rather than public buildings or universities, wives and daughters of scientists could make observations and even publish their own findings. (*Bibliothèque nationale de France.*)

cies of Louis XIV and was quickly banned in Paris and condemned in Rome. After attacking Louis XIV's anti-Protestant policies, Bayle took a more general stand in favor of religious toleration. No state in Europe officially offered complete tolerance, though the Dutch Republic came closest with its tacit acceptance of Catholics, dissident Protestant groups, and open Jewish communities. In 1697, Bayle published the *Historical and Critical Dictionary*, which cited all the errors and delusions that he could find in past and present writers of all religions. Even religion must meet the test of reasonableness: "Any particular dogma, whatever it may be, whether it is advanced on the authority of the Scriptures, or whatever else may be its origins, is to be regarded as false if it clashes with the clear and definite conclusions of the natural understanding [reason]."

Although Bayle claimed to be a believer himself, his insistence on rational investigation seemed to challenge the authority of faith. As one critic complained, "It is notorious that the works of M. Bayle have unsettled a large number of readers, and cast doubt on some of the most widely accepted principles of morality and religion." Bayle asserted, for example, that atheists might possess moral codes as effective as those of the devout. Bayle's *Dictionary* became a model of critical thought in the West.

Other scholars challenged the authority of the Bible by subjecting it to historical criticism. Discoveries in geology in the early eighteenth century showed that marine fossils dated immensely further back than the biblical flood. Investigations of miracles, comets, and oracles, like the growing literature against belief in witchcraft, urged the use of reason to combat superstition and prejudice. Comets, for example, should not be considered evil omens just because earlier generations had passed down such a belief. Defenders of church and state published books warning of the new skepticism's dangers. The spokesman for Louis XIV's absolutism, Bishop Bossuet, warned that "reason is the guide of their choice, but reason only brings them face to face with vague conjectures and baffling perplexities." Human beings, the traditionalists held, were simply incapable of subjecting everything to reason, especially in the realm of religion.

State authorities found religious skepticism particularly unsettling because it threatened to undermine state power too. The extensive literature of criticism was not limited to France, but much of it was published in French, and the French government took the lead in suppressing the more outspoken works. Forbidden books were then

TERMS OF HISTORY

Progress

Believing as they did in the possibilities of improvement, many Enlightenment writers preached a new doctrine about the meaning of human history. They challenged the traditional Christian belief that the original sin of Adam and Eve condemned human beings to unhappiness in this world and offered instead an optimistic vision: human nature, they claimed, was inherently good, and progress would be continuous if education developed human capacities to the utmost. Science and reason could bring happiness in this world. The idea of novelty or newness itself now seemed positive rather than threatening. Europeans began to imagine that they could surpass all those who preceded them in history, and they began to think of themselves as more "advanced" than the "backward" cultures they encountered in other parts of the world.

More than an intellectual concept, the idea of progress included a new conception of historical time and of Europeans' place within world history. Europeans stopped looking back, whether to a lost Garden of Eden or to the writings of Greek and Roman antiquity. Growing prosperity, European dominance overseas, and the scientific revolution oriented them toward the future. Europeans began to apply the word *modern* to their epoch, to distinguish it from the Middle Ages (a new term), and they considered their modern period superior in achievement. Consequently, Europeans took it as their mission to bring their modern, enlightened ways of progress to the areas they colonized.

The economic and ecological catastrophes, destructive wars, and genocides of the twentieth century cast much doubt on this rosy vision of continuing progress. As the philosopher George Santayana (1863–1952) complained, "The cry was for vacant freedom and indeterminate progress: *Vorwärts! Avanti! Onward! Full Speed Ahead!*, without asking whether directly before you was a bottomless pit." Historians are now chastened in their claims about progress. They would no longer side with the German philosopher Georg W. F. Hegel, who proclaimed in 1832, "The history of the world is none other than the progress of the consciousness of freedom." They worry about the nationalistic claims inherent, for example, in the English historian Thomas Babington Macaulay's insistence that "the history of England is emphatically the history of progress" (1843). As with many other historical questions, the final word is not yet in: Is there a direction in human history that can correctly be called progress? Or is history, as many in ancient times thought, a set of repeating cycles?

DOCUMENT

Voltaire, *Letters Concerning the English Nation* (1733)

In the 1720s, Voltaire (1694–1778) visited both the Dutch Republic and England. He learned English and came to admire English political institutions and customs, using comparison with them to criticize religious intolerance and Catholic censorship in France. In this selection from a letter on Locke, Voltaire develops the argument that religion should be considered a matter of faith and conscience and be separated from arguments concerning philosophy. He also shows his disdain for the common people.

We must not be apprehensive that any philosophical opinion will ever prejudice the religion of a country. Though our demonstrations clash directly with our mysteries, that's nothing to the purpose, for the latter are not less revered upon that account by our Christian philosophers, who know very well that objects of reason and those of faith are of a very different nature. Philosophers will never form a religious sect, the reason of which is, their writings are not calculated for the vulgar, and they themselves are free from enthusiasm. If we divide mankind into twenty parts, it will be found that nineteen of these consist of persons employed in manual labour, who will never know that such a man as Mr. Locke existed. In the remaining twentieth part how few are readers? And among such as are so, twenty amuse themselves with romances to one who studies philosophy. The thinking part of mankind are confined to a very small number, and these will never disturb the peace and tranquillity of the world.

Neither Montaigne, Locke, Bayle, Spinoza, Hobbes, Lord Shaftesbury, Collins nor Toland lightened up the firebrand of discord in their countries; this has generally been the work of divines, who, being at first puffed up with the ambition of becoming chiefs of a sect, soon grew very desirous of being at the head of a party. But what do I say? All the works of the modern philosophers put together will never make so much noise as even the dispute which arose among the Franciscans [a Catholic religious order] merely about the fashion of their sleeves and of their cowls.

Source: Peter Gay, ed., *The Enlightenment: A Comprehensive Anthology* (New York: Simon & Schuster, 1973), 166.

often published in the Dutch Republic, Britain, or Switzerland and smuggled back across the border to a public whose appetite was only whetted by censorship.

The Young Voltaire. The most influential writer of the early Enlightenment was a Frenchman born into the upper middle class, François-Marie Arouet, known by his pen name, **Voltaire** (1694–1778). Voltaire took inspiration from Bayle, noting: "He gives facts with such odious fidelity, he exposes the arguments for and against with such dastardly impartiality, he is so intolerably intelligible, that he leads people of only ordinary common sense to judge and even to doubt." In his early years, Voltaire suffered arrest, imprisonment, and exile, but he eventually achieved wealth and acclaim. His tangles with church and state began in the early 1730s, when he published his *Letters Concerning the English Nation* (the English version appeared in 1733), in which he devoted several chapters to Newton and Locke and used the virtues of the British as a way to attack Catholic bigotry and government rigidity in France (see Document, "Letters Concerning the English Nation," on this page). Impressed by British toleration of religious dissent (at least among Protestants), Voltaire spent two years in exile in Britain when the French state responded to his book with yet another order for his arrest.

Voltaire also popularized Newton's scientific discoveries in his *Elements of the Philosophy of Newton* (1738). The French state and many European theologians considered Newtonianism threatening because it glorified the human mind and seemed to reduce God to an abstract, external, rationalistic force. So sensational was the success of Voltaire's book on Newton that a hostile Jesuit reported, "The great Newton, was, it is said, buried in the abyss, in the shop of the first publisher who dared to print him. . . . M. de Voltaire finally appeared, and at once Newton is understood or is in the process of being understood; all Paris resounds with Newton, all Paris stammers Newton, all Paris studies and learns Newton." The

---

Voltaire: The pen name of François-Marie Arouet (1694–1778), who was the most influential writer of the early Enlightenment.

success was international, too. Before long, Voltaire was elected a fellow of the Royal Society in London and in Edinburgh, as well as to twenty other scientific academies. Voltaire's fame continued to grow, reaching truly astounding proportions in the 1750s and 1760s (see Chapter 18).

Travel Literature and the Challenge to Custom and Tradition

Just as scientific method could be used to question religious and even state authority, a more general skepticism also emerged from the expanding knowledge about the world outside of Europe. During the seventeenth and eighteenth centuries, the number of travel accounts dramatically increased as travel writers used the contrast between their home societies and other cultures to criticize the customs of European society.

Visitors to the new colonies sought something resembling "the state of nature," that is, ways of life that preceded sophisticated social and political organization—although they often misinterpreted different forms of society and politics as having no organization at all. Travelers to the Americas found "noble savages" (native peoples) who appeared to live in conditions of great freedom and equality; they were "naturally good" and "happy" without taxes, lawsuits, or much organized government. In China, in contrast, travelers found a people who enjoyed prosperity and an ancient civilization. Christian missionaries made little headway in China, and visitors had to admit that China's religious systems had flourished for four or five thousand years with no input from Europe or from Christianity. The basic lesson of travel literature in the 1700s, then, was that customs varied: justice, freedom, property, good government, religion, and morality all were relative to the place. One critic complained that travel encouraged free thinking and the destruction of religion: "Some complete their demoralization by extensive travel, and lose whatever shreds of religion remained to them. Every day they see a new religion, new customs, new rites."

Travel literature turned explicitly political in Montesquieu's *Persian Letters* (1721). Charles-Louis de Secondat, baron of Montesquieu (1689–1755), the son of an eminent judicial family, was a high-ranking judge in a French court. He published *Persian Letters* anonymously in the Dutch Republic, and the book went into ten printings in just one year—a best seller for the times. Montesquieu tells the story of two Persians, Rica and Usbek, who leave their country "for love of

knowledge" and travel to Europe. They visit France in the last years of Louis XIV's reign, writing of the king: "He has a minister who is only eighteen years old, and a mistress of eighty. . . . Although he avoids the bustle of towns, and is rarely seen in company, his one concern, from morning till night, is to get himself talked about." Other passages ridicule the pope. Beneath the satire, however, was a serious investigation into the foundation of good government and morality. Montesquieu chose Persians for his travelers because they came from what was widely considered the most despotic of all governments, in which rulers had life-and-death powers over their subjects. In the book, the Persians constantly compare France to Persia, suggesting that the French monarchy might verge on despotism.

The paradox of a judge publishing an anonymous work attacking the regime that employed him demonstrates the complications of the intellectual scene in this period. Montesquieu's anonymity did not last long, and soon Parisian society lionized him. In the late 1720s, he sold his judgeship and traveled extensively in Europe, staying eighteen months in Britain. In 1748, he published a widely influential work on comparative government, *The Spirit of Laws*. The Vatican soon listed both *Persian Letters* and *The Spirit of Laws* on its Index of forbidden books.

Raising the Woman Question

Many of the letters exchanged in *Persian Letters* focused on women, marriage, and the family because Montesquieu considered the position of women a sure indicator of the nature of government and morality. Although Montesquieu was not a feminist, his depiction of Roxana, the favorite wife in Usbek's harem, struck a chord with many women. Roxana revolts against the authority of Usbek's eunuchs and writes a final letter to her husband announcing her impending suicide: "I may have lived in servitude, but I have always been free, I have amended your laws according to the laws of nature, and my mind has always remained independent." Women writers used the same language of tyranny and freedom to argue for concrete changes in their status. Feminist ideas were not entirely new, but they were presented systematically for the first time during the Enlightenment and represented a fundamental challenge to the ways of traditional societies.

The most systematic of these women writers was the English author Mary Astell (1666–1731), the daughter of a businessman and herself a supporter of the Tory party and the Anglican religious establishment. In 1694, she published *A Serious Proposal to the Ladies*, in which she advocated founding a private women's college to remedy women's lack of education. Addressing women, she asked, "How can you be content to be in the World like Tulips in a Garden, to make a fine *shew* [show] and be good for nothing?" Astell argued for intellectual training based on Descartes's principles, in which reason, debate, and careful consideration of the issues took priority over custom or tradition. Her book was an immediate success: five printings appeared by 1701. In later works such as *Reflections upon Marriage* (1706), Astell criticized the relationship between the sexes within marriage: "If absolute sovereignty be not necessary in a state, how comes it to be so in a family? . . . *If all men are born free*, how is it that all women are born slaves?" Her critics accused her of promoting subversive ideas and of contradicting the Bible.

Astell's work inspired other women to write in a similar vein. The anonymous *Essay in Defence of the Female Sex* (1696) attacked "the Usurpation of Men; and the Tyranny of Custom," which prevented women from getting an education. In the introduction to the work of one of the best-known female poets, Elizabeth Singer Rowe, a friend of the author complained of the "notorious Violations on the Liberties of Freeborn English Women" that came from "a plain and an open design to render us meer [mere] Slaves, perfect Turkish Wives."

Most male writers unequivocally stuck to the traditional view of women, which held that women were less capable of reasoning than men and therefore did not need systematic education. Such opinions often rested on biological suppositions. The long-dominant Aristotelian view of reproduction held that only the male seed carried spirit and individuality. At the beginning of the eighteenth century, however, scientists began to undermine this belief. Physicians and surgeons began to champion the doctrine of *ovism* — that the female egg was essential in making new humans. During the decades that followed, male Enlightenment writers would continue to debate women's nature and appropriate social roles.

> **REVIEW:** What were the major issues in the early decades of the Enlightenment?

Conclusion

Europeans crossed a major threshold in the first half of the eighteenth century. They moved silently but nonetheless momentously from an economy governed by scarcity and the threat of famine to one of ever-increasing growth and the prospect of continuing improvement. Expansion of colonies overseas and economic development at home created greater wealth, longer life spans, and higher expectations for the future. In these better times for many, a spirit of optimism prevailed. People could now spend money on newspapers, novels, and travel literature as well as on coffee, tea, and cotton cloth. The growing literate public avidly followed the latest trends in religious debates, art, and music. Not everyone shared equally in the benefits, however: slaves toiled in misery for their masters in the Americas, eastern European serfs found themselves ever more closely bound to their noble lords, and rural folk almost everywhere tasted few fruits of consumer society.

Politics changed too as population and production increased and cities grew. Experts urged government intervention to improve public health, and states found it in their interest to settle many international disputes by diplomacy, which itself became more regular and routine. The consolidation of the European state system allowed a tide of criticism and new thinking about society to swell in Great Britain and France and begin to spill throughout Europe. Ultimately, the combination of the Atlantic system and the Enlightenment would give rise to a series of Atlantic revolutions.

FOR FURTHER EXPLORATION

- **For suggested references, including Web sites, for topics in this chapter,** see page SR-1 at the end of the book.

- **For additional primary-source material from this period,** see Chapter 17 in *Sources of THE MAKING OF THE WEST*, Third Edition.

- **For Web sites and documents related to topics in this chapter,** see *Make History* at bedfordstmartins.com/hunt.

MAPPING THE WEST

Europe in 1740

By 1740, Europe had achieved a kind of diplomatic equilibrium in which no one power predominated. But the relative balance should not deflect attention from important underlying changes: Spain, the Dutch Republic, Poland-Lithuania, and Sweden had all declined in power and influence while Great Britain, Russia, Prussia, and Austria had solidified their positions, each in a different way. France's ambitions had been thwarted, but its combination of a big army and rich overseas possessions made it a major player for a long time to come.

CHAPTER REVIEW

KEY TERMS AND PEOPLE

Atlantic system (520)

plantation (521)

mestizo (527)

buccaneers (527)

consumer revolution (528)

agricultural revolution (529)

rococo (534)

Pietism (536)

Peace of Utrecht (538)

Robert Walpole (539)

Peter the Great (540)

Westernization (540)

Enlightenment (545)

Voltaire (548)

MAKING CONNECTIONS

1. How did the rise of slavery and the plantation system change European politics and society?

2. Why was the Enlightenment born just at the moment that the Atlantic system took shape?

3. What were the major differences between the wars of the first half of the eighteenth century and those of the seventeenth century? (Refer to Chapters 15 and 16.)

> **For practice quizzes, a customized study plan, and other study tools,** see the Online Study Guide at bedfordstmartins.com/hunt.

REVIEW QUESTIONS

1. How was consumerism related to slavery in the early eighteenth century?

2. How were new social trends reflected in cultural life in the late 1600s and early 1700s?

3. What events and developments led to greater stability and less warfare in the European state system?

4. What were the major issues in the early decades of the Enlightenment?

IMPORTANT EVENTS

1690s	Beginning of rapid development of plantations in Caribbean
1694	Bank of England established; Mary Astell's *A Serious Proposal to the Ladies* argues for the founding of a private women's college
1697	Pierre Bayle publishes *Historical and Critical Dictionary,* detailing errors of religious writers
1699	Turks forced to recognize Habsburg rule over Hungary and Transylvania
1703	Peter the Great begins construction of St. Petersburg, founds first Russian newspaper
1713–1714	Peace of Utrecht
1714	Elector of Hanover becomes King George I of England
1715	Death of Louis XIV
1719	Daniel Defoe publishes *Robinson Crusoe*
1720	Last outbreak of bubonic plague in western Europe
1721	Treaty of Nystad; Montesquieu publishes *Persian Letters* anonymously in the Dutch Republic
1733	War of the Polish Succession; Voltaire's *Letters Concerning the English Nation* attacks French intolerance and narrow-mindedness
1741	George Frideric Handel composes *Messiah*

The Promise of Enlightenment
1740 — 1789

In the summer of 1766, Empress Catherine II ("the Great") of Russia wrote to Voltaire, one of the leaders of the Enlightenment:

> It is a way of immortalizing oneself to be the advocate of humanity, the defender of oppressed innocence. . . . You have entered into combat against the enemies of mankind: superstition, fanaticism, ignorance, quibbling, evil judges, and the powers that rest in their hands. Great virtues and qualities are needed to surmount these obstacles. You have shown that you have them: you have triumphed.

Over a fifteen-year period, Catherine corresponded regularly with Voltaire, a writer who, at home in France, found himself in constant conflict with authorities of church and state. Her admiring letter shows how influential Enlightenment ideals had become by the middle of the eighteenth century. Even an absolutist ruler such as Catherine endorsed many aspects of the Enlightenment call for reform; she too wanted to be an "advocate of humanity."

Catherine's letter aptly summed up Enlightenment ideals: progress for humanity could be achieved only by rooting out the wrongs left by superstition, religious fanaticism, ignorance, and outmoded forms of justice. Enlightenment writers used every means at their disposal — from encyclopedias to novels to personal interaction with rulers — to argue for reform. Everything had to be examined in the cold light of reason, and anything that did not promote the improvement of humanity was to be jettisoned. As a result, Enlightenment writers attacked the legal use of torture to extract confessions, supported religious toleration, favored the spread of education to eliminate ignorance, and criticized censorship by state or church. The book trade and new places for urban

Catherine the Great
In this portrait by the Danish painter Vigilius Eriksen, the Russian empress Catherine the Great is shown on horseback (c. 1762), much like any male ruler of the time. Born Sophia Augusta Frederika of Anhalt-Zerbst in 1729, Catherine was the daughter of a minor German prince. When she married the future tsar Peter III in 1745, she promptly learned Russian and adopted Russian Orthodoxy. Peter, physically and mentally frail, proved no match for her; in 1762 she staged a coup against him and took his place when he was killed. *(Erich Lessing/Art Resource, NY.)*

socializing, such as coffeehouses and learned societies, spread these ideas within a new elite of middle- and upper-class men and women.

The lower classes had little contact with Enlightenment ideas. Their lives were shaped more profoundly by an increasing population, rising food prices, and ongoing wars among the great powers. States had to balance conflicting social pressures: rulers pursued Enlightenment reforms that they believed might enhance state power, but they feared changes that might unleash popular discontent. For example, Catherine aimed to bring Western ideas, culture, and reforms to Russia, but when faced with a massive uprising of the serfs, she not only suppressed the revolt but also increased the powers of the nobles over their serfs. All reform-minded rulers faced similar potential challenges to their authority.

Even if the movement for reform had its limits, governments now needed to respond to a new force: "public opinion." Rulers wanted to portray themselves as modern, open to change, and responsive to the segment of the public that was reading newspapers and closely following political developments. Enlightenment writers appealed to public opinion, but they still looked to rulers to effect reform. Writers such as Voltaire expressed little interest in the future of peasants or the lower classes; they favored neither revolution nor political upheaval. Yet their ideas paved the way for something much more radical and unexpected. The American Declaration of Independence in 1776 showed how Enlightenment ideals could be translated into democratic political practice. After 1789, democracy would come to Europe as well.

FOCUS QUESTION: How did the Enlightenment influence Western politics, culture, and society?

The Enlightenment at Its Height

The Enlightenment emerged as an intellectual movement before 1740 but reached its peak in the second half of the eighteenth century. (See "Terms of History," page 565.) The writers of the Enlightenment called themselves **philosophes** (French for "philosophers"), but that term is somewhat misleading. Whereas philosophers concern themselves with abstract theories, the philosophes were public intellectuals dedicated to solving the real problems of the world. They wrote on subjects ranging from current affairs to art criticism, and they wrote in every conceivable format. The Swiss philosophe Jean-Jacques Rousseau, for example, wrote a political tract, a treatise on education, a constitution for Poland, an analysis of the effects of the theater on public morals, a best-selling novel, an opera, and a notorious autobiography. The philosophes wrote for a broad educated public of readers who snatched up every Enlightenment book they could find at their local booksellers, even when rulers or churches tried to forbid such works. Between 1740 and 1789, the Enlightenment acquired its name and, despite heated conflicts between the philosophes and state and religious authorities, gained support in the highest reaches of government.

Men and Women of the Republic of Letters

Although *philosophe* is a French word, the Enlightenment was distinctly cosmopolitan; philosophes could be found from Philadelphia to St. Petersburg.

---

philosophes (fee luh SAWF): Public intellectuals of the Enlightenment who wrote on subjects ranging from current affairs to art criticism with the goal of furthering reform in society. (The word in French means "philosophers.")

■ 1740–1748 War of the Austrian Succession

■ 1756–1763 Seven Years' War

| 1740 | 1750 | 1760 |

■ 1751–1772 Enlightenment writers publish *Encyclopedia*

■ 1762 Rousseau, *The Social Contract, Émile*

The philosophes considered themselves part of a grand "republic of letters" that transcended national political boundaries. They were not republicans in the usual sense, that is, people who supported representative government and opposed monarchy. What united them were the ideals of reason, reform, and freedom. In 1784, the German philosopher Immanuel Kant summed up the program of the Enlightenment in two Latin words: *sapere aude*, "dare to know" — have the courage to think for yourself.

The philosophes used reason to attack superstition, bigotry, and religious fanaticism, which they considered the chief obstacles to free thought and social reform. Voltaire took religious fanaticism as his chief target: "Once fanaticism has corrupted a mind, the malady is almost incurable. . . . The only remedy for this epidemic malady is the philosophical spirit." Enlightenment writers did not necessarily oppose organized religion, but they strenuously objected to religious intolerance. They believed that the systematic application of reason could do what religious belief could not: improve the human condition by pointing to needed reforms. Reason meant critical, informed, scientific thinking about social issues and problems. Many Enlightenment writers collaborated on a new multivolume *Encyclopedia* (published 1751–1772) that aimed to gather together knowledge about science, religion, industry, and society (see illustration at right). The chief editor of the *Encyclopedia*, Denis Diderot (1713–1784), explained the goal: "All things must be examined, debated, investigated without exception and without regard for anyone's feelings." (See Document, "Denis Diderot, 'Encyclopedia,'" page 559.)

Bookbinding

In this plate from the *Encyclopedia*, the various stages in bookbinding are laid out from left to right. Binding was not included in the sale of books; owners had to order leather bindings from a special shop. The man at (a) is pounding the pages to be bound on a marble block. The woman at (b) is stitching the pages with a special frame. The worker at (c) cuts the pages, and the one at (d) presses the volumes to prevent warping. In what ways is this illustration representative of the aims of the *Encyclopedia*?

The philosophes believed that the spread of knowledge would encourage reform in every aspect of life, from the grain trade to the penal system. Chief among their desired reforms was intellectual freedom — the freedom to use one's own reason and to publish the results. The philosophes wanted freedom of the press and freedom of religion, which they considered "natural rights" guaranteed by "natural law." In their view, progress depended on these freedoms.

Most philosophes, like Voltaire, came from the upper classes, yet Rousseau's father was a modest watchmaker in Geneva, and Diderot was the son of a cutlery maker. Although it was a rare

---

■ 1776 American Declaration of Independence; Smith, *Wealth of Nations*

■ 1787 U.S. Constitution

■ 1771 Louis XV attempts major court reform

■ 1785 Charter of the Nobility

1770   **1780**   **1790**

■ 1764 Voltaire, *Philosophical Dictionary*

■ 1772 First Partition of Poland

■ 1780 Joseph II's reforms

■ 1773 Pugachev rebellion

■ 1781 Kant, *The Critique of Pure Reason*

Madame Geoffrin's Salon in 1755
This 1812 painting by Anicet Charles Lemonnier claims to depict the best-known Parisian salon of the 1750s. Lemonnier was only twelve years old in 1755 and so could not have based his rendition on firsthand knowledge. Madame Geoffrin is the figure in blue on the right facing the viewer. The bust is of Voltaire. Rousseau is the fifth person to the left of the bust (facing right) and behind him (facing left) is Raynal. *(Bridgeman–Giraudon/Art Resource, NY.)*

phenomenon, some women were philosophes, such as the French noblewoman Émilie du Châtelet (1706–1749), who wrote extensively about the mathematics and physics of Gottfried Wilhelm Leibniz and Isaac Newton. (Her lover Voltaire learned much of his science from her.) Few of the leading writers held university positions, except those who were German or Scottish. Universities in France were dominated by the Catholic clergy and unreceptive to Enlightenment ideals.

Enlightenment ideas developed instead through printed books and pamphlets; through letters that were hand-copied, circulated, and sometimes published; and through informal readings of manuscripts. Salons — informal gatherings, usually sponsored by middle-class or aristocratic women — gave intellectual life an anchor outside the royal court and the church-controlled universities. Seventeenth-century salons had been tame affairs. In the Parisian salons of the eighteenth century, in contrast, the philosophes could discuss ideas they might hesitate to put into print, testing public opinion and even pushing it in new directions. Best known was the Parisian salon of Madame Marie-Thérèse Geoffrin (1699–1777), a wealthy middle-class widow who had been raised by her grandmother and married off at fourteen to a much older man (see Madame Geoffrin's Salon, above). She brought together the most exciting thinkers and artists of the time and provided a forum for new ideas and an opportunity to establish new intellectual contacts. Madame Geoffrin corresponded extensively with influential people across

Europe, including Catherine the Great. One Italian visitor commented, "There is no way to make Naples resemble Paris unless we find a woman to guide us, organize us, *Geoffrinize* us."

Women's salons provoked criticism from men who resented their power. (See "Contrasting Views," page 562.) Nevertheless, the gatherings helped galvanize intellectual life and reform movements all over Europe. Wealthy Jewish women created nine of the fourteen salons in Berlin at the end of the eighteenth century, and Princess Zofia Czartoryska gathered around her in Warsaw the reform leaders of Poland-Lithuania. Some of the aristocratic women in Madrid who held salons had lived in France, and they combined an interest in French culture and ideas with their efforts to promote the new ideas in Spain. Middle-class women in London used their salons to raise money to publish women's writings. Salons could be tied closely to the circles of power: in France, for example, Louis XV's mistress, Jeanne-Antoinette Poisson, first made her reputation as hostess of a salon frequented by Voltaire and Montesquieu. When she became Louis XV's mistress in 1745, she gained the title Marquise de Pompadour and turned her attention to influencing artistic styles by patronizing architects and painters.

Conflicts with Church and State

Madame Geoffrin did not approve of discussions that attacked the Catholic church, but elsewhere voices against organized religion could be heard.

DOCUMENT

Denis Diderot, "Encyclopedia" (1755)

Denis Diderot (1713–1784) led the multinational team that produced the Encyclopedia, *a work much more radical in its aims than its bland name suggests. Seventeen volumes of text and eleven volumes of illustrative plates were published between 1751 and 1772, despite the efforts of French authorities to censor it. The volumes covered every branch of human knowledge from the tools of artisans to the finest points of theology. Diderot and his collaborators used the occasion to lay out the principles of the Enlightenment as an intellectual movement and to challenge the authority, in particular, of the Catholic church. The article "Encyclopedia" summarized the goals of the project.*

ENCYCLOPEDIA (Philosophy). This word means the *interrelation of all knowledge*; it is made up of the Greek prefix *en*, in, and the nouns *kyklos*, circle, and *paideia*, instruction, science, knowledge. In truth, the aim of an *encyclopedia* is to collect all the knowledge scattered over the face of the earth, to present its general outlines and structure to the men with whom we live, and transmit this to those who will come after us, so that the work of the past centuries may be useful to the following centuries, that our children, by becoming more educated, may at the same time become more virtuous and happier, and that we may not die without having deserved well of the human race. . . .

We have seen that our *Encyclopedia* could only have been the endeavor of a philosophical century; that this age has dawned, and that fame, while raising to immortality the names of those who will perfect man's knowledge in the future, will perhaps not disdain to remember our own names. . . .

I have said that it could only belong to a philosophical age to attempt an *encyclopedia*; and I have said this because such a work constantly demands more intellectual daring than is commonly found in ages of pusillanimous [timid] taste. All things must be examined, debated, investigated without exception and without regard for anyone's feelings. . . . We must ride roughshod over all these ancient puerilities, overturn the barriers that reason never erected, give back to the arts and sciences the liberty that is so precious to them. . . . We have for quite some time needed a reasoning age when men would no longer seek the rules in classical authors but in nature.

Source: Margaret C. Jacob, *The Enlightenment: A Brief History with Documents* (Boston: Bedford/St. Martin's, 2001), 157–158.

Criticisms of religion required daring because the church, whatever its denomination, wielded enormous power in society, and most influential people considered religion an essential foundation of good society and government. Defying such opinion, the Scottish philosopher David Hume (1711–1776) boldly argued in *The Natural History of Religion* (1755) that belief in God rested on superstition and fear rather than on reason. Hume soon met kindred spirits while visiting Paris; he attended a dinner party consisting of "fifteen atheists, and three who had not quite made up their minds."

In the eighteenth century, most Europeans believed in God. After Newton, however, and despite Newton's own deep religiosity, people could conceive of the universe as an eternally existing, self-perpetuating machine, in which God's intervention was unnecessary. In short, such people could become either *atheists*, people who do not believe in God, or *deists*, people who believe in God but give him no active role in earthly affairs. For the first time, writers claimed the label *atheist* and disputed the common view that atheism led inevitably to immorality.

Deists continued to believe in a benevolent, all-knowing God who had designed the universe and set it in motion. But they usually rejected the idea that God directly intercedes in the functioning of the universe, and they often criticized the churches for their dogmatic intolerance of dissenters. Voltaire was a deist, and in his influential *Philosophical Dictionary* (1764) he attacked most of the claims of organized Christianity, both Catholic and Protestant. Christianity, he argued, had been the prime source of fanaticism and brutality among humans. Throughout his life, Voltaire's motto was *Écrasez l'infâme*— "Crush the infamous thing" (the "thing" being bigotry and intolerance). French authorities publicly burned his *Philosophical Dictionary*.

Criticism of religious intolerance involved more than simply attacking the churches. Critics also had to confront the states to which churches were closely tied. In 1762, a judicial case in

---

deists: Those who believe in God but give him no active role in human affairs. Deists of the Enlightenment believed that God had designed the universe and set it in motion but no longer intervened in its functioning.

Toulouse provoked an outcry throughout France that Voltaire soon joined. When the son of a local Calvinist was found hanged (he had probably committed suicide), magistrates accused the father, Jean Calas, of murdering him to prevent his conversion to Catholicism. (Since Louis XIV's revocation of the Edict of Nantes in 1685, it had been illegal to practice Calvinism publicly in France.) The all-Catholic parlement of Toulouse tried to extract the names of accomplices through torture — using a rope to pull up Calas's arm while weighing down his feet and then pouring water down his throat — and then executed him by breaking every bone in his body with an iron rod. Calas refused to confess. Voltaire launched a successful crusade to rehabilitate Calas's good name and to restore the family's properties, which had been confiscated after his death. Voltaire's efforts eventually helped bring about the extension of civil rights to French Protestants and encouraged campaigns to abolish the judicial use of torture.

Critics also assailed state and church support for European colonization and slavery. One of the most popular books of the time was the *Philosophical and Political History of European Colonies and Commerce in the Two Indies*, published in 1770 by Abbé Guillaume Raynal (1713–1796), a French Catholic clergyman. Raynal and his collaborators described in excruciating detail the destruction of native populations by Europeans and denounced the slave trade. Despite the criticism, the slave trade continued. So did European exploration. British explorer James Cook (1728–1779) charted the coasts of New Zealand and Australia, discovered New Caledonia, and visited the ice fields of Antarctica.

Cook's adventures captivated European readers. When he arrived on the Kona coast of Hawaii in 1779, Cook thought that the natives considered him godlike, but in a confrontation he fired and killed a man, provoking an attack that led to his death and those of some of his men. Like Cook, many Enlightenment writers held conflicting views of natives: to some, they were innocent because primitive, but to others they seemed untrustworthy because savage. Views of Africans could be especially negative. David Hume, for example, judged blacks to be "naturally inferior to the whites," concluding, "There never was a civilized nation of any other complexion than white."

Nevertheless, the Enlightenment belief in natural rights helped fuel the antislavery movement, which began to organize political campaigns against slavery in Britain, France, and the new United States in the 1780s. Advocates of the abo-

lition of slavery encouraged freed slaves to write the story of their enslavement. One such freed slave, Olaudah Equiano, wrote of his kidnapping and enslavement in Africa and his long effort to free himself. *The Interesting Narrative of the Life of Olaudah Equiano*, published in 1788, became an international best seller; it had appeared in English, Dutch, Russian, and French by the time Equiano died in 1797. Armed with such firsthand accounts of slavery, **abolitionists** began to petition their governments for the abolition of the slave trade and then of slavery itself.

Enlightenment critics of church and state usually advocated reform, not revolution. For example, though he resided near the French-Swiss border in case he had to flee, Voltaire made a fortune in financial speculations and ended up being celebrated in his last years as a national hero even by many former foes. Other philosophes also believed that published criticism, rather than violent action, would bring about necessary reforms. As Diderot said, "We will speak against senseless laws until they are reformed; and, while we wait, we will abide by them." The philosophes generally regarded the lower classes — "the people" — as ignorant, violent, and prone to superstition; as a result, they pinned their hopes on educated elites and enlightened rulers.

Despite the philosophes' preference for reform, in the long run their books often had a revolutionary impact. For example, Montesquieu's widely reprinted *Spirit of the Laws* (1748) warned against the dangers of despotism, opposed the divine right of kings, and favored constitutional government. His analysis of British constitutionalism inspired French critics of absolutism and would greatly influence the American revolutionaries.

The Individual and Society

The controversy created by the conflicts between the philosophes and the various churches and states of Europe drew attention away from a subtle but profound transformation in worldviews. In previous centuries, questions of theological doctrine and church organization had been the main focus of intellectual and even political interest. The Enlightenment writers shifted attention away from religious questions and toward the secular study of society and the individual's role in it. Religion did not drop out of sight, but the philosophes tended to make religion a private affair of individ-

---

abolitionists: Advocates of the abolition of the slave trade and of slavery.

ual conscience, even while rulers and churches still considered religion very much a public concern.

The Enlightenment interest in secular society produced two major results: it advanced the secularization of European political life that had begun after the Wars of Religion of the sixteenth and seventeenth centuries, and it laid the foundations for the social sciences of the modern era. Not surprisingly, then, many historians and philosophers consider the Enlightenment to be the origin of modernity, which they define as the belief that human reason, rather than theological doctrine, should set the patterns of social and political life. This belief in reason as the sole foundation for secular authority has often been contested, but it has also proved to be a powerful force for change.

Although most of the philosophes believed that human reason could understand and even remake society and politics, they disagreed about what reason revealed. Among the many different approaches were two that proved enduringly influential, those of the Scottish philosopher Adam Smith and the Swiss writer Jean-Jacques Rousseau. Smith provided a theory of modern capitalist society and devoted much of his energy to defending free markets as the best way to make the most of individual efforts. The modern discipline of economics took shape around the questions raised by Smith. Rousseau, by contrast, emphasized the needs of the community over those of the individual. His work, which led both toward democracy and toward communism, continues to inspire heated debate in political science and sociology.

Adam Smith.   Adam Smith (1723–1790) optimistically believed that individual interests naturally harmonized with those of the whole society. To explain how this natural harmonization worked, he published *An Inquiry into the Nature and Causes of the Wealth of Nations* in 1776. Smith insisted that individual self-interest, even greed, was quite compatible with society's best interest: the laws of supply and demand served as an "invisible hand" ensuring that individual interests would be synchronized with those of the whole society. Market forces—"the propensity to truck, barter, and exchange one thing for another"—naturally brought individual and social interests in line.

Smith rejected the prevailing mercantilist views that the general welfare would be served by accumulating national wealth through agriculture or the hoarding of gold and silver. Instead, he argued that the division of labor in manufacturing increased productivity and generated more wealth

for society and well-being for the individual. In his much-cited example of the manufacture of pins, Smith showed that when the manufacturing process was broken down into separate operations—one man to draw out the wire, another to straighten it, a third to cut it, a fourth to point it, and so on—workers who could make only one pin a day on their own could make thousands by pooling their labor.

To maximize the effects of market forces and the division of labor, Smith endorsed a concept called **laissez-faire** (that is, "to leave alone") to free the economy from government intervention and control. He insisted that governments eliminate all restrictions on the sale of land, remove restraints on the grain trade, and abandon duties on imports. Free international trade, he argued, would stimulate production everywhere and thus ensure the growth of national wealth: "The natural effort of every individual to better his own condition, when suffered to exert itself with freedom and security, is so powerful a principle that it is alone, and without any assistance, not only capable of carrying the society to wealth and prosperity, but of surmounting a hundred impertinent obstructions with which the folly of human laws too often encumbers its operations." Governments should restrict themselves to providing "security," that is, national defense, internal order, and public works. Smith recognized that government had an important role in providing a secure framework for market activity, but he placed most emphasis on freeing individual endeavor from what he saw as excessive government interference.

Jean-Jacques Rousseau.   Much more pessimistic about the relation between individual self-interest and the good of society was **Jean-Jacques Rousseau** (1712–1778). In Rousseau's view, society itself threatened natural rights or freedoms: "Man is born free, and everywhere he is in chains." Rousseau first gained fame by writing a prize-winning essay in 1749 in which he argued that the revival of science and the arts had corrupted social morals, not improved them. This startling conclusion seemed to oppose some of the Enlightenment's most cherished beliefs. Rather than

---

laissez-faire (LEH say FEHR): An economic doctrine developed by Adam Smith that advocated freeing the economy from government intervention and control. (The term is French for "to leave alone.")

Jean-Jacques Rousseau (zhahn zhahk roo SOH): One of the most important philosophes (1712–1778); he argued that only a government based on a social contract among the citizens could make people truly moral and free.

Women and the Enlightenment

During the Enlightenment, women's roles in society became the subject of heated debates. Some men resented what they saw as the growing power of women, especially in the salons. Rousseau railed against their corrupting influence: "Every woman at Paris gathers in her apartment a harem of men more womanish than she." Rousseau's Émile (Document 1) offered his own influential answer to the question of how women should be educated. The Encyclopedia ignored the contributions of salon women and praised women who stayed at home; in the words of one typical contributor, women "constitute the principal ornament of the world. . . . May they, through submissive discretion and through simple, adroit, artless cleverness, spur us [men] on to virtue." Many women objected to these characterizations. The editor of a prominent newspaper for women, Madame de Beaumer, wrote editorials blasting the masculine sense of superiority (Document 2). Many prominent women writers specifically targeted Rousseau's book because it proved to be the most influential educational treatise of the time (Document 3). Their ideas formed the core of nineteenth-century feminism.

1. Jean-Jacques Rousseau, *Émile* (1762)

Rousseau used the character of Émile's wife-to-be, Sophie, to discuss his ideas about women's education. Sophie is educated for a domestic role as wife and mother, and she is taught to be obedient, always helpful to her husband and family, and removed from any participation in the public world. Despite his insistence on the differences between men's and women's roles, many women enthusiastically embraced Rousseau's ideas, for he placed great emphasis on maternal affections, breast-feeding, and child rearing. Rousseau's own children, however, suffered the contradictions that characterized his life. By his own admission, he abandoned to a foundling hospital all the children he had by his lower-class common-law wife

because he did not think he could support them properly; if their fate was like that of most abandoned children of the day, they met an early death.

There is no parity between man and woman as to the importance of sex. The male is only a male at certain moments; the female all her life, or at least throughout her youth, is incessantly reminded of her sex and in order to carry out its functions she needs a corresponding constitution. She needs to be careful during pregnancy; she needs rest after childbirth; she needs a quiet and sedentary life while she nurses her children; she needs patience and gentleness in order to raise them; a zeal and affection that nothing can discourage. . . .

On the good constitution of mothers depends primarily that of the children; on the care of women depends the early education of men; and on women, again, depend their morals, their passions, their tastes, their pleasures, and even their happiness. Thus the whole education of women ought to be relative to men. To please them, to be useful to them, to make themselves loved and honored by them, to educate them when young, to care for them when grown, to counsel them, to console them, and to make life agreeable and sweet to them — these are the duties of women at all times, and should be taught them from their infancy.

Source: Susan Groag Bell and Karen M. Offen, *Women, the Family, and Freedom: The Debate in Documents*, vol. 1, *1750–1880* (Stanford: Stanford University Press, 1983), 46–49.

2. Madame de Beaumer, Editorial in *Le Journal des Dames* (1762)

Madame de Beaumer (d. 1766) was the first of three women editors of Le Journal des Dames *(The Ladies' Journal). She ran it for*

improving society, he claimed, science and art raised artificial barriers between people and their natural state. Rousseau's works extolled the simplicity of rural life over urban society. Although he participated in the salons, Rousseau always felt ill at ease in high society, and he periodically withdrew to live in solitude far from Paris. Paradoxically, his solitude was often paid for by wealthy upper-class patrons who lodged him on their estates, even as his writings decried the upper-class privilege that made his efforts possible.

Rousseau explored the tension between the individual and society in a best-selling novel (*The New Heloise*, 1761); in an influential work on education (*Émile*, 1762); and in a treatise on

political theory (*The Social Contract*, 1762). He wrote *Émile* in the form of a novel in order to make his educational theories easily comprehensible. Free from the supervision of the clergy, who controlled most schools, the boy Émile works alone with his tutor to develop practical skills and independent ways of thinking. After developing his individuality, Émile joins society through marriage to Sophie, who received the education Rousseau thought appropriate for women. (See "Contrasting Views," above.)

Whereas earlier Rousseau had argued that society corrupted the individual by taking him out of nature, in *The Social Contract* he aimed to show that the right kind of political order could make *two years and published many editorials defending women against their male critics.*

The success of the *Journal des Dames* allows us to triumph over those frivolous persons who have regarded this periodical as a petty work containing only a few bagatelles suited to help them kill time. In truth, Gentlemen, you do us much honor to think that we could not provide things that unite the useful to the agreeable. To rid you of your error, we have made our Journal historical, with a view to putting before the eyes of youth striking images that will guide them toward virtue. . . . An historical *Journal des Dames*! these Gentlemen reasoners reply. How ridiculous! How out of character with the nature of this work, which calls only for little pieces to amuse [ladies] during their toilette. . . . Please, Gentlemen *beaux esprits* [wits], mind your own business and let us write in a manner worthy of our sex; I love this sex, I am jealous to uphold its honor and its rights. If we have not been raised up in the sciences as you have, it is you who are the guilty ones.

Source: Bell and Offen, 27–28.

3. Catharine Macaulay, *Letters on Education* (1787)

Catharine Sawbridge Macaulay-Graham (1731–1791) was one of the best-known English writers of the 1700s. She wrote immensely popular histories of England and also joined in the debate provoked by Rousseau's Émile.

There is another prejudice . . . which affects yet more deeply female happiness, and female importance; a prejudice, which ought ever to have been confined to the regions of the east, because [of the] state of slavery to which female nature in that part of the world has been ever subjected, and can only suit with the notion of a positive inferiority in the intellectual powers of the female mind. You will soon perceive, that the prejudice which I mean, is that degrading difference in the culture of the understanding, which has prevailed for several centuries in all European societies. . . .

Among the most strenuous asserters of a sexual difference in character, Rousseau is the most conspicuous, both on account of that warmth of sentiment which distinguishes all his writing, and the eloquence of his compositions: but never did enthusiasm and the love of paradox, those enemies of philosophical disquisition, appear in more strong opposition to plain sense than in Rousseau's definition of this difference. He sets out with a supposition, that Nature intended the subjection of the one sex to the other; that consequently there must be an inferiority of intellect in the subjected party; but as man is a very imperfect being, and apt to play the capricious tyrant, Nature, to bring things nearer to an equality, bestowed on the woman such attractive graces, and such an insinuating address, as to turn the balance on the other scale. . . .

The situation and education of women . . . is precisely that which must necessarily tend to corrupt and debilitate both the powers of mind and body. From a false notion of beauty and delicacy, their system of nerves is depraved before they come out of the nursery; and this kind of depravity has more influence over the mind, and consequently over morals, than is commonly apprehended.

Source: Bell and Offen, 54–55.

QUESTIONS TO CONSIDER
1. Why would women in the eighteenth century read Rousseau with such interest and even enthusiasm?
2. Why does Madame de Beaumer address herself to male readers if the *Journal des Dames* is intended for women?
3. Why would Macaulay focus so much of her analysis on Rousseau? Why does she not just ignore him?
4. Was the Enlightenment intended only for men?

people truly moral and free. Individual moral freedom could be achieved only by learning to subject one's individual interests to "the general will," that is, the good of the community. Individuals did this by entering into a social contract not with their rulers, but with one another. If everyone followed the general will, then all would be equally free and equally moral because they lived under a law to which they had all consented.

These arguments threatened the legitimacy of eighteenth-century governments. Rousseau derived his social contract from human nature, not from history, tradition, or the Bible. He implied that people would be most free and moral under a republican form of government with direct democracy, and his abstract model included no reference to differences in social status. He roundly condemned slavery: "To decide that the son of a slave is born a slave is to decide that he is not born a man." Not surprisingly, authorities in both Geneva and Paris banned *The Social Contract* for undermining political authority. Rousseau's works would become a kind of political bible for the French revolutionaries of 1789, and his attacks on private property inspired the communists of the nineteenth century such as Karl Marx. Rousseau's rather mystical concept of the general will remains controversial. The "greatest good of all," according to Rousseau, was liberty combined with equality, but he also insisted that the individual could be

Jean-Jacques Rousseau
This eighteenth-century engraving of Rousseau shows him in his favorite place, outside in nature, where he walks, reads, and in this case collects plants. Rousseau claimed that he came to his most important insights while taking long walks, and in *Émile* he underlines the importance of physical activity for children. *(© Private Collection/The Bridgeman Art Library.)*

the *Decline and Fall of the Roman Empire* (1776–1788), in which he portrayed Christianity in a negative light, but when he served as a Member of Parliament he never even gave a speech. At the other extreme, in places with small middle classes, such as Spain and Russia, Enlightenment ideas did not get much traction because governments successfully suppressed writings they did not like. France was the Enlightenment hot spot because the French monarchy alternated between encouraging ideas for reform and harshly censuring criticisms it found too threatening.

The French Enlightenment.
French writers published the most daring critiques of church and state and often suffered harassment and persecution as a result. Voltaire, Diderot, and Rousseau all faced arrest, exile, or even imprisonment. The Catholic church and royal authorities routinely forbade the publication of their books, and the police arrested booksellers who ignored the warnings. Yet the French monarchy was far from the most autocratic in Europe, and Voltaire, Diderot, and Rousseau all ended their lives as cultural heroes. France seems to have been curiously caught in the middle during the Enlightenment: with fewer constitutional guarantees of individual freedom than Great Britain, it still enjoyed much higher levels of prosperity and cultural development than most other European countries. In short, French elites had reason to complain, the means to make their complaints known, and a government torn between the desires to censor dissident ideas and to appear open to modernity and progress. The French government controlled publishing—all books had to get official permissions—but not as tightly as in Spain, where the Catholic Inquisition made up its own list of banned books, or in Russia, where Catherine the Great allowed no opposition.

"forced to be free" by the terms of the social contract. He provided no legal protections for individual rights. In other words, Rousseau's version of democracy did not preserve the individual freedoms so important to Adam Smith.

Spreading the Enlightenment

The Enlightenment flourished in places where an educated middle class provided an eager audience for ideas of constitutionalism and reform. It therefore found its epicenter in the triangle formed by London, Amsterdam, and Paris and diffused outward to eastern and southern Europe and North America. Where constitutionalism and the guarantee of individual freedoms were most advanced, as in Great Britain and the Dutch Republic, the movement had less of an edge because there was, in a sense, less need for it. John Locke had already written extensively about constitutionalism in the 1690s. As a result, Scottish and English writers concentrated on economics, philosophy, and history rather than on politics or social relations. The English historian Edward Gibbon, for example, published an immensely influential *History of*

By the 1760s, the French government regularly ignored the publication of many works once thought offensive or subversive. In addition, a growing flood of works printed abroad poured into France and circulated underground. Private companies in Dutch and Swiss cities made fortunes smuggling illegal books into France over mountain passes and back roads. Foreign printers provided secret catalogs of their offerings and sold their products through booksellers who were willing to market forbidden books for a high price — among them not only philosophical treatises of the Enlightenment but also pornographic books and pamphlets (some by Diderot) lampooning the Catholic clergy and leading members of the royal court. In the 1770s and 1780s, lurid descriptions of sexual promiscuity at the French court helped undermine the popularity of the throne.

The German Enlightenment.   Whereas the French philosophes often took a violently anticlerical and combative tone, their German counterparts avoided direct political confrontations with authorities. Gotthold Lessing (1729–1781) complained in 1769 that Prussia was still "the most slavish society in Europe" in its lack of freedom to criticize government policies. As a playwright, literary critic, and philosopher, Lessing promoted religious toleration for the Jews and spiritual emancipation of Germans from foreign, especially French, models of culture, which still dominated. Lessing also introduced the German Jewish writer Moses Mendelssohn (1729–1786) into Berlin salon society. Mendelssohn labored to build bridges between German and Jewish culture by arguing that Judaism was a rational and undogmatic religion. He believed that persecution and discrimination against the Jews would end as reason triumphed.

Reason was also the chief focus of the most influential German thinker of the Enlightenment, Immanuel Kant (1724–1804). A university professor who lectured on everything from economics to astronomy, Kant wrote one of the most important works in the history of Western philosophy, *The Critique of Pure Reason* (1781). Kant admired Adam Smith and especially Rousseau, whose portrait he displayed proudly in his lodgings. Just as Smith founded modern economics and Rousseau modern political theory, Kant in *The Critique of Pure Reason* set the foundations for modern philosophy. In this complex book, Kant established the doctrine of idealism, the belief that true understanding can come only from examining the ways in which ideas are formed in the mind. Ideas are shaped, Kant argued, not just by sensory information (a position central to empiricism, a philosophy based on John Locke's writings) but also by the operation on that information of mental

TERMS OF HISTORY

Enlightenment

In 1784, in an essay titled "What Is Enlightenment?" the German philosopher Immanuel Kant gave widespread currency to a term that had been in the making for several decades. The term *enlightened century* had become common in the 1760s. The Enlightenment thus gave itself its own name, and the name clearly had propaganda value. The philosophes associated Enlightenment with philosophy, reason, and humanity; religious tolerance; natural rights; and criticism of outmoded customs and prejudices. They tied Enlightenment to "progress" and to the "modern," and it came into question, just as these other terms did, when events cast doubt on the benefits of progress and the virtues of modernity. Although some opposed the Enlightenment from the very beginning as antireligious, undermining of authority, and even atheistic and immoral, the French Revolution of 1789 galvanized the critics of Enlightenment who blamed every excess of revolution on Enlightenment principles.

For most of the nineteenth and twentieth centuries, condemnation of the Enlightenment came from right-wing sources. Some of the more extreme of these critics denounced a supposed "Jewish-Masonic conspiracy," believing that Jews and Freemasons benefited most from the spread of Enlightenment principles and worked in secret to jointly undermine Christianity and established monarchical authorities. Adolf Hitler and his followers shared these suspicions, and during World War II the Germans confiscated the records of Masonic lodges in every country they occupied. They sent the documents back to Berlin so that a special office could trace the links of this supposed conspiracy. They found nothing.

After the catastrophes of World War II, the Enlightenment came under attack from left-wing critics. They denounced the Enlightenment as "self-destructive" and even "totalitarian" because its belief in reason led not to freedom but to greater bureaucratic control. They asked why mankind was sinking into "a new kind of barbarism," and they answered, "Because we have trusted too much in the Enlightenment and its belief in reason and science." Reason provided the technology to transport millions of Jews to their deaths in scientifically sound gas chambers. Reason invented the atomic bomb and gave us the factories that pollute the atmosphere. These criticisms of the Enlightenment show how central the Enlightenment remains to the very definition of modern history.

categories such as space and time. In Kant's philosophy, these "categories of understanding" were neither sensory nor supernatural; they were entirely ideal and abstract and located in the human mind. For Kant, the supreme philosophical questions — Does God exist? Is personal immortality possible? Do humans have free will? — were unanswerable by reason alone. But like

MAJOR WORKS OF THE ENLIGHTENMENT

1748   Charles-Louis de Secondat, baron of Montesquieu, *Spirit of Laws*

1751   Beginning of publication of the French *Encyclopedia*

1755   David Hume, *The Natural History of Religion*

1762   Jean-Jacques Rousseau, *The Social Contract* and *Émile*

1764   Voltaire, *Philosophical Dictionary*

1770   Abbé Guillaume Raynal, *Philosophical and Political History of European Colonies and Commerce in the Two Indies*

1776   Adam Smith, *An Inquiry into the Nature and Causes of the Wealth of Nations*

1781   Immanuel Kant, *The Critique of Pure Reason*

Rousseau, Kant insisted that true moral freedom could be achieved only by living in society and obeying its laws.

The Limits of Reason: Roots of Romanticism and Religious Revival

As Kant showed, reason had its limits: it could not answer all of life's pressing questions. In reaction to what some saw as the Enlightenment's excessive reliance on the authority of human reason, a new artistic movement called **romanticism** took root. Although it would not fully flower until the early nineteenth century, romanticism traced its emphasis on individual genius, deep emotion, and the joys of nature to thinkers like Rousseau who had scolded the philosophes for ignoring those aspects of life that escaped and even conflicted with the power of reason. Rousseau's autobiographical *Confessions*, published posthumously in 1782, caused an immediate sensation because it revealed so much about his inner emotional life, including his sexual longings and his almost paranoid distrust of other Enlightenment figures.

A novel by the young German writer Johann Wolfgang von Goethe (1749–1832) captured the early romantic spirit with its glorification of emotion. *The Sorrows of Young Werther* (1774) told of a young man who loves nature and rural life and is unhappy in love. When the woman he loves marries someone else, he falls into deep melancholy and eventually kills himself. Reason cannot save him. The book spurred a veritable Werther craze: in addition to Werther costumes, engravings, em-

broidery, and medallions, there was even a perfume called Eau de Werther. The young Napoleon Bonaparte, who was to build an empire for France, claimed to have read Goethe's novel seven times.

Religious revivals underlined the limits of reason in a different way. Much of the Protestant world experienced an "awakening" in the 1740s. In the German states, Pietist groups founded new communities; and in the British North American colonies, revivalist Protestant preachers drew thousands of fervent believers in a movement called the Great Awakening. In North America, bitter conflicts between revivalists and their opponents in the established churches prompted the leaders on both sides to set up new colleges to support their beliefs. These included Princeton, Columbia, Brown, and Dartmouth, all founded between 1746 and 1769.

Revivalism also stirred eastern European Jews at about the same time. Israel ben Eliezer (1698–1760) laid the foundation for Hasidism in the 1740s and 1750s. He traveled the Polish countryside offering miraculous cures and became known as the Ba'al Shem Tov (meaning "Master of the Good Name") because he used divine names to effect healing and bring believers into closer personal contact with God. He emphasized mystical contemplation of the divine, rather than study of Jewish law, and his followers, the Hasidim (Hebrew for "most pious" Jews), often expressed their devotion through music, dance, and fervent prayer. Their practices soon spread all over Poland-Lithuania.

Most of the waves of Protestant revivalism ebbed after the 1750s, but in Great Britain one movement continued to grow through the end of the century. John Wesley (1703–1791), the Oxford-educated son of an Anglican cleric, founded **Methodism**, a term evoked by Wesley's insistence on strict self-discipline and a methodical approach to religious study and observance. In 1738, Wesley began preaching a new brand of Protestantism that emphasized an intense personal experience of salvation and a life of thrift, abstinence, and hard work. Traveling all over the British Isles, Wesley would mount a table or a box to speak to the ordinary people of the village or town. He slept in his followers' homes, ate their food, and treated their illnesses with various remedies, including small electric shocks for nervous diseases (Wesley eagerly followed Benjamin

---

romanticism: An artistic movement of the late eighteenth and early nineteenth centuries that glorified nature, emotion, genius, and imagination.

Methodism: A religious movement founded by John Wesley (1703–1791) that broke with the Anglican church in Great Britain and insisted on strict self-discipline and a "methodical" approach to religious study and observance.

George Whitefield

One of the most prominent preachers of the Great Awakening in the British North American colonies was the English Methodist George Whitefield, painted here by John Wollaston in 1742. Whitefield visited the North American colonies seven times, sometimes for long periods, and drew tens of thousands of people to his dramatic and emotional open-air sermons, which moved many listeners to tears of repentance. Whitefield was a celebrity in his time and is considered by many to be the founder of the Evangelical movement. *(National Portrait Gallery, London.)*

Franklin's experiments with electricity). In fifty years, Wesley preached forty thousand sermons, an average of fifteen a week. Not surprisingly, his preaching disturbed the Anglican authorities, who refused to let him preach in the churches. In response, Wesley began to ordain his own clergy. While radical in religious views, the Methodist leadership remained politically conservative during Wesley's lifetime; Wesley himself wrote many pamphlets urging order, loyalty, and submission to higher authorities.

REVIEW: What were the major differences between the Enlightenment in France, Great Britain, and the German states?

Society and Culture in an Age of Enlightenment

Religious revivals and the first stirrings of romanticism show that not all intellectual currents of the eighteenth century were flowing in the same channel. Some social and cultural developments, too, manifested the influence of Enlightenment ideas, but others did not. The traditional leaders of European societies—the nobles—responded to Enlightenment ideals in contradictory fashion: many simply reasserted their privileges and resis-

ted the influence of the Enlightenment, but an important minority embraced change and actively participated in reform efforts. The expanding middle classes saw in the Enlightenment a chance to make their claim for joining society's governing elite. They bought Enlightenment books, joined Masonic lodges, and patronized new styles in art, music, and literature. The lower classes were more affected by economic growth than by ideas. Trade boomed and the population grew, but people did not benefit equally. The ranks of the poor swelled, too, and with greater mobility, births to unmarried mothers also increased.

The Nobility's Reassertion of Privilege

Nobles made up about 3 percent of the European population, but their numbers and ways of life varied greatly from country to country. At least 10 percent of the population in Poland and 7 to 8 percent in Spain was noble, in contrast to only 2 percent in Russia and between 1 and 2 percent in the rest of western Europe. Many Polish and Spanish nobles lived in poverty; titles did not guarantee wealth. Still, the wealthiest European nobles luxuriated in almost unimaginable opulence. Many of the English peers, for example, owned more than ten thousand acres of land; invested widely in government bonds and trading companies; kept several country residences with scores of servants as well as houses in London; and occasionally even had their own private orchestras to complement libraries of expensive books, greenhouses for exotic plants, kennels of pedigreed dogs, and collections of antiques, firearms, and scientific instruments.

To support an increasingly expensive lifestyle in a period of inflation, European aristocrats sought to cash in on their remaining legal rights (called seigneurial dues, from the French *seigneur*, for "lord"). Peasants felt the squeeze as a result. French landlords required their peasants to pay dues to grind grain at the lord's mill, bake bread in his oven, press grapes at his winepress, or even pass on their own land as inheritance. In addition, peasants had to work without compensation for a specified number of days every year on the public roads. They also paid taxes to the government on salt, an essential preservative, and on the value of their land; customs duties if they sold produce or wine in town; and the tithe on their grain (one-tenth of the crop) to the church.

In Britain, the landed gentry could not claim these same onerous dues from their tenants, but they tenaciously defended their exclusive right to hunt game. The game laws kept the poor from eating meat and helped protect the social status of the rich. The gentry enforced the game laws themselves by hiring gamekeepers who hunted down poachers and even set traps for them in the forests. According to the law, anyone who poached deer or rabbits while armed or disguised could be sentenced to death. After 1760, the number of arrests for breaking the game laws increased dramatically. In most other countries, too, hunting was the special right of the nobility, a cause of deep popular resentment.

Even though Enlightenment writers sharply criticized nobles' insistence on special privileges, most aristocrats maintained their marks of distinction. The male court nobility continued to sport swords, plumed hats, makeup, and elaborate wigs, while middle-class men wore simpler and more somber clothing. Aristocrats had their own seats in church and their own quarters in the universities. Frederick II ("the Great") of Prussia (r. 1740–1786) made sure that nobles dominated both the army officer corps and the civil bureaucracy. Catherine II of Russia (r. 1762–1796) granted the nobility vast tracts of land, the exclusive right to own serfs, and exemption from personal taxes and corporal punishment. Her Charter of the Nobility of 1785 codified these privileges in exchange for the nobles' political subservience to the state. In Austria, Spain, the Italian states, Poland-Lithuania, and Russia, most nobles consequently cared little about Enlightenment ideas;

they did not read the books of the philosophes and feared reforms that might challenge their dominance of rural society.

In France, Britain, and the western German states, however, the nobility proved more open to the new ideas. Among those who personally corresponded with Rousseau, for example, half were nobles, as were 20 percent of the 160 contributors to the *Encyclopedia*. It had not escaped their notice that Rousseau had denounced inequality. In his view, it was "manifestly contrary to the law of nature . . . that a handful of people should gorge themselves with superfluities while the hungry multitude goes in want of necessities." The nobles of western Europe sometimes married into middle-class families and formed with them a new mixed elite, united by common interests in reform and new cultural tastes.

The Middle Class and the Making of a New Elite

The Enlightenment offered middle-class people an intellectual and cultural route to social improvement. The term *middle class* referred to the middle position on the social ladder; middle-class families did not have legal titles like the nobility above them, but neither did they work with their hands like the peasants, artisans, or workers below them. Most middle-class people lived in towns or cities and earned their living in the professions—as doctors, lawyers, or lower-level officials—or through investment in land, trade, or manufacturing. In the eighteenth century, the ranks of the middle class—also known as the bourgeoisie after *bourgeois*, the French word for "city dweller"—grew steadily in western Europe as a result of economic expansion. In France, for example, the overall population grew by about one-third in the 1700s, but the bourgeoisie nearly tripled in size. Although middle-class people had many reasons to resent the nobles, they also aspired to be like them.

Lodges and Learned Societies. Nobles and middle-class professionals mingled in Enlightenment salons and joined the new Masonic lodges and local learned societies. The Masonic lodges began as social clubs organized around elaborate secret rituals of stonemasons' guilds. They called their members **Freemasons** because that was the term given to apprentice masons when they were

---

Freemasons: Members of Masonic lodges, where nobles and middle-class professionals (and even some artisans) shared interest in the Enlightenment and reform.

deemed "free" to practice as masters of their guild. Although not explicitly political in aim, the lodges encouraged equality among members, and both aristocrats and middle-class men could join. Members wrote constitutions for their lodges and elected their own officers, thus promoting a direct experience of constitutional government.

Freemasonry arose in Great Britain and spread eastward: the first French and Italian lodges opened in 1726; Frederick II of Prussia founded a lodge in 1740; and after 1750, Freemasonry spread in Poland, Russia, and British North America. In France, women set up their own Masonic lodges. Despite the papacy's condemnation of Freemasonry in 1738 as subversive of religious and civil authority, lodges continued to multiply throughout the eighteenth century because they offered a place for socializing outside of the traditional channels and a way of declaring one's interest in the Enlightenment and reform. In short, Freemasonry offered a kind of secular religion. After 1789 and the outbreak of the French Revolution, conservatives would blame the lodges for every kind of political upheaval, but in the 1700s many high-ranking nobles became active members and saw no conflict with their privileged status.

Nobles and middle-class professionals also met in local learned societies, which greatly increased in number in this period. They gathered to discuss such practical issues as new scientific innovations or methods to eliminate poverty. The societies, sometimes called academies, brought the Enlightenment down from the realm of books and ideas to the level of concrete reforms. They sponsored essay contests, such as the one won by Rousseau in 1749, or the one set by the society in Metz in 1785 on the question "Are there means for making the Jews happier and more useful in France?" The Metz society approved essays that argued for granting civil rights to Jews.

New Cultural Styles. Shared tastes in travel, architecture, the arts, and even reading helped strengthen the links between nobles and members of the middle class. "Grand tours" of Europe often led upper-class youths to recently discovered Greek and Roman ruins at Pompeii, Herculaneum, and Paestum in Italy. These excavations aroused enthusiasm for the neoclassical style in architecture and painting, which began pushing aside the rococo and the long dominant baroque. Urban residences, government buildings, furniture, fabrics, wallpaper, and even pottery soon reflected the neoclassical emphasis on purity and clarity of forms. As one German writer noted, with considerable exaggeration, "Everything in Paris is in the Greek style." Employing neoclassical motifs, the English potter Josiah Wedgwood (1730–1795) almost single-handedly created a mass market for domestic crockery and appealed to middle-class desires to emulate the rich and royal. His designs of special tea sets for the British queen, for Catherine the

Neoclassical Style
In this Georgian interior of Syon House on the outskirts of London, various neoclassical motifs are readily apparent: Greek columns, Greek-style statuary on top of the columns, and Roman-style mosaics in the floor. The Scottish architect Robert Adam created this room for the duke of Northumberland in the 1760s. Adam had spent four years in Italy and returned in 1758 to London to decorate homes in the "Adam style," meaning the neoclassical manner.
(© The Fotomas Index, U.K./The Bridgeman Art Library.)

Jean-Baptiste Greuze, *Broken Eggs* (1756)
Greuze made his reputation as a painter of moralistic family scenes. In this one, an old woman (perhaps the mother) confronts the lover of a young girl and points to the eggs that have fallen out of a basket, a symbol of lost virginity. Diderot praised Greuze's work as "morality in paint," but the paintings often had an erotic subtext. *(© Francis G. Mayer/Corbis.)*

■ **For more help analyzing this image,** see the visual activity for this chapter in the Online Study Guide at bedfordstmartins.com/hunt.

Great of Russia, and for leading aristocrats allowed him to advertise his wares as fashionable. By 1767, he claimed that his Queensware pottery had "spread over the whole Globe," and indeed by then his pottery was being marketed in France, Russia, Venice, the Ottoman Empire, and British North America.

This period also supported artistic styles other than neoclassicism. Frederick II of Prussia built himself a palace outside of Berlin in the earlier rococo style, gave it the French name of Sanssouci ("worry-free"), and filled it with the works of French masters of the rococo. A growing taste for moralistic family scenes in painting reflected the same middle-class preoccupation with the emotions of ordinary private life that could be seen in novels. The middle-class public now attended the official painting exhibitions in France that were held regularly every other year after 1737. Court painting nonetheless remained much in demand. Marie-Louise-Élizabeth Vigée-Lebrun (1755–1842), who painted portraits at the French court, reported that in the 1780s "it was difficult to get a place on my waiting list. . . . I was the fashion."

Although wealthy nobles still patronized Europe's leading musicians, music, too, began to reflect the broadening of the elite and the spread of Enlightenment ideals as classical forms replaced the baroque style. Complex polyphony gave way to melody, which made the music more accessible to ordinary listeners. Large sections of string instruments became the backbone of professional orchestras, which now played to large audiences of well-to-do listeners in sizable concert halls. The public concert gradually displaced the private recital, and a new attitude toward "the classics" developed: for the first time in the 1770s and 1780s, concert groups began to play older music rather than simply playing the latest commissioned works.

This laid the foundation for what we still call classical music today—that is, a repertory of the greatest music of the eighteenth and early nineteenth centuries. Because composers now created works that would be performed over and over again as part of a classical repertory, rather than occasional pieces for the court or noble patrons, they deliberately attempted to write lasting works. As a result, the major composers began to produce fewer symphonies: the Austrian composer Franz Joseph Haydn (1732–1809) wrote more than one hundred symphonies, but his successor Ludwig van Beethoven (1770–1827) would create only nine.

The two supreme masters of the new musical style of the eighteenth century show that the transition from noble patronage to classical concerts was far from complete. Haydn and his fellow Austrian Wolfgang Amadeus Mozart (1756–1791) both wrote for noble patrons, but by the early 1800s their compositions had been incorporated into the canon of concert classics all over Europe. Incredibly prolific, both excelled in combining lightness, clarity, and profound emotion. Both also wrote numerous Italian operas, a genre whose popularity continued to grow: in the 1780s, the Papal States alone boasted forty opera houses. Haydn spent most of his career working for a Hungarian noble family, the Eszterházys. Asked once why he had written no string quintets (at which Mozart excelled), he responded simply: "No one has ordered any."

Interest in reading, like attending public concerts, took hold of the middle classes and fed a frenzied increase in publication. By the end of the eighteenth century, six times as many books were being published in the German states, for instance, as at the beginning. One Parisian author commented that "people are certainly reading ten times as much in Paris as they did a hundred years ago." Provincial towns in western Europe published their own newspapers; by 1780, thirty-seven English towns had local newspapers. Lending libraries and book clubs multiplied. Despite the limitations of women's education, which emphasized domestic skills, women benefited as much as men from the spread of print. As one Englishman observed, "By far the greatest part of ladies now have a taste for books." Women also wrote them. Catherine Macaulay (1731–1791) published bestselling histories of Britain, and in France Stéphanie de Genlis (1746–1830) wrote children's books — a genre that was growing in importance as middle-class parents became more interested in education. The universities had little impact on these new tastes. An Austrian reformer complained about the universities in his country: "Critical history, natural sciences — which are supposed to make enlightenment general and combat prejudice — were neglected or wholly unknown."

Life on the Margins

Booming foreign trade fueled a dramatic economic expansion — French colonial trade increased tenfold in the 1700s — but the results did not necessarily trickle all the way down the social scale. The population of Europe grew by nearly 30 percent, with especially striking gains in England, Ireland, Prussia, and Hungary. (See "Taking Measure" on this page.) Even though food production increased, shortages and crises still occurred periodically. Prices went up in many countries after the 1730s and continued to rise gradually until the early nineteenth century; wages in many trades rose as well, but less quickly than prices. Some people prospered — for example, peasants who produced surpluses to sell in local markets and shopkeepers and artisans who could increase their sales to meet growing demand. But those at the bottom of the social ladder — day laborers in the cities and peasants with small holdings — lived on the edge of dire poverty, and when they lost their land or work, they either migrated to the cities or wandered the roads in search of food and work. In France alone, 200,000 workers left their

homes every year in search of seasonal employment elsewhere. At least 10 percent of Europe's urban population depended on some form of charity.

The growing numbers of poor overwhelmed local governments. In some countries, beggars and vagabonds had been locked up in workhouses since the mid-1600s. The expenses for running these overcrowded institutions increased by 60 percent in England between 1760 and 1785. After 1740, most German towns created workhouses that were part workshop, part hospital, and part prison. Such institutions also appeared for the first time in Boston, New York, and Philadelphia. To

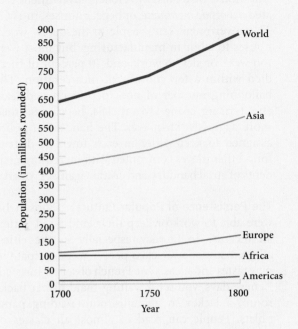

TAKING MEASURE

World Population Growth, 1700–1800

This graph gives a very crude comparison of regional population growth in the 1700s. Precise statistical data are impossible to develop for this period on a worldwide scale. Asia had many more people than Europe, and both Asia and Europe were growing much more rapidly in the 1700s than Africa or the Americas. The population stagnation in Africa has been the subject of much scholarly controversy; it seems likely that it was the result of the slave trade, which transported millions across the ocean to the Americas. The native population in the Americas died because of disease and was only partially replaced by the import of African slaves. What are the advantages of a growing population? What are the disadvantages? *(Adapted from Andre Gundar Frank, Reorient: Global Economy in the Asian Age (Berkeley: University of California Press), 1998.)*

supplement the inadequate system of religious charity, offices for the poor, public workshops, and workhouse hospitals, the French government created *dépôts de mendicité*, or beggar houses, in 1767. The government sent people to these new workhouses to labor in manufacturing, but most were too weak or sick to work, and 20 percent of them died within a few months of incarceration. The ballooning number of poor people created fears about rising crime. To officials, beggars seemed more aggressive than ever. The handful of police assigned to keep order in each town or district found themselves confronted with increasing incidents of rural banditry and crimes against property.

The Persistence of Popular Culture. Those who were able to work or keep their land fared better: an increase in literacy, especially in the cities, allowed some lower-class people to participate in new tastes and ideas. One French observer insisted, "These days, you see a waiting-maid in her backroom, a lackey in an ante-room reading pamphlets. People can read in almost all classes of society." In France, only 50 percent of men and 27 percent of women could read and write in the 1780s, but that was twice the rate of a century earlier. Literacy rates were higher in England and the Dutch Republic, much lower in eastern Europe. About one in four Parisians owned books, but the lower classes overwhelmingly read religious books, as they had in the past.

Whereas the new elite might attend salons, concerts, or art exhibitions, peasants enjoyed their traditional forms of popular entertainment, such as fairs and festivals, and the urban lower classes relaxed in cabarets and taverns. Sometimes pleasures were cruel. In Britain, bullbaiting, bearbaiting, dogfighting, and cockfighting were all common forms of entertainment that provided opportunities for organized gambling. "Gentle" sports frequented by the upper classes had their violent side too, showing that the upper classes had not become as different as they sometimes thought. Cricket matches, whose rules were first laid down in 1744, were often accompanied by brawls among fans (not unlike soccer matches today, though on a much smaller scale). Many Englishmen enjoyed what one observer called a "battle royal with sticks, pebbles and hog's dung."

Changes in Sexual Behavior. As population increased and villagers began to move to cities to better their prospects, sexual behavior changed too. The rates of births out of wedlock soared, from less than 5 percent of all births in the seventeenth century to nearly 20 percent at the end of the eigh-

teenth. Historians have disagreed about the causes and meanings of this change. Some detect in this pattern a sign of sexual liberation and the beginnings of a modern sexual revolution: as women moved out of the control of their families, they began to seek their own sexual fulfillment. Others view this change more bleakly, as a story of seduction and betrayal: family and community pressure had once forced a man to marry a woman pregnant with his child, but now a man could abandon a pregnant lover by simply moving away.

Increased mobility brought freedom for some women, but it also aggravated the vulnerability of those newly arrived in cities from the countryside. Desperation, not reason, often ruled their choices. Women who came to the city as domestic servants had little recourse against masters or fellow servants who seduced or raped them. The result was a startling rise in abandoned babies. Most European cities established foundling hospitals in the 1700s, but infant and child mortality was 50 percent higher in such institutions than for children brought up at home. Some women tried herbs, laxatives, or crude surgical means of abortion; a few, usually servants who would lose their jobs if their employers discovered they had borne a child, resorted to infanticide.

European states had long tried to regulate sexual behavior; every country had laws against prostitution, adultery, fornication, sodomy, and infanticide. Reformers criticized the harshness of laws against infanticide, but they showed no mercy for "sodomites" (as male homosexuals were called), who in some places, in particular the Dutch Republic, were systematically persecuted and imprisoned or even executed. Male homosexuals attracted the attention of authorities because they had begun to develop networks and special meeting places. The stereotype of the effeminate, exclusively homosexual male seems to have appeared for the first time in the eighteenth century, perhaps as part of a growing emphasis on separate roles for men and women.

The Enlightenment's emphasis on reason, self-control, and childhood innocence made parents increasingly anxious about their children's sexuality. Moralists and physicians wrote books about the evils of masturbation, "proving" that it led to physical and mental degeneration and even madness.

While the Enlightenment thus encouraged excessive concern about children being left to their own devices, it nevertheless taught the middle and upper classes to value their children and to expect their improvement through education. Writers such as de Genlis and Rousseau drew attention to children, who were no longer viewed only as little sinners in need of harsh discipline. Paintings now showed individual children playing at their favorite activities rather than formally posed with their families. Books about and for children became popular. *The Newtonian System of the Universe Digested for Young Minds*, by "Tom Telescope," was published in Britain in 1761 and reprinted many times. Toys, jigsaw puzzles, and clothing designed for children all appeared for the first time in the 1700s. Children were no longer considered miniature adults.

> **REVIEW:** What were the major differences in the impact of the Enlightenment on nobles, middle classes, and lower classes?

State Power in an Era of Reform

Rulers turned to Enlightenment-inspired reforms to improve life for their subjects and to gain commercial or military advantage over rival states. Historians label many of the sovereigns of this time **enlightened despots** or enlightened absolutists, for they aimed to promote Enlightenment reforms without giving up their absolutist powers. Catherine the Great's admiring relationship with Voltaire showed how even the most absolutist rulers championed reform when it suited their own goals. Foremost among those goals was the expansion of a ruler's territory.

War and Diplomacy

Europeans no longer fought devastating wars over religion that killed hundreds of thousands of civilians; instead, professional armies and navies battled for control of overseas empires and for dominance on the European continent. Rulers continued to expand their armies: the Prussian army, for example, nearly tripled in size between 1740 and 1789. Widespread use of flintlock muskets required deployment in long lines, usually three men deep, with each line in turn loading and firing on command. Military strategy became cautious and calculating, but this did not prevent the outbreak of hostilities. Between 1740 and 1775, the instability of the European balance of power re-

sulted in two major wars, a diplomatic reversal of alliances, and the partition of Poland-Lithuania among Russia, Austria, and Prussia.

War of the Austrian Succession, 1740–1748.

The difficulties over the succession to the Austrian throne typified the dynastic complications that repeatedly threatened the European balance of power. In 1740, Holy Roman Emperor Charles VI died without a male heir. Most European rulers recognized the emperor's chosen heiress, his daughter Maria Theresa, because Charles's Pragmatic Sanction of 1713 had given a woman the right to inherit the Habsburg crown lands. The new king of Prussia, Frederick II, who had just succeeded his father a few months earlier in 1740, saw his chance to grab territory and immediately invaded the rich Austrian province of Silesia. France joined Prussia in an attempt to further humiliate its traditional enemy Austria, and Great Britain

Maria Theresa and Her Family
In this portrait by Martin van Meytens (1695–1770), Austrian empress Maria Theresa is shown with her husband, Francis I, and twelve of their sixteen children. Their eldest son eventually succeeded to the Austrian throne as Joseph II, and their youngest daughter, Maria Antonia, or Marie-Antoinette, became the queen of France. *(Bridgeman–Giraudon/Art Resource, NY.)*

enlightened despots: Rulers—such as Catherine the Great of Russia, Frederick the Great of Prussia, and Joseph II of Austria—who tried to promote reform without giving up their own supreme political power; also called enlightened absolutists.

MAP 18.1 War of the Austrian Succession, 1740–1748

The accession of a twenty-three-year-old woman, Maria Theresa, to the Austrian throne gave the new king of Prussia, Frederick II, an opportunity to invade the province of Silesia. France joined on Prussia's side, Great Britain on Austria's. In 1745, the French defeated the British in the Austrian Netherlands and helped instigate an uprising in Scotland. The rebellion failed and British attacks on French overseas shipping forced the French to negotiate. The peace treaties guaranteed Frederick's conquest of Silesia, which soon became the wealthiest province of Prussia. France came to terms with Great Britain to protect its overseas possessions; Austria had to accept the peace settlement after a formal public protest.

Austria and allies
Prussia and allies
Seized from Austria
Main areas of fighting
Boundary of the Holy Roman Empire

allied with Austria to prevent the French from taking the Austrian Netherlands (Map 18.1). The War of the Austrian Succession (1740–1748) soon expanded to the overseas colonies of Great Britain and France. French and British colonials in North America fought each other all along their boundaries, enlisting native American auxiliaries. Britain tried but failed to isolate the French Caribbean colonies during the war, and hostilities broke out in India, too.

Maria Theresa (r. 1740–1780) survived only by conceding Silesia to Prussia in order to split the Prussians off from France. The Peace of Aix-la-Chapelle of 1748 recognized Maria Theresa as the heiress to the Austrian lands, and her husband, Francis I, became Holy Roman Emperor, thus reasserting the integrity of the Austrian Empire. The peace of 1748 failed to resolve the colonial conflicts between Britain and France, however, and fighting for domination continued unofficially.

Seven Years' War, 1756–1763. In 1756, a major reversal of alliances—what historians call the Diplomatic Revolution—reshaped relations among the great powers. Prussia and Great Britain signed a defensive alliance, prompting Austria to overlook two centuries of hostility and ally with France. Russia

and Sweden soon joined the Franco-Austrian alliance. When Frederick II invaded Saxony, an ally of Austria, with his bigger and better disciplined army, the long-simmering hostilities between Great Britain and France over colonial boundaries flared into a general war that became known as the **Seven Years' War** (1756–1763).

Fighting soon raged around the world (Map 18.2). The French and British battled on land and sea in North America (where the conflict was called the French and Indian War), the West Indies, and India. The two coalitions also fought each other in central Europe. At first, in 1757, Frederick the Great surprised Europe with a spectacular victory at Rossbach in Saxony over a much larger Franco-Austrian army. But in time, Russian and Austrian armies encircled his troops. Frederick despaired: "I believe all is lost. I will not survive the ruin of my country." A fluke of history saved him. Empress Elizabeth of Russia (r. 1741–1762) died and was succeeded by the mentally unstable Peter III, a fanatical admirer of Frederick and things Prussian. Peter withdrew Russia from the war. (This was

Seven Years' War: A worldwide series of battles (1756–1763) between Austria, France, Russia, and Sweden on one side and Prussia and Great Britain on the other.

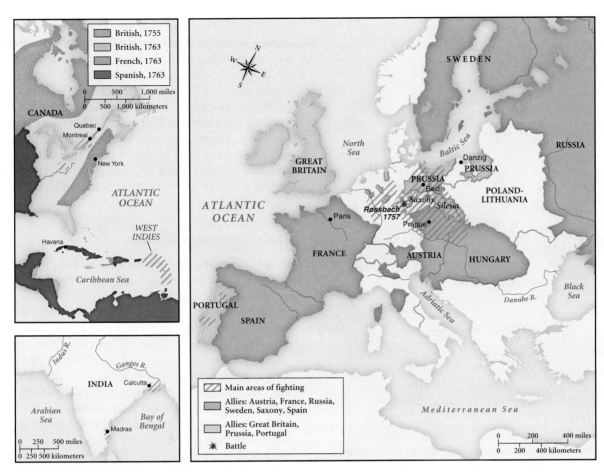

MAP 18.2 The Seven Years' War, 1756–1763
In what might justly be called the first worldwide war, the French and British fought each other in Europe, the West Indies, North America, and India. Skirmishing in North America helped precipitate the war, which became more general when Austria, France, and Russia allied to check Prussian influence in central Europe. The treaty between Austria and Prussia simply restored the status quo in Europe, but the changes overseas were much more dramatic. Britain gained control over Canada and India but gave back to France the West Indian islands of Guadeloupe and Martinique. Britain was now the dominant power of the seas.

practically his only accomplishment as tsar. He was soon mysteriously murdered, probably at the instigation of his wife, Catherine the Great.) In a separate peace treaty Frederick kept all his territory, including Silesia.

The Anglo-French overseas conflicts ended more decisively than the continental land wars. British naval superiority, fully achieved only in the 1750s, enabled Great Britain to rout the French in North America, India, and the West Indies. In the Treaty of Paris of 1763, France ceded Canada to Great Britain and agreed to remove its armies from India, in exchange for keeping its rich West Indian islands. Eagerness to avenge this defeat would motivate France to support the British North American colonists in their War of Independence just fifteen years later.

Prussia's Rise and the First Partition of Poland. Although Prussia suffered great losses in the Seven Years' War — some 160,000 Prussian soldiers died either in action or of disease — the army helped vault Prussia to the rank of leading powers. In 1733, Frederick II's father, Frederick William I, had instituted the "canton system," which enrolled peasant youths in each canton (or district) in the army, gave them two or three months of training annually, and allowed them to return to their family farms the rest of the year. They remained "cantonists" (reservists) as long as they were able-bodied. In this fashion, the Prussian military steadily grew in size; by 1740, Prussia had the third or fourth largest army in Europe even though it was tenth in population and thirteenth in land area. Under Frederick II, Prussia's military expenditures

Dividing Poland, 1772

In this contemporary depiction, Catherine the Great, Joseph II, and Frederick II point on the map to the portion of Poland-Lithuania each plans to take. The artist makes it clear that Poland's fate rested in the hands of neighboring rulers, not its own people. Can you infer the sentiments of the artist from the content of this engraving? *(Mansell/Time Life Pictures/Getty Images.)*

would spread "a stain over my whole reign," she agreed to the first **partition of Poland**, splitting one-third of Poland-Lithuania's territory and half of its people among the three powers. Austria feared growing Russian influence in Poland and in the Balkans, where Russia had been successfully battling the Ottoman Empire. Conflicts between Catholics, Protestants, and Orthodox Christians in Poland were used to justify this cynical move. Russia took over most of Lithuania, effectively ending the large but weak Polish-Lithuanian commonwealth.

State-Sponsored Reform

In the aftermath of the Seven Years' War, all the belligerents faced pressing needs for more money to fund their growing armies, to organize navies to wage overseas conflicts, and to counter the impact of inflation. To make tax increases more palatable to public opinion, rulers appointed reform-minded ministers and gave them a mandate to modernize government. As one adviser to the Austrian ruler Joseph II put it, "A properly constituted state must be exactly analogous to a machine . . . and the ruler must be the foreman, the mainspring . . . which sets everything else in motion." Such reforms always threatened the interests of traditional groups, however, and the spread of Enlightenment ideas aroused sometimes unpredictable desires for more change.

Administrative and Legal Reforms.   Reforming monarchs did not invent government bureaucracy, but they did insist on greater attention to merit, hard work, and professionalism, which made bureaucrats more like modern civil servants. In this view, the ruler should be a benevolent, enlightened administrator who worked for the general well-being of his or her people. Frederick II of Prussia, who drove himself as hard as he drove his officials, boasted, "I am the first servant of the state."

rose to two-thirds of the state's revenue. Virtually every nobleman served in the army, paying for his own support as officer and buying a position as company commander. Once retired, the officers returned to their estates, coordinated the canton system, and served as local officials. In this way, the military permeated every aspect of rural society, fusing army and agrarian organization. The army gave the state great power, but the militarization of Prussian society also had a profoundly conservative effect: it kept the peasants enserfed to their lords and blocked the middle classes from access to estates or high government positions.

Prussia's power grew so dramatically that in 1772 Frederick the Great proposed that large chunks of Polish-Lithuanian territory be divided among Austria, Prussia, and Russia. Despite the protests of the Austrian empress Maria Theresa that the partition

The First Partition of Poland, 1772

A freemason and supporter of religious toleration, Frederick abolished torture, reorganized taxation, and hosted leading French philosophes at his court. The Prussian king also composed more than a hundred original pieces of music.

Legal reform, both of the judicial system and of the often

---

partition of Poland: Division of one-third of Poland-Lithuania's territory between Prussia, Russia, and Austria in 1772.

disorganized and irregular law codes, was central to the work of many reform-minded monarchs. Like Frederick II, Joseph II of Austria (r. 1780–1790) ordered the compilation of a unified law code, a project that required many years for completion. Catherine II of Russia began such an undertaking even more ambitiously. In 1767, she called together a legislative commission of 564 deputies and asked them to consider a long document called the *Instruction*, which represented her hopes for legal reform based on the ideas of Montesquieu and the Italian jurist Cesare Beccaria. Montesquieu had insisted that punishment should fit the crime; he criticized the use of torture and brutal corporal punishment. In his influential book *On Crimes and Punishments* (1764), Beccaria argued that justice should be administered in public, that judicial torture should be abolished as inhumane, and that the accused should be presumed innocent until proven guilty. He also advocated eliminating the death penalty. Despite much discussion and hundreds of petitions and documents about local problems, little came of Catherine's commission because the monarch herself—despite her regard for Voltaire and his fellow philosophes—proved ultimately unwilling to see through far-reaching legal reform.

The Church, Education, and Religious Toleration.

Rulers everywhere wanted more control over church affairs, and they used Enlightenment criticisms of the organized churches to get their way. In Catholic countries, many government officials resented the influence of the Jesuits, the major Catholic teaching order. The Jesuits trained the Catholic intellectual elite, ran a worldwide missionary network, enjoyed close ties to the papacy, and amassed great wealth. Critics mounted campaigns against the Jesuits in many countries, and by the early 1770s the Society of Jesus had been dissolved in Portugal, France, and Spain. In 1773, Pope Clement XIV (r. 1769–1774) agreed under pressure to disband the order, an edict that held until a reinvigorated papacy restored the society in 1814. Joseph II of Austria not only applauded the suppression of the Jesuits but also required Austrian bishops to swear fidelity and submission to him. Joseph had become Holy Roman Emperor and co-regent with his mother, Maria Theresa, in 1765. After her death in 1780, he initiated a wide-ranging program of reform. Under him, the Austrian state supervised Catholic seminaries, abolished contemplative monastic orders, and confiscated monastic property to pay for education and poor relief.

Joseph II launched the most ambitious educational reforms of the period. In 1774, once the Jesuits had been disbanded, a General School Ordinance in Austria ordered state subsidies for local schools, which the state would regulate. By 1789, one quarter of the school-age children attended school. In Prussia, the school code of 1763 required all children between the ages of five and thirteen to attend school. Although not enforced uniformly, the Prussian law demonstrated Frederick II's belief that modernization depended on education. Catherine II of Russia also tried to expand elementary education—and the education of women in particular—and founded engineering schools.

No ruler pushed the principle of religious toleration as far as Joseph II of Austria, who in 1781 granted freedom of religious worship to Protestants, Orthodox Christians, and Jews. For the first time, these groups were allowed to own property, build schools, enter the professions, and hold political and military offices. The efforts of other rulers to extend religious toleration proved more limited. Louis XVI signed an edict in 1787 restoring French Protestants' civil rights—but still, Protestants could not hold political office. Great Britain continued to deny Catholics freedom of open worship and the right to sit in Parliament. Most European states limited the rights and opportunities available to Jews. In Russia, only wealthy Jews could hold municipal office, and in the Papal States, the pope encouraged forced baptism. Even in Austria, where Joseph encouraged toleration, the laws forced Jews to take German-sounding names. The leading philosophes opposed persecution of the Jews in theory but often treated them with undisguised contempt. Diderot's comment was all too typical: the Jews, he said, bore "all the defects peculiar to an ignorant and superstitious nation."

Limits of Reform

When enlightened absolutist leaders introduced reforms, they often ran into resistance from groups threatened by the proposed changes. The most contentious area of reform was agricultural policy. Whereas Catherine II reinforced the authority of nobles over their serfs, Joseph II tried to remove the burdens of serfdom in the Habsburg lands. In 1781, he abolished the personal aspects of serfdom: serfs could now move freely, enter trades, or marry without their lords' permission. Joseph abolished the tithe to the church, shifted more of the tax burden to the nobility, and converted peasants' labor services into cash payments.

The Austrian nobility furiously resisted these far-reaching reforms. When Joseph died in 1790, his brother Leopold II had to revoke most reforms to appease the nobles. Prussia's Frederick II, like Joseph, encouraged such agricultural innovations as planting potatoes and turnips (new crops that could help feed a growing population), experimenting with cattle breeding, draining swamplands, and clearing forests. But Prussia's noble landlords, the Junkers, continued to expand their estates at the expense of poorer peasants and thwarted Frederick's attempts to improve the status of serfs.

Reforming ministers also tried to stimulate agricultural improvement in France. Unlike most other western European countries, France still had about a hundred thousand serfs; though their burdens weighed less heavily than those in eastern Europe, serfdom did not entirely disappear until 1789. A group of economists called the physiocrats urged the French government to deregulate the grain trade and make the tax system more equitable to encourage agricultural productivity. In the interest of establishing a free market, they also insisted that urban guilds be abolished because the guilds prevented free entry into the trades. Their proposed reforms applied the Enlightenment emphasis on individual liberties to the economy; Adam Smith took up many of the physiocrats' ideas in his writing in favor of free markets. The French government heeded some of this advice and gave up its system of price controls on grain in 1763, but it had to reverse the decision in 1770 when grain shortages caused a famine.

A conflict with the parlements, the thirteen high courts of law, prompted Louis XV to go even further in 1771. He replaced the parlements with courts in which the judges no longer owned their offices and thus could not sell them or pass them on as an inheritance. Justice would then presumably be more impartial. The displaced judges of the parlements succeeded in arousing widespread opposition to what they portrayed as tyrannical royal policy. The furor calmed down only when Louis XV died in 1774 and his successor, Louis XVI (r. 1774–1792), yielded to aristocratic demands and restored the old parlements.

Louis XVI tried to carry out part of the program suggested by the physiocrats, and he chose one of their disciples, Jacques Turgot (1727–1781), as his chief minister. A contributor to the *Encyclopedia*, Turgot pushed through several edicts that again freed the grain trade, suppressed guilds, converted the peasants' forced labor on roads into a money tax payable by all landowners, and reduced court expenses. He also began making plans to in-troduce a system of elected local assemblies, which would have made government much more representative. Faced with broad-based resistance led by the parlements and his own courtiers, as well as with riots against rising grain prices, Louis XVI dismissed Turgot, and one of the last possibilities to overhaul France's government collapsed.

The failure of reform in France paradoxically reflected the power of Enlightenment thinkers; everyone now endorsed Enlightenment ideas but used them for different ends. The nobles in the parlements blocked the French monarchy's reform efforts using the very same Enlightenment language spoken by the crown's ministers. France's large and growing middle-class public felt increasingly frustrated by the failure to institute social change, a failure that ultimately helped undermine the monarchy itself. Where Frederick II, Catherine II, and even Joseph II used reform to bolster the efficiency of absolutist government, attempts at change in France backfired. French kings found that their ambitious programs for reform succeeded only in arousing unrealistic hopes.

> **REVIEW:** What prompted enlightened absolutists to undertake reforms in the second half of the eighteenth century?

Rebellions against State Power

Although traditional forms of popular discontent had not disappeared, Enlightenment ideals and reforms changed the rules of the game in politics. Governments had become accountable for their actions to a much wider range of people than ever before. In Britain and France, ordinary people rioted when they perceived government as failing to protect them against food shortages. The growth of informed public opinion had its most dramatic consequences in the North American colonies, where a struggle over the British Parliament's right to tax turned into a full-scale war for independence. The American War of Independence showed that once put into practice, Enlightenment ideals could have revolutionary implications.

Food Riots and Peasant Uprisings

Population growth, inflation, and the extension of the market system put added pressure on the already beleaguered poor. Seventeenth-century peasants and townspeople had rioted to protest new taxes. In the last half of the eighteenth century, the food supply became the focus of political and social conflict. Poor people in the villages and the towns believed that it was the government's responsibility to ensure they had enough food, and many governments did stockpile grain to make up for the occasional bad harvest. At the same time, in keeping with Adam Smith's and the French physiocrats' free-market proposals, governments wanted to allow grain prices to rise with market demand, because higher profits would motivate producers to increase the overall supply of food.

The Pugachev Rebellion, 1773

Free trade in grain meant selling to the highest bidder even if that bidder was a foreign merchant. In the short run, in times of scarcity, big landowners and farmers could make huge profits by selling grain outside their hometowns or villages. This practice enraged poor farmers, agricultural workers, and city wage workers, who could not afford the higher prices. Lacking the political means to affect policy, they could enforce their desire for old-fashioned price regulation only by rioting. Most did not pillage or steal grain but rather forced the sale of grain or flour at a "just" price and blocked the shipment of grain out of their villages to other markets. Women often led these "popular price fixings," as they were called in France, in desperate attempts to protect the food supply for their children.

Such food riots occurred regularly in Britain and France in the last half of the eighteenth century. One of the most turbulent was the so-called Flour War in France in 1775. Turgot's deregulation of the grain trade in 1774 caused prices to rise in several provincial cities. Rioting spread from there to the Paris region, where villagers attacked grain convoys heading to the capital city. Local officials often ordered merchants and bakers to sell at the price the rioters demanded, only to find themselves arrested by the central government for overriding free trade. The government brought in troops to restore order and introduced the death penalty for rioting.

Frustrations with serfdom and hopes for a miraculous transformation provoked the **Pugachev rebellion** in Russia beginning in 1773. An army

deserter from the southeast frontier region, Emelian Pugachev (1742–1775) claimed to be Tsar Peter III, the dead husband of Catherine II. Pugachev's appearance seemed to confirm peasant hopes for a "redeemer tsar" who would save the people from oppression. He rallied around him Cossacks like himself who resented the loss of their old tribal independence. Now increasingly enserfed or forced to pay taxes and endure army service, these nomadic bands joined with other serfs, rebellious mine workers, and Muslim minorities. Catherine dispatched a large army to squelch the uprising, but Pugachev eluded them and the fighting spread. Nearly three million people eventually participated, making this the largest single rebellion in the history of tsarist Russia. When Pugachev

A Cossack

Pugachev and many of his followers were Cossacks, Ukrainians who set up nomadic communities of horsemen to resist outside control, whether from Turks, Poles, or Russians. This eighteenth-century painting captures the common view of Cossacks as horsemen always ready for battle but with a fondness for music too. (© The Bridgeman Art Library.)

Pugachev (poo guh CHAWF) **rebellion:** A massive revolt of Russian Cossacks and serfs in 1773 against local nobles and the armies of Catherine the Great; its leader, Emelian Pugachev, was eventually captured and executed.

urged the peasants to attack the nobility and seize their estates, hundreds of noble families perished. Foreign newspapers called it "the revolution in southern Russia" and offered fantastic stories about Pugachev's life history. Finally, the army captured the rebel leader and brought him in an iron cage to Moscow, where he was tortured and executed. In the aftermath, Catherine tightened the nobles' control over their serfs with the Charter of the Nobility and harshly punished those who dared to criticize serfdom.

Public Opinion and Political Opposition

Peasant uprisings might briefly shake even a powerful monarchy, but the rise of public opinion as a force independent of court society caused more enduring changes in European politics. Across much of Europe and in the North American colonies, demands for broader political participation reflected Enlightenment notions about individual rights. Aristocratic bodies such as the French parlements, which had no legislative role like that of the British Parliament, insisted that the monarch consult them on the nation's affairs, and the new educated elite wanted more influence too. Newspapers began to cover daily political affairs, and the public learned the basics of political life, despite the strict limits on political participation in most countries. Monarchs turned to public opinion to seek support against aristocratic groups that opposed reform. Gustavus III of Sweden (r. 1771–1792) called himself "the first citizen of a free people" and promised to deliver the country from "insufferable aristocratic despotism." Shortly after coming to the throne, Gustavus proclaimed a new constitution that divided power between the king and the legislature, abolished the use of torture in the judicial process, and assured some freedom of the press.

The Wilkes affair in Great Britain showed that public opinion could be mobilized to challenge a government. In 1763, during the reign of George III (r. 1760–1820), John Wilkes, a member of Parliament, attacked the government in his newspaper, *North Briton*, and sued the crown when he was arrested. He won his release as well as damages. When he was reelected, Parliament denied him his seat, not once but three times.

The Wilkes episode soon escalated into a major campaign against the corruption and social exclusiveness of Parliament, complaints the Levellers had first raised during the English Revolution of the late 1640s. Newspapers, magazines, pamphlets, handbills, and cheap editions of Wilkes's collected works all helped promote his cause. Those who could not vote demonstrated for Wilkes. In one incident eleven people died when soldiers broke up a huge gathering of his supporters. The slogan "Wilkes and Liberty" appeared on walls all over London. Middle-class voters formed a Society of Supporters of the Bill of Rights, which circulated petitions for Wilkes; they gained the support of about one-fourth of all the voters. The more determined Wilkesites proposed sweeping reforms of Parliament, including more frequent elections, more representation for the counties, elimination of "rotten boroughs" (election districts so small that they could be controlled by one big patron), and restrictions of pensions used by the crown to gain support. These demands would be at the heart of agitation for parliamentary reform in Britain for decades to come.

Popular demonstrations did not always support reforms. In 1780, the Gordon riots devastated London. They were named after the fanatical anti-Catholic crusader Lord George Gordon, who helped organize huge marches and petition campaigns against a bill the House of Commons passed to grant limited toleration to Catholics. The demonstrations culminated in a seven-day riot that left fifty buildings destroyed and three hundred people dead. Despite the continuing limitation on voting rights in Great Britain, British politicians were learning that they could ignore public opinion only at their peril.

Political opposition also took artistic forms, particularly in countries where governments restricted organized political activity. A striking example of a play with a political message was *The Marriage of Figaro* (1784) by Pierre-Augustin Caron de Beaumarchais (1732–1799), who at one time or another worked as a watchmaker, a judge, a gunrunner in the American War of Independence, and a French spy in Britain. *The Marriage of Figaro* was first a hit at court, when Queen Marie-Antoinette had it read for her friends. But when her husband, Louis XVI, read it, he forbade its production on the grounds that "this man mocks at everything that should be respected in government." When finally performed publicly, the play caused a sensation. The chief character, Figaro, is a clever servant who gets the better of his noble employer. When speaking of the count, he cries, "What have you done to deserve so many rewards? You went to the trouble of being born, and nothing more." Two years later, Mozart based an equally famous but somewhat tamer opera on Beaumarchais's story.

Revolution in North America

Oppositional forms of public opinion came to a head in Great Britain's North American colonies, where the result was American independence and the establishment of a republican constitution that stood in stark contrast to most European regimes. Many Europeans saw the American War of Independence, or the American Revolution, as a triumph for Enlightenment ideas. As one German writer exclaimed in 1777, American victory would give "greater scope to the Enlightenment, new keenness to the thinking of peoples and new life to the spirit of liberty."

The American revolutionary leaders had been influenced by a common Atlantic civilization; they participated in the Enlightenment and shared political ideas with the opposition Whigs in Britain. Supporters demonstrated for Wilkes in South Carolina and Boston, and the South Carolina legislature donated a substantial sum to the Society of Supporters of the Bill of Rights. In the 1760s and 1770s, both British and American opposition leaders became convinced that the British government was growing increasingly corrupt and despotic. British radicals wanted to reform Parliament so that the voices of a broader, more representative segment of the population would be heard. The colonies had no representatives in Parliament, and colonists claimed that "no taxation without representation" should be allowed. Indeed, they denied that Parliament had any jurisdiction over the colonies, insisting that the king govern them through colonial legislatures and recognize their traditional British liberties. The failure of the "Wilkes and Liberty" campaign to produce concrete results convinced many Americans that Parliament was hopelessly tainted and that they would have to stand up for their rights as British subjects.

The British colonies remained loyal to the crown until Parliament's encroachment on their autonomy and the elimination of the French threat at the end of the Seven Years' War transformed colonial attitudes. Unconsciously, perhaps, the colonies had begun to form a separate nation; their economies generally flourished in the eighteenth

---

Overthrowing British Authority
The uncompromising attitude of the British government went a long way toward dissolving long-standing loyalties to the home country. During the American War of Independence, residents of New York City pulled down the statue of the hated George III. (*Lafayette College Art Collection, Easton, PA.*)

DOCUMENT

Thomas Jefferson, Declaration of Independence (July 4, 1776)

Although others helped revise the Declaration of Independence of the thirteen North American colonies from Great Britain, Jefferson wrote the original draft himself. A Virginia planter and lawyer, Jefferson went on to become governor of Virginia, minister to France, secretary of state, vice president and president of the United States (1801–1809). The Declaration begins with a stirring expression of the belief in natural or human rights.

When in the Course of human events, it becomes necessary for one people to dissolve the political bands which have connected them with another, and to assume among the powers of the earth, the separate and equal station to which the Laws of Nature and of Nature's God entitle them, a decent respect to the opinions of mankind requires that they should declare the causes which impel them to the separation.

We hold these truths to be self-evident, that all men are created equal, that they are endowed by their Creator with certain unalienable Rights, that among these are Life, Liberty and the pursuit of Happiness. — That to secure these rights, Governments are instituted among Men, deriving their just powers from the consent of the governed, — That whenever any Form of Government becomes destructive of these ends, it is the Right of the People to alter or to abolish it, and to institute new Government, laying its foundation on such principles and organizing its powers in such form, as to them shall seem most likely to effect their Safety and Happiness. Prudence, indeed, will dictate that Governments long established should not be changed for light and transient causes; and accordingly all experience hath shewn, that mankind are more disposed to suffer, while evils are sufferable, than to right themselves by abolishing the forms to which they are accustomed. But when a long train of abuses and usurpations, pursuing invariably the same Object evinces a design to reduce them under absolute Despotism, it is their right, it is their duty, to throw off such Government, and to provide new Guards for their future security. — Such has been the patient sufferance of these Colonies; and such is now the necessity which constrains them to alter their former Systems of Government. The history of the present King of Great Britain is a history of repeated injuries and usurpations, all having in direct object the establishment of an absolute Tyranny over these States.

Source: U.S. National Archives and Records Administration, Washington, D.C.

century, and between 1750 and 1776 their population almost doubled. With the British clamoring for lower taxes and the colonists paying only a fraction of the tax rate paid by the Britons at home, Parliament passed new taxes, including the Stamp Act in 1765, which required a special tax stamp on all legal documents and publications. After violent rioting in the colonies, the tax was repealed, but in 1773 a new Tea Act revived colonial resistance, which culminated in the so-called Boston Tea Party of 1773. Colonists dressed as Indians boarded British ships and dumped the imported tea (by this time an enormously popular beverage) into Boston's harbor.

Political opposition in the American colonies turned belligerent when Britain threatened to use force to maintain control. In 1774, the First Continental Congress convened, composed of delegates from the colonies, and unsuccessfully petitioned the crown for redress. The next year the Second Continental Congress organized an army with George Washington in command. After actual fighting had begun, in 1776, the congress issued the Declaration of Independence. An eloquent statement of the American cause written by Thomas Jefferson, the Declaration of Independence was couched in the language of universal human rights, which enlightened Europeans could be expected to understand. (See Document, "Declaration of Independence," above.) George III denounced the American "traitors and rebels." But European newspapers enthusiastically reported on every American response to "the cruel acts of oppression they have been made to suffer." In 1778, France boosted the American cause by entering on the colonists' side. Spain, too, saw an opportunity to check the growing power of Britain, though without actually endorsing American independence out of fear of the response of its Latin American colonies. Spain declared war on Britain in 1779; in 1780, Great Britain declared war on the Dutch Republic in retaliation for Dutch support of the rebels. The worldwide conflict that resulted was more than Britain could handle. The American colonies achieved their independence in the peace treaty of 1783.

The newly independent states still faced the challenge of republican self-government. The Articles of Confederation, drawn up in 1777 as a provisional constitution, proved weak because they gave the central government few powers. In 1787, a constitutional convention met in Philadelphia to draft a new constitution. It established a two-house legislature, an indirectly elected president, and an independent judiciary. The U.S. Constitution's preamble insisted explicitly, for the first time in history, that government derived its power solely from the people and did not depend on divine right or on the tradition of royalty or aristocracy. The new educated elite of the eighteenth century had now created government based on a "social contract" among male, property-owning, white citizens. It was by no means a complete democracy (women and slaves were excluded from political participation), but the new government represented a radical departure from European models. In 1791, the Bill of Rights was appended to the Constitution outlining the essential rights (such as freedom of speech) that the government could never overturn. Although slavery continued in the American republic, the new emphasis on rights helped fuel the movement for its abolition in both Britain and the United States.

Interest in the new republic was greatest in France. The U.S. Constitution and various state constitutions were published in French with commentary by leading thinkers. Even more important in the long run were the effects of the American war. Dutch losses to Great Britain aroused a widespread movement for political reform in the Dutch Republic, and debts incurred by France in supporting the American colonies would soon force the French monarchy to the edge of bankruptcy and then to revolution. Ultimately, the entire European system of royal rule would be challenged.

REVIEW: Why did public opinion become a new factor in politics in the second half of the eighteenth century?

Conclusion

When Thomas Jefferson looked back many years later on the Declaration of Independence, he said he hoped it would be "the signal of arousing men

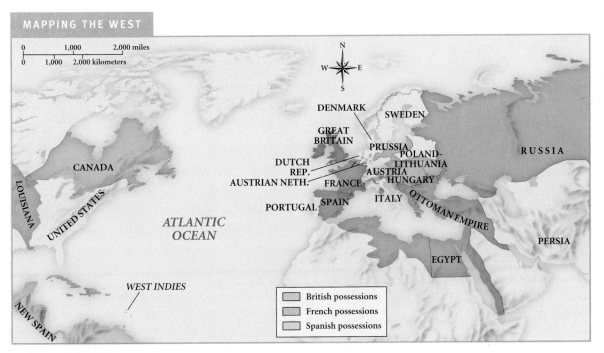

Europe and the World, c. 1780
Although Great Britain lost control over part of its North American colonies, which became the new United States, European influence on the rest of the world grew dramatically in the eighteenth century. The slave trade linked European ports to African slave-trading outposts and to plantations in the Caribbean, South America, and North America. The European countries on the Atlantic Ocean benefited most from this trade. Yet almost all of Africa, China, Japan, and large parts of India still resisted European incursion, and the Ottoman Empire, with its massive territories, still presented Europe with a formidable military challenge.

to burst the chains under which monkish igno-rance and superstition had persuaded them to bind themselves." What began as a cosmopolitan movement of a few intellectuals in the first half of the eighteenth century had reached a relatively wide audience among the educated elite of men and women by the 1770s and 1780s. The spirit of Enlightenment swept from the salons, coffee-houses, and Masonic lodges into the halls of gov-ernment from Philadelphia to Vienna. Scientific inquiry into the causes of social misery and laws defending individual rights and freedoms gained adherents even among the rulers and ministers re-sponsible for censoring Enlightenment works.

For most Europeans, however, the promise of the Enlightenment did not become a reality. Rulers such as Catherine the Great had every intention of retaining their full, often unchecked, powers, even as they corresponded with leading philosophes and entertained them at their courts. Moreover, would-be reformers often found themselves blocked by the resistance of nobles, by the priori-ties rulers gave to waging wars, or by popular re-sistance to deregulation of trade that increased the uncertainties of the market. Yet even the failure of reform contributed to the ferment in Europe after 1770. Peasant rebellions in eastern Europe, the "Wilkes and Liberty" campaign in Great Britain, the struggle over reform in France, and the revo-lution in America all occurred around the same time, and their conjunction convinced many Eu-ropeans that change was brewing. Just how much could change, and whether change made life bet-ter or worse, would come into question in the next ten years.

FOR FURTHER EXPLORATION

■ **For suggested references, including Web sites, for topics in this chapter,** see page SR-1 at the end of the book.

■ **For additional primary-source material from this period,** see Chapter 18 in *Sources of THE MAKING OF THE WEST,* Third Edition.

■ **For Web sites and documents related to topics in this chapter,** see *Make History* at **bedfordstmartins.com/hunt.**

CHAPTER REVIEW

KEY TERMS AND PEOPLE

philosophes (556)
deists (559)
abolitionists (560)
laissez-faire (561)
Jean-Jacques Rousseau (561)
romanticism (566)

Methodism (566)
Freemasons (568)
enlightened despots (573)
Seven Years' War (574)
partition of Poland (576)
Pugachev rebellion (579)

MAKING CONNECTIONS

1. Why would rulers feel ambivalent about the Enlightenment, supporting reform on the one hand, while clamping down on political dissidents on the other hand?

2. Which major developments in this period ran counter to the influence of the Enlightenment?

3. In what ways had politics changed, and in what ways did they remain the same during the Enlightenment?

REVIEW QUESTIONS

1. What were the major differences between the Enlightenment in France, Great Britain, and the German states?

2. What were the major differences in the impact of the Enlightenment on nobles, middle classes, and lower classes?

3. What prompted enlightened absolutists to undertake reforms in the second half of the eighteenth century?

4. Why did public opinion become a new factor in politics in the second half of the eighteenth century?

For practice quizzes, a customized study plan, and other study tools, see the Online Study Guide at bedfordstmartins.com/hunt.

IMPORTANT EVENTS

1740–1748	War of the Austrian Succession: France, Spain, and Prussia versus Austria and Great Britain
1751–1772	*Encyclopedia* published in France
1756–1763	Seven Years' War fought in Europe, India, and the American colonies
1762	Jean-Jacques Rousseau, *The Social Contract* and *Émile*
1764	Voltaire, *Philosophical Dictionary*
1771	Louis XV of France fails to break the power of the French law courts
1772	First partition of Poland

1773	Pugachev rebellion of Russian peasants
1776	American Declaration of Independence from Great Britain; Adam Smith, *The Wealth of Nations*
1780	Joseph II of Austria undertakes a wide-reaching reform program
1781	Immanuel Kant, *The Critique of Pure Reason*
1785	Catherine the Great's Charter of the Nobility grants nobles exclusive control over their serfs in exchange for subservience to the state
1787	Delegates from the states draft the U.S. Constitution

The Cataclysm of Revolution
1789–1799

On October 5, 1789, a crowd of several thousand women marched in a drenching rain twelve miles from the center of Paris to Versailles. They demanded the king's help in securing more grain for the hungry and his reassurance that he did not intend to resist the emerging revolutionary movement. Joined the next morning by thousands of men who came from Paris to reinforce them, they broke into the royal family's private apartments, killing two of the royal bodyguards. To prevent further bloodshed, the king agreed to move his family and his government to Paris. A dramatic procession of the royal family guarded by throngs of ordinary men and women made its slow way back to the capital. The people's proud display of cannons and pikes underlined the fundamental transformation that was occurring. Ordinary people had forced the king of France to respond to their grievances. The French monarchy was in danger, and if such a powerful and long-lasting institution could come under fire, then could any monarch of Europe rest easy?

Although even the keenest political observer did not predict its eruption in 1789, the French Revolution had its immediate origins in a constitutional crisis provoked by a growing government deficit, traceable to French involvement in the American War of Independence. The constitutional crisis came to a head on July 14, 1789, when armed Parisians captured the Bastille, a royal fortress and symbol of monarchical authority in the center of the capital. The fall of the Bastille, like the women's march to Versailles three months later, showed the determination of the common people to put their mark on events.

The French Revolution first grabbed the attention of the entire world because it seemed to promise universal human rights, constitutional government, and broad-based political participation. Its most

Women's March to Versailles
Thousands of prints broadcast the events of the French Revolution to the public in France and elsewhere. They varied from fine-art engravings signed by the artist to anonymous simple woodcuts. This colored engraving shows a crowd of armed women marching to Versailles on October 5, 1789, to confront the king. The sight of armed women frightened many observers and demonstrated that the Revolution was not only a men's affair. *(The Granger Collection, New York.)*

famous slogan pledged "Liberty, Equality, and Fraternity" for all. An enthusiastic German wrote, "One of the greatest nations in the world, the greatest in general culture, has at last thrown off the yoke of tyranny." The revolutionaries used a blueprint based on the Enlightenment idea of reason to remake all of society and politics: they executed the king and queen, established a republic for the first time in French history, abolished nobility, and gave the vote to all adult men.

Even as the Revolution promised democracy, however, it also inaugurated a cycle of violence and intimidation. When the revolutionaries encountered resistance to their programs, they set up a government of terror to compel obedience. Some historians therefore see in the French Revolution the origins of modern totalitarianism—that is, governments that try to control every aspect of life, including daily activities, while limiting all forms of political dissent. As events unfolded after 1789, the French Revolution became the model of modern revolution; republicanism, democracy, terrorism, nationalism, and military dictatorship all took their modern forms during the French Revolution.

The Revolution might have remained a strictly French affair if war had not involved the rest of Europe. After 1792, huge French republican armies, fueled by patriotic nationalism, marched across Europe, promising liberation from traditional monarchies but often delivering old-fashioned conquest and annexation. French victories spread revolutionary ideas far and wide, from Poland to the colonies in the Caribbean, where the first successful slave revolt established the republic of Haiti.

The breathtaking succession of regimes in France between 1789 and 1799 and the failure of the republican experiment after ten years of upheaval raised disturbing questions about the relationship between rapid political change and violence. Do all revolutions inevitably degenerate into terror or wars of conquest? Is a regime democratic if it does not allow poor men, women, or blacks to vote? The French Revolution raised these questions and many more. The questions resonated in many countries because the French Revolution seemed to be only the most extreme example of a much broader political and social movement at the end of the eighteenth century.

FOCUS QUESTION: What was so revolutionary about the French Revolution?

The Revolutionary Wave, 1787–1789

Between 1787 and 1789, revolts in the name of liberty broke out in the Dutch Republic, the Austrian Netherlands (present-day Belgium and Luxembourg), and Poland, as well as in France. At the same time, the newly independent United States of America prepared a new federal constitution. Historians have sometimes referred to these revolts as the Atlantic revolutions because so many protest movements arose in countries on both shores of the North Atlantic. These revolutions were the product of long-term prosperity and high expectations, created in part by the spread of the Enlightenment. Europeans in general were wealthier, healthier, more numerous, and better educated than they had ever been before; and the Dutch, Belgian, and French societies were among the wealthiest and best educated within Europe. The French Revolution nonetheless differed greatly from the others. Not only was France the richest, most powerful, and most

■ 1787 Dutch Patriot revolt stifled

■ 1788–1790 Austrian Netherlands' resistance

■ 1792 France and rest of Europe at war; second revolution of August 10

1787 | 1789 | 1791

■ 1789 French Revolution begins

■ 1791 St. Domingue slave revolt

populous state in western Europe, but its revolution was also more violent, more long-lasting, and ultimately more influential. (See "Terms of History," page 590.)

Protesters in the Low Countries and Poland

Political protests in the Dutch Republic attracted European attention because Dutch banks still controlled a hefty portion of the world's capital at the end of the eighteenth century, even though the Dutch Republic's role in international politics had diminished. Revolts also broke out in the neighboring Austrian Netherlands and Poland. Although none of these movements ultimately succeeded, they showed how quickly political discontent could boil over in this era of rising economic and political expectations.

The Dutch Patriot Revolt, 1787. The Dutch Patriots, as they chose to call themselves, wanted to reduce the powers of the prince of Orange, the kinglike stadholder who favored close ties with Great Britain. Government-sponsored Dutch banks owned 40 percent of the British national debt, and by 1796 they held the entire foreign debt of the United States. Relations with the British deteriorated during the American War of Independence, however, and by the middle of the 1780s, agitation in favor of the Americans had boiled over into an attack on the stadholder.

Building on support among middle-class bankers and merchants, the Patriots soon gained a more popular audience by demanding political reforms and organizing armed citizen militias of men, called Free Corps. Town by town the Patriots forced local officials to set up new elections to replace councils that had been packed with Orangist supporters through patronage or family

connections. Before long, the Free Corps took on the troops of the prince of Orange and got the upper hand. In response, Frederick William II of Prussia, whose sister had married the stadholder, intervened in 1787 with tacit British support. Thousands of Prussian troops soon occupied Utrecht and Amsterdam, and the house of Orange regained its former position.

The Low Countries in 1787

Social divisions among the rebels paved the way for the success of this outside intervention. Many of the Patriots from the richest merchant families feared the growing power of the Free Corps. The Free Corps wanted a more democratic form of government, and to get it they encouraged the publication of pamphlets and cartoons attacking the prince and his wife, promoted the rapid spread of clubs and societies made up of common people, and organized crowd-pleasing public ceremonies, such as parades and bonfires, that sometimes turned into riots. In the aftermath of the Prussian invasion in September 1787, the Orangists got their revenge: lower-class mobs pillaged the houses of prosperous Patriot leaders, forcing many to flee to the United States, France, or the Austrian Netherlands. Those Patriots who remained nursed their grievances until the French republican armies invaded in 1795.

The Belgian Independence Movement. If Austrian emperor Joseph II had not tried to introduce Enlightenment-inspired reforms, the Belgians of the ten provinces of the Austrian Netherlands might have remained tranquil. Just as he had done previously in his own crown lands (see Chapter 18), Joseph abolished torture, decreed toleration

■ **1793** Second partition of Poland; Louis XVI executed

■ **1795** Third partition of Poland; France annexes Austrian Netherlands

1793

1795

1797

■ **1794** French abolish slavery; Robespierre falls

■ **1797–1798** "Sister" republics established in Italian states and Switzerland

Revolution

Revolution had previously meant cyclical change that brought life back to a starting point, as a planet makes a revolution around the sun. Revolutions could come and go, by this definition, and change nothing fundamental in the structure of society. After 1789, *revolution* came to mean a self-conscious attempt to leap into the future by reshaping society and politics and even the human personality. A revolutionary official analyzed the meaning of the word in 1793: "A revolution is never made by halves; it must either be total or it will abort. . . . *Revolutionary* means outside of all forms and all rules." In short, *revolution* soon had an all-or-nothing meaning; you were either for the revolution or against it. There could be no in between.

Revolution still has the same meaning given it by the French revolutionaries, but it is now an even more contested term because of its association with communist theory. In the nineteenth century, Karl Marx incorporated the French Revolution into his new doctrine of communism. In his view, the middle-class French revolutionaries had overthrown the monarchy and the "feudal" aristocracy to pave the way for capitalist development. In the future, the proletariat (industrial workers) would overthrow the capitalist middle class to install a communist government that would abolish private property. Since Marxists claimed the French Revolution as the forerunner of the communist revolution in the nineteenth and twentieth centuries, it was perhaps inevitable that those who opposed communism would also criticize the French Revolution.

The most influential example of this view is that of the French scholar François Furet. An ex-communist, Furet argued that the French Revolution can be seen as the origin of totalitarianism because it incarnated what Furet calls "the illusion of politics," that is, the belief that people can transform social and economic relationships through political revolution. The French revolutionaries became totalitarian, in Furet's view, because they wanted to establish a kind of political and social utopia (a perfect society), in which reason alone determined the shape of political and social life. Because this dream is impossible given human resistance to rapid change, the revolutionaries had to use force to achieve their goals. In other words, revolution itself was a problematic idea, according to Furet. *Revolution* as a term remains as contested as the events that gave rise to it.

for Jews and Protestants (in this resolutely Catholic area), and suppressed monasteries. His reorganization of the administrative and judicial systems eliminated many offices that belonged to nobles and lawyers, sparking resistance among the upper classes in 1788.

Upper-class protesters intended only to defend historic local liberties against an overbearing government. Nonetheless, their resistance galvanized democrats, who wanted a more representative government and organized clubs to give voice to their demands. At the end of 1788, a secret society formed armed companies to prepare an uprising. By late 1789, each province had separately declared its independence, and the Austrian administration had collapsed. Delegates from the various provinces declared themselves the United States of Belgium, a clear reference to the American precedent.

Once again, however, social divisions doomed the rebels. When the democrats began to challenge noble authority, aristocratic leaders drew to their side the Catholic clergy and peasants, who had little sympathy for the democrats of the cities. Every Sunday in May and June 1790, thousands of peasant men and women, led by their priests, streamed into Brussels carrying crucifixes, nooses, and pitchforks to intimidate the democrats and defend the church. Faced with the choice between the Austrian emperor and "our current tyrants," the democrats chose to support the return of the Austrians under Emperor Leopold II (r. 1790–1792), who had succeeded his brother.

Polish Patriots.   A reform party calling itself the Patriots also emerged in Poland, which had been shocked by the loss of a third of its territory in the first partition of 1772. The Patriots sought to overhaul the weak commonwealth along modern western European lines and looked to King Stanislaw August Poniatowski (r. 1764–1795) to lead them. A nobleman who owed his crown solely to the dubious honor of being Catherine the Great's discarded lover but who was also a favorite correspondent of the Parisian salon hostess Madame Geoffrin, Poniatowski saw in moderate reform the only chance for his country to escape the consequences of a century's misgovernment and cultural decline. Ranged against the Patriots stood most of the aristocrats and the formidable Catherine the Great, determined to uphold imperial Russian influence.

Pleased to see Russian influence waning in Poland, Austria and Prussia allowed the reform movement to proceed. In 1788, the Patriots got their golden chance. Bogged down in war with the Ottoman Turks, Catherine could not block the summoning of a reform-minded parliament, which eventually enacted the constitution of May 3, 1791. It established a hereditary monarchy with somewhat strengthened authority, ended the veto power that each aristocrat had over legislation, granted townspeople limited political rights, and vaguely promised future Jewish emancipation. Abolishing serfdom was hardly mentioned. Within a year, however, Catherine II had turned her attention to Poland and engineered the downfall of the Patriots.

Origins of the French Revolution, 1787–1789

Many French enthusiastically greeted the American experiment in republican government and supported the Dutch, Belgian, and Polish patriots. But they did not expect the United States and the Dutch Republic to provide them a model. Montesquieu and Rousseau, the leading political theorists of the Enlightenment, taught that republics suited only small countries, not big ones like France. After suffering humiliation at the hands of the British in the Seven Years' War (1756–1763), the French had regained international prestige by supporting the victorious Americans, and the monarchy had shown its eagerness to promote reforms. In 1787, for example, the French crown granted civil rights to Protestants. Yet by the late 1780s, the French monarchy faced a serious fiscal crisis caused by a mounting deficit. It soon provoked a constitutional crisis of epic proportions.

Fiscal Crisis. France's fiscal problems stemmed from its support of the Americans against the British in the American War of Independence. About half of the French national budget went to paying interest on the debt that had accumulated. In contrast to Great Britain, which had a national bank to help raise loans for the government, the French government lived off relatively short-term, high-interest loans from private sources including Swiss banks, government annuities, and advances from tax collectors.

For years the French government had been trying unsuccessfully to modernize the tax system to make it more equitable. The peasants bore the greatest burden of taxes, whereas the nobles and clergy were largely exempt from them. Tax collection was also far from systematic: private contractors collected many taxes and pocketed a large share of the proceeds. With the growing support of public opinion, the bond and annuity holders from the middle and upper classes now demanded a clearer system of fiscal accountability.

In a monarchy, the ruler's character is always crucial. Many complained that **Louis XVI** (r. 1774–1792) showed more interest in hunting or in his hobby of making locks than in the problems of government. His wife, **Marie-Antoinette**, was blond, beautiful, and much criticized for her

extravagant taste in clothes, elaborate hairdos, and supposed indifference to popular misery. When confronted by the inability of the poor to buy bread, she was reported to have replied, "Let them eat cake." "The Austrian bitch," as underground writers called her, had been the target of an increasingly nasty pamphlet campaign in the 1780s. By 1789, the queen had become an object of popular hatred. The king's ineffectiveness and the queen's growing unpopularity helped undermine the monarchy as an institution.

Faced with a mounting deficit, in 1787 Louis submitted a package of reforms to the Assembly of Notables, a group of handpicked nobles, clergymen, and officials. When this group refused to

Queen Marie-Antoinette (detail)

Marie-Louise-Élizabeth Vigée-Lebrun painted this portrait of the French queen Marie-Antoinette and her children in 1788. The eldest son, Louis (not shown in this detail), died in 1789. When he died, her second son (on her lap here), also called Louis, became heir to the throne. Known to supporters of the monarch as Louis XVII, he died in prison in 1795 and never ruled. Vigée-Lebrun fled France in 1789 and returned only in 1805. (© Chateau de Versailles, France/The Bridgeman Art Library.)

Louis XVI: French King (r. 1774–1792) who was tried and found guilty of treason; he was executed on January 21, 1793.

Marie-Antoinette: Wife of Louis XVI and queen of France who was tried and executed in October 1793.

endorse his program, the king presented his proposals for a more uniform land tax to his old rival the parlement of Paris. When it too refused, he ordered the parlement judges into exile in the provinces. Overnight, the judges (members of the nobility because of the offices they held) became popular heroes for resisting the king's "tyranny"; in reality, however, the judges, like the notables, wanted reform only on their own terms. Louis finally gave in to demands that he call a meeting of the Estates General, which had last met 175 years before.

The Estates General. The calling of the Estates General electrified public opinion. Who would determine the fate of the nation? The **Estates General** was a body of deputies from the three estates, or orders, of France. The deputies in the First Estate represented some 100,000 clergy of the Catholic church, which owned about 10 percent of the land and collected a 10 percent tax (the tithe) on peasants. The deputies of the Second Estate represented the nobility, about 400,000 men and women who owned about 25 percent of the land, enjoyed many tax exemptions, and collected seigneurial dues and rents from their peasant tenants. The deputies of the Third Estate represented everyone else, at least 95 percent of the nation. In 1614, at the last meeting of the Estates General, each order had deliberated and voted separately. Before the elections to the Estates General in 1789, the king agreed to double the number of deputies for the Third Estate (making them equal in number to the other two combined), but he refused to mandate voting by individual head rather than by order. Voting by order (each order would have one vote) would conserve the traditional powers of the clergy and nobility; voting by head (each deputy would have one vote) would give the Third Estate an advantage since many clergymen and even some nobles sympathized with the Third Estate.

As the state's censorship apparatus broke down, pamphleteers by the hundreds denounced the traditional privileges of the nobility and clergy and called for voting by head rather than by order. In the most vitriolic of all the pamphlets, *What Is the Third Estate?*, the middle-class clergyman Abbé (Abbot) Emmanuel-Joseph Sieyès charged that the nobility contributed nothing at all to the nation's well-being; they were "a malignant disease which preys upon and tortures the body of a sick man." In the winter and spring of 1789, villagers

and townspeople alike held meetings to elect deputies and write down their grievances. The effect was immediate. Although educated men dominated the meetings at the regional level, the humblest peasants voted in their villages and burst forth with complaints, especially about taxes. As one villager lamented, "The last crust of bread has been taken from us." The long series of meetings raised expectations that the Estates General would help the king solve all the nation's ills.

These new hopes soared just at the moment France experienced an increasingly rare but always dangerous food shortage. Bad weather had damaged the harvest of 1788, causing bread prices to soar in many places in the spring and summer of 1789 and threatening starvation for the poorest people. In addition, a serious slump in textile production had been causing massive unemployment since 1786. Hundreds of thousands of textile workers were out of work and hungry, adding another volatile element to an already tense situation.

When some twelve hundred deputies journeyed to the king's palace of Versailles for the opening of the Estates General in May 1789, many readers avidly followed the developments in newspapers that sprouted overnight. Although most nobles insisted on voting by order, the deputies of the Third Estate refused to proceed on that basis. After six weeks of stalemate, on June 17, 1789, the deputies of the Third Estate took unilateral action and declared themselves and whoever would join them the National Assembly, in which each deputy would vote as an individual. Two days later, the clergy voted by a narrow margin to join them. Suddenly denied access to their meeting hall on June 20, the deputies met on a nearby tennis court and swore an oath not to disband until they had given France a constitution that reflected their newly declared authority. This "tennis court oath" expressed the determination of the Third Estate to carry through a constitutional revolution. A few days later, the nobles had no choice but to join too.

July 14, 1789: The Fall of the Bastille. At first, Louis appeared to agree to the new National Assembly, but he also ordered thousands of soldiers to march to Paris. The deputies who supported the Assembly feared a plot by the king and high-ranking nobles to arrest them and disperse the Assembly. "Everyone is convinced that the approach of the troops covers some violent design," one deputy wrote home. Their fears were confirmed when, on July 11, the king fired Jacques Necker, the Swiss Protestant finance minister and the one high official regarded as sympathetic to the deputies' cause.

Estates General: A body of deputies from the three estates, or orders, of France: the clergy (First Estate), the nobility (Second Estate), and everyone else (Third Estate).

Fall of the Bastille

The Bastille prison is shown here in all its imposing grandeur. When the fortress's governor Bernard René de Launay surrendered on July 14, 1789, he was marched off to city hall. The gathering crowd taunted and spat at him, and after he lashed out at one of the men nearest him, he was stabbed, shot, and then beheaded. The head was displayed as a trophy on a pike held high above the crowd. Royal authority had been successfully challenged and even humiliated. *(The Granger Collection, New York.)*

The popular reaction in Paris to Necker's dismissal and the threat of military force changed the course of the French Revolution. When the news spread, the common people in Paris began to arm themselves and attack places where either grain or arms were thought to be stored (Map 19.1). A deputy in Versailles reported home: "Today all of the evils overwhelm France, and we are between despotism, carnage, and famine." On July 14, 1789, an armed crowd marched on the Bastille, a fortified prison that symbolized royal authority. After a chaotic battle in which a hundred armed citizens died, the prison officials surrendered.

The fall of the Bastille (an event now commemorated as the French national holiday) set an important precedent. The common people showed themselves willing to intervene violently at a crucial political moment (see The Third Estate Awakens, at right). All over France, food riots turned into local revolts. The officials in one city wrote of their plight: "Yesterday afternoon [July 19] more than seven or eight thousand people, men and women, assembled in front of the two gates to the city hall. . . . We were forced to negotiate with them and to promise to give them wheat . . . and to reduce the price of bread." Local governments were forced out of power and replaced by committees of "patriots" loyal to the revolutionary cause. The king's government began to crumble. To restore order, the patriots relied on newly formed National Guard units composed of civilians. In

The Third Estate Awakens

This print, produced after the fall of the Bastille (note the heads on pikes outside the prison), shows a clergyman (First Estate) and a noble (Second Estate) alarmed by the awakening of the commoners (Third Estate). The Third Estate breaks the chains of oppression and arms itself. In what ways does this print draw attention to the social conflicts that lay behind the political struggles in the Estates General? *(Réunion des Musées Nationaux/Art Resource, NY.)*

■ **For more help analyzing this image,** see the visual activity for this chapter in the Online Study Guide at bedfordstmartins.com/hunt.

MAP 19.1 Revolutionary Paris, 1789
The French Revolution began with the fall of the Bastille prison on July 14, 1789. The huge fortified prison was located on the eastern side of the city in a neighborhood of working people. Before attacking the Bastille, crowds had torn down many of the customs booths located in the wall of the Farmers General (the private company in charge of tax collection), and taken the arms stored in the Hôtel des Invalides, a veterans' hospital on the western side of the city where the upper classes lived. During the Revolution, executions took place on the square or Place de la Révolution, now called Place de la Concorde.

Paris, the Marquis de Lafayette, a hero of the American War of Independence and a noble deputy in the National Assembly, became commander of the new National Guard. One of Louis XVI's brothers and many other leading aristocrats fled into exile. The Revolution thus had its first heroes, its first victims, and its first enemies.

> **REVIEW:** How did the beginning of the French Revolution resemble the other revolutions of 1787–1789?

From Monarchy to Republic, 1789–1793

Until July 1789, the French Revolution followed a course much like that of the protest movements in the Low Countries. Unlike the Dutch and Belgian uprisings, however, the French Revolution did not

come to a quick end. The French revolutionaries first tried to establish a constitutional monarchy based on the Enlightenment principles of human rights and rational government. This effort failed when the king attempted to raise a counterrevolutionary army. When war broke out in 1792, new tensions culminated in a second revolution on August 10, 1792, that deposed the king and established a republic in which all power rested in an elected legislature.

The Revolution of Rights and Reason

Before drafting a constitution, the deputies of the National Assembly had to confront growing violence in the countryside. Peasants made up 80 percent of the French population but owned only about 50 percent of the land. Most could barely make ends meet but still had to pay taxes to the state, the tithe to the Catholic church, and a host of seigneurial dues to their lords, whether for using the lords' mills to grind wheat or to ensure their ability to give their land as inheritance to their children. Peasants greeted the news of events in 1789 with a mixture of hope and anxiety. As food shortages spread, they feared that the beggars and vagrants crowding the roads might be part of an aristocratic plot to starve the people by burning crops or barns. In many places, the **Great Fear** (the term used by historians to describe this rural panic) turned into peasant attacks on aristocrats or on the records of

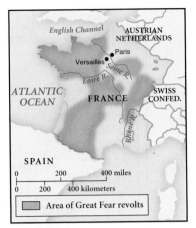

The Great Fear, 1789

peasants' dues kept in the lord's château. Peasants now refused to pay dues to their lords, and the persistence of peasant violence raised alarms about the potential for a general peasant insurrection.

The End of Feudalism. Alarmed by peasant unrest, the National Assembly decided to make sweeping changes. On the night of August 4, 1789, noble deputies announced their willingness to give up their tax exemptions and seigneurial dues. By the end of the night, amid wild enthusiasm, dozens of deputies had come to the podium to relinquish the tax exemptions of their own professional groups, towns, or provinces. The National Assembly decreed the abolition of what it called "the feudal regime" — that is, it freed the remaining serfs and eliminated all special privileges in matters of taxation, including all seigneurial dues on land. (A few days later the deputies insisted on financial compensation for some of these dues, but most peasants refused to pay.) Peasants had achieved their goals. The Assembly also mandated equality of opportunity in access to government positions. Talent, rather than birth, was to be the key to success. Enlightenment principles were beginning to become law.

The Declaration of the Rights of Man and Citizen. Three weeks later, the deputies drew up the **Declaration of the Rights of Man and Citizen** as the preamble to a new constitution. In words reminiscent of the American Declaration of Independence, whose author, Thomas Jefferson, was in Paris at the time, it proclaimed, "Men are born and

Great Fear: The term used by historians to describe the French rural panic of 1789, which led to peasant attacks on aristocrats or on seigneurial records of peasants' dues.

Declaration of the Rights of Man and Citizen: The preamble to the French constitution drafted in August 1789; it established the sovereignty of the nation and equal rights for citizens.

remain free and equal in rights." The Declaration granted freedom of religion, freedom of the press, equality of taxation, and equality before the law. It established the principle of national sovereignty: since "all sovereignty rests essentially in the nation," it said, the king derived his authority henceforth from the nation rather than from tradition or divine right.

By pronouncing all *men* free and equal, the Declaration immediately created new dilemmas. Did women have equal rights with men? What about free blacks in the colonies? How could slavery be justified if all men were born free? Did religious toleration of Protestants and Jews include equal political rights? Women never received the right to vote during the French Revolution, though Protestant and Jewish men did. Women were theoretically citizens under civil law but without the right to full political participation. (See Document, "The Rights of Minorities," page 597.)

Some women did not accept their exclusion, viewing it as a betrayal of the promised new order. In addition to joining demonstrations, such as the march to Versailles in October 1789, women wrote petitions, published tracts, and organized political clubs to demand more participation (see A Women's Club, below). In her Declaration of the

A Women's Club

In this gouache by the Lesueur brothers, *The Patriotic Women's Club*, the club president urges the members to contribute funds for poor patriot families. Women's clubs focused on philanthropic work but also discussed revolutionary legislation. The colorful but sober dress indicates that the women are middle class. *(Bridgeman-Giraudon/Art Resource, NY.)*

MAP 19.2 Redrawing the Map of France, 1789–1791

Before 1789, France had been divided into provinces named after the territories owned by dukes and counts in the Middle Ages. Many provinces had their own law codes and separate systems of taxation. As it began its deliberations, the new National Assembly determined to install uniform administrations and laws for the entire country. Discussion of the administrative reforms began in October 1789 and became law on February 15, 1790, when the Assembly voted to divide the provinces into eighty-three departments, with names based on their geographical characteristics: Basses-Pyrénées for the Pyrénées mountains, Haute-Marne for the Marne River, and so on. ■ How did this redrawing of the administrative map reflect the deputies' emphasis on reason over history?

Rights of Women of 1791, Olympe de Gouges (1748–1793) played on the language of the official Declaration to make the point that women should also be included. She announced in Article I, "Woman is born free and lives equal to man in her rights." She also insisted that since "woman has the right to mount the scaffold," she must "equally have the right to mount the rostrum." De Gouges linked her complaints to a program of social reform in which women would have equal rights to property and public office and equal responsibilities in taxes and criminal punishment.

The Constitution and the Church. Unresponsive to calls for women's equality, the National Assembly turned to preparing France's first written constitution. The deputies gave voting rights only to white men who passed a test of wealth. Despite these limitations, France became a constitutional monarchy in which the king served as the leading state functionary. A one-house legislature was responsible for making laws. The king could postpone enactment of laws but not veto them. The deputies abolished all the old administrative divisions of the provinces and replaced them with a national system of eighty-three departments with identical administrative and legal structures (Map 19.2). All officials were elected; no offices could be bought or sold. The deputies also abolished the old taxes and replaced them with new ones that were supposed to be uniformly levied. The National Assembly had difficulty collecting taxes, however, because many people had expected a substantial cut in the tax rate. The new administrative system survived, nonetheless, and the departments are still the basic units of the French state today.

DOCUMENT

The Rights of Minorities

When the National Assembly passed the Declaration of the Rights of Man and Citizen on August 26, 1789, it opened the way to discussion of the rights of various groups, from actors (considered ineligible for voting under the monarchy because they impersonated other people as part of their profession) to women, free blacks, mulattoes, and slaves. A nobleman, Count Stanislas de Clermont Tonnerre, gave a speech on December 23, 1789, in which he advocated ending exclusions based on profession or religion, though not gender or race.

Sirs, in the declaration that you believed you should put at the head of the French constitution you have established, consecrated, the rights of man and citizen. In the constitutional work that you have decreed relative to the organization of the municipalities, a work accepted by the King, you have fixed the conditions of eligibility that can be required of citizens. It would seem, Sirs, that there is nothing else left to do and that prejudices should be silent in the face of the language of the law; but an honorable member has explained to us that the non-Catholics of some provinces still experience harassment based on former laws, and seeing them excluded from the elections and public posts, another honorable member has protested against the effect of prejudice that persecutes some professions. This prejudice, these laws, force you to make your position clear. I have the honor to present you with the draft of a decree, and it is this draft that I defend here. I establish in it the principle that professions and religious creed can never become reasons for ineligibility. . . .

Every creed has only one test to pass in regard to the social body: it has only one examination to which it must submit, that of its morals. It is here that the adversaries of the Jewish people attack me. This people, they say, is not sociable. They are commanded to loan at usurious rates; they cannot be joined with us either in marriage or by the bonds of social interchange; our food is forbidden to them; our tables prohibited; our armies will never have Jews serving in the defense of the fatherland. The worst of these reproaches is unjust; the others are only specious. Usury is not commanded by their laws; loans at interest are forbidden between them and permitted with foreigners. . . .

But, they say to me, the Jews have their own judges and laws. I respond that is your fault and you should not allow it. We must refuse everything to the Jews as a nation and accord everything to Jews as individuals. We must withdraw recognition from their judges; they should only have our judges. We must refuse legal protection to the maintenance of the so-called laws of their Judaic organization; they should not be allowed to form in the state either a political body or an order. They must be citizens individually. But, some will say to me, they do not want to be citizens. Well then! If they do not want to be citizens, they should say so, and then, we should banish them. It is repugnant to have in the state an association of non-citizens, and a nation within the nation. . . . In short, Sirs, the presumed status of every man resident in a country is to be a citizen.

Source: *Archives parlementaires,* 10 (Paris, 1878): 754–57. Translation by Lynn Hunt.

When the deputies turned to reforming the Catholic church, they created enduring conflicts. Convinced that monastic life encouraged idleness and a decline in the nation's population, the deputies outlawed any future monastic vows and encouraged monks and nuns to return to private life by offering state pensions. Motivated partly by the ongoing financial crisis, the National Assembly confiscated all the church's property and promised to pay clerical salaries in return. The Civil Constitution of the Clergy, passed in July 1790, set pay scales for the clergy and provided that the voters elect their own parish priests and bishops just as they elected other officials. The impounded property served as a guarantee for the new paper money, called assignats, issued by the government. The assignats soon became subject to inflation because the government began to sell the church lands to the highest bidders in state auctions. The sales increased the landholdings of wealthy city dwellers and prosperous peasants but cut the value of the paper money.

Faced with resistance to these changes, in November 1790, the National Assembly required all clergy to swear an oath of loyalty to the Civil Constitution of the Clergy. Pope Pius VI in Rome condemned the constitution, and half of the French clergy refused to take the oath. The oath of allegiance permanently divided the Catholic population, which had to choose between loyalty to the old church and commitment to the Revolution with its "constitutional" church. The revolutionary government lost many supporters by passing laws against the clergy who refused the oath and by forcing them into exile, deporting them forcibly, or executing them as traitors. Riots and demonstrations led by women greeted many of the oath-taking priests who replaced those who refused.

The End of Monarchy

The reorganization of the Catholic church offended Louis XVI, who was reluctant to recognize the new limits on his powers. On June 20, 1791, the royal family escaped in disguise from Paris and fled to the eastern border of France, where they hoped to gather support from Austrian emperor Leopold II, the brother of Marie-Antoinette. The plans went awry when a postmaster recognized the king from his portrait on the new French money, and the royal family was arrested at Varennes, forty miles from the Austrian Netherlands border. The National Assembly tried to depict the departure as a kidnapping, but the "flight to Varennes" touched off demonstrations in Paris against the royal family, whom some now regarded as traitors. Cartoons circulated depicting the royal family as animals being returned "to the stable."

War with Austria and Prussia.   The constitution, finally completed in 1791, provided for the immediate election of the new Legislative Assembly. In a rare act of self-denial, the deputies of the National Assembly declared themselves ineligible for the new Assembly. Those who had experienced the Revolution firsthand now departed from the scene, opening the door to men with little previous experience in national politics. The status of the king might have remained uncertain if war had not intervened, but by early 1792 everyone seemed intent on war with Austria. Louis and Marie-Antoinette hoped that such a war would lead to the defeat of the Revolution, whereas the deputies who favored a republic believed that war would lead to the king's downfall. On April 21, 1792, Louis declared war on Austria. Prussia immediately entered on the Austrian side. Thousands of French aristocrats, including two-thirds of the army officer corps, had already emigrated, including both the king's brothers, and they were gathering along France's eastern border in expectation of joining a counterrevolutionary army.

When fighting broke out in 1792, all the powers expected a brief and relatively contained war. Instead, it would continue despite brief interruptions for the next twenty-three years. War had an immediate radicalizing effect on French politics. When the French armies proved woefully unprepared for battle, the authority of the Legislative Assembly came under fire. In June 1792, an angry crowd invaded the hall of the Assembly in Paris and threatened the royal family. The Prussian commander, the duke of Brunswick, issued a manifesto announcing that Paris would be totally destroyed if the royal family suffered any violence.

The Second Revolution of August 10, 1792.   The ordinary people of Paris did not passively await their fate. Known as *sans-culottes* (literally, "without breeches") — because men who worked with their hands wore long trousers rather than the knee breeches of the upper classes — they had followed every twist and turn in revolutionary fortunes. Faced with the threat of military retaliation and frustrated with the inaction of the Legislative Assembly, on August 10, 1792, the sans-culottes organized an insurrection and attacked the Tuileries palace, the residence of the king. The king and his

The King as a Farmyard Animal
This simple print makes a powerful point: King Louis XVI has lost not only his authority but also the respect of his subjects. Engravings and etchings like this one appeared in reaction to the attempted flight of the king and queen in June 1791.
(The Granger Collection, New York.)

The Execution of King Louis XVI
Louis XVI was executed by order of the National Convention on January 21, 1793. In this print, the executioner shows the severed head to the national guards standing in orderly silence around the scaffold. *(Mary Evans Picture Library.)*

family had to seek refuge in the meeting room of the Legislative Assembly, where the frightened deputies ordered elections for a new legislature. By abolishing the property qualifications for voting, the deputies instituted universal male suffrage for the first time.

When it met, the National Convention abolished the monarchy and on September 22, 1792, established the first republic in French history. The republic would answer only to the people, not to any royal authority. Many of the deputies in the Convention belonged to the devotedly republican **Jacobin Club**, named after the former monastery in Paris where the club first met. The Jacobin Club in Paris headed a national political network of clubs that linked all the major towns and cities. Lafayette and other liberal aristocrats who had supported the constitutional monarchy fled into exile.

Violence soon exploded again when early in September 1792 the Prussians approached Paris. Hastily gathered mobs stormed the overflowing prisons to seek out traitors who might help the enemy. In an atmosphere of near hysteria, eleven hundred inmates were killed, including many ordinary and completely innocent people. The princess of Lamballe, one of the queen's favorites, was hacked to pieces and her mutilated body displayed beneath the windows where the royal family was kept under guard. These "September massacres" showed the dark side of popular revolution, in which the common people demanded instant revenge on supposed enemies and conspirators.

The Execution of the King.　The National Convention faced a dire situation. It needed to write a new constitution for the republic while fighting a war with external enemies and confronting increasing resistance at home. Many thought the Revolution had gone too far when it confiscated the properties of the church, eliminated titles of nobility, and deposed the king. The French people had never known any government other than monarchy. Only half the population could read and write at even a basic level. In this situation, symbolic actions became very important. Any public sign of monarchy was at risk, and revolutionaries soon pulled down statues of kings and burned reminders of the former regime.

The fate of Louis XVI and the future direction of the republic divided the deputies elected to the

---

Jacobin Club: A French political club formed in 1789 that inspired the formation of a national network whose members dominated the revolutionary government during the Terror.

National Convention. Most of the deputies were middle-class lawyers and professionals who had developed their ardent republican beliefs in the network of Jacobin Clubs. After the fall of the monarchy in August 1792, however, the Jacobins divided into two factions. The Girondins (named after a department in southwestern France, the Gironde, which provided some of its leading orators) met regularly at the salon of Jeanne Roland, the wife of a minister. They resented the growing power of Parisian militants and tried to appeal to the departments outside of Paris. The Mountain (so called because its deputies sat in the highest seats of the National Convention), in contrast, was closely allied with the Paris militants.

The first showdown between the Girondins and the Mountain occurred during the trial of the king in December 1792. Although the Girondins agreed that the king was guilty of treason, many of them argued for clemency, exile, or a popular referendum on his fate. After a long and difficult debate, the National Convention supported the Mountain and voted by a very narrow majority to execute the king. Louis XVI went to the guillotine on January 21, 1793, sharing the fate of Charles I of England in 1649. "We have just convinced ourselves that a king is only a man," wrote one newspaper, "and that no man is above the law."

> REVIEW: Why did the French Revolution turn in an increasingly radical direction after 1789?

Terror and Resistance

The execution of the king did not solve the new regime's problems. The continuing war required even more men and money, and the introduction of a national draft provoked massive resistance in some parts of France. In response to growing pressures, the National Convention named the Committee of Public Safety to supervise food distribution, direct the war effort, and root out counterrevolutionaries. The leader of the committee, **Maximilien Robespierre** (1758–1794), wanted to go beyond these stopgap measures and create a "republic of virtue," in which the government would teach, or force, citizens to become virtuous republicans through a massive program of political reeducation. Thus began the **Terror**, in which the guillotine became the most terrifying instrument of a government that suppressed almost every form of dissent (see The Guillotine, page 601). These policies only increased divisions, which ultimately led to Robespierre's fall from power and to a dismantling of government by terror.

Robespierre and the Committee of Public Safety

The conflict between the more moderate Girondins and the more radical Mountain came to a head in spring 1793. Militants in Paris agitated for the removal of the deputies who had proposed a referendum on the king, and in retaliation the Girondins engineered the arrest of Jean-Paul Marat, a deputy allied with the Mountain who in his newspaper had been calling for more and more executions. Marat was acquitted, and Parisian militants marched into the National Convention on June 2, 1793, forcing the deputies to decree the arrest of their twenty-nine Girondin colleagues. The Convention consented to the establishment of paramilitary bands called "revolutionary armies" to hunt down political suspects and hoarders of grain. The deputies also agreed to speed up the operation of special revolutionary courts.

Setting the course for government and the war increasingly fell to the twelve-member Committee of Public Safety, set up by the National Convention on April 6, 1793. When Robespierre was elected to the committee three months later, he became in effect its guiding spirit and the chief spokesman of the Revolution. A lawyer from northern France known as "the incorruptible" for his stern honesty and fierce dedication to democratic ideals, Robespierre remains one of the most controversial figures in world history because of his association with the Terror. Although he originally opposed the death penalty and the war, he was convinced that the emergency situation of 1793 required severe measures, including death for those, such as the Girondins, who opposed the committee's policies.

Like many other educated eighteenth-century men, Robespierre had read the classics of republicanism from the ancient Roman writers Tacitus and Plutarch to the Enlightenment thinkers Mon-

---

Maximilien Robespierre (roh behs PYEHR): A lawyer from northern France who laid out the principles of a republic of virtue and of the Terror; his arrest and execution in July 1794 brought an end to the Terror.

Terror: The policy established under the direction of the Committee of Public Safety during the French Revolution to arrest dissidents and execute opponents in order to protect the republic from its enemies.

The Guillotine

Before 1789, only nobles were decapitated if condemned to death; commoners were usually hanged. Equalization of the death penalty was first proposed by J. I. Guillotin, a professor of anatomy and a deputy in the National Assembly. He also suggested that a mechanical device be constructed for decapitation, leading to the instrument's association with his name. The Assembly decreed decapitation as the death penalty in June 1791 and another physician, A. Louis, actually invented the guillotine. The executioner pulled up the blade by a cord and then released it. Use of the guillotine began in April 1792 and did not end until 1981, when the French government abolished the death penalty. The guillotine fascinated as much as it repelled. Reproduced in miniature, painted onto snuffboxes and china, worn as jewelry, and even serving as a toy, the guillotine became a part of popular culture. How could the guillotine be simultaneously celebrated as the people's avenger by supporters of the Revolution and vilified as the preeminent symbol of the Terror by opponents? *(Réunion des Musées Nationaux/Art Resource, NY.)*

tesquieu and Rousseau. But he took them a step further. He defined "the theory of revolutionary government" as "the war of liberty against its enemies." He defended the people's right to democratic government, while in practice he supported many emergency measures that restricted their liberties. He personally favored a free-market economy, as did almost all middle-class deputies, but in this time of crisis he was willing to enact price controls and requisitioning. In an effort to stabilize prices, the National Convention established the General Maximum on September 29, 1793, which set limits on the prices of thirty-nine essential commodities and on wages. In a speech to the Convention, Robespierre explained the necessity of government by terror: "The first maxim of your policies must be to lead the people by reason and the people's enemies by terror. . . . Without virtue, terror is deadly; without terror, virtue is impotent." *Terror* was not an idle term; it seemed to imply that the goal of democracy justified what we now call totalitarian means, that is, the suppression of all dissent.

Through a series of desperate measures, the Committee of Public Safety set the machinery of the Terror in motion. It sent deputies out "on mission" to purge unreliable officials and organize the war effort. Revolutionary tribunals set up in Paris and provincial centers tried political suspects. In October 1793, the Revolutionary Tribunal in Paris convicted Marie-Antoinette of treason and sent her to the guillotine. The Girondin leaders and Madame Roland were also guillotined, as was Olympe de Gouges. The government confiscated all the property of convicted traitors.

The new republic won its greatest success on the battlefield. As of April 1793, France faced war with Austria, Prussia, Great Britain, Spain, Sardinia, and the Dutch Republic—all fearful of the impact of revolutionary ideals on their own populations. The execution of Louis XVI, in particular, galvanized European governments; according to William Pitt, the British prime minister, it was "the foulest and most atrocious act the world has ever seen." To face this daunting coalition of forces, the French republic ordered the first universal draft of men in history. Every unmarried man and childless widower between the ages of eighteen and twenty-five was declared eligible for conscription. The government also tapped a new and potent source of power—nationalist pride—in decrees mobilizing young and old alike:

> The young men will go to battle; married men will forge arms and transport provisions; women will make tents and clothing and serve in hospitals; children will

make bandages; old men will get themselves carried to public places to arouse the courage of warriors and preach hatred of kings and unity of the republic.

Forges were set up in the parks and gardens of Paris to produce thousands of guns, and citizens everywhere helped collect saltpeter to make gunpowder. By the end of 1793, the French nation in arms had stopped the advance of the allied powers, and in the summer of 1794 it invaded the Austrian Netherlands and crossed the Rhine River. The army was ready to carry the gospel of revolution and republicanism to the rest of Europe.

The Republic of Virtue, 1793–1794

The program of the Terror went beyond pragmatic measures to fight the war and internal enemies to include efforts to "republicanize everything" — in other words, to effect a cultural revolution. While censoring writings deemed counterrevolutionary, the government encouraged republican art, set up civic festivals, and in some places directly attacked the churches in a campaign known as de-Christianization. In addition to drawing up plans for a new program of elementary education, the republic set about politicizing aspects of daily life, including even the measurement of space and time.

Republican Culture. Refusing to tolerate opposition, the republic left no stone unturned in its endeavor to get its message across. Songs — especially the new national anthem, "La Marseillaise" — and placards, posters, pamphlets, books, engravings, paintings, sculpture, even everyday crockery, chamberpots, and playing cards conveyed revolutionary slogans and symbols. Foremost among them was the figure of Liberty, which appeared on coins and bills, on letterheads and seals, and as statues in festivals. Hundreds of new plays were produced and old classics revised. To encourage the production of patriotic and republican works, the government sponsored state competitions for artists. Works of art were supposed to "awaken the public spirit and make clear how atrocious and ridiculous were the enemies of liberty and of the Republic."

At the center of this elaborate cultural campaign were the revolutionary festivals modeled on Rousseau's plans for a civic religion. The festivals

Representing Liberty
Liberty was represented by a female figure because in French the noun is feminine (*la liberté*). This painting from 1793–1794, by Jeanne-Louise Vallain, captures the usual attributes of Liberty: she is soberly seated, wearing a Roman-style toga and holding a pike with a Roman liberty cap on top. Her Roman appearance signals that she represents an abstract quality. The fact that she holds an instrument of battle suggests that women might be active participants. The Statue of Liberty in New York harbor, given by the French to the United States, is a late-nineteenth-century version of the same figure, but without any suggestion of battle. (*Musée de la Révolution française, Vizille; 1857#44.*)

first emerged in 1789 with the spontaneous planting of liberty trees in villages and towns. The Festival of Federation on July 14, 1790, marked the first anniversary of the fall of the Bastille. Under the National Convention, the well-known painter Jacques-Louis David (1748–1825), who was a deputy and an associate of Robespierre, took over festival planning. David aimed to destroy the mystique of monarchy and to make the republic sacred. His Festival of Unity on August 10, 1793, for example, celebrated the first anniversary of the overthrow of the monarchy. In front of the statue of Liberty built for the occasion, a bonfire consumed crowns and scepters symbolizing royalty while a cloud of three thousand white doves rose into the sky. This was all part of preaching the "moral order of the Republic . . . that will make us a people of brothers, a people of philosophers."

De-Christianization. Some revolutionaries hoped the festival system would replace the Catholic church altogether. They initiated a campaign of **de-Christianization** that included closing churches (Protestant as well as Catholic), selling many church buildings to the highest bidder, and trying to force even those clergy who had taken the oath of loyalty to abandon their clerical vocations and marry. Great churches became storehouses for arms or grain, or their stones were sold off to contractors. The medieval statues of kings on the facade of Notre Dame cathedral were beheaded. Church bells were dismantled and church treasures melted down for government use.

In the ultimate step in de-Christianization, extremists tried to establish what they called the Cult of Reason to supplant Christianity. In Paris in the fall of 1793, a goddess of Liberty, played by an actress, presided over the Festival of Reason in Notre Dame cathedral. Local militants in other cities staged similar festivals, which alarmed deputies in the National Convention, who were wary of turning rural, devout populations against the republic. Robespierre objected to the de-Christianization campaign's atheism; he favored a Rousseau-inspired deistic religion without the supposedly superstitious trappings of Catholicism. The Committee of Public Safety halted the de-Christianization campaign, and Robespierre, with David's help, tried to institute an alternative, the Cult of the Supreme Being, in June 1794. Neither the Cult of Reason nor the Cult of the Supreme Being attracted many followers, but both show the depth of the commit-

ment to overturning the old order and all its traditional institutions.

Politicizing Daily Life. In principle, the best way to ensure the future of the republic was through the education of the young. The deputy Georges-Jacques Danton (1759–1794), Robespierre's main competitor as theorist of the Revolution, maintained that "after bread, the first need of the people is education." The National Convention voted to make primary schooling free and compulsory for both boys and girls. It took control of education away from the Catholic church and tried to set up a system of state schools at both the primary and secondary levels, but it lacked trained teachers to replace those the Catholic religious orders had provided. As a result, opportunities for learning how to read and write may have diminished. In 1799, only one-fifth as many boys enrolled in the state secondary schools as had studied in church schools ten years earlier.

Although many of the ambitious republican programs failed, colors, clothing, and daily speech were all politicized. The tricolor—the combination of red, white, and blue that was to become the flag of France—was devised in July 1789, and by 1793 everyone had to wear a cockade (a badge made of ribbons) with the colors. Using the formal forms of speech—*vous* for "you"—or the title *monsieur* or *madame* might identify someone as an aristocrat; true patriots used the informal *tu* and *citoyen* or *citoyenne* ("citizen") instead. Some people changed their names or gave their children new kinds of names. Biblical and saints' names such as John, Peter, Joseph, and Mary gave way to names recalling heroes of the ancient Roman republic (Brutus, Gracchus, Cornelia), revolutionary heroes, or flowers and plants. Such changes symbolized adherence to the republic and to Enlightenment ideals rather than to Catholicism.

Even the measures of time and space were revolutionized. In October 1793, the National Convention introduced a new calendar to replace the Christian one. Its bases were reason and republican principles. Year I dated from the beginning of the republic on September 22, 1792. Twelve months of exactly thirty days each received new names derived from nature—for example, Pluviôse (roughly equivalent to February) recalled the rain (*la pluie*) of late winter. Instead of seven-day weeks, ten-day *décades* provided only one day of rest every ten days and pointedly eliminated the Sunday of the Christian calendar. The five days left at the end of the calendar year were devoted to special festivals called *sans-culottides*. The calendar remained in force for twelve years despite contin-

---

de-Christianization: During the French Revolution, the campaign of extremist republicans against organized churches and in favor of a belief system based on reason.

uing resistance to it. More enduring was the new metric system based on units of ten that was invented to replace the hundreds of local variations in weights and measures. Other countries in Europe and throughout the world eventually adopted the metric system.

Revolutionary laws also changed the rules of family life. The state took responsibility for all family matters away from the Catholic church: people now registered births, deaths, and marriages at city hall, not the parish church. Marriage became a civil contract and as such could be broken and thereby nullified. The new divorce law of September 1792 was the most far-reaching in Europe: a couple could divorce by mutual consent or for reasons such as insanity, abandonment, battering, or criminal conviction. Thousands of men and women took advantage of the law to dissolve unhappy marriages, even though the pope had condemned the measure. (In 1816, the government revoked the right to divorce, and not until the 1970s did French divorce laws return to the principles of the 1792 legislation.) In one of its most influential actions, the National Convention passed a series of laws that created equal inheritance among all children in the family, including girls. The father's right to favor one child, especially the oldest male, was considered aristocratic and hence antirepublican.

Resisting the Revolution

By intruding into religion, culture, and daily life, the republic inevitably provoked resistance. Shouting curses against the republic, uprooting liberty trees, carrying statues of the Virgin Mary in procession, hiding a priest who would not take the oath, singing a royalist song—all these expressed dissent with the new symbols, rituals, and policies. Resistance also took more violent forms, from riots over food shortages or religious policies to assassination and full-scale civil war.

Women's Resistance. Many women, in particular, suffered from the hard conditions of life that persisted in this time of war, and they had their own ways of voicing discontent. Long bread lines in the cities exhausted the patience of women, and police spies reported their constant grumbling, which occasionally turned into spontaneous demonstrations or riots over high prices

or food shortages. Women also organized their fellow parishioners to refuse to hear Mass offered by the "constitutional" priests, and they protected the priests who would not sign the oath of loyalty.

Other forms of resistance were more individual. One young woman, Charlotte Corday, assassinated the outspoken deputy Jean-Paul Marat in July 1793. Corday fervently supported the Girondins, and she considered it her patriotic duty to kill the deputy who, in the columns of his paper, had constantly demanded more heads and more blood. Marat was immediately eulogized as a great martyr, and Corday went to the guillotine vilified as a monster but confident that she had "avenged many innocent victims."

Rebellion and Civil War. Organized resistance broke out in many parts of France. The arrest of the Girondin deputies in June 1793 sparked insurrections in several departments. After the government retook the city of Lyon, one of the centers of the revolt, the deputy on mission ordered sixteen hundred houses demolished and the name of the city changed to Liberated City. Special courts sentenced almost two thousand people to death.

In the Vendée region of western France, resistance turned into a bloody and prolonged civil war. Between March and December 1793, peasants, artisans, and weavers joined under noble leadership to form a "Catholic and Royal Army." One rebel group explained its motives: "They [the republicans] have killed our king, chased away our priests, sold the goods of our church, eaten everything we have and now they want to take our bodies [in the draft]." The uprising took two different forms: in the Vendée itself, a counterrevolutionary army organized to fight the republic; in nearby Brittany, resistance took the form of guerrilla bands, which united to attack a target and then quickly melted into the countryside. Great Britain provided money and underground contacts for these attacks, which were almost always aimed at towns. In many ways this was a civil war between town and country, for the townspeople were the ones who supported the Revolution and bought church lands for themselves. The peasants had gained most of what they wanted in 1789 with the abolition of seigneurial dues, and they resented the government's demands for money and

The Vendée Rebellion, 1793

manpower and actions taken against their local clergy.

For several months in 1793, the Vendée rebels stormed the largest towns in the region. Both sides committed horrible atrocities. At the small town of Machecoul, for example, the rebels massacred five hundred republicans, including administrators and National Guard members; many were tied together, shoved into freshly dug graves, and shot. By the fall, however, republican soldiers had turned back the rebels. A republican general wrote to the Committee of Public Safety claiming, "There is no more Vendée, citizens, it has perished under our free sword along with its women and children. . . . Following the orders that you gave me I have crushed children under the feet of horses, massacred women who at least . . . will engender no more brigands." His claims of complete victory turned hollow soon afterward, as fighting continued.

"Infernal columns" of republican troops marched through the region to restore control, military courts ordered thousands executed, and republican soldiers massacred thousands of others. In one especially gruesome incident, the deputy Jean-Baptiste Carrier supervised the drowning of some two thousand Vendée rebels, including a number of priests. Barges loaded with prisoners were floated into the Loire River near Nantes and then sunk. Controversy still rages about the rebellion's death toll because no accurate count could be taken. Estimates of rebel deaths alone range from about 20,000 to 250,000 and higher. Many thousands of republican soldiers and civilians also lost their lives in fighting that continued on and off for years. Even the low estimates reveal the carnage of this catastrophic confrontation between the republic and its opponents.

The Fall of Robespierre and the End of the Terror

In an atmosphere of fear of conspiracy that these outbreaks fueled, Robespierre tried simultaneously to exert the National Convention's control over popular political activities and to weed out opposition among the deputies. As a result, the Terror intensified until July 1794, when a group of deputies joined within the Convention to order the arrest and execution of Robespierre and his followers. The Convention then ordered elections and drew up a new republican constitution that gave executive power to five directors. This "Directory government" maintained power during four years of see-saw battles between royalists and former Jacobins.

The Revolution Devours Its Own. In the fall of 1793, the National Convention cracked down on popular clubs and societies. First to be suppressed were women's political clubs. Founded in early 1793, the Society of Revolutionary Republican Women played a very active part in sans-culottes politics. The society urged harsher measures against the republic's enemies and insisted that women have a voice in politics even if they did not have the vote. Women had set up their own clubs in many provincial towns and also attended the meetings of local men's organizations. Using traditional arguments about women's inherent unsuitability for politics, the deputies abolished women's political clubs. The closing of women's clubs marked an important turning point in the Revolution. From then on, the sans-culottes and their political organizations came increasingly under the thumb of the Jacobin deputies in the National Convention.

In the spring of 1794, the Committee of Public Safety moved against its critics among leaders in Paris and deputies in the National Convention itself. First, a handful of "ultrarevolutionaries" — a collection of local Parisian politicians — were arrested and executed. Next came the other side, the "indulgents," so called because they favored a moderation of the Terror. Included among them was the deputy Danton, himself once a member of the Committee of Public Safety and a friend of Robespierre. Danton was the Revolution's most flamboyant orator and, unlike Robespierre, a high-living, high-spending, excitable politician. At every critical turning point in national politics, his booming voice had swayed opinion in the National Convention. Now, under pressure from the Committee of Public Safety, the Revolutionary Tribunal convicted him and his friends of treason and sentenced them to death.

"The Revolution," as one of the Girondin victims of 1793 had remarked, "was devouring its own children." Even after the major threats to the Committee of Public Safety's power had been eliminated, the Terror continued and even worsened. A law passed in June 1794 denied the accused the right of legal counsel, reduced the number of jurors necessary for conviction, and allowed only two judgments: acquittal or death. The category of political crimes expanded to include "slandering patriotism" and "seeking to inspire discouragement." Ordinary people risked the guillotine if they expressed any discontent. The rate of executions in Paris rose from five a day in the spring of 1794 to twenty-six a day in the summer. The political atmosphere darkened even though the military situation improved. At the end of June, the French armies decisively defeated the main Austrian army and advanced through the Austrian Netherlands to Brussels and Antwerp. The emergency measures for fighting the war were working, yet Robespierre and his inner circle had

MAJOR EVENTS OF THE FRENCH REVOLUTION

Date	Event
MAY 5, 1789	The Estates General opens at Versailles
JUNE 17, 1789	The Third Estate decides to call itself the National Assembly
JUNE 20, 1789	"Tennis court oath" shows determination of deputies to carry out a constitutional revolution
JULY 14, 1789	Fall of the Bastille
AUGUST 4, 1789	National Assembly abolishes "feudalism"
AUGUST 26, 1789	National Assembly passes Declaration of the Rights of Man and Citizen
OCTOBER 5–6, 1789	Women march to Versailles and are joined by men in bringing the royal family back to Paris
JULY 12, 1790	Civil Constitution of the Clergy
JUNE 20, 1791	Louis and Marie-Antoinette attempt to flee in disguise and are captured at Varennes
APRIL 20, 1792	Declaration of war on Austria
AUGUST 10, 1792	Insurrection in Paris and attack on Tuileries palace lead to removal of king's authority
SEPTEMBER 2–6, 1792	Murder of prisoners in "September massacres" in Paris
SEPTEMBER 22, 1792	Establishment of the republic
JANUARY 21, 1793	Execution of Louis XVI
MARCH 11, 1793	Beginning of uprising in the Vendée
MAY 31–JUNE 2, 1793	Insurrection leading to arrest of the Girondins
JULY 27, 1793	Robespierre named to the Committee of Public Safety
SEPTEMBER 29, 1793	Convention establishes General Maximum on prices and wages
OCTOBER 16, 1793	Execution of Marie-Antoinette
FEBRUARY 4, 1794	Slavery abolished in the French colonies
MARCH 13–24, 1794	Arrest, trial, and executions of so-called ultra-revolutionaries
MARCH 30–APRIL 5, 1794	Arrest, trial, and executions of Danton and his followers
JULY 27, 1794	Arrest of Robespierre and his supporters (executed July 28–29); beginning of end of the Terror
OCTOBER 26, 1795	Directory government takes office
APRIL 1796–OCTOBER 1797, 1795	Succession of Italian victories by Bonaparte

made so many enemies that they could not afford to loosen the grip of the Terror.

The Terror hardly touched many parts of France, but overall the experience was undeniably traumatic. Across the country, the official Terror cost the lives of at least 40,000 French people, most of them living in the regions of major insurrections or near the borders with foreign enemies, where suspicion of collaboration ran high. As many as 300,000 people — one out of every fifty French people — went to prison as suspects between March 1793 and August 1794. The toll for the aristocracy and the clergy was especially high. Many leading nobles perished under the guillotine, and thousands emigrated. Thirty thousand to forty thousand clergy who refused the oath left the country, at least two thousand (including many nuns) were executed, and thousands were imprisoned. The clergy were singled out in particular in the civil war zones: 135 priests were massacred at Lyon in November 1793, and 83 were shot in one day during the Vendée revolt. Yet many victims of the Terror were peasants or ordinary working people.

The final crisis of the Terror came in July 1794. Conflicts within the Committee of Public Safety and the National Convention left Robespierre isolated. On July 27, 1794 (the ninth of Thermidor, Year II, according to the revolutionary calendar), Robespierre appeared before the Convention with yet another list of deputies to be arrested. Many feared they would be named, and they shouted him down and ordered him arrested along with his followers on the committee, the president of the Revolutionary Tribunal in Paris, and the commander of the Parisian National Guard. An armed uprising led by the Paris city government failed to save Robespierre when most of the National Guard took the side of the Convention. Robespierre tried to kill himself with a pistol but only broke his jaw. The next day he and scores of followers went to the guillotine.

The Thermidorian Reaction and the Directory, 1794–1799. The men who led the attack on Robespierre in Thermidor (July 1794) did not intend to reverse all his policies, but that happened nonetheless because of a violent backlash known as the **Thermidorian Reaction.** As most of the instruments of terror were dismantled, newspapers attacked the Robespierrists as "tigers thirsting for human blood." The new government released hundreds of suspects and arranged a temporary truce

---

Thermidorian Reaction: The violent backlash against the rule of Robespierre that dismantled the Terror and punished Jacobins and their supporters.

in the Vendée. It purged Jacobins from local bodies and replaced them with their opponents. It arrested some of the most notorious "terrorists" in the National Convention, such as Carrier, and put them to death. Within the year, the new leaders abolished the Revolutionary Tribunal and closed the Jacobin Club in Paris. Popular demonstrations met severe repression. In southeastern France, in particular, the "White Terror" replaced the Jacobins' "Red Terror." Former officials and local Jacobin leaders were harassed, beaten, and often murdered by paramilitary bands who had tacit support from the new authorities. Those who remained in the National Convention prepared yet another constitution in 1795, setting up a two-house legislature and an executive body — the Directory, headed by five directors.

The Directory regime tenuously held on to power for four years, all the while trying to fend off challenges from the remaining Jacobins and the resurgent royalists. The puritanical atmosphere of the Terror gave way to the pursuit of pleasure — low-cut dresses of transparent materials, the reappearance of prostitutes in the streets, fancy dinner parties, and "victims' balls" where guests wore red ribbons around their necks as reminders of the guillotine. Bands of young men dressed in knee breeches and rich fabrics picked fights with known Jacobins and disrupted theater performances with loud antirevolutionary songs. All over France, people petitioned to reopen churches closed during the Terror. If necessary, they broke into a church to hold services with a priest who had been in hiding or a lay schoolteacher who was willing to say Mass.

Although the Terror had ended, the revolution had not. In 1794, the most democratic and most repressive phases of the Revolution both ended at once. Between 1795 and 1799, the republic endured in France, but it directed a war effort abroad that would ultimately bring to power the man who would dismantle the republic itself.

REVIEW: What factors can explain the Terror? To what extent was it simply a response to a national emergency or a reflection of deeper problems within the French Revolution?

Revolution on the March

War raged almost constantly from 1792 to 1815. At one time or another, and sometimes all at once, France faced every principal power in Europe. The French republic — and later the French Empire under its supreme commander, Emperor Napoleon Bonaparte — proved an even more formidable op-

ponent than the France of Louis XIV. New means of mobilizing and organizing soldiers enabled the French to dominate Europe for a generation. The influence of the Revolution as a political model and the threat of French military conquest combined to challenge the traditional order in Europe.

Arms and Conquests

The powers allied against France squandered their best chance to triumph in early 1793, when the French armies verged on chaos because of the emigration of noble army officers and the problems of integrating new draftees. By the end of 1793, the French had a huge and powerful fighting force of 700,000 men. But the army still faced many problems in the field. As many as a third of the recent draftees deserted before or during battle. At times the soldiers were fed only moldy bread, and if their pay was late, they sometimes resorted to pillaging and looting. Generals might pay with their lives if they lost a key battle and their loyalty to the Revolution came under suspicion.

France nevertheless had one overwhelming advantage: those soldiers who agreed to serve fought for a revolution that they and their brothers and sisters had helped make. The republic was their government, and the army was in large measure theirs too; many officers had risen through the ranks by skill and talent rather than by inheriting or purchasing their positions. One young peasant boy wrote to his parents, "Either you will see me return bathed in glory, or you will have a son who is a worthy citizen of France who knows how to die for the defense of his country."

When the French armies invaded the Austrian Netherlands and crossed the Rhine in the summer of 1794, they proclaimed a war of liberation. Middle-class people near the northern and eastern borders of France reacted most positively to the French invasion (Map 19.3). In the Austrian Netherlands, Mainz, Savoy, and Nice, French officers organized Jacobin Clubs that attracted locals. The clubs petitioned for annexation to France, and French legislation was then introduced, including the abolition of seigneurial dues. As the French annexed more and more territory, however, "liberated" people in many places began to view them as an army of occupation. Despite resistance, especially in the Austrian Netherlands, these areas remained part of France until 1815, and the legal changes were permanent.

The Directory government that came to power in 1795 launched an even more aggressive policy of creating semi-independent "sister republics" wherever the armies succeeded. When Prussia

MAP 19.3 French Expansion, 1791–1799
The influence of the French Revolution on neighboring territories is dramatically evident in this map. The French directly annexed the papal territories in southern France in 1791, Nice and Savoy in 1792, and the Austrian Netherlands in 1795. They set up a series of sister republics in the former Dutch Republic and in various Italian states. Local people did not always welcome these changes. For example, the French made the Dutch pay a huge war indemnity, support a French occupying army of 25,000 soldiers, and give up some southern territories. The sister republics faced a future of subordination to French national interests.

declared neutrality in 1795, the French armies swarmed into the Dutch Republic, abolished the stadholderate, and — with the revolutionary penchant for renaming — created the new Batavian Republic, a satellite of France. The brilliant young general Napoleon Bonaparte gained a reputation by defeating the Austrian armies in northern Italy in 1797 and then created the Cisalpine Republic. Next he overwhelmed Venice and then handed it over to the Austrians in exchange for a peace agreement that lasted less than two years. After the French attacked the Swiss cantons in 1798, they set up the Helvetic Republic and curtailed many of the Catholic church's privileges. They conquered the Papal States in 1798 and installed a Roman Republic, forcing the pope to flee to Siena.

The revolutionary wars had an immediate impact on European life at all levels of society. Thousands of men died in every country involved, with perhaps as many as 200,000 casualties in the French armies alone in 1794 and 1795. More soldiers died in hospitals as a result of their wounds than on the battlefields. Constant warfare hampered world commerce and especially disrupted French overseas shipping. Times were now hard almost everywhere, because the dislocations of internal and external commerce provoked constant shortages.

European Reactions to Revolutionary Change

The French Revolution profoundly transformed European politics and social relations. (See "Contrasting Views," page 610.) Many had greeted the events of 1789 with unabashed enthusiasm. The English Unitarian minister Richard Price had exulted, "Behold, the light . . . after setting AMERICA free, reflected to FRANCE, and there kindled into a blaze that lays despotism in ashes, and warms and illuminates EUROPE." Democrats and reformers from many countries flooded to Paris to witness events firsthand. Supporters of the French Revolution in Great Britain joined constitutional and reform societies that sprang up in many cities. The most important of these societies, the London Corresponding Society, founded in 1792, corre-

The English Rebuttal
In this caricature, James Gillray satirizes the French version of liberty. Gillray produced
thousands of political caricatures. How would you interpret the message of this print?

sponded with the Paris Jacobin Club and served as a center for reform agitation in England. Pro-French feeling ran even stronger in Ireland. Catholics and Presbyterians, both excluded from the vote, came together in 1791 in the Society of United Irishmen, which eventually pressed for secession from England.

European elites became alarmed when the French abolished monarchy and nobility and encouraged popular participation in politics. The British government, for example, quickly suppressed the corresponding societies and harassed their leaders, charging that their ideas and their contacts with the French were seditious (see the cartoon above for a negative English view). When the Society of United Irishmen timed a rebellion to coincide with an attempted French invasion in 1798, the British mercilessly repressed them, killing thirty thousand rebels. Twice as many regular British troops (seventy thousand) as fought in any of the major continental battles were required to put down the rebellion. Spain's royal gov-

ernment suppressed all news from France, fearing that it might ignite the spirit of revolt.

Elites sometimes found allies in opposing the French. Peasants in the German and Italian states fiercely resisted French occupation, often in the form of banditry. Because the French offered the Jews religious toleration and civil and political rights wherever they conquered, anti-French groups sometimes attacked Jews. One German traveler reported, "It is characteristic of the region in which the bandits are based that these two nations [the French and the Jews] are hated. So crimes against them are motivated not just by a wish to rob them but also by a variety of fanaticism which is partly political and partly religious."

Many leading intellectuals in the German states, including the philosopher Immanuel Kant, initially supported the revolutionary cause, but after 1793 most of them turned against the popular violence and military aggressiveness of the Revolution. One of the greatest writers of the age,

Perspectives on the French Revolution

Contemporaries instantly grasped the cataclysmic significance of the French Revolution and began to argue about its lessons for their own countries. A member of the British Parliament, Edmund Burke, ignited a firestorm of controversy with his Reflections on the Revolution in France *(Document 1). He condemned the French revolutionaries for attempting to build a government on abstract reasoning rather than taking historical traditions and customs into account; his book provided a foundation for the doctrine known as conservatism, which argued for "conserving" the traditional foundations of society and avoiding the pitfalls of radical or revolutionary change. Burke's views provoked a strong response from the English political agitator Thomas Paine. Paine's pamphlet* Common Sense *(1776) had helped inspire the British North American colonies to demand independence from Great Britain. In* The Rights of Man *(Document 2), written fifteen years later, Paine attacked the traditional order as fundamentally unjust and defended the idea of a revolution to uphold rights. Joseph de Maistre, an aristocratic opponent of both the Enlightenment and the French Revolution, put the conservative attack on the French Revolution into a deeply religious and absolutist framework (Document 3). In contrast, Anne-Louise-Germaine de Staël, an opponent of Napoleon and one of the most influential intellectuals of the early nineteenth century, took the view that the violence of the Revolution had been the product of generations of superstition and arbitrary rule, that is, rule by an absolutist Catholic church and monarchical government (Document 4).*

1. Edmund Burke, Reflections on the Revolution in France (1790)

An Irish-born supporter of the American colonists in their opposition to the British Parliament, Edmund Burke (1729–1797) opposed the French Revolution. He argued the case for tradition, continuity, and gradual reform based on practical experience— what he called "a sure principle of conservation."

Can I now congratulate the same nation [France] upon its freedom? Is it because liberty in the abstract may be classed amongst the blessings of mankind, that I am seriously to felicitate a madman, who has escaped from the protecting restraint and wholesome darkness of his cell, on his restoration to the enjoyment of light and liberty? Am I to congratulate an highwayman and murderer, who has broke prison, upon the recovery of his natural rights? . . .

Government is not made in virtue of natural rights, which may and do exist in total independence of it; and exist in much greater clearness, and in a much greater degree of abstract perfection: but their abstract perfection is their practical defect. By having a right to every thing they want every thing. . . . The science of constructing a commonwealth, or renovating it, or reforming it, is, like every other experimental science, not to be taught *a priori* [based on theory rather than on experience]. Nor is it a short experience that can instruct us in that practical science; because the real effects of moral causes are not always immediate; but that which in the first instance is prejudicial may be excellent in its remoter operation; and its excellence may arise even from the ill effects it produces in the beginning. . . .

In the groves of *their* academy, at the end of every visto [vista], you see nothing but the gallows. Nothing is left which engages the affections on the part of the commonwealth. . . . To make us love our country, our country ought to be lovely.

Source: Two Classics of the French Revolution: Reflections on the Revolution in France (Edmund Burke) and The Rights of Man (Thomas Paine) (New York: Doubleday Anchor Books, 1973), 19, 71–74, 90–91.

2. Thomas Paine, The Rights of Man (1791)

In his reply to Burke, The Rights of Man, *which sold 200,000 copies in two years, Thomas Paine (1737–1809) defended the idea of reform based on reason, advocated a concept of universal human rights, and attacked the excesses of privilege and tradition in Great Britain. Elected as a deputy to the French National Convention in 1793 in recognition of his writings in favor of the French Revolution, Paine narrowly escaped condemnation as an associate of the Girondins.*

Before anything can be reasoned upon to a conclusion, certain facts, principles, or data, to reason from, must be established, admitted, or denied. Mr. Burke, with his usual outrage, abuses the *Declaration of the Rights of Man*, published by the National Assembly of France, as the basis on which the Constitution of France is built. This he calls "paltry and blurred sheets of paper about the rights of man."

Does Mr. Burke mean to deny that *man* has any rights? If he does, then he must mean that there are no such things as rights any where, and that he has none himself; for who is there in the world but man? . . .

Hitherto we have spoken only (and that but in part) of the natural rights of man. We have now to consider the civil rights of man, and to show how the one originates from the other. Man did not enter into society to become *worse* than he was before, nor to have fewer rights than he had before, but to have those rights better secured. His natural rights are the foundation of all his civil rights. . . .

A constitution is not a thing in name only, but in fact. It has not an ideal, but a real existence; and wherever it cannot be produced in a visible form, there is none. A constitution is a thing *antecedent* to a government, and a government is only the creature of a constitution. The constitution of a country is not the act of its government, but of the people constituting a government. . . .

Can then Mr. Burke produce the English Constitution? If he cannot, we may fairly conclude, that though it has been so much talked about, no such thing as a constitution exists, or ever did exist, and consequently that the people have yet a constitution to form.

Source: *Two Classics of the French Revolution:* Reflections on the Revolution in France *(Edmund Burke) and* The Rights of Man *(Thomas Paine)* (New York: Doubleday Anchor Books, 1973), 302, 305–306, 309.

3. Joseph De Maistre, *Considerations on France* (1797)

An aristocrat born in Savoy, Joseph de Maistre (1753–1821) believed in reform but he passionately opposed both the Enlightenment and the French Revolution as destructive to good order. He believed that Protestants, Jews, lawyers, journalists, and scientists all threatened the social order because they questioned the need for absolute obedience to authority in matters both religious and political. De Maistre set the foundations for reactionary conservatism, a conservatism that defended throne and altar.

This consideration especially makes me think that the French Revolution is a great epoch and that its consequences, in all kinds of ways, will be felt far beyond the time of its explosion and the limits of its birthplace. . . .

There is a satanic quality to the French Revolution that distinguishes it from everything we have ever seen or anything we are ever likely to see in the future. Recall the great assemblies, Robespierre's speech against the priesthood, the solemn apostasy [renunciation of vows] of the clergy, the desecration of objects of worship, the installation of the goddess of reason, and that multitude of extraordinary actions by which the provinces sought to outdo Paris. All this goes beyond the ordinary circle of crime and seems to belong to another world.

Source: Joseph de Maistre, *Considerations on France*, trans. Richard A. Lebrun (Cambridge: Cambridge University Press, 1994), 21, 41.

4. Anne-Louise-Germaine de Staël, *Considerations on the Main Events of the French Revolution* (1818)

De Staël published her views long after the Revolution was over, but she had lived through the events herself. She was the daughter of Jacques Necker, Louis XVI's Swiss Protestant finance minister. Necker's dismissal in July 1789 had sparked the attack on the Bastille. De Staël published novels, literary tracts, and memoirs and became one of the best-known writers of the nineteenth century. In her writings she defended the Enlightenment; though she opposed the violence unleashed by the Revolution, she traced it back to the excesses of monarchical government. (See her portrait on page 627.)

Once the people were freed from their harness there is no doubt that they were in a position to commit any kind of crime. But how can we explain their depravity? The government we are now supposed to miss so sorely [the former monarchy] had had plenty of time to form this guilty nation. The priests whose teaching, example, and wealth were supposed to be so good for us had supervised the childhood of the generation that broke out against them. The class that revolted in 1789 must have been accustomed to the privileges of feudal nobility which, as we are also assured, are so peculiarly agreeable to those on whom they weigh [the peasants]. How does it happen, then, that the seed of so many vices was sown under the ancient institutions? . . . What can we conclude from this, then? — That no people had been as unhappy for the preceding century as the French. If the Negroes of Saint-Domingue have committed even greater atrocities, it is because they had been even more greatly oppressed.

Source: Vivian Folkenflik, ed., *An Extraordinary Woman: Selected Writings of Germaine de Staël* (New York: Columbia University Press, 1987), 365–66.

QUESTIONS TO CONSIDER

1. Which aspect of the French Revolution most disturbed these commentators?
2. How would you align each of these writers on a spectrum running from extreme right to extreme left in politics?
3. How would each of these writers judge the Enlightenment that preceded the French Revolution?

Friedrich Schiller (1759–1805), typified the turn in sentiment against revolutionary politics:

> Freedom is only in the realm of dreams
> And the beautiful blooms only in song.

The German states, still run by many separate rulers, experienced a profound artistic and intellectual revival, which eventually connected with anti-French nationalism. This renaissance included a resurgence of intellectual life in the universities, a thriving press (1225 journals were launched in the 1780s alone), and the multiplication of Masonic lodges and literary clubs.

Even far from France, echoes of revolutionary upheaval could be heard. In the United States, for example, opinion fiercely divided on the virtues of the French Revolution. In Sweden, King Gustavus III (r. 1771–1792) was assassinated by a nobleman who claimed that "the king has violated his oath . . . and declared himself an enemy of the realm." The king's son Gustavus IV (r. 1792–1809) was convinced that the French Jacobins had sanctioned his father's assassination, and he insisted on avoiding "licentious liberty." Despite government controls on news, 278 outbreaks of peasant unrest occurred in Russia between 1796 and 1798. One Russian landlord complained, "This is the self-same . . . spirit of insubordination and independence, which has spread through all Europe."

Poland Extinguished, 1793–1795

The spirit of independence made the Poles and Lithuanians especially discontent, for they had already suffered a significant loss of territory and population. Fearing French influence, Prussia joined Russia in dividing up generous new slices of Polish territory in the second partition of 1793 (Map 19.4). As might be expected, Poland's reform movement became even more pro-French. Some leaders fled abroad, including Tadeusz Kościuszko (1746–1817), an officer who had been a foreign volunteer in the War of American Independence and who now escaped to Paris. In the spring of 1794, Kościuszko returned from France to lead a nationalist revolt.

Cracow, Warsaw, and the old Lithuanian capital, Vilnius, responded with uprisings. Kościuszko faced an immediate, insoluble dilemma. He could win only if the peasants joined the struggle — highly unlikely unless villagers could be convinced that serfdom would end. But such a drastic step risked alienating the nobles who had started the revolt. So Kościuszko compromised. He promised the serfs a reduction of their obligations, but not freedom itself. A few peasant bands joined the insurrection, but most let their lords fight it out alone. Urban workers displayed more enthusiasm; at Warsaw, for example, a mob hanged several Russian collaborators, including an archbishop in his full regalia.

The uprising failed. Kościuszko won a few victories, but when the Russian empress Catherine the Great's forces regrouped, they routed the Poles and Lithuanians. Kościuszko and other Polish Patriot leaders languished for years in Russian and Austrian prisons. Taking no further chances, Russia, Prussia, and Austria wiped Poland completely from the map in the third partition of 1795. "The Polish question" would plague international rela-

---

MAP 19.4 The Second and Third Partitions of Poland, 1793 and 1795

In 1793, Prussia took over territory that included 1.1 million Poles while Russia gained 3 million new inhabitants. Austria gave up any claims to Poland in exchange for help from Russia and Prussia in acquiring Bavaria. In the final division of 1795, Prussia absorbed an additional 900,000 Polish subjects, including those in Warsaw; Austria incorporated 1 million Poles and the city of Cracow; Russia gained another 2 million Poles. The three powers determined never to use the term *Kingdom of Poland* again. ■ How had Poland become such a prey to the other powers?

Address on Abolishing the Slave Trade (February 5, 1790)

Founded in 1788, the Society of the Friends of Blacks agitated for the abolition of the slave trade. Among its members were many who became leaders of the French Revolution. In a pamphlet, titled Address to the National Assembly in Favor of the Abolition of the Slave Trade, *the Friends of Blacks denied that they wanted to abolish slavery altogether and argued only for the abolition of the slave trade. The pamphlet raised the prospect of a slave revolt, which in fact broke out in St. Domingue in 1791. As a consequence, many planters and their allies accused the society of fomenting the revolt.*

You have declared them, these rights; you have engraved on an immortal monument that all men are born and remain free and equal in rights; you have restored to the French people these rights that despotism had for so long despoiled; . . . you have broken the chains of feudalism that still degraded a good number of our fellow citizens; you have announced the destruction of all the stigmatizing distinctions that religious or political prejudices introduced into the great family of humankind. . . .

We are not asking you to restore to French blacks those political rights which alone, nevertheless, attest to and maintain the dignity of man; we are not even asking for their liberty. No; slander, bought no doubt with the greed of the shipowners, ascribes that scheme to us and spreads it everywhere; they want to stir up everyone against us, provoke the planters and their numerous creditors, who take alarm even at gradual emancipation. They want to alarm all the French, to whom they depict the prosperity of the colonies as inseparable from the slave trade and the perpetuity of slavery.

. . . The immediate emancipation of the blacks would not only be a fatal operation for the colonies; it would even be a deadly gift for the blacks, in the state of abjection and incompetence to which cupidity has reduced them. It would be to abandon to themselves and without assistance children in the cradle or mutilated and impotent beings.

It is therefore not yet time to demand that liberty; we ask only that one cease butchering thousands of blacks regularly every year in order to take hundreds of captives; we ask that henceforth cease the prostitution, the profaning of the French name, used to authorize these thefts, these atrocious murders; we demand in a word the abolition of the slave trade. . . .

In regard to the colonists, we will demonstrate to you that if they need to recruit blacks in Africa to sustain the population of the colonies at the same level, it is because they wear out the blacks with work, whippings, and starvation; that, if they treated them with kindness and as good fathers of families, these blacks would multiply and that this population, always growing, would increase cultivation and prosperity. . . .

If some motive might on the contrary push them [the blacks] to insurrection, might it not be the indifference of the National Assembly about their lot? Might it not be the insistence on weighing them down with chains, when one consecrates everywhere this eternal axiom: *that all men are born free and equal in rights.* So then therefore there would only be fetters and gallows for the blacks while good fortune glimmers only for the whites? Have no doubt, our happy revolution must re-electrify the blacks whom vengeance and resentment have electrified for so long, and it is not with punishments that the effect of this upheaval will be repressed. From one insurrection badly pacified will twenty others be born, of which one alone can ruin the colonists forever.

Source: *Adresse à l'Assemblée Nationale, pour l'abolition de la traite des noirs.* Par la Société des Amis des Noirs de Paris (Paris, February 1790), 1–4, 10–11, 17, 19–22. Translation by Lynn Hunt.

---

tions for more than a century as Polish rebels flocked to any international upheaval that might undo the partitions. Beyond all this maneuvering lay the unsolved problem of Polish serfdom, which isolated the nation's gentry and townspeople from the rural masses.

Revolution in the Colonies

The revolution that produced so much upheaval in continental Europe had repercussions in France's Caribbean colonies. These colonies were crucial to the French economy. Twice the size in land area of the neighboring British colonies, they also produced nearly twice as much revenue in exports. The slave population had doubled in the French colonies in the twenty years before 1789. St. Domingue (present-day Haiti) was the most important French colony. Occupying the western half of the island of Hispaniola, it was inhabited by 465,000 slaves, 30,000 whites, and 28,000 free people of color, whose primary job was to apprehend runaway slaves and ensure plantation security.

Despite the efforts of a Paris club called the Friends of Blacks, most French revolutionaries did not consider slavery a pressing problem. As one deputy explained, "This regime [in the colonies] is oppressive, but it gives a livelihood to several million Frenchmen. This regime is barbarous but a still greater barbarity will result if you interfere with it without the necessary knowledge." (See Document, "Address on Abolishing the Slave Trade," page 613.)

In August 1791, however, the slaves in northern St. Domingue, inspired by the slogan "Listen to the voice of Liberty which speaks in the hearts of all," organized a large-scale revolt. To restore authority over the slaves, the Legislative Assembly in Paris granted civil and political rights to the free

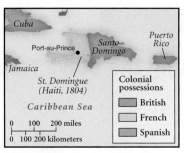

St. Domingue on the Eve of the Revolt, 1791

blacks. This action infuriated white planters and merchants, who in 1793 signed an agreement with Great Britain, now France's enemy in war, declaring British sovereignty over St. Domingue. To complicate matters further, Spain, which controlled the rest of the island and had entered on Great Britain's side in the war with France, offered freedom to individual slave rebels who joined the Spanish armies as long as they agreed to maintain the slave regime for the other blacks.

The few thousand French republican troops on St. Domingue were outnumbered, and to prevent complete military disaster, the French commissioner freed all the slaves in his jurisdiction in August 1793 without permission from the government in Paris. In February 1794, the National Con-

Toussaint L'Ouverture

The leader of the St. Domingue slave uprising appears in his general's uniform, sword in hand. This portrait appeared in one of the earliest histories of the revolt, Marcus Rainsford's *Historical Account of the Black Empire of Hayti* (London, 1805). Toussaint, a former slave who educated himself, fascinated many of his contemporaries in Europe as well as the New World by turning a chaotic slave rebellion into an organized and ultimately successful independence movement. *(North Wind Picture Archives.)*

vention formally abolished slavery and granted full rights to all black men in the colonies. These actions had the desired effect. One of the ablest black generals allied with the Spanish, the ex-slave François Dominique Toussaint L'Ouverture (1743–1803), changed sides and committed his troops to the French (see the illustration on page 614). The French eventually appointed Toussaint governor of St. Domingue as a reward for his efforts.

The vicious fighting and the flight of whites left St. Domingue's economy in ruins. In 1800, the plantations produced one-fifth of what they had in 1789. In the zones Toussaint controlled, army officers or government officials took over the great estates and kept all those working in agriculture under military discipline. The former slaves were bound to their estates like serfs and forced to work the plantations in exchange for an autonomous family life and the right to maintain personal garden plots.

Toussaint remained in charge until 1802, when Napoleon sent French armies to regain control of the island. They arrested Toussaint and transported him to France, where he died in prison. His arrest prompted the English poet William Wordsworth to write of him:

> There's not a breathing of the common wind
> That will forget thee; thou hast great allies;
> Thy friends are exultations, agonies,
> And love, and man's unconquerable mind.

Toussaint became a hero to abolitionists everywhere, a potent symbol of black struggles to win freedom. Napoleon attempted to restore slavery, as he had in the other French Caribbean colonies of Guadeloupe and Martinique, but the remaining black generals defeated his armies and in 1804 proclaimed the Republic of Haiti.

REVIEW: Why did some groups outside of France embrace the French Revolution while others resisted it?

Conclusion

Growing out of aspirations for freedom that also inspired the Dutch, Belgians, and Poles, the revolution that shook France permanently altered the political landscape of the Western world. Between 1789 and 1799, monarchy as a form of government had given way in France to a republic whose leaders were elected. Aristocracy based on rank and birth had been undermined in favor of civil equality and the promotion of merit. The people who marched in demonstrations, met in clubs, and, in the case of men, voted in national elections for the first time had insisted that government respond to them. Thousands of men had held elective office. A revolutionary government had tried to teach new values with a refashioned calendar, state festivals, and a civic religion. Its example inspired would-be revolutionaries everywhere, including in France's own colonies.

But the French Revolution also had its darker side. The divisions created by the Revolution within France endured in many cases until after World War II. Even now, French public-opinion surveys ask if it was right to execute the king in 1793 (most believe Louis XVI was guilty of treason but should not have been executed). The revolutionaries proclaimed human rights and democratic government as a universal goal, but they also explicitly excluded women, even though they admitted Protestant, Jewish, and eventually black men. They used the new spirit of national pride to inspire armies and then used them to conquer other peoples. Their ideals of universal education, religious toleration, and democratic participation could not prevent the institution of new forms of government terror to persecute, imprison, and kill dissidents. These paradoxes created an opening for Napoleon Bonaparte, who rushed in with his remarkable military and political skills to push France — and with it all of Europe — in new directions.

FOR FURTHER EXPLORATION

■ **For suggested references, including Web sites, for topics in this chapter,** see page SR-1 at the end of the book.

■ **For additional primary-source material from this period,** see Chapter 19 in *Sources of THE MAKING OF THE WEST,* Third Edition.

■ **For Web sites and documents related to topics in this chapter,** see *Make History* at bedfordstmartins.com/hunt.

MAPPING THE WEST

Legend:
- States established by revolutionary France
- Boundary of the Holy Roman Empire

Europe in 1799

France's expansion during the revolutionary wars threatened to upset the balance of power in Europe. A century earlier, the English and Dutch had allied and formed a Europe-wide coalition to check the territorial ambitions of Louis XIV. Thwarting French ambitions after 1799 would prove to be even more of a challenge to the other European powers. The Dutch had been reduced to satellite status, as had most of the Italian states. Even Austria and Prussia would suffer devastating losses to the French on the battlefield. Only a new coalition of European powers could stop France in the future.

CHAPTER REVIEW

KEY TERMS AND PEOPLE

Louis XVI (591)

Marie-Antoinette (591)

Estates General (592)

Great Fear (595)

Declaration of the Rights of Man and Citizen (595)

Jacobin Club (599)

Maximilien Robespierre (600)

Terror (600)

de-Christianization (603)

Thermidorian Reaction (606)

MAKING CONNECTIONS

1. Should the French Revolution be viewed as the origin of democracy or the origin of totalitarianism (a government in which no dissent is allowed)? Explain.

2. Why did other European rulers find the French Revolution so threatening?

> **For practice quizzes, a customized study plan, and other study tools,** see the Online Study Guide at bedfordstmartins.com/hunt.

REVIEW QUESTIONS

1. How did the beginning of the French Revolution resemble the other revolutions of 1787–1789?

2. Why did the French Revolution turn in an increasingly radical direction after 1789?

3. What factors can explain the Terror? To what extent was it simply a response to a national emergency or a reflection of deeper problems within the French Revolution?

4. Why did some groups outside of France embrace the French Revolution while others resisted it?

IMPORTANT EVENTS

1787	Dutch Patriot revolt is stifled by Prussian invasion		1792	Beginning of war between France and the rest of Europe; second revolution of August 10 overthrows monarchy
1788	Beginning of resistance of Austrian Netherlands against reforms of Joseph II; opening of reform parliament in Poland		1793	Second partition of Poland by Austria and Russia; Louis XVI of France executed for treason
1789	French Revolution begins		1794	Abolition of slavery in French colonies; Robespierre's government by terror falls
1790	Internal divisions lead to collapse of resistance in Austrian Netherlands		1795	Third (final) partition of Poland; France annexes the Austrian Netherlands
1791	Beginning of slave revolt in St. Domingue (Haiti)		1797–1798	Creation of "sister republics" in Italian states and Switzerland

Napoleon and the Revolutionary Legacy

1800–1830

I n her novel *Frankenstein* (1818), the prototype for modern thrillers, Mary Shelley tells the story of a Swiss technological genius who creates a humanlike monster in his pursuit of scientific knowledge. The monster, "so scaring and unearthly in his ugliness," terrifies all who encounter him and ends by destroying Dr. Frankenstein's own loved ones. Despite desperate chases across deserts and frozen landscapes, Frankenstein never manages to trap the monster, who is last seen hunched over his creator's deathbed.

Frankenstein's monster can be taken as a particularly horrifying incarnation of the fears of the postrevolutionary era, but which fears did Shelley have in mind? Did the monster represent the French Revolution, which had devoured its own children in the Terror? Shelley was the daughter of Mary Wollstonecraft, an English feminist who had defended the French Revolution and died in childbirth when Mary was born. Mary Shelley was also the wife of the romantic poet Percy Bysshe Shelley, who often wrote against the ugliness of contemporary life and in opposition to the conservative politics that had triumphed in Great Britain after Napoleon's fall. Whatever the meaning—and Mary Shelley may well have intended more than one—*Frankenstein* makes the forceful point that humans cannot always control their own creations. The Enlightenment and the French Revolution had celebrated the virtues of human creativity, but Shelley shows that innovation often has a dark and uncontrollable side.

Those who witnessed Napoleon Bonaparte's stunning rise to European dominance might have cast him as either Frankenstein or his monster. Like the scientist Frankenstein, Bonaparte created something

Napoleon as Military Hero
In this painting from 1800–1801, *Napoleon Crossing the Alps at St. Bernard*, Jacques-Louis David reminds the French of Napoleon's heroic military exploits. Napoleon is a picture of calm and composure while his horse shows the fright and energy of the moment. David painted this propagandistic image shortly after one of his former students went to the guillotine on a trumped-up charge of plotting to assassinate the new French leader. The former organizer of republican festivals during the Terror had become a kind of court painter for the new regime. (*Réunion des Musées Nationaux/Art Resource, NY.*)

dramatically new: the French Empire with himself as emperor. Like the former kings of France, he ruled under his first name. This Corsican artillery officer who spoke French with an Italian accent ended the French Revolution even while maintaining some of its most important innovations. Bonaparte transformed France from a republic with democratically elected leaders to an empire with a new aristocracy based on military service. But he kept the revolutionary administration and most of the laws that ensured equal treatment of citizens. Although he tolerated no opposition at home, he prided himself on bringing French-style changes to peoples elsewhere.

Bonaparte continued his revolutionary policy of conquest and annexation until it reached grotesque dimensions. His foreign policies made many see him as a monster hungry for dominion; he turned the sister republics of the revolutionary era into kingdoms personally ruled by his relatives, and he exacted tribute wherever he triumphed. Eventually, resistance to the French armies and the ever-mounting costs of military glory toppled Napoleon. The powers allied against him met and agreed to restore the monarchical governments that had been overthrown by the French, shrink France back to its prerevolutionary boundaries, and maintain this settlement against future demands for change.

Although the people of Europe longed for peace and stability in the aftermath of the Napoleonic whirlwind, they lived in a deeply unsettled world. Profoundly affected by French military occupation, many groups of people organized to demand ethnic and cultural autonomy, first from Napoleon and then from the restored governments after 1815. In 1830, a new round of revolutions broke out in France, Belgium, Poland, and some of the Italian states. The revolutionary legacy was far from exhausted.

FOCUS QUESTION: How did Napoleon Bonaparte's actions force other European rulers to change their policies?

The Rise of Napoleon Bonaparte

In 1799, a charismatic young general took over the French republic and set France on a new course. Within a year, **Napoleon Bonaparte** (1769–1821) had effectively ended the French Revolution and steered France toward an authoritarian state. As emperor after 1804, he dreamed of European integration in the tradition of Augustus and Charlemagne, but he also mastered the details of practical administration. To achieve his goals, he compromised with the Catholic church and with exiled aristocrats willing to return to France. His most enduring accomplishment, the new Civil Code, tempered the principles of the Enlightenment and the Revolution with an insistence on the powers of fathers over children, husbands over wives, and employers over workers. His influence spread into many spheres as he personally patronized scientific inquiry and encouraged artistic styles in line with his vision of imperial greatness.

A General Takes Over

It would have seemed astonishing in 1795 that the twenty-six-year-old son of a noble family from the island of Corsica off the Italian coast would within four years become the supreme ruler of France and

---

Napoleon Bonaparte: The French general who became First Consul in 1799 and emperor in 1804; after losing the battle of Waterloo in 1815, he was exiled to the island of St. Helena.

■ **1799** Coup against Directory; Napoleon named First Consul

■ **1801** Napoleon signs concordat with pope

■ **1805** Battle of Trafalgar; battle of Austerlitz

■ **1804** Napoleon crowned emperor; issues Civil Code

■ **1812** Napoleon invades Russia

■ **1814–1815** Congress of Vienna

■ **1815** Napoleon defeated at Waterloo, exiled to St. Helena

| 1800 | 1805 | 1810 | 1815 |

one of the greatest military leaders in world history. That year, Bonaparte was a penniless artillery officer, only recently released from prison as a presumed Robespierrist. Thanks to some early military successes and links to Parisian politicians, however, he was named commander of the French army in Italy in 1796.

Bonaparte's astounding success in the Italian campaigns of 1796–1797 launched his meteoric career. With an army of fewer than fifty thousand men, he defeated the Piedmontese and the Austrians. In quick order, he established client republics dependent on his own authority, negotiated with the Austrians himself, and molded the army into his personal force by paying the soldiers in cash taken as tribute from the newly conquered territories. He mollified the Directory government by sending home wagonloads of Italian masterpieces of art, which were added to Parisian museum collections (most are still there) after being paraded in victory festivals.

In 1798, the Directory set aside its plans to invade England, gave Bonaparte command of the army raised for that purpose, and sent him across the Mediterranean Sea to Egypt. The Directory government hoped that French occupation of Egypt would strike a blow at British trade by cutting the route to India. Although the French immediately defeated a much larger Egyptian army, the British admiral Lord Horatio Nelson destroyed the French fleet while it was anchored in Aboukir Bay, cutting the French off from home. In the face of determined resistance and an outbreak of the bubonic plague, Bonaparte's armies retreated from a further expedition in Syria. But the French occupation of Egypt lasted long enough for that largely Muslim country to experience the same kinds of Enlightenment-inspired legal reforms that had been introduced in Europe: the French abolished torture, introduced equality before the law, eliminated religious taxes, and proclaimed religious toleration.

Even the failures of the Egyptian campaign did not dull Bonaparte's luster. Bonaparte had taken France's leading scientists with him on the expedition, and his soldiers had discovered a slab of black basalt dating from 196 B.C.E. written in both hieroglyphic and Greek. Called the Rosetta stone after a nearby town, it enabled scholars to finally decipher the hieroglyphs used by the ancient Egyptians. With his army pinned down by Nelson's victory at sea, Bonaparte slipped out of Egypt and made his way secretly to southern France.

In October 1799, Bonaparte arrived home at just the right moment. The war in Europe was going badly. The territories of the former Austrian Netherlands had revolted against French conscription laws, and deserters swelled the ranks of rebels in western France. Amid increasing political instability, generals in the field had become virtually independent, and the troops felt more loyal to their units and generals than to the republic. Disillusioned members of the government saw in Bonaparte's return an occasion to overturn the constitution of 1795.

On November 9, 1799, the conspirators persuaded the legislature to move out of Paris to avoid an imaginary Jacobin plot. But when Bonaparte stomped into the new meeting hall the next day and demanded immediate changes in the constitution, he was greeted by cries of "Down with the dictator!" His quick-thinking brother Lucien, president of the Council of Five Hundred (the lower house), saved Bonaparte's coup by summoning troops guarding the hall and claiming that some deputies had tried to assassinate the popular general. The soldiers ejected those who opposed Bonaparte and left the remaining ones to vote to abolish the Directory and establish a new three-man executive called the consulate.

■ 1820 Revolt against Spanish crown

■ 1824 Beethoven, Ninth Symphony

■ 1830 Greece gains independence; Charles X overthrown; Louis-Phillipe installed; Polish revolt fails

| 1820 | 1825 | 1830 | 1835 |

■ 1818 Mary Shelley, *Frankenstein*

■ 1825 Decembrist Revolt in Russia

■ 1832 English Reform Bill; Goethe, *Faust*

Francisco de Goya, *The Colossus* (1808–1812)
The Spanish painter Goya might be imagined as portraying Frankenstein's monster or Napoleon himself as the new giant overwhelming much of Europe. Goya painted for the Spanish court before Napoleon invaded and occupied Spain; after an illness left him deaf, he turned toward darkly imaginative works such as this one.

Bonaparte became **First Consul**, a title revived from the ancient Roman republic. He promised to be a man above party and to restore order to the republic. A new constitution was submitted to the voters. Millions abstained from voting, and the government falsified the results to give an appearance of even greater support to the new regime. Inside France, political apathy had overtaken the original enthusiasm for revolutionary ideals. Altogether it was an unpromising beginning; yet within five years, Bonaparte would crown himself Napoleon I, emperor of the French. The French armies would recover from their reverses of 1799 to push the frontiers of French influence even farther eastward.

First Consul: The most important of the three consuls established by the French Constitution of 1800; the title, given to Napoleon Bonaparte, was taken from ancient Rome.

From Republic to Empire

Napoleon had no long-range plans to establish himself as emperor and conquer most of Europe. The deputies of the legislature who engineered the coup d'état of November 1799 picked him as one of three provisional consuls only because he was a famous general. Napoleon immediately asserted his leadership over the other two consuls in the process of drafting another constitution—the fourth since 1789. He then set about putting his stamp on every aspect of French life, building monuments and institutions that in some cases have endured to the present day.

The End of the Republic. The constitution of 1799 made Napoleon the First Consul with the right to pick the Council of State, which drew up all laws. He exerted control by choosing men loyal to him. Government was no longer representative in any real sense: the new constitution eliminated direct elections for deputies and granted no independent powers to the three houses of the legislature. Napoleon and his advisers chose the legislature's members out of a small pool of "notables." Almost all men over twenty-one could vote in the plebiscite (referendum) to approve the constitution, but their only option was to choose *yes* or *no*.

Napoleon's most urgent task was to reconcile to his regime Catholics who had been alienated by revolutionary policies. Although nominally Catholic, Napoleon held no deep religious convictions. "How can there be order in the state without religion?" he asked cynically. "When a man is dying of hunger beside another who is stuffing himself, he cannot accept this difference if there is not an authority who tells him: 'God wishes it so.'" In 1801, a concordat with Pope Pius VII (r. 1800–1823) ended a decade of church-state conflict in France. The pope validated all sales of church lands, and the government agreed to pay the salaries of bishops and priests who would swear loyalty to the state. Catholicism was officially recognized as the religion of "the great majority of French citizens." (The state also paid Protestant pastors' salaries.) Thus, the pope brought the huge French Catholic population back into the fold and Napoleon gained the pope's support for his regime.

Napoleon continued the centralization of state power that had begun under the absolutist monarchy of Louis XIV and resumed under the

Terror. As First Consul, he appointed prefects who directly supervised local affairs in every department in the country. He created the Bank of France to facilitate government borrowing and relied on gold and silver coinage rather than paper money. He made good use of budgets and improved tax collection, but he also frequently made ends meet by exacting tribute from the territories he conquered.

Napoleon promised order and an end to the upheavals of ten years of revolutionary turmoil, but his regime severely limited political expression. He never relied on mass executions to achieve control, but he refused to allow those who opposed him to meet in clubs, influence elections, or publish newspapers. A decree reduced the number of newspapers in Paris from seventy-three to thirteen (and then finally to four), and the newspapers that remained became government organs. Government censors had to approve all operas and plays, and they banned "offensive" artistic works even more frequently than their royal predecessors had. The minister of police, Joseph Fouché, once a leading figure in the Terror of 1793–1794, could impose house arrest, arbitrary imprisonment, and surveillance of political dissidents. Political contest and debate shriveled to almost nothing. When a bomb attack on Napoleon's carriage failed in 1800, Fouché suppressed the evidence of a royalist plot and instead arrested hundreds of former Jacobins. More than one hundred of them were deported and seven hundred imprisoned.

When it suited him, Napoleon also struck against royalist conspirators. In 1804, he ordered his police to kidnap from his residence in Germany Louis-Antoine-Henri de Bourbon-Condé, duc d'Enghien. Napoleon had intelligence, which proved to be false, that d'Enghien had joined a plot in Paris against him. Even when he learned the truth, he insisted that a military tribunal try d'Enghien, a close relative of the dead king Louis XVI. D'Enghien was shot on the spot after a summary trial. By then, Napoleon's political intentions had become clear. He had named himself First Consul for life in 1802, and in 1804, with the pope's blessing, he crowned himself emperor. Once again, plebiscites approved his decisions, but no alternatives were offered. The democratic political aims of the French Revolution had been trampled, but some aspects of daily life continued to be affected by those egalitarian ideals (see "Seeing History," page 624).

Imperial Rule. Napoleon's outsized personality dominated the new regime. His face and name adorned coins, engravings, histories, paintings, and public monuments. His favorite painters embellished his legend by depicting him as a warrior-hero of mythic proportions even though he was short and physically unimpressive in person. Believing that "what is big is always beautiful," Napoleon embarked on ostentatious building projects that would outshine even those of Louis XIV. Government-commissioned architects built the Arc de Triomphe, the Stock Exchange, fountains, and even slaughterhouses. Most of his new construction reflected his neoclassical taste for monumental buildings set in vast empty spaces.

Napoleon worked hard at establishing his reputation as an efficient administrator with broad intellectual interests: he met frequently with scientists, jurists, and artists, and stories abounded of his unflagging energy. When not on military campaigns, he worked on state affairs, usually until 10:00 p.m., taking only a few minutes for each meal. "Authority," declared his adviser Abbé Emmanuel-Joseph Sieyès, "must come from above and confidence from below." To establish his authority, Napoleon relied on men who had served with him in the army. His chief of staff Alexandre Berthier, for example, became minister of war, and the chemist Claude Berthollet, who had organized the scientific part of the expedition to Egypt, became vice president of the Senate in 1804. Napoleon's bureaucracy was based on a patron-client relationship, with Napoleon as the ultimate patron. Some of Napoleon's closest associates married into his family.

Combining aristocratic and revolutionary values in a new social hierarchy that rewarded merit and talent, Napoleon personally chose as senators the nation's most illustrious generals, ministers, prefects, scientists, rich men, and former nobles. Intending to replace both the old nobility of birth and the republic's strict emphasis on equality, in 1802 he took the first step toward creating a new nobility by founding the Legion of Honor. (Members of the legion received lifetime pensions along with their titles.) Napoleon usually equated honor with military success. By 1814, the legion had thirty-two thousand members, only 5 percent of them civilians.

In 1808, Napoleon introduced a complete hierarchy of noble titles, ranging from princes down to barons and chevaliers. All Napoleonic nobles had served the state. Titles could be inherited but had to be supported by wealth — a man could not be a duke without a fortune of 200,000 francs or a chevalier without 3,000 francs. To go along with their new titles, Napoleon gave his favorite gener-

SEEING HISTORY

The Clothing Revolution: The Social Meaning of Changes in Postrevolutionary Fashion

Some revolutions take place in the realm of social life and culture rather than politics. One of the most striking of these social and cultural revolutions was the wearing of trousers. Before the French Revolution of 1789, men of the middle classes and nobility wore knee breeches, stockings, and buckled shoes, as can be seen in the colored engraving from 1778. Trousers (long pants) were worn only by working-class men, who needed them to protect themselves on the job and from the mud in the streets.

From Napoleon onward, a shift toward trousers took place across Europe, not all at once but slowly and surely.

Napoleon himself wore close-fitting pantaloons (from which the word *pants* is derived) until he became too fat and reverted back to knee breeches. The colored engraving of a middle-class couple in 1830 shows how long pants had become the fashion for men. In line with political changes that installed equality under the law and careers open to merit rather than birth, men began to dress more alike; all men wore trousers. Taking a closer look at the men in both pictures, do you see any other changes in style and accessories that might reflect a less class-conscious society?

Women's dress, in contrast, maintained and even underlined social distinctions after the Revolution. In the nineteenth century, middle- and upper-class women continued to wear dresses with such long and full skirts that they could not possibly be imagined working. Working women wore simpler blouses and skirts that allowed the movements necessary to labor at home or in manufacturing. Compare the pre-Revolution fashion shown with that of the woman in the 1830 engraving. Does one outfit look more comfortable than the other? Why or why not? What other differences (or similarities) do you notice? Why do you think women's fashion failed to become more uniform the way men's did in the decades following the Revolution?

Gentleman Proposing to a Lady, 1778. (© Private Collection/The Stapleton Collection/The Bridgeman Art Library.)

Fashion for Men and Women, 1830. (© Musée de la Ville de Paris, Musée Carnavalet, Paris, France/Lauros/Giraudon/The Bridgeman Art Library.)

Napoleon's Coronation as Emperor
In this detail from *The Coronation of Napoleon and Josephine* (1805–1807), Jacques-Louis David shows Napoleon crowning his wife at the ceremony of 1804. Napoleon orchestrated the entire event and took the only active role in it: Pope Pius VII gave his blessing to the ceremony (he can be seen seated behind Napoleon), but Napoleon crowned himself. What is the significance of Napoleon crowning himself? *(Erich Lessing/Art Resource, NY.)*

■ **For more help analyzing this image,** see the visual activity for this chapter in the Online Study Guide at bedfordstmartins.com/hunt.

als huge fortunes, often in the form of estates in the conquered territories.

Napoleon's own family reaped the greatest benefits. He made his older brother, Joseph, ruler of the newly established kingdom of Naples in 1806, the same year he installed his younger brother Louis as king of Holland. He proclaimed his twenty-three-year-old stepson, Eugène de Beauharnais, viceroy of Italy in 1805 and established his sister Caroline and brother-in-law General Joachim Murat as king and queen of Naples in 1808 when he moved Joseph to the throne of Spain. Napoleon wanted to establish an imperial succession, but he lacked an heir. In thirteen years of marriage, his wife Josephine had borne no children, so in 1809 he divorced her and in 1810 married the eighteen-year-old princess Marie-Louise of Austria. The next year she gave birth to a son, to whom Napoleon immediately gave the title king of Rome.

The New Paternalism: The Civil Code

As part of his restoration of order, Napoleon brought a paternalist model of power to his state. Previous governments had tried to unify and standardize France's multiple legal codes, but only Napoleon successfully established a new one, partly because he personally presided over the commission that drafted the new **Civil Code**, completed in 1804. Called the Napoleonic Code as a way of further exalting his image, it reasserted the Old Regime's patriarchal system of male domination over women and insisted on a father's control over his children, which revolutionary legislation had limited. For example, if children under age sixteen refused to follow their fathers' commands,

Civil Code: The French legal code formulated by Napoleon in 1804; it ensured equal treatment under the law to all men and guaranteed religious liberty, but it curtailed many rights of women.

Emperor Napoleon in His Study
In this portrait painted by Jacques-Louis David in 1812, Napoleon is shown in his general's uniform, sword by his side. He stands by his desk covered with papers to show how hard he works for the country. *(Erich Lessing/Art Resource, NY.)*

Although the code maintained the equal division of family property between all children, both male and female, it sharply curtailed women's rights in other respects. Napoleon wanted to restrict women to the private sphere of the home. One of his leading jurists remarked, "Women need protection because they are weaker; men are free because they are stronger." The law obligated a husband to support his wife, but the husband alone controlled any property held in common; a wife could not sue in court, sell or mortgage her own property, or contract a debt without her husband's consent. Divorce was severely restricted. A wife could petition for divorce only if her husband brought his mistress to live in the family home. In contrast, a wife convicted of adultery could be imprisoned for up to two years. The code's framers saw these discrepancies as a way to reinforce the family and make women responsible for private virtue, while leaving public decisions to men. The French code was imitated in many European and Latin American countries and in the French colony of Louisiana, where it had a similar negative effect on women's rights. Not until 1965 did French wives gain legal status equal to that of their husbands.

Napoleon took little interest in girls' education, believing that girls should spend most of their time at home learning religion, manners, and such "female occupations" as sewing and music. For boys, by contrast, the government set up a new system of lycées, state-run secondary schools in which students wore military uniforms and drumrolls signaled the beginning and end of classes. The lycées offered wider access to education and thus helped achieve Napoleon's goal of opening careers to those with talent, regardless of their social origins. (Without the military trappings, the lycées are now coeducational and still the heart of the French educational system.)

The new paternalism extended to relations between employers and employees. The state required all workers to carry a work card attesting to their good conduct, and it prohibited all workers' organizations. The police considered workers without cards as vagrants or criminals and could send them to workhouses or prison. After 1806, arbitration boards settled labor disputes, but they took employers at their word while treating workers as minors, demanding that foremen and shop superintendents represent them. Occasionally strikes broke out, led by secret, illegal journeymen's associations, yet many employers laid off employees when times were hard, deducted fines from their wages, and dismissed them without

they could be sent to prison for up to a month with no hearing of any sort. Yet the code also required fathers to provide for their children's welfare. Moreover, the Civil Code protected many of the gains of the French Revolution by defining and assuring property rights, guaranteeing religious liberty, and establishing a uniform system of law that provided equal treatment for all adult males and affirmed the right of men to choose their professions. Napoleon wanted to discourage abortion and infanticide, not uncommon among the poorest classes in the fast-growing urban areas, so he helped set up private charities to help indigent mothers and made it easier for women to abandon their children anonymously to a government foundling hospital.

appeal for being absent or making errors. These limitations on workers' rights won Napoleon the support of French business.

Patronage of Science and Intellectual Life

Napoleon did everything possible to promote French scientific inquiry, especially that which could serve practical ends. He closely monitored the research institutes established during the Revolution, sometimes intervening personally to achieve political conformity. An impressive outpouring of new theoretical and practical scientific work rewarded the state's efforts. Experiments with balloons led to the discovery of laws about the expansion of gases, and research on fossil shells prepared the way for new theories of evolutionary change later in the nineteenth century. The surgeon Dominique-Jean Larrey developed new techniques of battlefield amputation and medical care during Napoleon's wars, winning an appointment as an officer in the Legion of Honor and becoming a baron with a pension.

Napoleon aimed to modernize French society through science, but he could not tolerate criticism. Napoleon considered most writers useless or dangerous, "good for nothing under any government." Some of the most talented French writers of the time had to live in exile. The best-known expatriate was Anne-Louise-Germaine de Staël (1766–1817), the daughter of Louis XVI's chief minister Jacques Necker. When explaining his desire to banish her, Napoleon exclaimed, "She is a machine in motion who stirs up the salons." While exiled in the German states, de Staël wrote a novel, *Corinne* (1807), whose heroine is a brilliant woman thwarted by a patriarchal system, and *On Germany* (1810), an account of the important new literary currents east of the Rhine. Her books were banned in France.

Although Napoleon restored the strong authority of state and religion in France, many royalists and Catholics still criticized him as an impious usurper. (See "Contrasting Views," page 634.) François-René de Chateaubriand (1768–1848) admired Napoleon as "the strong man who has saved us from the abyss," but he preferred monarchy. In his view, Napoleon had not properly understood the need to defend Christian values against the Enlightenment's excessive reliance on reason. Chateaubriand wrote his *Genius of Christianity* (1802) to draw attention to the power and mystery of faith. He warned, "It is to the vanity of knowledge that we owe almost all our misfor-

Germaine de Staël

One of the most fascinating intellectuals of her time, Anne-Louise-Germaine de Staël seemed to irritate Napoleon more than any other person did. Daughter of Louis XVI's Swiss Protestant finance minister, Jacques Necker, and wife of a Swedish diplomat, Madame de Staël frequently criticized Napoleon's regime. She published best-selling novels and influential literary criticism, and whenever allowed to reside in Paris she encouraged the intellectual and political dissidents from Napoleon's regime.

(Réunion des Musées Nationaux/Art Resource, NY.)

tunes. . . . The learned ages have always been followed by ages of destruction."

REVIEW: In what ways did Napoleon continue the French Revolution, and in what ways did he break with it?

"Europe Was at My Feet": Napoleon's Conquests

Building on innovations introduced by the republican governments before him, Napoleon revolutionized the art of war with tactics and strategy based on a highly mobile army. By 1812, he ruled a

European empire more extensive than any since ancient Rome (Map 20.1). Yet that empire had already begun to crumble, and with it went Napoleon's power at home. Napoleon's empire failed because it was based on a contradiction: Napoleon tried to reduce virtually all of Europe to the status of colonial dependents when Europe had long consisted of independent states. The result, inevitably, was a great upsurge in nationalist feeling that has dominated European politics to the present.

The Grand Army and Its Victories, 1800–1807

Napoleon attributed his military success "three-quarters to morale" and the rest to leadership and superiority of numbers at the point of attack. Con-

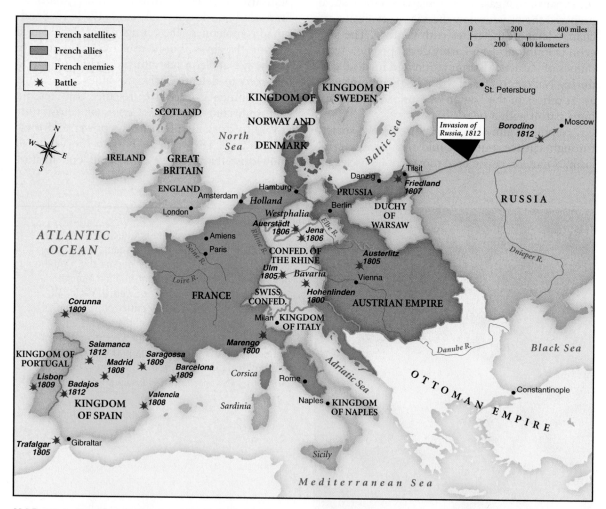

MAP 20.1 Napoleon's Empire at Its Height, 1812
In 1812, Napoleon had at least nominal control of almost all of western Europe. Even before he made his fatal mistake of invading Russia, however, his authority had been undermined in Spain and seriously weakened in the Italian and German states. His efforts to extend French power sparked resistance almost everywhere: as Napoleon insisted on French domination, local people began to think of themselves as Italian, German, or Dutch. Thus, Napoleon inadvertently laid the foundations for the nineteenth-century spread of nationalism.

scription provided the large numbers: 1.3 million men ages twenty to twenty-four were drafted between 1800 and 1812, another million in 1813–1814. Many willingly served because the republic had taught them to identify the army with the nation. Military service was both a patriotic duty and a means of social mobility. The men who rose through the ranks to become officers were young, ambitious, and accustomed to the new ways of war. Consequently, the French army had higher morale than the armies of other powers, most of which rejected conscription as too democratic and continued to restrict their officer corps to the nobility. Only in 1813–1814, when the military tide turned against Napoleon, did French morale plummet.

When Napoleon came to power in 1799, desertion was rampant, and the generals competed with one another for predominance. Napoleon ended this squabbling by uniting all the armies into one Grand Army under his personal command. By 1812, he commanded 700,000 troops; while 250,000 soldiers fought in Spain, others remained garrisoned in France. In any given battle, between 70,000 and 180,000 men, not all of them French, fought for France. Life on campaign was no picnic—ordinary soldiers slept in the rain, mud, and snow and often had to forage for food—but Napoleon nonetheless inspired almost fanatical loyalty. He fought alongside his soldiers in some sixty battles and had nineteen horses shot from under him. One opponent said that Napoleon's presence alone was worth 50,000 men.

A brilliant strategist who carefully studied the demands of war, Napoleon outmaneuvered virtually all his opponents. He had a pragmatic and direct approach to strategy: he went for the main body of the opposing army and tried to crush it in a lightning campaign. He gathered the largest possible army for one great and decisive battle and then followed with a relentless pursuit to break enemy morale altogether. His military command, like his rule within France, was personal and highly centralized. He essentially served as his own operations officer: "I alone know what I have to do," he insisted. This style worked as long as Napoleon could be on the battlefield, but he failed to train independent subordinates to take over in his absence. He also faced constant difficulties in supplying a rapidly moving army, which, because of its size, could not always live off the land.

One of Napoleon's greatest advantages was the lack of coordination among his enemies. Britain dominated the seas but did not want to field huge land armies. On the continent, the French republic had already set up satellites in the Netherlands and Italy, which served as a buffer against the big powers to the east, Austria, Prussia, and Russia. By maneuvering diplomatically and militarily, Napoleon could usually take these on one by one. After reorganizing the French armies in 1799, for example, Napoleon won striking victories against the Austrians at Marengo and Hohenlinden in 1800, forcing them to agree to peace terms. Once the Austrians had withdrawn, Britain agreed to the Treaty of Amiens in 1802, effectively ending hostilities on the continent. Napoleon considered the peace with Great Britain merely a truce, however, and it lasted only until 1803.

Napoleon used the breathing space not only to consolidate his position before taking up arms again but also to send an expeditionary force to the Caribbean colony of St. Domingue to regain control of the island. Continuing resistance among the black population and an epidemic of yellow fever forced Napoleon to withdraw his troops from St. Domingue and abandon his plans to extend his empire to the Western Hemisphere. As part of his retreat, he sold the Louisiana Territory to the United States in 1803.

France's Retreat from America

When war resumed in Europe, the British navy once more proved its superiority by blocking an attempted French invasion and by defeating the French and their Spanish allies in a huge naval battle at Trafalgar in 1805. France lost many ships; the British lost no vessels, but their renowned admiral Lord Horatio Nelson died in the battle. On land, Napoleon remained invincible. In 1805, Austria took up arms again when Napoleon demanded that it declare neutrality in the conflict with Britain. Napoleon promptly captured twenty-five thousand Austrian soldiers at Ulm, in Bavaria, in 1805. After marching on to Vienna, he again trounced the Austrians, who had been joined by their new ally, Russia. The battle of Austerlitz, often considered Napoleon's greatest victory, was fought on December 2, 1805, the first anniversary of his coronation.

After maintaining neutrality for a decade, Prussia now declared war on France. In 1806, the French routed the Prussian army at Jena and Auerstädt. In 1807, Napoleon defeated the Russians at Friedland. Personal negotiations between Napoleon and the young tsar Alexander I (r. 1801–1825) resulted in a humiliating settlement imposed on Prussia, which paid the price for temporary reconciliation between France and Russia; the Treaties of Tilsit turned Prussian lands west of

**Napoleon Visiting
the Battlefield**

Antoine-Jean Gros painted this scene of the battle of Eylau (now in northwestern Russia, then in East Prussia) shortly after Napoleon's victory against the Russian army in 1807. The painter aims to show the compassion of Napoleon for his men, but he also draws attention to the sheer carnage of war. Each side lost 25,000 men, killed or wounded, in this battle. What would you conclude from the way the ordinary soldiers are depicted here? (© Archivo Iconografico, S.A./Corbis.)

the Elbe River into the kingdom of Westphalia under Napoleon's brother Jerome, and Prussia's Polish provinces became the duchy of Warsaw. Napoleon once again had turned the divisions among his enemies in his favor.

The Impact of French Victories

Wherever the Grand Army conquered, Napoleon's influence followed soon after. By annexing some territories and setting up others as satellite kingdoms with much-reduced autonomy, Napoleon attempted to colonize large parts of Europe (see Map 20.1, page 628). But even where he did not rule directly or through his relatives, his startling string of victories forced the other powers to reconsider their own methods of rule.

Rule in the Colonized Territories. Napoleon brought the disparate German and Italian states together to rule them more effectively and to exploit their resources for his own ends. In 1803, he consolidated the tiny German states by abolishing some of them and attaching them

Consolidation of German and Italian States, 1812

to larger units. In July 1806, he established the Confederation of the Rhine, which soon included almost all the German states except Austria and Prussia. The Holy Roman Emperor gave up his title, held since the thirteenth century, and became simply the emperor of Austria. Napoleon established three units in Italy: the territories directly annexed to France and the satellite kingdoms of Italy and Naples. Italy had not been so unified since the Roman Empire.

Napoleon forced French-style reforms on both the annexed territories, which were ruled directly from France, and the satellite kingdoms, which were usually ruled by one or another of Napoleon's relatives but with a certain autonomy. French-style reforms included abolishing serfdom, eliminating seigneurial dues, introducing the Napoleonic Code, suppressing monasteries, and subordinating church to state, as well as extending civil rights to Jews and other religious minorities. Napoleon's chosen rulers often made real improvements in roads, public works, law codes, and education. The removal of internal tariffs fostered economic growth by opening up the domestic market for goods, especially textiles. By 1814, Bologna had five hundred factories and Modena four hundred. Yet almost everyone had some cause for complaint. Republicans regretted Napoleon's conversion of the sister republics into kingdoms. Tax increases and ever-rising conscription quotas fomented discontent as well. The annexed territories and satellite kingdoms paid half the cost of Napoleon's wars.

Almost everywhere, conflicts arose between Napoleon's desire for a standardized, centralized government and local insistence on maintaining customs and traditions. Sometimes his own relatives sided with the countries they ruled. Napoleon's brother Louis, for instance, would not allow conscription in the Netherlands because the Dutch had never had compulsory military service. When Napoleon tried to introduce an economic policy banning trade with Great Britain, Louis's lax enforcement prompted the frustrated emperor to complain that "Holland is an English province." In 1810, Napoleon annexed the satellite kingdom because his brother had become too sympathetic to Dutch interests.

Pressure for Reform in Prussia and Russia.

Napoleon's victories forced defeated rulers to rethink their political and cultural assumptions. After the crushing defeat of Prussia in 1806 left his country greatly reduced in territory, Frederick William III (r. 1797–1840) appointed a reform commission, and on its recommendation he abolished serfdom and allowed non-nobles to buy and enclose land. Peasants gained their personal independence from their noble landlords, who could no longer sell them to pay gambling debts, for example, or refuse them permission to marry. Yet the lives of the former serfs remained bleak; they were left without land, and their landlords no longer had to care for them in hard times. The king's advisers also overhauled the army to make the high command more efficient and to open the way to the appointment of middle-class officers. Prussia instituted these reforms to try to compete with the French, not to promote democracy. As one reformer wrote to Frederick William, "We must do from above what the French have done from below."

Reform received lip service in Russia. Tsar Alexander I had gained his throne after an aristocratic coup deposed and killed his autocratic and capricious father, Paul (r. 1796–1801), and in the early years of his reign the remorseful young ruler created Western-style ministries, lifted restrictions on importing foreign books, and founded six new universities; reform commissions studied abuses; nobles were encouraged voluntarily to free their serfs (a few actually did so); and there was even talk of drafting a constitution. But none of these efforts reached beneath the surface of Russian life, and by the second decade of his reign Alexander began to reject the Enlightenment spirit that his grandmother Catherine the Great had instilled in him.

The Continental System.

The one power always standing between Napoleon and total dominance of Europe was Great Britain. The British ruled the seas and financed anyone who would oppose Napoleon. In an effort to bankrupt this "nation of shopkeepers" by choking its trade, Napoleon inaugurated the **Continental System** in 1806. It prohibited all commerce between Great Britain and France or France's dependent states and allies. At first, the system worked: British exports dropped by 20 percent in 1807–1808, and manufacturing declined by 10 percent; unemployment and a strike of sixty thousand workers in northern England resulted. The British retaliated by confiscating merchandise on ships, even those of powers neutral in the wars, that sailed into or out of ports from which the British were excluded by the Continental System.

In the midst of continuing wars, moreover, the system proved impossible to enforce, and widespread smuggling brought British goods into the European market. British growth continued, despite some setbacks; calico-printing works, for example, quadrupled their production, and imports of raw cotton increased by 40 percent. At the same time, French and other continental industries benefited from the temporary protection from British competition.

Resistance to French Rule, 1807–1812.

Smuggling British goods was only one way of opposing the French. Almost everywhere in Europe, resistance began as local opposition to French demands for money or draftees, but it eventually prompted a more nationalistic patriotic defense. In southern Italy, gangs of bandits harassed the French army and local officials; thirty-three thousand Italian bandits were arrested in 1809 alone. But resistance continued via a network of secret societies, called the *carbonari* ("charcoal burners"), which got its name from the practice of marking each new member's forehead with a charcoal mark.

Continental System: The boycott of British goods in France and its satellites ordered by Napoleon in 1806; it had success but was later undermined by smuggling.

Throughout the nineteenth century, the carbonari played a leading role in Italian nationalism. In the German states, intellectuals wrote passionate defenses of the virtues of the German nation and of the superiority of German literature.

No nations bucked under Napoleon's reins more than Spain and Portugal. In 1807, Napoleon sent 100,000 troops through Spain to invade Portugal, Great Britain's ally. The royal family fled to the Portuguese colony of Brazil, but fighting continued, aided by a British army. When Napoleon got his brother Joseph named king of Spain in place of the senile Charles IV (r. 1788–1808), the Spanish clergy and nobles raised bands of peasants to fight the French occupiers. Even Napoleon's taking personal command of the French forces failed to quell the Spanish, who for six years fought a war of national independence that pinned down thousands of French soldiers. Germaine de Staël commented that Napoleon "never understood that a war might be a crusade. . . . He never reckoned with the one power that no arms could overcome—the enthusiasm of a whole people."

The Spanish War for Independence, 1807–1813

More than a new feeling of nationalism was aroused in Spain. Peasants hated French requisitioning of their food supplies and sought to defend their priests against French anticlericalism. Spanish nobles feared revolutionary reforms and were willing to defend the old monarchy in the person of the young Ferdinand VII, heir to Charles IV, even while Ferdinand himself was congratulating Napoleon on his victories. The Spanish Catholic church spread anti-French propaganda that equated Napoleon with heresy. As the former archbishop of Seville wrote to the archbishop of Granada in 1808, "You realize that we must not recognize as king a freemason, heretic, Lutheran, as are all the Bonapartes and the French nation." In this tense atmosphere, the Spanish peasant rebels, assisted by the British, countered every French massacre with atrocities of their own. They tortured their French prisoners (boiling one general alive) and lynched collaborators.

From Russian Winter to Final Defeat, 1812–1815

Despite opposition, Napoleon ruled over an extensive empire by 1812. He controlled more territory than any European ruler had since Roman times. Only two major European states remained fully independent—Great Britain and Russia—but once allied they would successfully challenge his dominion and draw many other states to their side. Britain sent aid to the Portuguese and Spanish rebels, while Russia once again prepared for war. Tsar Alexander I made peace with Turkey and allied himself with Great Britain and Sweden. In 1812, Napoleon invaded Russia with 250,000 horses and 600,000 men, including contingents of Italians, Poles, Swiss, Dutch, and Germans. This daring move proved to be his undoing.

Invasion of Russia, 1812. Napoleon followed his usual strategy of trying to strike quickly, but the Russian generals avoided confrontation and retreated eastward, destroying anything that might be useful to the invaders. In September, on the road to Moscow, Napoleon finally engaged the main Russian force in the gigantic battle of Borodino (see Map 20.1, page 628). French casualties numbered 30,000 men, including 47 generals; the Russians lost 45,000. The French soldiers had nothing to celebrate around their campfires: as one soldier wrote, "Everyone . . . wept for some dead friend." Once again the Russians retreated, leaving Moscow undefended. Napoleon entered the deserted city, but the victory turned hollow because the departing Russians had set the wooden city on fire. Within a week, three-fourths of it had burned to the ground. Still Alexander refused to negotiate, and French morale plunged with worsening problems of supply. Weeks of constant marching in the dirt and heat had worn down the foot soldiers, who were dying of disease or deserting in large numbers (see Document, "An Ordinary Soldier on Campaign with Napoleon," page 633).

In October, Napoleon began his retreat; in November came the cold. A German soldier in the Grand Army described trying to cook fistfuls of raw bran with snow to make something like bread. For him, the retreat was "the indescribable horror of all possible plagues." Within a week the Grand Army lost 30,000 horses and had to abandon most of its artillery and food supplies. Russian forces harassed the retreating army, now more pathetic than grand. By December only 100,000 troops remained, one-sixth the original number, and the retreat had turned into a rout: the Russians had captured 200,000 soldiers, including 48 generals and 3,000 other officers.

Napoleon had made a classic military mistake that would be repeated by Adolf Hitler in World War II: fighting a war on two distant fronts simultaneously. The Spanish war tied down 250,000

DOCUMENT

An Ordinary Soldier on Campaign with Napoleon

Jakob Walter (1788–1864) recorded his experience as a soldier in the Napoleonic armies marching to Moscow in 1812. He wrote his account sometime after the events took place, though exactly when is not known. Walter was a German conscripted into military service from one of the many west German states controlled by Napoleon. The selection here describes the Napoleonic armies still on the offensive moving toward Moscow. But the seeds of future problems are already germinating.

On August 19, the entire army moved forward, and pursued the Russians with all speed. Four or five hours' farther up the river another battle started, but the enemy did not hold out long, and the march now led to Moshaisk [near Borodino], the so-called "Holy Valley." From Smolensk to Moshaisk the war displayed its horrible work of destruction: all the roads, fields, and woods lay as though sown with people, horses, wagons, burned villages and cities; everything looked like the complete ruin of all that lived. In particular, we saw ten dead Russians to one of our men, although every day our numbers fell off considerably. In order to pass through woods, swamps, and narrow trails, trees which formed barriers in the woods had to be removed, and wagon barricades of the enemy had to be cleared away. . . . The march up to there, as far as it was a march, is indescribable and inconceivable for people who have not seen anything of it. The very great heat, the dust which was like a thick fog, the closed line of march in columns, and the putrid water from holes filled with dead people and cattle brought everyone close to death; and eye pains, fatigue, thirst, and hunger tormented everybody. God! How often I remembered the bread and beer which I had enjoyed at home with such an indifferent pleasure! Now, however, I must struggle, half wild, with the dead and living. How gladly would I renounce for my whole life the warm food so common at home if I only did not lack good bread and beer now! I would not wish for more all my life. But these were empty, helpless thoughts. Yes, the thought of my brothers and sisters so far away added to my pain! Wherever I looked, I saw the soldiers with dead, half-desperate faces.

Source: Marc Raeff, ed., *Jakob Walter: The Diary of a Napoleonic Foot Soldier* (New York: Doubleday, 1991), 52–53.

French troops and forced Napoleon to bully Prussia and Austria into supplying soldiers of dubious loyalty for the Moscow campaign. They deserted at the first opportunity. The fighting in Spain and Portugal also exacerbated the already substantial logistical and communications problems involved in marching to Moscow.

The End of Napoleon's Empire. Napoleon's humiliation might have been temporary if the British and Russians had not successfully organized a coalition to complete the job. Napoleon still had resources at his command; by the spring of 1813, he had replenished his army with another 250,000 men. With British financial support, Russian, Austrian, Prussian, and Swedish armies met the French outside Leipzig in October 1813 and defeated Napoleon in the Battle of the Nations. One by one, Napoleon's German allies deserted him to join the German nationalist "war of liberation." The Confederation of the Rhine dissolved, and the Dutch revolted and restored the prince of Orange. Joseph Bonaparte fled Spain, and a combined Spanish-Portuguese army under British command invaded France. In only a few months, the allied powers crossed the Rhine and marched toward Paris. In March 1814, the French Senate deposed Napoleon, who abdicated when his remaining generals refused to fight. Napoleon went into exile on the island of Elba off the Italian coast. His wife, Marie-Louise, refused to accompany him. The allies restored to the throne Louis XVIII (r. 1814–1824), the brother of Louis XVI, beheaded during the Revolution. (Louis XVI's son was known as Louis XVII even though he died in prison in 1795 without ever ruling.)

Napoleon had one last chance to regain power because Louis XVIII lacked a solid base of support. The new king tried to steer a middle course through a charter that established a British-style monarchy with a two-house legislature and guaranteed civil rights. But he was caught between nobles returning from exile who demanded a complete restoration of their lands and powers, and the vast majority of ordinary people who had supported either the republic or Napoleon during the previous twenty-five years. Sensing an opportunity, Napoleon escaped from Elba in early 1815 and, landing in southern France, made swift and unimpeded progress to Paris. Although he had left in ignominy, now crowds cheered him and former soldiers volunteered to serve him. The period eventually known as the Hundred Days (the length of time between

Napoleon: For and Against

After his final exile, Napoleon presented himself as a martyr to the cause of liberty whose goal was to create a European "federation of free people." Few were convinced by this "gospel according to St. Helena" (Document 1). Followers such as Emmanuel de Las Cases burnished the Napoleonic legend, but detractors such as Benjamin Constant viewed him as a tyrant (Document 2). For all his defects, Napoleon fascinated even those who were too young to understand his rise and fall. The French romantic poet Victor Hugo celebrated both the glory and the tragedy of Napoleonic ambitions (Document 3).

1. Napoleon's Own View from Exile

As might be expected, Napoleon put the most positive possible construction on his plans for France. In exile he wrote letters and talked at length to Emmanuel de Las Cases (1766–1842), an aristocratic officer in the royal navy who rallied to Napoleon in 1802, served in the Council of State, and later accompanied him to St. Helena. Much of what we know about Napoleon's views comes from a book published by Las Cases in 1821.

March 3, 1817:

In spite of all the libels, I have no fear whatever about my fame. Posterity will do me justice. The truth will be known; and the good I have done will be compared with the faults I have committed. I am not uneasy as to the result. Had I succeeded, I would have died with the reputation of the greatest man that ever existed. As it is, although I have failed, I shall be considered as an extraordinary man: my elevation was unparalleled, because unaccompanied by crime. I have fought fifty pitched battles, almost all of which I have won. I have framed and carried into effect a code of laws that will bear my name to the most distant posterity. I raised myself from nothing to be the most powerful monarch in the world. Europe was at my feet. I have always been of the opinion that the sovereignty lay in the people. In fact, the imperial government was a kind of republic. Called to the head of it by the voice of the nation, my maxim was, *la carrière est*

ouverte aux talents ["careers open to talent"] without distinction of birth or fortune, and this system of equality is the reason that your oligarchy hates me so much.

Source: R. M. Johnston, *The Corsican: A Diary of Napoleon's Life in His Own Words* (Boston: Houghton Mifflin, 1921), 492.

2. Benjamin Constant, Spokesman for the Liberal Opposition to Napoleon

Benjamin Constant (1767–1830) came from an old French Calvinist family that had fled to Switzerland to escape persecution. Constant spent the early years of the French Revolution in a minor post at a minor German court. He moved to Paris in 1795 and became active in French politics during the Directory. Under Napoleon he went into exile, where he published a romantic novel, Adolphe (1806), and pamphlets like this one attacking Napoleon. He reconciled to Napoleon during the Hundred Days and then opposed the restored Bourbon monarchy. In this selection, written during his exile, he expresses his hostility to Napoleon as a usurper dependent on war to maintain himself in power.

Surely, Bonaparte is a thousand times more guilty than those barbarous conquerors who, ruling over barbarians, were by no means at odds with their age. Unlike them, he has chosen barbarism; he has preferred it. In the midst of enlightenment, he has sought to bring back the night. He has chosen to transform into greedy and bloodthirsty nomads a mild and polite people: his crime lies in this premeditated intention, in his obstinate effort to rob us of the heritage of all the enlightened generations who have preceded us on this earth. But why have we given him the right to conceive such a project?

When he first arrived here, alone, out of poverty and obscurity, and until he was twenty-four, his greedy gaze wandering over the country around him, why did we show him a country in which any religious idea was the object of irony? [Constant refers here to de-Christianization during the French Revolution.]

Napoleon's escape and his final defeat) had begun. Louis XVIII fled across the border, waiting for help from France's enemies.

Napoleon quickly moved his reconstituted army of 74,000 men into present-day Belgium. At first, it seemed that he might succeed in separately fighting the two armies arrayed against him—a Prussian army of some 60,000 men and a joint force of 68,000 Belgian, Dutch, German, and

British troops led by British general Sir Arthur Wellesley (1769–1852), duke of Wellington. The decisive battle took place on June 18, 1815, at Waterloo, less than ten miles from Brussels. Napoleon's forces attacked Wellington's men first with infantry and then with cavalry, but the French failed to dislodge their opponents. Late in the afternoon, the Prussians arrived and the rout was complete. Napoleon had no choice but to abdicate

When he listened to what was professed in our circles, why did serious thinkers tell him that man had no other motivation than his own interest? . . .

Because immediate usurpation was easy, he believed it could be durable, and once he became a usurper, he did all that usurpation condemns a usurper to do in our century.

It was necessary to stifle inside the country all intellectual life: he banished discussion and proscribed the freedom of the press.

The nation might have been stunned by that silence: he provided, extorted or paid for acclamation which sounded like the national voice. . . . War flung onto distant shores that part of the French nation that still had some real energy. It prompted the police harassment of the timid, whom it could not force abroad. It struck terror into men's hearts, and left there a certain hope that chance would take responsibility for their deliverance: a hope agreeable to fear and convenient to inertia. How many times have I heard men who were pressed to resist tyranny postponing this, during wartime till the coming of peace, and in peacetime until war commences!

I am right therefore in claiming that a usurper's sole resource is uninterrupted war. Some object: what if Bonaparte had been pacific? Had he been pacific, he would never have lasted for twelve years. Peace would have re-established communication among the different countries of Europe. These communications would have restored to thought its means of expression. Works published abroad would have been smuggled into the country. The French would have seen that they did not enjoy the approval of the majority of Europe.

Source: Benjamin Constant, "Further Reflections on Usurpation," in *Political Writings*, trans. Biancamaria Fontana (Cambridge: Cambridge University Press, 1988), 161–63.

These Isles, where Ocean's shattered spray
Upon the ruthless rocks is cast,
Seem like two treacherous ships of prey,
Made by eternal anchors fast.
The hand that settled bleak and black
Those shores on their unpeopled rack,
And clad in fear and mystery,
Perchance thus made them tempest-torn,
That Bonaparte might there be born,
And that Napoleon there might die. . . .
He his imperial nest hath built so far and high,
He seems to us to dwell within that tranquil sky,
Where you shall never see the angry tempest break.
'Tis but beneath his feet the growling storms are sped,
And thunders to assault his head
Must to their highest source go back.
The bolt flew upwards: from his eyrie [nest] riven,
Blazing he falls beneath the stroke of heaven;
Then kings their tyrant foe reward—
They chain him, living, on that lonely shore;
And earth captive giant handed o'er
To ocean's more resistless guard. . . .
Shame, hate, misfortune, vengeance, curses sore,
On him let heaven and earth together pour:
Now, see we dashed the vast Colossus low.
May he forever rue, alive and dead,
All tears he caused mankind to shed,
And all the blood he caused to flow.

Source: Henry Carrington, *Translations from the Poems of Victor Hugo* (London: Walter Scott, 1885), 34–41.

3. Victor Hugo, "The Two Islands" (1825)

Victor Hugo (1802–1885) was France's greatest romantic poet and novelist, author of The Hunchback of Notre Dame *and* Les Misérables. *His father was a Napoleonic general, but his mother was an equally ardent royalist. In this early poem, Hugo compares Napoleon to one of Napoleon's favorite icons, the eagle, symbol of empire. The two islands of the title are Corsica, Napoleon's birthplace, and St. Helena, his place of final exile and death.*

QUESTIONS TO CONSIDER

1. Which of these views of Napoleon has the most lasting value as opposed to immediate dramatic effect?
2. According to these selections, what was Napoleon's greatest accomplishment? His greatest failure?
3. Victor Hugo called Napoleon "the vast Colossus." Why did he pick this larger-than-life metaphor even when writing lines critical of Napoleon's legacy of tears and bloodshed?

again. This time the victorious allies banished him permanently to the remote island of St. Helena, far off the coast of West Africa, where he died in 1821 at the age of fifty-two.

The cost of Napoleon's rule was high: 750,000 French soldiers and 400,000 others from annexed and satellite states died between 1800 and 1815. Yet his impact on world history was undeniable. (See "Contrasting Views," above.) Napoleon's plans

for a united Europe, his insistence on spreading the legal reforms of the French Revolution, his social welfare programs, and even his inadvertent awakening of national sentiment set the agenda for European history in the modern era.

REVIEW: Why was Napoleon able to gain control over so much of Europe's territory?

The "Restoration" of Europe

Even while Napoleon was making his last desperate bid for power, his enemies were meeting in the Congress of Vienna (1814–1815) to decide the fate of postrevolutionary, post-Napoleonic Europe. Although interrupted by the Hundred Days, the **Congress of Vienna** settled the boundaries of European states, determined who would rule each nation, and established a new framework for international relations based on periodic meetings, or congresses, between the major powers. The doctrine of conservatism bolstered this post-Napoleonic order and in some places went hand in hand with a revival of religion.

The Congress of Vienna, 1814–1815

The Vienna settlement established a new equilibrium that relied on cooperation among the major powers while guaranteeing the status of smaller states. The revolutionary and Napoleonic wars had produced a host of potentially divisive issues. In addition to determining the boundaries of France,

the congress had to decide the fate of Napoleon's duchy of Warsaw, the German province of Saxony, the Netherlands, the states once part of the Confederation of the Rhine, and various Italian territories. All had either changed hands or been created during the wars. These issues were resolved by face-to-face negotiations among representatives of the five major powers: Austria, Russia, Prussia, Britain, and France. With its aim to establish a long-lasting, negotiated peace endorsed by all parties, both winners and losers, the Congress of Vienna provided a model for the twentieth-century League of Nations and United Nations. The congress system, or "concert of Europe," helped prevent another major war until the 1850s, and no conflict comparable to the Napoleonic wars would occur again until 1914.

Austria's chief negotiator, Prince **Klemens von Metternich** (1773–1859), took the lead in devising the settlement and shaping the post-Napoleonic order. A well-educated nobleman who spoke five languages, Metternich served as a minister in the Austrian cabinet from 1809 to 1848. Although his penchant for womanizing made him a security risk in the eyes of the British Foreign Office (he even had an affair with Napoleon's younger

Congress of Vienna: Face-to-face negotiations (1814–1815) between the great powers to settle the boundaries of European states and determine who would rule each nation after the defeat of Napoleon.

Klemens von Metternich (KLAY mehnts fawn MEH tur nihk): An Austrian prince (1773–1859) who took the lead in devising the settlement arranged by the Congress of Vienna.

Congress of Vienna

An unknown French engraver caricatured the efforts of the diplomats at the Congress of Vienna, complaining that they used the occasion to divide the spoils of European territory. What elements in this engraving make it a caricature? *(Copyright Wien Museum.)*

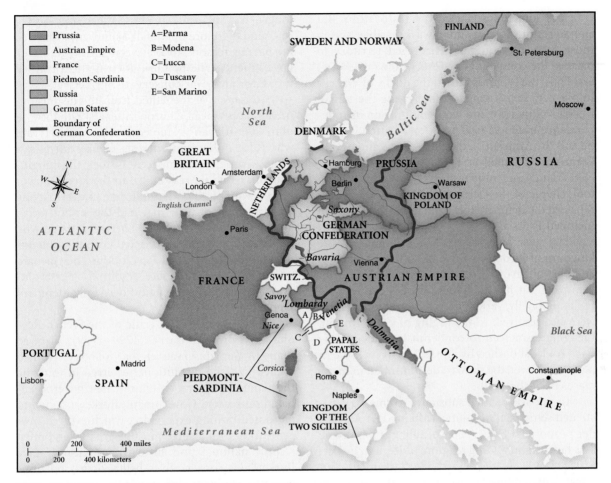

MAP 20.2 Europe after the Congress of Vienna, 1815

The Congress of Vienna forced France to return to its 1789 borders. The Austrian Netherlands and the Dutch Republic were united in a new kingdom of the Netherlands, the German states were joined in a German Confederation that built on Napoleon's Confederation of the Rhine, and Napoleon's duchy of Warsaw became the kingdom of Poland with the tsar of Russia as king. To compensate for its losses in Poland, Prussia gained territory in Saxony and on the left bank of the Rhine. Austria reclaimed the Italian provinces of Lombardy and Venetia and the Dalmatian coast.

sister), he worked with the British prime minister Robert Castlereagh (1769–1822) to ensure a moderate agreement that would check French aggression yet maintain France's great-power status. Metternich and Castlereagh believed that French aggression must be contained because it had threatened the European peace since the days of Louis XIV but at the same time that France must remain a major player to prevent any one European power from dominating the others. In this way, France could help Austria and Britain counter the ambitions of Prussia and Russia. Castlereagh hoped to make Britain the arbiter of European affairs, but he knew this could be accomplished only through adroit diplomacy because the British constitutional monarchy had little in common with most of its more absolutist continental counterparts.

The task of ensuring France's status at the congress fell to Prince Charles Maurice de Talleyrand (1754–1838), an aristocrat and former bishop who had embraced the French Revolution, served as Napoleon's foreign minister, and ended as foreign minister to Louis XVIII after helping to arrange the emperor's overthrow. Informed of Talleyrand's betrayal, Napoleon called him "excrement in silk stockings." When the French army failed to oppose Napoleon's return to power in the Hundred Days, the allies took away all territory conquered since 1790 and required France to pay an indemnity and support an army of occupation until it had paid.

The goal of the Congress of Vienna was to achieve postwar stability by establishing secure states with guaranteed borders (Map 20.2). Because the congress aimed to "restore" as many regimes as possible to their former rulers, this epoch is sometimes labeled the **restoration**. But simple restoration was not always feasible, and in those cases the congress rearranged territory to balance the competing interests of the great powers. Thus, the congress turned the duchy of Warsaw into a new Polish kingdom but made the tsar of Russia its king. (Poland would not regain its independence until 1918.) The former Dutch Republic and the Austrian Netherlands, both annexed to France, now united as the new kingdom of the Netherlands under the restored stadholder. Austria took charge of the German Confederation, which replaced the defunct Holy Roman Empire and also included Prussia.

The lesser powers were not forgotten. The kingdom of Piedmont-Sardinia took Genoa, Nice, and part of Savoy. Sweden obtained Norway from Denmark but had to accept Russia's conquest of Finland. Finally, various international trade issues were also resolved. At the urging of Great Britain, the congress agreed to condemn in principle the slave trade, abolished by Great Britain in 1807. In reality, however, the slave trade continued in many places until the 1840s.

To impart spiritual substance to this very calculated settlement of political affairs, Tsar Alexander proposed a Holy Alliance calling upon divine assistance in upholding religion, peace, and justice. Prussia and Austria signed the agreement, but Great Britain refused to accede to what Castlereagh called "a piece of sublime mysticism and nonsense." Despite the reassertion of traditional religious principle, the congress had in fact given birth to a new diplomatic order: in the future, the legitimacy of states depended on the treaty system, not on divine right.

The Emergence of Conservatism

The French Revolution and Napoleonic domination of Europe had shown contemporaries that government could be changed overnight, that the old hierarchies could be overthrown in the name of reason, and that even Christianity could be written off or at least profoundly altered with the stroke of a pen. The potential for rapid change raised many questions about the proper sources of authority. Kings and churches could be restored and former revolutionaries locked up or silenced, but the old order no longer commanded automatic obedience. The old order was now merely *old*, no

longer "natural" and "timeless." It had been ousted once and therefore might fall again. People insisted on having reasons to believe in their "restored" governments. The political doctrine that justified the restoration was **conservatism**.

Conservatives benefited from the disillusionment that permeated Europe after 1815. In the eyes of most Europeans, Napoleon had become a tyrant who ruled in his own interests. Conservatives saw a logical progression in recent history: the Enlightenment, based on reason, led to the French Revolution, with its bloody guillotine and horrifying Terror, which in turn spawned the authoritarian and militaristic Napoleon. Therefore, those who espoused conservatism rejected both the Enlightenment and the French Revolution. They favored monarchies over republics, tradition over revolution, and established religion over Enlightenment skepticism.

The original British critic of the French Revolution, Edmund Burke (1729–1799), inspired many of the conservatives that followed. He had argued that the revolutionaries erred in thinking they could construct an entirely new government based on reason. Government, Burke said, had to be rooted in long experience, which evolved over generations. All change must be gradual and must respect national and historical traditions. Like Burke, later conservatives believed that religious and other major traditions were an essential foundation for any society. Most of them took their resistance to change even further, however, and tried to restore the pre-1789 social order.

Conservatives blamed the French Revolution's attack on religion on the skepticism and anticlericalism of such Enlightenment thinkers as Voltaire, and they defended both hereditary monarchy and the authority of the church, whether Catholic or Protestant. Louis de Bonald, an official under the restored French monarchy, insisted that "the revolution began with the declaration of the rights of man and will only finish when the rights of God are declared." The declaration of rights, he asserted, represented the evil influence of Enlightenment philosophy and with it atheism, Protestantism, and freemasonry, which he lumped together. An enduring social order could only be constructed, in this view, on the foundations provided by the church, the state, and the patriarchal family. Faith, sentiment, history, and tradition

---

restoration: The epoch after the fall of Napoleon, in which the Congress of Vienna aimed to "restore" as many regimes as possible to their former rulers.

conservatism: A political doctrine that emerged after 1789 and rejected much of the Enlightenment and the French Revolution, preferring monarchies over republics, tradition over revolution, and established religion over Enlightenment skepticism.

must fill the vacuum left by the failures of reason and excessive belief in individual rights. Across Europe, these views were taken up and elaborated by government advisers, professors, and writers. Not surprisingly, they had their strongest appeal in ruling circles and guided the politics of men such as Metternich in Austria, Alexander I in Russia, and the restored Bourbons in France.

The restored French monarchy provided a major test for conservatism because the returning Bourbons had to confront the legacy of twenty-five years of upheaval. Louis XVIII tried to ensure a measure of continuity by maintaining Napoleon's Civil Code. He also guaranteed the rights of ownership to church lands sold during the revolutionary period and created a parliament composed of a Chamber of Peers nominated by the king and a Chamber of Deputies elected by very restricted suffrage (fewer than 100,000 voters in a population of 30 million). In making these concessions, the king tried to follow a moderate course of compromise, but the Ultras (ultraroyalists) pushed for complete repudiation of the revolutionary past. When Louis returned to power after Napoleon's final defeat, armed royalist bands attacked and murdered hundreds of Bonapartists and former revolutionaries. In 1816, the Ultras insisted on abolishing divorce and set up special courts to punish opponents of the regime. When an assassin killed Louis XVIII's nephew in 1820, the Ultras demanded even more extreme measures.

The Revival of Religion

The experience of revolutionary upheaval and nearly constant warfare prompted many to renew their religious faith once peace returned. In France, the Catholic church sent missionaries to hold open-air "ceremonies of reparation" to express repentance for the outrages of revolution. In Rome, the papacy reestablished the Jesuit order, which had been disbanded during the Enlightenment. In the Italian states and Spain, governments used religious societies of laypeople to combat the influence of reformers and nationalists such as the Italian carbonari.

Revivalist movements, especially in Protestant countries, could on occasion challenge the status quo rather than supporting it. In parts of Protestant Germany and Britain, religious revival had begun in the eighteenth century with the rise of Pietism and Methodism, movements that stressed individual religious experience rather than reason as the true path to moral and social reform.

The English Methodists followed John Wesley (1703–1791), who had preached an emotional, morally austere, and very personal "method" of gaining salvation. The Methodists, or Wesleyans, gradually separated from the Church of England and in the early decades of the nineteenth century attracted thousands of members in huge revival meetings that lasted for days.

Shopkeepers, artisans, agricultural laborers, miners, and workers in cottage industry, both male and female, flocked to the new denomination, even though at first Methodism seemed to emphasize conservative political views: Methodist statutes of 1792 had insisted that "none of us shall either in writing or in conversation speak lightly or irrever-

A Protestant Missionary in India
This colored engraving shows the English Baptist missionary William Carey (1761–1834) baptizing his first Hindu convert. Carey went to India in 1793 and spent forty years there as a teacher and a preacher. He led efforts to get the British governor general to outlaw the Hindu rite of sati, the burning of widows with their husbands. He became professor of Indian languages at Fort William College, established in Calcutta for training British officials and supervised the translation of the Bible into more than forty local languages. *(The Granger Collection, New York.)*

ently of the government." In their hostility to rigid doctrine and elaborate ritual and their encouragement of popular preaching, however, the Methodists fostered a sense of democratic community and even a rudimentary sexual equality. From the beginning, women preachers traveled on horseback to preach in barns, town halls, and textile dye houses. The Methodist Sunday schools that taught thousands of poor children to read and write eventually helped create greater demands for working-class political participation.

The religious revival was not limited to Europe. In the United States, the second Great Awakening began around 1790 with huge camp meetings that brought together thousands of worshippers and scores of evangelical preachers, many of them Methodist. (The original Great Awakening took place in the 1730s and 1740s, sparked by the preaching of George Whitefield, a young English evangelist and follower of John Wesley.) Men and women danced to exhaustion, fell into trances, and spoke in tongues. During this period, Protestant sects began systematic missionary activity in other parts of the world, with British and American missionary societies taking the lead in the 1790s and early 1800s. In the British colony of India, for example, Protestant missionaries argued for the reform of Hindu customs. *Sati*—the burning of widows on the funeral pyres of their husbands—was abolished by the British administration of India in 1829. Missionary activity by Protestants and Catholics would become one of the arms of European imperialism and cultural influence in the nineteenth century.

> **REVIEW:** To what extent was the old order restored by the Congress of Vienna?

Challenges to the Conservative Order

Conservatives hoped to clamp a lid on European affairs, but the lid kept threatening to fly off. Drawing on the turmoil in society and politics was romanticism, the burgeoning international movement in the arts and literature that dominated artistic expression in the first half of the nineteenth century. Although romantics shared with conservatives a distrust of the Enlightenment's emphasis on reason, romanticism did not translate into a unified political position. It did, however, heighten the general discontent with the conservative

Vienna settlement. Isolated revolts threatened the hold of some conservative governments in the 1820s, but most of these rebellions were quickly bottled up. Then in 1830, successive uprisings briefly overwhelmed the established order. Across Europe, angry protesters sought constitutional guarantees of individual liberties and national unity and autonomy. The revolutionary legacy came back to life again.

Romanticism

An artistic movement that encompassed poetry, music, painting, history, and literature, romanticism glorified nature, emotion, genius, and imagination. (See Chapter 18 for the origins of romanticism.) It proclaimed these as antidotes to the Enlightenment and to classicism in the arts, challenging the reliance on reason, symmetry, and cool geometric spaces. Classicism idealized models from Roman history; romanticism turned to folklore and medieval legends. Classicism celebrated orderly, crisp lines; romantics sought out all that was wild, fevered, and disorderly. Chief among the arts of romanticism were poetry, music, and painting, which captured the deep-seated emotion characteristic of romantic expression. Romantics might take any political position, but they exerted the most political influence when they expressed nationalist feelings.

Romantic Poetry. Romantic poetry celebrated overwhelming emotion and creative imagination. George Gordon, Lord Byron (1788–1824), explained his aims in writing poetry:

> For what is Poesy but to create
> From overfeeling, Good and Ill, and aim
> At an external life beyond our fate,
> And be the new Prometheus of new man.

Prometheus was the mythological figure who brought fire from the Greek gods to human beings. Byron did not seek the new Prometheus among political leaders or manufacturers of new wealth; he sought him within his own "overfeeling," his own intense emotions. Byron became a romantic hero himself when he rushed off to act on his emotions by fighting and dying in the Greek war for independence from the Turks. An English aristocrat, Byron nonetheless claimed, "I have simplified my politics into a detestation of all existing governments."

Romantic poetry elevated the wonders of nature almost to the supernatural. In a poem that became one of the most beloved exemplars of

Lord Byron

George Gordon, Lord Byron (1788–1824), lived a short, tumultuous life; wrote enduring romantic poetry; loved both women and young men; and died struggling for Greek independence. During the Napoleonic wars, he took a two-year trip through southern Europe. He visited Greece and Albania and collected souvenir costumes, such as the one he is wearing in this portrait by Thomas Philips (1813). As a result of this trip, he became passionately involved in things Greek; when the Greek rebellion broke out, he promptly joined the British Committee, which gathered aid for the Greeks. He died of a fever in Greece, where he had gone to distribute funds. How would viewers have reacted to the costume Byron is wearing? *(National Portrait Gallery, London.)*

romanticism, "Tintern Abbey" (1798), the English poet William Wordsworth (1770–1850) compared himself to a deer even while making nature seem filled with human emotions (see Document, "Wordsworth's Poetry," page 642). Like many poets of his time, Wordsworth greeted the French Revolution with joy; in his poem "French Revolution" (1809), he remembered his early enthusiasm: "Bliss was it in that dawn to be alive." But gradually he became disenchanted with the revolutionary experiment and celebrated British nationalism instead; in 1816, he published a poem to commemorate the "intrepid sons of Albion [England]" who died at the battle of Waterloo.

Their emphasis on authentic self-expression at times drew romantics to exotic, mystical, or even reckless experiences. Such transports drove one leading German poet to the madhouse and another to suicide. Some romantics depicted the artist as possessed by demons and obsessed with hallucinations. This more nightmarish side was captured, and perhaps criticized, by Mary Shelley in *Frankenstein*. The aged German poet Johann Wolfgang von Goethe (1749–1832) likewise denounced the extremes of romanticism, calling it "everything that is sick." In his epic poem *Faust* (1832), he seemed to warn of the same dangers Shelley portrayed in her novel. In Goethe's retelling of a sixteenth-century legend, Faust offers his soul to the devil in return for a chance to taste all human experience—from passionate love

to the heights of power—in his effort to reshape nature for humanity's benefit. Faust's striving, like Frankenstein's, leaves a wake of suffering and destruction.

Romantic Painting and Music. Romanticism in painting similarly idealized nature and the individual of deep feelings. The German romantic painter Caspar David Friedrich (1774–1840) depicted scenes—often far away in the mountains—that captured the romantic fascination with the sublime power of nature (see page 643). His melancholy individual figures looked lost in the vastness of an overpowering nature. Friedrich hated the modern world. His landscapes often had religious meaning as well, as in his controversial painting *The Cross in the Mountains* (1808), which showed a Christian cross standing alone in a mountain scene. It symbolized the steadfastness of faith but seemed to separate religion from the churches and attach it to mystical experience.

Many other artists developed similar themes. The English painter Joseph M. W. Turner (1775–1851) depicted his vision of nature in mysterious, misty seascapes, anticipating later artists by blurring the outlines of objects. The French painter Eugène Delacroix (1798–1863) chose contemporary as well as medieval scenes of great turbulence to emphasize light and color and break away from what he saw as "the servile copies repeated *ad nauseum* in academies of art." Critics

DOCUMENT

Wordsworth's Poetry

The son of a lawyer, William Wordsworth (1770–1850) studied at Cambridge University and then traveled to France during the early years of the French Revolution. He returned to England and began publishing the poetry that for many scholars marks the beginning of romanticism with its emphasis on the sublime beauties of nature. This excerpt from "Lines Composed a Few Miles above Tintern Abbey" (1798) shows the influence of his extensive walking tours through the English countryside. But the passage also captures the melancholy and nostalgia that characterized much of romantic poetry.

And now, with gleams of half-extinguished
   thought,
With many recognitions dim and faint,
And somewhat of a sad perplexity,
The picture of the mind revives again:
While here I stand, not only with the sense
Of present pleasure, but with pleasing
   thoughts
That in this moment there is life and food
For future years. And so I dare to hope,
Though changed, no doubt, from what I
   was when first
I came among these hills; when like a roe
I bounded o'er the mountains, by the
   sides
Of the deep rivers, and the lonely streams,
Wherever nature led: more like a man
Flying from something that he dreads,
   than one
Who sought the thing he loved. For nature
   then
(The coarser pleasures of my boyish days,
And their glad animal movements all gone
   by)
To me was all in all. — I cannot paint
What then I was. The sounding cataract
Haunted me like a passion: the tall rock,
The mountain, and the deep and gloomy
   wood,
Their colours and their forms, were then
   to me
An appetite; a feeling and a love,
That had no need of a remoter charm,
By thought supplied, nor any interest
Unborrowed from the eye. — That time is
   past.

Source: Paul Davis, ed., *Bedford Anthology of World Literature.* Book 5: *The Nineteenth Century, 1800–1900* (Boston: Bedford/St. Martin's, 2003), 246–47.

denounced his techniques as "painting with a drunken broom." To broaden his experience of light and color, Delacroix traveled in the 1830s to North Africa and painted many exotic scenes in Morocco and Algeria.

The towering presence of the German composer **Ludwig van Beethoven** (1770–1827) in early-nineteenth-century music helped establish the direction for musical romanticism. His music, according to one leading German romantic, "sets in motion the lever of fear, of awe, of horror, of suffering, and awakens just that infinite longing which is the essence of Romanticism." Beethoven transformed the symphony into a connected work with recurring and evolving musical themes. Romantic symphonies conveyed the impression of growth, a metaphor for the organic process with an emphasis on the natural that was dear to the romantics. For example, Beethoven's Sixth Symphony, the *Pastoral* (1808), used a variety of instruments to represent sounds heard in the country. Beethoven's work — ranging from reli-

gious works to symphonies, sonatas, and concertos — showed remarkable diversity. Some of his work was explicitly political; his Ninth Symphony (1824) employed a chorus to sing the German poet Friedrich Schiller's verses in praise of universal human solidarity. Beethoven had been an admirer of Napoleon and even dedicated his Third Symphony, the *Eroica* (1804), to him, but when he learned of Napoleon's decision to name himself emperor, he tore up the dedication in disgust.

Romantic Nationalism. If romantics had any common political thread, it was the support of nationalist aspirations, especially through the search for the historical origins of national identity. In the German states, the Austrian Empire, Russia and other Slavic lands, and Scandinavia, romantic poets and writers collected old legends and folktales that expressed a shared cultural and linguistic heritage stretching back to the Middle Ages. These collections showed that Germany, for example, had always existed even if it did not currently take the form of a single unified state. Romantic nationalism permeated *The Betrothed* (1825–1827), a novel by Alessandro Manzoni (1785–1873) that constituted a kind of bible for Italian nationalists. Manzoni, the grandson of the

---

Ludwig van Beethoven: The German composer (1770–1827) who helped set the direction of musical romanticism; his music used recurring and evolving themes to convey the impression of natural growth.

William Blake, *The Circle of the Lustful* **(1824)**
An English romantic poet, painter, engraver, and printmaker, Blake always sought his own way. Self-taught, he began writing poetry at age twelve and apprenticed himself to an engraver at fourteen. His works incorporate many otherworldly attributes; they are quite literally visionary—imagining other worlds. In this engraving of hell, the twisting, turning figures are caught up in a kind of spiritual ether. Can you find elements in this engraving that reflect a criticism of Enlightenment ideals? *(Birmingham Museums and Art Gallery.)*

Italian Enlightenment hero Cesare Beccaria, set his novel in the seventeenth century, when Spain controlled Italy's destiny, but his readers understood that he intended to attack the Austrians who controlled northern Italy in his own day. By writing this book (the first historical novel in Italian literature) in the Tuscan dialect, Manzoni achieved two aims: he helped create a standard national language and popularized Italian history for a people long divided by different dialects and competing rulers.

Manzoni had been inspired to write his novel by the most influential of all historical novelists, **Sir Walter Scott** (1771–1832). While working as a lawyer and then judge in Scotland, Scott first collected and published traditional Scottish ballads that he heard as a child. After achieving immediate success with his own poetry, especially *The Lady of the Lake* (1810), he switched to historical novels. His novels are almost all renditions of historical events, from *Rob Roy* (1817), with its account of Scottish resistance to the English in the early eighteenth century, to *Ivanhoe* (1819), with its tales of medieval England. One contemporary critic claimed that *Ivanhoe* was more historically true than any scholarly work: "There is more history in the novels of Walter Scott than in half of the historians."

Sir Walter Scott: A prolific author (1771–1832) of popular historical novels; he also collected and published traditional Scottish ballads and wrote poetry.

Caspar David Friedrich, *Wanderer above the Sea of Fog* **(1818)**
Friedrich, a German romantic painter, captured many of the themes most dear to romanticism: melancholy, isolation, and individual communion with nature. He painted trees reaching for the sky and mountains stretching into the distance. Nature to him seemed awesome, powerful, and overshadowing of human perspectives. The French sculptor David d'Angers said of Friedrich, "Here is a man who has discovered the tragedy of landscape." *(© Hamburg Kunsthalle, Hamburg, Germany / The Bridgeman Art Library.)*

Political Revolts in the 1820s

The restoration of regimes after Napoleon's fall disappointed those who dreamed of constitutional freedoms and national independence. Membership grew in secret societies such as the carbonari, attracting tens of thousands of members, including physicians, lawyers, officers, and students. Revolts broke out in the 1820s in Spain, Italy, Russia, and Greece (Map 20.3), as well as across the Atlantic in the Spanish and Portuguese colonies of Latin America. Most revolts failed, but those in Greece and Latin America succeeded, largely because they did not threaten the conservative order in Europe.

Uprisings in Spain and Italy. When Ferdinand VII regained the Spanish crown in 1814, he quickly restored the prerevolutionary nobility, church, and monarchy. He had foreign books and newspapers confiscated at the frontier and allowed the publication of only two newspapers. Not surprisingly, such repressive policies disturbed the middle class, especially the army officers who had encountered French ideas. Many responded by joining secret societies. In 1820, disgruntled soldiers demanded

that Ferdinand proclaim his adherence to the constitution of 1812, which he had abolished in 1814. When the revolt spread, Ferdinand convened the *cortes* (parliament), which could agree on virtually nothing. Ferdinand bided his time, and in 1823 a French army invaded and restored him to absolute power. The French acted with the consent of the other great powers. The restored Spanish government tortured and executed hundreds of rebels; thousands were imprisoned or forced into exile.

Hearing of the Spanish uprising, rebellious soldiers in the kingdom of Naples joined forces with the carbonari and demanded a constitution. When a new parliament met, it too broke down over internal disagreements. The promise of reform sparked rebellion in the northern Italian kingdom of Piedmont-Sardinia, where rebels urged Charles Albert, the young heir to the Piedmont throne, to fight the Austrians for Italian unification. He vacillated; but in 1821, after the rulers of Austria, Prussia, and Russia met and agreed on intervention, the Austrians defeated the rebels in Naples and Piedmont. Liberals were arrested in many Italian states, and the pope condemned the secret societies as "devouring wolves." Despite the opposition of Great Britain, which condemned the indiscriminate suppression of revolutionary

MAP 20.3 Revolutionary Movements of the 1820s

The revolts of the 1820s took place on the periphery of Europe, in Spain, Italy, Greece, Russia, and in the Spanish and Portuguese colonies of Latin America. Rebels in Spain and Russia wanted constitutional reforms. Although the Italian revolts failed, as did the uprisings in Spain and Russia, the Greek and Latin American independence movements eventually succeeded.

movements, Metternich convinced the other powers to agree to his muffling of the Italian opposition to Austrian rule.

Metternich never let discontent closer to home turn into revolt. The only sign of resistance within the new German Confederation came from university students, who formed nationalist student societies, or *Burschenschaften*. In 1817, they held a mass rally at which they burned books they did not like, including Napoleon's Civil Code. Their leader was Friedrich Ludwig Jahn, who hoped to created a nationally unified Germany through education. He advocated gymnastics (he invented the parallel bars, the balance beam, gymnastics rings, the vaulting horse, and the horizontal bar) and study of all things German in order to create a stronger German "breed." Jahn favored the formation of a huge, racially pure German nation encompassing Switzerland, the Low Countries, Denmark, Prussia, and Austria. He also spouted such xenophobic (antiforeign) slogans as "If you let your daughter learn French, you might just as well train her to become a whore." Metternich did not mind the anti-French slant, but he was convinced—incorrectly—that the Burschenschaften in the German states and the carbonari in Italy were linked in an international conspiracy. In 1819, when a student assassinated the playwright August Kotzebue because he had ridiculed the student movement, Metternich convinced the leaders of the biggest German states to pass the Karlsbad Decrees dissolving the student societies and more strictly censoring the press.

The Decembrist Revolt in Russia. Aspirations for constitutional government surfaced in Russia when Alexander I died suddenly in 1825. On a day in December when the troops assembled in St. Petersburg to take an oath of loyalty to Alexander's brother Nicholas as the new tsar, rebel officers insisted that the crown belonged to another brother, Constantine, whom they hoped would be more favorable to constitutional reform. Constantine, though next in the line of succession after Alexander, had refused the crown. The soldiers nonetheless raised the cry "Long live Constantine, long live the Constitution!" (Some troops apparently thought that "the Constitution" was Constantine's wife.) Soldiers loyal to Nicholas easily suppressed the Decembrists (so called after the month of their uprising), who were so outnumbered that they had no realistic chance to succeed. The subsequent trial, however, made the rebels into legendary heroes. Of their imprisonment at hard labor, the Russian poet Alexander Pushkin

(1799–1837) wrote:

> The heavy-hanging chains will fall,
> The walls will crumble at a word,
> And Freedom greet you in the light,
> And brothers give you back the sword.

Pushkin would not live to see this freedom. For the next thirty years, Nicholas I (r. 1825–1855) used a new political police, the Third Section, to spy on potential opponents and stamp out rebelliousness.

Greek Independence from the Turks. The Ottoman Turks faced growing nationalist challenges in the Balkans, but the European powers feared that supporting such opposition would encourage a rebellious spirit at home. The Serbs revolted against Turkish rule and won virtual independence by 1817. A Greek general in the Russian army, Prince Alexander Ypsilanti, tried to lead a revolt against the Turks in 1820 but failed when the tsar, urged on by Metternich, disavowed him. Metternich feared rebellion even by Christians against their Turkish rulers. A second revolt, this time by Greek peasants, sparked a wave of atrocities in 1821 and 1822. The Greeks killed every Turk who did not escape; in retaliation, the Turks hanged the Greek patriarch of Constantinople, and in the areas they still controlled

Nationalistic Movements in the Balkans, 1815–1830

they pillaged churches, massacred thousands of men, and sold the women into slavery.

Western opinion turned against the Turks; Greece, after all, was the birthplace of Western civilization. While the great powers negotiated, Greeks and pro-Greece committees around the world sent food and military supplies; like the English poet Byron, a few enthusiastic European and American volunteers joined the Greeks. The Greeks held on until the great powers were willing to intervene. In 1827, a combined force of British, French, and Russian ships destroyed the Turkish fleet at Navarino Bay; and in 1828, Russia declared war on Turkey and advanced close to Constantinople. The Treaty of Adrianople of 1829 gave Russia a protectorate over the Danubian principalities in the Balkans and provided for a conference among representatives of Britain, Russia, and France, all of whom had broken with Austria in support of

Greek Independence
From 1836 to 1839, the Greek painter Panagiotis Zographos worked with his two sons on a series of scenes from the Greek struggle for independence from the Turks. Response was so favorable that one Greek general ordered lithographic reproductions for popular distribution. Nationalistic feeling could be thus encouraged even among those who were not directly touched by the struggle. Here Turkish sultan Mehmet the Conqueror, exulting over the fall of Constantinople in 1453, views a row of Greeks under the yoke, a sign of submission. *(The Visual Connection.)*

the Greeks. In 1830, Greece was declared an independent kingdom under the guarantee of the three powers; in 1833, the son of King Ludwig of Bavaria became Otto I of Greece. Nationalism, with the support of European public opinion, had made its first breach in Metternich's system.

Wars of Independence in Latin America.   Across the Atlantic, national revolts also succeeded after a series of bloody wars of independence. Taking advantage of the upheavals in Spain and Portugal that began under Napoleon, restive colonists from Mexico to Argentina rebelled. One leader who stood out was **Simon Bolívar** (1783–1830), the son of a slave owner educated in Europe on the works of Voltaire and Rousseau. Although Bolívar fancied himself a Latin American Napoleon, he had to acquiesce to the formation of a series of independent republics between 1821 and 1823, even

in Bolivia, which is named after him. At the same time, Brazil (then still a monarchy) separated from Portugal (Map 20.4). The United States recognized the new states, and in 1823 President James Monroe announced his Monroe Doctrine, closing the Americas to European intervention—a prohibition that depended on British naval power and British willingness to declare neutrality. Great Britain dominated the Latin American economies, which had suffered great losses during the wars for independence.

Revolution and Reform, 1830–1832

In 1830, a new wave of liberal and nationalist revolts broke against the bulwark of conservatism. The revolts of the 1820s had served as warning shots but had been largely confined to the peripheries of Europe. Now revolution once again threatened the established order in western Europe.

The French Revolution of 1830.   Louis XVIII's younger brother and successor, Charles X

Simon Bolívar (1783–1830): The European-educated son of a slave owner who became one of the leaders of the Latin American independence movement in the 1820s. Bolivia is named after him.

Simon Bolívar
Known as "the Liberator," Simon Bolívar (1783–1830) is shown riding a white horse in this lithograph near the end of his life. Bolívar led the armies that gained independence from Spain in Venezuela, Colombia, Ecuador, Peru, and Bolivia. He had dreamed of creating a United States of Latin America but died of tuberculosis as factional fighting kept the various states separate from each other. (akg-images.)

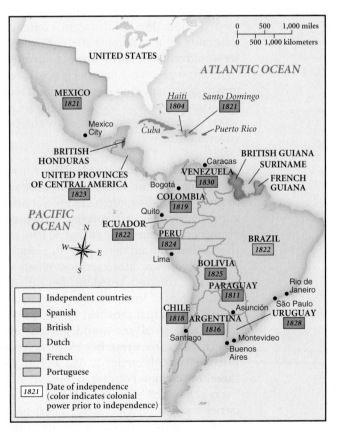

MAP 20.4 Latin American Independence, 1804–1830
Napoleon's occupation of Spain and Portugal seriously weakened those countries' hold on their Latin American colonies. Despite the restoration of the Spanish and Portuguese rulers in 1814, most of their colonies successfully broke away in a wave of rebellions between 1811 and 1830.

(r. 1824–1830), brought about his own downfall by steering the monarchy in an increasingly repressive direction. In 1825, a Law of Indemnity compensated nobles who had emigrated during the French Revolution for the loss of their estates, and a Law of Sacrilege in the same year imposed the death penalty for such offenses as stealing religious objects from churches. Charles enraged liberals when he dissolved the legislature, removed many wealthy and powerful voters from the rolls, and imposed strict censorship. Spontaneous demonstrations in Paris led to fighting on July 26, 1830. After three days of street battles in which 500 citizens and 150 soldiers died, a group of moderate liberal leaders, fearing the reestablishment of a republic, agreed to give the crown to Charles X's cousin Louis-Philippe, duke of Orléans.

Charles X went into exile in England, and the new king extended political liberties and voting rights. Although the number of voting men nearly doubled, it remained minuscule—approximately 170,000 in a country of 30 million. Such reforms did little for the poor and working classes, who had manned the barricades in July. Dissatisfaction with the 1830 settlement boiled over in Lyon in 1831, when a silk-workers' strike over wages turned into a rebellion that died down only when the army arrived. Revolution had broken the hold of those who wanted to restore the pre-1789 monarchy and nobility, but it had gone no further this time than installing a more liberal, constitutional monarchy.

Belgian Independence from the Dutch.   News of the July revolution in Paris ignited the Belgians, whose country had been annexed to the kingdom of the Netherlands in 1815. Differences in traditions, language, and religion separated the largely Catholic Belgians from the Dutch. An opera about a seventeenth-century insurrection in Naples provided the spark, and students in Brussels rioted, shouting "Down with the Dutch!"

The riot turned into revolt. King William of the Netherlands appealed to the great powers to intervene; after all, the Congress of Vienna had established his kingdom. But Great Britain and France opposed intervention and invited Russia, Austria, and Prussia to a conference that guaranteed Belgium independence in exchange for its neutrality in international affairs. Belgian neutrality would remain a cornerstone of European diplomacy for a century. After much maneuvering, the crown of the new kingdom of Belgium was offered to a German prince, Leopold of Saxe-Coburg, in 1831. Belgium, like France and Britain, now had a constitutional monarchy.

Revolts in Italy and Poland.   The Austrian emperor and the Russian tsar would have supported intervention in Belgium had they not been preoccupied with their own revolts. Anti-Austrian uprisings erupted in a handful of Italian states, but they fizzled without the hoped-for French aid. The Polish revolt was more serious. When set up in 1815, the "congress kingdom" (so called because the Congress of Vienna had created it) was given a constitution that provided for an elected parliament, a national army, and guarantees of free speech and a free press. But by 1818, its ruler, the Russian tsar Alexander I, had begun retracting these concessions. Polish students and military officers responded by forming secret nationalist societies to plot for change by illegal means. The government then cracked down, arresting student leaders and dismissing professors who promoted reforms. In 1830, in response to news of revolution in France, students raised the banner of rebellion. Polish aristocrats formed a provisional government, but it got no support from Britain

or France and was defeated by the Russian army. In reprisal, Tsar Nicholas abolished the Polish constitution that his brother Alexander had granted and ordered thousands of Poles executed or banished.

The British Reform Bill of 1832.   The British had long been preoccupied with two subjects: the royal family and elections for control of Parliament. In 1820, the domestic quarrels between the new king, George IV (r. 1820–1830), and his German wife, Caroline, seemed to threaten the future of the monarchy. When George IV came to the throne, he tried to divorce Caroline, and he refused to have her crowned queen. He hoped to use rumors of her love affairs on the continent to win his case, but the divorce trial provoked massive demonstrations in support of Caroline. Women's groups gathered thousands of signatures on petitions supporting her, and popular songs and satires portrayed George as a fat, drunken libertine. Caroline's death a few months after George's coronation ended the Queen Caroline Affair. The monarchy survived, but with a tarnished reputation.

The demonstrations in the Queen Caroline Affair followed on the heels of a huge political rally held just the year before. In August 1819, sixty thousand people attended an illegal political meeting held in St. Peter's Fields in Manchester. They wanted reform of Parliamentary elections, which had long been controlled by aristocratic landowners. When the local authorities sent the cavalry to arrest the speaker, panic resulted; eleven people were killed and many hundreds injured. Punsters called it the battle of Peterloo or the Peterloo massacre. An alarmed government passed the Six Acts, which forbade large political meetings and restricted press criticism.

In the 1820s, however, new men came into government. Sir Robert Peel (1788–1850), the secretary for home affairs, revised the criminal code to reduce the number of crimes punishable by death and introduced a municipal police force in London, called the Bobbies after him. In 1824, the laws prohibiting labor unions were repealed, and though restrictions on strikes remained, workers could now organize themselves legally to confront their employers collectively. In 1828, the appointment of the duke of Wellington, the hero of Waterloo, as prime minister kept the Tories in power, and his government pushed through a bill in 1829 allowing Catholics to sit in Parliament and hold most public offices.

When in 1830, and again in 1831, the Whigs in Parliament proposed an extension of the right to vote, Tory diehards, principally in the House of Lords, dug in their heels and predicted that even the most modest proposals would doom civilization itself. Even though the proposed law would not grant universal male suffrage, mass demonstrations in favor of it took place in many cities. One supporter of reform described the scene: "Meetings of almost every description of persons were held in cities, towns, and parishes; by journeymen tradesmen in their clubs, and by common workmen who had no trade clubs or associations of any kind." In this "state of diseased and feverish excitement" (according to its opponents), the **Reform Bill of 1832** passed, after the king threatened to create enough new peers to obtain its passage in the House of Lords.

Although the Reform Bill altered Britain's political structure in significant ways, the gains were not revolutionary. One of the bill's foremost backers, historian and member of Parliament Thomas Macaulay, explained, "I am opposed to Universal Suffrage, because I think that it would produce a destructive revolution. I support this plan, because I am sure that it is our best security against a revolution." Although the number of male voters increased by about 50 percent, only one in five Britons could now vote, and voting still depended on holding property. Nevertheless, the bill gave representation to new cities in the north for the first time and set a precedent for further widening suffrage. Exclusive aristocratic politics now gave way to a mixed middle-class and aristocratic structure that would prove more responsive to the problems of a fast-growing society. Those disappointed with the outcome would organize with renewed vigor in the 1830s and 1840s.

> **REVIEW:** Why were Austria and Russia able to thwart independence movements in Italy and Poland but not in Greece, Belgium, and Latin America?

Reform Bill of 1832: A measure passed by the British Parliament to increase the number of male voters by about 50 percent and give representation to new cities in the north; it set a precedent for widening suffrage.

Conclusion

The agitations and uprisings of the 1820s and early 1830s showed that the revolutionary legacy still smoldered and might erupt into flames again at any moment. Napoleon Bonaparte had kept the legacy alive by insisting on fundamental reforms wherever his armies triumphed. His imperial rule galvanized supporters and opponents alike; no one could be indifferent to his impact on European and even world affairs. He reshaped French institutions and left a lasting imprint in many European countries. Moreover, like Frankenstein's monster, he seemed to bounce back from every reversal; between the French retreat from Moscow in 1812 and his final defeat at Waterloo in 1815, Napoleon lost many battles and yet managed to raise an army again and again.

The French emperor's attempt to colonize much of Europe ultimately failed. Germans, Italians, Russians, and Spaniards all resisted and in the process discovered new national feelings that would have an impact throughout modern times. Unlike Frankenstein's monster, Napoleon could not hide from his enemies and was forced into exile until his death. The powers who eventually defeated Napoleon tried to maintain the European peace by shoring up monarchical governments and damping down aspirations for constitutional freedoms and national autonomy. They sometimes fell short. Belgium separated from the Netherlands, Greece achieved independence from the Turks, Latin American countries shook off the rule of Spain and Portugal, and the French installed a more liberal monarchy than the one envisioned by the Congress of Vienna. Yet Metternich's vision of a conservative Europe still held, and most efforts at revolt failed. In the next two decades, however, dramatic social changes would raise the stakes of political contests and prompt a new and much more deadly round of revolutions.

FOR FURTHER EXPLORATION

- **For suggested references, including Web sites, for topics in this chapter,** see page SR-1 at the end of the book.

- **For additional primary-source material from this period,** see Chapter 20 in *Sources of THE MAKING OF THE WEST,* Third Edition.

- **For Web sites and documents related to topics in this chapter,** see *Make History* at bedfordstmartins.com/hunt.

MAPPING THE WEST

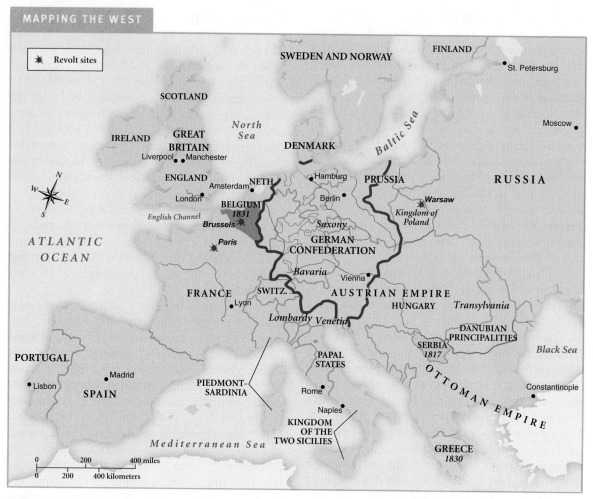

Europe in 1830

By 1830, the fragilities of the Congress of Vienna settlement had become apparent. Rebellion in Poland failed, but Belgium won its independence from the kingdom of the Netherlands, and a French revolution in July chased out the Bourbon ruler and installed Louis-Philippe, who promised constitutional reform. Most European rulers held on to their positions in this period of ferment, but they had to accommodate new desires for constitutional guarantees of rights and growing nationalist sentiment.

CHAPTER REVIEW

KEY TERMS AND PEOPLE

Napoleon Bonaparte (620)

First Consul (622)

Civil Code (625)

Continental System (631)

Congress of Vienna (636)

Klemens von Metternich (636)

restoration (638)

conservatism (638)

Ludwig van Beethoven (642)

Sir Walter Scott (643)

Simon Bolívar (646)

Reform Bill of 1832 (649) .

MAKING CONNECTIONS

1. What was the long-term significance of Napoleon for Europe?

2. In what ways did Metternich succeed in holding back the revolutionary legacy? In what ways did he fail?

> **For practice quizzes, a customized study plan, and other study tools,** see the Online Study Guide at bedfordstmartins.com/hunt.

REVIEW QUESTIONS

1. In what ways did Napoleon continue the French Revolution, and in what ways did he break with it?

2. Why was Napoleon able to gain control over so much of Europe's territory?

3. To what extent was the old order restored by the Congress of Vienna?

4. Why were Austria and Russia able to thwart independence movements in Italy and Poland but not in Greece, Belgium, and Latin America?

IMPORTANT EVENTS

1799	Coup against Directory government in France; Napoleon Bonaparte named First Consul	1818	Mary Shelley, *Frankenstein*
1801	Napoleon signs a concordat with the pope	1820	Revolt of liberal army officers against the Spanish crown
1804	Napoleon crowned as emperor of France; issues new Civil Code	1824	Ludwig van Beethoven, Ninth Symphony
1805	British naval forces defeat the French at the battle of Trafalgar; Napoleon wins his greatest victory at the battle of Austerlitz	1825	Russian army officers demand constitutional reform in the Decembrist Revolt
1812	Napoleon invades Russia	1830	Greece gains its independence from Ottoman Turks; rebels overthrow Charles X of France and install Louis-Philippe; rebellion in Poland against Russia fails
1814–1815	Congress of Vienna		
1815	Napoleon defeated at Waterloo and exiled to island of St. Helena, where he dies in 1821	1832	English Parliament passes Reform Bill; Johann Wolfgang von Goethe, *Faust*

Industrialization and Social Ferment
1830–1850

I n 1830, the Liverpool and Manchester Railway Line opened to the cheers of crowds and the congratulations of government officials, including the duke of Wellington, the hero of Waterloo and now the British prime minister. In the excitement, some of the dignitaries gathered on a parallel track. Another engine, George Stephenson's *Rocket*, approached at high speed—the engine could go as fast as twenty-seven miles per hour. Most of the gentlemen scattered to safety, but former cabinet minister William Huskisson fell and was hit. A few hours later he died, the first official casualty of the new-fangled railroad.

Dramatic and expensive, railroads were the most striking symbol of the new industrial age. Industrialization and its by-product of rapid urban growth fundamentally changed political conflicts, social relations, cultural concerns, and even the landscape. So great were the changes that they are collectively labeled the Industrial Revolution. Although this revolution did not take place in a single decade like the French Revolution, the introduction of steam-driven machinery, large factories, and a new working class transformed life in the Western world. Peasants and workers streamed into the cities. The population of London grew by 130,000 people in the 1830s alone. Berlin more than doubled between 1819 and 1849, and Paris expanded by 120,000 just between 1841 and 1846. To many observers, overcrowding, disease, prostitution, crime, and alcohol consumption all seemed to be on the increase as a result.

The shock of industrial and urban growth generated an outpouring of commentary on the need for social reforms. Painters, poets, and especially novelists joined in the chorus warning about rising tensions.

The New Railroad
This engraving by H. Pyall from 1831 shows the entrance of the Liverpool and Manchester Railway line at Edge Hill in Liverpool. The engines seem quaint to us now, but at the time they impressed everyone with their size and speed. Railroads immediately became the symbol as well as the driving force of the industrial age. The engraving shows that even upper-class men and women flocked to see the new engines in operation. *(Getty Images.)*

Many who wrote on social issues expected middle-class women to organize their homes as a domestic haven from the heartless process of upheaval. Yet despite the emphasis on domesticity, middle-class women participated in public issues too: they set up reform societies that fought prostitution and helped poor mothers, and they agitated for temperance (abstention from alcohol), and joined the campaigns to abolish slavery. Middle-class men and women frequently denounced the lower classes' appetites for drink, tobacco, and cockfighting, but they remained largely silent when British traders received government support in forcing the Chinese to accept imports of opium, an addictive drug.

Social ferment set the ideological pots to a boil. A word coined during the French Revolution, **ideology** refers to a coherent set of beliefs about the way the social and political order should be organized. The dual revolution of the French Revolution and the Industrial Revolution prompted the development of a whole spectrum of ideologies to explain the meaning of the changes taking place. Nationalists, liberals, socialists, and communists offered competing visions of the social order they desired: they all agreed that change was necessary, but they disagreed about both the means and the ends of change. Their contest came to a head in 1848 when the rapid transformation of European society led to a new set of revolutionary outbreaks, more consuming than any since 1789. As in 1789, food shortages and constitutional crises fueled rebellions, but now class tensions and nationalist impulses fanned the flames in capitals across Europe, not only in Paris. Because of internal quarrels and conflicts, however, the revolutionaries of 1848 eventually went down to defeat.

---

ideology: A word coined during the French Revolution to refer to a coherent set of beliefs about the way the social and political order should be organized.

FOCUS QUESTION: How did the Industrial Revolution create new social and political conflicts?

The Industrial Revolution

French and English writers of the 1820s invented the term **Industrial Revolution** to capture the drama of contemporary change and to draw a parallel with the French Revolution. The chief components of the Industrial Revolution, industrialization and urbanization, are long-term processes that have continued to the present; unlike the French upheaval, they do not have precise beginning and ending dates. The Industrial Revolution began in England in the 1770s and 1780s in textile manufacturing and spread from there across the continent. In the 1830s and 1840s, industrialization and urbanization both accelerated quite suddenly, as governments across Europe encouraged railroad construction and the mechanization of manufacturing. States exercised little control over the consequences of industrial and urban growth, however, and many officials, preachers, and intellectuals worried that unchecked growth would destroy traditional social relationships and create disorder. Some held out the constancy of rural life as an antidote to the ravages of industrialization and urbanization, but population growth produced new tensions in the countryside too.

Roots of Industrialization

British inventors had been steadily perfecting steam engines for five decades before George

---

Industrial Revolution: The transformation of life in the Western world over several decades in the late eighteenth and early nineteenth centuries as a result of the introduction of steam-driven machinery, large factories, and a new working class.

■ 1830–1832 Cholera epidemic

■ 1830 France invades Algeria

■ 1835 Belgium opens first continental railway

■ 1831 British and Foreign Temperance Society established

1830	1835	1840

■ 1832 George Sand, *Indiana*

■ 1833 British Factory Act; abolition of slavery

■ 1834 *Zollverein* established

■ 1839 Opium War begins; invention of photography

■ 1841 Dickens, *The Old Curiosity Shop*

Stephenson built his *Rocket*. A key breakthrough took place in 1776 when James Watt developed an efficient steam engine that could be used to pump water from coal mines or drive machinery in textile factories. Since coal fired the steam engines which drove new textile machinery, innovations tended to reinforce each other. This kind of synergy built on previous changes in the textile industry. In 1733, the Englishman John Kay had patented the flying shuttle, which enabled weavers to "throw" yarn across the loom rather than draw it back and forth by hand. When the flying shuttle came into widespread use in the 1760s, weavers began producing cloth more quickly than spinners could produce the thread. The resulting shortage of spun thread propelled the invention of the spinning jenny and the water frame, a power-driven spinning machine. In the following decades, water frames replaced thousands of women spinners working at home by hand. Using the engines produced by James Watt and his partner Matthew Boulton, Edmund Cartwright designed a mechanized loom in the 1780s that, when perfected, could be run by a small boy and yet yield fifteen times the output of a skilled adult working a handloom. By the end of the century, new power machinery was being assembled in large factories that hired semiskilled men, women, and children to replace skilled weavers.

Several factors interacted to make England the first site of the Industrial Revolution. Because population increased by more than 50 percent in England in the second half of the eighteenth century, manufacturers had an incentive to produce more and cheaper cotton cloth. England had a good supply of private investment capital from overseas trade and commercial profits, ready access to raw cotton from the plantations of its Caribbean colonies and the southern United States, and the necessary natural resources at home such as coal and iron. Good opportunities for social mobility and relative political stability in the eighteenth century provided an environment that fostered the pragmatism of the English and Scottish inventors who designed the machinery. These early industrialists shared a culture of informal scientific education through learned societies and popular lectures (one of the prominent forms of the Enlightenment in Britain). Manufacturers proved eager to introduce steam-driven machinery to increase output and gradually established factories to house the new machines and concentrate the labor of their workers. The agricultural revolution of the eighteenth century had enabled England to produce food more efficiently, freeing some agricultural workers to move to the new sites of manufacturing. Cotton textile production skyrocketed.

Elsewhere in Europe, textile manufacturing — long a linchpin in the European economy — expanded even without the introduction of new machines and factories because of the spread of the "putting-out," or "domestic," system. Under the putting-out system, manufacturers supplied the raw materials, such as woolen or cotton fibers, to families working at home. The mother and her children washed, carded, and combed the fibers. Then the mother and oldest daughters spun them into thread. The father, assisted by the children, wove the cloth. The cloth was then finished (bleached, dyed, smoothed, and so on) under the supervision of the manufacturer in a large workshop, located either in town or in the countryside. This system had existed in the textile industry for hundreds of years, but in the eighteenth century it grew dramatically, and the manufacture of other products, such as glassware, baskets, nails, and guns, followed suit. The spread of the domestic system of manufacturing is sometimes called proto-industrialization to signify that the process helped pave the way for the full-scale Industrial Revolution. Because of the increase in textile production,

■ **1848** Last Chartist demonstrations; Marx and Engels, *Communist Manifesto*; revolutions throughout Europe; French abolish slavery in remaining colonies; end of serfdom in Austrian Empire

1845	1850	1855

■ **1846** Famine in Ireland; Corn Laws repealed; insurrection in Galicia

■ **1851** Crystal Palace exhibition

ordinary people began to wear underclothes and nightclothes, both rare in the past. White, red, blue, yellow, green, and even pastel shades of cotton now replaced the black, gray, or brown of traditional woolen dress.

Workers in the textile industry, whether in the putting-out system or in factories, enjoyed few protections against fluctuations in the market. Whenever demand for cloth declined, manufacturers simply did not buy from the families producing it. Hundreds of thousands of families might be reduced to bankruptcy in periods of food shortage or overproduction. Handloom weavers sometimes violently resisted the establishment of factory power looms that would force them out of work. In England in 1811 and 1812, for example, bands of handloom weavers wrecked factory machinery and burned mills in the Midlands, Yorkshire, and Lancashire. To restore order and protect industry, the government sent in an army of twelve thousand regular soldiers and made machine wrecking punishable by death. The rioters were called Luddites after the fictitious figure Ned Ludd, whose signature appeared on their manifestos. (The term is still used to describe those who resist new technology.)

Engines of Change

Steam-driven engines took on a dramatic new form in the 1820s when the English engineer George Stephenson perfected an engine to pull wagons along rail tracks. In the 1830s and 1840s, every major country in Europe hurried to set up a railroad system, pushing industrialization from west to east across Europe (see "Taking Measure," below). Although the new industries employed only a small percentage of workers, the working class that took shape in them immediately attracted the attention of social commentators and government officials. Rulers could not afford to ignore the social problems that came from industrialization.

The Rise of the Railroad. The idea of a railroad was not new: iron tracks had been used since the seventeenth century to haul coal from mines in wagons pulled by horses. A railroad system as a mode of transport, however, developed only after Stephenson's invention of a steam-powered locomotive. Placed on the new tracks, steam-driven carriages could transport people and goods to the cities and link coal and iron deposits to the new factories. In the 1840s alone, railroad track mileage more than doubled in Great Britain, and British investment in railways jumped tenfold. The British also began to build railroads in India. Canal building waned in the 1840s: the railroad had won out. Britain's success with rail transportation led other countries to develop their own projects. Railroads grew spectacularly in the United States in the 1830s and 1840s, reaching

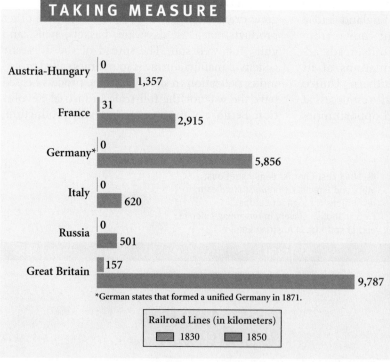

TAKING MEASURE

Austria-Hungary: 0 / 1,357
France: 31 / 2,915
Germany*: 0 / 5,856
Italy: 0 / 620
Russia: 0 / 501
Great Britain: 157 / 9,787

*German states that formed a unified Germany in 1871.

Railroad Lines (in kilometers)
■ 1830   ■ 1850

Railroad Lines, 1830–1850
Great Britain quickly extended its lead in the building of railroads. The extension of commerce and, before long, the ability to wage war would depend on the development of effective railroad networks. These statistics might be taken as predicting a realignment of power within Europe after 1850. What do the numbers say about the relative positions of Germany (the German states, including Prussia but excluding Austria), the Austrian Empire, and France? *(From B. R. Mitchell, European Historical Statistics 1750–1970 (New York: Columbia University Press, 1975), F1.)*

MAP 21.1 Industrialization in Europe, c. 1850

Industrialization (mainly mechanized textile production) first spread in a band across northern Europe that included Great Britain, northern France, Belgium, the northern German states, the region around Milan in northern Italy, and Bohemia. Although railroads were not the only factor in promoting industrialization, the map makes clear the interrelationship between railroad building and the development of new industrial sites of coal mining and textile production.

9,000 miles of track by midcentury. Belgium, newly independent in 1830, opened the first continental European railroad with state bonds backed by British capital in 1835. In all, the world had 23,500 miles of track by 1850, most of it in western Europe.

Railroad building spurred both industrial development and state power (Map 21.1). Governments everywhere participated in the construction of railroads, which depended on private and state funds to pay for the massive amounts of iron, coal, heavy machinery, and human labor required to build and run them. Demand for iron products accelerated industrial development. Until the 1840s, cotton had led industrial production; between 1816 and 1840, cotton output more than quadrupled in Great Britain. But from 1830 to 1850, Britain's output of iron and coal doubled (Table

21.1). Similarly, Austrian output of iron doubled between the 1820s and the 1840s. One-third of all investment in the German states in the 1840s went into railroads.

Steam-powered engines made Britain the world leader in manufacturing. By midcentury, more than half of Britain's national income came from manufacturing and trade. The number of steamboats in Great Britain rose from two in 1812 to six hundred in 1840. Between 1840 and 1850, steam-engine power doubled in Great Britain and increased even more rapidly elsewhere in Europe, as those adopting British inventions strove to catch up. The power applied in German manufacturing, for example, grew sixfold during the 1840s but still amounted to only a little more than a quarter of the British figure. German coal and iron outputs were only 6 or 7 percent of the British outputs.

TABLE 21.1 Coal Output, 1830–1850*

Like the numbers for railroad mileage, these figures for coal production show the economic dominance of Great Britain throughout the period 1830–1850. As long as coal remained the essential fuel of industrialization, Britain enjoyed a clear advantage.

	Austria	Belgium	France	German States (including Prussia)	Great Britain
1830	214	**	1,863	1,800	22,800
1835	251	2,639	2,506	2,100	28,100
1840	473	3,930	3,003	3,200	34,200
1845	689	4,919	4,202	4,400	46,600
1850	877	5,821	4,434	5,100	50,200

*In thousands of metric tons.

**Data not available.

Source: B. R. Mitchell, *European Historical Statistics, 1750–1970* (New York: Columbia University Press, 1975), D2.

Industrialization Moves Eastward. Although Great Britain consciously strove to protect its industrial supremacy, thousands of British engineers defied laws against the export of machinery or the emigration of artisans. Only slowly, thanks to the pirating of British methods and to new technical schools, did most continental countries begin closing the gap. Belgium became the fastest-growing industrial power on the continent: between 1830 and 1844, the number of steam engines in Belgium quadrupled, and Belgians exported seven times as many steam engines as they imported.

Industrialization spread slowly east from key areas in Prussia (near Berlin), Saxony, and Bohemia. Cotton production in the Austrian Empire tripled between 1831 and 1845, and coal production increased fourfold from 1827 to 1847. Both activities were centered in Bohemia, which was more productive than Prussia or Saxony. Even so, by 1850, continental Europe still lagged almost twenty years behind Great Britain in industrial development.

The advance of industrialization in eastern Europe was slow, in large part because serfdom still survived there, hindering labor mobility and tying up investment capital: as long as peasants were legally tied to the land as serfs, they could not migrate to the new factory towns and landlords felt little incentive to invest their income in manufacturing. The problem was worst in Russia, where industrialization would not take off until the end of the nineteenth century. Nevertheless, even in Russia signs of industrialization could be detected: raw cotton imports (a sign of a growing textile industry) increased sevenfold between 1831 and 1848, and the number of factories doubled along with the size of the industrial workforce.

Factories and Workers. Despite the spread of industrialization, factory workers remained a minority everywhere. In the 1840s, factories in England employed only 5 percent of the workers; in France, 3 percent; in Prussia, 2 percent. The putting-out system remained strong, employing two-thirds of the manufacturing workers in Prussia and Saxony, for example, in the 1840s. Many peasants kept their options open by combining factory work or putting-out work with agricultural labor. From Switzerland to Russia, people worked in agriculture during the spring and summer and in manufacturing in the fall and winter. Unstable industrial wages made such arrangements essential. In addition, some new industries idled periodically: for example, iron forges stopped for several months when the water level in streams dropped, and blast furnaces shut down for repairs several weeks every year.

Even though factories employed only a small percentage of the population, they attracted much attention. Already by 1830, more than a million people in Britain depended on the cotton industry for employment, and cotton cloth constituted 50 percent of the country's exports. Factories sprang up in urban areas, where the growing population provided a ready source of labor. The rapid expansion of the British textile industry had a colonial corollary: the destruction of the hand manufacture of textiles in India. The British put high import duties on Indian cloth entering Britain and kept such duties very low for British cloth entering India. The figures are dramatic: in 1813, the Indian city of Calcutta exported to England £2,000,000 of cotton cloth; by 1830, Calcutta was importing from England £2,000,000 of cotton cloth. When Britain abolished slavery in its

Factory Work
This 1836 depiction of mechanized spinning of cotton in England captures the dangers of child labor. The child is sweeping even while the machine works. The print does not portray the churning noise and swirling dust of the workplace, but it does show how machines could produce thread much more efficiently than individuals working on their own. Do you think the artist aimed to provide a positive or negative picture of factory work? *(Mary Evans Picture Library.)*

Caribbean colonies in 1833, British manufacturers began to buy raw cotton in the southern United States, where slavery still flourished.

Factories drew workers from the urban population surge, which had begun in the eighteenth century and now accelerated. The number of agricultural laborers also increased during industrialization in Britain, suggesting that a growing birthrate created a larger population and fed workers into the new factory system. The new workers came from several sources: families of farmers who could not provide land for all their children, artisans displaced by the new machinery, and children of the earliest workers who had moved to the factory towns. Factory employment resembled family labor on farms or in the putting-out system: entire families came to toil for a single wage, although family members performed different tasks. Workdays of twelve to seventeen hours were typical, even for children, and the work was grueling.

As urban factories grew, their workers gradually came to constitute a new socioeconomic class

with a distinctive culture and traditions. The term *working class*, like *middle class*, came into use for the first time in the early nineteenth century. It referred to the laborers in the new factories. In the past, urban workers had labored in isolated trades: water and wood carrying, gardening, laundry, and building. In contrast, factories brought working people together with machines, under close supervision by their employers. They soon developed a sense of common interests and organized societies for mutual help and political reform. From these would come the first labor unions.

Factories produced wealth without regard to the pollution they caused or the exhausted state of their workers; industry created unheard-of riches and new forms of poverty all at once. "From this foul drain the greatest stream of human industry flows out to fertilize the whole world," wrote the French aristocrat Alexis de Tocqueville after visiting the new English industrial city of Manchester in the 1830s. "From this filthy sewer pure gold flows. Here humanity attains its most complete

Statistics and the Standard of Living of the Working Class

From the very beginning of industrialization, experts argued about whether industrialization improved or worsened the standard of living of the working class. For every claim, there was a counterclaim, and most often these claims came in the form of statistics. Some experts argued that factories offered higher-paying jobs to workers; others countered that factories took work away from artisans such as handloom weavers and left them on the verge of starvation. Supporters of industrialization maintained that factories gave women paying work; opponents insisted that factories destroyed the family by taking women away from the home. Through mass production, industrialization made goods cheaper and therefore more available; by polluting the air, it destroyed health, lowered life expectancy, and ruined the environment. Karl Marx and Friedrich Engels would give the debate even more of an edge by tying it to the ideology of communism. In 1844, Engels described to Marx his aim in writing *The Condition of the Working Class in England*: "I shall present the English

with a fine bill of indictment. At the bar of world opinion I charge the English middle classes with mass murder, wholesale robbery and all the other crimes in the calendar." The stakes of the argument were not small.

The controversy about the benefits and costs of industrialization has continued right down to the present, in part because it is an argument directly inspired by the ideologies — liberalism, socialism, communism — that emerged as explanations of and blueprints for economic and social change. In the 1830s and 1840s, liberals insisted that industrialization would promote greater prosperity for everyone, whereas conservatives complained that it destroyed traditional ways of life and socialists warned that it exaggerated inequality and class division. In the 1950s and 1960s, defenders of capitalist free enterprise still advanced the argument about prosperity, but now they were opposed by communists who argued that state control of production could sidestep the horrors of early capitalist exploitation. Newly developing countries looked

to the history of the 1830s and 1840s for lessons about the likely impact of industrialization on their countries in the 1950s and beyond. The scholarly debates therefore attracted worldwide attention, and all sides called on statistics to make their competing cases.

Unfortunately, the statistics can be interpreted in many different ways. Did it matter more that wages for factory workers went up or that life expectancy went down? If an increase in sugar consumption in Great Britain from 207,000 tons in 1844 to 290,000 tons in 1847 meant an overall increase in the standard of living, how does that square with the hundreds of thousands of deaths in Ireland at the same time or the increasing disparity throughout Great Britain between rich and poor? Some convergence of opinion has taken place, however. Most now agree that by sometime between 1820 and 1845 (the exact date depending on the scholar), conditions in Great Britain had become better than before the Industrial Revolution. And there is no doubt that the debate itself has had one major positive

development and its most brutish, here civilization works its miracles and civilized man is turned almost into a savage." Studies by physicians set the life expectancy of workers in Manchester at just seventeen years (partly because of high rates of infant mortality), whereas the average life expectancy in England was forty years in 1840. (See "New Sources, New Perspectives," above.) One American visitor in Britain in the late 1840s described how "in the manufacturing town, the fine soot or *blacks* darken the day, give white sheep the color of black sheep, discolor the human saliva, contaminate the air, poison many plants, and corrode monuments and buildings." In some parts of Europe, city leaders banned factories, hoping to insulate their towns from the effects of industrial growth.

As factory production expanded, local and national governments collected information about the workers. Investigators detailed their pitiful condition. A French physician in the eastern town of Mulhouse described the "pale, emaciated women who walk barefooted through the dirt" to reach the factory. The young children who worked in the factory appeared "clothed in rags which are greasy with the oil from the looms and frames." A report to the city government in Lille, France, in 1832 described "dark cellars" where the cotton workers lived: "the air is never renewed, it is infected; the walls are plastered with garbage."

Government inquiries often focused on women and children. In Great Britain, the Factory Act of 1833 outlawed the employment of children under the age of nine in textile mills (except in the lace effect: since making one's point depends on having statistics to prove it, the debate itself has encouraged a staggering amount of research into quantitative measures of just about everything imaginable, from measures of wages and prices to rates of mortality and even average heights (height being correlated, it is thought, to economic well-being). British soldiers in the nineteenth century were taller on average than those in any other country except the United States, and people who believe that industrialization improved the standard of living are happy to seize on this as evidence for their case.

One example of a recently developed statistic shows both how powerful and how debatable such sources can be. The table shown at right, adapted from a recent study by Jeffrey G. Williamson, provides a simple measure—based on complex calculations—of the gap in wages between British farm and nonfarm laborers for the period 1797 to 1851. The index measures the attractiveness of non-farm (basically city, mining, and factory) work. It shows that nonfarm wages rose faster than farm wages, but only after 1820 or so. By 1851, nonfarm wages had far outstripped those on the farm. What can we conclude? Although these data seem to support the view that the standard of living of workers improved some-

time in the 1820s and continued to do so afterward, Williamson does not conclude that factory workers were better off than farmers; instead, he argues that the gap indicates that farm people did not migrate quickly enough to the city to satisfy urban labor demands. In short, he seems to consider the gap between farm and nonfarm wages to be a problem of "labor-market disequilibrium." The lesson to be learned is that all historians' conclusions depend on the questions they ask and the sources they use—and few other sources are as open to different interpretations as statistics.

Trends in the British Nominal-Wage Gap, 1797–1851

YEAR	INDEX	YEAR	INDEX
1797	100.0	1827	132.4
1805	86.6	1835	134.7
1810	96.7	1851	148.3
1815	105.1		

Source: Jeffrey G. Williamson, "Leaving the Farm to Go to the City: Did They Leave Quickly Enough?" in John A. James and Mark Thomas, *Capitalism in Context: Essays on Economic Development and Cultural Change in Honor of R. M. Hartwell* (Chicago: University of Chicago Press, 1994), 159–83; table on page 182.

QUESTIONS TO CONSIDER
1. What is a good measure of the standard of living in the first half of the nineteenth century? How would you measure the standard of living today?
2. How do you explain the initial decline in nonfarm wages relative to farm wages and the subsequent rise?
3. What are the virtues of using statistical measures to determine the standard of living? What are the defects?

FURTHER READING
Thompson, Noel W. *The Real Rights of Man: Political Economies for the Working Class, 1775–1850.* 1998.
Williams, Chris., ed. *Companion to Nineteenth-Century Britain.* 2004.

The gap is calculated as the difference between the weighted average of non-farm unskilled earnings (common laborers, porters, police, guards, watchmen, coal miners, and so on) and the farm-earnings rate, divided by the farm-earnings rate. Thus, it is the percentage differential by which nonfarm unskilled wages exceeded farm wages: below 100 = farm earnings exceed those of nonfarm earnings, whereas above 100 = nonfarm earnings exceed those of farm earnings.

and silk industries); it also limited the workdays for those aged nine to thirteen to nine hours a day, and those aged thirteen to eighteen to twelve hours. Adults worked even longer hours. Investigating commissions showed that women and young children, sometimes under age six, hauled coal trucks through low, cramped passageways in coal mines. One nine-year-old girl, Margaret Gomley, described her typical day in the mines as beginning at 7:00 a.m. and ending at 6:00 p.m.: "I get my dinner at 12 o'clock, which is a dry muffin, and sometimes butter on, but have no time allowed to stop to eat it, I eat it while I am thrusting the load. . . . They flog us down in the pit, sometimes with their hand upon my bottom, which hurts me very much." In response to the investigations, the British Parliament passed a Mines Act

in 1842 prohibiting the employment of women and girls underground. In 1847, the Central Short Time Committee, one of Britain's many social reform organizations, successfully pressured Parliament to limit the workday of women and children to ten hours. The continental countries followed the British lead, but since most did not insist on government inspection, enforcement was lax.

Urbanization and Its Consequences

Industrial development spurred urban growth, yet even cities with little industry grew as well. Here, too, Great Britain led the way: half the population of England and Wales was living in towns by 1850, while in France and the German states only about a quarter of the total population was urban. Both old and new cities teemed with rising numbers in the 1830s and 1840s; the population of Vienna ballooned by 125,000 between 1827 and 1847, and the new industrial city of Manchester grew by 70,000 just in the 1830s.

Massive rural emigration, rather than births to women already living in cities, accounted for this remarkable increase. Agricultural improvements had increased the food supply and hence the rural population, but the land could no longer support the people living on it. City life and new factories beckoned those faced with hunger and poverty, including emigrants from other lands: thousands of Irish emigrated to English cities, Italians went to French cities, and Poles flocked to German cities. Settlements sprang up outside the old city limits but gradually became part of the urban area. Cities incorporated parks, cemeteries, zoos, and greenways—all imitations of the countryside, which itself was being industrialized by railroads and factories. "One can't even go to one's land for the slightest bit of gardening," grumbled a French citizen, annoyed by new factories in town, "without being covered with a black powder that spoils every plant that it touches."

Overcrowding and Disease. The rapid influx of people caused serious overcrowding in the cities because the housing stock expanded much more slowly than population growth. In Paris, thirty thousand workers lived in lodging houses, eight or nine to a room, with no separation of the sexes. In 1847 in St. Giles, the Irish quarter of London, 461 people lived in just twelve houses. Men, women, and children huddled together on piles of filthy rotting straw or potato peels because they had no money for fuel to keep warm.

Severe crowding worsened already dire sanitation conditions. Residents dumped refuse into streets or courtyards, and human excrement collected in cesspools under apartment houses. At midcentury, London's approximately 250,000 cesspools were emptied only once or twice a year. Water was scarce and had to be fetched daily from nearby fountains. Despite the diversion of water from provincial rivers to Paris and a tripling of the number of public fountains, Parisians had enough water for only two baths annually per person (the upper classes enjoyed more baths, of course; the lower classes, fewer). In London, private companies that supplied water turned on pumps in the poorer sections for only a few hours three days a week. In rapidly growing British industrial cities such as Manchester, one-third of the houses contained no latrines. Human waste ended up in the

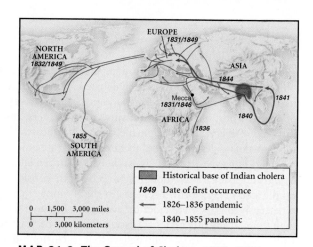

MAP 21.2 The Spread of Cholera, 1826–1855
Contemporaries did not understand the causes of the cholera epidemics in the 1830s and the 1840s in Europe. Western Europeans knew only that the disease marched progressively from east to west across Europe. Nothing seemed able to stop it. It appeared and died out for reasons that could not be grasped at the time. Nevertheless, the cholera epidemics prompted authorities in most European countries to set up public health agencies to coordinate the response and study sanitation conditions in the cities.

rivers that supplied drinking water. The horses that provided transportation inside the cities left droppings everywhere, and city dwellers often kept chickens, ducks, goats, pigs, geese, and even cattle, as well as dogs and cats, in their houses. The result was a "universal atmosphere of filth and stink," as one observer recounted.

Such conditions made cities prime breeding grounds for disease. In 1830–1832 and again in 1847–1851, devastating outbreaks of **cholera** swept across Asia and Europe, touching the United States as well in 1849–1850 (Map 21.2). Today we know that a waterborne bacterium causes cholera, but at the time no one understood the disease and everyone feared it. The usually fatal illness induced violent vomiting and diarrhea and left the skin blue, eyes sunken and dull, and hands and feet ice cold. While cholera particularly ravaged the crowded, filthy neighborhoods of rapidly growing cities, it also claimed many rural and some well-to-do victims. In Paris, 18,000 people died in the 1832 epidemic and 20,000 in that of 1849; in

---

cholera: An epidemic, usually fatal disease caused by a waterborne bacterium that induces violent vomiting and diarrhea; devastating outbreaks swept across Europe in 1830–1832 and 1847–1851.

London, 7,000 died in each epidemic; and in Russia, the epidemic was catastrophic, claiming 250,000 victims in 1831–1832 and 1 million in 1847–1851.

Rumors and panic followed in the wake of each cholera epidemic. Everywhere the downtrodden imagined conspiracies: in Paris in April 1832, a crowd of workers attacked a central hospital, believing the doctors were poisoning the poor but using cholera as a hoax to cover up the conspiracy. Eastern European peasants burned estates and killed physicians and officials. Although devastating, cholera did not kill as many people as tuberculosis, Europe's number-one deadly disease. But tuberculosis took its victims gradually, one by one, and therefore had less impact on social relations.

Middle-Class Fears. Epidemics revealed the social tensions lying just beneath the surface of urban life. The middle and upper classes lived in large, well-appointed apartments or houses with more light, more air, and more water than in lower-class dwellings. But the lower classes lived nearby, sometimes in the cramped upper floors of the same apartment houses. Middle-class reformers often considered the poor to be morally degenerate because of the circumstances of urban life. In their view, overcrowding led to sexual promiscuity and illegitimacy. They depicted the lower classes as dangerously lacking in sexual self-control. A physician visiting Lille, France, in 1835 wrote of "individuals of both sexes and of very different ages lying together, most of them without nightshirts and repulsively dirty. . . . The reader will complete the picture. . . . His imagination must not recoil before any of the disgusting mysteries performed on these impure beds, in the midst of obscurity and drunkenness."

Officials collected statistics on illegitimacy that seemed to bear out these fears: one-quarter to one-half of the babies born in the big European cities in the 1830s and 1840s were illegitimate, and alarmed medical men wrote about thousands of infanticides. Between 1815 and the mid-1830s in France, thirty-three thousand babies were abandoned at foundling hospitals every year; 27 percent of births in Paris in 1850 were illegitimate, compared with only 4 percent of rural births. By collecting such statistics, physicians and administrators in the new public health movement hoped to promote legislation to better the living conditions for workers, but at the same time they helped stereotype workers as immoral and out of control.

Sexual disorder seemed to go hand in hand with drinking and crime. Beer halls and pubs dotted the urban landscape. By the 1830s, Hungary's twin cities of Buda and Pest had eight hundred beer and wine houses for the working classes. One London street boasted twenty-three pubs in three hundred yards. Police officials estimated that London had seventy thousand thieves and eighty thousand prostitutes. In many cities, nearly half the population lived at the level of bare subsistence, and increasing numbers depended on public welfare, charity, or criminality to make ends meet.

Everywhere reformers warned of a widening separation between rich and poor and a growing sense of hostility between the classes. The French poet Amédée Pommier wrote of "These leagues of laborers who have no work, / These far too many arms, these starving mobs." Clergy joined the chorus of physicians and humanitarians in making dire predictions. A Swiss pastor noted: "A new spirit has arisen among the workers. Their hearts seethe with hatred of the well-to-do; their eyes lust for a share of the wealth about them; their mouths speak unblushingly of a coming day of retribution." In 1848, it would seem that that day of retribution had arrived.

Agricultural Perils and Prosperity

Rising population created increased demand for food and spurred changes in the countryside too. Peasants and farmers planted fallow land, chopped down forests, and drained marshes to increase their farming capacity. Still, Europe's ability to feed its expanding population remained questionable: although agricultural yields increased by 30 to 50 percent in the first half of the nineteenth century, population grew by nearly 100 percent. Railroads and canals improved food distribution, but much of Europe — particularly in the east — remained isolated from markets and vulnerable to famines.

Most people still lived on the land, and the upper classes still dominated rural society. Successful businessmen bought land avidly, seeing it not only as the ticket to respectability but also as a hedge against hard times. Hardworking, crafty, or lucky commoners sometimes saved enough to purchase holdings that they had formerly rented or slowly acquired slivers of land from less fortunate neighbors. In France at midcentury, almost two million economically independent peasants tended their own small properties. But in England, southern Italy, Prussia, and eastern Europe, large landowners, usually noblemen, consolidated and expanded their estates by buying up the land of less successful nobles or peasants. As agricultural prices rose, the big landowners pushed for legislation to allow them to continue converting common land to private property.

Wringing a living from the soil under such conditions put pressure on traditional family life. For example, men often migrated seasonally to earn cash in factories or as village artisans, while their wives, sisters, and daughters did the traditional "men's work" of tending crops. In France, Napoleon's Civil Code provided for an equal distribution of inheritance among all heirs; as a result, land was divided over generations into such small parcels that less than 25 percent of all French landowners could support themselves. In the past, population growth had been contained by postponing marriage (leaving fewer years for childbearing) and by high rates of death in childbirth as well as infant mortality. Now, as child mortality declined outside the industrial cities and people without property began marrying earlier, Europeans became more aware of birth control methods. Contraceptive techniques improved; for example, the vulcanization of rubber in the 1840s improved the reliability of condoms. When such methods failed and population increase left no options open at home, people emigrated, often to the United States. Some 800,000 Germans had moved out of central Europe by 1850, while in the 1840s famine drove hundreds of thousands of Irish abroad. Between 1816 and 1850, five million Europeans left their home countries for new lives overseas. When France colonized Algeria in the 1830s and 1840s, officials tried to attract settlers by emphasizing the fertility of the land; they offered the prospect of agricultural prosperity in the colony as an alternative to the rigors of industrialization and urbanization at home.

Despite all the challenges to established ways of life, rural political power remained in the hands of traditional elites. The biggest property owners dominated their tenants and sharecroppers, often demanding a greater yield without making improvements that would enhance productivity. They controlled the political assemblies as well and often personally selected local officials. Such power provoked resentment. One Italian critic wrote, "Great landowner is often the synonym for great ignoramus." Nowhere did the old rural social order seem more impregnable than in Russia. Most Russian serfs remained tied to the land, and troops easily suppressed serfs' uprisings in 1831 and 1842. By midcentury, peasant emancipation remained Russia's great unresolved problem.

REVIEW: What dangers did the Industrial Revolution pose to both urban and rural life?

Reforming the Social Order

In the 1830s and 1840s, Europeans organized to reform the social evils created by industrialization and urbanization. They acted in response to the outpouring of government reports, medical accounts, and literary and artistic depictions of new social problems. Middle-class women often took the lead in establishing new charitable organizations that tried to bring religious faith, educational uplift, and the reform of manners to the lower classes. Middle-class men, and middle-class women too, expected women to soften the rigors of a rapidly changing society, but this expectation led to some confusion about women's proper role: should they devote themselves to social reform in the world or to their own domestic spaces? Many hoped to apply the same zeal for reform to the colonial peoples living in places administered by Europeans.

Cultural Responses to the Social Question

The *social question*, an expression reflecting the widely shared concern about social changes arising from industrialization and urbanization, pervaded all forms of art and literature. The dominant artistic movement of the time, romanticism, generally took a dim view of industrialization. The English-born painter Thomas Cole (1801–1848) complained in 1836: "In this age . . . a meager utilitarianism seems ready to absorb every feeling and sentiment, and what is sometimes called improvement in its march makes us fear that the bright and tender flowers of the imagination shall all be crushed beneath its iron tramp." Yet culture itself underwent important changes as the growing capitals of Europe attracted flocks of aspiring painters and playwrights; the 1830s and 1840s witnessed an explosion in culture as the number of would-be artists increased dramatically and new technologies such as photography and lithography (see illustration, page 666) brought art to the masses. Many of these new intellectuals would support the revolutions of 1848.

Romantic Concerns about Industrial Life. Because romanticism tended to glorify nature and reject industrial and urban growth, romantics often gave vivid expression to the problems created by rapid economic and social transformation. The English poet Elizabeth Barrett Browning, best known for her love poems, denounced child labor in "The Cry of the Children" (1843). Architects of the period sometimes sought to recapture a preindustrial world. When the British Houses of Parliament were rebuilt after they burned down in 1834, the architect Sir Charles Barry constructed them in a Gothic style reminiscent of the Middle Ages. This medievalism was taken even further by A. W. N. Pugin, who contributed some of the designs for the Houses of Parliament. In his polemical book *Contrasts* (1836), Pugin denounced modern conditions and compared them unfavorably with those in the 1400s. To underline his view, Pugin wore medieval clothes at home.

Romantic painters specialized in landscape as a way of calling attention to the sublime wonders of nature, but sometimes even landscapes showed the power of new technologies. In *Rain, Steam, and Speed: The Great Western Railway* (1844), the leading English romantic painter, Joseph M. W. Turner

(1775–1851), portrayed the struggle between the forces of nature and the means of economic growth. Turner was fascinated by steamboats: in *The Fighting "Téméraire" Tugged to Her Last Berth to Be Broken Up* (1838; see illustration below), he featured the victory of steam power over more conventional sailing ships. An admirer described it as an "almost prophetic idea of smoke, soot, iron, and steam, coming to the front in all naval matters."

The Depiction of Social Conditions in Novels. Increased literacy, the spread of reading rooms and lending libraries, and serialization in newspapers and journals gave novels a large reading public. Unlike the fiction of the eighteenth century, which had focused on individual personalities, the great novels of the 1830s and 1840s specialized in the portrayal of social life in all its varieties. Manufacturers, financiers, starving students, workers, bu-

Joseph M. W. Turner, *The Fighting "Téméraire" Tugged to Her Last Berth to Be Broken Up* (1838)
In this painting a steamer belching smoke tows a wooden sailing ship to its last berth, where it will be destroyed. Turner muses about the passing of old ways but also displays his mastery of color in the final blaze of sunset, itself another sign of the passing of time. Turner was an avid reader of the romantic poets, especially Byron. British opinion polls have rated this painting the best of all British paintings. How does the painting capture the clash of old and new? *(© The National Gallery, London.)*

■ **For more help in analyzing this image**, see the visual activity for this chapter in the Online Study Guide at bedfordstmartins.com/hunt.

reaucrats, prostitutes, underworld figures, thieves, and aristocratic men and women filled the pages of works by popular writers. Hoping to get out of debt, the French writer Honoré de Balzac (1799–1850) pushed himself to exhaustion and a premature death by cranking out ninety-five novels and many short stories. He aimed to catalog the social types that could be found in French society. Many of his characters, like himself, were driven by the desire to climb higher in the social order.

The English fiction writer Charles Dickens (1812–1870) worked with a similar frenetic energy and for much the same reason. When his father was imprisoned for debt in 1824, the young Dickens took a job in a shoe-polish factory. In 1836, he published a series of literary sketches of daily life in London to accompany a volume of caricatures by the artist George Cruikshank. Dickens then produced a series of novels that appeared in monthly installments and attracted thousands of readers. In them, he paid close attention to the distressing effects of industrialization and urbanization. In *The Old Curiosity Shop* (1841), for example, he depicts the Black Country, the manufacturing region west and northwest of Birmingham, as a "cheerless region," a "mournful place," in which tall chimneys "made foul the melancholy air." In addition to publishing such enduring favorites as *Oliver Twist* (1838) and *A Christmas Carol* (1843), he ran charitable organizations and pressed for social reforms. For Dickens, the ability to portray the problems of the poor went hand in hand with a personal commitment to reform.

Novels by women often revealed the bleaker side of women's situations. Charlotte Brontë's *Jane Eyre* (1847) describes the difficult life of an orphaned girl who becomes a governess, the only occupation open to most single middle-class women. The French novelist **George Sand** (Amandine-Aurore Dupin, 1804–1876) took her social criticism a step further. She announced her independence in the 1830s by dressing like a man and smoking cigars. Like many other women writers of the time, she published her work under a male pseudonym while creating female characters who prevail in difficult circumstances through romantic love and moral idealism. Sand's novel *Indiana* (1832), about an unhappily married woman, was read all over Europe. Her notoriety—she be-

came the lover of the Polish pianist and composer Frédéric Chopin, among others, and threw herself into socialist politics—made the term *George-Sandism* a common expression of disdain for independent women.

The Explosion of Culture. As artists became more interested in society and social relations, ordinary citizens crowded cultural events. Museums opened to the public across Europe, and the middle classes began collecting art. Popular theaters in big cities drew thousands from the lower and middle classes every night; in London, for example, some twenty-four thousand people attended eighty "penny theaters" nightly. The audience for print culture also multiplied. In the German states, for example, the production of new literary works doubled between 1830 and 1843, as did the number of periodicals and newspapers and the number of booksellers. Thirty or forty private lending libraries offered books in Berlin in the 1830s, and reading rooms

George Sand
In this lithograph by Alcide Lorentz of 1842, George Sand is shown in one of her notorious male costumes. Sand published numerous works, including novels, plays, essays, travel writing, and an autobiography. She actively participated in the revolution of 1848 in France, writing pamphlets in support of the new republic. Disillusioned by the rise to power of Louis-Napoleon Bonaparte, she withdrew to her country estate and devoted herself exclusively to her writing. *(The Granger Collection, New York.)*

George Sand: The pen name of French novelist Amandine-Aurore Dupin (1804–1876), who showed her independence in the 1830s by dressing like a man and smoking cigars. The term *George-Sandism* became an expression of disdain for independent women.

in pastry shops stocked political newspapers and satirical journals. Young children and ragpickers sold cheap prints and books door-to-door or in taverns.

The advent of photography in 1839 provided an amazing new medium for artists. The daguerreotype, named after its inventor, French painter Jacques Daguerre (1787–1851), prompted one artist to claim that "from today, painting is dead." Although this prediction was highly exaggerated, photography did open up new ways of portraying reality. Visual images, whether in painting, on the stage, or in photography, heightened the public's awareness of the effects of industrialization and urbanization.

The number of artists and writers swelled. Estimates suggest that the number of painters and sculptors in France, the undisputed center of European art at the time, grew sixfold between 1789 and 1838. Not everyone could succeed in this hothouse atmosphere, in which writers and artists furiously competed for public attention. Their own troubles made some of them more keenly aware of the hardships faced by the poor. A satirical article in one of the many bitingly critical journals and booklets published in Berlin proclaimed: "In Ipswich in England a mechanical genius has invented a stomach, whose extraordinary efficient construction is remarkable. This artificial stomach is intended for factory workers there and is adjusted so that it is fully satisfied with three lentils or peas; one potato is enough for an entire week."

The Varieties of Social Reform

Lithographs, novels, and even joke booklets helped drive home the need for social reform, but religious conviction also inspired efforts to help the poor. Moral reform societies, Bible groups, Sunday schools, and temperance groups aimed to turn the poor into respectable people. In 1844, for example, 450 different relief organizations operated in London alone. States supported these efforts by encouraging education and enforcing laws against the vagrant poor.

The Religious Impulse for Social Reform.   Religiously motivated reformers first had to overcome the perceived indifference of the working classes. Protestant and Catholic clergy complained that workers had no interest in religion; less than 10 percent of the workers in the cities attended religious services. In a report on the state of religion in England and Wales in 1851, the head of the census, Horace Mann, commented that "the masses of our working population . . . are *unconscious secularists*. . . . These are never, or but seldom seen in our religious congregations." To combat such indifference, British religious groups launched the Sunday school movement, which reached its zenith in the 1840s. By 1851, more than half of all working-class children ages five to fifteen were attending Sunday school, even though very few of their parents regularly went to religious services.

The First Daguerreotype
Daguerre experimented extensively with producing an image on a metal plate before he came up with a viable photographic process in 1837. He called this first daguerreotype "Still Life," a common title for paintings. In 1839, the French government bought the rights and made the process freely available. *(Time & Life Pictures/Getty Images.)*

The Sunday schools taught children how to read at a time when few working-class children could go to school during the week.

Women took a more prominent role than ever before in charitable work. Catholic religious orders, which by 1850 enrolled many more women than men, ran schools, hospitals, leper colonies, insane asylums, and old-age homes. The Catholic church established new orders, especially for women, and increased missionary activity overseas. Protestant women in Great Britain and the United States established Bible, missionary, and female reform societies by the hundreds. Chief among their concerns was prostitution, and many societies dedicated themselves to reforming "fallen women" and castigating men who visited prostitutes. As a pamphlet of the Boston Female Moral Reform Society explained, "Our mothers, our sisters, our daughters are sacrificed by the thousands every year on the altar of sin, and who are the agents in this work of destruction: Why, our fathers, our brothers, and our sons."

Catholics and Protestants alike promoted the temperance movement. In Ireland, England, the German states, and the United States, temperance societies organized to fight the "pestilence of hard liquor." The first societies had appeared in the United States as early as 1813, and by 1835 the American Temperance Society claimed 1.5 million members. The London-based British and Foreign Temperance Society, established in 1831, matched its American counterpart in its opposition to all alcohol. In the northern German states, temperance societies drew in the middle and working classes, Catholic as well as Protestant. Temperance advocates saw drunkenness as a sign of moral weakness and a threat to social order. Industrialists pointed to the loss of worker productivity, and efforts to promote temperance often reflected middle- and upper-class fears of the lower classes' lack of discipline. One German temperance advocate insisted, "One need not be a prophet to know that all efforts to combat the widespread and rapidly spreading pauperism will be unsuccessful as long as the common man fails to realize that the principal source of his degradation and misery is his fondness of drink." Yet temperance societies also attracted working-class people who shared the desire for respectability.

Education and Reform of the Poor.

Social reformers saw education as one of the main prospects for uplifting the poor and the working class. In addition to setting up Sunday schools, British churches founded organizations such as the National Society for the Education of the Poor in the Principles of the Established Church and the British and Foreign School Society. Most of these emphasized Bible reading. More secular in intent were the Mechanics Institutes, which provided education for workers in the big cities.

In 1833, the French government passed an education law that required every town to maintain a primary school, pay a teacher, and provide free education to poor boys. As the law's author, François Guizot, argued, "Ignorance renders the masses turbulent and ferocious." Girls' schools were optional, although hundreds of women taught at the primary level, most of them in private, often religious schools. Despite these efforts, only one out of every thirty children went to school in France, many fewer than in Protestant states such as Prussia, where 75 percent of children were in primary school by 1835. Popular education remained woefully undeveloped in most of eastern Europe. Peasants were specifically excluded from the few primary schools in Russia, where Tsar Nicholas I blamed the Decembrist Revolt of 1825 on education.

Above all else, the elite sought to impose discipline and order on working people. Popular sports, especially blood sports such as cockfighting and bearbaiting, suggested a lack of control, and long-standing efforts in Great Britain to eliminate these recreations now gained momentum through organizations such as the Society for the Prevention of Cruelty to Animals. By the end of the 1830s, bullbaiting had been abandoned in Great Britain. "This useful animal," rejoiced one reformer in 1839, "is no longer tortured amidst the exulting yells of those who are a disgrace to our common form and nature." The other blood sports died out more slowly, and efforts in other countries generally lagged behind those of the British.

When private charities failed to meet the needs of the poor, governments often intervened. Great Britain sought to control the costs of public welfare by passing a new poor law in 1834, called by its critics the "Starvation Act." The law required that all able-bodied persons receiving relief be housed together in workhouses, with husbands separated from wives and parents from children. Workhouse life was designed to be as unpleasant as possible so that poor people would move on to regions of higher employment. British women from all social classes organized anti–poor law societies to protest the separation of mothers from their children in the workhouses.

Domesticity and the Subordination of Women.

Many women viewed charitable work as the extension of their domestic roles: they promoted virtu-

The Limits of Charity
In this lithograph from 1844, the French artist Honoré Daumier shows a middle-class philanthropist refusing to give aid to a poor mother and her children. The caption below explains his refusal: "I'm sorry, my good woman, I cannot do anything for you. I am a member of the Society of Philanthropists of the Nord [a region in northern France]. . . . I only give to the poor of Kamchatka!" (that is, the faraway poor rather than those at home). Daumier spared no one in his satires, and in the early 1830s, the artist's political cartoons landed him in prison for six months. *(Robert D. Farber Archives and Special Collections Department, Brandeis University Libraries. Donated by Benjamin A. and Julia M. Trustman, 1959. Forms part of the Trustman Daumier Collection.)*

ous behavior and morality in their efforts to improve society. In one widely read advice book, Englishwoman Sarah Lewis suggested in 1839 that "women may be the prime agents in the regeneration of mankind." But women's social reform activities concealed a paradox. According to the ideology that historians call **domesticity**, women were to live their lives entirely within the domestic sphere, devoting themselves to their families and the home. The English poet Alfred, Lord Tennyson, captured this view in a popular poem published in 1847: "Man for the field and woman for the hearth;/ Man for the sword and for the needle she. . . . All else confusion." Many believed that

domesticity: An ideology prevailing in the nineteenth century that women should devote themselves to their families and the home.

maintaining proper and distinct roles for men and women was critically important to maintaining social order in general.

Most women had little hope of economic independence. The notion of a separate, domestic sphere for women prevented them from pursuing higher education, work in professional careers, or participation in politics through voting or holding office — all activities deemed appropriate only to men. Laws everywhere codified the subordination of women. Many countries followed the model of Napoleon's Civil Code, which classified married women as legal incompetents along with children, the insane, and criminals. In Great Britain, which had no national law code, the courts upheld the legality of a husband's complete control. For example, a court ruled in 1840 that "there can be no doubt of the general dominion which the law of England attributes to the husband over the wife." In some countries, such as France and Austria, unmarried women enjoyed some rights over property, but elsewhere laws explicitly defined them as perpetual minors under paternal control.

Distinctions between men and women were most noticeable in the privileged classes. Whereas boys attended secondary schools, most middle- and upper-class girls still received their education at home or in church schools, where they were taught to be religious, obedient, and accomplished in music and languages. As men's fashions turned practical — long trousers and short jackets of solid, often dark colors; no makeup (previously common for aristocratic men), and simply cut hair — women continued to dress for decorative effect, now with tightly corseted waists that emphasized the differences between female and male bodies. Middle- and upper-class women favored long hair that required hours of brushing and pinning up, and they wore long, cumbersome skirts. Advice books written by women detailed the tasks that such women undertook in the home: maintaining household accounts, supervising servants, and organizing social events.

Scientists reinforced stereotypes. Once considered sexually insatiable, women were now described as incapacitated by menstruation and largely uninterested in sex, an attitude that many equated with moral superiority. Thus was born the "Victorian" woman (the epoch gets its name from England's Queen Victoria — see page 684), a figment of the largely male medical imagination. Physicians and scholars considered women mentally inferior. In 1839, Auguste Comte, an influential early French sociologist, wrote, "As for any functions of government, the radical inaptitude of the female sex is there yet more marked . . . and limited to the guidance of the mere family."

Some women denounced the ideology of domesticity; according to the English writer Ann Lamb, for example, "the duty of a wife *means* the obedience of a Turkish slave." Middle-class women who did not marry, however, had few options for earning a living; they often worked as governesses or ladies' companions for the well-to-do. Most lower-class women worked because of financial necessity; as the wives of peasants, laborers, or shopkeepers, they had to supplement the family's meager income by working on the farm, in a factory, or in a shop. Domesticity might have been an ideal for them, but rarely was it a reality. Families crammed into small spaces had no time or energy for separate spheres.

Abuses and Reforms Overseas

Like the ideal of domesticity, the ideal of colonialism often conflicted with the reality of economic interests. In the first half of the nineteenth century, those economic interests changed as European colonialism underwent a subtle but momentous transformation. Colonialism became **imperialism** — a word coined only in the mid-nineteenth century — as Europeans turned their interest away from the plantation colonies of the Caribbean and toward new colonies in Asia and Africa. Whereas colonialism most often led to the establishment of settler colonies, direct rule by Europeans, the introduction of slave labor from Africa, and the wholesale destruction of indigenous peoples, imperialism usually meant more indirect forms of economic exploitation and political rule. Europeans still profited from their colonies, but now they also aimed to re-form colonial peoples in their own image — when it did not conflict too much with their economic interests to do so.

Abolition of Slavery. Colonialism — as opposed to imperialism — rose and fell with the enslavement of black Africans. British religious groups, especially the Quakers, had taken the lead in forming antislavery societies. The contradiction between calling for more liberty at home and maintaining slavery in the West Indies seemed intolerable to them. One English abolitionist put the

---

imperialism: European dominance of the non-West through economic exploitation and political rule; the word (as distinct from *colonialism*, which usually implied establishment of settler colonies, often with slavery) was coined in the mid-nineteenth century.

matter in these terms: "[God] has given to us an unexampled portion of civil liberty; and we in return drag his rational creatures into a most severe and perpetual bondage." Agitation by such groups as the London Society for Effecting the Abolition of the Slave Trade succeeded in gaining a first victory in 1807 when the British House of Lords voted to abolish the slave trade. The new Latin American republics abolished slavery in the 1820s and 1830s after they defeated the Spanish with armies that included many slaves. British missionary and evangelical groups continued to condemn the conquest, enslavement, and exploitation of native African populations and successfully blocked British annexations in central and southern Africa in the 1830s.

British reformers finally obtained the abolition of slavery in the British Empire in 1833. Antislavery petitions to Parliament bore 1.5 million signatures, including those of 350,000 women on one petition alone. In France, the new government of Louis-Philippe took strong measures against clandestine slave traffic, virtually ending French participation during the 1830s. Slavery was abolished in the remaining French Caribbean colonies in 1848.

Slavery did not disappear immediately just because the major European powers had given it up. The transatlantic trade in slaves actually reached its peak in the early 1840s. Human bondage continued unabated in Brazil, Cuba (still a Spanish colony), and the United States. Some American reformers supported abolition, but they remained a minority. Like serfdom in Russia, slavery in the Americas involved a quagmire of economic, political, and moral problems that worsened as the nineteenth century wore on.

Economic and Political Imperialism. Despite the abolition of slavery, Britain and France had not lost interest in overseas colonies. Using the pretext of an insult to its envoy, France invaded Algeria in 1830 and, after a long military campaign, established political control over most of the country in the next two decades. By 1848, more than seventy thousand French, Italian, and Maltese colonists had settled there with government encouragement, often confiscating the lands of native peoples. In that year, the French government officially incorporated Algeria as part of France. Eventually, the French embarked on a policy of assimilating the native population into French culture, but their efforts proved less than completely successful. France also imposed a protectorate government over the South Pacific island of Tahiti.

Although the British granted Canada greater self-determination in 1839, they extended their dominion elsewhere by annexing Singapore (1819), an island off the Malay peninsula, and New Zealand (1840). They also increased their control in India through the administration of the East India Company, a private group of merchants chartered by the British crown. The British educated a native elite to take over much of the day-to-day business of administering the country, and they used native soldiers to augment their military control. By 1850, only one in six soldiers serving Britain in India was European.

The East India Company also tried to establish a regular trade with China in opium, a drug long known for its medicinal uses but increasingly bought in China as a recreational drug. The Chinese government forbade Western merchants to

---

Opium Den in London (c. 1870)
This woodcut by Gustave Doré shows that opium smoking persisted in Britain at least to the 1870s. Doré was a French book illustrator who came to London in 1869–1871 and produced illustrations of the poorer neighborhoods in the city. His taste for the grotesque is apparent in the figures watching the smokers. *(The New York Public Library/Art Resource, NY.)*

venture outside the southern city of Guangzhou (Canton) and banned the import of opium, but these measures failed. Through smuggling Indian opium into China and bribing local officials, British traders built up a flourishing market, and by the mid-1830s they were pressuring the British government to force an expanded opium trade on the Chinese. When the Chinese authorities expelled British merchants from southern China in 1839, Britain retaliated by bombarding Chinese coastal cities. The **Opium War** ended in 1842, when Britain dictated to a defeated China the Treaty of Nanking, by which four more Chinese ports were opened to Europeans and the British took sovereignty over the island of Hong Kong, received a substantial war indemnity, and were assured of a continuation of the opium trade. In this case, reform took a backseat to economic interest, despite the complaints of religious groups in Britain.

The Opium War, 1839–1842

> **REVIEW:** How did reformers try to address the social problems created by industrialization and urbanization? In which areas did they succeed, and in which did they fail?

Ideologies and Political Movements

Although reform organizations grew rapidly in the 1830s and 1840s, many Europeans found them insufficient to answer the questions raised by industrialization and urbanization. How did the new social order differ from the earlier one, which was less urban and less driven by commercial concerns? Who should control this new order? Should governments try to moderate or accelerate the pace of change? New ideologies such as liberalism and socialism offered competing answers to these questions and provided the platform for new political movements. Established governments faced challenges not only from liberals and socialists but

---

Opium War: War between China and Great Britain (1839–1842) that resulted in the opening of four Chinese ports to Europeans and British sovereignty over Hong Kong.

also from the most potent of the new doctrines, nationalism. Nationalists looked past social problems to concentrate on achieving political autonomy and self-determination for groups identified by ethnicity rather than by class.

The Spell of Nationalism

According to the doctrine of **nationalism**, all peoples derive their identities from their nations, which are defined by common language, shared cultural traditions, and sometimes religion. When such nations do not coincide with state boundaries, nationalism can produce violence and warfare as different national groups compete for control over territory (Map 21.3).

Nationalist aspirations were especially explosive for the Austrian Empire, which included a variety of peoples united only by their enforced allegiance to the Habsburg emperor. The empire included three main national groups: the Germans, who made up one-fourth of the population; the Magyars of Hungary (which included Transylvania and Croatia); and the Slavs, who together formed the largest group in the population but were divided into different ethnic groups such as Poles, Czechs, Croats, and Serbs. The Austrian Empire also included Italians in Lombardy and Venetia, and Romanians in Transylvania. Efforts to govern such diverse peoples preoccupied Prince Klemens von Metternich, chief minister to the weak Habsburg emperor Francis I (r. 1792–1835). Metternich's domestic policy aimed to restrain nationalist impulses, and it largely succeeded until the 1840s. He set up a secret police organization on the Napoleonic model that opened letters of even the highest officials. Censorship in the Italian provinces was so strict that even the works of Dante were expurgated. Metternich announced that "the Lombards must forget that they are Italians."

Metternich's policies forced the leading Italian nationalist, **Giuseppe Mazzini** (1805–1872), into exile in France in 1831. There Mazzini founded Young Italy, a secret society that attracted thousands with its message that Italy would touch off a European-wide revolutionary movement. The conservative order throughout Europe felt threatened by Mazzini's charismatic leadership and conspiratorial scheming, but he lacked both European allies against Austria and widespread support among the Italian masses.

Since so many different ethnic groups lived within the borders of the Austrian Empire, neither the emperor nor Metternich favored aspirations for German unification. Economic unification in the German states nonetheless took a step forward with the foundation in 1834, under Prussian leadership, of the *Zollverein*, or "customs union." Austria was not part of the Zollverein. German nationalists sought a government uniting German-speaking peoples, but they could not agree on its boundaries: Would the unified German state include both Prussia and the Austrian Empire? If it included Austria, what about the non-German territories of the Austrian Empire? And could the powerful, conservative kingdom of Prussia coexist in a unified German state with other, more liberal but smaller states? These questions would vex German history for decades to come.

Polish nationalism became more self-conscious after the collapse of the revolt in 1830 against Russian domination. Ten thousand Poles, mostly noble army officers and intellectuals, fled Poland in 1830 and 1831. Most of them took up residence in western European capitals, especially Paris, where they mounted a successful public relations campaign for worldwide support. Their intellectual hero was the poet Adam Mickiewicz (1798–1855), whose mystical writings portrayed the Polish exiles as martyrs of a crucified nation with an international Christian mission: "Your endeavors are for all men, not only for yourselves. You will achieve a new Christian civilization."

Mickiewicz formed the Polish Legion to fight for national restoration, but rivalries and divisions among the Polish nationalists prevented united action until 1846, when Polish exiles in Paris tried to launch a coordinated insurrection for Polish independence. Plans for an uprising in the Polish province of Galicia in the Austrian Empire collapsed when peasants instead revolted against their noble Polish masters. Slaughtering some two thousand aristocrats, a desperate rural population served the Austrian government's end by defusing the nationalist challenge. Class interests and national identity were not always the same.

In Russia, nationalism took the form of opposition to Western ideas. Russian nationalists, or Slavophiles (lovers of the Slavs), opposed the Westernizers, who wanted Russia to follow Western models of industrial development and constitutional government. The Slavophiles favored main-

---

nationalism: An ideology that arose in the nineteenth century and that holds that all peoples derive their identities from their nations, which are defined by common language, shared cultural traditions, and sometimes religion.

Giuseppe Mazzini: An Italian nationalist (1805–1872) who founded Young Italy, a secret society to promote Italian unity. He believed that a popular uprising would create a unified Italy.

MAP 21.3 Languages of Nineteenth-Century Europe

Even this detailed map of linguistic diversity understates the number of different languages and dialects spoken in Europe. In Italy, for example, few people spoke Italian as their first language. Instead, they spoke local dialects such as Piedmontese or Ligurian, and some might speak better French than Italian if they came from the regions bordering France. ■ How does the map underline the inherent contradictions of nationalism in Europe? What were consequences of linguistic diversity within national borders? Keep in mind that even in Spain, France, and Great Britain, linguistic diversity continued right up to the beginning of the 1900s.

taining rural traditions infused by the values of the Russian Orthodox church. Only a return to Russia's basic historical principles, they argued, could protect the country against the corrosion of rationalism and materialism. Slavophiles sometimes criticized the regime, however, because they believed the state exerted too much power over the church. The conflict between Slavophiles and Westernizers has continued to shape Russian cultural and intellectual life to the present day.

The most significant nationalist movement in western Europe could be found in Ireland. The Irish had struggled for centuries against English occupation, but Irish nationalists developed strong

organizations only in the 1840s. In 1842, a group of writers founded the Young Ireland movement, which aimed to recover Irish traditions and preserve the Gaelic language (spoken by at least one-third of the peasantry). Daniel O'Connell (1775–1847), a Catholic lawyer and landowner who sat in the British House of Commons, hoped to force the British Parliament to repeal the Act of Union of 1801, which had made Ireland part of Great Britain. In 1843, London newspapers reported "monster meetings" that drew crowds of as many as 300,000 people in support of repeal of the union. In response, the British government arrested O'Connell and convicted him of conspiracy.

Although his sentence was overturned, O'Connell withdrew from politics, partly because of a terminal brain disease. More radical leaders, who preached insurrection against the English, replaced him.

Liberalism in Economics and Politics

As an ideology, **liberalism** traced its origins to the writings of John Locke in the seventeenth century and the Enlightenment philosophy in the eighteenth. The adherents of liberalism defined themselves in opposition to conservatives on one end of the political spectrum and revolutionaries on the other. Unlike conservatives, liberals supported the Enlightenment ideals of constitutional guarantees of personal liberty and free trade in economics, believing that greater liberty in politics and economic matters would promote social improvement and economic growth. For that reason, they also generally applauded the social and economic changes produced by the Industrial Revolution, while opposing the violence and excessive state power promoted by the French Revolution. The leaders of the rapidly expanding middle class composed of manufacturers, merchants, and professionals favored liberalism.

British Liberalism. The rapid industrialization and urbanization of Great Britain created a receptive environment for liberalism. Its foremost proponent in the early nineteenth century was the philosopher and jurist Jeremy Bentham (1748–1832). He called his brand of liberalism utilitarianism because he held that the best policy is the one that produces "the greatest good for the greatest number" and is thus the most useful, or utilitarian. Bentham's criticisms spared no institution; he railed against the injustices of the British parliamentary process, the abuses of the prisons and the penal code, and the educational system. In his zeal for social engineering, Bentham proposed elaborate schemes for managing the poor and model prisons that would emphasize rehabilitation through close supervision rather than corporal punishment. British liberals like Bentham wanted government involvement, including deregulation of trade, but they shied away from any association with revolutionary violence.

British liberals wanted government to limit its economic role to maintaining the currency, enforcing contracts, and financing major enterprises like the military and the railroads. As historian and member of Parliament Thomas Macaulay (1800–1859) explained in 1830:

> Our rulers will best promote the improvement of the nation by strictly confining themselves to their own legitimate duties, by leaving capital to find its most lucrative course, commodities their fair price, industry and intelligence their natural reward, idleness and folly their natural punishment, by maintaining peace, by defending property, by diminishing the price of law, and by observing strict economy in every department of the State.

British liberals sought to lower or eliminate British tariffs, especially through repeal of the **Corn Laws**, which benefited landowners by preventing the import of cheap foreign grain. When landholders in the House of Commons thwarted efforts to lower grain tariffs, two Manchester cotton manufacturers set up the Anti–Corn Law League. The league appealed to the middle class against the landlords, who were labeled "a bread-taxing oligarchy" and "blood-sucking vampires," and attracted working-class backing by promising lower food prices. League members established local branches, published newspapers and the journal *The Economist* (founded in 1843 and now one of the world's most influential periodicals), and campaigned in elections. They eventually won the support of the Tory prime minister Sir Robert Peel, whose government repealed the Corn Laws in 1846.

Liberalism on the Continent. Free trade had less appeal in continental Europe than in England because continental industries needed protection against British industrial dominance. As a consequence, liberals on the continent focused on constitutional reform. French liberals, for example, agitated for greater press freedoms and a broadening of the vote. Louis-Philippe's government brutally repressed working-class and republican insurrections in Lyon and Paris in the early 1830s and forced the republican opposition underground. The French king's increasingly restrictive governments also thwarted liberals' hopes for reforms by suppressing many political organizations and reestablishing censorship.

Repression muted criticism in most other European states as well. Nevertheless, liberal reform movements grew up in pockets of industrializa-

---

liberalism: An economic and political ideology that emphasized free trade and the constitutional guarantees of individual rights such as freedom of speech and religion.

Corn Laws: Tariffs on grain in Great Britain that benefited landowners by preventing the import of cheap foreign grain; they were repealed by the British government in 1846.

tion in Prussia, the smaller German states, and the Austrian Empire. Some state bureaucrats, especially university-trained middle-class officials, favored economic liberalism. Hungarian count Stephen Széchenyi (1791–1860) personally campaigned for the introduction of British-style changes. He introduced British agricultural techniques on his own lands, helped start up steamboat traffic on the Danube, encouraged the importation of machinery and technicians for steam-driven textile factories, and pushed the construction of Hungary's first railway line, from Budapest to Vienna.

In the 1840s, however, Széchenyi's efforts paled before those of the flamboyant Magyar nationalist Lajos Kossuth (1802–1894). After spending four years in prison for sedition, Kossuth grabbed every opportunity to publicize American democracy and British political liberalism, all in a fervent nationalist spirit. In 1844, he founded the Protective Association, whose members bought only Hungarian products; to Kossuth, boycotting Austrian goods was crucial to ending "colonial dependence" on Austria. Born of a lesser landowning family without a noble title, Kossuth did not hesitate to attack "the cowardly selfishness of the landowner class."

Even in Russia, signs of liberal opposition appeared in the 1830s and 1840s. Small circles of young noblemen serving in the army or bureaucracy met in cities, especially Moscow, to discuss the latest Western ideas and to criticize the Russian state: "The world is undergoing a transformation, while we vegetate in our hovels of wood and clay," wrote one. Out of these groups came such future revolutionaries as Alexander Herzen (1812–1870), described by the police as "a daring free-thinker, extremely dangerous to society." Tsar Nicholas I (r. 1825–1855) banned Western liberal writings as well as all books about the United States. He sent nearly ten thousand people a year into exile in Siberia as punishment for their political activities.

Socialism and the Early Labor Movement

The newest ideology, **socialism**, took up where liberalism left off: socialists believed that the liberties advocated by liberals benefited only the middle class—the owners of factories and businesses—not the workers. They sought to reorganize society totally rather than to reform it piecemeal through political measures. They envisioned a future society in which workers would share a harmonious, cooperative, and prosperous life. Building on the theoretical and practical ideas laid out in the early nineteenth century by thinkers and reformers such as Count Henri de Saint-Simon, Charles Fourier, and Robert Owen, the socialists of the 1830s and 1840s hoped that economic planning and working-class organization would solve the problems caused by industrial growth, including the threat of increasingly mechanical, unfeeling social relations.

Origins of Socialism. Early socialists criticized the emerging Industrial Revolution for dividing society into two classes: the new middle class, or capitalists (who owned the wealth), and the working class, their downtrodden and impoverished employees. As their name suggests, the socialists aimed to restore harmony and cooperation through social reorganization. Robert Owen (1771–1858), a successful Welsh-born manufacturer, founded British socialism. In 1800, he bought a cotton mill in New Lanark, Scotland, and began to set up a model factory town, where workers labored only ten hours a day (instead of seventeen, as was common) and children between the ages of five and ten attended school rather than working. To put his principles once more into action, Owen moved to the United States in the 1820s and founded a community named New Harmony in Indiana. The experiment collapsed after three years, a victim of internal squabbling. But out of Owen's experiments and writings, such as *The Book of the New Moral World* (1820), would come the movement for producer cooperatives (businesses owned and controlled by their workers), consumers' cooperatives (stores in which consumers owned shares), and a national trade union.

Claude Henri de Saint-Simon (1760–1825) and Charles Fourier (1772–1837) were Owen's counterparts in France. Saint-Simon was a noble who had served as an officer in the War of American Independence and lost a fortune speculating in national property during the French Revolution. Fourier traveled as a salesman for a Lyon cloth merchant. Both shared Owen's alarm about the effects of industrialization on social relations. Saint-Simon—who coined the terms *industrialism* and *industrialist* to define the new economic order and its chief animators—believed that work was the central element in the new society and that

---

socialism: A social and political ideology that advocated the reorganization of society to overcome the new tensions created by industrialization and restore social harmony through communities based on cooperation.

it should be controlled not by politicians but by scientists, engineers, artists, and industrialists themselves. To correct the abuses of the new industrial order, Fourier urged the establishment of communities that were part garden city and part agricultural commune; all jobs would be rotated to maximize happiness. Fourier hoped that a network of small, decentralized communities would replace the state.

Socialism and Women. The emancipation of women was essential to Fourier's vision of a harmonious community: "The extension of the privileges of women is the fundamental cause of all social progress." After Saint-Simon's death in 1825, some of his followers established a quasi-religious cult with elaborate rituals and a "he-pope" and "she-pope," or ruling father and mother. Saint-Simonians lived and worked together in cooperative arrangements and scandalized some by advocating free love. They set up branches in the United States and Egypt. In 1832, some Saint-Simonian women founded a feminist newspaper, *The Free Woman*, asserting that "with the emancipation of woman will come the emancipation of the worker."

In Great Britain, many women joined the Owenites and helped form cooperative societies and unions. They defended women's working-class organizations against the complaints of men in the new societies and trade unions. As one woman wrote, "Do not say the unions are only for men. . . . 'Tis a wrong impression, forced on our minds to keep us slaves!" As women became more active, Owenites agitated for women's rights, marriage reform, and popular education. The French activist Flora Tristan (1801–1844) devoted herself to reconciling the interests of male and female workers. She had seen the "frightful reality" of London's poverty and made a reputation reporting on British working conditions. Tristan published a stream of books and pamphlets urging male workers to address women's unequal status, arguing that "the emancipation of male workers is *impossible* so long as women remain in a degraded state."

Collectivists and Communists. Even though most male socialists ignored Tristan's plea for women's participation, they did strive to create working-class associations. The French socialist Louis Blanc (1811–1882) explained the importance of working-class associations in his book *Organization of Labor* (1840), which deeply influenced the French labor movement. Similarly, Pierre-Joseph Proudhon (1809–1865) urged workers to form producers' associations so that the workers could control the work process and eliminate profits made by capitalists. His 1840 book *What Is Property?* argues that property is theft: labor alone is productive, and rent, interest, and profit unjust.

After 1840, some socialists began to call themselves **communists**, emphasizing their desire to replace private property by communal, collective ownership. The Frenchman Étienne Cabet (1788–1856) was the first to use the word *communist*. In 1840, he published *Travels in Icaria*, a novel describing a communist utopia in which a popularly elected dictatorship efficiently organized work, reduced the workday to seven hours, and made work tasks "short, easy, and attractive."

Out of the churning of socialist ideas of the 1840s emerged two men whose collaboration would change the definition of socialism and remake it into an ideology that would shake the world for the next 150 years. Karl Marx (1818–1883) had studied philosophy at the University of Berlin, edited a liberal newspaper until the Prussian government suppressed it, and then left for Paris, where he met Friedrich Engels (1820–1895). While working in the offices of his wealthy family's cotton manufacturing interests in Manchester, England, Engels had been shocked into writing *The Condition of the Working Class in England in 1844* (1845), a sympathetic depiction of industrial workers' dismal lives. In Paris, where German and eastern European intellectuals could pursue their political interests more freely than at home, Marx and Engels organized the Communist League, in whose name they published *The Communist Manifesto* in 1848 (see Document, "Marx and Engels," page 677). It eventually became the touchstone of Marxist and communist revolution all over the world. Communists, the *Manifesto* declared, must aim for "the downfall of the bourgeoisie [capitalist class] and the ascendancy of the proletariat [working class], the abolition of the old society based on class conflicts and the foundation of a new society without classes and without private property." Marx and Engels embraced industrialization because they believed it would eventually bring on the proletarian revolution and thus lead inevitably to the abolition of exploitation, private property, and class society.

Working-Class Organization. Socialism accompanied, and in some places incited, an upsurge in

---

communists: Those socialists who after 1840 (when the word was first used) advocated the abolition of private property in favor of communal, collective ownership.

DOCUMENT

Marx and Engels, *The Communist Manifesto*

Karl Marx (1818–1883) and Friedrich Engels (1820–1895) were both sons of prosperous German-Jewish families that had converted to Christianity. In the manifesto for the Communist League, they laid out many of the central principles that would guide Marxist revolution in the future: they insisted that all history is shaped by class struggle and that in future revolutions the working class would overthrow the bourgeoisie, or middle class, and replace capitalism and private property with a communist state in which all property is collectively rather than individually owned. As this selection shows, Marx and Engels always placed more emphasis on class struggle than on the state that would result from the ensuing revolution.

The history of all hitherto existing society is the history of class struggles.

Freeman and slave, patrician and plebeian, lord and serf, guild-master and journeyman, in a word, oppressor and oppressed, stood in constant opposition to one another, carried on an uninterrupted, now hidden, now open fight, a fight that each time ended, either in a revolutionary reconstitution of society at large, or in the common ruin of the contending classes. . . .

The modern bourgeois society that has sprouted from the ruins of feudal society has not done away with class antagonisms. It has but established new classes, new conditions of oppression, new forms of struggle in place of the old ones.

Our epoch, the epoch of the bourgeoisie, possesses, however, this distinctive feature: It has simplified the class antagonisms: Society as a whole is more and more splitting up into two great hostile camps, into two great classes directly facing each other: Bourgeoisie [middle class] and Proletariat [working class]. . . .

The weapons with which the bourgeoisie felled feudalism to the ground are now turned against the bourgeoisie itself.

But not only has the bourgeoisie forged the weapons that bring death to itself; it has also called into existence the men who are to wield those weapons— the modern working class—the proletarians. . . .

The essential condition for the existence, and for the sway of the bourgeois class, is the formation and augmentation of capital; the condition for capital is wage-labour. Wage-labour rests exclusively on competition between labourers. The advance of industry, whose involuntary promoter is the bourgeoisie, replaces the isolation of the labourers, due to competition, by their revolutionary combination, due to association. The development of Modern Industry, therefore, cuts from under its feet the very foundation on which the bourgeoisie produces and appropriates products. What the bourgeoisie, therefore, produces, above all, is its own gravediggers. Its fall and the victory of the proletariat are equally inevitable.

Source: Karl Marx and Friedrich Engels, *The Communist Manifesto.* Translated by Samuel Moore (New York: Penguin, 1985), 79–80, 87, 93–94.

---

working-class organization in western Europe. British workers founded cooperative societies, local trade unions, and so-called friendly societies for mutual aid—all of which frightened the middle classes. A newspaper exclaimed in 1834, "The trade unions are, we have no doubt, the most dangerous institutions that were ever permitted to take root."

Many British workers joined in **Chartism**, which aimed to transform Britain into a democracy. In 1838, political radicals drew up the People's Charter, which demanded universal manhood suffrage, vote by secret ballot, equal electoral districts, annual elections, and the elimination of property qualifications for and the payment of stipends to members of Parliament. Chartists denounced their opponents as seeking "to keep the people in social slavery and political degradation." Many women took part by founding female political unions, setting up Chartist Sunday schools, organizing boycotts of unsympathetic shopkeepers, and joining Chartist temperance associations. Nevertheless, the People's Charter refrained from calling for woman suffrage because the movement's leaders feared that doing so would alienate potential supporters.

The Chartists organized a massive campaign during 1838 and 1839, with large public meetings, fiery speeches, and torchlight parades. Presented with petitions for the People's Charter signed by more than a million people, the House of Commons refused to act. In response to this rebuff from middle-class liberals, the Chartists allied themselves in the 1840s with working-class strike movements in the manufacturing districts and associated with various European revolutionary movements. But at the same time they—like their British and continental allies—distanced themselves from women workers.

Chartism: The British movement of supporters of the People's Charter (1838), which demanded universal manhood suffrage, vote by secret ballot, equal electoral districts, and other reforms.

Continental workers were less well organized because trade unions and strikes were illegal everywhere except Great Britain. Nevertheless, artisans and skilled workers in France formed mutual aid societies that provided insurance, death benefits, and education. Workers in new factories rarely organized, but artisans in the old trades, such as the silk workers of Lyon, France, created societies to resist mechanization and wage cuts. In eastern and central Europe socialism and labor organization—like liberalism—had less impact than in western Europe. Cooperative societies and workers' newspapers did not appear in the German states until 1848.

REVIEW: Why did ideologies have such a powerful appeal in the 1830s and 1840s?

The Revolutions of 1848

Food shortages, overpopulation, and unemployment helped turn ideological turmoil into revolution. In 1848, demonstrations and uprisings toppled governments, forced rulers and ministers to flee, and offered revolutionaries an opportunity to put liberal, socialist, and nationalist ideals into practice (Map 21.4). In the end, however, all the revolutions failed because the various ideological movements quarreled, leaving an opening for rulers and their armies to return to power.

The Hungry Forties

Beginning in 1845, crop failures across Europe caused food prices to shoot skyward. In the best of times, urban workers paid 50 to 80 percent of their income for a diet consisting largely of bread; now even bread was beyond their means. Overpopulation hastened famine in some places, especially Ireland, where blight destroyed the staple crop, potatoes, first in 1846 and again in 1848 and 1851. Irish peasants had planted potatoes because a family of four might live off one acre of potatoes but would require at least two acres of grain. The Irish often sought security in large families, trusting that their children might help work the land and care for them in old age. By the 1840s, Ireland was especially vulnerable to the potato blight. Out of a population of eight million, as many as one million people died of starvation or disease. Corpses lay unburied on the sides of roads, and whole families were found dead in their cottages, half-eaten by dogs. Hundreds of thousands emigrated to England, the United States, and Canada.

The Irish Famine
Contemporary depictions such as this one from 1847 drew attention to the plight of the Irish peasants when a blight infected potato plants, destroying the single most important staple crop. In this illustration, a girl turns up the ground looking for potatoes while a starving boy looks dazed. The artist reported seeing six dead bodies nearby. *(The Granger Collection, New York.)*

Throughout Europe, famine jeopardized social peace. In age-old fashion, rumors circulated about large farmers hoarding grain to drive up prices. Believing that governments should ensure fair prices, crowds took to the streets to protest, often attacking markets or bakeries. They threatened officials with retribution. "If the grain merchants do not cease to take away grains . . . we will go to your homes and cut your throats and those of the three bakers . . . and burn the whole place down." So went one threat from French villagers in the hungry winter of 1847. Although harvests improved in 1848, by then many people had lost their land or become hopelessly indebted.

High food prices also drove down the demand for manufactured goods, resulting in increased unemployment. Industrial workers' wages had been rising—in the German states, for example, wages rose an average of 5.5 percent in the 1830s and 10.5 percent in the 1840s—but the cost of living rose about 16 percent each decade, canceling out wage increases. Seasonal work and regular unemployment were already the norm when the crisis of the late 1840s exacerbated the uncertainties of urban life. "The most miserable class that ever sneaked its way into history" is how Friedrich Engels described underemployed and starving workers in 1847.

Another French Revolution

The specter of hunger amplified the voices criticizing established rulers. A Parisian demonstration in favor of reform turned violent on February 23, 1848, when panicky soldiers opened fire on the crowd, killing forty or fifty demonstrators. The next day, faced with fifteen hundred barricades and a furious populace, King Louis-Philippe abdicated and fled to England. A hastily formed provisional government declared France a republic once again.

The new republican government issued liberal reforms—an end to the death penalty for political crimes, the abolition of slavery in the colonies, and freedom of the press—and agreed to introduce universal adult male suffrage despite misgivings about political participation by peasants and unemployed workers. The government allowed Paris officials to organize a system of "national workshops" to provide the unemployed with construction work. When women protested their exclusion, the city set up a few workshops for women workers, albeit with wages lower than men's. To meet a mounting deficit, the provisional government then levied a 45 percent surtax on property taxes, alienating peasants and landowners.

While peasants grumbled, scores of newspapers and political clubs inspired grassroots democratic fervor in Paris and other cities; meeting in concert halls, theaters, and government auditoriums, clubs became a regular evening attraction for the citizenry. Women also formed clubs, published women's newspapers, and demanded representation in national politics.

This street-corner activism alarmed middle-class liberals and conservatives. To ensure its control, the republican government paid some unemployed youths to join a mobile guard with its own uniforms and barracks. Tension between the government and the workers in the national workshops rose. Faced with rising radicalism in Paris and other big cities, the voters elected a largely conservative National Assembly in April 1848; most of the deputies chosen were middle-class professionals or landowners, who favored either a restoration

MAP 21.4 The Revolutions of 1848

The attempts of rulers to hold back the forces of change collapsed suddenly in 1848 when once again the French staged a revolution that inspired many others in Europe. This time, cities all over central and eastern Europe joined in as the spirit of revolt inflamed one capital after another. Although all of these revolutions eventually failed because of social and political divisions, the sheer scale of rebellion forced rulers to reconsider their policies.

of the monarchy or a moderate republic. The Assembly immediately appointed a five-man executive committee to run the government and pointedly excluded known supporters of workers' rights. Suspicious of all demands for rapid change, the deputies dismissed a petition to restore divorce and voted down women's suffrage, 899 to 1. When the numbers enrolled in the national workshops in Paris rocketed from a predicted 10,000 to 110,000, the government ordered the workshops closed to new workers, and on June 21 it directed that those already enrolled move to the provinces or join the army.

The workers exploded in anger. In the June Days, as the following week came to be called, the government summoned the army, the National Guard, and the newly recruited mobile guard to fight the workers. Alexis de Tocqueville (see Document, "Alexis de Tocqueville Describes the June Days in Paris (1848)," page 681) breathed a sigh of relief: "The Red Republic [red being associated

The Vésuviennes, 1848
This lithograph satirizes women's political ambitions, referring to a women's club named the Vésuviennes. The artist implies that women have left their children at home in the care of their hapless husbands so that they can actively participate in politics. Meetings of feminist clubs were often disrupted by men hostile to their aims. Can you compare the depiction of women in this lithograph to earlier depictions of women in the French Revolution of 1789 in Chapter 19? *(Bibliothèque nationale de France.)*

with demands for socialism] is lost forever; all France has joined against it. The National Guard, citizens, and peasants from the remotest parts of the country have come pouring in." The government forces crushed the workers; more than 10,000, most of them workers, were killed or injured, 12,000 were arrested, and 4,000 eventually were convicted and deported.

After the National Assembly adopted a new constitution calling for a presidential election in which all adult men could vote, the electorate chose **Louis-Napoleon Bonaparte** (1808–1873), nephew of the dead emperor. Bonaparte got more than 5.5 million votes out of some 7.4

Louis-Napoleon Bonaparte (1808–1873): Nephew of Napoleon I; he was elected president of France in 1848, declared himself Emperor Napoleon III in 1852, and ruled until 1870.

million cast. He had lived most of his life outside of France, and the leaders of the republic expected him to follow their tune. In uncertain times, the Bonaparte name promised something to everyone. Even many workers supported him because he had no connection with the blood-drenched June Days.

In reality, Bonaparte's election spelled the end of the Second Republic, just as his uncle had dismantled the first one established in 1792. In 1852, on the forty-eighth anniversary of Napoleon I's coronation as emperor, Louis-Napoleon declared himself Emperor Napoleon III, thus inaugurating the Second Empire. (Napoleon I's son died and never became Napoleon II, but Napoleon III wanted to create a sense of legitimacy and so used the Roman numeral III.) Political division and class conflict had proved fatal to the Second Republic. Although the revolution of 1848 never had a period of terror like that in 1793–1794, it nonetheless ended in similar fashion, with an authoritarian government that tried to play monarchists and republicans off against each other.

Nationalist Revolution in Italy

In January 1848, a revolt broke out in Palermo, Sicily, against the Bourbon ruler. Then came the electrifying news of the February revolution in Paris. In Milan, a huge nationalist demonstration quickly degenerated into battles between Austrian forces and armed demonstrators. In Venice, an uprising drove out the Austrians. Peasants in the south occupied large landowners' estates. Across central Italy, revolts mobilized the poor and unemployed against local rulers. Peasants demanded more land, and artisans and workers called for higher wages, restrictions on the use of machinery, and unemployment relief.

But class divisions and regional differences stood in the way of national unity. Property owners, businessmen, and professionals wanted liberal reforms and national unification under a conservative regime; intellectuals, workers, and artisans dreamed of democracy and social reforms. Some nationalists favored a loose federation; others wanted a monarchy under Charles Albert of Piedmont-Sardinia; still others urged rule by the pope; a few shared Mazzini's vision of a republic with a strong central govern-

The Divisions of Italy, 1848

Under Austrian control

Lombardy
Piedmont
Venetia
PAPAL STATES
Corsica (Fr.)
PIEDMONT-SARDINIA
Rome
Naples
Sardinia
KINGDOM OF THE TWO SICILIES
Sicily

0   100   200 miles
0 100 200 kilometers

DOCUMENT

Alexis de Tocqueville Describes the June Days in Paris (1848)

Alexis de Tocqueville (1805–1859) was a noble landowner, well-known writer, and deputy in the National Assembly elected in April 1848. As a political liberal, he supported the new republican government against the uprising of workers in the National Workshops. His description of the June Days comes from a memoir he wrote in 1850 about the events of the 1848 revolution. Although a fierce opponent of socialism, Tocqueville detected class struggle in the insurrection.

Now at last I have come to that insurrection in June which was the greatest and the strangest that had ever taken place in our history, or perhaps in that of any other nation: the greatest because for four days more than a hundred thousand men took part in it, and there were five generals killed; the strangest, because the insurgents were fighting without a battle cry, leaders, or flag, and yet they showed wonderful powers of co-ordination and a military expertise that astonished the most experienced officers.

Another point that distinguished it from all other events of the same type during the last sixty years was that its object was not to change the form of the government, but to alter the organization of so-ciety. In truth it was not a political strug-gle (in the sense in which we have used the word "political" up to now), but a class struggle, a sort of "Servile War." It stood in the same relation to the facts of the Feb-ruary Revolution as the theory of social-ism stood to its ideas; or rather it sprang naturally from those ideas, as a son from his mother; and one should not see it only as a brutal and blind, but as a powerful ef-fort of the workers to escape from the ne-cessities of their condition, which had been depicted to them as an illegitimate depression, and by the sword to open up a road towards that imaginary well-being that had been shown to them in the dis-tance as a right. It was this mixture of greedy desires and false theories that en-gendered the insurrection and made it so formidable. These poor people had been assured that the goods of the wealthy were in some way the result of a theft commit-ted against themselves. They had been as-sured that inequalities of fortune were as much opposed to morality and the inter-ests of society, as to nature. This obscure and mistaken conception of right, com-bined with brute force, imparted to it an energy, tenacity and strength it would never have had on its own.

One should note, too, that this ter-rible insurrection was not the work of a cer-tain number of conspirators, but was the revolt of one whole section of the popu-lation against another. The women took as much part in it as the men. While the men fought, the women got the ammunition ready and brought it up. And when in the end they had to surrender, the women were the last to yield. . . .

Down all the roads not held by the insurgents, thousands of men were pour-ing in from all parts of France to aid us. Thanks to the railways, those from fifty leagues [150 miles] off were already arriv-ing, although the fighting had begun only in the evening of the previous day. The next day and the days following, they were to arrive from one and two hundred leagues [300–600 miles] away. These men were drawn without distinction from all classes of society; among them there were great numbers of peasants, bourgeois, large landowners and nobles, all jumbled up together in the same ranks.

Source: Alexis de Tocqueville, *Recollections*, ed. J. P. Mayer and A. P. Kerr, trans. George Lawrence (Garden City, NY: Doubleday, 1970), 136–137, 152.

ment. Many leaders of national unification spoke standard Italian only as a second language; most Italians spoke regional dialects.

As king of the most powerful Italian state, Charles Albert (r. 1831–1849) inevitably played a central role. After some hesitation caused by fears of French intervention, he led a military campaign against Austria. It soon failed, partly because of dissension over goals and tactics among the na-tionalists. Although Austrian troops defeated Charles Albert in the north in the summer of 1848, democratic and nationalist forces prevailed at first in the south. In the fall, the Romans drove the pope from the city and declared Rome a republic. For the next few months, republican leaders, such as Giuseppe Mazzini and Giuseppe Garibaldi (1807–1882), congregated in Rome to organize the new republic. These efforts eventually faltered when foreign powers intervened. The new presi-dent of republican France, Louis-Napoleon Bona-parte, sent an expeditionary force to secure the papal throne for Pius IX. Mazzini and Garibaldi fled. Although revolution had been defeated in Italy, the memory of the Roman republic and the commitment to unification remained, and they would soon emerge again with new force.

Revolt and Reaction in Central Europe

News of the revolution in Paris also provoked pop-ular demonstrations in central and eastern Europe. When the Prussian army tried to push back a

Uprising in Milan, 1848
In this painting by an unknown artist, *Fighting at the Tosa Gate*, the Milanese are setting up barricades to oppose their Austrian rulers. Whole families are involved. The flag of green, white, and red is the flag of the Cisalpine Republic of the Napoleonic period, whose capital was Milan. The three colors would be incorporated into the national flag of Italy after unification. *(Scala/Art Resource, NY.)*

crowd gathered in front of Berlin's royal palace on March 18, 1848, their actions provoked panic and street fighting. The next day the crowd paraded wagons loaded with dead bodies under King Frederick William IV's window, forcing him to salute the victims killed by his own army. In a state of near collapse, the king promised to call an assembly to draft a constitution and adopted the German nationalist flag of black, red, and gold.

The goal of German unification soon took precedence over social reform or constitutional changes within the separate states. In March and April, most of the German states agreed to elect delegates to a federal parliament at Frankfurt that would attempt to unite Germany. Local princes and even the more powerful kings of Prussia and Bavaria seemed to totter. Yet the revolutionaries' weaknesses soon became apparent. The eight hundred delegates to the Frankfurt parliament had little practical political experience and no access to an army. Unemployed artisans and workers smashed machines; peasants burned landlords' records and occasionally attacked Jewish moneylenders; women set up clubs and newspapers to demand their emancipation from "perfumed slavery."

The advantage lay with the princes, who bided their time. While the Frankfurt parliament laboriously prepared a liberal constitution for a united Germany—one that denied self-determination to

Czechs, Poles, and Danes within its proposed German borders—the Prussian king Frederick William IV (r. 1840–1860) recovered his confidence. First, his army crushed the revolution in Berlin in the fall of 1848. Prussian troops then intervened to help other local rulers put down the last wave of democratic and nationalist insurrections in the spring of 1849. When the Frankfurt parliament finally concluded its work, offering the emperorship of a constitutional, federal Germany to the king of Prussia, Frederick William contemptuously refused this "crown from the gutter."

Events followed a similar course in the Austrian Empire. Just as Italians were driving the Austrians out of their lands in northern Italy and Magyar nationalists were demanding political autonomy for Hungary, on March 13, 1848, in Vienna, a student-led demonstration for political reform turned into rioting, looting, and machine breaking. Metternich resigned, escaping to England in disguise. Emperor Ferdinand promised a constitution, an elected parliament, and the end of censorship. The beleaguered authorities in Vienna could not refuse Magyar demands for home rule, and Széchenyi and Kossuth both became ministers in the new Hungarian government. The Magyars were the largest ethnic group in Hungary but still did not make up 50 percent of the population, which included Croats, Romanians, Slovaks, and

Revolution of 1848 in Eastern Europe
This painting by an unknown artist shows Ana Ipatescu leading a group of Romanian revolutionaries in Transylvania in opposition to Russian rule. In April 1848, local landowners began to organize meetings. Paris-educated nationalists spearheaded the movement, which demanded the end of Russian control and various legal and political reforms. By August, the movement had split between those who wanted independence only and those who pushed for the end of serfdom and for universal manhood suffrage. In response, the Russians invaded Moldavia and the Turks moved into Walachia. By October, the uprising was over. Russia and Turkey agreed to control the provinces jointly. *(The Art Archive.)*

Slovenes who preferred Austrian rule to domination by local Magyars.

The ethnic divisions in Hungary foreshadowed the many political and social divisions that would doom the revolutionaries. Fears of peasant insurrection prompted the Magyar nationalists around Kossuth to abolish serfdom. This measure alienated the largest noble landowners. The new government alienated the other nationalities when it imposed the Magyar language on them. In Prague, Czech nationalists convened a Slav congress as a counter to the Germans' Frankfurt parliament and called for a reorganization of the Austrian Empire that would recognize the rights of ethnic minorities. Such assertiveness by non-German peoples provoked German nationalists to protest on behalf of German-speaking people in areas with a Czech or Magyar majority.

The Austrian government took advantage of these divisions. To quell peasant discontent and appease liberal reformers, it abolished all remaining peasant obligations to the nobility in March 1848. Rejoicing country folk soon lost interest in the revolution. Military force finally broke up the revolutionary movements. The first blow fell in Prague in June 1848; General Prince Alfred von Windischgrätz, the military governor, bombarded the city into submission when a demonstration led to violence (including the shooting death of his wife, watching from a window). After another uprising in Vienna a few months later, Windischgrätz marched seventy thousand soldiers into the capital and set up direct military rule. In December, the Austrian monarchy came back to life when the

eighteen-year-old Francis Joseph (r. 1848–1916), unencumbered by promises extracted by the revolutionaries from his now feeble uncle Ferdinand, assumed the imperial crown after intervention by leading court officials. In the spring of 1849, General Count Joseph Radetzky defeated the last Ital-

REVOLUTIONS OF 1848	
1848	
JANUARY	Uprising in Palermo, Sicily
FEBRUARY	Revolution in Paris; proclamation of republic
MARCH	Insurrections in Vienna, German cities, Milan, and Venice; autonomy movement in Hungary; Charles Albert of Piedmont-Sardinia declares war on Austrian Empire
MAY	Frankfurt parliament opens
JUNE	Austrian army crushes revolutionary movement in Prague; June Days end in defeat of workers in Paris
JULY	Austrians defeat Charles Albert and Italian forces
NOVEMBER	Insurrection in Rome
DECEMBER	Francis Joseph becomes Austrian emperor; Louis-Napoleon elected president in France
1849	
FEBRUARY	Rome declared a republic
APRIL	Frederick William of Prussia rejects crown of united Germany offered by Frankfurt parliament
JULY	Roman republic overthrown by French intervention
AUGUST	Russian and Austrian armies combine to defeat Hungarian forces

ian challenges to Austrian power in northern Italy, and his army moved east, joining with Croats and Serbs to take on the Hungarian rebels. The Austrian army teamed up with Tsar Nicholas I, who marched into Hungary with more than 300,000 Russian troops. Hungary was put under brutal martial law. Széchenyi went mad, and Kossuth found refuge in the United States. Social conflicts and ethnic divisions weakened the revolutionary movements from the inside and gave the Austrian government the opening it needed to restore its position.

Aftermath to 1848

Although the revolutionaries of 1848 failed to achieve most of their goals, their efforts left a profound mark on the political and social landscape. Between 1848 and 1851, the French served a kind of republican apprenticeship that prepared the population for another, more lasting republic after 1870. In Italy, the failure of unification did not stop the spread of nationalist ideas and the rooting of demands for democratic participation. In the German states, the revolutionaries of 1848 turned nationalism from an idea of professors and writers into a popular enthusiasm and even a practical reality. The initiation of artisans, workers, and journeymen into democratic clubs increased political awareness in the lower classes and helped prepare them for broader political participation. Almost all the German states had a constitution and a parliament after 1850. The spectacular failures of 1848 thus hid some important underlying successes.

The absence of revolution in 1848 was just as significant as its presence. No revolution occurred in Great Britain, the Netherlands, or Belgium, the three places where industrialization and urbanization had developed most rapidly. In Great Britain, the prospects for revolution actually seemed quite good: the Chartist movement took inspiration from the European revolutions in 1848 and mounted several gigantic demonstrations to force Parliament into granting all adult males the vote. But Parliament refused and no uprising occurred, in part because the government had already proved its responsiveness. The middle classes in Britain had been co-opted into the established order by the Reform Bill of 1832, and the working classes had won parliamentary regulation of children's and women's work.

The other notable exception to revolution among the great powers was Russia, where Tsar Nicholas I maintained a tight grip through police surveillance and censorship. The Russian schools, limited to the upper classes, taught Nicholas's three most cherished principles: autocracy (the unlimited power of the tsar), orthodoxy (obedience to the church in religion and morality), and nationality (devotion to Russian traditions). These provided no space for political dissent. Social conditions also fostered political passivity: serfdom continued in force and the sluggish rate of industrial and urban growth created little discontent.

Although much had changed, the aristocracy remained the dominant power almost everywhere. As army officers, aristocrats put down revolutionary forces. As landlords, they continued to dominate the rural scene and control parliamentary bodies. They also held many official positions in the state bureaucracies. One Italian princess explained, "There are doubtless men capable of leading the nation . . . but their names are unknown to the people, whereas those of noble families . . . are in every memory." Aristocrats kept their authority by adapting to change: they entered the bureaucracy and professions, turned their estates into moneymaking enterprises, and learned how to invest shrewdly.

The reassertion of conservative rule hardened gender definitions. Women everywhere had participated in the revolutions, especially in the Italian states, where they joined armies in the tens of thousands and applied household skills toward making bandages, clothing, and food. As conservatives returned to power, all signs of women's political activism disappeared. The French feminist movement, the most advanced in Europe, fell apart after the June Days when the increasingly conservative republican government forbade women to form political clubs and arrested and imprisoned two of the most outspoken women leaders for their socialist activities.

In May 1851, Europe's most important female monarch presided over a midcentury celebration of peace and industrial growth that helped dampen the still-smoldering fires of revolutionary passion. Queen Victoria (r. 1837–1901), who herself promoted the notion of domesticity as women's sphere, opened the international Exhibition of the Works of Industry of All Nations in London on May 1. A huge iron-and-glass building housed the display. Soon people referred to it as the Crystal Palace; its nine hundred tons of glass created an aura of fantasy, and the abundant goods from all nations inspired satisfaction and pride. One German visitor described it as "this miracle which has so suddenly appeared to dazzle the inhabitants of our globe." In the place of revolutionary fervor, the

Crystal Palace offered a government-sponsored spectacle of what industry, hard work, and technological imagination could produce.

REVIEW: Why did the revolutions of 1848 fail?

Conclusion

Many of the six million people who visited the Crystal Palace display came on the new railroads, foremost symbol of this age of industrial transformation. The application of steam engines to textile manufacturing and the railroads set in motion a host of economic and social changes with cultural and political consequences: cities burgeoned with rapidly growing populations; factories concentrated laborers who formed a new working class; manufacturers now challenged landed elites for political leadership; and social problems galvanized reform organizations and governments alike. The Crystal Palace presented the rosy view of modern, industrial, urban life, but the housing shortages, inadequacy of water supplies, and recurrent epidemic diseases had not disappeared.

Although the revolutions of 1848 brought to the surface the profound tensions within a European society in transition toward industrialization and urbanization, they did not resolve those tensions. The Industrial Revolution continued, workers developed more extensive organizations, and

The Crystal Palace, 1851
George Baxter's lithograph (above) shows the exterior of the main building for the Exhibition of the Works of Industry of All Nations in London. It was designed by Sir Joseph Paxton to gigantic dimensions: 1,848 feet long by 456 feet wide; 135 feet high; 772,784 square feet of ground floor area covering no less than 18 acres. The view below, a lithograph by Peter Mabuse, offers a view of one of the colonial displays at the exhibition. The tented room and carved ivory throne are meant to recall India, Britain's premier colony. *(Top: © Maidstone Museum and Art Gallery, Kent, UK/The Bridgeman Art Library. Below: © Private Collection/The Stapleton Collection/The Bridgeman Art Library.)*

MAPPING THE WEST

Europe in 1850

This map of population growth between 1800 and 1850 reveals important trends that would not otherwise be evident. Although population growth correlated for the most part with industrialization, population also grew in more agricultural regions such as East Prussia, Poland, and Ireland. Ireland's rapid population growth does not appear on this map because the famine of 1846–1851 killed more than 10 percent of the population and forced many others to emigrate. ■ Compare this map to Map 21.1: Which areas experienced both industrialization and population increase?

liberals and socialists fought over the pace of reform. Confronted with the menace of revolution, elites now sought alternatives that would be less threatening to the established order and still permit some change. This search for alternatives became immediately evident in the question of national unification in Germany and Italy. National unification would hereafter depend not on speeches and parliamentary resolutions, but rather on what the Prussian leader Otto von Bismarck would call "iron and blood."

FOR FURTHER EXPLORATION

■ **For suggested references, including Web sites, for topics in this chapter,** see page SR-1 at the end of the book.

■ **For additional primary-source material from this period,** see Chapter 21 in *Sources of THE MAKING OF THE WEST*, Third Edition.

■ **For Web sites and documents related to topics in this chapter,** see *Make History* at bedfordstmartins.com/hunt.

CHAPTER REVIEW

KEY TERMS AND PEOPLE

ideology (654)

Industrial Revolution
    (654)

cholera (662)

George Sand (666)

domesticity (669)

imperialism (670)

Opium War (671)

nationalism (672)

Giuseppe Mazzini (672)

liberalism (674)

Corn Laws (674)

socialism (675)

communists (676)

Chartism (677)

Louis-Napoleon
    Bonaparte (680)

REVIEW QUESTIONS

1. What dangers did the Industrial Revolution pose to both urban and rural life?

2. How did reformers try to address the social problems created by industrialization and urbanization? In which areas did they succeed, and in which did they fail?

3. Why did ideologies have such a powerful appeal in the 1830s and 1840s?

4. Why did the revolutions of 1848 fail?

MAKING CONNECTIONS

1. Which of the ideologies of this period had the greatest impact on political events? How can you explain this?

2. In what ways might industrialization be considered a force for peaceful change rather than a revolution? (Hint: Think about the situation in Great Britain.)

For practice quizzes, a customized study plan, and other study tools, see the Online Study Guide at bedfordstmartins.com/hunt.

IMPORTANT EVENTS

1830–1832	Cholera epidemic sweeps across Europe
1830	France invades and begins conquest of Algeria
1831	British and Foreign Temperance Society established
1832	George Sand, *Indiana*
1833	Factory Act regulates work of children in Great Britain; abolition of slavery in the British Empire
1834	German *Zollverein* ("customs union") established under Prussian leadership
1835	Belgium opens first continental railway built with state funds
1839	Beginning of Opium War between Britain and China; invention of photography
1841	Charles Dickens, *The Old Curiosity Shop*
1846	Famine strikes Ireland; Corn Laws repealed in England; peasant insurrection in Austrian province of Galicia
1848	Revolutions of 1848 throughout Europe; last great wave of Chartist demonstrations in Britain; Karl Marx and Friedrich Engels, *The Communist Manifesto*; abolition of slavery in French colonies; end of serfdom in Austrian Empire
1851	Crystal Palace exhibition in London

TEATRO LA FENICE

VENEZIA

IN OCCASIONE DEL
CONGRESSO GEOGRAFICO INTERNAZIONALE

IMPRESA CESARE TREVISAN

DALL'11 AL 22 SETTEMBRE SI DARANNO 7 RAPPRESENTAZIONI DELLA GRANDIOSA OPERA-BALLO

AIDA

MUSICA DEL COMM. GIUSEPPE VERDI

ESEGUITA DAI SEGUENTI ARTISTI

PRIME DONNE

EMMA TUROLLA — GIUSEPPINA PASQUA

PRIMO TENORE

GIOVANNI SANI

PRIMO BARITONO

COMM. GOTTARDO ALDIGHIERI

PRIMI BASSI

ENRICO SERBOLINI ✦ FRANCESCO PANARI

MAESTRO DIRETTORE D'ORCHESTRA

CAV. FRANCO FACCIO

ALTRO MAESTRO

RAFAELE BRACÂLE

TENORE COMPRIMARIO	M'ISTRUTTORE DEI CORI	SUGGERITORE
GIUSEPPE CINQUANTA	LORENZO POLI	ANTONIO RENIER

COREOGRAFO

RINALDO ROSSI

N. 70 PROFESSORI D'ORCHESTRA, N. 80 CORISTI E CORISTE, N. 24 BALLERINE, N. 6 TROMBE EGIZIANE BANDA

Direttore della messa in scena	Direttore delle masse	Pittore Scenografo	Direttore al Macchinismo
RINALDO ROSSI	GAETANO ARCHINTI	CESARE RECANATINI	LUIGI CAPRARA
Vestiaria - proprietario L. ZAMPERONI della Scala di Milano	Attrezzista proprietà CROCE E FIGLIO della Scala di Milano	Fornitore della luce ANTONIO TREVISAN	Parrucchiere G. GASPEROTTO	Fornitore delle Calzari R. MAVEROFFER della Scala di Milano

GIRCA N. 100 COMPARSE, 6 CORIFEE, CORIFEI 12 PAGGI 8 BALLERINI STATISTI, STATISTE ECC. ECC.

Biglietto d'ingresso alla platea e palchi (in sere ordinarie)	L.	5.
detto al loggione (id)	»	2.—
Poltrona a bracciuoli, oltre l'ingresso	»	10.—
Posti riservati in platea (scanni in velluto)	»	5.—
Posti riservati in Galleria (Loggione)	»	1.50
Abbonamento per le sette rappresent. (compresa quella di gala)	»	25.—
detto limitato a N. 40 Poltrone	»	50.—
detto ai posti riservati (scanni)	»	25.—

Le suddette 7 rappresentazioni
sono finora stabilite nelle sere
del 11-13-15-17-18-20-22
Settembre

Proprietà dello spartito
Tito di Gio. Ricordi

Venezia 1 Agosto 1881

Politics and Culture of the Nation-State
1850–1870

I n 1859, the name *VERDI* suddenly appeared scrawled on walls across the disunited cities of the Italian peninsula. The graffiti seemed to celebrate the composer Giuseppe Verdi, whose operas made him a special hero among Italians. His stories of downtrodden groups struggling against tyrannical government seemed to refer specifically to them. As his operatic choruses thundered out calls to rebellion in the name of the nation, Italian audiences were sure that Verdi was telling them to throw off Austrian and papal rule and unite in a nation—the ancient Roman Empire reborn. The graffiti had a second political message: VERDI, an acronym for *Vittorio Emmanuele Re d'Italia* (Victor Emmanuel, King of Italy), summoned Italians to join together under Victor Emmanuel II, king of Sardinia and Piedmont—the one Italian leader with a nationalist, modernizing profile. The graffiti did its work, and the very next year a united Italy emerged, formed by warfare, popular uprisings, and hard bargaining by realist politicians.

In the wake of the failed revolutions of 1848, European statesmen and the politically conscious public increasingly abandoned the politics of idealism in favor of Realpolitik—a politics of tough-minded realism aimed at strengthening the state and tightening social order. Realpolitikers rejected the romanticism and high-minded ideologies of the revolutionaries. Instead, they believed in power politics and even the use of violence to attain their goals. Two particularly skilled practitioners of Realpolitik, the Italian Camillo di Cavour and the Prussian Otto von Bismarck, succeeded in unifying Italy and Germany, respectively, not by romantic rhetoric but by war and diplomacy. Most leading figures of the decades 1850–1870, enmeshed like Verdi's operatic heroes in violent

Aïda Poster
Aïda (1871), Giuseppe Verdi's opera of human passion and state power among people of different nations, became a staple of Western culture, bringing people across Europe into a common cultural orbit. Written to celebrate the opening of the Suez Canal, *Aïda* also celebrated the improvement of Europe's access to Asian resources provided by the new waterway. The opera was a prime example of the surge of interest in Egyptian styles and objects that followed the opening of the canal. *(Madeline Grimoldi.)*

political maneuverings, advanced state power by harnessing the forces of nationalism and liberalism that had led to earlier romantic revolts. Their achievements changed the face of Europe.

Nation building was the order of the day, but unifying people or territory was not just about winning wars. Economic development was crucial, as was using government policy and culture to create a sense of national identity and common purpose. As productivity and wealth increased, governments took vigorous steps to improve the urban environment, monitor public health, and promote national sentiment. State support for cultural developments ranging from public schools to public health programs made the citizenry as a whole better off, established a common fund of knowledge, and produced shared political beliefs and loyalties. Authoritarian leaders such as Bismarck and the new French emperor Napoleon III believed that a better quality of life would not only calm revolutionary impulses and build state power but also silence liberal reformers.

Shared culture helped build shared identity. Reading novels, viewing art exhibitions, keeping up-to-date at the newly fashionable world's fairs, and attending theater and opera performances gave ordinary people a stronger sense of being French or German or British. Also, the public consumed cultural works that increasingly rejected romanticism and portrayed harsher, more realistic aspects of everyday life. Artists painted nudes in shockingly blunt ways, eliminating romantic hues and poses. The Russian author Leo Tolstoy depicted the bleak life of soldiers in the Crimean War, which erupted in 1853 between the Russian and Ottoman empires, while his countryman Fyodor Dostoevsky wrote of ordinary people turning to crime in urban neighborhoods.

Alongside the tough-minded nation-building policies there arose tough-minded art, not just mirroring **Realpolitik** but encouraging it. Western politicians sent armies to distant areas to stamp out resistance to global expansion. At home, Realpolitikers destroyed people's neighborhoods to construct public buildings, roads, and parks. The process of nation building was thus often brutal, bringing arrests, protests, and outright civil war—all of these the centerpieces of Verdi's operas as well. In response to the pressures of nation building, an uprising of Parisians in 1871 challenged the central government's violent intrusion into everyday life and its failure to count the costs. Thus, for the most part, the powerful Western nation-state did not take shape automatically. Instead, national policymakers used warfare, the creation of new institutions, and often brutal uprooting of people around the world to create the modern nation-state. The Realpolitik approach to nation building also created a general climate of modern opinion that valued realism, hard facts, and tough-minded deeds.

FOCUS QUESTION: How did the creation and strengthening of nation-states change European politics, society, and culture in the mid-nineteenth century?

The End of the Concert of Europe

The revolutions of 1848 had weakened the concert of Europe, forcing its architect, Austrian foreign minister Klemens von Metternich, to resign and flee to England and allowing the forces of nation-

---

Realpolitik (ray AHL poh lih teek): Policies developed after the revolutions of 1848 and initially associated with nation building; they were based on realism rather than on the romantic notions of earlier nationalists. The term has come to mean any policy based on considerations of power alone.

Napoleon III and Eugénie Receive the Siamese Ambassadors, 1864

At a splendid gathering of their court, the emperor Napoleon III, his consort Eugénie, and their son and heir greet ambassadors from Siam, whose exoticism and servility before the imperial family are the centerpiece of this depiction by Jean-Léon Gerome. How might a middle-class French citizen react to this scene? *(Bridgeman-Giraudon/Art Resource, NY.)*

alism to flourish. Clashing national ambitions made it more difficult for countries to act together. In addition, the revival of Bonapartism in the person of Napoleon III destabilized international politics as France's Second Empire sought to reassert itself. One of Napoleon's targets was Russia, formerly a mainstay of the concert of Europe. Taking advantage of Russia's continuing drive to expand, France helped engineer the Crimean War. The war took a huge toll in human life and weakened Russia and Austria. Russia's defeat not only led to substantial reforms in the country but also changed the distribution of European power.

Napoleon III and the Quest for French Glory

Louis-Napoleon Bonaparte (Napoleon III) encouraged the cult of his famous uncle and the revival of French grandeur as part of nation building. "A

man of destiny," he called himself. Napoleon III acted as Europe's schoolmaster, showing its leaders how to combine economic liberalism and support from the people with authoritarian rule. To the public, he claimed to represent "your families, your property—rich and poor alike," but cafés where men might discuss politics were closed, and a rubber-stamp legislature (the Corps législatif) muffled the actual voices of the people. Imperial style replaced republican rituals (see the illustration on this page). Napoleon's opulent court dazzled the public, and the emperor (like his namesake) cultivated a masculine image of strength and majesty by wearing military uniforms and by conspicuously maintaining mistresses. Napoleon's wife, Empress Eugénie, however, followed middle-class conventions, playing up her domestic role as devoted mother to her only son and as volunteer worker in many charities. The authoritarian, apparently old-fashioned order imposed by Napoleon satisfied the

■ **1867** Second Reform Bill in England; Austro-Hungarian monarchy

■ **1871** German Empire proclaimed; Paris Commune

1865 | **1870** | **1875**

■ **1868** Meiji Restoration begins in Japan

■ **1869–1871** Women's colleges founded at Cambridge University

■ **1870–1871** Franco-Prussian War

many peasants who feared a flare-up of the urban radicalism of 1848.

Napoleon III was nonetheless a modernizer. He promoted a strong economy, public works programs, and jobs, luring the middle and working classes away from radical politics with the promise of employment. International trade fairs, artistic expositions, and the magnificent rebuilding of Paris helped make France prosper as Europe recovered from the hard times of the late 1840s. Empress Eugénie wore lavish gowns, encouraging French silk production and keeping Paris at the center of the lucrative fashion trade. The Second Empire also reached a free-trade agreement with Britain and backed the establishment of innovative investment banks. Such new institutions led the way in financing railroad expansion, and railway mileage increased fivefold during Napoleon III's reign. During the economic downturn of the late 1850s, he changed course by allowing working-class organizations to form and introducing democratic features into his governing methods. Although some historians have judged Napoleon III to be enigmatic and shifty because of these abrupt changes, his maneuvers were hardheaded responses to the fluid conditions.

On the international scene, Napoleon III's main goals were to overcome the containment of France imposed by the Congress of Vienna and acquire international glory like a true Bonaparte. To fracture the concert of Europe, Napoleon pitted France first against Russia in the Crimean War, then against Austria in the War of Italian Unification, and finally against Prussia in the Franco-Prussian War of 1870. Beyond Europe, Napoleon encouraged the construction of the Suez Canal to connect the Mediterranean and the Red Sea, while his army continued to enforce French rule in Algeria and Southeast Asia. His attempt to install Maximilian, the brother of Habsburg emperor Francis Joseph, as emperor of Mexico and ultimately of all Central America brought on rebellion in Mexico and ended with Maximilian's execution in 1867. Despite this glaring failure, Napoleon's foreign policy succeeded in breaking down the international system of peaceful diplomacy established at the Congress of Vienna. The consequences were the Crimean War, the end of serfdom in Russia, and the birth of new nations.

The Crimean War, 1853–1856: Turning Point in European Affairs

Napoleon first flexed his diplomatic muscle in the Crimean War (1853–1856), which began as a conflict between the Russian and Ottoman empires but ended as a war with long-lasting consequences for much of Europe. While professing to uphold the status quo, Russia had been expanding into Asia and the Middle East. In particular, Tsar Nicholas I wanted to absorb much of the Ottoman Empire, fast becoming known as "the sick man of Europe" because of its disintegrating authority. Napoleon III encouraged Nicholas to be even more aggressive in his expansionism — a maneuver that provoked war in October 1853 between the two eastern empires (Map 22.1). The war disrupted the united Austrian and Russian front that kept France — and Napoleon III — in check.

The war drew in other states and upset Europe's balance of power. To block Russia and thereby protect its Mediterranean routes to East Asia, Britain prodded the Ottomans to stand up to Russia. With the Austrian government still resenting its dependence on Russia in putting down Hungarian revolutionaries in 1849 and feeling threatened by continuing Russian expansion into the Balkans, Napoleon III managed to gain Austria's promise of neutrality during the war. Austrian neutrality split the conservative Russian-Austrian coalition that had blocked French ambitions for greater influence since 1815. In the fall of 1853, the Russians blasted the wooden Turkish ships to bits

MAP 22.1 The Crimean War, 1853–1856
The most destructive war in Europe between the Napoleonic Wars and World War I, the Crimean War drew attention to the conflicting ambitions around territories of the declining Ottoman Empire. Importantly for state building in these decades, the war fractured the alliance of conservative forces from the Congress of Vienna, allowing Italy and Germany to come into being as unified states.

The Mission of Mercy
Florence Nightingale organized British health care services during the Crimean War, inspiring a committed cadre of women to volunteer at the battlefront. The new sanitary measures Nightingale introduced into the care of the wounded and sick dramatically reduced the death rate of ailing soldiers. Jerry Barrett's romantic portrayal of her greeting the wounded at Scutari hardly captures the strenuous and tough-minded efforts involved in her work. Why would the artist portray Nightingale as a romantic, ladylike heroine? *(National Portrait Gallery, London.)*

at the Ottoman port of Sinope on the Black Sea; in 1854, France and Great Britain, enemies in war for more than a century, declared war on Russia to defend the Ottoman Empire's sovereignty and territories.

Faced with attacking the massive Russian Empire, the British and French allies settled for limited military goals focused on capturing the Russian naval base at Sevastopol, on the Crimea, a peninsula jutting into the Black Sea. Even so, the Crimean War was spectacularly bloody. British and French troops landed in the Crimea in September 1854, but it took a year of savage and costly combat before the fortified Sevastopol finally fell. Generals on both sides demonstrated their incompetence, and governments failed to provide combatants with even minimal supplies, sanitation, or medical care. Hospitals had no beds, no dishes, and no water. As a result, the war claimed a massive toll. Of the three-quarters of a million deaths, more than two-thirds were from disease and starvation.

In the midst of this unfolding catastrophe, **Alexander II** (r. 1855–1881) ascended the Russian throne following the death of Nicholas I, his father. With casualties mounting, the new tsar asked for peace. As a result of the Peace of Paris, signed in March 1856, Russia lost the right to base its navy

in the Straits of Dardanelles and the Black Sea, which were declared neutral waters. Moldavia and Walachia (which soon merged to form Romania) became autonomous Turkish provinces under victors' protection, drastically reducing Russian influence in that region too.

Some historians have called the Crimean War one of the most senseless conflicts in modern history because competing claims in southeastern Europe could have been settled by diplomacy had it not been for Napoleon III's driving ambition to disrupt the peace. Yet the war was full of consequence. New technologies were introduced into warfare: the railroad, shell-firing cannon, breech-loading rifles, and steam-powered ships. The relationship of the home front to the battlefront was beginning to change with the use of the telegraph and increased press coverage. Home audiences received news from the Crimean front lines more rapidly and in more detail than ever before. Reports of incompetence, poor sanitation, and the huge death toll outraged the public, inspiring a few to go to the front to help. The English nurse Florence Nightingale became the best known of these sojourners: she seized the moment to escape the confines of middle-class domesticity by organizing a battlefield nursing service to care for the British sick and wounded. Through her tough-minded organization of nursing units, she not only improved the sanitary conditions of the troops

---

Alexander II: Russian tsar (r. 1855–1881) who initiated the age of Great Reforms and emancipated the serfs in 1861.

Mrs. Seacole: The *Other* Florence Nightingale

Another highly skilled medical worker besides Florence Nightingale made an impact on the battlefields in Crimea. Mary Seacole (1805–1881), daughter of a free black Jamaican woman and a Scottish army officer, had learned about medicine from her mother and from doctors who passed through Kingston, staying at the family's boardinghouse. In addition to a gift for healing, Mrs. Seacole (as she was always called) had a passion for travel—to Europe, the United States, and Panama—which she supported by tending other travelers. When the Crimean War broke out, she chafed—like Nightingale herself—to be at the battlefront. Arriving in Crimea in 1855, Mrs. Seacole saved many desperately ill soldiers who lacked all medical care.

[Sick soldiers] could and did get at my store sick-comforts and nourishing food, which the heads of the medical staff would sometimes find it difficult to procure. These reasons, with the additional one that I was very familiar with the diseases which they suffered most from and successful in their treatment (I say this in no spirit of vanity), were quite sufficient to account for the numbers who came daily to the British Hotel for medical treatment.

That the officers were glad of me as a doctress and nurse may be easily understood. When a poor fellow lay sickening in his cheerless hut and sent down to me, he knew very well that I should not ride up in answer to his message empty-handed. And although I did not hesitate to charge him with the value of the necessaries I took him, still he was thankful enough to be able to *purchase* them. When we lie ill at home surrounded with com-

fort, we never think of feeling any special gratitude for the sick-room delicacies which we accept as a consequence of our illness; but the poor officer lying ill and weary in his crazy hut, dependent for the merest necessaries of existence upon a clumsy, ignorant soldier-cook, who would almost prefer eating his meat raw to having the troubles of cooking it (our English soldiers are bad campaigners), often finds his greatest troubles in the want of those little delicacies with which a weak stomach must be humoured into retaining nourishment.

Source: Mary Grant Seacole, *Wonderful Adventures of Mrs. Seacole in Many Lands* (New York: Oxford University Press, 1988), 125–26.

---

both during and after the war but also pioneered nursing as a profession. (See Document, "Mrs. Seacole: The *Other* Florence Nightingale," above.)

More immediately, the war accomplished Napoleon III's goal of severing the alliance between Austria and Russia, the two conservative powers on which the Congress of Vienna peace settlement had rested since 1815. It thus ended Austria's and Russia's grip on European affairs and undermined their ability to contain the forces of liberalism and nationalism. Russia's catastrophic defeat forced it to embark on some long-overdue reforms.

Reform in Russia

Defeat in the Crimean War not only thwarted Russia's territorial ambition but also made clear the need for meaningful reform. Hundreds of peasant insurrections had erupted during the decade before the Crimean War. Serf defiance ranged from malingering at forced labor to boycotting vodka to protest its heavy taxation. "Our own and neighboring households were gripped with fear," one aristocrat reported, because of potential serf

violence. Although economic development spread in parts of eastern Europe, the Russian economy stagnated compared with that of western Europe. Old-fashioned farming techniques depleted soil and led to food shortages, and the nobility was often contemptuous of the suffering malnutrition and hard labor caused. Artists made their own call for reform with their sympathetic portrayals of serfs and condemnation of brutal masters, as in the collection *A Hunter's Sketches* (1852) by novelist Ivan Turgenev. A Russian translation of Harriet Beecher Stowe's U.S. antislavery novel *Uncle Tom's Cabin* (1852) was also a "must-read" for reformers. When Russia lost the Crimean War, the educated public, including some government officials, found the poor performance of serf-conscripted armies a disgrace and the system of serf labor a glaring liability.

Emancipation of the Serfs. Confronted with the need for change, Tsar Alexander II acted. Well educated and more widely traveled than his father, Alexander ushered in what came to be known as the age of Great Reforms, granting Russians new rights from above as a way of ensuring that violent action from below would not force change. The most dramatic reform was the emancipation of almost fifty million serfs beginning in 1861. By the terms of emancipation, communities of newly freed serfs, headed by male village elders, received grants of land. The community itself, traditionally called a **mir**, had full power to allocate this land among individuals and to direct their economic activity. Although emancipation partially laid the groundwork for a modern labor force in Russia, communal landowning and decision making meant that individual peasants could not simply sell their parcel of land and leave their rural communities to work in factories as laborers had been doing in western Europe.

The condition attached to the so-called land grants in Russia was that peasants were not *given* land along with their personal freedom: they were forced to "redeem" the land they farmed by paying off long-term loans from the government, with which the government in turn compensated the original landowners. The best land remained in the hands of the nobility, and most peasants ended up owning less land than they had farmed as serfs. These conditions, especially the huge burden of debt and communal regulations, blunted Russian agricultural development for decades. But idealistic reformers believed that the emancipation of the serfs, once treated by the nobility virtually as livestock, had produced miraculous results. As one of them put it, "The people are without any exaggeration transfigured from head to foot. . . . The look, the walk, the speech, everything is changed."

The state also reformed local administration, the judiciary, and the military. The government compensated the nobility for loss of peasant services and set up zemstvos—regional councils through which aristocrats could control local affairs such as education, public health, and welfare. Aristocratic control assured that the zemstvos would remain a conservative structure, but they

Emancipation of the Russian Serfs
This trading card was used as a marketing gimmick to promote canned meat. Cards like these were given away by the thousands and traded just as baseball cards are today. Historical scenes were popular subjects for the cards—this one shows the emancipation of the serfs in Russia. Note that the caption is in French, the language of the European upper classes, including those in Russia, who would have consumed this product. The emancipation is presented as a wholly beneficial act with no strings attached. *(Mary Evans Picture Library.)*

became a new political force with the potential for challenging the authoritarian central government. Some aristocrats took advantage of newly relaxed rules on travel to see how the rest of Europe was governed. Their vision broadened as they observed new ways of solving social and economic problems. Judicial reform gave all Russians, even former serfs, access to modern civil courts, rather than leaving them at the mercy of a landowner's version of justice. The principle of equality of all persons before the law, regardless of social rank, was introduced in Russia for the first time. Military reform followed in 1874 when the government reduced the twenty-five-year term of conscription to a six-year term and began paying attention to education, efficiency, and humane treatment of recruits. These changes improved the fitness of Russian soldiers, bringing them closer to the level of soldiers in western Europe.

From Reform to Rebellion. Alexander's reforms benefited modern, market-oriented landowners in Russia just as enclosures had done much earlier for landowners in western Europe. At the same time, the changes weakened personal authority of the nobility and sparked intergenerational rebellion. "An epidemic seemed to seize upon [noble] chil-

---

mir (mihr): A Russian farm community that provided for holding land in common and regulating the movements of any individual by the group.

dren . . . an epidemic of fleeing from the parental roof," one observer noted. Rejecting aristocratic leisure, youthful rebels from the upper class valued practical activity and sometimes identified with peasants and workers. Some formed communes where they hoped to do humble manual labor, whereas others turned to higher education, especially the sciences. Rebellious daughters of the nobility opposed their parents by cutting their hair short, wearing black, and escaping from home through phony marriages so they could study in European universities. This repudiation of traditional society led these young people to be labeled as nihilists (from the Latin for "nothing"), those who do not believe in any values whatsoever. A defiant spirit was percolating not just at the bottom but also at the top of Russian society, and it would soon bring about a wave of violence.

Russian-dominated ethnic groups were inspired by the atmosphere of change, and in 1863 aristocratic and upper-class nationalist Poles rose up against the weakened Russian monarchy, demanding full national independence for their country. By 1864, however, Alexander II's army had regained control of the Russian section of Poland, using the promise of reform to win peasant support for defeating the rebels. Elsewhere among Russia's minorities, Alexander repressed nationalist unrest and intensified **Russification** — a tactic meant to reduce the threat of future rebellion by forcing the more than one hundred national minorities within the empire to adopt Russian language and culture. Despite these measures, the tsarist regime in this era of the Great Reforms only partially succeeded in developing the administrative, economic, and civic institutions that made the nation-state strong elsewhere in Europe. The tsar and his inner circle tightly held the reins of government, allowing few to share in power. Deliberate government policies in other European countries helped develop the sense of common citizenship, but in imperial Russia attempts to build a shared national loyalty were less successful.

> **REVIEW:** What were the main results of the Crimean War?

Russification: A program for the integration of Russia's many nationality groups that involved the forced learning of the Russian language and the practice of Russian Orthodox religion as well as the settlement of ethnic Russians among other nationality groups.

War and Nation Building

Politicians in the German and Italian states seized the opportunity provided by the weakened concert of Europe to unify their fragmented regions through warfare. Following a bloody civil war, the United States solidified its institutions for further national expansion. The rise of powerful **nation-states** such as Italy, Germany, and the United States was accompanied by a sense of pride in national identity — or nationalism — among their peoples (see "Terms of History, page 697). This was not an inevitable or universal trend in the West, however. Millions of individuals in the Austrian Empire, Ireland, and elsewhere maintained a regional, local, or separate ethnic identity despite the trend toward identifying with growing nation-states.

Cavour, Garibaldi, and the Process of Italian Unification

Even after the failure of the revolutions of 1848 in the Italian states, the call for Risorgimento (a term meaning "rebirth," associated with the rebirth of a united Italy) remained loud, aided by the disintegration of diplomatic stability across Europe. Leading the way toward Risorgimento was the kingdom of Piedmont-Sardinia, in the economically modernizing north of Italy. Italians thrilled to the operas of Verdi, but it was railroads, a modern army, and the military support of France against the Austrian Empire, which still dominated the peninsula, that made political unification possible.

Cavour, Architect of the New Italy. The pragmatic **Camillo di Cavour** (1810–1861), prime minister of the kingdom of Piedmont-Sardinia from 1852 until his death, had a Realpolitiker's vision of how to unify the Italian states. A rebel in his youth, Cavour as he matured organized steamship companies, played the stock market, and inhaled the heady air of modernization during his travels to Paris and London. He promoted economic development rather than idealistic uprisings as the means to achieve a united Italy. As skilled prime minister to a less capable king, Victor Emmanuel II (r. Italy 1861–1878), Cavour helped achieve a strong Piedmontese economy, a modern army, and a liberal political climate as the foundation for Piedmont's control of the unification process (Map 22.2).

---

nation-state: A sovereign political entity of modern times based on representing a united people.

Camillo di Cavour (1810–1861): Prime minister of the kingdom of Piedmont-Sardinia and architect of a united Italy.

To unify Italy, however, Piedmont would have to confront Austria, which governed the provinces of Lombardy and Venetia and exerted strong influence over most of the peninsula. Cavour turned for help to Napoleon III, who at a meeting in the summer of 1858 promised French assistance in exchange for the city of Nice and the region of Savoy. Napoleon III expected that France rather than Austria would influence the peninsula thereafter. Sure of French help, Cavour provoked the Austrians to invade northern Italy in April 1859. The cause of Piedmont now became the cause of nationalist Italians everywhere, even those who had supported romantic republicanism in 1848, and they rose up on the side of Piedmont. Using the newly built Piedmontese railroad to move troops, the French and Piedmontese armies achieved rapid victories. Suddenly fearing the growth of Piedmont as a potential competing force, Napoleon independently signed a peace treaty with Habsburg emperor Francis Joseph that seemed to end the war. Its terms gave Lombardy but not Venetia to Piedmont, and left the rest of Italy disunited. Nationalist ambitions were not yet realized.

Garibaldi, Emblem of Italian Freedom. Napoleon's plan to keep Italy disunited was soon derailed. Support for Piedmont continued to swell among Italians, while a financially strapped Austria stood by, unable to keep control of events on the peninsula. Ousting their rulers, citizens of the rest of the northern and central Italian states (except Rome, which French troops had occupied) elected to join Piedmont. In May 1860, Giuseppe Garibaldi (1807–1882), a committed republican, dedicated guerrilla fighter, and veteran of the revolutions of 1848, set sail from Genoa with a thousand red-shirted volunteers (many of them teenage boys) to liberate Sicily, where peasants were rebelling against their landlords and the corrupt government in anticipation of the Risorgimento. In the autumn of 1860, Victor Emmanuel II's victorious forces descending from the north and Garibaldi's moving up from the south met in Naples. Although some of his followers still clamored for a republic, Garibaldi threw his support to the king. In 1861, the kingdom of Italy was proclaimed with Victor Emmanuel at its head.

Exhausted by a decade of overwork, Cavour died within months of leading the unification, leaving lesser men to organize the new Italy. The task ahead was enormous and complex: 90 percent of the peninsula's inhabitants did not even speak a common language but rather local dialects. There were political difficulties too: consensus

TERMS OF HISTORY

Nationalism

The word *nationalism* is associated with a sense of a common identity among people within geographically defined nation-states. What is more important about nationalism is that it promotes the nation-state around which that common entity develops. A phenomenon of the past two to three centuries, it became increasingly important to politics from the nineteenth century on. Strongly held feelings of a common national identity grew in the years after 1750, and this sense of national identification increasingly competed in people's minds with religious, regional, and local loyalties.

In an early version of nationalism, the eighteenth-century British took pride in the fact that as Protestants they had defeated the Catholic French king in the global trade wars in Asia and the New World. At about the same time, the German author Johann Gottfried Herder concluded from his studies that a common language—along with its folktales, history, and laws—also served as the basis for a shared national identity. In 1789, French revolutionary politicians set out in the Declaration of the Rights of Man and Citizen that all men were citizens—not subjects—and that as citizens they had rights. This Declaration thus proclaimed that common identity could be based on the rule of law. By the beginning of the nineteenth century, some of the major components of nationalism had developed: pride in military conquest and in a common culture developed over centuries, along with citizenship and its guarantee of civil rights and other freedoms.

In the nineteenth century, nationalism became a force in domestic and international politics. From the 1820s on, nationalistic politicians took to the battlefield, as in the fight for Greek independence or in the wars of Italian and German unification. Some Italian nationalists expected that unification would strengthen national identity by providing the kind of common citizenship and freedom that the Americans and French had won through their revolutions.

After 1848, realists like Bismarck and Cavour promoted nationalism as the work of "iron and blood"—national strength backed by military might. Nationalism became a matter of pride in a people's toughness and realism in a competitive world. After their wars of unification, both Germany and Italy continued to promote the vision of the nation triumphant in battle. This differed from the French revolutionary ideal of being triumphant in battle in order to bring rights and constitutions to oppressed peoples. By the end of the nineteenth century, the basis of nationalism had shifted from pride in democratic institutions to pride in a nation's military power. Today, the word *nationalism* usually combines a wide array of ingredients, prompting politicians to appeal to common religion, laws, customs, language, ethnicity, race, and history to build national pride.

MAP 22.2 Unification of Italy, 1859–1870

The many states of the Italian peninsula had different languages, ways of life, and economic interests. The northern kingdom of Sardinia, which included the commercially advanced state of Piedmont, had much to gain from a unified market and a more extensive pool of labor. Although the armies of King Victor Emmanuel and Giuseppe Garibaldi brought these states together as a single country, it would take decades to construct a culturally, socially, and economically unified nation.

Seamstresses of the Red Shirts
Sewing uniforms and making battle flags, European women like these Italian volunteers saw themselves as contributors to the nation. Many nineteenth-century women participated in nation building as "republican mothers" by donating their domestic skills and raising the next generation of citizens to be patriotic.

among Italy's elected political leaders was often difficult to reach once the war was over, and admirers of Cavour, such as Verdi (who had been made senator), quit the quarrelsome political stage. Politicians from the wealthy commercial north and the impoverished agricultural south remained at odds over issues such as taxation and development, as they do even today. Finally, Italian borders did not yet seem complete because Venetia and Rome remained outside them, under Austrian and French control, respectively. Helping to overcome these difficulties and holding the new nation together was the romanticized retelling of the Italian struggle for freedom from foreign and domestic tyrants, under the daring leadership of Garibaldi and his Red Shirts. The legend of Garibaldi papered over Cavour's economic and military Realpolitik, which had made unification possible; but this story became the centerpiece of a new and unifying national pride.

Bismarck and the Realpolitik of German Unification

The most momentous act of nation building for Europe and the world was the creation of a united Germany in 1871. This too was the product of Realpolitik, undertaken once the concert of Europe was smashed and the champions of the status quo defeated. Employing the old military caste to wage war, yet enjoying support from industrialists, merchants, and financiers who saw profits in a single national market, the Prussian state brought a vast array of cities and kingdoms under its control within a single decade. From then on, Germany prospered, continuing to consolidate its economic and political might. By the end of the nineteenth century, it would be the foremost continental power.

Bismarck's Rise to Power.   The architect of the unified Germany was **Otto von Bismarck** (1815–1898). Bismarck came from a traditional Junker (Prussian landed nobility) family on his father's side; his mother's family included high-ranking bureaucrats and literati of the middle class. At university, the young Bismarck had gambled and womanized. After failing in the civil service, he worked to modernize operations on his landholdings while leading an otherwise decadent life. His marriage to a pious Lutheran woman worked a transformation and gave him new purpose. In the 1850s, his diplomatic service to the Prussian state made him increasingly angry at the Habsburg grip on the affairs of all the German states and the roadblock it created to the full flowering of Prussia. Bismarck determined to establish Prussia as a dominant power.

In 1862, William I (king of Prussia, r. 1861–1888; German emperor, r. 1871–1888; see the illustration at right) appointed Bismarck prime minister in hopes that he would quash the growing power of the liberals in the Prussian parliament. The liberals, representing the prosperous professional and business classes, had gained parliamentary strength at the expense of conservative landowners during the decades of industrial ex-

Emperor William I of Germany, 1871
The defeat of France in the Franco-Prussian War of 1870–1871 ended with the proclamation of the king of Prussia as emperor of a unified Germany. Otto von Bismarck, who had orchestrated the wars of unification, appropriately appears in Anton von Werner's rendering as the central figure attired in heroic white. *(akg-images.)*

pansion. Indeed, the liberals' wealth was crucial to the Prussian state's ability to augment its power, but liberals wanted Prussia to be like western Europe with political rights for citizens and increased civilian control of the military. William I, along with members of the traditional Prussian elite such as Bismarck, rejected the western European model. Acting on his conservative beliefs, Bismarck rammed through programs to build the army and prevent civilian control. "Germany looks not to Prussia's liberalism, but to its power," he preached. "The great questions of the day will not be settled by speeches and majority decisions—that was the great mistake of 1848 and 1849—but by iron and blood."

Prussia's Wars of Unification.   After his triumph over the parliament, Bismarck led Prussia into a series of wars, against Denmark in 1864, against Austria in 1866, and, finally, against France in 1870. Using war as a political tactic, he kept the disunited German states from choosing Austrian leadership and instead united them around Prussia. Bismarck drew Austria into a joint war along-

---

Otto von Bismarck (1815–1898): Leading Prussian politician and German prime minister who waged war in order to create a united German Empire, which was established in 1871.

MAP 22.3 Unification of Germany, 1862–1871
In a complex series of diplomatic maneuvers, Prussian leader Otto von Bismarck welded disunited kingdoms and small states into a major continental power independent of the other dominant German dynasty, the Habsburg monarchy. Almost immediately that unity unleashed the new nation's economic and industrial potential, but an aristocratic and agrarian elite remained firmly in power.

side Prussia against Denmark in 1864 over its proposed incorporation of the provinces of Schleswig and Holstein, with their partially German population. The Prussian-Austrian victory resulted in an agreement that Prussia would administer Schleswig, and Austria, Holstein. Such an arrangement stretched Austria's geographic interests far from its central European base: "We were very honorable, but very dumb," Emperor Francis Joseph later said of being drawn into the Schleswig-Holstein debacle.

Lagging in economic development and beset by the restlessness of its many national minorities, Austria proved weaker than Prussia. Bismarck, however, encouraged Austria's pretensions to grandeur and influence. He fomented disputes over the administration of Schleswig and Holstein, goading an overly confident Austria into declaring

war on Prussia itself. In the summer of 1866, Austria went to war with the support of most small states in the German Confederation. Within seven weeks, the modernized Prussian army, using railroads and breech-loading rifles against the outdated Austrian military, had won decisively. The masterful victory allowed Bismarck to drive Austria from the German Confederation and create a North German Confederation led by Prussia (Map 22.3).

To bring the remaining German states into the rapidly developing nation, Bismarck next moved to goad France into a war with Prussia. The atmosphere between France and Austria became charged when Spain proposed a Prussian prince to fill its vacant royal throne. This candidacy at once threatened France with Prussian rulers on two of its borders and inflated Prussian pride at the possibility

Bismarck Tricks the Public to Get His War

By 1870 Otto von Bismarck had gained the allegiance of most of the German states (excluding Austria) by waging two successful wars and thus showing the military muscle of Prussia. Defeating France, he believed, would pull in the remaining independent German states—most notably Bavaria—and unite Germany. To this end he doctored a document sent by the Prussian king to the French ambassador over the contested issue of succession to the Spanish throne and released the edited version to the press. He knew that its newly contrived imperious tone would offend the French parliament. Realpolitik, then as now, involved manipulating the press. Here Bismarck describes his actions.

All considerations, conscious and unconscious, strengthened my opinion that war could only be avoided at the cost of the honor of Prussia and of the national confidence in her. Under this conviction I made use of the royal authorization . . . to publish the contents of the telegram; and

in the presence of my two guests [General Moltke and General Roon] I reduced the telegram by striking out words, but without adding or altering anything, to the following form:

"After the news of the renunciation of the hereditary prince of Hohenzollern had been officially communicated to the imperial government of France by the royal government of Spain, the French ambassador at Ems made the further demand of his Majesty the king that he should authorize him to telegraph to Paris that his Majesty the king bound himself for all future time never again to give his consent if the Hohenzollerns should renew their candidature. His Majesty the king thereupon decided not to receive the French ambassador again, and sent to tell him, through the aid-de-camp on duty, that his Majesty had nothing further to communicate to the ambassador."

The difference in the effect of the abbreviated text of the Ems telegram as compared with that produced by the original

was not the result of stronger words, but of the form, which made this announcement appear decisive, while [the original] version would only have been regarded as a fragment of a negotiation still pending and to be continued at Berlin.

After I had read out the concentrated edition to my two guests, Moltke remarked: "Now it has a different ring; in its original form it sounded like a parley; now it is like a flourish of trumpets in answer to a challenge." I went on to explain: "If, in execution of his Majesty's order, I at once communicate this text, . . . not only to the newspapers, but also by telegraph to all our embassies, it will be known in Paris before midnight, and not only on account of its contents, but also on account of the manner of its distribution, will have the effect of a red rag upon the Gallic bull."

Source: Otto von Bismarck, *Memoirs* in James Harvey Robinson and Charles Beard, eds., *Readings in Modern European History* (Boston: Ginn, 1909), 2:158–59.

of its princely lines ruling grand states. Bismarck used the occasion to get nationalist sentiments onto the news pages in both countries by editing a diplomatic communication (the so-called Ems telegram, named after the spa town in which it was issued) to make it look as if the king of Prussia had insulted France over the issue of the vacant throne. Release of the revised version to journalists inflamed the French public into demanding war (see Document, "Bismarck Tricks the Public to Get His War," above). The parliament gladly declared it on July 19, 1870, setting in motion the alliances Prussia had created with the other German states and launching the Franco-Prussian War. The Prussians captured Napoleon III with his army on September 2, 1870, and France's Second Empire fell two days later.

Birth of the German Empire.　Prussian forces were still besieging Paris when, in January 1871 in the Hall of Mirrors at Versailles, King William of Prussia was proclaimed the kaiser, or emperor, of a new,

imperial Germany. The terms of the peace signed in May of that year ending the Franco-Prussian War required France to cede the rich industrial provinces of Alsace and Lorraine to Germany and to pay a multibillion-franc indemnity. Without French protection for the papacy, Rome became part of Italy. Germany was now poised to dominate continental politics.

Prussian military might served as the foundation for German nation building, and a complex constitution for the new German Empire ensured the continued political dominance of the aristocracy and monarchy—despite the growing wealth and influence of the liberal business classes. The kaiser, who remained Prussia's king, controlled the military and appointed Bismarck to the powerful position of chancellor for the Reich (empire). Individual German states were represented in the Bundesrat, while the Reichstag was an assembly elected by universal male suffrage. The Reichstag ratified all budgets but had little power to initiate programs. In framing this political settlement,

Bismarck accorded rights such as suffrage in the belief that the masses would uphold conservatism and the monarchy out of their fear of modernizing businessmen, whom Bismarck opposed as "liberal power." Taking no chances, he balanced this move with an electoral system in Prussia in which the votes from the upper classes counted more than those from the lower. He had little to fear from liberals, who, dizzy with German military success, came to support the blend of economic progress, constitutional government, and militaristic nationalism that Bismarck represented.

Francis Joseph and the Creation of the Austro-Hungarian Monarchy

The Austrian monarchy took a different approach to nation building, demonstrating that there was no one blueprint for the modern nation-state. Just as the Crimean War left Russia searching for solutions to its social and political problems, so the confrontations with Cavour and Bismarck left the Habsburg Empire struggling to keep its standing in a rapidly changing Europe. The Habsburg Empire had emerged from the revolutions of 1848 renewed by the ascension of the young monarch Francis Joseph (r. 1848–1916), who favored absolutist rule. A tireless worker, Francis Joseph enhanced his authority

The Austro-Hungarian Monarchy, 1867

through stiff court ceremonies, playing to the popular fascination with celebrity and power. Though the emperor stubbornly resisted reform, official standards of honesty and efficiency improved, and the government promoted local education. The German language was used by the administration and taught by the schools, but the government respected the rights of national minorities—Czechs and Poles, for instance—to receive education and communicate with officials in their native tongue. Above all, the government abolished most internal customs barriers, fostered a boom in private railway construction, and attracted foreign capital. The capital city of Vienna underwent extensive rebuilding, and people found jobs as industrialization progressed, if unevenly.

In the fast-moving age of the mid-nineteenth century, the absolutist emperor could not match Bismarck's pace in creating a modern nation-state. Too much of the old regime remained as a roadblock, while prosperous liberals wanting truly representative government and free speech prevented

other measures that would strengthen the state. They resented the police informers who swarmed around them, the Catholic church's control of education and civil institutions such as marriage, and their own lack of representation in such important policy matters as taxation and finance. Thus, liberals blocked funds for modernizing the military for fear of strengthening the reactionary government. Unlike in Prussia, there was no one to override them to bring about change.

After Prussia's 1866 victory over Austria, a vast, wealthy part of the empire, Hungary, became the key to the Habsburg Empire's existence. The leaders of the Hungarian agrarian elites forced the Austrian emperor to accept a **dual monarchy**— that is, one in which the Magyars had home rule over the Hungarian kingdom. This agreement restored the Hungarian parliament and gave it control of internal policy (including the right to decide how to treat Hungary's national minorities). Although the Habsburg emperor Francis Joseph was crowned king of Hungary and Austro-Hungarian foreign policy was coordinated from Vienna, the Hungarians mostly ruled themselves after 1867 and hammered out common policies such as tariffs with the government in Vienna. These negotiations were usually bitter, weakening the process of nation building in the empire.

A second weakness in the compromise that created the dual monarchy was that, although designed specifically to address the Hungarian demands, it led to claims by Czechs, Slovaks, and other national groups in the Habsburg Empire for a similar kind of self-rule. Czechs who had helped the empire advance industrially, for example, wanted Hungarian-style liberties. More of a menace, other leaders of dissatisfied ethnic groups turned to **Pan-Slavism**—that is, the transnational loyalty of all ethnic Slavs whose common heritage, they believed, transcended current national boundaries. Instead of looking toward Vienna, they turned to the largest Slavic country— Russia—as key to achieving the future unity of all Slavs outside the Habsburg Empire. With so many

dual monarchy: A shared power arrangement between the Habsburg Empire and Hungary after the Prussian defeat of the Austrian Empire in 1866–1867.

Pan-Slavism: A movement in the nineteenth century for the unity of all Slavs across national and regional boundaries.

Muslim Quarter and Bazaar
Nineteenth-century Europeans were a diverse people, composed of many religions, ethnicities, and ways of life. In the Balkans, many were Muslims, as this marketplace in Sarajevo, Bosnia, illustrates. The goal of finding a common cultural ground eluded the peoples of the Balkans. The Habsburg monarchy, which annexed Bosnia-Herzegovina in 1908, exerted its influence in the area to keep peoples divided and to play one against the other. *(Graphische Sammlung Albertina, Wien.)*

competing ethnicities, the Austro-Hungarian monarchy remained a dynastic state in which people could show loyalty to the Habsburg dynasty but had increasing difficulty relating to one another as members of a single nation.

Political Stability through Gradual Reform in Great Britain

In contrast to the nations in turmoil on the continent, Britain appeared the epitome of liberal progress. By the 1850s, the monarchy symbolized domestic tranquillity and propriety. Unlike their predecessors, Queen Victoria (r. 1837–1901) and her husband, Prince Albert, portrayed themselves as models of morality, British stability, and middle-class virtues (see "Seeing History," page 704). Britain's parliamentary system steadily brought more men into the political process. Economic prosperity supported peaceful political reform, except that politicians did little to relieve Ireland's continued suffering. A flexible party system helped smooth governmental decision making: the Tory Party evolved into the Conservatives, who favored a more status-oriented politics but still went along with the emerging liberal consensus around economic development and representative government. The Whigs became the Liberals, so named for their commitment to the same values on which the term *liberal* had taken shape in the first place: progress and free, expansive trade, and substituting active industrialists for the entrenched aristoc-

racy—the Stupid Party, as some called the Tories/Conservatives. In 1867, the Conservatives, led by Benjamin Disraeli (1804–1881), passed the Second Reform Bill, which extended voting rights to a million more men. Disraeli proposed, like Bismarck somewhat later, that the working classes would choose "the most conservative interests in the country"—not the radical ones. Thus more men voting and deferring to their aristocratic betters would build his party, not the Liberals.

Both political parties supported an array of reforms because pressure groups now influenced the party system. Women's groups advocated the Matrimonial Causes Act of 1857, which facilitated divorce, and the Married Women's Property Act of 1870, which allowed married women to own property and keep the wages they earned. The Reform League, another pressure organization, had held mass demonstrations in London to bring about passage of the Second Reform Bill. Plush royal ceremonies masked political conflict and united not only critics and activists but also, and more important, different social classes.

Whereas previous monarchs' sexual infidelities had incited mobs to riot, the monarchy of Queen Victoria and Prince Albert, with its newly devised celebrations of royal marriages, anniversaries, and births, drew respectful crowds. Promoting the monarchy in this way was so successful that the term *Victorian* came to symbolize almost the entire century and could refer to anything from manners to political institutions. The aristocracy,

SEEING HISTORY

Photographing the Nation: Domesticity and War

Fostering a common national identity among their citizens was important to many nineteenth-century European leaders, especially those, like Britain's Queen Victoria, who sought to build unity and loyalty among their subjects. The new technology of photography, developed in 1839, served this goal admirably by enabling a more immediate connection between the public and its leaders and their policies. For example, with the new medium, carefully staged photos of royal families became available for the first time, circulating in a small format like today's baseball cards among citizens who eagerly collected them. In the photo below, Queen Victoria and her husband Albert appear as an ordinary middle-class couple. Posing for many such photos, Victoria and Albert helped develop modern celebrity culture but also a national culture that transcended local identities. Why do you think they chose not to appear in royal regalia? What else is interesting about this image? What impression might viewers have formed about the royal couple based on it?

The Crimean War was another shared experience for Britons, many of whom avidly collected photos from the front, for the conflict was one of the first ever to be photographed. Crowds flocked to exhibitions in major cities to view battle scenes (usually staged) and portraits of soldiers, like the one below of officers of the Fifty-seventh regiment. How might this image have affected viewers? What could they learn from it about life on the front? How did it bring the war closer to home?

Both war photography and photography of national leaders, including U.S. president Abraham Lincoln with his wife, Mary Todd Lincoln, or France's Napoleon III and Eugénie, were major ingredients of nation building. The new technology made lofty leaders and the faraway wars they prosecuted accessible—indeed, a part of everyday life—to individuals across the West and beyond. As millions of eyes gazed on these images, the nation's people—wherever they lived—became one.

Portrait of Queen Victoria and Prince Albert at Buckingham Palace, May 15, 1860. *(Getty Images.)*

Roger Fenton, Officers of the 57th Regiment, 1855. *(Library of Congress, Prints and Photographs Division. LC-USZC4-9132.)*

maintaining power despite the rising wealth of liberal businessmen, built gigantic country houses in traditional English architectural styles such as Queen Anne and Georgian, thus using the monarchical heritage to anchor the modern age. Yet politicians in Britain were as devoted to Realpolitik as those in Germany, Italy, or France; their policies included the use of violence to expand their overseas empire and increasingly to control Ireland, where reform stopped short. This violence occurred beyond the view of most British people, however, allowing them to imagine their nation as peaceful, advanced, and united.

Nation Building in the United States and Canada

Nation building in the midcentury United States involved unprecedented and destructive upheaval. The young nation had a more democratic political culture than that of Europe, and nationalism was on the rise. Virtually universal white male suffrage, a rambunctiously independent press, and mass political parties reflected a common belief that sovereignty derived from the people. From the beginning, a combative public politics shaped America.

The United States continued to expand to the west (Map 22.4). In 1848, victory in its war with Mexico almost doubled the size of the country: Texas was officially annexed, and large portions of California and the Southwest extended U.S. borders into formerly Mexican land. Politicians and citizens alike favored banning the native Indian peoples from these western lands and confirming them to reservations. Complicating matters, however, was the question of whether slavery would be allowed in the new western territories. The issue polarized the country. In the North, politicians in the new Republican Party ran on a platform of "free soil, free labor, free men," although few Republicans endorsed the abolitionists' demand to end slavery.

After Republican Abraham Lincoln was elected president in 1860, most of the slaveholding states seceded to form the Confederate States of America. Civil war broke out in 1861 when, under Lincoln's leadership, the North fought to preserve the Union. The future of nation building in the United States hung in the balance. Lincoln did not initially aim to abolish slavery, but his Emancipation Proclamation of January 1863, issued as a wartime measure, officially freed all slaves in the Confederate states and turned the war into a fight not only for union but also for an end to human

bondage. After the summer of 1863, the North's superior industrial strength and military might overpowered and physically destroyed much of the South. By April 1865, the North had prevailed, even though a Confederate sympathizer assassinated Lincoln. Distancing the United States still further from the colonial plantation model, constitutional amendments ended slavery and promised full political rights to free African American men.

Northerners hailed their victory as the triumph of American values, but racism remained entrenched throughout the Union. By 1871, northern interest in promoting African American political rights was waning, and whites began regaining control of state politics in the South, often by organized violence and intimidation. The end of northern occupation of the South in 1877 put on hold the promise of rights for blacks. Nonetheless, in ending slavery, the Union victory opened the way to stronger national government and to economic advancement no longer tied to the old Atlantic system.

The North's triumph had profound effects elsewhere in North America. It allowed the reunited United States to contribute to Napoleon III's defeat in Mexico in 1867. The United States also demanded the annexation of Canada in retribution for Britain's partiality to the Confederacy because of its dependence on cotton. To block this possibility, the British government allowed Canadians to form a united dominion — that is, a self-governing unit of the empire — in 1867. Canadian activists had already appealed for home rule, and dominion status weakened domestic and increasingly powerful U.S. opposition to Britain's control of Canada.

> **REVIEW:** What role did warfare play in the various nineteenth-century nation-building efforts?

Establishing Social Order

Nineteenth-century nation building disrupted everyday life, bringing chaos to cities, death to soldiers, and sometimes dramatic public protest. Government officials sought to offset these disturbances with new social policies intended to build national unity. Confronted with growing populations and crowded cities, governments throughout Europe turned their attention to public health and safety. Many liberal theorists advocated a laissez-

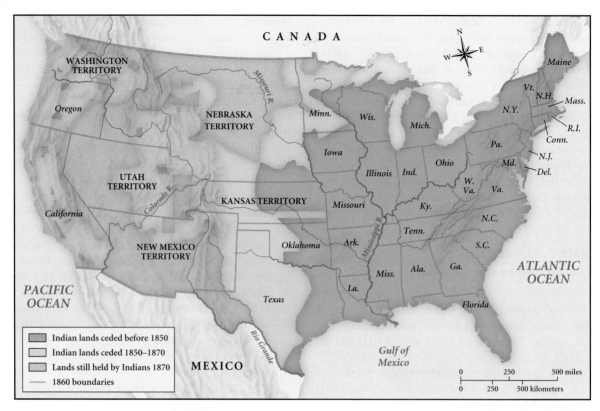

MAP 22.4 U.S. Expansion, 1850–1870
Like Russia, the United States expanded into adjacent regions to create a continental nation-state. In taking over territories, however, the United States differed from Russia by herding native peoples into small confined spaces called reservations so that settlers could acquire thousands of square miles for farming and other enterprises. The U.S. government granted full citizenship for all native Americans only in 1925.

faire government that left social and economic life largely to private enterprise. In contrast, bureaucrats and reformers paid more attention to citizens' lives and, along with missionaries and explorers, worked more actively to establish social order and to spread European influence to the farthest reaches of the globe. These policies did not always prevent protest, as evidenced by the development of Marxist socialism and a dramatic uprising of Parisian working people.

Bringing Order to the Cities

European cities became the backdrop for displays of state power and accomplishment. Governments focused on improving their capital cities, although many noncapital cities also acquired handsome parks, widened their streets, and erected stately museums and massive city halls. In 1857, Austrian emperor Francis Joseph ordered the old Viennese city walls to be replaced with concentric boulevards lined with major public buildings such as the opera house and government offices (see the illus-

tration on page 707). Opera houses and ministries tangibly represented national wealth and power, and the broad boulevards allowed crowds to observe royal pageantry. The wide roads were also easier for troops to navigate than the twisted, narrow medieval streets that in 1848 had concealed insurrectionists in cities like Paris and Vienna—an advantage that convinced some otherwise reluctant officials to approve the expense. Impressive parks and public gardens exemplified the state's control of nature while also helping to order people's leisure time. Revamped European cities inspired awe among the citizens of the various nation-states and throughout their empires.

One effect of refurbishing cities was to highlight class differences. Construction first required destruction, and officials chose to eliminate poor neighborhoods, dislocating tens of thousands of city dwellers. The new boulevards often served as boundaries marking rich and poor sections of the city. In Paris, the process of urban change was called Haussmannization, named for the city's prefect, Georges-Eugène Haussmann, who implemented a grand design that included eighty-five miles of new streets, many lined with showy dwellings for the wealthy. In London, many believed that improved architectural design, including Victorian ornamentation, would blot out the ugliness of commerce and industry. The size and spaciousness of the numerous new banks and insurance companies built there "help[ed] the impression of stability," as an architect put it. Urban renewal would also foster civic pride and make rebellion distasteful.

Refurbishing did not address all urban problems. Repeated epidemics of diseases such as cholera killed alarming numbers of city dwellers and gave the strong impression of social decay — not national power. Unregulated urban slaughterhouses and tanneries; heaps of animal excrement in chicken coops, pigsties, and stables; and piles of human waste alongside buildings were breeding grounds for disease. Typhoid bacteria also spread through sewage and into water supplies, infecting rich and poor alike. In 1861, Britain's Prince Albert — the beloved husband of Queen Victoria — reputedly died of typhus, commonly known as a "filth disease." Stench and disease in cities indicated such a degree of danger

and disorder that governments made sanitation a top priority.

Scientific research, increasingly undertaken in publicly financed universities and hospitals, provided the means to promote public health and control disease. France's Louis Pasteur, whose three young daughters had also died of typhus, advanced the germ theory of disease. Seeking a method to prevent wine from spoiling, Pasteur found that the growth of living organisms caused fermentation in wine, and he suggested that certain organisms — bacteria and parasites — might be responsible for human and animal diseases. Pasteur demonstrated that heating foods such as wine and milk to a certain temperature, a process that soon became known as pasteurization, killed these organisms and made food safe. English surgeon Joseph Lister applied Pasteur's germ theory of disease to infection and developed antiseptics for treating wounds and preventing puerperal fever, a condition that was caused by the dirty hands of physicians and midwives and that killed innumerable women after childbirth.

Governments undertook projects to modernize sewer and other sanitary systems — urban improvements prized by citizens, who often

---

Museums and Nation Building
The Kunsthistorisches Museum (Museum of Fine Arts) in Vienna was part of a huge rebuilding project that adorned the city with wide boulevards and grand public buildings. Art museums such as the one above represented the cultural wealth of the state and allowed citizens to take pride in this wealth while they routinely gathered collectively to view it. *(ullstein — imagebroker.net.)*

attributed them to national superiority. In Paris, huge underground collectors provided a watertight terminus for accumulated sewage (see the illustration of Paris sewers). In addition, Haussmann piped in water from uncontaminated sources in the countryside to provide each household with a secure supply. Widespread imitation followed: the Russian Empire's port city Riga (now in Latvia), for example, organized its first water company in 1863. Improved sanitation testified to the activist state's ability to bring about progress. Citizens responded sympathetically to government initiatives: when sanitary public toilets for men became a feature of modern cities, women petitioned governments for similar facilities. One Russian city dweller complained to a Moscow newspaper of "an enormous cloud of white dust constantly over the city" that injured the eyes and lungs. More aware of dirt, disease, and smells, the middle classes bathed more regularly, sometimes even once a week. Individual concerns for refinement and health mirrored the government's quest for order.

Expanding the Reach of Government

To build an orderly national community, government regulations reached far into the realm of everyday life. The regular censuses that Britain, France, and the United States had conducted since the early nineteenth century became routine in most other countries. Censuses provided the state with such personal details of its citizens' lives as age, occupation, marital status, residential patterns, and fertility. Governments then used these data for a variety of endeavors, ranging from setting quotas for military conscription to predicting the need for new prisons. Reformers like Florence Nightingale, who gathered medical and other statistics to support sanitary reform, believed that such quantitative information made government less susceptible to corruption and inefficiency. Decisions would be based on facts rather than on influence peddling or ill-informed hunches. In 1860, Sweden became the first country to introduce income taxes, which opened an area of private life—

Touring a National Treasure: The Sewers of Paris
The enlargement of sewage systems was so grand an undertaking in urban capitals that they attracted visitors. Many had a curiosity about what technology could achieve and flocked to the new sewers to enjoy tours—a pastime that continues to this day in cities like Paris. (© Leonard de Selva / Corbis.)

one's earnings from work or investment—to government scrutiny.

To bring about their vision of social order, most governments, including those of Britain, Italy, Austria, and France, also expanded their investigation and regulation of prostitution. Venereal disease, especially syphilis, infected individuals and whole families, and officials blamed prostitutes, not their clients, for its spread. The police picked up any suspect woman on the street, passed her to public health doctors who examined her for syphilis, and confined her for mandatory treatment if she was infected. As states began monitoring prostitution and other social matters like public health and housing, they had to add new departments and agencies. In 1867, Hungary's bureaucracy handled fewer than 250,000 public welfare cases; twenty years later, it dealt with more than a million.

Schooling and Professionalizing Society

Emphasis on empirical knowledge and objective standards of evaluation increased and enhanced the status of the professions. Growing numbers of middle-class doctors, lawyers, managers, professors, and journalists gained prestige for employing science, information, and standards in their work. The middle classes argued that civil service jobs should be awarded according to talent and skill rather than automatically go to those of aristocratic birth or political connections. In Britain, a civil service law passed in 1870 required competitive examinations to assure competency in government posts—a system long used in China. Governments began to allow professional people to influence state policy and to determine rules for who would and would not be admitted to their fields. Such legislation had both positive and negative effects: groups could set high standards, but otherwise qualified people were sometimes prohibited from working because they lacked the established credentials or connections. The medical profession, for example, gained the authority to license physicians, but it prevented experienced midwives from attending childbirths. Science became the province of the trained specialist rather than the experienced amateur. Newly employed at government-financed institutions, professors of science often viewed their work as part of a national struggle for prestige and excellence.

Nation building required major improvements in the education of all citizens, professional or not. "We have made Italy," one Italian official announced. "Now we have to make Italians." Education was one way of bringing citizens to think alike. Bureaucrats and professionals called for radical changes in the scope, curriculum, and faculty of schools—from kindergarten to university—to make the general population more unified, fit for citizenship, and useful in furthering economic progress. Expansion of the electorate and lower-class activism prompted one British aristocrat to say of the common people, whom he feared were gaining influence, "We must now educate our masters!" Governments introduced compulsory schooling to reduce illiteracy rates, which were more than 65 percent in Italy and Spain in the 1870s and even higher in eastern Europe. As ordinary people were allowed to participate in government, books taught them about the responsibilities of citizenship, along with practical knowledge necessary for an industrial society.

Educational reform was not always easy. At midcentury, religious authorities supervised schools and charged tuition, making primary education an option only for prosperous or religious parents. After the 1850s, national politicians felt that their states could not afford masses of ignorant peasants, whose backwardness one French official blamed on parish priests, specifically "their lack of intelligence, the narrowness of their views, and the vulgarity of their manners." His statement was extreme, but more measured opinion also questioned the relevance of religion in the curricula of modern schools. In 1861, an English commission on education concluded that instead of knowledge of the Bible, "the knowledge most important to a labouring man is that of the causes which regulate the amount of his wages, the hours of his work, the regularity of his employment, and the prices of what he consumes." As citizens of a nation, the young had to learn its language, literature, and history. Replacing religion was a challenge for the secular and increasingly knowledge-based state.

Enforcing school attendance was another challenge. Though the Netherlands, Sweden, and Switzerland had functioning primary-school systems before midcentury, rural parents in these and other countries did not automatically make use of the opportunity. They depended on their children to perform farm chores and often believed that young people would gain the knowledge they needed for life from working in the fields or the household. Urban homemakers from the lower classes depended on their children to help with domestic tasks such as fetching water, disposing of waste, tending younger children, and scavenging for household necessities such as stale bread from bakers or soup from local missions. Yet even the working poor developed a craze for learning, which made traveling lecturers, public forums, reading groups, and debating societies popular among the middle and working classes.

Secondary education also expanded through the creation of more lycées (high schools) and technical schools, yet it remained a luxury for the privileged few. In authoritarian countries such as Russia, advanced knowledge was suspect because it empowered the young with information and taught them to think objectively. Secondary schooling also expanded with the drive to allow young women access to high school courses in subjects such as history and science. The rationale was that modern knowledge would make them more interesting wives and better mothers. In Britain, the founders of two women's colleges—Girton (1869) and Newnham (1871)—at Cambridge University believed, and were later proved right, that exacting standards and a modern curriculum in women's higher education would inspire improvements in the men's colleges of Cambridge and Oxford. The need for highly competent leaders at all levels of society challenged the traditional idea that education merely served to indicate high social status rather than provide knowledge. Nonetheless, higher education for women remained a hotly contested issue as the vast majority of people felt that knowledge of religion, sewing, and deportment was adequate for women.

Education also opened professional doors to women, who came to attend universities—in particular, medical schools—in Zurich and Paris in the 1860s. Despite the complaint that their practicing medicine would weaken the system of separate spheres, women doctors thought that they could bring feminine values such as gentleness and understanding to health care. The growing need for educated citizens also offered the opportunity for large numbers of women to enter teaching, a field once dominated by men. They founded nursery schools and kindergartens based on the Enlightenment idea that developmental processes start at an early age. In Italy, these efforts coincided with the founding of a unified nation, and women there opened schools as a way to expand knowledge and teach civics lessons, thus providing a service to the fledgling state. Yet many men opposed the idea of women teaching. "I shudder at philosophic women," wrote one critic of female kindergarten teachers. Seen as radical because it enticed middle-class women out of the home, the kindergarten movement was as controversial as other educational reforms.

Spreading Western Order beyond the West

In an age of nation building, colonies took on new importance because they seemed to add to the political power of the state and not merely to economic prosperity. After midcentury, the governments of Great Britain and Russia began to rule colonies directly instead of through trading companies. Sometimes they offered social and cultural services, such as schools. For instance, in the 1850s and 1860s provincial governors and local officials promoted the extension of Russian borders to gain control over nomadic tribes in central and eastern Asia. Russian officials then instituted common educational and religious policies, such as instruction in the Russian language and in the principles of the Russian Orthodox church as a means to social order.

British Rule in India.   Great Britain, the era's mightiest colonial power, made a dramatic change of course toward direct political rule of India during these decades. Before the 1850s, British liberals desired commercial gain from colonies, but, believing in laissez-faire, they kept political involvement in colonial affairs to a minimum. In India, the East India Company directed Britain's interests, and many regional princes awarded the company commercial and other rights, such as the collection of taxes. Since the eighteenth century, the East India Company had gained control over various kingdoms on the Indian subcontinent and then began building railroads throughout the countryside to make commerce and revenue collecting more efficient. As commerce with Britain grew, many enterprising Indian merchants and financiers built fortunes by trading with the company and serving as its tax collectors. Local men served in the British-run Indian civil service and the colonial army, which became one of the largest standing armies in the world.

British rule met with resistance, however. In 1857, a contingent of Indian troops, both Muslim and Hindu, violently rebelled against the British presence. Ignoring the Hindu ban on beef and the Muslim prohibition of pork, the British had forced Indian soldiers to use cartridges greased with cow and pig fat. This was not the local soldiers' main grievance, however. More generally angered at tightening British control, they overran the old Moghul capital at Delhi and declared the inde-

An English View of the Indian Rebellion
Drawings such as this of the Indian Rebellion of 1857 show noble English families under savage attack by rebels. Artists emphasized the innocence of English victims and thus provided a rationale for the rule of superior Europeans over depraved non-Westerners. These drawings also united citizens around the expansion of the nation-state. *(The Granger Collection, New York.)*

pendence of the Indian nation—an uprising that became known as the Indian Rebellion.

Simultaneously, local rulers and their followers also rebelled, condemning "the tyranny and oppression of the infidel and treacherous English." The rani, or queen, Lakshmibai, widow of the ruler of the state of Jhansi in central India, led one of these revolts when the East India Company tried to take over her lands after her husband died—an example of the supposed oppression sparking the uprisings. In the end, the British crushed the Jhansi and other revolts, thus suppressing the Indian Rebellion of 1857. Great Britain then issued the Government of India Act of 1858, which established direct British control of India. In

Indian Resistance, 1857

1876, the British Parliament declared Queen Victoria the empress of India. Nonetheless, in reaction against foreign control and inspired by the revolts, Indian nationalism was born.

A system of rule took shape in which close to half a million South Asians, supervised by a few thousand British men, governed a region of once-independent states now called India. Local people also collected taxes and distributed patronage. Colonial rule meant both blatant domination and subtle intervention in everyday life. For example, the British aimed to divert the colonized Indian population away from its traditional, sophisticated production of textiles, which far surpassed the cheap British cottons and were much in demand. To cut the competition, the British colonial government closed down Indian manufacturing and forced Indians to farm raw materials such as wheat, cotton, and jute to supply British industry and feed its workers. Nevertheless, upper-class Indians came to admire British knowledge of medicine and science, and, following the British attack on their cultural practices, some rejected customs such as child marriage and *sati* — a widow's self-immolation on her husband's funeral pyre. British rule brought additional unity to what were once individual princedoms with separate allegiances. In so doing, it paradoxically promoted nationalism that would soon be used against Britain.

French Overseas Expansion. French political expansion was similarly complex. The French government pushed to establish its dominion over Cochin China (modern southern Vietnam) in the 1860s. Missionaries in the area, ambitious French naval officers, and even some local peoples — much like Indian merchants and financiers — urged the French government to bring the region under greater control. Like the British, the French made improvements: the Mekong Delta project increased both the amount of cultivated land and the available food supply. Sanitation and public health programs proved a mixed blessing, because they led to population growth that strained other local resources. Furthermore, landowners and French imperialists siphoned off most of the profits from economic improvement. The French also undertook a cultural mission to transform cities like Saigon with signs of Western urban life such as tree-lined boulevards similar to those of Paris. French literature, theater, and art were popular not only with colonial officials but also with upper-class local people.

Strategic commercial and military advantages motivated European overseas ventures in this age of Realpolitik. The Crimean War had shown the great powers the importance of the Mediterranean basin. Napoleon III, remembering his uncle's campaign in Egypt, took an interest in building the Suez Canal, which would connect the Mediterranean with the Red Sea and the Indian Ocean and thus dramatically shorten the route from Europe to Asia. Upon completion of the work in 1869, a mania erupted for all things Egyptian and associated with the canal. Verdi's opera *Aïda* was set in ancient Egypt, and Europeans applied Egyptian designs to textiles, furniture, architecture, and art.

The rest of the Mediterranean and the Ottoman Empire felt the heightened presence of the European powers. The French army occupied all of Algeria by 1870, and the number of European immigrants to the region reached one-quarter million. French rule in Algeria was aided by the attraction of local people to European goods and technology and the opportunity to make money. Merchants and local leaders cooperated in building railroads, sought trade with the French, and sent their children to European-style schools. Other local peoples, however, resisted the invasions by continuing to attack soldiers and settlers. European-spread diseases killed many others, and by 1872, the native population in Algeria had declined by more than 20 percent from five years earlier.

European Inroads in China. Its vastness allowed China to escape complete takeover, but the Qing Empire was rapidly losing its position as the world's most prosperous economy. Traders and Christian missionaries from European countries made inroads for the Western powers. Defeat in the Opium War, economic pressures from European trade, and interactions with western missionaries helped generate the mass movement known as the Taiping ("Heavenly Kingdom"). Its millions of adherents wanted an end to the ruling Qing dynasty, the expulsion of foreigners, more equal treatment of women, and land reform. By the mid-1850s, the Taiping controlled half of China. The Qing regime enlisted British and French military aid to help save the dynasty in exchange for greater influence. The result was a bloody civil war beginning in the 1840s and lasting until 1864 that killed some 20 million Chinese (compared with 600,000 dead in the U.S. Civil War). When peace finally came, Western governments controlled much of the Chinese customs service and had virtually unlimited access to the country.

The Meiji Restoration in Japan. Japan alone in East Asia escaped European domination. Dutch traders at Nagasaki had acquainted the Japanese with European industrial, military, and commercial innovations. By 1854, when a treaty opened Japan to trade with America, contacts with Europe had already given the Japanese a healthy appetite for Western goods, especially the superior weaponry. Trade agreements with Western governments followed, leading to concerted effort for reform. In 1867, Japanese reformers overthrew a government that resisted change and in 1868 enacted the Meiji Restoration — a change in regime aimed at establishing Japan as a modern, technologically powerful state free from Western control. The reformers used the restoration of the emperor, who had been marginalized under the earlier system, to make their other changes more acceptable. The word *Meiji*, the name given this new regime, meant "enlightened rule." Its goal was to combine "Western science and Eastern values" as a way of "making new" — hence, a combination of restoration and innovation.

Confronting the Nation-State's Order at Home

Europeans did not simply sit by as the growing nation-state disrupted their lives. A better-informed urban working class protested the upheavals in everyday life caused when cities were ripped apart for improvements and when the growth of factories destroyed artisans' livelihoods. Political theorists such as Pierre-Joseph Proudhon and Karl Marx analyzed what was wrong with society, and their ideas spread among disgruntled citizens. Unions sprang up, calling for strikes and other actions against both employers and the government. In the spring of 1871, the people of Paris, blaming the centralized state for the French surrender to the Prussians, declared Paris a commune — a community of equals without bureaucrats and politicians. Marx's accounts of the Paris Commune, the expansion of government, and the rise of big business, popular among ordinary people, spread fear among the middle classes and politicians for the stability of the social order as they built the nation-state.

The Rise of Marxism. New theories arose to explain the growing power of the nation-state and the spread of industry on which the state depended. Increasingly well-educated by public schools, urban workers frequented cafés and pubs to hear news and discuss economic and political changes. Unions gradually started to take shape after the post-1848 repression of worker organizations, sometimes in secret because of continuing opposition from the government. Many of the most outspoken labor activists were artisans, struggling to survive in the new industrializing climate and attracted at first by the ideas of former printer Pierre-Joseph Proudhon (1809–1865). In the 1840s, Proudhon proclaimed, "Property is theft," suggesting that ownership robbed propertyless people of their rightful share of the earth's benefits. He opposed the centralized state and proposed that society be organized instead around natural groupings

of men (but not women, who, he believed, should work in seclusion at home for their husbands' comfort) in artisans' workshops. These workshops and a central bank crediting each worker for his labor would replace government and would lead to a "mutualist" social organization.

As the nation-state expanded its power, workers were also drawn to **anarchism,** which maintained that the existence of the state was the root of social injustice. According to Russian nobleman and anarchist leader Mikhail Bakunin (1814–1876), the slightest infringement on freedom, especially by the central state and its laws, was unacceptable. Anarchism thus advocated the destruction of all state power. Its appeal grew alongside the growth of government in the second half of the nineteenth century.

Political theorist and labor organizer Karl Marx (1818–1883) opposed both mutualism and anarchism. These doctrines, he insisted, were emotional and wrongheaded, lacking the sound, scientific basis of his own theory, subsequently called **Marxism**. Marx's analysis, expounded most notably in *Das Kapital* ("Capital"), adopted the liberal idea, dating back to John Locke in the seventeenth century, that human existence was defined by the necessity to work to fulfill basic needs such as food, clothing, and shelter. Published between 1867 and 1894, *Das Kapital* was based on mathematical calculations of production and profit that would justify Realpolitik for the working classes. Marx held that the fundamental organization of any society, including its politics and culture, derived from the relationships arising from work or production. This idea, known as *materialism*, meant that the foundation of a society rested on class relationships — such as those between serf and medieval lord, slave and master, or worker and capitalist. Marx called the class relationships that developed around work the *mode of production* — for instance, feudalism, slavery, or capitalism. He rejected the liberal focus on individual rights and emphasized instead the unequal class relations caused by those who had taken from workers control of the means of production — that is, the capital, land, tools, or factories that allowed basic human needs to be met.

---

anarchism: The belief that people should not have government; it was popular among some peasants and workers in the last half of the nineteenth century and the first decades of the twentieth.

Marxism: A body of thought about the organization of production, social inequality, and the processes of revolutionary change as devised by the philosopher and economist Karl Marx.

Marx, like the politicians around him, took a tough-minded and realistic look at the economy, discarding the romantic views of the Utopian socialists. Unlike them, he saw struggle, not warmhearted cooperation, as the means for bringing about change. Workers' awareness of their oppression would produce class consciousness among those in the same predicament and ultimately lead them to revolt against their exploiters. Capitalism would be overthrown by these workers—the proletariat—who would then form a socialist society. Marx rejected the liberal Enlightenment view that society was basically harmonious, maintaining instead that social progress could occur only through conflict.

The Paris Commune versus the French State.

As the Franco-Prussian War ended, revolution and civil war erupted not only in Paris but also in other French cities—catching the attention of Marx as a sign that his predictions were coming true. One issue was the nation-state's takeover of city life in the Haussmannization of Paris. Urban renovation had displaced tens of thousands of workers from their homes in the heart of the city; homelessness and general chaos embittered many Parisians against the state. As the Prussians laid siege to Paris in the winter of 1870–1871, causing death from starvation and bitter cold, Parisians rose up against the state that did not protect them. They demanded new republican liberties, new systems of work, and a more balanced distribution of power between the central government and localities. To counter what they saw as the uncaring despotism of the centralized government, on March 28, 1871, they declared themselves a self-governing commune (Map 22.5). Other French municipalities did the same in an attempt to form a decentralized state of independent, confederated units run by local citizens.

In the Paris Commune's two months of existence, its forty-member council, its National Guard, and its many other improvised offices found themselves at cross-purposes. Trying to maintain "communal" instead of "national" values, Parisians quickly developed a wide array of political clubs, local ceremonies, and self-managed cooperative workshops. Women workers, for example, banded together to make National Guard uniforms on a cooperative rather than a profit-making basis. Beyond liberal political equality, the Commune proposed to liberate the worker and ensure "the absolute equality of women laborers." Thus, a *commune* in contrast to a *republic* was meant to bring about social revolution. But Communards often disagreed on what specific route to take to change society: mutualism, anticlericalism,

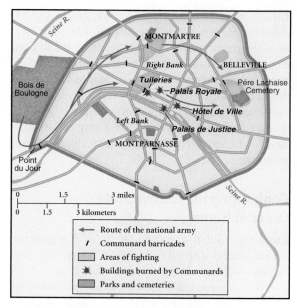

MAP 22.5 The Paris Commune, 1871
The war between the French government and the Paris Commune took place on the streets of Paris and resulted in widespread destruction of major buildings, most notably the Tuileries Palace adjacent to the Louvre. Combatants destroyed many government records in what some saw as a civil war; bitterness, like destruction of property, was great on both sides.

feminism, international socialism, and anarchism were but a few of the proposed avenues to social justice.

In the meantime, the provisional government that succeeded the defeated Napoleon III struck back to reinstitute national order. It quickly stamped out similar uprisings in other French cities. On May 21, the army entered Paris. In a week of fighting, both Communards and the army set the city ablaze (the Communards did so to slow the progress of government troops). Both sides executed hostages, but the well-supplied national army won. In the wake of victory, the army shot tens of thousands of citizens on the streets. One official commented that Parisian insurgents "deserved no better judge than a soldier's bullet." In an age of growing national power, the Communards had fatally promoted a kind of antistate. Soon a different interpretation of the Commune emerged: it was the work of the *pétroleuse*, or "woman incendiary"—a case of frenzied women running amok through the streets. Within a year, writers were blaming the burning of Paris on women—"shameless slatterns, half-naked women, who kindled courage and breathed life into arson." Revolutionary men often became heroes in the history books, but women in political

JUSTICE du PEUPLE

LA COMMUNE

The Commune
A sympathetic artist chose a ferocious woman to represent the Paris Commune. He shows her defending the people of France by driving off politicians who had negotiated the disastrous peace treaty with Germany and who wanted to bring back kings and emperors. The artist depicts those selling out the nation as wasps. (© *Bibliothèque Nationale, Paris, France/The Bridgeman Art Library.*)

situations were characterized as "sinister females, sweating, their clothing undone, [who] passed from man to man."

Defeat in the Franco-Prussian War, the Commune, and the civil war were all horrendous blows to the French state. Key to restoring order in France after 1870 were instilling family virtues, fortifying religion, and claiming that the Commune had resulted from the collapsed boundaries between the male political sphere and the female domestic sphere. Karl Marx disagreed: he analyzed the Commune as a class struggle of workers attacking the propertied capitalists. The centralized state grew larger, in his mind, to protect the interests of those wealthy citizens alone. In the struggle against the Commune, the nation-state once again showed its strengthening muscle. Executions and deportations by the thousands followed, and fear of workers smoldered across Europe.

REVIEW: How did Europe's expanding nation-states attempt to impose social order within and beyond Europe and what resistance did they face?

The Culture of Social Order

Artists and writers of the mid-nineteenth century had complex reactions to the state's expanding reach and the economic growth that sustained it. After 1848, many artists and writers expressed profound grievances about the resulting political repression as well as — paradoxically — the extension of the right to vote to working-class men. They saw daily life as tawdry, infused with commercial values and organized by mindless officials. Ordinary people were no longer deemed heroic as they had been during the revolutionary years. "How tired I am of the ignoble workman, the inept bourgeois, the stupid peasant, and the odious priest," wrote the French novelist Gustave Flaubert, who nonetheless described ordinary people in a new style called **realism** that reflected his disenchantment with romanticism. Intellectuals of the time proposed scientific theories that took a cold,

realism: An artistic style that arose in the mid-nineteenth century and was dedicated to depicting society realistically without romantic or idealistic overtones.

hard look at human life in society and used their new insights to challenge fervent religious belief. Cultural styles and intellectual ideas shared a claim to see society with a detached eye. The starkness of cultural realism was similar to that which statesmen applied to politics.

The Arts Confront Social Reality

The quest for national power enlisted culture in its cause. A hungry reading public devoured biographies of political leaders, past and present, and credited daring heroes with creating the triumphant nation-state. As the development of schooling spread literacy, all classes of readers responded to the mid-nineteenth-century novel and to an increasing number of artistic, scientific, and natural history exhibitions sponsored by the nation-state. While exalting hardheaded heroes of war and peace, citizens came to be schooled in the realism common to all the arts and, more generally, to embrace their shared national heritage.

The Realist Novel. A well-financed press and commercially minded publishers produced an age of best sellers out of the craving for realism. The novels of Charles Dickens appeared in serial form in magazines and periodicals, and each installment attracted buyers eager for the latest plot twist. Dickens's characters, from contemporary English society, include starving orphans, grasping lawyers, heartless bankers, and ruthless opportunists. *Hard Times* (1854) depicts the grinding poverty and ill health of workers alongside the

heartlessness of businessmen. The novelist **George Eliot** (the pen name of Mary Ann Evans) examined contemporary moral values and deeply probed private, real-life dilemmas in *The Mill on the Floss* (1860), *Middlemarch* (1871–1872), and other works. Describing rural society—high and low—Eliot allowed Britons to see one another's predicaments, wherever they lived. Eliot knew the pain of ordinary life from her own experience: she was a social outcast because she lived with a married man. Despite her fame, she was not received in polite society. Popular novels like hers showed readers a hard reality and thus helped form a shared culture among people in distant parts of a nation much as common state institutions like schools did.

French writers also scorned utopian dreams of perfect societies and transcendent beauty. Gustave Flaubert's novel *Madame Bovary* (1857) tells the story of a bored doctor's wife whose life is filled with romantic fantasies and longings for distraction. She has one love affair after another and becomes so hopelessly indebted buying gifts for her lovers that she commits suicide. *Madame Bovary* scandalized French society with its frank picture of women's sexuality, but the scandal brought it a nationwide readership. The poet Charles-Pierre Baudelaire, called satanic by his critics, wrote explicitly about sex; in *Les Fleurs du mal* (Flowers of Evil, 1857), he expressed sexual passion, described drug- and alcohol-induced fantasies, and spun out visions that critics condemned as perverse. Some of his verse explicitly describes the brown body of his mistress of African descent, using sexual terms that mirror colonizers' attitudes. French authorities brought charges of obscenity against both Flaubert and Baudelaire. At issue was social and artistic order: "Art without rules is no longer art," the prosecutor maintained, as both were found guilty.

During the era of the Great Reforms, Russian writers produced novels that debated the nature of both Russian culture and Russianness. Adopting one viewpoint, Ivan Turgenev created a powerful novel of Russian life, *Fathers and Sons* (1862), a story of nihilistic children rejecting not only parental authority but also their parents' spiritual values in favor of science and facts. Expressing another point of view, Fyodor Dostoevsky, in *The Possessed* (1871–1872) and other works, showed the dark, ridiculous, neurotic side of nihilists, thus

AGE OF GREAT BOOKS

1851	Auguste Comte, *System of Positive Politics*
1852	Harriet Beecher Stowe, *Uncle Tom's Cabin*
1854	Charles Dickens, *Hard Times*
1857	Gustave Flaubert, *Madame Bovary;* Charles Baudelaire, *Les Fleurs du mal*
1859	Charles Darwin, *On the Origin of Species;* John Stuart Mill, *On Liberty*
1866	Fyodor Dostoevsky, *Crime and Punishment*
1867	Karl Marx, *Das Kapital*
1869	John Stuart Mill, *The Subjection of Women*
1871–1872	George Eliot, *Middlemarch*

George Eliot: The pen name of English novelist Mary Ann Evans (1819–1880), who described the harsh reality of many ordinary people's lives in her works.

holding up Turgenev as a soft-headed romantic. Dostoevsky's highly intelligent characters in *Crime and Punishment* (1866) are personally tormented and condemned to lead absurd, even criminal lives. He used these antiheroes to emphasize spirituality and traditional Russian values but added a "realistic" spin by planting such values in ordinary people. Just as people were drawn together by the innovations of the nation-state, the Russian public was drawn together in discussing these novels and the issues they raised about Russian identity.

Painting. Visual artists had a different relationship to their governments than did writers, yet many still depicted society in harsh terms. Unlike novelists, painters depended on government patronage rather than sales to thousands of readers. Leaders such as Prince Albert of England actively patronized the arts and purchased works for official collections and for themselves. Another way for artists to earn a living was having their artwork displayed at government-sponsored exhibitions (called salons in Paris, the center of the art world). Officially appointed juries selected works of art to appear in the salon and then chose prize winners from among them. Hundreds of thousands from all social classes attended, though few could afford to buy the art.

Despite being dependent for their living on this patronage, after the revolutions of 1848 artists began rejecting the romantic idealizing of ordinary folk or grand historic events that government purchasers continued to favor. Instead, painters like Gustave Courbet portrayed groaning laborers at backbreaking work because he believed an artist should "never permit sentiment to overthrow logic." The renovated city, artists found, had become a visual spectacle, a setting whose wide new boulevards served as a stage on which urban residents performed. *Universal Exhibition* (1867) by Édouard Manet used the world's fair of 1867 as its background; figures from all social classes promenaded in the foreground, gazing at the Paris scene and observing one another to learn correct modern behavior. Manet also broke with romantic conventions of the nude. His *Olympia* (1865) depicted a white courtesan lying on her bed, attended by a black woman (see page 718). This disregard for the classical tradition of showing women in mythical or idealized settings was too much for the critics. "A sort of female gorilla," one wrote of *Olympia*, as debate raged. Although shocking at first, the graphic, realistic portrayals that shattered romantic illusions became a feature of modern art and the subject of discussion among a broad public.

Gustave Courbet, *Wrestlers* (1850)
Courbet painted his dirty, grunting wrestlers in the realist style, which rejected the hazy romanticism of revolutionary Europe. These muscular men embodied the resort to physical struggle during the nation-building decades and conveyed the art world's recognition that Realpolitik had triumphed in the governance of society. How does the depiction of people in this painting differ from the earlier nineteenth-century image on page 643? (© *Museum of Fine Arts, Budapest/The Bridgeman Art Library.*)

Opera. Unlike most of the visual arts, opera was commercially profitable, accessible to most classes of society, and thus an effective means of reaching the nineteenth-century public. Verdi used musical theater to contrast noble ideals with the corrosive effects of power, love of country with the inevitable call for sacrifice and death, and the lure of passion with the need for social order. The German Richard Wagner, the most musically innovative composer of the era, hoped to revolutionize opera by fusing music and drama to arouse the audience's fear, awe, and engagement with his productions. A gigantic cycle of four operas, *The Ring of the Nibelungen* reshaped ancient German myths into a modern, nightmarish story of a world doomed by its obsessive pursuit of money and power and saved only through unselfish love. His opera *The Mastersingers of Nuremberg* (*Die Meistersinger*, 1862–1867) was a tribute to German culture. The piece was said to be implicitly anti-

A Realist View of the Nude
Manet's *Olympia* (1865) was one of the most shocking works of art of its day. The central woman is not glamorously dressed or posed erotically; rather, she stares candidly and boldly at the viewer. The black maid offers the woman—obviously a courtesan—flowers from an admirer. This scene of modern life was far too modern in its style and subject matter for most critics. (*© Musée d'Orsay, Paris, France / The Bridgeman Art Library.*)

Semitic because of its rejection of influences other than German ones in the arts. Wagner's flair for publicity and musical innovation made him a major force in philosophy, politics, and the arts across Europe. To his fellow citizens, however, he stood for German opera and thus for Germany.

All of the arts, no matter how controversial, shaped the cultural attitudes of the decades 1850–1870. Employing the realist values of the nation builders, the arts provided visions that helped unite isolated individuals into a public with a shared, if debated, cultural experience. Artists both implicitly (like George Eliot) and more explicitly (like Richard Wagner) promoted nation building even as they experimented with new forms.

Religion and National Order

The expansion of state power set the stage for clashes over the role of organized religion in the nation-state. Should religion have the same hold on government and public life as in the past, thus competing with loyalty to the nation? In the 1850s, many politicians supported religious institutions and attended public church rituals because they were another source of order. Simultaneously, some nation builders, intellectuals, and economic liberals came to reject the religious worldview of established churches, particularly Roman Catholicism, as wrongheaded and even harmful to the nation because unrealistic. Bismarck was one of those who believed that religious loyalties also slowed the growth of nationalist sentiment.

Bismarck mounted a full-blown **Kulturkampf** ("culture war") against religion. The German government expelled the Jesuits from Germany in 1872, increased state power over the clergy in Prussia in 1873, and introduced obligatory civil marriage in 1875. Bismarck had bragged, "I am the master of Germany in all but name," but he miscalculated his ability to manipulate politics. The pope fought back, sending a public letter to bish-

---

Kulturkampf: Literally, "culture war"; in the 1870s, German chancellor Otto von Bismarck used the term to describe his fight to weaken the power of the Catholic church.

ops to resist Bismarck's attack: "One must obey God more than men," he ordered. German Catholics rebelled against policies of religious repression as part of nation building, and even conservative Protestants thought Bismarck wrongheaded in attacking religion. Competition between church and state for power and influence heated up in the age of Realpolitik.

Catholic Reaction. The Catholic church felt assaulted across Europe by the growing acceptance of rationalism and science. It saw nation building in Italy and Germany as competition for people's traditional loyalty to Catholicism. In addition, nation builders had extended liberal rights to Jews, whom Christians often considered enemies. Attacking reform, Pope Pius IX issued *The Syllabus of Errors* (1864), which found fault "with progress, with liberalism, and with modern civilization." In 1870, the First Vatican Council approved the dogma of papal infallibility. This teaching proclaimed that the pope, under certain circumstances, must be regarded by Catholics as speaking divinely revealed truth on issues of morality and faith. In 1878, a new pontiff, Leo XIII, began modernizing the church by encouraging up-to-date scholarship in Catholic institutes and universities and by accepting aspects of representative democracy. Leo's ideas marked a dramatic turn, ending the Kulturkampf between church and state and making it easier for the faithful to be both Catholic and patriotic.

Religion continued to have powerful popular appeal, but the place of organized religion in society at large was changing. On the one hand, church attendance declined among workers and artisans; on the other, many in the upper and middle classes and most of the peasantry remained faithful. There was a religious gender gap too. Women's spiritual beliefs became more intense, with both Roman Catholic and Russian Orthodox women's religious orders increasing in size and number; men, by contrast, were falling away from religious devotion. Many urban Jews assimilated to secular, national cultures, abandoning religious practice. The social composition of those faithful to religion had come to take a distinctly different shape from the days when it included everyone.

In 1854, the pope's announcement of the doctrine of the Immaculate Conception (stating that Mary, alone among all humans, had been born without original sin) was followed by an outburst of popular religious fervor, especially among women. In 1858, a young peasant girl, Bernadette Soubirous, began having visions of the Virgin Mary at Lourdes in southern France. In these visions, Mary told Bernadette to drink from the ground, at which point a spring appeared. Crowds comprised mostly of women flocked to Lourdes, believing that its waters could cure their ailments. In 1867, less than ten years later, a new railroad line to Lourdes enabled millions of pilgrims to visit the shrine on church-organized trips. The Catholic church thus showed that it too could use such modern means as railroads and medical verifications of miraculous cures to make holy places like Lourdes into thriving commercial and religious centers. Traditional institutions like churches began taking new steps to build cultural unity similar to that of the nation-state.

The Challenge from Natural Science. At about the time of Soubirous's vision, the English naturalist **Charles Darwin** (1809–1882) published *On the Origin of Species* (1859)—yet another challenge to the Judeo-Christian dogma that humanity was a unique creation of God. In this book and in later writings, Darwin argued that life had taken shape over countless millions of years before humans existed and that human life was but the result of this slow development, called evolution. Instead of God miraculously bringing the universe and all life into being in six days as described in the Bible, Darwin held that life developed from lower forms through a primal battle for survival and through the sexual selection of mates—processes called natural selection. A respectable Victorian gentleman, Darwin shockingly announced that the Bible gave a "manifestly false history of the world." Darwin's theories also undermined certain liberal, secular beliefs. Enlightenment principles, for example, had glorified nature as tranquil and noble and had viewed human beings as essentially rational. The theory of natural selection, in which the fittest survive, suggested a different kind of human society, one composed of warlike individuals and groups constantly fighting one another to triumph over hostile surroundings.

Darwin's findings and other innovative biological research placed religious views of reproduction under attack. Working with pea plants in his monastery garden in the 1860s, Gregor Mendel (1822–1884) discovered the principles of heredity, from which the science of genetics later developed. Investigation into the female reproductive cycle led German scientists to discover the principle of spontaneous ovulation—the automatic release of the

---

Charles Darwin (1809–1882): English naturalist who popularized the theory of evolution and thereby challenged the biblical story of creation.

Darwin Ridiculed, c. 1860

Charles Darwin's theories claimed that humans evolved from animal species and rejected the biblical explanation of a divine human origin. His scientific ideas so diverged from people's beliefs that cartoonists lampooned Darwin and his theory. What message might this cartoon have conveyed to a nineteenth-century viewer? *(Hulton Archive/Getty Images.)*

■ **For more help analyzing this image,** see the visual activity for this chapter in the Online Study Guide at **bedfordstmartins.com/hunt**.

egg by the ovary independent of sexual intercourse. This discovery caused theorists to conclude that men had aggressive and strong sexual drives because reproduction depended on their sexual arousal. In contrast, the spontaneous and cyclical release of the egg independent of arousal indicated that women were passive and lacked sexual feeling.

Darwin also tried to use biological findings to explain the way society worked. Even before Darwin, the influential writer Herbert Spencer (1820–1903) had written that the "unfit" should be allowed to perish in the name of progress—

thus challenging the biblical teaching that the poor were valued. On these grounds Spencer opposed public education, social reform, and any other attempt to soften the harshness of the struggle for existence. Darwin continued this line of argument when he claimed that white European men in the nineteenth century were wealthier and better because more highly evolved than white women or people of color. Despite recognizing a common ancestor for all humans, Darwin held that people of color, or "lower races," were far behind whites in intelligence and civilization. As for women, one could observe that they were in a lower state because any individual man achieved "a higher eminence in whatever he takes up." A school of thought known as Social Darwinism grew out of Darwin's and Spencer's ideas. In the years to come, Social Darwinists used their own version of evolutionary theory to lobby against traditional Christian charity and fairness and instead to promote racist, sexist, and other discriminatory policies as a way of strengthening the nation-state.

From the Natural Sciences to Social Science

In an age influenced by Realpolitik and by Darwin's revolutionary ideas, theorists devised scientific explanations of how society functioned to replace traditional ideas that the social order was created by God. French social philosopher Auguste Comte (1798–1857) developed **positivism**—a theory claiming that careful study of facts would generate accurate and useful, or "positive," laws of society. Comte's *System of Positive Politics, or Treatise on Sociology* (1851) proposed that social scientists construct knowledge of the political order as they would an understanding of the natural world—that is, through observation and objective study. This idea inspired people to believe they could solve the problems spawned by economic and social changes. To accomplish this goal, tough-minded reformers founded study groups and scientifically oriented associations to dig up social facts such as statistics on poverty or the conditions of working-class life. Comte encouraged women's participation in reform because he deemed "womanly" compassion and love as fundamental to social harmony as scientific public policy was. Positivism led not only to women's increased public activism but also to the development of the social sciences in this pe-

positivism: A theory developed in the mid-nineteenth century that the study of facts would generate accurate, or "positive," laws of society and that these laws could, in turn, help in the formulation of policies and legislation.

riod. Sociology was primary among the influential new disciplines that brought science and a new realism to the study of human society.

The celebrated English philosopher John Stuart Mill (1806–1873) used Comte's theories to advocate widespread reform and mass education. In his political treatise *On Liberty* (1859), Mill argued for the improvement of society generally, but he also expressed concern that superior people not be brought down by the will of the masses. Influenced not only by Comte but also by his wife, Harriet Taylor Mill, he advocated the extension of rights to women and introduced a woman suffrage bill into the House of Commons after her death. The bill's defeat led Mill to publish *The Subjection of Women* (1869), a work summarizing his studies with his wife. Translated into many languages and influential in eastern Europe, Scandinavia, and the Americas, *The Subjection of Women* showed the family as a despotic institution, lacking modern values such as rights and freedom. Mill exposed women's cheerful obedience in marriage as a sham. To make a woman appear "not a forced slave, but a willing one," he said, she was trained from childhood not to value her own talent and independence but to embrace "submission" and "the control of others." *The Subjection of Women* became an internationally celebrated guide for a growing movement committed to obtaining basic rights for women.

The progressive side of Mill's social thought was soon lost in a flood of social Darwinist theories and became one among several visions of social order — all of them believed to be scientific and thus true. The theories of Mill, Comte, Darwin, and others influenced later national debates over policy in the West. Inspired by the social sciences, policymaking came to rely on statistics and fact-gathering to produce realistic, hardheaded appraisals for the purpose of building strong, unified nations.

> **REVIEW:** How did cultural expression and scientific and social thought help produce the hardheaded and realistic values of the times?

Conclusion

Throughout modern history, the development of nation-states has been neither inevitable nor uniform nor peaceful. This was especially true in the nineteenth century, when ambitious politicians, shrewd monarchs, and determined bureaucrats used a variety of methods and policies to transform very different countries into centralized

states. Nation building was most dramatic in Germany and Italy, where states were unified through military force and where people of opposing political opinions ultimately agreed that national unity should be a primary goal. Compelled by military defeat to shake off centuries of tradition, the Austrian and Russian monarchs instituted reforms as a way of keeping their systems viable, with widely different results. The Habsburg Empire became a dual monarchy, an arrangement that gave the Hungarians virtual home rule and thus raised the level of disunity. Reforms in Russia left the authoritarian monarchy intact and only partially transformed the social order.

After decades of romantic fervor, hardheaded realism in politics — Realpolitik — became a much touted norm in other areas. Proponents of realism such as Darwin and Marx developed theories disturbing to those who maintained an Enlightenment faith in social and political harmony. Realist novels and artworks jarred polite society, and, like the operas of Verdi, portrayed dilemmas of the times. The policies of the growing state apparatus that were meant to bring order often brought disorder, such as the destruction of entire neighborhoods and violence toward people in far-off lands. Schooling, however, taught the lower classes to be orderly citizens, and urban renewal ultimately improved cities and public health to complement nation building. Yet when the ordinary people of the Paris Commune rose up to protest the loss of French power and prestige, they also aimed to defy the trend toward nation building. Their actions raised difficult questions. How far should the power of the state extend in both domestic and international affairs? Would nationalism be a force for war or for peace? As these issues ripened, the next decades saw extraordinary economic advances and an unprecedented surge in Europe's global power — much of it the result of successes in nation building.

FOR FURTHER EXPLORATION

- ■ For suggested references, including Web sites, for topics in this chapter, see page SR-1 at the end of the book.

- ■ For additional primary-source material from this period, see Chapter 22 in *Sources of THE MAKING OF THE WEST*, Third Edition.

- ■ For Web sites and documents related to topics in this chapter, see *Make History* at bedfordstmartins.com/hunt.

MAPPING THE WEST

Europe and the Mediterranean, 1871

European nation-states consolidated their power by building unified state structures and by developing the means for the diverse peoples within their borders to become socially and culturally integrated. Nation-states were also rapidly expanding outside their boundaries, extending their economic and political reach. North Africa and the Middle East—parts of the declining Ottoman Empire—particularly appealed to European governments because of their resources and their potential for further European settlement. They offered a gateway to the rest of the world. ■ Compare this map of Europe with that from two decades earlier (page 686) to explain the progress of nation building. What aspects of nation building do not appear on this map?

CHAPTER REVIEW

KEY TERMS AND PEOPLE

Realpolitik (690)

Alexander II (693)

mir (695)

Russification (696)

nation-state (696)

Camillo di Cavour (696)

Otto von Bismarck (699)

dual monarchy (702)

pan-Slavism (702)

anarchism (713)

Marxism (713)

realism (715)

George Eliot (716)

Kulturkampf (718)

Charles Darwin (719)

positivism (720)

MAKING CONNECTIONS

1. How did realism in social thought break with Enlightenment values?

2. Why did some nation-states tend toward secularism while the kingdoms that preceded them were based on religion?

3. How was the Paris Commune related to earlier revolutions in France? How did it differ from them? How was it related to nation building?

REVIEW QUESTIONS

1. What were the main results of the Crimean War?

2. What role did warfare play in the various nineteenth-century nation-building efforts?

3. How did Europe's expanding nation-states attempt to impose social order within and beyond Europe and what resistance did they face?

4. How did cultural expression and scientific and social thought help produce the hardheaded and realistic values of the times?

> **For practice quizzes, a customized study plan, and other study tools,** see the Online Study Guide at
> bedfordstmartins.com/hunt.

IMPORTANT EVENTS

1850s–1860s	Positivism, Darwinism become influential	1861–1865	U.S. Civil War
1850s–1870s	Realism in the arts	1867	Second Reform Bill in England; Austro-Hungarian monarchy
1853–1856	Crimean War	1868	Meiji Restoration begins in Japan
1857	British-led forces suppress Indian Rebellion	1869–1871	Women's colleges founded at Cambridge University
1861	Victor Emmanuel declared king of a unified Italy; abolition of serfdom in Russia	1870–1871	Franco-Prussian War
		1871	German Empire proclaimed at Versailles; self-governing Paris Commune established.

Industry, Empire, and Everyday Life
1870–1890

Between 1870 and 1890, Marianne North, an unmarried English-woman, traveled the globe several times. North was a botanical illustrator and "plant hunter," one of those energetic Europeans who on their own or under government sponsorship searched the world over for plants to classify, grow, and put to commercial use. She ventured to India, North and South America, Java, Borneo, South Africa, and many other distant points, setting up her easel and making scientific drawings of plants. She discovered at least five new species (officially named after her) and a new type of tree, and she collected thousands of plants to send back to botanical gardens in England. When North became too frail to travel, she organized a permanent museum in London to display her botanical drawings to the public (see the illustration, on page 726). Her goal was to promote ordinary people's knowledge of the British Empire: "I want them to know," she announced, "that cocoa doesn't come from the coconut."

North was just one of the millions of people who traveled vast distances in the nineteenth century—a time of greatly increased mobility and migration, much of which was made possible by an expansion of industry and colonization. Some, like North, who took advantage of the greater speed of travel, journeyed in pursuit of knowledge. Others migrated temporarily to the colonies to serve in colonial governments, for instance, or to find business opportunities. Still others relocated permanently within Europe or other places abroad in North and South America or Australia in search of work and a better life for themselves. Such migration changed the everyday life of both Europeans and non-Europeans: it uprooted tens of millions of people, it disrupted social

Thomas Roberts, *Coming South* (1886)
Most European migration occurred for political and economic reasons, with beleaguered segments of the population likely to cross thousands of miles by ship to find opportunity and political freedom. Other Western migration was temporary, like that of scientists, writers, soldiers, and missionaries. The Australian painter Thomas Roberts, who had himself migrated from London in 1869 at the age of thirteen, depicted these voyages on ship as so calm and boring as to test one's sanity, an atmosphere described similarly in migrants' diaries and letters. (*© National Gallery of Victoria, Melbourne, Australia / The Bridgeman Art Library.*)

and family networks, and often inflicted terrible violence on native peoples dislocated by European colonizers.

Like individual Europeans, Western nations looked beyond home borders from 1870 to 1890.

Marianne North, *Pitcher Plant*
Wealthy Europeans increasingly traveled overseas in the quest for knowledge and adventure. As the West prospered, travel and world tourism did too. An amateur artist, Marianne North initially gained an audience for her scientific drawings, reports, and specimens only because she traveled in the "best circles." Later her drawings, like this one of a pitcher plant, were prized by scientists. *(Reproduced with the kind permission of the Director and the Board of Trustees, Royal Botanic Gardens, Kew.)*

The Western powers were rapidly expanding their empires through the "new imperialism"—one name for the accelerated race for empire around the world and the seizure of political rather than just economic power. Europeans had been acquiring global territory since the late fifteenth century; the new imperialism was actually the final gulp in this process. In their rush for empire, Europeans explored and took political control of the interior of Africa and fought to dominate even more Asian lands until, by the beginning of the twentieth century, they claimed to control more than 80 percent of the world's surface. Influence and control went beyond political domination: with varying degrees of success, Europeans tried to stamp other continents with European-style place names, architecture, clothing, languages, and domestic customs. They used culture to create empires just as they used it to forge the nation-state.

The decades from 1870 to 1890 were an era of expanding industry in the West as well. Empire and industry fed on each other as raw materials from imperial conquest supplied Western industries. Industrial output soared in the West as industrialization spread from Britain to central and eastern Europe and brought a continuous new supply of products to the market. A growing appetite for these goods, many of them for household consumption, changed the fabric of everyday life for Europeans. New industry attracted people to cities, where common experiences of neighborhood and work life drew them closer together. They became more educated, both through formal schooling and through informal educators like Marianne North who helped them make connections between empire and their own lives. Citizens took pride in their nations' conquests and enjoyed a mushrooming array of new colonial goods. Newspapers covering political affairs expanded their sales to growing urban populations, and workers began demanding greater participation in the po-

■ **1860s–1890s** Impressionism flourishes; increased Asian influence in art

■ **1870s–1890s** Vast emigration; new imperialism

■ **1876** Victoria declared empress of India; invention of the telephone

1865

1870

1875

■ **1871** Franco-Prussian War ends

■ **1873** Recession begins with global impact

litical process. Proud of their imperial conquests and industrial growth, Europeans brimmed with confidence and hope, while the grimmer aspects of empire and industrialization played themselves out in distant colonies, urban slums, and declining standards of living in rural areas.

> **FOCUS QUESTION:** How were industrial expansion and imperial conquest related, and how did they affect Western society, culture, and politics in the late nineteenth century?

The Advance of Industry in an Age of Empire

The 1870s opened with a burst of prosperity as the Franco-Prussian War drew to a close. Fed by raw materials from around the world, industry turned out a cornucopia of new products, and many workers' wages increased. Beginning in 1873, however, a series of downturns in business threatened both entrepreneurs and the working class. Businesspeople sought remedies in new technology, managerial techniques, and a revolutionary marketing institution—the department store. Governments played their part by changing business law and supporting the drive for global profits. The steady advance of industry and the development of a consumer economy gave rise to the service sector, laying the foundation for further changes in work life.

Industrial Innovation

In the last third of the nineteenth century, Western industries turned out hundreds of new products ranging from the bicycle, the typewriter, and the telephone to the internal combustion engine.

In 1885, the German engineer Karl Benz devised a workable gasoline engine; six years later, France's Armand Peugeot constructed a car and tested it by chasing a bicycle race. Electricity became more widely used after 1880, providing power to light everything from private drawing rooms to government office buildings. The Eiffel Tower, constructed in Paris for the Universal Exposition of 1889, stood as a monument to the age's engineering wizardry; visitors rode to its summit in electric elevators. To fuel the West's explosive industrial growth, the leading industrial nations mined and produced massive quantities of coal, iron, and steel. Production of iron increased from 11 million to 23 million tons annually, and steel from 500,000 to 11 million tons annually in the 1870s and 1880s. Manufacturers used the metal to build the more than 100,000 locomotives that pulled trains—trains that transported two billion people a year.

Historians used to contrast a "second" Industrial Revolution, with a concentration on heavy industrial products like iron and steel, to the "first" one of the eighteenth and early nineteenth centuries, in which innovations in the manufacture of textiles and the use of steam energy predominated. Now, however, historians recognize that in most countries except Britain, where industrialization did rise in two stages, the development of textile, iron, and steel industries occurred at the same time and were a part of a single process of industrialization. For instance, numerous textile mills were installed on the continent at the same time as blast furnaces. Although industrialization led to the decline of traditional crafts like weaving, home industry—or **outwork**, the process of having some aspects of industrial work done outside factories in individual homes (similar to the putting-

---

outwork: The process of having some aspects of industrial work done outside factories in individual homes.

■ 1882 Triple Alliance formed; Britain invades Egypt

■ 1882–1884 Bismarck sponsors social welfare legislation

■ 1881 Tsar Alexander II assassinated

■ 1889 Japan adopts constitution; Second International established

1880	1885	1890

■ 1879 Dual Alliance formed

■ 1884 Reform Act doubles British male electorate

■ 1884–1885 Berlin conference on African imperialism

■ 1885 Invention of workable gasoline engine

■ 1891 Construction of Trans-Siberian Railroad begins

The Invention of Electric Lighting
By the 1890s, many new inventions could be seen in a single walk down the wide boulevards of major European cities. In this illustration of Piccadilly in London, electric lighting illuminates the way for modern bicycles and automobiles as well as horse-drawn carriages. By the turn of the century, streets had also become crowded with electric trams. *(Mary Evans Picture Library.)*

out system) — persisted in garment making, metalwork, and porcelain painting. Industrial production occurring simultaneously in homes, small workshops, and factories has continued through the entire history of modern manufacturing down to the present day.

Industrial innovations transformed agriculture. Chemical fertilizers boosted crop yields, and reapers and threshers mechanized harvesting. In the 1870s, Sweden produced a cream separator, a first step toward mechanizing dairy farming. Wire fencing and barbed wire replaced wooden fencing and stone walls, both of which required intensive labor to construct. Refrigeration allowed fruits, vegetables, and meat to be transported without spoiling, thus diversifying and increasing the urban food supply. Tin from colonial trade facilitated large-scale commercial canning, which made many foods available year-round to people in the cities.

Challenge to British Dominance. Britain's rate of industrial growth slowed as its entrepreneurs remained wedded to older technologies. Although Great Britain maintained its high output of industrial goods and profited from a multitude of worldwide investments, Germany and the United States began surpassing it in research, technical education, and innovation — and ultimately in overall rates of economic growth.

Following the Franco-Prussian War, Germany annexed Alsace and Lorraine, territories with both textile industries and rich iron deposits. Investing heavily in research, German businesses devised new industrial processes and began to mass-produce goods. Germany also spent as much money on education as on its military in the 1870s and 1880s. This investment resulted in highly skilled engineers and technical workers who sent German industrial productivity soaring.

The United States began intensive exploitation of its vast natural resources, including coal, metal ores, gold, and oil. The value of U.S. industrial goods jumped from $5 billion in 1880 to $13 billion by 1900. Whereas German productivity rested more on state promotion of industrial efforts, U.S. growth often involved innovative entrepreneurs, such as Andrew Carnegie in iron and steel and John D. Rockefeller in oil. The three-way industrial rivalry among Germany, the United States, and Great Britain would soon have political and diplomatic repercussions.

Areas of Slower Industrialization.

With the exception of Belgium, which had been the first continental country to industrialize, other countries trailed the three industrial leaders. Although France had some huge mining, textile, and metallurgical establishments, U.S. and German businesses soon surpassed French businesses in size. In Spain, Austria-Hungary, and Italy, industrial development was primarily concentrated in a few regions of each country. Austria-Hungary had densely industrialized areas around Vienna and in Styria and Bohemia, but the rest of the country remained tied to traditional, nonmechanized agriculture. Italy industrialized in the north while remaining rural and agricultural in the south. The Italian government spent more on building Rome into a grand capital than it invested in economic growth. A mere 1.4 percent of Italy's 1872 budget went to education and science, compared with 10.8 percent in Germany. Sweden and Norway, which were poor in coal and ore, became leaders in the use of hydroelectric power and the development of electrical products. Despite these innovations, Scandinavia retained its mostly rural character well into the twentieth century.

Russia's road to industrialization was tortuous, slowed partly by its relatively small urban labor force. The terms of serf emancipation bound many Russian peasants, who may have wished to find opportunities in factory work, to the mir, or landed community. Some villages sent men and women to cities, but on the condition that they return for plowing and harvesting. Nevertheless, by the 1890s,

Sukharev Market, Moscow (c. 1890)
For all their modernization, cities also offered their products in dozens of centuries-old food and flea markets such as this one in Russia. Rural farmers brought fresh produce to the cities, while urban market women sold clothing and household items.
(© Austrian Archives/Corbis.)

Moscow, St. Petersburg, and a few other cities had substantial working-class populations. The Russian minister of finance Sergei Witte attracted foreign capital, entrepreneurs, and engineers and used them to construct railroads, including the Trans-Siberian Railroad (1891–1916), which upon completion stretched 5,787 miles from Moscow to Vladivostok. Russia's industrial and military power increased, but its peasants bore the main burden of paying for the state's financing of industry, mostly in the form of higher taxes on vodka. Russia offered a prime example of the uneven benefits of industrialization: neither Russian peasants nor underpaid urban workers could afford to buy the goods their country produced.

Facing Economic Crisis

Economic conditions were far from rosy throughout the 1870s and 1880s despite industrial innovation. In 1873, prosperity abruptly gave way to a severe economic depression, followed by almost three decades of economic fluctuations, featuring sharp downturns whose severity varied from country to country. People of all classes lost their jobs or businesses and faced consequences ranging from long stretches of unemployment to bankruptcy. Because economic ties bound industrialized western Europe to international markets, the downturns affected the economies of such diverse regions as Australia, South Africa, California, Newfoundland, and the West Indies.

The dramatic fluctuations of the late nineteenth century differed from the economic cycles that were the rule before 1850, in which agricultural failure led to higher food prices and then to manufacturing decline. Agriculture was no longer so dominant that its fate determined the welfare of other parts of the economy. By the 1870s, industrial and financial setbacks were sending businesses into long-term tailspins. Innovation created new or modernized industries on an unprecedented scale, but economic uncertainty accompanied the forward march of Western industrial development.

Industrial progress was expensive and businesspeople faced real problems. First, the start-up costs of new enterprises skyrocketed. The early textile mills had required relatively small amounts of capital in comparison to the new factories producing steel and iron. **Capital-intensive industry**, which required huge financial investment for the purchase of expensive machinery, replaced labor-intensive production, which relied on the hiring of more workers. Second, the distribution and consumption of goods failed to keep pace with industrial growth. Increased productivity in both agriculture and industry led to rapidly declining prices. Wheat, for example, dropped to one-third its 1870 price by the 1890s. Consumers, however, did not always benefit from this deflation: wages were slashed and unemployment rose during the economic downturns, preventing the purchase of the new industrial goods. Industrialists had made their fortunes by emphasizing production, not consumption. The series of slumps refocused entrepreneurial policy on finding ways to enhance sales and distribution and to control markets and prices.

Governments took steps to address the economic crisis. New laws spurred the development of the **limited liability corporation**, which protected investors from personal responsibility for a firm's debt. Before limited liability, owners or investors were personally responsible for the debts of a bankrupt business. In one case in England, a former partner who had failed to have his name removed from a legal document after leaving the business remained responsible to creditors when the company went bankrupt. He lost everything he owned except a watch and the equivalent of one hundred dollars. By reducing personal risk, limited liability made investors more confident about financing business ventures.

Investing in stocks and bonds expanded with the need for more capital. Stock markets had existed prior to the changes in liability laws, but investors could trade only in government bonds and in shares of government-sponsored enterprises such as railroads. By the end of the century, stock market investors were trading heavily in stocks that financed a wide range of businesses and thus raised money from a larger pool of private capital than before. At the center of an international economy linked by telegraph, telephone, railways, and steamships, the London Stock Exchange in 1882 traded industrial shares worth £54 million, a value that surged to £443 million by 1900.

Another way in which businesses tried to resolve their financial difficulties was to band together in cartels and trusts to control prices and competition. Cartels (groups of industries organized into a monopoly for fixing prices) flourished particularly in German chemical, iron, coal, and electric industries. For example, the Rhenish-Westphalian Coal Syndicate, founded in 1893, eventually dominated more than 95 percent of coal production in Germany and could thus restrict output and set prices. Trusts appeared first in the United States. In 1882, John D. Rockefeller created the Standard Oil Trust by acquiring stock from many different oil companies and placing it under the direction of trustees. The trustees then controlled so much of the companies' stock that they could set prices for the entire industry and even dictate to the railroads the rates for transporting the oil.

While expressing their belief in free trade, the owners of cartels and trusts were actually restricting the free market. Governments did likewise by beginning to impose tariffs in the belief that doing so would help protect domestic industries. Much of Europe had adopted free trade after midcentury, but during the 1870s, huge trade deficits — caused when imports exceed exports — soured many Europeans on the concept. A country with a trade deficit had less capital available to invest internally; thus, business owners created fewer jobs and the chances of social unrest increased. Farmers in many European countries suffered when improvements

---

capital-intensive industry: A mid- to late-nineteenth-century development in industry that required great investments of money for machinery and infrastructure to make a profit.

limited liability corporation: A legal entity, developed in the second half of the nineteenth century, in which the amount that owners of a factory or other enterprise owed creditors was restricted (limited) in case of financial failure.

in transportation made it possible to import perishable food, such as cheap grain from the United States and Ukraine. The French and German governments were but two that approved tariffs to make foreign goods more expensive. Farmers, capitalists, and even many workers backed taxes on imports to prevent competition from outside. By the early 1890s, all but Belgium, Britain, and the Netherlands had ended free trade.

Revolution in Business Practices

Industrialists tried to minimize the damage of economic downturns by revolutionizing the everyday conduct of their businesses. A generation earlier, factory owners had been directly involved in every aspect of their businesses and often learned to run their firms through trial and error. In the late 1800s, industrialists began to hire managers to run their increasingly complex day-to-day operations. Managers who specialized in a particular aspect of a business such as sales and distribution, finance, or the purchase of raw materials made decisions, assisted by workers in the new "service sector."

The White-Collar Sector. A "white-collar" service sector composed of workers with mathematical skills and literacy acquired in the new public primary schools emerged as part of the development of management. Businesses employed secretaries, file clerks, and typists to guide the flow of business information. Banks that accepted savings from the general public and that invested those funds heavily in business needed tellers and clerks; railroads, insurance companies, and government-run telegraph and telephone companies all needed armies of office workers.

Women, responding to the availability of clean, respectable work, formed the bulk of service employees. At the beginning of the nineteenth century, middle-class women still tended businesses with their husbands. In the next few decades, however, the new ideology of domesticity became so strong that male employers were unwilling to hire women, and women in the lower-middle and middle classes were themselves ashamed to work outside the home. By the late nineteenth century, the costs of middle-class family life had increased, especially because children, who were now forced by law to get an education, were no longer working and contributing to family resources. Instead, the family needed more money to support them. Whether to help pay family expenses or to support themselves, both unmarried and married women of the respectable middle class increasingly took jobs despite the ideal of domesticity. Employers found, as

---

Copenhagen's Central Telephone Exchange (c. 1884)
European governments established telephone and telegraph services for individual customers late in the nineteenth century. These services were part of the rapid advance in transport and communications that characterized the modern West. Middle-class women, like these in Copenhagen's Telephone Exchange, staffed many white-collar positions that made up the new service sector and expanded job opportunities. *(Mary Evans Picture Library.)*

Interior of Au Coin de la Rue (c. 1870)
This Parisian department store, not the grandest or first of its kind, shows the typical cascade of goods displayed on railings and balconies. The abundance of textiles and carpets sparked the shopper's imagination, inciting her to let go of thrift and wander wherever her fancy took her among the many counters and displays until she had overspent. (© Stefano Bianchetti/Corbis.)

one put it, a "quickness of eye and ear, and the delicacy of touch" in the new women workers.

By hiring women for newly created clerical jobs, business and government contributed to a dual labor market in which certain categories of jobs were predominantly male and others were overwhelmingly female. Since society had come to believe that women were not meant to work and even not fit to work, businesses made greater profits by paying women in the service sector chronically low wages — much less than they would have had to pay men for doing the same tasks.

The Department Store. The drive to boost consumption led to a new development in merchandising — the emergence of the department store. Founded after midcentury in the largest cities, department stores gathered an impressive variety of goods in one place in imitation of the Middle Eastern bazaar. Created by daring entrepreneurs such as Aristide and Marguerite Boucicaut of the Bon Marché in Paris and John Wanamaker of Wanamaker's in Philadelphia, department stores eventually replaced stores selling single items such as dishware or fabrics.

Single-item stores that people entered knowing clearly what they wanted to purchase were of-

ten small, somber shops, miniature by comparison with the modern shopping palaces built of marble and filled with lights and mirrors. In the department store, luxurious silks, delicate laces, and richly embellished tapestries spilled over railings and counters, not in neat order reflecting rational, middle-class ideas, but in glorious disarray to stimulate consumer desires. Shoppers no longer restricted their purchases to what they needed but rather reacted to sales, a new marketing technique that could incite a buying frenzy. Because most men lacked the time for shopping, department stores became the domain of women, who came out of their domestic sphere into a new public role. Store owners hired attractive salesgirls, another variety of service workers, to inspire customers to buy. Department store shopping also took place outside of cities: enticing mail-order catalogs from the Bon Marché or Sears, Roebuck arrived regularly in rural areas, replete with all the luxuries and household items contained in the exotic, faraway dream world of the city.

Consumerism was shaped by empire and industry. Wealthy travelers like Marianne North journeyed on well-appointed ocean liners, carrying quinine, antiseptics, and other medicines as well as cameras, revolvers, and the latest in rubber goods and apparel. Consumption of colonial products such as coffee, tea, sugar, tobacco, cocoa, and cola became more widespread for the stimulation they offered hardworking Westerners. Tons of palm oil from Africa were turned into both margarine and fine soap, allowing even ordinary people in the West to see themselves as cleaner and more civilized than those in other parts of the world. Empire and industry jointly shaped everyday life by exciting the desire to own things—whether industrial goods or products from the colonies.

> **REVIEW:** What were the major economic changes in industry and business by the end of the nineteenth century?

The New Imperialism

Imperialism surged in the last third of the nineteenth century. Industrial demand for raw materials and heated business rivalry for new markets fueled competition for territory in Africa and Asia. The imperialism of these decades is called "new" because European nations, the United States, and Japan now aimed to rule vast regions of the world directly; they were no longer content with simply trading with them. The British government declared itself an empire in 1876 after taking control of India from the East India Company trading house, and other governments followed the British model. Champions of nation building connected industrial prosperity and imperial expansion with national identity. "Nations are not great except for the activities they undertake," declared a French advocate of imperialism in 1885. Conquering foreign territory and developing wealth through industry appeared to heap glory on the nation-state. Although some missionaries and reformers involved in the new imperialism aimed to spread Western religions and culture as a benefit to colonized peoples, the expansion of the West increased their subjugation, inflicted violence on them, and radically altered their lives.

Taming the Mediterranean

European countries had always viewed the African and Asian shores of the Mediterranean as areas where they could profit through trade and investment. In the late nineteenth century, they began to take political control of the region as well. Egypt, a convenient and profitable stop on the way to Asia, was an early target. Modernizing rulers had made Cairo into a bustling metropolis with lively commercial and manufacturing enterprises. Egyptians also increased the production of raw materials for its industry, such as cotton for its textile mills. Europeans invested heavily in the region, first in ventures such as building the Suez Canal in the 1860s, then in laying thousands of miles of railroad track, improving harbors, creating telegraph systems, and finally and most important, loaning money at exorbitant rates of interest.

In 1879, the British and the French took over the Egyptian treasury, allegedly to guarantee profits from their investments and the repayment of loans. In 1882, they invaded the country with the excuse of squashing Egyptian nationalists who protested the takeover of the treasury. The British next seized control of the government as a whole and forcibly reshaped the Egyptian economy from a system based on multiple crops that maintained the country's self-sufficiency to one that emphasized the production of a few crops— mainly cotton, raw silk, wheat, and rice—that cheaply fed both European manufacturing

The Suez Canal and British Invasion of Egypt, 1882

and the European working classes. Businessmen from the colonial powers, Egyptian landowners, and local merchants profited from these agricultural changes, while the bulk of the rural population barely eked out an existence.

To protect its colony of Algeria, France occupied neighboring Tunisia in 1881. Farther to the east, businessmen from Britain, France, and Germany flooded Asia Minor and the Levant (the portion of Asia at the eastern end of the Mediterranean) with cheap goods, driving artisans from their trades and into low-paid work building railroads or processing tobacco. Instead of basing wage rates on gender (as they did at home), Europeans used ethnicity and religion, paying Muslims less than Christians, and Arabs less than other ethnic groups. Such practices planted the seeds for anticolonial movements and long-lasting hatred.

Scramble for Africa

After the British takeover of the Egyptian government, Europeans turned their attention to sub-Saharan Africa. In the past, contact between the two continents had principally involved the trade of African slaves for manufactured goods from

The Violence of Colonization
King Leopold, ruler of the Belgian Congo, was so greedy and ruthless that his agents squeezed the last drop of rubber and other resources from local peoples. Missionaries reported and photographed such atrocities as the killing of workers whose quotas were even slightly short or the amputation of hands for the same offense. Belgian agents collected amputated hands and sent them to government officials to show Leopold that they were enforcing his kind of discipline. *(Anti-Slavery International.)*

around the world. The European slave trade had virtually ended by this time, and Europeans' principal objective was obtaining Africa's raw materials, such as palm oil, cotton, metals, diamonds, cocoa, and rubber. Additionally, Britain wanted the southern and eastern coasts of Africa for stopover ports on the route to Asia and its empire in India.

Except for the French conquest of Algeria, Europeans had rarely connected commerce with direct political control in Africa. Yet in the 1880s, European military forces conquered one African territory after another (Map 23.1). The British, French, Belgians, Portuguese, Italians, and Germans jockeyed to dominate peoples, land, and resources — "the magnificent cake of Africa," as King **Leopold II** of Belgium (r. 1865–1909) put it. Driven by insatiable greed, Leopold claimed the Congo region of central Africa, initiating competition with France for that territory and inflicting on its peoples unparalleled acts of cruelty. German chancellor Otto von Bismarck, who saw colonies mostly as political

Leopold II: King of Belgium (r. 1865–1909) who sponsored the takeover of the Congo in Africa, which he ran with great violence against native peoples.

bargaining chips, established German control over Cameroon and a section of East Africa. Faced with competition, the British poured millions of pounds into conquering the continent "from Cairo to Cape Town," as the slogan went, and the French cemented their hold on large portions of western Africa.

The scramble for Africa escalated tensions in Europe and prompted Bismarck to call a conference of European nations at Berlin. The fourteen nations at the conference, held in a series of meetings in 1884 and 1885, decided that control of settlements along the African coast guaranteed rights to internal territory. This agreement led to the strictly linear dissection of the continent; geographers and diplomats cut across indigenous boundaries of African culture and ethnic life. The Berlin conference also banned the sale of alcohol and controlled the sale of arms to native peoples. In theory, the meeting was supposed to reduce bloodshed and temper ambitions in Africa; in reality, European leaders awarded themselves the right to push even harder for control. Savagely greedy individuals like King Leopold continued to plunder the continent and terrorize its people (as shown in

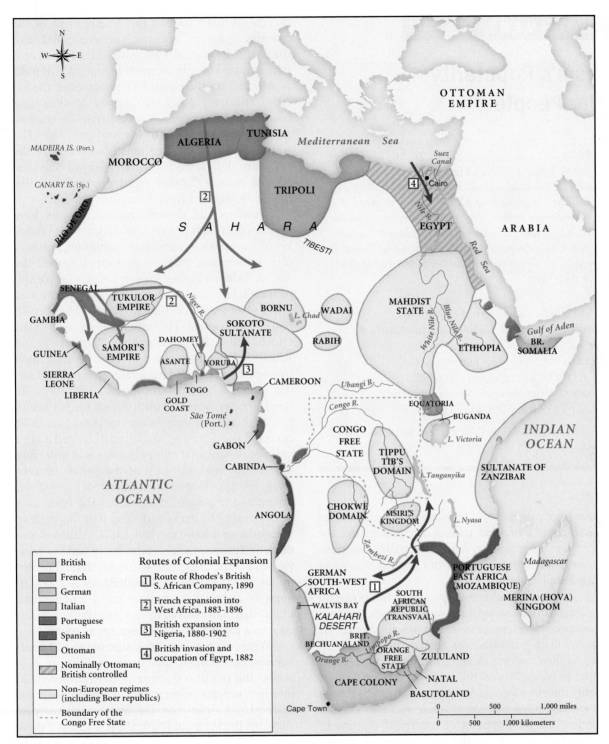

MAP 23.1 Africa, c. 1890

The "scramble for Africa" entailed a change in European trading practices, which generally had been limited to the coastline. Trying to penetrate economically and rule the interior ultimately resulted in a map of the continent that made sense only to the imperial powers, for it divided ethnic groups and made territorial unities that had nothing to do with Africans' sense of geography or patterns of settlement. This map shows the unfolding of that process and the political and ethnic groupings to be conquered.

DOCUMENT

Imperialism's Popularity among the People

Henry Stanley (1841–1904) was an unscrupulous English adventurer in Africa, who regularly killed and abused indigenous peoples to gain their land and wealth on behalf of such clients as Leopold of Belgium. Yet the press boosted sales by recounting his adventures as those of a brave and rugged soldier—an ambassador of civilized values. The celebratory tone infiltrated popular culture, as in the song below. Recounting Stanley's search for an important African leader, Emin Pasha, it brought London music-hall audiences to their feet in an orgy of thunderous applause for their hero.

Oh, I went to find Emin Pasha, and started away for fun,
With a box of weeds and a bag of beads, and some tracts and a Maxim
    gun . . .
I went to find Emin, I did, I looked for him far and wide;
I found him right, I found him tight, and a lot of folks beside,
Away through Darkest Africa, though it cost me lots of tin,
For without a doubt I'd rind him out, when I went to find Emin!

Source: Ernest Short, *Fifty Years of Vaudeville* (New York: Eyre and Spotteswoode, 1946), 43.

the photo on page 734). Newspaper accounts of vast chunks of land trading hands whetted the popular appetite for more imperialist ventures (See Document, "Imperialism's Popularity among the People," above).

Industrial technology provided the powerful guns, railroads, steamships, and medicines that accelerated Western penetration of all the continents. The gunboats that forced the Chinese to open their borders to opium in the 1830s continued to play a crucial role in European expansion, only this time forcing African ethnic groups to give up their independence. Quinine was also crucial. Before the development of medicinal quinine in the 1840s and 1850s, the deadly tropical disease malaria decimated many a European party embarking on exploration or military conquest, giving Africa the nickname "White Man's Grave." The use of quinine, extracted from cinchona bark from the Andes, to treat malaria radically cut death rates among soldiers, missionaries, adventurers, traders, and bureaucrats.

While quinine saved white lives, technology to take lives was also advancing. Improvements to the breech-loading rifle and the development of the machine gun, or "repeater," between 1862 and the 1880s dramatically increased firepower. Europeans carried on a brisk trade selling inferior guns to Africans on the coast, while peoples of the interior still used bows and arrows. Muslim slave traders and European Christians alike crushed African resistance with blazing gunfire: "The whites did not seize their enemy as we do by the body, but thundered from afar," claimed one local African resister. "Death raged everywhere—like the death vomited forth from the tempest."

Nowhere did this destructive capacity have greater effect than in southern Africa, where farmers of European descent and immigrant prospectors, rather than military personnel, battled the Xhosa, Zulu, and other African peoples for control of their land. The Dutch had moved into the area in the seventeenth century, but by 1815 the British had gained control. Thereafter, descendants of the Dutch, called Boers (Dutch for "farmers"), and British immigrants joined together in their fight to wrest farmland and mineral resources from native peoples. British businessman and politician Cecil Rhodes, sent to South Africa for his health just as diamonds were being discovered in 1870, cornered the diamond market and claimed a huge amount of African territory hundreds of miles into the interior with the help of the British government. His ambition for Britain and for himself was boundless: "I contend that we are the finest race in the world," he explained, "and that the more of the world we inhabit the better it is." Although notions of European racial superiority had been advanced before, Social Darwinism reshaped racism to justify converting trade with Africans into conquest of their lands. Within just a few decades, Darwinism had evolved from a contribution to science to a racist justification for imperialism.

Wherever necessary to ensure profit and domination, Europeans either destroyed African economic and political systems or transformed them into instruments of their rule. A British governor of the Gold Coast put the matter succinctly in 1886: the British would "rule the country as if there were no inhabitants." Indeed, most Europeans considered Africans barely civilized, despite the wealth local rulers and merchants accumulated in their international trade in raw materials and slaves, and despite individual Africans' accomplishments in fabric dyeing, road building, and architecture. Westerners claimed that Africans—unlike the Chinese and Indians, whom Europeans credited with a scientific and artistic heritage—were capable only of manual labor. Using this as

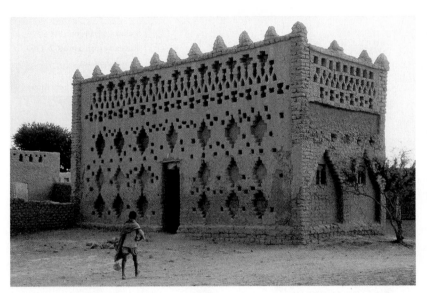

Malian Young Men's House
Europeans claimed that sub-Saharan Africans had no culture and especially no technical knowledge. Yet among Africans there were skilled road builders, textile designers, and manufacturers of weapons. Africans had also constructed intricate mosques, private dwellings, and communal buildings (such as this one for young men in Mali) long before the arrival of Europeans in the African interior. European painters, architects, and sculptors soon adapted features from African styles and even wholly modeled their designs on those of artists beyond the West. *(Photo: Carollee Pelos/ Jean-Louis Bourgeois.)*

an excuse, they confiscated Africans' land and then forced native peoples to work for them in order to pay the taxes they imposed. Agriculture to support families, often performed by women and slaves, declined in favor of mining and farming cash crops. Men were made to leave their homes to work in mines or to build railroads. Family and community networks, though upset by the new arrangements, helped support Africans during this upheaval in everyday life.

Acquiring Territory in Asia

Britain justified its invasion of African countries as strategically necessary to acquire stopover ports for resupplying ships bound for Asia and thus help to preserve its control over India's quarter of a billion people. But in reality from the 1870s on, the expansion of imperial power was occurring around the world. Much of Asia, with India as the centerpiece, was integrated into Western empires. At the same time, resistance to outside domination was also growing. Discriminated against but educated, the Indian elite in 1885 founded the Indian National Congress. Some of its members accepted British liberalism in economic and social policy, welcoming opportunities for trade, education, and social advancement. Others, however, challenged Britain's right to rule. In the next century, the Congress would develop into a mass movement.

To the east, British military forces took control of the Malay peninsula in 1874 and of the interior of Burma in 1885. In both areas, political instability often threatened secure trade. The British depended on the region's tin, oil, rice, teak,

and rubber as well as its access to the numerous interior trade routes of China. British troops guaranteed the order necessary to expand railroads for more efficient export of raw materials and the development of Western systems of communication. The British also built factories and hoped to use its base to expand industrially into China.

The British added to their holdings in Asia partly to counter Russian and French annexations. Since 1865, Russia had been absorbing the small Muslim states of central Asia, including provinces of Afghanistan (Map 23.2, page 738). Besides extending into the Ottoman Empire, Russian tentacles reached Persia, India, and China, often encountering British competition. The Trans-Siberian Railroad allowed Russia to begin integrating Siberia—considered a distant colony in the eighteenth and early nineteenth centuries. Hundreds of thousands of hungry peasants moved to the region, and trade routes to cities in the west expanded. France meanwhile used the threat of military action to negotiate favorable treaties with Indochinese rulers, creating the Union of Indochina from the ancient states of Cambodia, Tonkin, Annam, and Cochin China in 1887 (the latter three now constitute Vietnam). Laos was added to Indochina in 1893.

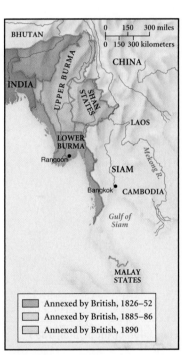

Annexed by British, 1826–52
Annexed by British, 1885–86
Annexed by British, 1890

British Colonialism in the Malay Peninsula and Burma, 1826–1890

MAP 23.2 Expansion of Russia in Asia, 1865–1895

Russian administrators and military men continued enlarging Russia, bringing in Asians of many different ethnicities, ways of life, and religions. Land-hungry peasants in western Russia followed the path of expansion into Siberia and Muslim territories to the south. In some cases they drove native peoples from their lands, but in others they settled unpopulated frontier areas. As in all cases of imperial expansion, local peoples resisted any expropriation of their livelihood, while the central government tried various policies for integration.

The Union of Indochina, 1893

To those who opposed this expansion as "spending our money on distant adventures," French advocates of imperialism pointed out, as did other Europeans, that whites had a "civilizing mission." The French thus taught some of their colonial subjects to speak French and learn French literature and history. The emphasis was always on European, not local people's, culture. In Africa, an exam for students in a school run by German missionaries asked them to write on "Germany's most important mountains" and "the reign of William I and the wars he waged." The deeds of Africa's great rulers and the accomplishments of its kingdoms disappeared from the curriculum. While Europeans believed in instructing colonial subjects, they did not believe that Africans and Asians were as capable as Europeans of achieving great things.

Japan's Imperial Agenda

Japan escaped European rule by its rapid transformation into a modern industrial nation with its own imperial agenda. A Japanese print of the late nineteenth century illustrates both traditional ways and the Western influence behind Japan's burgeoning power (opposite). The picture's small boats might have been rendered centuries earlier, but the steaming locomotive symbolizes change. The Japanese embraced foreign trade and industry. "All classes high and low shall unite in vigorously promoting the economy and welfare of the nation," ran one of the first pronouncements of the Meiji regime that had come to power in 1868. The Japanese government directed the country's turn toward modern industry, and state support led daring innovators like Iwasaki Yataro, founder of the Mitsubishi firm, to develop heavy industries such as mining and shipping. The Japanese had long acquired knowledge from other countries and now sent students, entrepreneurs, and government officials to the West to bring back as much new knowledge as they could. Unlike China, Japan endorsed Western-style modernization in preparation for gaining its own empire.

Change was the order of the day in Japan. Japanese legal scholars, following German models, helped draft a constitution in 1889 that emphasized state power rather than individual rights. Western dress became the rule at the imperial court, and when fire destroyed Tokyo in 1872, a European planner directed the rebuilding in Western architectural style. The Japanese adapted samurai traditions such as spiritual discipline for a large, technologically modern military, filled by universal conscription. In the 1870s, Japan ordered naval ships from Britain and began conquering adjacent islands, including Okinawa. In the 1880s, it used its new naval strength to begin imposing favorable trade treaties on Korea, preliminary to a more complete takeover on the horizon.

Modernization in Japan
Like the West, Japan bustled with commerce and industry thanks to improved and expanding transportation. Railroads, ships, and a range of new inventions such as the rickshaw speeded goods and individuals within cities, across the country, and ultimately to new, foreign destinations. The Japanese traveled widely to learn about ongoing technological innovation. *(Rue des Archives/The Granger Collection, New York.)*

The Paradoxes of Imperialism

Imperialism ignited constant, sometimes heated debate because of its many paradoxes. Although it was meant to make European nations more economically secure, imperialism intensified distrust in international politics and thus threatened everyone. Countries vied with one another for a share of world influence. In securing India's borders, for example, the British faced Russian expansion in Afghanistan and along the borders of China. Imperial competition even made areas of Europe more volatile than ever: Austria-Hungary, Russia, and rival ethnic groups disputed control of the Balkans as the Ottoman Empire's grip weakened in the region.

Politicians claimed that empire would bring great riches, but the costs of empire were great. Opponents claimed that empire was more costly than profitable to societies as a whole. Britain, for example, spent enormous amounts of tax revenue to maintain its empire even as its industrial lead began to slip. Yet for certain businesses, colonies provided crucial markets and great profits: late in the century, French colonies bought 65 percent of

France's exports of soap and 41 percent of its metallurgical exports. Imperialism provided huge numbers of jobs to people in European port cities, but taxpayers in all parts of a nation—whether they benefited or not—paid for colonial armies, increasingly costly weaponry, and administrators.

Even the final goals of imperialism were in conflict. French advocates argued that their nation "must keep its role as the soldier of civilization." But it was unclear whether imperialism should emphasize soldiering—that is, conflict, conquest, and murder of local peoples—or the exporting of culture and religion. The French tried both in Indochina, building a legacy of resistance that continued unabated until the mid-twentieth century. There was also the belief that through imperialist ventures "a country exhibits before the world its strength or weakness as a nation," as one French politician announced. Some in government, however, worried that imperialism—because of its expense and the constant possibility of war—might weaken rather than strengthen the nation-state.

The paradoxes of imperialism extended to the study of other cultures. Western scholars and travelers had long studied Asian and African lan-

***An ABC for Baby Patriots* (1899)**
Pride in empire began at an early age, when learning the alphabet from this kind of book helped develop an imperial sensibility. The subject of geography became important in schools during the decades between 1870 and 1890 and helped young people know what possessions they could claim as citizens. In British schools, the young celebrated the holiday Empire Day with ceremonies and festivities emphasizing imperial power. *(Bodleian Library, University of Oxford. Mary F. Ames, shelfmark 2523 c. 24 [1899].)*

guages, art, and literature, or, like Marianne North, had sought botanical and other scientific knowledge. Yet even the best scholars' study of foreign cultures was tinged with bias, misinterpretation, and error. European scholars of Islam characterized Muhammad as an inferior imitation of Jesus, for example. Confident in their cultural superiority, many Europeans considered Asians and Africans as low types, variously characterizing them as lying, lazy, self-indulgent, or irrational. One English official pontificated that "accuracy is abhorrent to the Oriental mind." At the height of imperialism, such beliefs offered still another justification for conquest: that inferior colonized peoples would ultimately be grateful for what Europe had brought them.

Hoping to spread their superior religion, European missionaries ventured to newly secured areas of Africa and Asia with attitudes that were full of contradictions. A woman missionary working among the Tibetans reflected a common view when she remarked that the native peoples were "going down, down into hell, and there is no one but me . . . to witness for Jesus amongst them." Christianizing colonized peoples often proved impossible, however. When that happened, "civilizers" such as missionaries often supported brutal military measures, willing to see native people slaughtered in the name of imparting Christian values.

Yet other Europeans—from novelists to military men—held quite opposite views of conquered peoples, considering them better than Europeans because they were unspoiled by civilization. "At last some local color," enthused one colonial officer, fresh from industrial cities of Europe, on seeing Constantinople. This romantic vision of an ancient center of culture, similar to eighteenth-century condescension toward the "noble savage," had little to do with the reality of conquered peoples' lives. The paradoxes of imperialism are clear in hindsight, but at the time European self-confidence hid many of them. The most glaring paradox of all was that Western peoples who believed in nation-building and national independence invaded the territory of others thousands of miles away and claimed the right to rule them.

REVIEW: What were the goals of the new imperialism, and how did Europeans accomplish those goals?

Imperial Society and Culture

The spread of empire not only made the world an interconnected marketplace but also transformed everyday culture and society. Success in manufacturing and foreign ventures created millionaires, and the expansion of a professional middle class and development of a service sector meant that more people were affluent enough to own property, see some of the world, and give their children a quality education. Many Europeans grew healthier, partly because of improved diet and partly because of government-sponsored programs aimed at promoting the fitness necessary for citizens of imperial powers. At the same time, the uncertainties of life in a rapidly changing society drove millions of poor Europeans to migrate in search of opportunities around the world—even in the colonies—while artists found exciting new subject matter in those same industrial and imperial changes around them.

The "Best Circles" and the Expanding Middle Class

The profits from empire and industry added new members to the upper class, or "best circles," so called at the time because of their members' wealth, education, and social status. People in the best circles often came from the aristocracy, which remained powerful and was still widely seen as a model of style. Increasingly, however, aristocrats had to share their social position with new millionaires from the ranks of the upper middle class, or bourgeoisie. In fact, the very distinction between aristocrat and bourgeois became blurred, as monarchs gratefully endowed millionaire industrialists and businesspeople with aristocratic titles for their contributions to national wealth. Moreover, financially strapped aristocrats approved marriages between their children and those of the newly rich. Such arrangements brought a much-needed infusion of money to old, established families and the prestige of an aristocratic title to newly wealthy families. Thus, Jeanette Jerome, daughter of a wealthy New York financier, married England's Lord Randolph Churchill (their son Winston later became England's prime minister). Millionaires discarded the thrifty ways of a century earlier to build palatial country homes and villas, engage in conspicuous displays of wealth, and wall themselves off from the poor in segregated neighborhoods. To justify their success, the wealthy often cited the Social Darwinist principle that their ability to accumulate money demonstrated the natural superiority of the rich over the poor.

Empire reshaped the way people in the best circles spent their leisure time. Under the influence of empire, big-game hunting in Asia and Africa became the rage, replacing age-old traditions of fox and bird hunting. European hunters forced native Africans, who had depended on hunting for income or food and for group unity, to work as guides, porters, and domestics for European hunters instead. Collectors on the hunts brought

exotic specimens back to Europe for zoological exhibits, natural history museums, and traveling displays, all of which flourished during this period. Wealthy Europeans brought empire into their homes with displays of stags' heads, elephant tusks, and animal skins.

People in the best circles saw themselves as an imperial elite, and upper-class women devoted themselves to maintaining its standards of social conduct, bearing its children, and directing staffs of servants. They took their role seriously, keeping detailed accounts of their expenditures and mon-

Tiger Hunting in the Punjab

Big-game hunting became the imperial sport of choice, as this Indian work of art shows. European and American hunters took the sport over from local Asians and Africans who had previously depended on the hunt for their livelihood. Western manliness was coming to depend on such seemingly heroic feats as big-game hunting, and imperialists scorned those who continued the old aristocratic fox hunt as effeminate. Though not apparent in this illustration, some Western women enjoyed hunting too. *(Victoria & Albert Museum, London/Art Resource, NY.)*

itoring their children's religious and intellectual development. They decorated their homes with imperial objects such as Persian-inspired textiles, Oriental carpets, wicker furniture, and Chinese porcelains. Although upper-class men chose plain garments, upper-class women wore elaborate costumes — featuring constricting corsets, voluminous skirts, bustles, and low-cut necklines for evening wear — that made them symbols of elite leisure. Women offset the grim side of imperial and industrial society with the rigorous practice of art and music. One Hungarian observer wrote, "The piano mania has become almost an epidemic in Budapest as well as Vienna." Its keys made of ivory from Africa, the piano symbolized the imperial elite's accomplishments and superiority.

Members of the upper class expected their families to be imperial leaders and hoped to perpetuate social and political dominance by controlling their children's social lives. Parents of marriageable women watched them closely to preserve their chastity and to keep them from socializing with lower-class men. Upper-class men regularly seduced lower-class women — part of the double standard that saw promiscuity as normal for men and as immoral for women — but few thought of marrying them. Parents arranged many marriages directly or arranged courtships that were initiated during visiting days, on which occasions prominent hostesses held an open house under formal conditions. This kind of monitored social scene could also be the setting for matrimonial decisions.

Below the best circles, or "upper crust," the "solid" middle class of businesspeople and professionals such as lawyers was expanding, most notably in western and central Europe. In eastern Europe, this expansion did not happen naturally, and the Russian government often sought out foreigners to build its professional and business classes. Although middle-ranked businessmen and professionals could sometimes mingle with those at the apex of society, their lives remained more modest. They did, however, employ at least one servant, to give the appearance of leisure to the middle-class woman in the home. Professional men working at home did so from the best-appointed, if not lavish, room. Middle-class domesticity substituted cleanliness and polish for the imperial grandeur of upper-class life.

Professional Sports and Organized Leisure

As nations competed for territory and economic markets, male athletes banded together to organize team sports that eventually replaced village games. Large audiences now backed a particular team, as soccer, rugby, and cricket drew mass followings that welded the lower and higher classes into a common, competitive culture. The reading public devoured newspaper accounts of competition, whether among nations for colonies or among participants in cross-country bicycle races sponsored by tire makers who wanted to prove the superiority of their product. These races evolved

Anglo-Indian Polo Team
Team sports underwent rapid development during the imperial years as spectators rooted for the success of their football team in the same spirit they rooted for their armies abroad. Some educators believed that team sports molded the male character so that men could be more effective soldiers against peoples of other races. In the instance of polo, as illustrated by the team photo here, the English learned what would soon be seen as a typically English sport from the Indians. *(Hulton Archive/Getty Images.)*

into an international competition in the Tour de France, first held in 1903. Competitive sports were seen as valuable to national strength and spirit. "The Battle of Waterloo was won on the playing fields of Eton," ran the wisdom of the day, suggesting that the games played in school could mold the strength of an army—an army that, as the nineteenth century drew to a close, competed with those of other nations in pursuit of empire.

Team sports—like civilian military service—helped differentiate male and female spheres and thus promoted a social order based on distinction between the sexes. Some women's teams emerged in sports such as soccer, field hockey, and rowing, but in general women interested in athletics were encouraged to engage in individual sports. "Riding improves the temper, the spirits and the appetite," wrote one sportswoman. Rejecting the idea of women's natural frailty, reformers introduced exercise and gymnastics into schools for girls, often with the idea that these would strengthen them for motherhood and thus help build the nation-state. As knowledge of the world developed, some women began to practice yoga.

The middle classes believed their leisure pursuits should strengthen the mind and fortify the body. Thus, mountain climbing became a popular middle-class hobby. As the editor of a Swedish publication of 1889 explained, "The passion for mountain-climbing can only be understood by those who realize that it is the step-by-step achievement of a goal which is the real pleasure of the world." Working-class people adopted middle-class habits by joining clubs for such pursuits as bicycling, touring, and hiking. Clubs that sponsored trips often had names like the Patriots or the Nationals, again associating physical fitness with national strength. The emphasis on healthy recreation gave people a greater sense of individual might and thereby contributed to a developing sense of imperial citizenship based less on constitutions and rights than on an individual nation's exercise of raw power. A farmer's son in the 1890s boasted that with a bicycle, "I was king of the road, since I was faster than a horse."

Working People's Strategies

For centuries, working people had migrated from countryside to city and from country to country to make a living. After the middle of the nineteenth century, empire and industry were powerful factors in migration. Older European cities like Riga, Marseille, and Hamburg offered secure new industrial jobs and opportunities for work in global trade, while new colonies provided land, jobs for soldiers and administrators, and the possibility of unheard-of wealth in diamonds, gold, and other natural resources.

Migration.   Europeans who left their native lands moved for a variety of reasons (see "Contrasting Views," page 744). In parts of Europe, the land simply could not produce enough to support a rapidly expanding population. For example, Greek shipbuilding in ancient times had stripped the vast forests of Sicily, leaving the soil eroded and nearly worthless. By the end of the nineteenth century, hundreds of thousands of Sicilians were leaving, often temporarily, to find work in the industrial cities of North and South America. One-third of all European immigrants came from the British Isles, especially Ireland between 1840 and 1920, first because of the potato famine and then because English landlords drove them from their farms to get higher rents from newcomers. Between 1886 and 1900, half a million Swedes out of a population of 4.75 million quit their country (Figure 23.1, page 746). Millions of rural Jews, especially from eastern Europe, left their villages for economic reasons, but Russian Jews also fled in the face of vicious anti-Semitism. Russian mobs brutally attacked Jewish communities, destroying homes and businesses and even murdering some Jews. These ritualized attacks, called pogroms, were scenes of horror. "People who saw such things never smiled anymore, no matter how long they lived," recalled one Russian Jewish woman who migrated to the United States in the early 1890s.

Commercial and imperial success determined destinations. Most migrants who left Europe went to North and South America, Australia, and New Zealand, as news of opportunity reached Europe. The railroad and steamship made journeys across and out of Europe more affordable and faster, though most workers traveled in steerage with few comforts. Once established elsewhere, migrants frequently sent money back home; the funds could be used to pay for education or set up family members in small businesses, thus improving their condition. European farm families often received a good deal of their income from husbands or grown sons and daughters who had left. Cash-starved peasants in eastern and central Europe welcomed the arrival of "magic dollars" from their kin. Migrants themselves appreciated the chance to begin anew without the harsh conditions of the Old World. One settler in the United States was relieved to escape the meager peasant fare of rye bread and

Experiences of Migration

In the nineteenth century, millions of migrants moved thousands of miles from their homelands. The vast distances traveled and the permanent relocation of these migrants were among the issues generating a wide range of responses. Among both migrants and those left behind, reactions varied from acceptance and enthusiasm to opposition and anger. The conflicting reactions appeared in official reports, local newspapers, poems, and very personal letters. While officials pointed with relief to the economic benefits of emigration (Document 1), people left behind were often heartbroken and destitute (Document 2). Migrants themselves had vastly differing experiences, adding to debate over migration (Documents 3 and 4).

1. The Government View

The preamble to the Hungarian census for 1890 was blunt and unambiguous on the subject. It saw emigration exclusively in financial terms.

Emigration has proved to be a veritable boom. The impoverished populace has been drawn off to where it has found lucrative employment; the position of those left behind, their work opportunities and standard of living, have undoubtedly improved thanks to the rise in wages, and thanks to the substantial financial aid coming into the country: sums of from 300,000 to 1,500,000 florints.

Source: Quoted in Julianna Puskas, "Consequences of Overseas Migration for the Country of Origin: The Case of Hungary," in Dirk Hoerder and Inge Blank, eds., *Roots of the Transplanted: Late 19th Century East Central and Southeastern Europe* (Boulder: East European Monographs, 1994), I:397.

2. Those Left Behind

Teofila Borkowska, from Warsaw, Poland, reacted to her husband's resettlement in the United States in two letters from 1893 and 1894. Stripped of a family group, Teofila had a difficult time surviving, and her husband, Wladyslaw Borkowski, never did return.

1893. Dear Husband: Up to the present I live with the Rybickis. I am not very well satisfied, perhaps because I was accustomed to live for so many years quietly, with you alone. And today you are at one end of the world and I at the other, so when I look at strange corners [surroundings], I don't know what to do from longing and regret. I comfort myself only that you won't forget me, that you will remain noble as you have been. . . . I have only the sort of friends who think that I own thousands and from time to time someone comes to me, asking me to lend her a dozen roubles.

1894. Up to the present I thought and rejoiced that you would still come back to Warsaw, but since you write that you won't come I comply with the will of God and with your will. I shall now count the days and weeks [until you take me to America]. . . . Such a sad life! I go almost to nobody, for as long as you were in Warsaw everything was different. Formerly we had friends, and everybody was glad to see us, while now, if I go to anybody, they are afraid I need something from them and they show me beforehand a different face.

Source: Letter from Teofila Borkowska to Wladyslaw Borkowski, in William Thomas and Florian Znaniecki, *The Polish Peasant in Europe and America* (New York: Dover, 1958), July 21, 1893, April 12, 1894, II: 874–75.

herring: "God save us from . . . all that is Swedish," he wrote home sourly.

Migration out of Europe often meant an end to the old way of life. Workers immediately had to learn new languages and compete for jobs in growing cities where they formed the cheapest pool of labor, often in factories or sweatshops. Emigrant women who worked as homemakers, however, tended to keep to themselves, preserving traditional ways. More insulated, they might never learn the new language or put their peasant dresses away. Their children and husbands more often cast aside their past as they were forced to build a life in schools and factories of the New World.

More common than international migration was internal migration from rural areas to European cities, accelerating the urbanization of Europe. The most urbanized countries were Great Britain and Belgium, followed by Germany, France, and the Netherlands. In Russia, only 7 percent of the population lived in cities of ten thousand or more; in Portugal the figure was 12 percent. Many who moved to the cities were seasonal migrants. In the cities, they worked as masons, cabdrivers, or factory hands to supplement declining income from agriculture; when they returned to the countryside, they provided hands for the harvest. In villages across Europe, independent artisans such as

3. Migration Defended

In some cases, emigrants were said to be unpatriotic and cowardly for leaving their homeland just to avoid hard economic times. To charges against Swedish emigrants, journalist Isador Kjelberg responded with the following defense.

Patriotism? Let us not misuse so fine a word! Does patriotism consist of withholding the truth from the workingman by claiming that "things are bad in America"? I want nothing to do with such patriotism! If patriotism consists of seeking, through lies, to persuade the poorest classes to remain under the yoke, like mindless beasts, so that we others should be so much better off, then I am lacking in patriotism! I love my country, as such, but even more I love and sympathize with the human being, the worker. . . . Among those who most sternly condemn emigration are those who least value the human and civic value of the workingman. . . . They demand that he remain here. What are they prepared to give him to compensate the deprivations this requires? . . . It is only cowardly, unmanly, heartless, to let oneself become a slave under deplorable circumstances which one *can* overcome.

Source: Quoted in H. Arnold Barton, *A Folk Divided: Homeland Swedes and Swedish Americans, 1840–1940* (Carbondale: Southern Illinois University Press, 1994), 72–73.

This anonymous Swedish poem combined a political defense of migration with an economic one.

I'm bound for young America,
Farewell old Scandinavia.
I've had my fill of cold and toil,
All for the love of mother soil.
You poets with your rocks and rills
Can stay and starve—on words, no frills.
There, out west, a man breathes free,
While here one slaves, a tired bee,
Gathering honey to fill the hive
Of wise old rulers, on us they thrive.

In toil we hover before their thrones,
While they take to slumber, like lazy drones.
Drunk with our nectar they've set us afright,
But opportunity has knocked, and we'll take our flight.

Source: Quoted in ibid., 137.

4. The Perils of Migration

A contrasting view of emigration to the United States appeared in the following Slovak song.

My fellow countryman, Rendek from Senica, the son of poor
  parents
Went out into the wide world. In Pittsburgh he began to toil.
From early morning till late at night he filled the furnaces with coal.
Faster, faster, roared the foreman, every day. . . .
Rendek toiled harder
So as to see his wife.
But alas! He was careless
And on Saturday evening late
He received his injuries. At home his widow waited
For the card which would never come.
I, his friend, write this song
To let you know
What a hard life we have here.

Source: Quoted in Frantisek Bielik, Horst Hogh, and Anna Stvrtecka, "Slovak Images of the New World: 'We Could Pay Off Our Debts'" in Dirk Hoerder and Inge Blank, eds., *Roots of the Transplanted: Late 19th Century East Central and Southeastern Europe* (Boulder: East European Monographs, 1994), I:388.

QUESTIONS TO CONSIDER
1. Did the vast nineteenth-century migration ultimately enrich or diminish European culture and society?
2. How would you characterize the experience of migration for families and individuals?
3. How did migration affect the national identity of both receiving countries and European countries of origin?

handloom weavers often supported their unprofitable livelihoods by sending their wives and daughters to work in industrial cities.

Adaptation to Industrial Change. Changes in technology and management practices eliminated outmoded jobs and often made factory work more difficult. Workers complained that new machinery sped up the pace of work to an unrealistic level. For example, employers at a foundry in suburban Paris required workers using new furnaces to turn out 50 percent more metal per day than they had produced using the old furnaces. Stepped-up productivity demanded much more physical exertion,

but workers received no additional pay for their extra efforts. Workers also grumbled about the proliferation of managers; many believed that foremen, engineers, and other supervisors interfered with their work. For women, supervision sometimes brought on-the-job harassment, as in the case of female workers in a German food-canning plant who kept their jobs only in return for granting sexual favors to the male manager.

Many in the urban and rural labor force continued to do outwork at home. In Russia, workers made bricks, sieves, shawls, lace, and locks during the slow winter season. Every branch of industry, from metallurgy to toy manufacturing to food

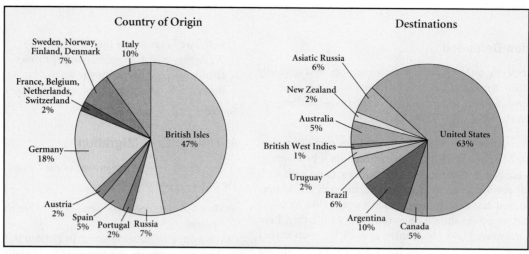

FIGURE 23.1 European Emigration, 1870–1890
The suffering caused by economic change and by political persecution motivated people from almost every European country to leave their homes for greater security elsewhere. North America attracted more than two-thirds of these migrants, many of whom followed reports of vast quantities of available land in both Canada and the United States. Both countries were known for following the rule of law and for economic opportunity in urban as well as rural areas. *(Theodore Hamerow,* The Birth of New Europe: State and Society in the Nineteenth Century *(Chapel Hill: University of North Carolina Press, 1983), 169.)*

processing, also employed urban women at home—and their work was essential to the family economy. They painted tin soldiers, wrapped chocolate, made cheese boxes, and polished metal. Factory owners liked the system because low piece rates made outworkers desperate for income under any conditions and thus willing to work extremely long days. A German seamstress at her new sewing machine reported that she "pedaled at a stretch from six o'clock in the morning until midnight. . . . At four o'clock I got up and did the housework and prepared meals." Owners could lay off women at home during slack times and rehire them whenever needed with little fear of organized protest.

Economic change and the periodic recurrence of hard times had uneven consequences for people's everyday lives. In the late nineteenth century, joblessness and destitution threatened. Some city workers prospered by comparison to those in rural areas, though a growing number lost the steadiness of traditional artisanal work. By and large, however, urban workers were better informed and more connected to the progress of industry and empire than their rural counterparts were.

Reform Efforts for Working-Class People

Many in the urban working class suffered under the uneven effects of industrial growth and the up-

heaval of migration. To address these problems and thereby strengthen their nations, middle- and upper-class reformers founded charities and other organizations for social improvement. Settlement houses, clinics, and maternal and child health centers became a common sight. Young men and women, often from universities, staffed these new organizations, especially the settlement houses, where the reformers took up residence in poor neighborhoods to study and help the people. Believing in the scientific approach, they thought that study would uncover the causes of social problems and point the way to solutions. One group devoted to this enterprise was the Fabian Society in London, a small organization established in 1884. It was committed to a kind of socialism based on study, state planning, and reform rather than revolution. In 1893, the Fabians helped found the Labour Party as a way of making social improvement a political cause. Still other reformers were motivated by a strong religious impulse. "There is Christ's own work to be done," wrote one woman who volunteered to inspect workhouse conditions.

Philanthropists and government officials influenced by Social Darwinism feared that ordinary Europeans would lack the fitness to survive in a competitive world. The poor, as one reformer put it, "were permanently stranded on lower levels of evolution." Reformers began to intervene more in the lives of working-class families as a way to "quicken evolution." They sponsored health clinics and milk centers to provide good medical care and food for children and instructed mothers in child-care techniques, including breast-feeding to promote infant health. Some schools distributed free lunches, medicine, and clothing and inspected the health and appearance of their students. Government officials or individual reformers pressured poor, overworked mothers to conform to new standards for their children — such as finding them respectable shoes — that they could ill afford. Reformers, considering themselves the creators of "wise social legislation," believed they had the right to enter working-class apartments whenever they chose to inspect them.

A few professionals began to make available birth-control information in the belief that smaller families could better survive the challenges of urban life. In the 1880s, Aletta Jacobs (1851–1929), a Dutch physician, opened the first birth-control clinic, which specialized in promoting the new, German-invented diaphragm. Jacobs wanted to help women in Amsterdam slums who were worn out by numerous pregnancies and whose lives, she believed, would be greatly improved by limiting their fertility. Working-class women used these clinics, and knowledge of birth-control techniques spread by word of mouth among workers. The churches adamantly opposed this trend, and even reformers wondered whether birth control would increase the sexual vulnerability of women if the threat of pregnancy and its responsibilities were removed.

Another government reform effort targeted at reproduction consisted of measures said to "protect" women from certain kinds of work. Legislation across Europe barred women from night work and from such "dangerous" trades as pottery making and bartending — allegedly for health reasons, even though medical statistics demonstrated that women became sick on the job less often than men. But lawmakers and workingmen claimed that women's work in pottery making and other trades endangered reproduction. The fear was not that families were too large but that women were not producing healthy enough children and were stealing jobs from men. Women who had worked in trades newly defined as "dangerous" were forced to find other, lower-paying jobs or remain at home. The new laws did not prevent women from holding jobs, but they made earning a living harder. Social Darwinists promoted such efforts in the name of producing a population most fit for the struggle to survive.

Artistic Responses to Empire and Industry

In the 1870s and 1880s, the arts explored the consequences of global expansion and economic innovation, often in the same gloomy Darwinistic terms that made reformers anxious. Darwin's theory held out the possibility that strong civilizations, if they failed to adapt to changing conditions, could weaken, decay, and collapse. French writer Émile Zola, influenced by fears of social decay, produced a series of novels set in industrializing France about a family plagued by alcoholism and madness. Zola's characters, who led violent strikes and in one case even castrated an oppressive grocer, raised questions about the future of civilization. Zola had a dark vision of how industrial society affected individuals: his novel *Women's Paradise* (1883) depicts the upper-class shopper who abandons rational, appropriate behavior for the frenzy of the new department stores. Other heroines were equally upsetting because they violated other long-standing rules. The character Nora in the drama *A Doll's House* (1879) by Norwegian playwright Henrik Ibsen threatens civilized values and the health of society as a whole by leaving an oppressive marriage (see Document, "From *A Doll's House*," page 748).

Writers envisioned a widespread deterioration of behavior pervading urban and rural life. The stories of Emilia Pardo Bazán are tales of incest and murder at work among wealthy landowning families in rural Spain. The heroine of Olive Schreiner's *The Story of an African Farm* (1889) rejects the role of submissive wife in rural Africa, describing the British Empire as a "dirty little world, full of confusion." Schreiner became celebrated among opponents of empire for her grim portrayals. Novelists addressed the burning issues of their times, but Social Darwinism made their realism even bleaker.

Decorative arts of this period featured a countertrend away from stark realism. Country people used mass-produced textiles to create traditional-looking costumes and developed ceremonies based on a mythical past. Such invented customs, romanticized as old and authentic, attracted city dwellers and brought tourist business to villages. So-called folk motifs caught the eye of modern urban architects and industrial designers, who copied rustic styles when creating household goods and decorative objects. The influence of empire is apparent in the traditional Persian and Indian motifs used by English designers William Morris (1834–1896) and his daughter May Morris (1862–1938) in their designs of fabrics, wallpaper, and household items based on such natural imagery as the silhouettes of plants. They wanted to replace "dead" and "ornate" styles of the early industrial years with the simple crafts of the past. Their work gave birth to the "arts and crafts" style, which paradoxically attracted consumers of the industrial age.

Industrial developments also influenced the work of painters, who by the 1870s felt intense competition from a popular industrial invention—the camera. Photographers could produce cheap copies of paintings and create more realistic portraits than painters could, at affordable prices. In response, painters altered their style, at times trying to make their work look as different from photographs as possible. Using thousands of dots and dabs, French painter Georges Seurat depicted the

DOCUMENT

Henrik Ibsen, From *A Doll's House*

Norwegian playwright Henrik Ibsen helped create the global marketplace of ideas with such plays as A Doll's House, *an 1879 work critical of traditional gender roles, as this selection reveals. With women like Marianne North traveling the globe, Ibsen increasingly believed that the middle-class housewife did not develop as a full human being. His plays were performed in many countries—not only in Europe but also in Egypt, the United States, and as far away as Japan—and always sparking fierce debate. If European artists and writers borrowed from other cultures, Europe's cultural influence also spread beyond its borders.*

Helmer: Nora, how can you be so unreasonable and ungrateful? Haven't you been happy here?

Nora: No; never. I used to think I was; but I haven't ever been happy.

Helmer: Not—not happy?

Nora: No. I've just had fun. You've always been very kind to me. But our home has never been anything but a playroom. I've been your doll-wife, just as I used to be Papa's doll-child. And the children have been my dolls. I used to think it was fun when you came in and played with me, just as they think it's fun when I go in and play games with them. That's all our marriage has been, Torvald.

Helmer: There may be a little truth in what you say, though you exaggerate and romanticize. But from now on it'll be different. Playtime is over. Now the time has come for education.

Nora: Whose education? Mine or the children's?

Helmer: Both yours and the children's, my dearest Nora.

Nora: Oh, Torvald, you're not the man to educate me into being the right wife for you.

Helmer: How can you say that?

Nora: And what about me? Am I fit to educate the children?

Helmer: Nora!

Nora: Didn't you say yourself a few minutes ago that you dare not leave them in my charge?

Helmer: In a moment of excitement. Surely you don't think I meant it seriously?

Nora: Yes. You were perfectly right. I'm not fitted to educate them. There's something else I must do first. I must educate myself. And you can't help me with that. It's something I must do by myself. That's why I'm leaving you.

Helmer (jumps up): What did you say?

Nora: I must stand on my own feet if I am to find out the truth about myself and about life. So I can't go on living here with you any longer.

Helmer: Nora, Nora!

Nora: I'm leaving you now, at once. Christine will put me up for tonight—

Helmer: You're out of your mind! You can't do this! I forbid you!

Nora: It's no use your trying to forbid me any more. I shall take with me nothing but what is mine. I don't want anything from you, now or ever.

Helmer: What kind of madness is this?

Nora: Tomorrow I shall go home—I mean, to where I was born. It'll be easiest for me to find some kind of a job there.

Helmer: But you're blind! You've no experience of the world—

Nora: I must try to get some, Torvald.

Helmer: But to leave your home, your husband, your children! Have you thought what people will say?

Nora: I can't help that. I only know that I must do this.

Helmer: But this is monstrous! Can you neglect your most sacred duties?

Nora: What do you call my most sacred duties?

Helmer: Do I have to tell you? Your duties towards your husband, and your children.

Nora: I have another duty which is equally sacred.

Helmer: You have not. What on earth could that be?

Nora: My duty towards myself.

Source: Henrik Ibsen, *A Doll's House* (New York: Anchor, 1966), 96–97.

Parisian suburbs' newly created parks with their Sunday bicyclists and white-collar workers in their store-bought clothing, carrying books or newspapers and parading like the well-to-do. Seurat and other painters used new and varying techniques to distinguish their art from the photographic realism of the camera.

This daring style of art came to be called **impressionism**. It emphasizes the artist's attempt to capture a single moment by focusing on the ever-changing light and color found in ordinary scenes. Using splotches and dots, impressionists moved away from the precise realism of earlier painters and challenged artistic norms. Claude Monet, for example, was fascinated by the way light transformed an object, and he often portrayed the same place—a bridge or a railroad station—at different times of day. Vincent Van Gogh used vibrant colors in great swirls to capture sunflowers, haystacks, and the starry evening sky. Such distortions of reality made the impressionists' visual style seem outrageous to those accustomed to re-

impressionism: A mid- to late-nineteenth-century artistic style that captured the sensation of light in images, derived from Japanese influences and in opposition to the realism of photographs.

alism, but a few enthusiastically greeted impressionism's luminous quality. Industry contributed to the new style, as factories produced a range of pigments that allowed artists to use a wider and more intense spectrum of colors than ever before. Both new industrial products such as the camera and industrial breakthroughs such as chemically based paints gave birth to the impressionist rebellion in the arts.

An increasingly global vision also influenced painting in the age of empire. In both composition and style, impressionists borrowed heavily from Asian art and architecture. The impressionist goal of portraying the fleetingness of light or human situations came from an ancient Japanese concept—*mono no aware* (sensitivity to the fleetingness of life). The color, line, and delicacy of Japanese art (which many impressionists collected) is evident, for example, in Monet's later paintings of water lilies, his studies of wisteria, and even his re-creation of a Japanese garden at his home in France as the subject for artistic study. Similarly, the American expatriate Mary Cassatt used the two-dimensionality of Japanese art in *The Letter* (1890–1891) and other paintings. Van Gogh filled the background of portraits with copies of intensely colored Japanese prints, even imitating

Mary Cassatt, *The Letter* (c. 1890)
Mary Cassatt, an American artist who spent much of her time in Europe, was one of the many Western artists smitten by Japanese prints. Like many other Western artists of her day, she learned Japanese techniques for printmaking, but she also reshaped her painting style to follow Japanese conventions in composition, perspective, and the use of color. Cassatt is known for her many depictions of Western mothers and children and of individual women. In this painting, the woman herself even looks Japanese. *(Mary Cassatt, The Letter, 1890/91. Drypoint and aquatint, 34.5 x 21.1 cm, Mr. and Mrs. M. A. Ryerson Collection, 1932. 1282, The Art Institute of Chicago Photography © The Art Institute of Chicago.)*

■ **For more help analyzing this image,** see the visual activity for this chapter in the Online Study Guide at bedfordstmartins.com/hunt.

classic Japanese woodcuts. The graphic arts advanced the West's ongoing borrowing from around the globe, while responding to the changes brought about by industry.

> REVIEW: How did empire and industry influence art and everyday life?

The Birth of Mass Politics

Amid the expansion of empire and the development of industry, ordinary people struggled for political voice, especially through the vote. By bringing more people into closer contact with one another, industrial growth and urban development strengthened networks of political communication and furthered the growth of national consciousness. The railroad, for example, took high-ranking officials such as prime minister William Gladstone on campaigns to win votes before national audiences, which thus spurred political involvement. As national consciousness grew among workers, they became politically aware and active, leading western European governments to allow more men to vote. Although only men profited from electoral reform, the era's expanding franchise marked the beginning of mass politics — a hallmark of the twentieth-century West. Women could not vote, but they participated in public life by forming auxiliary groups to support political parties. Among the authoritarian monarchies, Germany had male suffrage, but in more autocratic states to the east — for instance, Russia — violence and ethnic conflict shaped political systems. In such places, the harsh rule from above often resembled the control imposed on colonized peoples rather than participation of voting citizens.

Workers, Politics, and Protest

Workers in the 1870s–1890s joined together politically to exert pressure on governments and businesses. Strikes and worker activism were reactions to workplace hardships, but they depended on community bonds forged in neighborhoods. With the backing of their neighbors and fellow laborers, workers formed effective unions and powerful political parties — many of them based on a Marxist platform. Unions served to protect workers from the often brutal pace of industrial change and to guarantee that they received a fair wage. Workers banded together both in grassroots organizations

such as clubs and reading societies and in international organizations across their individual nation-state's boundaries. The Second International, founded in 1889, aimed to combat the growing nationalism and imperial competition that separated workers rather than binding them in a common cause.

Unions and Strikes. As the nineteenth century entered its final decades, workers organized formal unions, which attracted the allegiance of millions. Unions demanded a say in working conditions and aimed, as one union's rule book put it, "to ensure that wages never suffer illegitimate reductions and that they always follow the rises in the price of basic commodities." Businessmen and governments viewed striking workers as insubordinate, threatening political unrest and destructive violence. Even so, strong unions appealed to some industrialists because a union could make strikes more predictable (or even prevent them) and present worker demands coherently instead of piecemeal by groups of angry workers.

From the 1880s on, the pace of collective action for better pay, lower prices, and better working conditions accelerated. In 1888, for example, hundreds of young women who made matches, the so-called London matchgirls, struck to end the fining system, under which they could be penalized an entire day's wage for being a minute or two late to work. This system, the matchgirls maintained, helped companies reap profits of more than 20 percent. Newspapers and philanthropists picked up the strikers' story, condemning "respectable" owners "who suck wealth out of the starvation of helpless girls." In 1890, sixty thousand workers took to the streets of Budapest to agitate for safer working conditions and the vote; the next year, day laborers on Hungarian farms struck too. Across Europe between 1888 and 1890, the number of strikes and major demonstrations rose by more than 50 percent, from 188 to 289.

Housewives, who often acted in support of strikers, carried out their own protests against high food prices. They confiscated merchants' goods and sold them at what they considered a fair price. "There should no longer be either rich or poor," argued Italian peasant women. "All should have bread for themselves and for their children. We should all be equal." They took other kinds of action too: housewives often hid neighbors' truant children from school officials so that the children could continue to help with work at home. When landlords evicted tenants, women gathered in the streets to replace household goods as fast as they were removed from the rooms of ousted families. Meeting on doorsteps or at fountains, laundries, and markets, women initiated rural newcomers into urban ways. In doing so, they helped cement the working-class unity created by workers in the factory.

Governments increasingly responded to strikes by calling out troops or armed police, even though most strikes were about working conditions and not about political revolution. Even in the face of government force, unions did not back down or lose their commitment to solidarity. Craft-based unions of skilled artisans, such as carpenters and printers, were the most active and cohesive, but from the mid-1880s on, a movement known as **new unionism** attracted transport workers, miners, matchgirls, and dockworkers. These new unions were nationwide groups with salaried managers who could plan a widespread general strike across the trades, focusing on such common goals as the eight-hour workday and also paralyzing an entire nation through work stoppages. Although small, local workers' associations remained important, the large unions of the industrialized countries of western Europe had more potential for challenging large industries, cartels, and trusts.

Political Parties.   Workers joined new political parties that addressed working-class issues. Workingmen helped create the Labour Party in England, the Socialist Party in France, and the Social Democratic Parties of Sweden, Hungary, Austria, and Germany — most of them inspired by Marxist theories. Germany was home to the largest socialist party in Europe after 1890. Socialist parties held out hope that newly enfranchised male working-class voters who could become a collective force in national elections, even triumphing because of their numbers over the power of the upper class.

Those who accepted Marx's assertion that "workingmen have no country" went further, founding an international movement to address workers' common interests across national boundaries. In 1889, some four hundred socialists from across Europe met to form the **Second International**, a federation of working-class organizations and political parties that replaced the First International, founded by Marx before the Paris Commune. The Second International adopted a Marxist revolutionary program, but it also advocated suffrage where it still did not exist and better working conditions in the immediate future.

Members of the Second International determined to rid the organization of anarchists, who flourished in the less industrial parts of Europe — Russia, Italy, and Spain. In these countries, anarchism got heavy support from peasants, small property owners, and agricultural day laborers, for whom Marxist theories of worker-controlled factories had less appeal. In an age of crop failures and stiff international competition in agriculture, many rural people sought a life free from the domination of large landowners and governments that backed the landowners' interests. Many advocated extreme tactics, including physical violence and even murder. "We want to overthrow the government . . . with violence since it is by the use of violence that they force us to obey," wrote one Italian anarchist. In the 1880s, anarchists bombed stock exchanges, parliaments, and businesses. Members of the Second International felt that such random violence was counterproductive.

Workingwomen joined unions and workers' political parties, but in much smaller numbers than men. Unable to vote in national elections and usually responsible for housework in addition to their paying jobs, women had little time for party meetings. Furthermore, their low wages hardly allowed them to survive, much less pay party or union dues. Many workingmen opposed their presence, fearing women would dilute the union's masculine camaraderie. Contact with women would mean "suffocation," one Russian workingman believed, and end male union members' sense of being "comrades in the revolutionary cause." Unions glorified the heroic struggles of a male proletariat against capitalism. Marxist leaders maintained that capitalism alone caused injustice to women and thus that the creation of a socialist society would automatically end gender inequality. As a result, although the new political organizations encouraged women's support, most saw women's concerns about lower wages and sexual coercion in the workplace as basically unimportant.

Popular community activities that intertwined politics with everyday life also built worker solidarity. The gymnastics and choral societies that had once united Europeans in nationalistic fervor now served working-class goals. Songs emphasized worker freedom, progress, and eventual victory. "Out of the dark past, the light of the future shines forth brightly," went one Russian workers' song. Socialist gymnastics, bicycling, and marching societies rejected competition and prizes as middle-

new unionism: A nineteenth-century development in labor organizing that replaced local craft-based unions with those that extended membership to all kinds of workers.

Second International: A transnational organization of workers established in 1889, mostly committed to Marxian socialism.

class preoccupations, but they valued physical fitness because it could help workers in the "struggle for existence"—a reflection of the spread of Darwinian thinking to all levels of society. Workers also held festivals and cheerful parades, most notably on May 1—a centuries-old holiday that the Second International now claimed should honor working people. Like religious processions of an earlier time, parades were rituals that fostered unity. European governments frequently prohibited such public gatherings, fearing them as tools for agitators.

Expanding Political Participation in Western Europe

Ordinary people everywhere in the West were becoming aware of politics through newspapers, which, combined with industrial and imperial progress, were important in developing their sense of citizenship in a nation. Western European countries moved toward mass politics more rapidly than did countries to the east. In western Europe, people's access to newspapers and their political participation meant that the will of the people was increasingly important and the power of small cliques relatively less so in determining election outcomes. In eastern Europe, in contrast, conservative elites opposed the integration of citizens as active participants in a national community that was the trend in western Europe.

Mass Journalism.   The rise of mass journalism after 1880 was the product of imperial and industrial development. The invention of automatic typesetting and the production of newsprint from wood pulp lowered the costs of printing; the telephone allowed reporters to communicate news to their papers almost instantly. Once literary in content, many daily newspapers now emphasized sensational news, using banner headlines, dramatic pictures, and gruesome or lurid details—particularly about murders and sexual scandals—to sell papers. In the hustle and bustle of industrial society, one editor wrote, "you must strike your reader right between the eyes." A series of articles in 1885 in London's *Pall Mall Gazette* on the "white slave trade" warned the innocent not to read further. The author then proceeded to describe how young women were "snared, trapped," and otherwise forced into prostitution in distant lands through sexual violation and drugs. Stories of imperial adventurers and exaggerated accounts of wasted women workers and their unborn babies similarly drew ordinary people to the mass press.

Journalism created a national community of up-to-date citizens, whether or not they could vote. Unlike the book, the newspaper was meant not for quiet reflection at home or in the upper-class club but for quick reading of attention-grabbing stories on mass transportation and on the streets. Elites complained that the sensationalist press was a sign of social decay, but for up-and-coming people from the working and middle classes, journalism provided an avenue to success. As London, Paris, Vienna, Berlin, and St. Petersburg became centers not only of politics but also of news, a number of European politicians got their start working for daily newspapers. In western Europe, increasing political literacy opened the political process to wider participation.

British Political Reforms.   A change in political campaigning was one example of this widening participation. In the fall of 1879, **William Gladstone** (1809–1898), leader of the British Liberals, whose party was then out of power, took a train trip across Britain to campaign for a seat in the House of Commons. During his campaign, Gladstone addressed thousands of workers, arguing for the people of India and Africa to have more rights and summoning his audiences to "honest, manful, humble effort" in the middle-class tradition of "hard work." Newspapers around the country reported on his trip and these accounts, along with mass meetings, fueled public interest in politics. Queen Victoria, angered by Gladstone's novel tactic of speaking to ordinary people and by his attacks on her empire, vowed that he would never again serve as prime minister. Gladstone's campaign was successful, however; his Liberal Party won, and he did become prime minister.

Other changes fostered the growth of mass politics in Britain. The Ballot Act of 1872 made voting secret, a reform that reduced the ability of landlords and employers to control how their workers voted. The **Reform Act of 1884** doubled the electorate to around 4.5 million men, enfranchising many urban workers and artisans and thus further diminishing traditional aristocratic influence in the countryside. To win the votes of the newly enfranchised, Liberal and Conservative parties alike established national political clubs to build party loyalty. These clubs competed with the cliques of

---

William Gladstone (1809–1898): Liberal politician and prime minister of Great Britain who innovated in popular campaigning and who criticized British imperialism.

Reform Act of 1884: British legislation that granted the right to vote to a mass male citizenry.

parliamentary elites who had controlled party politics. Broadly based interest groups such as unions and national political clubs began to open up politics by appealing to many more voters.

British political reforms immediately affected Irish politics by arming disaffected tenant farmers with the secret ballot. The political climate in Ireland was explosive mainly because of the repressive tactics of absentee landlords, many of them English and Protestant, who drove tenants from their land in order to charge higher rents to newcomers. In 1879, opponents of these landlords' attacks on Irish well-being formed the Irish National Land League and launched fiery protests. Irish tenants elected a solid bloc of nationalist representatives to the British Parliament.

The Irish members of Parliament began voting as a group, which gave them sufficient strength to defeat legislation proposed by either the Conservatives or the Liberals. Irish leader **Charles Stewart Parnell** (1846–1891) demanded British support for **home rule**—a system giving Ireland its own parliament—in return for Irish votes (see Parnell's portrait on this page). Gladstone, who served four nonconsecutive terms as prime minister between 1868 and 1894, accommodated Parnell with bills on home rule and tenant security. But Conservatives called home rule "a conspiracy against the honor of Britain," and when they were in power (1885–1886 and 1886–1892), they cracked down on Irish activism. Scandals reported in the press, some of them totally invented, weakened Parnell's influence. In 1890, the news broke of his affair with a married woman, and he died in disgrace soon after. Parnell's leadership was sorely missed, and Irish home rule remained a heated political issue in the British Parliament as well as a fervent goal in Ireland.

France's Third Republic.

Prussia's defeat of Napoleon III in 1871 led to the creation of the **Third Republic** to replace the Second Empire. The republic was shaky at the start because the monarchist political factions—Bonapartist, Orléanist, and Bourbon—all struggled to restore their respective families to power. But the republican form

Charles Stewart Parnell, Irish Hero

Charles Stewart Parnell gained the support of both the moderates and the radicals working for Irish home rule. Many saw Ireland as the first of England's colonial conquests—a land that was both ruled and exploited economically like a colony. Son of a landowning Protestant and a skilled parliamentary politician, Parnell threw himself into the Irish cause by paralyzing the British Parliament's conduct of business. In retaliation, the government used forgeries and other unsavory means to destroy Parnell; but in the end, scandal in his personal life lost him the vital support of the public. *(Mary Evans Picture Library.)*

of government, which French supporters had been trying to solidify for almost a century, survived when the monarchists' compromise candidate for king, the comte de Chambord, stubbornly refused to accept the tricolored flag devised in the French Revolution. Associating the tricolor with regicide, he would accept only the white flag adorned with the fleur-de-lis of the Bourbons. He thus lost the chance to revive the monarchy, and in 1875, a new constitution created a ceremonial presidency and a premiership dependent on support from an elected Chamber of Deputies. An alliance of businessmen, shopkeepers, professionals, and rural property owners hoped the new system would prevent the kind of strongman politics that had seen previous republics give way to the rule of emperors and the return of monarchs.

Charles Stewart Parnell: Irish politician (1846–1891) whose advocacy of home rule was a thorn in the side of the British establishment.

home rule: The right to an independent parliament demanded by the Irish and resisted by the British from the second half of the nineteenth century on.

Third Republic: The government that succeeded Napoleon III's Second Empire after its defeat in the Franco-Prussian War of 1870–1871. It lasted until France's defeat by Germany in 1940.

Fragile at birth, the Third Republic would remain so until World War II. Economic downturns, widespread corruption, and growing anti-Semitism, fueled by a highly partisan press, kept the Third Republic on shaky ground. Newspaper stories about members of the Chamber of Deputies selling their votes to business interests and about the alleged trickery of Jewish businessmen manipulating the economy added to the instability. As a result, the public blamed Jews for the failures of republican government and the economy. Confidence in republican politics sank even further in 1887 when the president's son-in-law was discovered to have sold public honors. With the support of those disgusted by the messiness of parliamentary politics, Georges Boulanger, a dashing and highly popular general, began a coup to take over the government. He soon lost his nerve, however, saving the French from rule by another strongman. Nevertheless, Boulanger's popularity showed that in hard economic times, liberal politics—based on constitutions, elections, and the rights of citizens—could be called into question by someone promising easy solutions.

Republican leaders attempted to strengthen citizen loyalty by instituting compulsory and free public education in the 1880s. In public schools, secular teachers who supported republicanism replaced the Catholic clergy, who usually favored a restored monarchy. A centralized curriculum—identical in every schoolhouse in the country—featured patriotic reading books and courses in French geography, literature, and history. To perpetuate republican ideals, the government established secular public high schools for young women, seen as the educators of future citizens. Mandatory military service for men in the republic's army inculcated national pride in place of regional and rural loyalties that were often centered on the Catholic church. In short, schools and the army both turned peasants into Frenchmen.

Political Liberalism Rejected. Although many western European leaders believed in economic liberalism, constitutionalism, and efficient government, these ideals did not always translate into universal male suffrage, citizens' rights, and other forms of political liberalism in the less powerful western European countries. Spain and Belgium abruptly awarded suffrage to all men in 1890 and 1893, respectively, but both governments remained monarchies. An alliance of conservative landowners and the Catholic church dominated Spain, although there was increasingly lively urban ac-

tivism in the industrial centers of Barcelona and Bilbao. Denmark and Sweden continued to limit political participation, and reform in the Netherlands increased manhood suffrage to only 14 percent by the mid-1890s. An 1887 law in Italy gave the vote to all men who had a primary school education, something attained by only 14 percent of Italian men.

In Italy, the process of unification left a towering debt and huge pockets of discontented people, including Catholic supporters of the pope and impoverished citizens in the south. Without receiving the benefits of nation building—education, urban improvements, industrial progress, and the vote—the average Italian in the south felt less a loyalty to the new nation than a fear of the devastating effects of national taxes and the draft on the family economy. Italians' growing unhappiness with constitutional government would have dramatic implications in the twentieth century.

Power Politics in Central and Eastern Europe

Germany, Austria-Hungary, and Russia diverged from the political paths taken by western European countries in the deacdes 1870–1890. These countries industrialized at varying rates—Germany rapidly and Russia far more slowly. Literacy and the development of a civic, urban culture were more advanced in Germany and Austria-Hungary than in Russia (see "Taking Measure," page 755). Even Russia, however, saw the development of a modern press, although with a far smaller readership than elsewhere. In all three countries, conservative large landowners remained powerful, often blocking improvements in transport, sanitation, and tariff policy that would support a growing urban population.

Bismarck's Germany. Bismarck had upset the European balance of power, first by humiliating France in the Franco-Prussian War and then by creating a powerful, unified Germany, exemplified in the explosive economic growth and rapid development of every aspect of the nation-state, from transport to the thriving capital city of Berlin (Map 23.3). His goals achieved, Bismarck now desired stability and a respite from war and so turned to diplomacy instead of war. Fearing that France would soon seek revenge against the new Reich and needing peace to consolidate the nation, he pronounced Germany "satisfied," meaning that it sought no new territory. To ensure Germany's long-term security in Europe, in 1873 Bismarck

TAKING MEASURE

The Decline of Illiteracy
The development of mass politics and the consolidation of the nation-state depended on building a cohesive group of citizens, informed about the progress of the nation. Increasing literacy was thus a national undertaking but one with varying rates of success in different nations, ranging from low levels of illiteracy in Prussia to high levels in Austria-Hungary and Russia. Even in regions of high illiteracy, however, governments successfully encouraged people to read. In what ways does the decline of illiteracy reflect other developments in the countries represented above? *(Theodore Hamerow, The Birth of New Europe: State and Society in the Nineteenth Century (Chapel Hill: University of North Carolina Press, 1983), 85.)*

forged an alliance with Austria-Hungary and Russia, called the Three Emperors' League. The three conservative powers shared a commitment to maintaining the political status quo.

At home, Bismarck, who owned land and invested heavily in industry, joined with the liberals to create a variety of financial institutions, including a central bank to further German commerce and industry. Religious leaders mustered their political influence and defeated his Kulturkampf against religious institutions. Bismarck then stopped persecuting Catholics and turned to attacking socialists and liberals as enemies of the regime. He used unsuccessful assassination attempts on Emperor William I as a pretext to outlaw the workers' Social Democratic Party in 1878. Hoping to lure the working class away from socialism, between 1882 and 1884 Bismarck sponsored an accident and disability insurance program—the first of its kind in Europe and an important step in broadening the role of government to encompass social welfare. In 1879, he assembled a conservative Reichstag coalition that put through tariffs protecting German agriculture and industry from foreign competition but also raising the prices of consumer goods. This increased cost of basic necessities like food cut industrial profits because owners had to pay their workers more. Ending his support for laissez-faire

MAP 23.3 Expansion of Berlin to 1914
"A capital city is essential for the state to act as a pivot for its culture," the German historian Heinrich von Treitschke asserted. No other capital city grew as dramatically as Berlin after German unification in 1871. Industrialists and bankers set themselves up in the new capital, while workers migrated there for jobs, swelling the population. The city was newly dotted with military monuments and with museums to show off its culture.

economics, Bismarck severed his working relationship with political liberals while simultaneously increasing the power of the agrarian conservatives by attacking the interests of Germany's industrial sector.

Authoritarian Austria-Hungary.

Like Germany, Austria-Hungary frequently employed liberal economic policies and practices. From the 1860s, liberal businessmen succeeded in industrializing parts of the empire, and the prosperous middle classes erected conspicuously large homes, giving themselves a prominence in urban life that rivaled the aristocracy's. They persuaded the government to enact free-trade provisions in the 1870s and to search out foreign investment to build up infrastructure, such as railroads.

Despite these measures, Austria-Hungary remained resolutely monarchist and authoritarian. Liberals in Austria—most of them ethnic Germans—saw their influence weaken under the leadership of Count Edouard von Taaffe, Austrian prime minister from 1879 to 1893. Building a coalition of clergy, conservatives, and Slavic parties, Taaffe used its power to weaken the liberals. In Bohemia, for example, he designated Czech as an official language of the bureaucracy and school system, thus breaking the German speakers' monopoly on officeholding. Reforms outraged individuals at whose expense other ethnic groups received benefits, and those who won concessions, such as the Czechs, clamored for even greater autonomy. By playing nationalities off one another, the government ensured the monarchy's central role in holding together competing interest groups in an era of rapid change. Emperor Francis Joseph and his ministers still feared the influence of the most powerful Slavic nation—Russia—on the ethnic minorities living within Austria-Hungary.

Nationalists in the Balkans demanded independence from the declining Ottoman Empire, raising Austro-Hungarian fears and ambitions. In 1876, Slavs in Bulgaria and Bosnia-Herzegovina revolted against Turkish rule, killing Ottoman officials. As the Ottomans slaughtered thousands of Bulgarians in turn, two other small Balkan states, Serbia and Montenegro, rebelled against the sultan. Russian Pan-Slavic organizations sent aid to the Balkan rebels and so pressured the tsar's government that Russia declared war on Turkey in 1877 in the name of protecting Orthodox Christians. With help from Romania and Greece, Russia defeated the Ottomans and by the Treaty of San Stefano (1878) created a large, pro-Russian Bulgaria.

The Treaty of San Stefano sparked an international uproar that almost resulted in a general European war. Austria-Hungary and Britain feared that an enlarged Bulgaria would become a Russian satellite that would enable the tsar to dominate the Balkans. Austrian officials worried about an uprising of their own restless Slavs. British prime minister Benjamin Disraeli moved warships into position against Russia in order to halt the advance of Russian influence in the eastern Mediterranean, so close to Britain's routes through the Suez Canal. The public was drawn into foreign policy: the music halls and newspapers of England echoed a new jingoism, or political sloganeering, that throbbed with sentiments of war: "We don't want to fight, / but by Jingo if we do, / We've got the ships, / we've got the men, / we've got the money too!"

The other great powers, however, did not want a Europe-wide war, and in 1878 they attempted to revive the concert of Europe by meeting at Berlin under the auspices of Bismarck, who was a calming presence on the diplomatic scene. The Congress of Berlin rolled back the Russian victory by partitioning the large Bulgarian state that Russia had carved out of Ottoman territory and denying any part of Bulgaria full independence from the Ottomans (Map 23.4). Austria occupied (but did not annex) Bosnia and Herzegovina as a way of gaining clout in the Balkans; Serbia and Montenegro became fully independent. Nonetheless, the Balkans remained a site of political unrest, teeming ambition for independence, and great-power rivalries.

Following the Congress of Berlin, the European powers attempted to guarantee stability through a complex series of alliances and treaties. Anxious about Balkan instability and Russian aggression, Austria-Hungary forged a defensive alliance with Germany in 1879. The **Dual Alliance**, as it was called, offered protection against Russia, and its potential for inciting Slav rebellions. In 1882, Italy joined this partnership (henceforth called the Triple Alliance), largely because of Italy's imperial rivalries with France. Tensions between Russia and Austria-Hungary remained high, so Bismarck replaced the Three Emperors League with the Reinsurance Treaty (1887) with Russia to keep the Habsburgs from recklessly starting a war over Pan-Slavism.

Dual Alliance: A defensive alliance between Germany and Austria-Hungary in 1879 as part of Bismarck's system of alliances to prevent or limit war. It was joined by Italy in 1882 as a third partner and then called the Triple Alliance.

MAP 23.4 The Balkans, c. 1878
After midcentury, the map of the Balkans was almost constantly redrawn. This resulted in part from the weakness of the dominant Ottoman Empire, but also from the ambitions of inhabitants themselves and from great power rivalry. In tune with the growing sense of national identities based on shared culture, history, and ethnicity, various Balkan peoples sought to emphasize local, small-group identities rather than merging around a single dominant group such as the Serbs. Yet there was also a move by some intellectuals to transcend borders and create a southern Slav culture.

Unrest in Russia. Besides its expansionist moves and setbacks, Russia was beset by domestic problems in the 1870s and 1880s. It remained almost the only European country without a constitutional government, and young Russians were turning to revolutionary groups for solutions to political and social problems. One such group, the Populists, wanted to rouse debt-ridden peasants to revolt. Other people formed tightly coordinated terrorist bands with the goal of forcing change by assassinating public officials. The secret police, relying on informers, rounded up hundreds of members of one of the largest groups, Land and Liberty, and subjected them to brutal torture, show trials, and imprisonment. When in 1877 a young radical, Vera Zasulich, tried unsuccessfully to assassinate

the chief of the St. Petersburg police, the people of the capital city applauded her act and acquittal, so great was their horror at government treatment of young radicals from respectable families.

Writers added to the debate over Russia's future, often by specifically discussing these political issues and mobilizing public opinion. Novelists Leo Tolstoy, author of the epic *War and Peace* (1869), and Fyodor Dostoevsky, a former radical who changed position, believed that Russia above all required spiritual regeneration—not revolution. Tolstoy's novel *Anna Karenina* (1877) tells the story of an impassioned, adulterous love affair, but it also weaves in the spiritual quest of Levin, a former "progressive" landowner who, like Tolstoy, idealizes the peasantry's tradition of stoic

The Assassination of Alexander II
The assassination of Tsar Alexander II in St. Petersburg in 1881 was a shocking event, given that
the tsar had escaped unharmed from some half dozen previous attempts on his life. Even though
Alexander had emancipated the serfs and instituted a wave of reform, the young assassins
were mistakenly convinced that their deed would bring about a great serf uprising.
(The Granger Collection, New York.)

endurance. Dostoevsky satirized Russia's radicals in *The Possessed* (1871), a novel in which a group of revolutionaries murders one of its own members. In Dostoevsky's view, the radicals were simply destructive, offering no solutions whatsoever to Russia's ills.

Despite the influential critiques published by Tolstoy and Dostoevsky, violent action rather than spiritual uplift remained at the heart of radicalism. In 1881, the People's Will, a splinter group of Land and Liberty impatient with its failure to mobilize the peasantry, killed Tsar Alexander II in a bomb attack. His death, however, failed to provoke the general uprising the terrorists expected. Alexander III (r. 1881–1894), rejecting further liberal reforms, unleashed a new wave of oppression against religious and ethnic minorities and gave the police virtually unchecked power. Popular books and drawings depicted Tatars, Poles, Ukrainians, and

others as horrifying, uncivilized, or utterly ridiculous—and thus a menace to Russian culture. The five million Russian Jews, confined to the eighteenth-century Pale of Settlement (the name for the restricted territory in which they were permitted to live), endured particularly severe oppression. Local officials instigated pogroms against Jews, whose distinctive language, dress, and isolation in ghettos made them easy targets. Government administrators encouraged people to blame Jews for escalating living costs—though the true cause was the high taxes levied on peasants to pay for industrialization.

As the tsar inflicted even greater repression across Russia, Bismarck's delicate system of alliances of the three conservative powers was coming apart. A brash but deeply insecure young kaiser, William II (r. 1888–1918), came to the German throne in 1888. William resented Bismarck's power, and his advisers flattered

Russia: The Pale of Settlement in the Nineteenth Century

the young man into thinking that his own talent made Bismarck an unnecessary rival. William dismissed Bismarck in 1890 and, because he ardently supported Pan-German nationalism, let the Reinsurance Treaty with Russia lapse in favor of a strong relationship with the supposedly kindred Austria-Hungary. He thus destabilized the diplomatic scene just as imperial rivalries were intensifying antagonisms among the European nation-states and empires.

> **REVIEW:** What were the major changes in political life from the 1870s to the 1890s, and which areas of Europe did they most affect?

Conclusion

The period from the 1870s to the 1890s has been called the age of empire and industry because Western society pursued both these ends in a way that rapidly transformed Europe and the world. Much of Europe thrived due to industrial innovation, becoming more populous and more urbanized. The great powers undertook a new imperialism, carving up territory and establishing direct rule over foreign peoples. As they tightened connections with the rest of the globe, Europeans proudly spread their supposedly superior culture throughout the world, and like Marianne North, sought out whatever other peoples and places could offer in knowledge, experience, and wealth.

Imperial expansion and industrial change affected all social classes. The upper class attempted to maintain its position of social and political dominance while an expanding middle class was gaining new power and influence. Working-class people often suffered from the effects of rapid industrial change when their labor was replaced by machinery. Millions relocated to escape these poor conditions and to find new opportunities. Political reform, especially the expansion of suffrage, helped members of the working class gain a political voice. Workers formed unions and political parties to protect their interests, but governments often responded to workers' activism with repressive tactics.

As workers struck for improved wages and conditions and the impoverished migrated to find a better life, Western society showed that troubles existed in the new imperial and industrial age. Newspapers informed people about national and international events, and they also raised questions about poverty and social unrest. By the 1890s, the advance of empire and industry was bringing unprecedented tensions to national politics, the international scene, and everyday life. Racism, anti-Semitism, and ethnic chauvinism were spreading, and many were questioning the costs of empire both to their own nation and conquered peoples. Politics in the authoritarian countries of central and eastern Europe was taking a more conservative turn, resisting participation and reform while democratization advanced to the west. The rising tensions of modern life would soon have grave consequences for the West as a whole.

FOR FURTHER EXPLORATION

- **For suggested references, including Web sites, for topics in this chapter,** see page SR-1 at the end of the book.

- **For additional primary-source material from this period,** see Chapter 23 in *Sources of THE MAKING OF THE WEST*, Third Edition.

- **For Web sites and documents related to topics in this chapter,** see *Make History* at bedfordstmartins.com/hunt.

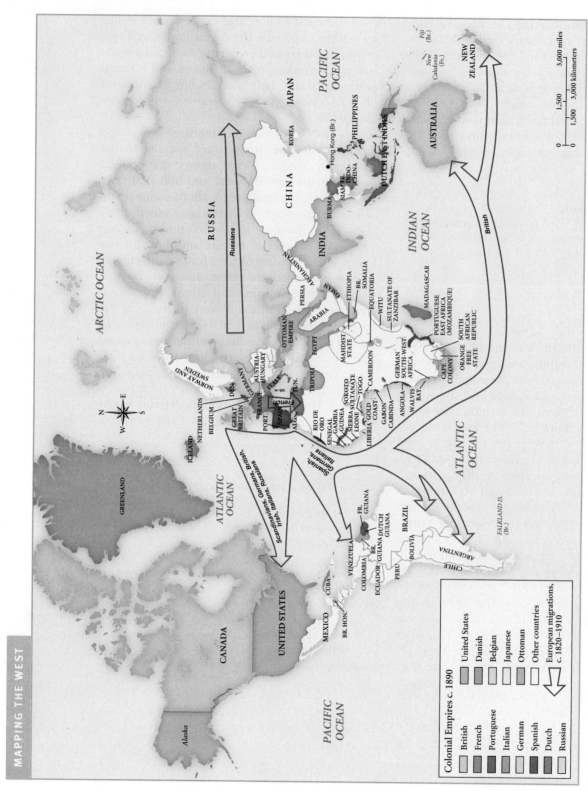

The West and the World, c. 1890

In the late nineteenth century, European trade and political reach spanned the globe. Needing markets for the vast quantities of goods that poured from European factories and access to raw materials to produce the goods, governments asserted that the Western way of life should be spread to the rest of the world and that resources would be best used by Europeans. Explorations and scientific discoveries continued both to build the knowledge base of Western nations and to enhance their ability for greater conquest. Simultaneously, millions of Europeans left their homes to find a better life elsewhere.

Colonial Empires c. 1890

- British
- French
- Portuguese
- Italian
- German
- Spanish
- Dutch
- Russian
- United States
- Danish
- Belgian
- Japanese
- Ottoman
- Other countries
- European migrations, c. 1820–1910

CHAPTER REVIEW

KEY TERMS AND PEOPLE

outwork (727)

capital-intensive industry (730)

limited liability corporation (730)

Leopold II (734)

impressionism (749)

new unionism (751)

Second International (751)

William Gladstone (752)

Reform Act of 1884 (752)

Charles Stewart Parnell (753)

home rule (753)

Third Republic (753)

Dual Alliance (756)

MAKING CONNECTIONS

1. Compare the political and social goals of the newly enfranchised male electorate with those of people from the "best circles."

2. Describe the effects of imperialism on European politics and society as a whole.

> **For practice quizzes, a customized study plan, and other study tools,** see the Online Study Guide at bedfordstmartins.com/hunt.

REVIEW QUESTIONS

1. What were the major changes in Western industry and business in the last third of the nineteenth century?

2. What were the goals of the new imperialism, and how did Europeans accomplish those goals?

3. How did empire and industry influence art and everyday life?

4. What were the major changes in political life from the 1870s to the 1890s, and which areas of Europe did they most affect?

IMPORTANT EVENTS

1860s–1890s	Impressionism flourishes in the arts; absorption of Asian influences	1882	Triple Alliance formed between Germany, Austria-Hungary, and Italy; Britain invades Egypt
1870s–1890s	Vast emigration from Europe continues; the new imperialism	1882–1884	Bismarck sponsors social welfare legislation
1871	Franco-Prussian War ends	1884	British Parliament passes the Reform Act, doubling the size of the male electorate
1873	Extended economic recession begins with global impact	1884–1885	European nations carve up Africa at the Berlin conference
1876	British Parliament declares Victoria empress; invention of the telephone	1885	Invention of workable gasoline engine
1879	Dual Alliance formed between Germany and Austria-Hungary	1889	Japan adopts constitution based on European models; Socialists meet in Paris and establish the Second International
1881	Tsar Alexander II assassinated	1891	Construction of Trans-Siberian Railroad begins

Modernity and the Road to War
1890–1914

I n the first decade of the twentieth century, a wealthy young Russian man traveled from one country to another to find relief from a common malady of the time called neurasthenia. Its symptoms included fatigue, lack of interest in life, depression, and sometimes physical illness. In 1910, the young man consulted Sigmund Freud, a Viennese physician whose unconventional treatment—eventually called psychoanalysis—took the form of a conversation about the patient's dreams, sexual experiences, and everyday life. Over the course of four years, Freud uncovered his patient's deeply hidden fear of castration, which was disguised as a fear of wolves—thus the name Wolf-Man by which he comes down to us. Freud worked his cure, as the Wolf-Man himself put it, "by bringing repressed ideas into consciousness" through extensive talking.

In many ways, the Wolf-Man was representative of his age. Born into a family that owned vast estates, he enjoyed Europe's growing prosperity, although on a grander scale than most. Despite being well-off, countless individuals like the Wolf-Man seemed anguished and mentally disturbed, and suicides abounded—the Wolf-Man's sister and father died from intentional drug overdoses. As the twentieth century opened, Europeans raised questions about family, gender relationships, empire, religion, and the consequences of technology. Every sign of imperial wealth brought on an apparently irrational sense of Europe's decline. British writer H. G. Wells saw in this era "humanity upon the wane . . . the sunset of mankind." Gloom filled the pages of many a book and seeped into the lives of individuals like the Wolf-Man.

Conflict reigned throughout Europe and the world, especially over empire. The nations of Europe had lurched from one diplomatic crisis

Edvard Munch, *The Scream* (1893)
In some of his paintings, Norwegian artist Edvard Munch captured a certain spirit of the turn of the century, depicting in soft pastel colors the newly leisured life of people strolling in the countryside. But modern life also had a tortured side, which Munch was equally capable of portraying. *The Scream* is taken as emblematic of the torments of modernity as the individual turns inward, beset by neuroses, self-destructive impulses, and even madness. It can also be suggested that the screamer, like Europe, travels the road to World War I. *(Scala/Art Resource, NY/© 2008 The Munch Museum/The Munch-Ellingsen Group/Artists Rights Society (ARS), NY.)*

to another over access to global resources and control of territory—both within Europe and outside it. As the great powers fought to dominate people around the world, the competition for empire fueled an arms race that threatened to turn Europe—the most civilized region of the world, according to its leaders—into a savage battleground. Militant nationalism fueled ethnic hatreds and anti-Semitism in public life grew intense, even leading to physical violence. Woman suffragists along with politically disadvantaged groups such as the Slavs and Irish demanded full rights, but tolerance for liberal values and claims weakened amid a wave of political assassinations and public brutality.

These were just some of the conflicts associated with modernity—a term often used to describe the faster pace of life, the rise of mass politics, and the decline of a rural social order that were so visible in the West from the late nineteenth century on (see "Terms of History," page 766). The word *modernity* also refers to the celebrated "modern" art, music, science, and philosophy of this period. Although many people today admire the brilliant, innovative qualities of modern art, music, and dance, people of the time were offended, even outraged, by the new styles and sounds. Freud's theory that sexual drives exist in even the youngest children shocked people. Every advance in science and the arts simultaneously had undermined middle-class faith in the stability of Western civilization.

That faith was further tested when the heir to the Austro-Hungarian throne was assassinated in June 1914. Few gave much thought to the global significance of the event, least of all the Wolf-Man, whose treatment with Freud was just ending. He viewed the fateful day of June 28 simply as the day he "could now leave Vienna a healthy man." Yet the assassination put the spark to the powder keg of international discord that had been building for

several decades. The resulting disastrous war, World War I, like the insights of Freud, would transform modern life.

FOCUS QUESTION: How did developments in social life, art, intellectual life and politics at the turn of the century produce instability and set the backdrop for war?

Public Debate over Private Life

At the beginning of the twentieth century, an increasing number of people could aspire to a comfortable family life because of Europe's improved standard of living. Yet as the twentieth century opened, traditional social norms such as heterosexual marriage and woman's domestic role as wife and mother came under attack by what were seen as the forces of modernity. The falling birthrate, rising divorce rate, and growing activism for marriage reform provoked heated accusations that changes in private life were endangering national health. Discussions about sexual identity led some elites to acknowledge homosexuality as a way of life, while others made it a political issue. Middle-class women took jobs and became active in public to such an extent that some feared the disappearance of distinct gender roles. Women's visibility in public life prompted one British songster in the late 1890s to write:

> Rock-a-bye baby, for father is near
> Mother is "biking" she never is here!
> Out in the park she's scorching all day
> Or at some meeting is talking away!

Discussions of gender roles and private life contributed to rising social tensions because they challenged so many traditional ideals. Freud and other scientists tried to study such phenomena—sexu-

---

■ 1894–1895 Sino-Japanese War

■ 1901 Irish National Theater established; Queen Victoria dies

1890	1895	1900

■ 1894–1899 Dreyfus Affair

■ 1899–1902 South African War

■ 1900 Freud, *The Interpretation of Dreams*

ality, for example—dispassionately and formulated new approaches to treating "modern" ailments such as those afflicting the Wolf-Man. Public discussions of private life—especially when they became intertwined with politics—demonstrated the close connection of private and public concerns.

Population Pressure

Urgent concerns over trends in population, marriage, and sexuality clogged the agendas of politicians and reformers from the 1890s on, and they continue to do so today. The staggering population increases of the eighteenth century persisted through the nineteenth, and rural people and migrants flooded into cities. Alarmed by the urban masses, often crowded into tenements and shacks, Social Darwinists became louder in their warnings about racial decay. Reformers, politicians, and critics of public life saw both the quantity and quality of population as looming national crises.

Soaring Population.   The European population continued to grow as the twentieth century opened. Germany increased in size from 41 million people in 1871 to 64 million in 1910, and tiny Denmark grew from 1.7 million people in 1870 to 2.7 million in 1911. Improvements in sanitation and public health that extended the human life span and reduced infant mortality contributed to the increase. To cope with their burgeoning populations, Berlin, Budapest, and Moscow were torn apart and rebuilt, following the earlier lead of Vienna and Paris. The German government pulled down eighteenth-century Berlin and reconstructed the city with new roadways and mass-transport systems as the capital's

Large Czech Family
This photograph of a rural family in Czechoslovakia shows the differences that were coming to distinguish urban from rural people. Although even a farm family, especially in eastern Europe, might proudly display technology such as a new phonograph, it might not practice family limitation, which was gradually reducing the size of urban households. In eastern Europe, several generations lived together more commonly in rural areas than in cities. How many generations do you see in this image? (© Scheufler Collection/Corbis.)

population grew to over 4 million. Rebuilding to absorb population growth was not confined to capitals of the most powerful states: tree-lined boulevards, new public buildings, and improved sanitation facilities graced the Balkan capitals of Sofia, Belgrade, and Bucharest. As the number of urban residents surpassed that of the rural population in many countries, some ruling elites from the countryside protested the independence and unruliness of urban dwellers.

■ 1905 Revolution erupts in Russia; Duma established; Einstein's special theory of relativity

■ 1914 Austrian archduke Francis Ferdinand and his wife assassinated, precipitating World War I

■ 1904–1905 Russo-Japanese War   ■ 1908 Young Turks revolt

1905   **1910**   **1915**

■ 1903 Women's Social and Political Union founded

■ 1911–1912 Qing dynasty overthrown; China declared a republic

■ 1906 Women receive the vote in Finland

■ 1907 Picasso, *Les Demoiselles d'Avignon*

TERMS OF HISTORY

Modern

The word *modernus* was introduced into Latin in the sixth century; after that, the claim to being modern occurred in many centuries and cultures. Shakespeare, for example, referred to "modern ideas" in his plays, and historians have long debated where "modern" history begins: with Abraham? with Charlemagne? or with the Renaissance?

Despite the claims of many ages to being modern, the term has fastened itself most firmly on the period from the end of the nineteenth century through the first half of the twentieth. Its most specific historical use has been to describe the art, music, and dance that flourished at that time. When used in this sense, *modern* indicates a sharp break with lyrical, romantic music and dance and with the tradition of realism in the arts. The blurred images of the impressionists and the jarring music of Arnold Schoenberg are part of modern art because they break with accepted forms. The sexual rawness of Gustave Flaubert's *Madame Bovary* (see Chapter 22) or of Sigmund Freud's analysis of the Wolf-Man's dreams added to the multifaceted meanings of the word *modern*. Sometimes this intellectual break with the cultural past is referred to as modernism.

At the end of the nineteenth century, the word *modern* also referred to social phenomena. Women who went to work or entered universities or began careers were called modern women. They believed that, by showing themselves capable and rational, they could end restrictions placed on them. They lived different lives from those women who confined themselves to the domestic sphere. This departure from tradition also made them appear modern.

In seeking an education, these women were invoking a meaning of the word *modern* dating back to the Enlightenment. Rational thought and science have also been taken as the bedrock of the modern. *Modernization*—another derivative of the word *modern*—refers to the kind of scientific and technological progress that rational observation produced. Industry and its products—indoor plumbing, electricity, telephones, and automobile—were signs of modernity.

The paradoxical meanings of the word *modern* make it a multipurpose term. While associated with the triumph of industry and science at the turn of the century, some artistic modernism glorified the so-called primitive and non-Western, whether in representational art, music, literature, or philosophy. Complex, paradoxical, and dense with meaning, *modern* may not always be precise. But its very breadth explains why *modern* remains a crucial—and debated—term of history.

Alarm over the Falling Birthrate. While the absolute size of the population was rising in much of the West, the birthrate (measured in births per thousand people) was falling. The birthrate had been decreasing in France since the eighteenth century; other European countries began experiencing the decline late in the nineteenth century. The Swedish rate dropped from thirty-five births per thousand people in 1859 to twenty-four per thousand in 1911; even populous Germany went from forty births per thousand in 1875 to twenty-seven per thousand in 1913.

Industrialization and urbanization helped to bring about this change. Farm families needed fewer hands because industry was turning out more efficient agricultural machinery. In cities, individual couples were free to make their own decisions about limiting family size, learning about new birth-control practices, including coitus interruptus—the withdrawal method of preventing pregnancy—from neighbors or, for those with enough money and education, from pamphlets and advice books. Industrial technology played a further role in curtailing reproduction: condoms, improved after the vulcanization of rubber in the 1840s, proved fairly reliable in preventing conception, as did the German-invented diaphragm. Abortions were also common.

The wider use of birth control stirred controversy. Critics accused middle-class women, whose fertility was falling most rapidly, of holding a "birth strike." Anglican bishops, meeting early in the twentieth century, condemned family limitation as "demoralizing to character and hostile to national welfare." Politicians claimed that the drop in the birthrate signaled a crisis in masculinity and that military strength was at risk. But U.S. president Theodore Roosevelt blamed middle-class women's selfishness for the population decline, calling family limitation "one of the most unpleasant and unwholesome features of modern life." The "quality" of those being born worried activists and politicians: If the "best" classes had fewer children, they asked, what would society look like if only the "worst" classes grew in number?

Racism and nationalism shaped the debate over population. The decline in fertility, one German nationalist warned, would fill the country with "alien peoples, above all Slavs and probably East European Jews as well." Nationalist groups promoting large, "racially fit" families sprang up in France, Germany, Britain, and elsewhere, and they inflamed the political climate with racial hatreds. Instead of building consensus to create an integrated political community, politicians won votes by raising fears of ethnic minorities, the poor, and women who limited family size.

Reforming Marriage

Reformers thought that improving both the quality of children born and the conditions within marriage would solve the population problem. Many believed in eugenics—a set of ideas about the importance of producing "superior" people through selective breeding and of preventing the disabled and others deemed inferior from polluting one's nation or "race." As a famed Italian criminologist put it, lower types of people were not humans but "orangutans." Eugenicists favored increased childbearing for "the fittest" and limitations on the fertility of "degenerates," including sterilization. Women of the "better" classes, reformers also believed, would be more inclined to reproduce if the traditional system of marriage were made more equal. Laws generally decreed that a married woman's wages and her other property belonged to her husband. Women had no legal rights to their own children and no financial support in the event of an abusive marriage. Given their lack of resources, women's reluctance to have more than one or two children was understandable, reformers suggested.

Reformers worked to improve marriage laws in order to boost the birthrate, while feminists sought to improve the lot of mothers and their children. Sweden made men's and women's control over property equal in marriage and allowed married women to work without their husband's permission. Other countries, among them France (1884), legalized divorce and made it less complicated, and thus less costly, to obtain. Reformers reasoned that divorce would allow unhappy couples to separate and undertake new, more loving, and thus more fertile marriages. By the early twentieth century, several countries had passed legislation that provided government subsidies for medical care and child support in order to improve motherhood among the lower classes. Concerns regarding population partially laid the foundations for the welfare state—that is, a nation-state whose policies addressed not just military defense, foreign policy, and political processes but also the social and economic well-being of its people.

The extent of changes in women's lives varied throughout Europe. For example, a greater number of legal reforms occurred in western Europe than in eastern Europe but even so, women could get university degrees in Austria-Hungary long before they could at Oxford or Cambridge. In much of rural eastern Europe, the father's power over the family remained almost dictatorial. According to a survey of family life in eastern Europe in the early 1900s, fathers married off their children so young that 25 percent

of women in their early forties had been pregnant more than ten times. Yet reform of everyday customs did occur. For instance, in some Balkan villages, there still existed a traditional family system called the *zadruga*, in which all individual families within an extended family shared a common great house. By the late nineteenth century, however, individual couples gained privacy by building small sleeping dwellings surrounding the great house. Among the middle and upper classes of eastern Europe, many grown children were coming to believe that they had a right to select a marriage partner instead of accepting the spouse their parents chose for them.

New Women, New Men, and the Politics of Sexual Identity

Rapid social change set the stage for even bolder behaviors among some middle-class women. Adventurous women traveled the globe on their own to promote Christianity, make money, or learn about cultures. Educated European women gained independence as they took on white-collar jobs. The so-called **new woman** dressed more practically, with fewer petticoats and looser corsets, biked and hiked through city streets and down country lanes, lived apart from her family in women's clubs or apartments, and supported herself (see The New Woman poster, below). Italian

---

new woman: A woman who, from the 1880s on, dressed practically, moved about freely, and often supported herself.

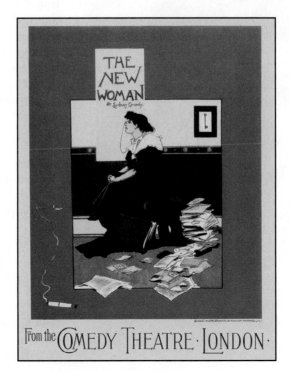

Sydney Grundy, *The New Woman* (1900)
By the opening of the twentieth century, the "new woman" had become a much-discussed phenomenon. Artists painted portraits of this independent creature, while novelists and playwrights like Henrik Ibsen depicted her ambition to throw off the wifely role—or at least to shape that role more to her own personality. In this lithograph, she also smokes. (© Private Collection/The Stapleton Collection/The Bridgeman Art Library.)

educator Maria Montessori (1870–1952), the first woman in Italy to earn a medical degree and the founder of an educational system that still bears her name, gave birth to an illegitimate child although she felt compelled to keep the child's existence a secret. Other new women lived openly with their lovers. The growing number of women freely moving in public, even across the globe, challenged accepted views of women's dependence and seclusion in the home. Not surprisingly, there was loud criticism: the new woman, German philosopher Friedrich Nietzsche wrote, had led to the "uglification of Europe."

Not just women's behavior but also men's and women's sexual identity fueled discussion. A popular book in the new field of "sexology," which studied sex scientifically, was *Sexual Inversion* (1894) by Havelock Ellis. Ellis, a British medical doctor, claimed that there was a new personality type—the homosexual—identifiable by such traits as effeminate behavior and attraction to the arts in males and physical affection for members of their own sex in both males and females. Homosexuals joined the discussion, calling for recognition that they composed a natural "third" or "intermediate" sex and were not just people behaving sinfully. Some believed that members of the intermediate sex, possessing both male and female traits, represented "a higher order" on the scale of human evolution, most often serving as society's "helpers and guides" because they were so highly evolved. The discussion of homosexuality started the trend toward considering sexuality in general a basic part of human identity.

The press condemned homosexuality as outrageous and perverse. In the spring of 1895, Irish playwright Oscar Wilde (1854–1900) was convicted of indecency—a charge that referred to his sexual affairs with young men (see the illustration on this page)—and sentenced to two years in prison. After Wilde's conviction one newspaper rejoiced, "Open the windows! Let in the fresh air!" Between 1907 and 1909, German newspapers publicized the scandal around the military men in Kaiser William II's closest circle who were condemned for homosexuality and transvestitism. Amid growing concern over population and family values, the government assured the public that William's own family life was "a fine model" for the German nation. Heterosexuality thus took on patriotic overtones: the accused homosexual elite in Germany was said by journalists to be out to "emasculate our courageous master race." These cases paved the way for growing sexual openness in the next generations; they also showed that sexual issues were becoming regular weapons in politics.

Oscar Wilde

The Irish-born writer Oscar Wilde symbolized the persecution experienced by homosexuals in the late nineteenth century. Convicted of indecency for having sexual relations with another man, Wilde served time in prison—a humiliation for a husband, father, acclaimed author, and witty playwright. *(Library of Congress, Prints and Photographs Division. LC-USZ62 914833.)*

Sciences of the Modern Self

Scientists and Social Darwinists found cause for alarm not only in the poor condition of the working class but also in modern society's host of mental complaints such as those of the Wolf-Man. Most of these illnesses originated in the "nerves," medical people decided, which were troubled by the hectic pace of urban living. New sciences of the mind such as psychology and psychoanalysis aimed to treat everyone, not just the insane.

New Approaches to Mental Ailments. A number of books in the 1890s presented arguments on causes and cures for modern nervous ailments. *De-*

Freud's Office

Sigmund Freud's therapy room, where his patients experienced the "talking cure," was filled with imperial trophies such as Oriental rugs and African art objects. Freud himself was fascinated by cures brought about through shamanism, trances, and other practices of non-Western medicine. In 1938, Freud fled to England to escape the Nazis. This photo shows his office re-created in London.

(Mary Evans Picture Library/Sigmund Freud copyrights.)

generation (1892–1893), by Hungarian-born physician Max Nordau, blamed overstimulation for both individual and national deterioration. According to Nordau, male and female nervous complaints and the increasingly bizarre art world reflected a general downturn in the human species. As a cure for mental and national decline, Social Darwinists recommended imperial adventure for men and the nation-state alike. Increased childbearing would cure mental disorders in both sexes, they contended, because it would restore men's virility and women's femininity.

Investigations into the working of the mind led to new fields of study. The field of criminology emerged as medical scientists attempted to identify and classify the "criminal mind." Other scientists developed intelligence tests that they said could measure the capacity of the human mind more accurately than a schoolteacher could. In Russia, physiologist Ivan Pavlov proposed that behavior could be controlled by conditioning mental reflexes. Pavlov's experiments in behavior modification, especially his success in getting a dog to salivate upon hearing a bell, became part of the toolkit of modern psychology.

Freud and Psychoanalysis. Sigmund Freud (1856–1939) devised an approach to understanding and treating modern anxieties and mental problems in which he argued that the human psy-

che is far from rational but is powerfully influenced by unconscious forces. Dreams, he explained in *The Interpretation of Dreams* (1900), reveal a repressed or hidden part of personality — the "unconscious"— where all sorts of desires are more or less buried. Freud also believed that the human psyche is made up of three competing parts: the ego, the part that is most in touch with the need to work and survive — that is, external reality; the id (or libido), the part that contains instinctive drives and sexual energies; and the superego, the part that serves as the conscience. Freud's theory of human mental processes and his method for treating their malfunctioning came to be called psychoanalysis. Freud's ideas challenged accepted liberal belief in a unified, rational self that acted in its own interest. Instead, as in Darwin's natural world, where species competed for survival, in Freud's view the different parts of an individual — ego, id, superego — warred with one another for control of an individual's personality.

Freud demanded that sexual life should be regarded objectively, free from religious or moral judgments. His views on sex, however, shocked many of his contemporaries. He insisted, for example, that sexual drives exist from the moment of birth. An individual, he said, has to repress many of these desires — such as impulses toward incest — in order to reach maturity and allow society to remain civilized. Freud claimed that adult gender identity does not result from anatomy alone but rather develops over the course of a person's life experiences. Although gender is more complicated than biology alone would suggest,

---

Sigmund Freud (1856–1939): Viennese medical doctor and founder of psychoanalysis, a theory of mental processes and problems and a method of treating them.

Psychohistory and Its Lessons

In the last fifty years, historians have radically changed the way they write history. In the nineteenth century, history books mostly recounted the deeds of kings and emperors, discussed royal genealogy, and listed wars and peace treaties. Determined to be factual, historians laid out the fine points of laws, charters, and treaties and they checked their sources in archives.

Much has changed since then, partly because of the rise of psychology and psychoanalysis as the twentieth century opened. Confronted with strikes, mass demonstrations, anarchist deeds, anti-Semitism, and other forms of political violence, some observers tried to explain a phenomenon they called crowd psychology. According to this view, psychic states are important factors in shaping some public events.

Not surprisingly, Sigmund Freud studied great historic figures like Leonardo da Vinci from a psychoanalytic perspective, exploring the connection between repressed childhood fantasies and later towering accomplishments. Freud also explained the outbreak of World War I as more of a psychic than a diplomatic event. He saw the war as a form of collective death wish. He subjected both individuals and entire societies to psychoanalytic probing. Few historians followed Freud's lead.

In 1957, William Langer, president of the American Historical Association, charged his fellow scholars with being foolishly backward in their methods. Unlike scientists, he claimed, historians did not try new systems or techniques such as psychoanalysis that might advance their understanding of the past. Others joined the debate, finding that traditional history sometimes attributed actions to traits such as ambition, greed, hate, and great intelligence. But what was the "scientific" depth in such characterizations? Another criticism of history by those interested in psychology and psychoanalysis was that, if it did take human agency into account, history usually saw people as acting rationally in their self-interest. Trauma, irrational or uncontrollable drives, and unconscious motivations played no role in understanding historical figures.

Psychohistory was born of these discussions. Psychoanalyst Erik Erikson, in *Young Man Luther* (1958), announced that the Protestant Reformation originated in the childhood traumas of Martin Luther. Identity crises stemming from his relationship with his father caused Luther to search for and reject father figures, including the pope. Erikson's book caused a stir among historians, changing the way people understood Luther and starting an entirely new school of historical thought.

Not surprisingly, some of the most compelling examples of psychohistory have focused on the lives of individuals and the development of political movements. Historians interested in psychoanalysis have examined Kaiser William II's childhood for explanations of his rejection of Bismarck, his turn to an aggressive foreign policy, and his participation in World War I. Analyses of Adolf Hitler's and Benito Mussolini's followers have attributed the blind worship of these dictators to mass psychic needs and traumas. The intense nationalism that most people in the modern world have increasingly felt for their countries has also become a phenomenon that psychohistorians investigate.

Psychohistory remains controversial to this day. While its practitioners expand the field of historical explanation, its critics find that fitting the behavior of historical characters into Freud's schema can be a formulaic process. Other critics find that certain aspects of gender roles—such as motherhood—are normal. Freud's psychoanalytic theory maintained that girls and women have powerful sexual feelings, an idea that broke sharply with existing beliefs in women's passionlessness.

The influence of psychoanalysis became pervasive in the twentieth century (see "New Sources, New Perspectives," above). For example, Freud's "talking cure," as his method of treatment was quickly labeled, gave rise to a general acceptance of talking out one's problems. As psychoanalysis gained respect as a means of restoring mental health, terms such as *neurotic* and *unconscious* came into widespread use. By way of paradox, Freud attributed girls' complaints about unwanted sexual advances or abuse to fantasy caused by "penis envy," an idea that led members of the new profession of social work to believe that most instances of such abuse had not actually occurred. A meticulous scientist, Freud closely observed symptoms and paid attention to the most minute evidence from everyday life. Like Darwin, he rejected optimistic scientific views of the world, claiming that humans were motivated by irrational drives toward death and destruction. These urges, he believed, shaped society's collective actions.

REVIEW: How did ideas about the self and about personal life change at the beginning of the twentieth century?

psychohistory is too imprecise and speculative because it is not based on the same kinds of hard, documentary evidence that historians have been trained to use. Nonetheless, psychohistorians have made a good case that if we are going to look at personalities, character, and relationships, we should do so in the most informed way possible. Their rationale makes psychohistory appear to be a necessity.

QUESTIONS TO CONSIDER
1. What are the advantages and disadvantages of psychohistory?
2. How would you set out to investigate the psychological reasons for the actions of William II, Emmeline Pankhurst, Marie Curie, or Gavrilo Princip? Would you look at their character, their childhood, their social background, or other parts of their lives?
3. Can we write history without talking about the emotions, mental habits, and human relationships of major figures? Should we avoid psychologizing when thinking about the past?

FURTHER READING
Binion, Rudolph. *Frau Lou: Nietzsche's Wayward Disciple.* 1968.

Erikson, Erik. *Young Man Luther: A Study in Psychoanalysis and History.* 1958.

Kohut, Thomas A. *Wilhelm II and the Germans: A Study in Leadership.* 1991.

Kaiser William and Edward VII's Family
Psychotherapy aimed to cure the individual in good part by discussing family relationships and the fantasies built around them. Psychohistory often draws its analyses from these same relationships. The royal families of Europe are ripe for such analysis because, as the photo shows, German and British monarchs (Edward VII, right; and William, second from right) were closely related; so too were the Russians, Germans, and British. Psychohistorians may therefore view the outbreak of World War I as the work of complex family dynamics. *(Hulton Archive/ Getty Images.)*

Modernity and the Revolt in Ideas

Toward the beginning of the twentieth century, intellectuals and artists so completely rejected long-standing beliefs and established artistic forms that they ushered in a new era. In science, the theories of Albert Einstein and other researchers established new truths in physics. Art and music became unrecognizable. Artists and musicians who produced deliberately shocking works were, like Freud, heavily influenced by advances in science and the progress of empire. Their blending of the scientific and the irrational, and of forms from the West and non-West, helped launch the disorienting revolution in ideas and creative expression that we now identify collectively as **modernism**.

The Opposition to Positivism

Late in the nineteenth century, many philosophers and social thinkers rejected the century-old faith in using scientific methods to discover enduring social laws. This belief, called positivism, had emphasized the permanent nature of fundamental laws and had motivated reformers' attempts to perfect legislation based on studies of society.

---

modernism: Artistic styles around the turn of the twentieth century that featured a break with realism in art and literature and with lyricism in music.

Challenging positivism, some critics declared that because human experience is ever changing, there are no constant or enduring social laws. German political theorist Max Weber (1864–1920) maintained that the sheer number of facts involved in policymaking would often make decisive action by bureaucrats impossible. In times of crisis, a charismatic leader might usurp power because of his ability to act simply on intuition. These turn-of-the-century thinkers, called relativists and pragmatists, posed a challenge to entrenched ideas about policymaking, reform, and the conduct of government.

The most radical among the scholars was the German philosopher **Friedrich Nietzsche** (1844–1900), who called himself neither a relativist nor a pragmatist but a nihilist. In his theory of human nature, he distinguished between the "Apollonian," or rational, side of human existence and the "Dionysian" side, with its expression of more primal urges. Nietzsche believed that people generally prefer the rational, Apollonian explanations of life because the powerful Dionysian sense of death and love such as that found in Greek tragedy is too disturbing.

Much of Nietzsche's writing consisted of aphorisms — short, disconnected statements of truth or opinion — rather than the long, sustained argument common to traditional Western philosophy. Nietzsche used aphorisms to convey the impression that his ideas were a single individual's unique perspective, not universal truths that thinkers since the Enlightenment had claimed were attainable. Nietzsche was convinced that late-nineteenth-century Europe was witnessing the decline of absolute truths such as those found in religion. Thus, he announced, "God is dead, we have killed him." Far from arousing dread, however, the death of God, according to Nietzsche, would give birth to a joyful quest for new "poetries of life" to replace worn-out religious and middle-class rules. Nietzsche believed that an uninhibited, dynamic "superman," free from traditional religious and moral values, would replace the rule-bound middle-class person.

Nietzsche thought that each individual had within a vital life energy that he called "the will to power." The idea inspired many at the time, even his students. As a teacher, Nietzsche was so vibrant — like his superman — that his first students thought they were hearing another Socrates. Nietzsche contracted syphilis and was insane in the last eleven years of his life, cared for by his sister. She edited his attacks on middle-class values into attacks on Jews, and after his death, she revised his complicated concepts of the will to power and of superman to appeal to nationalists and anti-Semites. Nietzsche's legacy was thus mixed: he influenced not only the works of avant-garde artists and thinkers but also the ideas of militarist and racist right-wing political parties.

Revolutionizing Science

While Nietzsche and other philosophers questioned the ability of traditional science to provide timeless truths, scientific inquiry itself flourished and the scientific method gained authority. Technological breakthroughs and improvements in public hygiene earned science prestige in the population at large even as discoveries by pioneering researchers shook the foundations of scientific certainty. In 1896, French physicist Antoine Becquerel discovered radioactivity. He also suggested the mutability of elements by the rearrangement of their atoms. French chemist Marie Curie and her husband, Pierre Curie, isolated the elements polonium and radium, which are more radioactive than the uranium Becquerel used. From these and other discoveries, scientists concluded that atoms are not solid, as had long been believed, but are composed of subatomic particles moving about a core. In a paper published in 1900, German physicist Max Planck announced his quantum theory, stating that energy does not flow in a steady stream but rather is delivered in discrete packets that he later called quanta.

It was in this atmosphere of discovery that physicist **Albert Einstein** (1879–1955) proclaimed his special theory of relativity in 1905. According to this theory, space and time are not absolute categories but instead vary according to the vantage point of the observer. Only the speed of light is constant. That same year, Einstein suggested that the solution to problems in Planck's theory lay in considering light both as little packets *and* as waves. Einstein later proposed yet another blurring of two distinct physical properties, mass and energy. He expressed this equivalence in the equation $E = mc^2$, or energy equals mass times the square of the speed of light. In 1916, Einstein published his general theory of relativity, which connected

---

Friedrich Nietzsche (1844–1900): German philosopher who called for a new morality in the face of the death of God at the hands of science and whose theories were reworked by his sister to emphasize militarism and anti-Semitism.

Albert Einstein (1879–1955): Scientist whose theory of relativity revolutionized modern physics and other fields of thought.

Marie Curie and Her Daughter
Recipient of two Nobel Prizes, Marie Curie came from Poland to western Europe to study science. Curie's extraordinary career made her the epitome of new womanhood; her daughter, Irene Joliot-Curie, followed her mother into the field and also won a Nobel Prize. Both women died of leukemia caused by their exposure to radioactive materials. *(ACJC—Archives Curie et Joliot-Curie.)*

the force, or gravity, of an object with its mass and postulated a fourth mathematical dimension to the universe. Much more lay ahead once Einstein's theories of energy were applied to technology: television, nuclear power, and, within forty years, nuclear bombs.

The findings of Planck, Einstein, and others were not readily accepted, largely because long-standing scientific truths were at stake. Einstein, like Planck, struggled against mainstream science and its professional institutions. Other factors were at work: Marie Curie faced such resistance from the scientific establishment that even after she became the first person ever to receive a second Nobel Prize (1911), the prestigious French Academy of Science turned down her candidacy for membership. They claimed that as a woman she could not have done such outstanding work. More widespread acceptance gradually came, however, as Max Planck Institutes were established in German cities, streets across Europe were named after Marie Curie, and Einstein's name became synonymous with genius. These scientists achieved what historians call a paradigm shift — that is, in the face of considerable resistance, they transformed the foundations of science as their findings and theories came to replace those of earlier pioneers.

Modern Art

Conflicts between traditional values and new ideas also raged in the arts as artists distanced themselves still further from classical Western styles. Some modern artists defied the historic and realistic scenes still favored, for example, by the powerful German monarchy and by buyers for public museums. Modernism in the arts not only challenged time-honored standards but also led to the proliferation of competing artistic styles that continues today.

A Variety of Styles. Some artists addressed city people caught up in the rush of modern life. Abandoning the soft colors of impressionism as too subtle for a dynamic industrial society, a group of Parisian artists exhibiting in 1905 combined blues, greens, reds, and oranges so intensely that they were called *fauves,* or "wild beasts." A leader of the short-lived fauvism, Henri Matisse soon struck out in a new direction, targeting the expanding class of white-collar workers. Matisse saw his art as meant "for every mental worker, be he businessman or writer, like an appeasing influence, like a mental soother, something like a good armchair in which to rest from physical fatigue." His colorful depictions of domestic interiors, North African scenes, and family life departed from strict realism, yet they continue to appeal to modern viewers in part because of their calming qualities.

French artist Paul Cézanne initiated one of the most powerful and enduring trends in modern art by emphasizing structure in painting. Cézanne used rectangular daubs of paint to create geometric visions of dishes, fruit, drapery, and the human body. Cézanne's art accentuated the lines and planes found in nature instead of presenting

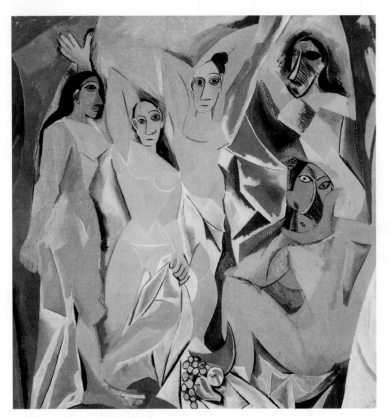

Pablo Picasso, *Les Demoiselles d'Avignon* (1907)
Impressionists had borrowed heavily from Asian art, but many artists in Pablo Picasso's generation leaned on Africa for inspiration. In *Les Demoiselles d'Avignon*, Picasso used the elongated, angular limbs found in African carvings, while the faces resemble African masks. He borrowed these forms even as Europeans were extolling the superiority of their civilization to that of Africa. *(Digital Image © The Museum of Modern Art/Licensed by Scala/Art Resource, NY. © 2008 Estate of Pablo Picasso/Artists Rights Society (ARS), NY.)*

nature as people saw it in everyday life. Following in Cézanne's footsteps, Spanish artist Pablo Picasso (1881–1973) developed a style called cubism. Its radical emphasis on planes and surfaces converted people into bizarre, inhuman, almost unrecognizable forms. Picasso's painting *Les Demoiselles d'Avignon* (1907), for example, showed the bodies of the *demoiselles*, or "young ladies" (prostitutes in this case), as angular, with their heads modeled on African masks. Picasso's work showed the profound influences of African, Asian, and South American arts, but his use of these features was less decorative and more brutal than Matisse's, for example. Some critics say that his jarring style captured in art the uncertain, at times brutal, atmosphere of society and politics.

Art as Political Criticism. Across Europe, artists mixed political criticism with the radical stylistic

changes in their work. "Show the people how hideous is their actual life," challenged the anarchists. Picasso, who had spent his youth in working-class Barcelona, a hotbed of anarchist thought, aimed to present the plain truth about industrial society. In 1912, Picasso and French painter Georges Braque devised a new kind of collage that incorporated bits of newspaper stories, string, and various useless objects. The effect was a work of art that appeared to be made of trash. The newspaper clippings Picasso included described battles and murders, suggesting that Western civilization was not as refined as it claimed to be. In eastern and central Europe, artists criticized the growing nationalism that determined official purchases of sculpture and painting: "The whole empire is littered with monuments to soldiers and monuments to Kaiser William of the same conventional type," one German artist complained. Groups of avant garde artists in Vienna and Berlin produced other types of art, much of it critical of boastful nationalism.

Scandinavian and eastern European artists produced works expressing the torment many felt at the time. Like the ideas of Freud, their style of portraying inner feelings—called expressionism—broke with middle-class optimism. Norwegian painter Edvard Munch aimed "to make the emotional mood ring out again as happens on a gramophone." His painting *The Scream* (1893) used twisting lines and a tortured skeletal human form to convey the horror of modern life that many artists perceived. The "Blue Rider" group of artists, led by German painter Gabriele Münter and Russian painter Wassily Kandinsky used geometric forms and striking colors to express an inner, spiritual truth. Kandinsky is often credited with producing the first fully abstract paintings around 1909; shapes in these paintings no longer bear any resemblance to physical objects or reality but are meant to express deep feelings. The expressionism of Oskar Kokoschka, who worked in Vienna, was even more intense, displaying ecstasy, horror, and hallucinations. As a result, his work— like that of other expressionists and cubists before World War I—was a commercial failure in an increasingly complex marketplace run by museum curators, professional dealers, and art "experts." Trade in art became professionalized, as had medicine and government work before it, even as modern artists rebelled against traditional norms.

Art Nouveau. Only one innovative style of this period was an immediate commercial success:

art nouveau ("new art") won approval from government, critics, and the masses. Creating everything from dishes, calendars, and advertising posters to streetlamps and even entire buildings in this new style, designers manufactured beautiful objects for the general public. As one French official said about the first art nouveau coins issued in 1895, "Soon even the most humble among us will be able to have a masterpiece in his pocket." Art nouveau, adapting elements from Asian design, attempted to offset the harshness of industrial work and office routine with images depicting the unified forms of nature. The impersonality of machines was replaced by intertwined vines and flowers and the softly curving bodies of female nudes intended to soothe the individual viewer. This idea directly contrasted with Picasso's artistic vision. Art nouveau was the notable exception to the public outcries over innovations in the visual arts.

The Revolt in Music and Dance

"Astonish me!" was the motto of modern dance and music, both of which shocked audiences in the concert halls of Europe. American dancer Isadora Duncan took Europe by storm at the turn of the century when, draped in a flowing garment, she danced barefoot in one of the first performances of modern dance. Her sophisticated style was called primitive and scandalous because it no longer followed the steps of classical ballet. Experimentation with forms of bodily expression animated the Russian Ballet's 1913 performance of *The Rite of Spring*, by Igor Stravinsky, the tale of an orgiastic dance to the death performed to ensure a plentiful harvest. The dance troupe struck awkward poses and danced to rhythms intended to sound primitive. At the work's premiere in Paris, one journalist reported that "the audience began shouting its indignation. . . . Fighting actually broke out among some of the spectators." Such controversy made *The Rite of Spring* a box-office hit, although critics called its choreographer a "lunatic" and the music itself "the most discordant composition ever written."

Composers had been rebelling against musical standards for several decades, producing music that was disturbing rather than pretty. Having heard Asian musicians at international expositions, French composer Claude Debussy trans-

Léon Bakst, *Nijinsky in* L'Après-Midi d'un Faune (*The Afternoon of a Faun*, 1912)
Léon Bakst, a Russian painter and set designer, used the art nouveau style to depict the graceful human form of ballet star and choreographer Vaslav Nijinsky. Yet on the eve of World War I, Nijinsky was part of a revolution in ballet that introduced jerky, awkward, pounding movements to indicate the primal nature of dance. *(Wadsworth Atheneum Museum of Art, Hartford, CT. The Ella Gallup Sumner and Mary Catlin Sumner Collection Fund.)*

formed his style to reflect non-European musical patterns and wrote articles in praise of Asian harmonies. Italian composer Giacomo Puccini used non-Western subject matter for his opera *Madame Butterfly*, which debuted in 1904. Listeners were jarred when they also heard non-Western tonalities. Austrian composer Richard Strauss added to the revolution in music by using several musical keys simultaneously in his compositions. Like the bizarre representation of reality in cubism, several tonalities at once distorted familiar harmonic patterns. Strauss's operas *Salome* (1905) and *Elektra* (1909) reflected a modern fascination with violence and obsessive passion. A newspaper critic

---

art nouveau: An early-twentieth-century artistic style in graphics, fashion, and household design that featured flowing, sinuous lines, borrowed in large part from Asian art.

claimed that Strauss's dissonant works "spit and scratch and claw each other like enraged panthers."

The early orchestral work of Austrian composer Arnold Schoenberg, who also wrote cabaret music to earn a living, shocked even Strauss. In *Theory of Harmony* (1911), Schoenberg proposed eliminating tonality altogether; a decade later, he devised a new twelve-tone scale. "I am aware of having broken through all the barriers of a dated aesthetic ideal," Schoenberg wrote of his music. But new aesthetic models distanced artists like Schoenberg from their audiences, who found this music unpleasant and incomprehensible. The artistic elite and the social elite parted ranks. "Anarchist! Nihilist!" shouted Schoenberg's audiences, expressing their distaste for modernism and joining conflicts in the arts with politics.

REVIEW: How did modernism transform the arts and the world of ideas?

Growing Tensions in Mass Politics

Alongside modernist disturbances in intellectual life, the political atmosphere grew charged. On the one hand, liberal opinions led to growing tolerance and political representation for workingmen. Networks of communication, especially the development of journalism, created a common fund of political knowledge that made mass politics possible. On the other hand, even as working-class men got the vote, political activists were no longer satisfied with the liberal rights sought by reformers a century earlier, and some strenuously opposed them. Militant nationalists, anti-Semites, socialists, suffragists, and others demanded changes that challenged the liberal status quo. Traditional elites, resentful of the rising middle classes and urban peoples, aimed to overturn constitutional processes and crush city life. Politics soon threatened national unity, especially in central and eastern Europe, where governments often answered reformers' demands with repression.

Labor's Expanding Power

European leaders worried about the rise of working-class political power late in the nineteenth century. Laboring people's growing confidence came in part from expanding educational opportunities. Workers in England, for example, avidly read

works by Shakespeare and took literally his calls for political action in the cause of justice that rang out in plays such as *Julius Caesar*. Unions gained members among factory workers, while the labor and socialist parties won seats in parliaments as men in the lower classes received the vote. In Germany, Kaiser William II had allowed antisocialist laws to lapse after dismissing Bismarck as chancellor in 1890. Through grassroots organizing at the local level, the Social Democratic Party, founded by German socialists in 1875, became the largest parliamentary group in the Reichstag by 1912. Other socialist parties across Europe helped elect workers' representatives into parliaments, where they focused on passing legislation that benefited workers and their families.

Growing strength, especially winning elections, actually raised problems among socialists. Some felt uncomfortable sitting in parliaments alongside the upper classes — in Marxism, the enemies of working people. Others worried that accepting high public offices such as heads of governmental ministries would compromise their ultimate goal of revolution. These issues divided socialists from one another. Between 1900 and 1904, the Second International wrestled with the question of revisionism — that is, whether socialists should serve in governments and work from within to improve the daily lives of laborers or push for a violent revolution to overthrow governments. Powerful German Marxists argued that settling for reform rather than revolution would only buttress capitalism. The wealthy would continue to rule unchallenged while throwing small crumbs to a few working-class politicians. Stormy discussions divided these German purists, who as a group were consistently blocked from holding high positions by conservatives in the military and aristocracy, from the socialist delegates of France, England, and Belgium who had gained influential government posts.

Police persecution forced some working-class parties to operate in exile. The Russian government, for instance, outlawed political parties, imprisoned activists, and gave the vote to only a limited number of men when it finally introduced a parliament in 1905. Thus, Russian activist V. I. Lenin (1870–1924), who would take power during the Russian Revolution of 1917, moved to western Europe after his release from exile in Siberia in 1900 and earned a reputation among Marxists for hard-hitting journalism and political intrigue. Lenin advanced the theory that a highly disciplined socialist elite — rather than the working class as a whole — would lead a lightly industrialized Russia immediately into socialism. At a 1903 party meeting of Russian Marxists, he maneuvered his opponents into walking out of the proceedings so that his supporters gained control of the party. Thereafter, his faction was known as the Bolsheviks, so named after the Russian word for "majority" (which they had temporarily formed), and they made it their goal to suppress the Mensheviks ("minority"), who had been the dominant voice in Russian Marxism until Lenin outmaneuvered them. Neither of these factions, however, had as large a constituency within Russia as the Socialist Revolutionaries, whose objective was to politicize peasants, rather than industrial workers, as the foundation of a populist revolution. All of these groups prepared for the revolutionary moment through study, propaganda efforts, and organizing—not through the electoral politics successfully employed elsewhere in Europe.

During this same period, anarchists, along with some trade union members known as syndicalists, kept Europe in a panic with their terrorist acts. In the 1880s, anarchists had bombed stock exchanges, parliaments, and businesses; by the 1890s, they were assassinating heads of state: the Spanish premier in 1897, the empress of Austria-Hungary in 1898, the king of Italy in 1900, and the president of the United States in 1901, to name a few famous victims. Syndicalists advocated the use of direct action, such as general strikes and sabotage, to paralyze the economy and give labor unions more power. Not unexpectedly, the upper and middle classes watched these developments with alarm, while politicians from the old landowning and military elites of eastern and central Europe tried to figure out how to reverse the trend toward constitutionalism and mass political participation.

Rights for Women and the Battle for Suffrage

Women continued to agitate for the benefits of liberalism such as the right to own their wages and to be represented in parliaments. In most countries, women could not vote or own property if married; in some, they could not exercise free speech. Laws in France, Austria, and Germany even made women's attendance at political meetings a crime. There were many battlefields besides the one for legal rights. German women focused on widening opportunities for female education. Their activism aimed to achieve the German cultural ideal of *Bildung*—the belief that education can build character and that individual development has public importance. In several countries,

women monitored the regulation of prostitution. Their goal was to prevent prostitutes from being imprisoned on suspicion of having syphilis when men with syphilis faced no such incarceration. Other women took up the cause of pacifism. Many of them were inspired by Bertha von Suttner's popular book *Lay Down Your Arms* (1889), which emphasized how war inflicted terror on women and families. (Later, von Suttner would influence Alfred Nobel to institute a peace prize and then win the prize herself in 1903.)

By the 1890s, many activists decided to focus their efforts on a single issue — the right to vote — as the most effective way to correct the many problems caused by male privilege. Thereafter, suffragists created major organizations involving millions of activists, paid officials, and permanent offices out of the earlier reform groups and women's clubs. British suffrage leader Millicent Garrett Fawcett (1847–1929) pressured members of Parliament for women's right to vote and participated in national and international congresses on behalf of suffrage. Across the Atlantic, American Susan B. Anthony (1820–1906) traveled the country to speak at mass suffrage rallies, edited a suffragist newspaper, and founded the International Woman Suffrage Alliance in 1904. Its leadership argued that despite men's promises to protect women in exchange for their inequality, the system of male chivalry had led to exploitation and abuse. "So long as the subjection of women endures, and is confirmed by law and custom, . . . women will be victimized," a leading British suffragist claimed. Other activists believed that women had attributes needed to balance masculine qualities that dominated society. The characteristics associated with mothering were as necessary in shaping a country's destiny as were qualities that stemmed from industry and commerce, they asserted.

Women's rights activists were predominantly, though not exclusively, from the middle class. Free from the need to earn a living, they simply had more time to be activists and to read the works of feminist theorists such as Harriet Taylor and John Stuart Mill. They attended theater productions of Norwegian playwright Henrik Ibsen's jarring plays about rebellious middle-class heroines and partly saw feminism in terms of their experience of middle-class life. But working-class women also participated in the suffrage movement, though many distrusted the middle class and believed suffrage to be less crucial than women's pressing economic concerns. Textile workers of Manchester, England, for example, put together a vigorous

Woman Suffrage in Finland
In 1906, Finnish women became the first in Europe to receive the vote in national elections when the socialist party there—usually opposed to feminism as a middle-class rather than a working-class project—supported woman suffrage. The Finnish vote encouraged activists in the West, now linked together by many international organizations and ties, because it showed that more than a century of lobbying for reform could lead to gains. *(Mary Evans Picture Library.)*

carried little hammers in their hand-warming muffs to smash the plate-glass windows of department stores and shops. Parades and demonstrations made suffrage a public spectacle, and outraged men responded by attacking the marchers. Arrested for disturbing the peace, the marchers went on hunger strikes in prison. Like striking workers, these women were willing to use confrontational tactics to obtain rights, and like anarchists they were not afraid to damage property. The struggle for and against women's right to vote added to the tensions of urban life.

Liberalism Tested

Governments in western Europe, where liberal institutions were seemingly well entrenched, sought to control the turn-of-the-century conflicts of the late nineteenth century with pragmatic policies that often struck at liberalism's very foundations. Beyond ending the policy of free trade at the heart of economic liberalism, politicians decided that government needed to expand social welfare programs—another break with the liberal idea that societies should develop freely without government interference. Although the programs were few and addressed urban needs only in part, they added to the growing apparatus of the welfare state in which governments actively promoted social well-being.

movement for the vote, seeing it as essential to improved working conditions.

In 1906 in Finland, suffragists achieved their first major victory when the Finnish parliament granted women the vote. But the failure of parliaments elsewhere in Europe to enact similar legislation provoked some suffragists to violence. British suffragist **Emmeline Pankhurst** (1858–1928) and her daughters founded the Women's Social and Political Union (WSPU) in 1903 in the belief that women would accomplish nothing unless they threatened men's property. Starting in 1907, members of the WSPU held parades in English cities, and in 1909 they began a campaign of violence, blowing up railroad stations, slashing works of art, and chaining themselves to the gates of Parliament. Disguising themselves as ordinary shoppers, they

Revising Liberalism in Britain. Political parties in Britain discovered that the recently enfranchised voter wanted solid benefits in exchange for his support. In 1905, the British Liberal Party won a majority in the House of Commons and pushed for social legislation aimed at the working class. "We are keenly in sympathy with the representatives of Labour," one Liberal politician announced. "We have too few of them in the House of Commons." The National Insurance Act of 1911 instituted a program of unemployment assistance funded by new taxes on the wealthy. When Conservatives in the House of Lords resisted the higher taxation, the Liberal government threatened to add to the number of lords and thus dilute the power of the nobility. The newcomers, unlike the defiant Conservatives, would be sure to vote for reform. Under this threat, the lords ap-

---

Emmeline Pankhurst (1858–1928): Organizer of a militant branch of the British suffrage movement, working actively for women's right to vote.

proved the Parliament Bill of 1911, which eliminated their veto power.

The Irish question further tested Britain's commitment to such liberal values as autonomy, opportunity, and individual rights. In the 1890s, new groups formed to foster Irish culture as a way of heightening the political challenge to what they saw as Britain's continuing colonization of the country. In 1901, the circle around poet William Butler Yeats and actress Maud Gonne founded the Irish National Theater to present Irish rather than English plays. Gonne took Irish politics into everyday life by opposing British efforts to gain the loyalty of the young. Every time an English monarch visited Ireland, he or she held special receptions for children. Gonne and other Irish volunteers sponsored competing events, handing out candies and other treats for patriotic youngsters. "Dublin never witnessed anything so marvelous," enthused one home rule supporter, "as the procession . . . of thirty thousand school children who refused to be bribed into parading before the Queen of England."

Promoters of an "Irish way of life" encouraged speaking Gaelic instead of English, singing Gaelic songs, and rallying in support of Catholicism instead of the Anglican church. This cultural agenda gained political force with the founding in 1905 of Sinn Fein ("We Ourselves"), a group that strove for complete Irish independence. In 1913, Parliament approved home rule for Ireland, but the outbreak of World War I prevented the legislation from taking effect though it hardly killed dreams of independence.

Unrest in Italy.   Italian nation builders, left with a towering debt from unification and with widespread pockets of discontent, drifted rapidly from liberalism's moorings in solid industrial development and the rule of law. Corruption plagued Italy's constitutional monarchy, which had not yet developed either the secure parliamentary system of England or the authoritarian monarchy of Germany to guide its growth. To forge a national consensus in the 1890s, prime ministers used patriotic rhetoric and imperial adventure, culminating in a second unsuccessful attempt to conquer Ethiopia in 1896. Riots and strikes, followed by armed government repression, erupted, until Giovanni Giolitti, who served as prime minister for three terms between 1903 and 1914, adopted a policy known as *trasformismo* (from the word for "transform"). Following this policy, he used bribes, public works programs, and other benefits to localities to gain support from their deputies in parliament. Political opponents called Giolitti the "Minister of the Underworld" and accused him of preferring to buy the votes of local bosses rather than spend money to develop the Italian economy. In a wave of protest, urban workers in the industrial cities of Turin and Milan and rural laborers in the depressed agrarian south demanded change, especially of the suffrage laws that allowed only three million of more than eight million adult men to vote. Giolitti appeased the protesters by instituting social welfare programs and, in 1912, virtually complete manhood suffrage. These reforms, however, did not signal a full commitment either to a liberal constitutional system or to economic development across the nation.

Anti-Semitism, Nationalism, and Zionism in Mass Politics

The real crisis for liberal political values of equal citizenship and tolerance came in the two decades leading up to World War I when politicians used anti-Semitism and militant nationalism to win elections. They told voters that Jews were responsible for the difficulties of everyday life and that anti-Semitism and increased patriotism would fix all problems. Voters from all levels of society responded enthusiastically, agreeing that Jews were villains and the nation-state was the hero in the armed struggle to survive. In both republics and monarchies, anti-Semitism and militant nationalism played key roles in mass politics by providing those on the radical right with a platform to gain working-class votes and thus combat the radical left of social democracy. This new radical right shattered the older notion of nationalism based on liberal ideas of the rule of law and the equality of all citizens. Liberals had hoped that voting by the masses would make politics more harmonious as parliamentary debate and compromise smoothed out class differences. The new politics as shaped by right-wing leaders — usually representatives of the agrarian nobility, aristocrats who controlled the military, and highly placed clergy — dashed those hopes by making politics loud, emotional, and hateful.

Authoritarianism in Russia.   A strong tradition of anti-Semitism existed in Russian politics. Russian tsar **Nicholas II** (r. 1894–1917) believed firmly in Russian orthodox religion, autocratic politics, and anti-Semitic social values. Taught as a child to hate Jews, Nicholas blamed them for any failure in

---

Nicholas II: Tsar of Russia (r. 1894–1917) who promoted anti-Semitism and resisted reform in the empire.

Russian policy. Many high officials eagerly endorsed anti-Semitism to gain the tsar's favor. Pogroms became a regular threat to Russian Jews, especially as Nicholas was adamant that he would never order soldiers to "fire on Christians to protect Jews." Nicholas increasingly limited where Jews could live and how they could earn a living. This tradition of anti-Semitism was integral to Russian autocracy and religion, but it was not yet a tool in modern party politics.

The Dreyfus Affair in France. Principles of equal citizenship and tolerance were sorely tested in France, where the most notorious instance of anti-Semitism in mass politics occurred in the Dreyfus Affair. The Third Republic was fragile, with the liberal alliance of businessmen, shopkeepers, professionals, and rural property owners who backed republican government opposed by powerful forces in the aristocracy, military, and Catholic church who hoped that it, like earlier republics, could be brought down. Economic downturns, widespread corruption, and attempted coups made the republic even more vulnerable, and the press attributed failures of almost any kind to Jews, who, it said, controlled all businesses and even the republic itself. Despite an excellent system of primary education promoting literacy and rational thinking, the public tended to agree, while the clergy and monarchists kept hammering the message that the republic was nothing but a conspiracy of Jews.

Amid rising anti-Semitism, a Jewish captain in the French army, Alfred Dreyfus, was charged with spying for Germany in 1894. From a well-respected family, Dreyfus had worked his way through the military, whose upper echelons were traditionally aristocratic, Catholic, and monarchist. The military produced "evidence"—later proved to be false—to gain Dreyfus's conviction and exile to the harsh fortress on Devil's Island. Even though the espionage continued, the republican government adamantly upheld Dreyfus's guilt. Then several newspapers received proof that the army had used perjured testimony and fabricated documents to convict Dreyfus. In 1898, the celebrated French novelist Émile Zola published an article titled *"J'accuse"* (I accuse) on the front page of a Paris daily. Zola cited a list of military lies and government cover-ups that had created the impression of Dreyfus's guilt.

The article named the truly guilty parties and called for a return to government based on honesty, tolerance, and the rule of law. "I have but one passion, that of Enlightenment," wrote Zola. His piece led to public riots, quarrels among families and friends, and denunciations of the army, eroding public confidence in the republic and in French institutions. The government finally pardoned Dreyfus in 1899, dismissed the aristocratic and Catholic officers held responsible, and ended religious teaching orders to ensure a secular public school system that promoted tolerance and honored the rule of law. In the final analysis, however, the Dreyfus Affair made anti-Semitism a standard tool of politics by showing the effectiveness of hate-filled slogans in shaping public opinion.

Nationalist and Anti-Semitic Politics in Germany. The ruling elites in Germany also used anti-Semitism to win support from those caught up in the confusion of Germany's sudden industrialization. The

The Humiliation of Alfred Dreyfus
French captain Alfred Dreyfus was sent to a harsh exile after being convicted of spying for Germany. Before he was taken to Devil's Island, he was subjected to the extreme humiliation of having his officer's insignia and ribbons stripped from his uniform and his sword broken before hundreds of troops and a mob of screaming anti-Semites. We imagine what this meant to a man in his mid-thirties, who despite being Jewish had worked his way through an elite military school and up the ranks of the army. What do you see in his bearing? *(The Granger Collection, New York)*

agrarian elites still controlled the highest reaches of government and influenced the kaiser's policy, but the basis of their power was rapidly eroding. Agriculture, from which they drew their fortunes, declined as a percentage of gross national product from 37 percent in the 1880s to only 25 percent early in the 1900s. New opportunities drew rural workers to the cities, where they would be free from the landowner's grip. As industrialists grew wealthier, the agrarian elites came to loathe industry for challenging their traditional authority. As a Berlin newspaper noted, "The agrarians' hate for cities . . . blinds them to the simplest needs and the most natural demands of the urban population." In contrast to Bismarck's astute wooing of the masses through social programs, William II's aristocracy often encouraged anti-Semitism, both in the corridors of power and in the streets.

Conservatives and a growing radical right claimed that Jews, who made up less than 1 percent of the German population, were responsible for destroying traditional society. In the 1890s, nationalist and anti-Semitic political pressure groups flourished, hurling diatribes against Jews, "new women," and Social Democrats, whom they branded as internationalist and unpatriotic. In the 1890s, agrarian conservatives played to the fears of small farmers by accusing Jews of causing agricultural booms and busts. Political campaigns came to feature hate-filled speeches against an array of groups rather than rational programs to meet the problems of economic change. The politics of this new right invented a modern politics that rejected the liberal value of parliamentary consensus, relying instead on mouthing slogans and inventing enemies within what was supposed to be a unified nation-state.

Ethnic Politics in Austria-Hungary.

Politicians in the dual monarchy of Austria-Hungary also used militant nationalism and anti-Semitism to win votes, but here the presence of many ethnic groups meant competing nationalisms and thus greater complexity in the politics of hate. Foremost among the nationalists were the Hungarians, who wanted autonomy for themselves while forcibly imposing Hungarian language and culture on all other, supposedly inferior, ethnic groups in Hungary. Nationalist claims for greater Hungarian influence (or Magyarization, from Magyars, the principal ethnic group) rested on two pieces of evidence: Budapest was a thriving industrial city, and the export of Hungarian grain from the vast estates of the Magyar nobility saved the monarchy's finances. The nationalist Independence Party dis-

rupted the Hungarian parliament so regularly that it weakened the orderly functioning of the government.

Although capable of causing trouble for the empire, Hungarian nationalists, who mostly represented agrarian wealth, were themselves vulnerable. Exploited ethnic groups — Slovaks, Romanians, and Ruthenians — formed their own political alliances to resist Magyarization. Industrial workers struck to protest horrendous labor conditions, and in the fall of 1905, 100,000 activists gathered in front of the Hungarian parliament to demonstrate for the

Principal Ethnic Groups in Austria-Hungary, c. 1900

vote. In response, Hungarians intensified Magyarization, even decreeing that all tombstones be engraved in Magyar. Emperor Francis Joseph temporarily quieted the Hungarian nationalists by threatening to introduce universal manhood suffrage, which would allow both the Magyars' lower-class and non-Magyar opponents to vote. Although numerous ethnic groups and many Jews assimilated Magyar ways, the chauvinist nature of Hungarian policies toward both the other ethnic groups and the imperial government in Vienna made for instability throughout Austria-Hungary.

Hungarian nationalism roused other nationalities to intensify their demands for rights. Croats, Serbs, and other Slavic groups in the south called for equality with the Hungarians. The central government allowed the Czechs a greater number of Czech officials in the government because of the growing industrial prosperity of their region. But every step favoring the Czechs provoked outrage from the traditionally dominant ethnic Germans. When Austria-Hungary decreed in 1897 that government officials in the Czech region of the empire would have to speak Czech as well as German, the Germans rioted — further straining the stability and unity in the empire.

Tensions mounted as German politicians in Vienna linked the growing power of Hungarians and Czechs to Jews. Karl Lueger, whose newly formed Christian Social Party attracted members from among the aristocracy, Catholics, artisans, shopkeepers, and white-collar workers, had great success with this new brand of politics. In hate-filled speeches that hurled abuse at Jews and other non-German groups, Lueger appealed to those groups for whom modern life meant a loss of privilege and security — and was elected mayor of Vienna in 1895. Lueger's ethnic nationalism and anti-Semitism threatened the multinationalism on which Austria-Hungary was based. His attacks were so effective at getting votes, however, that a widening group of politicians made anti-Semitism an integral part of their election campaigns, calling Jews the "sucking vampire" of modernity and blaming them for the tumult of migration, the economy, and just about anything else people found disturbing. Politics became a thing not of debate in parliaments but of violent racism in the streets.

The Jewish Response to Anti-Liberal Politics.

Like Christians and people of other religions, Jews often differed from one another, separated by social class and education. Jews in western Europe had responded to increased legal tolerance in the nineteenth century by moving out of Jewish neighborhoods, intermarrying with Christians, and in some cases converting to Christianity — practices known as assimilation. Many well-educated Jews favored the classical culture of the German Em-

pire because it seemed more rational and liberal than the ritualistic Catholicism of Austria-Hungary. Still, many accomplished and prosperous Jews, like the pioneer of psychoanalysis, Sigmund Freud, flourished amid the cosmopolitan urban culture of Vienna or Budapest despite escalating anti-Semitism. By contrast, less educated and less prosperous Jews, such as those in Russia and Romania, were increasingly singled out for persecution, legally disadvantaged, and forced to live in ghettos. Jews from these countries might seek refuge in the nearby cities of central and eastern Europe where they could eke out a living as day laborers or artisans. Jewish migration to the United States and other countries also swelled (Map 24.1). By 1900, many Jews were prominent in cultural and economic affairs in cities across the continent even as far more were discriminated against and victimized elsewhere.

Amid vast migration and continued persecution, a spirit of Jewish nationalism arose. "Why should we be any less worthy than any other . . . people," one Jewish leader asked. "What about our nation, our language, our land?" Jews

MAP 24.1 Jewish Migrations in the Late Nineteenth Century

Pogroms in eastern Europe, increasingly violent anti-Semitism across the continent, and the search for opportunity motivated Jews to migrate to many parts of the world. Between 1890 and 1914, some five million Jews left Russia alone. They moved to European cities; to North and South America; and, as Zionism progressed, to Palestine.

Leon Pinsker Calls for a Jewish State

In 1882, the Ukrainian physician Leon Pinsker published a pamphlet called Auto-Emancipation *in which he analyzed the situation of the Jews in Europe. This pamphlet convinced some in Europe—most notably Theodor Herzl—that Jews could never be assimilated to European culture no matter how many dropped their religion in favor of Christian ways. This pamphlet ultimately led some Jews to migrate to Palestine, despite Pinsker's own conviction that the Middle East was not necessarily the right place for creating a Jewish nation.*

This is the kernel of the problem, as we see it: *the Jews comprise a distinctive element among the nations under which they dwell, and as such can neither assimilate nor be readily digested by any nation....*

A fear of the Jewish ghost has passed down the generations and the centuries. First a breeder of prejudice, later ... it culminated in Judeophobia. Judeophobia is a psychic aberration. As a psychic aberration it is hereditary, and as a disease transmitted for two thousand years it is incurable....

The Jews are aliens who can have no representatives, because they have no country. Because they have none, because their home has no boundaries within which they can be entrenched, their misery too is boundless....

... If we would have a secure home, give up our endless life of wandering and rise to the dignity of a nation in our own eyes and in the eyes of the world, we must, above all, not dream of restoring ancient Judaea. We must not attach ourselves to the place where our political life was once violently interrupted and destroyed. The goal of our present endeavors must be not the "Holy Land," but a land of our own. We need nothing but a large tract of land for our poor brothers, which shall remain our property and from which no foreign power can expel us. There we shall take with us the most sacred possessions which we have saved from the shipwreck of our former country, the *God-idea* and the *Bible*. It is these alone which have made our old fatherland the Holy Land, and not Jerusalem or the Jordan. Perhaps the Holy Land will again become ours. If so, all the better, but *first of all*, we must determine—and this is the crucial point—what country is accessible to us, and at the same time adapted to offer the Jews of all lands who must leave their homes a secure and indisputed refuge, capable of productivization.

Source: Robert Chazan and Marc Lee Raphael, eds., *Modern Jewish History: A Source Reader* (New York: Schocken Books, 1974), 161, 163, 165–66, 169–71, 171–74.

began organizing resistance to pogroms and anti-Semitic politics, and intellectuals drew on Jewish folklore, language, customs, and history to establish a national identity parallel to that of other Europeans. In the 1880s, the Ukrainian physician Leon Pinsker, seeing the Jews' lack of national territory as fundamental to the persecution heaped on them, advocated the migration of Jews to Palestine. (See Document, "Leon Pinsker Calls for a Jewish State," above.) In 1896, Theodor Herzl, strongly influenced by Pinsker, published *The Jewish State*, which called not simply for migration but for the creation of a Jewish nation-state, the goal of a movement known as **Zionism**. A Hungarian-born Jew, Herzl experienced anti-Semitism firsthand as a Viennese journalist and a writer in Paris during the Dreyfus Affair. He scoured Europe for financial backing, but many prosperous Jews who had assimilated thought his ideas mad. However, backed by poorer eastern European Jews, he organized the first International Zionist Congress (1897). By 1914, some eighty-five thousand Jews had moved into Palestine.

> **REVIEW:** What were the points of tension in European political life at the beginning of the twentieth century?

European Imperialism Challenged

Anti-Semitism was only one sign that the conditions of modern life were deeply troubling and that the rule of law and other liberal values like tolerance were now threatened. Militant nationalism across the West made it difficult for nations to calm domestic politics and ease the tensions caused by rapid industrial and social change. The political atmosphere heated up, as imperialism made relations among the European powers alarmingly worse and as colonized peoples challenged European control. Japan's growth as an Asian power also threatened:

Zionism: A movement that began in the late nineteenth century among European Jews to found a Jewish state.

in 1904–1905, Japanese expansionism came close to toppling the mighty Russian Empire.

The Trials of Empire

After centuries of global expansion, imperial adventure soured for Britain and France at the beginning of the twentieth century. Newcomers Italy and Germany now fought for a place at the imperial table, and the tense atmosphere among nations raised questions about the future. "Where thirty years ago there existed one sensitive spot in our relations with France, or Germany, or Russia," the British economist J. A. Hobson wrote in 1902, "there are a dozen now; diplomatic strains are of almost monthly occurrence between the Powers."

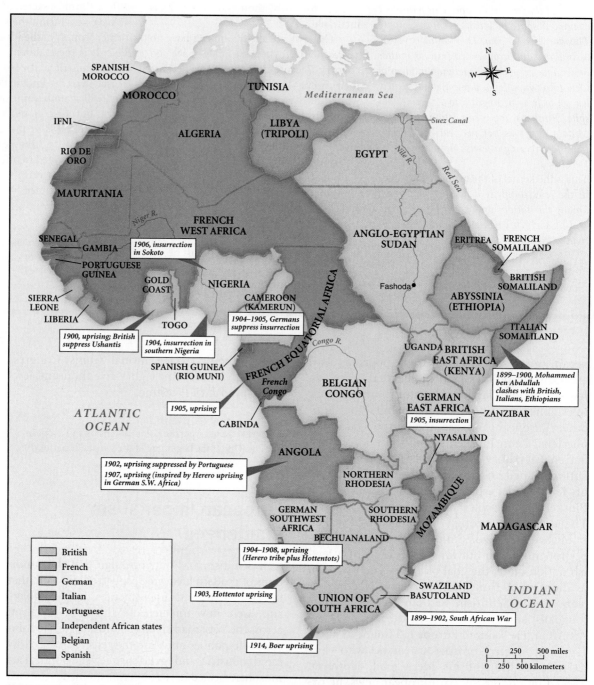

MAP 24.2 Africa in 1914

Uprisings intensified in Africa in the early twentieth century as Europeans tried both to consolidate their rule and to extract more wealth from the Africans. As Europeans were putting down rebellions against their rule, a pan-African movement arose, attempting to unite Africans as one people.

Mounting tensions exploded violently when Japan and Russia went to war in 1904.

The South African War.

The imperial tide turned for Britain in the **South African War** (or Boer War) of 1899–1902. In 1896, Cecil Rhodes, then prime minister of the Cape Colony in southern Africa, directed a raid into the neighboring territory of the Transvaal in hopes of stirring up trouble between the Boers, descendants of early Dutch settlers, and the more recent immigrants from Britain who had come to southern Africa in search of gold and other riches. In Rhodes's scheme, the turmoil caused by the raid would justify a British takeover of the Transvaal and the Orange Free State, which the Boers independently controlled. The Boers, however, easily routed the raiders, dealing Britain a bloody defeat and forcing Rhodes to resign in disgrace.

The stunned British government did not accept defeat easily, especially when other Europeans gloated over the British loss. Kaiser William II telegraphed his congratulations to the Transvaal president for "maintaining the independence of the country against attacks from without." In 1899, Britain began full-scale operations against the Boers. Foreign correspondents covering the South African War reported on appalling bloodshed, heavy casualties, and the unfit condition of the average British soldier. Most alarmingly to those who liked to think of Britain as the most civilized country in the world, news arrived back in London of rampant disease and inhumane treatment of South Africans herded into an unfamiliar institution—the concentration camp, which became the graveyard of tens of thousands. Britain finally annexed the area after defeating the Boers in 1902, but the cost of war in money, destruction, demoralization, and loss of life was enormous (Map 24.2, page 784). Prominent citizens began to call imperialism not the work of civilization but an act of barbarism.

Newcomers Face Setbacks.

Nearly simultaneously with the South African War, the United States defeated Spain in the Spanish-American War in 1898 and took Cuba, Puerto Rico, and the Philippines as its trophies. Not a novice to imperialism, the United States had successfully crushed native Americans, killing many and confining survivors to reservations. Its imperial reach had generally been continental until its annexation of Hawaii in 1898. Both Cuba and the Philippines had begun

vigorous efforts to free themselves from Spanish rule before the war. Urged on by the expansionist-minded Theodore Roosevelt (then assistant secretary of the navy) and the inflammatory daily press, the United States went to war, claiming it was doing so to help the independence movements. Instead of allowing the independence that victory promised, however, the U. S. government annexed Puerto Rico and Guam and bought the Philippines from Spain. Cuba was theoretically independent, but the United States monitored its activities.

Both Spain and the United States found the fortunes of imperialism unpredictable. Spain lost its territories, and the triumphant United States next had to wage a bloody war against the Filipinos, who wanted independence, not another imperial ruler. British poet Rudyard Kipling had encouraged the United States to "take up the white man's burden" by bringing the benefits of Western civilization to those liberated from Spain. However, reports of American brutality in the Philippines, where some 200,000 local people were slaughtered, further disillusioned the Western public, who liked to imagine native peoples joyously welcoming the bearers of civilization.

Despite these setbacks, newly powerful countries had an emotional stake in gaining colonies. In the early twentieth century, Italian public figures bragged about Italians becoming Nietzschean supermen by conquering Africa and restoring Italy to its ancient position of world domination. After a disastrous war against Ethiopia in 1896, Italy won a costly victory over the Ottoman Empire in Libya. These wars stirred the military spirit in Italians, and hopes rose for imperial grandeur in the future.

Germany likewise joined the imperial contest, demanding an end to British-French domination as colonial powers. Under Bismarck, Germany had begun its imperial expansion, and German bankers and businessmen were ensconced throughout Asia, the Middle East, and Latin America. By the turn of the century, Germany had colonies in Southwest Africa, the Cameroons, Togoland, and East Africa and sent linguists, ethnographers, and museum curators to study other cultures and obtain their treasures. Despite these successes, there was no easy road to colonial might. Germany, too, met humiliation and faced constant problems, especially

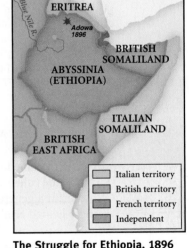

The Struggle for Ethiopia, 1896

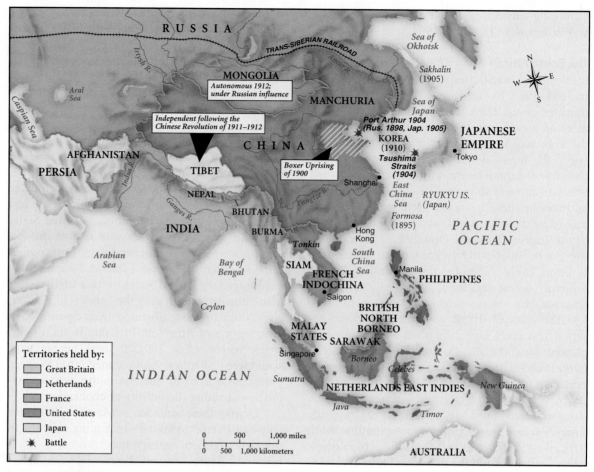

MAP 24.3 Imperialism in Asia, 1894–1914
The established imperialists came to blows in East Asia as they struggled for influence in China and as they met a formidable new rival—Japan. Simultaneously, liberation groups like the Boxers were taking shape, committed to throwing off restraints imposed by foreign powers and eliminating these interlopers altogether. In 1911, revolutionary Sun Yat-Sen overthrew the Qing dynasty, which had left China unprepared to resist foreign takeover, and started the country on a different course.

in its dealings with Britain and France and with local peoples in Africa and elsewhere who resisted the German takeover of their lands. As Italy and Germany joined the aggressive pursuit of new territory, the rules set for imperialism at the Congress of Berlin a generation earlier gave way to increasingly heated rivalry and nationalist passion.

Japan Victorious. Japan's rise as an imperial power further ate into Europeans' confident approach to imperialism. Continuing its expansion in the region, in 1894, Japan defeated China in the Sino-Japanese War, which ended China's domination of Korea. The European powers, alarmed at Japan's victory, forced it to relinquish most gains, a move that outraged and affronted the Japanese. Japan's insecurity had risen with Russian expansion to the east and south in Asia. Pushing into

eastern Asia, the Russians had built the Trans-Siberian Railroad through Manchuria, sent millions of Russian settlers eastward, and sponsored anti-Japanese groups in Korea, making the Korean peninsula appear, as a Japanese military leader put it, like "a dagger thrust at the heart of Japan." Angered by the continuing presence of Russian troops in Manchuria, the Japanese attacked the tsar's forces at Port Arthur in 1904 (Map 24.3).

The conservative Russian military proved inept in the ensuing Russo-Japanese War, even though it often had better equipment or strategic advantage. Russia's Baltic Fleet sailed halfway around the globe only to be completely destroyed by Japan in the battle of Tsushima Straits (1905). Opening an era of Japanese domination in East Asian politics, the victory was the first by a non-European nation over a European great power in the modern age, and it gave the West reason to fear the future. As one English general observed of the Russian defeat: "I have today seen the most stupendous spectacle it is possible for the mortal brain to conceive — Asia advancing, Europe falling back." Japan annexed Korea in 1910 and began to target other areas for colonization.

The Russian Empire Threatened

Following the humiliating loss to Japan, revolution erupted in Russia in 1905, and the empire tottered on the brink of chaos. A mighty empire that had expanded southward in Asia and settled much of Siberia during the nineteenth century, Russia concealed its weaknesses well. State-sponsored industrialization in the 1890s had made the country appear modern to outside observers, and the Russification policy imitated Western-style state building by attempting to impose a unified, national culture on Russia's diverse population. Burdened by heavy taxes to pay for industrialization and by debts owed for the land they acquired during emancipation, peasants revolted in isolated uprisings at the turn of the century. Unrest occurred in the cities, too, as Marxist and union activists incited workers to demand better conditions. In 1903, skilled workers led strikes in Baku; the united demonstration of Armenians and Tatars there showed how urbanization and Russification made unified political action possible among the lower classes. These and other worker protests challenged the autocratic regime, which was weakened further by Japan's victory.

The Revolution of 1905. On a Sunday in January 1905, a crowd gathered outside the tsar's Winter Palace in St. Petersburg to march in a demonstration to make Nicholas II aware of the brutal working conditions they suffered. Nicholas had often traveled the empire, displaying himself as the divinely ordained "father" of his people, and thus appealing to him seemed natural to his "children." Leading the demonstration was a priest who, unknown to the crowd, was a police informant and agitator. Instead of allowing the marchers to pass, troops guarding the palace shot into the trusting crowd, killing hundreds and wounding thousands. Thus began the Revolution of 1905, and news of "Bloody Sunday" moved outraged workers elsewhere to rebel.

In almost a year of turmoil across Russia, urban workers struck over wages, hours, and factory conditions and demanded political representation

in the government. Delegates from revolutionary parties such as the Social Democrats and the Socialist Revolutionaries encouraged more direct blows against the central government, but workers rejected their leadership and organized their own councils, called soviets. In February, the uncle of the tsar was assassinated; in June, sailors on the battleship *Potemkin* mutinied; in October, a massive railroad strike ground rail transportation to a halt; and in November, uprisings broke out in Moscow. The tsar's forces kept killing protesters, but their deaths only produced more protest.

Russian Revolution of 1905

Anger at Nicholas II's absolute rule brought together an opposition of artisans and industrial workers, peasants, professionals, and upper-class reformers. Women joined the fray, many demanding an end to discriminatory laws such as those firing women teachers who married. Using the unrest to press their goals, liberals from the zemstvos (local councils) and the intelligentsia (a Russian word for well-educated elites) demanded political reform, in particular the creation of a constitutional monarchy and representative legislature. They believed that the reliance on censorship and the secret police, characteristic of Romanov rule, relegated Russia to the ranks of the most backward states. Nicholas's halfhearted responses triggered more street fighting. In the words of one protester, the tsar's attitude turned "yesterday's benighted slaves into decisive warriors."

Attempts at Political Reform. The tsar finally yielded to the violence by creating a representative body called the **Duma.** Although very few Russians could vote for representatives to the Duma, its mere existence, along with the new right of open public debate, liberalized government and allowed people to present their grievances to a responsive body. Political parties committed to parliamentary rather than revolutionary programs also took shape during this time. When these newly formed constitutional parties threw their support to the reorganized government, revolutionary activity finally stopped.

Duma: The Russian parliament set up in the aftermath of the outbreak of the Revolution of 1905.

People soon wondered, however, if anything had really changed. From 1907 to 1917, the Duma convened, but twice when the tsar disliked its recommendations he simply sent the delegates home and forced new elections. Nicholas did have an able administrator in Prime Minister Pyotr Stolypin (1863–1911), who was determined to eliminate the sources of discontent. He ended the mir system of communal farming and taxation, and canceled the land redemption payments that had burdened the peasants since their emancipation in 1861. He also made government loans available to peasants, who were then able to purchase land and thus to own farms outright. Although these reforms did not eradicate rural poverty, they did allow people to move to the cities in search of jobs and created a larger group of independent peasants.

Stolypin succeeded only partially in his other goal of restoring law and order. He clamped down on revolutionary organizations, executing their members by hanging them with "Stolypin neckties." The government urged more pogroms and stifled ethnic unrest by stepping up Russification. But rebels continued to assassinate government officials—four thousand were killed or wounded in 1906–1907. Stolypin himself was assassinated in 1911. Stolypin's reforms had promoted peasant well-being, which encouraged what one historian has called a "new peasant assertiveness." The industrial workforce also grew, and another round of strikes broke out, culminating in a general strike in St. Petersburg in 1914. The imperial government and the conservative nobility still had no solution to the ongoing turmoil, and their refusal to share power and produce true political reform left the way open to an even greater upheaval in 1917.

Growing Resistance to Colonial Domination

Japanese military victories over the Qing in China and the Romanovs in Russia upset the status quo in both countries. In addition, colonized peoples gained confidence from the Japanese victory to act more forcefully against imperialism. Moreover, the ability of Russian revolutionaries to force a great European power to reform, however slightly, encouraged nationalist protests throughout the globe, further challenging Western imperialists.

Revolution in China. Uprisings began in China after its 1895 loss to Japan forced the ruling Qing dynasty to grant more economic concessions to Western powers. Humiliated by these events and driven to despair by famine, peasants organized

into secret societies to expel the foreigners and restore Chinese autonomy. One organization was the Society of the Righteous and Harmonious Fists (or Boxers), whose members maintained that ritual boxing would protect them from a variety of evils, including bullets. Encouraged by the Qing ruler, Dowager Empress Tz'u-hsi (Cixi; 1835–1908), the Boxers rebelled in 1900, massacring the missionaries and Chinese Christians to whom they attributed China's troubles. Seven of the colonial powers united to put down the Boxer Uprising and encouraged their troops to ravage the areas in which the Boxers operated. Defeated once more, the Chinese were compelled to pay a huge indemnity for damages done to foreign property and to allow even greater foreign military occupation.

The Boxer Uprising thoroughly discredited the Qing dynasty, leading a group of revolutionaries to overthrow the dynasty in 1911 and to declare China a republic the next year. Their leader, Sun Yat-Sen (1866–1925), who had been educated in Hawaii and Japan, combined Western ideas and Chinese values in his "Three Principles of the People": "nationalism, democracy, and socialism." For example, Sun Yat-Sen's socialism included the Chinese belief that all people should have enough food. Sun Yat-Sen's Nationalist Party called for revival of the Chinese tradition of correctness in behavior between governors and the governed, modern economic reform, and an end to Western domination of trade. Sun's stirring leadership and the changes brought about by the 1911 revolution helped weaken Western imperialism.

Nationalists in India. In India, the Japanese victory over Russia and the Revolution of 1905 stimulated politicians to take a more radical course than that offered by the Indian National Congress. The anti-British Hindu leader B. G. Tilak, less moderate than Congress reformers, urged noncooperation: "We shall not give them assistance to collect revenue and keep peace. We shall not assist them in fighting beyond the frontiers or outside India with Indian blood and money." Tilak promoted Hindu customs, asserted the distinctiveness of Hindu values from British ways, and inspired violent rebellion against the British. This brand of nationalism broke with that based on assimilating to British culture and promoting gradual change. Trying to repress Tilak, the British sponsored a rival nationalist group, the Muslim League, in a blatant attempt to divide Muslim nationalists from Hindus in the Congress.

Faced with political activism on many fronts, however, Britain conceded to Indians representa-

The Foreign Pig Is Put to Death
The Boxers used brightly colored placards to spread information about their movement in order to build wide support among the Chinese population. They felt that the presence of foreigners had caused a series of disasters, including the defection of the Chinese from traditional religion, the flow of wealth from the country, and a string of natural disasters such as famine. This depiction shows the harsh judgment of the Boxers toward foreigners and their Chinese allies — they are pigs to be killed.
(© The Bridgeman Art Library.)

■ **For more help analyzing this image,** see the visual activity for this chapter in the Online Study Guide at **bedfordstmartins.com/hunt**.

tion in ruling councils and the right to vote based on property ownership. Because the independence movement had not fully reached the masses, these small concessions to the elites temporarily maintained British power by appeasing the best-educated and most influential people in the upper and middle classes. But the British hold on India was weakening.

Young Turks in the Ottoman Empire. Revolutionary nationalism was simultaneously weakening the Ottoman Empire, which for centuries had controlled much of the Mediterranean. Rebellions plagued Ottoman rule, and this resistance, along with Ottoman deterioration as an effective state, allowed European influence to grow. Just as the Habsburgs used the transnational appeal of Catholicism to quash nationalist aspirations, Sultan Abdul Hamid II (r. 1876–1909) tried to revitalize the multiethnic empire by using Islam to counteract the rising nationalism of the Serbs, Bulgarians, and Macedonians. Instead, he unintentionally provoked Turkish nationalism in Constantinople itself. Turkish nationalists rejected the sultan's pan-Islamic solution and built their movement on the uniqueness of their culture, history, and language, as many European ethnic groups were doing. Using the findings of Western scholarship, they first traced the history and culture of the group they called Turks to change the word *Turk* from one of derision to one of pride.

The Japanese defeat of Russia in 1904–1905 electrified these nationalists with the vision of a modern Turkey becoming "the Japan of the Middle East," as they called it. In 1908, a group of nationalists called the Young Turks took control of the government in Constantinople, which had been fatally weakened by nationalist agitation and by the empire's economic dependence on Western financiers and businessmen.

The Young Turks' triumph motivated other ethnic groups in the Middle East and the Balkans to demand self-rule, thus ending Ottoman domination in their regions. These nationalists adopted Western values and platforms, and some, such as the Egyptians, had strong contingents of feminist-nationalists who mobilized women to work for independence. But the Young Turks, often aided by European powers with financial and political interests in the region, brutally tried to repress nationalist uprisings in Egypt, Syria, and the Balkans that their own success had encouraged.

The rebellions became part of the tumult shaping international relations in the decade before World War I. Empires, whether old or young, were the scene of growing opposition in the wake of Japanese, Russian, and Turkish events. In German East Africa, colonial forces responded to native resistance in 1905 with a scorched-earth policy of destroying homes, livestock, food, and other resources, eventually killing more than 100,000 Africans there. To maintain their grip on Indochina, the French closed the University of Hanoi, executed Indochinese intellectuals, and deported thousands of suspected nationalists. A French general stationed there summed up the fears of many colonial rulers: "The gravest fact of our actual political situation in Indochina is not the recent trouble in Tonkin [or] the plots undertaken against us but in the muted but growing hatred that our subjects show toward us." At home and abroad, Western political ambitions had given birth to political violence.

REVIEW: How and why did events in overseas empires from the 1890s on challenge Western faith in imperialism?

Roads to War

International developments intensified competition among the great powers and drove Western nationalism to become more aggressive. In the spring of 1914, U.S. president Woodrow Wilson (1856–1924) sent his trusted adviser Colonel Edward House to Europe to assess the rising tensions there. "It is militarism run stark mad," House reported, adding that he foresaw an "awful cataclysm" ahead. Government spending on what people called the arms race had stimulated European economies; but while stockpiles of arms temporarily promoted economic growth, they menaced the future. As early as the mid-1890s, one socialist had called the situation a "cold war" because the hostile atmosphere made physical combat seem imminent. By 1914, the air was even more charged, with militant nationalism in the Balkan states and conflicts in domestic politics propelling Europeans toward mass destruction.

Competing Alliances and Clashing Ambitions

As the twentieth century opened, the Triple Alliance that Bismarck had negotiated among Germany, Austria-Hungary, and Italy confronted an opposing alliance between France and Russia, created in the 1890s. The wild card in the diplomatic scenario was Great Britain, traditional enemy of France, especially in the contest for global power. Constant rivals in Africa, Britain and France edged to the brink of war in 1898 over competing claims to Fashoda, a town in the Sudan. France withdrew, however, and both nations were frightened into getting along for mutual self-interest. To prevent another Fashoda, they entered into secret agreements, the first of which (1904) recognized British claims in Egypt and French claims in Morocco. This agreement marked the beginning of the British-French alliance called the **Entente Cordiale**. Despite the alliance, Britain's response to a European war remained in question; even French statesmen feared that, should war break out, their ally might decide to remain neutral.

Germany's Imperial Demands. Kaiser William II inflamed the diplomatic atmosphere just as France and Britain were reaching these diplomatic understandings. After victory in the Franco-Prussian War, Bismarck had proclaimed Germany a "satisfied" nation and worked to balance great-power interests, generally avoiding imperial battles. William II, in contrast, was emboldened by Germany's growing industrial might and announced in 1901 that Germany needed world power achieved by "friendly conquests." But his actions were far from friendly. Convinced of British hostility toward France, William II used the opportunity presented by the defeat of France's ally Russia in 1904–1905 to contest French claims in Morocco. A boastful, blustery man who was easily prodded to rash actions by his advisers, William landed in Morocco in 1905, challenging French claims there. To resolve what became known as the First Moroccan Crisis, an international conference met in Spain in 1906. Germany confidently expected to gain concessions and new territories, but instead the powers, now including the United States, decided to uphold the French claims. France and Britain, seeing German aggression in Morocco, drew closer together.

Germany found itself weak internationally and strong economically, a situation that made its leaders more determined to compete for territory abroad. When the French took over Morocco completely in 1911, Germany triggered the Second Moroccan Crisis by sending a gunboat to the port of Agadir and demanding concessions from the French. This time no power—not even Austria-Hungary—backed the German move. No one acknowledged this dominant country's might, nor did its insistence on recognition encourage anyone to do so. The British and French now made binding military provisions for the deployment of their forces in case of war, thus strengthening the Entente Cordiale. Smarting from its setbacks on the world stage, Germany refocused its sights on its continental role and on its own alliances.

Entente Cordiale: An alliance between Britain and France that began with an agreement in 1904 to honor colonial holdings.

Crises in the Balkans.   Germany's bold territorial claims, along with public uncertainty about the binding force of alliances, unsettled Europe, particularly the Balkans. German statesmen began envisioning the creation of a **Mitteleuropa** — a term that literally meant "central Europe" but that in their minds also included the Balkans and Turkey. The Habsburgs, now firmly backed by Germany, judged that expansion into the Balkans and the resulting addition of even more ethnic groups would weaken the claims of any single ethnic minority in the Dual Monarchy. Russia, however, saw itself as the protector of Slavs in the region and wanted to replace the Ottomans as the dominant Balkan

---

Mitteleuropa (miht el oy ROH pah): Literally, "central Europe," but used by military leaders in Germany before World War I to refer to land in both central and eastern Europe that they hoped to acquire.

power, especially since Japan had crushed Russian hopes for expansion to the east. Austria's swift annexation of Bosnia-Herzegovina during the Young Turk revolt in 1908 enraged not only the Russians but the Serbs as well, who wanted Bosnia as part of an enlarged Serbia. The Balkans thus whetted many appetites (Map 24.4).

Even without the greedy eyes cast on the Balkans, the situation would have been extremely volatile. The nineteenth century had seen the rise of nationalism and ethnicity as the basis for the unity of the nation-state, and by late in the century, ethnic loyalty challenged dynastic power in the Balkans. Greece, Serbia, Bulgaria, Romania, and Montenegro emerged as autonomous states, almost all of them composed of several ethnicities as well as Orthodox Christians, Roman Catholics, and Muslims. All these states sought more Ottoman and Habsburg territory that included their

MAP 24.4 The Balkans, 1908–1914
Balkan peoples—mixed in religion, ethnicity, and political views—were successful in asserting their desire for independence, especially in the First Balkan War, which claimed territory from the Ottoman Empire. Their increased autonomy sparked rivalries among them and continued to attract attention from the great powers. Three empires in particular—the Russian, Ottoman, and Austro-Hungarian—simultaneously wanted influence for themselves in the region, which became a powder keg of competing ambitions.

own ethnic group—a complicated desire given the intermingling of ethnicities throughout the region. War for territory was on these nationalists' agenda.

In the First Balkan War, in 1912, Serbia, Bulgaria, Greece, and Montenegro joined forces to gain Macedonia and Albania from the Ottomans. The victors divided up their booty, with Bulgaria gaining the most territory, but in a Second Balkan War in 1913, Serbia, Greece, and Montenegro contested Bulgarian gains. The quick victory of these allies increased Austria's dismay at Serbia's rising power. Grievances between the Habsburgs and the Serbs now seemed irreconcilable as each aimed for greater influence in the Balkans. The region had become perilous as both Austria-Hungary (as ruler of many Slavs) and Russia (as their protector) stationed increasing numbers of troops along the borders. The situation tempted strategists to think hopefully that a quick war there—something like Bismarck's wars—could resolve tension and uncertainty.

The Race to Arms

In the nineteenth century, global rivalries and aspirations for national greatness made constant readiness for war seem increasingly necessary. On the seas and in foreign lands, the colonial powers battled to establish control, and they developed railroad, telegraph, and telephone networks everywhere to link their conquests and to move troops as well as commercial goods. Governments began to draft ordinary citizens for periods of two to six years into large standing armies, in contrast to smaller eighteenth-century forces that had served the more limited military goals of the time. By 1914, escalating tensions in Europe boosted the annual intake of draftees: Germany, France, and Russia called up 250,000 or more troops each year. The per capita expenditure on the military rose in all the major powers between 1890 and 1914; the proportion of national budgets devoted to defense in 1910 was lowest in Austria-Hungary at 10 percent, and highest in Germany at 45 percent.

The modernization of weaponry also transformed warfare. Swedish arms manufacturer Alfred Nobel patented dynamite and developed a kind of gunpowder that improved the accuracy of guns and produced a less clouded battlefield environment by reducing firearm smoke. Breakthroughs in the chemical industry led to improvements in long-range artillery, which by 1914 could fire on targets as far as six miles away. Munitions factories across Europe manufactured ever-growing stockpiles of howitzers, Mauser rifles, and Hotchkiss machine guns. Used in the Russo-Japanese and South African wars, these new weapons had shown that military offensives were more difficult to win than in the past because neither side could overcome such accurate firepower. Military leaders devised new strategies to protect their armies from the heavy firepower and deadly accuracy of the new weapons: in the Russo-Japanese War, trenches and barbed wire blanketed the front around Port Arthur.

Naval construction figured in both the arms race and the rising nationalism in politics. To defend against the new powerful, accurate weaponry, ships built after the mid-nineteenth century were made of metal rather than wood. Launched in 1905, the H.M.S. *Dreadnought*, a warship with unprecedented firepower, was the centerpiece of the British navy's plan to construct at least seven battleships per year. Germany also built up its navy and made itself a great land and sea power. The German military encouraged William II to view the navy as the essential ingredient in making Germany a world power and directed him to the writings of the American naval theorist Alfred Thayer Mahan. Mahan's argument that command of the seas determined international power encouraged Germany to plan for naval bases as far away as the Pacific. The German drive to build battleships strengthened Britain's alliance with France in the Entente Cordiale, as all the powers dramatically raised their annual naval spending (Figure 24.1). The Germans described their fleet buildup as "a peaceful policy," but, like British naval expansion, it led only to a hostile international climate and intense competition in weapons manufacture.

Public relations campaigns encouraged military buildup (see Document, "A Historian Promotes Militant Nationalism," page 795). When critics of the arms race suggested a temporary "naval holiday" to stop British and German building, British officials sent out news releases warning that such a cutback "would throw innumerable men on the pavement." Advocates of imperial expansion and nationalist groups lobbied for military spending, while enthusiasts in government promoted large navies as beneficial to international trade, domestic industry, and national pride. When Germany's Social Democrats questioned the use of taxes and their heavy burden on workers, the press criticized the party for lack of patriotism. The Conservative Party in Great Britain, eager for more battleships, made popular the slogan "We want eight and we won't wait." Public enthusiasm for arms buildup and militant nationalism

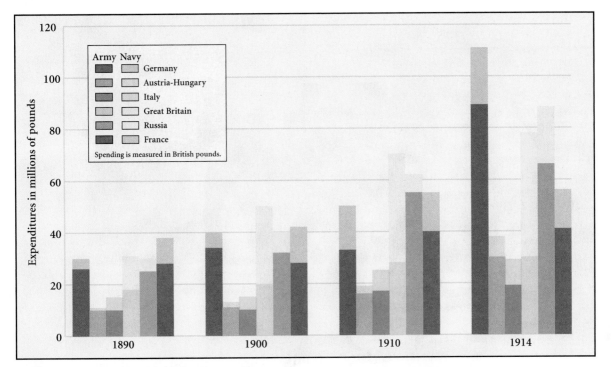

FIGURE 24.1 The Growth in Armaments, 1890–1914
At the beginning of the twentieth century, the European powers engaged in a massive arms race.
Several comparisons offer themselves, particularly the resources newly devoted to navies and the
soaring defense spending of the Germans. Historians often ask whether better diplomacy could
have prevented the outbreak of world war in 1914. The enormous military buildup, however, made
some people living in the early twentieth century, as well as some later historians, see war as
inevitable. *(The Hammond Atlas of the Twentieth Century* (London: Times Books, 1996), *29.)*

amid growing international competition set the
stage for the outbreak of war. The remarks of a
French military leader typified the sentiments of
the time, even among the public at large. When
asked in 1912 about his predictions for war and
peace, he responded enthusiastically, "We shall
have war. I will make it. I will win it."

1914: War Erupts

June 28, 1914, began as an ordinary, even happy
day not only for Freud's patient the Wolf-Man but
also for the Austrian archduke Francis Ferdinand
and his wife, Sophie, as they ended a state visit to
Sarajevo in Bosnia. The archduke, in full military
regalia, was riding in a motorcade to bid farewell
to various officials when a group of young Serb
nationalists threw bombs in an unsuccessful assassination attempt. The danger did not register; after a stop, the archduke and his wife set out again.
In the crowd was another nationalist, Gavrilo Princip, who had traveled in secret for several weeks to
reach this destination, dreaming of reuniting his

homeland of Bosnia-Herzegovina with Serbia and
smuggling weapons with him to accomplish his
end. The unprotected and unsuspecting Austrian
couple became Princip's victims, as he shot both
dead.

Some in the Habsburg government saw the assassination as an opportunity to put down the Ser-
bians once and for all. Evidence showed that
Princip had received arms and information from
Serbian officials, who directed a terrorist organization from within the government. Endorsing a
quick defeat of Serbia, German statesmen and military leaders urged the Austrians to be unyielding
and promised support in case of war. The Austrians sent an ultimatum to the Serbian government,
demanding public disavowals of terrorism, suppression of terrorist groups, and the participation
of Austrian officials in an investigation of the
crime. "You are setting Europe ablaze," the Russian foreign minister remarked of the Austrians' humiliating demands made on a sovereign state. Yet
the Serbs were conciliatory, accepting all the terms
except the presence of Austrian officials in the in-

Arrest of the Assassin
Gavrilo Princip belonged to the Young Bosnians, a group devoted to killing Habsburgs in revenge for the Austro-Hungarian monarchy's having sent workers to colonize their homeland. In June 1914, at the age of nineteen, Princip lived out his dream, killing the heir to the Habsburg throne and his wife. Here Princip is shown being apprehended. He spent the rest of his life in prison and was appalled at the carnage of World War I. *(© Bettmann/Corbis.)*

vestigation. Kaiser William was pleased: "A great moral success for Vienna! All reason for war is gone." His relief proved unfounded. Austria-Hungary, confident of German backing, used the Serbs' resistance to one demand as the pretext for declaring war against Serbia on July 28.

Some statesmen tried desperately to avoid war. The tsar and the kaiser sent pleading letters to one another not to start a European war. The British foreign secretary proposed an all-European conference, but without success. Germany displayed firm support for Austria in hopes of convincing the French and British to shy away from the war. The failure of either to fight, German officials believed, would keep Russia from mobilizing. Additionally, German military leaders had become fixed on fighting a short, preemptive war that would provide territorial gains leading toward the goal of a Mitteleuropa. As conservatives, they planned to impose martial law as part of such a war, using it as a pretext for arresting the leadership of the German Social Democratic Party, which threatened their rule.

The European press caught the war fever of expansionist, imperialist, and other pro-war or-ganizations, even as many governments were torn over what to do. Military leaders, especially in Germany and Austria-Hungary, promoted mobilization rather than diplomacy in the last days of July. The Austrians declared war and then ordered mobilization on July 31 without fear of a Russian attack. They did so in full confidence of German military aid, because as early as 1909 Germany had promised to defend Austria-Hungary, even if that country took the offensive. The thought was that Russia would not dare to intervene against an Austria-Hungary backed by Germany military power, but Nicholas II ordered the mobilization in defense of the Serbs — Russia's Slavic allies. Encouraging the Austrians to attack Serbia, the German general staff mobilized on August 1. France declared war by virtue of its agreement to aid its ally Russia, and when Germany violated Belgian neutrality on its way to invade France, Britain entered the war on the side of France and Russia.

REVIEW: What were the major factors leading to the outbreak of World War I?

DOCUMENT

A Historian Promotes Militant Nationalism

As the nineteenth century came to an end, competitive nationalism in preparation for war was everywhere, even in classrooms. History had developed into a "science" by this time, and historians were supposed to be neutral, basing their conclusions on solid, documentary evidence and erasing all trace of religious or national bias from their work. In the climate of military buildup, competition for empire, and a pro-war spirit, the goal of dispassionate objectivity weakened. Supporting his nation was a driving force in the writing and teaching, of, among others, Heinrich von Treitschke of the University of Berlin, who delivered his lectures glorifying Germany's wars to throngs of cheering students and army officers.

The next essential function of the State is the conduct of war. The long oblivion into which this principle had fallen is a proof of how effeminate the science of government had become in civilian hands. . . .

Without war no State could be. All those we know of arose through war, and the protection of their members by armed force remains their primary and essential task. War, therefore, will endure to the end of history, as long as there is multiplicity of States. The laws of human thought and of human nature forbid any alternative, neither is one to be wished for. The blind worshipper of an eternal peace falls into the error of isolating the State, or dreams of one which is universal, which we have already seen to be at variance with reason.

Even as it is impossible to conceive of a tribunal above the State, which we have recognized as sovereign in its very essence, so it is likewise impossible to banish the idea of war from the world. It is a favourite fashion of our time to instance England as particularly ready for peace. But England is perpetually at war; there is hardly an instant in her recent history in which she has not been obliged to be fighting somewhere. The great strides which civilization makes against barbarism and unreason are only made actual by the sword.

Source: Heinrich Treitschke, *Politics*, Hans Kohn, ed., Blanche Duddale and Torben de Bille, trans. (New York: Harcourt, 1965), 37–38.

Conclusion

Rulers soon forgot their last-minute hesitations when in some capitals celebration erupted with the declaration of war. "A mighty wonder has taken place," wrote a Viennese actor after watching the troops march off amid public enthusiasm. "We have become *young*." Both sides exulted, certain of victory—a triumph of the militant nationalism that led many Europeans to favor war over peace. There were other advantages. Disturbances in private life and challenges to established certainties in ideas would disappear, it was believed, in the crucible of war. A short conflict, people maintained, would resolve tensions ranging from the rise of the working class to political problems caused by global imperial competition. German military men saw war as an opportune moment to round up social democrats and reestablish the traditional deference of an agrarian society. Liberal government based on rights and constitutions, some believed, had simply gone too far in allowing new groups full citizenship and political influence.

Modernity helped blaze the path to war. New technology, mass armies, and new techniques of persuasion supported the military buildup. *The Rite of Spring*, the ballet that opened in Paris on the eve of war in 1913, had taken as its theme the ritualistic attraction of death. Facing continuing violence in politics, chaos in the arts, and problems in the industrial order, many Europeans had come to believe that war would save them from the modern perils they faced. The pessimism that characterized the years before 1914 would end. "Like men longing for a thunderstorm to relieve them of the summer's sultriness," wrote an Austrian official, "so the generation of 1914 believed in the relief that war might bring." Tragically, any hope of relief soon faded. Instead of bringing the refreshment of summer rain, war opened an era of political turmoil, widespread suffering, massive human slaughter, and even greater doses of modernity.

FOR FURTHER EXPLORATION

■ **For suggested references, including Web sites, for topics in this chapter,** see page SR-1 at the end of the book.

■ **For additional primary-source material from this period,** see Chapter 24 in *Sources of THE MAKING OF THE WEST*, Third Edition.

■ **For Web sites and documents related to topics in this chapter,** see *Make History* at bedfordstmartins.com/hunt.

MAPPING THE WEST

Triple Alliance, 1882–1915

Triple Entente, 1907–1917

Europe at the Outbreak of World War I, August 1914

All the powers expected a great, swift victory when war broke out. Many saw war as a chance to increase their territories; as rivals for trade and empire, almost all believed that war would bring them many advantages. But if European nations appeared well prepared and invincible at the start of the war, relatively few would survive the conflict intact.

CHAPTER REVIEW

KEY TERMS AND PEOPLE

new woman (767)
Sigmund Freud (769)
modernism (771)
Friedrich Nietzsche (772)
Albert Einstein (772)
art nouveau (775)
Emmeline Pankhurst
  (778)

Nicholas II (779)
Zionism (783)
South African War (785)
Duma (787)
Entente Cordiale (790)
Mitteleuropa (791)

MAKING CONNECTIONS

1. How did changes in society at the turn of the century affect the development of mass politics?

2. How was culture connected to the world of politics in the years 1890–1914?

3. How had nationalism changed since the French Revolution?

> **For practice quizzes, a customized study plan, and other study tools,** see the Online Study Guide at bedfordstmartins.com/hunt.

REVIEW QUESTIONS

1. How did ideas about the self and about personal life change at the beginning of the twentieth century?

2. How did modernism transform the arts and the world of ideas?

3. What were the points of tension in European political life at the beginning of the twentieth century?

4. How and why did events in overseas empires from the 1890s on challenge Western faith in imperialism?

5. What were the major factors leading to the outbreak of World War I?

IMPORTANT EVENTS

1894–1895	Japan defeats China in the Sino-Japanese War
1894–1899	Dreyfus Affair exposes anti-Semitism in France
1899–1902	South African War fought between Dutch descendants and the British in South African states
1900	Sigmund Freud publishes *The Interpretation of Dreams*
1901	Irish National Theater established by Maud Gonne and William Butler Yeats; death of Queen Victoria
1903	Emmeline Pankhurst founds the Women's Social and Political Union to fight for women's suffrage in Great Britain
1904–1905	Japan defeats Russia in the Russo-Japanese War
1905	Revolution erupts in Russia; violence forces Nicholas II to establish an elected body, the Duma; Albert Einstein publishes his special theory of relativity
1906	Women receive the vote in Finland
1907	Pablo Picasso launches cubist painting with *Les Demoiselles d'Avignon*
1908	Young Turks revolt against rule by the sultan in the Ottoman Empire
1911–1912	Revolutionaries overthrow the Qing dynasty and declare China a republic
1914	Assassination of the Austrian archduke Francis Ferdinand and his wife by a Serbian nationalist precipitates World War I

World War I and Its Aftermath
1914–1929

Jules Amar found his true vocation in World War I. A French expert on improving the efficiency of industrial work, Amar switched his focus after 1914. As hundreds of thousands of men returned from the battlefront missing body parts, plastic surgery and the construction of masks and other devices to hide deformities developed rapidly. Amar devised artificial limbs and appendages to "make up for a function lost, or greatly reduced" that would allow the wounded soldier to return to normal life. The arms he designed featured hooks, magnets, and other mechanisms with which the veteran could hold a cigarette, play a violin, and, most important, work with tools such as typewriters. Mangled by the weapons of modern technological warfare, the survivors of World War I would be made whole, it was thought, by technology such as Amar's.

Amar dealt with the human tragedy of the Great War, so named by contemporaries because of its staggering human toll—forty million wounded or killed in battle. The Great War did not settle problems or restore social order as the European powers hoped it would. Instead, the war produced political chaos, overturning the Russian, German, Ottoman, and Austro-Hungarian empires. The crushing burden of war on the European powers accelerated the rise of the United States, while service in the war intensified the demands of colonized peoples for independence. Many soldiers remained actively fighting long into what was supposed to be peacetime, while others had been so militarized that they longed for a life that was more like wartime.

World War I transformed society too, sometimes building on trends under way before the war started. A prewar feeling of doom and decline gave way to a more pervasive postwar cynicism. Many Westerners turned

Grieving Parents
Before World War I, the German artist Käthe Kollwitz gained her artistic reputation with woodcuts of handloom weavers whose livelihoods were threatened by industrialization. From 1914 on, she depicted the suffering and death that swirled around her and never with more sober force than in these two monuments to her son Peter, who died on the western front in the first months of battle. Today one can still travel to his burial place in Vladslo, Belgium, to see this father and mother mourning their loss, like millions across Europe in those heartbreaking days. (© *John Parker Picture Library.* © *2008 Artists Rights Society (ARS), New York/VG Bild-Kunst, Bonn.*)

their backs on politics and attacked life with frenzied gaiety in the Roaring Twenties, shopping for new consumer goods, drinking in entertainment provided by films and radio, and enjoying once forbidden personal freedoms. Others found reason for hope in the new political systems the war made possible: Soviet communism and Italian fascism. Modern communication technologies such as radio gave politicians the means to promote a utopian mass politics that, paradoxically, was antidemocratic, militaristic, and violent—like the war itself. Total war further weakened the gentlemanly political tone of British prime minister William Gladstone's day and perhaps even totally devastated it.

A war that was long anticipated and even welcomed in some quarters as a solution to the conflicts of modernity destabilized Europe and the world long after the fighting ended. From statesmen to ordinary citizens, many Europeans, like Jules Amar, would spend the next decade dealing with the aftermath of war. While some tried to make war-ravaged society function normally, others were planning to tap into the forces of militarism that the war had so glorified. It became clear that the prewar normality was gone forever and that the war and its values were shaping the 1920s.

> **FOCUS QUESTION:** What political, social, and economic impact did World War I have during the conflict, immediately after it, and through the 1920s?

The Great War, 1914–1918

When war erupted in August 1914, there already existed long-standing alliances, well-defined strategies, and built-up military technologies such as heavy artillery, machine guns, and airplanes. Most people felt that this would be a short, decisive conflict similar to Prussia's rapid victories in the 1860s and 1870 and Japan's swift defeat of Russia in 1904–1905. In fact, the unexpected happened: this war lasted for more than four long years. It was also what historians call a **total war**, meaning one built on the full mobilization of entire societies—soldiers and civilians—and the complete technological capacities of the nations involved. It was the war's unexpected and unprecedented horror that made World War I "great."

Blueprints for War

World War I pitted two sets of opponents formed roughly out of the alliances developed during the previous fifty years. On one side stood the Central Powers (Austria-Hungary and Germany), which had evolved from Bismarck's Triple Alliance. On the other side were the Allies (France, Great Britain, and Russia), which had emerged as a bloc from the Entente Cordiale between France and Great Britain and the 1890s treaties between France and Russia. In 1915, Italy, originally part of the Triple Alliance, switched sides and joined the Allies in hopes of postwar gain. The war became worldwide almost from the start: in late August 1914, Japan, eager to extend its empire into China, went over to the Allies, while in the fall the Ottoman Empire united with the Central Powers against its traditional enemy, Russia (Map 25.1).

The antagonists fought with the same ferocious hunger for power, prestige, and prosperity that had inspired imperialism. Of the Central Powers, Germany wanted a bigger empire, to be gained by annexing Russian territory and incorporating parts of Belgium, France, and Luxembourg. Some German leaders wanted to annex Austria-Hungary

---

total war: A war built on the full mobilization of soldiers, civilians, and technology of the nations involved. The term also refers to a highly destructive war of ideologies.

■ 1914 August World War I begins

■ 1918 November World War I armistice

■ 1917 March Russian Revolution
April United States enters World War I
November Bolshevik Revolution

1912	1915	1918

■ 1913–1915 Suffrage for women expands in Europe

■ 1918–1922 Civil war in Russia

■ 1916 Easter Uprising in Ireland

■ 1919 Weimar Republic begins

■ 1919–1920 Paris Peace Conference

A French Regiment Leaves for the Front, August 1914
Bands played, crowds cheered, and bicyclists led the way as bayonet-equipped soldiers marched eagerly to war. But some viewed the outbreak of war more soberly, and this mood became more common as machine guns and poison chemicals brought the bravest men down. People in cities, working to provide munitions and supplies, soon felt the pinch of inflation; later, many lacked food. Countless men returned physically disabled or mentally deranged from their experience. *(Roger Viollet/Getty Images.)*

as well. Austria-Hungary hoped to keep its great-power status despite the competing nationalisms of ethnic groups within its borders. Among the Allies, Russia wanted to reassert its status as a great power and as the protector of the Slavs by adding a reunified Poland to the Russian Empire and by taking formal leadership of other Slavic peoples. The French, too, craved territory, especially the return of Alsace and Lorraine, ceded to Germany after the Franco-Prussian War of 1870–1871. The

British wanted to cement their hold on Egypt and the Suez Canal and keep the rest of their world empire secure. By the Treaty of London (1915), France and Britain promised Italy territory in Africa, Asia Minor, the Balkans, and elsewhere in return for joining the Allies.

The war involved more than the major European nations and Japan; their colonies participated too, providing massive assistance and serving as battlegrounds. Some one million Africans, one

■ 1924 Lenin dies; Stalin and
Trotsky contend for power

■ 1924–1929 Economic prosperity and stability

■ 1929 October U.S.
stock market crash

| 1921 | 1924 | 1927 | 1930 |

■ 1922 Ireland gains independence;
Fascists march on Rome;
Eliot, "The Waste Land";
Joyce, *Ulysses*

MAP 25.1 The Fronts of World War I, 1914–1918
Because the western front remained relatively stationary, devastation of land and resources was intense. All fronts, however, destroyed segments of Europe's hard-won industrial and agricultural capacity, while the immobile trenches increased military casualties whenever heavy artillery fire pounded them. Men engaged in trench warfare for so long developed an intense camaraderie based on their mutual suffering and deprivation.

million Indians, and more than a million members of the British commonwealth countries fought in the battles. The imperial powers also conscripted still uncounted numbers of colonists as forced laborers both at home and on the battlefront: a million Kenyans and Tanzanians alone are estimated to have been conscripted for menial labor in the battle for East Africa. Colonial troops played a major role in the fighting across north

and sub-Saharan Africa. Using Arab, African, and Indian troops, the British waged successful war in the Ottoman lands of the Middle East. When the Russian Revolution broke out in 1917, the war moved beyond the Black Sea into the Caucasus in a fight for the rich Baku oilfields. In sub-Saharan Africa, the vicious campaign for East Africa cost many lives, not only among the African troops used against one another on behalf of the imperialist powers but also among the civilian population whose resources were confiscated and whose villages were burned. The Japanese seized German-controlled territories in China to enlarge their influence on the mainland.

Unprecedented use of machinery also determined the course of war. In August 1914, machine guns and rifles, airplanes, battleships, submarines, and motorized transport — cars and trains — were at the disposal of armies; other technologies like chlorine gas, tanks, and bombs developed between 1914 and 1918. Countries differed, however, in their experience with and quantities of weapons. British generals who had fought in the South African War (1899–1902) knew the destructive capacity of these weapons, while the Germans were far more advanced in strategy and weaponry than either the Russians or the Austrians. The war itself became a lethal testing ground as both new and old weapons were used, often ineffectively. Nonetheless, officers on both sides believed in a **cult of the offensive**, which called for continuous attacks against the enemy and sustained high troop morale. Despite the availability of newer, more powerful war technology, an old-fashioned vision of war made many officers unwilling to abandon the more familiar sabers, lances, and bayonets. In the face of massive firepower, the cult of the offensive would cost millions of lives.

The Battlefronts

The first months of the war crushed hope of quick victory. All the major armies mobilized rapidly. The Germans were guided by the **Schlieffen Plan**, named after its author, Alfred von Schlieffen, a former chief of the general staff. The plan essentially outlined a way to combat enemies on two fronts by concentrating on one foe at a time. It called for a rapid and concentrated blow to the west against France, which would lead to that nation's defeat in six weeks, accompanied by a light holding action against Russia to

The Schlieffen Plan

the east. The attack on France was to proceed through Belgium, whose neutrality was guaranteed by the European powers. Once France had fallen, Germany's western armies would be deployed against Russia, which, it was believed, would mobilize far more slowly. The great powers were not prepared for the unexpected, especially the prolonged massacre of their nations' youth with no hint of a victory in sight.

Indecisive Offensives: 1914–1915. When German troops reached Belgium and Luxembourg at the beginning of August 1914, the Belgian government rejected an ultimatum to allow the uncontested passage of the German army through the country. Instead, the Belgians put up spirited resistance. Meanwhile, the main body of French troops, tricked by German diversionary tactics, attacked the Germans in Alsace and Lorraine instead of meeting the main invasion from the north. Belgian resistance slowed the German advance, allowing British and French troops to reach the northern front. In September, the British and French armies engaged the Germans along the Marne River in France. Neither side could defeat the other, and casualties were shocking: in the first three months of war, more than 1.5 million men fell on the western front alone. Guns like the 75-millimeter howitzer, accurate at long range, turned what was supposed to be an offensive war of movement into a stationary standoff along a line that stretched from the North Sea through Belgium and northern France to Switzerland (Map 25.2). Deep within opposing lines of trenches dug along this front, millions of soldiers lived in nightmarish homes.

On the eastern front, the "Russian steam-roller" — named thus because of the number of men mobilized, some twelve million in all — drove far more quickly than expected into East Prussia on August 17. The Russians believed that no army could stand up to their massive numbers, regardless of how badly equipped and poorly trained they were. Their success was short-lived. The Germans crushed the tsar's army in East Prussia and then turned south to Galicia. Victory made heroes of the military leaders Paul von Hindenburg (1847–1934) and Erich Ludendorff (1865–1937), who demanded more troops for the eastern front. Despite victories, German triumphs

---

cult of the offensive: A military strategy of constantly attacking the enemy that was believed to be the key to winning World War I but that brought great loss of life while failing to bring decisive victory.

Schlieffen Plan: The Germans' strategy in World War I that called for attacks on two fronts — concentrating first on France to the west and then turning east to attack Russia.

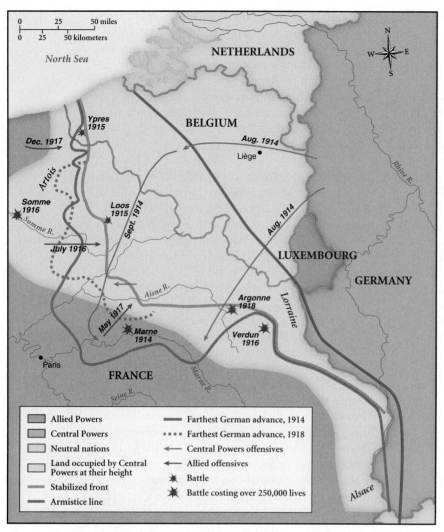

MAP 25.2 The Western Front
The western front occupied some of the richest parts of France, with long-lasting consequences. Destruction of French villages, roads, bridges, livestock, and property was the worst in Europe, while the trauma of the French people endured for generations. The effects of horrendous casualties, ever-present artillery fire, provisioning and hospital needs, and the demands of military and medical personnel changed everyone's way of life.

tained a policy of neutrality; Germany, unwilling to provoke Wilson further, called off unrestricted submarine warfare. In May 1916, the navies of Germany and Britain finally clashed in the North Sea at Jutland. This inconclusive battle demonstrated that the German fleet could not master British seapower.

Ideas of a negotiated peace were discarded: "No peace before England is defeated and destroyed," William II railed against his cousin King George V. "Only amidst the ruins of London will I forgive Georgy." French leaders called for a "war to the death." General staffs on both sides continued to prepare fierce attacks several times a year. Indecisive campaigns opened with heavy artillery pounding enemy trenches and gun emplacements. Troops then responded to the order to go "over the top" by scrambling out of their trenches and into battle, usually to be mowed down by machine-gun fire from defenders secure in their own trenches. On the western front throughout 1915, the French assaulted the Germans in the north to drive them from industrial regions; they accomplished little, however, and casualties of 100,000 and more for a single campaign became commonplace. On the eastern front, Russian armies captured parts of Galicia in the spring of 1915 and lumbered toward Hungary. The Central Powers struck back in Poland later that year, bringing the front closer to Petrograd (formerly St. Petersburg), the Russian capital. The Austro-Hungarian armies routed the Serbs and then engaged the newly mobilized Italian army.

in the east had failed to knock out the Russians by year's end and had also misdirected the Schlieffen Plan by removing forces from the west before the western front had been won.

War at sea proved equally indecisive. Confident in Britain's superior naval power, the Allies blockaded ports to prevent supplies from reaching Germany and Austria-Hungary. Kaiser William II and his advisers planned a massive submarine campaign against Allied and neutral shipping around Britain and France. In May 1915, a German U-boat (*Unterseeboot*, "underwater boat") sank the British passenger ship *Lusitania* and killed 1,198 people, including 124 Americans. Despite U.S. outrage, President Woodrow Wilson main-

Mounting Catastrophe: 1916. The next year's battles were even more disastrous and futile. To cripple French morale, the Germans launched massive assaults on the fortress at Verdun, firing as many as a million shells in a single day. Combined French and German losses totaled close to a million men. Nonetheless, the French held. Hoping to relieve their allies, the British unleashed an artillery pounding of German trenches in the Somme region in June 1916. In several months of battle at the Somme, 1.25 million men were killed or wounded, but the final result was a draw. By the end of 1916, the French had absorbed more than 3.5 million casualties. To help the Allies engaged at Verdun and the Somme, the Russians struck again, driving once more into the Carpathian Mountains, recouping territory, and menacing Austria-Hungary until stopped by the German army. Amid huge losses, the Austrian army recruited men in their mid-fifties, and the German general staff decided it would take over Austrian military operations. The war was sapping Europe's strength and individual sovereignty.

The Soldiers' War. Had the military leaders thoroughly dominated the scene, historians judge, all armies would have been utterly demolished by the end of 1915. Yet ordinary soldiers in this war were not automatons in the face of what seemed to them suicidal orders. Informal agreements among troops to avoid battles allowed some battalions to go for long stretches with hardly a casualty. Enemies facing each other across the trenches frequently ate their meals in peace, even though the trenches were within hand-grenade reach. Throughout the war, soldiers on both fronts fraternized with one another. They played an occasional game of soccer, shouted across the trenches, and made gestures of agreement not to fight. A British veteran of the trenches explained to a new recruit that the Germans "don't want to fight any more than we do, so there's a kind of understanding between us. Don't fire at us and we'll not fire at you." Burying enemy dead in common graves with their own fallen comrades, many ordinary soldiers came to feel more warmly toward enemies who shared the trench experience than toward civilians back home.

Newly forged bonds of male camaraderie alleviated some of the misery of trench life and aided survival. Sharing the danger of death and the deprivations of frontline experience weakened tradi-

War in the Skies (1914)
As the war started, aviators and the machines they piloted became symbols of the human potential to transcend time and space. The Great War, however, featured the airplane as the new weapon in what British writer H. G. Wells called the "headlong sweep to death." Daring pilots, or "aces," took the planes on reconnaissance flights and guided them in the totally new practice of aerial combat, as shown in this engraving from an Italian newspaper of a French airplane shooting down a German one. *(The Art Archive/ Domenica del Corriere/Dagli Orti.)*

War in the Trenches
Men at the front developed close friendships while they lived with daily discomfort, death, and the horrors of modern technological warfare. Some of the complexities of trench warfare appear in this image showing soldiers rescuing their fallen comrades after fighting at Bagatelle in northern France. *(Getty Images.)*

tional class distinctions. In some cases, upper-class officers and working-class recruits became friends in that "wholly masculine way of life uncomplicated by women," as another British soldier put it. Soldiers picked lice from one another's bodies and clothes, revered section leaders who tended their blistered feet, and came to love one another, sometimes even passionately. Positive memories of this frontline community survived the war and influenced postwar politics.

Troops of colonized soldiers from Asia and Africa had different experiences. Often these soldiers were put in the very front ranks, where the risks were greatest. They suffered particularly from the rigors of an unfamiliar climate and strange food as well as from the devastation inflicted by Western war technology. Yet, as with class divisions, racial barriers sometimes fell, for instance, whenever a European understood enough to alleviate the distress caused by severe cold. Colonial troops' perspectives changed, too, as they saw their "masters" completely undone and "uncivilized." For when fighting did break out, trenches became a veritable hell of shelling and sniping, flying body parts, rotting cadavers, and blinding gas. Some soldiers became hysterical or succumbed to shell shock through the sheer stress and violence of battle. Alienation and cynicism rose: "It might be me tomorrow," a young British soldier wrote his mother in 1916. "Who cares?" Many had gone to war to escape ordinary life in industrial society; however, they learned, as one German put it, "that in the modern war . . . the triumph of the machine over the individual is carried to its most extreme form." They took this hard-won knowledge into battle, pulling their comrades back when an offensive seemed lost or too costly.

The Home Front

World War I took place off the battlefield too. Total war meant the indispensable involvement of civilians in the war industry: manufacturing the shells and machine guns, the poisonous gases, the bombs and airplanes, and eventually the tanks that were the backbone of technological warfare. Increased production of coffins, canes, wheelchairs, and artificial limbs (devised by the likes of Jules Amar) was also a wartime necessity. Because soldiers would have utterly failed without them, civilians had to work overtime, believe in, and sacrifice for victory. To keep the war machine operating smoothly, governments oversaw factories, transportation systems, and resources ranging from food to coal to textiles. Such dictatorial government control would have outraged many liberals before the war but was now accepted as a necessary condition for victory.

Politics Suspended. Initially, all political parties on both sides put aside their differences. Many socialists and working-class people who had formerly criticized the military buildup announced their support for the war. For decades, socialist parties had preached that "the worker has no country" and that nationalism was mere ideology meant to keep workers disunited and subjected to the will of their employers. In August 1914, however, most socialists became as patriotic as the rest of society. Feminists divided over whether to maintain their traditional pacifism or to support the war. Although many feminists actively opposed the conflict, the British suffrage leader Emmeline Pankhurst and her daughter Christabel were among the many activists who became militant nationalists, even changing the name of their suffrage paper to *Britannia*. Parties representing the middle classes shelved their distrust of the socialists and working classes. In the name of victory, national leaders wanted to end political division of all kinds: "I no longer recognize [political] parties," William II declared on August 4, 1914. "I recognize only Germans." Ordinary people, even those who had been at the receiving end of discrimination, came to believe that a new day of unity was dawning. One rabbi proudly echoed the kaiser: "In the German fatherland there are no longer any Christians and Jews, any believers and disbelievers, there are only Germans."

Governments Mobilize the People. Governments mobilized the home front with varying degrees of success. All countries were caught without ready replacements for their heavy losses of weapons and military equipment and soon felt the shortage of food and labor. War ministries set up boards to allocate labor on both the home front and the battlefront and to give industrialists financial incentives to encourage productivity. But the Russian bureaucracy only reluctantly and ineffectively cooperated with industrialists and other groups that could aid the war effort. In several countries, emergency measures allowed the drafting of both men and women for military or industrial service. Desperate for factory workers, the Germans forced Belgian citizens to move to Germany, housing them in prison camps. In the face of rationing, municipal governments set up canteens and day-care centers. Rural Russia, Austria-Hungary, Bulgaria, and Serbia, where youths, women, and old men struggled to sustain farms, had no such relief programs.

Governments throughout Europe passed sedition laws that made it a crime to criticize official policies. To ensure civilian acceptance of longer working hours and shortages of consumer goods, governments created propaganda agencies to tout the war as a patriotic mission to resist villainous enemies (see the propaganda posters in "Seeing History," page 808). British propagandists fabricated atrocities that the Germans, whom they called "Huns," supposedly committed against Belgians, and German propagandists warned that French African troops would rape German women if Germany were defeated. In Russia, Tsar Nicholas II changed the German-sounding name of St. Petersburg to the Russian Petrograd in 1914. Efforts were often clumsy: though civilians found it riveting, the British film *The Battle of the Somme* (1916) was so obviously sanitized of the war's horrors that soldiers in the audience roared with laughter.

Despite widespread popular support for the war, some individuals and groups worked to end the fighting and urged a negotiated peace. In 1915, activists in the international women's movement met in The Hague to call for an end to the war.

"We can no longer endure . . . brute force as the only solution of international disputes," declared Dutch physician Aletta Jacobs. The women had no success, however, in bringing about negotiations. In Austria-Hungary, nationalist groups agitating for ethnic self-determination hampered the empire's war effort. The Czechs undertook a vigorous anti-Habsburg campaign at home, while in the Balkans, Croats, Slovenes, and Serbs formed a committee to plan a South Slav state independent of Austria-Hungary or any other power. The Allies encouraged such independence movements as part of their strategy to defeat Austria-Hungary.

The Civilians' War. The war upset the social order as well as the political one. In the war's early days, many women lost their jobs when luxury shops, textile factories, and other nonessential businesses closed. With men at the front, many women headed households with little support and few opportunities to work. But governments and businesses soon recognized the amount of labor it would take to wage technological war. As more and more men left for the trenches, women who had lost their jobs in nonessential businesses as well as many low-paid domestic workers took over

---

A New Workforce in Wartime

With men at the front, women moved into factory work at jobs from which they had been unofficially barred before the war, as shown in this French photograph. In addition, tens of thousands of forced laborers from the colonies were moved to Europe also to replace men sent to the front. The European experience of forced labor and service at the front politicized colonial subjects, fortifying independence movements in the postwar period. *(Roger Viollet/Getty Images.)*

Demonizing the Enemy: Italian Propaganda Posters from World War I

Propaganda was a major ingredient of World War I, crucial in mobilizing civilian populations to work overtime and to sacrifice willingly food, health, and even the lives of their men. Propaganda specialists who had promoted arms buildup before the war now joined with graphic artists to produce emotionally compelling images of the dangers posed by the enemy.

Although Italy joined the war only in 1915, after being promised postwar compensation by the Allies, Italian propaganda demonized the enemy just as forcefully as that of the early combatant powers. To inspire Italians to buy bonds that financed the war effort, the classically dressed woman in the poster shown below represents Italy holding back the savage "Hun," who symbolizes the collective Germanic enemy. What elements in the poster create the impression of German wartime savagery? By contrast, what messages about Italy and the Allies does the woman portray? Why do you think the opposition of male and female figures was a particularly powerful one? The second image, (see below right) employs creatures—two giant squids, according to the Italian caption—to depict the enemy. Part of the boxed text reads, "'We do not threaten small nations' declared the German Chancellor on December 10th 1915." What is happening in this image? What feelings do these grasping tentacled creatures call up in your mind? How might Italians have responded at the time? How do you account for the different expressions of the two beasts? This particular image was printed in several versions, including both English and Italian. Why might interchangeable propaganda work just as well as nation-specific posters, as in the first image?

Propaganda posters from World War I ranged from showing actual people in danger to depictions of the enemy as various forms of animals, including reptiles and octopuses. Why do you think that both kinds of representations were effective?

"Subscribe to the Bond Program," 1915–1918. *(Imperial War Museum.)*

"The Prussian Squid or 'Sea Demon,'" 1916. *(Imperial War Museum.)*

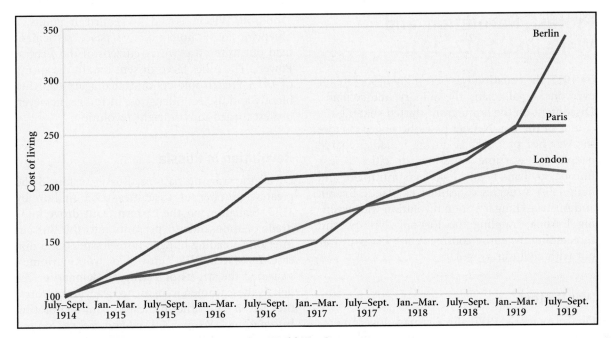

FIGURE 25.1 The Rising Cost of Living During World War I
The diversion of resources to the military resulted in a soaring cost of living for civilians. As men went to the front and as some remaining agricultural workers could find higher pay in factories, a decline in agricultural output led to scarcity and thus rising prices for food. Finally, housing came to be in short supply as resources were directed to the war effort rather than used to construct needed buildings. Even after the war, prices rose in Germany because the Allies maintained their blockade to keep the pressure on the peacemaking process. *(Jay Winter and Jean-Louis Robert,* Capital Cities at War: Paris, London, Berlin, 1914–1919 *(Cambridge: Cambridge University Press, 1997), 259.)*

higher-paying jobs in munitions and metallurgical industries. In Warsaw they drove trucks, and in London they conducted streetcars. Some young women drove ambulances and nursed the wounded near the front lines.

The press praised women's patriotism in adapting to the wartime emergency, but women's assumption of men's jobs looked to many like a sign of social disorder. In the words of one metalworker, women were "sending men to the slaughter." Men feared that women would remain in the workforce after the war, robbing men of the breadwinner role. Many people, even some women, objected to women's loss of femininity. "The feminine in me decreased more and more, and I did not know whether to be sad or glad about this," wrote one Russian nurse about adopting rough male clothing near the battlefield. But others criticized young female munitions workers for squandering their pay on ribbons and jewelry. The heated prewar debates over gender roles returned.

Whereas soldiers from different backgrounds often felt bonds of solidarity in the trenches, difficult wartime conditions increasingly pitted civilians against one another on the home front. Workers toiled long hours with less to eat, while many in the upper classes bought fancy food and fashionable clothing on the black market (outside the official system of rationing). Governments allowed many businesses high rates of profit, a policy that made the cost of living surge and thus contributed to social tensions (see Figure 25.1). Shortages of staples like bread, sugar, and meat occurred across Europe; the Germans, in fact, called the brutal winter of 1916–1917 the turnip winter, after what was often their only available food. A German roof workers' association pleaded for relief: "We can no longer go on. Our children are starving." Dredging up prewar hatred, some blamed Jews for the shortages. Civilians in the colonies suffered severely. Both sides simply deported or conscripted able-bodied people in territories they occupied. The French forcibly transported some 100,000 Vietnamese to work in France for the war effort. Africans also faced grueling forced labor along with skyrocketing taxes and prices. Their suffering during wartime laid the groundwork for ordinary people, whether in the colonies or at home in Europe, to take political action.

REVIEW: In what ways was World War I a total war?

Protest, Revolution, and War's End, 1917–1918

By 1917, the situation was becoming desperate for everyone — politicians, the military, and civilians. Discontent on the home front started shaping the course of the war. Neither patriotic slogans before the war nor propaganda during it had prepared people for wartime suffering. In cities across Europe, civilians revolted; soldiers mutinied, and nationalist struggles continued to plague Britain and Austria-Hungary. Soon revolution was sweeping Europe, toppling the Russian dynasty, and threatening the entire continent not just with war but with civil war as well.

War Protest

On February 1, 1917, the German government, hard-pressed by the public clamor over mounting casualties and by the military's growing power, resumed full-scale submarine warfare. The military promised that this campaign would end the war in six months by cutting off supplies to Britain and thus forcing the island nation to surrender before the United States could come to its rescue. The British responded by mining its harbors and the surrounding seas, and by developing the convoy system of shipping, in which a hundred or more warships and freighters traveling the seas together could drive off the submarines. The Germans' submarine gamble not only failed to defeat the British but also brought the United States into the war in April 1917, after German U-boats had sunk several American ships.

Political opposition increased in Europe: Irish republicans attacked government buildings in Dublin on Easter Monday 1916 in an effort to wrest Ireland's independence from Britain. Ill prepared, the Irish were easily defeated, and many of them were executed. Civilians in other countries revolted against food shortages and high prices. "We are living on a volcano," warned an Italian politician in the spring of 1917. In the cities of Italy, Russia, Germany, and Austria, women rioted to get food for their families. As inflation mounted, tenants conducted rent strikes, and factory hands and white-collar workers alike walked off the job.

Amid these protests, Austria-Hungary secretly asked the Allies for a negotiated peace to avoid a total collapse of the empire. In the summer of 1917, the German Reichstag made overtures for a "peace of understanding and permanent reconciliation of peoples." In January 1918, President Woodrow Wilson issued his Fourteen Points, a blueprint for a nonvindictive peace settlement held out to the war-weary citizens of the Central Powers. The Allies faced dissent too. In the spring of 1917, French soldiers mutinied against further bloody and useless offensives. In Russia, however, protest turned into outright revolution.

Revolution in Russia

Of all the warring nations, Russia sustained the greatest number of casualties — 7.5 million by 1917. Slaughter on the eastern front drove hundreds of thousands of peasants into the Russian interior, spreading hunger, homelessness, and disease. In March 1917,[1] crowds of workingwomen swarmed the streets of Petrograd demanding relief. As these women were turned away from stores, they fell in with other protesters commemorating International Women's Day and began looting shops for food. Factory workers and other civilians joined them. Russia's comparative economic underdevelopment overwhelmed the government's ability to provide basic necessities on the home front. Many in the army, instead of remaining loyal to the tsar, were embittered by the massive casualties caused by their inferior weapons and their leaders' foolhardy tactics.

Government incompetence and Nicholas II's stubborn resistance to change had made the war even worse in Russia than elsewhere. Unlike other heads of state, Nicholas failed to unite the bureaucracy and his people in a single-minded wartime effort. Grigori Rasputin, a combination of holy man and charlatan, manipulated Nicholas and his wife, Alexandra, by claiming to control the hemophilia of their son and heir. Rasputin's disastrous influence on state matters led influential leaders to question rather than support the government. "Is this stupidity or treason?" one member of the Duma asked of the corrupt wartime administration. When the riots erupted in March 1917, Nicholas finally realized the situation was hopeless. He abdicated, bringing the three-hundred-year-old Romanov dynasty to a sudden end.

The Provisional Government. Politicians from the moderate aristocracy and the middle classes

---

[1]Until February 1918, Russia observed the Julian calendar, which was thirteen days behind the Gregorian calendar used by the rest of Europe. Hence, the first phase of the revolution occurred in March according to the Gregorian calendar (but February in the Julian calendar), the later phase in November on the Gregorian calendar (October according to the Julian). All dates used in this book follow the Gregorian calendar.

in the old Duma formed a new administration called the Provisional Government. At first, hopes were high that under the Provisional Government, as one revolutionary poet put it, "our false, filthy, boring, hideous life should become a just, pure, merry, and beautiful life." To survive, the Provisional Government had to pursue the war successfully, manage internal affairs better, and set the government on a firm constitutional footing to establish its credibility. However, it did not rule alone, because other political forces had also strengthened during the revolution. Among them, the **soviets**—councils elected from workers and soldiers—competed with the government for political support. Born during the Revolution of 1905, the soviets in 1917 campaigned to end the deference usually given to the wealthy and to military officers, urged respect for workers and the poor, and temporarily gave an air of celebration and carnival to this political cataclysm. The peasantry, also competing for power, began to confiscate gentry estates and withheld produce from the market because there were no consumer goods for which to exchange food. Increasing urban food shortages opened the Provisional Government to further opposition.

In hopes of adding to the turmoil in Russia, the Germans in April 1917 provided safe rail transportation through German territory for **V. I. Lenin** (1870–1924) and other prominent Bolsheviks to return to their homeland from exile. Lenin had devoted himself to bringing about socialism through the force of his small band of Bolsheviks. Upon his return to Petrograd, he issued the April Theses, a document that called for Russia to withdraw from the war, for the soviets to seize power on behalf of workers and poor peasants, and for all private land to be nationalized. Announcing their platform with such slogans as "All power to the soviets" and "Peace, land, and bread," the Bolsheviks aimed to oust the Provisional Government.

Time was running out for the Provisional Government, which saw a battlefield victory as the only way to ensure its position. On July 1, the Russian army attacked the Austrians in Galicia but was defeated once again. The new prime minister, Aleksandr Kerensky, used his commanding oratory to arouse patriotism, but he lacked the polit-

REVOLUTION IN RUSSIA		
1917	March 8	International Women's Day, strikes and demonstrations
	March 12	Establishment of Provisional Government
	March 15	Nicholas II abdicates
	April	Lenin and other Bolshevik leaders return to Russia
	May	Turmoil in the Provisional Government
	Late June–early July	Russian offensive against Germany fails
	Mid-July	Attempted popular uprising fails; Kerensky is prime minister
	September	Military coup fails
	November 6–7	Bolsheviks seize power on behalf of soviets
	November 25	Constituent assembly elections held
1918	January	Constituent assembly closed down by Bolsheviks
	March 2	Treaty of Brest-Litovsk
1918–1922		Civil war
1923		Union of Soviet Socialist Republics established
1924		Death of Lenin
1928–1929		Stalin takes full power

ical skills needed to create an effective wartime government. In Petrograd, groups of workers, soldiers, and sailors—many of them Bolsheviks—agitated for the soviets to replace the Provisional Government. Unable to clamp down on the protesters, the Provisional Government had to call on the people to put down a military coup. Depending on its sworn enemies, the Provisional Government had shown itself to be helpless—unable to enact reforms, summon a constituent assembly to plan a new permanent government, or win the war. The army had become, as one critic put it, "a huge crowd of tired, poorly clad, poorly fed, embittered men"—eager for radical change.

The Bolshevik Takeover. The Bolshevik leadership, urged on by Lenin, attacked and overthrew the weakened Provisional Government in November 1917, an event called the **Bolshevik Revolution**. In January 1918, elections for a constituent assembly failed to give the Bolsheviks a plurality, so the party used troops to take over the new government

---

soviets: Councils of workers and soldiers first formed in Russia in the Revolution of 1905; they were revived to represent the people in the early days of the 1917 Russian Revolution.

V. I. Lenin (1870–1924): Bolshevik leader who executed the Bolshevik Revolution in the fall of 1917, took Russia out of World War I, and imposed communism in Russia.

Bolshevik Revolution: The overthrow of Russia's Provisional Government in the fall of 1917 by V. I. Lenin and his Bolshevik forces.

Lenin Addressing the Second All-Russian Congress of Soviets
In the spring of 1917, the German government craftily let Lenin and other Bolsheviks travel from their exile in Switzerland back to the scene of the unfolding revolution in Russia. A committed revolutionary instead of a political reformer, Lenin used his oratory and skilled maneuvering to convince many in the soviets to follow him in overthrowing the Provisional Government, taking Russia out of the war, and implementing his brand of communism. *(RIA Novosti.)*

completely. The Bolsheviks also seized town and city administrations, and in the winter of 1918–1919, their new government, observing Marxist doctrine, abolished private property and nationalized factories in order to rebuild production (see Document, "Outbreak of the Russian Revolution," page 813). The Provisional Government had allowed both men and women to vote in 1917, making Russia the first great power to legalize universal suffrage. The vote soon became a hollow privilege when the Bolsheviks limited the candidates to chosen members of the Communist Party.

The Bolsheviks asked Germany for peace and agreed to the Treaty of Brest-Litovsk (March 1918), which placed vast regions of the old Russian Empire under German occupation. Because the loss of millions of square miles to the Germans put Petrograd at risk, the Bolsheviks relocated the capital to Moscow and formally adopted the name Communists (taken from Karl Marx's writings) to distinguish themselves from the socialists/social democrats who had voted for the disastrous war in the first place. Lenin agreed to the catastrophic terms of the treaty not only because he had promised to bring peace to Russia but also because he believed that the rest of Europe would soon rebel against the war and overthrow the capitalist order.

Civil War in Russia. A full-fledged civil war now broke out with the pro-Bolsheviks (the "Reds") pitted against an array of forces (the "Whites") who wanted to turn back the revolution (Map 25.3). Among the Whites, the tsarist military leadership, composed mainly of landlords and supporters of aristocratic rule, took to the field whatever troops it could muster. Businessmen whose property had been nationalized and the liberal educated classes soon lent their support. Many non-Russian nationality groups who had been incorporated into the empire through force and Russification fought the Bolsheviks because they saw their chance for independence. Before World War I ended, Russia's former allies—notably the United States, Britain, France, and Japan—also landed troops in the country both to block the Germans and to fight the Bolsheviks. The counterrevolutionary groups lacked a strong leader and unified goals, however. Instead, the groups competed with one another: the pro-tsarist forces, for example, alienated groups seeking independence, such as the Ukrainians, Estonians, and Lithuanians, by stressing the goal of restoring Russian imperial power. Without a common purpose or an effective, unified command, the opponents of revolution were doomed.

Outbreak of the Russian Revolution

It is clear only in retrospect when a full-fledged and sustainable revolution has broken out. Here an eighteen-year-old student describes what happened when news of the St. Petersburg revolt reached Moscow in the late winter of 1917. Crowds had already formed when the young man decided to see what was happening in the streets.

In the crowd were many students who explained that a revolution had begun in St. Petersburg. The news swept through them like a breeze and created an extraordinary atmosphere. People began to embrace and kiss; strangers became close friends; some wept for joy. In five to ten minutes people seemed reborn. A pretty girl came up to me and took me by the hand, as though we had known each other for ages. Then hand-in-hand, in a warm embrace, and without asking each other's name, we proceeded toward the Krutitskie barracks. . . .

The crowd grew bigger and bigger, and somewhere in the distance one could hear the well-known refrain of a revolutionary song. By this time it was so crowded that it was quite impossible to get to one side or the other. We continued to hold hands, as though we might get lost. Slowly, barely perceptibly, the human stream moved toward the Red Gates, where I knew there was another barracks. It was the same scene there, except that the soldiers were shouting loudly, waving and greeting us. We couldn't make out what they said. Near Pokrovka we ran into a group of police officers, but instead of greeting them with good-natured jokes, thousands of voices yelled fierce, threatening cries: "Pharaohs! Your time is up! Get away for your own good!"

. . . We moved slowly and could see neither the front nor the back of the crowd, for the street was blocked solid. For the first time in my life I sensed that atmosphere of joy, when everyone you meet seems close to you, your flesh and blood, when people look at one another with eyes full of love. To call it mass hypnosis is not quite right, but the mood of the crowd was transmitted from one to another like conduction, like a spontaneous burst of laughter, joy, or anger.

The majority of the crowd consisted of people who that morning had been praying for the good health of the imperial family. Now they were shouting, "Down with the Tsar!" and not disguising their joyful contempt. My companion was a good example. She showered me with questions: Where are we going? Why are we marching? Why is there a revolution? How will we manage without a tsar? It seemed like a mere holiday to her—Sunday's carnival procession, complete with mass participation. Tomorrow—Monday—humdrum working life would begin again, just as usual. Without asking a question, as though talking to herself, she suddenly said: "How good it would be if there was another revolution tomorrow!" What could I say? Tomorrow? Probably tomorrow the police would arrest us. But today there was a festival on the streets.

Source: Eduard Dune, *Notes of a Red Guard*, trans. and ed. Dianne Koenker and S. A. Smith (Champaign: University of Illinois Press, 1993), 32, 34.

The civil war shaped Russian communism. Leon Trotsky (1879–1940), Bolshevik commissar of war, built a highly disciplined army by ending democratic procedures, such as the election of officers, that had originally attracted soldiers to Bolshevism. Lenin and Trotsky introduced the policy of war communism, whereby urban workers and troops moved through the countryside, seizing grain from the peasantry to feed the civil war army and workforce. The Cheka (secret police) imprisoned political opponents and black marketers and often shot them without trial. The bureaucracy, the Cheka, and the Red Army all grew in size and strength. The result was a more authoritarian government—a development that broke with Marx's promise that revolution would bring a "withering away" of the state.

The Bolsheviks clamped down on their opponents during the bloody civil war, and they organized their supporters to foster revolutionary Marxism across Europe. In March 1919, they founded the Third International, also known as the Comintern (Communist International), for the explicit purpose of replacing the Second International with a centrally run organization dedicated to preaching communism. By mid-1921, the Red Army had defeated the Whites in the Crimea, the Caucasus, and the Muslim borderlands in central Asia. The Japanese withdrew from Siberia in 1922, ending the civil war in central and east Asia. The Bolsheviks were now in charge of a state as complex and multinational as the old Russian Empire had been. But although the revolution had turned out the inept Romanovs and the privileged aris-

MAP 25.3 The Russian Civil War, 1917–1922
Nationalists, aristocrats, middle-class citizens, and property-owning peasants tried to combine their interests to defeat the Bolsheviks, but they failed to create an effective political consensus. As fighting covered the countryside, ordinary people suffered, especially when their grain was confiscated by armies on both sides. The Western powers and Japan also sent in troops to put down this threatening revolution.

tocracy, the civil war and the resulting hunger and disease took millions of lives. Meanwhile, the Bolsheviks had made brutality their political style, one at odds with socialist promises for a humane and flourishing society.

Ending the War, 1918

With Russia out of World War I, Europe's leaders faced a new balance of forces. Added to war protest was the new fear that communism might lie in their future. Desperate for victory before revolution took over, the Central Powers made one final attempt to smash through the Allied lines using a new offensive strategy. It consisted of concentrated forces piercing single points of the enemy's defense lines and then wreaking havoc from the rear. Using these tactics, the Central Powers overwhelmed the Italian army at Caporetto in the fall of 1917.

In the spring of 1918, however, a similar offensive on the western front ground to a bloody halt within weeks. By then, the British and French had started making limited but effective use of tanks supported by airplanes. The first tanks were cumbersome, but their ability to withstand machine-gun fire made offensive attacks possible. In the summer of 1918, the Allies, now fortified by the Americans, pushed back the Germans all along the western front and headed toward Germany. The German armies, suffering more than two million casualties between spring and summer, rapidly disintegrated.

By October 1918, the German command recognized defeat and helped create a civilian government to take over rule of the home front. As these inexperienced politicians took power, they were also taking blame for the defeat. The generals, knowing victory was hopeless, still proclaimed themselves fully capable of winning the war. Weak-willed civilians, they announced, had dealt the military a "stab in the back" by forcing a surrender. Amid this blatant lying, naval officers called for a final sea battle. Having spent years watching high-ranking officers enjoy champagne-filled meals while they themselves survived on turnips and thin soup, sailors rebelled against what they saw as a suicide mission. The sailors' revolt spread to the workers, who demonstrated in Berlin, Munich, and other major cities. The situation was no better in Austria-Hungary, where combat units had to be pulled from the front to maintain order at home. The uprisings provoked Social Democratic politicians to declare a German republic in an effort to prevent revolution, while Czechs and Slovaks joined to declare themselves an independent state. On November 9, 1918, Kaiser William II fled as the Central Powers collapsed on all fronts.

Finally, on the morning of November 11, 1918, delegates from the two sides signed an armistice. The guns fell silent on the western front six hours later. In the course of four years, European civilization had been sorely tested, if not shattered. Conservative figures put the battlefield toll at a minimum of ten million dead and thirty million wounded, incapacitated, or doomed eventually to die of their wounds. In every European combatant country, industrial and agricultural production had plummeted, and much of the reduced output had been sent to the military. Asia, Africa, and the Americas, which depended on European trade, also felt the painful impact of Europe's declining production. From 1918 to 1919, the weakened global population suffered an influenza epidemic that left as many as one hundred million more dead worldwide.

Besides illness, hunger, and death, the war also provoked tremendous moral questioning. Soldiers returning home in 1918 and 1919 flooded the book market with their memoirs, trying to give meaning to their experiences. Some twenty-five hundred war poets published in Britain alone. Whereas many had begun by emphasizing heroism and glory, others were cynical and bitter by war's end. They insisted that the fighting had been absolutely meaningless. Total war had drained society of resources and population and had sown the seeds of further catastrophe.

> **REVIEW:** Why did people rebel during World War I, and what turned rebellion into outright revolution in Russia?

The Search for Peace in an Era of Revolution

World War I, like many other wars in the past, had unforeseen and dramatic consequences. Even before the war ended, revolutionary fervor swept the continent, especially in the former empires of Germany and Austria-Hungary. In Moscow, Lenin welcomed the emperors' downfall as part of a larger world revolution that would bring the triumph of working-class internationalism. Until 1921, socialist victory seemed plausible; many of the newly independent peoples of eastern and central Europe fervently supported socialist principles. The revolutionary mood captured workers and peasants in Germany too. In contrast, many liberal and right-wing opponents hoped for a political order based on military authority of the kind they had relied on during the war. Faced with uprisings by radicals from both right and left, diplomats from around the world arrived in Paris in January 1919 to negotiate the terms of peace, though without fully recognizing that the war was still going on not only in city streets, where soldiers were bringing the war home, but also in people's hearts.

Europe in Turmoil

Urban citizens and returning soldiers ignited the protests that swept Europe in 1918 and 1919. In January 1919, the red flag of socialist revolution flew from the city hall in Glasgow, Scotland, while in cities of the collapsing Austro-Hungarian monarchy, workers set up councils to take over factory production and direct politics. Many soldiers did not disband at the armistice but formed volunteer armies, preventing the return to peacetime politics. Germany was especially unstable, partly because of the shock of defeat. Independent socialist groups and workers' councils fought for control of the government, and workers and veterans took to the streets to demand food and back pay. Whereas the revolutionaries of 1848 had marched to city hall or the king's residence, these protesters took over newspapers and telegraph offices to control the flow of information. One of the most radical socialist factions was the Spartacists, led by cofounders Karl Liebknecht (1871–1919) and Rosa Luxemburg (1870–1919). Unlike Lenin, the two Spartacist leaders favored uprisings that would give workers political experience instead of simply following an all-knowing party leadership as in Russia.

German conservatives had believed that the war would put an end to Social Democratic influence. Instead it brought German socialists to power. Social Democratic leader Friedrich Ebert, who headed the new German government, backed the creation of a parliamentary republic to replace the kaiser's rule. He appeared to support the idea of settling political differences with violence by calling on the German army and the Freikorps — a roving paramilitary band of students, demobilized soldiers, and others — to suppress the workers' councils and demonstrators. "The enthusiasm is marvelous," wrote one young soldier. "No mercy's shown. We shoot even the wounded. . . . We were much more humane against the French in the field." Members of the Freikorps hunted down Luxemburg and Liebknecht, among others, and murdered them.

Violence continued even as an assembly meeting in the city of Weimar in February 1919 approved a constitution and founded a parliamentary republic called the **Weimar Republic**. This time the right rebelled, for the military leadership dreamed of a restored monarchy: "As I love Germany, so I hate the Republic," wrote one officer. To defeat a

---

Weimar Republic: The parliamentary republic established in 1919 in Germany to replace the monarchy.

military coup by Freikorps officers, Ebert called for a general strike. This action cut short a takeover of the new republic by showing the clear lack of popular support for a military regime. But in so doing, the Weimar Republic had set a dangerous precedent: it had relied on street violence, paramilitary groups, and protests rather than parliaments to solve political problems.

Revolutionary activism surged and was smashed in many parts of Europe. In the late winter of 1919, leftists proclaimed soviet republics—governments led by workers' councils—in Bavaria and Hungary. Volunteer armies and troops soon put the soviets down. The Bolsheviks tried to establish a Marxist regime in Poland in the belief that its people wanted a workers' revolution. Instead, the Poles resisted and drove the Red Army back in 1920, while the Allied powers rushed supplies and advisers to Warsaw. Though this and other revolts failed, they provided further proof that total war had let loose the forces of political chaos.

The Paris Peace Conference, 1919–1920

As political turmoil engulfed peoples from Berlin to Moscow, a peace conference opened in Paris in January 1919. Visions of communism spreading westward haunted it, but the assembled statesmen were focused on the reconstruction of a secure Europe and the status of Germany. Leaders such as French premier Georges Clemenceau had to satisfy their angry citizens' demands for revenge or, at the very least, money to rebuild. France had lost 1.3 million people—almost an entire generation of young men—and more than a million buildings, six thousand bridges, and thousands of miles of railroad lines and roads. Great Britain's representative, Prime Minister David Lloyd George, caught the mood of the British public by campaigning in 1918 with such slogans as "Hang the kaiser." Italians arrived on the scene demanding the territory promised to them in the 1915 Treaty of London. Meanwhile, U.S. president Woodrow Wilson (1856–1924), head of the new world power that had helped achieve the Allied victory, had his own agenda. His **Fourteen Points**, on which the truce had been based, were steeped in the language of freedom and called for open diplomacy, arms reduction, an "open-minded" settlement of colonial issues, and the self-determination of peoples.

The Fourteen Points did not represent the mood of all the victors (see "Contrasting Views," page 818). Allied propaganda had made the Germans seem like inhuman monsters, and many citizens demanded a harsh peace. Some military experts feared that Germany was using the armistice only to regroup for more warfare. Indeed, Germans widely refused to admit that their army had lost the war. Eager for army support, Ebert had given returning soldiers a rousing welcome: "As you return unconquered from the field of battle, I salute you." Wilson's former allies thus campaigned to make him look naive and unrealistic. "Wilson bores me with his Fourteen Points," Clemenceau complained. "Why, the good Lord himself has only ten."

Nevertheless, Wilson's Fourteen Points persuaded Germans that the settlement would not be vindictive. His commitment to *settlement* as opposed to *surrender* wisely recognized that Germany was still the strongest state on the continent. Wilson pushed for a treaty that balanced the strengths and interests of various European powers. Economists and other specialists accompanying Wilson to Paris agreed that, harshly dealt with and humiliated, Germany might soon become vengeful and chaotic—a combination that might be more lethal than the war just ended.

The Peace of Paris Treaties. After six months, the statesmen and their teams of experts produced the **Peace of Paris** (1919–1920), composed of a cluster of individual treaties. These treaties shocked the countries that had to accept them: the treaties separated Austria from Hungary, reduced Hungary by almost two-thirds of its inhabitants and three-quarters of its territory, broke up the Ottoman Empire, and treated Germany severely. They replaced the Habsburg Empire with a group of small, internally divided states: Czechoslovakia, Poland, and the Kingdom of the Serbs, Croats, and Slovenes, soon renamed Yugoslavia. After a century and a half of partition, Poland was reconstructed from parts of Russia, Germany, and Austria-Hungary, with one-third of its population ethnically non-Polish. The statesmen in Paris also created a Polish Corridor that connected Poland to the Baltic Sea and separated East Prussia from the rest of Germany (Map 25.4). Austria and Hungary were both left reeling at their drastic loss of territory and resources. In general, the new states were economically and politically weak.

Fourteen Points: U.S. president Woodrow Wilson's World War I peace proposal; based on settlement rather than on conquest, it encouraged the surrender of the Central Powers.

Peace of Paris: The series of peace treaties that provided the settlement of World War I.

MAP 25.4 Europe and the Middle East after the Peace Settlements of 1919–1920
The political landscape of central, east, and east-central Europe changed dramatically as a result of the Russian Revolution and the Peace of Paris. The Ottoman, German, Russian, and Austro-Hungarian empires were either broken up altogether into multiple small states or territorially reduced. The settlement left resentments among Germans and Hungarians and created a group of weak, struggling nations in the heartland of Europe. The victorious powers took over much of the oil-rich Middle East. ■ Why is it significant that the postwar geopolitical changes were so concentrated in one section of Europe?

The Treaty of Versailles with Germany was the centerpiece of the Peace of Paris. France recovered Alsace and Lorraine, and the victors would temporarily occupy the left, or western, bank of the Rhine and the coal-bearing Saar basin. Wilson accepted his allies' expectations that Germany would pay substantial reparations for civilian damage during the war. The specific amount was set in 1921 at the crushing sum of 132 billion gold marks. Germany also had to re-duce its army, almost eliminate its navy, stop manufacturing offensive weapons, and deliver a large amount of free coal each year to Belgium and France. Furthermore, it was forbidden to have an air force and had to give up its colonies. The average German saw in these terms an un-merited humiliation that was compounded by Article 231 of the treaty, which described Germany's "responsibility" for damage caused "by the aggression of Germany and her allies."

CONTRASTING VIEWS

Arguing with the Victors

The end of World War I aroused hopes around the world. The conquered expected a fair-minded treaty based on Wilson's Fourteen Points, while a variety of other peoples saw in that same document the promise of self-determination. In particular, men living under colonial domination, such as many in Africa and the Arab states, had taken part in the conflict because the Allies had promised new rights in return for fighting this bloody and destructive war. The emir Faisal had led troops to bring about freedom and Arab unity (Document 1). Like some representatives at the Pan-African Congress, even those Africans who had not fought saw peacemaking as a process that should forge a better future. Many wanted full political rights and parliamentary representation if not outright independence (Document 2).

In Paris in 1919, representatives of the victorious powers were besieged by outsiders to Western government, each making a claim for special attention to their needs or for concrete action to realize the noble rhetoric of the Fourteen Points. Feminist-pacifists wanted to ensure the pacifist cause (Document 3), while a Polish representative articulated a concern that Jews had taken too many good jobs in the new Poland (Document 4). The proposals to the peacemakers produced few results.

1. Claiming Independence for the Middle East

Arabs had hotly debated whether to join with the Allied colonizers in World War I, but promises of independence won them over. Some Arabs argued for independence of individual areas in the Middle East and for resolutions to competing claims of the Arabs and of new Jewish settlers in the region. Emir Faisal, who had commanded Arab forces in the war, presented the pan-Arab ideal.

The aim of the Arab nationalist movement is to unite the Arabs eventually into one nation.... I came to Europe on behalf of my father and the Arabs of Asia to say that they are expecting the powers at the Conference not to attach undue importance to superficial differences of condition among us and not to consider them only from the low ground of existing European material interests and supposed spheres of influence. They expect the powers to think of them as one potential people, jealous of their language and liberty, and they ask that no step be taken inconsistent with the prospect of an eventual union of these areas under one sovereign government.

Source: Stephen Bonsal, *Suitors and Suppliants: The Little Nations at Versailles* (Port Washington: Kennikat Press, 1969), 32–33.

2. The Voice of Pan-Africanists

African and African American leaders believed it would be opportune for them to meet in a Pan-African Congress while the Paris Peace Conference was going on. For some time an idea of a single African people had been forming among leading black intellectuals, and Pan-African meetings had taken place from the late nineteenth century on. The demands were legion, but above all the congress, by mid-February 1919, had resolved to seek better treatment from the colonial powers.

Resolved

That the Allied and Associated Powers establish a code of law for the international protection of the natives of Africa....

The Negroes of the world demand that hereafter the natives of Africa and the peoples of African descent be governed according to the following principles:

1. The land: the land and its natural resources shall be held in trust for the natives and at all times they shall have effective ownership of as much land as they can profitably develop....
3. Labor: slavery and corporal punishment shall be abolished and forced labor except in punishment for crime....
5. The state: the natives of Africa must have the right to participate in the government as fast as their development permits,

Outraged Germans interpreted this as a **war guilt clause**, which blamed Germany for the war and allowed the victors to collect reparations from economically developed Germany rather than from ruined Austria. War guilt made Germans feel like outcasts in the community of nations.

The League of Nations. Besides redrawing the map of Europe, the Peace of Paris set up an organization called the **League of Nations**, whose members had a joint responsibility for maintaining peace — a principle called collective security. It was supposed to replace the divisive secrecy of prewar power politics. As part of Wilson's vision, the league

---

war guilt clause: The part of the Treaty of Versailles that assigned blame for World War I to Germany.

League of Nations: The international organization set up following World War I to maintain peace by arbitrating disputes and promoting collective security.

in conformity with the principle that the government exists for the natives, and not the natives for the government.

source">**Source:** Quoted in W. E. B. Du Bois, *The World and Africa* (New York: International Publishers, 1946), 11–12.

3. Pacifists' Goals for the Peace Process

Pacifist women were angered that the peace conference would be held in Paris instead of in a noncombatant or neutral country. Situating it where wartime hatred was at a fevered pitch, they argued, would not allow the conquered to receive a fair hearing. The continuing blockade of the Central Powers after the armistice was increasing suffering and causing deaths. Themselves meeting in neutral Switzerland, pacifist women speeded the dispatch of their resolutions to Paris when the Treaty of Versailles was announced.

The International Congress of Women regards the famine, pestilence, and unemployment extending throughout great tracts of central and eastern Europe and into Asia as a disgrace to civilization.

It therefore urges the Governments of all the Powers assembled at the Peace Conference immediately to develop the inter-allied organizations formed for purposes of war into an international organization for purposes of peace, so that the resources of the world — food, raw materials, finance, transport — shall be made available for the relief of the peoples of all countries from famine and pestilence.

To this end it urges that immediate action be taken . . . to raise the blockade.

The terms of the peace tacitly sanction secret diplomacy, deny the principles of self-determination, recognize the rights of victors to the spoils of war, and create all over Europe discords and animosities, which can only lead to future war. . . . By the financial and economic proposals a hundred million people of this generation in the heart of Europe are condemned to poverty, disease, and despair, which must result in the spread of hatred and anarchy within each nation.

Source: James Weber Linn, *Jane Addams: A Biography* (New York: Greenwood, 1968), 342–43.

4. Anti-Semitism at the Peace Table

Some of the new nations of eastern Europe were using anti-Semitism to focus their unity and independence. A Polish leader lobbied the Allies to exercise a police power in the newly independent Poland, where a major problem after the war came to be rural crowding. Nonetheless, Poles had the idea that Jews controlled the professions and commercial wealth and needed to be knocked down a peg or two.

We have too many Jews, and those who will be allowed to remain with us must change their habits. I recognize that this will be difficult and will take time. The Jew must produce and not remain devoted exclusively to what we regard as parasitical pursuits. Unless restrictions are imposed upon them soon, all our lawyers, doctors, and small merchants will be Jews. They must turn to agriculture, and they must at least share small business and retail stores with their Polish neighbors. I readily admit that there is some basis in the Jewish contention that in days past it was difficult for them to own land or even to work the fields of others as tenants; that they were often compelled by circumstances beyond their control to gain their livelihood in ways which are hurtful to Polish economy. Under our new constitution all this will be changed, and for their own good I hope the Jews will avail themselves of their new opportunities. I say this in their own interest as well as in the interest of restored Poland.

Source: Bonsal, *Suitors and Suppliants*, 124.

QUESTIONS TO CONSIDER
1. Describe the various contending claims beyond those of the official combatant powers. Did the victorious powers heed these voices when forging the peace?
2. How were the various demands at the peace conference related to the politics and conditions of World War I?
3. Do any of the demands seem more justifiable in addressing the peacetime needs of Europe and the world?

---

would guide the world toward disarmament and arbitrate its members' disputes. The U.S. Senate, in a humiliating defeat for the president, failed to ratify the peace settlement and refused to join the league. Both Germany and Russia initially were excluded from the league and were thus discouraged from cooperating with other nations. The absence of these three important powers weakened the league as a global peacekeeper from the outset.

The League of Nations also organized the administration of the colonies and territories of Ger-

many and the Ottoman Empire through a system of mandates. The victorious powers exercised political control over mandated territory, but local leaders retained limited authority. The league covenant justified the **mandate system** as providing governance by "advanced nations" over territories "not yet able to stand by themselves under the

---

mandate system: The political control over the former colonies and territories of the German and Ottoman empires granted to the victors of World War I by the League of Nations.

strenuous conditions of the modern world." However, colonized people, who had served and fallen on the battlefield, began to challenge the claims of their European masters. They had seen how savage were these people who claimed to be racially superior and politically advanced. "Never again will the darker people of the world occupy just the place they had before," the African American leader W. E. B. Du Bois predicted in 1918. The mandate system continued the practice of apportioning the globe among European powers at a time when those powers were bankrupt and weak. Like the Peace of Paris, it aroused anger and resistance.

Economic and Diplomatic Consequences of the Peace

Just as wartime conditions—including outright military action—continued long after the armistice, so the Peace of Paris generated problems into the 1920s and beyond. Western leaders faced two intertwined issues in the aftermath of the war. The first was economic recovery and its relationship to war debts and German reparation payments. The second was ensuring that peace actually came about and lasted.

Economic Dilemmas. France, hardest hit by wartime destruction and billions of dollars in debt

to the United States, estimated that Germany owed it at least $200 billion. Britain, by contrast, had not been physically devastated; its concern was restoring trade with Germany, not exacting huge reparations. Nevertheless, both France and Britain depended on some monetary reparations to pay their war debts to the United States because Europe's income from world trade had plunged during the war. Germany claimed that the demand for reparations strained its government, already beset by political upheaval. But Germany's economic problems had begun when the kaiser refused to raise taxes, especially on the rich, to pay for the war, thus leaving the new republic with a staggering war debt. As an experiment in democracy, the Weimar Republic needed to woo the citizenry, not alienate it by hiking taxes. In 1921, when Germans refused to present a realistic plan for paying reparations, the French occupied several cities in the Ruhr until a settlement was reached.

Embroiled with powers to the west, the German government mended its economic and diplomatic fences in eastern Europe. It reached an agreement to foster economic ties with Russia, which was desperate for Western trade, in the Treaty of Rapallo (1922). Germany's relations with powers to the west, however, continued to deteriorate. In 1923, after Germany defaulted on coal deliveries, the French and the Belgians sent troops into the

Inflation in Germany (1923)
The German government resisted paying reparations by slowing down the shipments of manufactured goods that were a condition of the reparations program. French troops were sent into the Ruhr manufacturing region to take goods by force, but angry workers refused to work for the occupiers. To pay the workers and service its debt, the government printed money so rapidly that inflation brought the value of the German mark from 4.2 marks to the dollar to 4.2 trillion marks to the dollar, which destroyed savings and increased resentment in Germany. As children played with worthless marks, shown in this picture, a new administration came to power in the summer and resolved the issue. *(akg-images.)*

■ **For more help in analyzing this image,** see the visual activity for this chapter in the Online Study Guide at **bedfordstmartins.com/hunt**.

Ruhr basin, planning to seize its resources to pay for wartime expenditures. Urged on by the government, Ruhr citizens shut down industry by staying home from work. The German government printed trillions of marks to support the workers and to pay its own war debts with practically worthless currency. Soon Germany was in the midst of a staggering inflation that gravely threatened the international economy: at one point, a single U.S. dollar cost 4.42 trillion marks, and wheelbarrows of money were required to buy a turnip. Negotiations to resolve this economic chaos resulted in the Dawes Plan (1924) and the Young Plan (1929), which reduced reparations to more realistic levels and restored the value of German currency. Nonetheless, the inflation had wiped out people's savings and ruined those living on fixed incomes. The experience of losing everything continued the Germans' wartime trauma and turned many more people against democratic government.

Ensuring Peace.   In addition to economic recovery, a second pressing issue involved ensuring that peace would take hold and last. Statesmen recognized that peace demanded disarmament, a return of Germany to the fold, and security for the new countries of eastern Europe. Diplomatic negotiations produced two plans in Germany's favor. At the Washington Conference in 1921, the United States, Great Britain, Japan, France, and Italy agreed to reduce their number of battleships and to stop constructing new ones for ten years. Four years later, in 1925, the League of Nations sponsored a meeting of the great powers, including Germany, at Locarno, Switzerland. The Treaty of Locarno provided Germany with a seat in the league as of 1926. In return, Germany agreed not to violate the borders of France and Belgium and to keep the nearby Rhineland demilitarized — that is, unfortified by troops.

To the east, statesmen feared a German attempt to regain territory lost to Poland, to form a merger with Austria, or to attack the states spun off from Austria-Hungary. To meet the threat, Czechoslovakia, Yugoslavia, and Romania formed the Little Entente in 1920–1921, a collective security agreement intended to protect them from Germany and Russia. Between 1924 and 1927, France allied itself with the Little Entente and with Poland. Sixty nations, including

The Little Entente

the major European powers, Japan, and the United States, also signed the Kellogg-Briand Pact (1928), which formally rejected international violence. Lacking any measures to enforce its provisions, however, this idealistic agreement was powerless to prevent the outbreak of war.

The public international agreements of the 1920s sharply contrasted with old-style diplomacy, which had been conducted in secret and subject to little public scrutiny. The development of a system of open, collective security suggested a diplomatic revolution that would promote peace in international relations. Yet openness allowed diplomats of the era to feed the press information calculated to arouse the masses. For example, the press and opposition parties whipped the German populace into a nationalist frenzy whenever Germany's diplomats, who were successfully working to reduce reparation payments, seemed to compromise. Although international meetings such as the one at Locarno aimed to promote peace, they also exposed the diplomatic process to rabble-rousers who wanted to inflame political passions rather than contribute to rational public discussion.

REVIEW: What were the major outcomes of the postwar peacemaking process?

The Aftermath of War: Europe in the 1920s

The armistice brought an end to the war's fighting, and treaties established the terms of peace, but the wartime spirit endured. Words and phrases from the battlefield punctuated everyday speech. Before the war the word *lousy* had meant "lice-infested," but English-speaking soldiers returning from the trenches now applied it to anything bad. Raincoats became *trenchcoats*, and terms like *bombarded* and *rank and file* entered peacetime usage. Maimed, disfigured veterans were present everywhere, and while some gained prostheses designed by Jules Amar, others without limbs were sometimes carried in baskets — hence the expression *basket case*.

Total war had generally strengthened the military spirit and authoritarian government.

WOMEN GAIN SUFFRAGE IN THE WEST

1906	Finland
1913	Norway
1915	Denmark, Iceland
1917	Netherlands, Russia
1918	Czechoslovakia, Great Britain (limited suffrage)
1919	Germany
1920	Austria, United States
1921	Poland
1925	Hungary (limited suffrage)
1945	Italy, France
1971	Switzerland

Although four autocratic governments had collapsed as a result of the war, whether they would become workable democracies remained a burning question. During the war, the European economy lost many of its international markets to India, Canada, Australia, Japan, and the United States. Now worldwide economic competition with these new players also threatened European recovery. Returning veterans crowded hospitals and mental institutions, and family life centered on their care. Although contemporaries referred to the 1920s as the Roaring Twenties or the Jazz Age, the sense of cultural release masked the serious problem of restoring stability. The real challenge of the 1920s was coming to terms with the political, economic, and social legacy of the war.

Changes in the Political Landscape

Some Europeans saw the collapse of autocratic governments and the extension of suffrage to women, widely granted at the war's end, as opportunities for a rebirth of democracy. Woman suffrage resulted in part from decades of activism, but many governments claimed that suffrage was a "reward" for women's war efforts. In the first postwar elections, women in some countries were voted into parliaments, and the impression grew that

they had also made extraordinary gains in the workplace. French men pointedly denied women the vote, however, threatening that women voters would bring back the rule of kings and priests. (Only at the end of World War II would France and Italy extend suffrage to women.) Governments continued building the welfare state by expanding payments to veterans, families with children, and workers who were unemployed or injured. New government benefits demonstrated a belief that more evenly distributed wealth—sometimes referred to as economic democracy—was important to social stability in a climate where revolution threatened.

The slow trend toward economic democracy was not easy to maintain, however, because the cycles of boom and bust that had characterized the late nineteenth century reemerged. A short postwar economic boom prompted by reconstruction and consumer spending was followed by an economic downturn that was most severe between 1920 and 1922. By the mid-1920s, many of the economic opportunities for women had disappeared and women made up a smaller percentage of the workforce than in 1913. Skyrocketing unemployment produced more discontent with governments.

Eastern Europe. The new republics of eastern Europe were unprepared for the hard economic times and ill equipped to compete in the world market. None but Czechoslovakia had a mature industrial sector, and agricultural techniques were often primitive. But more pressing problems hampered them: vast migrations occurred as some one million people escaped the civil war in Russia; as 800,000 soldiers from the defeated Whites searched for safety; and as two million more fled Turkey, Greece, and Bulgaria because the postwar settlement called for the new nations to be built along ethnic lines—"a great unmixing of populations" one statesman called the settlement. Hundreds of thousands thus landed in new nations with a population most closely representing their own ethnic group: Hungary, for example, had to receive 300,000 people of Magyar ethnicity who were no longer welcome in Romania, Czechoslovakia, or Yugoslavia. Most refugees lacked land or jobs. They had nothing to do "but loaf

▨ Polish	▨ German
▨ Czech	▨ Latvian
▨ Slovak	▨ Lithuanian
☐ Belorussian	▨ Magyar (Hungarian)
▨ Ukrainian	▨ Romanian

National Minorities in Postwar Poland

and starve," an English reporter observed of refugees in Bulgaria. The influx of people brought more conflict in various parts of eastern Europe. Romania, Czechoslovakia, and the Kingdom of the Serbs, Croats, and Slovenes invaded Hungary, for instance, to gain more land.

Poland provides an example of how postwar chaos destroyed the new nation's parliamentary democracy. One-third of the reunified Poland consisted of Ukrainians, Belorussians, Germans, and other ethnic minorities—many of whom had grievances against the dominant Poles. There were also varying religious, dynastic, and cultural traditions dividing the new nation, which for 150 years had been split among Austria, Germany, and Russia. Polish independence and reunification occurred without a common currency, political structure, or language—even the railroad tracks were not a standard size.

The Polish constitution professed equal rights for all ethnicities and religions, and the Sejm (parliament) tried to legislate the redistribution of large estates to the peasantry. However, declining crop prices and overpopulation (two-thirds of the population lived by subsistence farming) made life in the countryside difficult. Urban workers were better off than the peasantry but worse off than laborers across Europe. The economic downturn brought strikes and violence in 1922–1923, and the inability of the government to bring about economic prosperity led to a coup in 1926 by strongman and former military leader Jozef Pilsudski. In postwar east-central Europe, military solutions to economic hardship became common, demonstrating the influence of war long after the peace had officially begun.

Central Europe. Germany was a different case, though it too felt the flood of refugees from the east. Although the German economy picked up and Germany became a center of experimentation in the arts, political life remained unstable because so many people felt nostalgia for imperial glory and associated defeat with the new Weimar Republic. Extremist politicians heaped daily abuse on Weimar's parliamentary political system. A wealthy newspaper and film magnate deemed anyone who cooperated with the parliamentary system "a moral cripple." Right-wing parties favored violence rather than consensus building, and nationalist thugs murdered democratic leaders and Jews.

Support for the far right came from wealthy landowners and businessmen, white-collar workers whose standard of living had dropped during the war, and members of the lower-middle and middle classes hurt by inflation. Bands of disaffected youth and veterans multiplied, among them a group called the Brown Shirts, led by ex-soldier and political newcomer Adolf Hitler (1889–1945). A riveting speaker, Hitler gradually became a favorite of antigovernment political groups that collected donations from the enthusiastic crowds he drew. In the wake of the Ruhr occupation of 1923, Hitler and German military hero Erich Ludendorff launched a coup d'état—or *putsch* in German—from a beer hall in Munich. Government troops suppressed the Beer Hall Putsch and arrested its leaders, but Ludendorff was acquitted and Hitler spent less than a year in jail. For conservative judges, former aristocrats, and most of the prewar bureaucrats who still staffed government offices, such men were national heroes.

Western Europe. In France and Britain, where parliamentary institutions were better established and the upper classes were not plotting to restore an authoritarian monarchy, parties of the right had less effect. In France, politicians from the conservative right and moderate left successively formed coalitions and rallied general support to rebuild war-torn regions and to force Germany to pay for the reconstruction. Hoping to stimulate population growth after the devastating loss of life, members of the French parliament made the distribution of birth-control information illegal and abortion a severely punished crime.

Britain encountered postwar boom and bust, and strife continued in Ireland. Ramsay MacDonald (1866–1937), elected the first Labour prime minister in 1924, represented the political strength of workers. Like other postwar British leaders, he had to face the unpleasant truth that although Britain had the largest world empire, many of its industries were obsolete or in poor condition. A showdown came in the ailing coal industry, where prices fell and wages plunged once the Ruhr mines again offered tough postwar competition to British mines. On May 3, 1926, workers launched a nine-day general strike against wage cuts and dangerous conditions in the mines. The strike provoked unprecedented middle-class resistance. University students, homemakers, and businessmen shut down the strike by driving trains, working on docks, and replacing workers in other jobs. Thus, citizens from many walks of life revived the wartime spirit to defeat those who appeared to attack the weakening national economy.

In Ireland, the continuing failure to implement home rule provoked bloody confrontations. In January 1919, republican leaders announced

The Irish Free State and Ulster, 1921

Ireland's independence from Britain and created a separate parliament. The British government refused to recognize the parliament and sent in the Black and Tans, a volunteer army of demobilized soldiers named after the color of their uniforms. Terror reigned in Ireland, as both the pro-independence forces and the Black and Tans waged guerrilla warfare, taking hostages, blowing up buildings, and even shooting into crowds at soccer matches. By 1921, public outrage forced the British to negotiate a treaty. It reversed the Irish declaration of independence and made the Irish Free State a self-governing dominion owing allegiance to the British crown. Northern Ireland, a group of six northern counties containing a majority of Protestants, gained a separate status: it was self-governing but still had representation in the British Parliament. This settlement left bitter discontent, especially over the rights of religious minorities; violence soon erupted again.

The Colonies. War changed everything in the colonies too. Colonized peoples who had fought in the war expected more rights and even independence. Indeed, European politicians and military recruiters had actually promised the vote and many other reforms in exchange for support. But colonists' political activism, now enhanced by increasing education, trade, and experience with the West, mostly met a brutal response. Fearful of losing India, British forces massacred protesters at Amritsar in 1919 and put down revolts against the mandate system in Egypt and Iran in the early 1920s. The Dutch jailed political leaders in Indonesia; the French punished Indochinese nationalists. For many Western governments, maintaining empires abroad was crucial to ensuring democracy at home, as agitators railed at any hint of declining national prestige.

Despite resistance, the 1920s marked the high tide of imperialism. Britain and France, enjoying new access to Germany's colonies in Africa and to territories of the fallen Ottoman Empire in the Middle East, were at the height of their global power. No matter how battered by the war, all the imperial powers took advantage of the growing profitability that enterprises around the world could bring. Middle Eastern and Indonesian oil,

for instance, heated homes and fueled the growing number of automobiles, airplanes, trucks, ships, and buses. Products like chocolate and tropical fruit became regular items in the diet, and by extracting them from the colonies, some Westerners built fortunes.

The balance of power among the imperial nations was shifting, however. The most important change was Japan's surging competition for markets, resources, and influence. During the war, Japanese output of industrial goods such as metal and ships grew dramatically because the Western powers outsourced their wartime needs for such products. As Japan took business from Britain and France, its prosperity skyrocketed, allowing the country to edge out Britain as the dominant power in China. The Japanese government touted its success as a sign of hope for non-Westerners. Japan's prosperity, the country's politicians claimed, would end oppression by the West. Ardently nationalist, the Japanese government was not yet strong enough to challenge the Western powers militarily. Thus, although outraged that the Western powers at Paris had refused a nondiscrimination clause in the charter of the League of Nations, Japan cooperated in the Anglo-American–dominated peace. It agreed to the settlement at the naval conference in Washington that set the ratio of English, American, and Japanese shipbuilding at 5:5:3. "Rolls Royce, Rolls Royce, Ford," a Japanese official commented bitterly.

Reconstructing the Economy

The war had so weakened the traditional European powers that newcomers and rivals — Japan, India, the United States, Australia, and Canada — flourished in their place. At the same time, the war had forced many European manufacturers to become more efficient and had expanded the demand for automotive and air transport, electrical products, and synthetic goods. The prewar pattern of mergers and cartels continued after 1918, giving rise to gigantic food-processing firms such as Nestlé in Switzerland and petroleum enterprises such as Royal Dutch Shell. Owners of these large manufacturing conglomerates wielded more financial and political power than entire small countries. By the late 1920s, Europe had overcome the wild economic swings of the immediate postwar years and was enjoying renewed economic prosperity.

European businesspeople acknowledged that the United States had become the trendsetter in economic modernization, and they made pilgrimages to the Ford Motor Company's Detroit assembly line, which by 1929 produced a Ford automobile every ten seconds. Increased productivity, founder Henry Ford pointed out, resulted in a lower cost of living and thus increased workers' purchasing power. American workers could afford such expensive goods as cars: whereas French, German, and British citizens in total had fewer than two million cars, some seventeen million cars were on U.S. streets in 1925.

Scientific management also aimed to raise productivity. American efficiency expert Frederick Taylor (1856–1915) developed methods to streamline workers' tasks and motions for maximum productivity. European industrialists adopted Taylor's methods during the war and after, but they were also influenced by European psychologists who emphasized the mental aspects of productivity and the need to balance of work and leisure activities, for both workers and managers. In theory, increased productivity not only produced prosperity for all but also aimed to bind workers and management together, avoiding Russian-style worker revolution. Streamlining helped reduce working hours in many industries, causing union leaders to embrace modernization and the "cult of efficiency." For many workers, however, the emphasis on efficiency seemed inhuman, with restrictions so severe that often they were allowed to use the bathroom only on a fixed schedule. "When I left the factory, it followed me," wrote one worker. "In my dreams I was a machine."

The managerial sector in industry had expanded during the war and continued to do so thereafter. Workers' initiative became devalued, with managers alone seen as creative and innovative. Managers reorganized work procedures and classified workers' skills. They categorized "female" jobs as those requiring less skill and therefore deserving of lower wages, thus adapting the old segmentation of the labor market to the new working conditions. With male workers' jobs increasingly threatened by labor-saving machinery, unions usually agreed that women should receive lower wages to keep them from competing with men for scarce high-paying jobs. Like the managerial sector, a complex union bureaucracy had ballooned during World War I to help monitor labor's part in the war. Playing a key role in everyday political life, unions could mobilize masses of people for displays of worker power such as stopping the coups against the Weimar government in the 1920s and organizing the 1926 general strike in Great Britain.

Restoring Society

Postwar society met the returning millions of brutalized, incapacitated, and shell-shocked veterans with combined joy and apprehension. Civilian anxieties were often valid. Tens of thousands of German, central European, and Italian soldiers refused to disband; a few British veterans even vandalized university classrooms and assaulted women streetcar conductors and factory workers. For their part, many veterans were angry that civilians had rebelled against wartime conditions instead of patriotically enduring them. The world to which the veterans returned differed from the home they had left: the war had blurred class distinctions, giving rise to expectations that life would be fairer afterward. The massive casualties had fostered social mobility by allowing commoners to move up to the ranks of officers, positions often monopolized by the prewar aristocracy. His son killed on the battlefield, author Rudyard Kipling was among those who influenced the decision that all memorials to individual soldiers would be the same for rich and poor, just as the experience of the trenches had been. Wealth, he maintained, should not allow some to "proclaim their grief above other people's grief" when rich and poor had died for the same cause. The identical, evenly spaced crosses of military cemeteries kept all the dead equal, as did the mass "brothers' graves" at the battlefront where all ranks lay side by side in a single burial pit.

In contrast to expectations, veterans often had few or no jobs open to them; and some soldiers found that their wives and sweethearts had abandoned them—a wrenching betrayal for most of them. Veterans faced other changes as well: middle-class women did their own housework because former servants could earn more money in factories; middle-class daughters began to work outside the home, too. Women of all classes cut their hair short, wore sleeker clothes, smoked, and had money of their own. In the United States, this postwar version of the "new woman" was called the flapper. Patriotic when the war erupted, civilians, especially women, sometimes felt estranged from these returning warriors who had inflicted so much death and who had lived daily with filth, rats, and decaying human flesh. Women who had served on the front could empathize with the soldiers' woes. But many suffragists in England, for instance, who had fought for an end to separate spheres before the war, now embraced gender segregation, so fearful were they of returning veterans.

New Housing in Vienna
Politicians saw to the building of "homes for heroes" across postwar Europe, and Vienna was one leader in constructing modern housing for the working class. With many veterans enraged by the war experience and with socialist revolution a looming threat, new housing, it was hoped, would help return men to peaceful civilian life. *(© Bettmann/Corbis.)*

Governments tried to make civilian life as comfortable as possible to reintegrate men into society and reduce the appeal of communism. Politicians believed in the stabilizing power of traditional family values and supported social programs such as pensions, unemployment benefits, and housing for veterans. The new housing—"homes for heroes," as politicians called the program—was a considerable improvement over nineteenth-century working-class tenements. In Vienna, Frankfurt, Berlin, and Stockholm, modern housing projects provided collective laundries, day-care centers, and rooms for group socializing; they featured gardens, terraces, and balconies to provide a soothing, country ambience that offset the hectic nature of industrial life. Inside, they boasted modern kitchens, indoor plumbing, central heating, and electricity.

Despite government efforts to restore traditional family values, war had dissolved many middle-class conventions, among them attempts to keep unmarried young men and women apart. Freer relationships and more open discussions of sex characterized the 1920s. Middle-class youth of both sexes visited jazz clubs and attended movies together. Revealing bathing suits, short skirts, and body-hugging clothing emphasized women's sexuality, seeming to invite men and women to join together and replenish the postwar population. The context for sexuality, however, remained marriage. British scientist Marie Stopes published the best seller *Married Love* in 1918, and the wildly successful *Ideal Marriage: Its Physiology and Technique* by Dutch author Theodor van de Velde appeared in 1927. Both described sex in glowing terms and offered precise information about birth control and sexual physiology. Changing ideas about sex were not limited to the middle and upper classes; one Viennese reformer described working-class marriage as "an erotic-comradely relationship of equals" rather than the economic partnership of past centuries. Meanwhile, such writers as the Briton D. H. Lawrence and the American Ernest Hemingway glorified men's sexual vigor in, respectively, *Women in Love* (1920) and *The Sun Also Rises* (1926). Mass culture's focus on heterosexuality encouraged the return to normality after the gender disorder that had troubled the prewar and war years.

As images of men and women changed, people paid more attention to bodily improvement. The increasing use of toothbrushes and toothpaste,

The Flapper
This modern workingwoman smoking her cigarette stood for all that had changed—or was said to have changed—in the postwar world. Women had worked and had money of their own, they were out in public and could vote in many countries, and they were liberated from old constraints on their sexual and other behavior. *(Getty Images.)*

safety and electric razors, and deodorants reflected new standards for personal hygiene and grooming. For Western women, a multibillion-dollar cosmetics industry sprang up almost overnight. Women went to beauty parlors regularly to have their short hair cut, set, dyed, conditioned, straightened, or curled. They also tweezed their eyebrows, applied makeup, and even submitted to cosmetic surgery. Ordinary women painted their faces as formerly only prostitutes had done and competed in beauty contests that judged physical appearance. Instead of wanting to look plump and prosperous, people aimed to become thin and tan, often through exercise and playing sports. Consumers' new focus on personal health coincided with industry's need for a physically fit workforce.

As prosperity returned in the mid-1920s, people could afford to buy more consumer goods. Middle- and upper-class families snapped up sleek modern furniture, washing machines, and vacuum cleaners. Other modern conveniences such as electric irons and gas stoves appeared in better-off working-class households. Installment buying, popularized from the 1920s on, helped people finance these purchases. Housework became more mechanized, and family intimacy increasingly depended on machines of mass communication like radios, phonographs, and even automobiles. These new products not only transformed private life but

also brought changes in the public world of mass culture and mass politics.

> **REVIEW:** What were the major political, economic, and social problems facing postwar Europe, and how did governments attempt to address them?

Mass Culture and the Rise of Modern Dictators

Wartime propaganda had aimed to unite all classes against a common enemy. In the 1920s, new technology made the process of integrating diverse groups into a single Western or mass culture easier and more thorough. The instruments of mass culture—primarily radio, film, and newspapers—expanded their influence in the 1920s. Whereas some intellectuals urged elites to form an experimental avant-garde that refused to cater to "the drab mass of society," others wanted to use modern media and art to reach and even control the masses. The media had the potential for creating an informed citizenry and thus strengthening democracy. At the same time, it had the potential for allowing dictators to use it as a tool to keep war and revolution foremost in people's minds. Benito

Mussolini, Joseph Stalin, and ultimately Adolf Hitler used mass media to control citizens far beyond the hopes of wartime military leaders.

Culture for the Masses

The media had received a big boost from the war. Bulletins from the battlefront had whetted the public's craving for news and real-life stories, and sales of nonfiction books soared. After years of deprivation, people were driven to achieve material success, and they devoured books that advised how to gain it. A biography of Henry Ford, telling his story of upward mobility and technological accomplishment, became a best seller in Germany. With postwar readers avidly pursuing practical knowledge, institutes and night schools became popular, and school systems promoted the study of geography, science, and history. Phonographs, radio programs, and movies also widened the scope of national culture.

The war years, when the U.S. film industry began to outstrip the European, gave rise to specialization: directors, producers, marketers, film editors, and many others subdivided the process. Then, during the 1920s, film evolved from an experimental medium to a thriving international business in which large corporations set up theater chains and marketed movies worldwide. A "star" system, promoted by professional publicity, turned film personalities into celebrities. Films of literary classics and political events developed people's sense of a common heritage and were often sponsored by governments. Bolshevik leaders actively supported filmmaking. In particular, two films by innovative director Sergei Eisenstein, *Potemkin* (1925) and *Ten Days That Shook the World* (1927–1928), presented a Bolshevik view of history to Russian and international audiences.

Films incorporated familiar elements from everyday life. The piano accompaniment of silent films derived from music halls; comic characters, farcical plots, and slapstick humor were borrowed from street or burlesque shows and from trends in postwar living. The popular comedies of the 1920s made the flapper more visible to the masses and satirized men and women inept at marriage and emotional intimacy. Lavish cinema houses attracted some hundred million weekly viewers, the majority of them women. As popular films and books crossed national borders, a global culture for an international audience flourished.

Films also played to postwar fantasies and fears. In Germany, where filmmakers used expressionist sets and costumes to make films frightening, the in-fluential hit *The Cabinet of Doctor Caligari* (1919) depicted events in an insane asylum as horrifying symbols of state power. Popular detective and cowboy films portrayed heroes who could restore wholeness to the disordered world of murder, crime, and injustice. The plight of gangsters appealed to war veterans, who had been exposed to the cheap value of life in the modern world. English comedian, actor, and producer Charlie Chaplin (1889–1977) created the character of the Little Tramp, who won international popularity as the down-and-out hero, the anonymous soldier who struggled to keep his dignity in a postwar society. All of these films played in theaters internationally, reflecting the restoration of global culture. Many featured a global cast of characters and were often set in North Africa or the Middle East, whose deserts became a common backdrop. Sporting events like cricket and boxing became internationalized in the 1920s and 1930s, and clips from these matches were shown worldwide in newsreels before feature films.

Like film, radio evolved from an experimental medium to an instrument of mass culture during the 1920s. Developed from the wireless technology of Italian inventor Guglielmo Marconi, which had been introduced at the turn of the century, radio broadcasts in the first half of the 1920s were heard by mass audiences in public halls (much like movie houses) and featured orchestra performances and songs followed by audience discussion. The radio quickly became a relatively inexpensive consumer item, allowing the public concert or lecture to penetrate the individual's private living space. Specialized programming for men (such as sports reporting) and for women (such as advice on home management) soon followed. By the 1930s, radio was available for politicians to reach the masses wherever they might be — even alone at home (see "Taking Measure," page 829).

Cultural Debates over the Future

Cultural leaders in the 1920s either were haunted by the horrendous experience of war or held high hopes for creating a fresh, utopian future that would have little relation to the past. German artists, especially, produced bleak or violent visions. The sculpture and woodcuts of German artist Käthe Kollwitz (1867–1945), whose son died in the war, portrayed bereaved parents, starving children, and other heart-wrenching antiwar images (see page 798). Others thought that Europeans needed to search for answers in far-off cultures. Seeing Europe as decadent, some turned

TAKING MEASURE

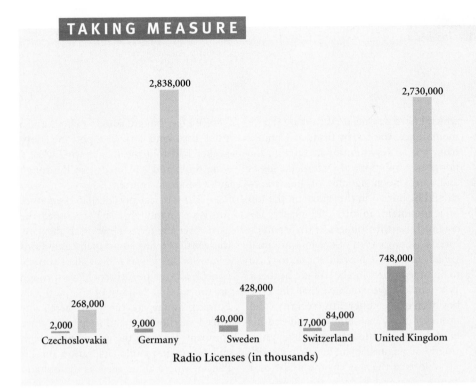

2,838,000

2,730,000

748,000

268,000

428,000

2,000
Czechoslovakia

9,000
Germany

40,000
Sweden

17,000 84,000
Switzerland

United Kingdom

Radio Licenses (in thousands)

The Growth of Radio, 1924–1929
The spread of radio technology, like the earlier development of printing, advanced the cultural and political unity of citizens in a nation-state. The most industrially and commercially developed societies witnessed the most rapid diffusion of radios, which were both programmed and taxed by governments. Because of this centralized control, historians can compare the country-by-country use of radio in Europe and in much of the rest of the world. Of the five countries represented here, which experienced the most rapid spread of radio technology? Can you suggest reasons for their lead in accepting radio?

■ 1924   □ 1929

to the spiritual richness of Asian philosophies and religions, fixing on the pacifist leader for Indian independence Mohandas Gandhi. An "Asiatic fever" seemed to grip intellectuals, including the writer Virginia Woolf, who drew on ideas of reincarnation in her novel *Orlando* (1928), and the filmmaker Sergei Eisenstein, who modeled the new techniques of juxtaposing shots (montage) on Japanese ideograms.

Other artists employed satire, irony, and flippancy to express postwar rage and revulsion at civilization's apparent failure. George Grosz (1893–1959), stunned by the war's carnage, joined Dada, an artistic and literary movement that had

George Grosz, "Twilight" from the Series *Ecce Homo*, 1922
George Grosz's series of postwar art was named after a book by Friedrich Nietzsche, *Ecce Homo* (*Behold the Man*). The "man" to behold was the veteran, opportunistically called a "hero" by postwar politicians to get their votes but in fact living a grim reality, as Grosz saw it. Surrounded by prosperous businessmen, fashionable women, and strutting military officers, the veteran was pushed to the background, gray and lonely amid the colorful peacetime society. *(Bildarchiv Preussischer Kulturbesitz/Art Resource, NY/© Estate of George Grosz/Licensed by VAGA, New York, NY.)*

Battlefield Tourism

World War I left deep wounds in the sur-vivors, including the families of those who had died. Like the English writer Vera Brittain, many relatives roamed the battlefields of Europe, in hopes of understanding what had happened to their loved ones—and to Western civilization as a whole. During the war, Brittain had served as a nurse while suffering the loss of her brother, fiancé, and friends. There was no organized tour of Italian battlefields in 1921 as there was of those in northwestern Europe, so Brittain went on her own to find her brother's grave high up in the remote mountains. She later recounted this visit in a memoir of her early life.

"How strange, how strange it is," I reflected, as I looked, with an indefinable pain stabbing my chest, for Edward's name among those neat rows of oblong stones, "that all my past years—the childhood of which I have no one, now, to share the remembrance, the bright fields at Uppingham, the restless months in Buxton, the hopes and ambitions of Oxford, the losses and long-drawn agonies of the War—should be buried in this grave on the top of a mountain, in the lofty silence, the singing unearthly stillness, of these remote forests! At every turn of every future road I shall want to ask him questions, to recall to him memories, and he will not be there. Who could have dreamed that the little boy born in such uneventful security to an ordinary provincial family would end his brief days in a battle among the high pine-woods of an unknown Italian plateau?"

Close to the wall, in the midst of a group of privates from the Sherwood Foresters who had all died on June 15th, I found his name: "Captain E. H. Brittain, M.C., 11th Notts. And Derby Regt. Killed in action June 15th, 1918. Aged 22." In Venice I had bought some rosebuds and a small asparagus fern in a pot; the shop-keeper had told me that it would last a long time, and I planted it in the rough grass beside the grave.

"How trivial my life has been since the War!" I thought, as I smoothed the earth over the fern. "How mean they are, these little strivings, these petty ambitions of us who are left, now that all of you are gone! How can the future achieve, through us, the sombre majesty of the past? Oh, Edward, you're so lonely up here; why can't I stay for ever and keep your grave company, far from the world and its vain endeavours to rebuild civilisation, on this Plateau where alone there is dignity and peace?"

Source: Vera Brittain, *Testament of Youth* (London: Virago, 1978 [1933]), 525–27.

---

emerged during the war. With a meaningless name, Dada produced works marked by nonsense and shrieks of alienation. Grosz's paintings and cartoons of maimed soldiers and brutally murdered women reflected his wartime trauma and his self-proclaimed desire "to bellow back." In the postwar years, the modernist tradition of shocking audiences became more savage and often more contemptuous of ordinary people. Portrayals of seedy everyday life flourished in cabarets and theaters in the 1920s and reinforced veterans' beliefs in civilian decadence.

The art world itself became a battlefield, especially in defeated Germany, where it paralleled the Weimar Republic's contentious politics. Popular writers such as Ernst Jünger glorified life in the trenches and called for the militarization of society to restore order. In contrast, Erich Maria Remarque cried out for an end to war in *All Quiet on the Western Front* (1928). This international best seller depicted the life shared by enemies on the battlefield, thus aiming to overcome the national hatred aroused by wartime propaganda.

Remarque's novel was part of a flood of popular, and often bitter, literature appearing on the tenth anniversary of the war's end. It coincided with new interest in visiting battlefields and other "Great War tourism." (See Document, "Battlefield Tourism," above.)

Poets reflected on postwar conditions in more general terms, using styles that rejected the comforting rhymes or accessible metaphors of earlier verse. T. S. Eliot, an American-born poet who for a time worked as a banker in Britain, portrayed postwar life as petty and futile in "The Waste Land" (1922) and "The Hollow Men" (1925). The Irish poet William Butler Yeats joined Eliot in mourning the end of traditional society and moral values and the rise of a new, superficial generation gaily dancing to jazz and engaging in promiscuous sex. Both poets had an uneasy relationship with the modern world and at times advocated authoritarianism rather than democracy.

The postwar arts produced many a utopian fantasy turned upside down; dystopias of life in a war-traumatized Europe multiplied. In the bizarre expressionist stories of Franz Kafka, an employee of a large insurance company in Prague, the world is a vast, impersonal machine. His novels *The Trial* (1925) and *The Castle* (1926) evoked the hopeless condition of individuals caught between the cogs of society's relentlessly turning gears. His themes seemed to capture for civilian life the helplessness that soldiers had felt at the front. As an old social order collapsed in the face of political and technological innovation, other writers depicted the complex, sometimes nightmarish inner life of individuals.

Irish writer James Joyce and British writer Virginia Woolf portrayed this interior self built on memories and sensations, many of them from the war. Joyce's *Ulysses* (1922) and Woolf's *Mrs. Dalloway* (1925) illuminated the fast-moving inner lives of their characters in the course of a single day. In one of the most celebrated passages in *Ulysses*, a long interior monologue traces a woman's lifetime of erotic and emotional sensations. The technique of using a character's thoughts to propel a story was called stream of consciousness. For Woolf, the war had dissolved the solid society from which absorbing stories and fascinating characters were once fashioned. Her characters experience fragmented conversations and incomplete relationships. Woolf's novel *Orlando* also reflected the current interest in Eastern ideas of reincarnation and the postwar attention to women. In the novel, the hero Orlando lives hundreds of years and in the course of his long life is eventually transformed into a woman.

There was another side to the postwar story, one based not on the interior life of a traumatized society but on the promise of technology. Avant-garde artists before the war had celebrated the new, the futuristic, the utopian. Like Jules Amar crafting prostheses for shattered limbs, they were optimistic that technology could make an entire society whole after the slaughter. The aim of art, observed one of them, "is not to decorate our life but to organize it." The group of German artists called the Bauhaus (after the idea of a craft association, or *Bauhütte*) created streamlined office buildings and designed functional furniture and utensils, many of them inspired by forms from "untainted" East Asia and Africa. Russian artists, temporarily entranced by communism, wrote novels about cement factories and ballets about steel.

Artists fascinated by technology and machinery were drawn to the most modern of all countries—the United States. Hollywood films, glossy advertisements, and the bustling metropolis of New York tempted careworn Europeans. They loved films and stories about the Wild West or the carefree "modern American girl." They were especially attracted to jazz, the improvisational music that emanated from New York's Harlem. Performers like Josephine Baker (1906–1976) and Louis Armstrong (1900–1971) became international sensations when they toured Europe's capital cities. Like jazz, the New York skyscraper pointed to the future, not to the grim wartime past.

The Communist Utopia

Communism also promised a shining future and a modern, technological culture. But as the Bolsheviks met powerful resistance, they became ever more ruthless and authoritarian. In the early 1920s, peasant bands called Green Armies revolted against the policy of war communism that confiscated their crops. Industrial production stood at only 13 per-

The New Man
There was a sense in the postwar world that people were entering a new age after the horrors of war. Nowhere was this feeling stronger than among Communists in Russia, where it was also believed that communism would also create "The New Man," the subtitle of this work by Eli Lissitsky ("Victory over the Sun: The New Man," 1923). Note the energy in the figure, as it stretches its reach in all directions. The use of pure lines and geometric forms symbolized the higher reality that the new man would reach once the messiness and corruption of ordinary reality had been eliminated. *(Tate, London/Art Resource, NY/© 2008 Artists Rights Society (ARS), NY.)*

cent of its prewar output, shortages of housing affected the entire population, and millions of refugees clogged the cities and roamed the countryside. In the early spring of 1921, workers in Petrograd and sailors at the nearby naval base at Kronstadt revolted, protesting their short rations and the privileged standard of living that Bolshevik supervisors enjoyed. They called for "soviets without Communists"—that is, a return to the early promises of a worker state without elite leaders.

The Bolsheviks had many of the rebels shot, but the Kronstadt revolt pushed Lenin to institute reform. His New Economic Policy (NEP) returned parts of the economy to the free market, a temporary retreat to capitalist methods that allowed peasants to sell their grain and others to trade consumer goods freely. Although the state still controlled large industries and banking, the NEP encouraged people to produce, sell, and even, in the spirited slogan of one official, "get rich." As a result, consumer goods and more food to eat soon became available. Although many remained impoverished, some peasants and merchants prospered. The rise of these wealthy "NEPmen," who bought and furnished splendid homes, again broke the Bolshevik promise of a classless utopia.

Further protest erupted within Communist ranks. At the 1921 party congress, a group called the Worker Opposition objected to the party's usurpation of economic control from worker organizations and pointed out that the NEP was an agrarian program, not a proletarian one for workers. In response, Lenin suppressed the Worker Opposition and set up procedures for purging opponents—a policy that would become a deadly feature of Communist rule. Bolshevik leaders also worked to make the Communist revolution a cultural reality in people's lives and thinking. Party leaders set up classes in a variety of political and social subjects throughout the countryside, and volunteers struggled to improve the rate of literacy—which was only 40 percent on the eve of World War I. To facilitate social equality between the sexes, which had been part of the Marxist vision of the future, the state made birth control, abortion, and divorce readily available. As commissar for public welfare, **Aleksandra Kollontai** (1872–1952) promoted birth-control education for adults and day care for children of working parents. To encourage literacy, she wrote simply

worded novels about love and work in the new socialist state for ordinary readers.

The bureaucracy swelled to bring modern ways to every corner of life, and *hygiene* and *efficiency* became watchwords, as they were in the rest of Europe. Such agencies as the Zhenotdel (Women's Bureau) taught women about their rights under communism and about sanitary housekeeping. Efficiency experts aimed to replace tsarist backwardness with technological modernity based on the techniques of Americans Henry Ford and Frederick Taylor. The short-lived government agency Proletkult tried to develop proletarian culture through such undertakings as workers' universities, a workers' theater, and workers' publishing. Russian artists experimented with blending high art and technology in mass culture: poet Vladimir Mayakovsky wrote verse praising his Communist passport and essays promoting toothbrushing, and composers punctuated their music with the sound of train or factory whistles. The early days of Bolshevik rule saw interesting experiments in all of the arts and in mass culture.

As with war communism, many resisted attempts to change everyday life and culture. As Zhenotdel workers moved into the countryside, for example, they attempted to teach women to behave as men's equals. Peasant families, still strongly patriarchal, often resisted. In Islamic regions of central Asia, incorporated from the old Russian Empire into the new Communist one, Bolsheviks urged Muslim women to remove their veils, but fervent Muslims often attacked both Zhenotdel workers and women who followed their advice.

Lenin suffered a debilitating stroke in the spring of 1922, and amid ongoing cultural experimentation and factional fighting, the architect of the Bolshevik Revolution died in January 1924. The party congress declared the day of his death a permanent holiday, changed the name of Petrograd to Leningrad, and elevated the deceased leader into a secular god. After Lenin's death, no one was allowed to criticize anything associated with his name, a situation that paved the way for future abuses of power by Communist leaders.

Joseph Stalin (1879–1953), who served in the powerful post of general secretary of the Communist Party, was the chief mourner at Lenin's funeral. Stalin organized the Lenin cult, which included the public display of Lenin's embalmed corpse—still on view today. He dealt with thousands of local party officials, which gave him enormous national patronage, and in 1923 welded both Russian and non-Russian regions into the Union of Soviet Socialist Republics (USSR). Wary of

---

Aleksandra Kollontai (1872–1952): Russian activist and minister of public welfare in the Bolshevik government; she promoted social programs such as birth control and day care for children of working parents.

Stalin's growing influence and ruthlessness, Lenin in his last will and testament had asked that "the comrades find a way to remove Stalin." Stalin, however, prevented Lenin's will from being publicized and discredited his chief rival, Trotsky, as an unpatriotic internationalist who was unwilling to concentrate on the tough job of modernizing the Soviet Union. With the blessing of Trotsky's other rivals, Stalin had him exiled. Bringing in several hundred thousand new party members who owed their positions in government and industry to him, Stalin built a loyal base of supporters. By 1928–1929, he had achieved virtually complete control of the USSR.

Fascism on the March in Italy

In Italy, the war remained alive in the rise to power of **Benito Mussolini** (1883–1945), who, like the Bolsheviks, promised an efficient military utopia. Italian anger boiled over when the Allies at Paris refused to honor the territorial promises of the Treaty of London. Domestic unrest swelled when peasants and workers protested their economic plight during the slump of the early 1920s. Since the late nineteenth century, many Europeans had come to blame parliaments and constitutions for their problems, so Italians approved when Mussolini, a socialist journalist who turned to the radical right, built a personal army (the Black Shirts) of veterans and the unemployed to overturn parliamentary government. In 1922, his supporters, known as Fascists, started a march on Rome, forcing King Victor Emmanuel III (r. 1900–1946) to make Mussolini prime minister.

The Fascist movement flourished in the soil of poverty, social unrest, and wounded national pride. It attracted to its bands of Black Shirts many young men who felt cheated of wartime glory by the Allies and veterans who missed the vigor of military life. The fasces, an ancient Roman symbol depicting a bundle of sticks wrapped around an ax with the blade exposed, served as the movement's emblem; it represented both unity and force to Mussolini's supporters. Unlike Marxism, Fascism had no coherent ideology: "Fascism is not a church," Mussolini announced upon taking power in 1922. "It is more like a training ground." **Fascism** was thus defined by its promotion of male violence and its opposition to parliamentary rule and the antinationalist socialist movement.

Benito Mussolini (1883–1945): Leader of Italian fascist movement and, after the March on Rome in 1922, dictator of Italy.

fascism: A doctrine that emphasized violence and glorified the state over the people and their individual or civil rights.

Mussolini consolidated his power by making criticism of the state a criminal offense and by violently wiping out parliamentary opposition. His Fascist bands demolished socialist newspaper offices, attacked striking workers, used their favorite tactic of forcing castor oil (which caused diarrhea) down the throats of socialists, and even murdered certain powerful opponents. Yet this brutality and the sight of the Black Shirts marching through the streets like disciplined soldiers signaled to many Italians that their country was orderly and modern. Large landowners and businessmen approved Fascist attacks on strikers, and they supported the movement financially. Their generous funding allowed Mussolini to build a large staff by hiring the unemployed, creating the illusion that Fascists could rescue the economy when no one else could.

Like a wartime leader, Mussolini used mass propaganda to build support for a kind of military campaign to remake Italy by uniting rich and poor, peasant and worker. Peasant men huddled around radios to hear him call for a "battle of wheat" to enhance farm productivity. Peasant women, responding to his praise for maternal duty, idolized him for appearing to value womanhood. In the cities the government launched avant-garde architectural projects and used public relations promoters to advertise its achievements. The modern city became a stage set for Fascist spectacle: old residential neighborhoods fell to the wrecking machines, allowing roadbuilders to put in broad avenues for Fascist parades, captured by newsreel cameras and broadcast by radio. Mussolini claimed that he made the trains run on time, and this additional triumph of modern technology fanned people's hopes that he could restore order even if it were a warlike kind of order.

Mussolini added a strong dose of traditional values and prejudices to his modern order. Although an atheist, he recognized the importance of Catholicism to most Italians. In 1929, the Lateran Agreement between the Italian government and the church made the Vatican an independent state under papal sovereignty. The government recognized the church's right to determine marriage and family policy and supported its role in education. In return, the church ended its criticism of Fascist tactics. Mussolini also introduced a "corporate" state that denied individual political rights in favor of duty to the state, as in wartime. Corporatist decrees in 1926 outlawed independent labor unions and peasant groups, replacing them with organized groups or corporations of employers, workers, and professionals to settle grievances and determine conditions of work. Mussolini drew more praise from business leaders when he announced cuts in women's wages; and then in the late 1920s he won the approval of civil servants, lawyers, and professors by banning women from those professions. Mussolini did not want women out of the workforce altogether but aimed to confine them to low-paying jobs as part of his scheme for reinvigorating men.

Mussolini's admirers were numerous across the West and included Adolf Hitler, who throughout the 1920s had been building a paramilitary group of storm troopers and a political organization called the National Socialist German Workers' Party, or Nazis. During his brief stint in jail for the Beer Hall Putsch in 1923, Hitler wrote *Mein Kampf* (My Struggle, 1925), which articulated both a vicious

anti-Semitism and a political psychology for manipulating the masses. Hitler was fascinated by the specifics of Mussolini's success: the dramatic Fascist march on Rome, Mussolini's legal accession to power, and the triumph over socialist and trade unionist opposition. But the poor economic conditions that had allowed Mussolini to rise to power in 1922 no longer existed in Germany. Although Hitler was welding the Nazi Party into a strong political instrument, the Weimar parliamentary government was actually working as the decade wore on.

> **REVIEW:** How did the postwar atmosphere influence cultural expression and encourage the trend toward dictatorship?

Mussolini and the Black Shirts

For movements like Mussolini's Fascism, the best society was one controlled by militarized politics that killed its critics and political opponents. Fascism saw parliamentary democracies as effeminate and doomed in the modern world, which would need dictators and obedient warriors to make it strong, efficient, and machinelike. Thus, in the name of promoting state power, Mussolini gained adherents both within and outside of Italy. *(Farabolafoto.)*

Conclusion

The year 1929 was to prove just as fateful as 1914 had been. In 1914, World War I began an orgy of death, causing tens of millions of casualties, the destruction of major dynasties, and the collapse of aristocratic classes. For four years war promoted military technology, virulent nationalism, and the control of everyday life by bureaucracy. While dynasties fell, the centralization of power increased the scope of the nation-state. The Peace of Paris treaties of 1919–1920 left Germans bitterly resentful, while in eastern and central Europe the intense intermingling of ethnicities, religions, and languages in the new states created by the treaties failed to guarantee a peaceful future. Massive migrations provoked additional chaos, as some new nations expelled minority groups.

War furthered the development of mass society. It leveled social classes on the battlefield and in the graveyard, standardized political thinking through wartime propaganda, and extended many political rights to women for their war effort. Production techniques, improved during wartime, turned in peacetime toward churning out consumer goods and technological innovations like the prostheses built by Jules Amar, air transport, cinema, and radio transmission for greater numbers of people. Modernity in the arts intensified after the war, as artists and writers probed the nightmarish cataclysm that continued to haunt the population.

By the end of the 1920s, the legacy of war had been to so militarize politics that strongmen had come to power in several countries, including the Soviet Union and Italy, with Adolf Hitler waiting in the wings in Germany. These strongmen kept alive the wartime commitment to violence. Many Westerners were impressed by their tough, modern efficiency. Fascists and Communists especially worked to make parliaments and citizen rule seem out-of-date, even effeminate. When the U.S. stock market crashed in 1929 and economic disaster circled the globe, authoritarian solutions and militarism continued to look appealing. What followed was a series of catastrophes even more devastating than World War I.

FOR FURTHER EXPLORATION

- **For suggested references, including Web sites, for topics in this chapter,** see page SR-1 at the end of the book.

- **For additional primary-source material from this period,** see Chapter 25 in *Sources of THE MAKING OF THE WEST*, Third Edition.

- **For Web sites and documents related to topics in this chapter,** see *Make History* at bedfordstmartins.com/hunt.

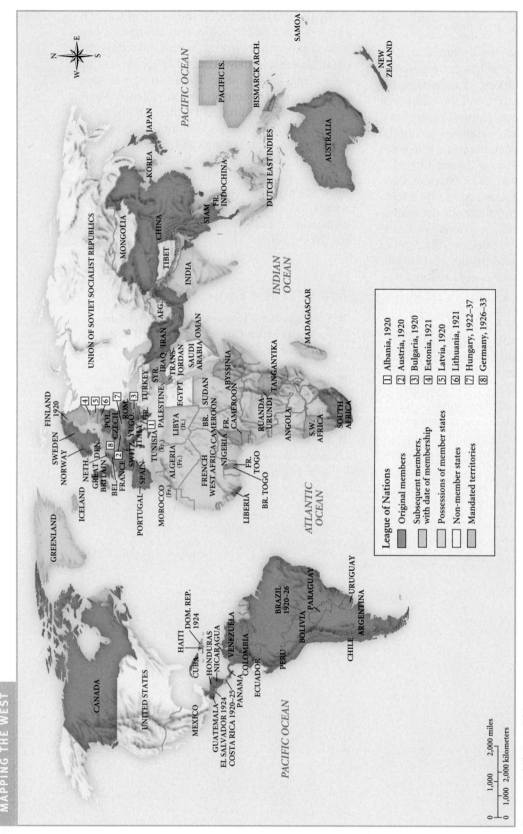

Europe and the World in 1929

The map reflects the partitions and nations that came into being as a result of war and revolution, while it obscures the increasing movement toward throwing off colonial rule. This was the true high point of empire: the drive for empire would diminish after 1929 except for Italy, which still craved colonies, and Japan, which continued searching for more land and resources to fuel its rapid growth. ■ Observe the League of Nations membership as depicted in the map. What common bonds, if any, united these member nations?

CHAPTER REVIEW

KEY TERMS AND PEOPLE

total war (800)
cult of the offensive (803)
Schlieffen Plan (803)
soviets (811)
V. I. Lenin (811)
Bolshevik Revolution (811)
Weimar Republic (815)

Fourteen Points (816)
Peace of Paris (816)
war guilt clause (818)
League of Nations (818)
mandate system (819)
Aleksandra Kollontai (832)
Benito Mussolini (833)
fascism (833)

REVIEW QUESTIONS

1. In what ways was World War I a total war?

2. Why did people rebel during World War I, and what turned rebellion into outright revolution in Russia?

3. What were the major outcomes of the postwar peacemaking process?

4. What were the major political, social, and economic problems facing postwar Europe, and how did governments attempt to address them?

5. How did the postwar atmosphere influence cultural expression and encourage the trend toward dictatorship?

MAKING CONNECTIONS

1. How did the experience of war shape postwar mass politics?

2. What social changes from the war carried over into the postwar years and why?

For practice quizzes, a customized study plan, and other study tools, see the Online Study Guide at bedfordstmartins.com/hunt.

IMPORTANT EVENTS

1913–1925	Suffrage for women expands in much of Europe
1914 August	World War I begins
1916	Irish nationalists stage Easter Uprising against British rule
1917 March	Revolution in Russia overturns tsarist autocracy
April	The United States enters World War I
November	Bolshevik Revolution in Russia
1918 November	Armistice ends fighting of World War I; revolutionary turmoil throughout Germany; the kaiser abdicates
1918–1922	Civil war in Russia
1919	The Weimar Republic established
1919–1920	Paris Peace Conference redraws the map of Europe
1922	Ireland is split in two: the independent Irish Free State in the south and British-affiliated Ulster in the north; Fascists march on Rome; Mussolini becomes Italy's prime minister; T. S. Eliot publishes "The Waste Land"; James Joyce publishes *Ulysses*
1924	Lenin dies; Stalin and Trotsky contend for power
1924–1929	Period of general economic prosperity and stability
1929 October	Stock market crash in United States

The Great Depression and World War II
1929–1945

When Etty Hillesum moved to Amsterdam from the Dutch provinces in 1932 to attend law school, an economic depression gripped the world. A resourceful young woman, Hillesum pieced together a living as a housekeeper and part-time language teacher so that she could continue her studies. Absorbed by the pressures and pleasures of her life as a bookworm, she took little note of Adolf Hitler's spectacular rise to power in Germany, even when he demonized her fellow Jews as responsible for the economic slump and for virtually every other problem Germany faced. In 1939, the outbreak of World War II awakened her to the reality of what was happening. The German conquest of the Netherlands in 1940 led to the persecution of Dutch Jews, bringing Hillesum to a shattering realization, noted in her diary: "What they are after is our total destruction." The Nazis started relocating Jews to camps in Germany and Poland. Hillesum went to work for Amsterdam's Jewish Council, which was forced to organize the transport of Jews to the death camps in eastern Europe. Changing from self-absorbed student to heroine, she did what she could to help other Jews and began meticulously recording the deportations. When she and her family were captured and deported in turn, she smuggled out letters from the transit camps along the route to Poland, bearing witness to the inhumane conditions and brutal treatment of the Jews. "I wish I could live for a long time so that one day I may know how to explain it," she wrote. Etty Hillesum never got her wish: she died at Auschwitz in November 1943.

The economic recovery of the late 1920s came to a crashing halt with the collapse of the U.S. stock market in 1929. Financial collapse in

Nazis on Parade
By the time Hitler came to power in 1933, Germany was mired in the Great Depression. Hated by Communists, Nazis, and conservatives alike, the Weimar Republic had few supporters. Hitler took his cue from Mussolini by promising an end to democracy and tolerance and by using the visual power of Nazi soldiers marching through the streets during the depression to win support for overthrowing the government. *(Time & Life Pictures/Getty Images.)*

■ **For more help analyzing this image,** see the visual activity for this chapter in the Online Study Guide at **bedfordstmartins.com/hunt**.

the United States soon became a worldwide Great Depression. Economic distress intensified social grievances. In Europe, many people turned to military-style strongmen for solutions to their problems. Chief among these dictators, Adolf Hitler roused the masses to restore the German glory that had been tarnished by defeat in 1918. He urged Germans to scorn democratic rights and ideas of equal citizenship by joining him in rooting out what he considered to be inferior people: Jews, Slavs, and Gypsies, among others. Authoritarian and militaristic regimes spread to Spain, Poland, Hungary, Japan, and elsewhere, tramping on representative institutions. In the Soviet Union, Joseph Stalin justified the killing of millions of citizens as necessary for the USSR's industrialization and the survival of communism. For millions of hard-pressed people in the difficult 1930s, dictatorship had great appeal.

Elected leaders in the democracies reacted cautiously to both economic depression and the new dictators' aggressive actions and policies. Fearful of conflict and following democratic procedures, these leaders appeared weak while dictators sporting uniforms looked bold and decisive. Only the German invasion of Poland in 1939 finally pushed the democracies to strong action, as World War II erupted in Europe. By 1941, the war had spread across the globe with the United States, Great Britain, the Soviet Union, and many other nations united in combat against Germany, Italy, Japan, and their allies. Tens of millions would perish in this war because both technology and ideology had become more deadly than they had been just two decades earlier. More than half the dead were civilians, among them Etty Hillesum, whose only crime was being a Jew.

> **FOCUS QUESTION:** What were the main economic, social, and political challenges of the years 1929–1945, and how did governments and individuals respond to them?

The Great Depression

The U.S. stock market crash of 1929 and economic developments around the world triggered the Great Depression of the 1930s. Rural and urban folk alike suffered as tens of millions lost their jobs and livelihoods. The whole world felt the depression's impact: commerce and investment in industry fell off, social life and gender roles were upset, and the birthrate plummeted. From peasants in Asia to industrial workers in Germany and the United States, the Great Depression shattered the lives of millions.

Economic Disaster Strikes

In the 1920s, U.S. corporations and banks as well as millions of individual Americans had not only invested all their money but also borrowed money to invest in the stock market, which seemed to deliver endless profits. Confident that stock prices would continue to rise, they used easy credit to buy shares in popular companies based on electric, automotive, and other new technologies. By the end of the decade, the Federal Reserve Bank—the nation's central bank, which controlled financial policy—tried to slow speculation by tightening available credit. To meet the new restrictions, brokers had to demand that their clients immediately pay back the money they had borrowed to buy stock. As stocks were sold to cover the borrowed funds, the market collapsed. Between early October and mid-November 1929, the value of businesses listed on the U.S. stock market dropped from $87 billion to $30 billion. For individuals and for the economy as a whole, it was the beginning of catastrophe.

The crash helped bring on a global depression because the United States, a leading international creditor, had financed the economic growth of the previous five years. Suddenly strapped for credit, U.S. banks cut back on loans and called in debts,

■ **1929** U.S. stock market crashes; global depression begins; Soviet war against kulaks

■ **1933** Hitler comes to power

1930

■ **1931** Japan invades Manchuria; Spanish republicans overthrow monarchy

■ **1935** Nuremburg Laws; Italy invades Ethiopia

■ **1936** Purges and show trials in USSR begin

1935

■ **1936–1939** Spanish Civil war

■ **1937** Japan attacks China

undermining businesses at home and abroad. The recent U.S. lead in industrial production and the rise of Japanese manufacturing made the collapse in Europe even worse. From the aging industries of Britain to the fledgling factories of eastern Europe, a decline in investment and consumer buying further wore down the European economy.

The Great Depression left no sector of the world economy unscathed, but government actions made the depression worse. Governments instituted budget cuts and high tariffs against foreign goods to spur their economies, but these policies further discouraged spending and international trade. By 1933, almost six million German workers, or about one-third of the workforce, were unemployed, and many others were underemployed. Even in France, which had a more self-sufficient economy based on small businesses, firms began to fail, and by the mid-1930s more than 800,000 French people had lost their jobs. Great Britain—with its textile, steel, and coal industries near ruin because of out-of-date techniques and foreign competition—had close to three million unemployed in 1932.

Agricultural prices had been declining for several years because of technological advances and abundant harvests around the world. Now creditors confiscated farms and equipment. With their incomes slashed, millions of small farmers had no money to buy the chemical fertilizers and motorized machinery they needed to remain competitive, and they too went under. Eastern and southern European peasants, who had pressed for the redistribution of land after World War I, could not afford to operate their newly acquired farms. In Poland, many of the 700,000 new landowners fell into debt trying to upgrade their farms—a situation that was widespread across eastern Europe. Eastern European governments often ignored the farmers' plight as they poured available funds into industrialization—a policy that increased tensions in rural society.

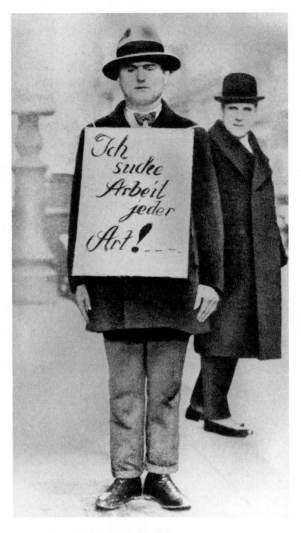

Unemployed in Germany (1932)
"I'm looking for work of any kind," this respectably dressed unemployed man announces on his sign. Germans were among those hardest hit by the Great Depression, and when demogogues pointed to such sights as evidence that democracy didn't work, it helped pull down the rule of constitutions, representative government, and guaranteed rights.
(ullstein bild / The Granger Collection, New York.)

■ **1941** Germany invades USSR; Japan attacks Pearl Harbor; United States enters war

■ **1939** Germany invades Poland; World War II begins

■ **1942–1943** Siege of Stalingrad

1940

1945

■ **1938** Kristallnacht; Germany annexes Austria

■ **1940** France falls to the German army

■ **1944** Allied forces land at Normandy

■ **1940–1941** Battle of Britain

■ **1941–1945** The Holocaust

■ **1945** Fall of Berlin; United States drops atomic bombs on Japan; World War II ends

DOCUMENT

A Family Copes with Unemployment

Austria and Germany were incredibly hard hit by the depression and the trauma was made worse because of the catastrophic defeat, reparations, and dismemberment of both the Austrian and German empires. In 1931, sociologists visited a small industrial town called Marienthal, an hour outside of Vienna, to report on the psychological and physical condition of the hundreds of families left penniless by the closing of the textile mills.

The father was sitting on a low stool with a pile of worn-out children's shoes in front of him that he was trying to mend with roofing felt. The children were sitting together motionless on a box, in stockinged feet, waiting for their shoes to be finished. The father explained with embarrassment, ". . . On Sundays I have to patch the shoes up a bit so that the children can go to school again on Monday." He held up the completely dilapidated shoes of the eldest boy. "I just don't know what I can do with these. On holidays he can't go out of the house any more. . . ."

The youngest child caught our attention. His face was feverish and puffy and swollen around the nose. He breathed heavily with his mouth open. The mother explained: "He always has a cold. He ought to have his tonsils and adenoids out, but we can't afford the trip to the hospital. . . ." The father told us that things had been going terribly badly these last few days. All they had been able to buy was bread, and not enough of that. The children kept coming into the kitchen asking for another piece; they were always hungry. His wife sat in the kitchen crying.

Source: Marie Jahoda et al., eds., *Marienthal: The Sociography of an Unemployed Village*, trans. John Reginall and Thomas Elsaesser (Chicago: Aldine-Atherton, 1971 [1933]), 87–88.

Social Effects of the Depression

The picture of society during the Great Depression was more complex than utter ruin, however. First, the situation was not uniformly bleak. Despite the slump, modernization proceeded. Bordering English slums, one traveler in the mid-1930s noticed, were "filling stations and factories that look like exhibition buildings, giant cinemas and dance halls and cafés, bungalows with tiny garages, cocktail bars, Woolworth's [and] swimming pools." Municipal and national governments continued road construction and sanitation projects. Running water, electricity, and sewage pipes were installed in many homes for the first time. New factories manufactured synthetic fabrics, electrical products such as stoves, and automobiles—all of them in demand. With government assistance, eastern European industry developed: Romanian industrial production, for example, increased by 55 percent between 1929 and 1939.

Second, the majority of Europeans and Americans had jobs throughout the 1930s, and people with steady employment benefited from a drastic drop in prices. Service workers, managers, and business magnates often enjoyed considerable prosperity. On the other hand, in towns with heavy industry, sometimes more than half the population was out of work. In England in the mid-1930s, close to 20 percent of the population lacked adequate food, clothing, or housing. In a 1932 school assignment, a German youth wrote: "My father has been out of work for two and a half years. He thinks that I'll never find a job." Despite the prosperity of many people, the Great Depression spread fear beyond the unemployed. (See Document, "A Family Copes with Unemployment," above.)

Economic catastrophe upset gender relations and weakened social ties. Women could often find low-paying jobs doing laundry and cleaning house for others, while unemployed men sometimes stayed home all day and took over housekeeping chores. Some, however, felt that this "women's work" demeaned their masculinity. As many women became breadwinners, albeit for low wages, men could be seen standing on street corners begging—a change in gender expectations that fed discontent. Young men in cities faced severe unemployment; with nothing to do but loiter in parks, they became ripe for movements like Nazism. As the number of farmworkers in western Europe decreased, rural men also faced a decline in male authority, once central to the organization of labor and to decisions about distributing property to children. Demagogues everywhere railed against democracy's failure to stop the collapse of traditional life. Their complaints helped clear the way for Nazi and Fascist politicians who promised to create jobs and thus restore male dignity.

After a brief postwar upturn, the birthrate had been steadily declining. The reason for the decline was clear: in difficult economic times, which had plagued the West on and off since the war, people chose to have fewer children. In addition, mandatory education and more years of required schooling, enforced more strictly after World War I, reduced the income once earned by children. Working-class children were no longer wage earners; they now cost their families money while they went to school. Family-planning centers opened, receiving a warm reception, and knowledge of birth control spread across the working and lower-middle classes.

Politicians of all stripes jumped on the declining birthrate, claiming that it, along with a depressed economy, would lead to national collapse. Many politicians also used the population "crisis" to gain votes by igniting racism: "superior" peoples were selfishly failing to breed, politicians charged, while "inferior" peoples were just waiting to take their place. This sort of racism was particularly heated in eastern Europe, where the rural population rose because of increased life expectancy despite the declining birthrate, adding to financial hardships. Throughout eastern Europe, peasant political parties blamed Jewish bankers for farm foreclosures and Jewish civil servants (of whom there were actually very few) for inadequate relief programs. Thus, population issues along with economic misery produced divisiveness, especially in the form of anti-Semitism, once again opening the way for dictators who promised that eliminating such undesirables as Jews would restore prosperity.

The Great Depression beyond the West

The effects of the depression extended beyond the West, spreading discontent in European empires. World War I and postwar investment had produced economic growth, a rising population, and explosive urbanization in Asia, Africa, and Latin America. Japan in particular had become a formidable industrial rival. The depression, however, cut the demand for copper, tin, and other raw materials and for the finished products made in urban factories worldwide. Rising agricultural productivity drove down the price of foodstuffs like rice and coffee, a disastrous consequence for colonial peoples who had been forced to grow a single cash crop. One French official in Algeria said that the crash in agricultural prices there "endangers the entire colonial project." Just as in Europe, however,

the economic picture in the colonies was uneven. For instance, established Indian industries such as the textile business gained strength, with India achieving virtual independence from British cloth.

Economic distress fueled anger, and anger led to action. Colonial farmers withheld produce like cocoa from imperial trade, and colonial workers went on strike to protest the wage cuts imposed by imperial landlords. Discontent ran deep. Millions of African and Asian colonial troops had fought for Britain and France in World War I, but the imperialist countries had given little back to their colonial populations. In fact, the League of Nations charter had pointedly omitted any reference to the principle of racial equality demanded by people of color at the Paris peace conference. Fortified by these wrongs, by the model of Japan's power, and by their own industrial development, more colonial peoples than ever before resolved to win independence.

In India, anger toward colonialism boiled over. Millions of working people, including hundreds of thousands of veterans, joined with the upper-class Indians, who had organized to gain rights from Britain in the late nineteenth century. Mohandas Gandhi (1869–1948; called Mahatma, or "great-souled") emerged as the charismatic leader for Indian independence. Trained in England as a Western-style lawyer, Gandhi preached Hindu self-denial and rejected elaborate British ceremonies and manners. He wore simple clothing made of thread he had spun and advocated **civil disobedience** — deliberately but peacefully breaking the law — a tactic he claimed to have taken from the British suffragists and from the teachings of spiritual leaders like Jesus and Buddha. Boycotting British-made goods and disobeying British laws, Gandhi aimed to end Indian deference to the British. The British jailed Gandhi repeatedly and tried to split the independence movement by promoting Hindu-Muslim antagonism. Instead, commitment to independence grew.

The end of the Ottoman Empire following World War I led to efforts to build new independent nations in the Middle East. Mustafa Kemal (1881–1938), who later took the name Atatürk ("first among Turks"), led the Turks to found an independent republic in 1923 and to craft a capitalist economy. In an effort to Westernize Turkish

---

civil disobedience: The act of deliberately but peacefully breaking the law, a tactic used by Mohandas Gandhi in India and earlier by British suffragists to protest oppression and obtain political change.

Gandhi Leading the Salt March (1930)
Mohandas Gandhi appealed to the masses, not just to the middle- and upper-class constituency of the Indian National Congress, which had emphasized gaining rights under British rule. Instead, Gandhi addressed the entire colonial system that prevented ordinary Indian people from using their own national resources such as salt. Violating British laws, which prohibited Indians from gathering this natural product, Gandhi led the people in an act of civil disobedience — his march to the sea to harvest the salt. *(© Bettmann/Corbis.)*

ing the depression depended increasingly on the profits it could take from its colonies. Thus, France's trade with its colonies increased as that with Europe lagged. France also depended on the colonies for sheer numbers of people, and the rising colonial population bolstered French optimism. One official estimated what colonial numbers could mean for national security: "One hundred and ten million strong, France can stand up to Germany." Ho Chi Minh, founder of the Indochinese Communist Party, rallied his people to protest French imperialism, but in 1930 the French government brutally crushed the peasant uprising he led. Needing their empires, Britain and France increased the number of their troops stationed around the world. As a result, totalitarianism spread largely unchecked throughout Europe during the 1930s.

> **REVIEW:** How did the Great Depression affect society and politics?

Totalitarian Triumph

Representative government collapsed in many countries under the sheer weight of social and economic crisis. After 1929, Mussolini in Italy, Stalin in the USSR, and Hitler in Germany were able to mobilize vast support for their regimes. Many admired Mussolini and Hitler for the discipline they brought to social and economic life. Desperate for economic relief, many citizens supported political violence as key to restoring well-being and guaranteeing the future. The common use of violence has led scholars to apply the term *totalitarianism* to the Fascist, Nazi, and Communist regimes of the 1930s (see "Terms of History," page 845). The term refers to highly centralized systems of government that attempt to control society and ensure obedience through a single party and police terror. Born during World War I and gaining support in its aftermath, totalitarian governments broke with liberal principles of freedom and natural rights and came to wage war on their own citizens.

The Rise of Stalinism

In the 1930s, **Joseph Stalin** (1879–1953) led the transformation of the USSR from a rural society into a formidable industrial power. Stalin ended

culture and the new Turkish state, Kemal moved the capital from Constantinople to Ankara in 1923, officially changed the name Constantinople to the Turkish name Istanbul in 1930, mandated Western dress for men and women, introduced the Latin alphabet, and abolished polygamy. In 1936, women received the vote and were made eligible to serve in the parliament. Persia, which changed its name to Iran in 1935, similarly loosened the European grip on its economy by updating its government and by forcing the negotiation of oil contracts that kept Western countries from taking the oil virtually free. In 1936, Britain agreed to end its military occupation of Egypt (though not yet the Suez Canal), moving toward fulfilling the promise of Egyptian self-rule it had made in 1922.

The French made fewer concessions in their colonies. Like all imperial countries, France dur-

Joseph Stalin (1879–1953): Leader of the USSR who, with considerable backing, formed a brutal dictatorship and forcefully converted the country into an industrial power.

Lenin's New Economic Policy, which had allowed free private trade and agriculture, and in 1929 laid out the first of several ambitious five-year plans for industrializing the country. Coercion and violence were crucial components of this gigantic undertaking.

Transforming the Economy. Stalin's **five-year plans** outlined a program for huge increases in the output of coal, iron ore, steel, and industrial goods over successive five-year periods. Without an end to economic backwardness, Stalin warned, "the advanced countries . . . will crush us." He thus established central economic planning—a policy used on both sides in World War I and increasingly favored by bureaucrats around the world. Between 1928 and 1940, the number of Soviet workers in industry, construction, and transport grew from 4.6 million to 12.6 million and factory output soared. Stalin's first five-year plan helped make the USSR a leading industrial nation.

A new elite of bureaucrats implemented the plans, and the number of managers—mostly party officials and technical experts—in heavy industry grew by almost 500 percent between 1929 and 1935. Despite limited rights to change jobs or even move from place to place, skilled workers benefited from the privileges that went along with their new industrial role. Compared with people working the land, both managers and industrial workers had better housing and wages. Communist officials received additional rewards such as country homes, better food, and luxurious vacations.

New or unskilled workers enjoyed no such benefits. Newcomers from the countryside were herded into barrack-style dwellings or tents and subjected to dangerous factory conditions. Despite the hardships, many took pride in their new skills. "We mastered this profession—completely new to us—with great pleasure," a female lathe operator recalled. More often, however, workers fresh from the countryside lacked the technical skills necessary to accomplish goals of the five-year plans. Because meeting these goals had top priority as a measure of progress toward a Communist utopia, official lying about productivity became part of the economic system. The attempt to turn an illiterate peasant society into an advanced industrial economy in a single decade brought intense suffering, but hardship was tolerated because, as one worker put it, Soviet workers believed in the need for "con-

---

five-year plans: Centralized programs for economic development first used by Joseph Stalin and copied by Adolf Hitler; these plans set production priorities and gave production targets for individual industries and agriculture.

TERMS OF HISTORY

Totalitarianism

When the word *totalitarianism* was first introduced in Italy, Mussolini's government adopted it as a mark of pride. In 1923, Mussolini proposed a law by which the political party that had the most votes would gain 75 percent of the seats in Italy's parliament. One journalist protested, claiming that this proposal would eliminate both majority rule and minority coalitions in favor of a "totalitarian" system. He was beaten to death by Mussolini's thugs. The Fascists then embraced the term, proclaiming the superiority of a "total state" especially needed when conditions of "total war" demanded efficient military rule that would stamp out effeminate principles of rights and freedom. The Nazis also adopted the term, hailing the effective totalitarian party that could make workers and soldiers like steel in body and in spirit.

During the 1930s, critics of totalitarian regimes turned the meaning to a negative one. They saw totalitarianism as originating in the scientific revolution and the Enlightenment of the seventeenth and eighteenth centuries, both of which aimed to dominate nature. Industrialization likewise aimed at domination of the economy and resources. By this negative view, Stalin's Soviet Union was as totalitarian as Mussolini's Fascists and Hitler's Nazis. But as the cold war took shape in 1945, people who defended the USSR and hailed its role in defeating Hitler and Mussolini in World War II turned against the term as a common definition for all three dictatorships. During the cold war, however, the United States wanted to view the Soviet system as identical to Nazism, while the USSR's defenders now regarded the word *totalitarianism* as cold war propaganda and rejected its use.

Now that the cold war is over, some scholars believe that the term merits rethinking. A totalitarian state, as its definition evolved late in the twentieth century, was one that intensified government's concern with private life and individual thought, leaving no realm of existence outside the state's will. Besides censorship, suppression of parliamentary government, and one-party rule, laws regulating reproduction and family life were also central to totalitarianism. Hitler, Mussolini, Stalin, and later Mao Zedong of China all made state control of reproduction pivotal to their regimes. Totalitarian regimes also relied on violence of various kinds and control of mass communications to define proper ways of thinking and to eliminate enemies, including those who simply had different ideas.

Nonetheless, it is important to note the vast differences among totalitarian states: the socialist economy of the Soviet Union differed from the economies of both Nazi Germany and Fascist Italy. Nationalism was key in the rise of fascism and Nazism, whereas communism began as an international workers' movement and forced people of many ethnicities to live together. Anti-Semitism also infected totalitarian societies in varying degrees: German Nazism had the elimination of the Jews as central to its mission, whereas Italian fascism and Soviet communism did not.

stant struggle, struggle, and struggle" to achieve a Communist society.

In country and city alike, politics influenced work. Stalin demanded more output from industry and more grain from peasants both to feed the urban workforce and to provide exports whose sale abroad would finance industrialization. Some peasants resisted government demands by withholding produce from the market, prompting Stalin to demand a "liquidation of the kulaks." The word *kulak*, which literally means "fist," was a negative term for prosperous peasants, but in practice it applied to anyone who opposed Stalin's plans to end independent farming. Party workers began searching villages, seizing grain, and forcing villagers to identify the kulaks among them. Propagandists followed to stir up hatred. One Russian remembered believing the kulaks were "bloodsuckers, cattle, swine, loathsome, repulsive: they had no souls; they stank." Denounced as "enemies of the state," whole families were robbed of their possessions, left to starve, or even murdered outright. Confiscated kulak land formed the basis for the new collective farms, or kolkhoz, where the remaining peasants were forced to share facilities and modern machinery. Traditional peasant life was brought to a violent end.

Transforming Society. Once the state had defined work life as central to communism, economic failure took on political meaning. Such failure was common because factory workers, farmers, and party officials alike were too inexperienced with advanced industrialization to meet quotas. The experiment with collectivization, combined with the murder of farmers, resulted in a drop in the grain harvest from 83 million tons in 1930 to 67 million in 1934. Soviet citizens starved. Blaming failure on "wreckers" deliberately plotting against communism, Stalin instituted **purges**—that is, state violence in the form of widespread arrests, imprisonments in labor camps, and executions—to rid society of these "villains." The purges touched all segments of society, beginning with engineers who were condemned for causing low productivity.

Beginning in 1936, the government charged prominent Bolshevik leaders with conspiring to overthrow Soviet rule. In a series of "show trials"—trials based on trumped-up charges, fabricated evidence, and coerced confessions—Bolshevik leaders were tortured and forced to

---

purges: The series of attacks on citizens of the USSR accused of being "wreckers," or saboteurs of communism, in the 1930s and later.

confess in court. Most of those found guilty were shot. Some of the top leaders accepted their fate, seeing the purges as good for the future of socialism. Just before his execution, one Bolshevik loyalist and former editor of the party newspaper *Pravda* wrote to Stalin praising the "great and bold political idea behind the general purge" that was clearly part of achieving communist democracy. While there was resistance to Stalin, there were also sincere believers who sought to please their cruel master and serve his noble work.

The spirit of purge swept through society, eventually reaching the Soviet power structure. One woman poet described the scene in towns and cities: "Great concert and lecture halls were turned into public confessionals. . . . People did penance for [everything]. . . . Beating their breasts, the 'guilty' would lament that they had 'shown political short-sightedness' and 'lack of vigilance' . . . and were full of 'rotten liberalism.'" In 1937 and 1938, military leaders were arrested and executed without public trials; some ranks were entirely wiped out. Although the massacre of military leaders appeared suicidal at a time when Hitler threatened war, thousands of high military posts became open to new talent. Stalin would not have to worry about an officer corps wedded to old ideas, as had happened in World War I. Simultaneously, the government expanded the system of prison camps, founded under Lenin, into an extensive network stretching several thousand miles from Moscow to Siberia. Called the Gulag—an acronym for the government department that ran the camps—the system held millions of prisoners under lethal conditions. Prisoners aided the economy by doing every kind of work from digging canals to building apartment buildings. Some one million died annually as a result of the harsh conditions, which included insufficient food, inadequate housing, and twelve- to sixteen-hour days of crushing physical labor. Regular beatings and murders of prisoners rounded out Gulag life, as it too became another aspect of totalitarian violence.

The 1930s marked an end to toleration in Soviet social life, as social and sexual freedom began to disappear. As in the rest of Europe, the birthrate in the USSR declined rapidly in the 1930s. The Soviet Union also needed to replace the millions of people lost since 1914. To meet this need, Stalin restricted access to birth-control information and abortion. More lavish wedding ceremonies came back into fashion, divorces became difficult to obtain, and the state made homosexuality a crime. Whereas Bolsheviks had once attacked the family as a capitalist institution, propaganda now referred to the family as a "school for socialism." At the same time, women in rural areas made gains in literacy and received improved health care. Positions in the lower ranks of the party opened to women as the purges continued, and more women were accepted into the professions. However, women in the industrial workforce faced new and increased stress. After long hours in factories, workingwomen stood in lines for scarce consumer goods and still performed all household and child-care tasks.

Avant-garde experimentation in the arts ended under Stalin. He called artists and writers "engineers of the soul" and, thus recognizing their influence, controlled their output through the Union of Soviet Writers. The union not only assigned housing, office space, equipment, and secretarial help but also determined the types of books authors could write. In return, the "comrade artist" adhered to the official style of "socialist realism," derived from the 1920s focus on the common worker as a social hero. Although some writers and artists went underground, secretly creating works that are still coming to light, many others found ways to adjust their talents to the state's demands. The composer Sergei Prokofiev, for example, composed scores both for the delightful *Peter and the Wolf* and for Sergei Eisenstein's 1938 film *Alexander Nevsky*, a work that flatteringly compared Stalin to the medieval rulers of the Russian people. Aided by adaptable artists, workers, and bureaucrats, Stalin stood triumphant as the 1930s drew to a close. He was, as two different workers put it, "our beloved Leader" and "a god on earth."

Hitler's Rise to Power

A different but ultimately no less violent system emerged when **Adolf Hitler** (1889–1945) put an end to democracy in Germany. Since the early 1920s, he had harangued the German masses to destroy the Weimar Republic and drummed at a message of anti-Semitism and the rebirth of the German "race." When the Great Depression struck Germany in 1929, his Nazi Party began to outstrip its rivals in elections, thanks in part to financial support from big business. Other influential businesspeople, such as film and press tycoon Alfred Hugenberg, boosted Hitler in other ways. Hugenberg's press relentlessly slammed the Weimar government, blaming it for the disastrous economy

Adolf Hitler (1889–1945): Chancellor of Germany who, with considerable backing, overturned democratic government, created the Third Reich, persecuted millions, and ultimately led Germany and the world into World War II.

and for the loss of German pride after World War I. Nazi supporters took to the streets, attacking young Communist groups who agitated just as loudly on behalf of the new Soviet experiment. Hugenberg's press always reported such incidents as the work of Communist thugs who had assaulted blameless Nazis, thus building sympathy for the Nazis among the middle classes.

Parliamentary government ground to a halt during the depression, adding to the social disorder. The Reichstag, or German assembly, failed to approve emergency plans to improve the economy, first because its members disagreed over policies and second because Nazi and Communist deputies disrupted its sessions. The failure to act discredited democracy among the German people. Hitler's followers made parliamentary government look even worse — incapable of providing basic law and order — by rampaging unchecked through the streets and attacking Jews, Communists, and Social Democrats. By targeting all these as a single, monolithic group of "Bolshevik" enemies, the Nazis won wide approval. Hitler was seen as fearlessly confronting those responsible for the depression. Many thought it was time to replace democratic government with a bold new leader who would take on these enemies militarily, without concern for constitutions, laws, or individual rights.

Every age group and class of people supported Hitler, though like Stalin, he especially attracted young people. In 1930, 70 percent of Nazi Party members were under forty. Full of idealism, the young had faith that a better world was possible if Hitler took control. The largest number of supporters came from the industrial working class, but many white-collar workers and members of the lower-middle class also joined the party in percentages out of proportion with their numbers in the population. The inflation that had wiped out savings left them especially bitter and open to Hitler's rhetoric. In the deepening economic crisis, the Nazi Party, which had received little more than 2 percent of the vote in 1928, won almost 20 percent in the Reichstag elections of 1930 and more than twice that in 1932.

Hitler used modern propaganda techniques to build up his following. Nazi Party members passed out thousands of recordings of Hitler's speeches and other Nazi mementos to German citizens. Teenagers painted their fingernails with swastikas, and soldiers flashed metal match covers with Nazi insignia. Nazi rallies were carefully planned displays in which Hitler captivated the crowds, who saw him as their strong, vastly superior *Führer*, or

Toys Depicting Nazis
As a totalitarian ideology, Nazism was part of everyday life. Nazi insignia decorated clothing, dishes, cigarette lighters, and even fingernails. People sent young people to Nazi clubs and organizations and bought Nazi toys like these for their children's playtime. Nazi songs, Nazi parades and festivals, and Nazi radio programs filled leisure hours.
(Imperial War Museum, London.)

"leader." Frenzied and inspirational, he seemed neither a calculating politician nor a wooden bureaucrat but a "creative element," as one poet put it. In actuality, however, Hitler regarded the masses with contempt, and in *Mein Kampf* he discussed how to deal with them:

> The receptivity of the great masses is very limited, their intelligence is small. In consequence of these facts, all effective propaganda must be limited to a very few points and must harp on those in slogans until the last member of the public understands what you want him to understand.

Hitler's media techniques were to endure, influencing today's political style — some believe — of sound bites and simple, often hate-filled and threatening, messages.

In the 1932 Reichstag elections, both Nazis and Communists did very well, making the leader of one of these two parties the logical choice as chancellor. Influential conservative politicians loathed the Communists for their opposition to private property and favored Hitler as someone they could easily control. When he was invited to become chancellor in January 1933, Hitler accepted.

The Nazification of German Politics

Millions celebrated Hitler's ascent to power. "My father went down to the cellar and brought up our best bottles of wine. . . . And my mother wept for joy," one German recalled. "Now everything will be all right," she said. Tens of thousands of Hitler's paramilitary supporters, called storm troopers (SA or Stürmabteilung), paraded through the streets with blazing torches. Instead of being easy to control, Hitler took command brutally, quickly closing down representative government with an ugly show of force.

Terror in the Nazi State. Within a month of Hitler's taking power, the Nazi state was in place. When the Reichstag building was gutted by fire in February 1933, Nazis used the fire as the excuse for suspending civil rights, censoring the press, and prohibiting meetings of other political parties. Hitler had always claimed to hate democracy and diverse political opinions. "Our opponents complain that we National Socialists, and I in particular, are intolerant," he declared. "They are right, we are intolerant! I have set myself one task, namely to sweep those parties out of Germany."

The SA's political violence became a way of life, silencing many democratic politicians. At the end of March, intimidated Reichstag delegates let pass the **Enabling Act**, which suspended the constitution for four years and allowed Nazi laws to take effect without parliamentary approval. Solid middle-class Germans approved the Enabling Act as a way to advance the creation of a *Volksgemeinschaft* ("people's community") of like-minded, racially pure Germans — Aryans in Nazi terminology. Heinrich Himmler headed the elite Schutzstaffel (SS), an organization that protected Hitler, and he commanded the Reich's political police system. The Gestapo, the political police force run by Hermann Goering, also enforced complete obedience to Nazism. These organizations had vast powers to arrest people and either execute them or imprison them in concentration camps, the first of which opened at Dachau, near Munich, in March 1933. The Nazis filled it and later camps with political enemies like socialists, and then with Jews, homosexuals, and others said to interfere

---

Enabling Act: The legislation passed in 1933 suspending constitutional government for four years in order to meet the crisis in the German economy.

with the Volksgemeinschaft. As one Nazi leader proclaimed:

> [National socialism] does not believe that one soul is equal to another, one man equal to another. It does not believe in rights as such. It aims to create the German man of strength, its task is to protect the German people, and all . . . must be subordinate to this goal.

Hitler deliberately blurred authority in the government and party to encourage confusion and competition. He then settled disputes, often with violence. When Ernst Roehm, leader of the SA and Hitler's longtime collaborator, called for a "second revolution" to end the business and military elites' continuing influence on top Nazis, Hitler ordered Roehm's assassination. The bloody Night of the Long Knives (June 30, 1934), during which hundreds of SA leaders and innocent civilians were killed, enhanced Hitler's support among conservatives. They saw that he would deal ruthlessly with those favoring a leveling-out of social privilege. Nazism's terrorist politics served as the foundation of Hitler's Third Reich, which succeeded the First Reich of Charlemagne and the Second Reich of Bismarck and William II.

Nazi Economic and Social Programs. Like violence, new economic programs, especially those putting people back to work, were crucial to the survival of Hitler's regime. Economic revival built popular support, strengthened military industries, and provided the basis for German expansion. The Nazi government pursued **pump priming**—that is, stimulating the economy through public works programs such as building the Autobahn, or highway system, and military spending on the production of tanks and airplanes. Unemployment declined from a peak of almost 6 million in 1932 to 1.6 million by 1936. As labor shortages began to appear in certain areas, the government drafted single women into forced service as farmworkers and domestics. The Nazi Party closed down labor unions, and government managers determined work procedures and set pay levels, rating women's jobs lower than men's regardless of the level of expertise required. Imitating Stalin, Hitler announced a four-year plan in 1936 with the secret aim of preparing Germany for war by 1940. His programs produced large budget deficits, but he was already planning to conquer and loot neighboring countries in order to fill the German treasury.

The Nazi government set policies to control everyday life, including gender roles. In June 1933, a bill took effect that encouraged Aryans (those people defined as racially German) to marry and have children. The bill provided for loans to Aryan newlyweds, but only to couples in which the wife left the workforce. The loans were forgiven on the birth of the pair's fourth child. The ideal woman gave up her job, gave birth to many children, and completely surrendered her will to that of men, allowing her husband to feel powerful despite military defeat and economic depression. A good wife "joyfully sacrifices and fulfills her fate," as one Nazi leader explained.

The government also controlled culture, destroying the rich creativity of the Weimar years. Although 70 percent of households had radios by 1938, programs were severely censored. Books like Erich Maria Remarque's *All Quiet on the Western Front* were banned, and in May 1933 a huge bookburning ceremony rid libraries of works by Jews, socialists, homosexuals, and modernist writers. Modern art in museums and private collections was either destroyed or confiscated. In the Hitler Youth, a mandatory organization for boys and girls over age ten, children learned to report those adults they suspected of disloyalty to the regime, even their own parents. People boasted that they could leave their bicycles out at night without fear of robbery, but their world was also filled with informers—some 100,000 of them on the Nazi payroll. In general, the improved economy led many to believe that Hitler was working an economic miracle while restoring pride in Germany and the harmonious community of an imaginary past. For hundreds of thousands if not millions of Germans, however, Nazi rule in the 1930s brought anything but harmony and community.

Nazi Racism

The Nazis defined Jews as an inferior "race" dangerous to the superior Aryan or Germanic "race" and responsible for most of Germany's problems, including defeat in World War I and the economic depression. Hitler's reasons for targeting Jews were, he insisted, scientific. "National Socialism is a cool and highly reasoned approach to reality based on the greatest of scientific knowledge," he declared in a 1938 speech. Hitler attacked many ethnic and social groups, but he took anti-Semitism to new and frightening heights. In the rhetoric of Nazism, Jews were "vermin," "abscesses," "parasites," and "Bolsheviks," whom the Germans would have to eliminate to become

---

pump priming: An economic policy used by governments to stimulate the economy through public works programs and other infusions to public funds.

Stalin and Hitler: For and Against

Today Hitler and Stalin are widely regarded as dictators who perpetrated great harm on their societies, especially by causing the deaths of tens of millions of people. In the 1930s, however, there was a division of opinion about these two men even as they rose to be dictators in their countries and beyond.

1. A German against Hitler

Victor Klemperer was a professor of literature and a Protestant, though his father had been a Jewish rabbi. Once Hitler came to power, Klemperer, a veteran of World War I who was married to an "Aryan" woman, found himself unable to publish his writings and dismissed from his teaching position. During the Third Reich, he kept a journal tracking not only his own mounting difficulties but also the emigration, dismissals, poverty, and suicides of his family and friends. He had clear opinions about Hitler, whom he listened to on the radio, and firm beliefs about the Nazis and Communists.

November 11, 1933 . . . more than forty minutes of Hitler. A mostly hoarse, strained, agitated voice, long passages in the whining tone of the sectarian preachers. . . . "Jews!" want to set nations of millions at one another's throat. I want only peace, I have risen from the common people. I want nothing for myself. . . . Etc. in no proper order, impassioned; every sentence mendacious, but I almost believe unconsciously mendacious. The man is a blinkered fanatic. November 14, 1933 . . . All Germany prefers Hitler to the Communists. And I see no difference between either of the two movements; both are materialistic and lead to slavery.

Source: Victor Klemperer, *I Will Bear Witness: A Diary of the Nazi Years, 1933–1941,* trans. Martin Chalmers (New York: Random House, 1998), 41–42.

2. Praise for Hitler

A year after Hitler came to power, Paula Müller-Otfried, a former deputy to the Reichstag who had opposed both communism and liberalism, sent out this New Year's card.

When I wrote a year ago and saw only a glimmer of hope, I could not possibly have believed . . . my plea would be so richly fulfilled. . . . The vast majority of the *Volk* joyfully summoned the national regime, with its drive to purify public life, to combat unemployment, hunger, and need. . . . We prayed and the answer arrived. May God grant our rulers wisdom. May the "steel-hardened man" for whom we cried out a year ago . . . retain his power.

Source: Quoted in Claudia Koonz, *Mothers in the Fatherland: Women, the Family, and Nazi Politics* (New York: St. Martin's, 1987), 234.

3. Hitler in Prayers

Children in Germany recited the following bedtime prayer, addressed not to God but to Hitler. It expressed a clear view of who Hitler was and what he meant to Germany:

Führer, my Führer, sent to me from God, protect and maintain me throughout my life. Thou who has saved Germany from Deepest need, I thank thee today for my daily bread. Remain at my side and never leave me, Führer, my Führer. My Faith. My light. *Heil, mein Führer!*

Source: Quoted in Claudia Koonz, *Mothers in the Fatherland: Women, the Family, and Nazi Politics* (New York: St. Martin's, 1987), 287.

4. Poetry Denouncing the Stalinist Regime

Some artists, such as the poet Anna Akhmatova (1889–1966), refused to accept the Stalinist system, including its direction of writing, music, and painting. While waiting in line in the mid-1930s to visit her son, whom the government had imprisoned, she began composing "Requiem," a poem that is now one of the classics of Russian literature.

INTRODUCTION
This happened when only the dead wore smiles—
They rejoiced at being safe from harm.
. . . .
Stars of death stood overhead,

a true Volksgemeinschaft. By branding the Jews both as evil businessmen and as working-class Bolsheviks, Hitler created an enemy that many segments of the population could hate passionately.

Nazis insisted that terms such as *Aryan* and *Jewish* (a religious category) were scientific racial classifications that could be determined by physical characteristics such as the shape of the nose.

In 1935, the government enacted the **Nuremberg Laws**, legislation that deprived Jews of citizenship and prohibited marriage between Jews and other Germans. Abortions and birth-control information were readily available to outcast groups,

---

Nuremberg Laws: Legislation enacted by the Nazis in 1935 that deprived Jewish Germans of their citizenship and imposed many other hardships on them.

And guiltless Russia, that pariah,
Writhed under boots, all blood-bespattered,
And the wheels of many a black maria.[1]

Source: "Requiem," in Anna Akhmatova, *Poems,* ed. and trans. Lyn Coffin (New York: W. W. Norton, 1983).

5. Defense of the Purges

Playwright Alexander Afinogenov's work interested Stalin, who often wrote comments on the manuscripts of Afinogenov's plays. During the era of the purges, both the Communist Party and the writers' union ousted Afinogenov for seeming to deviate from correct Communist thinking. He was eventually reinstated. Afinogenov kept a diary in these years; in this entry from 1937, he remarks on the value of the purges.

Oh what a gigantic turn: genuine History is upon us, and we are granted the joy of witnessing these turns, when Stalin mercilessly chops off all and everything, all the unfit and weakened, the decaying and empty. . . . — Life has now taken a turn onto the new, the real: in this way and no other will we march forward to genuine Communism. Whoever says otherwise is lying.

Source: Quoted in Jochen Hellbeck, *Revolution on My Mind: Writing a Diary under Stalin* (Cambridge: Harvard University Press, 2006), 304.

6. Stalin as Beneficent Creator

One worker wrote this poem to Stalin and sent it to the Communist Party Congress in 1939.

Heroes grow all over our land.
And if you suddenly ask each one:
"Tell me, who inspired your exploits?"
With a happy smile, he will joyfully reply:
"He who is the creator of all that is wonderful,
The masterful architect, our friend and father
Comrade Stalin. We are Stalin's children."

Source: Lewis Siegelbaum and Andrei Sokolov, eds., *Stalinism as a Way of Life: A Narrative in Documents* (New Haven: Yale University Press, 2000), 207.

---

[1]Police wagon.

1. What are the positive qualities that supporters attribute to Hitler and Stalin?
2. What are the major criticisms of Hitler's and Stalin's opponents?
3. To what do you attribute the different opinions about these dictators?

N. J. Altman, *Anna Akhmatova*
This modernist painting portrays the poet Anna Akhmatova in 1914, when she was a centerpiece of literary salon life in Russia and the subject of several avant-garde portraits. In the 1930s and 1940s, Akhmatova gave poetic voice to Soviet suffering, recording in her verse ordinary people's endurance of purges, deprivation, and warfare. As she encouraged people to resist the Nazis during World War II, Stalin allowed her to revive Russian patriotism instead of socialist internationalism. *(State Russian Museum, St. Petersburg/The Bridgeman Art Library. © Estate of N. J. Altman/RAO, Moscow/VAGA, New York, NY.)*

---

including Jews, Gypsies, Slavs, and mentally or physically disabled people, but were forbidden to women classified as Aryan. In the name of improving the Aryan race, doctors helped organize the T4 project, which used carbon monoxide poisoning and other means to kill large numbers of people — 200,000 handicapped and elderly — late in the 1930s. The murder of the disabled aimed to eliminate those whose disability or "racial inferiority" endangered the Aryans. These murders prepared the way for even larger mass exterminations in the future.

Jews were forced into slave labor, evicted from their apartments, and prevented from buying most clothing and food. In 1938, a Jewish teenager, reacting to such harassment of his parents, killed a German official. In retaliation, Nazis attacked some two hundred synagogues, smashed windows of Jewish-owned stores, ransacked apartments of known or suspected Jews, and threw more than twenty thousand Jews into prisons and camps. The night of November 9–10 became known as Kristallnacht, or the Night of Broken Glass. Faced with this relentless persecution, more than half of Germany's 500,000 Jews had emigrated by the outbreak of World War II in 1939. Their enormous emigration fees helped finance Germany's economic revival, while neighbors and individual Nazis redoubled their anti-Semitism because they got emigrants' jobs and personal property. Identifying a group as a permanent and menacing foe had been an ideological tactic used to bring unity in wartime, but it now became a political and economic tactic in peacetime to build support for Nazism.

> **REVIEW:** What role did violence play in the Soviet and Nazi regimes?

Democracies on the Defensive

Nazism, communism, and fascism offered bold new approaches to modern politics. These ideologies maintained that democracy was effeminate and that it wasted precious time in building consensus among all citizens. Totalitarian leaders' military style of mobilizing the masses made representative government and the democratic values of the United States, France, and Great Britain appear feeble—a sign that these societies were on the decline. The appeal of totalitarianism to citizens of Britain, the United States, France and elsewhere put democracies on the defensive as they aimed to restore the well-being of citizens while still upholding individual rights and the rule of law.

Confronting the Economic Crisis

As the depression wore on through the 1930s, some governments experimented with ways to solve social and economic crises in a democratic fashion. The United States and Sweden were among the most successful in facing the double-barreled assault of economic depression and fascism. Other countries, such as France, had less consistently good results, but its short-lived Popular Front government made antifascism and the preservation of democracy its special cause. In the new nations of eastern Europe, however, the economic crisis took such a toll on individual lives

that parliamentary government and the rule of law often gave way to dictatorship and worse.

The United States.   In the early days of the slump, U.S. president Herbert Hoover opposed direct help to the unemployed and even ordered the army to drive away jobless veterans who had marched on Washington, D.C. With unemployment close to fifteen million, Franklin Delano Roosevelt (1882–1945), the wealthy, patrician governor of New York, defeated Hoover in the presidential election of 1932 on the promise of relief and recovery. Roosevelt, or FDR as he became known, pushed through a torrent of legislation: relief for businesses, price supports for hard-pressed farmers, and public works programs for unemployed youth. The Social Security Act of 1935 set up a fund to which employers and employees contributed. It provided retirement benefits for workers, unemployment insurance, and payments to dependent mothers, their children, and people with disabling physical conditions.

These programs advanced the trend toward the welfare state—that is, a government that guarantees a certain level of economic well-being for individuals and businesses—that was taking shape not only in the United States but elsewhere across the West. Roosevelt's "New Deal" angered businesspeople and the wealthy, who saw it as socialist. But even though the depression remained severe, Roosevelt maintained widespread support. Like other successful politicians of the 1930s, he was an expert at using the new mass media, especially in his series of "fireside chats" broadcast by radio to the American people. In sharp contrast to Mussolini and Hitler, however, Roosevelt's public statements promoted rather than attacked faith in democratic rights and popular government. The participation of First Lady Eleanor Roosevelt sharply contrasted with the antiwoman stance of the fascists, and the Roosevelts as a political team insisted that justice and human rights for all must not be surrendered in difficult times. "We Americans of today . . . are characters in the living book of democracy," Roosevelt told a group of teenagers in 1939. "But we are also its author." Lynchings and other racial violence continued to cause great suffering in the United States during the Roosevelt administration, and the economy did not fully recover. But the president's new programs and media success kept most Americans committed to democracy.

Sweden.   Sweden also developed a coherent program for solving economic and population problems, assigning the government a central role in

A Fireside Chat with FDR
President Franklin Delano Roosevelt
was a master of words, inspiring
Americans during the depression and
World War II. Aware of growing media
power in making politicians look
dynamic, the press never showed
that Roosevelt was actually confined
to a wheelchair (after being
paralyzed by polio). Instead, FDR
became a symbol of U.S. resolve and
might. Here he addresses the nation
on August 23, 1938, over a radio
hookup while Eleanor Roosevelt and
the president's mother, Sarah,
observe — a far different image from
that of Hitler and Mussolini. *(Hulton
Archive/Getty Images.)*

promoting social welfare and economic democracy. Sweden instituted central planning in the
1930s and devalued the currency to make Swedish
exports more attractive on the international market. Thanks to pump-priming programs, Swedish
productivity rose by 20 percent between 1929 and
1935, a time when other democracies were still experiencing decline.

Sweden addressed the population problem
with government programs, but without the
racism and coercion of totalitarianism. Alva
Myrdal, a leading member of parliament, believed
that boosting childbirth depended on both the
economy and individual well-being. It was un-
democratic, she maintained, that "the bearing of a
child should mean economic distress" to parents.
Acting on Myrdal's advice to promote "voluntary
parenthood," the government introduced prenatal
care, free childbirth in a hospital, a food relief program, and subsidized housing for large families. By
the end of the decade, almost 50 percent of all
mothers in Sweden received government aid, most
importantly in the form of a **family allowance** to
help cover the costs of raising children. Long a concern of feminists and other social reformers, support of families became one of the tasks of the

modern state, which became increasingly responsible for citizen welfare in hard times. Because all
families — rural and urban, poor or prosperous —
received these social benefits, there was widespread
approval for developing a welfare state.

Britain and France.   The most powerful democracy, the United States, had withdrawn from world
leadership by refusing to participate in the League
of Nations, leaving Britain and France with greater
responsibility for international peace and well-
being than their postwar resources could sustain.
When the Great Depression hit, British prime
minister Ramsay MacDonald faced a drop in government income. Though leader of the Labour
Party, he reduced payments to the unemployed,
and Parliament denied unemployment insurance
to women even though they had contributed to
the unemployment fund. To protect jobs, the government imposed huge tariffs on imported goods,
but these only discouraged a revival of international trade and did not relieve British misery.
Finally, in 1933, with the economy continuing to
worsen, the government began to take effective
steps with massive programs of slum clearance,
new housing construction, and health insurance
for the needy. British leaders saw pump-priming
methods of stimulating the economy as untested
and thus resorted to them only when all else had
failed.

---

family allowance: Government funds given to families with children to boost the birthrate in totalitarian and democratic countries alike.

Depression struck later in France, but the country endured a decade of public strife in the 1930s due to severe postwar demoralization and stagnant population growth. Deputies with opposing solutions to the economic crisis frequently came to blows in the Chamber of Deputies, and administrations were voted in and out with dizzying speed. Parisians took to the streets to protest the government's budget cuts, and Nazi-style paramilitary groups flourished, attracting the unemployed, students, and veterans to the cause of ending representative government. In February 1934, the paramilitary groups joined Communists and other outraged citizens in riots around the parliament building. "Let's string up the deputies," chanted the crowd. "And if we can't string them up, let's beat in their faces, let's reduce them to a pulp." Hundreds of demonstrators were wounded and killed, but the antirepublican right, despite its promises that ending democracy would restore prosperity, lacked both substantial support outside Paris and a charismatic leader like Hitler or Mussolini.

Shocked into action by fascist violence, French liberals, socialists, and Communists established an antifascist coalition known as the **Popular Front**. Until that time, such a merging of groups had been impossible because Stalin directed Communist parties in European democracies not to cooperate with liberals and socialists, who opposed Communist-style revolution. As fascism spread throughout Europe, however, Stalin reversed himself and allowed Communists to join efforts to protect democracy. For just over a year in 1936–1937 and again briefly in 1938, the French Popular Front led the government, with the socialist leader Léon Blum as premier. Like the American New Dealers and the Swedish reformers, the Popular Front instituted social-welfare programs, including family subsidies. Blum appointed women to his government (though women still were not allowed to vote). In June 1936, the government guaranteed workers two-week paid vacations, a forty-hour workweek, and the right to collective bargaining. Working people would long remember Blum as the man who improved their living standards and provided them with the right to vacations.

During its brief life, the Popular Front offered the masses a youthful but democratic political culture. "In 1936 everyone was twenty years old," one man recalled, evoking the atmosphere of idealism.

Popular Front: An alliance of political parties (initially led by Léon Blum in France) in the 1930s to resist fascism despite philosophical differences.

To express their opposition to fascism, citizens celebrated democratic holidays like Bastille Day with new enthusiasm. But not everyone liked the Popular Front, and despite the support from workers, Léon Blum's government was politically weak. Fearing for their investments, bankers and industrialists sent their money out of the country, leaving France financially strapped. "Better Hitler than Blum" was the slogan of the upper classes. Blum's government fell when it lost crucial support for refusing to aid the fight against fascism in Spain. Because of antiwar sentiment, France, like Britain, kept military budgets small and refused any form of military confrontation, even to help the cause of republican government in Spain. The collapse of the antifascist Popular Front showed the difficulties that democratic societies had facing economic crisis and the revival of militarism.

Central and Eastern Europe. Fledgling democracies in central Europe, hit hard by the depression, also fought the twin struggle for economic survival and representative government, but with little success. In 1932, Engelbert Dollfuss came to power in Austria, dismissing the parliament and ruling briefly as a dictator. Despite his authoritarian stance, Dollfuss would not submit to the Nazis, who stormed his office and assassinated him in 1934 in an unsuccessful coup attempt. In Hungary, where outrage over the Peace of Paris remained intense, a crippled economy allowed right-wing general Gyula Gömbös to take over in 1932. Gömbös reoriented his country's foreign policy toward Mussolini and Hitler. He stirred up anti-Semitism and ethnic hatreds and left considerable pro-Nazi feeling after his death in 1936. In democratic Czechoslovakia, the Slovaks, who were both poorer and less educated than the urbanized Czechs, built a strong Slovak Fascist Party. In many of the new states created by the Peace of Paris, ethnic tensions simmered and the appeal of fascism grew during the Great Depression.

Cultural Visions in Hard Times

Responding to the crisis of hard times and political menace, cultural leaders produced art that captured the spirit of everyday struggle. Some empathized with the situations of factory workers, homemakers, and shopgirls straining to support themselves and their families; others looked to interpret the lives of an ever-growing number of unemployed and destitute. Artists portrayed the inhuman, regimented side of modern life. In 1931, French director René Clair's film *Give Us Liberty* related the routine of prison to work on a factory assembly line. In the film *Modern Times* (1936), the Little Tramp character created by **Charlie Chaplin** is a factory worker so molded by his monotonous job that he assumes anything he can see, even a coworker's body, needs mechanical adjustment.

Media sympathy poured out to victims of the economic crisis, with women portrayed alternately as the cause and as the cure for society's problems. *The Blue Angel* (1930), a German film starring Marlene Dietrich, contrasted a powerfully seductive woman with an impractical, bumbling professor, showing how mixed-up gender roles could destroy men—and civilization. Such films worked to strengthen fascist claims. In comedies and musicals, by comparison, heroines behaved bravely, pulling their men out of the depths of despair and setting things right again. In such films as *Keep Smiling* (1938), the British comedienne Gracie Fields portrayed spunky working-class women who remained cheerful despite the challenges of living in hard times. Two years later, Chaplin mocked Hitler in his classic satire *The Great Dictator* (1940), which sympathetically took a beleaguered Jewish woman as its heroine.

To drive home their antifascist, pacifist, or pro-worker beliefs, writers created realistic studies of human misery and the threat of war that haunted life in the 1930s. The British writer George Orwell described his experiences among the poor of Paris and London, wrote investigative pieces about the unemployed in the north of England, and published an account of atrocities committed by both sides during the Spanish Civil War (1936–1939). German writer Thomas Mann was so outraged at Hitler's ascent to power that he went into voluntary exile. Mann's series of novels based on the Old Testament hero Joseph convey

Gracie Fields Keeps Smiling
Like Roosevelt and many cultural leaders during the Great Depression, British star Gracie Fields in the hit film *Shipyard Sally* (1939) urged viewers to be courageous and maintain their respect as workers and citizens despite hard times. This was in stark contrast to fascist advocacy of conquest, war, and violence toward neighbors at home and abroad. *(20th Century Fox/The Kobal Collection.)*

the struggle between humane values and barbarism. The fourth volume, *Joseph the Provider* (1944), praised Joseph's welfare state, in which the granaries were full and the rich paid taxes so that the poor might live decent lives. In *Three Guineas* (1938), one of her last works, English writer Virginia Woolf attacked militarism, poverty, and the oppression of women, claiming they were interconnected parts of a single, devastating ethos undermining Europe in the 1930s.

While writers rekindled moral concerns, scientists in research institutes and universities pointed out limits to human understanding—limits that seemed at odds with the megalomaniacal pronouncements of dictators. Astronomer Edwin Hubble in California determined in the early 1930s that the universe was an expanding entity and thus an unpredictably changing one. Czech mathematician Kurt Gödel maintained that all mathematical systems contain some propositions that are undecidable. The German physicist Werner Heisenberg

---

Charlie Chaplin (1889–1977): Major entertainment leader, whose satires of Hitler and sympathetic portrayals of the common man helped preserve democratic values.

developed the uncertainty, or indeterminacy, principle in physics. Scientific observation of atomic behavior, according to this theory, itself disturbs the atom and thereby makes precise formulations impossible. Even scientists, Heisenberg asserted, had to settle for statistical probability. Approximation, probability, and limits to understanding were not concepts that military dictators welcomed, and even people in democracies had a difficult time reconciling these new ideas with science's reputation for certainty.

Religious leaders helped foster a spirit of resistance to dictatorship among the faithful. Some prominent clergymen hoped for a re-Christianization of ordinary people so that they might choose religious values rather than fascist ones. The Swiss theologian Karl Barth encouraged opposition to the Nazis, teaching that religious people had to take seriously biblical calls for resistance to oppression. In his 1931 address to the world on social issues, Pope Pius XI (r. 1922–1939) condemned the failure of modern societies to provide their citizens with a decent, moral life. To critics, the proclamation seemed an endorsement of the heavy-handed intervention of the fascists. In Germany, nonetheless, German Catholics opposed Hitler, and religious commitment inspired many other individuals to oppose the rising tide of fascism.

> **REVIEW:** How did the democracies' responses to the twin challenges of economic depression and the rise of fascism differ from those of totalitarian regimes?

THE ROAD TO WORLD WAR II

1929	Global depression begins with U.S. stock market crash
1931	Japan invades Manchuria
1933	Hitler comes to power in Germany
1935	Italy invades Ethiopia
1936	Civil war breaks out in Spain; Hitler remilitarizes the Rhineland
1937	Japan invades China
1938	Germany annexes Austria; European leaders meet in Munich to negotiate with Hitler
1939	Germany seizes Czechoslovakia; Hitler and Stalin sign nonaggression pact; Germany invades Poland; Britain and France declare war on Germany

The Road to Global War

The economic crash intensified competition among the major powers and made external colonies more important than ever. Governments did not let up on the collection of taxes and other charges in the colonies and in some cases increased them to make up for shortfalls at home. As Britain, France, and other imperial powers struggled to protect their holdings, Hitler, Mussolini, and Japan's military leaders believed that their nations deserved to rule a far larger territory as part of their special destiny. At first, statesmen in Britain and France hoped that sanctions imposed by the League of Nations would stop these aggressors. Other people, still traumatized by memories of the past war, turned a blind eye both to Japanese, Italian, and German expansionism and to the fascist attack on the Spanish republic. The unchecked brutality of these states in the 1930s would lead to another, more deadly global war.

A Surge in Global Imperialism

The global imperialism of the 1930s ultimately produced a thoroughly global war. While the French, Dutch, British, and Belgians increased their control over their colonies, in Palestine European Jews continued to arrive and claim the area from local peoples. The numbers of immigrants escalated sharply as Hitler enacted his harsh anti-Jewish policies in 1933 and as people across Europe and Asia felt the impact of the economic slump. To prevent the arrival of Jews in their own countries, the major European states encouraged emigration to Palestine. Local politicians in the region regarded the soaring number of immigrants as a major threat. Hard-pressed like the colonial powers for resources, Japan, Germany, and Italy escalated the competition for land and wealth— both close at hand and far away.

Japan's Expansionism. Japan, which had once borrowed from European institutions to become modern and powerful, now decided to chase Europeans from Asia. Japan's military and business leaders longed to control more of Asia and saw China, Russia, the United States, and other Western powers as obstacles to the empire's prosperity and the fulfillment of its destiny. Japan suffered from a weak monarchy in the person of Hirohito, just twenty-five years old when he became emperor in 1926, leading military and other groups to seek control of the government. Nationalists encouraged these leaders to pursue military success for Japan as the basis of a new world order. They viewed an expanded empire as key to pulling agriculture and small business from the depths of economic depression. Japan's claims to racial superiority and to the right to take the lands of inferior peoples linked it with Germany and Italy in the 1930s. The groundwork was being laid for a powerful global alliance.

The army swung into action in order to make these claims a reality: in September 1931, Japanese officers blew up a railroad train in the Chinese province of Manchuria, where Japanese businesses had invested heavily. Making the explosion look to be a Chinese plot, the army then used the explosion as an excuse to take over the territory totally and, from there, push farther into China (Map 26.1). The Japanese public agreed with journalistic calls for aggressive expansion, and from 1931 on, Japan continued to attack China, angering the United States, on which Japan depended for natural resources and markets. Ideologically, the Japanese military leadership saw itself as fully justified in its expansionism because of unfair Western domination in East Asia. "Unequal distribution of land and resources causes war," an adviser to Hirohito announced to an enthusiastic Japanese public. Advocating Asian conquest as part of Japan's "divine mission," the military extended its influence in the government. By 1936–1937, Japan was spending 47 percent of its budget on arms.

The situation in East Asia affected international politics. Japanese military success added to the threat Japan posed to the West, because the conquest of new regions gave Japanese goods bigger markets in Asia. The League of Nations condemned the invasion of Manchuria, but it imposed no economic sanctions to back up its condemnation. Meanwhile, the public condemnation outraged Japanese citizens and goaded the government to ally with Hitler and Mussolini. In 1937, Japan undertook another major attack on China, justifying its offensive as a first step toward liberating the region from Western imperialism. Hundreds of thousands of Chinese were massacred in the "Rape of Nanjing"—an atrocity so named because of the brutality toward girls and women and other acts of torture perpetrated by the Japanese. President Roosevelt immediately an-

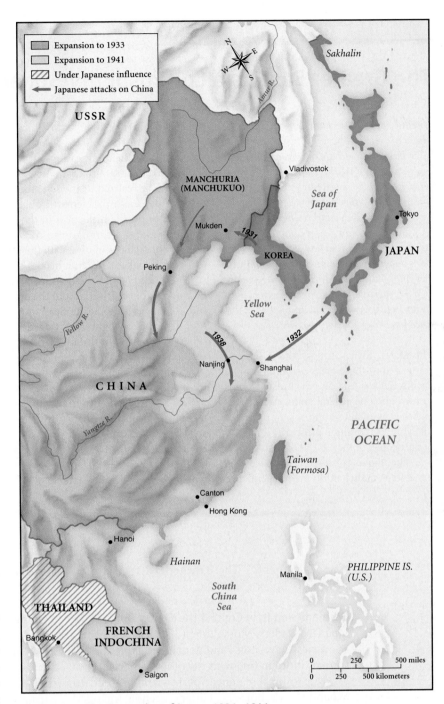

MAP 26.1 The Expansion of Japan, 1931–1941
Japanese expansion in the twentieth century approximated that of Russia and the United States in the nineteenth century: that is, it incorporated neighboring regions of Korea, Taiwan, and Manchuria with the vast area of China an inviting target. Japan's ambition upset the United States's own Pacific goals and made these two powers suddenly become deadly rivals.

nounced an embargo on U.S. export of airplane parts to Japan and later drastically cut the flow of the crucial raw materials that supplied Japanese industry. Nonetheless, the Western powers, including the Soviet Union, did not effectively resist Japan's territorial expansion in Asia and the Pacific

DOCUMENT

The Greater East Asia Co-Prosperity Sphere

During the 1930s, Japan entered a new phase of imperial expansion in the Pacific, after having already taken over Korea and Formosa before World War I. To keep pace with its rapidly developing industrial and military capacities, Japan needed access to raw materials and markets blocked by the U.S. and European powers. Japan justified its expansion in China and other Pacific nations as a move to liberate Asians from Western imperialism and form an independent "Co-Prosperity Sphere" for the region. This secret 1942 government planning paper outlines Japan's expansionist goals.

The states, their citizens, and resources, comprised in those areas pertaining to the Pacific, Central Asia, and the Indian Oceans formed into one general union are to be established as an autonomous zone of peaceful living and common prosperity on behalf of the peoples of the nations of East Asia. . . .

The above purpose presupposes the inevitable emancipation or independence of Eastern Siberia, China, Indo-China, the South Seas, Australia, and India. . . . It is intended that the unification of Japan, Manchoukuo, and China in neighborly friendship be realized by the settlement of the Sino-Japanese problems through the crushing of hostile influences in the Chinese interior, and through the construction of a new China in tune with the rapid construction of the Inner Sphere. Aggressive American and British influences in East Asia shall be driven out of the area of Indo-China and the South Seas, and this area shall be brought into our defense sphere. The war with Britain and America shall be prosecuted for that purpose.

The Russian aggressive influence in East Asia will be driven out. Eastern Siberia shall be cut off from the Soviet regime and included in our defense sphere. For this purpose, a war with the Soviets is expected. It is considered possible that this Northern problem may break out before the general settlement of the present Sino-Japanese and the Southern problems if the situation renders this unavoidable. Next the independence of Australia, India, etc. shall gradually be brought about. For this purpose, a recurrence of war with Britain and her allies is expected. . . . Occidental individualism and materialism shall be rejected and a moral world view, the basic principle of whose morality shall be the Imperial Way, shall be established. The ultimate object to be achieved is not exploitation but co-prosperity and mutual help, not competitive conflict but mutual assistance and mild peace, not a formal view of equality but a view of order based on righteous classification, not an idea of rights but an idea of service, and not several world views but one unified world view.

Source: Ryusaku Tsunoda, William Theodore de Bary, and Donald Keene, *Sources of Japanese Tradition* (New York: Columbia University Press, 1958) 802–3, 805.

(see Document, "The Greater East Asia Co-Prosperity Sphere," above).

Germany and Italy Contest the Status Quo.   Like Japanese leaders, Mussolini and Hitler called their countries "have-nots" and demanded land and resources more in line with the other imperial powers. Mussolini threatened "permanent conflict" to expand Italy's borders. Hitler's agenda included disregarding the Versailles treaty's restrictions and gaining more **Lebensraum**, or living space, in which "superior" Aryans could thrive, and supplanting the "inferior" Slavic peoples and Bolsheviks, who would be moved to Siberia or would serve as slaves. Both dictators portrayed themselves as peace-loving men who resorted to extreme measures only to benefit their country and hu-

manity. Their anticommunism appealed to statesmen across the West, and Hitler's anti-Semitism also had widespread support. Some thus favored giving in to these two dictators' demands to take land at the expense of others.

Both leaders moved to plunder other countries openly and audaciously. In the autumn of 1933, Hitler announced Germany's withdrawal from the League of Nations. In 1935, Hitler loudly rejected the clauses of the Treaty of Versailles that limited German military strength and openly started rearming. (Germany had been rearming in secret for years.) Mussolini also chose 1935 to invade Ethiopia, one of the few African states not overwhelmed by European imperialism. He wanted to demonstrate his regime's youth and vigor and to raise Italy's standing in the world. "The Roman legionnaires are again on the march," one soldier exulted. The poorly equipped Ethiopians resisted, but their capital, Addis Ababa, fell in the spring of 1936. Although the League of

---

Lebensraum: Literally, "living space"; the land that Hitler proposed to conquer so that true Aryans might have sufficient space to live their noble lives.

Nations voted to impose sanctions against Italy, Britain and France opposed an embargo with teeth in it—one on oil—and thus kept the sanctions from being effective while also suggesting a lack of resolve to fight aggression. The fall of Ethiopia and Italy's boastful assertions of African racial inferiority strengthened the resolve of African nationalists.

Profiting from the world's focus on Italy's Ethiopian campaign, in March 1936 Hitler defiantly sent his troops into what was supposed to be a permanently demilitarized zone in the Rhineland bordering France. The inhabitants greeted the Germans with wild enthusiasm, and the French, whose security was most endangered by this action, protested to the League of Nations instead of occupying the region, as they had done in the Ruhr in 1923. The British simply accepted the German military move, and the two dictators thus appeared as powerful heroes forging, in Mussolini's muscular phrase, a "Rome–Berlin Axis." Next to them, the politicians of France and Great Britain looked timid and defeatable.

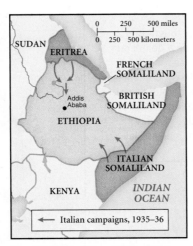

The Ethiopian War, 1935–1936

The Spanish Civil War, 1936–1939

Spain seemed to be headed toward democracy early in the 1930s. In 1931, Spanish republicans overthrew the monarchy and the dictatorship that ruled in its name. For centuries, the Spanish state had backed the domination of large landowners and the Catholic clergy over the countryside. With some cities, like Barcelona and Bilbao, industrializing, these ruling elites kept an impoverished peasantry in their grip, making Spain a country of economic extremes. Urban groups reacted enthusiastically to the end of the dictatorship and began debating the course of change, with Communists, socialists, anarchists, constitutionalists, and other splinter groups all disagreeing on how to create a democratic nation. For republicans, the air was electric with promise. As public debate developed, one woman recalled, people sat for hours dreaming dreams: "We saw a backward country suddenly blossoming out into a modern state. We saw peasants living like decent human beings. We saw men allowed freedom of conscience. We saw life, instead of death, in Spain."

Democratic groups so battled one another to get their way, however, that the republic had a hard

time putting in place a political program that would gain it widespread support in the countryside. Instead of building popular loyalty and reducing the strength of the right wing by enacting land reform, the various antimonarchist factions struggled among themselves to dominate the new government. Although they wanted political and economic modernization, they failed to mount a unified effort against their reactionary opponents. The republicans resorted instead to symbolic acts such as releasing political prisoners and doling out coveted municipal jobs to the urban unemployed. In 1936, pro-republican forces temporarily banded together in a Popular Front coalition to win elections and prevent the republic from collapsing altogether in the face of growing monarchist opposition.

In response to the Popular Front victory, the forces of the right drew closer together, using their considerable wealth to undermine the government. In 1936, a group of army officers led by General **Francisco Franco** (1892–1975) staged an uprising against the republican government in Madrid. The rebels, who included monarchists, landowners, the clergy, and the fascist Falange Party, soon had the help of fascists in other parts of Europe. Citizens—male and female—took up arms in turn on behalf of the republic and formed volunteer fighting units to meet the grave military challenge. In their minds, citizen armies symbolized republicanism, while professional troops followed the aristocratic rebels. As civil war gripped the country, the republicans generally held Madrid, Barcelona, and other commercial and industrial areas. The right-wing rebels took the agricultural west and south (Map 26.2).

Spain became a training ground for World War II. Hitler and Mussolini sent military personnel in support of Franco, gaining the opportunity to test new weapons and to practice the terror bombing of civilians. In 1937, German planes attacked the town of Guernica, mowing down civilians in the streets. This useless slaughter inspired Pablo Picasso's memorial mural to the dead, *Guernica* (1937), in which the intense suffering is

---

Francisco Franco (1892–1975): Right-wing military leader who successfully overthrew the democratic republic in Spain and instituted a repressive dictatorship.

MAP 26.2 The Spanish Civil War, 1936–1939

Republican and antirepublican forces bitterly fought one another to determine whether Spain would be a democracy or an authoritarian state. Germany and Italy sent military assistance to the rebels, notably airplanes to experiment with bombing civilians, while volunteers from around the world arrived to fight for the republic. Defeating the ill-organized republican groups, General Francisco Franco instituted a pro-fascist government that sent many to jail and into exile.

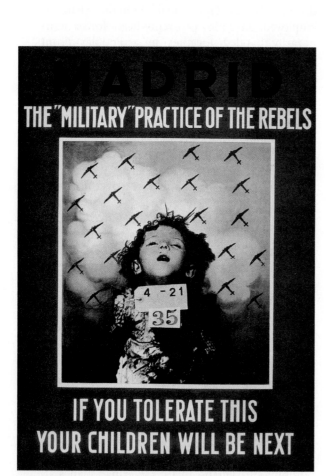

The Spanish Republic Appeals for Aid

The government of the Spanish Republic sent out modernist advertising to attract support from the remaining democracies — especially Great Britain and France. Antiwar sentiment remained high among the British and French, however. Thus, despite the horrifying and deliberate bombing of civilians by Franco's German allies, aid for the republic failed to arrive. *(Imperial War Museum, London.)*

starkly displayed in monochromatic grays and whites. The Spanish republican government appealed everywhere for assistance, but only the Soviet Union answered. Stalin withdrew his troops and tanks in 1938 as the republican ranks floundered, however. Britain and France refused to provide aid despite the outpouring of popular support for the cause of democracy. Instead, a few thousand volunteers from a variety of countries — including many students, journalists, and artists — fought for the republic. With Hitler and Mussolini on a rampage in Europe, "Spain was the place to stop fascism," these volunteers believed. The conflict was bitter and bloody, with widespread atrocities committed on both sides. But the splinter groups and random armies with which the Republic defended itself could not hold, while the aid Franco received ultimately proved decisive. His troops defeated the republicans in 1939, strengthening the cause of military authoritarianism in Europe. Tens of thousands fled Franco's brutal revenge; remaining critics found themselves jailed and worse.

Hitler's Conquest of Central Europe, 1938–1939

The next step toward World War II was Germany's annexation of Austria in 1938. Many Austrians had actually wished for a German-Austrian merger, or *Anschluss*, after the Paris peace settlement stripped them of their empire. So Hitler's troops simply entered Austria, and the elation of Nazi sympathizers among the Austrians made the Anschluss appear an example of the Wilsonian idea of self-determination. The annexation began the so-called unification of Aryan peoples into one greater German nation, and Hitler's seizure of Austria's gold supplies marked the next step in taking over the resources of central and eastern Europe. Austria was declared a German province, and Nazi thugs ruled once-cosmopolitan Vienna. An observer later commented on the scene:

> University professors were obliged to scrub the streets with their naked hands, pious white-bearded Jews were dragged into the synagogue by hooting youths and forced to do knee-exercises and to shout "Heil Hitler" in chorus.

Nazis gained additional support in Austria by solving the stubborn problem of unemployment—especially among the young and out-of-work rural migrants to the cities. Factories sprang up overnight, mostly to foster rearmament, and new "Hitler housing" was made available to workers. "We were given work!" Austrians continued to say long afterward, defending their enthusiasm for the Third Reich. German policies eliminated some of the pain Austrians had suffered when their empire had been reduced to a small country after World War I.

Flush with success, Hitler next targeted Czechoslovakia and its rich resources. Conquering this democracy looked more difficult, however, because Czechoslovakia had a large army, strong border defenses, and efficient armament factories—and most Czech citizens were prepared to fight for their country. The Nazi propaganda machine swung into action, accusing Czechoslovakia of persecuting its German minority. By October 1, 1938, Hitler warned, Czechoslovakia would have to grant autonomy (amounting to Nazi rule) to the German-populated border region, the Sudetenland, or face German invasion.

Hitler gambled correctly that the other Western powers would not interfere, for as the October deadline approached, British prime minister Neville Chamberlain, French premier Edouard Daladier, and Mussolini met with Hitler at Munich and agreed not to oppose Germany's claim to the Sudetenland. The strategy of preventing a war by making concessions for grievances (in this case, the supposed insult to Germans in the Peace of Paris) was called **appeasement**. At the time, these concessions were widely seen as positive, and the Munich Pact among Germany, Great Britain, France,

and Italy prompted Chamberlain to announce that he had secured "peace in our time." Having portrayed himself as a man of peace, Hitler waited until March 1939 to invade the rest of Czechoslovakia (Map 26.3). Britain and France responded by promising military support to Poland, Romania, Greece, and Turkey in case of Nazi invasion. In May 1939, Hitler and Mussolini countered this agreement by signing a pledge of mutual support called the Pact of Steel.

Some historians have sharply criticized the Munich Pact because it bought Hitler time to build his army and seemed to give him the green light for further aggression. They believe that a confrontation might have stopped Hitler and that even if war had resulted, the democracies would have triumphed at less cost than they later did. According to this view, each military move by Germany, Italy, and Japan should have been met with stiff opposition, and the Soviet Union should have been made a partner to this resistance. Others counter that appeasement provided France and Britain precious time to beef up their own armies, which the Munich Pact caused them to begin doing.

Stalin, excluded from the Munich deliberations, saw that the democracies were not going to fight to protect eastern Europe. He took action. To the astonishment of public opinion in the West, on August 23, 1939, Germany and the USSR signed a nonaggression agreement. The **Nazi-Soviet Pact** provided that if one country became embroiled in war, the other country would remain neutral. Moreover, the two dictators secretly agreed to divide Poland and the Baltic States—Latvia, Estonia, and Lithuania—at some future date. The Nazi-Soviet Pact ensured that, should war come, the democracies would be fighting a Germany that feared no attack on its eastern borders. The pact also benefited the USSR. Despite Hitler's threats to wipe Bolshevism off the face of the earth, the pact allowed Stalin extra time to reconstitute his officer corps destroyed in the purges. In the belief that Great Britain and perhaps even France would continue not to resist him, Hitler now moved to enlarge his empire further and aimed his forces at Poland. The contest for territory and resources was set to become another world war.

> **REVIEW:** How did the aggression of Japan, Germany, and Italy create the conditions for global war?

---

appeasement: The strategy of preventing a war by making concessions for legitimate grievances.

Nazi-Soviet Pact: The agreement reached in 1939 by Germany and the Soviet Union in which both agreed not to attack the other in case of war and to divide any conquered territories.

MAP 26.3 The Growth of Nazi Germany, 1933–1939
German expansion was rapid and surprising, as Hitler's forces and Nazi diplomacy achieved the annexation of several new states of central and eastern Europe. Although committed to defending the independence of these states through the League of Nations, French and British diplomats were more concerned with satisfying Hitler in the mistaken belief that doing so would prevent his claiming more of Europe. In the process, Hitler acquired the human and material resources of adjacent countries to support his Third Reich. ■ What is the relationship between Germany's expansion during the 1930s and the terms of the Treaty of Versailles after World War I?

World War II, 1939–1945

World War II opened when Hitler launched an all-out attack on Poland on September 1, 1939. In contrast to 1914, no jubilation in Berlin accompanied the invasion; when Britain and France declared war two days later, the mood in those nations was similarly grim. Although Japan, Italy, and the United States did not join the battle immediately, their eventual participation spread the fighting and mobilized civilians around the world. By the time World War II ended in 1945, millions were starving; countries lay in ruins; and unparal-

leled atrocities, including technological genocide, had killed six million Jews and six million Slavs, Gypsies, homosexuals, and other civilian enemies of fascism.

The German Onslaught

German ground forces quickly defeated the ill-equipped Polish troops by launching an overpowering **Blitzkrieg** ("lightning war"), in which they

---

Blitzkrieg: Literally, "lightning war"; a strategy for the conduct of war in which motorized firepower quickly and overwhelmingly attacks the enemy, leaving it unable to resist psychologically or militarily.

concentrated airplanes, tanks, and motorized infantry to encircle Polish defenders and capture the capital, Warsaw, with blinding speed. Allowing the army to conserve supplies, Blitzkrieg assured Germans at home that the human costs of gaining Lebensraum would be low. On September 17, 1939, the Soviets invaded Poland from the east. By the end of the month, the Polish army was in shambles and the victors had divided the country according to the Nazi-Soviet Pact. Within the Reich, Hitler sold the war as one of self-defense, especially from what German propagandists called the "warlike menace" of world Jewry.

Hitler ordered an attack on France for November 1939, but his generals, who feared that Germany was ill prepared for total war, convinced him to postpone the offensive until the spring of 1940. In April 1940, the Blitzkrieg crushed Denmark and Norway; the battles of Belgium, the Netherlands, and France followed in May and June. On June 5, Mussolini, eyeing future spoils for Italy, invaded France from the southeast. The French defense and its British allies could not withstand the German onslaught. Trapped on the beaches of Dunkirk in northern France, 370,000 British and French soldiers were rescued in a heroic effort by an improvised fleet of naval ships, fishing boats, and pleasure craft. A dejected French government surrendered on June 22, 1940, leaving Germany to rule the northern half of the country, including Paris. In the south, named Vichy France after the spa town where the government sat, the reactionary and aged World War I hero Henri Philippe Pétain was allowed to govern. Stalin used the diversion in western Europe to annex the Baltic States of Estonia, Latvia, and Lithuania.

Britain now stood alone. Blaming Germany's rapid victories on Chamberlain's policy of appeasement, the British swept him out of office and installed as prime minister Winston Churchill (1874–1965), an early advocate of resistance to Hitler. After Hitler ordered the bombardment of Britain in the summer of 1940, Churchill rallied the nation by radio — now in millions of British homes — to protect the ideals of liberty with their "blood, toil, tears, and sweat." In the battle of Britain — or Blitz, as the British called it — the German Luftwaffe (air force) bombed monuments, public buildings,

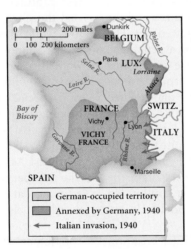

The Division of France, 1940

weapons depots, and industry. Using the wealth of its colonies, Britain poured resources into antiaircraft weapons, its highly successful code-detecting group called Ultra, and development of its advantage in radar. At year's end, the British air industry was outproducing that of the Germans by 50 percent.

By the fall of 1940, German air losses forced Hitler to abandon his plan for a naval invasion of Britain. Forcing Hungary, Romania, and Bulgaria to ally with him, Hitler gained access to their food, oil, and other resources. He then made his fatal decision to attack the Soviet Union — the "center of judeobolshevism," he called it. In June 1941, the German army crossed the Soviet border, breaking the Nazi-Soviet Pact while Hitler boasted of "razing Moscow and Leningrad to the ground." Three million German and other troops quickly penetrated Soviet lines along a two-thousand-mile front, and by July, the German army had rolled to within two hundred miles of Moscow. Using a strategy of rapid encirclement, German troops killed, captured, or wounded more than half the 4.5 million Soviet soldiers defending the borders.

Amid success, Hitler blundered. Considering himself a military genius and the Slavic people inferior, he proposed attacking Leningrad, the Baltic States, and the Ukraine simultaneously, whereas his generals wanted to concentrate on Moscow. Hitler's grandiose strategy wasted precious time without achieving a decisive victory, and driven by Stalin and local party members, the Soviet people fought back. The onset of winter turned Nazi soldiers to frostbitten wretches because Hitler had feared that equipping his army for Russian conditions would suggest to civilians that a long campaign lay in store, as in fact it did. Yet Hitler remained so convinced of imminent victory in the USSR that he switched German production from making tanks and artillery to making battleships and airplanes for war beyond the Soviet Union. Consequently, Germany's poorly supplied armies succumbed not only to the weather but also to a shortage of equipment. As the war became worldwide, Germany had an inflated view of its power and a poorly calculated understanding of wartime reality.

War Expands: The Pacific and Beyond

With the outbreak of war in Europe, Japan took territories of the British Empire, bullied the Dutch in Indonesia, and invaded French Indochina to procure raw materials for its industrial and military expansion. The militarist Japanese government then decided that it should settle matters with the United States, which was blocking Japan's access to technology and resources in an attempt to stop its expansionism, and launched an all-out attack on the United States at Pearl Harbor in Hawaii on December 7, 1941. After bombing Pearl Harbor, Japanese planes then decimated a fleet of airplanes in the Philippines. Roosevelt summoned the U.S. Congress to declare war on Japan. By the spring of 1942, the Japanese had conquered Guam, the Philippines, Malaya, Burma, Indonesia, Singapore, and much of the southwestern Pacific. Like Hitler's early conquests, the Japanese victories strengthened the military's confidence: "The era of democracy is finished," the foreign minister announced. Officials marketed Emperor Hirohito to the region as the pan-Asian monarch who would liberate Asians everywhere.

Germany quickly joined its Japanese ally and declared war on the United States — an enemy, Hitler proclaimed, that was "half Judaized and the other half Negrified." Mussolini followed suit. The United States was not prepared for a prolonged struggle at the time, partly because isolationist sentiment remained strong: its armed forces numbered only 1.6 million, and no plan existed for producing the necessary guns, tanks, and airplanes. Also, the United States and the Soviet Union mistrusted each other. Yet despite these obstacles to cooperation, Hitler's four enemies came together in the Grand Alliance of Great Britain, the Free French (an exile government in London led by General Charles de Gaulle), the Soviet Union, and the United States.

The Grand Alliance and the larger coalition with twenty other countries — known collectively as the Allies — had to overcome animosity and competing interests in their struggle against the Axis powers — Germany, Italy, and Japan. Yet in the long run, the Allies had real advantages. Their manpower and resources were greater than those of the Axis powers, and the extensive terrain the Allies controlled gave them access to more goods from around the world. The globalization of the war brought into play Britain's traditional naval strength and its leaders' and troops' experience in combat on many continents. Meeting frequently, Allied leaders worked hard to wage effective war against the Axis powers, whose rulers were fanatically committed to global conquest at any price.

The War against Civilians

Far more civilians than soldiers died in World War II. The Axis powers and Allies alike bombed cities to destroy civilian will to resist — a tactic that seemed to backfire by inspiring defiance rather than surrender. Allied firebombing of Dresden and Tokyo were but two instances that killed tens of thousands of civilians, but Axis attacks far outweighed these. The British people, not British soldiers, were the target of the battle of Britain, and as the German army swept through eastern Europe, it slaughtered Jews, Communists, Slavs, and others Nazi ideology deemed "racial inferiors" and enemies. In Poland, the SS murdered hundreds of thousands of Polish citizens or relocated them in forced-labor camps. Confiscated Polish land and homes were given to "racially pure" Aryans from Germany and other central European countries. Literate people in conquered areas were the most vulnerable, because Hitler, like Stalin, saw them as leading members of the civil society that he wanted to destroy. A ploy of the Nazis was to test captured people's reading skills, suggesting that those who could read would be given clerical jobs while those who could not would be relegated to hard labor. Those who could read, however, were lined up and shot. Because many in the German army initially rebelled at this inhuman mission, special Gestapo forces took up the charge of herding their victims into woods, to ravines, or even against town walls where they would be shot en masse. The Japanese did the same in China, southeast Asia, and on the islands in the Pacific. The number of casualties in China alone has been estimated at thirty million, with untold millions murdered elsewhere.

The Holocaust.   On the eve of war in 1939, Hitler had predicted "the destruction of the Jewish race in Europe." The Nazis' initial plan for reducing the Jewish population included herding Jews into urban ghettos, stripping them of their possessions, and making people live on minimal rations until they died of starvation or disease. There was also direct murder. Around Soviet towns, Jews were usually shot in pits, some of which they had been forced to dig themselves. After making people shed their clothes, which were put in ordered piles for later use, the Nazis killed ten thousand or more at a time, often with the help of local anti-Semitic people. In Jedwabne, Poland, and surrounding towns in 1941, some eight hundred citizens on their own initiative beat and burned their Jewish neighbors to death and took their property — evidence that the Holocaust was not simply a Nazi initiative. However, the "Final Solution" — the Nazis' diabolical plan to murder all of Europe's Jews systematically — was not yet fully under way.

A more organized, technological system for rounding up Jews and transporting them to extermination sites had taken shape by the fall of 1941. Although no clear order written by Hitler exists, his responsibility for it is clear: he discussed the Final Solution's progress, issued oral directives for it, and made violent anti-Semitism a basis for Nazism from the beginning. Efficient scientists, doctors, lawyers, and government workers also made the Holocaust work. Six camps in Poland were developed specifically for the purposes of mass murder, though some, like Auschwitz-Birkenau, served as both extermination and labor camps (Map 26.4). Using techniques developed in the T4 project, which killed disabled and elderly people, the camp at Chelmno first gassed Christian Poles and Soviet prisoners of war. Specially designed crematoria for the mass burning of corpses started functioning in 1943. By then, Auschwitz had the capacity to burn 1.7 million bodies per year. About 60 percent of new arrivals — particularly children, women, and old people — were selected for immediate murder in the gas chambers; the other 40 percent labored until, utterly used up, they too were gassed.

MAP 26.4 Concentration Camps and Extermination Sites in Europe
This map shows the major extermination sites and concentration camps in Europe, but the entire continent was dotted with thousands of lesser camps to which the victims of Nazism were transported. Some of these lesser camps were merely way stations on the path to ultimate extermination. In focusing on the major camps, historians often lose sight of the ways in which evidence of deportation and extermination blanketed Europe.

Death and Life in the Camps.

Victims from all over Europe were sent to extermination camps. In the ghettos of various European cities, councils of Jewish leaders, such as the one in Amsterdam where Etty Hillesum worked, were ordered to determine those to be "resettled in the east" — a phrase used to mask the Nazis' true plans. For weakened, poorly armed ghetto inhabitants, open resistance meant certain death. When Jews rose up against their Nazi captors in Warsaw in 1943, they were mercilessly butchered. The Nazis also took pains to cloak the purpose of the extermination camps. Bands played to greet incoming trainloads of victims; some new arrivals were given postcards with reassuring messages to mail home. Survivors later noted that the purpose of the camps was so unthinkable that potential victims could not begin to imagine that they were to be killed en masse. Those not chosen for immediate murder had their heads shaved, were showered and disinfected, and were then given prison garments — many of them used and so thin that they offered no protection

against winter cold and rain. So began life in "a living hell," as one survivor wrote.

The camps were scenes of struggle for life in the face of torture and death. Instead of the minimum two thousand calories needed to keep an adult alive, overworked inmates usually received less than five hundred calories per day, leaving them vulnerable to the diseases that swept through the camps. Prisoners sometimes went mad, as did many of the guards. In the name of advancing "racial science," doctors performed unbelievably cruel medical experiments with no anesthesia on pregnant women, twins, and other innocent people. Despite the harsh conditions, however, some people maintained their spirit: prisoners forged new friendships, and women in particular observed religious holidays and celebrated birthdays — all of which helped the struggle for survival. Thanks to those sharing a bread ration, wrote the Auschwitz survivor Primo Levi, "I managed not to forget that I myself was a man." In the end, six million Jews, the vast majority from eastern Europe, along with an estimated five to six million Gypsies, homosexuals, and Slavs, and countless others were murdered in the Nazi genocidal fury. The planned, bureaucratic organization of this vast and unspeakable crime perpetrated by apparently civilized people still shocks and outrages. (See "New Sources, New Perspectives," page 867.)

Societies at War

Even more than World War I, World War II depended on industrial productivity aimed totally toward war and mass killings. The Axis countries remained at a disadvantage throughout the war despite their initial conquests, for the Allies simply outproduced them (Figure 26.1). Even while Germany occupied the Soviet industrial heartland and besieged many of its cities, the USSR increased its production of weapons. Both Japan and Germany made the most of their lower output, especially in the use of Blitzkrieg, but they faced other problems: Hitler had to avoid imposing wartime austerity because he had come to power promising to end economic suffering, not increase it. The use of millions of slave laborers said to be

inferior helped, but both Japan's and Germany's belief in their racial superiority worked against them by preventing them from accurately assessing the capabilities of an enemy they held in contempt.

Allied governments were overwhelmingly successful in mobilizing civilians, especially women. In Germany and Italy, where government policy particularly exalted motherhood and kept women from good jobs, officials began to realize that women were desperately needed in the workforce. Nazis changed their propaganda to emphasize the need for everyone to take a job, but they could not convince women to take the low-paid work offered them. In contrast, Soviet women constituted more than half the workforce by war's end, and 800,000 volunteered for the military, even serving as pilots. As the Germans invaded, Soviet citizens moved entire factories eastward. In a dramatic about-face, the government encouraged devotion to the Russian Orthodox church as a way of boosting morale and patriotism.

Even more than in World War I, civilians faced huge amounts of propaganda when they listened to the radio or went to the movies. People were

---

Life in the Warsaw Ghetto
The occupying Nazis resettled Warsaw's Jews into a minuscule area of the city in order, the Germans explained, to bring moral purification and to keep Germans from being infected by these "carriers of the bacteria of epidemics." Living with bare amounts of food, Warsaw's Jews died daily on the streets. Corpses were a regular sight for the average citizen—young or old. (ullstein bild/The Granger Collection, New York.)

Museums and Memory

Historical monuments and museums that house historical artifacts are testimonials to historical events because they provide records of those events and show that people were deeply moved by them. But is the impression conveyed by a tragic photo or the memory of an event the same as its history? For the most part, historians regard photographs and oral testimony as legitimate kinds of evidence. However, many judge such institutions as Holocaust museums as only partially about the history of the Holocaust. Instead, a Holocaust museum tells a great deal about the nation or group that builds it. It tells about the "memory" that the nation or group wants people to have of the Holocaust.

The complicated development of Holocaust memorials is instructive to historians. Some Holocaust memory sites sprang up spontaneously in concentration camps as memorials constructed by survivors themselves. Stones, writings, plaques, flowers and plants, and other objects were used to testify to what had happened in the camp. In many cases, these initial memorials were replaced when local and national governments stepped in to take over the site, sometimes waiting years between destroying the spontaneous memorials and replacing them with an official one. The concentration camp at Dachau, near Munich, fell into disrepair until a group of survivors, including many Catholic clergy, demanded that the camp be made into a permanent museum and memorial, with the crematorium and other grisly features preserved. Although townspeople and local government resisted, Dachau and its crematorium became one of the most visited camps and indeed came to symbolize the Holocaust in all its horror. Yet Dachau was not primarily an extermination site for Jews, Slavs, and Gypsies but rather a grim concentration camp where Hitler put political prisoners, many of them Catholic clergy. It is so often visited because it is on the tourist route, close to a beautiful city. Indeed, one of the plaques in this on-site museum invites visitors to tour other cultural institutions and scenery of the area while another asks them to remember that vast numbers of those interned at Dachau were Polish and Catholic. All of these factors in the politics of memories—official and unofficial, competing and contested—need to be taken into account by historians.

In the case of Holocaust museums, official memories can clash with memories of actual survivors who, for instance, may not like what is often the most aesthetic or avant-grade in terms of art and architecture. Survivors generally reject abstract art, feeling that a more realistic depiction of their suffering is more authentic. The architectural design of the American Holocaust Museum was redone so that it would not look grimly out of place but would instead fit in with the tranquil style of the central museum mall in Washington, D.C., and thus be another nice tourist attraction. Historians question the way certain objects like shoes or eyeglasses are displayed to create a certain memory effect. They note that costume designers puff up prison uniforms to make them look more lifelike and to stir people emotionally.

Holocaust museums offer a powerful, vivid, and emotionally charged experience of history. In contrast, historians pride themselves on eliminating emotions and biases in ascertaining facts, calculating cause and effect, and reaching historical judgments. Though each provides an important representation of the past, the relationship between memory and history remains fraught with questions—and never more so than in the case of the Holocaust.

Jewish Museum Berlin
Among the latest of the museums dedicated to the Holocaust was this one, which opened in 2001 in Berlin—the heart of Nazi Germany. Architect Daniel Libeskind, a Polish Jew who lost many family members in the Holocaust, hoped the museum would serve not only as a memorial to Jewish deaths but also as a celebration of Jewish life and culture. What features on the museum's exterior stand out? (© Jewish Museum Berlin. Photo: Jens Ziehe.)

QUESTIONS TO CONSIDER

1. What is the difference between a historical textbook and a historical monument?
2. Do you trust a history book more than you trust a museum? How do people compare and evaluate the presentation of the past in either one?
3. Why do museums and public exhibitions of art and artifacts arouse more debate than do history books?

FURTHER READING

Marcuse, Harold. *Legacies of Dachau: The Uses and Abuses of a Concentration Camp, 1933–2001.* 2001.

Sherman, Daniel J., and Irit Rogoff, eds. *Museum Culture: Histories, Discourses, Spectacles.* 1994.

Young, James Edward. *At Memory's Edge: After-Images of the Holocaust in Contemporary Art and Architecture.* 2000.

FIGURE 26.1 Weapons Production of the Major Powers, 1939–1945

World War II devoured people and weapons, necessitating dramatic changes in the workforce and everyday life. Because agricultural production was often hit hard by invading forces, people lived on reduced rations. Raw materials were channeled into the manufacture of weapons, and it was the real difference in productivity that spelled victory for the Allies: Germany and Japan were outproduced in almost every category.

(*From* The Hammond Atlas of the Twentieth Century (London: Times Books, 1996), 103.)

	1939	1940	1941	1942	1943	1944	1945
Aircraft							
Great Britain	7,940	15,049	20,094	23,672	26,263	26,461	12,070
United States	5,856	12,804	26,277	47,826	85,998	96,318	49,761
USSR	10,382	10,565	15,735	25,436	34,900	40,300	20,900
Germany	8,295	10,247	11,776	15,409	24,807	39,807	7,540
Japan	4,467	4,768	5,088	8,861	16,693	28,180	11,066
Major Vessels							
Great Britain	57	148	236	239	224	188	64
United States	——	——	544	1,854	2,654	2,247	1,513
USSR	——	33	62	19	13	23	11
Germany (U-boats only)	15	40	196	244	270	189	0
Japan	21	30	49	68	122	248	51
Tanks							
Great Britain	969	1,399	4,841	8,611	7,476	5,000	2,100
United States	——	c. 400	4,052	24,997	29,497	17,565	11,968
USSR	2,950	2,794	6,590	24,446	24,089	28,963	15,400
Germany	c. 1,300	2,200	5,200	9,200	17,300	22,100	4,400
Japan	c. 200	1,023	1,024	1,191	790	401	142

glued to their radios for war news, but much of it was tightly controlled. The totalitarian powers often withheld news of military defeats and large casualty numbers in order to keep civilian support. Wartime films focused on aviation heroes and infantrymen as well as on the self-sacrificing workingwomen and wives on the home front. Filmmakers were subject to censorship by government agencies that allocated supplies only to films whose scripts they liked.

Between 1939 and 1945, governments organized many aspects of everyday life, a necessity because resources such as food had to be shifted away from civilians toward soldiers and military production. In most countries, it was simply taken for granted that civilians would not receive what they needed to survive in good health. Soviet children and old people were at the greatest risk of being among the one million residents who starved to death during the siege of Leningrad. Statisticians and other specialists regulated the production and distribution of food, clothing, and household products, all of which were rationed and generally of lower quality than before the war. They gave hints for meals without meat, sugar, and fat, and urged women and children to embrace deprivation so that their fighting men would have more. With governments standardizing such items as food, clothing, and entertainment, World War II furthered the development of mass society in which people lived and thought in identical ways.

On both sides, propaganda and government policies promoted racial thinking. Since the early 1930s, the German government had published ugly caricatures of Jews, Slavs, and Gypsies. Similarly, Allied propaganda during the war depicted Germans as perverts and the "Japs" as insectlike fanatics. The U.S. government forced citizens of Japanese origin into internment camps, while Muslims and minority ethnic groups in the Soviet Union were uprooted and relocated away from the front lines as potential Nazi collaborators. Both sides drew colonized peoples into the war through forced labor and conscription into the armies. Some two million Indian men served the Allied cause, as did several hundred thousand Africans. As the Japanese swept through the Pacific and parts of East Asia, they too conscripted local men into their army.

From Resistance to Allied Victory

Resistance to fascism began early in the war. Having escaped from France to London in 1940, General Charles de Gaulle directed from a distance the Free French government and its forces—a mixed

MAP 26.5 World War II in Europe and Africa
World War II inflicted massive loss of life and destruction of property on civilians, armies, and all the
infrastructure—including factories, equipment, and agriculture—needed to wage total war. Thus, the
war swept the European continent as well as areas in Africa colonized by or allied with the major powers.
Ultimately the Allies crushed the Axis by moving from east, west, and south to inflict a total defeat.

organization of troops of colonized Asians and
Africans, soldiers who had escaped via Dunkirk,
and volunteers from other occupied countries.
Then Allied forces started tightening a noose
around the Axis powers in mid-1942 (Map 26.5),
and Allied victory began to look certain by 1943.
At the same time, civilian resistance in the Nazi-
occupied areas further pressured the Axis. Still Hitler
and his minions continued to promote an unrealistic expectation of German victory, announcing,
for example, that the United States was "a big
bluff." But bluster could not win the war, and the
Allies, squeezing Germany from east and west and

crushing the Japanese in the Pacific, brought the
war to an end in 1945.

Civilian Resistance.   Less well-known than the
Free French, resisters in occupied Europe fought
in Communist-dominated groups, some of which
gathered information to aid the Allied invasion of
the continent. Rural groups called partisans, or the
maquis, not only planned assassinations of traitors
and German officers but also bombed bridges, rail
lines, and military facilities. Although the Catholic
church supported Mussolini in Italy and endorsed
the Croatian puppet government's slaughter of a

Hidden Revolver
Resistance to Nazism took many forms, from the uprising in Warsaw to small acts of protest to assassinations of Nazi officers and collaborators. In a militarized state with informers everywhere, retaliation against Nazis sparked human ingenuity, whether in obtaining enough food or killing the enemy. Weapons were hidden in baby carriages, under clothing, or in books—as in this example from the Dutch resistance. *(Erich Lessing/Art Resource, NY.)*

million Serbs, Catholic and Protestant clergy and their parishioners were among those who set up resistance networks, often hiding Jews and fugitives. The Polish resistance worked tirelessly against the Nazis, as did renowned individuals such as Swedish diplomat Raoul Wallenberg, whose dealings with Nazi officials saved thousands of Hungarian Jews.

People also fought back through everyday activities. Homemakers circulated newsletters urging demonstrations at prisons where civilians were detained. In central Europe, hikers smuggled Jews and others over dangerous mountain passes. Danish villagers created vast escape networks, and countless thousands across Europe volunteered to be part of local escape routes. Women resisters used stereotypes to good advantage, often carrying weapons to assassination sites in the correct belief that Nazis would rarely suspect or search them. They also seduced and murdered enemy officers. "Naturally the Germans didn't think that a woman could have carried a bomb," explained one Italian resister, "so this became the woman's task." Resistance kept alive the liberal ideal of individual political action in the face of tyranny.

Both invisible and dramatically visible resistance took place in the fascist countries. Couples in Germany and Italy limited family size in defiance of pro-birth policies. German teenagers danced the forbidden American jitterbug, thus disobeying the Nazis and forcing the police to monitor their groups. More spectacularly, in July 1944, a group of German military officers, fearing their country's military humiliation, tried and failed to assassinate Hitler—one of several such attempts. Wounded but shaken, Hitler mercilessly tortured and killed hundreds of conspirators, innocent friends, and family members. Some ask whether the assassina-

tion attempt came too late in the war to count as resistance. However, some five million Germans alone, and millions more of other nationalities, lost their lives in the last nine months of the war. Had Hitler died even as late as the summer of 1944, the relief to humanity would have been considerable.

The Axis Crushed in Europe.
Beginning with the battle of Stalingrad in 1942–1943, the Allies turned the frontline war against the Axis powers. In August 1942, the German army began a siege of this city, whose capture would give Germany access to Soviet oil. Months of ferocious house-to-house fighting ended when the Soviet army captured the ninety thousand German survivors in February 1943. Meanwhile, the British army in North Africa held against German troops under Erwin Rommel, an adept practitioner of the new kind of mobile warfare. Although Rommel let his tanks improvise creatively, moving hundreds of miles from supply lines, the Allies' access to secret German communication codes ultimately helped them capture Morocco and Algeria in the fall of 1942. After driving Rommel out of Africa, the Allies landed in Sicily in July 1943, provoking a German invasion during which they took over the war effort from the Italians. A slow, bitter fight for the Italian peninsula followed, lasting until April 1945, when Allied forces finally triumphed. After Italy's liberation, partisans shot Mussolini and his mistress and hung their dead bodies for public display.

The victory at Stalingrad marked the beginning of the Soviet drive westward, during which the Soviets bore the brunt of the Nazi war machine. From the air, Britain and the United States bombed German cities, aiming to demoralize ordinary Germans and destroy war industries. But it was an invasion from the west that Stalin wanted from his allies. Finally, on June 6, 1944, known as D-Day, the combined Allied forces, under the command of U.S. general Dwight Eisenhower, attacked the heavily fortified French beaches of Normandy and then fought their way through the German-held territory of western France. In late July, Allied forces broke through German defenses and a month later helped liberate Paris. The Soviets meanwhile captured the Baltic States and entered Poland, pausing for desperately needed supplies. The Germans took advantage of the pause to put down an uprising of the Polish resistance in August 1944. German elimination of the Polish resistance allowed the Soviets a freer hand in east-

The Battle of Stalingrad
These soldiers fight in what was left of Stalingrad after almost nine months of bitter struggle (June 1942–February 1943) between the German and Soviet armies. Hitler allowed no surrender, leading to greater losses than necessary. The Russian military was so angry at the continuing bloodshed, despite the German defeat, that many units simply shot the final German survivors when they surrendered. Stalingrad is seen as the true turning point in World War II. *(Getty Images.)*

ern Europe after the war. Facing more than twice as many troops as on the western front, the Soviet army took Bulgaria and entered Romania at the end of August, then faced fierce German fighting in Hungary during the winter of 1944–1945. British, Canadian, U.S., and other Allied forces were simultaneously fighting their way eastward to join the Soviets in squeezing the Third Reich to its final defeat.

As the Allies advanced, Hitler decided that Germans were proving themselves unworthy of his greatness and deserved to perish in a total and bloody downfall. He thus refused to surrender and thereby spare Germans further death and destruction from the relentless bombing. As the Soviet army took Berlin, Hitler committed suicide with his wife, Eva Braun. Although many soldiers re-

mained committed to the Third Reich, Germany finally surrendered on May 8, 1945.

The Atomic Bomb and the Defeat of Japan.   The Allies had followed a "Europe first" strategy for conducting the war. They had nonetheless pursued the Japanese in the Pacific without pause. In 1940 and 1941, Japan had ousted the Europeans from many colonial holdings in Asia, but the Allies turned the tide in 1942 by destroying some of Japan's formidable navy in battles at Midway Island and Guadalcanal (Map 26.6). Japan had far less industrial capacity and manpower than the United States alone, while the Allies as a group had not only their own productive power but also access to matériel from Australia, India, and elsewhere around the world. The Allies stormed one

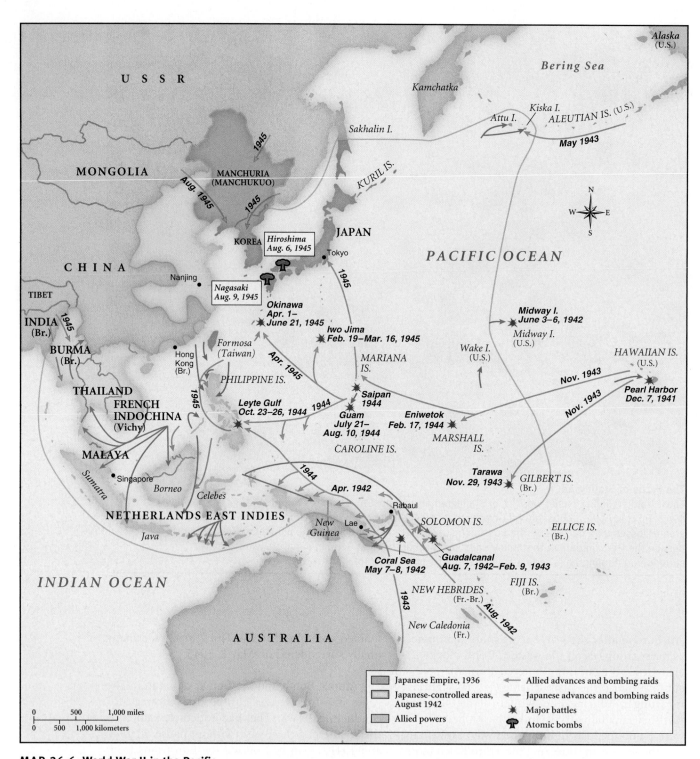

MAP 26.6 World War II in the Pacific

As in Europe, the early days of World War II gave the advantage to the Axis power Japan as it took the offensive in conquering islands in the Pacific and territories in Asia—many of them colonies of European states. Britain countered by mobilizing a vast Indian army, while the United States, after the disastrous losses at Pearl Harbor and in the Philippines, gradually gained the upper hand by costly assaults, island by island. The Japanese strategy of fighting to the last person instead of surrendering when a loss was in sight was one factor in President Truman's decision to drop the atomic bomb in August 1945.

Pacific island after another, gaining more bases from which to cut off the import of supplies and to launch bombers toward Japan itself. Short of men and weapons, the Japanese military resorted to kamikaze tactics, in which pilots deliberately crashed their planes into Allied ships, killing themselves in the process. In response, the Allies stepped up their bombing of major cities, killing more than 100,000 civilians in their spring 1945 firebombing of Tokyo. The Japanese leadership still ruled out surrender.

Meanwhile a U.S.-based international team of more than 100,000 workers, including scientists and technicians, had been working on the Manhattan Project, the code name for a secret project to develop an atomic bomb. The Japanese practice of dying almost to the man rather than surrendering caused Allied military leaders to calculate that defeating Japan might cost the lives of hundreds of thousands of Allied soldiers (and even more Japanese). On August 6 and 9, 1945, the U.S. government thus unleashed its new atomic weapons on Hiroshima and Nagasaki, respectively, killing 140,000 people instantly; tens of thousands later died from burns, wounds, and other afflictions. Although hardliners in the Japanese military wanted to continue the war, on August 14, 1945, Japan surrendered.

An Uneasy Postwar Settlement

Throughout the war, Allied leaders had met not only to plan strategy but also to resolve postwar issues. Unlike World War I, however, there would be neither a celebrated peace conference nor a formal agreement among all the Allies about the final terms for peace. Yet peace and recovery were more important than ever: Europe lay in ruins, and tens of millions were starving, many of them wandering the continent in search of food, shelter, and personal safety. Because the victorious Allies distrusted one another in varying degrees, with the United States and the Soviet Union moving to

---

Hiroshima
This photo captures the few remains of the city of Hiroshima after the United States dropped an atomic bomb on August 6, 1945. Without the bomb, the U.S. military foresaw a long and costly struggle to defeat Japan, given its overall strategy of fighting to the last person and in the process inflicting as many casualties on the enemy as possible. Some claim that the bomb was dropped to menace the Soviet Union, with which the United States was embarking on the cold war. *(© Corbis.)*

the brink of another war, the future for most Europeans looked grim.

Wartime Agreements about the Peace. Wartime agreements among members of the Grand Alliance about the future reflected their differences and would be the subject of intense postwar debate. In 1941, Roosevelt and Churchill crafted the Atlantic Charter, which condemned aggression and endorsed collective security and the right of all people to choose their governments. Not only did the Allies come to support these ideals, but so did colonized peoples to whom, Churchill said, the charter was not meant to apply. In October 1944, Churchill and Stalin agreed on the postwar distribution of territories. The Soviet Union would control Romania and Bulgaria, Britain would control Greece, and they would jointly oversee Hungary and Yugoslavia. These agreements went against Roosevelt's faith in collective security, self-determination, and open doors in trade. In February 1945, the "Big Three"—Roosevelt, Churchill, and Stalin—met in the Crimean town of Yalta. Roosevelt advocated the institution of an organization to be called the United Nations to replace the League of Nations as a global peace mechanism, and he supported future Soviet influence in Korea, Manchuria, and

the Sakhalin and Kurile Islands. The last meeting of the Allied leaders, with President Harry S. Truman replacing Roosevelt, who had died in April, took place at Potsdam, Germany, in the summer of 1945, where they agreed to give the Soviets control of eastern Poland, to cede a large stretch of eastern Germany to Poland, and to adopt a temporary four-way occupation of Germany that included France as one of the supervising powers.

The War's Grim Legacy. The Great Depression had inflicted global suffering, while the Second World War left an estimated 100 million dead, more than 50 million refugees without homes, and one of the most abominable moral legacies in human history. Forced into armies or into labor camps for war production, colonial peoples were in full rebellion or close to it. For a second time in three decades, they had seen their imperial masters killing one another, slaughtered by the very technology that was supposed to make European civilization superior. Deference to Europe was virtually finished, with independence a matter of time.

The war weakened and even destroyed standards of decency and truth. Democratic Europe had succumbed to economic hardship and wartime values, and it was this Europe that George Orwell

---

Alberto Giacometti, *The Square II*, 1948–1949
Swiss Artist Alberto Giacometti began making sculptures featuring thin, elongated figures in the 1940s. They appear to be moving forward, striving and active, but at the same time their spareness evokes the skeletal shape of concentration camp survivors. What kind of statement do you see Giacometti making about the times? *(Bildarchiv Preussischer Kulturbesitz/Art Resource, NY/Artists Rights Society (ARS), NY.)*

captured in his novel *1984* (1949). Orwell had worked for the wartime Ministry of Information (called the Ministry of Truth in the novel) and made up phony news for wartime audiences. Truth hardly mattered, and words changed meaning during the war to sound better: *battle fatigue* substituted for *insanity*, and *liberating* a country could mean invading it and slaughtering its civilians. Poor food, ragged clothing, and careworn people walking grimy streets—all characterized both wartime London and Orwell's fictional state of Oceania. Millions cheered the demise of Nazi evil in 1945, but Orwell saw the war as ending prosperity, deadening creativity, and bringing big government into everyday life. For Orwell, bureaucratic domination depended on continuing conflict, and fresh conflict was indeed brewing even before the war ended. As Allied powers competed for territory, a new struggle called the cold war was taking root.

REVIEW: How and where was World War II fought and won, and what were its major consequences?

Conclusion

The Great Depression, which brought fear, hunger, and joblessness to millions, created a setting in which dictators thrived because they promised to restore economic prosperity by destroying democracy and representative government. Desperate people believed the promises of these dynamic new leaders—Mussolini, Stalin, and Hitler—often forgiving the brutality of their regimes. In the USSR, Stalin's program of rapid industrialization cost the lives of millions as he inspired Communist believers to purge enemies—real and imagined. With the democracies preoccupied with economic recovery while preserving the rule of law and still haunted by memories of World War I, Hitler and Mussolini went on to menace Europe unchallenged. At the same time, Japan embarked on a program of conquest aimed at ending West-

ern domination in Asia and taking control of more of Asia for itself. The coalition of Allies that finally formed to stop the Axis powers of Germany, Italy, and Japan, was an uneasy alliance among Britain, Free France, the Soviet Union, and the United States. World War II ended European dominance. Its economies were shattered, its colonies were on the verge of independence, and its peoples were starving and homeless.

The costs of a bloody war—one waged against civilians as much as armies—taught the victorious powers different lessons. The United States, Britain, and France were convinced that a minimum of citizen well-being was necessary to prevent a recurrence of fascism. The devastation of the USSR's population and resources made Stalin increasingly obsessed with national security and compensation for the damage inflicted by the Nazis. Britain and France faced the end of their imperial might, underscoring Orwell's insight that the war had utterly transformed society. The militarization of society and the deliberate murder of millions of innocent citizens like Etty Hillesum were tragedies that permanently injured the West's claims to being an advanced civilization. Nonetheless, backed by vast supplies of sophisticated weaponry, the United States and the Soviet Union used their opposing views on a postwar settlement to justify threatening one another—and the world—with another horrific war.

FOR FURTHER EXPLORATION

■ **For suggested references, including Web sites, for topics in this chapter,** see page SR-1 at the end of the book.

■ **For additional primary-source material from this period,** see Chapter 26 in *Sources of THE MAKING OF THE WEST,* Third Edition.

■ **For Web sites and documents related to topics in this chapter,** see *Make History* at bedfordstmartins.com/hunt.

MAPPING THE WEST

Percent of population killed

- Over 10%
- 5–10%
- 1–5%
- Under 1%

- ■ Military dead
- ▲ Civilian dead (does not include 12 million death camp victims)
- ✳ City substantially damaged

FINLAND
■ 79,047

NORWAY
■ 4,780

SWEDEN

Leningrad

ESTONIA

LATVIA

LITHUANIA

Baltic Sea

Königsberg

North Sea

IRELAND

GREAT BRITAIN
■ 271,311
▲ 60,595

DENMARK
■ 4,339

USSR
■ 14,500,000
▲ Over 7,000,000

Coventry

London

Rotterdam

NETH.
■ 13,700
▲ 236,300

Hamburg

Bremen

Hanover

Warsaw

Kiev

Düsseldorf

Dortmund

Berlin

POLAND
■ 850,000
(169,822 as Allies)
▲ 5,778,000

BELG.
■ 9,561
▲ 75,000

Cologne

GERMANY
■ 2,850,000
▲ 2,300,000

Dresden

Caen

Frankfurt

Würzburg

CZECHOSLOVAKIA
■ 6,683
▲ 310,000

FRANCE
■ 210,671
▲ 173,260

SWITZ.

Munich

AUSTRIA
■ 380,000
▲ 145,000

HUNGARY
■▲ 750,000

ROMANIA
■ 519,822
▲ 465,000

Ploesti

Milan

Genoa

Bologna

YUGOSLAVIA
■▲ 1,700,000

Black Sea

SPAIN
■ 4,500 (For Axis)
7,500 (For Allies)
■▲ 10,000
(in concentration camps)

Corsica

ITALY
■ 279,820
▲ 17,400 (as Allies)

BULGARIA
■ 18,500
▲ 1,500

Sardinia

GREECE
■ 16,357
▲ 155,300

0   200   400 miles
0   200   400 kilometers

Europe at War's End, 1945

The damage of World War II left scars that would last for decades. Major German cities were bombed to bits, while the Soviet Union suffered an unimaginable toll of perhaps as many as forty-five million deaths due to the war alone. In addition to the vast civilian and military losses shown on this map, historians estimate that no less than twelve million people were murdered in the Nazi death camps. Everything from politics to family life needed rebuilding, adding to the chaos. (*From The Hammond Atlas of the Twentieth Century (London: Times Books, 1996), 102.*)

CHAPTER REVIEW

KEY TERMS AND PEOPLE

civil disobedience (843)
Joseph Stalin (844)
five-year plans (845)
purges (846)
Adolf Hitler (847)
Enabling Act (848)
pump priming (849)
Nuremberg Laws (850)

family allowance (853)
Popular Front (854)
Charlie Chaplin (855)
Lebensraum (858)
Francisco Franco (859)
appeasement (861)
Nazi-Soviet Pact (861)
Blitzkrieg (862)

MAKING CONNECTIONS

1. Compare fascist ideas of the individual with the idea of individual rights that inspired the American and French revolutions.

2. What are the major differences between World War I and World War II?

> **For practice quizzes, a customized study plan, and other study tools,** see the Online Study Guide at bedfordstmartins.com/hunt.

REVIEW QUESTIONS

1. How did the Great Depression affect society and politics?

2. What role did violence play in the Soviet and Nazi regimes?

3. How did the democracies' responses to the twin challenges of economic depression and the rise of fascism differ from those of totalitarian regimes?

4. How did the aggression of Japan, Germany, and Italy create the conditions for global war?

5. How and where was World War II fought and won, and what were its major consequences?

IMPORTANT EVENTS

1929	The U.S. stock market crashes; global depression begins; Soviet leadership initiates war against prosperous farmers, the kulaks; Stalin's first five-year plan officially begins
1931	Japan invades Manchuria; Spanish republicans overthrow monarchy
1933	Hitler comes to power in Germany
1935	German government enacts Nuremberg Laws; Italy invades Ethiopia
1936	Show trials begin in the USSR; Stalin purges top Communist Party officials and military leaders; the Spanish Civil War begins
1937	Japan attacks China
1938	Kristallnacht (Night of the Broken Glass) in Germany; Germany annexes Austria
1939	Nazi-Soviet Pact; Germany invades Poland; World War II begins; the Spanish Civil War ends
1940	France falls to the German army
1940–1941	The British air force fends off German attacks in the battle of Britain
1941	Germany invades the Soviet Union; Japan attacks Pearl Harbor; the United States enters the war
1941–1945	The Holocaust
1942–1943	Siege of Stalingrad
1944	Allied forces land at Normandy, France
1945	The fall of Berlin; United States drops atomic bombs on Hiroshima and Nagasaki; World War II ends

A LOVE CAUGHT IN THE FIRE OF REVOLUTION

Turbulent were the times and fiery was the love story of Zhivago, his wife... and the passionate, tender Lara.

METRO-GOLDWYN-MAYER PRESENTS A CARLO PONTI PRODUCTION

DAVID LEAN'S FILM OF BORIS PASTERNAKS

DOCTOR ZHIVAGO

STARRING

GERALDINE CHAPLIN · JULIE CHRISTIE · TOM COURTENAY
ALEC GUINNESS · SIOBHAN McKENNA · RALPH RICHARDSON
OMAR SHARIF (AS ZHIVAGO) · ROD STEIGER · RITA TUSHINGHAM

SCREEN PLAY BY   DIRECTED BY
ROBERT BOLT · DAVID LEAN   IN PANAVISION® AND METROCOLOR

WINNER OF 6 ACADEMY AWARDS!

The Cold War and the Remaking of Europe
1945–1960s

L ate in 1945, with the USSR still reeling from the devastation of World War II, Soviet poet Boris Pasternak set out on a new project — *Doctor Zhivago,* a novel about a contemplative medical man caught up in the whirlwind of the Russian Revolution. Like most others in the USSR, Pasternak expected the postwar era to usher in, as he put it, "a great renewal of Russian life," ending the violence, terror, and famine of the past three decades, and so he struggled on with his complex epic even as the cold war tensions between the United States and the USSR began. In 1953, Stalin's sudden death raised Pasternak's hopes that a more tolerant political climate would allow his masterpiece to receive a warm reception; those hopes were dashed, however, when the Soviets forbade the book's publication. A determined Pasternak bypassed the Soviet authorities and allowed *Doctor Zhivago* to come out first in 1957 in Italy — now an anti-Soviet ally of the United States in the cold war. The book became a best seller, showing its readers that the Russian Revolution was far from perfect and so angering the Soviet establishment that Stalin's successor, Nikita Khrushchev, forced Pasternak to decline the Nobel Prize for Literature awarded him in 1958. But if the Soviets tried to suppress *Doctor Zhivago* so that the U.S. bloc could not use it to create cold war propaganda, it was the cold war that allowed *Doctor Zhivago* to live on. Soon after the novel appeared, the famed Hollywood studio MGM bought the rights to the book and turned it into a blockbuster film (1965), seen by tens of millions. By that time, however, Pasternak was dead — a broken victim of cold war persecutions that haunted the world long after the calamitous years of war and genocide had ended.

As the cold war opened, Europe and Japan were prostrate, their people were starving and homeless; evidence of genocide and other

Doctor Zhivago

As soon as Boris Pasternak's forbidden novel *Doctor Zhivago* was published in Italy in 1957, Hollywood's MGM studio went after the rights for the film. Finally completed in 1965, it was a cold war blockbuster—an epic of life and love in postrevolutionary Russia. The opening scene, invented for the movie, was a grim Soviet factory, while the story itself was more or less symbolized in this advertising poster of two incredibly attractive people who fall in love and are torn apart by the crushing Bolshevik system. *(MGM/The Kobal Collection.)*

inhumanity came to the fore; the menace of nuclear annihilation loomed. The old international order was gone, replaced by the rivalry of the United States and the Soviet Union for control of Europe, whose political, social, and economic order was shattered. The nuclear arsenals of these two superpowers — a term coined in 1947 — grew massively in the 1950s, but they were enemies who did not fight outright. Thus, their terrifying rivalry was called the **cold war**. The cold war divided the West and led to political persecution in many areas, even in the wealthy and secure United States.

At the same time, the defeat of Nazism inspired optimism and a revival of thoughtful reflection like Pasternak's. Heroic effort had defeated fascism, and that defeat raised hopes that a new age would begin. Atomic science promised advances in medicine, and nuclear energy was trumpeted as a replacement for coal and oil. The creation of the United Nations in 1945 heralded an era of international cooperation. Around the globe, colonial peoples won independence from European masters, while in the United States the civil rights movement gained new momentum. The welfare state expanded, and by the end of the 1950s, economic rebirth had made much of Europe more prosperous than ever before. An "economic miracle" had occurred; just a decade after the war, many Europeans and Americans were beginning to enjoy the highest standard of living they had ever known, which included the ability to buy quantities of consumer goods and to enjoy simple pleasures such as films like *Doctor Zhivago*.

The postwar period was one of open redefinition, as the experience of total war transformed both society and the international order. Gone was the definition of a West comprising Europe and its

---

cold war: The rivalry between the United States and the Soviet Union following World War II that led to massive growth in nuclear weapons on both sides.

cultural offshoots such as the United States and of an East comprising Asian countries like India, China, and Japan. During the cold war, the word *West* came to stand for the United States and its dependent allies in western Europe, while *East* meant the Soviet Union and its tightly controlled bloc in eastern Europe. Still another set of terms arose in the 1950s, one that divided the globe into the first world, or capitalist bloc of countries; the second world, or socialist bloc; and the third world, or countries emerging from imperial domination — a characterization that initially was meant to refer to the Third Estate of the French Revolution but that is now considered an insulting term. As the world's people redefined themselves, the superpowers took the world to the brink of nuclear disaster when the United States discovered Soviet missile sites on the island of Cuba. From the dropping of the atomic bomb on Japan in 1945 to the Cuban missile crisis of 1962, fear and personal anguish like that suffered by Pasternak gripped much of the world, albeit in the midst of prosperity and Europe's rebirth.

> **FOCUS QUESTION:** How did the cold war shape the politics, economy, social life, and culture of post–World War II Europe?

World Politics Transformed

World War II ended Europe's global leadership. Many countries lay in ruins in the summer of 1945, and conditions would deteriorate before they got better. Though victorious, bombed and bankrupt Britain could not feed its people, and continuing turmoil destroyed the lives of millions in central and eastern Europe. In contrast, the United States, whose territory was virtually untouched in the war, emerged as the world's sole economic giant,

---

■ **1945** Cold war begins

■ **1947** India, Pakistan win independence from Britain

■ **1948** State of Israel established

■ **1953** Stalin dies

1945   **1950**

■ **1949** Communist revolution in China; Beauvoir, *The Second Sex*

■ **1950–1953** Korean War

while the Soviet Union, despite suffering immense devastation, retained formidable military might. Occupying Europe as part of the victorious alliance against Nazism and fascism, the two superpowers used Germany—at the heart of the continent and its politics—to divide Europe in two. By the late 1940s, the USSR had imposed Communist rule throughout most of Eastern Europe, and Western Europeans found themselves at least partially controlled by the very U.S. economic power that helped them rebuild, especially because the United States maintained air bases and nuclear weapons sites on their soil. The new age of bipolar world politics made Europe its testing ground.

Chaos in Europe

In contrast to the often stationary trench warfare of World War I, armies in World War II had fought a war of movement on the ground and in the air. Massive bombing had leveled thousands of square miles of territory, whole cities were clogged with rubble, and homeless survivors wandered the streets. In Sicily and on the Rhine River, almost no bridge remained standing; in the Soviet Union, seventy thousand villages and more than a thousand cities lay in shambles. Everywhere people were suffering. In the Netherlands, the severity of Nazi occupation left the Dutch population close to death, relieved only by a U.S. airlift of food. In Britain, many died in the bitterly cold winter of 1946–1947 because of a shortage of fuel. To control scarce supplies, Italian bakers sold bread by the slice. Allied troops in Germany were almost the sole source of food: "To see the children fighting for food," remarked one British soldier handing out supplies, "was like watching animals being fed in a zoo." There was social disarray, even chaos, at the war's end but no mass uprisings as after World War I. Until the late 1940s, people were too absorbed by the struggle for bare survival.

The tens of millions of refugees suffered the most, as they wandered a continent where resources were slim and the dangers of assault and robbery great. An estimated thirty million Europeans, many of German ethnicity, were forcibly expelled from Poland, Czechoslovakia, and Hungary. Many refugees fled to western Europe, but others ultimately found homes in countries that experienced little or no war damage, such as Denmark, Sweden, Canada, and Australia. Following the exodus of refugees from the east, western Europe became one of the world's most densely populated regions (Map 27.1). The USSR lobbied hard for the return of several million Soviet prisoners of war and forced laborers, and the Allies transported millions of Soviet refugees home. The Allies slowed the process when they discovered that Soviet leaders had ordered the execution of many of the returnees for being "contaminated" by Western ideas. Hundreds of thousands of Soviets thus joined the ocean of disoriented refugees in western Europe.

Survivors of the concentration camps discovered that their suffering had not ended with Germany's defeat. Many returned diseased and disoriented, while others had no home to return to, as property had been confiscated. Anti-Semitism—official policy under the Nazis—lingered in popular attitudes, and people used it to justify their claim to Jewish property and to jobs vacated by Jews. The use of violence as a way to maintain the upward mobility gained from fascism was common throughout eastern Europe. In the summer of 1946, a vicious crowd in Kielce, Poland, assaulted some 250 Jewish survivors, killing at least 40. Meanwhile, some officials across Europe even denied that unprecedented atrocities had been committed and wanted to refuse Jews any help. Survivors thus fled to the port cities of Italy and other Mediterranean countries, eventually leaving Europe for Palestine, where Zionists had been settling for half a century. Unwilling or unable to help

■ **1954** *Brown v. Board of Education*; French defeat at Dien Bien Phu

■ **1958** Fifth Republic begins in France

■ **1956** Suez Canal nationalized; Hungarian uprising

1955   **1960**   **1965**

■ **1957** *Sputnik* launched; EEC established; Pasternak, *Doctor Zhivago*

■ **1962** Cuban missile crisis

Zones of occupation

- Lost by Germany to Poland, 1945
- Territory gained by Soviet Union
- Allied occupation of Germany and Austria, 1945–55
- Lost by Italy to Yugoslavia, 1945
- Lost by Romania to Bulgaria, 1940–47

Zones of occupation
- American
- British
- French
- Soviet
- Jointly occupied cities

Refugee movements and repatriated armed forces
- Germans
- Finns
- Baltic peoples
- Russians
- Poles
- Czechs
- People settled by the International Refugee Organization

◀ **MAP 27.1 The Impact of World War II on Europe**
European governments, many of them struggling
to provide food and other necessities for their
populations, found themselves responsible for
hundreds of thousands, if not millions, of new
refugees. Simultaneously, millions of prisoners of
war, servicemen, and slave laborers were returned
to the Soviet Union, many of them by force. This
situation unfolded amid political instability and
even violence. ■ What does the movement of
peoples shown on the map suggest about social
conditions in post–World War II Europe?

Hitler's victims, many European countries had
simply lost their moral bearings.

New Superpowers: The United States and the Soviet Union

Only two powerful countries were left in 1945: the
United States and the Soviet Union. The United
States was now the richest nation in the world. Its
industrial output had increased by a remarkable
15 percent annually between 1940 and 1944. By
1947, the United States controlled almost two-
thirds of the world's gold bullion and launched
more than half of the world's commercial shipping. Continued spending on industrial and military research added to postwar prosperity, building
still further the victorious mood that now swept
the United States. In contrast to the post–World
War I policy of isolationism, Americans embraced
global leadership. Many had learned about the
world while tracking the war's progress; hundreds
of thousands of soldiers, government officials, and
relief workers had direct experience of Europe,
Africa, and Asia. Despite the fear of nuclear annihilation that troubled many, a wave of suburban
housing development and consumer spending
kept the economy buoyant. Temporarily reversing
the trend toward lower birthrates, a baby boom exploded from the late 1940s through the early 1960s
in response to prosperity.

The Soviets also emerged from the war with a
well-justified sense of accomplishment. Despite horrendous losses, they had resisted the most massive
onslaught ever launched against a nation. Instead of
being shunned as they had been after World War I,
Soviet officials expected respect and influence on
the world stage, and indeed many Europeans and
Americans gratefully acknowledged the Soviet
contribution to Hitler's defeat. Ordinary Soviet
citizens believed that a victory that had cost the
USSR as many as forty-five million lives would

bring improvement in their everyday conditions
and a continuation of the war's relatively relaxed
politics. Rumors spread among the peasants that
the collective farms would be divided and returned
to them as individual property now that the war
had been won and agriculture modernized. "Life
will become pleasant," one writer prophesied.
"There will be much coming and going, and a lot
of contacts with the West." The Stalinist goals of
industrialization and defense against Nazism had
been won, and thus many Soviets, among them
Boris Pasternak, expected an end to decades of
hardship and repression.

Stalin took a different view and, despite his
personal exhaustion, moved ruthlessly to reassert
control. In 1946, his new five-year plan set increased production goals and mandated more
stringent collectivization of agriculture. For him,
rapid recovery meant more work, not less, and
more order, not greater freedom. Stalin cut back
the army by two-thirds to beef up the labor force
and also turned his attention to the low birthrate,
a result of wartime male casualties and women's
long, arduous working days, which discouraged
them from adding child care to their already heavy
responsibilities. He introduced an intense propaganda campaign emphasizing that women should
hold down jobs and also fulfill their "true nature"
by producing many children. A crackdown on freedom took place, and a new round of purges began
in which people were told that enemies among
them were threatening the state. Jews were especially targeted, and in 1953 the government announced that doctors — most of them Jews — had
long been assassinating Soviet leaders, murdering
newborns and patients in hospitals, and plotting
to poison water supplies. Hysteria gripped the nation, as people feared for their lives. "I am a
simple worker and not an anti-Semite," one Moscow
resident wrote, "but I say . . . it's time to clean these
people out." With this rebirth of Stalinism, an atmosphere of fear returned to feed the cold war.

Origins of the Cold War

The cold war between the United States and the
Soviet Union, which began immediately after
World War II, would afflict the world for more
than four decades. No peace treaty officially ended
the conflict with Germany as a written record of
contest and compromise or of things gone wrong,
as in the Peace of Paris of 1919–1920. As a result,
the origins of the cold war remain a matter of debate, with historians faulting both sides for starting the fearsome rivalry (see "New Sources, New

Perspectives," page 885). Some point to consistent U.S., British, and French hostility to the Soviets that began as far back as the Bolshevik Revolution of 1917 and continued through the Depression and World War II. These powers opposed the Communists' abolition of private property and Russia's withdrawal from World War I. Others stress the Soviets' aggressive policies, notably the 1939 Nazi-Soviet Pact and Stalin's quick claims on the Baltic States and Polish territory when World War II broke out. In this view, other countries naturally feared Soviet expansionism.

Suspicion ran deep among the Allied leadership during World War II, and the alliance was always a troubled one. Stalin believed that Churchill and Roosevelt were deliberately letting the USSR bear the brunt of Hitler's onslaught on the continent as part of their anti-Communist policy. He rightly viewed Churchill in particular as interested primarily in preserving Britain's imperial power, no matter what the cost in lives of Soviet citizens. At the time, some Americans believed that dropping the atomic bomb on Japan would also frighten the Soviets from land grabs, and the new U.S. president, Harry Truman, was far tougher than Roosevelt with regard to Soviet needs. He cut

off aid to the USSR almost the instant the last gun was fired, fueling Stalin's belief that the United States was aiming for the Soviet Union's utter collapse. Seeing a threat from the West, especially from a revived Germany, Stalin concluded that a temporary military occupation would not be a sufficient safeguard for his own exhausted country; what the USSR needed was a permanent "buffer zone" of European states loyal to the Soviet Union. Across the Atlantic, Truman viewed the Soviet occupation of eastern Europe as opening an era of Communist takeovers around the world. Members of the U.S. State Department fueled U.S. fears by depicting Stalin as another in a long line of neurotic Asian tyrants thirsting for world domination.

The cold war thus became a series of moves and countermoves in the shared occupation of a rich European heartland that had fallen into chaos. In line with the view of its geopolitical needs, the USSR repressed democratic coalition governments of liberals, socialists, Communists, and peasant parties in central and eastern Europe between 1945 and 1949. It imposed Communist rule almost immediately in Bulgaria and Romania. In Romania, Stalin cited citizen violence in 1945 as the excuse to demand an ouster of all non-Communists from the civil service and cabinet. In Poland, the Communists fixed the election results of 1945 and 1946 to create the illusion of approval for communism. Nevertheless, the Communists had to share power between 1945 and 1947 with the popular Peasant Party, which had a large constituency of rural workers and peasant landowners. The Allies protested many of these moves by the Communists as the cold war advanced.

The United States put its new interventionist spirit to work, promoting American influence. It acknowledged Soviet authority in USSR-occupied areas of central and eastern Europe but worried that Communist power would spread to western Europe. The Communists' promises of better conditions appealed to hungry workers, while memories of Communist leadership in the resistance to fascism made the party additionally attractive. In Greece, Communist insurgents had enough of a following to threaten the right-wing monarchy the British had installed in 1944. In March 1947, Truman reacted to the Communist threat in Greece by announcing what quickly became known as the **Truman Doctrine**, the countering of political crises with economic and military aid. The president requested $400 million in military

THE COLD WAR

1945–1949	USSR establishes satellite states in eastern Europe
1947	Truman Doctrine announces American commitment to contain communism; U.S. Marshall Plan provides massive aid to rebuild Europe
1948–1949	Soviet troops blockade Berlin; United States airlifts provisions to Berliners
1949	West Germany and East Germany formed; Western nations form North Atlantic Treaty Organization (NATO); Soviet bloc establishes Council for Mutual Economic Assistance (COMECON); USSR tests its first nuclear weapon
1950–1953	Korean War
1950–1954	U.S. senator Joseph McCarthy leads hunt for American Communists
1953	Stalin dies
1955	USSR and Eastern bloc countries form military alliance, the Warsaw Pact
1956	Khrushchev denounces Stalin in "secret speech" to Communist Party Congress; Hungarians revolt unsuccessfully against Soviet domination
1959	Fidel Castro comes to power in Cuba
1961	Berlin Wall erected
1962	Cuban missile crisis

Truman Doctrine: The United States's policy to limit communism after World War II by countering political crises with economic and military aid.

NEW SOURCES, NEW PERSPECTIVES

Government Archives and the Truth about the Cold War

As the modern nation-state grew in the nineteenth century, historians came increasingly to rely on official government archives to answer questions arising from ideological disputes. The cold war was one such battle of charges and countercharges. Government archives have thrown light on the accusations of both sides. Participants and eyewitnesses, it is believed, are not reliable because of their bias. Instead, trained scholars, ridding themselves of bias, carefully examine government records, preserved in official repositories where tampering cannot take place.

The opening of the Soviet Union's archives in the late 1980s and 1990s after the fall of Soviet communism gave answers to many cold war questions. In 1956, in the midst of superpower rivalry, Nikita Khrushchev first threw official light on the slaughter connected with Stalin's regime. In Khrushchev's partial revelation of truths, V. I. Lenin and Joseph Stalin were presented as distinctly different political beings, with Lenin an ideologue and benefactor, and Stalin a creature of excess. The Soviet archives, however, revealed a more vicious Lenin, one who demanded from the start of the Bolshevik regime the kind of brutality that Khrushchev had pinned on Stalin alone. Lenin and his contemporaries started the reliance on wholesale massacre of the upper classes, peasants, dissenters, and even ordinary citizens. At the same time, the archives discredited the U.S. claim that the Soviet Union in the 1950s was out to conquer the world. Instead, scholars found both Stalin and Khrushchev fearful of a U.S. nuclear attack and eager to come to terms.

Much official U.S. archival material still remains closed to scholars, but the Freedom of Information Act (1966, amended 1974) allows historians to press for access and at times to obtain it. Official U.S. documents have opened up debate about the dropping of the atomic bomb, with some scholars concluding that it was not merely a matter of ending the war with Japan in the most expeditious way. Instead, brandishing atomic weapons served the United States's desire to scare the Soviets. Tapes released from John F. Kennedy's administration have shown the president differing from his generals, most of whom wanted a nuclear war during the Cuban missile crisis. Kennedy, far from being the consistent cold warrior he sought to portray, pulled back from the brink.

For all that new archival evidence can reveal, reliance on this material has many pitfalls. First, one train of thought leads to the mistaken belief that if an archive contains no written evidence of an event, the event is open to question. For instance, if there is no written order from Adolf Hitler to start the Holocaust, some have argued, it means that he did not know about the event or even that it did not occur. Second, archives are susceptible to evidence tampering, including forgery and document planting, as has happened with some Russian documents of the 1990s. Finally, excessive faith in archival documents, some critics say, skews history by suggesting that the most important kind of history comes from official government sources. Important historical evidence lies as well in sources ranging from newspapers, family account books, diaries, and personal letters to novels, paintings, and architecture, especially when many kinds of sources are used to verify one another.

QUESTIONS TO CONSIDER

1. Are archives overseen by government officials more or less likely to be biased than other sources? How can we know the extent to which archives contain the truth?

Russian Secret Archives
The opening of archives across the former Soviet bloc had many consequences. In the former East Germany, for instance, names of secret police informers were made public and many people had their reputations utterly tarnished. The opening of the archives also exposed the cases of those convicted with trumped-up evidence (some pictured here), most of them sent to camps and to their deaths long since. The probable existence of such secret archives around the world has made historians and the families of victims fight for access. Simultaneously, politicians in the democracies are struggling to keep their archives closed, especially to scholars trained to assess them. (*Sovfoto/Eastfoto.*)

2. What are the most reliable sources for discovering historical truth? Make a list and provide reasons for your counting these sources as reliable.

FURTHER READING

Andrew, Christopher, and Vasili Mitrokhin. *The Mitrokhin Archive: The KGB in Europe and the West.* 1999.

Courtois, Stephane, et al. *The Black Book of Communism: Crimes, Terror, Repression,* trans. Jonathan Murphy and Mark Kramer. 1999.

Zubok, Vladislav, and Constantine Pleshakov. *Inside the Kremlin's Cold War: From Stalin to Khrushchev.* 1996.

aid for Greece and Turkey, where the Communists were also exerting pressure. Fearing that Americans would balk at backing Greece, the U.S. Congress said it would agree to the program only if, as one congressman put it, Truman would "scare the hell out of the country." Truman thus publicized an expensive aid program as a necessary first step to prevent Soviet conquest of the world. The show of American support made the Communists back off, and in 1949 the Greek rebels declared a cease-fire.

In 1947, the United States also devised the **Marshall Plan**—a program of massive economic aid to Europe—to relieve ordinary people of the hardships that were making communism attractive. "The seeds of totalitarian regimes are nurtured by misery and want," the president warned in the same speech that introduced the Truman Doctrine. Named after Secretary of State George C. Marshall, who proposed the plan, the program's direct aid would immediately improve everyday life, while loans and financial credits would restart international trade. The government claimed that the Marshall Plan, also known as the European Recovery Program, was not directed "against any country or doctrine but against hunger, poverty, desperation, and chaos." By the early 1950s, the United States had sent Europe more than $12 billion in food, equipment, and services, reducing communism's appeal in the countries of western Europe that received the aid.

Stalin saw the Marshall Plan as a U.S. political ploy because the devastated USSR had little aid to offer client countries in eastern and central Europe. He thus clamped down still harder on eastern European governments, preventing them from responding to the U.S. offer of assistance and eliminating the last remnants of democracy in Hungary and Poland. In the autumn of 1947, a purge of non-Communist officials began in Czechoslovakia; by June 1948, Czechoslovakia's socialist president, Edvard Beneš, had resigned and been replaced by a Communist figurehead. The populace accepted the change so passively that Communist leaders said the takeover was "like cutting butter with a knife."

Yugoslavia after the Revolution

The only exception to the Soviet sweep in eastern Europe came in Yugoslavia, under the Communist ruler known as Tito (Josip Broz, 1892–1980). During the war, Tito had led the powerful anti-Nazi Yugoslav "partisans." After the war, he drew on support from Serbs, Croats, and Muslims to mount a Communist revolution. His revolution, however, was explicitly meant to avoid Soviet influence. Eager for Yugoslavia to develop industrially rather than simply serve Soviet needs, Tito remarked, "We study and take as an example the Soviet system, but we are developing socialism in our country in somewhat different forms." Stalin was furious; in his eyes, commitment to communism meant obedience to him. Nonetheless, Yugoslavia emerged from its Communist revolution as a culturally diverse federation of six republics and two independent provinces within Serbia. Tito's break with Stalin further fueled the purges in the USSR because the Soviet government could point to Tito as a vivid example of the treachery supposedly at work even in the heart of the Communist world. Holding diverse groups of southern Slavs together until his death in 1980, Tito used his forceful personality and strong organization to also hold the Soviets at bay.

The Division of Germany

The superpower struggle for control of Germany took the cold war to a highly menacing level. The agreements reached at the February 1945 conference at Yalta provided for Germany's division into four zones, each of which was controlled by one of the four principal victors in World War II—the United States, the Soviet Union, Britain, and France—and occupied by troops from those nations. However, the superpowers disagreed on fundamental matters in German history. Many in the United States had come to believe that there was something inherently wrong with the character of Germans—a fatal, evil flaw responsible for two world wars and the Holocaust. After the war, the U.S. occupation forces undertook a reprogramming of German cultural attitudes by controlling the press and censoring all media in the U.S. zone to ensure that they did not express fascist values. In contrast, Stalin believed that Nazism was merely an extreme form of capitalism. His solution was to confiscate and redistrib-

---

Marshall Plan: A post–World War II program funded by the United States to get Europe back on its feet economically and thereby reduce the appeal of communism. It played an important role in the rebirth of European prosperity in the 1950s.

ute the estates of wealthy Germans to ordinary people and supporters.

A second disagreement, concerning economic potential, led to Germany's partition. According to the American plan for coordinating the various segments of the German economy, surplus crops from the Soviet-occupied areas would feed urban populations in the western zones; in turn, industrial goods would be sent to the USSR. The Soviets upset this plan. Following the Allied agreement that the USSR would receive reparations from German resources, the Soviets dismantled industries and seized German equipment, shipping it all to the Soviet Union. They transported skilled workers, engineers, and scientists to the USSR to work virtually as slave laborers. The Soviets also manipulated the currency in their zone, enabling the USSR to buy German goods at low prices.

The struggle between the superpowers escalated when the western Allies agreed to merge their zones into a West German state. Instead of limiting German power, as wartime agreements called for, the United States began an economic buildup under the Marshall Plan to make the western zone of Germany a strong buffer against the Soviets. By 1948, notions of a permanently weakened Germany had ended, and the United States enlisted many former Nazi officials as spies and bureaucrats to jump-start the economy and pursue the cold war. On July 24, 1948, Stalin retaliated by using Soviet troops to blockade Germany's capital, Berlin. Like Germany as a whole, the city had been divided into four occupation zones, even though it was located more than one hundred miles deep into the Soviet zone and was thus cut off from western territory. Expecting the United States and its allies to capitulate, the Soviets declared that Berlin was now part of their zone of occupation and refused to allow western vehicles to travel through the Soviet zone to reach the city. The United States responded decisively, flying in millions of tons of provisions. During the winter of 1948–1949, the Berlin airlift—Operation Vittles, as U.S. pilots called it—even funneled in coal to warm some two million isolated Berliners (Map 27.2). Given the immense quantities of fuel and food needed and the limited number of transport planes, pilots kept the plane engines on to achieve a rapid turnaround that would ensure the necessary number of flights each day. The Soviets ended their blockade in May 1949, but cold war rhetoric made the divided city of Berlin an enduring symbol of the capitalist-communist divide—of good versus evil.

MAP 27.2 Divided Germany and the Berlin Airlift, 1946–1949
Berlin—controlled by the United States, Great Britain, France, and the Soviet Union—was deep in the Soviet zone of occupation and became a major point of contention among the former allies. When the USSR blockaded the western half of the city, the United States responded with a massive airlift. To stop movement between the two zones, the USSR built a wall in 1961 and used troops to patrol it.

The formation of competing institutions, military alliances, and entirely new countries added to cold war tensions (Map 27.3). In response to the creation of a West German state by the Western allies in 1948, the USSR established an East German state a few months later. In 1949, the United States, Canada, and their allies in western Europe and Scandinavia formed the **North Atlantic Treaty Organization (NATO)**. NATO provided a unified military force for its member countries. In 1955, after the United States forced France and Britain to invite West Germany to join NATO, the Soviet Union retaliated by establishing with its satellite countries the military organization commonly called the **Warsaw Pact**. By that time, both the United States and the USSR had accelerated their arms buildups: the Soviets had exploded their own

North Atlantic Treaty Organization (NATO): The security alliance formed in 1949 to provide a unified military force for the United States, Canada, and their allies in western Europe and Scandinavia.

Warsaw Pact: A security alliance of the Soviet Union and its allies formed in 1955 when NATO admitted West Germany.

MAP 27.3 European NATO Members and the Warsaw Pact in the 1950s
The two superpowers intensified their rivalry by creating large military alliances: NATO, formed in 1949, and the Warsaw Pact, formed in 1955 after NATO invited West German membership. International politics revolved around these two alliances, which faced off in the heart of Europe. War games for the two sides often assumed a massive war concentrated in central Europe over control of Germany.

atomic bomb in 1949, and each nation had tested highly destructive hydrogen bombs and then increasingly powerful nuclear weapons. These two massive regional alliances, armed to the teeth, backed cold war politics with military muscle, definitively outstripping the individual might of other European powers.

REVIEW: What were the major events in the development of the cold war?

Political and Economic Recovery in Europe

The clash between the United States and the Soviet Union served as a background to the remarkable recovery that took place in Europe. The first two items on the political agenda were the eradication of the Nazi past and the inauguration of peacetime governments. While western Europe revived its democratic political structures, its individualistic culture, and its productive capabilities, eastern Europe was far less prosperous and far more repressive under the Stalinism of the immediate postwar period. Even to the east, however, the conditions of everyday life improved as peasant societies were forced to modernize and some consumer goods industries and basic health services were restored. By 1960, people across the continent were enjoying a higher standard of living than ever before in their history. Governments

took increasing responsibility for the health and well-being of citizens, making the cold war era also the age of the welfare state.

Dealing with Nazism

In May 1945, Europeans lived under a confusing system in which local resistance leaders, Allied armies of occupation, international relief workers, and the remnants of bureaucracies—among them Nazi sympathizers—vied for authority. The goals of feeding civilians, dealing with millions of refugees, purging Nazis, and setting up new governments all needed attention. Governments-in-exile returned to reclaim power, but they often ran up against occupying armies that were a law unto themselves. The Soviets were especially feared for inflicting rape and robbery on Germans—abuses they justified by pointing to the tens of millions of worse atrocities committed by the Nazis. Adding to the sense of disorder was the lively trade in food for sex among well-supplied soldiers in all armies and starving civilians. The desire for revenge against Nazis hardened with the discovery of the death camps' skeletal survivors and the remains of the millions murdered there. Employing swift vigilante justice, civilians released pent-up rage and punished collaborators for their complicity in genocide and occupation crimes. In France, villagers often shaved the heads of women suspected of associating with Germans and made some of them parade naked through the local streets. Members of the resistance executed tens of thousands of Nazi officers and collaborators on the spot and without trial.

Allied representatives undertook what they claimed to be a more systematic "denazification" that ranged from forcing German civilians to view the death camps to investigating and bringing to trial suspected local collaborators. The trials conducted at Nuremberg, Germany, by the victorious Allies in the fall of 1945 used the Nazis' own documents to reveal a horrifying panorama of crimes by Nazi leaders. Although international law lacked a precedent for defining genocide as a crime, the judges at Nuremberg found sufficient cause to impose death sentences on half of the twenty-four defendants, among them Hitler's closest associates, and to give prison terms to the remainder. The Nuremberg trials introduced today's notion of prosecution for crimes against humanity.

Polish Refugees
These refugees, a handful among millions, are waiting for a train that might carry them to a safer destination. The refugee situation was appalling, as ethnic Poles, Germans, Hungarians, Croats, Czechs, and others were driven from areas where in some cases their families had lived for centuries. The goal of many postwar governments was to "ethnically cleanse" regions along the line of thought that grew up with Wilson's Fourteen Points: that national ethnicities should determine the kind of society and government they would have.
(Getty Images.)

Allied prosecution of the Axis leadership was hardly thorough, however; some of those most responsible for war crimes disappeared and were not pursued, leaving many Germans skeptical about Allied intentions. As women in Germany faced violence at the hands of occupying troops, endured starvation, and were forced to do the rough manual labor of clearing rubble, Germans came to believe that they themselves were the main victims of the war. German civilians also interpreted the trials of Nazis as simple payback by victors rather than a just punishment of the guilty. Distrust mounted when Allied officials, eager to restore government services and make western Europe more efficient than Soviet-controlled eastern Europe, began to hire former high-ranking Fascists and Nazis. Soon the new West German government proclaimed that the war's real casualties were the German prisoners of war held in Soviet camps.

Rebirth of the West

Following the immediate postwar chaos, Europe's revival accelerated in the 1950s. In western Europe, reform-minded civilian governments reflected the broad coalitions of the resistance movements and other opposition to the Axis. They conspicuously emphasized democratic values to show their rejection of the totalitarian regimes that had earlier attracted so many Europeans. Rebuilding devastated towns and cities spurred industrial recovery, while

bold projects for economic cooperation — like the European Common Market and the conversion of wartime technology to peacetime use — produced a brisk trade in consumer goods and services in western Europe by the late 1950s. Memories of the war remained vivid, but prosperity restored confidence and hope for a better future.

Democratic Politics Restored. Resistance leaders made the first claims on political office in postwar western Europe. In France, the leader of the Free French, General Charles de Gaulle, governed briefly as chief of state, and the French approved a constitution in 1946 that established the Fourth Republic and finally granted the vote to French women. De Gaulle wanted a more conservative political system with a strong executive and, failing to get that, soon resigned in favor of centrist and left-wing parties. Meanwhile, Italy replaced its constitutional monarchy with a republic that also allowed women the vote for the first time. As in France, a resistance-based government initially took control. Then, late in 1945, the socialist and labor politicians were replaced by a coalition headed by the conservative **Christian Democrats**, descended from the traditional Catholic centrist parties of the prewar period. Other countries likewise saw the

---

Christian Democrats: Powerful center to center-right political parties that evolved in the late 1940s from former Catholic parties of the pre–World War II period.

growing influence of Christian politicians because of their participation in the resistance.

Many voters in western Europe also favored the Communist Party. Symbol of the common citizen, the Soviet soldier was a hero to many western Europeans outside occupied Germany. So were the resistance leaders, who were themselves often Communist until more establishment politicians decided late in the war to join what looked to be a certain resistance victory. People still remembered the hardships of the depression of the 1930s. Thus, in Britain, despite the wartime successes of Winston Churchill's Conservative Party leadership, the Labour government of Clement Attlee—though not Communist—appeared more likely to fulfill promises to share prosperity equitably among the classes through expanded social welfare programs. The extreme difficulties of the immediate postwar years provided further support for governments that would represent the millions of ordinary citizens who had suffered, fought, and worked incredibly hard during the war.

In West Germany, however, with the Communist takeovers going on directly to the east, communism and the left in general had little appeal. In 1949, centrist politicians helped create a new state, the German Federal Republic, whose constitution aimed to prevent the emergence of a dictator and to guarantee individual rights. West Germany's first chancellor was the seventy-three-year-old Catholic anti-Communist Konrad Adenauer, who allied himself with the economist Ludwig Erhard. Erhard stabilized the postwar German currency so that

people would have enough confidence in its soundness to resume normal trade, manufacturing, and other economic activity crucial to society's revival. Successfully guiding Germany away from both fascism and communism, the economist and the politician restored the representative government that Hitler had overthrown.

Paradoxically, given its leadership in the fight against fascism, the United States was a country in which individual freedom and democracy were imperiled after the war. Two events in 1949—the Soviet Union's successful test of an atomic bomb and the Communist revolution in China—brought to the fore Joseph McCarthy, a U.S. senator foreseeing a reelection struggle. To strengthen his following and win the election, McCarthy warned of a great conspiracy to overthrow the United States. As during the Soviet purges, people of all occupations, including government workers, film stars, and union leaders, were called before congressional panels to confess, testify against friends, and to admit whether they had ever had Communist sympathies. The atmosphere was electric with confusion, for only five years before the mass media had run glowing stories about Stalin and the Soviet system. During the war, the American public was told to think of Stalin as a friendly "Uncle Joe." By 1952, however, more than six million Americans had been investigated, imprisoned, or fired from their jobs. McCarthy had books like Thomas Paine's *Common Sense*, written in the eighteenth century to support the American Revolution, removed from U.S. agency shelves at home

Women Clearing Berlin
The amount of destruction caused by World War II was staggering, requiring the mobilization of the civilian population in Berlin, where women were conscripted to sort the rubble and clear it away. Scenes like this were ultimately used as propaganda in the cold war to make it seem as if the Germans were the victims rather than the perpetrators of the war. That German soldiers held in Soviet camps were only slowly repatriated added to the image of Soviet rather than German aggression in World War II. *(akg-images.)*

■ **For more help analyzing this image,** see the visual activity for this chapter in the Online Study Guide at bedfordstmartins.com/hunt.

and abroad, and he personally oversaw book burnings. Although the Senate finally voted to censure McCarthy in the winter of 1954, the assault on freedom had been devastating and anticommunism had come to dominate political life.

An Economic Surge.   Given the wartime destruction, the economic rebirth of western Europe was even more surprising than the revival of democracy. In the first weeks and months after the war, the job of rebuilding often involved menial physical labor that mobilized entire populations for such jobs as clearing massive urban rubble by hand. Initially, governments diverted labor and capital into rebuilding infrastructure—transportation, communications, industrial capacity—and away from producing consumer goods. However, the scarcity of household goods sparked unrest; communism held some attraction because it seemed less interested in the revival of big business and more concerned with ensuring ordinary people a decent standard of living. In the midst of this growing discontent, the Marshall Plan suddenly boosted recovery with American dollars; food and consumer goods became more plentiful; and demand for automobiles, washing machines, and vacuum cleaners accelerated economic growth. Increased productivity wiped out most unemployment.

The postwar recovery also featured the adaptation of wartime technology to consumer industry and the continuation of military spending. Civilian travel expanded as nations organized their own airline industries based on improved airplane technology. Developed to relieve wartime shortages, synthetic goods such as nylon now became part of peacetime civilian life. Factories churned out a vast assortment of plastic products, ranging from pipes to household goods to rainwear. In the climate of cold war, however, military needs remained high: governments ordered bombs, fighter planes, tanks, and missiles (Figure 27.1) and sponsored military research. The outbreak of the Korean War in 1950 increased U.S. orders for manufactured goods to wage that war, further sustaining economic growth in Europe. Ultimately, the cold war prevented a repeat of the 1920s, when reduced military spending threw people out of jobs and fed the growth of fascism.

Large and small states alike developed modern economies in short order. In the twelve principal countries of western Europe, the annual rate of economic growth had been 1.3 percent per inhabitant between 1870 and 1913. Those countries almost tripled that rate between 1950 and 1973,

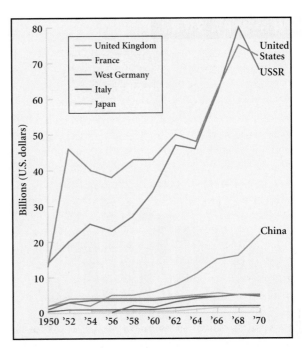

FIGURE 27.1 Military Spending and the Cold War Arms Race, 1950–1970
As soon as the war ended, the United States and the Soviet Union started a massive arms buildup that would continue into the 1980s. Because it had not suffered destruction during the war, the United States could afford to spend hundreds of billions of dollars on weapons. The Soviet Union could not, so its military expenditures deprived Soviet citizens of consumer goods. By the end of the twentieth century, the United States and Russia held vast arsenals of nuclear and other weapons and, along with France, led the way in selling arms that fueled war and genocide around the world.

attaining an annual rate of growth per capita of 3.8 percent. Among the larger powers, West Germany surprisingly became the economic leader, achieving by the 1960s a stunning revival called the "economic miracle." The smaller Scandinavian countries also achieved a notable recovery: Sweden succeeded in the development of automobile, truck, and shipbuilding industries. Finland modernized its industry in order to pay the reparations demanded by the Soviet Union for resisting its invasion; it also modernized its agriculture, which in turn forced the surplus farm population to seek factory work. Scandinavian women joined the workforce in record numbers, which also boosted economic growth and expanded prosperity. The thirty years after World War II were a golden age of European economic growth. (See "Taking Measure," page 892.)

TAKING MEASURE

1963=100

World Manufacturing Output, 1950–1970
During the long boom from the 1950s to the early 1970s, the world experienced increased industrial output, better agricultural production, and rising consumer spending. This era of prosperity resulted not only from the demand generated by the need to rebuild Europe and other areas affected by the war but also from the adaptation of war technology to peacetime uses. A General Agreement on Trade and Tariffs (GATT) was also implemented after the war, lowering tariffs and thus advancing trade. *(From* Hammond Atlas of the Twentieth Century *(London: Times Books, 1987), 127.)*

Birth of the Common Market. The creation of the Common Market, which evolved over time to become the European Union, was a final ingredient in the postwar recovery. The Marshall Plan demanded as a condition for assistance that recipient nations undertake far-reaching economic cooperation. In 1951, Italy, France, West Germany, Belgium, Luxembourg, and the Netherlands took a major step toward cooperation when they formed the European Coal and Steel Community (ECSC) — an organization to manage the joint production of basic resources. Importantly, it arranged for West Germany's abundant output of coal and steel to benefit all of western Europe. According to the ECSC's principal architect, Robert Schuman, the cooperation created by the organization would make another war "materially impossible." Simply put, the bonds of common productivity and trade would keep France and Germany from another cataclysmic war. (See Document, "The Schuman Plan on European Unity, 1950," page 893.)

The success of the ECSC led to the next momentous step: In 1957, the six ECSC members signed the Treaty of Rome, which provided for a more general trading partnership called the **European Economic Community (EEC)**, known popularly as the **Common Market**. The EEC reduced tariffs among the six partners and developed common trade policies. It brought under one cooperative economic umbrella more than two hundred million consumers and would eventually add several hundred million more. According to one of its founders, the EEC aimed to "prevent the race of nationalism, which is the true curse of the modern world." Increased cooperation produced great economic rewards for the six members, whose rates of economic growth soared. Britain pointedly refused to join the partnership at first, since membership would have required surrendering certain imperial trading rights among its Commonwealth partners such as Australia, New Zealand, and Canada. Since 1945, British politicians had shunned the developing continental trading bloc because, as one of them put it, participation would make Britain "just another European country." Even without Britain, the rising prosperity of a new western Europe joined in the Common Market was striking.

Economic planning and coordination by specialists (as developed during wartime) shaped the Common Market. Called technocrats, specialists working for the Common Market were to base decisions on expertise rather than on personal interest and on the goals of the Common Market as a whole rather than on the demands of any one nation. The aim was to reduce the potential for irrationality and violence in politics, both domestic and international. Administered by a commission of technocrats in Brussels, Belgium, the Common Market transcended the borders of the nation-state and thus exceeded the power of elected politicians. Some critics insisted (and some still insist

European Economic Community (EEC or Common Market): A consortium of six European countries established to promote free trade and economic cooperation among its members. Since its founding in 1957, its membership and activities have expanded.

The Schuman Plan on European Unity (1950)

One method of reviving European productivity and well-being after the devastation of World War II was for countries to pool natural resources such as coal and steel. Robert Schuman, French foreign minister from 1948 to 1953, was an architect of the European Coal and Steel Community, instituted after the war to share resources among France, West Germany, and other nations. Schuman, however, foresaw more long-term benefits, including lasting peace and the unification of all of Europe. The Schuman Plan, excerpted here, is widely viewed as a blueprint for today's European Union.

World peace can only be safeguarded if constructive efforts are made proportionate to the dangers which threaten it. . . . Europe will not be made all at once, nor according to a single, general plan. It will be formed by taking measures which work primarily to bring about real solidarity.

The gathering of the European nations requires the elimination of the age-old opposition of France and Germany. The action to be taken must first of all concern these two countries.

With this aim in view, the French Government proposes to take immediate action on one limited but decisive point. The French Government proposes that Franco-German production of coal and steel be placed under a common high authority within an organisation open to the participation of the other European nations.

The pooling of coal and steel production will immediately ensure the establishment of common bases for economic development as a first step in the federation of Europe, and will change the destinies of those regions which have long been devoted to the manufacture of arms, to which they themselves were the constant victims.

The common production thus established will make it plain that any war between France and Germany becomes not only unthinkable, but materially impossible. The establishment of this powerful entity, open to all countries willing to take part, and eventually capable of making available on equal terms the fundamental elements of industrial production, will give a real foundation to their economic unification. . . .

By pooling basic production and by creating a new high authority whose decisions will be binding on France, Germany and the other countries that may subsequently join, these proposals will lay the first concrete foundation for a European Federation which is so indispensable to the preservation of peace.

Source: U.S. Department of State Bulletin, June 12, 1959, 936–37. Reprinted in *Documents on European Union,* eds., A. G. Harryvan and J. van der Harst (New York: St. Martin's, 1997), 61–62.

---

today) that expert planning would diminish democracy by putting massive control in the hands of a bureaucracy instead of legislatures. Defenders were just as insistent that planning and cooperation would be the surest tools of prosperity and lasting peace.

The Welfare State: Common Ground East and West

On both sides of the cold war divide, governments channeled new resources into state-financed programs such as pensions, disability insurance, and national health care. These social programs taken as a whole became known as the **welfare state**, indicating that states were no longer interested solely in maintaining order and augmenting their power. Veterans' pensions and programs were primary, but the welfare state extended beyond those who

---

welfare state: A system comprising government-sponsored programs aimed to bring economic democracy by providing health care, family allowances, and pensions for veterans and retired workers.

---

had sacrificed in wartime. Because the European population had declined during the war, almost all countries now desperately wanted to boost the birthrate and thus gave couples direct financial aid for having children. Imitating the social security programs initiated under Bismarck and the more sweeping Swedish programs of the 1930s, nations expanded or created family allowances, health care and medical benefits, and programs for pregnant women and new mothers. The French gave larger family allowances for each birth after the first; for many French families, this allowance provided as much as a third of the household income.

Some welfare-state policies had a strong gender bias against women. Britain's maternity benefits and child allowances favored women who did not work outside the home by providing little coverage for workingwomen. The West German government passed strict legislation that forced employers to give women maternity leave, thus discouraging them from hiring women. It also cut back or eliminated pensions and benefits to married women. In fact, West Germans bragged about

The Welfare State in Action, 1947
The Danish creche or daycare center here shows the welfare state in action. Government programs to maintain the well-being of citizens became almost universally available in Europe, Canada, and (to a lesser extent) the United States. Children were seen as particularly important given the loss of the life in the war. So governments encouraged couples to reproduce through up-to-date health care systems, day-care centers, and generous family allowances to support family growth. *(Getty Images.)*

programs, family allowances, and maternity benefits were designed to encourage pregnancies by workingwomen. A national health program provided medical services, as in most countries to the west, but the hardships of everyday life undermined the drive to increase population. The scarcity of consumer goods, the housing shortages, and the lack of household conveniences discouraged workingwomen in Communist countries from having large families no matter what the government wanted. Because women bore the sole burden of domestic duties under such conditions on top of their paying jobs, they hardly welcomed additional children. As a result, birthrates in the eastern bloc stagnated.

Across Europe, welfare-state programs aimed to improve people's health. State-funded health care systems covered medical needs in most industrial nations except the United States. The combination of better material conditions and state provision of health care dramatically extended life expectancy and lowered rates of infant mortality. Contributing to the overall progress, the number of doctors and dentists more than doubled between the end of World War I and 1950, and vaccines greatly reduced the death toll from such diseases as tuberculosis, diphtheria, measles, and polio. In England, schoolchildren stood an inch taller, on average, than children the same age had a decade earlier.

State initiatives in other areas played a role in raising the standard of living. A growing network of government-built atomic power plants brought more thorough electrification of eastern Europe and the Soviet Union. Governments legislated more leisure time for workers. Beginning in 1955, Italian workers received twenty-eight paid holidays annually; in Sweden, workers received twenty-nine vacation days, a number that grew in the 1960s. Housing shortages brought on by three decades of economic depression and destructive war meant that postwar Europeans often lived with three generations sharing one or two rooms. To rebuild, governments sponsored a postwar housing boom. New suburbs and even entire cities formed around the edges of major urban areas in both East and West. Many buildings went up slapdash, and although some suburbs ultimately were seen as a blight on the environment, they dramatically improved living conditions for postwar refugees, workers, and immigrants.

removing women from the workforce, claiming that doing so distinguished democratic practices from Communist ones. The refusal to build day-care centers or to allow stores to remain open in the evening so that workingwomen could buy food for their families led West Germany to have among the lowest rate of female employment of any industrial country. Another result of West Germany's discriminatory policies was a high rate of female poverty in old age.

By contrast, in eastern Europe and the Soviet Union, where wartime loss of life had been enormous, women worked nearly full-time and usually outnumbered men in the workforce. As in many western European countries, however, child-care

Recovery in the East

To create a Soviet bloc according to Stalin's prewar vision of industrialization, Communists revived the crushing methods that had served before to transform peasant economies. In eastern Europe, Stalin enforced collectivized agriculture and badly needed industrialization through the nationalization of private property. In Hungary, for example, Communists seized and reapportioned all estates over twelve hundred acres. Having gained support of the poorer peasants through this redistribution, Communists later dispossessed many of their prized lands and pushed them into cooperative farming, though less thoroughly than in the USSR. In Poland, a substantial number of private farms remained. The process of collectivization was brutal, and rural people looked back on the 1950s as dreadful. But some among those in the countryside felt that ultimately their lives and their children's lives had improved. "Before we peasants were dirty and poor, we worked like dogs. . . . Was that a good life? No sir, it wasn't. . . . I was a miserable sharecropper and my son is an engineer," said one Romanian peasant. Despite modernization, government investment in agriculture was never high enough to produce the bumper crops of western Europe, and even the USSR depended on produce from the small plots that enterprising farmers cultivated on the side.

Constructing the Soviet Bloc. Stalin admired American industrial know-how and prodded the Communist economies to match U.S. productivity. The Soviet Union formed regional organizations like those in the West, instituting the Council for Mutual Economic Assistance (COMECON) in 1949 to coordinate economic relations among the satellite countries and Moscow. The terms of the COMECON relationship worked against the satellite states, for the USSR was allowed to buy goods from its clients at bargain prices and sell goods to them at exorbitant ones. Nonetheless, these formerly peasant states became oriented toward technology and bureaucratically directed industrial economies. Modernization of production created new technical and bureaucratic careers, and modernizers in the satellite states touted the virtues of steel plants and modern transport. Tired of the struggles on the land, rural people moved to cities, where they received better education, health care, and ultimately jobs, albeit at the price of repression. The Roman Catholic church, which often protested the imposition of communism, was crushed as much as possible or infiltrated by government agents. Elites, including professionals, were discriminated against or imprisoned, sometimes forced into hard labor in uranium and other dangerous mines. This policy cleared away opposition—real and imagined—to the Communist takeover of eastern Europe.

Science and culture were the building blocks of Stalinism in the satellite countries as well as in the USSR. State-instituted programs aimed to build loyalty to the modernizing regime; thus, citizens were obliged to attend adult education classes, women's groups, and public ceremonies. An intense program of Russification and de-Christianization forced students in eastern Europe to read histories of the war that ignored their own country's resistance and gave the Red Army sole credit for fighting the Nazis. Rigid censorship resulted in what even one Communist writer in the USSR characterized as "a dreary torrent of colorless, mediocre literature." Stalin also purged

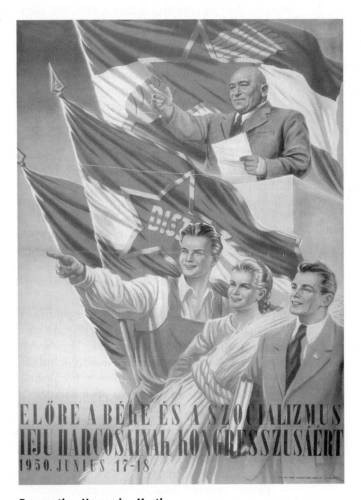

Re-creating Hungarian Youth
People across Europe focused on the well-being of young people after World War II, and in the Soviet sphere this took the form of education in Communist ways. Youth groups, such as those in the early Stalinist USSR, served this end, and vivid posters in the Soviet realist style carried inspirational messages: "Forward for the Congress of the Young Fighters of Peace and Socialism," reads this typical message to Hungarian youth in 1950. Why was the condition of youth so important a concern after World War II? Why was youth so prominent in popular culture during this period? *(Magyar Nemzeti Múzeum, Budapest [Hungarian National Museum].)*

prominent wartime leaders to ensure obedience and conformity. Marshal Zhukov, a popular architect of the Soviet wartime victory, was shipped to a distant command, while Anna Akhmatova, the widely admired poet who championed wartime resistance to the Nazis, was confined to a crowded hospital room because she refused to glorify Stalin in her postwar poetry.

The Death of Stalin. In March 1953, amid looming troubles, Stalin died, and it soon became clear that the old ways would not hold. Political prisoners in the labor camps rebelled, leading to the release of more than a million people from the Gulag. At the other end of the social order, Soviet officials, despite enjoying luxury goods and plentiful food, had come to distrust Stalinism and now favored change. As protests took place across the Soviet bloc, governments stepped up the production of consumer goods—a policy called goulash communism (after the Hungarian stew) because it resulted in more food for ordinary people. The future after Stalin remained uncertain, however.

In 1955, **Nikita Khrushchev** (1894–1971), an illiterate coal miner before the Bolshevik Revolution, outmaneuvered other rivals to emerge the undisputed leader of the Soviet Union—but he did so without resorting to the Stalinist practice of executing his opponents. Khrushchev listened to popular complaints in both city and countryside about conditions and then made the surprising move of attacking Stalin. At a party congress in 1956, Khrushchev denounced the "cult of personality" Stalin had built about himself and announced that Stalinism did not equal communism. Khrushchev thus cagily attributed problems with communism to a single individual. The "secret speech"—it was not published in the USSR but became known fairly quickly—was a bombshell. People experienced, in the words of one writer, "a holiday of the soul." Debates broke out in public, and books appeared championing the ordinary worker against the party bureaucracy. The climate of relative tolerance for free expression after Stalin's death was called the thaw.

Protest erupted once more in early summer 1956, when discontented Polish railroad workers struck for better wages. Popular support for their cause ushered in policies providing more resources for ordinary people's needs. Inspired by the Polish

example and angry at living under communism, Hungarians rebelled against forced collectivization in October 1956—"the golden October," they would call their uprising. As in Poland, economic issues, especially announcements of reduced wages, contributed to the outbreak of violence, but the protest soon targeted the entire Communist system. Tens of thousands of protesters filled the streets of Budapest and succeeded in returning a popular hero, Imre Nagy, to power. When Nagy announced that Hungary might leave the Warsaw Pact, however, Soviet troops moved in, killing tens of thousands and causing hundreds of thousands more to flee to the West. Nagy was hanged. The crushing of the Hungarian Revolution thus vividly displayed the limits to the thaw. Despite a rhetoric of democracy, the United States refused to intervene in Hungary, choosing not to risk another world war by challenging the Soviet sphere of influence.

The failure of eastern European uprisings overshadowed significant changes since Stalin's death. While defeating his rivals, Khrushchev ended the Stalinist purges and reformed the courts, which came to function according to procedures instead of staging the show trials of the past. The gates of the Gulag opened further, and the secret police lost many of its arbitrary powers. "It has become more interesting to visit and see people," Boris Pasternak said of the changes. "It has become easier to work." In 1957, the Soviets successfully launched the first artificial earth satellite, *Sputnik*, and in 1961 they put the first cosmonaut, Yuri Gagarin, in orbit around the earth. The Soviets' edge in space technology shocked the Western bloc and motivated the creation of the U.S. National Aeronautics and Space Administration (NASA). For Soviets, such successes indicated that the USSR had achieved Stalin's goal of modernization and might inch further toward freedom.

Khrushchev, however, was erratic and crude, showing himself open to changes in Soviet culture at one moment and then bullying honest writers at another. After assaulting Pasternak because his novel *Doctor Zhivago* cast doubt on the glory of the Communist revolution and affirmed the value of the individual, in 1961 he allowed the publication of Aleksandr Solzhenitsyn's *One Day in the Life of Ivan Denisovitch*. This chilling account of life in the Gulag was useful, however, in confirming Khrushchev's denunciation of Stalin's crimes and excesses. Under the thaw, Khrushchev himself made several trips to the West and was more widely seen by the public than Stalin. More confident and more affluent, the Soviets took steps to reduce their diplomacy's paranoid style and to expand

---

Nikita Khrushchev (nyih KEE tuh kroosh CHAWF): Leader of the USSR from c. 1955 until his dismissal in 1964; known for his speech denouncing Stalin, creation of the "thaw," and participation in the Cuban missile crisis.

communism's appeal in the emerging nations of Asia, Africa, and Latin America. Despite the USSR's more relaxed posture, however, the cold war advanced and the superpowers moved the world to the nuclear brink.

REVIEW: What factors drove recovery in western Europe? In eastern Europe?

Decolonization in a Cold War Climate

After World War II, activists in colonized regions used the postwar chaos in Europe and the uncertainties of the cold war to achieve their long-held goal of liberation. At war's end, Britain, France, the Netherlands, and other colonial powers repressed nationalist groups and futilely attempted to reimpose their control. As in World War I, colonized peoples had been on the front lines defending the West; and as before, they had witnessed the full barbarism of Western warfare. Like African American soldiers in the U.S. army, they experienced discrimination even while saving the West. Excluded from victory parades so that the great powers could maintain the illusion of white and Western supremacy, colonial veterans returning home still did not receive the rights of citizenship promised them. Moreover, successive wars had allowed local industries in the colonies to develop, while industry in the imperial homelands fell into decline. As a result of the war, people in Asia, Africa, and the Middle East, often led by individuals steeped in Western values and experienced in war and business, sped toward independence.

The path to independence—a process called **decolonization**—was paved with difficulties. In Africa, a continent whose peoples spoke more than five thousand languages and dialects, the European creation of convenient administrative units such as Nigeria and Rhodesia had cut across ethnic lines and undermined local cultures. Religion played a divisive role in independence movements. In India, Hindus and Muslims battled one another even though they shared the goal of eliminating the British. In the Middle East and North Africa, pan-Arab and pan-Islamic movements—that is, those wanting to bring together all Arabs or all

---

decolonization: The process—both violent and peaceful—by which colonies gained their independence from the imperial powers after World War II.

Jawaharlal Nehru, Prime Minister of India (1952)
Jawaharlal Nehru (1889–1964) led his newly independent country of India from 1947 to 1964, during its first years of freedom from British rule. Both sides in the cold war rivalry competed to make India an ally, but U.S. presidents and diplomats hesitated to woo this crucial leader in part because of their suspicions about the toughness of a man who wore what appeared to them a dress along with a rose pinned to it. Nehru and his compatriots were thought to be too "feminine" to be reliable in an age of robust cold war heroes like the fictional James Bond. Nehru chose to maintain India, though a populous Asian democracy, as a neutral country. *(© Bettmann/Corbis.)*

Muslims as the basis for decolonization—might seem to have been unifying forces. Yet many Muslims were not Arab, not all Arabs were Muslim, and Islam itself encompassed many competing beliefs and sects. Differences among religious beliefs, ethnic groups, and cultural practices—many of them invented or promoted by the colonizers to divide and rule—worked against political unity. Despite these complications, various peoples in what was coming to be called the third world succeeded in overthrowing imperialism, while the United States and the Soviet Union rushed in to co-opt them for the cold war.

The End of Empire in Asia

At the end of World War II, leaders in Asia succeeded in mobilizing mass discontent to drive out foreign rulers. Declining from an imperial power to a small island nation, Britain was the biggest loser. In 1947, it parted with India, whose independence it had promised in the 1930s. While some two million Indian men were mobilized to fight in the Middle East and Asia, local Indian industry became an important supplier of war goods, and Indian business leaders bought out British entrepreneurs short of cash. Now, armed with economic might and an effective military, Indians began to face off with the British in strikes and other protests.

Britain quickly faced the inevitable, decreeing that two countries should emerge from the old colony, so great was the mistrust the British had sown between the Indian National Congress and Muslim League parties. Thus, in 1947 India was created for Hindus, and Pakistan—itself later divided into two parts—for Muslims. During the independence year, political tensions exploded among opposing members of the two religions. Hundreds of thousands were massacred in the great shift of populations between India and Pakistan. In 1948, a radical Hindu assassinated Gandhi, who though a Hindu himself had continued to champion religious reconciliation. As some half a billion Asians gained their independence, Britain's sole notable Asian colony was Hong Kong.

In 1949, a Communist takeover in China brought in a government led by Mao Zedong (1893–1976) that was no longer the plaything of the traditional colonial powers. Chinese communism in the new People's Republic of China emphasized above all the welfare of the peasantry rather than the industrial proletariat and was thus distinct from Marxism and Stalinism. At the same time, backed by Stalin, Mao instituted reforms such as civil equality for women but also imposed Soviet-style collectivization, rapid industrialization, and brutal repression of the privileged classes.

The United States and the Soviet Union were deeply interested in East Asia, the United States be-

The Korean War, 1950–1953

Indochina, 1954

cause of the region's economic importance and the USSR because of its shared borders. The victory of the Chinese Communists spurred both superpowers to increase their involvement in Asian politics, where they faced off first in Korea, which had been split at the thirty-eighth parallel after World War II. In 1950, the North Koreans, with the support of the Soviet Union, invaded U.S.-backed South Korea, whose agents had themselves been stirring up tensions with incursions across the border. The United States maneuvered the Security Council of the United Nations into approving a "police action" against the North, and its forces quickly drove well into North Korean territory, where they were met by the Chinese army. After two and a half years of a horribly destructive stalemate, the opposing sides finally agreed to a settlement in 1953: Korea would remain split at its prewar border, the thirty-eighth parallel. As a result of the Korean War, the United States increased its military spending from $10.9 billion in 1948 to almost $60 billion in 1953. The expansion of the cold war to Asia prompted the creation of an Asian counterpart to NATO: the U.S.-backed Southeast Asia Treaty Organization (SEATO), established in 1954. An important effect of the Korean War was the rapid reindustrialization of Japan to provide the United States with supplies.

The cold war then spread to Indochina, where nationalists had been struggling against the postwar revival of French imperialism. Their leader, the European-educated Ho Chi Minh (1890–1969), preached both nationalism and socialism and built a powerful organization, the Viet Minh, to fight colonial rule. He advocated the redistribution of land held by big landowners, especially in the rich agricultural area in southern Indochina where some six thousand owners possessed more than 60 percent of the land. Viet Minh peasant guerrillas ultimately defeated the technologically superior French army, which was receiving aid from the United States, in the bloody battle of Dien Bien Phu in 1954. Later that year, the Geneva Conference carved out an independent Laos and divided Vietnam along the seventeenth parallel into North and South, each free from French control. The Communist-backed Viet Minh, under Ho Chi Minh as president, ruled in the north, while the United States supported the repressive regime of Ngo Dinh Diem (1901–1963) in the south. Superpower intervention undermined the peace agreement while risking nuclear war at any moment.

The Struggle for Identity in the Middle East

Independence struggles in the Middle East highlighted the world's growing need for oil and showed the ability of small countries to maneuver between the superpowers. As in other regions dominated by the West, Middle Eastern peoples resisted attempts to reimpose imperial control after 1945. Weakened by the war, British oil companies wanted to tighten their grip on profits, as the value of this energy source soared. But the British leaders arrogantly behaved as if they were still dominant. For example, Winston Churchill, paying a visit to Saudi Arabia during negotiations over the renewal of Britain's oil rights in the country, insisted that he be served drinks and cigars, sneering at the Islamic prohibitions against alcohol and tobacco. Outraged by this insult, Saudi Arabia turned to the United States, saying that the superpower could take over the oil consortium so long as Britain was kept out. By playing the powers against one another, Middle Eastern leaders gained their independence and built their economic clout.

The legacy of the Holocaust, however, complicated the Middle Eastern political scene. Western commitment to secure a Jewish settlement in the Middle East stirred up Arabs' determination not to be pushed out of their ancient homeland. When World War II broke out, six hundred thousand Jewish settlers and twice as many Arabs lived, in intermittent conflict, in British-controlled Palestine. In 1947, an exhausted Britain ceded Palestine to the newly created United Nations, which voted to partition Palestine into an Arab region and a Jewish one (Map 27.4). Conflicting claims, however, led to war, and Jewish military forces prevailed. On May 14, 1948, the state of Israel came into being. "The dream had come true," Golda Meir, the future prime minister of Israel, remembered, but "too late to save those who

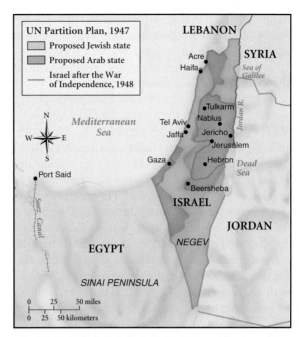

MAP 27.4 The Partition of Palestine and the Creation of Israel, 1947–1948
The creation of the Jewish state of Israel in 1948 against a backdrop of ongoing wars among Jews and indigenous Arab peoples made the Middle East a powder keg, a situation that has lasted until the present day. The struggle for resources and for securing the borders of viable nation-states was at the heart of these bitter contests, threatening to pull the superpowers into a third world war.

had perished in the Holocaust." Israel opened its gates to immigrants, pitting its expansionist ambitions against those of its Arab neighbors.

One of those neighbors, Egypt, gained its independence from Britain at the end of the war. Britain, however, retained its dominance in shipping to Asia through control of the Suez Canal, which was owned by a British-run company. In 1952, Colonel Gamal Abdel Nasser (1918–1970) became Egypt's president on a platform of economic modernization and true national independence — meaning Egyptian control of the canal. In July 1956, Nasser nationalized the canal: "I am speaking in the name of every Egyptian Arab," he remarked in his speech explaining the takeover, "and in the name of all free countries and of all those who believe in liberty and are ready to defend it." Nasser became a heroic figure to Arabs in the region, especially when Britain, supported by Israel and France, attacked Egypt, bringing the Suez crisis to a head while the Hungarian revolt was in full swing. The British branded Nasser another Hitler and hoped that the Hungarian revolt would distract the superpowers. But the United States, fearing that Egypt would turn to the USSR, made the British back down. Nasser's triumph inspired confidence that colonized peoples around the world could gain their independence.

New Nations in Africa

In sub-Saharan Africa, nationalist leaders roused their people to challenge Europe's increasing demand for resources and labor, which resulted only in poverty for African peoples. "The European Merchant is my shepherd, and I am in want," went one African version of the Twenty-third Psalm. Many Africans flocked to shantytowns in cities during the war, where they kept themselves alive through doing menial labor for whites and scavenging. At war's end, veterans returned home and protest mounted. Kwame Nkrumah (1909–1972), for example, led the inhabitants of the British-controlled West African Gold Coast in Gandhian-style passive re-

sistance, finally driving the British to withdraw and bringing the state of Ghana into being in 1957. Nigeria, the most populous African region, achieved independence in 1960, and many other African states also became free (see Map 27.5).

Where the population was almost entirely black, independence came less violently than in mixed-race territory with large settler populations. The eastern coast and southern and central areas of Africa had numerous European settlers, who violently resisted giving up their control. In British East Africa, where white settlers ruled in splendor and where blacks lacked both land and economic opportunity, fighting erupted in the 1950s. African men formed rebel groups named the Land Freedom Army but nicknamed Mau Mau. With women serving as provisioners, messengers, and weapon stealers, Mau Mau bands, composed mostly of war veterans from the Kikuyu ethnic group, tried to recover land from whites. In 1964, the Land Freedom Army's resistance helped Kenya gain formal inde-

MAP 27.5 The Decolonization of Africa, 1951–1990

The liberation of Africa from European rule was an uneven process, sometimes occurring peacefully and at other times demanding armed struggle to drive out European settlers, governments, and armies. The difficult—and costly—process of nation building following liberation involved setting up state institutions, including educational and other services. Creating national unity out of many ethnicities also took work, except where the struggle against colonialism had already brought people together.

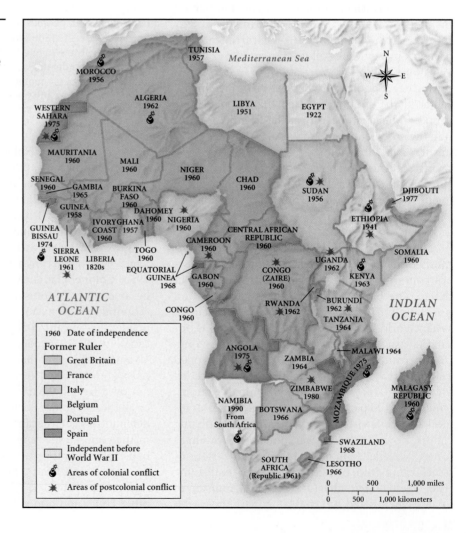

pendence, but only after the British had put hundreds of thousands of Kikuyus in concentration camps — called a "living hell" and a "British gulag" by those tortured there. The British slaughtered tens of thousands more.

France — although eager to regain its great-power status after its humiliating defeat and occupation in World War II — followed the British pattern of granting independence with relatively little bloodshed to territories such as Tunisia, Morocco, and West Africa, where there were few white settlers. In Algeria, however, the French fought bitterly to keep control, not only because the French army took such pride in its conquest of Algeria but also because a huge European population prospered there. In the final days of World War II, the French army massacred tens of thousands of Algerian nationalists seeking independence; however, the liberation movement resurfaced with ferocious intensity as the Front for National Liberation (FNL) in 1954. The French dug in, sending more than four hundred thousand troops. Neither side fought according to the rules of warfare: the French savagely tortured Algerian Arabs; Algerian women, shielded by gender stereotypes, planted bombs in European cafés and carried weapons to assassination sites. "The loss of Algeria," warned one statesman, defending French savagery, "would be an unprecedented national disaster," while the FNL, far less powerful and smaller in number, took its case to the court of world opinion. Reports of the French army's barbarous practices against Algeria's Muslim population prompted protests in Paris and around the globe.

France's Fourth Republic collapsed over Algeria, and Charles de Gaulle returned to power in 1958. While promising an end to the Algerian quagmire, he demanded the creation of a new republican government, one with a strong president who chose the prime minister and could exercise emergency power. As de Gaulle's plans to decolonize Algeria unfolded, the French military launched a campaign of terrorism within France itself. By 1962, de Gaulle had negotiated independence with the Algerian nationalists, and hundreds of thousands of *pieds noirs* — or "black feet," as the French condescendingly called Europeans in Algeria — as well as their Arab supporters fled to France.

Violent resistance to the reimposition of colonial rule also ended the Dutch and Belgian empires, and as newly independent nations emerged in Asia, Africa, and the Middle East, structures arose to promote international security and worldwide deliberations that included representation from the new states. Foremost among these was

the **United Nations (UN)**, convened for the first time in 1945. One notable change ensured the UN a greater chance of success than the League of Nations: both the United States and the Soviet Union were active members from the outset. The UN's charter outlined a collective global authority that would resolve conflicts and provide military protection if any members were threatened by aggression. In 1955, the Indonesian president Sukarno, who had succeeded in wrenching Indonesian independence from the Dutch, sponsored the Bandung Convention of nonaligned nations to set a common policy for achieving modernization and facing the superpowers. Newly independent countries viewed the future with hope but still had to contend with the high costs of nation building and problems left from decades of colonial exploitation. Both UN deliberations and meetings of emerging nations such as the Bandung Conference began raising major global issues such as human rights and inequities between the countries of the north, which had prospered through colonial plunder, and those of the south, which had been plundered.

Newcomers Arrive in Europe

Amid the uncertainties of wars of liberation and independence, people from the former colonies began migrating to Europe — a reversal of the nineteenth-century trend of migration out of Europe. The first influx of non-Europeans came from Britain's Caribbean possessions right after the war. Next, labor shortages in Germany, France, Switzerland, and elsewhere drove governments to negotiate with southern European countries for temporary workers. The German situation was particularly dire; in 1950, the working-age population (people between the ages of fifteen and sixty-four) was composed of 15.5 million men and 18 million women. In an ideological climate that kept women out of the workforce, the government desperately needed immigrants. Germany and France next turned to North African and then to sub-Saharan countries in the 1960s. Countries in the Soviet bloc took refugees from war-torn Southeast Asia. Then, in the late 1970s, clandestine workers from Africa and Asia began entering countries like Italy that had formerly exported labor. Scandinavia received immigrants from around the world who flocked there because of reportedly greater opportunity and social pro-

---

United Nations (UN): An organization set up in 1945 for collective security and for the resolution of international conflicts through both deliberation and the use of force.

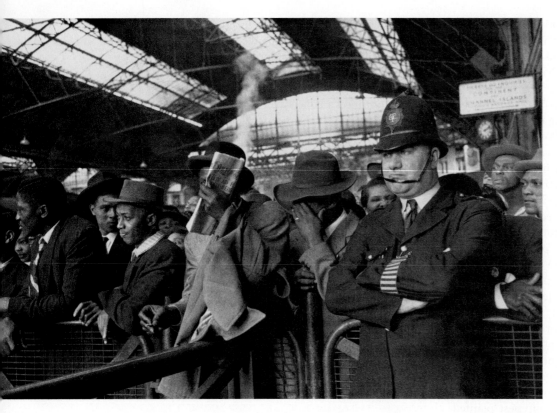

Newcomers to Europe
World War II disrupted everyday life and patterns of trade not only in Europe but also around the globe. Some of the first people to immigrate to Europe in search of postwar opportunity were from the Caribbean (like these men photographed in London in 1956) and South Asia. An expanding welfare state hired some of them to do menial work in hospitals, clinics, and construction, no matter what their qualifications. Governments and businesses in western Europe needed these new laborers to rebuild after World War II, and though some objected, many of these workers—and their wives and children—became not only citizens but political, economic, and cultural leaders as well.
(© Hulton-Deutsch Collection/Corbis.)

grams to integrate newcomers. By the 1980s, some 8 percent of the European population was foreign-born, compared to 6 percent in the United States.

The negotiated agreements stipulated that immigrant workers would have only temporary resident status, with a regular process of emigration back to their homeland. Turks and Algerians would arrive in Germany or France, for example, to work for a set period of time, return home temporarily to see their families, then head back to Europe for another period as guest workers. Initially, these workers were housed in barracks-like dormitories and few Europeans paid any attention to the quality of their lives. They were welcomed because they took few social services, not even needing education because they came as adults. For businesspeople and policymakers alike, temporary workers made good economic sense. Virtually none of the welfare-state benefits would apply to them; often their menial work was off the books. "As they are young," one French business publication explained, "the immigrants often pay more in taxes than they receive in allowances." Most immigrants did jobs that people in the West were not likely to want: they collected garbage, built roads, and cleaned homes. Although men predominated among migrant workers, women performed similar chores for even less pay.

Seeing Europe as a land of relatively good government, wealth, and opportunity, many immigrants were determined to stay. They simply appreciated having jobs and decent living conditions. As one Chinese immigrant to Spain put it: "If you want to be a millionaire, you must go to Singapore; if you want to be rich, you must go to Germany; but if you want good weather and an easy life, go to Spain." The advantages of living in Europe, especially the higher wages, became so overwhelming that clandestine workers began arriving. As empires collapsed, European populations became more diverse in terms of race, religion, ethnicity, and social life. As in the United States, many of these newcomers eventually became citizens and their children achieved high positions in government, business, education, and the professions.

REVIEW: What were the results of decolonization?

Daily Life and Culture in the Shadow of Nuclear War

Both World War II and the cold war shaped postwar culture. People engaged in heated debate over the responsibility for Nazism, the matter of ethnic and racial justice, and the merits of the two superpowers. During this period of intense self-scrutiny, Europeans discussed the Americanization that seemed to accompany the influx of U.S. dollars, consumer goods, and cultural media. Were they becoming too materialistic, like the Americans, or too intolerant like the Soviets? As Europeans examined their war-filled past and their newfound prosperity, the cold war menaced hopes for peace and stability. In 1961, the USSR demanded the construction of a massive wall that physically divided the city of Berlin in half. In October 1962, the world held its breath while the leaders of the Soviet Union and the United States nearly provoked nuclear conflagration over the issue of missiles on the island of Cuba. In hindsight, the existence of extreme nuclear threat in an age of unprecedented prosperity seems utterly bewildering, but for those who lived with the threat of global annihilation, the dangers were all too real.

Restoring "Western" Values

After the depravity of fascism, cultural currents in Europe and the United States reemphasized universal values and spiritual renewal. Some saw the churches as central to the restoration of values through an active commitment to "re-Christianizing" both the West and the world without concern for national boundaries or imperial interests. Responding to what he saw as a crisis in faith caused by affluence and secularism, Pope John XXIII (r. 1958–1963) in 1962 convened the Second Vatican Council, known as **Vatican II**. The Council modernized the liturgy, democratized many church procedures, and at the last session in 1965 renounced church doctrine that condemned the Jewish people as guilty of killing Jesus. Vatican II promoted ecumenism — that is, mutual cooperation among the world's faiths — and outreach to the world different from the old spirit of missionary crusading on behalf of imperialism.

The trend toward a more secular culture continued despite reform in the churches. In the early postwar years, people in the U.S. bloc emphasized the triumph of a Western heritage, a Western civilization, and Western values over fascism, and they characterized the war as one "to defend civilization [from] a conspiracy against man." This definition of *West* often emphasized the heritage of Greece and Rome and the rise of national governments in England, France, and western Europe as they encountered "barbaric" forces, be these no-

madic tribes, Nazi armies, Communist agents, or national liberation movements in Asia and Africa. Many white Europeans looked back nostalgically on their imperial history and produced exotic films and novels about conquest and its pageantry. University courses in Western civilization flourished after the war to reaffirm Western values.

Holocaust and Resistance Literature. Readers around the world snapped up memoirs of the death camps and tales of the resistance. Rescued from the Third Reich in 1940, Nelly Sachs won the Nobel Prize for Literature in 1966 for her poetry about the Holocaust. Anne Frank's *Diary of a Young Girl* (1947), the poignant record of a teenager hidden with her family in the back of an Amsterdam house, showed the survival of Western values in the face of Nazi persecution. Amid the menacing evils of Nazism, Anne wrote that she never stopped believing that "people are really good at heart." Governments erected permanent plaques at spots where resisters had been killed, and biographies of resistance leaders filled magazines and bookstalls. Although resistance efforts were publicized, discussion of collaboration was suppressed because it threatened to open old wounds. Thus, French filmmakers, for instance, avoided the subject for decades after the war. Many a politician with a Nazi past returned easily to the new cultural mainstream even as the stories of resistance took on mythical qualities.

Existential Philosophy. By the end of the 1940s, **existentialism** became the rage among the cultural elites and students in universities. This philosophy explored the meaning of human existence in a world where evil flourished. Two of existentialism's leaders, Albert Camus and Jean-Paul Sartre, had written for the resistance during the war, and in its aftermath they confronted the question of "being," given what they perceived as the absence of God and the tragic breakdown of morality. Their answer was that being, or existing, was not the automatic process either of God's creation or of birth into the natural world. One was not born with spiritual goodness in the image of a creator, but instead one created an "authentic" existence through action and choice. Camus's novels, such as *The Stranger* (1942) and *The Plague* (1947), pondered the responsibility of humans living under an evil and corrupt political order. Sartre's writings emphasized political activism and resistance under

---

Vatican II: A Catholic Council held between 1962 and 1965 to modernize some aspects of church teachings (such as condemnation of Jews), to update the liturgy, and to promote cooperation among the faiths (i.e., ecumenism).

---

existentialism: A philosophy prominent after World War II developed primarily by Jean-Paul Sartre to stress the importance of action in the creation of an authentic self.

Jean-Paul Sartre and Simone de Beauvoir
The postwar period saw the rise of glossy, richly illustrated weekly magazines featuring news and pop culture. The faces of even the most complex philosophers became well known to the public, while their private lives intrigued readers. The public story of these two existentialists, who were seen to promote the revival of human values after the nightmare of fascism, hid the twisted relationship Sartre and Beauvoir actually had. Does the photo give any hints as to why Sartre and Beauvoir and their circle received such media attention? *(Editions Gallimard.)*

totalitarianism. Even though they had never confronted the enormous problems of making choices while living under fascism, young people in the 1950s found existentialism compelling and made it the most fashionable philosophy of the day.

In 1949, **Simone de Beauvoir,** Sartre's lifetime companion, published the twentieth century's most important work on the condition of women, *The Second Sex.* Beauvoir believed that most women had failed to take the kind of action necessary to lead authentic lives. Instead, they lived in the world of biological necessity, devoting themselves exclusively to having children. Failing to create an authentic self through action and accomplishment, they had become its opposite — an object, or "Other." Moreover, instead of struggling to define themselves and assert their freedom, women passively accepted their lives as defined by men. Beauvoir's classic book was a smash hit, in large part because people thought Sartre had writ-

***

Simone de Beauvoir (see MAWN duh bohv WAHR): Author of *The Second Sex,* a globally influential work that created an interpretation of women's age-old inferior status from existentialist philosophy.

ten it. Both writers were celebrities, for the media spread the new commitment to humane values just as it had previously spread support for Nazism or for other political ideas.

Race and Human Rights. People of color in Africa and Asia contributed new theories of humanity by exploring the topics of liberation and racial difference. During the 1950s, Frantz Fanon, a black psychiatrist from the French colony of Martinique, began analyzing liberation movements. He wrote that the mental functioning of the colonized person was "traumatized" by the brutal imposition of outside values. Ruled by guns, the colonized person knew only violence and would thus naturally decolonize by means of violence. Translated into many languages, Fanon's *Black Skin, White Masks* (1952) and *The Wretched of the Earth* (1961) posed the question of how to decolonize one's culture and mind.

Simultaneous with decolonization, the commitment of such long-standing organizations as the National Association for the Advancement of Colored People (NAACP, founded 1909) to the cause of civil rights intensified in the 1950s. African Americans had fought in the war to defeat the Nazi idea of white racial superiority; as civilians, they now hoped to advance that ideal in the United States. With its ruling in *Brown v. Board of Education* (1954), the U.S. Supreme Court declared that segregated education violated the U.S. Constitution. The next step in the civil rights movement came in December 1955, in Montgomery, Alabama, when Rosa Parks, a part-time secretary for the local branch of the NAACP, boarded a city bus and took the first available seat, in the so-called white section. By sitting in that section, Parks violated discriminatory and often brutal Southern laws toward African Americans. When a white man found himself without a seat, the driver screamed at Parks, "Nigger, move back." She refused to move, and her action led to a boycott of public transportation in Montgomery and eventually to widespread nonviolent civil disobedience among African Americans throughout the South.

Civil rights groups boycotted discriminatory businesses, held sit-ins at segregated facilities, and registered black voters disfranchised by local regulations. Many talented leaders emerged, foremost among them Martin Luther King Jr. (1929–1968), a Baptist pastor from Georgia whose speeches roused activists to nonviolent resistance despite brutal white retaliation. Strongly influenced by Gandhi's life and practice of nonviolent resistance, King advocated "soulforce" — Gandhi's *satya-*

Consumerism, Youth, and the Birth of the Generation Gap

Young people were at the cutting edge of consumerism and other aspects of Americanization and economic revival. The generation gap, so much talked about in the 1960s, was taking shape earlier because of youthful openness on matters of the body and sexuality. Not so mired in the war as their parents, the young were ready for adventure—and adults worried about the consequences. Here an Austrian working-class woman (born in 1933) who sewed for a living describes her youth around 1955.

I bought myself records, American blues and jazz, Benny Goodman and Louis Armstrong. I was happy dancing the boogie-woogie. . . .

In fashion I was always very much in opposition to my mother. First, there was the craze around nylon stockings, which were very expensive, and which almost everyone bought. We wore long checked skirts, not made of sheep's wool but of a "mixed" wool that was produced out of rags. Then came a short skirt, just above the knee. When I went dancing, however, everyone wore tight, fashionable skirts. One really had to get oneself into them with a shoehorn, and one's backside stood out. I then sewed a kind of cascade on one side, and thus attired, I proudly went dancing.

At first one wore hair long. But my boss was at me so much about it that I had it cut. Then with the new permanents from America one got a totally new look which was flat in the back with a garland of curls around the rest. But fashion changed fast, at one minute such a hairdo was modern, but then one had to put a comb in to push it up higher.

My home was very nice, with a great deal of love, and because of that my parents gave me a lot of freedom although my mother was always concerned. Above everything she always worried: "What will the neighbors think?"

We only spoke about sex with our schoolmates. Certainly nothing about it came from my parents, nothing either from the school. No, one could not ask about such things. . . . Everything was taboo. And boys and girls were strictly segregated from one another in the school. I remember at carnival time a boy came to school dressed as a girl and was sent right home.

Source: Birgit Bolognese-Leuchtenmüller et al., eds., *Frauen der ersten Stunde 1945–1955.* (Vienna: Medieninhaber Europaverlag, 1985), 20–21. Translation by Bonnie G. Smith.

---

graha, or "holding to truth"—to counter aggression. The postwar culture of nonviolence shaped the early years of the civil rights movement until the influence of Fanon and other third world activists turned it toward more violent activism in pursuit of rights.

Consumerism and Shifting Gender Norms

Government spending on Europe's reconstruction and welfare helped prevent the kind of upheaval that had followed World War I. A rising birthrate and bustling youth culture made for an upsurge in consumer spending that contrasted with the absence of spending in wartime because of a lack of anything to consume. Increased emphasis on consumer needs created jobs for veterans. Nonetheless, the war affected men's roles and sense of themselves. Young men who had missed World War II adopted the rough, violent style of soldiers, and roaming gangs posed as tough military types.

While Soviet youth admired aviator aces, elsewhere groups such as the "teddy boys" in England (named after their Edwardian style of dressing) and the *gamberros* ("hooligans") in Spain took their cues from pop culture in rock-and-roll music and film. (See Document, "Consumerism, Youth, and the Birth of the Generation Gap," above.)

The leader of rock-and-roll style was the American singer Elvis Presley. Sporting slicked-back hair and an aviator-style jacket, Presley bucked his hips and sang sexual lyrics to screaming and devoted fans. Rock-and-roll concerts and movies galvanized youth across Europe, including the Soviet bloc, where teens demanded the production of blue jeans and leather jackets. In a German nightclub late in the 1950s, members of a British rock group of Elvis fans called the Quarrymen performed, yelling at and fighting with one another as part of their show. They would soon become known as the Beatles. Rebellious young American film stars like James Dean in *Rebel Without a Cause* (1955) and Marlon Brando in *The Wild One* (1953)

Zbigniew Cybulski, the Polish James Dean
Zbigniew Cybulski depicted a tortured young resistance fighter in the film *Ashes and Diamonds* (1958) by Andrzej Wajda. Cybulski's character is to assassinate a Communist resistance leader on what turns out to be the last day of World War II, and his human dilemma around the act is set amid the chaos in Poland at war's end. Like existentialist philosophers and other film directors at the time, Wajda captured the debate over human values and the interest in young heroes of the postwar era. *(Photofest.)*

created the beginnings of a conspicuous postwar youth culture in which the ideal was to be a bad boy. The rebellious and rough masculine style appeared also in literature, for example in James Watson's autobiography, *The Double Helix* (1968), in which he described how he and Francis Crick had discovered the structure of the DNA molecule by stealing other people's findings. The German novelist Heinrich Böll, who decades later admitted to having been a Nazi soldier, protested that West Germany's postwar goal of respectability had allowed the reappearance of those groups of people who had produced Nazism. In Böll's novel *The Clown* (1963), the young middle-class hero leaves home and takes up life as a vagabond clown, amusing audiences with clever pantomimes about the folly of their lives. Not a breadwinner but a bum, he ends up a model bad boy begging in a railroad station. American "beat" poets and writers vehemently rejected the traditional ideals of the upright male breadwinner and family man.

Both high and low culture revealed that two horrendous world wars had weakened the Enlightenment view of men as rational, responsible achievers. The 1953 inaugural issue of the American magazine *Playboy*, and the hundreds of magazines that came to imitate it, ushered in a startling depiction of a changed male identity. This new media presented modern man as sexually aggressive and independent of dull domestic life—just as he had been in the war. Breadwinning for a family destroyed a man's freedom and sense of self, this new male culture claimed. The notion of men's citizen-

Rock and Roll
Rock and roll, born in the 1950s, swept cities around the world with unprecedented energy and speed. Teen women wore the voluminous skirts that the "new look" had made fashionable in the late 1940s, and young men sported hairdos like those of Elvis Presley or Zbigniew Cybulski. East and west, teens thronged and even rioted to attend rock concerts and would continue to do so despite public criticism and even police action against the movement. *(ullstein bild/The Granger Collection, New York.)*

ship had come to include not just political and economic rights but also freedom of sexual expression outside the restrictions of the family.

In contrast, Western society promoted a postwar model for women that differed from their wartime roles, adopting instead the fascist notion of women's inferiority. Rather than being essential workers and heads of families in the absence of their men, postwar women were to symbolize the return to normalcy by leading a domestic and submissive life at home. Late in the 1940s, the fashion house of Christian Dior launched a clothing style called the "new look." It featured a pinched waist, tightly fitting bodices, and voluminous skirts. This restoration of the nineteenth-century female silhouette invited a renewal of clearly defined gender roles. Women's magazines publicized the new look and urged women to give up ambitions for themselves. Even in the hard-pressed Soviet Union, domesticity flourished; recipes for homemade face creams, for example, passed from woman to woman, and beauty parlors did a brisk business. In the West, household products such as

refrigerators and washing machines raised standards for housekeeping by giving women the means to be "perfect" housewives.

However, new-look propaganda did not necessarily mesh with reality or even with all social norms. Dressmaking fabric was still being rationed in the late 1940s; even in the next decade, women could not always get enough of it to make voluminous skirts. In Europe, where people had barely enough to eat, the underwear needed for new-look contours simply did not exist—although the semistarved look was, for many, easy enough to achieve. In Spain, women were said to perform their role best by being religious and concerned with the spiritual well-being of their families. Spanish advertising, however, emphasized the physical beauty available through cosmetics and clothing; it urged women to buy things that would make their families look better too. European women continued to work outside the home after the war; indeed, mature women and mothers were working more than ever before—especially in the Soviet bloc (Figure 27.2). The female workforce

FIGURE 27.2 Women in the Workforce, 1950–1960
In contrast to the situation after World War I, women did not leave the workforce in great numbers after World War II. In fact, Europe faced labor shortages. In Soviet-bloc countries, women vastly outnumbered men because so many men had died in the war, and the task of rebuilding demanded every available worker. In western Europe, women's workforce participation was lower, and countries like West Germany tried to keep women out of the labor pool to distinguish themselves from the Communist bloc. Note the increase in women's service-sector employment in just one decade. *(From* World Employment 1996–1997: National Policies in a Global Context *(Geneva: International Labour Office, 1996), 7.)*

	Member Countries of Council of Mutual Economic Assistance[1]		Member Countries of European Economic Community[2]	
	1950	1960	1950	1960
Female as % of total population	54.9	53.9	51.8	51.6
Female labor force as % of total labor force	48.5	48.7	31.1	31.4
Distribution of female labor force (%):				
Agriculture	63.3	50.0	26.1	16.8
Industry	16.9	22.6	29.3	31.3
Services	19.8	27.4	44.6	51.9

[1] Albania, Bulgaria, Czechoslovakia, East Germany, Hungary, Poland, Romania, and USSR

[2] Belgium, Denmark, France, West Germany, Ireland, Italy, Luxembourg, Netherlands, and United Kingdom

was going through a profound revolution as it gradually became populated by wives and mothers who would hold jobs all their lives despite being bombarded with images of nineteenth-century femininity.

The advertising business presided over the creation of these cultural messages as well as over the rise of more widespread consumerism that accompanied recovery. Guided by marketing experts, western Europeans imitated Americans by driving some forty million motorized vehicles, including motorbikes, cars, buses, and trucks. They drank Coca-Cola and used American detergents, toothpaste, and soap. The number of radios in homes grew steadily and even as radio remained the most influential medium, television loomed on the horizon. In the United States, two-thirds of the population had TV sets in the early 1950s, while in Britain only one-fifth did. Only in the 1960s did

television become an important consumer item for most Europeans. In the 1950s, radio was still king and consumerism a growing mass phenomenon.

The Culture of Cold War

Films, books, and other cultural productions promoted the cold war even when they conveyed an antiwar message. Books like George Orwell's *1984* (1949) were claimed by both sides in the cold war as supporting their position. Ray Bradbury's popular *Fahrenheit 451* (1953), whose title refers to the temperature at which books would burn, condemned curtailment of intellectual freedom on both sides of the cold war divide. In the USSR, official writers churned out spy stories, and espionage novels topped bestseller lists in the West. *Casino Royale* (1953), by the British author Ian Fleming, introduced the

Barbara Hepworth, *Single Form* (1961–1964)
Like others in the West, British sculptor Barbara Hepworth was strangely buoyed by the war, hoping that it meant the dawn of a new age. Full of renewed energy, Hepworth believed that art should follow pure forms, which some called "primitive," as a way of expressing enduring values. Her twenty-one-foot abstract sculpture *Single Form*, shown here as a plaster cast, was installed at the United Nations building in New York to commemorate the life of her friend Dag Hammarskjöld, who served as secretary-general of the United Nations from 1953 until his death in 1961. "[We] depend on the pure courage of the UN," Hepworth wrote of the sculpture created to honor Hammarskjöld's life and work. *(Photo Morgan-Wells, London/© Bowness, Hepworth Estate.)*

fictional British intelligence agent James Bond, who tested his wit and physical prowess against Communist and other political villains. Soviet pilots would not take off for flights when the work of Yulian Simyonov, the Russian counterpart of Ian Fleming, was playing on radio or television. Reports of Soviet- and U.S.-bloc characters—fictional or real—facing one another down became part of everyday life.

High and low culture alike contributed to the cold-war climate. Even as Europe's major cities rebuilt their war-ravaged opera houses and museums, they could not hold back "Americanization." Americans had money to spend, and American businesses produced an array of tempting products. While many Europeans were proponents of American business practices, the Communist Party in France led a successful campaign to ban Coca-Cola for a time in the 1950s. Soviet magazines carried fashion photos praised for their "decency," in contrast to the highly sexualized garments for women to the west. Both sides also tried to win the cold war by pouring vast sums of money into high culture, though the United States did it by secretly channeling government money into foundations to award fellowships to artists or promote favorable journalism around the world. As leadership of the art world passed to the United States, art became part of the cold war. Abstract expressionists such as American artist Jackson Pollock produced nonrepresentational works by dripping and spattering paint; they also spoke of the importance of the artist's self-discovery in the process of painting. "If I stretch my arms next to the rest of myself and wonder where my fingers are, that is all the space I need as a painter," commented Dutch-born artist Willem de Kooning on his relationship with his canvas. Said to exemplify Western freedom, such painters were awarded commissions at the secret direction of the U.S. Central Intelligence Agency.

The USSR openly promoted an official Communist culture. When a show of abstract art opened in the Soviet Union, Khrushchev yelled that it was "dog shit." Pro-Soviet critics in western Europe saw U.S.-style abstract art as "an infantile sickness" and supported socialist realist art with "human content," showing the condition of the workers and the oppressed races in the United States. The Italian filmmakers Roberto Rossellini, in *Open City* (1945), and Vittorio De Sica, in *The Bicycle Thief* (1948), developed the neorealist technique that challenged Hollywood-style sets and costumes by using ordinary characters living in devastated, impoverished cities. By depicting stark conditions, neorealist directors conveyed their distance both from middle-class prosperity and from fascist bombast. "We are in rags? Let's show everyone our rags," said one Italian director. Many of these left-leaning directors associated support for the suffering masses with the Communist cause, while on the pro-American side, the film *Doctor Zhivago* became a hit celebrating individualism and condemning the Communist way of life. Overtly or covertly, the cold war affected virtually all aspects of cultural life.

The Atomic Brink

Radio was also at the center of the cold war, conveying messages about the threat of nuclear annihilation at the hands of the villainous superpower enemy. As superpower rivalry heated up, radio's propaganda function remained as strong as it had been in wartime. During the late 1940s and early 1950s, the Voice of America, with its main studio in Washington, D.C., broadcast in thirty-eight languages from one hundred transmitters and provided an alternative source of news for people in eastern Europe. Its Soviet counterpart broadcast in Russian around the clock but initially spent much of its wattage jamming U.S. programming. Russian programs stressed a uniform Communist culture and values; the United States, by contrast, emphasized diverse programming and promoted debate about current affairs. The contrast was meant to show the dictatorial nature of Communist values versus the democratic ones of choice and free speech. The public also heard reports of nuclear buildups and tests of emergency power facilities sent them scurrying for cover. Children rehearsed at school for nuclear war, while at home families built bomb shelters in their backyards.

It was in this pervasive climate of cold war that **John Fitzgerald Kennedy** (1917–1963) became U.S. president in 1960. Kennedy represented American affluence and youth yet also the nation's commitment to cold war. Kennedy's media advisers and ghostwriters recognized how perfect a match their articulate, good-looking president was for the power of television. A war hero and an early fan of the fictional cold war spy James Bond, Kennedy escalated the cold war. Some of this escalation occurred over the nearby island of Cuba, where in 1959 the Communist leader Fidel Castro

---

John Fitzgerald Kennedy: U.S. president, from 1961 to 1963, who faced off with Soviet leader Nikita Khrushchev in the Cuban missile crisis.

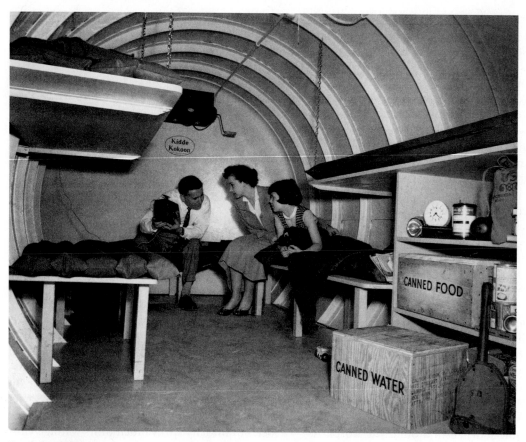

Bomb Shelter
Americans expressed their fear of nuclear annihilation by building tens of thousands of individual bomb shelters. Stocked with several months' supply of canned food and other goods, the shelters were to protect a family from the nuclear blast itself and from the disorder that might follow nuclear war. The government also prepared shelters to shield top officials and to ensure the continuation of civil society despite vast casualties and massive destruction. (© Corbis.)

(1926–) had come to power by overthrowing the corrupt government of the dictator Fulgencio Batista. After being rebuffed by the United States, Castro aligned his new government with the Soviet Union. In the spring of 1961, Kennedy, assured by the Central Intelligence Agency (CIA) of success, launched an invasion of Cuba at the Bay of Pigs intended to overthrow Castro. The invasion failed miserably and humiliated the United States.

Cold war rivalries continued to escalate. In the summer of 1961, East German workers, supervised by police and the army, stacked bales of barbed wire across miles of the city's east–west border as the beginning of the Berlin Wall. The divided city had served as an escape route by which some three million people, including skilled workers and professionals, had fled to the West. Meanwhile, Kennedy called for increased

defense spending. In October 1962, tensions came to a head in the **Cuban missile crisis**, when the CIA reported the installation of silos to house Soviet medium-range missiles in Cuba (Map 27.6). Kennedy responded forcefully, ordering a naval blockade of ships headed for Cuba and demanding removal of the installations. For several days, the world stood on the brink of nuclear war. Then, between October 25 and 27, Khrushchev and Kennedy negotiated an end to the crisis. Kennedy spent the remainder of his short life working to improve nuclear diplomacy; Khrushchev did the same. In the summer of 1963, less than a year after the shock of the Cuban missile crisis, the United States and the Soviet Union signed a test-

Cuban missile crisis: The confrontation in 1962 between the United States and the USSR over Soviet installation of missile sites off the U.S. coast in Cuba.

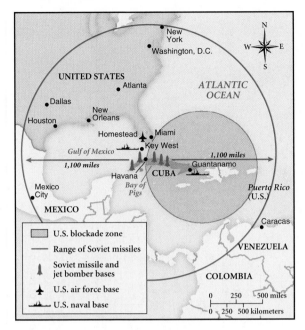

MAP 27.6 The Cuban Missile Crisis, 1962
Just off the coast of the southeastern United States,
Cuba posed a threat to North American security once
the Soviet Union began stocking the island with silos
for missiles. The United States reacted vigorously,
insisting on the dismantling of the missile sites.
Although his generals were prepared for nuclear war
with the Soviet Union, President Kennedy refused
to take this step, and Soviet premier Khrushchev
similarly backed down from a military confrontation.
■ Explain the placement of missiles in Cuba and the
U.S. reaction to it.

ban treaty outlawing the explosion of nuclear
weapons in the atmosphere and in the seas. Allowing the superpowers to back away from the
brink, the treaty held out hope that the cold war
and its culture would give way to something
better.

REVIEW: How did the cold war affect everyday culture
and social life?

Conclusion

Nikita Khrushchev was ousted in 1964 for his erratic policies and for the Cuban missile crisis. In
his forced retirement, he expressed regret at his
brutal treatment of Boris Pasternak: "We should-
n't have banned [*Doctor Zhivago*]. There's nothing anti-Soviet in it." But the postwar decades
were grim times. Two superpowers, the Soviet

Union and the United States, each controlling
atomic arsenals, overshadowed European leadership and engaged in a menacing cold war, complete with the threat of nuclear annihilation. The
cold war saturated everyday life, giving birth to
bomb shelters, spies, purges, and witch hunts —
all of them creating a culture of anxiety that kept
people in constant fear of imminent war. Postwar
diplomacy divided Europe into an eastern bloc
dominated by the Soviets and a freer western bloc
mostly allied with the United States. In this omi-
nous atmosphere, starving, homeless, and refugee
people joined the task of rebuilding a devastated
Europe.

Despite the chaos at the end of 1945, both
halves of Europe recovered almost miraculously
in little more than a decade. Eastern Europe,
where wartime devastation and ongoing violence
were greatest, experienced less prosperity, while in
western Europe wartime technology served as the
basis for new consumer goods and welfare-state
planning improved health. Spurred on by aid
from the United States, western Europe formed
the successful Common Market, which became
the foundation for greater European unity. As a
result of the war, Germany recovered as two countries, not one, and the weakened European powers shed their colonies. Newly independent
nations emerged in Asia and Africa, leaving in
question whether there would be further redistribution of global power. Often serving as pawns in
the cold war, these new countries faced the problems of creating stable political structures and a
sound economic future. As the West as a whole
grew in prosperity, its cultural life focused paradoxically on eradicating the evils of Nazism while
enjoying the new phenomenon of mass consumerism. But above all, the West — and the rest
of the world — had to survive the atomic rivalry
of the superpowers.

FOR FURTHER EXPLORATION

■ **For suggested references, including Web sites,
for topics in this chapter,** see page SR-1 at the
end of the book.

■ **For additional primary-source material from
this period,** see Chapter 27 in *Sources of THE
MAKING OF THE WEST,* Third Edition.

■ **For Web sites and documents related to
topics in this chapter,** see *Make History*
at **bedfordstmartins.com/hunt.**

MAPPING THE WEST

The Cold War World, c. 1960

Superpower rivalry between the United States and the Soviet Union resulted in the division of much of the industrial world into cold war alliances. Simultaneously, the superpowers vied for the allegiance of the newly decolonized countries of Asia and Africa by providing military, economic, and technological assistance. Wars such as those in Vietnam and Korea were also products of the cold war. ■ How might this map be said to convey the idea that a first, second, and third world existed? How does this map differ from the map on page 760?

Decolonized (with date), 1945–1962

1 Tunisia
2 Senegal
3 Gambia
4 Guinea
5 Sierra Leone
6 Ivory Coast
7 Burkina Faso
8 Ghana
9 Togo
10 Dahomey
11 Cameroon
12 Gabon
13 Central African Republic
14 Uganda
15 Rwanda
16 Burundi

Warsaw Pact members

NATO members

CHAPTER REVIEW

KEY TERMS AND PEOPLE

cold war (880)

Truman Doctrine (884)

Marshall Plan (886)

North Atlantic Treaty Organization (NATO) (887)

Warsaw Pact (887)

Christian Democrats (889)

European Economic Community (EEC or Common Market) (892)

welfare state (893)

Nikita Khrushchev (896)

decolonization (897)

United Nations (UN) (901)

Vatican II (903)

existentialism (903)

Simone de Beauvoir (904)

John Fitzgerald Kennedy (909)

Cuban missile crisis (910)

MAKING CONNECTIONS

1. What was the political climate after World War II, and how did it differ from the political climate after World War I?

2. What were the relative strengths of the two European blocs in the cold war?

3. What were the main developments of postwar cultural life?

4. Why did decolonization follow the war so immediately?

> **For practice quizzes, a customized study plan, and other study tools,** see the Online Study Guide at bedfordstmartins.com/hunt.

REVIEW QUESTIONS

1. What were the major events in the development of the cold war?

2. What factors drove recovery in western Europe? In eastern Europe?

3. What were the results of decolonization?

4. How did the cold war affect everyday culture and social life?

IMPORTANT EVENTS

1945	Cold war begins
1947	India and Pakistan win independence from Britain
1948	State of Israel established
1949	Mao Zedong leads Communist revolution in China; Simone de Beauvoir publishes *The Second Sex*
1950	Korean War begins
1953	Stalin dies; Korean War ends
1954	*Brown v. Board of Education* prohibits segregated schools in the United States; Vietnamese forces defeat the French at Dien Bien Phu

1956	Egyptian leader General Abdel Nasser nationalizes the Suez Canal; uprising in Hungary against USSR
1957	Boris Pasternak publishes *Doctor Zhivago*; USSR launches *Sputnik*; Treaty of Rome establishes the European Economic Community (Common Market)
1958	Fifth Republic begins in France
1962	The United States and USSR face off in the Cuban missile crisis

Postindustrial Society and the End of the Cold War Order

1960s–1989

I n January 1969, Jan Palach, a twenty-one-year-old philosophy student, drove to a main square in Prague, doused his body with gasoline, and set himself on fire. Before that, he had put aside his coat with a message in it demanding an end to Communist repression in Czechoslovakia. It promised more such suicides unless the government lifted state censorship. The manifesto was signed: "Torch No. 1." Jan Palach's suicide stunned his nation. Black flags hung from windows, and close to a million people flocked to Palach's funeral. In the next months, more Czech youth followed Palach's grim example, setting themselves ablaze for freedom.

Before his self-immolation, Jan Palach was an ordinary, well-educated citizen of an increasingly technological society. Having recovered from World War II, the West shifted from a manufacturing economy based on heavy industry to a service economy that depended on technical knowledge in such fields as engineering, health care, and finance. This new service economy has been labeled "postindustrial." To staff it, institutions of higher education sprang up at a dizzying rate and attracted more students than ever before. Young men like Jan Palach—along with women, minorities, and many other activists in the 1960s and 1970s—far from being satisfied with their rising status, struck out against war and cold war, inequality and repression, and even against technology itself. From Czechoslovakia to the United States and around the world, protesters warned that postindustrial nations in general and the superpowers in particular were becoming technological and political monsters. Before long, countries in both the Soviet and U.S. blocs were on the verge of political revolution.

Shrine to Jan Palach
Jan Palach was a martyr to the cause of an independent Czechoslovakia. His self-immolation on behalf of that cause roused the nation. As makeshift shrines sprang up and multiplied throughout the 1970s and 1980s, they served as common rallying points that ultimately contributed to the overthrow of Communist rule. Václav Havel, the future president of a liberated Czechoslovakia, was arrested early in the momentous year of 1989 for commemorating Palach's sacrifice at the shrine. In light of so many other deaths in the Soviet bloc, why did Jan Palach's death become so powerful a force? (© Marc Garanger/Corbis.)

The challenges posed by young reformers came at a bad time for the superpowers and other leading European states. An agonizing war in Vietnam weakened the United States, and China confronted the Soviet Union on its borders. In a dramatic turn of events, the oil-producing states of the Middle East formed a cartel and reduced the export of oil to the leading Western nations in the 1970s. The resulting price increases helped bring on a recession, threatening the ballooning postindustrial economy. Extremists turned to terrorism to achieve their goals, while despite their wealth and military might, the superpowers could not guarantee that they would emerge victorious in this age of increasingly global competition. As the USSR experienced invisible economic decay, a reform-minded leader—Mikhail Gorbachev—directed his nation to change course and initiated new policies of economic and political freedom. It was too late: in 1989, the Soviet bloc collapsed, helped by countless acts of protest, not least of them the individual heroism of Jan Palach and his fellow human torches.

> **FOCUS QUESTION:** How did technological, economic, and social change contribute to increased activism, and what were the political results of that activism?

The Revolution in Technology

The protests of the 1960s began in the midst of astonishing technological advances. These advances steadily boosted prosperity and changed daily life in the West, where people awoke to instantaneous radio and television news, worked with computers, and used new forms of contraceptives to control reproduction. Satellites orbiting the earth relayed telephone signals and collected military intelligence, while around the world nuclear energy powered economies. Smaller gadgets—electric popcorn poppers, portable radios and tape players, automatic garage door openers—made life more pleasant. The increased use of machines led one philosopher to insist that people were no longer self-sufficient individuals, but rather cyborgs—that is, humans who needed machines to sustain ordinary life processes.

The Information Age: Television and Computers

Information technology powered change in the postindustrial period that began in the 1960s just as innovations in textile making and the spread of railroads had in the nineteenth century. This technology's ability to transmit knowledge, culture, and political information globally made it even more revolutionary. In the first half of the twentieth century, mass journalism, film, and radio had begun to forge a more uniform society based on shared information and images; in the last third of the century, television, computers, and telecommunications made information even more accessible and, some critics said, made culture more standardized. Once-remote villages were linked to urban capitals on the other side of the world thanks to videocassettes, satellite television, and telecommunications. Because of technology, protests became media events worldwide.

Television. Americans embraced television in the 1950s; following the postwar recovery, it was Europe's turn. Between the mid-1950s and the mid-1970s, Europeans rapidly adopted television as a major entertainment and communications medium. In 1954, just 1 percent of French households had television; by 1974, almost 80 percent did. With the average viewer tuning in about four and a half hours a day, the audience for newspapers and theater declined. "We devote more . . .

■ 1963 Friedan, *The Feminine Mystique*

■ 1966 Brandt's Ostpolitik

■ 1967 First successful human heart transplant

■ 1968 Revolution in Czechoslovakia; widespread student uprisings

■ 1969 U.S. moon landing

■ 1972 SALT I

■ 1973 North Vietnam and the United States sign peace treaty; OPEC oil embargo

■ 1973–1976 Solzhenitsyn, *The Gulag Archipelago*

| 1965 | 1970 | 1975 |

hours per year to television than [to] any other single artifact," one sociologist commented in 1969. As with radio, European governments funded television broadcasting with tax dollars and controlled TV programming to avoid what they perceived as the substandard fare offered by American commercial TV; instead they featured drama, ballet, concerts, variety shows, and news. The welfare state, in Europe at least, thereby gained more power to shape daily life.

The emergence of communications satellites and video recorders in the 1960s brought competition to state-sponsored television. Worldwide audiences enjoyed broadcasts from throughout the West as satellite technology allowed for the global transmission of sports broadcasts and other programming. What statesmen and intellectuals considered the junk programming of the United States — soap operas, game shows, sitcoms — arrived dubbed in the native language. Feature films on videotape became readily available to television stations (although not yet to individuals) and competed with made-for-television movies and other programs. The competition increased in 1969 when the Sony Corporation introduced the first affordable color videocassette recorder to the consumer market. Critics complained that, although TV provided more information than had ever been available before, the resulting shared culture represented the lowest common denominator.

East and west, television exercised a powerful political and cultural influence. Even in a rural area of the Soviet Union, more than 70 percent of the inhabitants watched television regularly in the late 1970s. Educational programming united the far-flung population of the USSR by broadcasting shows designed to advance Soviet culture. At the same time, with travel impossible or forbidden to many, shows about foreign lands were among the most popular — as were postcards from these lands,

which became household decorations. Heads of state could usually bump regular programming. In the 1960s, French president Charles de Gaulle appeared frequently on television, using the grandiose gestures of an imperial ruler to stir patriotism. As electoral success in western Europe increasingly depended on cultivating a successful media image, political staffs needed media experts as much as they did policy experts.

Computers.   Just as revolutionary as television, the computer reshaped work in science, defense, and ultimately industry. Computers had evolved dramatically since the first electronic ones, like the Colossus used by the British in 1943 to decode Nazi military and diplomatic messages. Several countries had devised these machines for processing information, all of them primitive by later standards in being gigantic, slow, noisy, and able only to decode. With growing use in civilian industry and business after the war, computing machines shrank from the size of a gymnasium in the 1940s to that of an attaché case in the mid-1980s. They also became both far less expensive and fantastically more powerful, thanks to the development of increasingly sophisticated digital electronic circuitry implanted on tiny silicon chips, which replaced the clumsy radio tubes used in 1940s and 1950s computers. Within a few decades, the computer could perform hundreds of millions of operations per second and the price of the integrated circuit at the heart of computer technology would fall to less than a dollar.

Computers changed the pace and patterns of work not only by speeding up and easing tasks but also by performing many operations that workers had once done themselves. In garment making, for example, experienced workers no longer painstakingly figured out how to arrange patterns on cloth for maximum economy. Instead, a computer specified instructions for the best positioning of pat-

THE SPACE AGE

1957	Soviet Union launches the first artificial satellite, *Sputnik*
1961	Soviet cosmonaut Yuri Gagarin orbits the earth; capsule carrying Alan Shepard Jr. makes first U.S. suborbital flight
1965	United States launches first commercial communications satellite, *Intelsat I*
1969	U.S. astronauts Neil Armstrong and Edwin Aldrin walk on moon's surface
1970s–present	Soviet Union and United States individually and in collaboration with various countries perform space station maneuvers, lunar probes, and other scientific experiments
1971	Soviet Union attempts unsuccessfully to put the space station *Salyut 1* into orbit
1973	United States puts the experimental space station *Skylab* into orbit
1976	*Viking* spacecraft explores Mars
1979–1986	Spacecraft *Voyager* makes successful flybys of Jupiter, Saturn, and Uranus

Valentina Tereshkova, Russian Cosmonaut
People sent into space were heroes, representing modern values of courage, strength, and well-honed skills. Insofar as the space age was part of the cold war race for superpower superiority, the USSR held the lead during the first decade. The Soviets trained both women and men, and the 1963 flight of Valentina Tereshkova—the first woman in space—supported Soviet claims of gender equality in contrast to the all-male superstar image of the early U.S. space program. *(Hulton Archive/Getty Images.)*

tern pieces, and trained workers, usually women, followed the machine's directions. Soon, like outworkers of the eighteenth century, people could work for large industries at home, connected to a central mainframe. In 1981, the French phone company launched a public Internet server, the Minitel—a forerunner of the World Wide Web—through which individuals could make reservations, perform stock transactions, and obtain information.

Whereas during the Industrial Revolution mechanical power replaced human energy, the computer technology of the information revolution added to brain power. Many observers believed that computers would profoundly expand mental capacity, providing, in the words of one scientist, "boundless opportunities . . . to resolve the puzzles of cosmology, of life, and of the society of man." Others countered that computers programmed people, reducing human initiative and the ability to solve problems. As the 1970s closed, such predictions were still untested and the information revolution was just beginning.

The Space Age

The "space race" between the United States and the Soviet Union began when the Soviets launched the satellite *Sputnik* in 1957. The competition led to in-

creasingly complex space flights that tested humans' ability to survive the process of space exploration, including weightlessness. Astronauts walked in space, endured weeks (and later months) in orbit, docked with other craft, fixed satellites, and carried out experiments for the military and private industry. In addition, a series of unmanned rockets launched weather, television, intelligence, and other communications satellites into orbit around the earth.

In July 1969, a worldwide television audience watched as U.S. astronauts Neil Armstrong and Edwin "Buzz" Aldrin walked on the moon's surface—the climactic moment in the space race. The space race also drove Western cultural developments. Astronauts and cosmonauts were perhaps the era's most admired heroes: Yuri Gagarin, John Glenn, and Valentina Tereshkova—the first woman in space—topped the list. A whole new fantasy world developed. Children's toys and games revolved increasingly around space. Films such as *2001: A Space Odyssey* (1968) portrayed space explorers answering questions about life that were formerly the domain of church leaders. Polish author Stanislaw Lem's popular novel *Solaris* (1961), later made into a film, described space-age individuals engaged in personal quests and drew readers and ultimately viewers into a futuristic fantasy.

The space age grew out of cold war concerns, and advances in rocket technology not only launched vehicles into space but also powered destructive missiles. At the same time, the space age promoted global cooperation. From the 1960s on, U.S. spaceflights often involved the participation of other countries such as Great Britain and the Netherlands. In 1965, an international consortium headed by the United States launched the first commercial communications satellite, *Intelsat I*; by the 1970s, some 150 countries worked together at more than four hundred stations worldwide to maintain global satellite communications. Although some 50 percent of satellites were for spying purposes, the rest made international communication possible and transnational collaboration a necessity.

Pure science flourished amid the space race. Astronomers used mineral samples from the moon to calculate the age of the solar system with unprecedented precision. Unmanned spacecraft provided data on cosmic radiation, magnetic fields, and infrared sources. Although the media depicted the space age as one of warrior astronauts conquering space, breakthroughs in space exploration and astronomy depended on the products of technology, including the radio telescope, which depicted space by receiving, measuring, and calculating nonvisible rays. These findings reinforced the so-called big bang theory of the origin of the universe, first outlined in the 1930s by American astronomer Edwin Hubble and given crucial support in the 1950s by the discovery of a low level of radiation permeating the universe in all directions. The big bang theory proposes that the universe originated from the explosion of superdense, superhot matter some ten to twenty billion years ago.

The Nuclear Age

Scientists, government officials, and engineers put the force of the atom to economic use, especially in the form of nuclear power, and the dramatic boost in available energy helped continue postwar economic expansion into the 1960s and beyond. The USSR built the first nuclear plant to produce electricity in Obinsk in 1954, followed by Britain and the United States. During the 1960s and 1970s, nuclear power for industrial and household use

multiplied a hundredfold — a growth that did not include the nuclear-powered submarines and aircraft carriers, which also multiplied in this period.

Because of the vast costs and complex procedures involved in building, supplying, running, and safeguarding nuclear reactors, governments provided substantial aid and even financed nuclear power plants almost entirely. "A state does not count," announced French president Charles de Gaulle, "if it does not . . . contribute to the technological progress of the world." The watchword for all governments building nuclear reactors was technological development — a new function for the modern state. The USSR sponsored plants throughout the Soviet bloc as part of the drive to modernize, but it was not alone — Western nations, too, continued to rely on nuclear power. In 2006, France produced some 80 percent of its energy, and the United States 20 percent, via nuclear power plants. More than thirty countries had substantial nuclear installations in the twenty-first century, with more under construction.

Revolutions in Biology and Reproductive Technology

A revolution in the life sciences brought about dramatic new health benefits and ultimately changed reproduction itself. In 1952, scientists Francis Crick, an Englishman, and James Watson, an American, discovered the structure of **DNA**, the material in a cell's chromosomes that carries hereditary information. Simultaneously, other scientists were working on "the pill" — an oral contraceptive for women that capped more than a century of scientific work in the field of birth control. Still other breakthroughs lay ahead, including ones that revolutionized conception and made scientific duplication of species possible.

Understanding DNA.   Crick and Watson solved the mystery of biological inheritance when they demonstrated the structure of DNA. They showed how the double helix of the DNA molecule splits in cellular reproduction to form the basis of each new cell. This genetic material, biologists concluded, provides a chemical pattern for an individual organism's life. Beginning in the 1960s, genetics and the new field of molecular biology progressed rapidly. Growing understanding of nucleic acids and proteins led to increased knowledge about

---

DNA: The genetic material that forms the basis of each cell; the discovery of its structure in 1952 revolutionized genetics, molecular biology, and other scientific and medical fields.

viruses and bacteria and almost completely ended such diseases as polio, tetanus, syphilis, mumps, and measles in the West through the development of new vaccines.

Scientists used their understanding of DNA both to alter the makeup of plants and to bypass natural animal reproduction in a process called cloning—obtaining the cells of an organism and dividing or reproducing them in an exact copy in a laboratory. In 1997, one group of British researchers produced a cloned sheep named Dolly, though the breakthrough was marred by the fact that Dolly suffered an array of disabilities and died six years later. Questions about whether scientists should interfere with so basic and essential a process as reproduction became increasingly urgent as cloning progressed. Similarly, the possibility of genetically altering species and even creating new ones (for instance, to control agricultural pests) led to concern about how such actions would affect the balance of nature. In 1967, Dr. Christiaan Barnard of South Africa performed the first successful heart transplant, and U.S. doctors later developed an artificial heart. As major

breakthroughs like these occurred, commentators began to ask whether the enormous cost of new medical technology to save a few people would be better spent on helping the many who lacked even basic medical and health care.

Transforming Reproduction.   Technology also influenced the most intimate areas of human relations—sexuality and procreation. Matching family size to agricultural productivity no longer shaped sexual behavior in the industrialized and urbanized West. With reliable birth-control devices more readily available, young people began sexual relations earlier, with less risk of pregnancy. These trends accelerated in the 1960s when the birth-control pill, first produced in the United States and tested on women in developing areas, came on the Western market. By 1970, its use was spreading around the world. Millions also sought out voluntary surgical sterilization through tubal ligations and vasectomies. New techniques brought abortion, traditionally performed by amateurs, into the hands of medical professionals, making it a safe procedure for the first time.

Thalidomide Children
In the last third of the twentieth century, increasingly destructive side effects of powerful medicines became apparent. Women who had taken the drug thalidomide gave birth to children with severe disabilities, a result of the race to profit from scientific and technological developments. Children affected by thalidomide, once they became adults, were among those who launched the disability rights movement. *(Deutsche Presse Agentur.)*

■ **For more help analyzing this image,** see the visual activity for this chapter in the Online Study Guide at bedfordstmartins.com/hunt.

The First Test-Tube Baby
The birth in Britain in 1978 of Louise Brown, the first baby conceived by in vitro fertilization, caused a sensation worldwide. The new procedure was just one of the many medical breakthroughs of the late twentieth century and gave hope to would-be parents around the world that science might make infertility a thing of the past. *(Getty Images.)*

Childbirth and conception itself were similarly transformed. Whereas only a small minority of Western births took place in hospitals in 1920, more than 90 percent did by 1970. Obstetricians now performed much of the work midwives had once done. As pregnancy and birth became a medical process, innovative new procedures and equipment made it possible to monitor women and fetuses throughout pregnancy, labor, and delivery. The number of medical interventions such as cesarean births rose. In 1978, the first "test-tube baby," Louise Brown, was born to an English couple. She had been conceived when her mother's eggs were fertilized with her father's sperm in a laboratory dish and then implanted in her mother's uterus—a complex process called **in vitro fertilization**. If a woman could not carry a child to term, the laboratory-fertilized embryo could be implanted in the uterus of a surrogate, or substitute, mother. Researchers even began working on an artificial womb to allow for reproduction entirely outside the body—from storage bank to artificial embryonic environment. In reproductive technology, as in other areas, the revolution in biology was dramatically changing human life, improving health, and even making new life possible.

REVIEW: What were the technological and scientific advances of the 1960s and 1970s, and how did they change human life and society?

Postindustrial Society and Culture

Soaring investments in science and the spread of technology put Western countries on what has been labeled a postindustrial course. Instead of being centered on manufacturing and heavy industry, a postindustrial economy emphasized the distribution of services such as health care and education. The dominance of the service sector meant that intellectual work, not industrial or manufacturing work, was central to creating jobs and profits. Moreover, all parts of society and industry interlocked, forming a system constantly in need of complex analysis, as in the nuclear industry, leading to new cultural trends. The characteristics of postindustrial society and culture would carry over from the 1960s and 1970s into the next century.

Multinational Corporations

One of the major developments of the postindustrial era was the growth of the **multinational corporation**. Multinationals produced goods and services for a global market and conducted business worldwide, but unlike older kinds of international firms, they established major factories in countries other than their home base. For example, of the five hundred largest businesses in the

---

in vitro fertilization: A process developed in the 1970s by which eggs are fertilized with sperm outside the human body and then implanted in a woman's uterus.

multinational corporation: A business that operates in many foreign countries by sending large segments of its manufacturing, finance, sales, and other business components abroad.

MAP 28.1 The Airbus Production System
The international consortium Airbus marked an important step in the economic and industrial integration of Europe and the revitalization of individual national economies. Today, Airbus is a global enterprise with locations offering parts and service around the world, including the United States, China, and India, but coordinating production in so many sites has proved difficult recently.

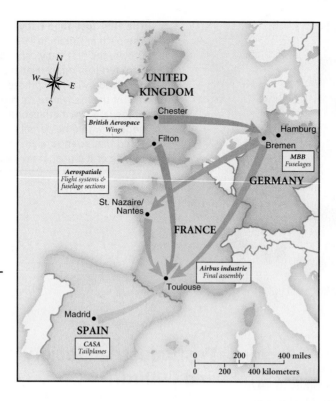

specializing in all phases of construction—a wise move given the postwar building boom. European firms increased their investment in research and used international cooperation to produce major new products. The British-French Concorde supersonic aircraft, which, beginning with its first flight in 1976, flew from London to New York in under four hours, was one result. Another venture was the Airbus, a more practical series of passenger jets inaugurated in 1972 by a consortium of European firms. Both projects attested to the strong relationships among government, business, and science as well as to the international cooperation in manufacturing among members of the Common Market (Map 28.1). Such relationships allowed European businesses to compete successfully with U.S.-based multinational giants.

United States in 1970, more than one hundred did over a quarter of their business abroad, with IBM operating in more than one hundred countries. Although U.S.-based corporations led the way, European and Japanese multinationals like Volkswagen, Shell, Nestlé, and Sony also had a broad global reach.

Some multinational corporations had bigger revenues than entire nations. They appeared to burst the bounds of the nation-state as they set up shop in whatever part of the world offered cheap labor. In the first years after World War II, multinationals preferred European employees, who constituted a highly educated labor pool and had well-developed consumer habits. Then, beginning in the 1960s, multinationals moved more of their operations to the emerging economies of formerly colonized states to reduce labor costs and avoid taxes. Although multinational corporations provided jobs in developing areas, profits usually went out of those areas to enrich foreign stockholders. Multinational corporations lacked the interest in the well-being of localities or nations that earlier industrialists had often shown. Thus, this system of business looked to some like imperialism in a new form.

Firms believed that they could stay competitive only by expanding, merging with other companies, or partnering with government. In France, for example, a massive glass conglomerate merged with a metallurgical company to form a new group

The New Worker

In the early years of industry, workers often labored to exhaustion and lived in such poor conditions that they sometimes resorted to violence to improve their lot. These conditions changed fundamentally in postwar Europe with the reduction of the blue-collar workforce, the growth of off-shore manufacturing, and increased automation in industrial processes. Work in manufacturing was simply cleaner and less dangerous than ever before. Within firms, the relationship of workers to bosses shifted as management started grouping workers into teams that set their own production quotas, organized and assigned tasks, and competed with other teams to see who could produce more. As workers took on responsibilities once assigned to managers, union membership declined.

In both the U.S. and Soviet blocs, a new working class of white-collar service personnel emerged. Its rise undermined economic distinctions based on the way a person worked, for those who performed service work or had managerial titles were not necessarily better paid than blue-collar laborers. The ranks of service workers swelled with researchers, planners, health care and medical staff, and government functionaries. As emphasis on service

TAKING MEASURE

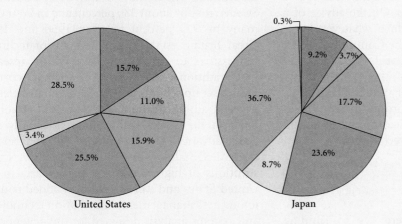

United States   Japan   Average of 12 European Countries[1]

[1]Austria, Belgium, West Germany, Denmark, Spain, Finland, Greece, Ireland, Netherlands, Norway, Portugal, and Sweden

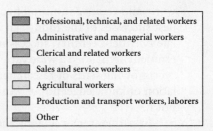

□ Professional, technical, and related workers
□ Administrative and managerial workers
□ Clerical and related workers
□ Sales and service workers
□ Agricultural workers
□ Production and transport workers, laborers
□ Other

Postindustrial Occupational Structure, 1984

Striking changes occurred in the composition of the workforce in the postwar period. Agriculture continued to decline as a source of jobs; by the 1980s, the percentage of agricultural workers in the most advanced industrial countries had dropped well below 10 percent. The most striking development was the expansion of the service sector, which came to employ more than half of all workers. In the United States, the agricultural and industrial sectors (represented by production and transportation workers), which had dominated a century earlier, now offered less than a third of all jobs. What difference does it make to ordinary people that jobs in service work predominate? (*Yearbook of Labour Statistics (Geneva: International Labour Office, 1992), Table 2.7).*

grew, entire categories of employees such as flight attendants devoted much of their skill to the psychological well-being of customers. The consumer economy provided more jobs in restaurants and personal health, fitness and grooming, and hotels and tourism. By 1969, the percentage of service-sector employees had passed that of manufacturing workers in several industrial countries: 61.1 percent versus 33.7 percent in the United States; and 48.8 percent versus 41.1 percent in Sweden (see "Taking Measure," above).

Postindustrial work life differed somewhat in the Soviet bloc. There, the percentage of farmers remained higher than in western Europe. A huge difference between professional occupations and those involving physical work also remained in socialist countries because of declining investment in advanced machinery and cleaner work processes. Men in both blocs generally earned higher pay for better jobs; uniquely in the Soviet

bloc, however, women's badly paying jobs included street cleaning, garbage collection, heavy labor on farms, and medicine (both as doctors and dentists). Somewhere between 80 and 95 percent of women worked in socialist countries, mostly under difficult conditions.

Farming changed as well, consolidating and becoming more scientific. Small landowners sold family plots to farmers engaged in agribusiness—that is, vast acreage devoted to commercial rather than peasant farming. Governments, farmers' cooperatives, and planning agencies shaped the decision making of the individual farmer; they set production quotas and handled an array of marketing transactions. Genetic research that yielded pest-resistant seeds and the skyrocketing use of pesticides, fertilizers, and machinery contributed to economic growth. Between 1965 and 1979, the number of tractors in Germany more than tripled from 384,000 to 1,340,000.

Technicians played a crucial role in transforming agriculture. For example, in the 1970s, a woman named Fernande Pelletier owned a hundred-acre farm in southwestern France. On the advice of a government expert to produce whatever foods might sell competitively in the Common Market, she switched from lamb and veal to foie gras and walnuts, and she joined with other farmers in her region to buy heavy machinery and to bring products to market. Agricultural prosperity required as much managerial and technical know-how as did success in other parts of the economy.

The Boom in Education and Research

Education and research were key to running postindustrial society and were the means by which nations maintained their economic and military might. In the West, common sense, hard work, and creative intuition had launched the earliest successes of the Industrial Revolution. By the late twentieth century, success in business or government demanded a wide variety of expertise and ever-growing staffs of researchers — "the accumulation of knowledge, not of wealth," as one official put it.

Investment in research fueled military and industrial leadership. The United States funneled more than 20 percent of its gross national product into research in the 1960s, attracting many of Europe's leading intellectuals and technicians to move to the United States in a so-called brain drain. Complex systems — for example, nuclear power generation with its many components, from scientific conceptualization to plant construction to the publicly supervised disposal of radioactive waste — required intricate coordination and professional oversight. Scientists and bureaucrats frequently made more crucial decisions than did elected politicians in the realm of space programs, weapons development, and economic policy. Here east–west differences are telling: Soviet-bloc nations proved less adept at linking their considerable achievements in science to real-life applications because of bureaucratic red tape. In the 1960s, some 40 percent of scientific findings in the Soviet bloc became obsolete before the government approved them for application to technology. An invisible backsliding from superpower effectiveness and leadership had begun in the USSR — much of it due to the lack of systems coordination and cooperation.

The centrality of sophisticated knowledge to success in postindustrial society led to unprece-

dented growth in education, especially in universities, scientific institutes, and other postsecondary institutions. The number of university students in Sweden rose by about 580 percent and in West Germany by 250 percent between 1950 and 1969. Great Britain established a network of technical universities to encourage the practical research that traditional elite universities often scorned. France set up schools to train future high-level experts in administration. The scientific establishment in the Soviet Union grew so rapidly that Soviet advanced researchers outnumbered those in the United States by the late 1970s. Meanwhile, institutions of higher learning, particularly in the United States and western Europe, added courses in business management, information technology, and systems analysis designed for the new pool of postindustrial workers.

Changing Family Life and the Generation Gap

Just as education changed to meet the needs of postindustrial society, family structures and parent–child relationships shifted from what they had been a century earlier. Households became more varied, headed by a single parent, by remarried parents merging two sets of unrelated children, by unmarried couples cohabiting, or by traditionally married couples who had few — or no — children. Households of same-sex partners became more common. By the end of the 1970s, the marriage rate in the West had fallen by 30 percent from its 1960s level, and after almost two decades of baby boom, the birthrate dropped significantly. On average, Belgian women, for example, bore 2.6 children in 1960 but only 1.8 by the end of the 1970s. In the Soviet bloc, the birthrate was even lower. Although the birthrate fell, the percentage of children born outside of marriage soared.

Daily life within the family also changed. Technological consumer items filled the home, with radio and television often forming the basis of the household's common social life. Appliances such as dishwashers, washing machines, and clothes dryers became more affordable and more widespread, raising standards of cleanliness and reducing (in theory) the time women had to devote to household work. More women worked outside the home during these years to pay for the prolonged economic dependence of children, but working mothers still did the housework and provided child care almost entirely themselves.

Whereas earlier the family had organized labor, taught craft skills, and monitored reproductive behavior, the modern family seemed to have a primarily psychological mission, providing emotional nurturance for children who acquired their intellectual skills in school. Parents turned to psychologists, social workers, and other social service experts for advice on rearing their children. Television and other media also offered much-heeded advice and models of how people should deal with life in postindustrial society.

Teenagers' lives changed dramatically, creating strong differences between adolescents and adults. A century earlier, teens had been full-time wage earners like their parents; now, in the new knowledge-based society, most were students, financially dependent on their parents into their twenties. Despite teenagers' prolonged financial childhood, sexual activity began at an ever younger age, and people talked more openly about sex, prompting the Western media to announce the arrival of a "sexual revolution" where young people were concerned. Youth simultaneously gained new roles as consumers. Seeing baby boomers as a multibillion-dollar market, advertisers and industrialists wooed them with consumer items associated with rock music—records, portable radios, stereos, and so on. Rock music celebrated youthful rebellion against adult culture in biting, critical, and often explicitly sexual lyrics. Sex roles for the young did not change, however. Despite the popularity of a few individual women rockers, promoters focused on men, whom they depicted as heroic, surrounded by worshipping female "groupies." The new models for youth such as the Beatles were themselves the products of advanced technology and savvy marketing for mass consumption. "What's your message for American teenagers?" the Beatles were asked. "Buy some more Beatles records," they responded. The mixture of high-tech music, pop-star marketing, and the sexual openness of fans contributed to a sense that there was a unique youth culture separating the young from their parents—a so-called generation gap.

Art, Ideas, and Religion in a Technocratic Society

Artists and scholars of the postindustrial age addressed the growing consumerism and the new world of space, electronics, and computers in their art and thought. As colonies threw off the imperialist yoke and became new nations, the influence of their culture on the West remained strong. Like the new multinational corporations, many artists and scholars enjoyed increasing international recognition and reached global markets. Social sci-

The Rolling Stones (1976)
The Rolling Stones were more energetic, sexual, and flamboyant than the earlier British rock sensation, the Beatles. Astute marketing experts for big record companies helped such rock groups target youth successfully. What exactly was the appeal of the Beatles, the Rolling Stones, and the other celebrated rock stars who followed in their wake? *(Getty Images.)*

entists added to their prestige and influence by employing complex statistical and other scientific methods made possible by increasingly sophisticated and powerful computers.

The Visual Arts. A new trend in the visual arts was called **pop art**. It featured images from everyday life and employed the glossy techniques and products of what these artists called admass, or mass advertising. Robert Rauschenberg, a leading U.S. practitioner, made collages from comic strips, magazine clippings, and fabric to fulfill his vision

---

pop art: A style in the visual arts that mimicked advertising and consumerism and that used ordinary objects as a part of paintings and other compositions.

that "a picture is more like the real world when it's made out of the real world." The movement had become a financial success by the early 1960s, propelled by such maverick American artists as Andy Warhol (1928–1987), who parodied modern commercialism. Through images of actress Marilyn Monroe and former first lady Jacqueline Kennedy, Warhol showed, for example, how depictions of women were used to sell everything mass culture had to offer in the 1960s and 1970s. He depicted Campbell's soup cans as they appeared in advertisements and sold these works as elite artistic creations.

Swedish-born artist Claes Oldenburg (1929–) portrayed the grotesque aspects of ordinary consumer products in *Giant Hamburger with Pickle*

Claes Oldenberg, *Trowel* (1971)

Claes Oldenberg captured the playful mood of pop art when he began duplicating ordinary objects such as vacuum cleaners, telephones, and even raisin bread on a larger-than-life scale. Pop art seemed to make a mockery of consumerism and everyday life, but museums and wealthy collectors snapped it up, eventually making celebrities of the artists and paying tens of millions of dollars for these works. *(Nicolas Sapieha/Art Resource, NY.)*

Attached (1962) and *Lipstick Ascending on Caterpillar Tractor* (1967). Capturing this mocking world of art, German artist Sigmar Polke did cartoon-like drawings of products and of those who craved them. Others practicing this "high art" picked up "low" objects such as scraps of metal, cigarette butts, dirt, and even excrement. The Swiss sculptor Jean Tinguely used rusted parts of old machines—the junk of industrial society—to make fountains that could move. His partner Niki de Saint Phalle (1930–2002) then decorated them with huge, gaudy figures—many of them inspired by the folk traditions of the Caribbean and Africa. Their colorful, mobile fountains adorned main squares in Stockholm, Paris, and other cities.

Music. The American composer John Cage (1912–1992) worked in a similar vein when he added to his musical scores sounds produced by such everyday items as combs, pieces of wood, and radio noise. Buddhist influence led Cage to incorporate silence in music and to compose by randomly tossing coins and then choosing notes by the corresponding numbers in the ancient Chinese *I Ching* (Book of Changes). These techniques continued the trend away from classical melody that had begun with modernism. Other composers, called minimalists, simplified music by featuring repetition and sustained notes instead of producing the lush melodies of nineteenth-century symphonies and piano music. Estonian composer Arvo Pärt wrote minimalist pieces in the 1970s using only three or four notes in total; he called this style "starvation" music to emphasize the lack of both freedom and goods in the Soviet bloc.

German composer Karlheinz Stockhausen introduced electronic music into classical composition in 1953; Cage also used it soon after. Influenced by his own travels, Stockhausen continued the modern style of fully exploring non-Western tonalities in such 1970s pieces as *Ceylon*. Even though this music echoed the familiar technology of everyday life, many listeners hated what seemed unpleasant sounds. Yet improved recording technology and mass marketing brought music of all varieties to a wider home audience than ever before.

Social Science. The social sciences reached the peak of their prestige in the postindustrial era, often because of the increasing use of statistical models made possible by advanced electronic computations. Sociologists and psychologists produced detailed empirical studies that claimed to demonstrate rules for understanding individual and group behavior. Anthropology was among the most exciting of the social sciences, for it exposed the young university student to societies that seemed immune to modern technology and industry. Fieldwork and colorful ethnographic films revealed alternative lifestyles and seemingly exotic practices. While studying people who came to be called "the other," these young experts had their sense of freedom reinforced by the vision of going back to nature. Whatever their discipline, social scientists announced that, like technicians and engineers, their specialized methods and factual knowledge were key to managing the complexities of postindustrial society and developing nations alike.

Yet at the same time, the social sciences undermined Enlightenment beliefs that individuals had true freedom. French anthropologist Claude Lévi-Strauss (1908–) developed a theory called structuralism, which insisted that rigid, rule-bound structures—kinship and exchange, for example—control the functioning of all societies. By challenging existentialism's claim that humans could create a free existence, structuralism shook the social sciences' faith in rationality. Lévi-Strauss's book *The Savage Mind* (1966) also demonstrated that people outside the West, even though they did not use scientific methods, had their own extremely effective systems of problem solving. In the 1960s and 1970s, the findings of some social scientists echoed concerns that technology was creating a society of automatons and that bureaucracies were destroying individuality and freedom.

Religion. Religious leaders and parishioners responded to the changing times in a variety of ways. Pope Paul VI (1963–1978) opposed artificial birth control as it became more prevalent, but he also became the first pontiff to carry out the new global vision of Vatican II by visiting Africa, Asia, and South America. In some places, religious fervor at the grass roots surged in the face of advancing science and the threat of nuclear annihilation. Growing numbers of U.S. Protestants, for example, joined sects that stressed the literal truth of the Bible and denied the validity of past scientific discoveries such as the age of the universe and the evolution of the species. In western Europe, however, Christian churchgoing remained at a low ebb. In the 1970s, for example, only 10 percent of the British population went to religious services—about the same number that attended live soccer matches. Most striking was the changing composition of the Western religious public. Immigration of people from former colonies and other parts of the world increased the strength of non-Christian religions such as Islam and varieties of Hindu faiths. Cities and towns came to house mosques, Buddhist temples, and shrines to other creeds. New religious values sometimes mixed tensely with both Western European Judeo-Christianity and the antireligious culture of the Soviet bloc.

> **REVIEW:** How did Western society and culture change in the postindustrial age?

Protesting Cold War Conditions

The United States and the Soviet Union reached new heights of power in the 1960s, but trouble was brewing for the superpowers. By 1965, the six nations of the Common Market had replaced the United States as the leader in worldwide trade and the marketing of new technologies, and they often acted in their own self-interest, not in the interests of the superpowers. In 1973, Britain's membership in the Common Market, followed by Ireland and Denmark, boosted the market's exports to almost three times those of the United States. The USSR faced challenges too. Communist China, along with countries in eastern Europe, contested Soviet leadership, and many decolonizing regions refused to ally with either of the superpowers. By the mid-1960s, the United States was enmeshed in a devastating war in Vietnam in order to block the Communist independence movement there. At the end of the 1970s, the USSR became embroiled in an equally devastating war in Afghanistan. Rising citizen discontent, sometimes expressed in dramatic acts of protest like that of Jan Palach, presented another serious challenge to the cold war order. From the 1960s until 1989, people rose up against technology, the lack of fundamental rights, and the potential for nuclear holocaust.

Cracks in the Cold War Order

Across the social and political spectrum came calls to at least soften the effects of the cold war in this age of unprecedented technological advance. In the Soviet Union, the new middle class of bureaucrats and managers demanded a better standard of living and a reduction in the cold war animosity that made everyday life so menacing. Voters in western European countries elected politicians who promoted an increasing array of social programs designed to ensure the economic democracy of the welfare state and to promote technological development. A significant minority of voters shifted their allegiance from the centrist Christian Democratic coalitions that supported U.S. political goals to Socialist, Labor, and Social Democratic parties that endorsed policies to bridge the cold war divide.

Germany and France.   The German and French governments both made solid and highly visible changes in policy, which, though different, unsettled cold war divisiveness. In Germany, Social Democratic politicians had enough influence to shift money from defense spending to domestic programs. Willy Brandt (1913–1992), the Socialist mayor of West Berlin, became foreign minister in 1966 and pursued an end to frigid relations with Communist East Germany in order to open up commerce across borders. This policy, known as **Ostpolitik**, gave West German business leaders what they wanted: "the depoliticization of Germany's foreign trade," as one industrialist put it, and an opening of consumerism in the Soviet bloc. West German trade with eastern Europe grew rapidly; however, it left the relatively poorer countries of the Soviet bloc strapped with mounting debt—some $45 billion annually by 1970. Nonetheless, commerce had built a bridge across the U.S.-Soviet cold war divide.

To break the superpowers' stranglehold on international politics, French president Charles de Gaulle poured huge sums into French nuclear development, withdrew French forces from NATO, and signed trade treaties with the Soviet bloc. Communist China and France also drew closer through trade and diplomatic ties. However, de Gaulle also maintained France's good relations with Germany to prevent further encroachments from the Soviet bloc. At home, de Gaulle's government sponsored construction of modern housing and mandated the exterior cleaning of all Parisian buildings—a massive project taking years—to wipe away more than a century of industrial grime. With his haughty and stubborn pursuit of French grandeur, de Gaulle offered the European public an alternative to submission to the superpowers.

The Soviet Union.   Brandt's Ostpolitik and de Gaulle's assertiveness, especially in economic development, had their echoes in Soviet-bloc reforms. After Soviet premier Nikita Khrushchev's ouster in 1964, the new leadership of Leonid Brezhnev (1909–1982) and Alexei Kosygin (1904–1980) ini-

tially continued attempts at reform, encouraging plant managers to turn a profit and allowing the production of televisions, household appliances, and cheap housing to alleviate the discontent of an increasingly better-educated and better-informed citizenry. The government also loosened restrictions to allow cultural and scientific meetings with Westerners, another move that relaxed the cold war atmosphere in the mid-1960s. Like the French, the Soviets set up "technopoles"—new cities devoted to research and technological innovation. The Soviet satellites in eastern Europe seized the economic opportunity presented by Moscow's relaxed posture. For example, Hungarian leader János Kádár introduced elements of a market system into the national economy by encouraging small businesses and trade to develop outside the Communist-controlled state network.

In the arts, Soviet-bloc writers sought to halt the slavish praise for the Soviet past and loosen the hold of socialist realism as the dominant style. Dissident artists' paintings subverted the brightly attired and heroic figures of socialist realism and depicted Soviet citizens as worn and tired in grays and other monochromatic color schemes (see "Seeing History," page 929). Ukrainian poet Yevgeny Yevtushenko exposed Soviet complicity in the Holocaust in *Babi Yar* (1961), a passionate protest against the slaughter of tens of thousands of Jews near Kiev during World War II. Challenging the celebratory nature of socialist art, East Berlin writer Christa Wolf showed a couple tragically divided by the Berlin Wall in her novel *Divided Heaven* (1965). Repression of expression returned in the later 1960s and 1970s, as the Soviet government took to bulldozing outdoor art shows, thereby forcing visual artists to hold secret exhibitions or public ones announced at the very last minute by word of mouth. For their part, writers relied on **samizdat** culture, a form of dissident activity in which uncensored publications were reproduced by hand and passed from reader to reader, thus building a foundation for the successful resistance of the 1980s.

The United States.   Other issues challenged U.S. leadership of the free world during the cold war. The assassination of President John F. Kennedy in November 1963 shocked the nation and the world, but only momentarily did it halt the escalating demands for civil rights for African Americans and other minorities. White segregationists mur-

---

Ostpolitik: A policy initiated by Willy Brandt in the late 1960s in which West Germany sought better economic relations with the Communist countries of eastern Europe.

samizdat: A key form of dissident activity across the Soviet bloc; individuals reproduced uncensored publications by hand and passed them from reader to reader, thus building a foundation for the successful resistance of the 1980s.

Critiquing the Soviet System: Dissident Art in the 1960s and 1970s

Artists, writers, composers, and performers in the USSR were supposed to follow Communist Party directives, creating uplifting works that spread Communist ideals, despite the political repression and economic hardships that plagued the system. Numerous dissident artists sought to undermine the Communist message and criticize the regime through their work, thus helping to preparing the ground for a full-scale revolt against the Soviet system in the late 1980s. The Soviet government persecuted these artists and their families and often destroyed subversive works that were displayed in public. Yet dissident artists bravely forged ahead, displaying their art and even selling it to foreign dealers to smuggle out of the country.

Dissident artists employed a range of techniques, both subtle and explicit, to critique the Soviet regime. Eric Bulatov often made use of the officially approved Soviet style of "socialist realism" in his works to slyly criticize the system. His painting *Krasikov Street,* shown here, refers to Lenin's much-repeated motto meant to inspire Soviet citizens: "Always forward, never backward." How does Bulatov use motion and color here to comment on both Soviet society and the Communist establishment? What messages is he conveying?

In his work *The General,* Boris Orlov used sculpture to lampoon one of the mainstays of Soviet society during the cold war. As the heroes of World War II and protectors of communism, generals were officially revered, parading on Soviet holidays and at commemorative events. What are the general's main features as portrayed by Orlov? What adjectives would you use to describe this work? How would you characterize the tone and purpose of Orlov's depiction?

As you reflect on these two works of art, what in your opinion would have made them dangerous to the survival of Soviet communism?

Boris Orlov, *The General,* 1970. *(Collection of the Jane Voorhees Zimmerli Art Museum, Rutgers, The State University of New Jersey, The Norton and Nancy Dodge Collection of Nonconformist Art from the Soviet Union. Photograph by Jack Abraham. 14194 © Boris Orlov/RAO, Moscow/VAGA, New York, NY.)*

Eric Bulatov, *Krasikov Street,* 1977. *(Collection of the Jane Voorhees Zimmerli Art Museum, Rutgers, The State University of New Jersey, The Norton and Nancy Dodge Collection of Nonconformist Art from the Soviet Union. Photograph by Jack Abraham. 05125/© 2008 Artists Rights Society (ARS), NY/ADAGP, Paris.)*

dered, maimed, and arrested those attempting to integrate lunch counters, register black voters, or simply march on behalf of freedom. This violent racism was a weak link in the American claim to moral superiority in the cold war. In response to the murders and destruction, Kennedy had introduced civil rights legislation and forced the desegregation of schools and universities. Lyndon B. Johnson (1908–1973), Kennedy's successor, steered the Civil Rights Act through Congress in 1964. This legislation forbade segregation in public facilities and created the Equal Employment Opportunity Commission (EEOC) to fight job discrimination based on "race, color, national origin, religion, and sex." Southern conservatives had tacked on the provision outlawing discrimination against women in the vain hope that it would doom the bill. Modeling himself on his hero Franklin Roosevelt, Johnson envisioned what he called a Great Society, in which new government programs would improve the lot of the forty million Americans living in poverty. Johnson's myriad reform programs included Project Head Start for educating disadvantaged preschool children and the Job Corps for training youth. Black novelist Ralph Ellison called Johnson "the greatest American president for the poor and the Negroes."

Still, the cold war remained, and the United States became increasingly embroiled in Vietnam (Map 28.2). After the Geneva Conference of 1954, which divided Vietnam into North and South, the United States increased its support for the corrupt and incompetent leaders of non-Communist South Vietnam. North Vietnam, China, and the Soviet Union backed the rebel Vietcong, or South Vietnamese Communists. The strength of the Vietcong seemed to grow daily, and by 1966, the United States had more than half a million soldiers in South Vietnam. Early in the war, Johnson's advisers appeared on television, predicting imminent victory despite mounting U.S. casualties and the need to draft young men, many of them unwilling to go. Faced with growing antiwar sentiment and increasing military costs, Johnson announced in March 1968 that he would not run for president again.

The Growth of Citizen Activism

In the midst of cold war conflict and technological advance, a new activism emerged. Prosperity and the rising benefits of a postindustrial, service-oriented

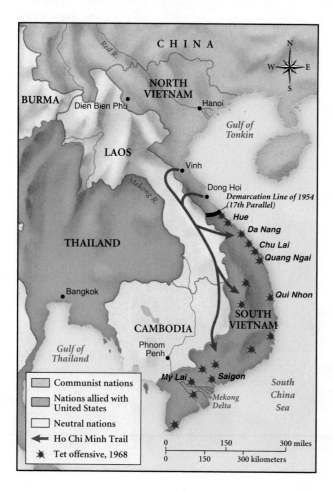

MAP 28.2 The Vietnam War, 1954–1975
The local peoples of Southeast Asia had long resisted incursions by their neighbors. The Vietnamese beat the French colonizers in the battle of Dien Bien Phu in 1954. But the Americans soon became involved, trying to stem what they saw as the tide of Communist influence behind the Vietnamese liberation movement. The ensuing war in Vietnam in the 1960s and 1970s spread into neighboring countries, making the region the scene of vast destruction.

economy made people ever more eager for peace. University students did not want their lives to end on faraway battlefields. Other activists — among them minorities, women, and homosexuals — simply wanted a fair chance at education, jobs, and some political voice. Students, blacks and other minorities, Soviet-bloc citizens, women, environmentalists, and homosexuals brought their societies to the brink of revolution during what became increasingly fiery protests in the late 1960s.

Civil Rights. The U.S. civil rights movement broadened, as other minorities joined African Americans in demanding fair treatment. In 1965, César Chávez (1927–1993) led Mexican American migrant workers in the California grape agribusiness to strike for better wages and working conditions. Meanwhile, urban riots erupted across the United States in 1965 and subsequent summers as frustrated and angry African Americans turned their struggle for equal rights into a militant celebration of their race under the banner "Black is beautiful." The issue they faced was one they felt they had in common with decolonizing people: how to shape an identity different from that imposed on them by white oppressors. Some urged a push for "black power" to reclaim rights forcefully instead of begging for them nonviolently. Separatism, not integration, became the goal of still others; small cadres of militants like the Black Panthers took up arms, believing that, like decolonizing people elsewhere, they needed to protect themselves against the violent whites around them.

Student Activism. As a result of the new turn in black efforts for change, white American university students who had participated in the early stages of the civil rights movement found themselves excluded from leadership positions. Many of them soon joined the swelling protest against technological change, consumerism, and the Vietnam War. European youth were also feverish for reform. In the mid-1960s, university students in Rome occupied an administration building after right-wing opponents assassinated one of their number during a protest against the 200-to-1 student–teacher ratio. In 1966, Prague students, chanting "The only good Communist is a dead one," held carnival-like processions to commemorate the tenth anniversary of the 1956 Hungarian uprisings. The "situationists" in France called on students to wake up from the slumbering pace of mass society by jolting individuals to action with shocking graffiti and street theater.

Throughout the 1960s, students criticized the traditional university curriculum and flaunted their own countercultural values. They questioned how studying Plato or Dante would help them after graduation. "How to Train Stuffed Geese" was French students' satirical version of the teaching methods inflicted on them. "No professors over forty" and "Don't trust anyone over thirty" were powerful slogans of the day. Long hair, communal living, scorn for personal cleanliness, and ridicule for sexual chastity were part of students' rejection of middle-class values. Widespread use of the pill made abstinence unnecessary as a method of birth control, and open promiscuity made the sexual revolution explicit and public. Marijuana use became common among students, and amphetamines and barbiturates added to the drug culture, which had its own rituals, music, and gathering places. Disdained by students, big business nonetheless made billions of dollars by selling blue jeans, natural foods, and drugs as well as by packaging and managing the rock stars of the counterculture.

The Women's Movement. Women's activism erupted across the political spectrum (see "Contrasting Views," page 932). Working for reproductive rights, women in France helped end the nation's ban on birth control in 1965. More politically conventional middle-class women eagerly responded to the international best seller *The Feminine Mystique* (1963) by American journalist Betty Friedan. Pointing to the stagnating talents of many housewives, Friedan helped organize the National Organization for Women (NOW) in 1966 "to bring women into full participation in the mainstream of American society now." NOW advocated equal pay for women and a variety of other legal and economic reforms. In Sweden, women lobbied to make tasks both at home and in the workplace less gender-segregated, and in these same years a few Soviet women began speaking out against their low-paid and unpaid work that kept the USSR running.

Those engaged in the civil rights and student movements soon realized that many of those protest organizations devalued women just as society at large did. Male activists adopted the leather-jacketed machismo style of their film and rock heroes, but women in the movements were often judged by the status of their male-protester lovers. "A woman was to 'inspire' her man," African American activist Angela Davis complained, adding that women seeking equality were accused of wanting "to rob [male activists] of their manhood." West German women students tossed tomatoes at male protest leaders in defiance of male domination of the movement and of standards for ladylike behavior.

Feminist Debates

The feminist movement of the late twentieth century provoked the most pronounced and widespread debate over gender in recorded history. Discussion often reached a heated pitch, as it did in other reform movements of the day. Hardly the single movement described by journalists, feminism had a variety of concerns, often depending on nationality, ethnicity, sexual orientation, and class. Opinion on these issues could produce conflict among activists and serious divisions on goals and policies, as the authors of the Combahee River Statement demonstrated (Document 1). At times, concerns over issues like equal opportunity in the workplace were directed at government policies, as in the case of the Soviet worker (Document 2). Italian feminists saw all the disabilities imposed by government as characteristic of larger problems (Document 3), while Germans explicitly connected the cause of feminism to that of environmentalism (Document 4).

1. Criticizing Feminism

In the United States, black women, like several other minority groups, found themselves marginalized in both the feminist and civil rights movements. In 1977, some of them issued the Combahee River Statement.

Black, other third world, and working women have been involved in the feminist movement from its start, but both outside reactionary forces and racism and elitism within the movement itself have served to obscure our participation. . . .

Black feminist politics also have an obvious connection to movements for Black liberation, particularly those of the 1960s and 1970s. . . . It was our experience and disillusionment within these liberation movements, as well as experience on the periphery of the white male left, that led to the need to develop a politics that was antiracist, unlike those of white women, and antisexist, unlike those of Black and white men. . . .

Above all else, our politics initially sprang from the shared belief that Black women are inherently valuable, that our liberation is a necessity not as an adjunct to somebody else's but because of our need as human persons for autonomy.

Source: "The Combahee River Collective Statement," in *Feminism in Our Time: The Essential Writings, World War II to the Present,* ed. Miriam Schneir (New York: Vintage, 1994), 177–79.

2. Criticizing Socialism

Official policy in the Soviet Union stated that socialism had brought women full equality, eliminating the need for feminism. In the 1970s, however, clusters of Russian women announced their dissatisfaction with so-called equality under socialism. Tatyana Mamonova, the editor of a collection of Russian women's writings such as this from a railroad worker, was ultimately expelled from the USSR.

It is becoming increasingly clear that the current equality means only giving women the right to perform heavy labor. . . . [I]n our day the woman, still not freed from the incredible burden of the family, strains herself even harder in the service of society. The situation . . . is true not only in large cities but also in villages. On collective and state farms, women do the hardest and most exhausting work while the men are employed as administrators, agronomists, accountants, warehouse managers, or high-paid

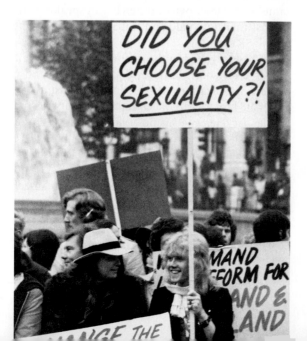

Women also took to the streets on behalf of such issues as abortion rights or the decriminalization of gay and lesbian sexuality. Many flouted social conventions in their attire, language, and

Campaign for Homosexual Equality Rally, London 1974
The reformist spirit of the 1960s and 1970s changed homosexuals' activism. Instead of concentrating mostly on legal protection from criminal prosecution, gays and lesbians began affirming a special and positive identity. Critics charged that constitutional rights were sufficient and that homosexuals and others constituted special-interest groups. Gays, women, and ethnic or racial minorities countercharged that the universal values and constitutional rights first put forth in the Enlightenment seemed to apply only to a privileged few. (© Hulton-Deutsch Collection/Corbis.)

tractor and combine drivers. In other words, men do the work that is more interesting and more profitable and does not damage their health.

Source: Tatyana Mamonova, ed., *Women and Russia: Feminist Writings from the Soviet Union* (Boston: Beacon Press, 1984), 8.

3. Policy and Patriarchy

In Italy, as in the Soviet Union, feminism had an underground quality involving mimeographed tracts and graffiti on buildings; women formed their own bookshops and published small newspapers. But others lobbied hard to get legislation on divorce and abortion changed, while in 1976 the Feminist Movement of Rome issued this article in its paper.

Patriarchal society is based on authoritarian-exploitative relationships, and its sexuality is sadomasochistic. The values of power, of the domination of man over the other [woman], are reflected in sexuality, where historically woman is given to man for his use. . . .

The idea of woman as man's property is fundamental to her oppression and she is often the only possession that dominant men allow exploited men to keep. . . .

In other words woman is given to the (exploited) man as compensation for his lack of possessions. . . .

We denounce as the latest form of woman's oppression the idea of a "sexual revolution" where woman is forced to go from being one man's object to being everybody's object, and where sadomasochistic pornography in films, in magazines, in all the forms of mass media that brutalize and violate woman, is bandied about as a triumph of sexual liberty.

Source: "Male Sexuality—Perversion," *Movimento Femminista Romano* (1976), quoted in *Italian Feminist Thought: A Reader*, eds. Paola Bono and Sandra Kemp (Oxford: Blackwell, 1991), 68–69.

4. Feminism and Environmentalism

"Green" feminists took a different approach, such as announced in this "Manifesto of the 'Green' Women." It was originally a 1975 speech made in West Germany in the context of the moon landing and other accomplishments in space.

Man has actually landed on the moon—an admirable feat. . . . We "Green" women . . . believe that men belong to our environment. In order to rescue that environment for our children, we want to confront this man, this adventurer and moon explorer. A female cosmonaut from a so-called socialist republic doesn't justify this energy-wasting enterprise for us at a time when three-fourths of the earth's population is suffering from malnutrition.

Our inability to solve immediate problems may tempt us into escape—to the moon, into careerism, escape into ideologies, into alcohol or other drugs. But one group cannot escape completely: women, society's potential mothers, who must give birth to children, willingly or unwillingly, in this polluted world of ours.

Source: Delphine Brox-Brochot, "Manifesto of the 'Green' Women," in *German Feminism: Readings in Politics and Literature*, eds. Edith Hoshino Altbach et al. (Albany: State University of New York Press, 1984), 314.

QUESTIONS TO CONSIDER

1. Was the feminist movement of the 1960s and 1970s primarily an offshoot of other reform movements of the day, or did it have a character of its own?
2. In what ways was feminism in these decades a unified movement, and in what ways was it a set of multiple movements?
3. What issues do these activists raise?

---

attitudes. Renouncing brassieres, high-heeled shoes, cosmetics, and other adornments, they spoke openly about taboo subjects such as their sexual feelings and even announced that they had resorted to illegal abortions. This brand of feminist activism was meant to shock polite society—and it did. Many women of color, however, broke with feminist solidarity and spoke out against the "double jeopardy" of being "black and female." Soon there were concrete changes. In Catholic Italy, feminists won the rights to divorce, to gain access to birth-control information, and to obtain legal abortions. The demand for equal pay, job opportunities, and protection from rape, incest, and battering framed the major legal struggles of thousands of women's groups into the 1970s.

1968: Year of Crisis

Calls for reform finally boiled over in 1968. In January, on the first day of Tet, the Vietnamese New Year, the Vietcong and the North Vietnamese attacked more than one hundred South Vietnamese towns and American bases, inflicting heavy casualties. The Tet offensive, as it came to be called, led many to conclude that the war might be unwinnable and gave crucial momentum to the antiwar movement around the world. Students in Paris, Tokyo, Mexico City, and other major capitals took to the streets, often in violent protest. Meanwhile, in Czechoslovakia, a quieter movement against Soviet cold war domination had taken shape, but the atmosphere in that country, as elsewhere, became explosive when the Soviets invaded to put down reform.

Violence Erupts. On April 4, 1968, a white racist assassinated civil rights leader Martin Luther King Jr. Riots erupted in more than a hundred cities in the United States as African Americans vented their anguish and rage. Rejecting King's policy of nonviolence, black leaders turned from rhetoric to violence: "Burn, baby, burn," chanted rioters as they rampaged through grim inner cities. On campuses, strident confrontation over the intertwined issues of war, technology, racism, and sexism closed down classes.

Student dissent escalated, with the most dramatic protests occurring in France. In January, students at Nanterre, outside of Paris, had gone on strike, invading administration offices to protest their inferior education and status. They called themselves a proletariat—an exploited working class—as labor activists had done for more than a century. They did not embrace Soviet communism but rather considered themselves part of a New Left, not the old Communist or Socialist left. When in the spring students at the prestigious Sorbonne in Paris took to the streets in protest, police assaulted them. The Parisian middle classes reacted with unexpected, if temporary, sympathy to the student uprising because of their own resentment of bureaucracy.

They were also horrified at seeing the police force beating middle-class students and even passersby who expressed their support.

French workers joined in the protest: some nine million went on strike, occupying factories and calling not only for higher wages but also for participation in everyday decision making. The combined revolt of youth and workers looked as if it might spiral into another French revolution, so unified were the expressions of political alienation. The normally decisive president Charles de Gaulle seemed paralyzed at first, but he soon sent tanks into Paris. In June, he announced a raise for workers, and businesses offered them a strengthened voice in decision making. Many citizens, having grown tired of the street violence, the destruction of so much private property, and the breakdown of services (for example, the garbage was not collected for weeks), began to sympathize with the government instead of the students. Although demonstrations continued throughout June, the student movement in France at least had been closed down. The revolutionary moment had passed.

The Prague Spring. The 1968 revolt in Prague began within the Czechoslovak Communist Party itself. At a party congress in the autumn of 1967,

Invasion Puts Down the Prague Spring
When the Soviet Union and other Warsaw Pact members cracked down on the Prague Spring, they met determined citizen resistance. People refused assistance of any kind to the invaders and personally talked to them about the Czech cause. Despite the repression, protests small and large continued until the final fall of Communist rule two decades later. (© Bettmann/Corbis.)

Alexander Dubček, head of the Slovak branch of the party, had called for more social and political openness. Attacked as an inferior Slovak by the Communist leadership, Dubček nonetheless struck a chord among frustrated party officials, technocrats, and intellectuals; Czech citizens began to dream of creating a new society—one based on "socialism with a human face." Reform-minded party delegates elevated Dubček to the top position, and he quickly changed the Communist style of government by ending censorship, instituting the secret ballot for party elections, and allowing competing political groups to form. "Look!" one little girl in the street remarked as the new government took power. "Everyone's smiling today." The Prague Spring had begun—"an orgy of free expression," one Czech journalist called it. People bought uncensored publications, flocked to uncensored theater productions, and engaged in nonstop political debate.

Dubček faced the enormous problem of negotiating policies acceptable to the USSR, the entrenched party bureaucracy, and reform-minded citizens. Reforms were handed down with warnings about maintaining "discipline" and showing "wise behavior." Fearing change, the Polish, East German, and Soviet regimes threatened the reform government daily. When Dubček failed to attend a meeting of Warsaw Pact leaders, Soviet threats intensified until finally, in August 1968, Soviet tanks rolled into Prague in a massive show of force. Citizens tried to halt the return to Communist orthodoxy through sabotage: they painted graffiti on the tanks and removed street signs to confuse invading troops. Illegal radio stations broadcast testimonials of resistance, and merchants refused to sell food or other commodities to Soviet troops. These actions could not stop the determined Soviet leadership, which gradually removed reformers from power. Jan Palach and other university students immolated themselves, and protests of one type or another continued. Nonetheless, the moment of reform-minded change eventually ended here too. Around the world, governments worked to stamp out criticism of the cold war status quo.

The Superpowers Restore Order. The protests of 1968 challenged the political direction of Western societies, but little turned out the way reformers

Prague Spring, 1968

hoped as governments turned to conservative solutions. In November 1968, the Soviets announced the Brezhnev Doctrine, which stated that reform movements, as a "common problem" of all socialist countries, would face swift repression. In the early 1970s, the hard-liner Brezhnev clamped down on critics, crushing the morale of dissidents in the USSR. "The shock of our tanks crushing the Prague Spring . . . convinced us that the Soviet colossus was invincible," explained one pessimistic liberal. Other voices persisted, however. In 1974, Brezhnev expelled author Aleksandr Solzhenitsyn from the USSR after the publication of the first volume of *The Gulag Archipelago* (1973–1976) in the U.S.-led bloc. Composed from biographies, firsthand reports, and other sources of information about prison camp life, Solzhenitsyn's story of the Gulag (the Soviet system of internment and forced-labor camps) documented the brutal conditions Soviet prisoners endured under Stalin and his successors. More than any other single work, *The Gulag Archipelago* disillusioned many loyal Communists around the world.

The USSR also persecuted many ordinary citizens who did not have Solzhenitsyn's international reputation. Soviet psychologists, complying with the government, certified the "mental illness" of people who did not play by the rules; thus, dissidents wound up as virtual prisoners in mental institutions. In a revival of tsarist Russia's anti-Semitism, Jews faced educational restrictions (especially in university admissions), severe job discrimination, and constant assault on their religious practice. Soviet officials commonly charged that Jews were "unreliable, they think only of emigrating. . . . It's madness to give them an education, because it's state money wasted." Ironically, even dissidents blamed Jews for the Bolshevik Revolution and for the terror of Stalinist collectivization. As attacks intensified in the 1970s, Soviet Jews sought to emigrate to Israel or the United States, often unsuccessfully.

The brain drain of eastern European intellectuals to the West had become significant and continued into the 1970s and beyond. The modernist composer Gyorgy Ligeti had left Hungary in 1956, after which his work was celebrated in concert halls and in such classic films as *2001: A Space Odyssey*. From exile in Paris, Czech writer Milan Kundera enthralled audiences with *The Book of Laughter and Forgetting* (1979) and *The Unbearable Lightness of Being* (1984). His novels chronicled his own descent from enthusiasm for communism to a despair characterized by bitter humor. Kundera claimed the Soviet regime in Czechoslovakia depended on making people forget. The memory of fallen leaders was ruthlessly erased from history books, for instance, and individuals tried to forget grim reality with lots of sexual activity. Like the migrants from fascist Germany and Italy in the 1930s, newcomers—from noted intellectuals to skilled craftspeople and dancers—enriched the culture of those countries in the West that welcomed them.

In the United States, the reaction against activists was different, though the impulse to restore order prevailed there too. Elected in 1968, President **Richard Nixon** (1913–1994) promised to bring peace to Southeast Asia, but in 1970, he ordered U.S. troops to invade Cambodia, the site of North Vietnamese bases. Campuses erupted again in protest, and on May 4 the National Guard killed four students and wounded eleven others at a demonstration at Kent State University in Ohio. Nixon called the victims "bums," and a growing reaction against the counterculture led many Americans to agree with him that the guardsmen "should have fired sooner and longer." The United States and North Vietnam agreed to peace in January 1973, but hostilities continued. In 1975, a determined North Vietnamese offensive defeated South Vietnam and its U.S. allies and forcibly reunified the country. The United States reeled from the defeat, having suffered loss of young lives, turbulence at home, vast military costs, and a weakening of its reputation around the world. Yet a strong current of public opinion turned against activists, born of the sense that somehow they—not the war, government corruption, or a spiraling war debt—had brought the United States down. Both superpowers were being tested, almost to the limits, and in a climate of political volatility, the future of postindustrial prosperity was uncertain.

REVIEW: What were the main issues for protesters in the 1960s, and how did governments address them?

Richard Nixon: U.S. president from 1969 to 1974 who escalated the Vietnam War, worked for accommodation with China, and resigned from the presidency after trying to block free elections.

The Testing of Superpower Domination and the End of the Cold War

Protesters like Jan Palach left a lasting legacy that continued to motivate those seeking political change, particularly in the Soviet bloc. As order was restored, some disillusioned reformers in the West turned to open terrorism. New forces were also emerging from beyond the West to challenge superpower dominance. The 1970s brought an era of détente—a lessening of tensions—during which both superpowers limited the nuclear arms race in order to meet crises at home. Despite this relaxation in the cold war, internal corruption, the threat of terrorism, competition from the oil-producing states, and attempts to control the world beyond their borders threw the superpowers and their allies off balance, allowing reform-minded heads of state to come to the fore. The two most famous innovators were Margaret Thatcher in Britain and Mikhail Gorbachev in the USSR, who introduced drastic new policies in the 1980s to keep their economies moving forward. But in the Soviet bloc, postindustrial prosperity was simply unattainable under the old system. Gorbachev's reforms actually contributed to the collapse of the Soviet system and the end of the cold war in 1989.

A Changing Balance of World Power

After being tested by protest at home, the superpowers next confronted a changing world. In 1972, the United States pulled off a foreign policy triumph over the USSR when it opened relations with the other Communist giant—China. But it was hit hard by a Middle Eastern oil embargo that followed on the heels of that victory. As the situation in the Middle East grew ever bloodier, militants in Iran took U.S. embassy personnel hostage. The relationship of the United States to the Middle East began to weaken the U.S. bloc and overtake the cold war as a major global issue.

From Nixon in China to Détente. In the midst of turmoil at home and the draining war in Vietnam, Henry Kissinger, Nixon's secretary of state and a believer—like Otto von Bismarck—in Realpolitik, decided to take advantage of the ongoing USSR-Chinese rivalry. After the Communist Revolution in 1949, Mao Zedong, China's new leader, undertook foolish experiments in both manufacturing and agriculture that caused famine and massive suffering. In the Cultural Revolution of the 1960s, Mao encouraged students to attack officials, teachers, and other authorities to prevent — he claimed — the development of a Soviet-style bureaucracy. As internal problems grew in both the Soviet Union and China, the two Communist giants skirmished along their shared borders and in diplomatic arenas. In 1972, in the midst of turmoil at home and the draining war in Vietnam, President Nixon visited China, linking, if only tentatively, two very different great nations both facing disorder at home. In China, Nixon's visit helped slow the brutality and excesses of Mao's Cultural Revolution and advanced the careers of Chinese pragmatists interested in technology, trade, and relations with the West.

The diplomatic success of the visit also sped up the process of détente between the United States and the Soviet Union. Fearful of the Chinese diplomatic advantage and similarly confronted by popular protest, the Soviets made their own overtures to the U.S.-led bloc. In 1972, the superpowers signed the first Strategic Arms Limitation Treaty (SALT I), which set a cap on the number of antimissile defenses each country could have. In 1975, in the Helsinki accords on human rights, the Western bloc officially acknowledged Soviet territorial gains in World War II in exchange for the Soviet bloc's guarantee of basic human rights.

Despite these diplomatic successes, rising purchases for the war in Vietnam left the United States billions of dollars in debt to other countries. The international currency system collapsed under the weight of the dollars flooding the global markets. In the face of this global chaos, Common Market countries united to force the United States to relinquish its single-handed direction of Western economic strategy. Another blow to U.S. leadership followed when it was revealed that Nixon's office had threatened to undermine free elections by authorizing the burglary and wiretapping of Democratic Party headquarters at Washington's Watergate building during the 1972 presidential campaign. The Watergate scandal forced Nixon to resign in disgrace in the summer of 1974 — the first U.S. president ever to do so. The Watergate scandal was one

Israel after the Six-Day War, 1967

Map legend:
- Israel after independence, 1948
- Israeli conquests, 1967

Map labels: LEBANON, SYRIA, Golan Heights, Mediterranean Sea, Tel Aviv, West Bank, Jerusalem, Gaza, ISRAEL, JORDAN, Suez Canal, SINAI PENINSULA (returned to Egypt 1981), Gulf of Suez, EGYPT, SAUDI ARABIA, Red Sea. 0 25 50 miles / 0 50 kilometers

more weak spot in U.S. superpower status in the 1960s and 1970s.

Oil and Stagflation.

Amid the instability in the United States in the 1960s and 1970s, the Middle East's oil-producing nations dealt Western dominance still another major blow. Tensions between Israel and the Arab world provided the catalyst. In 1967, Israeli forces, responding to Palestinian guerrilla attacks, quickly seized Gaza and the Sinai peninsula from Egypt, the Golan Heights from Syria, and the West Bank from Jordan. Israel's stunning victory in this action, which came to be called the Six-Day War, was followed in 1973 by a joint Egyptian and Syrian attack on Israel on Yom Kippur, the most holy day in the Jewish calendar. Israel, with material assistance from the United States, stopped the assault.

Having failed militarily, the Arabs turned to economic clout. They struck at the West's weakest point — its dependence on Middle Eastern oil for its advanced industries and postindustrial lifestyle. Arab nations in the **Organization of Petroleum Exporting Countries (OPEC)**, a relatively loose consortium before the Yom Kippur War, combined to quadruple the price of their oil and impose an embargo, cutting off all exports of oil to the United States and its allies because they backed Israel. For the first time since imperialism's heyday, the producers of raw materials — not the industrial powers — controlled the flow of commodities and set prices to their own advantage. The West was now mired in an oil crisis.

Throughout the 1970s, oil-dependent Westerners watched in astonishment as OPEC upset the balance of economic power and helped provoke a recession in the West (Figure 28.1). The oil embargo and price hike not only caused unemployment to rise by more than 50 percent in Europe and the United States but also caused inflation to soar. By the end of 1973, the inflation rate jumped

---

Organization of Petroleum Exporting Countries (OPEC): A consortium that regulated the supply and export of oil and that acted with more unanimity after the United States supported Israel against the Arabs in the wars of the late 1960s and early 1970s.

The Middle East and the Politics of Oil

When Middle Eastern countries took control of the price and volume of oil they sold, Western leaders were taken aback, so thoroughly accustomed were the United States and its allies to setting the conditions of trade. OPEC leaders were lampooned in cartoons as the global economic crisis unfolded. Stagflation hit Western economies hard, while everyone came to terms with the new force of oil in international politics. *(Rosen/Albany Times-Union/Rothco.)*

"AND ANYWHERE KHALID WENT, THE LAMB WAS SURE TO GO!"

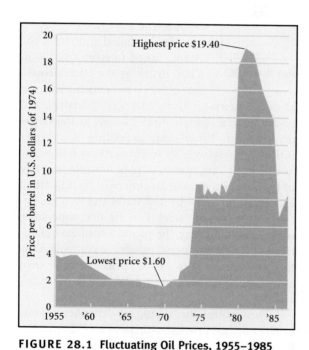

FIGURE 28.1 Fluctuating Oil Prices, 1955–1985
Colonization allowed the Western imperial powers to obtain raw materials at advantageous prices or even without paying at all. OPEC's oil embargo and price hikes of the 1970s were signs of change, which included the exercise of decolonized countries' control over their own resources. OPEC's action led to a decade of painful economic downturn, but it also encouraged some European governments to improve public transportation, encourage the production of fuel-efficient cars, and make individual consumers cut back their dependence on oil.

to over 8 percent in West Germany, 12 percent in France, and 20 percent in Portugal. Eastern-bloc countries, dependent on Soviet oil, fared little better because the West could no longer afford their products and the Soviets boosted the price of their own oil. Skyrocketing interest rates discouraged both industrial investment and consumer buying. With prices, unemployment, and interest rates all rising—an unusual combination of economic conditions dubbed **stagflation**—some in the West came to realize that both energy resources and economic growth had limits. Western Europe drastically cut back on its oil dependence by undertaking conservation, enhancing public transportation, and raising the price of gasoline to encourage the development of fuel-efficient cars.

The U.S. bloc had further to fall. Elected U.S. president in 1976, Jimmy Carter, a wealthy farmer and former governor of Georgia, was unable to return the economy to its pre–Vietnam War and pre–oil embargo prosperity. His administration also faced an insurmountable crisis in the Middle East. Late in the 1970s, students, clerics, shopkeepers, and unemployed men in Iran began a religious agitation that brought to power the Islamic religious leader Ayatollah Ruhollah Khomeini (1902–1989). Employing audiocassettes to spread his message, he called for a transformation of the country into a truly Islamic society, which meant the renunciation of the

stagflation: The combination of a stagnant economy and soaring inflation; a period of stagflation occurred in the West in the 1970s as a result of an OPEC embargo on oil.

Soldiers and Civilians in Northern Ireland
Separatist, civil rights, and terrorist movements increasingly directed their violence against ordinary people, following the lead of soldiers in World War II. In Northern Ireland, British troops fought to put down the Irish Republican Army, but civilians were also their target. However, this image from Derry in 1969 shows that civilians resisted, fighting with homemade weapons. It was only late in the 1990s that both sides called a halt to the killing and agreed to negotiate. *(Getty Images.)*

Western ways advocated by the American-backed shah, who as a result was deposed. In the autumn of 1979, revolutionary supporters of Khomeini took hostages at the U.S. embassy in Teheran and would not release them. The United States was essentially paralyzed in the face of both Islamic militancy and a downwardly spiraling economy.

The Western Bloc Meets Challenges with Reform

As the 1980s opened, the first agenda item for non-Communist governments in the West was to put their economic houses in order. On top of the economic challenge was the growing phenomenon of terrorism—that is, coordinated and targeted political violence by opposition groups at home. The unprecedented mix of terrorism, the energy crisis, soaring unemployment, and double-digit inflation sparked the election of conservative politicians, who maintained that decades of supporting a welfare state were at the heart of economic problems. Across the West, people came to feel that the unemployed and new immigrants from around the world were responsible for the downturn in the postindustrial economy. Nineteenth-century emphases on competitiveness, individualism, and revival of privilege for the "best circles" replaced the twentieth-century trend toward advancing economic democracy to combat totalitarianism. Postindustrial society changed political course.

Terrorism. The terrorism at the U.S. embassy in Iran was part of a trend that had actually begun in the West. In the 1970s, terrorist bands in Europe responded to the suppression of activism and the worsening economic conditions with kidnappings, bank robberies, bombings, and assassinations. Disaffected and well-to-do youth, steeped in extreme theories that claimed Western society was decaying, often joined these groups. In West Germany throughout the 1970s, the Red Army Faction assassinated prominent businessmen, judges, and other public officials. Practiced in assassinations of public figures and random shootings of pedestrians, Italy's Red Brigades kidnapped and then murdered the head of the dominant Christian Democrats in 1978. Advocates of independence for the Basque nation in northern Spain assassinated Spanish politicians and police officers.

In the 1970s, Catholics in Northern Ireland pitted themselves against the dominant Protestants to protest job discrimination and a lack of civil rights. Demonstrators urged

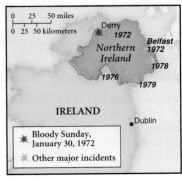

Nationalist Movements of the 1970s

union with the Irish Republic, and with protest escalating, the British government sent in troops. On January 30, 1972, which became known as Bloody Sunday, British troops fired at demonstrators and killed thirteen, setting off a cycle of violence that left five hundred dead in that single year. Protestants fearful of losing their dominant position combated a reinvigorated Irish Republican Army (IRA), which carried out bombings and assassinations to press for the union of the two Irelands and an end to the oppression of Catholics.

Terrorists failed in their goal of overturning the existing democracies, and, battered as it was, parliamentary government scored a few important successes in the 1970s. Spain and Portugal, suffering under dictatorships since the 1930s, regained their freedom and set out on a course of greater prosperity. The death of Spain's Francisco Franco in 1975 ended more than three decades of dictatorial rule. Franco's handpicked successor, King Juan Carlos, surprisingly steered his nation to Western-style constitutional monarchy, facing down threatened military coups. Portugal and Greece also ousted right-wing dictators, thus paving the way for their integration into western Europe and for substantial economic growth. Despite these democratic advances, a consensus emerged — given the economic crisis, political ter-

rorism, and failures in leadership — that the West was in trouble.

Thatcher Reshapes Politics. More than anyone else, **Margaret Thatcher**, the leader of Britain's Conservative Party and prime minister from 1979 to 1990, reshaped the West's political and economic ideas to meet the crisis. Coming to power amid continuing economic decline, revolt in Northern Ireland, and labor unrest, the combative prime minister rejected the politics of consensus building. Believing that only business could revive the sluggish British economy, Thatcher lashed out at union leaders, Labour Party politicians, and people who received welfare-state benefits, calling them enemies of British prosperity. Her anti-welfare-state policies struck a revolutionary chord, and she called herself "a nineteenth-century liberal" in reference to the economic individualism of that age. In her view, business leaders were the key members of society. Although immigrants often worked for the lowest wages and contributed to profits, she characterized migrants and the unemployed as inferior, saying that neither group contributed to national wealth. Even workers blamed labor leaders or newcomers for Britain's troubles.

The policies of "Thatcherism" were based on monetarist, or supply-side, theories of U.S. economists. According to monetarist theory, inflation results when government pumps money into the economy at a rate higher than the nation's economic growth rate. Thus, government should keep a tight rein on the money supply to prevent prices from rising rapidly. Supply-side economists maintain that the economy as a whole flourishes when businesses grow and their prosperity "trickles down" throughout the society. To implement such theories, the British government cut income taxes on the wealthy to spur new investment, increasing sales taxes to compensate for the lost revenue. The result was a greater burden on working people, who bore the brunt of the sales tax. Thatcher also vigorously cut government's role in the economy: she sold publicly owned businesses and utilities such as British Airways, refused to prop up "outmoded" industries such as coal mining, and slashed education and health programs. As their influence spread through the West and the world, Thatcher's economic policies came to be known as

Margaret Thatcher at Conservative Party Conference (1983)
As British prime minister for more than a decade, Margaret Thatcher profoundly influenced the course of modern government by rolling back the welfare state. Thatcher was convinced, and convinced others, that the welfare state did not advance society and its citizens but made them lazy when it rewarded useless people with handouts. Her tenure in office encouraged other politicians, from Ronald Reagan to Helmut Kohl, to execute similar cuts in social programs. (© Bettmann/Corbis.)

Margaret Thatcher: Prime minister of Britain from 1979 to 1990; she set a new tone for British politics by promoting neoliberal economic policies and criticizing poor people, union members, and racial minorities as worthless, even harmful citizens.

Margaret Thatcher's Economic Vision

Margaret Thatcher, Britain's longest-serving prime minister, changed Western thinking about the welfare state. Many Europeans saw the welfare state as a mainstay of democracy, which would alleviate the hardships that had turned workers toward either socialism, from Bismarck's time onward, or toward Mussolini's and Hitler's fascism during the difficult interwar years. Thatcher, however, believed that programs to provide health care, education, and housing coddled the lazy. She thought the money for such programs should be invested in private industry, to produce a profit and to encourage more investment and greater productivity. Here she outlines her thoughts on public spending to members of the Conservative Party.

I and my colleagues say that to add to public spending takes away the very money and resources that industry needs to stay in business, let alone to expand. Higher public spending, far from curing unemployment, can be the very vehicle that loses jobs and causes bankruptcies in trade and commerce. That is why we warned local authorities that since rates [taxes] are frequently the biggest tax that industry now faces, increases in them can cripple local businesses. . . .

That is why I stress that if those who work in public authorities take for themselves large pay increases, they leave less to be spent on equipment and new buildings. That in turn deprives the private sector of the orders it needs, especially some of those industries in the hard pressed regions. Those in the public sector have a duty to those in the private sector not to take out so much in pay that they cause others' unemployment. That is why we point out that every time high wage settlements in nationalised monopolies lead to higher charges for telephones, electricity, coal, and water, they can drive companies out of business and cost other people their jobs.

If spending money like water was the answer to our country's problems, we would have no problems right now. If ever a nation has spent, spent, spent, and spent again, ours has. Today that dream is over. All of that money has got us nowhere, but it still has to come from somewhere. Those who urge us to relax the squeeze, to spend yet more money indiscriminately in the belief that it will help the unemployed and the small businessman, are not being kind or compassionate or caring. They are not the friends of the unemployed or the small business. They are asking us to do again the very things that caused the problems in the first place. . . .

I am accused of lecturing or preaching about this. I suppose it is a critic's way of saying, "Well, we know it is true, but we have to carp at something." I do not care about that. But I do care about the future of free enterprise, the jobs and exports it provides, and the independence it brings to our people.

Source: Juliet S. Thompson and Wayne C. Thompson, ed., *Margaret Thatcher: Prime Minister Indomitable* (Boulder: Westview, 1994), 230–31.

---

neoliberalism (see Document, "Margaret Thatcher's Economic Vision," above).

In the first three years of Thatcher's government, the British economy did not respond well to her shock treatment. The quality of universities, public transportation, highways, and hospitals deteriorated, and leading scholars and scientists left the country in a renewal of the brain drain. In addition, social unity fragmented as she pitted the lower classes against one another. In 1981, blacks and Asians rioted in major cities. Thatcher revived her sagging popularity with a nationalist war against Argentina in 1982 over ownership of the Falkland Islands off the Argentinian coast. Stagflation ultimately dissipated, although historians and economists debated whether the change resulted from Thatcher's policies or from the lack of spending power that burdened the poor and unemployed. In any case, Thatcher's program became the standard for those facing the challenge of stagflation and economic decline. Britain had been one of the pioneers of the welfare state, and now it pioneered in changing course.

In Thatcher's Footsteps. In the United States, Ronald Reagan, who served as president between 1981 and 1989, followed a similar road to combat the economic crisis. Dividing U.S. citizens into the good and the bad, Reagan vowed to promote the values of the "moral majority," which included commitment to Bible-based religion, dedication to work, and unquestioned patriotism. He blasted so-called spendthrift and immoral "liberals" when introducing "Reaganomics"—a program of whopping income tax cuts for the wealthy combined with massive reductions in federal spending for student loans, school lunch programs, and mass transit. Like Thatcher, Reagan believed that tax cuts would lead to investment and a reinvigorated

---

neoliberalism: A theory first promoted by British minister Margaret Thatcher, calling for a return to liberal principles of the nineteenth century, including the reduction of welfare-state programs and the cutting of taxes for the wealthy to promote economic growth.

economy; federal outlays for social programs, he felt, only encouraged bad Americans to be lazy.

In foreign policy, Reagan spent most of his time in office warning of the Communist threat from the "evil empire" (USSR) and rolling back détente. He demanded huge military budgets to counter the Soviets and announced the Strategic Defense Initiative (SDI), known popularly as Star Wars, a costly plan to put lasers in space to defend the United States against a nuclear attack. The combination of tax cuts and military expansion had pushed the federal budget deficit to $200 billion by 1986.

Other western European leaders also limited welfare-state benefits in the face of stagflation, though without Thatcher's and Reagan's socially divisive rhetoric. West German leader Helmut Kohl, who took power in 1982, reduced welfare spending, froze government wages, and cut corporate taxes. By 1984, the inflation rate was only 2 percent and West Germany had acquired a 10 percent share of world trade. Unlike Thatcher, Kohl did not fan class and racial hatreds. The politics of divisiveness was particularly unwise in Germany, where terrorism on the left and on the right continued to flourish. Moreover, the legacy of Nazism loomed menacingly. When an unemployed German youth said of immigrant Turkish workers, "Let's gas 'em," the revival of Nazi language appalled many in Germany's middle class.

By 1981, stagflation had put more than 1.5 million people out of work in France, but the French took a different political path to deal with the economic crisis. They elected a socialist president, François Mitterrand, who nationalized banks and certain industries and increased wages and social spending to stimulate the economy—the opposite of Thatcherism. New public buildings like museums and libraries arose along with new subway lines and improved public transport. When conservative Jacques Chirac succeeded Mitterrand as president in 1995, he adopted neoliberal policies. The same divisive politics that had unfolded during hard economic times continued as the government changed. From the 1980s on, the racist National Front Party won 10 percent and sometimes more of the vote with promises to deport African and Middle Eastern immigrants.

Prosperity in Smaller States.   At the same time, smaller European states without heavy defense commitments began to thrive, some of them by slashing away at welfare programs. Spain joined the Common Market in 1986 and used Common Market investment and tourist dollars to help re-

build its sagging infrastructure such as the southern cities of Granada and Córdoba. In Ireland, a surge of investment in education for high-tech jobs combined with low wage rates to attract much new business to the country in the 1990s. Prosperity and the increasingly unacceptable death toll led to a political rapprochement between Ireland and Northern Ireland in 1999. Austria prospered too, in part by reducing government pensions and aid to business. Austrian chancellor Franz Vranitsky summed up the changed focus of government in the 1980s and 1990s: "In Austria, the shelter that the state has given to almost everyone—employee as well as entrepreneur—has led . . . a lot of people [to] think not only what they can do to solve a problem but what the state can do. . . . This needs to change." The century-long growth of the welfare state slowed by the 1990s as new economic and political theories took hold.

Almost alone, Sweden maintained a full array of social programs for everyone. The government also offered each immigrant a choice of subsidized housing in neighborhoods inhabited primarily by Swedes or primarily by people from the immigrant's native land. Such programs were expensive: the tax rate on income over $46,000 was 80 percent. Despite a highly productive workforce, Sweden dropped from fourth to fourteenth place among nations in per capita income by 1998. Although the Swedes reduced their costly dependence on foreign oil by cutting consumption in half between 1976 and 1986, their welfare state came to seem extreme to many citizens. As elsewhere, immigrants were cast as the source of the country's problems—past, present, and future: "How long will it be before our Swedish children will have to turn their faces toward Mecca?" ran one politician's campaign speech in 1993.

Collapse of Communism in the Soviet Bloc

Beginning in 1985, reform came to the Soviet Union as well, but instead of fortifying the economy, it helped bring about the collapse of the Soviet bloc. Other causes were global communications, international trade, and the ongoing protests of workers, artists, and intellectuals. Moreover, a corrupt system of political and economic management prevented any kind of cure for the ailing economy. Years of stagnant and then negative growth led to a deteriorating standard of living. After working a full day, Soviet homemakers stood in long lines to obtain basic commodities; shortages necessitated the three-generation household, in which grandparents took over tedious homemaking tasks from their working children and grandchildren. "There is no special skill to this," a seventy-three-year-old grandmother and former garbage collector remarked. "You just stand in line and wait." Even so, people often went away empty-handed as basic household supplies like soap disappeared instantly from stores. One cheap and readily available product—vodka—often formed the center of people's social lives. Alcoholism reached crisis levels, diminishing productivity and tremendously straining the nation's morale.

Mikhail Gorbachev, Soviet Reformer. In 1985, a new leader, **Mikhail Gorbachev,** unexpectedly opened an era of change in hopes of remedying all these ills. The son of peasants, Gorbachev had risen through Communist Party ranks as an agricultural specialist and had traveled abroad to observe life in the West. At home, he saw the consequences of that economic stagnation: in much of the USSR ordinary people decided not to have children. The Soviet Union was forced to import massive amounts of grain because 20 to 30 percent of the grain that was produced in the USSR rotted before it could be harvested or shipped to market, so great was the inefficiency of the state-directed economy. Industrial pollution reached scandalous proportions because state-run enterprises cared only about meeting production quotas. A massive and privileged party bureaucracy feared innovation and failed to achieve socialism's professed goal of a decent standard of living for working people. To match U.S. military growth, the Soviet Union diverted 15 to 20 percent of its gross national product (more than double the U.S. proportion) to armaments, further crippling the economy's chances of raising living standards. As these problems grew, a new cynical generation was coming of age that had no memory of World War II or Stalin's purges. "They believe in nothing," a mother said of Soviet youth in 1984.

Gorbachev knew from experience and from his travels to western Europe that the Soviet system was completely inadequate, and he quickly proposed several unusual programs. A crucial economic reform, **perestroika** ("restructuring"),

Mikhail and Raisa Gorbachev
Mikhail Gorbachev and his wife, Raisa, gave a fresh look to Soviet politics. They traveled, made friends abroad, and were fashionable and modern. While the Gorbachevs became part of Western celebrity culture, however, average citizens back home in the USSR saw the Gorbachevs' privileged lifestyle as simply the continuation of the Communist government's disregard for ordinary people. *(© Peter Turnley/Corbis.)*

aimed to reinvigorate the Soviet economy by improving productivity, increasing investment, encouraging the use of up-to-date technology, and gradually introducing such market features as prices and profits. The complement to economic change was the policy of **glasnost** (usually translated as "openness" or "publicity"), which called for disseminating "wide, prompt, and frank information" and for allowing Soviet citizens new measures of free speech. When officials complained that glasnost threatened their status, Gorbachev replaced more than a third of the Communist Party's leadership in the first months of his administration. The pressing need for glasnost became most evident after the Chernobyl catastrophe in 1986, when a nuclear reactor exploded and spewed radioactive dust into the atmosphere. Bureaucratic cover-ups delayed the spread of information about the accident, with lethal consequences for people living near the plant.

Mikhail Gorbachev: Leader of the Soviet Union from 1985 to 1991; he instituted reforms such as glasnost and perestroika, thereby contributing to the collapse of Communist rule in the Soviet bloc and the USSR.

perestroika: Literally, "restructuring"; an economic policy instituted in the 1980s by Soviet premier Mikhail Gorbachev calling for the introduction of market mechanisms and the achievement of greater efficiency in manufacturing, agriculture, and services.

glasnost: Literally "openness" or "publicity"; a policy instituted in the 1980s by Soviet premier Mikhail Gorbachev calling for greater openness in speech and in thinking, which translated to the reduction of censorship in publishing, radio, television, and other media.

DOCUMENT

Criticizing Gorbachev

Some people—especially in the U.S. bloc—interpreted Gorbachev's reforms as noble and enlightened, opening the way to free markets and free speech. Others, especially in the Soviet Union, saw him as simply another member of the Communist establishment, hoping to prop up a rotten system. "A flatterer," one critic called him, "who can live for free in luxurious villas at our expense." For such critics, Gorbachev's reforms were merely machinations by a Soviet leader hoping to boost productivity so that there would be more to siphon off. Journalist Tatyana Tolstoya appraised Gorbachev with a critical eye, proposing that her opinions represented those of Soviet citizens. The first passage here was written in response to a book published about Gorbachev in 1990. The second passage was written in 1991 just after an attempted coup against his regime in August 1991.

We do not know who proposed Gorbachev for the top and who supported him (our analysts now think that it was the military-industrial complex) but his initial behavior, when you look back on what happened, bears the mixed traits of boldness and indecision, ignorance and a fine knowledge of human nature (in its Party version), recklessness and cold calculation. Having grown up under conditions of Brezhnev's stagnation Gorbachev knew his small world [of the Party] extremely well, and supposed that he knew how to change it. But he did not know the larger world and its problems; and when he destroyed the habitual structures with his own hands, he ceased to understand his immediate surroundings and took one false step after another. . . .

One judges a man by his actions, and all of Gorbachev's actions showed that he desperately tried to stop the reforms in which he did not wish to participate any longer. The logic of democratic development, after all, required that he, too, be swept from his post and stripped of his position, his perquisites, his glory.

Perestroika was started largely to provide a better life for the Party authorities, but things got out of hand. Instead of feeding the Party more fully, perestroika saw the people moving—awkwardly, looking nervously over their shoulders, fighting bitterly with one another—toward democracy. (Gorbachev liked to speak not of democracy but of democratization, which prompted the joke that the difference between democracy and democratization is like the difference between a canal and canalization—i.e. a sewer system.) When the dangerous question of party privileges inevitably arose, Gorbachev tried to avoid it in every way.

Source: Tatyana Tolstaya, *Pushkin's Children: Writings on Russia and Russians*, trans. Jamey Grambrell (New York: Houghton Mifflin, 2003), 46, 51.

After Chernobyl, even the Communist Party and Marxism-Leninism were opened to public criticism. Party meetings suddenly included complaints about the highest leaders and their policies. Television shows adopted the outspoken methods of American investigative reporting; one program exposed the plight of Leningrad's homeless children—an admission of communism's failings. Instead of publishing made-up letters praising the great Soviet state, newspapers were flooded with real ones complaining of shortages and abuse. One outraged "mother of two" protested that the cost-cutting policy of reusing syringes in hospitals was a source of AIDS. "Why should little kids have to pay for the criminal actions of our Ministry of Health?" she asked. Debate and factions arose across the political spectrum (see Document, "Criticizing Gorbachev," above). In the fall of 1987, one of Gorbachev's allies, Boris Yeltsin, quit the government after denouncing perestroika as insufficient to produce real reform. Yeltsin's political daring, which in the past would have consigned him to oblivion (or Siberia), inspired others to organize in opposition to crumbling Communist rule. In the spring of 1989, in a remarkably free balloting in Moscow's local elections, not a single Communist was chosen.

Glasnost and perestroika dramatically changed superpower relations. Recognizing how severely the cold war arms race was draining Soviet resources, Gorbachev almost immediately began scaling back missile production. His unilateral actions gradually won over Ronald Reagan. In 1985, the two leaders initiated a personal relationship and began defusing the cold war. "I bet the hard-liners in both our countries are bleeding when we shake hands," said the jovial Reagan at the conclusion of one meeting. In early 1989, Gorbachev withdrew the last of his country's forces from the debilitating war in Afghanistan, and the United States started to cut back its own vast military buildup by the end of the year.

Rebellion in Poland. As Gorbachev's reforms in the USSR started spiraling out of his control, they did so in an atmosphere of rising dissent across the Soviet bloc, most notably in Poland. Already in the summer of 1980, Poles had gone on strike to protest government-increased food prices. As the protest spread, workers at the Gdańsk shipyards, led by electrician Lech Walesa and crane operator Anna Walentynowicz, created an independent labor movement called **Solidarity**. The organization soon embraced much of the adult population, including a million members of the Communist Party. Both intellectuals and the Catholic church, long in the forefront of opposition to antireligious communism, supported Solidarity workers as they occupied factories in protest against inflation, the scarcity of food, and other deteriorating conditions of everyday life. The members of Solidarity waved Polish flags and paraded giant portraits of the Virgin Mary and Pope John Paul II—a Polish native.

Having achieved mass support at home and worldwide sympathy through media coverage, Solidarity leaders insisted that the government recognize it as an independent union—a radical demand under communism. As food became scarce and prices rose, tens of thousands of women marched in the streets crying, "We're hungry!" They, too, protested working conditions, but as both workers and the only caretakers of home life, it was the scarcity of food that sent them into the streets. The Communist Party teetered on the edge of collapse, until the police and the army, with Soviet support, imposed a military government and in the winter of 1981 outlawed Solidarity. Stern and puritanical, General Wojciech Jaruzelski took over as the head of Poland's new regime in 1981, but the general could not push repression too far: he needed new loans from the U.S.-led bloc to keep the sinking Polish economy afloat. Using global communications, dissidents kept Solidarity alive both inside and outside of Poland. Workers kept meeting, creating a new culture outside the official Soviet arts and newscasts. Poets read dissident verse to overflow crowds, and university professors lectured to Solidarity members on such forbidden topics as Polish resistance in World War II. Activism in Poland set the stage for communism's downfall throughout the Soviet bloc.

The Revolutions of 1989.

The year 1989 saw the sudden and unexpected disintegration of Communist power in eastern Europe, but first came a surprising attack on the Communist state in China. Inspired by Gorbachev's visit to Beijing, in the spring of 1989 thousands of Chinese students massed in the city's Tiananmen Square, the world's largest public square, to demand democracy. They used telex machines and e-mail to rush their messages to the international community, and they effectively conveyed their goals through the cameras that Western television trained on them. China's aged Communist leaders, while pushing economic modernization, refused to consider the introduction of democracy. As workers began joining the pro-democracy forces, the government crushed the movement and executed as many as a thousand rebels.

The protests in Tiananmen Square were galvanizing. In June 1989, the Polish government, weakened by its own bungling of the economy and lacking Soviet support for further repression, held free parliamentary elections. Solidarity candidates overwhelmingly defeated the Communists, and in early 1990, Walesa became president, hastening Poland's rocky transition to a market economy. Gorbachev openly reversed the Brezhnev Doctrine in the Polish case, refusing to interfere in the political course of another nation. When it became clear that the Soviet Union would not intervene in Poland, the fall of communism repeated itself across the Soviet bloc.

Communism collapsed first in Poland and then in Hungary because of those countries' early introduction of free-market measures. In Hungary, which had experimented with "market socialism" since the 1960s, even officials began to realize that political democracy had to accompany economic freedom. Citizens were already protesting the government, lobbying, for example, against ecologically unsound projects like the construction of a new dam. They encouraged boycotts of Communist holidays, and on March 15, 1989, they boldly commemorated the anniversary of the Hungarian uprising. Finally, these popular demands for liberalization led the Parliament in the fall of 1989 to dismiss the Communist Party as the official ruling institution; people across the country tore down Soviet and Communist symbols.

The most potent symbol of a divided Europe—the Berlin Wall—stood in the midst of a divided Germany. East Germans had attempted to escape over the wall for decades, and since the early 1980s dissidents had held peace vigils in cities across East Germany. In the summer of 1989, crowds of East Germans flooded the borders to escape the crumbling Soviet bloc, and hundreds of thousands of protesters rallied throughout the fall against the regime. Satellite television brought them visions of

---

Solidarity: A Polish labor union founded in 1980 by Lech Walesa and Anna Walentynowicz that contested Communist Party programs and eventually succeeded in ousting the party from the Polish government.

Reunited Berliners Welcome the New Year
On New Year's Eve, 1989, Berliners—and indeed supporters from around the world—celebrated the fall of the Berlin Wall and the prospect of a new Germany. The exuberant crowd tore the Communist seal from the flag and then hoisted it above the Brandenburg Gate as fireworks added to the intense emotion of the moment. The difficult transition, which included disposing of the remnants of communism, lay in the future. *(ullstein bild–Boening.)*

postindustrial prosperity and of free and open public debate in West Germany. Crowds of demonstrators greeted Gorbachev, taken as a hero by many, when he visited the country in October. On November 9, guards at the Berlin Wall allowed free passage to the west, turning protest into a festive holiday: West Berliners greeted the Easterners with bananas, a consumer good that had been in short supply in the Eastern zone, and that fruit became the unofficial symbol of a newfound liberation. As they strolled freely in the streets, East Berliners saw first-hand the goods available in a successful postindustrial society. Soon thereafter, citizens—east and west—released years of frustration by assaulting the Berlin Wall with sledgehammers. The government finished the wall's destruction in 1990.

In Czechoslovakia, which after 1968 had been firmly restored to Soviet-style rule, people also watched the progress of glasnost expectantly. Persecuted dissidents had maintained their critique of Communist rule. In an open letter to the

Czechoslovak Communist Party leadership, playwright Václav Havel accused Marxist-Leninist rule of making people materialistic and indifferent to civic life. In 1977, Havel, along with a group of fellow intellectuals and workers, signed Charter 77, a public protest against the regime that resulted in the arrest of the signers. In the mid-1980s, these dissidents watched Gorbachev on television calling for free speech, though never mentioning reform in Czechoslovakia. Protesters clamored for democracy, but the government turned the police on them, arresting activists in January 1989 for commemorating the death of Jan Palach. The turning point came in November 1989 when, in response to police beatings of students, Alexander Dubček, leader of the Prague Spring of 1968, addressed the crowds in Prague's Wenceslas Square with a call to oust the Stalinists from the government. Almost immediately, the Communist leadership resigned. Capping the country's "velvet revolution," as it became known for its lack of bloodshed, the formerly Communist-dominated parliament elevated Havel to the presidency.

The world's attention next fastened on the unfolding political drama in Romania. From the mid-1960s on, Nicolae Ceaușescu had ruled as the harshest dictator in Communist Europe since Stalin. In the name of modernization, he destroyed whole villages; to build up the population, he outlawed contraceptives and abortions, a restriction that led to the abandonment of tens of thousands of children. He preached the virtues of a very slim body so that he could cut rations and use the savings on his pet projects such as buying up private castles and other property. Most Romanians lived in utter poverty as Ceaușescu channeled almost all the country's resources into building himself an enormous palace in Bucharest. To this end, he tore down entire neighborhoods and dozens of historical buildings and crushed opponents of the gaudy project to make it appear popular. Yet in early December 1989, an opposition movement rose up: workers demonstrated against the dictatorial government, and the army turned on Ceaușescu loyalists. On Christmas Day, viewers watched on television as the dictator and his wife were tried by a military court and then executed. For many, the death of Ceaușescu meant that the very worst of communism was over.

Homeless Romanian Children (1995)
These children were among the many who lived without families around the railroad station in Romania's capital city, Bucharest. Nicolae Ceaușescu's regime prohibited birth control and abortion in order to increase the supply of workers while simultaneously cutting back on food rations. Children were the victims of this policy, even after Ceaușescu was overthrown, as families simply abandoned children they could not support. In order to survive, the children scavenged, stole, and begged. (© Barry Lewis/Corbis.)

REVIEW: How and why did the balance of world power change during the 1980s?

Conclusion

The fall of the Berlin Wall in 1989 symbolized the end of the cold war, even though the USSR still stood as a bulwark of communism. Collapse of communism in the Soviet satellites was an utter surprise, for U.S.-bloc analysts had reported throughout the 1980s that the Soviet empire was in dangerously robust health. But no one should have been unaware of dissent or economic discontent. Since the 1960s, rebellious youth, ethnic and racial minorities, and women had all been condemning conditions across the West, along with criticizing the threat posed by the cold war. By the early 1980s, wars in Vietnam and Afghanistan, protests against privations in the Soviet bloc, the power of oil-producing states, and the growing political force of Islam had cost the superpowers their resources and reputations. Margaret Thatcher in Britain, Ronald Reagan in the United States, and Mikhail Gorbachev in the Soviet Union tried with varying degrees of success to put their postindus-

trial and cold war houses in order. The first two were successful, while Gorbachev's policies of glasnost and perestroika — aimed at political and economic improvements — brought on collapse.

Glasnost and perestroika were supposed to bring about the high levels of postindustrial prosperity enjoyed outside the Soviet bloc. Across the West, including the USSR, an unprecedented set of technological developments had transformed businesses, space exploration, and the functioning of government. Technological advances also had an enormous impact on everyday life. Work changed as society reached a stage called postindustrial, in which the service sector predominated. New patterns of family life, new relationships among the generations, and revised standards for sexual behavior also characterized these years. But it was only in the United States and western Europe that the consumer benefits of postindustrialization reached ordinary people, for the attainment of a thoroughgoing consumer, service, and high-tech society demanded levels of efficiency, coordination, and cooperation unknown in the Soviet bloc.

Many complained, nonetheless, about the dramatic changes resulting from postindustrial development. The protesters of the late 1960s addressed

MAPPING THE WEST

The Collapse of Communism in Europe, 1989–1990
The 1989 overthrow of the Communist party in the USSR satellite countries of Eastern Europe occurred with surprising rapidity. The transformation began in Poland when Polish voters tossed out Communist Party leaders in June 1989, and then accelerated in September when thousands of East Germans fled to Hungary, Poland, and Czechoslovakia. Between October and December, Communist regimes were replaced in East Germany, Czechoslovakia, Bulgaria, and Romania. Within three years, the Baltic States would declare their independence, the USSR itself would dissolve, and the breakup of Yugoslavia would lead to war in the Balkans.

postindustrial society's stubborn problems: concentrations of bureaucratic and industrial power, social inequality, environmental degradation, and even uncertainty about humankind's future. In the Soviet sphere, these protests were continuous but were little heeded until the collapse of Soviet domination of eastern Europe in 1989. Soon communism would be overturned in the USSR itself. However, the triumph of democracy in the former Soviet empire opened an era of painful adjustment, impoverishment, and even violence for hundreds of millions of people. Ending the cold war also accelerated the process of globalization.

FOR FURTHER EXPLORATION

■ **For suggested references, including Web sites, for topics in this chapter,** see page SR-1 at the end of the book.

■ **For additional primary-source material from this period,** see Chapter 28 in *Sources of THE MAKING OF THE WEST,* Third Edition.

■ **For Web sites and documents related to topics in this chapter,** see *Make History* at bedfordstmartins.com/hunt.

CHAPTER REVIEW

KEY TERMS AND PEOPLE

DNA (919)

in vitro fertilization (921)

multinational corporation (921)

pop art (925)

Ostpolitik (928)

samizdat (928)

Richard Nixon (936)

Organization of Petroleum Exporting Countries (OPEC) (937)

stagflation (938)

Margaret Thatcher (940)

neoliberalism (941)

Mikhail Gorbachev (943)

perestroika (943)

glasnost (943)

Solidarity (945)

REVIEW QUESTIONS

1. What were the technological and scientific advances of the 1960s and 1970s, and how did they change human life and society?

2. How did Western society and culture change in the postindustrial age?

3. What were the main issues for protesters in the 1960s, and how did governments address them?

4. How and why did the balance of world power change during the 1980s?

MAKING CONNECTIONS

1. What were the differences between industrial society of the late nineteenth century and postindustrial society of the late twentieth century?

2. Why were there so many protests, acts of terrorism, and uprisings across the West in the decades between 1960 and 1990?

3. What have been the long-term consequences of Communist rule between 1917 and 1989?

> **For practice quizzes, a customized study plan, and other study tools,** see the Online Study Guide at bedfordstmartins.com/hunt.

IMPORTANT EVENTS

1963	Betty Friedan publishes *The Feminine Mystique*
1966	Willy Brandt becomes West German foreign minister and develops Ostpolitik, a policy designed to bridge tensions between the two Germanies
1967	South Africa's Dr. Christiaan Barnard performs first successful human heart transplant
1968	Revolution in Czechoslovakia against communism; student uprisings throughout Europe and the United States
1969	U.S. astronauts walk on the moon's surface
1972	SALT I between the United States and Soviet Union
1973	North Vietnam and the United States sign treaty ending war in Vietnam; OPEC raises price of oil and imposes oil embargo on the West
1973–1976	Aleksandr Solzhenitsyn publishes *The Gulag Archipelago*
1978	The first test-tube baby is born in England
1978–1979	Islamic revolution in Iran; hostages taken at U.S. embassy in Teheran
1980	The independent trade union Solidarity organizes resistance to Polish communism; British prime minister Margaret Thatcher begins dismantling the welfare state
1981	Ronald Reagan becomes U.S. president
1985	Mikhail Gorbachev comes to power in the USSR
1986	Explosion at Soviet nuclear plant at Chernobyl; Spain joins the Common Market
1989	Chinese students revolt in Tiananmen Square and government suppresses them; Communist governments ousted in eastern Europe; Berlin Wall demolished

A New Globalism
1989 TO THE PRESENT

Therese is a Congolese immigrant to Paris who arrived there in the late 1970s with the help of a brother who worked for an airline. Therese had been well-known in Africa as the teenage girl-friend of pop singer Bozi Boziana, who wrote a hit song about her. But Congo's political instability made her search for safety in Paris. Once there, Therese remained famous among African immigrants, for whom she began running *nganda*, or informal bars. Like Therese, the immigrants who frequent her nganda are often Congolese and other Africans who, because of problems in their home countries, have settled in Paris, many of them illegally. They flock to her nganda because they like her stylish dress, the African food she cooks, the African music she plays, and the African products she sells. Many of Therese's small bars and eateries have flourished, only to be closed down by landlords who want more of her handsome profits or who object to her running an unlicensed café. Despite such obstacles, Therese keeps business going by moving her faithful clientele around her Paris neighborhood from basement to shop front to spare room. Therese is a new global citizen, working networks back home for supplies, constantly on the move because she lives on the margins of legality, and always striving to make a good living for herself and her family.

Therese is just one concrete example of the ease with which people in the post–cold war world crossed national boundaries while maintaining crucial ties around the globe. The end of the cold war rivalry between the superpowers and their allies paved the way for a more intimately connected world. In the 1990s, globalization advanced further with the dramatic collapse of communism in Yugoslavia and then of the Soviet Union itself. The world was no longer divided in two, with all the guarded borders and burdensome restrictions of the cold war

Global Citizens
The world's migrants at the turn of the millennium sought safety, education, or jobs in the West's manufacturing and service occupations. Like these young immigrants from Senegal who are sharing a meal at a café in Paris, they also appreciated Western amenities. Children of immigrants were sometimes disillusioned, however, not wanting the life of extreme sacrifice that their parents had lived. Their frustrations at not being accepted as full citizens occasionally erupted into protest and even violence. (© Directphoto.org /Alamy.)

division. Now, instead of being forced to follow one superpower or the other, nations around the world had more opportunity to trade and interact freely. The former Common Market transformed itself into the European Union and in 2004 and 2007 admitted many states from the former Soviet bloc. The telecommunication systems put in place in the 1960s contributed to the process of **globalization,** binding peoples and cultures together in an ever-denser social and economic web.

The global age brought the vast national and international migration of tens of millions of people, an expanding global marketplace, and an accelerated cultural exchange of popular music, books, films, and television entertainment. On the negative side, the new globalization also brought lethal disasters such as epidemic diseases, environmental deterioration, genocide, and terrorism. Cutting their own welfare state programs, nations in the West faced competition from the rising economic power of Japan, China, India, and Latin America. International business mergers accelerated from the 1990s on, advancing efficiencies but often threatening jobs. As millions of workers found new but sometimes unsatisfying jobs in an interlinked economy, they discovered that the global age was one of opportunities but also unprecedented dilemmas.

While the end of superpower rivalry made global exchange easier, it also resulted in the dominance of a single power, the United States, in world affairs. As the United States sought to exercise global power through warfare, however, the West itself seemed to fragment. European states started to resist the United States just as the Soviet

satellites had pulled away from the USSR. New forces arose to rival those of the West: not only the economic power of Asian, Middle Eastern, and other countries but also the cultural might of Islam created new centers of influence. Some observers predicted a huge "clash of civilizations" because of sharp differences between Western civilization and cultures beyond the West. Others, however, saw a different clash — one between a Europe reborn after decades of disastrous wars as a peace-seeking group of nations confronting an imperial United States that, like Europe in the nineteenth century, was increasingly at war around the world. Instead of bringing connections and understanding, globalization in either of these scenarios could bring global warfare.

For historians, understanding the recent past is a challenge in itself. Every day since 1989 has been filled with news, and never more so than after September 11, 2001. Global communication technology makes possible the virtually instantaneous reporting of news. Unlike journalists, historians do not choose from this mass the most sensational story of the moment or the one that will attract the biggest readership. Rather, they are interested in judging which items from the unfiltered mass of instant news are actually true and, of these, which will be important in the long run. Historians identify social, cultural, and political events that are uniquely important or generally significant for people's everyday lives, and they need time to collect facts from more than one source. They make the most reliable evaluations when events are no longer "news" — that is, after a substantial period of time has shown the events' lasting influence and importance.

When we wrote the first edition of this book, we held our breath in the face of rapidly changing events and judged that the fall of communism and the increasing interconnectedness of the world's peoples and cultures were the challenges not only

---

globalization: The interconnection of labor, capital, services, ices, and goods around the world. Although globalization has existed for hundreds of years, the late twentieth and early twenty-first centuries are seen as more global because of the speed with which people, goods, and ideas travel the world.

■ **1989** Tiananmen Square uprising; Berlin Wall falls

■ **1990–1991** Persian Gulf War

■ **1992** Soviet Union dissolves

■ **1994** Mandela elected in South Africa; Russia invades Chechnya; EU formed

1985   **1990**   **1995**

■ **1990s** Internet revolution   ■ **1993** Toni Morrison wins Nobel Prize; splitting of Czechoslovakia

■ **1991** Civil war in Yugoslavia; failed coup in the Soviet Union of the moment but also of history. In this third edition we have persisted in that judgment even though the fall of communism and the coming of globalism have brought greater perils than we saw only a few years earlier. Today, more than a decade after we made our first selections of important trends, we judge the potential for the unification of the entire European continent as momentous. We also see both the rising economic development around the world and the forces of terrorism as having historical staying power. As an experiment in history, you might note the important events during the months in which you take this course, put your list away for several years or more, and then see if they — along with the events discussed in this chapter — stand the test of time.

> **FOCUS QUESTION:** How has globalization been both a unifying and a divisive influence on the West in the twenty-first century?

Collapse of the Soviet Union and Its Aftermath

Rejection of communism spread in the 1990s, turning events in unpredictable, even violent directions. Yugoslavia and then the Soviet Union itself fell apart. Like Hungarians and Czechs in the early-twentieth-century Habsburg Empire, nationality groups in the USSR began to demand independence. The Soviet bloc had contained more than one hundred ethnic groups, and the five republics of Soviet Central Asia were home to fifty million Muslims. For more than a century, successive governments had attempted to instill Russian and Soviet culture, although some cultural autonomy was allowed. The policy of Russification shakily held the vast multiethnic empire together but

failed to build full allegiance. The USSR fragmented quickly. In Yugoslavia, Communist rulers had also enforced unity among religious and ethnic groups. From the unstable years of the early 1990s on, ambitious politicians seeking to build a following whipped up ethnic hatred (Map 29.1). The collapse of Communist regimes and the use of ethnic violence as a political tool raised questions about what new forms of government would take shape and what types of people might come to control the massive Soviet arsenal of nuclear weapons.

The Breakup of Yugoslavia

Ethnic nationalism shaped the post-Communist future in Yugoslavia. Tensions erupted there in 1990 when Serb Communist **Slobodan Milosevic** won the presidency of Serbia and began to promote Serb control as a replacement for communism in the Yugoslav federation as a whole. Other ethnic groups in Yugoslavia resisted Milosevic's militant pro-Serb nationalism and called for secession. "Slovenians . . . have one more reason to say they are in favor of independence," warned one of them in the face of mounting Serb claims to rule the other small republics that comprised Yugoslavia. Slovenia, Croatia, and Bosnia, opposed to Milosevic's desire to maintain a centralized state dominated by Serbia, hoped for a confederation of independent republics (Map 29.2). In the spring of 1991, Slovenia and Croatia seceded, but Croatia lost almost a quarter of its territory when the Serb-dominated Yugoslav army, eager to enforce Serbian supremacy, invaded. A devastating civil war broke out in Bosnia-Herzegovina when the republic's Muslim majority tried to create a multicultural and multiethnic state. With the covert military

---

Slobodan Milosevic: Serb leader of post-Communist Yugoslavia; he was tried for crimes against humanity in the ethnic cleansing that accompanied the dissolution of the Yugoslav state.

- 1999 Euro introduced; world population reaches six billion
- 2000 Putin becomes Russian president
- 2004 Ten countries join the European Union
- 2005 Emissions reductions of Kyoto Protocol go into effect

2000	2005	2010

- 2001 September 11 terrorist attack; United States launches war against terrorism
- 2003 United States invades Iraq; the West divides
- 2007 Bulgaria and Romania admitted to the European Union

MAP 29.1 Eastern Europe in the 1990s
In the 1990s, the countries of eastern Europe tried to forge their own destiny free from the direction of either Russia or the United States. The transition was far from easy. States like Czechoslovakia fragmented, and many state borders were contested. Turning from Russia, the leadership of these countries began to look to western Europe, most of them eventually opting for membership in the European Union.

support of Milosevic's government, Bosnian Serb men formed a guerrilla army and gained the upper hand. A United Nations (UN) arms embargo prevented the Bosnian Muslims from equipping their forces adequately to defend themselves even though the Serbs at the time were massacring them.

Violence in the Balkans was relentless—inflicted on neighbors in the name of creating "ethnically pure" states in a region where ethnic mixture, not ethnic purity, was the norm. During the 1990s, civilians died by the tens of thousands, as Serbs under Milosevic's leadership pursued a policy they called **ethnic cleansing**—that is, genocide—against the other ethnicities or nationalities. They raped women to leave them pregnant with Serb babies as another form of conquest. In 1995, Croatian forces massacred Serbs who had helped seize land from Croatia; that same year, the Serbs retaliated by slaughtering eight thousand Muslim boys and men in the town of Srebrenica, burying them

in mass graves, then re-interring them to conceal the massacre. "Kill the lot," the commander of the Serb forces ordered at Srebrenica. Military units on all sides destroyed libraries and museums, architectural treasures like the Mostar Bridge, and cities rich with history such as Dubrovnik. Ethnic cleansing thus entailed eliminating both actual people and all traces of their complex past. Many in the West explained violence in the Balkans as part of "age-old" blood feuds typical of a backward, almost "Asian" society. Others saw using genocide to achieve national power as nothing more than a modern political practice that had been employed by other politicians, including Adolf Hitler.

As with German, Italian, and Japanese aggression in the 1930s, no one stepped in to impose effective sanctions against such violence. Late in the 1990s, Serb forces moved to attack Muslims of Albanian ethnicity living in the Yugoslav province of Kosovo. From 1997 to 1999, crowds of Albanian Kosovars fled their homes as Serb militias and the Yugoslav army slaughtered the civilian population. North Atlantic Treaty Organization (NATO) pilots bombed the region in an attempt to drive back the army and Serb militias. UN peacekeeping forces finally intervened to enforce an interethnic truce,

---

ethnic cleansing: The mass murder—genocide—of people according to ethnicity or nationality, beginning with the post–World War I elimination of minorities in eastern and central Europe and continuing with the rape and murders that resulted from the breakup of Yugoslavia in the 1990s.

MAP 29.2 The Former Yugoslavia, c. 2000
After a decade of destructive civil war, UN forces and UN-brokered agreements attempted to protect the civilians of the former Yugoslavia from the brutal consequences of post-Communist rule. Ambitious politicians, most notably Slobodan Milosevic, used the twentieth-century Western strategy of fostering ethnic and religious hatred as a powerful tool to build support for themselves while making those favoring peace look softhearted and unfit to rule. ■ What issues of national identity does the breakup of Yugoslavia indicate?

but people throughout the world felt that this intervention came far too late and reflected the self-interest of the great powers rather than a true commitment to maintaining peace and protecting human rights. Alongside the decimated independent republics of Slovenia, Bosnia, and Croatia, a new regime emerged in Serbia, and Milosevic was turned over to the International Court of Justice, or World Court, in the Netherlands to be tried for crimes against humanity. In 2003, Milosevic loyalists, many of them in line to be rounded up for trial in the World Court, assassinated the new Serbian president. Across both western and eastern Europe, hateful racial, ethnic, and religious rhetoric influenced political agendas, nowhere more violently than in the former Communist states.

Destruction of the Mostar Bridge in Yugoslavia, 1990
In modern history, the construction of a nation-state has depended on the growth of institutions such as armies and bureaucracies and the promotion of a common national culture. In an effort to dominate Bosnia and Croatia, Serbs in the 1990s destroyed non-Serb art, books, and architecture, including such symbols as the sixteenth-century bridge. *(Top and bottom:* © Cardinale Stephane/Corbis Sygma.)

The Soviet Union Comes Apart

In 1992, amid deteriorating conditions and the threat of violence, the Soviet Union itself collapsed. By 1990, perestroika had failed to revitalize the Soviet economy; people confronted soaring prices, the specter of unemployment, and even greater scarcity of goods than they had endured in the past. That year, Soviet leader Mikhail Gorbachev announced that there was "no alternative to the transition to the market [economy]," but his plan was too little, too late and satisfied no one. In 1991, the Russian parliament elected Boris Yeltsin as president of the Russian Republic over a Communist candidate, prompting a group of eight antireform hard-liners, including the powerful head of the Soviet secret police, or KGB, to attempt to overthrow the government. Holding Gorbachev under house arrest, coup leaders claimed to be rescuing the Soviet Union from the "mortal danger" posed by "extremist forces." Yeltsin, defiantly standing atop a tank outside the Russian Republic's parliament building, called for mass resistance. Residents of Moscow and Leningrad filled the streets, and units of the army defected to protect Yeltsin's headquarters. People used fax machines and computers to coordinate internal resistance and send messages to the rest of the world. The coup collapsed as citizens overwhelmingly rejected a return to Communist orthodoxy.

Yeltsin Defeats the Communists. After the failed coup, the Soviet Union disintegrated. People tore down statues of Soviet heroes; Yeltsin outlawed the Communist Party newspaper, *Pravda*, and sealed the KGB's files. At the end of August 1991, the Soviet parliament suspended operations of the Communist Party itself. The Baltic States of Estonia, Latvia, and Lithuania declared their independence in September, and one republic after another followed their lead. Bloody ethnic conflicts erupted in the disintegrating Soviet world. In the Soviet republic of Tajikistan, native Tajiks rioted against Armenians living there; in the Baltic States, anti-Semitism revived as a political tool. The USSR finally dissolved on January 1, 1992. Twelve of the fifteen former Soviet republics banded together as the Commonwealth of Independent States (CIS), but that hardly ended the disintegration of Russian power (Map 29.3).

Weakened by the coup, Gorbachev abandoned politics. Yeltsin stepped in and accelerated the change to a market economy, introducing new problems as he did so. Plagued by corruption, the Russian economy entered an ever-deepening crisis. Yeltsin's political allies bought up national resources, stripped them of their value, and sent billions of dollars out of the country. By 1999, Yeltsin's own family appeared to be deeply implicated in stealing the wealth once seen as belonging to all the people. Managers, military officers, and bureaucrats took whatever goods they could lay their hands on, including weaponry, and sold it. Attempting to consolidate support and appealing to nationalist anti-ethnic sentiments in Russia, Yeltsin launched a destructive military action against the resource-rich province of Chechnya, which wanted independence. Social disorder added to the political upheaval when organized criminals interfered in the distribution of goods and services and assassinated legitimate entrepreneurs, legislators, and anyone who criticized them. As the Russian parliament pursued an investigation into the business dealings of Yeltsin, his family, and his allies, Yeltsin resigned on December 31, 1999. He appointed a new protégé, **Vladimir Putin**, as interim president.

Vladimir Putin Takes Charge. Putin was a little-known functionary in Russia's new security apparatus, which had evolved from the old KGB. In the presidential elections of spring 2000, Putin surprised everyone when the electorate voted him in. Though associated with the Yeltsin family corruption, he declared himself committed to legality. "Democracy," he announced, "is the dictatorship of law." With a solid mandate, Putin proceeded to drive from power the biggest figures in regional government, usually the henchmen of the robber barons, and he fired their associates who held high positions in the central government. Faced with a desperate economic situation, Putin claimed to restore "strong government" and end the influence of a "handful of billionaires with only egotistical concerns." Putin's popularity rose even higher when the government arrested the billionaire head of the Yukos Oil Company in 2003. The pillaging of the country—the source of ordinary citizens' recent suffering—was finally being punished. According to some insiders, however, Putin was merely transferring Russia's natural resources and other assets to his own cronies, and he also continued the destructive war in Chechnya to quell the independence movement. Casualties, atrocities, disease, and the physical devastation of

---

Vladimir Putin: President of Russia elected in 2000; he has worked to reestablish Russia as a world power through control of the country's resources and military capabilities.

MAP 29.3 Countries of the Former Soviet Union, c. 2000
Following an agreement of December 1991, twelve of the countries of the former Soviet Union formed the Commonwealth of Independent States (CIS). Dominated by Russia and with Ukraine often disputing this domination, the CIS worked to bring about common economic and military policies. As nation-states dissolved rapidly in the late twentieth century, regional alliances and coordination were necessary to meet the political and economic challenges of the global age.

Chechen cities continued to plague Russians and rebels alike.

Toward a Market Economy

Developing a free market and a republican government initially brought misery to Russia and the rest of eastern Europe. The conditions of everyday life grew increasingly dire as salaries went unpaid, food remained in short supply, and essential services disintegrated. In 1994, inflation soared at a rate of 14 percent a month in Russia, while industrial production dropped by 15 percent. People took drastic steps to stay alive. Hotel lobbies became clogged with prostitutes because women were the first people fired as governments privatized industry and cut service jobs. Unpaid soldiers sold their services to the Russian Mafia. Ordinary citizens lined the sidewalks of major cities selling their household possessions. "Anything and everything is for sale," one critic noted at the time. Simultaneously, a pent-up demand was unleashed for items never before available. An enormous underground economy existed in goods such as automobiles stolen from people in other countries and then driven or shipped to Russia.

There were, of course, many pluses: people were able to travel freely for the first time, and the media were more open than ever before. Some workers, many of them young and highly educated, profited from contacts with technology and business. However, their frequent emigration to more prosperous parts of the world further depleted the human resources of the former Communist states. "I knew in my heart that communism would collapse," said one Romanian ex-dissident, commenting sadly on the exodus of youth from his country, "but it never crossed my mind that the future would look like this." At the same time, as the different republics that had once comprised the Soviet Union became independent, the hundreds of thousands of ethnic Russians who had earlier been sent by the state to colonize these regions returned to Russia as refugees, putting further demands on the chaotic Russian economy. The dismantling of communism was more complicated and painful than anyone had imagined it would be.

The Economic Agenda. For many in the former Soviet bloc, the first priority was getting economies running again—but on new terms. Replacing a

Aftermath of Communism's Collapse
The collapse of communism and the Soviet Union created financial disaster, particularly for women, who represented more than two-thirds of the unemployed. Some of the unemployed resorted to prostitution; others tried to sell whatever they had, as these Muscovites did in 1992. The streets of Russian cities filled with destitute citizens, such as the homeless man sleeping in a broken store window. As crime escalated, calls for more law and order paved the way for tougher political candidates—not the liberal-minded reformers of the Gorbachev and Yeltsin years. *(AFP/Getty Images.)*

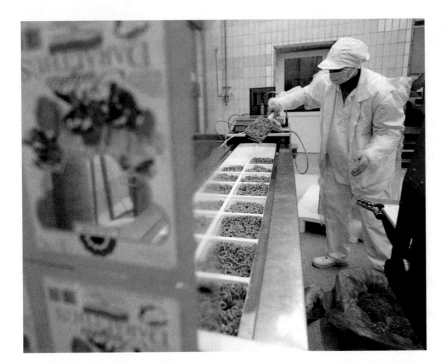

Hungarian Meat Packing Plant, 2007
The economy of the former Soviet bloc changed dramatically after the fall of Communist rule. Megastores were built at an astonishing pace and were filled with eager consumers. Western firms bought up out-of-date factories and installed modern labor-saving equipment, as in this meat-packing plant in Hungary, which processed food for sale across the European Union. *(AFP/Getty Images.)*

state-controlled economy with a market one could not happen naturally or automatically but rather required government planning. Given the spiraling misery, however, many opposed the introduction of new market-oriented measures. In Russia, members of collective farms fought to preserve them as a means of security in a rapidly changing world. With the farms up for sale, most collective farmers faced landlessness and starvation. The countries that experienced the most success were those in which administrators had earlier introduced ingredients of free trade, such as allowing farmers to sell their produce on the open market or encouraging independent entrepreneurs or even government factories to deal in international trade. Hungary and Poland thus emerged from the transition with less strain, because both had favored market elements early on and had hired advisers to speed the transformation of the economy. They set up business schools and worked to attract foreign capital, anchoring these two countries securely to the world economy.

Elsewhere, however, the transition happened differently. The former Soviet Union itself became, in the words of one critic, a vast "kleptocracy" in the 1990s as the country's resources — theoretically the property of all the people — were stolen for individual gain. An economist described the new scene as "piratization" rather than privatization. In this regard, one Polish adviser noted, democracy and a successful transition went hand in hand, for unless the people were institutionally powerful enough to prevent it, former leaders and administrators would simply operate as criminals. In addition to the problem of corruption, the Soviet practice of removing the economy from global developments further hindered the transition to a market economy. Industry had not benefited from technological change, and plants and personnel were hopelessly out of date, even worthless. The introduction of competition and free trade often meant closing plants and firing all the workers.

Talent Flees the Region. A final element in post-Soviet economic difficulties was a brain drain that plagued the region. The economic chaos that followed the fall of communism set off a rush of migration from eastern Europe to western Europe, often involving those with marketable skills. Migrants left for several reasons, including the lack of jobs, the upsurge of ethnic hatreds, and the availability of higher salaries for well-educated workers in other countries. Escaping anti-Semitism also played a role: post-Communist politicians used the rallying cry of hatred of Jews to build a following, just as Hitler and many others had done so effectively in the past. Banditry and violence inflicted by organized crime added to the disadvantages of remaining in eastern Europe. Some migrants from the east, fearful of reprisals from the Russian Mafia and others, sought political asylum.

The everyday amenities of western Europe included safe water, better housing, better roads, and at least a minimal level of social services. Although western Europe was now on a firm neoliberal course of cutting the social programs of the welfare state, most benefits had disappeared entirely in former Communist countries. Pensions for veterans and retired workers were rarely paid, and even when paid were often worthless given the soaring inflation; day-care centers, kindergartens, and homes for the elderly closed their doors; hospitals and health care deteriorated. In these circumstances, the benefits of citizenship in western European countries seemed almost irresistibly desirable.

International Politics and the New Russia

Although Gorbachev had pulled the Soviet Union out of its disastrous war with Afghanistan, his successors opened another war to prevent the secession of oil-rich Chechnya and to provide a nationalist rallying cry to shore up domestic support for the administration. For decades, Chechens had been integrated into the Soviet bureaucracy and military, but in the fall of 1991, the National Congress of the Chechen People took over the government of the region from the USSR, moving toward the same kind of independence sought by the Baltic nations and other former Soviet states. In June 1992, Chechen rebels got control of massive numbers of Russian weapons, including airplanes, tanks, and some forty thousand automatic weapons and machine guns. In December 1994, the Russian government sealed the Chechen borders and invaded. A high Russian official defended the war as crucial to bolstering Yeltsin's position: "We now need a small victorious war. . . . We must raise the President's rating." To counteract the Russian population's opposition to the war, Yeltsin, prompted by his advisers, announced the impossibility of negotiating with the Chechens. As the war dragged on, Chechnya's capital city of Grozny was pounded to bits. Casualties mounted not only among Chechen civilians but among Russians too. Protest against continuing the conflict increased. In 2002, Chechen loyalists took hundreds of hostages in a Moscow theater; Chechen suicide bombers blew up airplanes, buses, and apartment buildings. Putin pursued the Chechen war into the twenty-first century,

Chechnya, 1999
Russia justified its war in Chechnya in the 1990s and early 2000s as part of a struggle against Muslim terrorists. During the war, the Russian military kidnapped and murdered Chechen rebels while pummeling cities with gunfire and harassing the population, as this photo of civilians being checked shows. In retaliation, Chechens brought terrorism to Russia, setting off bombs and blowing up planes. Even with the new administration of Vladimir Putin, the bloodshed continued. (© Reuters/Corbis.)

compounding the problem of establishing a credible post-Communist government.

Putin expanded Soviet influence in Ukraine, Belarus, India, and China as well by taking advantage of the politics of oil. Russia had the commodities—especially oil and gas—needed to sustain the fantastic growth of emerging industries around the world, and by 2005 surging commodity prices were making Russia once again a real player in global politics—now because of its economic strength. Achieving democratic values remained a more elusive goal. Putin's critics were mercilessly assassinated, newspapers and radios were closed down, and a general apathy toward politics persisted, especially as wealth from the now healthy economy was used to refurbish cities and everyday life grew easier.

REVIEW: What were the major issues facing the former Soviet bloc in the 1990s and early 2000s?

The Nation-State in a Global Age

While the end of the Soviet system fractured one large regional economy, European unification progressed in the rest of Europe. The European Community was economically robust compared to former Soviet-bloc countries, many of which applied for membership to benefit from tying themselves to a powerful transnational organization. The relatively harmonious operation of the European Community stood in marked contrast to the wars and civil strife that plagued many other regions of the world, and its economic success provoked the formation of the North American Free Trade Agreement (NAFTA), which established a free-trade zone of the United States, Canada, and Mexico. The nationalist function of cities diminished as major urban areas like London and Paris became packed with people from other countries, who brought with them new ideas and new customs. These trends, however, aroused resistance from those who wanted to preserve their own traditions and who felt the loss of a secure, face-to-face, local way of life.

Europe Looks beyond the Nation-State

The peoples of Europe took immense strides in the 1990s to strengthen their shared institutions beyond those of the traditional nation-state. The

Common Market had opened the pathway to unified supranational policy in economic matters; its evolution into the European Union (EU) in the 1990s extended cooperation in political and cultural matters. Then, in 2004 and 2007, nations from the former Soviet bloc joined the EU, suggesting that power might shift eastward as some of these new EU members built thriving economies too.

From Common Market to European Union. The Common Market changed dramatically after the demise of European communism. In 1992, the twelve countries of the Common Market ended national distinctions in the spheres of business activity, border controls, and transportation, effectively closing down passport controls at most of their shared borders. Citizens of the member countries carried a common burgundy-colored passport, and governments, whether municipal or national, had to treat all member nations' firms the same. In 1994, by the terms of the **Maastricht Treaty**, the European Community (EC) became the **European Union (EU)**, and in 1999 a common currency—the **euro**—came into being, first for transactions among financial institutions and then in 2002 for general use by the public. Common policies governed everything from the number of American soap operas aired on television to pollution controls on automobiles to the health warnings on cigarette packages. The EU parliament convened regularly in Strasbourg, France, while subgroups met to negotiate further cultural, economic, and social policies. With the adoption of a common currency, an EU central bank came into being to guide interest rates and economic policy.

The EU was seen as the key to a peaceful Europe. "People with the same money don't go to war with one another," said a French nuclear scientist about the introduction of the euro. Greece pushed for the admission of its traditional enemy Turkey in 2002 and 2003 despite the warnings of a former

Maastricht Treaty: The agreement among the members of the European Community to have a closer alliance, including the use of common passports and eventually the development of a common currency; by the terms of this treaty, the European Community became the European Union (EU) in 1994.

European Union (EU): Formerly the European Economic Community (EEC, or Common Market), and then the European Community (EC); formed in 1994 by the terms of the 1992 Maastricht Treaty. Its members have political ties through the European parliament as well as long-standing common economic, legal, and business mechanisms.

euro: The common currency accepted by twelve members of the European Union. It went into effect gradually, used first in business transactions in 1999 and entering public circulation in 2002.

The Euro

These new bills went into circulation on January 1, 2002. The bills' designer used architectural imagery of windows and bridges to suggest openness, light, connectedness, and boundary crossing. Reflecting the compromise between Europe and individual states, the head sides of euro coins bear a common image, while the tail sides contain symbols chosen by individual nations within the euro zone. *(Royalty Free/Corbis.)*

MAP 29.4 The European Union in 2007

The European Union (EU) appeared to increase the economic health of its members despite the rocky start of its common currency, the euro. The EU helped end the traditional competition between its members and facilitated trade and worker migration by providing common passports and business laws, and open borders. But many critics feared a loss of cultural distinctiveness among peoples in an age of mass communications.

president of France that a predominantly Muslim country could never fit in with the Christian traditions of EU members. Both Greece and Turkey stood to benefit by having their disputes adjudicated by the larger body of European members, principally by being able to cut that part of their defense budget used for weaponry against the other country. Like the rivalry between Germany and France, that between Turkey and Greece, it was hoped, would dissolve if bound by the strong economic and political ties of the EU.

Drawbacks to EU membership remained, however. The EU enforced no common regulatory practices, and the common economic policies demanding cooperation among its members were not always observed. Individual governments set up hurdles and barriers for businesses: for instance, obstructing transnational mergers they did not like.

One government might block the acquisition of a company based on its own soil no matter what the advantages to shareholders, the economy, the workforce, or the consumers of unified Europe. Nonetheless, countries of eastern Europe clamored to join, working hard to meet not only the EU's fiscal requirements but also those pertaining to human rights and social policy (Map 29.4).

East Joins West. The EU's attractions became clear to eastern Europe, as demonstrated in the case of Greece, long considered the poor relative of the other member countries. Greece joined the European Community in 1981; its per capita gross domestic product was 64 percent of the European average in 1985. However, Greek leaders and the EU made a real effort during the 1990s to bring the country closer to EU norms. By the early

DOCUMENT

Václav Havel, "Czechoslovakia Is Returning to Europe"

Czech playwright and longtime anti-Communist activist Václav Havel became the first president of his country after the Communist Party was ousted in 1989. Havel was an idealist who believed that the people of eastern Europe had gained important insights from their experience of Soviet domination. This speech provides a backdrop to the admission of eastern European countries to the European Union in 2004. Despite fears among more prosperous EU countries that the lower standard of living in eastern Europe will drag the EU down, there is also a strong sense that the EU is incomplete without them. Havel details what eastern Europeans have to offer, even to those who have long enjoyed greater freedom and prosperity.

Czechoslovakia is returning to Europe. . . . We are doing what we can so that Europe will be capable of really accepting us, its wayward children. Which means that it may open itself to us, and may begin to transform its structures — which are formally European but de facto Western European. . . .

The Communist type of totalitarian system has left . . . all the nations of the Soviet Union and the other countries the Soviet Union subjugated in its time, a legacy of countless dead, an infinite spectrum of human suffering, profound economic decline, and above all enormous human humiliation. It has brought us horrors that fortunately you have not known.

At the same time, however — unintentionally, of course — it has given us something positive: a special capacity to look, from time to time, somewhat further than someone who has not undergone this bitter experience. A person who cannot move and live a somewhat normal life because he is pinned under a boulder has more time to think about his hopes than someone who is not trapped that way. . . .

For this reason, the salvation of the human world lies nowhere else than in the human heart, in the human power to reflect, in human meekness and in human responsibility. . . . If we are no longer threatened by world war, or by the danger that the absurd mountains of accumulated nuclear weapons might blow up the world, this does not mean that we have definitively won. We are in fact far from the final victory. . . .

In other words, we still don't know how to put morality ahead of politics, science and economics. We are still incapable of understanding that the only genuine backbone of all our actions — if they are to be moral — is responsibility. Responsibility to something higher than my family, my country, my company, my success. Responsibility to the order of Being, where all our actions are indelibly recorded. . . .

I end where I began: history has accelerated. I believe that once again it will be the human mind that will notice this acceleration, give it a name, and transform those words into deeds.

Source: From speech delivered to the Joint Session of Congress, Washington, D.C., on February 21, 1990. Reprinted in *Vital Speeches of the Day*, March 15, 1990, 329–30.

---

twenty-first century, thanks to advice from the EU and an infusion of funds, Greece had reached 80 percent of the EU per capita gross domestic product. The benefits of EU membership were clear to national leaders.

Hoping for similar gains, the countries to the east moved toward EU membership throughout the 1990s. The collapse of the Soviet system advanced privatization of eastern European industry, as governments sold basic services to the highest bidder. Often, only companies in the wealthy western countries of the EU could afford to purchase eastern European assets. For example, the Czech Republic in 2001 sold its major energy distributor Transgaz and eight other regional distributors for 4.1 billion euros to a German firm. Lower wages and costs of doing business in eastern Europe attracted foreign investment, especially to Poland, the Czech Republic, Hungary, and Slovenia — the most developed state spun off from Yugoslavia. There were hopes that membership would encourage further investment and advance modernization. (See Document, "Václav Havel, 'Czechoslovakia Is Returning to Europe.'")

Ten new members — Estonia, Latvia, Lithuania, Poland, the Czech Republic, Slovakia, Hungary, Slovenia, Malta, and Cyprus — joined the European Union in 2004, and Romania and Bulgaria were admitted in 2007. Just before Poland's admission to the EU, its standard of living was 39 percent of EU standards, up from 33 percent in 1995. The Czech Republic and Hungary enjoyed 55 and 50 percent, respectively, but in all three cases these figures masked the discrepancy between the ailing countryside and thriving cities. Citizens in eastern Europe were not always happy at the prospect of joining the EU. A retiree fore-saw the cost of beer going up and added, "If I wanted to join anything in the West, I would have defected." Still others felt that having just estab-lished an independent national identity, it was pre-mature to join yet another body that would swallow them up. People in older member states were having second thoughts too: in the spring of 2005, a majority of voters in France and the Netherlands rejected a complex draft constitution that would have strengthened EU ties. Commen-tators attributed the rejection to popular anger at the EU bureaucracy's failure to consult ordinary people in its decision making.

Although still weak by comparison with most of western Europe, the economic life of eastern Eu-rope had in fact picked up considerably by 2000. In contrast to the massive layoffs, soaring inflation, and unpaid salaries of the first post-Communist years, in 2002 residents of Poland, Slovenia, and Estonia had purchasing power some 40 percent higher than in 1989. Outsourcing began to flour-ish across the region, increasing opportunities for those with language and commercial skills. Even in countries with the weakest economies — Latvia, Bulgaria, and Romania — a greater number of res-idents enjoyed such modern conveniences as freez-ers, computers, and portable telephones. Shopping malls sprang up mostly around capital cities, tes-tifying both to the urban nature of the benefits of the free economy and to the allure of this great new market of 100 million customers. Superstores like the furniture giant IKEA or the electronics firm Electroworld were a consumer's paradise to those long starved of goods. "When Electroworld opened in Budapest [April 2002], it provoked a riot. Two hundred thousand people crowded to get in the doors," reported one amazed observer. Crit-ics worried that eastern Europeans had fallen prey to uncontrolled materialism and frenzied shop-ping, a Western disease they called "consumania." Consumers themselves, however, saw shopping as "a social act, indicating that one had joined con-sumer society," as one eastern European business-man put it. Joining the consumer world was a sign of belonging to a global community of those free and prosperous enough to consume. They had left the isolation of communist poverty behind.

Globalizing Cities and Fragmenting Nations

After the collapse of communism, the West changed still further. It both fragmented into more nation-states than it had had even fifty years ear-

lier and developed new characteristics — most no-tably the globalization of major cities. These were cities whose institutions, functions, and visions were overwhelmingly global rather than regional or national. They contained stock markets, legal firms, insurance companies, financial service or-ganizations, and other enterprises that operated worldwide, transcending all borders and bound-aries and linking to similar enterprises in other global cities. Within these cities high-level decision makers set global economic policy and enacted global business. The high-powered and high-priced nature of such global business operatives made life in global cities extremely costly, driving middle managers and engineers to lower-priced living quarters in the suburbs, which nonetheless provided good schools and other amenities for well-educated white-collar earners. However, liv-ing in squalid conditions in the global cities were the very lowest paid of service providers — the maintenance, domestic, and other workers whose menial labor was essential around the clock to the needs and comfort of those at the top.

Global cities often had the best transport or telecommunication facilities and thus became cen-ters for migration, of highly skilled as well as more modest workers. Paris, London, Moscow, and New York were not just cosmopolitan but global, with direct and constant contact around the world. As a result, citizens of other cities who took pride in maintaining a distinctive national culture or local sense of community denounced them. Global cities also drew criticism for their concentrated wealth, seen to be taken at the expense of poorer people in southern countries. In other cases, however, glob-alization produced diasporas of prosperous mi-grants, such as the estimated ninety thousand Japanese in England in the mid-1990s who staffed Japan's thriving global businesses. Because these migrants did not aim to become citizens, they made no economic or political claims on the adopted country and were thus sometimes called invisible migrants. Global cities were said to produce a "de-territorialization of identities" — meaning that many city dwellers lacked both a national and a lo-cal sense of themselves, so much did they travel the world or deal worldwide.

Ironically, as globalization took hold econom-ically and culturally, there came to be more nation-states in Europe in 2000 than there had been in 1945. Claims of ethnic distinctiveness caused in-dividual nation-states to fragment and separatist movements to grow. Despite two centuries aimed at unification of the Slavs, for example, and the trend toward larger nation-states, Slavs separated themselves from one another in the 1990s and early twenty-first century. In 1993, Czechoslovakia split into the Czech Republic and Slovakia (see Map 29.1, page 954). Yugoslavia came apart into several states, and Russia fought to keep Chechnya from becoming independent as had many other states of the former Soviet Union.

Activists launched movements for regional autonomy in France, Italy, and Spain. Some Bretons (residents of the historical French province of Brittany) and Corsicans demanded independence from France, the Corsicans violently attacking national officials. Basque nationalists in northern Spain assassinated tourists, police, and other public servants in an effort to gain autonomy, and although in 2005 they publicly renounced terrorism, the violence did not stop completely. The push for an independent northern Italy began somewhat halfheartedly, but when politicians saw its attractiveness to voters, they became adamant in their demands and the movement grew. As cities globalized and nations fragmented, new combinations of local, national, and global identities took shape. Nganda manager Therese enjoyed her neighborhood in Paris, her identity as a migrant to France, and continuing contact with friends and family in Congo. Basque separatists divorced themselves emotionally from Spain, while promoting a common identity with Basques in France and in other parts of the world. These developments, plus the overall expansion in the functioning of the EU, called into question the future of the nation-state.

Global Organizations

Supranational organizations, some of them regulating international finance and trade and others addressing social issues, had been in place for decades. By the twenty-first century, the interconnectedness of industry, finance, and government had made these organizations even more powerful and influential. Sponsored by large numbers of individual nations, the World Bank, International Monetary Fund, and World Trade Organization, for example, dealt with the terms of trade among countries and the economic well-being of individual peoples. The International Monetary Fund made loans to developing countries on the condition that they restructure their economies according to neoliberal principles. Other supranational organizations were charitable foundations, investigative think tanks, or service-based organizations acting independently of governments, many of them based in Europe and the United States; they

were called **nongovernmental organizations** (**NGOs**). Because some—the Rockefeller, Ford, and Open Society Foundations, for example—controlled so much money, these NGOs often had considerable international power. After the fall of the Soviet bloc, NGOs used their resources to shape economic and social policy and the course of political reform. Some charitable and activist NGOs, like the French-based Doctors Without Borders, gained money through global contributions and used it to provide medical attention in such places as the former Yugoslavia, where people facing war otherwise had no medical help. Small, locally based NGOs excelled at inspiring grassroots activism. All of these organizations, small and large, were in tune with the globalization process. As with the EU, the larger NGOs were often criticized for influencing government policies with no regard for democratic processes.

Not everyone supported or was pleased with the process of globalization. Activists formed local or supranational groups to attack globalization itself or to influence its course. In 1998, the Association for the Benefit of Citizens (or ATTAC, after its French name) worked to block the control of globalization by the forces of high finance: "Commercial totalitarianism is not free trade." ATTAC had as its major policy goal to tax international financial transactions (just as the purchase of household necessities were taxed) and to create with the tax a fund for people living in underdeveloped countries. With members from more than forty countries, the organization held well-attended conferences to find new directions for countries suffering from global development. A globally known activist, French farmer José Bové, protested the opening of McDonald's chains in France and destroyed genetically modified seeds: "The only regret I have now," Bové claimed at his trial in 2003, "is that I didn't destroy more of it." Bové went to jail for his protests, but he remained a hero to antiglobalism activists, who saw him as a simple champion of, in his own words, "good food" and an enemy of standardization.

REVIEW: What trends suggest that the nation-state was a declining institution at the beginning of the twenty-first century?

---

nongovernmental organizations (NGOs): Charitable foundations and activist groups such as Doctors Without Borders that work outside of governments, often on political, economic, and relief issues; also, philanthropic organizations such as the Rockefeller, Ford, and Open Society Foundations that shape economic and social policy and the course of political reform.

Challenges from an Interconnected World

The rising tide of globalization ushered in as many challenges as opportunities. First, the health of the world's peoples and their environment came under a multipronged attack from nuclear disaster, acid rain, and surging population. Second, economic prosperity and physical safety continued to elude great masses of people, especially in the southern half of the globe. Third, as suprastate organizations developed, transnational allegiances and religious and ethnic movements also vied for power and influence. Growing prosperity in regions outside the West challenged the traditional economic lead of the United States and Europe. This newfound wealth gave leaders in Asia, the Middle East, and Latin America confidence to assert that it was time for the West to surrender some of its power.

The Problems of Pollution

By the early years of the twenty-first century, many people had become aware of the dangers of industrial growth — once seen as an unqualified blessing. Despite growing ecological awareness, technological development continued to threaten the environment. In the aftermath of the 1986 nuclear explosion at Chernobyl, levels of radioactivity rose for hundreds of miles in all directions, thirty-one people died instantly, and some fifteen thousand perished more slowly from the effects of radiation. Moreover, as Russia opened up, it became clear that Soviet managers and officials had left thousands of square miles of the Asian continent rife with toxic waste in major lakes and rivers, had dumped used nuclear fuel in neighboring seas, and had so poisoned the environment of many parts of Asia by nuclear and other testing that entire regions were unfit for human and other life.

Other environmental problems had devastating global effects. Fossil-fuel pollutants such as those from natural gas, coal, and oil mixed with atmospheric moisture to produce acid rain, a poisonous brew that destroyed forests in industrial areas. In eastern Europe, the unchecked use of fossil fuels ravaged forests, leaving their trees brown skeletons, and inflicted ailments such as chronic bronchial disease on children. In less industrial areas, the world's rain forests were hacked down at an alarming rate to develop the land for cattle grazing or for cultivation of cash crops. Clearing the forests depleted the global oxygen supply and threatened the biological diversity of the planet. By

the late 1980s, scientists determined that the use of chlorofluorocarbons (CFCs), chemicals found in aerosol and refrigeration products, had blown a hole in the earth's ozone layer, the part of the blanket of atmospheric gases that prevents harmful ultraviolet rays from reaching the planet. Simultaneously, automobile and industrial emissions of chemicals were adding to that thermal blanket. The buildup of CFCs, carbon dioxide, and other atmospheric pollutants produced what is known as a greenhouse effect that results in **global warming**, an increase in the temperature of the earth's lower atmosphere. Climatic extremes and dramatic weather cycles of drought or drenching rain indicated that a greenhouse effect might be permanently warming the earth. Already in the 1990s, the Arctic pack ice was breaking up, allowing Finland by 2002 to ship oil along a once-iced-over route. Scientists predicted dire consequences: the rate of global ice melting, which had more than doubled since 1988, would raise sea levels by more than ten inches by 2100, flooding coastal areas, disturbing fragile ecosystems, and harming the freshwater supply.

Activism against unbridled industrial growth took decades to develop as an effective political force. An escapee from Nazi Germany, E. F. "Fritz" Schumacher, produced one of the bibles of the environmental movement, *Small Is Beautiful* (1973), which spelled out how technology and industrialization threatened the earth and its inhabitants. Rachel Carson's powerful critique, *Silent Spring* (1962), advocated the immediate rescue of rivers, forests, and the soil from the ravages of factories and chemical farming in the United States. In West Germany, environmentalism united members of older and younger generations around a political tactic called citizen initiatives, in which groups of people blocked plans for urban growth that menaced forests and farmland. In 1979, the **Green Party** was founded in West Germany, and soon after, the emergence of Green Party candidates across Europe forced other politicians to voice their concern for the environment. (See Document, "The European Green Party Becomes Transnational," page 967.)

Spurred by successful Green Party campaigns, Europeans attacked environmental problems on local and global levels. Some European cities — Frankfurt, for example — developed car-free zones,

global warming: An increase in the temperature of the earth's lower atmosphere resulting from a buildup of chemical emissions.

Green Party: A political party first formed in West Germany in 1979 to bring about environmentally sound policies. It spread across Europe and around the world thereafter.

The European Green Party Becomes Transnational (2006)

In 1993, members of Green parties across Europe formed the European Federation of Green Parties, which came to include members from twenty-nine European countries. The federation also made global connections with parties in Australia, Taiwan, the United States, and elsewhere in the world. In 2004, the federation formally became the European Green Party, which in 2006 adopted a charter endorsing not only environmental responsibility but a range of other values as well. Following is the opening statement of the charter.

The European Greens proudly stand for the sustainable development of humanity on planet Earth, a mode of development respectful of human rights and built upon the values of environmental responsibility, freedom, justice, diversity and non-violence.

Green political movements emerged in Europe while the continent was divided by the Cold War and amidst the energy crises of the mid-seventies. At that time, it became clear that the pattern of economic development was unsustainable and was putting the planet and its inhabitants in grave environmental, social and economic dangers. Existing political parties were incapable of dealing with this challenge.

Our origins lie in many social movements: environmentalists and anti-nuclear activists concerned with the growing damages to our planet; non-violent peace activists promoting alternative ways to resolve conflicts; feminists, struggling for real equality between women and men; freedom and human rights movements fighting against dictatorial and authoritarian regimes; third-world solidarity movements supporting the end of colonization and more economically balanced relations between the North and the South of our planet; activists campaigning against poverty and for social justice within our own societies.

From these origins, European Greens have come together to form our own political family. We stand for a free, democratic and social Europe in a peaceful, equitable and environmentally sustainable world. We defend values like justice, human and citizen's rights, solidarity, sustainability and the right of each individual to lead their own lives, free from fear.

and Venice operated completely without the use of automobiles because of the threat they pose to the city's very existence. In Paris, whenever automobile emissions reached dangerous levels, cars were banned from city streets until the emission levels receded. The Smart, a very small car using reduced amounts of fuel, became a fashionable way in Europe to reduce dependence on fossil fuels. Cities also developed bicycle lanes on major city streets. To reduce dependence on fossil fuels, parts of Europe developed wind power to such an extent that 20 percent of some countries' electricity was generated by wind. Many cities in the West began to recycle waste materials. These were success stories, involving changing habits and dependencies in some of the most industrialized countries in the world. By 1999, some eighty-four countries, including EU members, had signed the Kyoto Protocol, an international treaty whose signatories agreed to reduce their levels of emissions and other pollutants to specified targets. The Kyoto emissions reductions finally went into effect in February 2005, but with the world's leading polluter — the United States — still refusing to join either its former allies or developing nations in the

Smart Cars in Europe
The havoc caused by the oil crisis of the 1970s spurred many European states to encourage the development of alternate sources of energy and transportation. Thus, by the twenty-first century, the landscape was dotted not only with windmills but also with tiny, highly fuel-efficient automobiles like the Smart car shown here. European governments also heavily taxed gasoline with the result that it cost twice as much or more than in the United States, thus further encouraging people to buy the Smart car rather than an SUV — a far rarer sight in Europe than in the United States. *(© David Cooper/Toronto Star/ZUMA/Corbis.)*

TAKING MEASURE

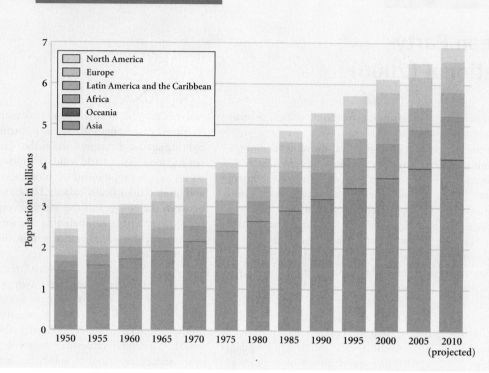

Legend:
- North America
- Europe
- Latin America and the Caribbean
- Africa
- Oceania
- Asia

World Population Growth, 1950–2010
In the twenty-first century, a major question is whether the global environment can sustain billions of people indefinitely. In the early modern period, local communities had lived according to unwritten rules that balanced population size with the productive capacities of individual farming regions. Centuries later, the same need for balance had reached global proportions. As fertility dropped around the planet because of contraception, population continued to grow because of improved health.

effort. Here was a sign that the West was fragmenting, with cooperation on the environment one of the first defining issues.

Population, Health, and Disease

The issue of population was as staggering in the early twenty-first century as it had been in the 1930s. Nations with less-developed economies struggled with the pressing problem of surging population, while Europe experienced negative growth (that is, more deaths than births) after 1995. The less industrially developed countries accounted for 98 percent of worldwide population growth, in part because the spread of Western medicine enabled people there to live much longer than before. By late 1999, the earth's population had reached six billion, with a doubling forecast for 2045 (see "Taking Measure," above). Yet many European countries were not replacing their population, leading to an aging of the citizenry and a shortage of people to bring new ideas and promote change. In fact, Europe as a region had the lowest fertility in the world. The fertility rate in Italy and Spain was only 1.3 children per woman of reproductive age, far below the replacement level of 2.1 needed to maintain a steady popula-

tion number. Some forecasters predicted that this low rate meant that by 2050 the population of Europe would fall from 725 to 600 million. Economists saw as a consequence fewer young workers paying into the social security system to fund retirees' pensions.

Population problems were especially dire in former Soviet-bloc countries, where life expectancy was declining at a catastrophic rate from a peak of seventy years for Russian men in the mid-1970s to fifty-three in 1995 and to fifty-one at the beginning of the twenty-first century. Heart disease and cancer were the leading causes of male death, and these stark death rates were generally attributed to increased drinking (one in seven men was an alcoholic in Russia), smoking, drug use, poor diet, and general stress. Meanwhile, fertility rates were also declining: the lowest levels of fertility in 2003 were in the Czech Republic and Ukraine with a rate of 1.1 children, and children in eastern Europe lived on average twelve years less than their counterparts in western Europe. Between 1992 and 2002, the Russian population declined from 149 to 144 million, with predictions that by 2050 it would fall below 100 million.

Good health was spread unevenly around the world. Western medicine brought better health to many in the less-developed world through the increased use of vaccines and drugs for diseases such as malaria and smallpox. However, half of all Africans lacked access to basic public health facilities such as safe drinking water. Drought and poverty, along with the maneuvers of politicians in some cases, spread famine in Sudan, Somalia, Ethiopia, and elsewhere. Around the world, the poor and the unemployed suffered more chronic illnesses than those who were better off, but they received less care. Whereas in many parts of the world people still died from malnutrition and infectious diseases, in the West noncontagious illnesses—heart and autoimmune diseases, stroke, cancer, and depression—were more lethal. The distribution of health services—heart transplants for the wealthy versus preventive health care for a wider range of clients—became a hotly debated issue in the general argument about whether technological solutions could remedy global problems.

Disease, like population and technology, operated on a global terrain, though there were many regional differences. In the early 1980s, both Western values and Western technological expertise were challenged by the spread of a global epidemic disease: acquired immunodeficiency syndrome (AIDS). An incurable, highly virulent killer that effectively shuts down the body's entire immune system, AIDS initially afflicted heterosexuals in central Africa; the disease later turned up in Haitian immigrants to the United States and in homosexual men worldwide. Within a decade, AIDS became a global epidemic. The disease spread especially quickly and widely among the heterosexual populations of Africa and Asia, passed mainly by men to and through women. By the late 1990s, no cure had yet been discovered, though protease-inhibiting drugs helped alleviate the symptoms. The mounting death toll made some equate AIDS with the Black Death. Treatment was often not forthcoming for some forty million victims because most of them, living in sub-Saharan Africa and the slums of Asian cities, were too poor. On top of the AIDS pandemic, the deadly Ebola virus and dozens of other viruses smoldered like a global conflagration in the making. In 2003, an unknown respiratory illness traveled the world: in the space of a month, severe acute respiratory syndrome (SARS) caused hundreds of deaths despite quarantines and surveillance of travelers. Incidences of avian flu virus—potentially deadly to humans—appeared in Asian chickens in 2002 and by 2006 had shown up in Turkey, Romania, and in other Mediterranean countries. Disease as much as environmental dangers underscored the interconnectedness of the world's peoples.

North versus South?

During the 1980s and 1990s, world leaders tried to address the growing schism between the earth's northern and southern regions. Other than Australians and New Zealanders, southern peoples generally suffered lower living standards and measures of health than northerners. Recently emerging from colonial rule and economic exploitation by northerners, citizens in the southern regions could not yet count on their new governments to provide welfare services or education. Their funds generally coming from the wealth of the northern countries, international organizations like the World Bank and the International Monetary Fund provided loans for economic development. However, the conditions tied to those loans, such as cutting government spending for education and health care, led to criticism that ordinary citizens gained no real benefit. Some twenty-first-century leaders from both north and south advocated that wealthy countries simply give southern countries the money they needed as reparation for centuries of imperial plunder.

Southern regions experienced different kinds of barriers to economic development. Latin American nations grappled with government corruption, multibillion-dollar debt, widespread crime, and grinding poverty, though some countries—prominent among them Mexico—began to strengthen their economies by marketing their oil and other natural resources more effectively. Africa suffered from drought, famine, and civil war. In countries such as Rwanda, Somalia, and Sudan, the military rule, ideological factionalism, and ethnic antagonism encouraged under imperialism produced a lethal mixture of conflict and genocide in the 1990s and early 2000s. Millions perished; others were left starving and homeless due to kleptocracies that drained revenues. Although African countries began turning away from military dictatorship and toward parliamentary government, global economic advance was uneven on the continent, and in the twenty-first century the scourge of AIDS and other unchecked diseases added to the weight of Africa's problems.

Islam Meets the West

North–south antagonisms became evident in the rise of militant Islam, which often flourished where democracy and prosperity for the masses were missing. The Iranian hostage crisis that began in 1979 showed religion, nationalism, and anti-Western sentiment commanding the world's attention. The charismatic leaders of the 1980s and 1990s—Iran's Ayatollah Ruhollah Khomeini; Libya's Muammar Qaddafi; Iraq's Saddam Hussein; and **Osama bin Laden**, leader of the al-Qaeda transnational terrorist organization—variously promoted a pan-Arabic or pan-Islamic world order that gathered increasing support. Khomeini's program—"Neither East, nor West, only the Islamic Republic"—had wide appeal. Renouncing the Westernization that had flourished under the shah, Khomeini's regime in Iran required women once again to cover their bodies almost totally in special clothing, restricted their access to divorce, and eliminated a range of other rights. Buoyed by the prosperity that oil had brought, Islamic revolutionaries believed that a strict theocracy would restore the pride and Islamic identity that imperialism had stripped from Middle Eastern men. Khomeini built widespread support among Shi'ite Muslims by proclaiming the ascendancy of the Shi'ite clergy. Although they were numerous, even constituting the majority in parts of the Middle East, the Shi'ites had long been discriminated against by the Sunnis.

Power in the Middle East remained dispersed, however, and Islamic leaders did not achieve their unifying goals. Instead, war plagued the region, as

Osama bin Laden: Wealthy leader of the militant Islamic group al-Qaeda, which executed terrorist plots, including the attacks on the United States in 2001, to rid Islamic countries of infidel influence.

Saddam Hussein, fearing a rebellion from Shi'ites in Iraq, attacked Iran in 1980, hoping to channel Shi'ite discontent with a patriotic crusade against non-Arab Iranians. The United States provided Iraq with massive aid in the struggle against Iran. But eight years of combat, with extensive loss of life on both sides, ended in stalemate. The Soviet Union had become embroiled against Islam in Afghanistan when it supported a coup by a Communist faction against the government in 1979. Tens of thousands of Soviets fought in Afghanistan, using the USSR's most advanced missiles and artillery to combat a powerful group of Muslim resisters. The United States, China, Saudi Arabia, and Pakistan provided aid to this resistance movement, some of whose members later coalesced into the Taliban—a militant Islamic political group. The losing war in Afghanistan so riled the Soviet population and drained resources that the Soviet leaders withdrew the troops in 1989. In the late 1990s, the Taliban took over the government of Afghanistan and imposed a regime that forbade girls from attending schools and women from leaving their homes without a male escort.

The Middle East remained in turmoil, as Saddam Hussein tested the post–cold war waters by invading Kuwait in 1990 in hopes of annexing the oil-rich country to debt-ridden Iraq. A UN coalition quickly stopped the invasion and defeated the Iraqi army, but discontent mounted in the region (Map 29.5). Conflict between the Israelis and the Palestinians continued. As Israeli settlers began taking more Palestinian land, Palestinian suicide bombers began murdering Israeli civilians in the late 1990s. The Israeli government retaliated with

Europeans React to 9/11 Terror
On September 11, 2001, terrorists killed thousands of people from dozens of countries in airplane attacks on the World Trade Center and the Pentagon. Throughout the world, people expressed their shock and sorrow in vigils, and like this British tourist in Rome, they remained glued to the latest news. Terrorism, which had plagued Europeans for several decades, easily traveled the world in the days of more open borders, economic globalization, and cultural exchange. (© Pizzoli Alberto/Corbis Sygma.)

■ **For more help analyzing this image,** please see the visual activity for this chapter in the Online Study Guide at bedfordstmartins.com/hunt.

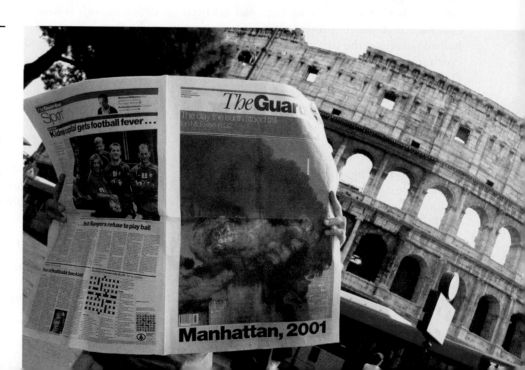

missiles, machine guns, and tanks, often killing Palestinian civilians in turn. In 2006, the Israelis, responding to the political militia Hezbollah's kidnapping of Israeli soldiers, attacked Lebanon, destroying infrastructure, sending missiles into its capital city of Beirut, and killing hundreds of civilians. Throughout the 1980s and 1990s and into the twenty-first century, terrorists from the Middle East and North Africa planted bombs in many European cities, blew airplanes out of the sky, and bombed the Paris subway system. These attacks, causing widespread destruction and loss of life, were said to be punishment for the West's support

for both Israelis and the repressive regimes in the Middle East.

On September 11, 2001, the ongoing terrorism in Europe and around the world finally caught the full attention of the United States. In an unprecedented act, Muslim militants hijacked four planes in the United States and flew two of them into the World Trade Center in New York City and one into the Pentagon in Virginia. The fourth plane, en route to the Capitol, crashed in Pennsylvania when passengers forced the hijackers to lose control of the aircraft. The hijackers, most of whom were from Saudi Arabia, were inspired by

MAP 29.5 The Middle East in the Twenty-first Century

Tensions among states in the Middle East, especially the ongoing conflict between the Palestinians and Israelis and animosities among Shi'ites and Sunnis, became more complicated from the 1990s on. The situation in the Middle East grew more uncertain in 2003 when a U.S.- and British-led invasion of Iraq deteriorated into escalating violence among competing religious and ethnic groups in the country. Additionally, for thirty-four days in the summer of 2006, Israel bombed Lebanon, including its capital city and refugee camps, with fire returned by Hezbollah and Hamas forces in the region.

War Protest in Seville, Spain 2003
Hundreds of thousands of demonstrators around the world protested the invasion of Iraq in March 2003, including these in Seville, Spain, whose signs condemned the alliance of Spanish prime minister José Maria Anzar with U.S. president George W. Bush as producing "war crimes" and "the dead for oil." Some 92 percent of Spaniards objected to the invasion of Iraq in March 2003, but the prime minister sent 1300 troops anyway.
(© Felipe Rodriguez/Alamy.)

Terrorist Attacks on Spanish Commuter Trains, 2004
Terrorism became more widespread from the 1970s onward, taking many forms and espousing many causes. Although terrorists of the 1970s and early 1980s often targeted prominent individuals, later ones engineered wider attacks on random citizens to increase the loss of life. On March 11, 2004, foreign terrorists who opposed Spain's participation in the Iraq War used bombs planted on commuter trains to kill 191 people and injure more than 2000. Spanish voters ousted the prime minister and installed one who pulled Spanish forces out of Iraq.
(AFP/Getty Images.)

the wealthy radical leader Osama bin Laden, who sought to end the presence of U.S. forces in Saudi Arabia. The hijackers had trained in bin Laden's terrorist camps in Afghanistan and learned to pilot planes in the United States. The loss of more than three thousand lives led the United States to declare a "war against terrorism." The administration of U.S. president George W. Bush forged a multinational coalition, which included the vital cooperation of Islamic countries such as Pakistan. The coalition enjoyed initial successes in driving the ruling Taliban out of Afghanistan, though it failed in its major goal of capturing bin Laden and permanently crushing the Taliban.

At first, the September 11 attacks and other lethal bombings around the world promoted global cooperation. European countries rounded up terrorists and conducted the first successful trials of them in the spring of 2003. Ultimately, however, the West became divided when the United States claimed that Saddam Hussein was concealing weapons of mass destruction in Iraq and suggested ties between Saddam Hussein and bin Laden's terrorist group. Great Britain, Spain, and Poland were among those who joined the U.S. invasion of Iraq in March 2003, but powerful European states, including Germany, Russia, and France, refused. Many people in the United States were furious, sporting bumper stickers with the demand "First Iraq, Next France" and joining happy hours to participate in "French bashing." U.S. war fever mounted with the suggestion that Syria and Iran should also be invaded, while the rest of the world condemned what seemed a sudden American blood lust. Europeans in general, including the British public, accused the United States of becoming a world military dictatorship in order to preserve its only remaining value—wasteful consumerism. The United States countercharged that the Europeans were too selfishly enjoying their democracy and creature comforts to help fund the military defense of freedom under attack. The Spanish withdrew from the U.S. occupation of Iraq after terrorists linked to al-Qaeda bombed four Madrid commuter trains on March 11, 2004. The British, too, reeled when terrorists exploded bombs in three subway cars and a bus in central London in July 2005. As the war in Iraq dragged on into its fourth year, there was a sense that the West was coming apart.

World Economies on the Rise

Amid these confrontations, an incredible rise in industrial entrepreneurship and development of technology took place outside the West, especially in Asia. Just as economic change in the early modern period had redirected European affairs from the Mediterranean to the Atlantic, so explosive productivity from Japan to Singapore in the 1980s and 1990s spread economic power from the Atlantic region to the Pacific. In 1982, the Asian Pacific nations accounted for 16.4 percent of global gross domestic product, a figure that had doubled since the 1960s. By 1989, East Asia's share of world production had grown to more than 25 percent as that of the West declined. By 2006, China alone was achieving economic growth rates of over 10 percent per year, while Japan had developed the second largest national economy after the United States, with Germany in third place and China poised to overtake it.

South Korea, Taiwan, Singapore, and Hong Kong were popularly called **Pacific tigers** for the ferocity of their growth in the 1980s and 1990s. By the 1990s,

China, pursuing a policy of economic modernization and market orientation, had joined the surge in productivity. Japan, however, led the initial charge of Asian economies with investment in high-tech consumer industries driving the Japanese economy. For example, in 1982, Japan had thirty-two thousand industrial robots in operation; western Europe employed only nine thousand, and the United States had seven thousand. In 1989, the Japanese government and private businesses invested $549 billion to modernize industrial capacity, a full $36 billion more than U.S. public and private investment. Such spending paid off substantially, as buyers around the world snapped up automobiles, televisions, videocassette recorders, and computers from Japanese or other Asian Pacific companies. As the United States poured vast sums into its military budgets and a series of wars, Asian and Middle Eastern governments purchased U.S. government bonds, thus financing America's ballooning national debt. Forty years after its total defeat in World War II, Japan was bankrolling its former conqueror.

Despite rising national prosperity, individual workers, particularly outside of Japan, often paid dearly for this newly created wealth. For example, safety standards in China were abominable, leading to horrendous mining disasters. Women in South Korea, Taiwan, and Central America labored in sweatshops to produce clothing for such U.S.-based companies as JCPenney and Calvin Klein. Using the lure of a low-paid and docile female workforce, governments were able to attract electronics and other industries. However, educational standards rose, along with access to birth control and other medical care for these women.

Other emerging economies in the Southern Hemisphere as a whole continued to increase their share of the world's gross domestic product during the 1980s and 1990s, and some achieved political gains as well. In South Africa, native peoples began winning the struggle for political rights when, in 1990, the moderate government of F. W. de Klerk released political leader Nelson Mandela, imprisoned for almost three decades because of his antiapartheid activism. After holding

Tigers of the Pacific Rim, c. 1995

Pacific tigers: Countries of East Asia so named because of their massive economic growth, much of it from the 1980s on; foremost among these were Japan and China.

free elections in 1994, which Mandela won, South Africa—like Russia, Brazil, Iran, Saudi Arabia, Nigeria, and Chile—profited from the need for vast quantities of raw materials such as oil and ores to feed global expansion. India made strides in education, women's rights, and local cooperation (calming bitter rivalries), but assassinations of prime ministers raised the question of whether India would continue to have the strong leadership necessary to attract investment and thus to continue modernization. After the brief rule of a Hindu nationalist government that often blocked development, India's economy also achieved soaring growth early in the twenty-first century, taking business from Western firms and making global acquisitions that gave it, for example, the world's largest steel industry. Although Western firms faced the challenge of competition, they also profited from prosperity that was more widely spread around the world.

> **REVIEW:** What were the principal challenges facing the West at the beginning of the twenty-first century?

Global Culture and Society in the Twenty-first Century

At the beginning of the twenty-first century, increased migration and growing global communications were changing culture and society, prompting many to ask what would become of national cultures and Western civilization itself. Would the world become a homogeneous mass with everyone wearing the same kind of clothing, eating the same kind of food, and watching the same films (on their cell phones)? Some critics predicted a clash of civilizations in which increasingly incompatible religions and cultures would lead to a global holocaust. Others asked whether the West would collapse as the United States wore itself down waging war while much of Europe distanced itself from its former ally.

The migration that had accelerated since the 1990s, the spread of disease, global climate change, the information revolution, and the global sharing of culture argued against the cultural purity of any group, Western or otherwise. "Civilizations," Indian economist and Nobel Prize winner Amartya Sen wrote after the terrorist attacks of September 11, "are hard to partition . . . given the diversities within each society as well as the linkages among different countries and cultures." Western society

changed even more rapidly in the 1980s and 1990s than it had hundreds of years earlier when it came into intense contact with the rest of the globe through migration and communications. Moreover, national boundaries in the traditional European center of the West were weakening, given the growing strength of the EU and the influx of migrants. Culture transcended national boundaries, as East, West, North, and South became saturated with one another's cultural products. Some observers labeled the new century an era of denationalization—meaning that national cultures as well as national boundaries were becoming less distinct. There is no denying that even while the West absorbed peoples and cultures, it continued to exercise not only economic but also cultural influence over the rest of the globe. Yet Western influence was also being debated and contested.

Redefining the West: The Impact of Global Migration

The global movement of people was massive in the last third of the twentieth century and into the twenty-first. Uneven economic development, political persecution, and warfare (which claimed more than 100 million victims after 1945) sent tens of millions in search of opportunity and safety. By 2001, France had some six million Muslims within its borders and Europe as a whole had between thirty-five and fifty million. Other parts of the world were as full as the West of migrants from other cultures. The oil-producing nations of the Middle East employed millions of foreign workers, who generally constituted one-third of the labor force. Violence in Africa sent Rwandans, Congolese, and others to South Africa, as its government became dominated by blacks. Wars in Afghanistan increased the number of refugees to Iran to nearly two million in 1995, while the Iraq-Iran war and successive attacks on Iraq by the West sent millions more fleeing. By 2000, there were some 120 million migrants worldwide, many of them headed to the West.

Migrants often earned desperately needed income for family members who remained in the native country, and in some cases they propped up the economies of entire nations. In countries as different as Yugoslavia (before its breakup), Egypt, Spain, and Pakistan, money sent home from abroad constituted up to 60 percent of national income. Sometimes migration was coerced; many eastern European and Asian prostitutes were held in international sex rings that controlled their passports, wages, and lives. Others came to the

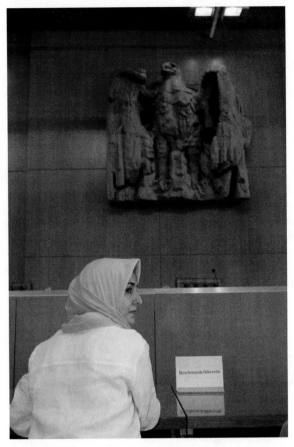

Headscarf Controversy in Germany
Western countries have long debated the relationship between religion and the nation-state. In particular, that debate targeted the need for religiously neutral education in order to develop citizens with undivided national loyalties. In an age of global migration, the issue of religion in the schools resurfaced, this time focusing on the headscarfs worn by many Muslim women. Although in 2003 Germany upheld the right of the teacher Fereshta Ludin, pictured here, to wear her headscarf while teaching on the grounds of religious freedom, it simultaneously asserted the right of children to a religiously neutral education. *(Michael Latz/ddp Berlin.)*

Foreign workers were often scapegoats for native peoples suffering from economic woes such as unemployment caused by downsizing. On the eve of EU enlargement in 2004, the highly respected weekly magazine *The Economist* included an article entitled "The Coming Hordes," which warned of Britain's being overrun by Roma (Gypsies) from eastern Europe. Political parties with racist programs sprang to life in Europe, aided by celebrities: the Moscow rock band Corroded Metals campaigned for anti-immigrant candidates with hate-filled songs and chants in English of "Kill, kill, kill, kill the bloody foreigners" running in the background. Even citizens of immigrant descent often had a difficult time being accepted. In Austria, France, the Netherlands, Sweden, and many other Western countries, thriving anti-immigrant and white supremacist politicians challenged centrist parties. In Austria and the Netherlands, anti-immigration candidates were elected to head the government. (See "Contrasting Views," page 976.) Nonetheless, especially as employers sought out illegal immigrants for the work they performed and the low wages they could be paid, the West remained a place of opportunity.

Global Networks and the Economy

Like migration, rapid technological change also weakened traditional political, cultural, and economic borders—if it did not make them altogether obsolete. In particular, the world's economy became far more global than ever before. In 1969, the U.S. Department of Defense developed a computer network to carry communications in case of nuclear war. This system and others like it in universities, government, and business grew into an unregulated system of more than ten thousand networks globally. These came to be known as the Internet—shorthand for *internetworking*. By 1995, users in more than 137 countries were connected to the Internet, creating new "communities" based on business needs, shared cultural interests, or other factors that transcended common citizenship in a particular nation-state. An online global marketplace emerged, offering goods and services ranging from advanced weaponry to organ transplants. While enthusiasts claimed that the Internet could promote world democracy, critics charged that communications technology favored elites and disadvantaged those without computer skills.

By 2000, as postindustrial skills spread, the Internet brought service jobs to countries that had heretofore suffered unemployment and real

West voluntarily, seeking opportunity and a better life: "I do not want to go back to China," said one woman restaurant owner in Hungary in the 1990s. "Some of my relatives there also have restaurants. . . . They have to have good relations with officials, . . . and sometimes they have to bribe somebody. . . . I would not be happy living like that." Like the illegal Congolese café proprietor Therese, whose story opens this chapter, many lived on the margins of the law, supporting networks of family and maintaining global economic ties from a new base in the West.

Muslim Immigrants and Turkey in the EU: The Dutch Debate Globalization

Early in the twenty-first century, Westerners debated a series of intertwined issues springing from conditions created by the new globalized world. The issue of immigration and the accommodation of peoples from outside the West was one of them. The Netherlands was one of the European countries that began debating whether globalization hadn't gone too far in this direction. The debate came to the fore in the Netherlands after an animal rights activist in 2002 assassinated Pim Fortuyn, a candidate for prime minister who ran on a popular anti-immigrant platform and proclaimed, "Holland is full." When, in 2004, a Muslim radical assassinated filmmaker Theo van Gogh, who took special pride in insulting Islam, the Dutch debate over globalization fixated on the presence of foreigners, especially Muslims, in the Netherlands and the admission of Turkey to the European Union.

1. The View from Everyday Life

Leon was a Rotterdam window cleaner who did not want his last name revealed. Here is his opinion of the main problem of Dutch life brought about by globalization.

There are too many people coming here who don't want to work. Before long there will be more foreigners than Dutch people, and Dutch people won't be the boss of their own country. That's why this has to be stopped.

Source: Jennifer Ehrlich, "Liberal Netherlands Grows Less So on Immigration," *Christian Science Monitor*, December 19, 2003.

2. Too Much Islamic Architecture

Many immigrants and their descendants, all of whom could become Dutch citizens, often lived in cities where there was economic opportunity. Although mosques existed in many cities, most were tucked away in obscure and shabby parts of town near the ghettos where many Muslim immigrant families lived. When the Muslim community in Rotterdam proposed building a stately mosque with 164-foot minarets, many in Rotterdam opposed the project. Ronald Sorenson, a member of Rotterdam's city council, objected in particular to the design of the proposed mosque and its cultural connotations.

There's no reason the minarets have to be that high — it will not be Rotterdam; it will be Mecca on the Maas [river].

Source: Jennifer Ehrlich, "Liberal Netherlands Grows Less So on Immigration," *Christian Science Monitor*, December 19, 2003.

3. Opposing Immigration and Turkey's Membership in the European Union

Acceptance of new members has made the EU the largest economic power in the world. In the first decade of the twenty-first century, some Europeans looked to the integration of Turkey into the EU as further expansion of EU influence. Others, however, opposed it, as the issue of EU enlargement had implications for

poverty. One of the first countries to recognize the possibilities of computing and help-desk services was Ireland, which pushed computer literacy to attract business. In 2003, U.S. firms spent $8.3 billion on outsourcing to Ireland and $7.7 billion on outsourcing to India. The Internet allowed for jobs to be apportioned anywhere. Moroccans did help-desk work for French or Spanish speakers, and in the twenty-first century Estonia, Hungary, and the Czech Republic as well as India and the Philippines were rebuilding their economies successfully by providing call-center and other business services. The Internet allowed service industries to globalize just as the manufacturing sector had done much earlier through multinational corporations.

Globalization of the economy affected the West in complex ways. Those who worked in outsourc-

ing enterprises were more likely than those in domestic firms to participate in the global consumer economy, much of it for Western goods. Benefiting from the booming global economy of the 1990s, the Irish and eastern Europeans became integrated into the Western consumer economy. Their new disposable income allowed them to purchase luxury automobiles, CD players, and personal computers that would have been far beyond their means a decade earlier. Non-Westerners may have taken jobs from the West, but they often sent funds back. A twenty-one-year-old Indian woman, working for a service provider in Bangalore under the English name Sharon, used her salary to buy Western consumer items, such as a cell phone from the Finnish company Nokia. "As a teenager I wished for so many things," she said. "Now I'm my own Santa *immigration. Geert Wilders, member of Dutch parliament, voiced his opposition.*

Turkey is an Islamic country and as such doesn't belong in the EU. The flow [of Turks] is already too big. . . . There is a big problem with the integration of immigrants already in Holland. They top the list in terms of criminality, unemployment, welfare payments, domestic violence . . . Let us concentrate on solving the problems with the immigrants already here properly.

Source: *Expatica*, October 5, 2004.

4. An Evaluation of Dutch Values

Popular Amsterdam actress Funda Müjde admitted to being called a "filthy Turk" during the debates over immigration and ethnic violence in the city.[1] Nonetheless, in her online stage performances and journalism, she gave sharp-witted responses to the anti-immigration furor around her.

"Do aliens actually love Holland?" This question woke me up with a start. After work (a workshop at the Employment Office) I traveled back with a colleague because he needed to be in Amsterdam. We have been working together for a while now and I notice that our conversations are always about something substantial.

Now it seemed as if he was even bolder in asking all kinds of questions.

Hurray! Do we aliens (read: mainly the first-generation Moroccans and Turks) really love Holland? Immediately I want to

---

[1] Ian Buruma, *Murder in Amsterdam: The Death of Theo van Gogh and the Limits of Tolerance* (New York: Penguin, 2006), 175.

answer this question with another question. "Does Holland really love aliens?" Just in time, I bite my tongue.

Source: Funda Müjde Web site: http//:www.fundam.nl/English/fundas-column-telegraaf-daily-newspaper-04.htm

5. Encouragement for Religious Tolerance in the EU

On July 21, 2004, Dutch prime minister Jan Peter Balkenende gave a speech before the European Parliament that called on Europeans to reconsider their position on immigration.

We must not allow ourselves to be guided by fear, for example, of Islam. The raising of barriers to any particular religion is not consistent with Europe's shared values. Our opposition should be directed not against religions, but against people and groups misusing their religion to get their way by force. Islam is not the problem.

Source: European Stability Initiative, "Speech by the President, Jan Peter Balkenende, to the European Parliament, in Strasbourg on 21 July 2004," http://www.esiweb.org.

QUESTIONS TO CONSIDER

1. What are the main points of view in the debate over immigration and the admission of Turkey to the European Union?
2. How do you evaluate the strength of each position?
3. Given that globalization brought about a wide variety of changes, why would immigration and Turkish EU membership become such heated issues?

Claus." Ordinary Western workers often discovered that this global revolution threatened their jobs. In Germany, where taxes for social security and other welfare-state financing comprised 42 percent of payroll costs in 2003, the incentive for businesses to downsize or to move to countries with lower costs was strong. Globalization redistributed jobs across the West and revamped economic networks.

A Global Culture?

As far back as the first millennium of human history, culture has transcended political boundaries. In the ancient world, Greek philosophers and traders knew distant Asian beliefs, while in the eighteenth and nineteenth centuries, Western scholars immersed themselves in Asian languages.

In the post–World War II period, tourism had become the largest single industry in Britain and in many other Western countries by the early 1990s, promoting cultural exchange. Chinese students in Tiananmen Square in 1989 testified to the power of the West in the world's imagination when in the name of freedom they rallied around their own representation of the Statue of Liberty (which itself was a gift from France to the United States). In Japan, businesspeople wore Western-style clothing and watched soccer, baseball, and other Western sports using English terms, while Europeans and Americans wore flip-flops, carried umbrellas, and used the "thumbs up" sign — all imports from beyond the West.

Remarkable innovations in communications integrated cultures and made the earth seem a

Tourism, Migration, and the Mixing of Cultures
Tourism was a major economic boon to the West, and Western countries were the top tourist destinations in the world. Spreading prosperity allowed for greater leisure and travel to distant spots. Curiosity grew about other cultures. This Scottish bagpiper in London clearly arouses the interest of passersby, whether visitors from afar or citizens of his own country.
(© Will van Overbeek. All Rights Reserved.)

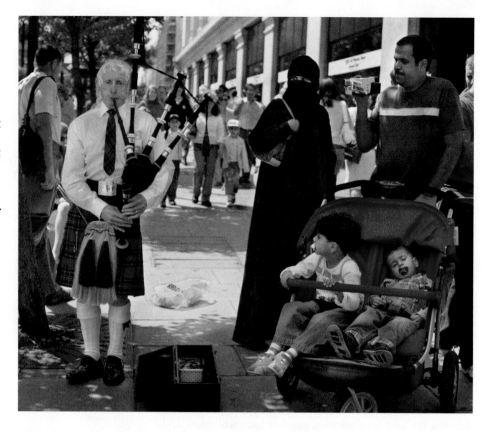

much smaller place, though possibly one with a Western flavor. Videotapes and satellite-beamed telecasts transported American television shows to Hong Kong and Japanese movies to Europe and North America. American rock music sold briskly in Russia and elsewhere in the former Soviet bloc. When more than 100,000 Czechoslovakian rock fans, including President Václav Havel, attended a Rolling Stones concert in Prague in 1990, it was clear that despite half a century of supposedly insular Communist culture, Czechs and Slovaks had tuned in to the larger world. Young black immigrants forged transnational culture when they created hip-hop and other pop music styles by combining elements of Africa, the Caribbean, Afro-America, and Europe. Athletes like the Brazilian soccer player Ronaldo, the American golf hero Tiger Woods, and Japanese baseball star Ichiro Suzuki became better known to countless people than their own national leaders were. Film entrepreneurs marketed such international blockbusters as the Chinese *Crouching Tiger, Hidden Dragon* (2000). With their messages conveyed around the world, even today's moral leaders—the Nobel Peace Prize winners Nelson Mandela, former president of South Africa; the Dalai Lama, the spiritual leader of Tibet; and Aung San Suu Kyi, opposition leader in Burma—are global figures.

Culture from beyond the West. As it had done for centuries, the West continued to devour material from other cultures—whether Hong Kong films, African textiles, Indian music, or Latin American pop culture. Publishers successfully marketed written work by major non-Western artists and intellectuals, and Hollywood made many of their novels into internationally distributed films. Egyptian Naguib Mahfouz, the author of more than forty books and recipient of the Nobel Prize for Literature in 1988, gained critical acclaim and a wide readership in the West. His celebrated *Cairo Trilogy*, written in the 1950s, describes a middle-class family—from its practice of Islam and seclusion of women to the business and cultural life of men in the family. British colonialism forms the trilogy's backdrop; it impassions the protagonists and shapes their lives and destinies. In the eyes of Arab critics, Mahfouz was a safe choice for the Nobel Prize because he had adopted a European style. "He borrowed the novel from Europe; he imitated it," charged one fellow Egyptian writer. "It's not an Egyptian art form. Europeans . . . like it very much because it is their own form." After author Gao Xingjian was harassed in China as an example of "intellectual pollution," his searing *Soul Mountain* (1990) about a ten-month contemplative trip by foot through his homeland, became a European best seller. Gao finished writing his masterpiece from exile in Paris, and in 2000 the Norwegian Nobel Prize Committee awarded him its prize for literature—the first Chinese author to be so honored. Non-Western literature's global appeal did not guarantee a warm welcome in an author's homeland.

Immigrants to Europe described how the experience of Western culture felt to the transnational person. Nigerian writer Buchi Emecheta, in her novel *In the Ditch* (1972), explored the experiences of a newcomer to Britain, critiquing colonialism and the welfare state from a non-Western perspective. Her book *The New Tribe* (2000) looked at the next generation's search for an identity; the hero, of Nigerian descent, finds that he is a total outsider when he visits Nigeria. Emecheta, like many other immigrants, felt the lure of Western education and values, but this new allegiance could become dangerous. The novel *The Satanic Verses* (1988) by **Salman Rushdie**, an immigrant to Great Britain from India, ignited outrage among Muslims around the world because it appeared to blaspheme the prophet Muhammad. From Iran, the Ayatollah Khomeini issued a fatwa, promising both a monetary reward and salvation in the afterlife to anyone who would assassinate the writer. Rushdie's Norwegian publisher was shot and his Italian and Japanese translators murdered, but in a display of Western cultural unity, international leaders took bold steps to protect Rushdie until the threat to his life was lifted a decade later.

The mainstream became fraught with conflict as groups outside the accepted circles engaged in artistic production. From within the West, novelist **Toni Morrison** became, in 1993, the first African American woman to win the Nobel Prize for Literature. Her works such as *Beloved* (1987) and *Jazz* (1992) describe the nightmares, daily experiences, achievements, and dreams of the descendants of men and women who had been brought as slaves to the United States. But some parents objected to the inclusion of Morrison's work in school curricula alongside Shakespeare and other white authors. Critics charged that, unlike Shakespeare's universal Western truth, the writing of African Americans, Native Americans, and women represented only a partial vision, not great literature. In both the United States and Europe, politicians on the right saw the presence of multiculturalism as a sign of deterioration similar to that brought about by immigration.

Building Post-Soviet Culture. In the former Soviet bloc, artists and writers faced unique challenges. After the Soviet Union collapsed, classical writers like Mikhail Bulgakov (1891–1940), famous in the West for his novel *The Master and Margarita* (published posthumously in 1966–1967), became known in his homeland. At the same time, the collapse put literary dissidents out of business, because, having helped bring down the Soviet regime, they had lost their subject matter—the critique of a tyrannical system. State-sanctioned authors, suddenly deprived of their jobs, had to sell their products on the free market in countries where economic conditions were so harsh that books were an unaffordable luxury. Eastern-bloc writers who formerly found both critical and financial success in the West seemed less heroic—and less talented—in the wide-open post-Soviet world. The work of Czech writer Milan Kundera, for example, lost its luster. It had been, according

Toni Morrison, Recipient of the Nobel Prize
The first African American woman to receive the Nobel Prize, Toni Morrison has used her literary talent to depict the condition of blacks under slavery and after emancipation. Morrison has also published cogent essays on social, racial, and gender issues in the United States. *(Time & Life Pictures/Getty Images.)*

Salman Rushdie: Immigrant British author, whose novel *The Satanic Verses* led the Ayotallah Ruhollah Khomeini of Iran to issue a fatwa calling for Rushdie's murder.

Toni Morrison: The first African American woman to win the Nobel Prize for Literature; her works include *Beloved* and *Jazz*.

to one critic, merely about Western publishers' hype, that is, not literature but merely a "line of business." To make matters worse, there was no idea of what the post-Communist arts should be, sending artists in the former Soviet bloc scurrying for solutions.

Talented fresh voices rang out, however. Andrei Makine, an expatriate Russian author, became popular worldwide for his poignant yet disturbing novels of the collapse of communism, many of them showing the attraction of western European culture and the resonance of the war and the Gulag on the imaginations of eastern-bloc people, including teenagers and older people. Both *Dreams of My Russian Summers* (1995) and *Once Upon the River Love* (1994) describe young people bred to fantasize about the wealth, sexiness, and material goods of western Europe and America. Victor Pelevin wrote more satirically and bitingly in such works as *The Life of Insects* (1993), in which insect-humans buzz around Russia trying to discover who they are in the post-Soviet world. Pelevin, a Buddhist and former engineer, wrote hilarious send-ups of politicians and the almost sacred Soviet space program, depicting it as a media sham run from the depths of the Moscow subway system in which hundreds of cosmonaut-celebrities are killed to prevent the truth from getting out. For him, "any politician is a TV program, and this doesn't change from one government to another." So one simply judged them by haircuts, ties, and other aspects of personal style, as he showed in his novel *Homo Zapiens*, in which politicians were all "virtual"—that is, produced by technical effects and scriptwriters.

In music and the other arts, much energy was spent on recovering and absorbing all the underground works that had been hidden since 1917. The situation was utterly astonishing as the work of literally dozens of first-rate composers, for example, emerged. They had written their classical works in private for fear that they might contain phrasings, sounds, and rhythms that would be called subversive. Meanwhile, they had often earned a living writing for films, as did Giya Kancheli, who wrote immensely popular music for more than forty films but was in addition a gifted composer of classical music. Other work could now become even better known. Alfred Schnittke (1934–1998) produced rich compositions—dozens of operas, symphonies, chamber music pieces, concertos, and other works—that were extremely sad, punctuated with anger in loud bursts of dissonance, and set in a somber bass register.

U.S. Cultural Dominance.   The political and economic power of the United States gave its culture an edge. U.S. success in "marketing" culture, along with the legacy of British imperialism, helped make English the dominant international language by the end of the twentieth century. Such English words as *stop, shopping, parking, okay, weekend,* and *rock* infiltrated dozens of non-English vocabularies. English became one of the official languages of the European Union; across Europe it served as the main language of higher education, science, and tourism. In the 1960s, French president Charles de Gaulle, fearing the corruption of the French language, had banned such new words as *computer* in government documents, and succeeding administrations followed his path; but such a directive did not stop the influx of English into scientific, diplomatic, and daily life. Nonetheless, in another sign of cultural divide, the EU's parliament and national cultural ministries regulated the amount of American programming on television and in cinemas.

American influence in film was dominant: films such as *Titanic* (1997) and *The Matrix Reloaded* (2003) earned hundreds of millions of dollars from global audiences. Simultaneously, however, the United States itself welcomed films from around the world—whether the Mexican *Y Tu Mamá También* (2001) or the Italian *Life Is Beautiful* (1997). "Bollywood" films—happy, lavish films from the Indian movie industry—had a huge following in all Western countries, even influencing the plots of some American productions. The fastest-growing medium in the United States in the twenty-first century was Spanish-language television, just one more indication that even in the United States culture was based on mixture and global exchange.

Postmodernism.   Some have called the global culture of the late twentieth and early twenty-first centuries **postmodernism**, defined in part as intense stylistic mixing in the arts without a central unifying theme or elite set of standards guiding the art. Striking examples of postmodern art abounded in Western society, including the AT&T building (now known as the Sony Building) in New York City, the work of architect Philip Johnson. Although the structure itself, designed in the

---

postmodernism: A term applied in the late twentieth century to both an intense stylistic mixture in the arts without a central unifying theme or elite set of standards and a critique of Enlightenment and scientific beliefs in rationality and the possibility of certain knowledge.

The German Reichstag: Reborn and Green
Nothing better symbolizes the end of the postwar era and the new millennium than the restoration of the Reichstag, the parliament building in Berlin. Like other manifestations of postmodernism, the restoration—designed by a British architect—preserves the old, while adding a new dome of glass, complete with solar panels that make the building self-sufficient in its energy needs. Visitors can walk around the glass dome, looking at their elected representatives deliberating below. (© Svenja-Foto/zefa/Corbis.)

political postmodernism included the decline of the Western nation-state. A structure like the Bilbao Guggenheim was simply an international tourist attraction rather than an institution reflecting Spanish traditions or national purpose. It embodied consumption, global technology, mass communications, and international migration rather than citizenship, nationalism, and rights. These qualities made it a rootless structure, unlike the Louvre in Paris, for example, which was built by the French monarchy to serve its own purposes. Critics saw it as drifting, more like the nomadic businesswoman Therese, who moved between nations and cultures with no set identity. Cities and nations alike were losing their function as places providing social roots, personal identity, or human rights. For postmodernists of a political bent, computers had replaced the autonomous, free self and bureaucracy had rendered representative government obsolete.

The issues raised by postmodernism—whether in architecture, political thought, or the popular media—focused on the basic ingredients of Western identity as it had been defined over the past two hundred years. Postmodernism was part of the rethinking and questioning that accompanied globalization. Such critical thinking—whatever its tentative conclusions may be—is today, as in the past, a key ingredient in the making of the West.

> **REVIEW:** What social and cultural questions has globalization raised?

late 1970s, looks sleek and modern, its entryway is a Roman arch, and its cloud-piercing top suggests eighteenth-century Chippendale furniture. Buildings designed by Johnson and other postmodernists appealed to the human past and drew from cultural styles that spanned millennia and continents without valuing one style above others. The Guggenheim Museum in Bilbao, Spain, designed by American Frank Gehry, was considered bizarre by classical or even "modern" standards as it represented forms, materials, and perspectives that, by rules of earlier decades, did not belong together. Architects from around the world working in a variety of hybrid styles completed the postunification rebuilding of Berlin.

Other intellectuals defined postmodernism in political terms as part of the decline of the eighteenth-century Enlightenment ideals of human rights, individualism, and personal freedom, which were seen as "modern" (see page 766). This

Conclusion: The Making of the West Continues

Postmodernism has not fully eclipsed modern values in the global age, however. Although some postmodernists have proclaimed an end to centuries of faith in progress, they themselves have worked within the modern Western tradition of constant criticism and reevaluation. Moreover, said their critics, the daunting problems of contemporary life—population explosion, scarce resources, North–South inequities, global pollution, ethnic hatred, and global terrorism—demanded, more than ever, the exercise of humane values and rational thought. Postmodernists and other philosophers countered that attempts at rational decision-making fall short because of the issue of "unintended consequences"—that is, one cannot know in advance the consequences of an act. Who would have predicted, for example, the human misery and rising criminality resulting initially from the fall of the Soviet empire?

The years since 1989 have proved both sides of the postmodernist debate correct. The collapse of communism signaled the eclipse of an ideology that was perhaps noble in intent but deadly in practice. Events from South Africa and Northern Ireland, for example, indicated that certain long-feuding groups could rationally put aside decades of bloodshed and work toward peace. In contrast, those reformers rationally seeking improved conditions by bringing down Soviet and Yugoslav communism unleashed bloodshed, sickness, and even genocide. The global age ushered in by the Soviet collapse has unexpectedly brought denationalization to many regions of the world.

The consequences of increasing globalization are still being determined. While the Internet and migration suggest that people will and often do have empathy for one another worldwide, militants from Saudi Arabia, Egypt, Indonesia, the Philippines, North Africa, Britain, and elsewhere have unleashed unprecedented terrorism on the world in an attempt to push back global forces. Even as globalization has raised standards of living and education in many parts of the world, in other areas—such as poorer regions in Africa and Asia—people face disease and the dramatic social and economic deterioration associated with the global age. Rational results of planning and inexplicable consequences coexist in our present world.

Western traditions of democracy, human rights, and economic equality have much to offer. Given that these were initially intended for a limited number of people—white men in powerful Western nations—global debates about their value and relevance abound. The nation-state, which protected those values for the privileged and denied them to many others, is another legacy of the West that must be rethought in an age of transnationalism. Migrants, for example, demand the dignity of citizenship and these demands are often resisted even though migrants' work and taxes are welcomed. Moreover, it is often supranational organizations rather than the nation-state that have advocated for worldwide prosperity and human values. At the same time, the West faces questions of its own unity and cultural identity—an identity that more than ever includes people from Asia, Africa, and the Americas—areas far from Europe, the traditional center of the West. Non-Westerners of all kinds have challenged, criticized, refashioned, and made enormous contributions to Western culture; they have also served the West's citizens as slaves, servants, and menial workers. One of the greatest challenges to the West and the world in this global millennium is to determine how diverse peoples and cultures can live together on terms that are fair for everyone. Supranational organizations, both governmental and nongovernmental, have attempted to meet the challenges created by increased globalism, but the long-term effects of these efforts are not yet known.

A final challenge to the West involves the inventive human spirit. Over the past five hundred years, the West has benefited from its scientific and technological advances. Longevity and improved material well-being spread to many places. In the past century, communication and information technology brought people closer to one another than ever before. Simultaneously, through the use of technology, the period from the last century to the present one has become the bloodiest era in human history—and one during which the use of technology threatens the future of the earth as a home for the human race. War, genocide, terrorism, and environmental deterioration are among technology's hallmarks, posing perhaps the greatest challenge to the West and to the world. The making of the West has been a constantly inventive undertaking, but also a deadly one. The question is, How will the West and the world manage both the promises and challenges of technology to protect the creativity of the human race in the years ahead?

FOR FURTHER EXPLORATION

■ **For suggested references, including Web sites, for topics in this chapter,** see page SR-1 at the end of the book.

■ **For additional primary-source material from this period,** see Chapter 29 in *Sources of THE MAKING OF THE WEST,* Third Edition.

■ **For Web sites and documents related to topics in this chapter,** see *Make History* at bedfordstmartins.com/hunt.

The World's Wealth
Income bands

High

Middle

Low

No data available

Internet Use by Percent
of Country Population

76–100%

51–75%

26–50%

0–25%

No data available

The World in the New Millennium

By the twenty-first century, the Internet had transformed communications and economic organization into an interconnected global network. People in the so-called north had greater access to this network in 2007 and for the most part enjoyed greater wealth. Despite inequalities and lower Internet usage compared to the north, the rate of growth of the Internet accelerated in Africa, the Middle East, and Latin America. ■ In what ways does this map indicate a closely connected world? *(From www.internetworldstats.com. Copyright © 2007, Miniwatts Marketing Group.)*

CHAPTER REVIEW

KEY TERMS AND PEOPLE

globalization (952)

Slobodan Milosevic (953)

ethnic cleansing (954)

Vladimir Putin (956)

Maastricht Treaty (961)

European Union (EU) (961)

euro (961)

nongovernmental organizations (NGOs) (965)

global warming (966)

Green Party (966)

Osama bin Laden (970)

Pacific tigers (973)

Salman Rushdie (979)

Toni Morrison (979)

postmodernism (980)

MAKING CONNECTIONS

1. In what ways were global connections at the beginning of the twenty-first century different from the global connections at the beginning of the twentieth century?

2. How did the Western nation-state of the early twenty-first century differ from the Western nation-state at the opening of the twentieth century?

> **For practice quizzes, a customized study plan, and other study tools,** see the Online Study Guide at bedfordstmartins.com/hunt.

REVIEW QUESTIONS

1. What were the major issues facing the former Soviet bloc in the 1990s and early 2000s?

2. What trends suggest that the nation-state was a declining institution at the beginning of the twenty-first century?

3. What were the principal challenges facing the West at the beginning of the twenty-first century?

4. What social and cultural questions has globalization raised?

IMPORTANT EVENTS

1989	Chinese students revolt in Tiananmen Square and government suppresses them; fall of the Berlin Wall
1990s	Internet revolution
1990–1991	War in the Persian Gulf
1991	Civil war erupts in the former Yugoslavia; failed coup by Communist hard-liners in the Soviet Union
1992	Soviet Union is dissolved
1993	Toni Morrison is the first African American woman to win the Nobel Prize; Czechoslovakia splits into Czech Republic and Slovakia
1994	Nelson Mandela elected president of South Africa; Russian troops invade Chechnya; European Union (EU) officially formed
1999	Euro introduced in the European Union; world population reaches six billion
2000	Vladimir Putin becomes president of Russia
2001	Terrorist attack on the United States and declaration of a "war against terrorism"
2003	United States invades Iraq; the West divides on this policy
2004	Ten countries join the European Union
2005	Emissions reductions of Kyoto Protocol go into effect
2007	Bulgaria and Romania admitted to the European Union

Appendix
USEFUL FACTS AND FIGURES

PROMINENT ROMAN EMPERORS

Julio-Claudians

27 B.C.E.–14 C.E.	Augustus
14–37	Tiberius
37–41	Gaius (Caligula)
41–54	Claudius
54–68	Nero

Flavian Dynasty

69–79	Vespasian
79–81	Titus
81–96	Domitian

Golden Age Emperors

96–98	Nerva
98–117	Trajan
117–138	Hadrian
138–161	Antoninus Pius
161–180	Marcus Aurelius

Severan Emperors

193–211	Septimius Severus
211–217	Antoninus (Caracalla)
217–218	Macrinus
222–235	Severus Alexander

Period of Instability

235–238	Maximinus Thrax
238–244	Gordian III
244–249	Philip the Arab
249–251	Decius
251–253	Trebonianus Gallus
253–260	Valerian
270–275	Aurelian
275–276	Tacitus
276–282	Probus
283–285	Carinus

Dominate

284–305	Diocletian
306	Constantius
306–337	Constantine I
337–340	Constantine II
337–350	Constans I
337–361	Constantius II
361–363	Julian
363–364	Jovian
364–375	Valentinian I
364–378	Valens
367–383	Gratian
375–392	Valentinian II
378–395	Theodosius I (the Great)

The Western Empire

395–423	Honorius
406–407	Marcus
407–411	Constantine III
409–411	Maximus
411–413	Jovinus
412–413	Sebastianus
423–425	Johannes
425–455	Valentinian III
455–456	Avitus
457–461	Majorian
461–465	Libius Severus
467–472	Anthemius
473–474	Glycerius
474–475	Julius Nepos
475–476	Romulus Augustulus

PROMINENT BYZANTINE EMPERORS

Dynasty of Theodosius

395–408	Arcadius
408–450	Theodosius II
450–457	Marcian

Dynasty of Leo

457–474	Leo I
474	Leo II
474–491	Zeno
475–476	Basiliscus
484–488	Leontius
491–518	Anastasius

Dynasty of Justinian

518–527	Justin
527–565	Justinian I
565–578	Justin II
578–582	Tiberius II
578–582	Tiberius II (I) Constantine
582–602	Maurice
602–610	Phocas

Dynasty of Heraclius

610–641	Heraclius
641	Heraclonas
641	Constantine III
641–668	Constans II
646–647	Gregory
649–653	Olympius
669	Mezezius
668–685	Constantine IV
685–695	Justinian II (banished)
695–698	Leontius
698–705	Tiberius III (II)
705–711	Justinian II (restored)
711–713	Bardanes
713–716	Anastasius II
716–717	Theodosius III

Isaurian Dynasty

717–741	Leo III
741–775	Constantine V Copronymus
775–780	Leo IV

780–797	Constantine VI
797–802	Irene
802–811	Nicephorus I
811	Strauracius
811–813	Michael I
813–820	Leo V

Phrygian Dynasty

820–829	Michael II
821–823	Thomas
829–842	Theophilus
842–867	Michael III

Macedonian Dynasty

867–886	Basil I
869–879	Constantine
887–912	Leo VI
912–913	Alexander
913–959	Constantine VII Porphrogenitos
920–944	Romanus I Lecapenus
921–931	Christopher
924–945	Stephen
959–963	Romanus II
963–969	Nicephorus II Phocas
976–1025	Basil II
1025–1028	Constantine VIII (IX) alone
1028–1034	Romanus III Argyrus
1034–1041	Michael IV the Paphlagonian
1041–1042	Michael V Calaphates
1042	Zoe and Theodora
1042–1055	Constantine IX Monomachus
1055–1056	Theodora alone
1056–1057	Michael VI Stratioticus

Prelude to the Comnenian Dynasty

1057–1059	Isaac I Comnenos
1059–1067	Constantine X (IX) Ducas
1068–1071	Romanus IV Diogenes

1071–1078	Michael VII Ducas
1078–1081	Nicephorus III Botaniates
1080–1081	Nicephorus Melissenus

Comnenian Dynasty

1081–1118	Alexius I
1118–1143	John II
1143–1180	Manuel I
1180–1183	Alexius II
1183–1185	Andronieus I
1183–1191	Isaac, Emperor of Cyprus

Dynasty of the Angeli

1185–1195	Isaac II
1195–1203	Alexius III
1203–1204	Isaac II (restored) with Alexius IV
1204	Alexius V Ducas Murtzuphlus

Lascarid Dynasty in Nicaea

1204–1222	Theodore I Lascaris
1222–1254	John III Ducas Vatatzes
1254–1258	Theodore II Lascaris
1258–1261	John IV Lascaris

Dynasty of the Paleologi

1259–1289	Michael VIII Paleologus
1282–1328	Andronicus II
1328–1341	Andronicus III
1341–1391	John V
1347–1354	John VI Cantancuzenus
1376–1379	Andronicus IV
1379–1391	John V (restored)
1390	John VII
1391–1425	Manuel II
1425–1448	John VIII
1449–1453	Constantine XI (XIII) Dragases

PROMINENT POPES

314–335	Sylvester	1227–1241	Gregory IX	1831–1846	Gregory XVI
440–461	Leo I	1243–1254	Innocent IV	1846–1878	Pius IX
590–604	Gregory I (the Great)	1294–1303	Boniface VIII	1878–1903	Leo XIII
687–701	Sergius I	1316–1334	John XXII	1903–1914	Pius X
741–752	Zachary	1447–1455	Nicholas V	1914–1922	Benedict XV
858–867	Nicholas I	1458–1464	Pius II	1922–1939	Pius XI
1049–1054	Leo IX	1492–1503	Alexander VI	1939–1958	Pius XII
1059–1061	Nicholas II	1503–1513	Julius II	1958–1963	John XXIII
1073–1085	Gregory VII	1513–1521	Leo X	1963–1978	Paul VI
1088–1099	Urban II	1534–1549	Paul III	1978	John Paul I
1099–1118	Paschal II	1555–1559	Paul IV	1978–2005	John Paul II
1159–1181	Alexander III	1585–1590	Sixtus V	2005–	Benedict XVI
1198–1216	Innocent III	1623–1644	Urban VIII		

THE CAROLINGIAN DYNASTY

687–714	Pepin of Heristal, Mayor of the Palace	877–879	Louis II, King	**East Francia**	
715–741	Charles Martel, Mayor of the Palace	879–882	Louis III, King	840–876	Ludwig, King
		879–884	Carloman, King	876–880	Carloman, King
741–751	Pepin III, Mayor of the Palace	**Middle Kingdoms**		876–882	Ludwig, King
751–768	Pepin III, King	840–855	Lothair, Emperor	876–887	Charles the Fat, Emperor
768–814	Charlemagne, King	855–875	Louis (Italy), Emperor		
800–814	Charlemagne, Emperor	855–863	Charles (Provence), King		
814–840	Louis the Pious	855–869	Lothair II (Lorraine), King		
West Francia					
840–877	Charles the Bald, King				
875–877	Charles the Bald, Emperor				

GERMAN KINGS CROWNED EMPEROR

Saxon Dynasty		1198–1215	Otto IV (Welf)	1493–1519	Maximilian I
		1220–1250	Frederick II	1519–1556	Charles V
962–973	Otto I	1250–1254	Conrad IV	1556–1564	Ferdinand I
973–983	Otto II			1564–1576	Maximilian II
983–1002	Otto III	**Interregnum, 1254–1273:**		1576–1612	Rudolf II
1002–1024	Henry II	**Emperors from Various Dynasties**		1612–1619	Matthias
				1619–1637	Ferdinand II
Franconian Dynasty		1273–1291	Rudolf I (Habsburg)	1637–1657	Ferdinand III
		1292–1298	Adolf (Nassau)	1658–1705	Leopold I
1024–1039	Conrad II	1298–1308	Albert I (Habsburg)	1705–1711	Joseph I
1039–1056	Henry III	1308–1313	Henry VII (Luxemburg)	1711–1740	Charles VI
1056–1106	Henry IV	1314–1347	Ludwig IV (Wittelsbach)	1742–1745	Charles VII (not a Habsburg)
1106–1125	Henry V	1347–1378	Charles IV (Luxemburg)		
1125–1137	Lothair II (Saxony)	1378–1400	Wenceslas (Luxemburg)	1745–1765	Francis I
		1400–1410	Rupert (Wittelsbach)	1765–1790	Joseph II
Hohenstaufen Dynasty		1410–1437	Sigismund (Luxemburg)	1790–1792	Leopold II
				1792–1806	Francis II
1138–1152	Conrad III	**Habsburg Dynasty**			
1152–1190	Frederick I (Barbarossa)				
1190–1197	Henry VI	1438–1439	Albert II		
1198–1208	Philip of Swabia	1440–1493	Frederick III		

RULERS OF FRANCE

Capetian Dynasty

987–996	Hugh Capet
996–1031	Robert II
1031–1060	Henry I
1060–1108	Philip I
1108–1137	Louis VI
1137–1180	Louis VII
1180–1223	Philip II (Augustus)
1223–1226	Louis VIII
1226–1270	Louis IX (St. Louis)
1270–1285	Philip III
1285–1314	Philip IV
1314–1316	Louis X
1316–1322	Philip V
1322–1328	Charles IV

Valois Dynasty

1328–1350	Philip VI
1350–1364	John
1364–1380	Charles V
1380–1422	Charles VI
1422–1461	Charles VII
1461–1483	Louis XI
1483–1498	Charles VIII
1498–1515	Louis XII
1515–1547	Francis I
1547–1559	Henry II
1559–1560	Francis II
1560–1574	Charles IX
1574–1589	Henry III

Bourbon Dynasty

1589–1610	Henry IV
1610–1643	Louis XIII
1643–1715	Louis XIV
1715–1774	Louis XV
1774–1792	Louis XVI

After 1792

1792–1799	First Republic
1799–1804	Napoleon Bonaparte, First Consul
1804–1814	Napoleon I, Emperor
1814–1824	Louis XVIII (Bourbon Dynasty)
1824–1830	Charles X (Bourbon Dynasty)
1830–1848	Louis Philippe
1848–1852	Second Republic
1852–1870	Napoleon III, Emperor
1870–1940	Third Republic
1940–1944	Vichy government, Pétain regime
1944–1946	Provisional government
1946–1958	Fourth Republic
1958–	Fifth Republic

MONARCHS OF ENGLAND AND GREAT BRITAIN

Anglo-Saxon Monarchs

829–839	Egbert
839–858	Ethelwulf
858–860	Ethelbald
860–866	Ethelbert
866–871	Ethelred I
871–899	Alfred the Great
899–924	Edward the Elder
924–939	Ethelstan
939–946	Edmund I
946–955	Edred
955–959	Edwy
959–975	Edgar
975–978	Edward the Martyr
978–1016	Ethelred the Unready
1016–1035	Canute (Danish nationality)
1035–1040	Harold I
1040–1042	Hardicanute
1042–1066	Edward the Confessor
1066	Harold II

Norman Monarchs

1066–1087	William I (the Conqueror)
1087–1100	William II
1100–1135	Henry I

House of Blois

1135–1154	Stephen

House of Plantagenet

1154–1189	Henry II
1189–1199	Richard I
1199–1216	John
1216–1272	Henry III
1272–1307	Edward I
1307–1327	Edward II
1327–1377	Edward III
1377–1399	Richard II

House of Lancaster

1399–1413	Henry IV
1413–1422	Henry V
1422–1461	Henry VI

House of York

1461–1483	Edward IV
1483	Edward V
1483–1485	Richard III

House of Tudor

1485–1509	Henry VII
1509–1547	Henry VIII
1547–1553	Edward VI
1553–1558	Mary
1558–1603	Elizabeth I

House of Stuart

1603–1625	James I
1625–1649	Charles I

Commonwealth and Protectorate (1649–1660)

1653–1658	Oliver Cromwell
1658–1659	Richard Cromwell

House of Stuart (Restored)

1660–1685	Charles II
1685–1688	James II
1689–1694	William III and Mary II
1694–1702	William III (alone)
1702–1714	Anne

House of Hanover

1714–1727	George I
1727–1760	George II
1760–1820	George III
1820–1830	George IV
1830–1837	William IV
1837–1901	Victoria

House of Saxe-Coburg-Gotha

1901–1910	Edward VII

House of Windsor

1910–1936	George V
1936	Edward VIII
1936–1952	George VI
1952–	Elizabeth II

PRIME MINISTERS OF GREAT BRITAIN

Term	Prime Minister	Government
1721–1742	Sir Robert Walpole	Whig
1742–1743	Spencer Compton, Earl of Wilmington	Whig
1743–1754	Henry Pelham	Whig
1754–1756	Thomas Pelham-Holles, Duke of Newcastle	Whig
1756–1757	William Cavendish, Duke of Devonshire	Whig
1757–1761	William Pitt (the Elder), Earl of Chatham	Whig
1761–1762	Thomas Pelham-Holles, Duke of Newcastle	Whig
1762–1763	John Stuart, Earl of Bute	Tory
1763–1765	George Grenville	Whig
1765–1766	Charles Watson-Wentworth, Marquess of Rockingham	Whig
1766–1768	William Pitt, Earl of Chatham (the Elder)	Whig
1768–1770	Augustus Henry Fitzroy, Duke of Grafton	Whig
1770–1782	Frederick North (Lord North)	Tory
1782	Charles Watson-Wentworth, Marquess of Rockingham	Whig
1782–1783	William Petty FitzMaurice, Earl of Shelburn	Whig
1783	William Henry Cavendish Bentinck, Duke of Portland	Whig
1783–1801	William Pitt (the Younger)	Tory
1801–1804	Henry Addington	Tory
1804–1806	William Pitt (the Younger)	Tory
1806–1807	William Wyndham Grenville (Baron Grenville)	Whig
1807–1809	William Henry Cavendish Bentinck, Duke of Portland	Tory
1809–1812	Spencer Perceval	Tory
1812–1827	Robert Banks Jenkinson, Earl of Liverpool	Tory
1827	George Canning	Tory
1827–1828	Frederick John Robinson (Viscount Goderich)	Tory
1828–1830	Arthur Wellesley, Duke of Wellington	Tory
1830–1834	Charles Grey (Earl Grey)	Whig
1834	William Lamb, Viscount Melbourne	Whig
1834–1835	Sir Robert Peel	Tory
1835–1841	William Lamb, Viscount Melbourne	Whig
1841–1846	Sir Robert Peel	Tory
1846–1852	John Russell (Lord)	Whig
1852	Edward Geoffrey–Smith Stanley Derby, Earl of Derby	Whig

Term	Prime Minister	Government
1852–1855	George Hamilton Gordon Aberdeen, Earl of Aberdeen	Peelite
1855–1858	Henry John Temple Palmerston, Viscount Palmerston	Tory
1858–1859	Edward Geoffrey–Smith Stanley Derby, Earl of Derby	Whig
1859–1865	Henry John Temple Palmerston, Viscount Palmerston	Tory
1865–1866	John Russell (Earl)	Liberal
1866–1868	Edward Geoffrey–Smith Stanley Derby, Earl of Derby	Tory
1868	Benjamin Disraeli, Earl of Beaconfield	Conservative
1868–1874	William Ewart Gladstone	Liberal
1874–1880	Benjamin Disraeli, Earl of Beaconfield	Conservative
1880–1885	William Ewart Gladstone	Liberal
1885–1886	Robert Arthur Talbot, Marquess of Salisbury	Conservative
1886	William Ewart Gladstone	Liberal
1886–1892	Robert Arthur Talbot, Marquess of Salisbury	Conservative
1892–1894	William Ewart Gladstone	Liberal
1894–1895	Archibald Philip–Primrose Rosebery, Earl of Rosebery	Liberal
1895–1902	Robert Arthur Talbot, Marquess of Salisbury	Conservative
1902–1905	Arthur James Balfour, Earl of Balfour	Conservative
1905–1908	Sir Henry Campbell-Bannerman	Liberal
1908–1915	Herbert Henry Asquith	Liberal
1915–1916	Herbert Henry Asquith	Coalition
1916–1922	David Lloyd George, Earl Lloyd-George of Dwyfor	Coalition
1922–1923	Andrew Bonar Law	Conservative
1923–1924	Stanley Baldwin, Earl Baldwin of Bewdley	Conservative
1924	James Ramsay MacDonald	Labour
1924–1929	Stanley Baldwin, Earl Baldwin of Bewdley	Conservative
1929–1931	James Ramsay MacDonald	Labour
1931–1935	James Ramsay MacDonald	Coalition
1935–1937	Stanley Baldwin, Earl Baldwin of Bewdley	Coalition
1937–1940	Neville Chamberlain	Coalition
1940–1945	Winston Churchill	Coalition
1945	Winston Churchill	Conservative
1945–1951	Clement Attlee, Earl Attlee	Labour
1951–1955	Sir Winston Churchill	Conservative
1955–1957	Sir Anthony Eden, Earl of Avon	Conservative
1957–1963	Harold Macmillan, Earl of Stockton	Conservative

(Continued)

PRIME MINISTERS OF GREAT BRITAIN (CONTINUED)

Term	Prime Minister	Government	Term	Prime Minister	Government
1963–1964	Sir Alec Frederick Douglas-Home, Lord Home of the Hirsel	Conservative	1976–1979	James Callaghan, Lord Callaghan of Cardiff	Labour
1964–1970	Harold Wilson, Lord Wilson of Rievaulx	Labour	1979–1990	Margaret Thatcher (Baroness)	Conservative
1970–1974	Edward Heath	Conservative	1990–1997	John Major	Conservative
1974–1976	Harold Wilson, Lord Wilson of Rievaulx	Labour	1997–2007	Tony Blair	Labour
			2007–	Gordon Brown	Labour

RULERS OF PRUSSIA AND GERMANY

1701–1713	*Frederick I
1713–1740	*Frederick William I
1740–1786	*Frederick II (the Great)
1786–1797	*Frederick William II
1797–1840	*Frederick William III
1840–1861	*Frederick William IV
1861–1888	*William I (German emperor after 1871)
1888	Frederick III
1888–1918	*William II
1918–1933	Weimar Republic
1933–1945	Third Reich (Nazi dictatorship under Adolf Hitler)
1945–1952	Allied occupation
1949–1990	Division of Federal Republic of Germany in west and German Democratic Republic in east
1990–	Federal Republic of Germany (reunited)

*King of Prussia

RULERS OF AUSTRIA AND AUSTRIA-HUNGARY

1493–1519	*Maximilian I (Archduke)
1519–1556	*Charles V
1556–1564	*Ferdinand I
1564–1576	*Maximilian II
1576–1612	*Rudolf II
1612–1619	*Matthias
1619–1637	*Ferdinand II
1637–1657	*Ferdinand III
1658–1705	*Leopold I
1705–1711	*Joseph I
1711–1740	*Charles VI
1740–1780	Maria Theresa
1780–1790	*Joseph II
1790–1792	*Leopold II
1792–1835	*Francis II (emperor of Austria as Francis I after 1804)
1835–1848	Ferdinand I
1848–1916	Francis Joseph (after 1867 emperor of Austria and king of Hungary)
1916–1918	Charles I (emperor of Austria and king of Hungary)
1918–1938	Republic of Austria (dictatorship after 1934)
1945–1956	Republic restored, under Allied occupation
1956–	Free Republic

*Also bore title of Holy Roman Emperor

LEADERS OF POST–WORLD WAR II GERMANY

West Germany (Federal Republic of Germany), 1949–1990

Years	Chancellor	Party
1949–1963	Konrad Adenauer	Christian Democratic Union (CDU)
1963–1966	Ludwig Erhard	Christian Democratic Union (CDU)
1966–1969	Kurt Georg Kiesinger	Christian Democratic Union (CDU)
1969–1974	Willy Brandt	Social Democratic Party (SPD)
1974–1982	Helmut Schmidt	Social Democratic Party (SPD)
1982–1990	Helmut Kohl	Christian Democratic Union (CDU)

LEADERS OF POST–WORLD WAR II GERMANY (CONTINUED)

East Germany (German Democratic Republic), 1949–1990

Years	Communist Party Leader
1946–1971	Walter Ulbricht
1971–1989	Erich Honecker
1989–1990	Egon Krenz

Federal Republic of Germany (reunited), 1990–

Years	Chancellor	Party
1990–1998	Helmut Kohl	Christian Democratic Union (CDU)
1998–2005	Gerhard Schroeder	Social Democratic Party (SPD)
2005–	Angela Merkel	Christian Democratic Union (CDU)

RULERS OF RUSSIA, THE USSR, AND THE RUSSIAN FEDERATION

c. 980–1015	Vladimir
1019–1054	Yaroslav the Wise
1176–1212	Vsevolod III
1462–1505	Ivan III
1505–1553	Vasily III
1553–1584	Ivan IV
1584–1598	Theodore I
1598–1605	Boris Godunov
1605	Theodore II
1606–1610	Vasily IV
1613–1645	Michael
1645–1676	Alexius
1676–1682	Theodore III
1682–1689	Ivan V and Peter I
1689–1725	Peter I (the Great)
1725–1727	Catherine I
1727–1730	Peter II
1730–1740	Anna
1740–1741	Ivan VI
1741–1762	Elizabeth
1762	Peter III
1762–1796	Catherine II (the Great)
1796–1801	Paul
1801–1825	Alexander I
1825–1855	Nicholas I
1855–1881	Alexander II
1881–1894	Alexander III
1894–1917	Nicholas II

Union of Soviet Socialist Republics (USSR)*

1917–1924	Vladimir Ilyich Lenin
1924–1953	Joseph Stalin
1953–1964	Nikita Khrushchev
1964–1982	Leonid Brezhnev
1982–1984	Yuri Andropov
1984–1985	Konstantin Chernenko
1985–1991	Mikhail Gorbachev

Russian Federation

1991–1999	Boris Yeltsin
1999–	Vladimir Putin

*USSR established in 1922

RULERS OF SPAIN

1479–1504	Ferdinand and Isabella
1504–1506	Ferdinand and Philip I
1506–1516	Ferdinand and Charles I
1516–1556	Charles I (Holy Roman Emperor Charles V)
1556–1598	Philip II
1598–1621	Philip III
1621–1665	Philip IV
1665–1700	Charles II
1700–1746	Philip V
1746–1759	Ferdinand VI
1759–1788	Charles III
1788–1808	Charles IV
1808	Ferdinand VII
1808–1813	Joseph Bonaparte
1814–1833	Ferdinand VII (restored)
1833–1868	Isabella II
1868–1870	Republic
1870–1873	Amadeo
1873–1874	Republic
1874–1885	Alfonso XII
1886–1931	Alfonso XIII
1931–1939	Republic
1939–1975	Fascist dictatorship under Francisco Franco
1975–	Juan Carlos I

RULERS OF ITALY

1861–1878	Victor Emmanuel II
1878–1900	Humbert I
1900–1946	Victor Emmanuel III
1922–1943	Fascist dictatorship under Benito Mussolini (maintained in northern Italy until 1945)
1946 (May 9–June 13)	Humbert II
1946–	Republic

SECRETARIES-GENERAL OF THE UNITED NATIONS

		Nationality
1946–1952	Trygve Lie	Norway
1953–1961	Dag Hammarskjöld	Sweden
1961–1971	U Thant	Myanmar
1972–1981	Kurt Waldheim	Austria
1982–1991	Javier Pérez de Cuéllar	Peru
1992–1996	Boutros Boutros-Ghali	Egypt
1997–2006	Kofi A. Annan	Ghana
2007–	Ban Kimoon	South Korea

UNITED STATES PRESIDENTIAL ADMINISTRATIONS

Term(s)	President	Political Party	Term(s)	President	Political Party
1789–1797	George Washington	No party designation	1889–1893	Benjamin Harrison	Republican
1797–1801	John Adams	Federalist	1893–1897	Grover Cleveland	Democratic
1801–1809	Thomas Jefferson	Democratic-Republican	1897–1901	William McKinley	Republican
1809–1817	James Madison	Democratic-Republican	1901–1909	Theodore Roosevelt	Republican
1817–1825	James Monroe	Democratic-Republican	1909–1913	William H. Taft	Republican
1825–1829	John Quincy Adams	Democratic-Republican	1913–1921	Woodrow Wilson	Democratic
1829–1837	Andrew Jackson	Democratic	1921–1923	Warren G. Harding	Republican
1837–1841	Martin Van Buren	Democratic	1923–1929	Calvin Coolidge	Republican
1841	William H. Harrison	Whig	1929–1933	Herbert C. Hoover	Republican
1841–1845	John Tyler	Whig	1933–1945	Franklin D. Roosevelt	Democratic
1845–1849	James K. Polk	Democratic	1945–1953	Harry S. Truman	Democratic
1849–1850	Zachary Taylor	Whig	1953–1961	Dwight D. Eisenhower	Republican
1850–1853	Millard Filmore	Whig	1961–1963	John F. Kennedy	Democratic
1853–1857	Franklin Pierce	Democratic	1963–1969	Lyndon B. Johnson	Democratic
1857–1861	James Buchanan	Democratic	1969–1974	Richard M. Nixon	Republican
1861–1865	Abraham Lincoln	Republican	1974–1977	Gerald R. Ford	Republican
1865–1869	Andrew Johnson	Republican	1977–1981	Jimmy Carter	Democratic
1869–1877	Ulysses S. Grant	Republican	1981–1989	Ronald W. Reagan	Republican
1877–1881	Rutherford B. Hayes	Republican	1989–1993	George H. W. Bush	Republican
1881	James A. Garfield	Republican	1993–2001	William J. Clinton	Democratic
1881–1885	Chester A. Arthur	Republican	2001–	George W. Bush	Republican
1885–1889	Grover Cleveland	Democratic			

MAJOR WARS OF THE MODERN ERA

1546–1555	German Wars of Religion	1796–1815	Napoleonic wars
1526–1571	Ottoman wars	1846–1848	Mexican-American War
1562–1598	French Wars of Religion	1853–1856	Crimean War
1566–1609, 1621–1648	Revolt of the Netherlands	1861–1865	United States Civil War
1618–1648	Thirty Years' War	1870–1871	Franco-Prussian War
1642–1648	English Civil War	1894–1895	Sino-Japanese War
1652–1678	Anglo-Dutch Wars	1898	Spanish-American War
1667–1697	Wars of Louis XIV	1904–1905	Russo-Japanese War
1683–1697	Ottoman wars	1914–1918	World War I
1689–1697	War of the League of Augsburg	1939–1945	World War II
1702–1714	War of Spanish Succession	1946–1975	Vietnam wars
1702–1721	Great Northern War	1950–1953	Korean War
1714–1718	Ottoman wars	1990–1991	Persian Gulf War
1740–1748	War of Austrian Succession	1991–1997	Civil War in the former Yugoslavia
1756–1763	Seven Years' War	2003–	Iraq War
1775–1781	American Revolution		

Glossary of Key Terms and People

This glossary contains definitions of terms and people that are central to your understanding of the material covered in this textbook. Each term or person in the glossary is in boldface in the text when it is first defined, then listed again in the corresponding Chapter Review section to signal its importance. We have also included the page number on which the full discussion of the term or person appears so that you can easily locate the complete explanation to strengthen your historical vocabulary.

For words or names not defined here, two additional resources may be useful: the index, which will direct you to many more topics discussed in the text, and a good dictionary.

abolitionists (560): Advocates of the abolition of the slave trade and of slavery.

absolutism (484): A system of government in which the ruler claims sole and uncontestable power.

agricultural revolution (529): Increasingly aggressive attitudes toward investment in and management of land that increased production of food in the 1700s.

Alexander II (693): Russian tsar (r. 1855–1881) who initiated the age of Great Reforms and emancipated the serfs in 1861.

Anabaptists (436): Sixteenth-century Protestants who believed that only adults could truly have faith and accept baptism.

anarchism (713): The belief that people should not have government; it was popular among some peasants and workers in the last half of the nineteenth century and the first decades of the twentieth.

appeasement (861): The strategy of preventing a war by making concessions for legitimate grievances.

art nouveau (775): An early-twentieth-century artistic style in graphics, fashion, and household design that featured flowing, sinuous lines, borrowed in large part from Asian art.

Atlantic system (520): The network of trade established in the 1700s that bound together western Europe, Africa, and the Americas. Europeans sold slaves from western Africa and bought commodities that were produced by the new colonial plantations in North and South America and the Caribbean.

baroque (472): An artistic style of the seventeenth century that featured curves, exaggerated lighting, intense emotions, release from restraint, and even a kind of artistic sensationalism.

Beauvoir, Simone de (904): Author of *The Second Sex*, a globally influential work that created an interpretation of women's age-old inferior status from existentialist philosophy.

Beethoven, Ludwig van (642): The German composer (1770–1827) who helped set the direction of musical romanticism; his music used recurring and evolving themes to convey the impression of natural growth.

bin Laden, Osama (970): Wealthy leader of the militant Islamic group al-Qaeda, which executed terrorist plots, including the attacks on the United States in 2001, to rid Islamic countries of infidel influence.

Bismarck, Otto von (699): 1815–1898. Leading Prussian politician and German prime minister who waged war in order to create a united German Empire, which was established in 1871.

Blitzkrieg (862): Literally, "lightning war"; a strategy for the conduct of war in which motorized firepower quickly and overwhelmingly attacks the enemy, leaving it unable to resist psychologically or militarily.

Bolívar, Simon (646): 1783–1830. The European-educated son of a slave owner who became one of the leaders of the Latin American independence movement in the 1820s. Bolivia is named after him.

Bolshevik Revolution (811): The overthrow of Russia's Provisional Government in the fall of 1917 by V. I. Lenin and his Bolshevik forces.

Bonaparte, Louis-Napoleon (680): 1808–1873. Nephew of Napoleon I; he was elected president of France in 1848, declared himself Emperor Napoleon III in 1852, and ruled until 1870.

Bonaparte, Napoleon (620): The French general who became First Consul in 1799 and emperor in 1804; after losing the battle of Waterloo in 1815, he was exiled to the island of St. Helena.

buccaneers (527): Pirates of the Caribbean who governed themselves and preyed on international shipping.

bureaucracy (489): A network of state officials carrying out orders according to a regular and routine line of authority.

Calvin, John (432): French-born Christian humanist (1509–1564) and founder of Calvinism, one of the major branches of the Protestant Reformation; he led the reform movement in Geneva, Switzerland, from 1541 to 1564.

capital-intensive industry (730): A mid- to late-nineteenth-century development in industry that required great investments of money for machinery and infrastructure to make a profit.

Catherine de Médicis (453): Italian-born mother of French king Charles X; she served as regent and tried but failed to prevent religious warfare between Calvinists and Catholics.

Cavour, Camillo di (696): 1810–1861. Prime minister of the kingdom of Piedmont-Sardinia and architect of a united Italy.

Chaplin, Charlie (855): 1889–1977. Major entertainment leader, whose satires of Hitler and sympathetic portrayals of the common man helped preserve democratic values.

Charles V (430): Holy Roman Emperor (r. 1519–1556) and the most powerful ruler in sixteenth-century Europe; he reigned over the Low Countries, Spain, Spain's Italian and New World dominions, and the Austrian Habsburg lands.

Chartism (677): The British movement of supporters of the People's Charter (1838), which demanded universal manhood suffrage, vote by secret ballot, equal electoral districts, and other reforms.

cholera (662): An epidemic, usually fatal disease caused by a waterborne bacterium that induces violent vomiting and diarrhea; devastating outbreaks swept across Europe in 1830–1832 and 1847–1851.

Christian Democrats (889): Powerful center to center-right political parties that evolved in the late 1940s from former Catholic parties of the pre–World War II period.

Christian humanism (427): A general intellectual trend in the sixteenth century that coupled love of classical learning, as in Renaissance humanism, with an emphasis on Christian piety.

Civil Code (625): The French legal code formulated by Napoleon in 1804; it ensured equal treatment under the law to all men and guaranteed religious liberty, but it curtailed many rights of women.

civil disobedience (843): The act of deliberately but peacefully breaking the law, a tactic used by Mohandas Gandhi in India and earlier by British suffragists to protest oppression and obtain political change.

classicism (510): A style of painting and architecture that reflected the ideals of the art of antiquity; in classicism, geometric shapes, order, and harmony of lines take precedence over the sensuous, exuberant, and emotional forms of the baroque.

cold war (880): The rivalry between the United States and the Soviet Union following World War II that led to massive growth in nuclear weapons on both sides.

Columbus, Christopher (421): An Italian sailor (1451–1506) who opened up the New World by sailing west across the Atlantic in search of a route to Asia.

communists (676): Those socialists who after 1840 (when the word was first used) advocated the abolition of private property in favor of communal, collective ownership.

Congress of Vienna (636): Face-to-face negotiations (1814–1815) between the great powers to settle the boundaries of European states and determine who would rule each nation after the defeat of Napoleon.

conservatism (638): A political doctrine that emerged after 1789 and rejected much of the Enlightenment and the French Revolution, preferring monarchies over republics, tradition over revolution, and established religion over Enlightenment skepticism.

constitutionalism (484): A system of government in which rulers share power with parliaments made up of elected representatives.

consumer revolution (528): The rapid increase in consumption of new staples produced in the Atlantic system as well as of other items of daily life that were previously unavailable or beyond the reach of ordinary people.

Continental System (631): The boycott of British goods in France and its satellites ordered by Napoleon in 1806; it had success but was later undermined by smuggling.

Corn Laws (674): Tariffs on grain in Great Britain that benefited landowners by preventing the import of cheap foreign grain; they were repealed by the British government in 1846.

Cortés, Hernán (425): A Spanish explorer (1485–1547) who captured the Aztec capital, Tenochtitlán (present-day Mexico City), in 1519.

Council of Trent (439): A general council of the Catholic church that met at Trent between 1545 and 1563 to set Catholic doctrine, reform church practices, and defend the church against the Protestant challenge.

Cuban missile crisis (910): The confrontation in 1962 between the United States and the USSR over Soviet installation of missile sites off the U.S. coast in Cuba.

cult of the offensive (803): A military strategy of constantly attacking the enemy that was believed to be the key to winning World War I but that brought great loss of life while failing to bring decisive victory.

Darwin, Charles (719): 1809–1882. English naturalist who popularized the theory of evolution and thereby challenged the biblical story of creation.

de-Christianization (603): During the French Revolution, the campaign of extremist republicans against organized churches and in favor of a belief system based on reason.

Declaration of the Rights of Man and Citizen (595): The preamble to the French constitution drafted in August 1789; it established the sovereignty of the nation and equal rights for citizens.

decolonization (897): The process—both violent and peaceful—by which colonies gained their independence from the imperial powers after World War II.

deists (559): Those who believe in God but give him no active role in human affairs. Deists of the Enlightenment believed that God had designed the universe and set it in motion but no longer intervened in its functioning.

DNA (919): The genetic material that forms the basis of each cell; the discovery of its structure in 1952 revolutionized genetics, molecular biology, and other scientific and medical fields.

domesticity (669): An ideology prevailing in the nineteenth century that women should devote themselves to their families and the home.

Dual Alliance (756): A defensive alliance between Germany and Austria-Hungary in 1879 as part of Bismarck's system of alliances to prevent or limit war. It was joined by Italy in 1882 as a third partner and then called the Triple Alliance.

dual monarchy (702): A shared power arrangement between the Habsburg Empire and Hungary after the Prussian defeat of the Austrian Empire in 1866–1867.

Duma (787): The Russian parliament set up in the aftermath of the outbreak of the Revolution of 1905.

Edict of Nantes (455): The decree issued by French king Henry IV in 1598 that granted the Huguenots a large measure of religious toleration.

Einstein, Albert (772): 1879–1955. Scientist whose theory of relativity revolutionized modern physics and other fields of thought.

Eliot, George (716): The pen name of English novelist Mary Ann Evans (1819–1880), who described the harsh reality of many ordinary people's lives in her works.

Elizabeth I (458): English queen (r. 1558–1603) who oversaw the return of the Protestant Anglican church and, in 1588, the successful defense of the realm against the Spanish Armada.

Enabling Act (848): The legislation passed in 1933 suspending constitutional government for four years in order to meet the crisis in the German economy.

enlightened despots (573): Rulers — such as Catherine the Great of Russia, Frederick the Great of Prussia, and Joseph II of Austria — who tried to promote reform without giving up their own supreme political power; also called enlightened absolutists.

Enlightenment (545): The eighteenth-century intellectual movement whose proponents believed that human beings could apply a critical, reasoning spirit to every problem.

Entente Cordiale (790): An alliance between Britain and France that began with an agreement in 1904 to honor colonial holdings.

Estates General (592): A body of deputies from the three estates, or orders, of France: the clergy (First Estate), the nobility (Second Estate), and everyone else (Third Estate).

ethnic cleansing (954): The mass murder — genocide — of people according to ethnicity or nationality, beginning with the post–World War I elimination of minorities in eastern and central Europe and continuing with the rape and murders that resulted from the breakup of Yugoslavia in the 1990s.

euro (961): The common currency accepted by twelve members of the European Union. It went into effect gradually, used first in business transactions in 1999 and entering public circulation in 2002.

European Economic Community (EEC or Common Market) (892): A consortium of six European countries established to promote free trade and economic cooperation among its members. Since its founding in 1957, its membership and activities have expanded.

European Union (EU) (961): Formerly the European Economic Community (EEC, or Common Market), and then the European Community (EC); formed in 1994 by the terms of the 1992 Maastricht Treaty. Its members have political ties through the European parliament as well as long-standing common economic, legal, and business mechanisms.

existentialism (903): A philosophy prominent after World War II developed primarily by Jean-Paul Sartre to stress the importance of action in the creation of an authentic self.

family allowance (853): Government funds given to families with children to boost the birthrate in totalitarian and democratic countries alike.

fascism (833): A doctrine that emphasized violence and glorified the state over the people and their individual or civil rights.

First Consul (622): The most important of the three consuls established by the French Constitution of 1800; the title, given to Napoleon Bonaparte, was taken from ancient Rome.

five-year plans (845): Centralized programs for economic development first used by Joseph Stalin and copied by Adolf Hitler; these plans set production priorities and gave production targets for individual industries and agriculture.

Fourteen Points (816): U.S. president Woodrow Wilson's World War I peace proposal; based on settlement rather than on conquest, it encouraged the surrender of the Central Powers.

Franco, Francisco (859): 1892–1975. Right-wing military leader who successfully overthrew the democratic republic in Spain and instituted a repressive dictatorship.

Frederick William of Hohenzollern (493): The Great Elector of Brandenburg-Prussia (r. 1640–1688) who brought his nation through the end of the Thirty Years' War and then succeeded in welding his scattered lands into an absolutist state.

Freemasons (568): Members of Masonic lodges, where nobles and middle-class professionals (and even some artisans) shared interest in the Enlightenment and reform.

Freud, Sigmund (769): 1856–1939. Viennese medical doctor and founder of psychoanalysis, a theory of mental processes and problems and a method of treating them.

Gladstone, William (752): 1809–1898. Liberal politician and prime minister of Great Britain who innovated in popular campaigning and who criticized British imperialism.

glasnost (943): Literally, "openness" or "publicity"; a policy instituted in the 1980s by Soviet premier Mikhail Gorbachev calling for greater openness in speech and in thinking, which translated to the reduction of censorship in publishing, radio, television, and other media.

globalization (952): The interconnection of labor, capital, ideas, services, and goods around the world. Although globalization has existed for hundreds of years, the late twentieth and early twenty-first centuries are seen as more global because of the speed with which people, goods, and ideas travel the world.

global warming (966): An increase in the temperature of the earth's lower atmosphere resulting from a buildup of chemical emissions.

Glorious Revolution (504): The events of 1688 when Tories and Whigs replaced England's monarch James II with his Protestant daughter, Mary, and her husband, Dutch ruler William of Orange; William and Mary agreed to a Bill of Rights that guaranteed rights to Parliament.

Gorbachev, Mikhail (943): Leader of the Soviet Union from 1985 to 1991; he instituted reforms such as glasnost and perestroika, thereby contributing to the collapse of Communist rule in the Soviet bloc and the USSR.

Great Fear (595): The term used by historians to describe the French rural panic of 1789, which led to peasant attacks on aristocrats or on seigneurial records of peasants' dues.

Green Party (966): A political party first formed in West Germany in 1979 to bring about environmentally sound policies. It spread across Europe and around the world thereafter.

heliocentrism (475): The view articulated by Polish clergyman Nicolaus Copernicus that the earth and planets revolve around the sun.

Henry VIII (433): The English king (r. 1509–1547) who first opposed the Protestant Reformation and then broke with the Catholic church, naming himself head of the Anglican church in the Act of Supremacy of 1534.

Hitler, Adolf (847): 1889–1945. Chancellor of Germany who, with considerable backing, overturned democratic government, created the Third Reich, persecuted millions, and ultimately led Germany and the world into World War II.

home rule (753): The right to an independent parliament demanded by the Irish and resisted by the British from the second half of the nineteenth century on.

ideology (654): A word coined during the French Revolution to refer to a coherent set of beliefs about the way the social and political order should be organized.

imperialism (670): European dominance of the non-West through economic exploitation and political rule; the word (as distinct from *colonialism*, which usually implied establishment of settler colonies, often with slavery) was coined in the mid-nineteenth century.

impressionism (749): A mid- to late-nineteenth-century artistic style that captured the sensation of light in images, derived from Japanese influences and in opposition to the realism of photographs.

Industrial Revolution (654): The transformation of life in the Western world over several decades in the late eighteenth and early nineteenth centuries as a result of the introduction of steam-driven machinery, large factories, and a new working class.

in vitro fertilization (921): A process developed in the 1970s by which eggs are fertilized with sperm outside the human body and then implanted in a woman's uterus.

Jacobin Club (599): A French political club formed in 1789 that inspired the formation of a national network whose members dominated the revolutionary government during the Terror.

Jesuits (439): Members of the Society of Jesus, a Catholic religious order founded by Ignatius of Loyola (1491–1556) and approved by the pope in 1540. Jesuits served as missionaries and educators all over the world.

Kennedy, John Fitzgerald (909): U.S. president, from 1961 to 1963, who faced off with Soviet leader Nikita Khrushchev in the Cuban missile crisis.

Khrushchev, Nikita (896): Leader of the USSR from c. 1955 until his dismissal in 1964; known for his speech denouncing Stalin, creation of the "thaw," and participation in the Cuban missile crisis.

Kollontai, Aleksandra (832): 1872–1952. Russian activist and minister of public welfare in the Bolshevik government; she promoted social programs such as birth control and day care for children of working parents.

Kulturkampf (718): Literally, "culture war"; in the 1870s, German chancellor Otto von Bismarck used the term to describe his fight to weaken the power of the Catholic church.

laissez-faire (561): An economic doctrine developed by Adam Smith that advocated freeing the economy from government intervention and control. (The term is French for "to leave alone.")

League of Nations (818): The international organization set up following World War I to maintain peace by arbitrating disputes and promoting collective security.

Lebensraum (858): Literally, "living space"; the land that Hitler proposed to conquer so that true Aryans might have sufficient space to live their noble lives.

Lenin, V. I. (811): 1870–1924. Bolshevik leader who executed the Bolshevik Revolution in the fall of 1917, took Russia out of World War I, and imposed communism in Russia.

Leopold II (734): King of Belgium (r. 1865–1909) who sponsored the takeover of the Congo in Africa, which he ran with great violence against native peoples.

Lepanto (455): A site off the Greek coast where, in 1571, the allied Catholic forces of Spain's king Philip II, Venice, and the papacy defeated the Ottoman Turks in a great sea battle; the victory gave the Christian powers control of the Mediterranean.

Levellers (499): Disgruntled soldiers in Cromwell's New Model Army who wanted to "level" social differences and extend political participation to all male property owners.

liberalism (674): An economic and political ideology that emphasized free trade and the constitutional guarantees of individual rights such as freedom of speech and religion.

limited liability corporation (730): A legal entity, developed in the second half of the nineteenth century, in which the amount that owners of a factory or other enterprise owed creditors was restricted (limited) in case of financial failure.

Louis XIV (484): French king (r. 1643–1715) who personified the absolutist ruler; in theory he shared his power with no one, but in practice he had to gain the cooperation of nobles, local officials, and even the ordinary subjects who manned his armies and paid his taxes.

Louis XVI (591): French King (r. 1774–1792) who was tried and found guilty of treason; he was executed on January 21, 1793.

Luther, Martin (429): A German monk (1483–1546) who started the Protestant Reformation in 1517 by challenging the practices and doctrines of the Catholic church and advocating salvation through faith alone.

Maastricht Treaty (961): The agreement among the members of the European Community to have a closer alliance, including the use of common passports and eventually the development of a common currency; by the terms of this treaty, the European Community became the European Union (EU) in 1994.

mandate system (819): The political control over the former colonies and territories of the German and Ottoman empires granted to the victors of World War I by the League of Nations.

Marie-Antoinette (591): Wife of Louis XVI and queen of France who was tried and executed in October 1793.

Marshall Plan (886): A post–World War II program funded by the United States to get Europe back on its feet economically and thereby reduce the appeal of communism. It played an important role in the rebirth of European prosperity in the 1950s.

Marxism (713): A body of thought about the organization of production, social inequality, and the processes of revolutionary change as devised by the philosopher and economist Karl Marx.

Mazzini, Giuseppe (672): An Italian nationalist (1805–1872) who founded Young Italy, a secret society to promote Italian unity. He believed that a popular uprising would create a unified Italy.

mercantilism (490): The doctrine that governments must intervene to increase national wealth by whatever means possible.

mestizo (527): A person born to a Spanish father and a native American mother.

Methodism (566): A religious movement founded by John Wesley (1703–1791) that broke with the Anglican church in Great Britain and insisted on strict self-discipline and a "methodical" approach to religious study and observance.

Metternich, Klemens von (636): An Austrian prince (1773–1859) who took the lead in devising the settlement arranged by the Congress of Vienna.

Milosevic, Slobodan (953): Serb leader of post-Communist Yugoslavia; he was tried for crimes against humanity in the ethnic cleansing that accompanied the dissolution of the Yugoslav state.

mir (695): A Russian farm community that provided for holding land in common and regulating the movements of any individual by the group.

Mitteleuropa (791): Literally, "central Europe," but used by military leaders in Germany before World War I to refer to land in both central and eastern Europe that they hoped to acquire.

modernism (771): Artistic styles around the turn of the twentieth century that featured a break with realism in art and literature and with lyricism in music.

Morrison, Toni (979): The first African American woman to win the Nobel Prize for Literature; her works include *Beloved* and *Jazz*.

multinational corporation (921): A business that operates in many foreign countries by sending large segments of its manufacturing, finance, sales, and other business components abroad.

Mussolini, Benito (833): 1883–1945. Leader of Italian fascist movement and, after the March on Rome in 1922, dictator of Italy.

nationalism (672): An ideology that arose in the nineteenth century and that holds that all peoples derive their identities from their nations, which are defined by common language, shared cultural traditions, and sometimes religion.

nation-state (696): A sovereign political entity of modern times based on representing a united people.

Nazi-Soviet Pact (861): The agreement reached in 1939 by Germany and the Soviet Union in which both agreed not to attack the other in case of war and to divide any conquered territories.

neoliberalism (941): A theory first promoted by British prime minister Margaret Thatcher, calling for a return to liberal principles of the nineteenth century, including the reduction of welfare-state programs and the cutting of taxes for the wealthy to promote economic growth.

new unionism (751): Nineteenth-century development in labor organizing that replaced local craft-based unions with those that extended membership to all kinds of workers.

new woman (767): A woman who, from the 1880s on, dressed practically, moved about freely, and often supported herself.

Nicholas II (779): Tsar of Russia (r. 1894–1917) who promoted anti-Semitism and resisted reform in the empire.

Nietzsche, Friedrich (772): 1844–1900. German philosopher who called for a new morality in the face of the death of God at the hands of science and whose theories were reworked by his sister to emphasize militarism and anti-Semitism.

Nixon, Richard (936): U.S. president from 1969 to 1974 who escalated the Vietnam War, worked for accommodation with China, and resigned from the presidency after trying to block free elections.

nongovernmental organizations (NGOs) (965): Charitable foundations and activist groups such as Doctors Without Borders that work outside of governments, often on political, economic, and relief issues; also, philanthropic organizations such as the Rockefeller, Ford, and Open Society Foundations that shape economic and social policy and the course of political reform.

North Atlantic Treaty Organization (NATO) (887): The security alliance formed in 1949 to provide a unified military force for the United States, Canada, and their allies in western Europe and Scandinavia.

Nuremberg Laws (850): Legislation enacted by the Nazis in 1935 that deprived Jewish Germans of their citizenship and imposed many other hardships on them.

Opium War (671): War between China and Great Britain (1839–1842) that resulted in the opening of four Chinese ports to Europeans and British sovereignty over Hong Kong.

Organization of Petroleum Exporting Countries (OPEC) (937): A consortium that regulated the supply and export of oil and that acted with more unanimity after the United States supported Israel against the Arabs in the wars of the late 1960s and early 1970s.

Ostpolitik (928): A policy initiated by Willy Brandt in the late 1960s in which West Germany sought better economic relations with the Communist countries of eastern Europe.

outwork (727): The process of having some aspects of industrial work done outside factories in individual homes.

Pacific tigers (973): Countries of East Asia so named because of their massive economic growth, much of it from the 1980s on; foremost among these were Japan and China.

Pankhurst, Emmeline (778): 1858–1928. Organizer of a militant branch of the British suffrage movement, working actively for women's right to vote.

Pan-Slavism (702): A movement in the nineteenth century for the unity of all Slavs across national and regional boundaries.

Parnell, Charles Stewart (753): Irish politician (1846–1891) whose advocacy of home rule was a thorn in the side of the British establishment.

partition of Poland, first (576): Division of one-third of Poland-Lithuania's territory between Prussia, Russia, and Austria in 1772.

Peace of Augsburg (446): The treaty of 1555 that settled disputes between Holy Roman Emperor Charles V and his Protestant princes. It recognized the Lutheran church and established the principle that all Catholic or Lutheran princes enjoyed the sole right to determine the religion of their lands and subjects.

Peace of Paris (816): The series of peace treaties that provided the settlement of World War I.

Peace of Utrecht (538): Treaties drawn up in 1713–1714 that ended the War of the Spanish Succession.

Peace of Westphalia (463): The settlement (1648) of the Thirty Years' War; it established enduring religious divisions in the Holy Roman Empire by which Lutheranism would dominate in the north, Calvinism in the area of the Rhine River, and Catholicism in the south.

perestroika (943): Literally, "restructuring"; an economic policy instituted in the 1980s by Soviet premier Mikhail Gorbachev calling for the introduction of market mechanisms and the achievement of greater efficiency in manufacturing, agriculture, and services.

Peter the Great (540): Russian tsar Peter I (r. 1689–1725), who undertook the Westernization of Russia and built a new capital city named after himself, St. Petersburg.

Philip II (455): King of Spain (r. 1556–1598) and the most powerful ruler in Europe; he reigned over the western Habsburg lands and all the Spanish colonies recently settled in the New World.

philosophes (556): Public intellectuals of the Enlightenment who wrote on subjects ranging from current affairs to art criticism with the goal of furthering reform in society. (The word in French means "philosophers.")

Pietism (536): A Protestant revivalist movement of the early eighteenth century that emphasized deeply emotional individual religious experience.

plantation (521): A large tract of land that produced staple crops such as sugar, coffee, and tobacco; was farmed by slave labor; and was owned by a colonial settler.

politiques (455): Political advisers during the sixteenth-century French Wars of Religion who argued that compromise in matters of religion would strengthen the monarchy.

pop art (925): A style in the visual arts that mimicked advertising and consumerism and that used ordinary objects as a part of paintings and other compositions.

Popular Front (854): An alliance of political parties (initially led by Léon Blum in France) in the 1930s to resist fascism despite philosophical differences.

positivism (720): A theory developed in the mid-nineteenth century that the study of facts would generate accurate, or "positive," laws of society and that these laws could, in turn, help in the formulation of policies and legislation.

postmodernism (980): A term applied in the late twentieth century to both an intense stylistic mixture in the arts without a central unifying theme or elite set of standards and a critique of Enlightenment and scientific beliefs in rationality and the possibility of certain knowledge.

predestination (432): John Calvin's doctrine that God preordained salvation or damnation for each person before creation; those chosen for salvation were considered the "elect."

Pugachev rebellion (579): A massive revolt of Russian Cossacks and serfs in 1773 against local nobles and the armies of Catherine the Great; its leader, Emelian Pugachev, was eventually captured and executed.

pump priming (849): An economic policy used by governments to stimulate the economy through public works programs and other infusions to public funds.

purges (846): The series of attacks on citizens of the USSR accused of being "wreckers," or saboteurs of communism, in the 1930s and later.

Puritans (458): Strict Calvinists who opposed all vestiges of Catholic ritual in the Church of England.

Putin, Vladimir (956): President of Russia elected in 2000; he has worked to reestablish Russia as a world power through control of the country's resources and military capabilities.

raison d'état (464): French for "reason of state," the political doctrine, first proposed by Cardinal Richelieu of France, which held that the state's interests should prevail over those of religion.

Razin, Stenka (496): The head of a powerful band of pirates and outlaws in southern Russia, who in 1667 led a rebellion that promised peasants liberation from noble landowners and officials; Razin was captured by the tsar's army in 1671 and publicly executed in Moscow.

realism (715): An artistic style that arose in the mid-nineteenth century and was dedicated to depicting society realistically without romantic or idealistic overtones.

Realpolitik (690): Policies developed after the revolutions of 1848 and initially associated with nation building; they were based on realism rather than on the romantic notions of earlier nationalists. The term has come to mean any policy based on considerations of power alone.

Reform Act of 1884 (752): British legislation that granted the right to vote to a mass male citizenry.

Reform Bill of 1832 (649): A measure passed by the British Parliament to increase the number of male voters by about 50 percent and give representation to new cities in the north; it set a precedent for widening suffrage.

restoration (638): The epoch after the fall of Napoleon, in which the Congress of Vienna aimed to "restore" as many regimes as possible to their former rulers.

revocation of the Edict of Nantes (489): French king Louis XIV's decision to eliminate the rights of Calvinists granted in the edict of 1598; Louis banned all Calvinist public activities and forced those who refused to embrace the state religion to flee.

Robespierre, Maximilien (600): A lawyer from northern France who laid out the principles of a republic of virtue and of the Terror; his arrest and execution in July 1794 brought an end to the Terror.

rococo (534): A style of painting that emphasized irregularity and asymmetry, movement and curvature, but on a smaller, more intimate scale than the baroque.

romanticism (566): An artistic movement of the late eighteenth and early nineteenth centuries that glorified nature, emotion, genius, and imagination.

Rousseau, Jean-Jacques (561): One of the most important philosophes (1712–1778); he argued that only a government based on a social contract among the citizens could make people truly moral and free.

Rushdie, Salman (979): Immigrant British author, whose novel *The Satanic Verses* led the Ayotallah Ruhollah Khomeini of Iran to issue a fatwa calling for Rushdie's murder.

Russification (696): A program for the integration of Russia's many nationality groups that involved the forced learning of the Russian language and the practice of Russian Orthodox religion as well as the settlement of ethnic Russians among other nationality groups.

salon (513): An informal gathering held regularly in private homes and presided over by a socially eminent woman; salons spread from France in the seventeenth century to other countries in the eighteenth century.

samizdat (928): A key form of dissident activity across the Soviet bloc; individuals reproduced uncensored publications by hand and passed them from reader to reader, thus building a foundation for the successful resistance of the 1980s.

Sand, George (666): The pen name of French novelist Amandine-Aurore Dupin (1804–1876), who showed her independence in the 1830s by dressing like a man and smoking cigars. The term *George-Sandism* became an expression of disdain for independent women.

Schlieffen Plan (803): The Germans' strategy in World War I that called for attacks on two fronts—concentrating first on France to the west and then turning east to attack Russia.

scientific method (475): The combination of experimental observation and mathematical deduction that was used to determine the laws of nature and became the secular standard of truth.

Scott, Sir Walter (643): A prolific author (1771–1832) of popular historical novels; he also collected and published traditional Scottish ballads and wrote poetry.

Second International (751): A transnational organization of workers established in 1889, mostly committed to Marxian socialism.

secularization (471): The trend toward making religious faith a private domain rather than one directly connected to state power and science; it prompted a search for nonreligious explanations for political authority and natural phenomena.

Seven Years' War (574): A worldwide series of battles (1756–1763) between Austria, France, Russia, and Sweden on one side and Prussia and Great Britain on the other.

social contract (504): The doctrine that all political authority derives not from divine right but from an implicit contract between citizens and their rulers.

socialism (675): A social and political ideology that advocated the reorganization of society to overcome the new tensions created by industrialization and restore social harmony through communities based on cooperation.

Solidarity (945): A Polish labor union founded in 1980 by Lech Walesa and Anna Walentynowicz that contested Communist Party programs and eventually succeeded in ousting the party from the Polish government.

South African War (785): The war between Britain and the Boer (originally Dutch) inhabitants of South Africa for control of the region (1899–1902); also called the Boer War.

soviets (811): Councils of workers and soldiers first formed in Russia in the Revolution of 1905; they were revived to represent the people in the early days of the 1917 Russian Revolution.

stagflation (938): The combination of a stagnant economy and soaring inflation; a period of stagflation occurred in the West in the 1970s as a result of an OPEC embargo on oil.

Stalin, Joseph (844): 1879–1953. Leader of the USSR who, with considerable backing, formed a brutal dictatorship and forcefully converted the country into an industrial power.

Suleiman the Magnificent (443): Sultan of the Ottoman Empire (r. 1520–1566) at the time of its greatest power.

Terror (600): The policy established under the direction of the Committee of Public Safety during the French Revolution to arrest dissidents and execute opponents in order to protect the republic from its enemies.

Thatcher, Margaret (940): Prime minister of Britain from 1979 to 1990; she set a new tone for British politics by promoting neoliberal economic policies and criticizing poor people, union members, and racial minorities as worthless, even harmful citizens.

Thermidorian Reaction (606): The violent backlash against the rule of Robespierre that dismantled the Terror and punished Jacobins and their supporters.

Third Republic (753): The government that succeeded Napoleon III's Second Empire after its defeat in the Franco-Prussian War of 1870–1871. It lasted until France's defeat by Germany in 1940.

total war (800): A war built on the full mobilization of soldiers, civilians, and technology of the nations involved. The term also refers to a highly destructive war of ideologies.

Truman Doctrine (884): The United States's policy to limit communism after World War II by countering political crises with economic and military aid.

United Nations (UN) (901): An organization set up in 1945 for collective security and for the resolution of international conflicts through both deliberation and the use of force.

Vatican II (903): A Catholic Council held between 1962 and 1965 to modernize some aspects of church teachings (such as condemnation of Jews), to update the liturgy, and to promote cooperation among the faiths (i.e., ecumenism).

Voltaire (548): The pen name of François-Marie Arouet (1694–1778), who was the most influential writer of the early Enlightenment.

Walpole, Robert (539): The first, or "prime," minister of the House of Commons of Great Britain's Parliament. Although appointed initially by the king, through his long period of leadership (1721–1742) he effectively established the modern pattern of parliamentary government.

war guilt clause (818): The part of the Treaty of Versailles that assigned blame for World War I to Germany.

Warsaw Pact (887): A security alliance of the Soviet Union and its allies formed in 1955 when NATO admitted West Germany.

Weimar Republic (815): The parliamentary republic established in 1919 in Germany to replace the monarchy.

welfare state (893): A system comprising government-sponsored programs aimed to bring economic democracy by providing health care, family allowances, and pensions for veterans and retired workers.

Westernization (540): The effort, especially in Peter the Great's Russia, to make society and social customs resemble counterparts in western Europe, especially France, Britain, and the Dutch Republic.

William, prince of Orange (504): Dutch ruler who, with his Protestant wife, Mary (daughter of James II), ruled England after the Glorious Revolution of 1688.

Zionism (783): A movement that began in the late nineteenth century among European Jews to found a Jewish state.

Suggested References

CHAPTER 14

Widening Horizons

The study of European voyages of exploration and conquest has been reshaped by a more global historical perspective, which pays as much attention to indigenous peoples' reactions to the newcomers as it does to the conditions experienced by the Europeans.

Buisseret, David. *The Mapmakers' Quest: Depicting New Worlds in Renaissance Europe*. 2003.
Christopher Columbus: **http://www.ibiblio.org/expo/1492.exhibit/ Intro.html**
Crosby, Alfred. *The Colombian Exchange: Biological and Cultural Consequences of 1492*. 1972.
Fritze, Ronald. *New Worlds: The Great Voyages of Discovery, 1400–1600*. 2005.
Subrahmanyam, Sanjay. *The Career and Legend of Vasco da Gama*. 1997.
*Symcox, Geoffrey, and Blair Sullivan. *Christopher Columbus and the Enterprise of the Indies: A Brief History with Documents*. 2005.

The Protestant Reformation

While continuing to refine our understanding of the leading Protestant reformers, recent scholars have also offered new interpretations that take into consideration the popular impact of the reformers' teachings.

Bernard, G. W. *The King's Reformation: Henry VIII and the Remaking of the English Church*. 2005.
Eisenstein, Elizabeth. *The Printing Revolution in Early Modern Europe*. 2005.
Essential Works of Erasmus. Ed. W. T. H. Jackson. 1965.
*Hillerbrand, Hans J., ed. *The Protestant Reformation*. 1969.
Hsia, R. Po-chia, ed. *Cambridge History of Christianity*. Vol. 6, *Reform and Expansion 1500–1660*. 2006.
Jardine, Lisa. *Erasmus: Man of Letters*. 1993.
Martin Luther's writings: **http://www.ctsfw.edu/etext/luther**
Rublack, Ulinka. *Reformation Europe*. 2005.

Reshaping Society through Religion

The most important trend in recent scholarship has been the consideration of the impact of the Reformation on society and culture. Many studies have shown the limited influence of the ideas of reformers; others document the persistence of traditional religious habits and practices well past the sixteenth century.

Bagchi, David, and David Steinmetz. *The Cambridge Companion to Reformation Theology*. 2004.
Collinson, Patrick. *The Reformation: A History*. 2004.

Koenigsberger, H. B. *Early Modern Europe 1500–1789*. 1999.
Marshall, Sherrin, ed. *Women in Reformation and Counter-Reformation Europe: Public and Private Worlds*. 1989.
*Müntzer, Thomas. *Revelation and Revolution: Basic Writings of Thomas Müntzer*. 1993.
O'Malley, John W. *Trent and All That*. 2000.
Wiesner, Merry. *Christianity and the Regulation of Sexuality in the Early Modern World*. 2000.

A Struggle for Mastery

Still focused on the struggle between the Habsburg and Valois dynasties, historical scholarship has also moved out in the direction of cultural and military history.

*Guicciardini, Francesco. *The History of Italy*. Trans. Sidney Alexander. 1969.
Kleinschmidt, Harald. *Charles V: The World Emperor*. 2004.
Levin, Carole, Debra Barrett-Graves, and Jo Eldridge Carney, eds. *"High and Mighty Queens" of Early Modern England: Realities and Representations*. 2003.
MacHardy, Karin. *War, Religion, and Court Patronage in Habsburg Austria, 1521–1622*. 2003.
Shaw, Christine, ed. *Italy and the European Powers: The Impact of War, 1500–1530*. 2006.
Tanner, Marie. *The Last Descendant of Aeneas: The Hapsburgs and the Mythic Image of the Emperor*. 1993.

CHAPTER 15

Religious Conflicts and State Power, 1560–1618

The personalities of rulers such as Elizabeth I of England and Philip II of Spain remain central to the religious and political conflicts of this period.

Benedict, Philip. *Christ's Churches Purely Reformed: A Social History of Calvinism*. 2002.
Elizabeth I: **http://englishhistory.net/tudor/monarchs/eliz1.html**
Holt, Mack P. *The French Wars of Religion, 1562–1629*. 1995.
Kamen, Henry. *Spain, 1469–1714: A Society of Conflict*. 2005.
Mattingly, Garrett. *The Defeat of the Spanish Armada*. 2nd ed. 1988.
Philip II: **http://www.historylearningsite.co.uk/Phillip.htm**
*Pryor, Felix. *Elizabeth I: Her Life in Letters*. 2003.

The Thirty Years' War, 1618–1648

As ethnic conflicts erupt again in eastern Europe, historians have traced their roots back to the intertwined religious, ethnic, and dynastic struggles of the Thirty Years' War.

*Primary source.

Bonney, Richard. *The Thirty Years' War 1618–1648*. 2002.

Parker, Geoffrey. *The Military Revolution: Military Innovation and the Rise of the West, 1500–1800*. 1996.

Parrott, David. *Richelieu's Army: War, Government and Society in France, 1624–1642*. 2001.

Pursell, Brennan C. *The Winter King: Frederick V of the Palatinate and the Coming of the Thirty Years' War*. 2003.

Economic Crisis and Realignment

Painstaking archival research has enabled historians to reconstruct the demographic, economic, and social history of the period discussed in this chapter. Recently, attention has shifted to the competition for empire in the New World.

Ashton, Trevor H., ed. *Crisis in Europe*. 1965.

Braudel, Fernand. *The Mediterranean and the Mediterranean World in the Age of Philip the Second*. 2 vols. Trans. Siân Reynolds. 1972–1973.

*Greer, Allan, ed. *Jesuit Relations: Natives and Missionaries in Seventeenth-Century North America*. 2000.

Seymour, M. J. *The Transformation of the North Atlantic World, 1492–1763: An Introduction*. 2004.

Wiesner, Merry E. *Women and Gender in Early Modern Europe*. 2nd ed. 2000.

The Rise of Secular and Scientific Worldviews

The transformation of intellectual and cultural life has long fascinated scholars. Recent works have developed a new kind of study called microhistory, which focuses on one person (like Ginzburg's Italian miller).

Briggs, Robin. *Witches & Neighbors: The Social and Cultural Context of European Witchcraft*. 1996.

The Galileo Project: **http://riceinfo.rice.edu/ Galileo**

Ginzburg, Carlo. *The Cheese and the Worms: The Cosmos of a Sixteenth-Century Miller*. Trans. John Tedeschi and Anne Tedeschi. 1992.

Isaac Newton: **http://www.newtonproject.ic.ac.uk/prism.php?id'1**

Thomas, Keith. *Religion and the Decline of Magic*. 1971.

CHAPTER 16

Louis XIV: Absolutism and Its Limits

Recent studies have insisted that absolutism could never be entirely absolute because the king depended on collaboration and cooperation to enforce his policies. Some of the best sources for Louis XIV's reign are the letters written by important noblewomen.

*Beik, William. *Louis XIV and Absolutism: A Brief Study with Documents*. 2000.

*Forster, Elborg, trans. *A Woman's Life in the Court of the Sun King: Elisabeth Charlotte, Duchesse d'Orléans*. 1984.

Rowlands, Guy. *The Dynastic State and the Army under Louis XIV: Royal Service and Private Interest, 1661 to 1701*. 2002.

*Sévigné, Madame de. *Selected Letters*. Trans. Leonard Tancock. 1982.

Treasure, G. R. R. *Louis XIV*. 2001.

Versailles: **http://www.chateauversailles.fr**

Absolutism in Central and Eastern Europe

Too often central and eastern European forms of state development have been characterized as backward in comparison with those of western Europe. Now historians emphasize the patterns of ruler-elite cooperation shared with western Europe, but they also underscore the weight of serfdom in eastern economies and political systems.

Barkey, Karen. *The Ottoman Route to State Centralization*. 1994.

Çiçek, Kemal, ed. *The Great Ottoman-Turkish Civilisation*. 4 vols. 2000.

Kotilaine, Jarmo, and Marshall Poe, eds. *Modernizing Muscovy: Reform and Social Change in Seventeenth-Century Russia*. 2004.

Vierhaus, Rudolf. *Germany in the Age of Absolutism*. Trans. Jonathan B. Knudsen. 1988.

Wilson, Peter H. *German Armies: War and German Politics, 1648–1806*. 1998.

Constitutionalism in England

Though recent interpretations of the English revolutions emphasize the limits on radical change, Hill's portrayal of the radical ferment of ideas remains fundamental.

Cromwell: **http://www.olivercromwell.org**

*Graham, Elspeth, et al., eds. *Her Own Life: Autobiographical Writings by Seventeenth-Century English Women*. 1989.

*Haller, William, and Godfrey Davies, eds. *The Leveller Tracts, 1647–1653*. 1944.

Hill, Christopher. *The World Turned Upside Down: Radical Ideas during the English Revolution*. 1972.

*Pincus, Steven C. A. *England's Glorious Revolution, 1688–1689*. 2006.

Outposts of Constitutionalism

Studies of the Dutch Republic emphasize the importance of trade and consumerism. Recent work on the colonies has begun to explore the intersecting experiences of settlers, native Americans, and African slaves.

France in America: **http://international.loc.gov/intldl/fiahtml/ fiatheme.html#track1**

Gragg, Larry. *Englishmen Transplanted: The English Colonization of Barbados, 1627–1660*. 2003.

Price, J. L. *The Dutch Republic in the Seventeenth Century*. 1998.

Schama, Simon. *The Embarrassment of Riches: An Interpretation of Dutch Culture in the Golden Age*. 1988.

Thornton, John. *Africa and Africans in the Making of the Atlantic World, 1400–1800*. 1992.

The Search for Order in Elite and Popular Culture

Historians do not always agree about the meaning of popular culture: Was it something widely shared by all social classes or a set of activities increasingly identified with the lower classes, as Burke argues? Was discipline of the lower classes increasing as members of the court learned the new emphasis on manners, as Elias argues?

Burke, Peter. *Popular Culture in Early Modern Europe*. 1978.

Davis, Natalie Zemon. *Women on the Margins: Three Seventeenth-Century Lives*. 1995.

*Primary source.

Elias, Norbert. *The Civilizing Process.* Trans. Edmund Jephcott. 2000.

*Fitzmaurice, James, ed. *Margaret Cavendish: Sociable Letters.* 1997.

*Molière (Jean-Baptiste Poquelin). *The Bourgeois [Middle-Class] Gentleman.* Trans. Bernard Sahlins. 2000.

CHAPTER 17

The Atlantic System and the World Economy

It is easier to find sources on individual parts of the system than on the workings of the interlocking trade as a whole, but work has been rapidly increasing in this area. The Dunn book remains one of the classic studies of how the plantation system took root.

Blackburn, Robin. *The Making of New World Slavery: From the Baroque to the Modern, 1492–1800.* 1997.

Dunn, Richard S. *Sugar and Slaves: The Rise of the Planter Class in the English West Indies, 1624–1713.* 1972.

Harms, Robert. *The Diligent: A Voyage Through the Worlds of the Slave Trade.* 2003.

McKendrick, Neil, John Brewer, and J. H. Plumb. *The Birth of a Consumer Society: The Commercialization of Eighteenth-Century England.* 1982.

Slave movement during the eighteenth and nineteenth centuries: **http://dpls.dacc.wisc.edu/slavedata**

New Social and Cultural Patterns

Many of the novels of the early eighteenth century provide fascinating insights into the development of new social attitudes and customs. In particular, see Daniel Defoe's *Robinson Crusoe* (1719) and *Moll Flanders* (1722); the many novels of Eliza Haywood; and Antoine François Prévost's *Manon Lescaut* (1731), a French psychological novel about a nobleman's fatal love for an unfaithful woman, which became the basis for an opera in the nineteenth century.

Earle, Peter. *The Making of the English Middle Class: Business, Society, and Family Life in London, 1660–1730.* 1989.

Eighteenth-Century Resources: **http://andromeda.rutgers.edu/ ~jlynch/18th/index.html**

Handel's Messiah: The New Interactive Edition. CD-ROM. 1997.

Roche, Daniel. *The People of Paris: An Essay in Popular Culture in the Eighteenth Century.* Trans. Marie Evans. 1987.

Consolidation of the European State System

Studies of rulers and states can be supplemented by works on public health.

Black, Jeremy, ed. *The Origins of War in Early Modern Europe.* 1987.

Brewer, John. *The Sinews of Power: War, Money, and the English State, 1688–1783.* 1990.

Brockliss, Laurence, and Colin Jones. *The Medical World of Early Modern France.* 1997.

Cracraft, James. *The Petrine Revolution in Russian Culture.* 2004.

Hughes, Lindsey. *Peter the Great: A Biography.* 2002.

Porter, Roy. *Madness: A Brief History.* 2002.

War of the Spanish Succession: **http://www.historyworld.net/wrldhis/ PlainTextHistories.asp?historyid=ad06**

The Birth of the Enlightenment

The definitive study of the early Enlightenment is the book by Hazard, but many others have contributed biographies of individual figures or, more recently, studies of women writers.

Besterman, Theodore. *Voltaire.* 1969.

Grendy, Isobel. *Lady Mary Wortley Montagu.* 1999.

Hazard, Paul. *The European Mind: The Critical Years, 1680–1715.* 1990.

*Hill, Bridget, ed. *The First English Feminist: Reflections upon Marriage and Other Writings by Mary Astell.* 1986.

*Jacob, Margaret C. *The Enlightenment: A Brief History with Selected Readings.* 2000.

Women Writers Online: **http://www.wwp.brown.edu/texts/wwoentry .html**

CHAPTER 18

The Enlightenment at Its Height

The interpretive study by Gay remains useful even though it is over thirty years old, but the Kors volumes give the most up-to-date views. The Lessing play focuses on the question of toleration for the Jews.

*Allison, Robert J., ed. *The Interesting Narrative of the Life of Olaudah Equiano (Written by Himself).* 2nd ed. 2006.

Gay, Peter. *The Enlightenment: An Interpretation.* 2 vols. 1966, 1969.

Immanuel Kant: **http://www.manchester.edu/kant**

Kors, Alan Charles, ed. *Encyclopedia of the Enlightenment.* 4 vols. 2003.

*Lessing, Gotthold Ephraim. *Nathan the Wise.* Ed. Ronald Schechter. 2004.

Porter, Roy. *The Creation of the Modern World: The Untold Story of the British Enlightenment.* 2000.

*Voltaire. *Candide.* Ed. and trans. Daniel Gordon. 1999.

Society and Culture in an Age of Enlightenment

Recent work has drawn attention to the lives of ordinary people. The personal journal of the French glassworker Ménétra is a rarity: it offers extensive documentation of the inner life of an ordinary person during the Enlightenment. Ménétra claimed to have met Rousseau. Even if not true, the claim shows that Rousseau's fame was not limited to the upper classes.

Darnton, Robert. *The Great Cat Massacre and Other Episodes in French Cultural History.* 1984.

Hull, Isabel V. *Sexuality, State, and Civil Society in Germany, 1700–1815.* 1996.

*Ménétra, Jacques Louis. *Journal of My Life.* Trans. Arthur Goldhammer. Intro. Daniel Roche. 1986.

Mozart Project: **http://www.mozartproject.org**

Smith, Douglas. *Working the Rough Stone: Freemasonry and Society in Eighteenth-Century Russia.* 1999.

Stone, Lawrence. *The Family, Sex, and Marriage in England, 1500–1800.* Abridged ed. 1979.

State Power in an Era of Reform

Biographies and general histories of this period tend to overemphasize the individual decisions of rulers. Although these decisions are incontestably important, the relentless growth of armies impacted virtually every European society.

*Primary source.

Blanning, T. C. W. *Joseph II and Enlightened Despotism.* 1994.
Catherine the Great: **http://russia.nypl.org/level4.html**
*Frederick II, King of Prussia. *Frederick the Great on the Art of War.* Ed. and trans. Jay Luvaas. 1999.
Gorbatov, Inna. *Catherine the Great and the French Philosophers of the Enlightenment: Montesquieu, Voltaire, Rousseau, Diderot and Grimm.* 2006.
Showalter, Dennis E. *The Wars of Frederick the Great.* 1996.
Venturi, Franco. *The End of the Old Regime in Europe, 1768–1776: The First Crisis.* Trans. R. Burr Litchfield. 1989.

Rebellions against State Power

Historians have recently shown great interest in the riots and rebellions of this era, but most have focused on one national case. Palmer's overview of political movements therefore remains valuable for its comparative aspects.

Alexander, John T. *Autocratic Politics in a National Crisis: The Imperial Russian Government and Pugachev's Revolt, 1773–1775.* 1969.
Cash, Arthur H. *John Wilkes: The Scandalous Father of Civil Liberty.* 2006.
Palmer, R. R. *The Age of Democratic Revolution: A Political History of Europe and America, 1760–1800.* Vol. 1, *The Challenge.* 1959.
*Rakove, Jack N. *Declaring Rights: A Brief History with Documents.* 1998.
Thompson, E. P. *Whigs and Hunters: The Origin of the Black Act.* 1975.
John Wilkes: **http://www.spartacus.schoolnet.co.uk/PRwilkes.htm**

CHAPTER 19

The Revolutionary Wave, 1787–1789

In the 1950s and 1960s, historians debated vehemently about whether the French Revolution should be considered part of a more general phenomenon of Atlantic revolutions, as R. R. Palmer argues. The most influential book on the meaning of the French Revolution is still the classic study by Tocqueville, who insisted that the Revolution continued the process of state centralization undertaken by the monarchy.

*Censer, Jack R., and Lynn Hunt. *Liberty, Equality, Fraternity: Exploring the French Revolution.* 2001. (Includes a CD-ROM with images, songs, and documents.) See also the accompanying Web site: **http://www.chnm.gmu.edu/revolution**
Lefebvre, Georges. *The Coming of the French Revolution.* Trans. with a new preface, R. R. Palmer. 1989.
Palmer, R. R. *The Age of the Democratic Revolution: A Political History of Europe and America, 1760–1800.* Vol. 2, *The Struggle.* 1964.
Polasky, Janet L. *Revolution in Brussels, 1787–1793.* 1987.
Te Brake, Wayne. *Regents and Rebels: The Revolutionary World of an Eighteenth-Century Dutch City.* 1989.
Tocqueville, Alexis de. *The Old Regime and the French Revolution.* Trans. Stuart Gilbert. 1955. Originally published 1856.

From Monarchy to Republic, 1789–1793

From 1789 onward, commentators on the French Revolution have differed over its meaning: Was it a struggle for human rights and democracy or a dangerous experiment in implementing reason and destroying religion and tradition? Among the most important

additions to the debate have been new works on women, Jews, Protestants, and slaves.

*Hunt, Lynn, ed. *The French Revolution and Human Rights: A Brief Documentary History.* 1996.
*Levy, Darline Gay, Harriet Branson Applewhite, and Mary Durham Johnson, eds. *Women in Revolutionary Paris, 1789–1795.* 1979.
Schama, Simon. *Citizens: A Chronicle of the French Revolution.* 1989.
*Two Classics of the French Revolution: *Reflections on the Revolution in France* (Edmund Burke) *and* The Rights of Man (Thomas Paine). 1973.
*Wollstonecraft, Mary. *A Vindication of the Rights of Woman.* Ed. Miriam Brody. 1992.

Terror and Resistance

The most controversial episode in the French Revolution has, not surprisingly, provoked conflicting interpretations. Not to be overlooked, however, are studies of broader underlying processes, such as Desan's study of women and the family.

Andress, David. *The Terror: The Merciless War for Freedom in Revolutionary France.* 2006.
Desan, Suzanne. *The Family on Trial in Revolutionary France.* 2004.
Furet, François. *Interpreting the French Revolution.* Trans. Elborg Forster. 1981.
Hunt, Lynn. *Politics, Culture, and Class in the French Revolution.* 1984.
Palmer, R. R. *Twelve Who Ruled: The Year of the Terror in the French Revolution.* 1989.
Scurr, Ruth. *Fatal Purity: Robespierre and the French Revolution.* 2006.

Revolution on the March

In the past, controversy about the Revolution in France raged while its influence on other places was relatively neglected. This imbalance is now being redressed.

Blanning, T. C. W. *The French Revolutionary Wars, 1787–1802.* 1996.
Dubois, Laurent. *Avengers of the New World: The Story of the Haitian Revolution.* 2004.
———, and John D. Garrigus. *Slave Revolution in the Caribbean, 1789–1804: A Brief History with Documents.* 2006.
Haitian Revolution: **http://www.ci.miami.fl.us/haiti2004/history.htm**
Irish Rebellion of 1798: **http://www.iol.ie/~98com**
Elliot, Marianne. *Partners in Revolution: The United Irishmen and France.* 1982.
Forrest, Alan I. *The Soldiers of the French Revolution.* 1990.

CHAPTER 20

The Rise of Napoleon Bonaparte

Much has been written about Napoleon as a military leader, but only recently has his regime within France attracted interest. Historians now emphasize the mixed quality of Napoleon's rule. He carried forward some revolutionary innovations and halted others.

*Arnold, Eric A., Jr., ed. *A Documentary Survey of Napoleonic France.* 1994.
*Blaufarb, Rafe. *Napoleon: A Symbol for an Age. A Brief History with Documents.* 2008.
Englund, Steven. *Napoleon: A Political Life.* 2004.

*Primary source.

Kafker, Frank A., and James M. Laux. *Napoleon and His Times: Selected Interpretations.* 1992.

Napoleon Foundation: **http://www.napoleon.org**

Wilson-Smith, Timothy. *Napoleon and His Artists.* 1996.

Woloch, Isser. *Napoleon and His Collaborators: The Making of a Dictatorship.* 2001.

"Europe Was at My Feet": Napoleon's Conquests

Napoleon's armies affected every European state. Whether annexed, allied, or simply defeated, every nation had to come to terms with this dynamo of activity.

*Brunn, Geoffrey. *Napoleon and His Empire.* 1972.

Connelly, Owen. *Napoleon's Satellite Kingdoms.* 1965.

Forrest, Alan. *Napoleon's Men: The Soldiers of the Revolution and Empire.* 2002.

Simms, Brendan. *The Impact of Napoleon: Prussian High Politics, Foreign Policy, and the Crisis of the Executive, 1797–1806.* 1997.

The "Restoration" of Europe

Diplomatic historians have shown how events in this period shaped European affairs for decades. Domestic politics have been relatively understudied.

Johnson, Paul. *The Birth of the Modern: World Society, 1815–1830.* 1991.

Laven, David, and Lucy Riall, eds. *Napoleon's Legacy: Problems of Government in Restoration Europe.* 2000.

Schroeder, Paul W. *The Transformation of European Politics, 1763–1848.* 1994.

Seward, Desmond. *Metternich: The First European.* 1991.

Challenges to the Conservative Order

In general, the early nineteenth century is an understudied period of European history. Unsuccessful revolts attract less attention than successful ones, but even the Greek, Latin American, and Belgian independence movements need to be better integrated into European history.

Berlin, Sir Isaiah. *The Roots of Romanticism.* 1999.

Betley, J. A. *Belgium and Poland in International Relations, 1830–1831.* 1960.

*Breckman, Warren. *European Romanticism. A Brief History with Documents.* 2008.

Brewer, David. *The Flame of Freedom: The Greek War of Independence, 1821–1833.* 2001.

Kroen, Sheryl. *Politics and Theater: The Crisis of Legitimacy in Restoration France, 1815–1830.* 2000.

*Leader, Zachary, and Ian Haywood, eds. *Romantic Period Writings, 1798–1832: An Anthology.* 1998.

Romantic Chronology: **http://english.ucsb.edu:591/rchrono**

Sir Walter Scott digital archives: **http://www.walterscott.lib.ed.ac .uk/home.html**

CHAPTER 21

The Industrial Revolution

The spread of industrialization has elicited much more historical interest than the process of urbanization because the analysis of industrialization occupied a central role in Marxism.

Berend, Ivan T. *History Derailed: Central and Eastern Europe in the Long Nineteenth Century.* 2003.

Industrial Revolution: **http://www.victorianweb.org/technology/ ir/irov.html**

Morgan, Kenneth. *The Birth of Industrial Britain: Social Change, 1750–1850.* 2004.

*Pollard, S., and C. Holmes. *Documents of European Economic History.* Vol. 1, *The Process of Industrialization, 1750–1870.* 1968.

Thompson, E. P. *The Making of the English Working Class.* 1964.

Reforming the Social Order

There is no shortage of materials on social and cultural life in this era, but what is lacking is broader integration of them into the general historical narrative. The Web site Gallica, produced by the National Library of France, offers a wealth of imagery and information on French cultural history.

Davidoff, Leonore, and Catherine Hall. *Family Fortunes: Men and Women of the English Middle Class, 1780–1850.* 1987.

The Dickens Project: **http://humwww.ucsc.edu/dickens**

Gallica: Images and Texts from Nineteenth-Century French-Speaking Culture: **http://gallica.bnf.fr**

Townsend, Mary Lee. *Forbidden Laughter: Popular Humor and the Limits of Repression in Nineteenth-Century Prussia.* 1992.

Ideologies and Political Movements

Ideologies are too often studied in an exclusively national context, so broader generalizations are especially welcome.

Anderson, Benedict. *Imagined Communities: Reflections on the Origin and Spread of Nationalism.* 1983.

Blom, Ida, Karen Hagemann, and Catherine Hall, eds. *Gendered Nations: Nationalisms and Gender Order in the Long Nineteenth Century.* 2000.

Hobsbawm, E. J. *The Age of Revolution, 1789–1848.* 1996.

*Mather, F. C., ed. *Chartism and Society: An Anthology of Documents.* 1980.

Sewell, William H., Jr. *Work and Revolution in France: The Language of Labor from the Old Regime to 1848.* 1980.

Taylor, Barbara. *Eve and the New Jerusalem: Socialism and Feminism in the Nineteenth Century.* 1983.

The Revolutions of 1848

Interest in the revolutions of 1848 has revived of late, perhaps because the recent upsurge of ethnic violence in the Balkans has prompted scholars to look again at this critical period.

Dowe, Dieter, ed. *Europe in 1848: Revolution and Reform.* Trans. David Higgins. 2001.

Evans, Robert, and Hartmut Pogge von Strandmann, eds. *The Revolutions in Europe, 1848–1849.* 2000.

Lincoln, W. Bruce. *Nicholas I: Emperor and Autocrat of All the Russias.* 1978.

Sperber, Jonathan. *The European Revolutions, 1848–1851.* 1994.

Toíbín, Colm, and Diarmaid Ferriter. *The Irish Famine: A Documentary.* 2002.

*Walker, Mack. *Metternich's Europe.* 1968.

*Primary source.

CHAPTER 22

The End of the Concert of Europe

Historians have often neglected the inglorious Crimean War despite its impact on European politics. Much of the best new literature focuses not only on political changes but also on the war's social impact in Russia. Worobec's and Stites's books give a searching look at the lives of Russian serfs in this age of transition.

Baumgart, Winfried. *The Crimean War, 1853–1856.* 1999.

Hazareesingh, Sudhir. *From Subject to Citizen: The Second Empire and the Emergence of Modern French Democracy.* 1998.

Stites, Richard. *Serfdom, Society, and the Arts in Imperial Russia: The Pleasure and the Power.* 2005.

Worobec, Christine. *Peasant Russia: Family and Community in the Post-Emancipation Period.* 1991.

Wortman, Richard S. *Scenarios of Power: Myth and Ceremony in Russian Monarchy.* 2 vols. 1995–2000.

War and Nation Building

Nation building has produced a varied literature ranging from biographies to studies of ceremonials and the presentation of royalty as celebrities and unifying figures. Two Web sites show the complexities of this process: Brown University's Victorian Web demonstrates the connections among royalty, politicians, religion, and culture; and Bucknell University's Russian Studies site opens to the strains of the Russian national anthem, composed in the reign of Nicholas I to foster reverence for the dynasty and homeland.

Ascoli, Albert Russell, and Krystyna Von Henneberg, eds. *Making and Remaking Italy: The Cultivation of National Identity around the Risorgimento.* 1991.

Blackbourn, David. *Fontana History of Germany, 1780–1918: The Long Nineteenth Century.* 1997.

Breuilly, John. *The Formation of the First German Nation-State, 1800–1871.* 1996.

Homans, Margaret. *Royal Representations: Queen Victoria and British Culture, 1837–1876.* 1998.

Russian Studies: **http://www.departments.bucknell.edu/Russian**

Smith, Paul. *Disraeli: A Brief Life.* 1996.

The Victorian Web: **http://landow.stg.brown.edu/victorian/victov.html**

Wetzel, David. *A Duel of Giants: Bismarck, Napoleon III, and the Origins of the Franco-Prussian War.* 2001.

Establishing Social Order

Nation building entailed state-sponsored activities stretching from promoting education to rebuilding cities. New histories show the process of creating a sense of nationality through government management of people's environment, such that citizenship became part of everyday life. Hine and Faragher show the intersection of U.S. expansionism and nation building, while works by Megill and Eichner interpret Marx and the Paris Commune. Northwestern University has digitized its collection on the Siege of Paris and the Commune.

Chakravarty, Gautam. *The Indian Mutiny and the British Imagination.* 2005.

Eichner, Carolyn. *Surmounting the Barricades: Women in the Paris Commune.* 2004.

Hamm, Michael F. *Kiev: A Portrait, 1800–1917.* 1993.

Hine, Robert V., and John Mack Faragher. *The American West: A New Interpretative History.* 2001.

Hoffenberg, Peter H. *An Empire on Display: English, Indian, and Australian Exhibitions from the Crystal Palace to the Great War.* 2001.

Johanson, Christine. *Women's Struggle for Higher Education in Russia, 1855–1900.* 1987.

Jordan, David. *Transforming Paris: The Life and Labor of Baron Haussmann.* 1995.

Keene, Donald. *Emperor of Japan: Meiji and His World, 1852–1912.* 2002.

Megill, Allan. *Karl Marx: The Burden of Reason (Why Marx Rejected Politics and the Market).* 2002.

Rotenberg, Robert. *Landscape and Power in Vienna.* 1995.

Siege of Paris Collection, Northwestern University: **http://www.library.northwestern.edu/spec/siege**

The Culture of Social Order

Like the biographies of politicians, the biographies of artists and intellectuals have proved crucial to understanding the period of realism and Realpolitik. Eldredge's book on Darwin examines his notebooks to see at what point he switched from believing the religious story of creation to proposing evolution. Kaufman's book shows how the Catholic church harnessed the modern forces of tourism and transportation to religious fervor.

Bordenheimer, Rosemarie. *The Real Life of Mary Ann Evans: George Eliot, Her Letters and Fiction.* 1994.

Eldredge, Niles. *Darwin: Discovering the Tree of Life.* 2005.

Kaufman, Suzanne. *Consuming Visions: Mass Culture and the Lourdes Shrine.* 2005.

Nord, Philip. *Impressionists and Politics: Art and Democracy in the Nineteenth Century.* 2000.

*Turgenev, Ivan. *A Hunter's Sketches.* 1852.

CHAPTER 23

The Advance of Industry

Industry in the 1870s–1890s advanced on every front, from the development of new products and procedures to the reorganization of work life and consumption. Crouzet's sweeping new work on the creation of economic structures contrasts with other recent studies (such as Rappaport's) on the impact of consumers and taste in driving economic change.

Crossick, Geoffrey, and Serge Jaumin, eds. *Cathedrals of Consumption: The European Department Store, 1850–1939.* 1999.

Crouzet, Francois. *A History of the European Economy, 1000–2000.* 2001.

Franzoi, Barbara. *At the Very Least She Pays the Rent: Women and German Industrialization.* 1985.

Malone, Carolyn. *Women's Bodies and Dangerous Trades in England, 1880–1914.* 2003.

Marks, Steven G. *Road to Power: The Trans-Siberian Railroad and the Colonization of Asian Russia, 1850–1917.* 1991.

Morris, Charles B. *The Tycoons: How Andrew Carnegie, John D. Rockefeller, Jay Gould, and J. P. Morgan Invented the American Supereconomy.* 2005.

Smith, Michael S. *The Emergence of Modern Business Enterprise in France, 1800–1930.* 2006.

*Primary source.

Rappaport, Erika. *Shopping for Pleasure: Women in the Making of London's West End.* 2000.

The New Imperialism

New studies of imperialism show not only increasing conquest and the creation of an international economy but also the cultural impulses behind it. Cannadine offers a readable—and debatable—interpretation of the social relations involved. Headrick connects the advance of industry with both peaceful activities and imperial expansion and warfare. The University of Pennsylvania's African studies Web site offers vivid depictions of African art and architecture, such as that confiscated for Western museums, while the Chrétien book investigates the long-term effects of European imperialism in Africa.

African Studies Center: **http://www.sas.upenn.edu/African_Studies/ AS.html**

Cannadine, David. *Ornamentalism: How the British Saw Their Empire.* 2001.

Chrétien, Jean-Pierre, *The Great Lakes of Africa: 2,000 Years of History.* 2003.

Crosby, Alfred W. *Ecological Imperialism: The Biological Expansions of Europe, 900–1900.* 1993.

Ferro, Marc. *Colonization: A Global History.* 1997.

Headrick, Daniel R. *The Invisible Weapon: Telecommunications and International Politics, 1851–1945.* 1991.

Keene, Donald. *Emperor of Japan: Meiji and His World.* 2002.

*Stanley, Sir Henry. *Autobiography.* 1909.

Wildenthal, Lora. *German Women for Empire, 1884–1945.* 2001.

Imperial Society and Culture

Historians have come to see that industrial development and the spread of imperialism affected the smallest details of everyday life as well as the larger phenomena of class formation and massive regional and global migration. Blakely gives particularly rich portrayals of cultural mixture, exploitation, motivation, and resistance under the colonial regime.

Blakely, Allison. *Blacks in the Dutch World: The Evolution of Racial Imagery in Modern Society.* 1993.

*Bonnell, Victoria, ed. *The Russian Worker.* 1983.

Callen, Anthea. *The Art of Impressionism: Painting Technique and the Making of Modernity.* 2000.

Hoerder, Dirk. *Cultures in Contact: World Migrations in the Second Millennium.* 2002.

Maynes, Mary Jo. *Taking the Hard Road: Life Course in French and German Workers' Autobiographies in the Era of Industrialization.* 1995.

McReynolds, Louise. *Russia at Play: Leisure Activities at the End of the Tsarist Era.* 2003.

Moch, Leslie Page. *Moving Europeans: Migration in Western Europe since 1650.* 2003.

Reeder, Linda. *Widows in White: Migration and the Transformation of Rural Italian Women, Sicily, 1880–1920.* 2003.

The Birth of Mass Politics

Historical study of politics in this period entails looking at both government policies and the activism based on neighborhood solidarity, the growth of unions, and the rise of the mass media. The Avalon Project at the Yale Law School provides access to major treaties and conventions, making it an excellent resource for this period.

Applegate, Celia. *A Nation of Provincials: The German Idea of Heimat.* 1990.

Avalon Project at Yale Law School: **http://www.yale.edu/lawweb/ avalon/avalon.htm**

Eley, Geoff. *Forging Democracy: A History of the Left in Europe, 1850–2000.* 2002.

Glassheim, Eagle. *Noble Nationaists: The Transformation of the Bohemian Aristocracy.* 2005.

Hoppen, K. Theodore. *Ireland since 1800: Conflict and Conformity.* 1999.

Jenkins, Jennifer. *Provincial Modernity: Local Culture and Liberal Politics in Fin-de-Siècle Hamburg.* 2003.

McDonough, Terrence, ed. *Was Ireland a Colony?: Economics, Politics, and Culture in Nineteenth-Century Ireland.* 2005.

Mazower, Mark. *The Balkans: A Short History.* 2000.

Ross, Ellen. *Love and Toil: Motherhood in Outcast London, 1870–1918.* 1993.

CHAPTER 24

Private Life in the Modern Age

Historians are engaged in serious study of the transformations of everyday life brought about by industrial and imperial advance in the early twentieth century. Women's striving for personal autonomy was expressed in dozens of novels about the "new woman," including the famous *Keys to Happiness*, now available in an English translation.

Forth, Christopher. *The Dreyfus Affair and the Crisis of French Manhood.* 2004.

Roberts, Mary Louise. *Disruptive Acts: The New Woman in Fin-de-Siècle France.* 2002.

*Verbitskaya, Anastasia. *The Keys to Happiness.* Trans. Beth Holmgren and Helen Goscilo. 1999. Originally published 1908–1913.

Vicinus, Martha. *Intimate Friendships: Women Who Loved Women, 1778–1928.* 2004.

Walkowitz, Judith. *City of Dreadful Delight: Narratives of Sexual Danger in Late-Victorian London.* 1993.

Modernity and the Revolt in Ideas

Some of the most controversial historical writing sees the road to World War I as paved with cultural conflict. Many of the studies here suggest that new forms of art, music, dance, and philosophy were as central to the challenges Europe faced as were ethnic, economic, and international turmoil. The Web offers good cultural sites for this important period.

Art nouveau: **http://www.nga.gov/feature/nouveau/nouveau.htm**

Eksteins, Modris. *Rites of Spring: The Great War and the Birth of the Modern Age.* 1989.

Everdell, William R. *The First Moderns: Profiles in the Origins of Twentieth-Century Thought.* 1997.

Gibson, Mary. *Born to Crime; Cesare Lombroso and the Origins of Biological Criminology.* 2002.

Marchand, Suzanne, and David Lindenfeld, eds. *Germany at the Fin de Siècle: Culture, Politics, and Ideas.* 2004.

Marks, Steven. *How Russia Shaped the Modern World: From Art to Anti-Semitism, Ballet to Bolshevism.* 2003.

Nineteenth- and twentieth-century philosophy: **http://www .epistemelinks.com/index.asp**

Safranski, Rüdiger. *Nietzsche: A Philosophical Biography.* 2002.

*Primary source.

Staller, Natasha. *A Sum of Destructions: Picasso's Cultures and the Creation of Cubism.* 2001.

Growing Tensions in Mass Politics

Historians are uncovering the dramatic changes in political life and the rise of mass politics across Europe, including the development of suffragist movements. Rose shows that mass education gave the working class a foundation in the works of Shakespeare and other classical writers. Another major phenomenon was a growing political hatred and the rise of militant nationalism to replace nationalism based on constitutional values.

Dennis, David B. *Beethoven in German Politics, 1870–1989.* 1996.

Forth, Christopher E. *The Dreyfus Affair and the Crisis of French Manhood.* 2004.

Frankel, Richard E. *Bismarck's Shadow: The Cult of Leadership and the Transformation of the German Right, 1898–1945.* 2005.

Kent, Susan. *Gender and Power in Britain, 1640–1990.* 1999.

Lendavi, Paul. *The Hungarians: A Thousand Years of Victory in Defeat.* 2003.

Lindemann, Albert. *Anti-Semitism before the Holocaust.* 2000.

Robertson, Ritchie, and Edward Timms. *Theodor Herzl and the Origins of Zionism.* 2005.

Rose, Jonathan. *Intellectual Life of the British Working Class.* 2001.

European Imperialism Challenged

In the midst of raucous political and social debate, the European powers faced growing resistance to their domination and increasingly serious setbacks. Many historians now judge Europe to have played a less commanding role in the rest of the world than the leading empires claimed. Imperial instability, as some studies show, paved the road to war. The fascination with the major non-Western contender — Japan — can be traced on the Japanese history Web site.

Japanese history: **http://www.csuohio.edu/history/japan/index.html**

Conklin, Alice. *A Mission to Civilize: The Republican Idea of Empire in France and West Africa, 1895–1930.* 1997.

Gooch, John, ed. *The Boer War: Direction, Experiences, Image.* 2000.

Hull, Isabel. *Absolute Destruction: Military Culture and the Practices of War in Imperial Germany.* 2005.

Kansu, Aykut. *The Revolution of 1908 in Turkey.* 1997.

Sinha, Mrinalini. *Colonial Masculinity: The "Manly Englishman" and the "Effeminate Bengali" in the Late Nineteenth Century.* 1995.

South African War: **http://www.anglo-boer.co.za**

Weeks, Theodore R. *Nation and State in Late Imperial Russia: Nationalism and Russification on the Western Frontier.* 1996.

Roads to War

Why World War I broke out remains a widely debated topic. There are always newcomers to the discussion devoted to assessing the responsibility for the war's beginning, some fixing on a single country and others investigating the full range of diplomatic, military, social, and economic conditions.

Ascher, Abraham. *The Revolution of 1905: Russia in Disarray.* 1988.

Clark, Christopher. *William II.* 2000.

Cornwall, Mark, ed. *The Last Years of Austria-Hungary: A Multi-National Experiment in Early Twentieth-Century Europe.* 2002.

Hermann, David G. *The Arming of Europe and the Making of the First World War.* 1996.

Hewitson, Mark. *Germany and the Causes of the First World War.* 2004.

Hobson, Rolf. *Imperialism at Sea: Naval Strategic Thought, the Ideology of Sea Power, and the Tirpitz Plan, 1875–1914.* 2002.

Manning, Roberta. *The Crisis of the Old Order in Russia.* 1982.

Nolan, Michael E. *The Inverted Mirror: Mythologizing the Enemy in France and Germany, 1898–1914.* 2005.

CHAPTER 25

The Great War, 1914–1918

The most recent histories of the Great War consider its military, technological, psychic, social, and economic aspects. This vision of the war as a phenomenon occurring beyond the battlefield as well as on it characterizes the newest scholarship.

Davis, Belinda. *Home Fires Burning: Food, Politics, and Everyday Life in World War I Berlin.* 2000.

Echenberg, Myron. *Colonial Conscripts: The "Tirailleurs Sénégalais" in French West Africa, 1857–1960.* 1990.

Healy, Maureen. *Vienna and the Fall of the Habsburg Empire: Total War and Everyday Life in World War I.* 2004.

Leed, Eric J. *No Man's Land: Combat and Identity in World War I.* 1979.

Panchasi, Roxanne. "Reconstructions: Prosthetics and the Rehabilitation of the Male Body in World War I." *Differences.* 1995.

Roshwald, Aviel, and Richard Stites, eds. *European Culture in the Great War: The Arts, Entertainment, and Propaganda, 1914–1918.* 1999.

Schmitt, Bernadotte E., and Harold C. Vederler. *The World in the Crucible, 1914–1919.* 1984.

World War I Documents Archive: **http://www.lib.byu.edu/%7Erdh/wwi.**

Protest, Revolution, and War's End, 1917–1918

Histories of the war's end account for the cataclysmic setting: deprivation, ongoing mass slaughter, and the eruption of revolution. Peacemaking also occurred, and that too was complex. In all, the violence of the postwar scene has made historians call into question the idea that wars end with an armistice.

Barry, John. *The Great Influenza: The Epic Story of the Greatest Plague in History.* 2004.

Fitzpatrick, Sheila. *The Russian Revolution, 1917–1932.* 1995.

Holquist, Peter. *Making War, Forging Revolution: Russia's Continuum of Crisis, 1914–1921.* 2002.

Horne, John, ed. *State, Society and Mobilization in Europe during the First World War.* 2000.

Lewis, David Levering. *W. E. B. Du Bois: The Fight for Equality and the American Century, 1919–1963.* 2000.

Smith, Leonard V., et al. *France and the Great War 1914–1918.* 2003.

Welch, David. *Germany, Propaganda, and Total War, 1914–1918: The Sins of Omission.* 2000.

The Search for Peace in an Era of Revolution

Peacemaking was a fraught process, occurring amid revolution, the flu pandemic, and starvation. Many aspired to a lasting peace and to social justice. Both dreams were to be dashed, as the story of individuals and the fate of institutions like the League of Nations show. Thompson investigates the new mandates.

*Primary source.

Cooper, John Milton. *Breaking the Heart of the World: Woodrow Wilson and the Fight for the League of Nations.* 2001.

Marks, Sally. *The Ebbing of European Ascendency: An International History of the World.* 2002.

Thompson, Elizabeth. *Colonial Citizens: Republican Rights, Paternal Privilege, and Gender in French Syria and Lebanon.* 2000.

Wrigley, Chris, ed. *The First World War and the International Economy.* 2000.

The Aftermath of War: Europe in the 1920s

Two themes shape the history of the 1920s: recovery from the trauma of war and revolution and ongoing modernization of work and social life. The great technological innovations of the prewar period such as films and airplanes receive sophisticated treatment by historians for their impact on people's imagination. The radio is another phenomenon just beginning to find its historians.

African American Culture and its influence in the Jazz Age: **http://www.nypl.org/research/sc/sc.html**

Hau, Michael. *The Cult of Health and Beauty in Germany: A Social History, 1890–1930.* 2003.

Kent, Susan. *Making Peace: The Reconstruction of Gender in Postwar Britain.* 1994.

Lerner, Paul. *Hysterical Men: War, Psychiatry, and the Politics of Trauma in Germany, 1890–1930.* 2003.

Makaman, Douglas, and Michael Mays, eds. *World War I and the Cultures of Modernity.* 2000.

Roshwald, Aviel. *Ethnic Nationalism and the Fall of Empires: Central Europe, Russia and the Middle East, 1914–1923.* 2001.

Schwartz, Vanessa, and Leo Charney, eds. *Cinema and the Invention of Modern Life.* 1995.

Mass Culture and the Rise of Modern Dictators

Mass communications advances in cinema and radio provided new tools for the rule of modern dictators who arose from the shambles of war and revolution. Many of the most interesting recent studies look at the cultural components of the consolidation of dictatorial power, while Kollontai's novel is an example of fiction being used to teach literacy and Soviet citizenship.

Ben-Ghiat, Ruth. *Fascist Modernities: Italy, 1922–1945.* 2001.

Helstosky, Carol. *Garlic and Oil: The Politics of Food in Italy.* 2004.

*Kollontai, Aleksandra. *Love of Worker Bees.* 1923.

Northrop, Douglas. *Veiled Empire: Gender and Power in Stalinist Central Asia.* 2004.

Russian Revolution documents and links: **http://www.fordham.edu/halsall/mod/modsbook39.html**

Sneeringer, Julia. *Winning Women's Votes: Propaganda and Politics in Weimar Germany.* 2002.

Tumarkin, Nina. *Lenin Lives! The Lenin Cult in Soviet Russia.* 1997.

CHAPTER 26

The Great Depression

Historians look to the depression as a complex event with economic, social, and cultural consequences, but in addition they see its impact as yet another indication of the tightening of global economic connections. To follow some of the political implications for European empires, see in particular Columbia University's South Asia

Web site, which explores Gandhi's economic resistance to British colonialism.

Balderston, Theo, ed. *The World Economy and National Economics in the Interwar Slump.* 2003.

Clavin, Patricia. *The Great Depression in Europe, 1929–1939.* 2000.

Evans, Richard J., and Dick Geary. *The German Unemployed: Experiences and Consequences of Mass Unemployment from the Weimar Republic to the Third Reich.* 1987.

South Asia and Gandhi: **http://www.columbia.edu/cu/libraries/indiv/area/sarai**

Strachura, Peter D. *Poland, 1918–1945.* 2004.

Totalitarian Triumph

The vicious dictators Stalin, Hitler, and Mussolini are among the most popular subjects for historians and readers alike. Recent histories study their mobilization of art and the media and consider people's complex participation in totalitarian regimes. Studies like those by Engel and Posadskaya-Vanderbeck, Gellately and Stolzfus, and Kaplan have provided us with fascinating if grim insights into everyday life.

Ben-Ghiat, Ruth. *Fascist Modernities: Italy, 1922–1945.* 2001.

Burleigh, Michael. *The Third Reich: A New History.* 2000.

*Engel, Barbara Alpern, and Anastasia Posadskaya-Vanderbeck, eds. *A Revolution of Their Own: Voices of Women in Soviet History.* 1998.

Fritzsche, Peter. *Germans into Nazis.* 1998.

Gellately, Robert, and Nathan Stolzfus, eds. *Social Outsiders in Nazi Germany.* 2001.

Hellbeck, Jochen. *Revolution on My Mind: Writing a Diary under Stalin.* 2006.

Kaplan, Marion. *Between Dignity and Despair: Jewish Life in Nazi Germany.* 1998.

Viola, Lynn, ed. *Contending with Stalinism: Soviet Power and Popular Resistance in the 1930s.* 2003.

Democracies on the Defensive

The democracies attacked the depression from a variety of perspectives, ranging from state policy to film and the arts, yet another indication of how complex politics can be. Further departures from liberal policies, whether in trade or in the development of the activist welfare state, also have attracted historical study.

Bok, Sissela. *Alva Myrdal: A Daughter's Memoir.* 1991.

Cook, David A. *A History of Narrative Film.* 2004.

Lebovics, Herman. *True France: The Wars over Cultural Identity, 1900–1945.* 1992.

Kennedy, David M. *Freedom from Fear: The American People in Depression and War, 1929–1945.* 1999.

Pawlowski, Merry M. *Virginia Woolf and Fascism: Resisting the Dictators' Seduction.* 2001.

Rearick, Charles. *The French in Love and War: Popular Culture in the Era of the World Wars.* 1997.

The Road to Global War

The road to war encircled the globe, involving countries seemingly peripheral to the struggles among the antagonists. The perennial question for many historians is whether Hitler could have been stopped, but with globalization there is new attention to the beginnings of war beyond the West as a prelude to decolonization.

*Primary source.

Bix, Herbert P. *Hirohito and the Making of Modern Japan.* 2000.

Chickering, Roger, and Stig Förster, eds. *The Shadows of Total War: Europe, East Asia, and the United States, 1919–1939.* 2003.

Imlay, Talbot C. *Facing the Second World War: Strategy, Politics, and Economics in Britain and France 1938–1940.* 2003.

Martin, Benjamin. *France in 1938.* 2005.

Peattie, Mark R. *Sunburst: The Rise of Japanese Naval Air Power, 1909–1940.* 2002.

Seidman, Michael. *Republic of Egos: A Social History of the Spanish Civil War.* 2002.

World War II, 1939–1945

In a vast literature historians have charted the war's innumerable and global horrors, with issues of the Holocaust, industrial killing, and the nature of racial thinking drawing particular attention. The U.S. Holocaust Memorial Museum provides online exhibits giving the history of the Holocaust in different locations, while an online collection by Soviet war photographers reveals every aspect of the Soviet defense and offense, down to the capture of Berlin in May 1945. While looking at the social aspects of war, historians have intensely debated the development of the cold war within the hot war.

Browning, Christopher. *The Origins of the Final Solution: The Evolution of Nazi Jewish Policy, September 1939–March 1942.* 2004.

Dower, John W. *War without Mercy: Race and Power in the Pacific War.* 1986.

Holocaust Museum: **http://usholocaustmuseum.org**

Gross, Jan. *Neighbors: The Destruction of the Jewish Community in Jedwabne, Poland.* 2001.

Miner, Steven Merritt. *Stalin's Holy War: Religion, Nationalism, and Alliance Politics, 1941–1945.* 2003.

Slaughter, Jane. *Women in the Italian Resistance, 1943–1945.* 1997.

Soviet War Photography: **http://www.shicklerart.com/exh/sovietwar/index.html**

Weinberg, Gerhard. *A World at Arms: A Global History of World War II.* 2005.

CHAPTER 27

World Politics Transformed

In the past decade, both the opening of Soviet archives and closer research in American records have allowed for more informed views of the diplomacy and politics of the cold war in Europe and around the world. Although few defend Stalin, we now benefit from balanced assessments of superpower rivalry. Several Web sites on the cold war contain biographies of the main players, time lines, and descriptions of how nuclear weapons actually work and how they cause destruction.

Cold War Files: Interpreting History through Documents: **http://coldwarfiles.org**

The Cold War Museum: **http://www.coldwar.org**

Cronin, James. *The World the Cold War Made: Order, Chaos, and the Return of History.* 1996.

Eisenberg, Carolyn Woods. *Drawing the Line: The American Decision to Divide Germany, 1944–1949.* 1996.

Gaddis, John. *The Cold War: A New History.* 2006.

Leffler, Melvyn P., and David S. Painter. *Origins of the Cold War: An International History.* 2005.

Trachtenberg, Marc. *A Constructed Peace: The Making of a European Settlement, 1945–1963.* 1999.

Zubkova, Elena. *Russia after the War: Hopes, Illusions, and Disappointments, 1945–1957.* 1998.

Political and Economic Recovery in Europe

Though painstaking and complex, recovery in its material and political forms yielded a distinctly new Europe whose characteristics historians are still uncovering. Because of the opening of the archives, historical attention has focused on charting Soviet occupation, Communist takeover, and the ethnic cleansing that were part of postwar recovery.

Crowley, David, and Susan E. Reid, ed. *Socialist Spaces: Sites of Everyday Life in the Eastern Bloc.* 2002.

Frommer, Benjamin. *National Cleansing: Retribution against Nazi Collaborators in Postwar Czechoslovakia.* 2005.

Herf, Jeffrey. *Divided Memory: The Nazi Past in the Two Germanies.* 1997.

Hitchcock, William. *The Struggle for Europe: The Turbulent History of a Divided Continent, 1945–2002.* 2003.

Kenney, Padraic. *Rebuilding Poland: Workers and Communists, 1945–1950.* 1997.

Milward, Alan S. *The United Kingdom and the Economic Community.* 2002.

Moeller, Robert. *War Stories: The Search for a Usable Past in the Federal Republic of Germany.* 2001.

Taubman, William. *Khrushchev: The Man and His Era.* 2003.

Van Hook, James C. *Rebuilding Germany: The Creation of the Social Market Economy, 1945–1957.* 2004.

Decolonization in a Cold War Climate

Novelists, philosophers, and historians debate the impact and issues of decolonization. Powerful evocations of the brutality of the process appear most often in novels such as Sidwha's *Cracking India*, which was made into the film *Earth*.

Connelly, Matthew. *A Diplomatic Revolution: Algeria's Quest for Independence and the Origins of the Post–Cold War Era.* 2002.

Elkins, Caroline. *Imperial Reckoning: The Untold Story of Britain's Gulag in Kenya.* 2005.

*Fanon, Frantz. *The Wretched of the Earth.* 1961.

The Korean War Educator: **http://www.koreanwar-educator.org**

Macey, David. *Frantz Fanon: A Biography.* 2000.

Marsh, Steve. *Anglo-American Relations and Cold War Oil.* 2003.

Shepard, Todd. *The Invention of Decolonization: The Algerian War and the Remaking of France.* 2006.

*Sidhwa, Bapsi. *Cracking India: A Novel.* 1992.

Cultural Life on the Brink of Nuclear War

Cold war culture, including the growth of consumerism, make the 1950s a fertile field for research, especially as new sources become available. Jobs's work shows the concern for youth and their culture, while Herzog's study describes the importance of sexual norms to the creation of West Germany.

Engel, Barbara Alpern. *Women in Russia, 1700–2000.* 2004.

Heineman, Elizabeth D. *What Difference Does a Husband Make? Women and Marital Status in Nazi and Postwar Germany.* 1999.

*Primary source.

Herzog, Dagmar. *Sex after Fascism: Memory and Morality in Twentieth-Century Germany.* 2005.

Jobs, Richard I. *Riding the New Wave: Youth and the Rejuvenation of France after World War II.* 2007.

Poiger, Ute G. *Jazz, Rock, and Rebels: Cold War Politics and American Culture in a Divided Germany.* 2000.

Rowley, Hazel. *Tête-à-Tête: Simone de Beauvoir and Jean-Paul Sartre.* 2005.

When Bomb Shelters Were All the Rage: **http://detnews.com/history/shelters/shelters.htm**

CHAPTER 28

The Revolution in Technology

Wartime technological development came to have profound consequences for the peacetime lives of individuals and for society. The works listed here describe the new technologies and analyze their importance, with authors divided on whether the new developments should be feared or embraced. The International Atomic Energy Agency site has all the facts about nuclear energy, including the percentage of energy generated by nuclear reactors, construction of new plants, and international monitoring.

Bauer, Martin W., and George Gaskell, eds. *Biotechnology: The Making of a Global Controversy.* 2002.

Edwards, Jeannette. *Born and Bred: Idioms of Kinship and New Reproductive Technologies in England.* 2000.

Harvey, Brian. *Europe's Space Program: To Ariane and Beyond.* 2003.

Hecht, Gabrielle. *The Radiance of France: Nuclear Power and National Identity after World War II.* 1998.

International Atomic Energy Agency: **http://www.iaea.org**

Natalicchi, Giorgio. *Wiring Europe: Re-Shaping the European Telecommunications Regime.* 2001.

Postindustrial Society and Culture

Changes in the way people worked became striking in the 1960s, causing social observers to analyze the social and cultural meaning of the transformation. Many critics agree that technology's creation of a postindustrial workplace changed not only the way people worked but also how they lived in families and interacted with peers.

Chandler, Alfred D., Jr., and Bruce Mazlish, eds. *Leviathans: Multinational Corporations and the New Global History.* 2005.

Evans, Christopher. *The Micro Millennium.* 1979.

Ramet, Sabrina P., and Gordana P. Crnković, eds. *Kazaaam! Splat! Ploof! The American Impact on European Culture since 1945.* 2003.

Roulleau-Berger, Laurence. *Youth and Work in the Post-Industrial City of North America and Europe.* 2003.

Wakeman, Rosemary. *Modernizing the Provincial City: Toulouse 1945–1975.* 1997.

Protesting Cold War Conditions

Historians look to domestic politics, international events, and social change to capture the texture of the tumultuous 1960s. The momentous changes on so many fronts are beginning to receive synthetic treatment in books such as Suri's, which connects the move for détente with domestic protest around the world. The Martin Luther King Web site introduces visitors to the biography, speeches, sermons, and major life events of the slain civil rights leader.

*Dubček, Alexander. *Hope Dies Last: The Autobiography of Alexander Dubček.* 1993.

Fink, Carole, et al., eds. *1968: The World Transformed.* 1998.

*Guy-Sheftall, Beverly, ed. *Words of Fire: An Anthology of African-American Feminist Thought.* 1995.

*Lévi-Strauss, Claude. *Tristes Tropiques.* 1961.

The Martin Luther King Jr. Papers Project: **http://www.stanford.edu/group/King/mlkpapers**

Suri, Jeremi. *Power and Protest: Global Revolution and the Rise of Détente.* 2003.

Varon, Jeremy. *Bringing the War Home: The Weather Underground, the Red Army Faction, and Revolutionary Violence in the Sixties and Seventies.* 2004.

Williams, Kieran. *The Prague Spring and Its Aftermath: Czechoslovak Politics, 1968–1970.* 1997.

The Testing of Superpower Domination and the End of the Cold War

As the superpowers continued their standoff, historians found that myriad global changes affected their status and that protest continued at home. The dissident art of the Soviet Union is striking for its deft and moving critique of life under communism. Attempts at reform succeeded in the United States and western Europe, but eastern Europe saw the surprising collapse of communism and the end of the cold war in 1989.

*Gorbachev, Mikhail. *Memoirs.* 1996.

Kenney, Padraic. *A Carnival of Revolution: Central Europe 1989.* 2002.

Kligman, Gail. *The Politics of Duplicity: Controlling Reproduction in Ceausescu's Romania.* 1998.

Reiton, Earl A. *The Thatcher Revolution: Margaret Thatcher, John Major, Tony Blair, and the Transformation of Modern Britain.* 2002.

Rosenfeld, Alla, and Norton T. Dodge. *From Gulag to Glasnost: Nonconformist Art from the Soviet Union.* 1995.

Rothschild, Joseph, and Nancy M. Wingfield. *Return to Diversity: A Political History of East Central Europe.* 2000.

*Solzhenitsyn, Aleksandr Isaevich. *The Gulag Archipelago.* 1973–1976.

Sternhal, Suzanne. *Gorbachev's Reforms: De-Stalinization through Demilitarization.* 1997.

Weigel, George. *Witness to Hope: The Biography of Pope John Paul II.* 1999.

CHAPTER 29

Collapse of the Soviet Union and Its Aftermath

Historians will be telling and retelling this story, for the full consequences of communism's collapse are still unfolding. As new information becomes available, scholars like Goldman explain the post-Communist situation in terms of long-standing trends. Balkansnet gives documents and testimony on one of the massacres as Yugoslavia fell apart.

Balkansnet: Srebrenica. **http://balkansnet.org/srebrenica.html**

Benson, Leslie. *Yugoslovia: A Concise History.* 2004.

Engel, Barbara. *Women in Russian History, 1700–2000.* 2004.

Goldman, Marshall. *The Piratization of Russia: Russian Reform Goes Awry.* 2003.

*Primary source.

*Gorbachev, Mikhail. *Memoirs*. 1996.

Humphrey, Caroline. *The Unmaking of Soviet Life: Everyday Economies after Socialism*. 2002.

Kotkin, Stephen. *Armageddon Averted: The Soviet Collapse, 1970–2000*. 2001.

Mazower, Mark. *The Balkans: A Short History*. 2000.

Naimark, Norman. *Fires of Hatred: Ethnic Cleansing in Twentieth-Century Europe*. 2001.

The Nation-State in a Global Age

The many new institutional forms, such as global cities and rising regionalism, are outlined in both Applegate and Sassen, among others. The advance of the European Union is one of the transnational stories of the 1990s and the twenty-first century.

Applegate, Celia. "A Europe of Regions: Reflections on the Historiography of Sub-National Places in Modern Times." *The American Historical Review*. 1999.

European Union: **http://europa.eu.int**

Ried, T. R. *The United States of Europe: The New Superpower and the End of American Supremacy*. 2005.

Sassen, Saskia. *Cities in a World Economy*. 2006.

Wilson, Andrew. *Ukraine's Orange Revolution*. 2005.

Challenges from an Interconnected World

The international scene is politically challenging and often dangerous. The forces of overpopulation, disease, and pollution remain potentially destructive. Kagan pictures the West as losing its unity.

Baldwin, Peter. *Disease and Democracy: The Industrialized World Faces AIDS*. 2005.

Bess, Michael. *The Light-Green Society: Economic and Technological Modernity in France*. 2003.

*Primary source.

Frieden, Jeffry A. *Global Capitalism: Its Fall and Rise in the Twentieth Century*. 2006.

Kagan, Robert. *Of Paradise and Power: America and Europe in the New World Order*. 2003.

Prunier, Gérard. *Darfur: The Ambiguous Genocide*. 2005.

Rashid, Ahmed. *Jihad: The Rise of Militant Islam in Central Asia*. 2002.

Rosefielde, Steven. *Russia in the 21st Century: The Prodigal Superpower*. 2006.

United Nations. *State of the World Population: People, Poverty, and Possibilities*. 2003.

Global Culture and Society in the Twenty-first Century

The fate of cultural identity in an age of globalization engages a wide range of studies. This age of migration and the Internet requires a rethinking of long-standing identities and individual relationships, as Turkle, among others, suggests. New technology both enhances and challenges Western prosperity. The Public Broadcasting Service's Web site offers a wide array of information on current issues.

Agre, Philip. *Computation and Human Experience*. 1997.

*Emecheta, Buchi. *The New Tribe*. 2000.

Forrester, Sibelan, et al., eds. *Over the Wall/After the Fall: Post-Communist Cultures through an East-West Gaze*. 2004.

Hoerder, Dirk. *Cultures in Contact: World Migrations in the 2nd Millennium*. 2002.

Iriye, Akira. *Cultural Internationalism and World Order*. 1997.

MacGaffey, Janet, et al. *Congo-Paris: Transnational Traders on the Margins of the Law*. 2000.

*Morrison, Toni. *Paradise*. 1998.

Public Broadcasting Service: **http://www.pbs.org**

Smith, Andrea, ed. *Europe's Invisible Migrants*. 2002.

Turkle, Sherry. *Life on the Screen: Identity in the Age of the Internet*. 1995.

Additional Credits

Index

Charles V (Spain, r. 1519–1556), 426, 446
  court of, 419
  Erasmus instruction of, 428
  German princes and, 436
  Habsburg-Valois-Ottoman wars and, 443, 444, 448
  Schmalkaldic League and, 446
  Truce of Nice and, 443(i)
Charles VI (Holy Roman emperor, r. 1711–1740), 573
Charles IX (France, r. 1560–1574), 453, 454
Charles X (France, r. 1824–1830), 646–647
Charles XII (Sweden, r. 1697–1718), 543
Charles Albert (Piedmont-Sardinia, r. 1831–1849), 644, 680–681
Charter 77 (Czechoslovakia), 946
Charter of the Nobility (Russia), 568, 580
Chartism, 677, 684
Chateaubriand, François-René de (1768–1848), 627–628
Châtelet, Émilie du (1706–1749), 558
Chávez, César (1927–1993), 931
Chechen rebels, 960(i), 960–961
Chechnya, 965
  Russia and, 956–958, 960(i), 960–961
Cheka (secret police), 813
Chernobyl catastrophe, 943, 944, 966
Childbirth, 921
  test-tube babies and, 921(i)
Child labor, in factories, 659(i), 660–661
Children
  in 18th century, 572–573
  in Great Depression, 843
  illegitimate, 768
  in 1960s, 925
  in Romania, 947(i)
  thalidomide and, 920(i)
  World War I and, 767
China
  Britain and, 737
  civil service in, 709
  Communists in, 890, 898
  economic growth in, 973
  Europeans, and, 527, 549, 712–713
  France and, 928
  industrial safety in, 973
  Japan and, 786, 857, 864
  Mongols and, 420
  Nixon in, 937
  porcelain from, 421
  printing in, 426
  revolution in (1911), 788
  revolution in (1949), 890, 898
  riots in, 945
  Russia and, 737, 961
  Taiping in, 712
  U.S. relations with, 936
  World War I and, 803
Chirac, Jacques, 942
Chlorine gas, World War I and, 803
Chlorofluorocarbons (CFCs), 966
Cholera, 662, 662(m)
Chopin, Frédéric (1810–1849), 666
Christian IV (Denmark, r. 1596–1648), 461
Christian Democrats, 889, 928
Christianity
  Christian humanism and, 427
  in 1960s, 927
  popular piety and, 427
Christianization, 439–440

Christian Social Party (Austria-Hungary), 781–782
Christmas Carol, A (Dickens), 666
Church(es)
  Great Awakening and, 566
  social order and, 718
  tithes and, 468
Church and state, in 19th century, 719
Churchill, Randolph (1849–1895), 741
Churchill, Winston (1874–1965), 741, 874, 884, 899
Church of England. See Anglican church (Church of England)
CIA. See Central Intelligence Agency (CIA)
Circle of the Lustful, The (Blake), 643(i)
Circumnavigation, 420–421
CIS. See Commonwealth of Independent States (CIS)
Cisalpine Republic, 608, 682(i)
Cities and towns. See also Urban areas
  culture in, 529
  in Enlightenment, 568
  in Fascist Italy, 833
  globalization of, 964
  illegitimacy in, 663
  industrialization and, 659
  migration to, 653, 659
  population growth in, 765
  rural aspects of, 662
  social life in, 531–534
  social order in, 706–708
  in Soviet Union, 928
Citizens and citizenship. See also Democracy
  activism in 1960s and 1970s, 930–936
  education for, 709
  for native Americans, 706(m)
City-states. See also Citizens and citizenship
  Geneva as theocratic, 433
Civil Code (Napoleonic), 620, 625–627, 630
  land ownership and, 664
  Louis XVIII and, 639
  women under, 669
Civil Constitution of the Clergy (France, 1790), 597
Civil disobedience
  in India, 843, 844(i)
  in U.S. civil rights movement, 904–905
Civilians
  in Chechnya, 960
  World War I and, 807–809
  World War II and, 864–866, 869–870
Civilization(s). See also Culture; Geography; Western world
  "clash of," 952
Civil rights
  legislation for, 930
  movements, 904, 928–930, 931
  in Nazi Germany, 848
  in Northern Ireland, 939–940
Civil Rights Act (U.S., 1964), 930
Civil service, 709. See also Bureaucracy
Civil war(s)
  in Bosnia-Herzegovina, 953–954
  in China (1840s–1864), 712
  in Russia, 812–814, 814(m)
  in Spain (1936–1939), 859–860, 860(i), 860(m)
  in United States, 696, 705
Clair, René, 854–855
Clandestine workers, in Europe, 902

Classes. See also Aristocracy
  in cities, 706–707
  education for, 709
  hostility between, 663, 681(b)
  World War I and, 805–806, 825
Classical music, 570–571
Classicism, 510
  French, 509
  vs. romanticism, 640
Clemenceau, Georges (1841–1929), 816
Clement VII (Pope, r. 1523–1534), 434
Clement XIV (Pope, r. 1769–1774), 577
Clergy
  French Terror and, 606
  indigenous people as, 440
  Methodist, 567
  in 1930s, 856
  in Prussia, 718
  in revolutionary France, 597
  roles of, 427, 448
  in Spanish colonies, 527
  training of, 439
  World War II resistance by, 870
Clermont Tonnerre, Stanislas de (1757–1792), 597(b)
Climate
  global warming and, 966
  little ice age of 1600–1850, 466–467(b)
Cloning, 920
Clothing
  gender differences in, 669
  industrialization and, 655–656
  Napoleonic revolution in, 624(i)
  social status of, 533
Clown, The (Böll), 906
Coal and coal industry, 727
  in Britain, 657
  child labor in, 661
  in Germany, 657
  output of (1830–1850), 658(f)
  strikes in England (1926), 823
  World War I and, 820
  World War II and, 892
Cochin China, 712, 737
Cochlaeus, Johannes, 432(b)
Cockade (French badge), 603
Code of Laws (Muscovy, 1649), 469
Codes, World War II and, 863
Codes of law. See Law(s); Law codes
Coffee (kavah), 519
Coffeehouses, 518(i), 519, 528, 534
Colbert, Jean-Baptiste (1619–1683), 486(i), 490, 511
Cold war, 880, 927–936
  in Asia, 898
  culture of, 908–909
  decolonization during, 897–902
  end of, 947
  government archives and truth about, 885(b)
  lifestyle and culture during, 902–911
  military spending during, 891(f)
  origins of, 883–886
  space age and, 919
  totalitarianism and, 845(b)
  world during (1960), 912(m)
Cole, Thomas (1801–1848), 664
Collaborators, World War II and, 888
Collage, 774
Collective action, by workers, 750

Mediterranean region–Movies

Mediterranean region (*Continued*)
  new imperialism in, 733
  Spanish control of, 455
Mehmed II (Sultan, r. 1451–1481), 646(*i*)
Meiji Restoration (Japan), 712–713
Mein Kampf (Hitler), 834, 848
Meir, Golda, 899
Memoirs of the Life of Colonel Hutchinson
  (1664–1671) (Hutchinson), 500–501(*b*)
Men. *See also* Gender
  earnings of, 923
  in Great Depression, 842
  in postwar society, 906–907
Mendel, Gregor (1822–1884), 719–720
Mendelssohn, Moses (1729–1786), 565
Mensheviks, 777
Mental illness, 768–770, 851
Mercantilism
  Colbert and, 490
  in England, 502
  science and, 511–512
Mercenaries
  in Habsburg-Valois-Ottoman wars, 443
  Ottoman peasants as, 495
  in Thirty Years' War, 461, 462–463
Merian, Maria Sibylla (1646–1717),
  510–511, 512(*i*)
Merian, Matthäus (1593–1650), 450(*i*)
Messiah (Handel), 535
Mestizos, 527
Metacomet (King Philip), 508
Metal and metallurgy, 727
Methodism, 566–567, 639–640
Metric system, 604
Metternich, Klemens von (1773–1859),
  636–637, 639, 644–645, 672, 682, 690
Meulen, Adam Frans van der (1632–1690),
  482(*i*)
Mexican Americans, protests by, 931
Mexican Ecclesiastical Provincial Council
  (1555), 440
Mexico, 418(*i*), 692, 969
Michelangelo Buonarroti (1475–1564), 441,
  441(*i*)
Mickiewicz, Adam (1798–1855), 672
Middle class, 659. *See also* Bourgeoisie; Classes
  arts and, 535
  attitudes toward lower classes, 654
  courtly manners and, 513
  in Dutch Republic, 506–507
  in England, 703
  Enlightenment and, 564, 568–571
  expansion of, 741–742
  joining elite, 567
  lifestyle of, 532
  literacy and, 534
  professions and civil service in, 709
  as Prussian officers, 631
  social fears of, 663
  socialist view of, 675
  sports and, 743
  Wilkes affair and, 580
  woman suffrage movement and, 777
  women and, 664, 670
Middle-Class Gentleman, The (Molière), 513
Middle East
  colonies in, 824
  decolonization in, 897
  England and, 802
  foreign workers in, 974
  independence struggles in, 899–900

Islamic theocracy in, 967
Jewish nation in, 783(*b*)
in 1930s, 843–844
oil policy and, 937–938, 938(*f*), 938(*i*)
in 21st century, 971(*m*)
World War I peace settlements and
  (1919–1920), 817(*m*), 818(*b*)
Middlemarch (Eliot), 716
Midway Island, battle at, 871
Midwives, 709
Migration. *See also* Immigrants and
  immigration
  cultural globalization and, 978(*i*)
  by Europeans, 741
  experiences of, 744–745(*b*)
  globalization and, 950(*i*), 952, 964, 974
  Jewish, 782(*m*)
  in 19th century, 664, 724(*i*), 725–727
  of rural poor, 571
  in Western world, 974–975
  by workers, 743–745
  World War I and, 822
  World War II and, 881, 889(*i*)
Milan, 680
  uprising in, 682(*i*)
Militance. *See also* Activism
  by blacks, 931
  Islamic, 939
  promotion of, 795(*b*)
  World War I and, 776
Militarism, World War I and, 821–822
Military. *See* Armed forces
Military dictatorship, French Revolution and,
  588
Military draft. *See also* Conscription
  World War I and, 792
Military intelligence, in 1960s, 916
Military spending, under Reagan, 942
Military technology
  of conquistadores, 426
  in 16th century, 444
Mill, Harriet Taylor, 721, 777
Mill, John Stuart (1806–1873), 721, 777
Mill on the Floss (Eliot), 716
Milosevic, Slobodan, 953, 955
Milton, John (1608–1674), 509–510
Mines Act (Britain, 1842), 661
Minimalist composers, 926
Minorities
  activism of, 931
  in Austria-Hungary, 781
  fears of, 766
  rights for, 764
  World War II and, 868
Mir (Russian community), 695
Miseries and Misfortunes of War, The
  (Callot), 461(*i*)
Missiles
  Cuban missile crisis and, 910, 911(*m*)
  Soviet reduction in, 944
Missions and missionaries
  in Asia, 440, 440(*i*)
  Calvinist, 452, 453(*m*)
  in Europe, 419
  European imperialism and, 740
  in India, 639(*i*), 640
  Jesuit, 439
  in New Spain, 419, 439–440
  in Philippines, 470–471
Mitteleuropa, 791, 794
Mitterrand, François (1916–1996), 942

Mobilization
  World War I and, 794, 806–807
  World War II and, 862
Modernism, 547(*b*), 771
  in dance and music, 775–776
  in painting, 773–775
Modernity
  Enlightenment and, 561
  ideas and, 771–776
  World War I and, 764, 766(*b*)
Modernization
  in eastern Europe, 895
  of French armed forces, 490
  of government, 576–578
  of Japan, 738, 739(*i*)
  in Russia, 497, 540–541, 541(*i*)
Mohács, battle of (1526), 443
Moldavia, 693
Molecular biology, 919–920
Molière (Jean-Baptiste Poquelin)
  (1622–1673), 487, 512
Monarchs and monarchies. *See also* specific
  monarchs and monarchies
  Austro-Hungarian, 702–703
  Bodin on, 474
  divine right and, 464–465
  in England, 703–705, 704(*b*), 704(*i*)
  in France, 598–600
  royal images and, 464–465
Monasticism and monasteries. *See also*
  Religious orders
  Jesuits, 439, 577
  under Napoleon, 630
  in revolutionary France, 597
Monet, Claude (1840–1926), 749
Monetarism, 940
Money markets
  Amsterdam as, 458
  Dutch Republic and, 506
Mongols and Mongol Empire, 420, 421
Monroe, James, 646
Monroe Doctrine, 646
Montagu, Mary Wortley (1689–1762), 545
Montaigne, Michel de (1533–1592), 474, 478
Montenegro, 756, 791, 792
Montespan, Madame de, 487
Montesquieu, Charles-Louis de Secondat
  (Baron de, 1689–1755), 549, 560, 577,
  591, 600–601
Montessori, Maria, 768
Monteverdi, Claudio (1567–1643), 472
Moon landing (1969), 918
Morality, in 1930s, 855
Moral majority (U.S.), 941
More, Thomas (1478–1535), 427, 428–429, 434
Moriscos, 455–456
Morocco, 790, 901
Morris, May (1862–1938), 747
Morris, William (1834–1896), 747
Morrison, Toni, 979, 979(*i*)
Mortality, infant, 572, 894
Moscow, 729(*i*), 863, 964
Mostar Bridge, Yugoslavia, 954, 955(*i*)
Mountain (French political faction), 600
Movies
  global culture and, 978
  about Holocaust, 903
  neorealist, 909
  in 1930s, 854–855
  U.S. influence on, 980
  World War I and, 828

Elevation

Feet	Meters
Over 13,120	Over 4,001
6,561–13,120	2,001–4,000
1,641–6,560	501–2,000
661–1640	201–500
0–660	0–200
Below sea level	Below sea level

⊛ National capital
• Major city

0   150   300 miles
0   150   300 kilometers

NORWAY
Bergen
SWEDEN
Oslo ⊛
Stockholm ⊛
Göteborg
SCOTLAND
Glasgow
Edinburgh
North Sea
Aarhus
DENMARK
Copenhagen ⊛
Baltic Sea
Kaliningra
Gdańsk
NORTHERN IRELAND
Belfast
IRELAND
Dublin ⊛
Liverpool
UNITED
KINGDOM
WALES
Birmingham
ENGLAND
Thames R.
London
Cork
English Channel
NETHERLANDS
Amsterdam ⊛
Rotterdam
Antwerp
Brussels ⊛
BELGIUM
Berlin ⊛
GERMANY
Frankfurt
Elbe R.
POLAND
Oder R.
Cracov
Prague ⊛
CZECH REP.
Brno
SLOV.
Bratislava ⊛
Vistula
Rhine R.
Paris ⊛
Seine R.
Luxembourg ⊛
LUXEMBOURG
Loire R.
ATLANTIC OCEAN
FRANCE
LIECHTENSTEIN
Zürich
Vaduz ⊛
Munich
Vienna ⊛
Danube R.
Bern ⊛
SWITZERLAND
Innsbruck
AUSTRIA
Graz
Budapest
HUNGAR
Bay of Biscay
Lyon
A L P S
Milan
SLOVENIA
Ljubljana ⊛
Zagreb ⊛
CROATIA
Belgrad
Po R.
ANDORRA
PYRENEES
Andorra la Vella ⊛
Oporto
PORTUGAL
Ebro R.
Madrid ⊛
SPAIN
Barcelona
Marseille
MONACO
San Marino ⊛
SAN MARINO
A P E N N I N E S
Adriatic Sea
Split
BOSNIA AND HERZEGOVINA
Sarajevo ⊛
Podgorica
MONTENEGRO
Tiran
ALBAN
Corsica
Rome ⊛
ITALY
Naples
Lisbon
Seville
BALEARIC IS.
Sardinia
Tyrrhenian Sea
Ionian Sea
Gibraltar (Br.)
Palermo
Sicily
Valletta ⊛
MALTA
Algiers ⊛
Tunis ⊛
Rabat ⊛
MOROCCO
TUNISIA
Mediterranean
ALGERIA
Tripoli ⊛
LIBYA

80°N

Greenland
(Den.)

Alaska

ICELAND

60°N

UNITED
KINGDOM
IRELAND

CANADA

FRANCE

SPAIN

40°N

UNITED STATES

PORTUGAL

Azores
(Port.)

ATLANTIC
OCEAN

MOROCCO

Canary Is.
(Sp.)

Hawaii

BAHAMAS
DOMINICAN
REPUBLIC

Western Sahara
(Mor.)

20°N

MEXICO

CUBA

HAITI

Puerto Rico (U.S.)

CAPE
VERDE

MAURITANIA

JAMAICA

ST. KITTS AND NEVIS
ANTIGUA AND BARBUDA

BELIZE

Guadeloupe (Fr.)

DOMINICA

SENEGAL

MALI

GUATEMALA

HONDURAS

Martinique (Fr.)

ST. VINCENT AND THE GRENADINES

GAMBIA

EL SALVADOR

NICARAGUA

ST. LUCIA

BARBADOS

GUINEA-BISSAU

GRENADA

COSTA RICA

TRINIDAD AND TOBAGO

GUINEA

PANAMA

VENEZUELA

GUYANA

SURINAME

SIERRA LEONE

French Guiana (Fr.)

LIBERIA

COLOMBIA

CÔTE D'IVOIRE

PACIFIC OCEAN

0°

Equator

Galápagos Is.
(Ec.)

ECUADOR

BURKINA FASO

GHANA

PERU

BRAZIL

SAMOA

BOLIVIA

20°S

TONGA

PARAGUAY

Easter I.
(Chile)

CHILE

ATLANTIC
OCEAN

URUGUAY

0		1,500		3,000 miles

0	1,500	3,000 kilometers

ARGENTINA

40°S

Falkland Is.
(U.K.)

60°S

80°S

160°W   140°W   120°W   100°W   80°W   60°W   40°W   20°W

ARCTIC OCEAN

NORWAY
SWEDEN
FINLAND
ESTONIA
LATVIA
LITHUANIA
DEN.
NETH.
GERMANY POLAND BELARUS
BEL. LUX.
CZ. REP.
SLK. UKRAINE
AUS. HUNG. MOLDOVA
SLN. ROMANIA
SWITZ. SERB.
CR. BULGARIA
ITALY B.H. MAC.
MONT.
ALB. GREECE
TUNISIA MALTA

RUSSIAN FEDERATION

KAZAKHSTAN

MONGOLIA

N. KOREA
S. KOREA   JAPAN

PACIFIC OCEAN

GEORGIA
ARMENIA
TURKEY
AZERBAIJAN
CYPRUS SYRIA LEBANON
ISRAEL IRAQ
JORDAN
KUWAIT
SAUDI ARABIA
QATAR
UNITED ARAB
EMIRATES

UZBEKISTAN   KYRGYZSTAN
TURKMENISTAN TAJIKISTAN
AFGHANISTAN

CHINA

IRAN
BAHRAIN
OMAN

PAKISTAN

NEPAL BHUTAN
BANGLADESH

TAIWAN

ALGERIA LIBYA EGYPT

INDIA

MYANMAR
(BURMA)
THAILAND
CAMBODIA

VIETNAM
LAOS

PHILIPPINES

Mariana Is.
(U.S.)

Guam
(U.S.)

MARSHALL
IS.

NIGER CHAD SUDAN
NIGERIA
BENIN
TOGO
CENTRAL
AFRICAN REP.
CAMEROON
EQ.
GUINEA
GABON
SÃO TOMÉ
& PRÍNCIPE

ERITREA
YEMEN
DJIBOUTI

ETHIOPIA

SOMALIA

MALDIVES

SRI
LANKA

BRUNEI

MALAYSIA

PALAU

FEDERATED STATES
OF MICRONESIA

NAURU   KIRIBATI
TUVALU

CONGO
RWANDA UGANDA
DEM. REP. OF KENYA
THE CONGO
BURUNDI TANZANIA
COMOROS

SINGAPORE

INDONESIA

PAPUA
NEW
GUINEA

SOLOMON
IS.

SEYCHELLES

INDIAN OCEAN

EAST TIMOR

ANGOLA
ZAMBIA MALAWI
ZIMBABWE
NAMIBIA MADAGASCAR
BOTSWANA
MAURITIUS

VANUATU   FIJI

New Caledonia
(Fr.)

AUSTRALIA

SOUTH
AFRICA
MOZAMBIQUE
SWAZILAND
LESOTHO

NEW
ZEALAND

Tasmania
(Aust.)

N
W   E
S

Abbreviations	
ALB.	ALBANIA
AUS.	AUSTRIA
BEL.	BELGIUM
B.H.	BOSNIA AND HERZEGOVINA
CR.	CROATIA
CZ. REP.	CZECH REPUBLIC
DEN.	DENMARK
HUNG.	HUNGARY
LUX.	LUXEMBOURG
MAC.	MACEDONIA
MONT.	MONTENEGRO
NETH.	NETHERLANDS
SERB.	SERBIA
SLK.	SLOVAKIA
SLN.	SLOVENIA
SWITZ.	SWITZERLAND

ANTARCTICA

20°E   40°E   60°E   80°E   100°E   120°E   140°E   160°E